# BOOKS ABOUT DESIGN AND PROGRAMMING

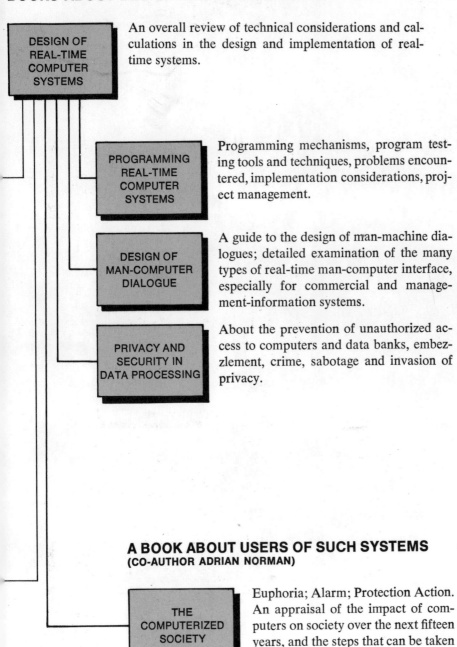

**DESIGN OF REAL-TIME COMPUTER SYSTEMS**

An overall review of technical considerations and calculations in the design and implementation of real-time systems.

**PROGRAMMING REAL-TIME COMPUTER SYSTEMS**

Programming mechanisms, program testing tools and techniques, problems encountered, implementation considerations, project management.

**DESIGN OF MAN-COMPUTER DIALOGUE**

A guide to the design of man-machine dialogues; detailed examination of the many types of real-time man-computer interface, especially for commercial and management-information systems.

**PRIVACY AND SECURITY IN DATA PROCESSING**

About the prevention of unauthorized access to computers and data banks, embezzlement, crime, sabotage and invasion of privacy.

# A BOOK ABOUT USERS OF SUCH SYSTEMS
## (CO-AUTHOR ADRIAN NORMAN)

**THE COMPUTERIZED SOCIETY**

Euphoria; Alarm; Protection Action. An appraisal of the impact of computers on society over the next fifteen years, and the steps that can be taken to direct it into the most beneficial channels.

# SYSTEMS ANALYSIS
# FOR DATA TRANSMISSION

Prentice-Hall Series in Automatic Computation

*George Forsythe, editor*

# SYSTEMS ANALYSIS
# FOR DATA TRANSMISSION

## JAMES MARTIN

IBM SYSTEMS RESEARCH INSTITUTE

Prentice-Hall, Inc.,   Englewood Cliffs, New Jersey

© 1972 by
PRENTICE-HALL, INC.
Englewood Cliffs, N. J.

10 9 8 7 6 5 4

ISBN: 0-13-881300-0


Library of Congress Catalog Card Number: 75-37761

Printed in the United States of America

PRENTICE-HALL INTERNATIONAL, INC., *London*
PRENTICE-HALL OF AUSTRALIA, PTY., LTD., *Sydney*
PRENTICE-HALL OF CANADA, LTD., *Toronto*
PRENTICE-HALL OF INDIA PRIVATE LIMITED, *New Delhi*
PRENTICE-HALL OF JAPAN, INC., *Tokyo*

TO CHARITY

# ACKNOWLEDGMENTS

Any book about the state of the art in a complex technology draws material from a vast number of sources. While many of these are referenced in the text, it is impossible to include all of the pioneering projects that have contributed to the new uses of telecommunications. To the many systems engineers who contributed to this body of knowledge, the author is indebted.

I am very grateful for the time spent reviewing and criticizing the manuscript by Mr. J. W. Greenwood, Mr. T. A. Puorro, various members of the IBM technical staff, and my wife.

Mr. E. J. Moore of Bell Canada pointed out that the name Baudot code is commonly misused in the industry for the CCITT Telegraph Alphabet No. 2, which was in fact designed by Donald Murray and which bears little resemblance to Baudot's earlier code. The name "Baudot code" has been used in this book.

Miss Toby Kosloff converted the author's original PL/I programs, written for this book, into FORTRAN. Her excellent work is much appreciated.

I am immensely grateful to my wife for compiling the index.

Last, and perhaps most important, I am indebted to Dr. E. S. Kopley, Director of the IBM Systems Research Institute for his constant encouragement. Without the environment that he created, this work would not have been completed.

# STRUCTURE

## VI. Design Calculations

## Appendices

# EXAMPLES IN THE DESIGN CALCULATIONS

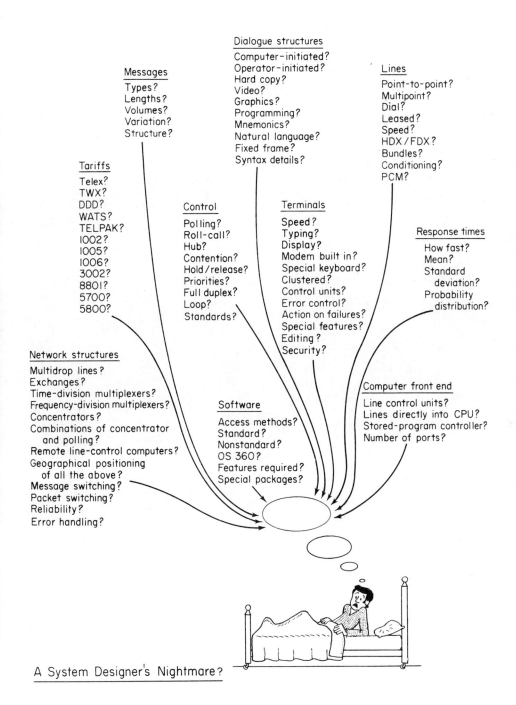

Dialogue structures
Computer–initiated?
Operator–initiated?
Hard copy?
Video?
Graphics?
Programming?
Mnemonics?
Natural language?
Fixed frame?
Syntax details?

Messages
Types?
Lengths?
Volumes?
Variation?
Structure?

Lines
Point-to-point?
Multipoint?
Dial?
Leased?
Speed?
HDX / FDX?
Bundles?
Conditioning?
PCM?

Tariffs
Telex?
TWX?
DDD?
WATS?
TELPAK?
1002?
1005?
1006?
3002?
8801?
5700?
5800?

Control
Polling?
Roll-call?
Hub?
Contention?
Hold/release?
Priorities?
Full duplex?
Loop?
Standards?

Terminals
Speed?
Typing?
Display?
Modem built in?
Special keyboard?
Clustered?
Control units?
Error control?
Action on failures?
Special features?
Editing?
Security?

Response times
How fast?
Mean?
Standard
   deviation?
Probability
   distribution?

Network structures
Multidrop lines?
Exchanges?
Time-division multiplexers?
Frequency-division multiplexers?
Concentrators?
Combinations of concentrator
   and polling?
Remote line-control computers?
Geographical positioning
   of all the above?
Message switching?
Packet switching?
Reliability?
Error handling?

Software
Access methods?
Standard?
Nonstandard?
OS 360?
Features required?
Special packages?

Computer front end
Line control units?
Lines directly into CPU?
Stored-program controller?
Number of ports?

A System Designer's Nightmare?

SECTION **I**

**SYSTEMS**
**CONSIDERATIONS**

# 1  INTRODUCTION

The most rapidly growing use of the world's telecommunication links is for data transmission. The most rapidly growing area in the exploding data processing industry is teleprocessing. The reason is the power and versatility that the interlinking of computers can bring, plus the potential benefits to the individual of having this power at his fingertips. In all walks of life and in all areas of industry, the devices connected to distant computers will change the realms of what is possible for man to do. In centuries hence, historians will look back on the coming of computer data transmission as a fundamental step forward in civilization, perhaps eventually having a greater effect on the human condition than even the invention of the printing press.

Data transmission will become as indispensable to city-dwelling man as his electricity supply. He will employ it in his home, in his office, in shops, and in his car. He will use it to pay for goods, to teach his children, to obtain information, transportation, stock prices, items from stores, and sports scores; he will use it to seek protection in the crime-infested streets. The best potentials of data transmission will give man more knowledge, more power, more leisure time; he will have less mandatory travel; his job will be more interesting. In many ways his life will be richer. The worse potentials of data transmission conjure up visions of George Orwell's *1984* and will cause us to look harder at issues involving privacy, security and the democratic process.

Data transmission will drop in cost. Long-distance costs will drop much more than short-distance costs, thereby having an effect on the organization of nationwide corporations. The cost of intercontinental links will drop much more than that of national links, and the international corporation will be bound together via satellite communication.

3

Computers are also dropping in cost and their rate of drop is greater than that of communication lines. To some extent this trend will go against the trend toward increased use of data transmission. In some cases, it will be increasingly cheaper to obtain computing power locally rather than at a distance. The era of the mini-computer is upon us, and many people will have one in their office. And yet, there will be an increasing need to use *very* complex machines. The need to employ a million-dollar computer will remain, and people will not have that in their office—they will have a terminal. The ways in which the computer is used will, in some cases, become more specialized, and highly elaborate programs will be executed only infrequently by each user. The program storage will be centralized to some extent. Often the small local computers will obtain their programs from the larger centralized machines.

Although simple computing may be decentralized with the mini-computers, data storage will become more and more centralized. There are two reasons for this situation. First, the quantity of data stored and the complexity of its organization are going up by leaps and bounds. The addressing and searching operation to locate data becomes, at times, so complex that it requires a centralized computer. Second, the information in the data banks is often updated from terminals or from peripheral computers. The reading and writing of the data often occur in real-time, thus requiring that the information be kept in one place. An airline, for example, does not keep multiple copies of its reservation data; if it did, the same seat could be sold at the same instant by computers using different sets of seat-availability data. Instead, reservation agents around the world are linked to a central computer system. In the business world, files on customer orders, manufacturing data, parts inventories, bank accounts, and so on will be centralized for the same reason.

*Data transmission, then, may be used more for gaining access to data than to computing power.*

Having said that, it is still predictable that the use of data transmission to obtain computing power will increase greatly from today's level. Programming and remote job entry at terminals are increasing rapidly. Load-sharing networks are being constructed so that overloaded or faulty computers are bypassed and turnaround time to the user is fast. With a load-sharing network, the user waits for access not to one computer but to one of many, and as we shall see in our calculations, the decrease in waiting time can be disproportionately great. Computer networks will be one of the major developments of the years ahead.

Like computers, logic circuits are fast dropping in cost and will continue to do so with the maturing of *large-scale integration* technology. For this reason, the devices attached to data transmission links will contain an increasing quantity of logic circuits. The "intelligence" in a teleprocessing network will tend to be less centralized and will spread outward to the peripheral machines. The possibilities as to how this peripheral logic can be used are numerous, and we will see a greater range of options for the systems designer. In addition, the telecommunication companies are offering a greater diversity of transmission facilities, especially in North America, where some measure of competition is permitted. The design, or systems analysis, for data transmission will become increasingly complex, and that is why this book is large.

Although it is true that the cost of telecommunication links is not dropping as fast as that of computers, nevertheless, there is scope for using these links with vastly improved efficiency. As we shall illustrate at the start of Chapter 18, telephone lines are sometimes used today for data transmission with an efficiency as low as 0.0001. There is scope for a ten-thousandfold improvement. It is commonly the case that scope for a four-hundredfold improvement exists. In general, learning to use existing communication facilities with high efficiency for data transmission portends a drop in cost that by itself drastically changes what is economically feasible. The telephone line (especially the PCM telephone line) could stay the same price, and yet, in the short term, the cost of data transmission could spiral downward faster than the drop in computer costs. To make this happen, as we shall explain later, requires extensive use of mass-produced logic circuits, which the advent of large-scale integration makes possible; it also requires much entrepreneurial courage and initiative.

This book is concerned with the calculations that should be done and the system decisions that are necessary when designing data transmission systems.

Frequently, one sees systems today in which these calculations are not done, or they are done in a short sighted manner. Indeed, in many systems they are not straightforward calculations because there are intricate trade-offs between one aspect of the design and another—trade-offs, for example, between line cost and logic cost, between system centralization and decentralization, between response time and network complexity, between data accuracy and transmission speed, and between network cost and psychological considerations in the man-machine dialogue. The trade-offs that involve user psychology are subjective. They can only be made confidently by a systems analyst who is experienced, and probably also well read, in the art of designing man-computer dialogue.

There are many interlocking questions in this aspect of system design and many types of technique that one can use in answer to the questions—so many, in fact, that one often sees valuable approaches being overlooked in the design and vital questions not being asked. It is the intention of this book to make the reader familiar with the questions that should be asked, and to survey the types of answers that are possible. It is necessary to appreciate how the questions interlock. At first it may not be apparent that an improvement in the psychology of the terminal dialogue could change the concentrator philosophy or that a high-speed modem may give a worse response time than a low-speed one because of line turnaround time for polling. The relationship between these diverse aspects of the system must be understood. The different aspects are often the province of different experts, but as in all systems engineering, *the man responsible for the design should understand all the possible trade-offs, quantitatively.*

In the future, systems analysis for data transmission will be a much more professional operation than it is today. At present a great deal of money is wasted in many organizations because systems analysis is not handled in a sufficiently professional manner. Eventually there will be new tariffs and new communication facilities. The network proposed by the Datran Corporation, for example, will provide a new form of switched transmission [1]. There will be new computers, new terminals, and new devices. The details of the calculations in this book will change, but most of the principles will remain. Therefore the reader should concentrate on the principles. The computer programs in Section VI, for instance, apply to the tariffs at the time of writing. The tariffs may have changed by the time the book is published, but the methodology will remain applicable if used with intelligence. Most users of data transmission have different situations and different problems. Consequently, the systems analyst must be able to *adapt* the techniques illustrated to his own needs.

The ability to adapt is the most vital ability in the turbulent world ahead.

## REFERENCE

1. James Martin: *Future Developments in Telecommunications.* Prentice-Hall, Inc., Englewood Cliffs, N. J., 1971.

# 2 CATEGORIES OF DATA TRANSMISSION SYSTEMS

Data transmission systems are built for a wide variety of purposes and differ accordingly in the way they function.

The most common form of system in the future will probably be one in which people at terminals communicate with a distant computer. The computer will usually respond to them quickly. Often a dialogue takes place between the terminal user and the remote computer. This type of application did not exist for the first hundred years of data transmission, and thus many traditional ideas are being rethought. Indeed, when a person whose background is data processing approaches transmission, he does so with a point of view fundamentally different from that of the traditional telecommunications man.

**THE MAN-MACHINE INTERFACE**  In order to bring the power of computers and the information in their data banks to the maximum number of people, careful attention must be paid to the man-machine interface. Increasingly, in the years ahead, *man* must become the prime focus of systems design. The computer is there to serve him, to obtain information for him and to help him do his job. The ease with which he communicates with it will determine the extent to which he uses it. Whether or not he uses it powerfully will depend on the man-machine language available to him and how well he is able to understand it. For the ordinary manager, and for many other types of computer users, remarkably little has been done to provide an efficient man-machine interface as yet.

The interface is going to differ greatly from one man to another and from one machine to another. Different applications will need fundamentally different types of dialogue structures. Some are very complex and need a high level of

7

intelligence; others are simple. In some applications today, one can observe the "man-in-the-street" who has never touched a terminal before sitting down at one and carrying on a successful, if simple, dialogue with a computer. On the other hand, one also finds terminals being discarded a few months after installation because the intended user never learned to communicate successfully with the system.

The man-computer dialogue will be a starting point in the design of the data communication facilities in many real-time systems.

**ON-LINE AND OFF-LINE SYSTEMS**    Many systems are not real-time in nature but are required merely to move a quantity of data from one point to another. The communication links in this case may be *on-line* to a computer or *off-line*. *On-line* means that they go directly into the computer, with the computer controlling the transmission. *Off-line* means that telecommunication data do not go directly into the computer but are written onto magnetic tape or disk, or punched into paper tape or cards for later processing.

*An on-line system may be defined as one in which the input data enter the computer directly from the point of origination and/or output data are transmitted directly to where they are used. The intermediate stages of punching data onto cards or paper tape or of writing magnetic tape or off-line printing are avoided.*

**INTERACTIVE AND NONINTERACTIVE SYSTEMS**    Off-line systems are not "interactive." As no computer is directly connected at the location the data are sent to, no data response will be received from that location, although simple control signals may be received to control the mechanical functioning of the devices and to indicate whether the transmission has been found free of errors.

Moreover, some on-line systems are also noninteractive. The computer may merely receive a batch transmission and may have no need to respond to it. Sometimes it may take a hash total at the end of a batch transmission to ensure that no data have been garbled; therefore, the only interactive response is confirmation of correct receipt of the transmission.

Most transmissions from human operators at terminals are interactive; in fact, it is bad design *not* to give a response to an operator and to leave him wondering whether or not his input has reached the computer. In inexpensive terminals, however, there may be no mechanism for responding. Such is the case with some factory data-collection terminals into which a worker may insert a machine-readable badge and set some keys or dials. The system may respond with a light or mechanical action simply indicating that it has received the message.

For noninteractive systems or systems that give a very rudimentary response, the data will flow in one direction only. Normally the transmission system is not designed to be entirely one way because a small trickle of control signals are needed going in the other direction. Occasionally, in telemetry, the use of radio makes two-way transmission difficult and a purely one-way link is used. An interactive system, on the other hand, can have a high flow of data in both directions. Factors such as this will sometimes affect the data transmission techniques used.

Figure 2.1 lists some common categories of data transmission systems.

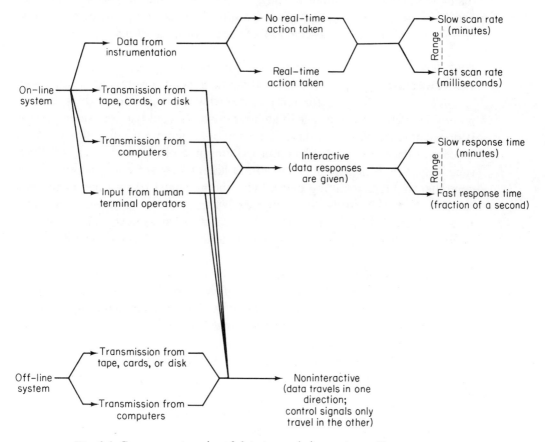

*Fig. 2.1.* Common categories of data transmission systems. Human interactive dialogue systems are becoming the most common category.

**QUANTITY OF DATA TRANSMITTED**    The quantity of data to be transmitted varies enormously from one system to another. At one extreme we find whole files being transmitted, and at the other all that is needed is to indicate a YES/NO condition and one bit would suffice. Sometimes a single transaction is transmitted, sometimes a batch of many transactions. When no immediate action is required on data that are gathered, the information may be collected and transmitted in a batch, which is less expensive than sending it a transaction at a time. Occasionally the contents of entire magnetic tapes or disks are sent. Payroll data or machine shop schedules, for example, may be transmitted from one location to another. Often a "dialogue" takes place between a terminal user and a computer. The message sizes then depend on the design of the dialogue structure: the input to the computer being one statement by the user, and the output being the computer's response, which may range from a one-character confirmation to a screenfull of data or printed listing.

**TIME FOR TRANSMISSION**
Sometimes it is necessary to transmit the data quickly. The speed required depends on the system. A system for relaying one-way messages, like cables, may be required to deliver the message in an hour or so. It would be convenient to have it done more quickly, but there is no major economic need to do so. When batches of data are sent for batch processing on a distant computer, a delivery time longer than one hour is sometimes acceptable. However, where a man-computer dialogue is taking place, the responses must be returned to the man sufficiently quickly so as not to impede his train of thought. Response times between 1 and 5 seconds are typical. In "real-time" systems in which a machine or process is being controlled, response times can vary from a few milliseconds to many minutes.

Response time for a terminal operator can be defined as *that time interval from the operator's pressing the last key of the input to the terminal's typing or displaying the first character of the response.* For different types of situations, response time can be defined similarly: *the interval between an event and the system's response to the event.*

Systems differ widely in their response-time requirements, and the response time needed can, in turn, have a major effect on the design of the data transmission networks.

Where systems are not interactive, we might specify a "delivery time" rather than a response time. Delivery time refers to situations in which the data are flowing in one direction, and it can be defined as *that time interval from the start of transmission at the transmitting terminal to the completion of reception at the receiving terminal.*

The question of how fast the response time must be can have a major effect on the cost of the network, as we shall see later. The need for different response times in different dialogue structures is discussed in Chapter 7. For a dialogue in which the operator must maintain a continuing chain of thought, responses in

2 seconds or less are usually needed. Where the input is a simple inquiry, or a request for a listing, or for a program to be run, the response time may be longer, sometimes much longer. Where machinery is being controlled, a faster response is necessary at times; and where one computer is requesting data from another computer, it may be needed very quickly so that the requesting computer itself can achieve a specified response time.

Figure 2.2 shows some of the common requirements for delivery time or

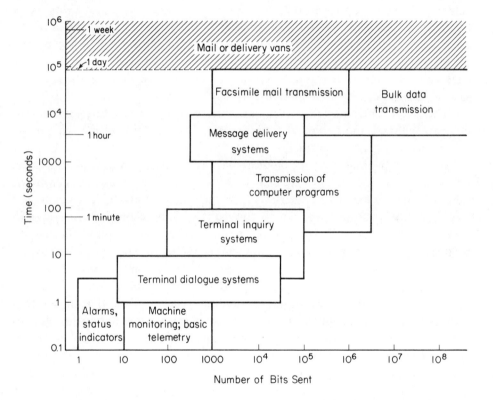

*Fig. 2.2.* Desirable delivery time or response time and quantity of data for typical uses of data transmission.

response time and for quantities of data transmitted. It is probable that the most common use of data transmission in the years ahead will be the block labeled "terminal dialogue systems." This block indicates a response-time requirement of from 1 to 10 seconds, and a message size ranging from one character (usually 7 or 8 bits) to about 4000 characters (around 30,000 bits). A few exceptional cases will extend beyond the block shown (as with all of the blocks on the diagram).

The block labeled "terminal inquiry systems" extends on the time scale to 100 seconds. A wait of this duration would be quite inacceptable in a dialogue situation; but where a storekeeper or foreman, for example, is making a simple request for a listing, a wait of a minute may not cause much inconvenience. In all such cases, the cost of providing different response times must be related to the requirements of the user.

Systems for delivering messages or cables, commonly called *message-switching systems*, are referred to with the block labeled "message-delivery systems." With the apparent deterioration of the mail services, it seems likely that facsimile mail transmission will grow in popularity. Certainly it will be the fastest way of delivering mail, but delivery times up to one day will be acceptable. The same delivery times will often be acceptable for the bulk transmission of data. Bulk transmission of data extends to the extreme right of the diagram because sometimes very large quantities of data are sent.

There is not much point in using data transmission over a line so slow that the delivery time is more than 24 hours. In these cases, mail, delivery van, or air transportation is usually cheaper.

It is probable that in the near future data transmission will be used in areas outside the blocks shown in Fig. 2.2. To some extent the areas in which it has been used to date have been determined by the speeds of available transmission lines. The transmission speed equals the delivery time of one-way messages in Fig. 2.2 (vertical axis), divided by the number of bits transmitted (horizontal axis). For most of the applications shown in the figure, the speeds of teletype and telephone lines—speeds up to, say, 4800 bits per second—are sufficient. Lines of higher speed today are mainly required when a very large bulk of data must be sent.

The computer industry changes swiftly, and it seems likely that those areas in which a computer responds to a machine or another computer, rather than to a person, will require different transmission facilities. One computer may ask a second, distant computer for a program or data for immediate processing. One computer will pass jobs on to another because it does not have the capability to handle them itself, or for load-sharing reasons. The requirement for access time in obtaining data from disks—the time taken to "seek" and read a record—may become the time requirement for obtaining data from a distant computer over telecommunication links in the future. Small local computers will sometimes pass their compiling work on to bigger, distant machines with better facilities. The initial program loading of small local computers will sometimes be done by a large remote computer.

The computers and file units that are connected by cabling in the machine room today may be connected by telecommunication links tomorrow if channels of suitable speed are available.

**TIME–SHARING SYSTEMS**
Most systems with manually operated terminals are time-shared, meaning that more than one user is using them at the same time. When the machine pauses in the processing of one user's item, it switches its attention to another user.

The term *time sharing*, however, generally refers to a system in which the users are *independent*, each using the terminal as though it were the console of a computer and entering, testing, and executing programs of their own at the terminal. The work on programs of one terminal user is quite unrelated to that of other users.

In many systems the users do not *program* the system at the terminal, nor are the users entirely independent. Each is *using* the programs in the computer in a related manner. The users may, for example, be insurance or railroad clerks who are perhaps using the same programs and possibly the same file areas. In many time-shared systems, however, the computing facility is being divided between separate users who can program *whatever they wish* on it, independently of one another. Four categories of on-line systems, differing by the degree of independence of the users, are in common use.

1. Systems that carry out a carefully specified and limited function—for example, banking systems, in which all terminal users can update the same files.

2. Systems for a specific, limited function, in which the user has personal independent files or in which shared files can be read but not updated by general terminal users.

3. Systems in which programmers can program anything they wish at the terminals, providing that they all use the same language, an interpreter or compiler for this purpose being in the machine. Normally each user has the same type of terminal.

4. Systems in which programmers can program anything by using a variety of different languages. Often a wide variety of terminals is also permitted.

The last two types of system are, in effect, dividing up the computing facility "timewise" and giving the pieces to different programmers to do what they like with them. The files are also divided according to use. It cannot be known beforehand how much space in the files the various users will occupy. This situation is quite different from category 1, in which the file size and organization are planned in detail.

**TIME–SHARING COMMUNICATION LINES**   The reason why time sharing is so important in computers is that the human keying rate and reading rate are much slower than computer speeds. Furthermore, the human being requires lengthy pauses to think between transactions. The key to using the computer efficiently for real-time dialogue operations is to make it divide its time between many users. *The same is true with telecommunications.* A voice line could transmit many more bits than a terminal operator employs in an alphanumeric dialogue with a computer. The key to using it efficiently is to time share the line between many users. There are many ways of doing this, as we shall find in later chapters.

The need to share communication lines will become greater in the future, for facilities capable of transmitting higher bit rates will be employed. Today's telephone lines are normally made to carry data rates of 2400 or 4800 bits per second. However, in the Bell System T1 carrier, of which millions of miles are already installed, the telephone voice channel is equivalent to 56,000 bits per second.

As with computers, the degree of independence of users on a shared communication facility varies. On some shared lines, all users must employ the same terminal type with the same line-control procedure. On other lines, these items can be different, but the same character code must be used. With some systems, the users can be entirely independent and use different codes. The users may all be of one type, in one organization—reservation agents linked to an airline system, for example. On the other hand, they may be different types of users who are sharing communication facilities installed within one organization. Finally, they might be entirely independent users who share public data-transmission facilities. It is in the latter case that the greatest savings may result, and eventually public data networks will play a vital part in a nation's data processing.

**TYPES OF SYSTEM**   Table 2.1 shows some of the types of system that use data transmission, indicating whether they are likely to be on-line or off-line, in-plant or out-plant, and interactive or not. Some exceptional systems differ from the categorization shown in this table. The two bottom lines may remain the largest categories and have been expanded in Tables 2.2 and 2.3.

Details of a variety of real-time systems and the economic justification for them are given in the author's *Design of Real-Time Computer Systems.*[1]

[1] Prentice-Hall, Englewood Cliffs, N. J., 1968.

**Table 2.1.** A CATEGORIZATION OF COMMON DATA TRANSMISSION SYSTEMS*

| | On-Line or Off-Line | Interactive? | Typical Response Time | Typical Delivery Time | In-Plant or Out-Plant |
|---|---|---|---|---|---|
| Data-collection system | ON or OFF | YES or NO | 1–5 sec | | IN |
| Alarm system | ON | YES or NO | 1–20 sec | | IN or OUT |
| Machine monitoring | ON or OFF | YES or NO | Wide variation | | IN or OUT |
| Telemetry | ON or OFF | YES or NO | | Short | IN or OUT |
| Process control | ON | YES or NO | 1 sec–10 min | | IN |
| Batch transmission | ON or OFF | NO | | Dependent on batch or job size | OUT |
| Load-sharing batch system | ON | NO | | Dependent on batch or job size | OUT |
| Remote job entry | ON | YES | | Dependent on batch or job size | IN or OUT |
| Intercomputer transmission | ON | YES | 0.1–1 sec | | OUT |
| Interactive programming | ON | YES | 1–5 sec | | IN or OUT |
| Message switching | ON or OFF | NO | | ½ to 8 hr | OUT |
| Commercial real-time systems | ON | YES | 1–5 sec | | IN or OUT |
| Information utilities | ON | YES | 1–5 sec | | OUT |

* The two bottom lines are expanded on in Tables 2.2 and 2.3.

**Table 2.2.** SOME OF THE MANY TYPES OF COMMERCIAL REAL-TIME SYSTEMS

| | |
|---|---|
| Airline reservations systems | Information-retrieval systems |
| Banking systems | Library catalog systems |
| Sales inquiry systems | Museum catalog systems |
| Sales-order entry systems | Hotel-booking systems |
| Point-of-sale data collection systems | Stores and inventory control systems |
| Credit-information systems | Production data collection systems |
| Electronic fund-transfer systems | Management inquiry systems |
| Stockbroker-information systems | Engineering design aids |
| Hospital-information systems | Terminals for statistical services |
| Text-editing systems | Terminals for financial analysis |
| Document-retrieval systems | Terminals for specialized professional functions |

**Table 2.3.** A FEW OF THE MANY POSSIBLE CATEGORIES OF INFORMATION UTILITIES*

| Type | General Purpose or Subscriber Oriented | Retrieval or Processing | Digital or Graphical | Small, Medium, or Large Subscriber | Local, Regional, or National |
|---|---|---|---|---|---|
| 1. Savings account processing | S | P | D | S, M, L | L, R |
| 2. Stockbrokerage information | S | R | D | S, M, L | N |
| 3. Travel service | S | P | D | S, M, L | N |
| 4. Professional billing | S | P | D | S | L |
| 5. Engineering problem solving | G | P | D, G | S, M, L | L, R, N |
| 6. Graphical design | G | P | G | S, M, L | L, R, N |
| 7. Document retrieval | G | R | G | S, M, L | N |
| 8. Data retrieval | G | R | D | S, M, L | L, R, N |
| 9. General purpose | G | P | D, G | S, M, L | L |
| 10. Credit information | S | R | D | S, M, L | L, R, N |
| 11. Financial exchange | Multiple S | P | D | S, M, L | L, R, N |
| 12. Hospital and medical | S | P | D, G | S, M, L | L, R |
| 13. Educational and teaching | G, S | P | D, G | S, M, L | L, R, N |
| 14. Hotel reservations | S | P | D | S, M, L | N |
| 15. Interairline reservations | S | P | D | S, M, L | N |
| 16. Railroad information | S | P | D | S, M, L | N |
| 17. Publishing | S | P | D, G | S, M, L | L, R, N |
| 18. Radio and TV time brokerage | S | R | D | S, M | N |
| 19. Retail and distribution | S | P | D | S, M | L, R |
| 20. Insurance | S | P | D | S, M | L, R |
| 21. Merchandising and advertising | G | P | D | S, M | N |
| 22. Public survey and polling | G | P | D | S | N |
| 23. Sport and theater tickets | S | P | D | S | L, R, N |
| 24. Tax service | G | P | D | S, M | L |
| 25. Labor negotiations | S | P | D | S, M, L | N |
| 26. Career and employment information | G | P | D | S, M, L | N |
| 27. Legal citation service | S | P | D | S, M, L | N |
| 28. Post office | S | P | D | L | N |

| | | | | | |
|---|---|---|---|---|---|
| 29. Marketing research | G | R | D | M, L | N |
| 30. Criminal intelligence | S | P | D | L | ' N |
| 31. Typing and editing service | G | P | D | S, M, L | N |
| 32. Personal data services | G | P | D | S | L, R, N |
| 33. Library catalogs | G | R | D | S, M, L | L, R, N |
| 34. Lottery service | S | P | D | M, L | L, R, N |
| 35. Terminals for surveyors | G, S | P, R | D, G | S | N |
| 36. Terminals for engineers | G, S | P, R | D, G | S | N |
| 37. Terminals for electronics designers | G, S | P, R | D, G | S | N |
| 38. Terminals for architects | G, S | P, R | D, G | S | N |
| 39. Terminals for lawyers | G, S | P, R | D | S | N |
| 40. Terminals for statisticians | G, S | P, R | D | S | N |
| 41. Terminals for doctors | G, S | P, R | D | S | N |
| 42. Terminals for other professional groups | G, S | P, R | D, G | S | N |

*Reproduced with permission in modified form from Richard E. Sprague, *Information Utilities*, Prentice-Hall, Englewood Cliffs, N.J., 1969.

# 3 FACTORS AFFECTING THE DESIGN

The systems analyst has a wide variety of alternatives in his design of communication systems. In this chapter we will review the factors that affect his choice.

**OPERATOR CONSIDERATIONS**   A first and major factor will be whether the system is designed for human terminal operators. If it is for batch transmission, telemetry, intercomputer communication, or other interlinking of mechanical devices, then all the design decisions that must be made depend upon the mechanisms. On the other hand, where human operators generate the input or carry on a dialogue with the system, the psychology and organization of these users will have a major effect on the design decisions. The starting point in the design of such a system should be concern for the human factors and human organization. For this reason, the next section of this book is called "User Considerations," and it precedes "Terminal Considerations," "Network Considerations," "Programming Considerations," or "Design Calculations."

The users come in a variety of types. Some can program; some cannot. Some can be highly trained; some are too busy. Some are intelligent; some are not. Some have a natural ability to communicate with computers; some have only to sit at a terminal for a form of paralysis to set in. (Worse, some seem to cause paralysis in the system!) There is a big difference between a factory worker entering data into a shop-floor terminal and a statistician entering data into his office terminal. There is a big difference between an airline agent sorting out changes in a passenger's journey and a high-level manager wanting to sort out changes in a customer's order. The airline agent spends her whole day operating the terminal; the manager, if he operates it at all, only does so occasionally in the midst of a harassing schedule.

These differences will lead to differences in the structure of the terminal dialogue. As will be illustrated in Section II, terminal dialogues differ *very* widely in their structure. Furthermore, in the future when more varied communication facilities are available, they will differ still more widely.

The type of dialogue structure that is designed has, in turn, a major influence on the design of the telecommunication facilities. If the communication lines are long, and thus expensive, this factor, with today's tariffs, will be a constraining one on the permissible dialogue structures. Conversely, some effective but seemingly expensive dialogue structures can be employed by restructuring the communication network to make use of "intelligent" line-control computers, terminal-control units, or concentrators. The considerations of user psychology, then, can permeate all aspects of the network design.

**OPERATOR ERRORS**     All terminal operators make errors occasionally. The errors will be particularly serious if the operator is *entering* data that are then used for further processing or that reside in the system's data bank. How many errors are made can be affected to a major degree by the structure of the man-machine dialogue. Once again we have an important relationship between psychological factors and system design.

Where the operators enter data, it is particularly important that facilities for correcting their errors be well thought out. If possible, the system should be programmed to catch the error at the time it is made. An error message will then be sent to the operator. In those cases where the operator does not have an interactive terminal (e.g., many factory data-collection terminals), the errors will be referred to a special operator or staff with facilities to correct them. Sometimes the errors will be detected long after they are made by continuing or periodic checks. In this case, a mechanism must be constructed for sending an unsolicited message about the errors either to the operator who originated them or to a special operator or group charged with the responsibility for correcting errors.

**SECURITY**     A subject that will be of increasing concern in data processing is security. The data banks contain data that corporations wish to keep confidential, plus a wide variety of personal information about private individuals. Keeping such information out of the reach of unauthorized personnel is extremely important. Still more important is the need to prevent unauthorized persons from changing data on the files;

otherwise a rich variety of new forms of embezzlement and sabotage would be possible. Many techniques are available for maintaining security. An inter-linking set of measures that cover many aspects of the design is required. For the data transmission network, these can include a positive identification of the terminal being used, means to prevent wiretapping, a positive identification of the individual using the terminal by means of identification cards, passwords, and other measures, a lock on the terminals, authorization tables, security logs, and surveillance techniques and, in some cases, the use of cryptography.

In some cases, one of the procedures will be to notify a security officer immediately of any suspected breach in security. Security officers may be used at terminal locations, or, as with the control of errors, a specially trained person or group may be used in a central location.

**THIRD-PARTY OPERATORS**   Where a system is designed to provide information, the person needing the information need not necessarily operate the terminal. There are a variety of circumstances in which it would be better if he did not. They are not always recognized as such by the systems analyst. First, giving everyone terminals may be too expensive. Second, the job of obtaining adequate results from the terminal may be too difficult for the people in question. Systems analysts usually tend to overestimate the ability of laymen to operate terminals. Young people learn to operate them easily, but people set in their ways usually do not, particularly when, like most managers, they cannot afford the time and patience needed to learn. Third, it may be undesirable for security reasons to allow *any* person to be able to operate the terminal.

Where a system is designed to *gather* information, as well as *give* it, the same arguments apply. Sometimes it is even more necessary that the data which will reside on the files for commercial use be entered by a person trained to be accurate rather than by someone who only uses the terminal infrequently.

The person, then, who does not operate a terminal may gain access to a computer either by having an assistant who does operate one or by telephoning a specialist terminal operator. He may obtain information in this way, or he may cause information to be entered into the system. This is exactly what you do when you telephone an airline to make a reservation. You speak to a specialist terminal operator who obtains details of flights and seat availability for you; then when you decide on your trip, you give her details that she causes to be recorded in the computer files. You do not have a terminal yourself; and if you did, you probably could not operate it because the airline reservation language is very precise. The same reasoning can apply to management and other persons in an organization who will interact with an information system.

**LOCATION
OF TERMINALS**

When the terminals are not in the office of the person originating or requiring information, the question arises: Where should they best be positioned? If the user has a telephone link to the person with the terminal, that person could be almost anywhere. It is up to the systems analyst to decide where to put the terminals. He may group them together in such a way as to minimize the probability of the user not receiving immediate service, or to minimize queuing delays. He may gather together in one room different types of terminals connected to different types of systems, thus gathering, perhaps, different types of expertise in the operators. He may build "information rooms" having a variety of functions. Given the constraints imposed by these factors, he will locate the terminals so as to minimize the overall system cost.

**LOCATION OF
COMPUTERS**

The computers may also be positioned so as to minimize the overall cost. If a system covering a large geographical area is to have one central computer, this computer may be positioned in such a way as to minimize the network cost. (Often, in actuality, it is not.) Another factor is whether one computer should be used with lines linking distant terminals to it or whether several computers with shorter-distance lines should be used. If several computers are decided on, how many should there be and where should they be located? What is the optimum balance between computer cost and network cost?

In order to provide a nationwide time-sharing or information service, a computer in each city may be used, or a computer covering a group of cities. On the other hand, groups of computers in the same building may serve many locations, the grouping being designed to minimize the probability of a user not having access to a machine when he needs one. Again a load-sharing network may be designed; and when one computer is fully loaded, jobs are switched to a different machine. The balance in cost between having many local machines with short-distance transmission or fewer machines with long-distance transmission needs to be evaluated. This cost balance will steadily change in the future as both long-distance transmission costs and computer costs drop and transmission efficiency increases. The Datran System, for example, has proposed a long-distance tariff independent of distance. If adopted, this proposal would swing the balance in favor of using a single distant computer center with interswitchable computers.

**DUPLICATION OF
DATA BANKS?**

Just as we may have a choice between many localized computers and one centralized one, so there is a choice on some systems between localized data banks with duplicate data and one centralized data bank. Sometimes one single data file is desirable because of simultaneous updating from many sources. On other systems, however, the updating may be done at preplanned intervals, which makes it possible to have multiple identical data banks at different places, thus reducing transmission cost. The systems analyst should evaluate which is lower in cost, as well as where to position his data banks.

**COMMUNICATION NETWORK FACTORS**    The choice of communication line types, network structures, and equipment to be used depends on a number of factors, which are primarily derived from the foregoing considerations. There are three main factors.

1. *Space.* The distance between the transmitting and receiving devices, or if there are many of them, their geographical distribution.

2. *Time.* The time within which the transmission or message should be received, or within which a response should be received.

3. *Quantity.* The number of bits to be sent in a single transmission or "message."

In some cases, an examination of these three factors may lead a systems analyst to conclude that data transmission should not be used at all. In addition to these points, there are a number of secondary but important considerations, such as accuracy of transmission, line-failure probability, probability of obtaining a "busy" signal, whether a device should be connectable to one, or many, other devices, and how many times the transmission reverses direction (as when many terminals used for man-computer dialogue are connected to the same line).

Let us examine these parameters in more detail.

**GEOGRAPHICAL DISTRIBUTION**    Some data transmission links simply interconnect two points, as shown in Fig. 3.1.

More commonly, more than two places have to be linked. They may be linked with a leased line, privately operated, or a public dial-up line. As will be discussed later, a leased line is cheaper if the line is to be in use for a high enough proportion of the time. The leased line in Fig. 3.2 connects three links, and there must be some form of switch at *B* to enable *A* to be connected to *B*, *B* to *C*, or *A* to *C*.

When more than a few terminals are used, some form of logic is needed to establish interconnections between them automatically. Consider the seven terminals shown in Fig. 3.3. One way to connect them would be as in Fig. 3.4. Here the shortest line interconnecting all seven terminals has been used. A line like this, with more than one device attached to it, is referred to as a *multidrop* line.

This line may be designed so that when a message is transmitted by A, the electrical impulses that travel on the line are received by all the other six. However, only one of the six takes any notice of them, for it has been informed that the message is meant for it. The others, not so informed, ignore. This process may be achieved by sending an addressing message before the data message or, alternately, tagging an address on to the front of the data message itself. Each terminal then has a logic circuit that searches for its own address. In such a scheme, only one terminal may be permitted to transmit at once; and so it is normal for one of the locations to have a controlling device, which, like a traffic policeman, instructs the terminals when they may transmit.

Another way of interconnecting the seven terminals is illustrated in Fig. 3.5. Here all the terminals are connected to a switch, like a telephone exchange. Any terminal user can dial any other terminal, like a telephone subscriber. The total line distance in Fig. 3.5 is greater than that in Fig. 3.4, which may not matter if the lines are short. If they are long, it will mean that the Fig. 3.5 configuration is substantially more expensive than that of Fig. 3.4. However, the exchange

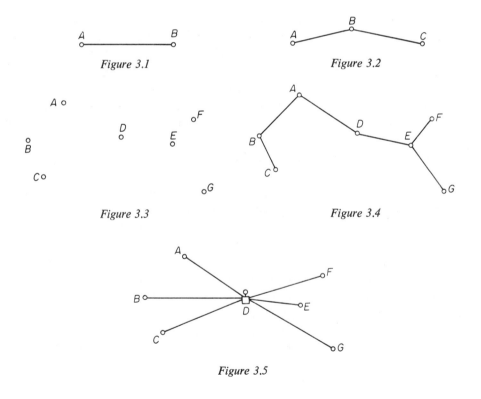

Figure 3.1

Figure 3.2

Figure 3.3

Figure 3.4

Figure 3.5

at $D$ will have more than one path through it, so that more than one pair of terminals can be interconnected at once. $A$ can transmit to $F$, while $E$ transmits to $C$.

When large numbers of terminals are connected by leased communication lines, the network configuration becomes complex. Figure 3.6 shows terminals in more than 100 cities on the eastern side of the United States, connected to a computer center at Chicago. In designing such a network, it is desirable to

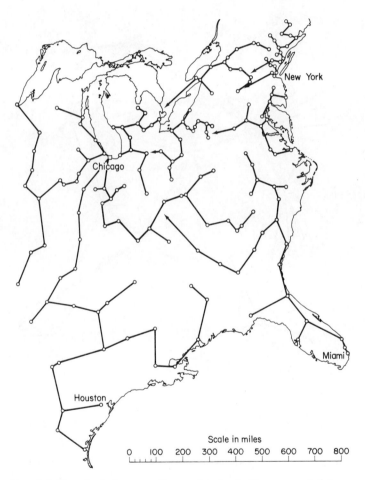

*Fig. 3.6.* Terminals in more than a hundred cities connected to a computer center at Chicago via multidrop lines. The layout results from a minimum-cost calculation. *Note:* Lines with C4 conditioning can only have up to three segments in series. Lines in certain countries other than North America cannot have as many drop points as are shown here.

achieve the minimum line cost within the constraints of the other requirements, such as response time, which are discussed in this chapter. Lines with C4 conditioning (explained later) can only have up to three line segments in series. Certain countries other than North America place restrictions on the number of drop points that a multidrop line can have.

A wide variety of network configurations can be used in a system like the one illustrated in Fig. 3.6. Figure 3.7 shows the same terminals connected to

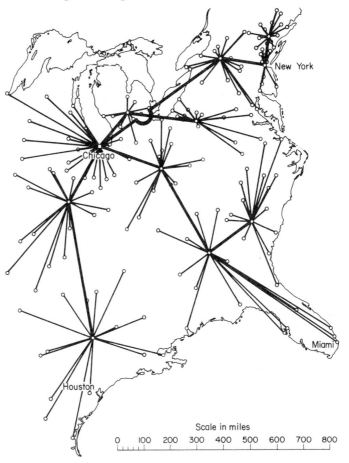

*Fig. 3.7.* The same terminals as in Fig. 3.6 connected to Chicago by means of a network with concentrators. Here, again, a minimum-cost calculation that meets the design constraints must be performed.

concentration locations with point-to-point rather than multipoint lines. We will discuss the pros and cons of different types of network organizations, and the calculations needed for designing them, later on.

In many systems no network is laid down as in the figures cited because the terminal users always *dial* the computer center on a public network. Several different line types and tariffs are available for public dial-up use. A consideration of them will always form part of the problem of how the system is interconnected.

**IN-PLANT AND OUT-PLANT LINES**  Communication lines that run exclusively within a user's premises can be laid down by the user rather than leased from a telephone company. These lines are referred to as *in-plant* lines and those going outside the premises are called *out-plant* lines.

The user thus has three categories: in-plant lines, which have been privately installed; private out-plant lines, which are leased from a common carrier; and public lines, such as the public or telegraph networks.

An organization, or perhaps a group of organizations, that frequently needs to transmit over long distances will often use private leased lines, for such lines are cheaper than dial-up public lines, with today's tariffs. An illustration of how this trade-off is calculated will be given in Chapter 41. On the other hand, if the lines are short (i.e., within one city), or their usage is low, it may be cheaper to use the public network.

Table 3.1 illustrates the line categories that might be used in different situations; the bold face letters indicate the preferred alternative.

**Table 3.1.** POSSIBLE LINE CATEGORIES *

| | Lines within One Organization | Lines Shared by Several Organizations | Public Utilities |
|---|---|---|---|
| Within one building or complex | **I**, *L*, *P* | **I**, *L*, *P* | **I**, *L*, *P* |
| Within one city | *L*, **P** | *L*, **P** | **P** |
| Nationwide links | **L**, *P* | **L**, *P* | **P** |
| International links | **L**, *P* | **L**, *P* | **P** |

* I = In-plant;  L = Leased, out-plant;  P = Public.

**TIME AND QUANTITY**  As we commented in the previous chapter, both the quantity of data in a single transmission and the time available to deliver it vary enormously. These two factors determine the speed of transmission line that is necessary. We can, in fact, take Fig. 2.2 from the previous chapter and draw line speeds that are available on the chart. This is done in Fig. 3.8.

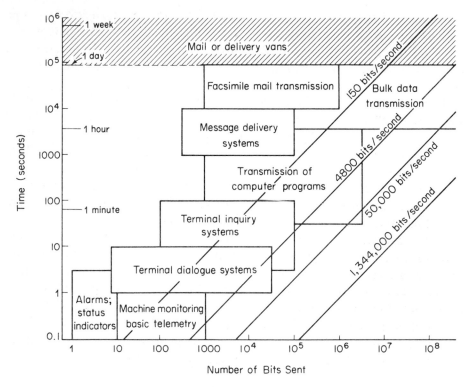

*Fig. 3.8.* Desirable delivery time or response time and quantity of data for typical uses of data transmission today as it relates to four available line speeds. The speed requirements of the computer industry are likely to change, however.

Four line speeds are shown: a teletype line of 150 bits per second, a voice-grade line used at 4800 bits per second, a wideband line of 50,000 bits per second, and, the basic bit rate of the T1 carrier line[1] 1,344,000 bits per second.

Most of the blocks representing today's uses of data transmission do not intersect the line speed of 50,000 bits per second. This fact is perhaps not surprising because the 50,000-bits-per-second speed has not been generally available; it has been available only on a limited basis. If a switched network at this speed had been widely available for the last ten years at appropriate cost, the utilization of teleprocessing would probably have developed differently. It is a chicken-and-egg argument: Which comes first, the line facility or the market demand for it? Future uses of data transmission will be mentioned in Chapter 17.

[1] See James Martin, *Future Developments in Telecommunications*, Prentice-Hall, Englewood Cliffs, N.J., 1971.

**SWITCHING**
**REQUIREMENTS**
In many systems a terminal is installed for one purpose only; it will communicate with only one computer system. This is the case with many terminals for special commercial functions, such as those in banks, airlines, stockbrokers, and those forming parts of specialized information systems. Sometimes terminals on general-purpose time-sharing systems are installed to communicate with one computer only. In other cases, however, a terminal can be linked to many different computers. If such is the case, there must be some means of switching the connection between the different machines. The most common way of doing so today is to use the public telephone network. The operator dials the telephone number of the computer he needs, and his terminal is then connected to it. A terminal used by one person for programming in APL on one computer may be used by another for PL/I on a different computer. A secretary may dial a text-editing computer on it. Another person dials statistical services, and so on.

Although the public telephone network is useful for switching the connection, because of the ubiquitousness of the telephone connections, other switching means may be used to give access to machines within a building complex or within a corporation. The latter are constructed from leased or privately installed facilities. The need for communication with more than one computer center is a parameter that will affect the design.

**BUSY**
**SIGNAL**
In a switched network there will be a certain probability of receiving a "busy" signal. The busy signal may occur because the computer dialed has no more free ports or because there are no free trunks or paths through an exchange. The systems analyst must determine what probability of being denied access to the computer is acceptable and must then design the trunks, exchanges, and computer facilities so as to achieve this condition.

**AVAILABILITY**
**OF TERMINALS**
A somewhat similar question arises where a user community is provided with a terminal room. In a laboratory, for example, each person may not have his own terminal but may instead go to a communal group of terminals. What is the probability that he will not find a terminal free when he wants one? Again the systems analyst must determine what grade of service he wants to achieve and on this basis do a probability calculation to determine the number of terminals he will employ.

**LINE CONTENTION**
**AND QUEUING**
Where several terminals are attached to one line, as in Fig. 3.4, not all of them can transmit at the same time. When the line is in use and another terminal wants it, there will be no busy signal. Instead there will be a waiting time. The terminal wanting the line waits until it becomes free. If the messages are short and the line speed is high, the waiting times will be short. The organization of the line will affect the terminal response times. The systems analyst should evaluate the probabilities of obtaining different response times and should adjust the line configuration so that it is in keeping with his users' time requirements.

**LINE**
**TURNAROUND**
**TIME**
If a conventional roll-call polling mechanism is used, as will be explained in Chapter 19, there will be a large number of line turnarounds in the organization of a line, such as that in Fig. 3.4. In other words, the direction of transmission will frequently be reversed as the polling messages travel backward and forward. The response time in this case will become dependent on the line turnaround time. Some of the modems that enable data to be transmitted over a telephone or other line have a lengthy turnaround time. This is an additional factor to be considered in the network design.

**ERROR**
**RATES**
A certain number of errors will occur in data transmitted over telecommunication lines. For most types of lines, statistics are available giving the distributions of error rates that can be expected. On some systems the numbers of errors that can be expected from the terminal operators far exceed those caused by line errors, and the same checking means may be used for dealing with both operator errors and line errors. When the data originate from a machine, however, we generally expect their transmission to be correct. Error-detecting or error-correcting codes will be employed. Error-detecting codes give the higher measure of safety. When they are used and an error is detected, the message containing it will be retransmitted. If a large number of errors occur, a large amount of time will be spent in retransmission. This situation can be controlled by adjusting the block size that is transmitted and by selecting transmission means with appropriate speed and error characteristics. Such factors are also under the control of the system designer.

**NETWORK**
**AVAILABILITY**
In some systems it is necessary to have a high degree of certainty of obtaining access to the computer. This is true in military systems and it is important on some commercial systems as well. In order to achieve a high system avail-

ability, the computers, and sometimes the data on the files, are duplicated. It is also necessary to design a communication network that will not fail to establish the necessary connection.

In such cases, leased lines which do not pass through switching equipment are normally used. Several terminals are often connected to one leased line, as in Figs. 3.4 or 3.6, or concentrators may be used, as in Fig. 3.7. Every such line will enter the computer so that there is no possibility of blocking. In this way, the possibility of receiving busy signals is eliminated.

A further problem remains—that of line failure. If the probability of leased-line failure is deemed inacceptably high, then alternative routing must be planned. The public network may be used to provide backup to a leased-line system.

**MULTIPLE**
**USAGE**
Leased communication lines and equipment are used for many systems in commercial and other organizations. Many different types of computer system are in use in some organizations, and it is becoming increasingly desirable that they should *share* the leased communication facilities, because doing so is a key to cost reduction. There are a variety of ways in which a leased network can be constructed in order that it can be shared by different systems. These methods will be discussed in Section IV.

# 4 THE MASTER PLAN

A corporation using data transmission extensively today is likely to have a wide diversity of needs. It will use both real-time systems and batch data transmission. It may use many of the categories of system shown in Fig. 2.2. Different real-time systems may have fundamentally different modes of operation. And these operational methods may carry out entirely separate functions and be largely unrelated in their structure and design.

Ideally and theoretically, it would be better to have one integrated network that carries out all the corporation's information transmission. Voice and data could travel over the same network. A method of carrying telephone transmission is being used increasingly in which the sound is converted into a stream of bits (pulse code modulation). Under certain circumstances, there are major economic advantages in pulse code modulation, and the arguments in favor of it will increase as the cost of digital logic drops. (See the author's *Future Developments in Telecommunications*.) An integrated network could consist of either (1) analog telephone lines in which the data have to be converted into an analog form by means of a modem at each end of the line (discussed in Chapter 14) or (2) digital lines in which telephone transmission is converted into a digital form (pulse code modulation) by telephone company equipment. Today most lines are analog in construction and data have to be converted into an analog form. In the future, an increasing proportion of lines will be digital, thus requiring no modems. A corporate network will probably have both lines that are analog in construction and lines that are digital. Eventually, when more advanced public data-transmissions facilities are working and when pulse code modulation is the rule rather than the exception, the corporation may have one integrated system.

For the years immediately ahead, however, an increasing proliferation seems more likely.

**REASONS**
**FOR SEPARATE**
**NETWORKS**
Many large corporations today have a proliferation of separate networks. The proliferation has grown up over a period of years with a variety of reasons for installing new facilities without dismantling the old. A new computer system is installed with its own particular requirements. It is economic for it to use new transmission facilities rather than an extension of the old ones, but the old ones are still in use for a different purpose and are not dismantled. There are also *current* reasons for using separate networks, and these are based on the cost of contemporary technology. In particular, they are dependent on the tariff structures. Some computer systems need the speed of wideband links (40,800 bits per second or more). Others can operate at voice-line speeds (4800 bits per second, typically). Many require only teletype speeds (less than 150 bits per second). Use of multiplexers, concentrators, and message-switching systems at these different speeds can be combined, but often it is more economical or more convenient to have separate networks.

Again, some data transmission devices need the communication line continuously or very frequently, and it is economic for them to have a private leased line. Others need the connection only occasionally, so that the lowest-cost answer is a dial-up line.

Where a corporation has many calls, data or voice, between certain locations, it will use a mechanism for switching separate calls onto leased lines connecting these points. This step can be handled either by switching the lines themselves with private exchanges, as in a tie-line network, or it can be done by a message-switching network. It can be done by data networks using multiplexing or packet-switching (explained in Section IV). We thus have several alternative methods of interconnecting terminals and computers.

1. Permanently connected leased lines
2. Message switching on a leased-line network
3. Dial-up on a switched network constructed with leased lines
4. A data network using multiplexing or packet-switching
5. Dial-up on the public network
6. Privately installed in-plant lines

Relative costs, as well as response-time requirements, should determine which method is used (see Section VI).

Many corporations make a substantial use of leased voice lines. In this case, the voice tie-line network may become a major factor in designing the data transmission facilities. Often, however, the data transmission network is set up independently.

Probably, however, the most important reason for the growth of separate transmission networks concerns the difficulty of implementing complex computer systems. A data processing team does not implement all the systems required by a large corporation in one gigantic integrated step. Doing so would be far too complex. Instead, the corporate data processing facilities evolve step by step, each step being a new system or a change to an existing system, which can be implemented by the available staff. If the staff attempt to bite off more than they can chew at any one step, then grave difficulties lie ahead. On the other hand, in a large corporation, several steps may be proceeding simultaneously. The result is a patchwork of different computer systems interlinked in a variety of different ways.

**MASTER PLAN**     Although the different systems will evolve separately, it is desirable that, as far as possible, the data processing designers have a master plan for the future evolution of data processing in their organization. Only in this way can there be an adequate measure of compatibility between the systems. This is particularly important in systems for performing commercial or administrative operations. Without such advanced planning, the systems become more difficult to link together, often more difficult for the terminal operators to use, more cumbersome in the data base planning, and more expensive in application of resources and in telecommunication costs.

Adherence to a neatly conceived master plan has rarely been achieved in reality. The state of the art is moved by unpredictable tides and their pressures are strong enough to distort the best-laid plans. A certain machine or software package suddenly becomes available. One approach works and another fails. Natural selection takes over, and we have a process of evolution dominated by the survival of whatever is the most practical.

The master plan, then, must not be too rigid. It must be permissible for different systems to evolve in their own ways. The master plan may call for defined interfaces between separately evolving systems. The separate systems should each be of a level of complexity that is currently practicable.

Components of the plan should be designed, as far as possible, with proliferation in mind. System $X$ in Fig. 4.1 is developed in isolation of other systems, perhaps at a plant location. It is then linked to system B. This step works successfully, and each of eight plants then installs a version of system $X$

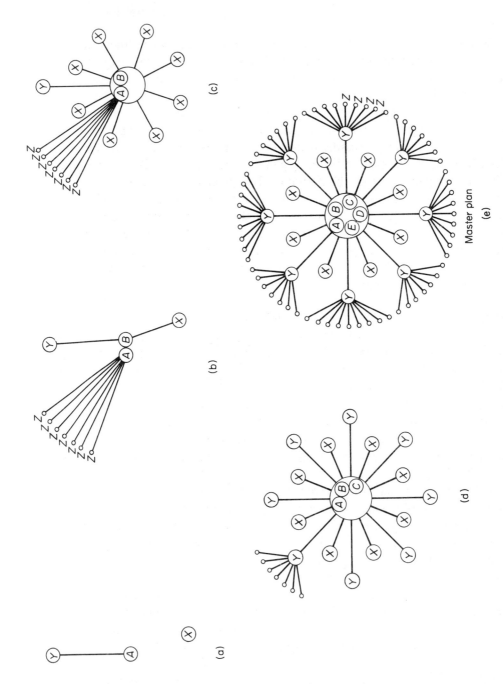

*Fig. 4.1.* As far as possible, the individual computer systems should be developed with an overall master plan in mind.

with a link to the central installation. Each system $X$ will be modified appropriately for local conditions, and it is important to design the original so as to facilitate this modification. The connection of the locations labeled $Z$ to $A$ is superseded by an improvement that links them via system $Y$. This improvement is allowed to take place before the other $Z$ locations are connected.

Systems in real life sometimes evolve conceptually like Fig. 4.1 but certainly do not have its artificial neatness. The figures in the following chapter piece together the systems using data transmission that typically coexist in a large progressive corporation today.

A master plan for the communication network may exist separately from a master plan for the evolution of systems. Its purpose would be to lower the overall cost of the corporation's data transmission and other telecommunication links. Designers of new systems would be expected to use the planned communication facilities where it was reasonable for them to do so. The saving can be worthwhile, especially in large nationwide corporations, which often spend many millions of dollars per month on telecommunications. A large part of the saving comes from the "bulk-buying" of bundles of lines.

As Section IV will indicate, there are a variety of different ways in which a data network can be constructed to meet the needs of different types of users.

This problem is similar in some ways to the problem of how best to construct a *public* switched data network. A variety of designs for public data networks have been proposed. Most of the design alternatives could also be incorporated into a private corporate network.

# 5 THE TRANSMISSION NETWORKS IN A LARGE CORPORATION

With the comments of the preceding chapter in mind, let us now sketch the types of transmission networks in use in a large American corporation. The figures in this chapter show the separate systems using data transmission that have been separately designed. (The systems described are fictional but are based on the systems of an existing corporation, simplified somewhat for reasons of clarity.)

The systems shown cover the information needs of the corporation from selling the products and maintaining them, to deciding what to manufacture, giving instructions to the plants, and controlling the manufacturing process. They handle accounting operations, provide networks for relaying administrative messages between most corporate locations and data between computer locations, and gather together many types of information for management, which they endeavor to make conveniently accessible. In addition, they provide terminal services for staff ranging from scientists to secretaries and give remote batch access to large computers.

There is little doubt that the proliferation of networks shown will be tidied up eventually. However, doing so is not easy and is unlikely to happen in the next few years. The evolutionary growth of complex systems is becoming untidy and, for reasons concerned with practical implementation, often deviates from theoretically neat concepts. As in nature, entropy tends to increase.

### 1. *Administrative Message Switching Network (Fig. 5.1)*

Figure 5.1 shows the first of the corporation's separate data networks. This network was the first to be installed and remains separate from those

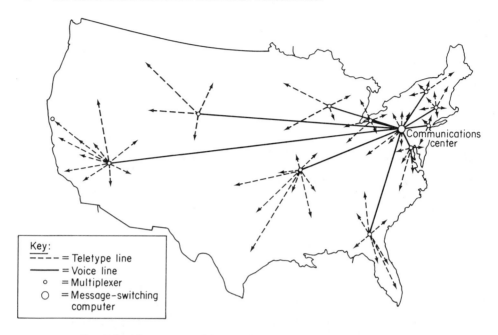

*Fig. 5.1. Administrative Message-Switching Network.* A system linking leased teletype lines from major corporate locations to a communications center, in which administrative messages are forwarded by a message-switching computer. Several teletype channels are multiplexed onto the leased voice lines, and many terminals may be "multidropped" on each teletype channel.

installed later. Its purpose is to relay messages from any major location in the corporation to any other, at high speed. Such locations have machines like teleprinters for receiving or transmitting the messages. A message will normally reach its destination in a few minutes. The sending of a message is equivalent to the sending of a commercial cable except that it is quicker and more accurate, and the messages are stored for future reference and can be broadcast to many locations. More important, the overall cost per message is substantially lower than that of commercial cables.

### 2. *Switched Wideband Network* (*Fig. 5.2*)

While the network in Fig. 5.1 is primarily for *people* sending messages to *people*, the one in Fig. 5.2 is for computers sending data to computers. Some but not all of the main computer installations are linked to this network. It differs from Fig. 5.1 in two major respects. First, it uses line switching, not message switching. In other words, the lines are *physically* switched at the

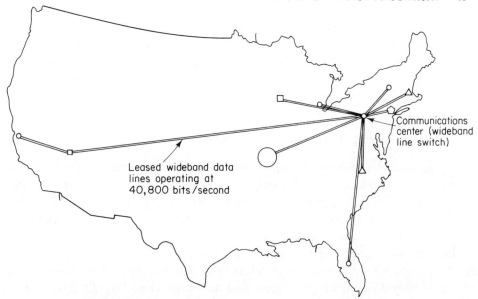

*Fig. 5.2. Switched Wideband Network.* Major computer centers can establish a high-capacity link between one another by dialing on a private leased wideband network, with a small, private exchange.

communications center. Second, the speed of transmission is high: 40,800 bits per second, whereas the teletype lines of Fig. 5.1 transmit at less than 150 bits per second. The mode of transmission between the computers is typically from magnetic tape to magnetic tape, or disk to disk.

Large quantities of information have to be transferred, hence the line speed used. Switched public transmission facilities at these speeds do not yet exist except between a small number of city locations.

Any computer installation on this network can dial any other just like dialing a telephone number; and when the connection is obtained, transmission can begin. The switching is done by a small and inexpensive wideband exchange.

### 3. *The Telephone Tie-Line Network*

A network of switched private lines exists for telephone calls. This tie-line network is accessed from an office telephone by dialing 8, next a three-digit code identifying the location, and then the extension number at that location. The reason for using leased lines instead of the public telephone service is that this process lowers the overall cost of telephone calls, just as the network in Fig. 5.1 lowers the overall cost of sending cables.

Telephone lines, either public or on the tie-line network, can carry data at a speed of 2400 bits per second or more by using appropriate modems (data sets). Thus a terminal location can dial any computer that will accept its call, via the public network or the tie-line network. The number of tie lines between certain points has been substantially increased as a result of data usage.

### 4. *Engineering Division System (Fig. 5.3)*

In addition to general-purpose facilities, such as the preceding three, there are telecommunication-based computer systems for carrying out specific functions. Often these are real-time systems in which certain response-time criteria have to be met—a concern of much of the remainder of the book. Such systems are likely to have their own data transmission network, constructed from leased lines and used for that application exclusively.

Figure 5.3 shows systems installed in the three regions of the corporation's engineering division to give support to field engineers. Initially a system was installed in one region on a pilot basis and, when successful, was duplicated in the other two regions. The field engineers can obtain a variety of services from the

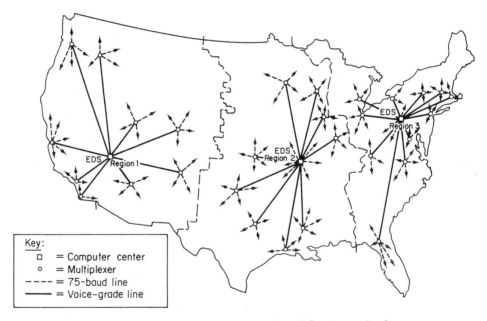

Key:
- □ = Computer center
- ○ = Multiplexer
- ---- = 75-baud line
- ——— = Voice-grade line

*Fig. 5.3. Engineering Division System.* A real-time network of typewriter-like terminals for field engineers giving them technical assistance, assuring the maintenance schedules are met, and for maintaining inventory control of spare parts required. Engineers send detailed reports of failures and repair activity to the regional computers.

low-speed terminals. For instance, they can make inquiries about technical information and, in some cases, receive lengthy instructions.

They can order components that are needed and obtain delivery-time estimates. They report full details of all failures. The computers analyze the failure reports and the repair activity. They maintain inventory control of the spare parts kept at all the locations in each region, with terminals being used for this purpose in all the stores, where spare parts are kept.

### 5. *Sales Administration System (Fig. 5.4)*

A separate real-time system providing display screen terminals in the branch offices was installed by the sales division.

These terminals are used to enter details of all orders taken, of all customer payments, and of all customer requirements, such as training course bookings.

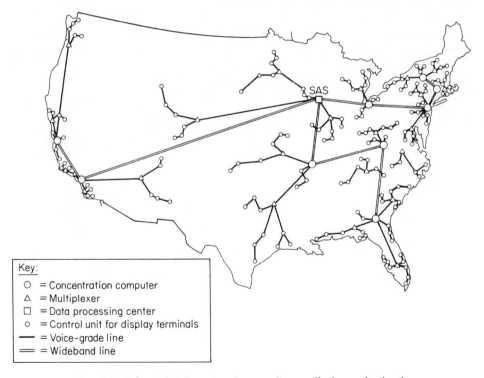

Key:
- ○ = Concentration computer
- △ = Multiplexer
- □ = Data processing center
- o = Control unit for display terminals
- — = Voice-grade line
- = = Wideband line

*Fig. 5.4. Sales Administration System.* Screen-display units in the branch offices give a response time from the data processing center of about 2 seconds. The screens are used for customer-proposed planning, for sales-order entry, for filing details about customer payments and requirements, and for inquiries about customer or order status.

The sales staff can inquire about the status of all orders. The branch offices now have little of the paperwork that they required before this system was installed, and much clerical and administrative manpower has been saved. Customer inquiries can be answered immediately. Details of sales proposals can be planned, priced, and varied—with the aid of the computer—before the proposal is made. This process is valuable, for the proposals are highly complex. The computer will check that the items proposed conform to regulations and constraints applicable at that time. The availability of the computer screens in the branch offices means that more complex selling can be contemplated in future plans. The communications network again consists of permanently leased lines; however, the configuration is very different from the one in Fig. 5.3. Voice lines link the screen units to concentration computers, and the latter are linked to the Sales Administration System computers with wideband lines. The network is designed so that the terminal users receive a response time of about 2 seconds to most of their terminal actions.

6. *Evening Transmission on the SAS Wideband Lines (Fig. 5.5)*

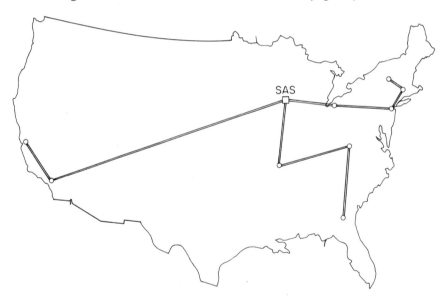

Fig. 5.5. *Sales Administration System (evening transmission).* After the branch offices shut down, the concentration computers of this diagram, at district centers, become batch-processing machines with direct-access files and high-speed printers. The wideband links to the Sales Administration System data processing center are used for transmitting data to them for customer mailings and for back-up purposes.

When the branch offices close down, the concentration computers are no longer needed to service them and therefore are used for general data processing.

These computers, shown in Fig. 5.5, have direct-access files and high-speed printers. The wideband lines linking these devices to the central installation of the Sales Administration System are used for batch transmission. Invoices and other documents are composed, mailed, and controlled at the district centers where the concentration computers are located. Backup information in case of failure is stored at the district centers, and this information is transmitted to them at night from the data processing center.

### 7. The Manufacturing Central System (Fig. 5.6)

The corporation has several manufacturing plants. The planning of what should be manufactured takes place centrally at the location of one of the largest plants and is handled with the aid of a data processing system called the Manufacturing Central System.

The input for the decision of what to manufacture comes from market forecasts, and from day-to-day knowledge of what orders have been taken and what spare parts are needed. The latter two are kept by the Sales Administra-

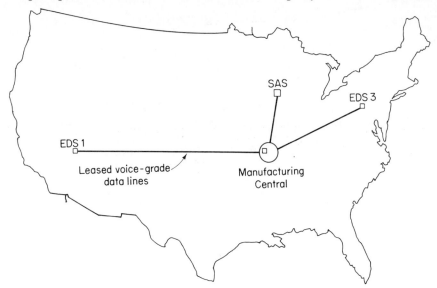

Fig. 5.6. Manufacturing Central System. Central planning of what is to be manufactured is carried out by this system. The Sales Administration System and the Engineering Division Systems are linked to the Manufacturing Central location by leased voice-grade data lines.

tion System (SAS) and the Engineering Division Systems (EDS). These are transmitted, once daily, to the Manufacturing Central System.

The Manufacturing Central System, in return, transmits details of the manufacturing status of orders and when they will be completed to the SAS and EDS systems.

Voice lines are used for these transmissions. The transmissions are sufficiently long that leased lines give a lower telecommunication cost than the use of public telephone lines. The leased voice lines shown in Fig. 5.6 are therefore permanently connected.

### 8. *Transmission to the Plant Information Systems* (*Fig. 5.7*)

The Manufacturing Central System does a breakdown or "explosion" of orders received and spare parts required, into requirements for separate machines or subsystems. These requirements, together with the sales forecast and knowledge of the manufacturing lead time, enable it to calculate orders to be placed on the manufacturing plants.

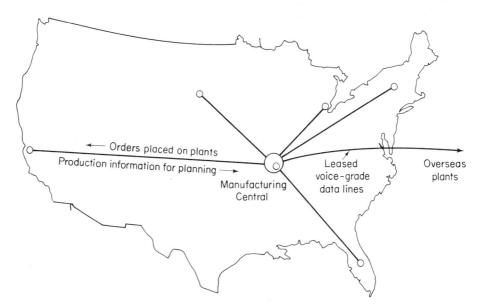

*Fig. 5.7. Leased Lines to Plant Information Systems.* Leased voice-grade lines carry orders of what to manufacture to the plant computers. The Manufacturing Central System has determined these orders. Production information for planning is transmitted from the plant computers to the Central system. The staff at the Manufacturing Central location can interrogate the data files kept at the plant locations.

A two-way interchange takes place between the Manufacturing Central System and the data processing systems at the plants. The former sends the plants orders of what to manufacture. The plants return progress details, estimates of completion dates, and information about plant schedules which will aid the central planning process.

The orders are now processed by the plant computer. Here breakdowns into individual components are fed into the production shop schedules. The plant computers maintain files giving order and stock status, plus other files that can be interrogated by the staff at the manufacturing central location.

The information interchange between the plant computers and the Manufacturing Central System again takes place over leased voice lines, for reasons of cost.

### 9. *The Plant Production Control System (Fig. 5.8)*

A real-time system exists in each plant to collect data from the shop floor on the status of each job, worker, machine tool, or other facility. This system operates side by side with the batch-processing system, which plans the production schedules, handles the payroll, and so on. The shop-floor workers enter

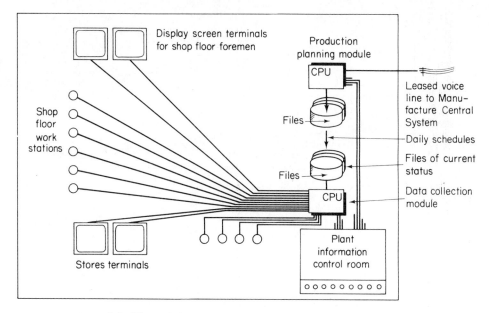

*Fig. 5.8. Plant Information Systems.* The production planning module primarily executes batch runs to determine what components to manufacture and to establish daily production schedules. The other, real-time, computer collects data from the shop floor that are used in controlling the production.

details of each job as they start and finish it, or if they leave it for any reason. Foremen with display screens see the work schedules that the computer has planned and modify them, using their terminal, if they have reason to. The work allocated to the machine tools is reshuffled by the computer when circumstances necessitate a change.

An information control room has terminals linked to each computer and a skilled staff who assist in controlling the flow of work through the factory. The staff deal with exceptions and answer management questions.

The communication links used in the plant are privately installed and maintained. The only common carrier link is the leased line between the batch computer and the Manufacturing Central System.

10. *The Corporate Management Data Bank* (*Fig. 5.9*)

A large data bank of corporate information is kept at the corporate headquarters in New York. This bank contains details of personnel salaries, sales,

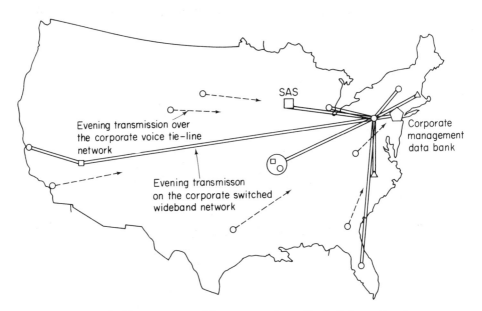

*Fig. 5.9. The Corporate Management Data Bank.* Information is transmitted daily from various data processing locations to the corporate headquarters building, which houses the corporate management data bank. This information is then processed, summarized, statistically analyzed, and stored for ready access. The data are transmitted over the switched wideband network (Fig. 5.2), where this network serves the location in question. Otherwise it is sent over the corporate voice tie-line network.

forecasts, customers, suppliers, and other relevant information. It is organized in such a way that a variety of management questions can be answered as quickly as possible, and this necessitates a file organization quite different to that of the separate systems, where the information is compiled (e.g., the Sales Administration System). Much of the data are processed to provide summaries and statistical digests in anticipation of management needs.

The corporate management data bank is built up from information transmitted daily from the plant locations, the Manufacturing Central System, the Sales Administration System, the laboratory locations, and several other sources. Transmission to this system takes place over the switched wideband network, where possible. Some locations, however, are not connected to this network. In general, such sites have smaller quantities of information to send, so it is transmitted over the corporate voice tie lines.

### 11. *The Corporate Information Center (Fig. 5.10)*

The mission of the Corporate Information Center is to provide the information needed by functional and strategic management. Much of this information

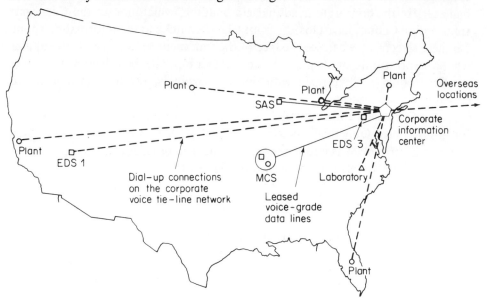

*Fig. 5.10. Corporate Information Center.* The corporate information center, set up to provide immediate information for functional and strategic management, frequently needs real-time access to other systems. The staff of the center need to converse with the staff of the other information centers. The volume of this traffic warrants two leased lines, as shown. Other such interchanges are via dial-up connections on the corporate voice tie-line network.

is needed "immediately" or at least very quickly by the management in question. A group of specialists in the center are familiar with all the sources designed to satisfy this need. Much of the information comes from the files maintained at the information center, such as the management data bank mentioned above. However, for many queries, it is necessary to go farther afield and inspect other files or question the staff of other information centers.

Each plant has an information center for its own management (see Fig. 5.10). The Manufacturing Central System has a group of specialists who are able to interrogate its files, and so has the Sales Administration System. The staff of the Corporate Information Center call on these specialists when necessary, converse with them, and link their terminals into their systems.

In some cases, the staff of the specialized systems do the file interrogation with their own terminals and then switch the results on to the terminals of the Corporate Information Center. The staff here, in turn, display the information they have located on the screens or terminals used by management. Several mechanisms for doing so exist. The manager in question may have a compatible terminal, and so the data are switched for display on it. There may be a low-speed printer in his locality, thus providing him with a print-out. Many of the managers in the corporate headquarters building, which houses the Corporate Information Center, have closed-circuit television links to the information room. On these screens they can see the face of the staff member who assists them, plus whatever print-outs or displays he may generate. The boardroom and other meeting rooms are equipped with display terminals, printing terminals, and closed-circuit television.

The Corporate Information Center needs real-time links to other systems for this purpose. Only the links to the SAS and MCS are used frequently enough to make a permanent leased line economical. The other locations are accessed by a dial-up telephone line, as shown in Fig. 5.10.

### 12. *Time-Sharing Computer Services* (*Fig. 5.11*)

Time-sharing computers provide a variety of services to corporate employees by means of typewriterlike terminals operating at below 150 bits per second. Included are text-editing and document preparation services for secretaries, elaborate desk calculator facilities, a statistical analysis package, and on-line computer programming facilities. Users can maintain their own files at the computer center. Some scientists and secretaries have such terminals at their desks, and in many locations there is a room with communally used terminals.

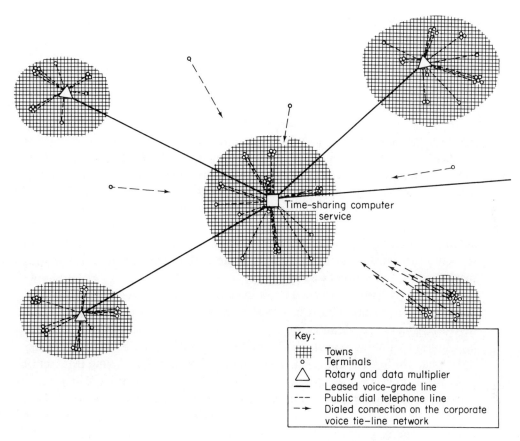

*Fig. 5.11. Time-Sharing Computer Services.* Terminals that may dial a time-sharing computer provide services which include text editing, document-preparation facilities, elaborate desk calculator facilities, a statistical analysis package, and on-line programming.

The computer, and occasionally different computers, can be dialed from the terminals. At present such computer systems cover a community of users in a limited geographical area. Several such systems exist in different parts of the country. Users in the same city as the computer location dial it on the public telephone network or, sometimes, on tie lines. Users in certain distant cities dial a number that connects them to a leased voice line shared among many users by means of time-division multiplexing (Fig. 5.11). The dialed call reaches a scanning device that searches for a free data channel on the multiplexed link (shown as a Δ symbol on Fig. 5.11). This leased-line facility serves only those locations with a suitably high density of users. Locations without such a line may dial the computer directly, either on the public network or on the corporate tie-line network.

**INTEGRATION OF THE NETWORKS**

All the systems described are rapidly evolving. It is possible, for example, that the time-sharing systems may become nationwide. They will probably also become hierarchical with a lesser local computer attached to the terminals having the ability to request help from a higher-level machine. The lesser computer may obtain specialized programs from the higher-level machine; it may pass lengthy calculations on to a powerful "number cruncher"; or it may request up-to-date information from a central data bank.

For "job shop" batch processing also, a network of computers may be used. An experimental system that links a number of very large machines for load sharing is in use. If one computer is heavily loaded, certain jobs will automatically be transferred to distant computers. The user will not know which machine his job was processed on.

Eventually there must be a "rationalization" of these assorted data transmission requirements. One form that it might take is a corporate-wide data network, which all systems can use, consisting of high-capacity data trunks and high-speed switching facilities. Computer-controlled switching facilities exist today that are fast enough to give automatic switching of real-time transactions and still achieve very short response times. If public networks that give fast enough switching or high enough transmission capacity to the locations in question do not exist, a network may be built with private leased lines and privately operated exchanges or switching computers. In time public data transmission facilities will no doubt develop to a stage where they can be used to provide the transmission for the applications described in this chapter. Such facilities, however, seem to be many years in the future. Even when available, it may still be less expensive for a corporation to build its own data transmission "utility" from leased lines. Corporate networks of this type are discussed in Section IV.

SECTION

USER CONSIDERATIONS

# 6 TERMINAL-USER CONSIDERATIONS

When the terminal is manned, human operating factors must always be taken into consideration. In some systems they are not a dominating consideration; they would not be, for example, with a terminal designed for the batch transmission of punched cards. In some real-time systems, however, the human factors become all important because success or failure depends on how well men can communicate with the system and it with them.

Where the system is primarily oriented toward communication with human beings, the design may well *begin* with the planning of the man-machine interface. This will determine the types of terminal used, the communication line speeds, the probability of obtaining the desired service at the first attempt, and the response times to be achieved. These factors, in turn, will lead, as we shall see, to different choices in the *structure* of the data transmission network.

In this chapter we will summarize some of the user considerations and then will discuss them in more detail in the remainder of this section. The author's book *Design of Man-Computer Dialogue* deals with this vital topic in more detail. Our conclusions concerning the man-machine interface will influence many of the more technical decisions discussed in subsequent sections of this book.

### 1. Dedicated or Casual Operator?

On some real-time systems, the operator spends the whole of her working day sitting in front of the terminal. This operator can be specially trained for the job, perhaps with a lengthy training program. She will have plenty of time to practice her interaction with the machine, to learn its language, and to become accustomed to its idiosyncrasies.

On other systems, the terminal is used only occasionally by someone, like a salesman or a manager, who spends most of his day doing entirely different work. This person is not highly trained in terminal usage. He will be easily confused by unclear terminal responses and easily frustrated by lengthy response times. It is probable that an increasing proportion of terminal operators will fall into this category in the years ahead. For them, the man-machine interface must be designed to appear as *natural* as possible; otherwise bewilderment will quickly turn into annoyance, criticism, or behavior that amounts to rejection of the system.

As we shall see, the man-machine conversation is often designed very differently for these two categories, and the difference in design will affect the organization of the communication line network.

### 2. *Operator with Programming Skills?*

On some terminals, the operator uses a programming language. It may be one of the standard programming languages and a set of program statements devised for the application. On the majority of terminals for commercial use, however, programming is not used.

Operator skills might be categorized as in Table 6.1, and for each division of the table the conversation structure would be different.

**Table 6.1.** OPERATOR SKILLS

|  | Dedicated Operator | Casual Operator |
|---|---|---|
| Operator with programming skills |  |  |
| Nonprogrammer operator with high IQ and detailed training |  |  |
| Nonprogrammer operator without high IQ but with detailed training |  |  |
| Operator with little training |  |  |
| Totally untrained operator |  |  |

## 3. *Media Used*

The most common means for input at a terminal for human interaction are a keyboard, switches, knobs, a badge reader, or a light pen. The most common means for output are printing, display of characters on a screen, display of lines or curves of a screen, display of photographic images—for example, from slides or film frames at the terminal—voice answerback, and combinations of these devices.

The systems analyst must select the most suitable media for his particular application, taking into consideration terminal cost, communication network cost, and user psychology.

## 4. *Language and Response Structure*

Having selected the media, the analyst then plans the language and response structure. What exactly will the man say to the machine and in what form, exactly, will it respond?

There are endless possible structures for terminal conversations. The choice will depend on the nature of the application, the terminal, and the categories of operator. In the planning of terminal applications, other than the simplest, it has generally taken many months to define the input and response structure. The more successfully this is done, the greater the chance of the system being widely accepted and efficiently employed by its users.

If we narrow our observations to a system on which the input and the responses are alphanumeric, we can categorize a variety of techniques for facilitating man-machine conversation. It will usually be true that techniques designed to make the terminal as easy as possible to use will result in many more characters being transmitted. On a far-flung system, this situation can result, as we shall see, in a much more expensive communication network.

## 5. *Speed of Terminal*

The speed of the terminal has a major effect on its possible interactive users. Suppose that a response of 500 characters must be sent. This might be a well-formatted table, so that many of the characters are blanks. With a teleprinter operating at 7.5 characters per second, the time taken to print this response would be more than 1 minute and 6 seconds. With a visual-display unit operating on a 4800 bit-per-second line, the time could be less than a second. A conversation involving many lengthy responses would be prohibitively slow with the teleprinter. Even with faster printing devices operating at 15 or 30 characters per second, it would be very frustrating and would often inhibit creative thought at the terminal. The high speed of the visual-display screen is needed for applications with multiple lengthy responses.

### 6. *Response Time*

Certain applications are very sensitive to the response time at the terminal. For some terminal uses, a very fast response time is necessary; for others it is not. For the applications needing it, fast response time is not simply a luxury. Research by behavioral psychologists has shown that it is essential for certain terminal actions, including problem solving, creative processes, complex interrogation, and, in many cases, plain business uses of terminals. This subject is discussed in the next chapter.

### 7. *Availability*

This category refers to the probability that the terminal is usable at the time the operator wishes to use it. With some forms of system design, he may obtain a busy signal occasionally, just as he may on the telephone. Such a signal could be caused by full occupancy of all the lines or all the "ports" into the computer, or all the paths through or registers in an exchange. It might also be caused by overload in a computer or concentrator.

The probability of not obtaining service when it is requested is sometimes referred to as "the grade of service." Some systems are designed so that the terminals will always receive service when they request it, except in a period of equipment failure. This, however, may be unnecessarily expensive, especially when the terminals have low utilization. A figure for "grade of service" should be decided on by the systems analyst and the data transmission facilities should be planned so as to achieve that figure. Too low a system availability will demoralize its users and sometimes cause them to avoid using the system. In some installations, utilization of the system has grown more rapidly than anticipated and the grade of service has dropped severely. If this condition can be anticipated, the designer can take steps to protect the system from degradation.

### 8. *Control of Errors*

When files of data are being built up on a real-time system, the information often comes from large numbers of terminal operators. In many cases, the terminal operator is less trained and less accurate than the keypunch operator on a batch system. Unless measures are taken for controlling their accuracy, substantial erroneous data could be entered into the system.

Again, the likelihood of error will depend to a large extent on human factors. A well-designed conversation structure minimizes errors; and an on-line system has the great advantage that many errors can be caught when they are made, and the operator notified immediately. Error-detecting formats can be devised, and the information being entered can be checked against existing files. On-line data collection systems have been installed in factories to give a fraction of the errors that equivalent off-line systems had. Besides notifying the operator of suspected errors, the system can inform a control center or supervisor if desirable.

### 9. *Privacy and Security*

When data on files can be read or changed by persons at terminals, it is necessary to prevent unauthorized persons from reading information that does not concern them and from modifying data or creating new records. The unauthorized reading of records can constitute an invasion of privacy on some systems—a situation that, understandably, has caused concern in the press and Congress. Unauthorized modification of records provides opportunities for crime or for tampering with the system.

Steps should be taken to prevent this form of access to a system. Improper access could originate from terminals, from the computer room, by wire tapping, by means of programs, or by entry into tape or disk stores. Access by wire-tapping or terminal misuse can be controlled by appropriate design of terminal procedures. Security might add 5 percent to the overall system cost, or more if very tight controls are needed. Some users have been willing to spend this money to prevent the possibility of embezzlement. Terminal access by a wide variety of people can offer temptations for tampering with the records. Yet, some users have been unwilling to spend money to secure privacy of personal information. This attitude may have to change as increasing personal information is stored in computer data banks.

It is important that the public, the press, and political authorities understand that computer data banks and data transmission *can* be made secure. Data *can* be locked up in computer systems just as it can in a bank vault, but the system becomes more expensive. In devising electronic locks and procedures, computer technology ultimately works on the side of security rather than on the side of the invader.

# 7 RESPONSE-TIME REQUIREMENTS

One of the main parameters in the design of a data transmission system is the required response time or turnaround time. This factor is especially important in real-time systems. When a response to a human at a terminal is needed, the permissible time for the response will affect in a major way the network organization and the equipment selected. The details of this relationship will emerge in subsequent chapters. In this chapter we will discuss the varying requirements for response time.

Response time, as discussed earlier, is the time a system takes to respond to a given input. We defined it for an operator using a terminal keyboard as *the interval between the operator's pressing the last key of the input message and the terminal's switching on lights or typing the first character of the reply.* It is similarly defined for different kinds of systems: *the interval between an event and the system's response to the event.* In a chemical plant it may be the interval between reading instruments and making appropriate adjustments to valves, heaters, and so on; in a factory it may be the interval between management's requesting certain information and receiving it, or the interval between facts becoming available and their being processed; in a laboratory it may be the interval between a scientist or engineer's completing a FORTRAN program and seeing its results.

It should be noted that some authorities define it differently. The defined response time may, for example, include the total time for transmission and display of the response. It does not really matter how it is defined on a given system providing that the definition is perfectly clear and that the design calculations are done accordingly. The definition used in this book is the one given in the preceding paragraph.

The response time achieved will be the sum of three major time elements: the time associated with the data transmission network, the time associated with accessing the file system, and the time associated with the computer. The last two categories are discussed in the author's *Design of Real-Time Computer Systems.*[1] The present book will give detailed calculations concerning the first category—the transmission time, delays, queuing, and so on.

In some computer systems, the terminal response time is almost entirely dependent on the computer and its files. The communication lines may have a single terminal attached to each line and thus have little effect on response time. In other systems, especially those with large numbers of terminals or geographically extensive networks, the communication system may make a much greater contribution to the overall response time than the computer system. Where the network is other than a simple point-to-point network, response time will figure substantially in our design procedure.

The cost of having a very short response time can be high. This may be true because of computer and file considerations. It will often be true because of the communications network, as will emerge in the calculations in Section VI. Let us discuss, therefore, what response time is needed in different situations.

Ideally one would like a very fast response at a computer terminal. In many cases, however, such a response may not be necessary for the efficient functioning of the system. The network cost for different response times could be calculated, if considered worthwhile, and plotted as in Fig. 7.1. The curve would have discontinuities in it caused by a switch to different line types or different equipment, such as concentrators, multiplexers, or terminals. Faced with a curve such as the one in the figure, the systems analyst should think carefully about designing a system with a response time less than, say, 2 seconds. Many systems *are* installed with this tight response-time criterion. Some corporations have demanded contractually that 90 percent of the responses be less than 3 seconds, which usually requires, as we shall see, a *mean* response time of 1.5 seconds or less. It has been demonstrated that such fast responses are necessary to achieve an efficient man-machine conversation in many systems.

**DIFFERING RESPONSE TIMES IN ONE SYSTEM**

All response times on a system need not be identical. Sometimes certain terminals will be given a higher response time than others. Sometimes—and this case is often important—different operations at one terminal will be given a higher response time than other operations.

[1] Prentice-Hall, Englewood Cliffs, N. J., 1968.

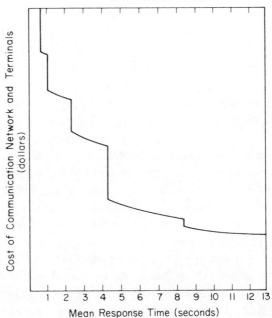

*Fig. 7.1.* The cost of different response times should be evaluated. Sometimes the cost of a very short response time is high.

An enquiry about certain data may be given a much faster response time than the updating of that data. A manager asking for information needs a quick answer. However, it does not matter if that answer is 5 minutes out of date. Sometimes it does not matter if it is 24 hours out of date.

Similarly, if he instructs the system to execute an operational command, he should receive confirmation in a few seconds that the command has been accepted, understood, and can be complied with. However, the processing can be stacked for later action. The execution response is quite separate from the response saying that the command is accepted.

The systems analyst needs to go through all the functions his system will perform and write down the desired response time for each of them, recognizing that they can be different.

**SPEED OF RESPONSE**      There can be a variety of reasons why a system is designed to have a *fast* response time. Four of them, in order of decreasing viability, are listed below.

1. Considerations of behavioral psychology indicate that a fast response time is necessary for an acceptable and efficient man-machine interaction in certain situations.

2. A fast response time may result in economic savings that can be calculated in a tangible manner.

3. Fast response time is impressive. It pleases management or is a desirable "public relations" consideration.

4. It is desirable to keep up with the Joneses.

**ECONOMIC**
**SAVINGS**
If the processing of a real-time transaction needs several "conversation" elements—that is, messages to the computer followed by responses to them—a lengthy response time will delay the overall transaction processing. The longer a transaction takes, the more terminals will be needed to handle a given volume of work. A lengthy response time may tie up other equipment, such as buffers or components in the communications network. A lengthy response time may result in people being kept waiting and it may be possible to place an economic value on this. A shop foreman making entries many times per day may lose a significant proportion of his time. Lengthy transaction processing may result in queues developing. Customers may be kept waiting and, in some cases, may be lost. If an airline customer is kept waiting more than 5 minutes on the telephone when trying to make a reservation, the probability of his choosing the same airline again is reduced by, say, 20 percent—the figure might be established by a market survey.

Tangible cash values may be attached to differences in response time in such cases. In actual practice, however, the cash values established in this way are usually small. A 5-minute conversation for airline reservations or sales-order entry might typically have, say, ten responses to input messages. The difference between a 1.5-second response time and a 4.5-second response time gives only $10 \times 3 = 30$ seconds in overall conversation time. If the costs are as in Fig. 7.1, this 10 percent time saving has been expensive. Simple economic calculations would suggest using the 4.5-second response time. Again, if a warehouseman makes one stock enquiry per hour (with one transaction), it does not matter much in economic terms if he has to wait 20 seconds for a response.

In practice, then, economic calculations alone would often lead us away from the 2-second response time to larger figures. The psychological factors, however, in man-machine interaction are very important.

**PSYCHOLOGICAL**
**REACTION**
The terminals of a real-time system should be as easy and natural to use as possible. If the man-machine interface is well designed, the operators will accept it and use it efficiently. If it is badly designed, they may reject it and seek other methods of operating.

Behavioral psychologists have identified two requirements concerned with terminal response time.[2] First, there is the user's expectancy of a response. In human conversation one expects a response within about 2 seconds; in a slower conversation, the figure may be higher. The response may be no more than a grunt or a facial expression, but lack of response for 4 seconds would be an unnatural break in the conversation. One would want to know the reason for the delay. There would be a break in the chain of conversational thought. In conditioning experiments, a response within 2 seconds has been shown to constitute an important boundary in the effectiveness of feedback.

Second, human beings spontaneously organize their activity into "clumps" that can easily be completed. There is a sense of completion when such a clump of activity is terminated. Writing one sentence, or occasionally two, of this book is one such "clump." Dialing a telephone number would also be followed by a temporary sense of completion, or "closure" as psychologists call it. In the same way, segments of a terminal conversation are followed by a "closure." The main reason is that a certain amount of information—the telephone number being dialed, for example—must be held in "short-term memory," a sort of human buffer storage. When a person is dialing a telephone number, for instance, he retains it in his "buffer" until the number is dialed and then, on "closure," it becomes erased. Similarly, when a person is entering information into a computer terminal, throughout the action he is holding the data in his short-term memory. During this period he does not want to be interrupted, otherwise he will lose what he is remembering in his "buffer." An interruption or a delay in achieving "closure" is frustrating.

In complex problem-solving or complex activity at a terminal, the short-term memory is heavily filled. Psychologists generally agree that the degree of complexity of problems that can be solved in the head is related to the quantity and form of information that can be held in this memory. The short-term memory is constantly in danger of losing all or part of its contents due to "noise," distractions, or mind-wandering. These effects increase severely when the person is aware of waiting an unnaturally long time, as at a terminal with a lengthy response time.

The result of these factors is that the functions which humans can perform and are willing to perform with machines change their character if the response delays are greater than 2 or 3 seconds. For simple uses, such as single enquiries, a lengthy response time will suffice. For uses involving continuity of thinking, or the retention of substantial information in human short-term memory for the duration of a response, a fast reply is necessary. A 10-second response when doing something elaborate with a terminal is insufferably frustrating.

[2] The following conclusions are drawn from an excellent study of response time by Miller (Reference 1).

Psychologist Robert B. Miller [1] concludes:

There is not a straight-line decrease in efficiency as the response increases; rather, sudden drops in mental efficiency occur when delays exceed a given point. These sudden drops at given points can be thought of as psychological step-down discontinuities.

There are different degrees of psychological "closure." Completing the dialing of a telephone number is a simple closure. Completing the entry of a detailed transaction into a system is more elaborate, and completing a problem-solving operation is a much more final closure. Miller concludes that

The greater the closure, the longer the acceptable delay in preparing for and receiving the next response following that closure. A general rule for guidance would be: for good communication with humans, response delays of more than 2 seconds should follow only a condition of task closure as perceived by the human, or as structured for the human.

Different elements in a terminal conversation may, then, require different response times, and it is sometimes possible to take advantage of this fact in the design of the system. For example, when data are being entered into a computer system at a terminal, many conversation elements are often present in the entry process. This is true in booking a journey on an airline system, for example. The last action the operator may take may be to indicate that the entry sequence is complete, perhaps by pressing an END TRANSACTION key on the terminal. This action represents a major "closure," and the response to it may be longer than with the other terminal actions. The other terminal actions may merely result in the items being stored in the computer with no updating of files; and because this action is simple, a response of less than 2 seconds may be achieved easily. On receiving the "END TRANSACTION," however, the computer performs new types of checks on the entire sequence of entries and updates the files, perhaps with many lengthy seeks. The response time here can be permitted to rise well above 2 seconds.

In general, it is not necessary to have the same response time to every operation. Different types of actions may have responses of different speeds, if this variation helps in the system design.

**USES OF DIFFERENT RESPONSE TIMES**   The acceptability of different response times can be summarized as follows:

1. *Greater than 15 seconds*. In general, delays greater that 15 seconds rule out conversational interaction. Certain types of employees may be content to sit at a terminal for more than 15 seconds waiting for the answer to a single simple enquiry. However, for a busy man captivity for more than 15 seconds seems intolerable. If a terminal user has

something else to do, his attention can leave the terminal and return to it after a "closure" with his other work. As Miller puts it [1]: "if delays of more than 15 seconds will occur, the system had better be designed to free the user from physical and mental captivity, so that he can turn to other activities and get his displayed answer when it is *convenient to him* to do so."

2. *Greater than 4 seconds.* Responses greater than 4 seconds are generally too large for a conversation requiring the operator to retain information in his short-term memory. They would be very inhibiting in problem-solving activity and frustrating in data-entry activity. After a major "closure," the operator is prepared to wait longer, almost in relief at the closure. If he keys "EXECUTE" at the end of entering a sequence of instructions, he will usually be content to wait for up to a quarter of a minute or so. Any period longer than this and he may wander away from the terminal or carry out some other activity, perhaps losing his problem-solving frame of mind.

3. *2 to 4 seconds.* A delay longer than 2 seconds can be inhibiting to those terminal operations demanding a high level of concentration. A wait of 2 seconds at a terminal can be surprisingly long when the user is absorbed and emotionally committed to complete what he is doing.

4. *Less than 2 seconds.* When the terminal user has to remember information throughout several responses, the response must be short. The more detailed the information remembered, the greater the need for responses of less than 2 seconds. For elaborate terminal activities, 2 seconds represents one of Miller's "step-down discontinuities" in the capability of most terminal users.

   People involved in creative and other highly motivated complex activities can accomplish relatively large amounts of work during a single session of intense concentration. This is particularly noticeable with certain uses of terminals, and here the terminal interaction must be designed to maintain the intensity. In some elaborate applications, particularly those using graphics, a response of less than 1 second seems desirable to preserve the mental heat of the man-machine process.

5. *Almost instantaneous.* A response to the pressing of a key, such as a click or the typing of a character, needs to be almost instantaneous—say within 0.1 second of the action. The motion of a light pen drawing a curve or positioning a symbol must be followed almost immediately by the appearance of the curve or symbol on the screen. These and other control actions would normally be built into the design of the terminal itself.

**TOO SHORT A RESPONSE TIME**

In some cases it has been claimed that too *short* a response time is psychologically bad. It can have a harassing effect on a slow-thinking operator if every machine response comes back instantaneously. Subconsciously he feels coerced into an attempt to keep up with the machine. On some systems a built-in delay has been used to ensure that no response occurs in less than 1.5 seconds. On telecommunication-based systems, however, the designer is more likely to be worried about long response times than short ones.

**INTERIM RESPONSES**

There are two main reasons for demanding a response within 2 seconds. One is concerned with the user's continuity of thinking, in particular with short-term memory and "closures." The other is concerned with response expectancies and frustration at not receiving a response in the time the user would receive one if this were a human conversation. The latter situation can be ameliorated somewhat by giving an interim response—saying, in effect, "I heard what you said; wait a minute while I think about it!" This would appear as a word or a phrase on the terminal. If the terminal operates at teletype speed, the phase may take 2 seconds or so to print, giving the rest of the system that much more time to reply. IBM's QUIKTRAN system, for example, prints back a three-digit line number and a remark such as +READY, +REJECT, or a program statement number at the start of each line.[3] If the terminal then pauses for several seconds before giving the wanted response, the wait does not seem quite so long.

If the delay in response is primarily caused by the telecommunications network, as with many of the examples in this book, the interim response may originate at a control unit, programmed concentrator, or other device sufficiently close to the terminal to avoid the major delay.

An interim response produced in this way does not, of course, solve the problem when the reason for requiring a fast response is continuity of the user's thinking.

**SPECIFIC RESPONSE SITUATIONS**

Using the results of research on these topics—short-term memory, psychological closure, and expectancies—Miller [1] goes on to comment on certain situations in man-terminal interaction. Some of these situations are listed below.

---

[3] See the author's *Design of Real-Time Computer Systems*, Fig. 8.14.

1. *Response to "System, are you Listening?"*

When we pick up the telephone and listen for the dial tone, we are in effect asking this question. We expect to hear the dial tone within 1 second because that is what we are accustomed to. When a session with a computer is being *initialized*, a wait of 3 seconds or longer would generally be acceptable. This will affect the design of automatic dialing and switching on data networks. If the system is *not* listening, some form of busy signal is desirable, as on the telephone networks.

2. *Response to Initialization*

When the user is taking initialization action, his capacity for annoyance at delay is not yet as great as when he is locked into conversation or problem solving. Sometimes the initialization or sign-on procedure may involve a wait of many seconds in the computer while facilities are being set up or programs are being read into storage. Here a fairly quick interim response, followed by a wait of up to half a minute would usually be acceptable.

3. *Error Messages*

When the user makes a mistake that is detected by the system, an error message will be sent back to him. He should always be allowed to complete his segment of thought before being informed of his error. It is offensive to be interrupted in midthought and abruptly told of an error. It is, in fact, desirable to have a brief pause after this temporary "closure" rather than bang back the error message instantly. Miller recommends that the response time of the error message be between 2 and 4 seconds. The error message, he finds, is more acceptable after the sense of completion that comes with the 2-second pause.

4. *Badge-Reader Response*

The user of a badge-reader terminal for brief data entry needs two kinds of response. First, an almost immediate indication that the badge is correctly inserted in the machine. This indication, a click or snap, should come from the machine itself. Second, a light or other response indicating that it has reached the computer, or terminal-control machine, should appear within 2 seconds. The average worker is apt to be impatient with delays at this machine, especially when clocking out, and, again, 2 seconds can seem a long time to him.

### 5. *Response to a Single-Step Enquiry*

When there is a solitary response to a simple question like "Part No. 574138: How many in stock?" or "What is the last traded price of CDC stock?" a response time of lengthy duration may be acceptable. It may be made more acceptable if there is an interim quick response. If, however, a person uses his terminal frequently (several times per hour), he may become frustrated with it, or wasteful of time if the response time is, say, 15 seconds.

Much depends on the reason for the enquiry and, in particular, on whether other work has to stop until the response is received. If the terminal user is talking to a customer when he makes his enquiry, normally he will want a quick response. A stockbroker would become very annoyed with a terminal giving a 6-second response and would usually feel that he needed a response in less than 2 seconds. The reason is because of the sense of urgency with which he makes his inquiry. A storekeeper, on the other hand, might be reasonably unconcerned about a 10-second response.

### 6. *Response to Chained Questions*

When the user is attempting to answer a question that needs a linked series of enquiries, then the fast response time becomes necessary for his continuity of attention. The more complex the thought process, the more important this point is. It is particularly important where there is ambiguity in the results. Suppose, for example, that an airline agent is using a terminal for booking a journey from New York to Rome and that the passenger wants to stop at some Caribbean island on the way. What are the best flights? There are many possible answers to this question, and most of them involve flying with more than one carrier. He will use his terminal to explore the alternatives. This is a simple example of enquiries that, because they are linked, should have a 2-second response time.

### 7. *Browsing*

Suppose that the user is leafing through information looking for a particular fact or item, much as a person looks through a telephone directory or list of technical reports. This "browsing" operation may proceed very rapidly at a screen, the screen, perhaps, being filled at a voice-line speed of 4800 bits per second. The screen might contain 600 characters and be filled in 1 second. The user will probably not read every word on the screen before he requests the next screen; rather, his eye will scan the information very quickly. In this circumstance, he will want the next screen very quickly, preferably with a response time of no longer than 1 second. If his requests for the next frame are sequential, the data transmission system may anticipate them, sending them to a buffer in a control unit near the terminal.

### 8. *Request for "Next Page"*

At times the screen of a visual display unit will not be large enough to hold the whole of a response. The user, when he has assimilated the information displayed, will ask for the next page. The "page turning" should be very fast—again, if possible, not longer than 1 second. The annoyance of longer delays will be considerable, as well as inhibiting to thought processes. The communication network may be organized in such a way that the next page cannot be delivered in 1 second; in this case, again, a buffer may be used in the terminal control unit, or concentrator, that can store a response of more than one screenful and so facilitate fast page flipping.

### 9. *Keyboard Entry vs. Light-Pen Entry*

An operator using a light pen often expects a quicker response than an operator using a keyboard. Part of the reason is that there may be an adaptation time of as long as $1\frac{1}{2}$ seconds when a user shifts his attention from the keyboard to the screen. A 2-second delay in response to a light-pen selection of a screen item can seem *very* long. Often a 1-second response to light-pen actions would be preferable if it can be achieved.

### 10. *Graphic Response to a Light Pen*

A graphic response to a light-pen action (as opposed to an alphanumeric response) can take a variety of different forms.

1. Lines are drawn on the screen with the pen. Here the line should appear on the screen in about 0.1 second or less. There should be no perceivable variability in delay.
2. The image is built up from a menu of image parts selected by the pen. The user may place his pen over one of the symbols and move it to the required position. Here a delay of a second may be acceptable.
3. An entire new image may be called for. In this case, the considerations are much the same as the preceding ones requiring a nongraphic response. In order to avoid a break in continuity of thinking, the image should appear in 2 seconds or less. If continuity of thinking is not involved, the user can wait longer.

### 11. *Graphic Manipulation of Models and Structures*

Advanced graphic applications can become complicated, with the user carrying out manipulations that require him to retain much information in his short-term memory. A fast response time is needed in order to permit this type of man-machine "thinking." It is possible to maintain a high level of mental activity at a computer terminal for short periods. Responses of 1 second or so are needed for such activity. The need for fast responses and elaborate displays will necessitate the use of large buffers and considerable logic circuitry close to the terminals. Often it is necessary to have a small computer close to the terminals. If the terminals are linked to a distant computer by means of a telecommunication line, the line will either be of high bandwidth or the distant computer will only be used occasionally—not for every response. It will be used for loading programs into the screen control computers, or it will be used when a major "closure" occurs in the user's thinking.

This is an example of "intelligence" in the network being distributed to points away from the central computer. The need for peripheral intelligence may also occur in nongraphic applications where the terminal usage is other than simple, and we will see illustrations of it in subsequent chapters.

### 12. *Response to "Go" Command*

The user may key a lengthy series of entries into a system with some interactive dialogue and then, at the end of this operation, instruct the machine to execute a complex operation with these entries. He may be typing in the details of a problem, the parameters of a file search that is required, or the instructions of a program to be executed. When he finally says "Go" at the end of such a sequence, this is usually a point at which he is prepared to sit back and relax. His "short-term" memory clears. A fast response to the problem is not required, although an acknowledgement of the "Go" command should be sent.

**VARIATION IN RESPONSE TIME**   Many systems will not give the same response time to each request of the same type. Some, in fact, because of the nature of the system design, will give a wide dispersion of response times. The mean response time might be 2 seconds; but 10 percent of the response times are more than 4 seconds, 5 percent more than 6 seconds, and 1 percent more than 8 seconds. The distribution of response times might typically be as shown in Fig. 7.2.

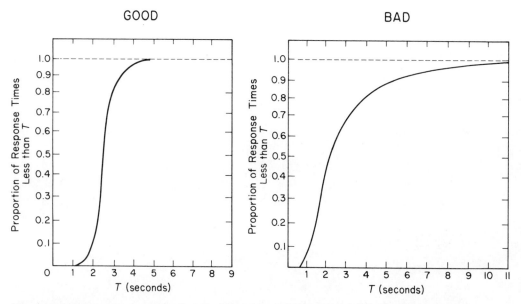

*Fig. 7.2.* A system with too high a standard deviation of response times will be frustrating for the terminal operator.

Ideally, for most applications, we would like the dispersion of response times to be low. Too high a standard deviation means that the operator will occasionally become frustrated. If an operator is accustomed to a 2-second response and the system sometimes takes 6 seconds, he may wonder whether the computer is going to respond at all this time. The 6 seconds will seem unnaturally long. He may even initiate the action again or pummel some key on the terminal, which could cause problems.

Again, when the load on the system increases, its response time may go up severely. These are effects we must know about during the system design and must attempt to control. Some of the calculations in Section VI indicate how to do so.

## REFERENCE

1. Robert B. Miller, *Response Time in Man-Computer Conversational Transactions*: AFIPS Conference Proceedings for Joint Computer Conference. 1968.

# 8 DESIGN OF THE MAN-MACHINE DIALOGUE

Still more important than response time in producing a good man-machine interface is the structure of the dialogue. What *exactly* does the man say to the machine and what *exactly* does it say to him? What medium and what format are used for these statements? These are questions that the systems analyst has to answer in planning a teleprocessing or real-time system. At times answering them has been surprisingly complex and has consumed an unexpectedly large slice of the implementation effort. The nature of the answer can make a major difference to the user acceptance of the system and hence, in some cases, to its efficiency.

The structure of the terminal dialogue can differ widely on seemingly similar systems. There are many approaches to man-computer dialogue. In this chapter we will discuss 12 types of approach using alphanumeric dialogue (as opposed to graphics). Some of these approaches are valuable in certain kinds of situations only. Within each of the following types, wide variations in syntax are possible.[1] As we shall see, the choice of structure for the terminal dialogue can have a major effect on the structure—plus the cost—of the data transmission network. It is important that the overall system designer understand this relationship.

The twelve types of approach are

1. Programming languages
2. Natural language dialogue
3. Limited English input

[1] See James Martin, *Design of Man-Computer Dialogue*, Prentice-Hall, Englewood Cliffs, N. J., 1972.

4. Dialogue using mnemonics

5. Program-like statements

6. Computer-initiated dialogue

7. Form-filling

8. Hybrid dialogue

9. Special terminal hardware

10. Dialogue with a totally untrained operator

11. Fixed-frame responses

12. Dialogue with pictures

## TWELVE TYPES OF DIALOGUE

### 1. *Programming Languages*

Many systems analysts, when they first think of man-computer dialogue, think of time-sharing systems and of programming. Most computer languages are now available in an appropriate form at terminals, and several new languages have been devised specifically for terminal use. The time-sharing user can program *interactively* and in so doing he finds several advantages. First, he obtains his results quickly. If he has been accustomed to waiting half a day or more for the turnaround from a job shop, this is indeed a welcome feature. Second, he can debug his program at the terminal. Some errors are caught as he keys in the statements and others when he attempts to execute them. Previously a program with a dozen errors in it might have dragged on for several days before it was debugged because of the slow job-shop turnaround. Third, he can sometimes obtain help at the terminal when he forgets or misunderstands an element of the language. The terminal may instruct him in language usage when he so requires.

Figure 8.1 shows a typical example of terminal dialogue using a programming language.

Unfortunately, the majority of persons whom we would like to see using terminals are not programmers. Most of them do not want to program; many have little aptitude for it, and would make a mess of it if they tried. The answer, say the enthusiasts, is to make the program dialogue simple, like BASIC (in Fig. 8.1) or JOSS. If this step is too restricting on what the user can do, another alternative is to provide an elementary and easily learned subset of a more versatile language like PL/I or APL. APL is particularly noteworthy as a concise and powerful language for interactive use, which is nevertheless easy for beginners to learn [1].

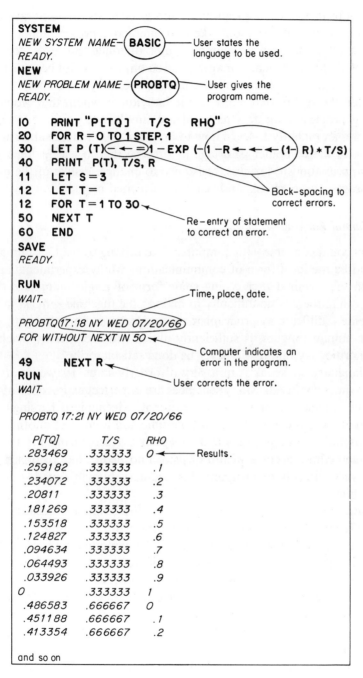

```
SYSTEM
NEW SYSTEM  NAME—( BASIC )——— User states the
READY.                          language to be used.
NEW
NEW PROBLEM NAME —(PROBTQ)——— User gives the
READY.                          program name.

10     PRINT "P[TQ]    T/S    RHO"
20     FOR R = 0 TO 1 STEP. 1
30     LET P (T)(— ← =)1 – EXP (–(1 –R ← ← ←(1–) R) ∗ T/S)
40     PRINT  P(T), T/S, R
11     LET  S = 3
12     LET  T =
12     FOR T = 1 TO 30
50     NEXT T
60     END
SAVE
READY.

RUN
WAIT.                          Time, place, date.

PROBTQ(17:18 NY  WED  07/20/66)
FOR WITHOUT NEXT IN 50

49        NEXT R
RUN                            Computer indicates an
WAIT.                          error in the program.
                               User corrects the error.

PROBTQ 17:21 NY  WED  07/20/66

  P[TQ]       T/S      RHO
 .283469     .333333    0 ←——— Results.
 .259182     .333333    .1
 .234072     .333333    .2
 .20811      .333333    .3
 .181269     .333333    .4
 .153518     .333333    .5
 .124827     .333333    .6
 .094634     .333333    .7
 .064493     .333333    .8
 .033926     .333333    .9
 0           .333333    1
 .486583     .666667    0
 .451188     .666667    .1
 .413354     .666667    .2

and so on
```

Back-spacing to correct errors.

Re–entry of statement to correct an error.

*Fig. 8.1.* A calculation being done at a teletypewriter with the BASIC language.

No doubt in the years ahead many more scientists, accountants, financial analysts, and such will become hooked on interactive programming languages. We need a different form of man-computer dialogue, however, for the vast numbers of clerks, salesmen, managers, and so on, who do not become proficient at programming. There are many alternatives. Some systems analysts have not yet accepted the reality that many of the individuals whom they would like to have using programming at a terminal are simply not going to do so. Their reason is not an inability to learn how to program, but a more subtle mixture of pride, fear of the computer, shortage of time needed to learn, dread of being made to appear foolish, laziness, resistance to change, dislike of the machine's error messages, future shock, and years of cultivated prejudice.

## 2. *Natural-Language Dialogue*

If you could converse with computers like talking to another human being, that would be the ideal form of communication. Many experiments have been made with the terminal user typing some form of English-language dialogue. However, while there is no difficulty in making the machine *respond* in English, it is extremely difficult to program it to comprehend English input. English, and other human tongues, is sufficiently difficult to decipher by machine that some authorities say that it will never be done satisfactorily.

The language we speak is in a very disorderly state. Its words are ambiguous; its syntax confused. Many sentences are imperfect expressions of thought because the language is only partially rational. Mechanized parsing is difficult because many words can be a verb at one time and a noun at another, and the language is full of irregularities and exceptions. Recognizing the meaning of sentences sometimes needs a wealth of prior knowledge, like recognizing faces, and it is very difficult to program this ordinary human function in today's serial machines.

Certain simple words are ambiguous to the computer because they can assume different shades of meaning. Take the word "nothing," for example. If "A is better than B and B is better than C," a computer could be expected to conclude that A is better than C. However, if we say "Nothing is better than a good square meal, but a sandwich is better than nothing," the machine concludes that "a sandwich is better than a good square meal." [2] Again, the answer to the question "Can anyone walk over Niagara Falls on a tightrope?" is "yes," but it does not follow that "Anyone can walk over Niagara Falls on a tightrope."

Because of the alternate meanings of words, some sentences are very difficult to parse by programming. For example, in the sentence "Time flies like an arrow" it is possible that either "time," "flies," or "like" could be the verb. (Fruit flies *like* a banana!) And even many sentences that appear unambiguous at first sight can lead to subtle problems that would be extremely difficult to solve by computer.

A problem still more difficult to program for is that of presupposition. The mental processes of the hearer must be reasonably close to those of the speaker for him to give the correct meaning to what he hears. Statements that have been made, or beliefs that are held, prior to the speaking of the current sentence will condition the interpretation of it. The English we speak presupposes an immensely elaborate web of interconnections between the words that are used. Human beings grasp the meaning of sentences because they have an internal encyclopedia to which the sentences are relevant. As a result, the sentence need not necessarily be grammatical or even complete in some cases. A person checks a partially heard sentence against his view of the world and establishes a meaning for it. It is extremely difficult to give a computer such an internal encyclopedia except when the subject matter is restricted to a very narrow area.

The difficulties with natural language are an extreme case of a more general dilemma with man-computer dialogue. We need to design the dialogue structure so that it is as easy as possible for humans to use. The degree to which we achieve this condition will determine the acceptability of the systems we create. However, the more freedom we give the operator in his phrase structuring, the more complexity will be necessary in the programming to interpret what he says. In practice, we very quickly find the requirements for the interpretation program surpassing acceptable commercial levels for software expenditure and/or machine time. Furthermore, the objective of making the dialogue as fluid as possible is generally at odds with the objective of making the input from the human operator as precise as possible. This is not surprising if fluidity means addressing the computer in normal conversational terms because our language is so imprecise and ambiguous.

Exploration of natural-language dialogue in the research laboratories deserves the maximum encouragement; however, the commercial systems analyst should be warned to steer clear of any temptations luring him into this quagmire.

### 3. Limited English Input

Although natural-language input suffers from an imprecision that defeats the simple-minded computer, input with a small number of English words can be used provided that the key words are defined with exactness. The advantage is that the user is employing words which are familiar to him. The disadvantage is that he will be tempted to overestimate the intelligence of the machine he is communicating with and to overstep the tight restrictions on input wording.

An example of limited English input is found in some systems for searching files to extract certain categories of information. The input statement must contain key words that the system has in its dictionary, such as file names, field names, report names, verbs, search parameters, and types of comparison. A request for information on a typical system might be as follows:

PERSONNEL FILE
LOCATION = CHICAGO
SALARY LESS THAN 1200
EDUCATION GREATER THAN 7

This means: "Search the Personnel File for people in Chicago with an education grade greater than 7 but a salary less than 1200 ($ per month)."

In some systems it is permissible to pad out the input statements with "null" words that have no effect but that make the input statements closer to English. Thus in the statement

PLEASE GIVE ME THE <u>DISTRICT STAFF</u> REPORT FOR THOSE PEOPLE WITH A <u>SALARY GREATER</u> THAN <u>1200</u>

only the words underlined are recognized by the system. The others are ignored, and

DISTRICT STAFF SALARY GREATER 1200

would have exactly the same meaning.

DISTRICT STAFF is recognized by the program as the name of a report for which the system has a stored definition of the format required and the file to be searched.

Although "null words" permit attractive Englishlike input and sometimes encourage a diffident user to employ the terminal, they can also cause confusion. The system may fail to recognize what appears a reasonable request to the user. For example, in

LIST ALL EMPLOYEES WHO HAVE BEEN WITH THE COMPANY MORE THAN 20 YEARS

the computer may have in its dictionary LIST, EMPLOYEES, MORE THAN, and 20, but not WHO HAVE BEEN WITH THE COMPANY. The user may try MORE THAN 20 YEARS STANDING, EMPLOYED FOR MORE THAN 20 YEARS, OF 20 YEARS DURATION WITH THE COMPANY, and so on, with equal lack of success. He may give up before thinking of a wording that *would* contain relevant key words:

"<u>LIST EMPLOYEES</u> WHOSE DATE OF <u>HIRE</u> IS <u>LESS</u> THAN <u>1952</u>"

Worse, in some cases he may obtain an incorrect answer because he uses a word or phrase that, although it has meaning to him, is not in the dictionary. Thus the request "LIST ALL CHICAGO BRANCH MANAGERS WITH POLICE CONVICTIONS" would give all innocent Chicago branch managers because "POLICE CONVICTIONS" is not in the dictionary. A misspelled word would similarly be ignored.

The problem of misinterpretation might be overcome in part by displaying on the screen the condensed version of the request (i.e., LIST CHICAGO BRANCH MANAGERS). Another school of thought advocates that *no* word should be permitted that is not in the dictionary. If null words are to be permitted, then an acceptable set of them should be in the dictionary along with the key words.

A language of this type is likely to acquire abbreviations to lessen the number of characters the user has to key in. Thus IBM's MIS system includes the following abbreviations:

| | |
|---|---|
| EQ | Equal to |
| NE | Not equal to |
| GT | Greater than |
| NG | Not greater than |
| LT | Less than |
| NL | Not less than |
| WL | Within limits |
| OL | Outside limits |
| SEQ/H | Sequence, high to low, of all records meeting the criteria |
| SEQ/L | Sequence, low to high, of all records meeting the criteria |
| TOP | Top number of records that meet the criteria |
| LOW | Lowest number of records that meet the criteria. |

In addition, a file can be defined either with its full name or with an abbreviation: thus PERSONNEL or PS. Misspelled names may also be equated to this definition: PERSONEL

Thus the experienced user may type in highly abbreviated statements such as

PS NM SE SL GT 800 YH LT 70 PROMOTABLE

while the inexperienced user would type this statement in the nonabbreviated form

PERSONNEL NAME SERIAL SALARY GREATER THAN 800 YEAR OF HIRE LESS THAN 1970 PROMOTABLE

or possibly in a form with extra padded words

DISPLAY FROM THE PERSONNEL FILE THE NAME AND SERIAL NUMBER OF THOSE WHOSE SALARY IS GREATER THAN 800 AND YEAR OF HIRE IS LESS THAN 1970 AND WHO ARE PROMOTABLE.

The result will be the same in each case.

### 4. *Dialogue Using Mnemonics*

The English input in the previous example has been largely condensed into a set of mnemonics. Many forms of dialogue are built entirely out of mnemonics.

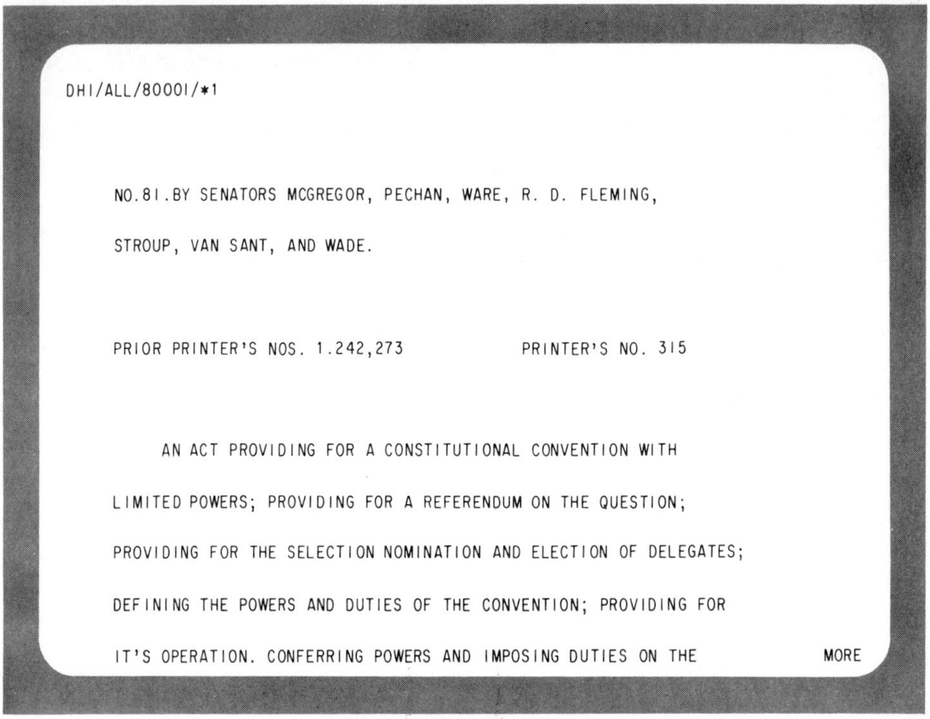

```
DHI/ALL/80001/*1


    NO.81.BY SENATORS MCGREGOR, PECHAN, WARE, R. D. FLEMING,

    STROUP, VAN SANT, AND WADE.


    PRIOR PRINTER'S NOS. 1.242,273          PRINTER'S NO. 315


       AN ACT PROVIDING FOR A CONSTITUTIONAL CONVENTION WITH

    LIMITED POWERS; PROVIDING FOR A REFERENDUM ON THE QUESTION;

    PROVIDING FOR THE SELECTION NOMINATION AND ELECTION OF DELEGATES;

    DEFINING THE POWERS AND DUTIES OF THE CONVENTION; PROVIDING FOR

    IT'S OPERATION. CONFERRING POWERS AND IMPOSING DUTIES ON THE          MORE
```

*Figure 8.2*

It is often the case that terminal-based systems are built for handling a particular application. A specific set of mnemonics can be devised for this application. The disadvantage of using mnemonics is that the user has to remember them. This disadvantage becomes prohibitive if there are a large number of them. It can also be a severe disadvantage if the operators are "casual" (as discussed in Chapter 6) rather than "dedicated." The dedicated operator can become entirely familiar with a set of mnemonics because he has so much practice with them. The casual operator will need help, perhaps via a list of mnemonics pasted on the terminal.

In a few areas, mnemonic codes have been in use for a long time. The airlines, for example, have an international code for cabling information relating to seat reservations, and this code has been incorporated into some parts of the dialogue used on real-time reservation systems. The majority of systems analysts, however, will have to make up their own mnemonics if they decide to use them.

As an illustration of a mnemonic system in operation with "casual" users, we will give some typical dialogue from the Pennsylvania Legislative System [2], which is designed to provide the Pennsylvania General Assembly with real-time access to information about bills, resolutions, executive communications and actions, committee members, and so on. In order to use the system, a legislator or other person keys in a statement with four or five segments. The following statement relates to the *history* of a bill and asks for *all* its history to be displayed:

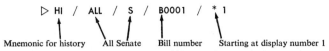

▷ HI  /  ALL  /  S  /  B0001  /  * 1

Mnemonic for history    All Senate    Bill number    Starting at display number 1

The system responds as shown in Fig. 8.2.

By pressing a given key, he can now "turn the page" to the next screen of information on this bill. If he wishes, he can "page flip" very quickly through the data until he finds the page that interests him. He could start at a given page by keying its number in at the end of the initial statement. For example, if he wished to start at page 12 he would key

▷ HI  /  ALL  /  S  /  B0001  /  * 12

If a user wishes to know the bills and resolutions sponsored by a given legislator, he keys in one of the following two statements:

▷ ME  /  SPO  /  H or S  /  Name or title of legislator    or

▷ ME  /  SPO  /  H or S  /  Seat number of legislator

Mnemonic for member    Sponsored    House or senate

What he sees on the screen is shown in Fig. 8.3.

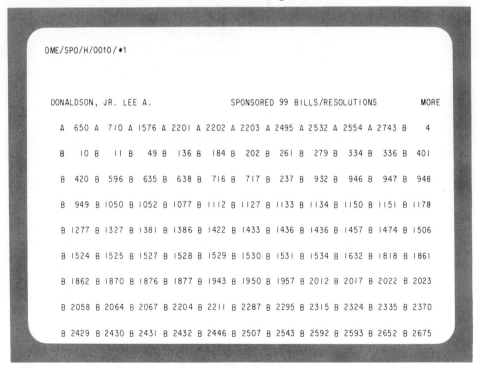

```
DME/SPO/H/0010/*1


   DONALDSON, JR. LEE A.              SPONSORED 99 BILLS/RESOLUTIONS        MORE

      A  650  A  710 A 1576 A 2201 A 2202 A 2203 A 2495 A 2532 A 2554 A 2743 B    4

      B   10 B   11 B   49 B  136 B  184 B  202 B  261 B  279 B  334 B  336 B  401

      B  420 B  596 B  635 B  638 B  716 B  717 B  237 B  932 B  946 B  947 B  948

      B  949 B 1050 B 1052 B 1077 B 1112 B 1127 B 1133 B 1134 B 1150 B 1151 B 1178

      B 1277 B 1327 B 1381 B 1386 B 1422 B 1433 B 1436 B 1436 B 1457 B 1474 B 1506

      B 1524 B 1525 B 1527 B 1528 B 1529 B 1530 B 1531 B 1534 B 1632 B 1818 B 1861

      B 1862 B 1870 B 1876 B 1877 B 1943 B 1950 B 1957 B 2012 B 2017 B 2022 B 2023

      B 2058 B 2064 B 2067 B 2204 B 2211 B 2287 B 2295 B 2315 B 2324 B 2335 B 2370

      B 2429 B 2430 B 2431 B 2432 B 2446 B 2507 B 2543 B 2592 B 2593 B 2652 B 2675
```

*Figure 8.3*

If he wishes to know a given committee's membership, he keys in

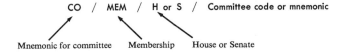

He receives the information shown in Fig. 8.4.

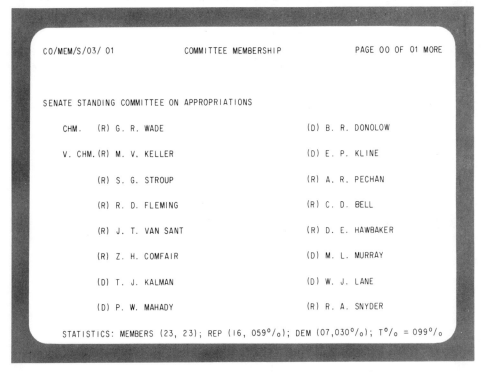

CO/MEM/S/03/ 01                COMMITTEE MEMBERSHIP                PAGE 00 OF 01 MORE


SENATE STANDING COMMITTEE ON APPROPRIATIONS

   CHM.   (R) G. R. WADE                     (D) B. R. DONOLOW

   V. CHM.(R) M. V. KELLER                   (D) E. P. KLINE

      (R) S. G. STROUP                       (R) A. R. PECHAN

      (R) R. D. FLEMING                      (R) C. D. BELL

      (R) J. T. VAN SANT                     (R) D. E. HAWBAKER

      (R) Z. H. COMFAIR                      (D) M. L. MURRAY

      (D) T. J. KALMAN                       (D) W. J. LANE

      (D) P. W. MAHADY                       (R) R. A. SNYDER

   STATISTICS: MEMBERS (23, 23); REP (16, 059%); DEM (07,030%); T% = 099%

*Figure 8.4*

It will be seen that these mnemonics are all designed to be fairly simple to remember. A large variety of other types of enquiries can be made, including the investigation of legislation or executive actions that have been taken on a bill, the request for personal biographic information about a member, details of what bills have been referred to a given committee, and so on.

It is possible that the user could make a mistake keying in the mnemonics, or could forget the correct mnemonic. When this happens, the screen automatically gives him a list of all of the valid mnemonics (Fig. 8.5).

Again, he may use correct mnemonics but enter insufficient data. This step could happen, for example, because there are two members of the same name. The screen would then instruct him as to the correct action (Fig. 8.6).

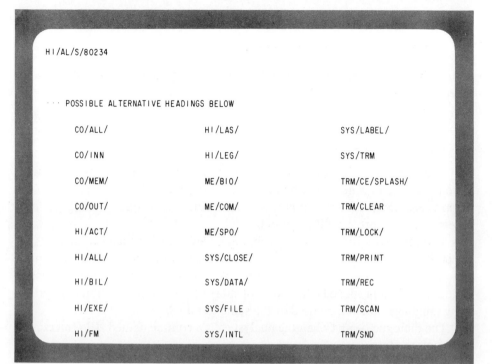

HI/AL/S/80234


···  POSSIBLE ALTERNATIVE HEADINGS BELOW

| | | |
|---|---|---|
| CO/ALL/ | HI/LAS/ | SYS/LABEL/ |
| CO/INN | HI/LEG/ | SYS/TRM |
| CO/MEM/ | ME/BIO/ | TRM/CE/SPLASH/ |
| CO/OUT/ | ME/COM/ | TRM/CLEAR |
| HI/ACT/ | ME/SPO/ | TRM/LOCK/ |
| HI/ALL/ | SYS/CLOSE/ | TRM/PRINT |
| HI/BIL/ | SYS/DATA/ | TRM/REC |
| HI/EXE/ | SYS/FILE | TRM/SCAN |
| HI/FM | SYS/INTL | TRM/SND |

*Figure 8.5*

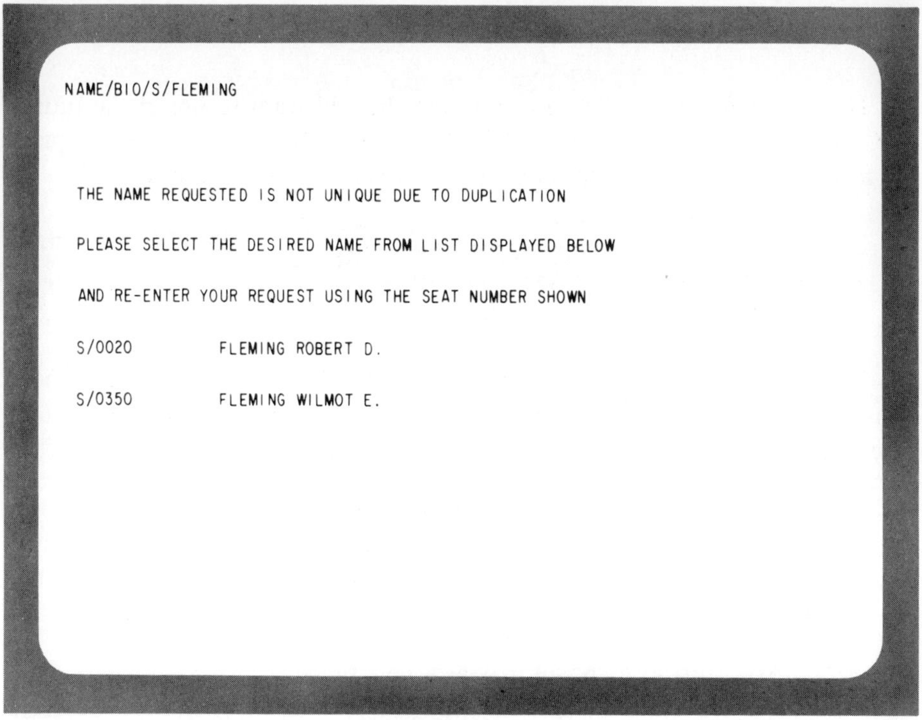

NAME/BIO/S/FLEMING


THE NAME REQUESTED IS NOT UNIQUE DUE TO DUPLICATION

PLEASE SELECT THE DESIRED NAME FROM LIST DISPLAYED BELOW

AND RE-ENTER YOUR REQUEST USING THE SEAT NUMBER SHOWN

S/0020        FLEMING ROBERT D.

S/0350        FLEMING WILMOT E.

*Figure 8.6*

85

A differently structured example of the use of mnemonics in dialogue is given in Chapter 10.

### 5. *Programlike Statements*

The preceding dialogue looks nothing like programming, but on some systems the use of mnemonics builds up into programlike statements. There are diverse examples of this situation. Some data-based query languages use mnemonics in a programlike fashion.

The following illustration of a dialogue designed for financial analysts [4] looks like an interactive program. It is, however, designed for a specific application and does not have the flexibility of a programming language. Such a dialogue is often produced in the form of subroutines in a conventional programming language that can be used at the same terminal.

The dialogue begins when the analyst calls a routine named IIR (Interactive Information Retriever).

```
ANALYST:    CALL IIR;
COMPUTER:   IIR. PROCEED:
ANALYST:    R1 = 100*NFC/EQUITY;
COMPUTER:   PROCEED:
```

Here the analyst is defining a ratio that he will want to use in the future. NFC (Net For Common) and EQUITY are already defined. The computer will store the definition R1 in its dictionary. The analyst proceeds:

```
ANALYST:    GET R1 (MCDONNELL) FOR 1968 to 1972;
COMPUTER:   1968   1969   1970   1971   1972
            18.24  16.91  15.13  17.31  20.12
```

The computer has calculated the ratio R1 for McDonnell Aircraft. (Fictitious figures are used in this illustration.) The analyst would now like to compare it with the rest of this industry. He defines a group of 12 corporations:

```
ANALYST:    AEROIND = AEROJET, BENDIX, BOING, DOUGLAS, GRUMMAN, LOCKHEED,
            MCDONNELL, NORTH AMERICAN, NORTHROP, REPUBLIC, THIKOL, UTD AIRCRAFT;
COMPUTER:   BOING NOT IN FILE. PLEASE MAKE CHANGE:
ANALYST:    BOEING;
COMPUTER:   CHANGE ACCEPTED. PROCEED:
ANALYST:    GET R1 (MCDONNELL)/AVERAGE (R1(AEROIND));
```

| **COMPUTER:** | FOR WHAT DATES? | | | | |
|---|---|---|---|---|---|
| **ANALYST:** | 1968 TO 1972; | | | | |
| **COMPUTER:** | 1968 | 1969 | 1970 | 1971 | 1972 |
| | 1.41 | 1.32 | 1.63 | 1.84 | 2.01 |
| **ANALYST:** | R2 = SALES/EQUITY; | | | | |
| **COMPUTER:** | PROCEED: | | | | |
| **ANALYST:** | T1 = 1968 TO 1972; | | | | |
| **COMPUTER:** | PROCEED: | | | | |
| **ANALYST:** | GET R2 (MCDONNELL) AND R2 (AVERAGE(AEROIND)) FOR T1; | | | | |

| **COMPUTER:** | | 1968 | 1969 | 1970 | 1971 | 1972 |
|---|---|---|---|---|---|---|
| | MCDONNELL: | 7.29 | 4.60 | 4.93 | 3.82 | 6.91 |
| | AVERAGE (AEROIND): | 1.21 | 0.82 | 0.86 | 1.34 | 1.70 |
| **ANALYST:** | END IIR; | | | | | |

A language of this type is fairly simple for a financial analyst to learn and use. It enables him to display quickly comparisons, averages, ratios, statistic functions, and a variety of different facts about the corporations in the accessible data base.

### 6. Computer-Initiated Dialogue

One way to avoid making the operator learn mnemonics or program statements is to design the dialogue so that it is always the computer rather than the operator that leads.

A dialogue consists of pairs of messages—a question or statement (sometimes a set of statements) followed by a response. In any man-computer dialogue, the first message of each pair can come either from the man or from the computer. We will call the former *operator-initiated* dialogues and the latter *computer-initiated*. If the dialogue is operator-initiated, as in all the preceding examples, the operator has to know exactly what to do. He must be familiar with the necessary mnemonics, procedures, and formats. If it is computer-initiated, the computer can tell him precisely what to do. The computer-initiated dialogue is less flexible in that the operator has to follow a predetermined path of operations. The path can, however, have many branches in it, at each step if necessary. The operator works his way down a multiple-branching tree.

The following dialogue (Figs. 8.7 to 8.10) at a visual-display unit illustrates this process. Note that the computer tells the operator exactly what to do at each step.

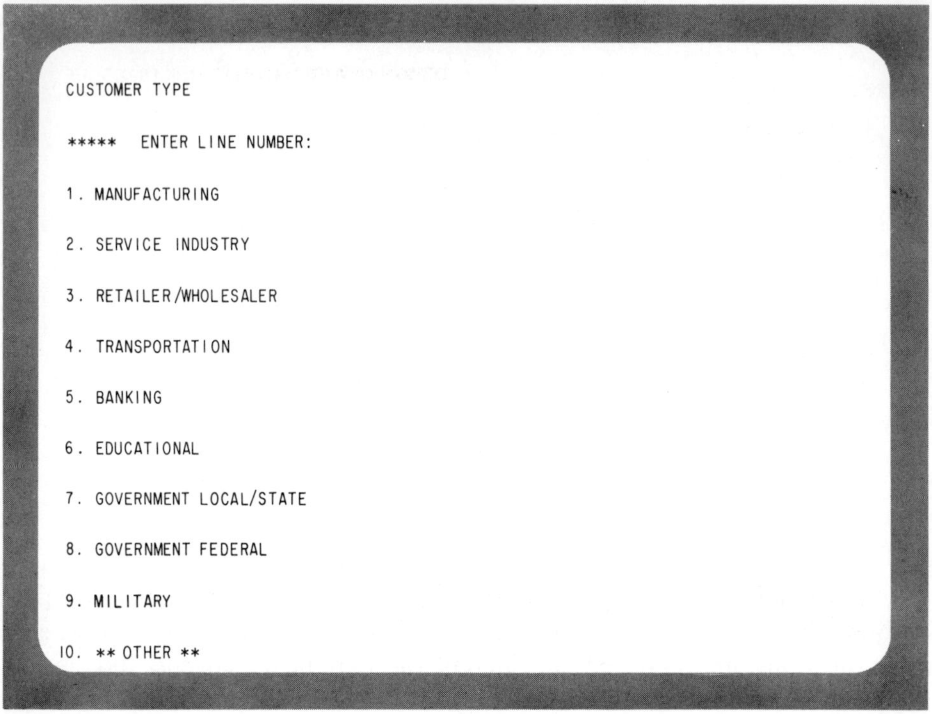

```
CUSTOMER TYPE

*****   ENTER LINE NUMBER:

1.  MANUFACTURING

2.  SERVICE  INDUSTRY

3.  RETAILER/WHOLESALER

4.  TRANSPORTATION

5.  BANKING

6.  EDUCATIONAL

7.  GOVERNMENT LOCAL/STATE

8.  GOVERNMENT FEDERAL

9.  MILITARY

10.  ** OTHER **
```

The operator enters: 4                    *Figure 8.7*

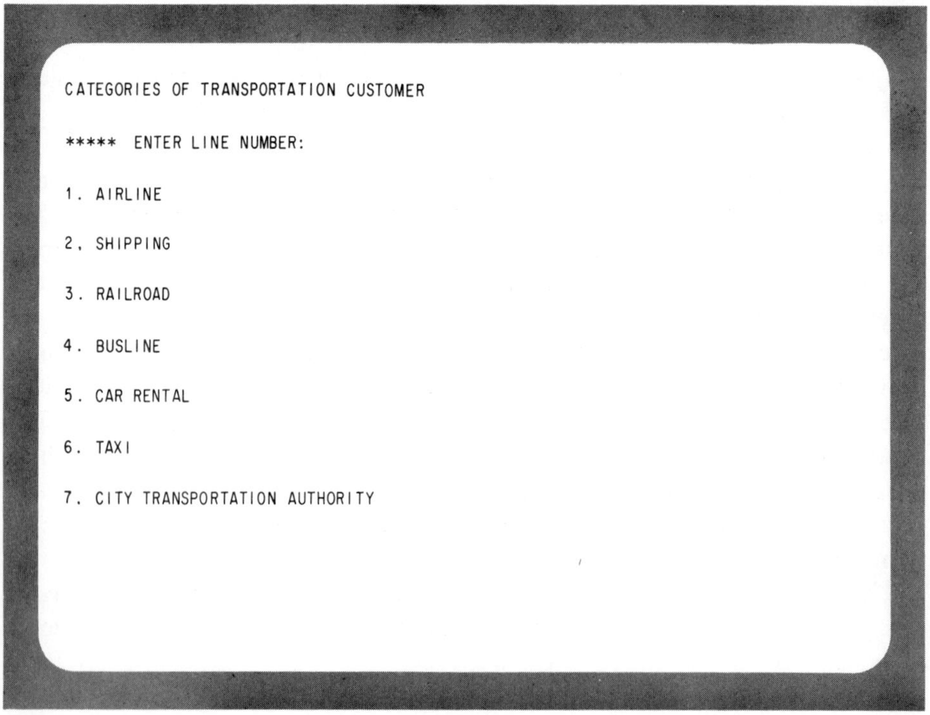

```
CATEGORIES OF TRANSPORTATION CUSTOMER

*****   ENTER LINE NUMBER:

1.  AIRLINE

2.  SHIPPING

3.  RAILROAD

4.  BUSLINE

5.  CAR RENTAL

6.  TAXI

7.  CITY TRANSPORTATION AUTHORITY
```

The operator types: 1                     *Figure 8.8*

```
AIRLINE CUSTOMERS

***** ENTER LINE NUMBER:

1. DOMESTIC AIRLINE

2. FOREIGN AIRLINE
```

The operator types: 1

*Figure 8.9*

```
DOMESTIC AIRLINES

*****  ENTER LINE NUMBER:


1. ALLEGHENY          10. NORTHWEST

2. AMERICAN           11. PAN AMERICAN

3. BRANIFF            12. PIEDMONT

4. CONTINENTAL        13. SOUTHERN

5. DELTA              14. TRANSCARIBBEAN

6. EASTERN            15. TWA

7. MOWHAWK            16. UNITED

8. NATIONAL           17. WESTERN

9. NORTHEAST          18. **OTHER**
```

The operator types: 15

*Figure 8.10*

The technique referred to in the previous illustration is sometimes called "menu selection," the operator choosing one item from a menu of alternatives. Complete and complex applications have been implemented using this technique. The operator needs little training and cannot go far wrong. Such a method is very useful for the "casual" operator.

Often computer-initiated dialogue permits types of answers other than simple selection from a menu. In the following illustration, the computer asks questions or gives commands that can be answered with digits or predetermined words. *The words are all truncated by the computer to four letters*, which permits the operator to type in shortened responses and simplifies the computer's dictionary look-up.

The example is taken from a scheme devised for the ICL Atlas computer in which a small peripheral machine assists the engineer in fault diagnosis [5]. The peripheral machine is attached to the large computer and its store. It records fault histories in its own store. It can help in locating solid faults, but its special value is with intermittent faults, these being particularly difficult and time consuming to find in a computer of great complexity.

**COMPUTER:**   TYPE DIRECTIVE
**OPERATOR:**   guide main store

**COMPUTER:**   ARE ALL STACKS BROKEN? 'YES' OR 'NO'.
**OPERATOR:**   no

**COMPUTER:**   IS FAILURE 'TOTAL' OR 'INTERMITTENT'?
**OPERATOR:**   total

**COMPUTER:**   IS TOTAL FAILURE EVIDENT IN 'LOSS OR PREPULSE', 'ADDRESS TEST',
                OR ANY 'OTHER' TEST?
**OPERATOR:**   address

**COMPUTER:**   TYPE AS TEST RESULT 'SINGLE' DIGIT FAULT, 'BOTH HALVES' OR 'ONE HALF' FAILING
**OPERATOR:**   both

**COMPUTER:**   RUN ADDRESS TEST ON FAILING STACK. LOOK DOWN 970 AND 971 MONITORS
                TO SEE MOVEMENT. TYPE 970,971, 'STOPPED' OR 'MONITORS ALL MOVING'
**OPERATOR:**   monitors

**COMPUTER:**   CHECK ALL 972 CURRENT WAVEFORMS, THEN TYPE FOR PULSE 'O/K', 'HALF-
                SIZE' OR 'NONE'
**OPERATOR:**   half

**COMPUTER:**   PULL OUT VOLTAGE 964'S ONE BY ONE UNTIL PULSES GO FULL-SIZE.
                REPLACE FAILING 964
                IS A CASE HISTORY OF SIMILAR FAULTS REQUIRED?
**OPERATOR:**   yes

**COMPUTER:**   TYPE STACK NUMBER
**OPERATOR:**   11

**COMPUTER:** THE CASE HISTORY WILL BE OUTPUT ON THE LINEPRINTER. IF STILL U/S CHECK VOLTAGE LEVELS. TYPE DIRECTIVE

**OPERATOR:** finish

## 7. Form-Filling

Many different types of computer-initiated dialogue are in use, just as are many different types of operator-initiated dialogue. One approach to computer-initiated dialogue is to make the operator "fill in a form" on the screen of a display unit. A display is presented with blanks, which the operator fills in. The operator's having to position the curser on the screen can be avoided if the spaces to be filled are on the left-hand side of the screen, as in the following example (Figs. 8.11 and 8.12).

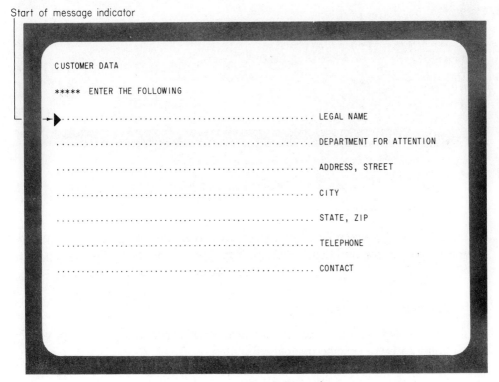

Fig. 8.11. Computer-generated screen of information.

The message transmitted to the computer in this case is not the whole screen but merely ANDERS CHARITIES INC ◢ ADVERTISING ◢ 432E34TH ST ◢ NEW YORK ◢ NY 10016 ◢ 212-MU4-0832 ◢ JOHN ABRAHAM

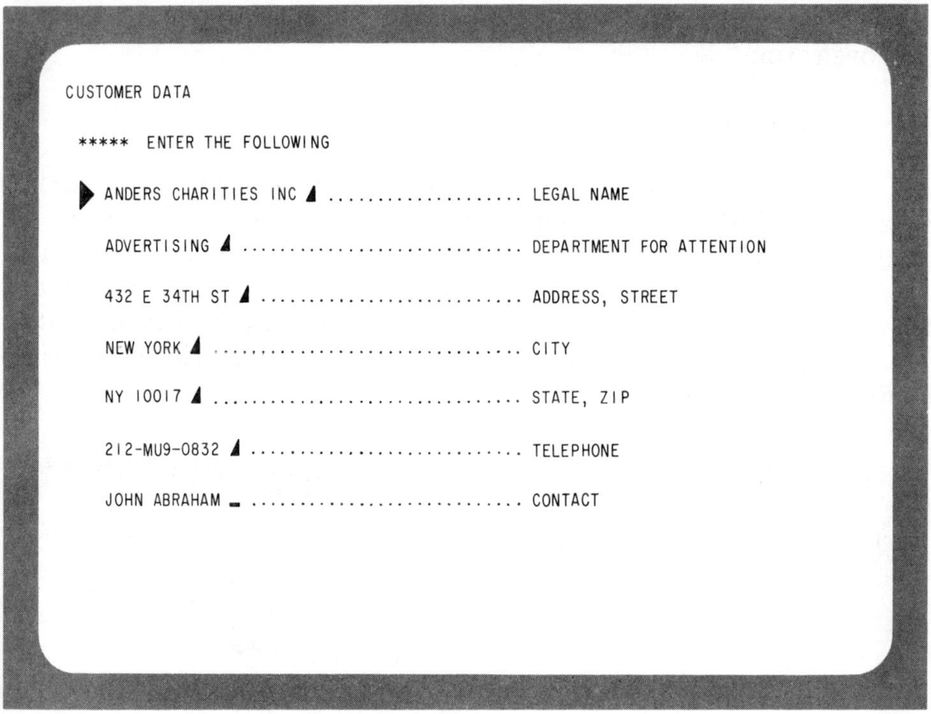

```
CUSTOMER DATA

*****  ENTER THE FOLLOWING

▶  ANDERS CHARITIES INC ◢ ...................  LEGAL NAME

   ADVERTISING ◢ ...........................  DEPARTMENT FOR ATTENTION

   432 E 34TH ST ◢ .........................  ADDRESS, STREET

   NEW YORK ◢ .............................  CITY

   NY 10017 ◢ .............................  STATE, ZIP

   212-MU9-0832 ◢ ..........................  TELEPHONE

   JOHN ABRAHAM ▬ ..........................  CONTACT
```

Start of message indicator: ▶   New line indicators: ◢   Cursor: ▬

*Fig. 8.12.* The screen when the operator has filled in the necessary spaces.

8. *Hybrid Dialogue*

Although the majority of dialogues are either entirely computer-initiated or entirely operator-initiated, some are a mixture of the two. This is the case in the following illustration, which again is designed for a financial analyst [4].

**OPERATOR:**  CALL SAM;

The operator asks for a set of statistical analysis programs (SAM) of which he is going to use a specific one called scatter.

**COMPUTER:**  PROCEED:
**OPERATOR:**  CALL SCATTER;
**COMPUTER:**  DEFINE DATA:
**OPERATOR:**  STOCK LIST A23;
**COMPUTER:**  DEFINE Y AXIS:
**OPERATOR:**  PE = PRICE FOR MAR 22 1972/EPS FOR 1972;
**COMPUTER:**  DEFINE X AXIS:

**OPERATOR:**    EPSG = GROWTH (EPS);
**COMPUTER:**    FOR WHAT DATES?
**OPERATOR:**    1968–1972;
**COMPUTER:**    SPECIFY CONSTRAINTS:
**OPERATOR:**    EPSG GREATER THAN 0;
**COMPUTER:**

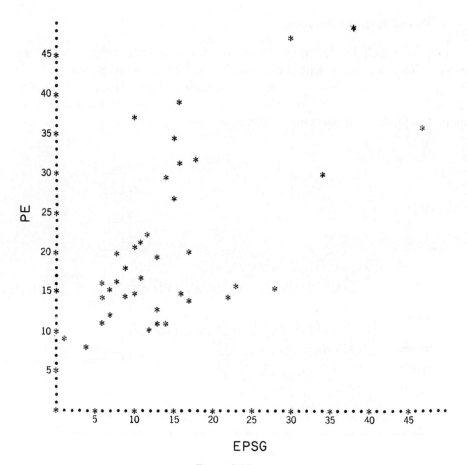

*Figure 8.13*

**COMPUTER:**    PROCEED:
**OPERATOR:**    CALL LINEAR FIT;
**COMPUTER:**    DO THE PREVIOUS DEFINITIONS HOLD?
**OPERATOR:**    YES;
**COMPUTER:**    PE = 10.7+0.67*EPSG
                 PROCEED:
**OPERATOR:**    CALL CORRELATION COEF;

**COMPUTER:** DO THE PREVIOUS DEFINITIONS HOLD?
**OPERATOR:** Y;
**COMPUTER:** R = 0.61
            PROCEED:
**OPERATOR:** END;


### 9. *Special Terminal Hardware*

One approach to designing a dialogue for a specific purpose is to use specially built hardware with keys and lights labeled with elements of the dialogue. Often other devices are also used, such as badge readers and matrix card holders; this has been done on many systems. The temptation to have unique terminals for a particular application appears to be strong. Figure 8.14

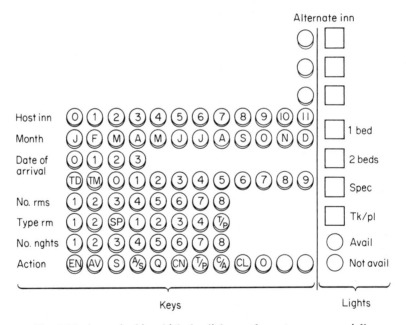

*Fig. 8.14.* A terminal in which the dialogue elements are on specially labeled keys. This terminal is for hotel reservations.

shows a typical example. In some cases, the special-purpose terminal has been much more complex (and expensive) than this one. It seems likely that we will see many more attempts to use special terminals in the future. It can be predicted that at most of the forthcoming symposia on the man-machine interface someone will have a new device in which special dialogue features are built into the hardware.

A major disadvantage in many uses is cost. If the large numbers of terminals predicted are to be in use, it is important that the terminal cost be as low as possible. This condition will be achieved by making a mass-produced standard product, as the success of machines like AT&T's teletypewriters has shown. Machines that are specially constructed and that have small sales will be expensive, particularly when reliability and maintenance are taken into consideration. The cost penalty can be partially overcome, however, by modular keyboard construction.

The second disadvantage is that of inflexibility. Commercial computer applications are subject to a high rate of change. It is often difficult for the systems analyst to anticipate what change will occur or how rapidly it will come. If he designs his dialogue around a custom-built keyboard, he is building resistance to change into the system. Indeed, most dialogues other than the simplest have changed drastically even before cutover—this is the rule rather than the exception. The difficulty of changing terminal hardware three months before cutover is much greater than that of changing programs.

Terminals will be discussed further in Chapter 12. Let us merely note here that in most cases where the dialogue has been built into the hardware, as on the early airline terminals, the same result could have been achieved with a cheaper off-the-shelf terminal and a suitably structured man-machine dialogue.

### 10. *Dialogue with a Totally Untrained Operator*

We have much in our favor if we can *train* the terminal operator, even if only for a fairly brief time. However, there are *many* potential applications for which we would like a totally untrained, naive, and often unintelligent person to use the terminal. This condition has been achieved with great success on certain systems. The key to success again lies in the dialogue design.

The first essential for dialogue with a totally untrained operator is to stop him from saying anything that the computer cannot interpret. There are several ways to do so. The most effective is to restrict his means of input by giving him only certain keys. If we do not give him an alphabetic keyboard, he cannot compose verbal messages. Dialogues for totally untrained operators will almost always be "computer-initiated," not "operator-initiated" dialogues.

The simplest keyboard the author has seen is one with only three keys: YES, NO, and ?. The system in question was used at a hospital for interviewing outpatients before they see a doctor. It was desirable that the terminal should be inexpensive and that it should use a standard time-sharing service, and so a normal teletype machine was fitted with a specially designed mask to simplify the keyboard.

Another way of restricting the user's input is to confine the dialogue to "menu selection" techniques. A terminal with keys at the side of the screen designed for "menu selection" dialogue would have a wide range of applications.

An additional essential for dialogue with an untrained operator is to design the computer responses so that they have the utmost clarity. They should leave the operator with no doubt about what he is supposed to key in. The design of this type of dialogue requires a basic literacy that appears conspicuously absent in the designers of some of today's systems.

## 11. *Fixed-Frame Responses*

In some systems with computer-initiated dialogue, it is possible to carry out the entire operation with a set of unvarying computer responses. The computer, in other words, does not *compose* a response; it merely *selects* one from a predetermined set. The set, in some cases, is large.

This approach simplifies the programming and raises the possibility of avoiding transmission of the actual computer responses over expensive communication links. The responses could be stored in small local machines near the terminal locations, or they could be stored at the concentrator location. The computer would indicate which response was to be sent to a terminal by transmitting only a coded identification—possibly a four-digit number. The local machine would generate the requisite response.

A feature of computer-initiated dialogues that makes this scheme attractive is that the dialogue is usually very one-sided. The computer gives lengthy responses and the operator very short ones, sometimes only one character, as in the examples in Figs. 8.7 to 8.10. A full-duplex line capable of transmitting equal numbers of characters in each direction would be partially wasted in this case.

On some schemes using visual display units, the computer-generated displays have been referred to as "frames." Although the frames may be stored ready for use at peripheral locations, they can also be maintained centrally. If the peripheral storage is of a read/write nature, such as drums or disks, the system may be designed so that a new or changed frame may be transmitted from the central computer to the peripheral device. Each day of operation may start or end with frame maintenance. The day's date may be changed, for example. Inventory levels or other working data may be updated, or codes used for security reasons may be altered.

It is worth noting that a disk used for peripheral dialogue storage need be neither large nor fast. It could be less expensive than most disk units used in data processing today.

### 12. *Dialogue with Pictures*

In some applications in operation today, a picture is needed in the computer response, as well as alphanumeric data. We are not talking here about applications of graphics but simply the displaying to the terminal operator of a photograph or other picture as a response to what he keyed in. It is possible that this scheme may become an important form of man-computer dialogue in the future. There are innumerable potential applications in which the capability to have picture responses could be used to good effect.

The difficulty with pictures is that they generally need a greater transmission bandwidth than alphanumeric data. One Picturephone® frame, for example, can be encoded with 200,000 bits. Alphanumeric data displayed on the same frame could be encoded with about 2000 bits. It is unlikely, therefore, that such pictures as photographs will be transmitted to terminals over conventional telecommunications in the near future. The CATV coaxial cable into the home *could* be used in this way to provide a still-picture dialogue using the TV set [6]. It is more probable, however, that the pictures, like the "fixed-frame" alphanumeric responses discussed above, will be stored at the terminal locations. They can be stored in the form of slides, film frames, microfiche, or other photographic media. Such storage is done on some terminals today, notably those used for computer-assisted instruction. A most promising candidate for future systems is the EVR method of recording. One EVR cartridge contains 180,000 black-and-white frames or 90,000 color. With the addition of an addressing and searching mechanism, the EVR set could form the basis of a most versatile computer dialogue. The computer would transmit variable alphanumeric data and details of which frame the terminal should display. In many cases, there would be no variable data but merely a "fixed-frame" dialogue.

In addition to its use in computer-assisted instruction, this form of dialogue can have many uses where a document, drawing, or photograph must be examined. It is likely to be used, for example, for engineering or architectural drawings, for maps or town plans, for real-estate systems, or systems for purchasing industrial items. In the years ahead when we have terminals in the home (which probably make use of the television set), it will be used for consumer information. Catalogs such as the Sears Roebuck catalog for example, could be on EVR. One cartridge would be enough for a greatly expanded catalog. Home "shopping" could use such cartridges in conjunction with the transmission of a small amount of information to and from a computer using the telephone line for interrogation, indexing, and searching for the appropriate frame. Here we have the possibility of a "yellow pages" like that issued by the telephone company, but with 180,000 frames of information, each frame having a picture if necessary and a computer to assist in finding information. There are endless potential uses of such a technology—encyclopedias, sports history, vacation planning, career information, stock market history, and far more versatile forms of computer-assisted instruction. We can expect a major growth in the knowledge industry.

Where it is necessary to change the contents of the still-picture frames, a medium may be used in which changes can be made at an appropriate cost. Replaceable microfiche cards may be suitable for this purpose. Microfilm reels may be employed with a new reel being distributed each week or month.

On some present-day systems, *off-line* video devices are used. The reason is because equivalent on-line devices are still expensive. The New England Real-Estate Clearing House, for example, places microfilm viewers alongside a teletype machine in its clients' offices. Brokers carry on a dialogue with a time-sharing system at the terminals, asking the computer to search for property that fulfills the clients' requirements. A wide diversity of search parameters can be used. The computer gives the answer in the form of numbers referring to microfilm frames. The broker then scans through the microfilm manually to find the frame in question. A new "listing" in the form of a new reel of microfilm is sent to each subscribing broker periodically.

It is perhaps in this off-line form that we will see many dialogues with pictures in the near future. Eventually, when the on-line linkage drops sufficiently in cost, the pictures will appear without manual intervention.

## REFERENCES

1. Katzan, Harry, Jr., *APL Programming and Computer Techniques*, Van Nostrand Reinhold Co., New York, 1970. A good text for beginners with APL.

2. C. Languet-Higgins and S. D. Isard, *The Monkey's Paw*, Conference on Man-Computer Interaction organized by the IEEE, England, September 1970.

3. "The Commonwealth of Pennsylvania Computerized Legislative Information Processing and Retrieval System," *IBM Manual K20-0273*, White Plains.

4. J. J. Gal, Man-Machine Interactive Systems and Their Application to Financial Analysis, *Financial Analysts Journal*, May–June 1966. The dialogue illustrations from this article used in this chapter are given with minor modifications.

5. M. H. J. Baylis, *Maintenance of Large Computer Systems—The Engineer's Assistant.* A paper published in *Machine Intelligence 3*, edited by Donald Michie, American Elsevier Publishing Company, New York, 1968.

6. James Martin, *Future Developments in Telecommunications*, Prentice-Hall, 1971.

# 9 CONTROL OF
# USER ERRORS

Terminal operators will always make errors. It is essential to protect the computer system and its data from these errors, as far as possible, and to do so without antagonizing the operators.

On systems in which the operator does not modify the data stored, system protection presents little difficulty. The files will be "locked" so that they cannot be overwritten; and if the terminal operator writes programs, these will be confined to a partition so that they cannot interfere with any other programs. The main problem is to help the operator find the information he wants when he uses the terminal incorrectly.

The control of errors is of much greater concern when the operators modify the data base or are responsible for building up the information in the data base. In some systems all information stored originates from the terminal operators. Sometimes the terminal operators work in a fairly casual manner compared with the card-punch operators and verifiers of batch data processing. The error controls used in batch data processing are largely inapplicable. Clearly, the whole idea of building up a data base in this way depends on whether we can control the accuracy of the terminal input, catching the errors that occur.

On certain systems, the errors are cumulative. The files contain information about a set of items that is kept for several months and updated periodically by terminal operator actions. If occasional operator actions cause errors in the files, as the months pass the files will steadily collect more and more inaccuracies. This situation could obviously bring the system into disrepute, and controls *must* be devised to prevent it.

A number of factors make real-time systems worse than batch systems for the control of accuracy. First, there are likely to be more terminal operators creating the input and these people are scattered over many areas. They tend to be more diverse and less controllable than the girls in a keypunch room. Second, the verification operation found in a keypunch room is usually not employed. Third, batch totals and other batch controls often cannot be used, for the transactions originate singly, not in batches. Fourth, equipment failures will occur. Frequently it is when a terminal, line, or computer fails, or during the recovery period, that operator errors originate.

We do, however, have one factor strongly in our favor on real-time systems: the fact that in an appropriately designed dialogue most of the errors made can be caught *in real time*—as the operator makes them. The mistake or discrepancy is then corrected on the spot. The effectiveness of such real-time error detection is highly dependent on the design of the man-machine dialogue.

The battle for accuracy on real-time systems has six vital aspects:

1. The psychological considerations in dialogue design must be planned so as to minimize the probability of human errors.
2. The dialogue must be structured in such a way as to catch as many errors as possible immediately.
3. The system must be planned so as to facilitate immediate correction of errors caught.
4. The real-time, error-detection process must be backed up with off-line file inspection and, if applicable, balancing routines.
5. Self-checking operations must be built into both the real-time dialogue and the linkage of this dialogue to the file-inspection routines.
6. Procedures must be worked out to bridge all periods of system failure and recovery in such a way that errors are not introduced here.

In this chapter we are concerned only with those aspects of accuracy control that affect the man-machine dialogue. The aspects concerned with hardware and lines are discussed in Chapters 15 and 21.

**ERROR PSYCHOLOGY**   It is desirable in the dialogue design to steer a course between operator boredom and bewilderment. Operator "channel overload," on the one hand, and lack of motivation on the other will lead to errors.

When errors occur, the operator should be notified immediately rather than later. Studies of the human–learning process have shown that positive response to correct actions and admonition of incorrect actions *within seconds* give by far the best reinforcement. The conscientious operator will learn from the response to his incorrect actions. The response, however, should not be overly abrupt. A split-second error response in midthought is jarring and "rude." The operator should be permitted to finish his thought before the error response is sent. A dedicated operator may tolerate and learn from abrupt, abbreviated error messages, although Miller [1] recommends a response time of not less than 2 seconds. A casual operator is likely to require more dignified treatment. Figure 9.1 shows a typical error message to legislators on the Pennsylvania Legislative System [2] discussed in Chapter 8.

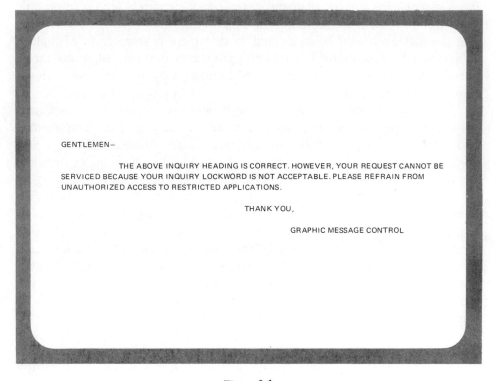

GENTLEMEN–

   THE ABOVE INQUIRY HEADING IS CORRECT. HOWEVER, YOUR REQUEST CANNOT BE SERVICED BECAUSE YOUR INQUIRY LOCKWORD IS NOT ACCEPTABLE. PLEASE REFRAIN FROM UNAUTHORIZED ACCESS TO RESTRICTED APPLICATIONS.

     THANK YOU,

      GRAPHIC MESSAGE CONTROL

*Figure 9.1*

There is one danger in giving real-time error responses: the operator may develop the attitude that he does not need to be careful because the system picks up all his mistakes anyway. This attitude must clearly be discouraged, and in many systems an appropriate way to do so is to log the error messages sent and then analyze them. When the operator knows that the system is keeping track of the mistakes he makes, he will normally try to improve his performance.

**TYPES OF**
**CONTROLS**
Controls on card and tape systems are mainly based on taking batch totals. Checks, invoices, or other documents may pass through a control point where a girl groups them into batches and adds up on an adding machine the total sum of money in the batch. Or a hash total may be taken by adding all the account numbers or customer numbers, or those of other fields.

These batch totals accompany the group of work as it goes to the punch room and later into the computer. The computer will check the totals to make sure that all the items have been correctly punched into cards. Where these small batches are combined to form large decks of work, appropriate totals will be built up and used to ensure that no items are lost—for example, in sorts or merges—and that all the required documents are printed.

On many, but not all, dialogue systems, batch controls are inappropriate. Instead some form of *single-transaction* check must be devised. The transaction, and the dialogue, must be structured so that there is some form of built-in redundancy or some means of comparing the transaction with what was anticipated. There is a wide veriety of ways of doing so, varying, of course, with the nature of the application.

The single-transaction checks will be backed up by a periodic check on a *group of transactions* where possible. In a bank, for example, the cash handled and entered by a teller will be balanced periodically to ensure that it is still correct. In a lengthy data-entry dialogue relating to a single complex item, the status will be summarized at intervals to ensure that all appears correct.

These transaction checks will themselves be backed up by off-line accuracy controls, and the structure of the system and its processing must be designed to make these controls as effective as possible. Again taking the example of a bank, an end-of-day file scan will balance the cash from each teller and each branch, ensuring that it is correct. This procedure will take place on other systems in which cash is involved. On still other systems, the file scan will ensure that no record has been accidentally deleted; it will check for given types of undesirable circumstances and will police certain of the operator actions.

**SINGLE-TRANSACTION**
**CHECKS**
Let us list a number of types of single-transaction checks. The list is illustrative, not exhaustive, for there is a wide difference in what is possible on different applications. The dialogue designer should survey all the possibilities he can and select a set that will make his dialogue as secure as possible.

### 1. *Self-Checking Numbers*

Account numbers, part numbers, and similar items can be made self-checking. The last digit or digits will be an arithmetical combination of the previous ones. They may, for example, be obtained by taking the digits in the unchecked number, dividing by a prime, and using the low-order digits of the remainder as the check digits. If the operator miskeys the number—for example, accidentally interposes two digits—then the check digits will usually catch the error. One or more check digits may be used, depending on the level of safety desired.

### 2. *Descriptive Print-Back*

Where the operator keys in a number or a mnemonic, an alphabetic print-back should be given saying what it relates to, if possible. If he keys in tour 193 instead of 192, he will see immediately that it is going to Athens, New York, not Athens, Greece. The computer would no doubt be blamed if it delivered an unhappy tourist to Athens, New York, by mistake!

Where a menu-selection technique is used, as in Figs. 8.7 to 8.10, the operator keys in one digit. The following screen should state what he has selected. The screen following that in Fig. 8.7 begins with a heading which says TRANSPORTATION CUSTOMER, for example.

### 3. *Link to Earlier Transaction*

Sometimes a transaction can be linked to an earlier transaction for error-control purposes. When a customer takes his passbook into a savings bank, for example, it should contain the balance at the end of the previous transaction. This redundant information may be keyed in by the teller. The computer checks the previous balance on the record for this customer. If it is not in agreement, this may indicate that the teller has made a mistake; it may indicate that something has gone astray earlier. If the latter, it should be sorted out there and then. There are many other examples of dialogue that is designed to give continuity between separate transactions relating to the same account or same entity.

### 4. *Check for a Valid Sequence of Transactions*

Sometimes events should happen only in a certain fixed sequence. A deviation from this sequence will indicate an error, and so sequence checks will be made when each transaction is entered. Such is the case in a production-control system. Workers on a factory shop floor enter into terminals details of jobs they start, complete, or, for some reason, leave. They may enter their man number, the job number, and the number of the machine tool that they are using. If they leave a job, they may indicate that it is 20 percent complete or whatever. The computer may maintain three sets of records, each of which is updated at this point—a record for the man, a record for the job, and a record for the machine tool. When an entry is made, the computer will check that *that* man should have been working on *that* job, using *that* machine tool. If he reports that the job is 20 percent complete, it will check that that is a viable figure. If the job had not been reported as started, or had already been reported 50 percent complete, then an error message would result. These continuity checks, in practice, result in most data-entry errors being detected. As soon as the computer's picture of what is occurring on the shop floor deviates from what is reported, action is taken.

### 5. *Use of Machine-Readable Documents*

On production-control and data-entry systems, badges with information punched into them are commonly used. A badge is used to give the employee number. Sometimes a badge travels around the factory with the job, giving the job number. Sometimes a badge is used for giving the machine tool number. The use of such badges ensures that no mistake is made in the entry of these numbers, as it might be if the worker keyed them in.

A number of other forms of portable documents are in use for similar reasons. It is possible that we may see a massive use of machine-readable credit cards in the future. Credit cards with data about their owners encoded on a machine-readable magnetic stripe are now in use.

### 6. *Check for Internal Contradictions*

A false entry may be detected by the fact that it contradicts other known data, or a set of entries may contain some inconsistancy. In a system controlling railroad cars, a terminal entry stating the movement of a car would first be checked to ensure that *that* car was in *that* location and, possibly, that it *was* loaded with the goods stated. If an entry on a airline system is made to change a booking, the computer will first check that the passenger *was* booked on the stated flight.

Often the dialogue can be designed to enhance the checks that can be made. In an airline reservation dialogue, for example, in which a multistop journey is being booked, it is desirable to do a location continuity check and also a date-time continuity check. Unfortunately, however, many passengers do not book continuous journeys. For instance, a man might make a reservation from New York to Los Angeles, drive to San Francisco, and then fly back from there to New York. The airline knows nothing about how he travels from Los Angeles to San Francisco, and so the continuity checks may seem valueless at first sight. The airline overcomes this problem by booking a false segment to bridge the gap; it is known as an ARUNK segment, meaning ARRIVAL UN-KNOWN. The ARUNK segment is booked from Los Angeles to San Francisco and then the computer can check the whole booking for location continuity and date-time continuity. A device like an ARUNK segment would be worthwhile in other types of application as well.

There are many ways of building doublechecks into a dialogue structure. It is up to the designer to find them.

### 7. *Check That All Facts Have Been Entered*

The facts about a situation will often be entered in a variable rather than a fixed sequence. This will often be true when the facts are being obtained from a potential customer over the telephone. The computer must then check that all the facts have been entered. Usually the entry of a subset of facts is mandatory. If the operator attempts to close the dialogue before this information has been entered, he must be asked by the computer for the missing data. If one item of the set is not applicable—for example, if the customer does not have a telephone number—then a NIL entry should be made.

**GROUP-TRANSACTION CHECKS**   The error checks may be applicable to a group of transactions rather than to single transactions.

### 8. *Periodic Cash Balances*

On systems in which cash is handled, an interim balance may be taken at fairly small intervals. On some systems, several different accumulators are used to give a multiple balance.

### 9. *Running Totals*

On certain systems, running totals are kept. The terminal maintains a print-out giving the totals of certain items entered. The totals may be broken down by category. At intervals, or at the end of the day, the totals will be compared with totals obtained by the computer.

Running totals are especially valuable during periods of equipment failure. The terminal goes dead, but customers still have to be dealt with. At some later time, hopefully not too much later, the terminal returns to life, and the transactions made in some makeshift manner while it was out are entered into the system. The running totals are maintained during the period of outage. When the transactions are then entered into the system, these totals will be compared with those obtained by the computer. In this way the running totals bridge the gap of terminal outage.

### 10. *Checkpoints*

Where an operator is entering separate related items, each perhaps requiring some decision-making dialogue, he may be made to inspect a summary of his progress at intervals. At this checkpoint, he must inspect the status summary and verify that he thinks it is correct. The checkpoint procedure may be designed to be optional so that the operator can use it when he thinks fit. It is probably better, however, to make it mandatory, forcing him to check at intervals that no misunderstanding or omission has occurred.

**ERRORS CAUGHT AT A LATER TIME**  On occasions an error may not be caught at the time it is made, but it becomes apparent at some later time. It should, in fact, be given every opportunity to make itself manifest later. When an operator is given a display of a set of previously stored facts, he should be asked to verify that they are correct.

If the operator makes a correction entry at this stage, it is often advisable to keep a copy of the original, particularly if the operator making the correction is not the one who made the original entry. On airline reservation systems, the passenger records are kept in two parts: one part gives details of the current status for that passenger, and the other is a "history record" showing what changes in the record have been made.

There are some types of real-time system in which a discrepancy is unlikely to survive undetected for long, provided that the data on the files are checked against each succeeding entry. As each change in status of an entity is recorded, it is compared with the previous information the computer had about that entity.

**ERRORS CORRECTED
BY A SPECIALIZED
OPERATOR**
Occasionally when an entry triggers off an error indication, the best person to deal with it would not be the operator who originated the entry but a different person who has overall knowledge of the situation. In other words, it pays on some systems to have a specialist, or group of specialists, for dealing with certain types of errors.

The error-handling staff would sit at terminals through which they would receive notification of discrepancies. In some cases, they will be close to the computer room and may use listings prepared each night on file-scanning runs. They will use their terminals for making corrections to the files when necessary.

Each major file may have a man assigned to it who would be responsible for its accuracy. He may also be responsible for its security, ensuring that unauthorized persons do not read items they should not and that they do not make changes in the records. We will call this person the "file owner." One person may have responsibility for more than one file. He will understand its structure, addressing, and the on-line and off-line checks that are made on it. He will receive real-time notification of suspected discrepancies and will investigate them, making such changes as are appropriate.

The file owners may be gathered together in a room, which we will call the "information control room." A variety of other operations are likely to take place in such a room, and it is an essential adjunct to many real-time systems. We will explore this theme further in Chapter 11.

**INDIRECT
FEEDBACK**
The majority of errors are best dealt with by the operator making the transaction. The feedback to this operator is of great importance. In some systems, however, direct and immediate feedback is not possible. The two main cases in which this is so are, first, when the operator is off line and, second, when the operator has an inexpensive terminal not capable of giving verbal feedback. The first case occurs when messages are sent by teletype to the computer in a machine-readable code, but from an off-line operator, perhaps in a different organization. This case occurs, for example, when one airline sends a teletype message to another about reservations. If the message turns out to be machine-unreadable or if it contains a detectable error, it will be referred to an operator. Sometimes the operator will be able to see an obvious miscoding that can be corrected on the spot. Sometimes he must compose a message to the originator requesting clarification.

The most common use of terminals that cannot give a detailed error message involves applications in which data are collected at stations in a factory, warehouse, or other work locations. Such applications often use a large number of terminals, and it is desirable to make the terminal as inexpensive as possible. For this reason, no printing or other character–response mechanism is used. Figure 9.2 illustrates a typical terminal of this type.

*Fig. 9.2.* A 2790 terminal.

The user of such a terminal will make errors; therefore the systems designer must construct a mechanism for dealing with them. One solution is to place a terminal that *is* capable of dialogue in the vicinity of the work stations. It might be situated in a foreman's office, for example, and the foreman would sort out the problems. Another possibility is to have a shop-floor expediter, or roving problem solver, who is directed from the information control room.

Figure 9.3 shows a configuration that worked particularly well in practice in a factory data-collection system. Erroneous transactions from the workstation terminals are detected by the computer and details of them are printed at the terminals in the information control room. The specialists there investigate the errors and can sometimes take care of them themselves. When they

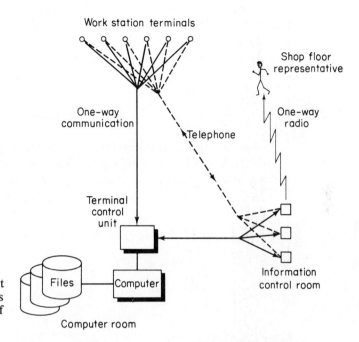

*Fig. 9.3.* A three-way dialogue at the information control room is used to improve the accuracy of data entered on the shop floor.

need the help of the roving shop-floor representative, they send a radio signal to him. He has a radio "beeper" in his belt; when it sounds, he goes to the nearest terminal, which has a telephone jack wired to the information control room. The control room specialist tells the shop-floor man what is wrong, and the latter goes to the worker in question, finds out the correct situation, and makes appropriate corrections at the terminal.

This three-way linkage works well because it is highly flexible and because the workers know that if they make mistakes at the terminal they will be visited by the shop-floor representative. Normally they try to avoid such visits. They can, however, ask for help at the terminal and, in effect, call for the representative.

**MORAL**     Effective error control requires three interlinked system elements.

1. A dialogue designed to catch the maximum possible number of errors with effective feedback to the operators.
2. Off-line file balancing, scanning, and policing operations.
3. Intelligent and flexible *human action* to detect and correct errors that do slip through.

Designing the man-machine interface to avoid errors will require perhaps 10 percent more programming and 10 percent more operator actions; sometimes a greater percentage than this is required. The moral of systems in operation today is that this extra effort is very well worthwhile.

## REFERENCES

1. Robert B. Miller, *Response Time in Man-Computer Conversational Transactions.* IBM Technical Report TR00-1660. IBM Corporation, Poughkeepsie, N.Y., 1968.
2. "The Commonwealth of Pennsylvania Computerized Legislative Information Processing and Retrieval System," *IBM Manual K20-0273*, White Plains.

# 10 THE TRADE-OFF BETWEEN PSYCHOLOGICAL FACTORS AND NETWORK COST

The designers of the man-machine dialogue would often like to concentrate on user psychology alone and forget about constraints imposed by the mechanics of the system beyond the terminal and dialogue programs. Unfortunately, these constraints sometimes assume great importance because of cost; this is true in the telecommunication network. The calculations in Section 6 of this book are intended to find the optimum structure for any particular network. As we shall see, the optimum network structure for a particular system differs considerably, depending on the design of the man-machine dialogue. For a system with a far-flung network, then, different dialogue approaches result in different network costs.

On many systems a team has worked on the dialogue design, adjusting it so that the operators find it as simple and unconfusing as possible and so that the number of operator errors tends to be as low as possible. Such a team sometimes works for an extensive period with live operators and a simulated system, polishing the dialogue structure. The result of this process has usually been to increase the number of characters that are transmitted by the computer and to increase the number of dialogue "pairs"—in other words, the number of times the direction of transmission reverses. Both steps can increase the cost of the terminal network.

There is a trade-off between the psychological considerations in the dialogue and the network cost. For a small network, the differences in cost may be insignificant. For a nationwide system, they can be great.

113

**TWO TYPICAL**
**EXAMPLES**

The structure of the terminal dialogue can differ widely on seemingly similar systems. Let us examine two typical cases chosen to illustrate how great this difference can be.

Both relate to a similar problem. A central data base of order or booking information is being kept. The desired information about customers and their "orders" is entered via terminals at sales offices. Some of the orders are taken over the telephone. The customer is quite likely to change his order or possibly cancel it, and such changes, as they occur, must be entered correctly into the data base. In both examples, a change is required in the time of execution. The first example is of an airline reservations system; the time of one of the flights booked is to be changed. The second example relates to an order of engineering components; the delivery date is to be changed. The problems seem similar, on the face of it, and one would expect that the conversation structure would be broadly similar. In reality, there is no resemblance between the two cases.

The airline conversation proceeds as follows:

A Mr. Goldsmith telephones the airline to say that he wants to modify his reservation. The agent he speaks to instructs her terminal to display his record—Flight 21 on March 25. The entry is as follows (Fig. 10.1):

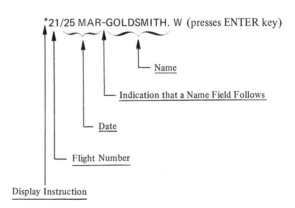

*Figure 10.1*

The computer gives details of his record (Fig. 10.2).

The operator checks that this record is indeed the required one, and the passenger indicates that he wishes to change the second flight of his journey. He wants to fly back from Los Angeles (LAX) to New York's Kennedy Airport (JFK) on the 26th of March rather than the 25th.

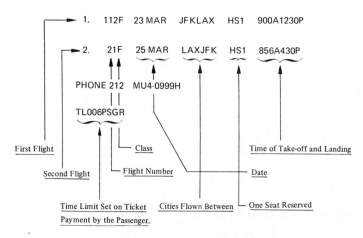

Fig. 10.2. The record displayed.

The girl informs the computer that the second flight of the journey is to be changed. She types (Fig. 10.3):

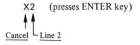

The computer types:

NEXT SEG ENTRY REPLACES 2

She responds:

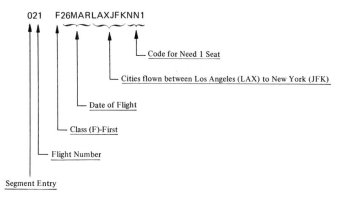

Figure 10.3

This statement is a request for a seat on the 26th of March rather than the 25th. NN is a code meaning that the agent needs one seat. The computer replies with a replacement for line 2 above:

    2.  21F  26MAR  LAXJFK  HS1  845A430P

The operator attempts to book this seat by pressing the E key, meaning END TRANSACTION:

    E

The computer asks who requested this modification:

    WHO MADE CHANGE

The operator replies that the passenger himself requested it. The 6 key means "change made by . . .":

    6  PSGR
    ↑         ↖
    Change      Passenger
    Made by

The computer indicates that this message has been received by placing an asterisk at the end of it.

    6  PSGR*

The operator again presses the E key, and this time the computer carries out the END TRANSACTION operation and updates the appropriate files. It responds:

    OK  1232A
    ↑        ↖
    Booking      Time
    Made

This "conversation" makes a heavy use of abbreviations and mnemonics. The operator must know the precise format for each message she keys in. She must be familiar with the abbreviations used. In practice, there are a large number, only a few of which have been shown here. A typical airline needs to send its terminal operators to a 3-week training course to learn to communicate with the system in this way.

Our second example is very different in that the operator does not need to know any mnemonics, abbreviations, or formats. He simply does what he is told by the computer. Here he is attempting to change the delivery data on an order for engineering components:

| | |
|---|---|
| **SCREEN:** | ENTER CUSTOMER NUMBER IF KNOWN. IF NOT TYPE "N" |
| **USER:** | N |
| **SCREEN:** | TYPE FIRST TWO LETTERS OF CUSTOMER'S NAME |
| **USER:** | GO |
| **SCREEN:** | WHICH CUSTOMER? ENTER LINE NUMBER |
| | 1. GOLDBERG SIDNEY & CO. |
| | 2. GOLDEN KAUFMAN SALES CO. |
| | 3. GOLDSMITH WALTER & CO. |
| | 4. GOODMAN ABE |
| | 5. NONE OF THE ABOVE |
| **USER:** | 3 |
| **SCREEN:** | CUSTOMER NUMBER: 17-8341 |
| | GOLDSMITH WALTER & CO. |
| | 745, OLD STONE HIGHWAY, SPRINGS, |
| | EAST HAMPTON, N. Y., 11937 |
| | REPRESENTATIVE E. S. ROPLEY #543271 |
| | PRESS ENTER IF CORRECT |
| **USER:** | *Presses "Enter" key.* |
| **SCREEN:** | WHICH INFORMATION IS TO BE CHANGED? |
| | ENTER LINE NUMBER |

| | |
|---|---|
| 1. NEW ORDER | 9. INVOICE TO ADDRESS |
| 2. CANCEL ORDER | 10. SHIP TO ADDRESS |
| 3. ORDER QUANTITY | 11. CUSTOMER ADDRESS |
| 4. DELIVERY DATE | 12. CUSTOMER NAME |
| 5. PRIORITY CODE | 13. MISC. INSTRUCTIONS |
| 6. ORDER DETAILS | 14. REPRESENTATIVE DETAILS |
| 7. DISCOUNT | 15. BRANCH OFFICE |
| 8. TAX DETAILS | 16. OTHER |

| | |
|---|---|
| **USER:** | 4 |
| **SCREEN:** | WHICH ORDER IS TO BE CHANGED? |
| | ENTER LINE NUMBER |

| | ORDER # | ITEMS | | | ORDER DATE | DEL. DATE |
|---|---|---|---|---|---|---|
| 1 | 573824 | 87289 | 00241 | 00029 | 4/1/69 | 4/1/70 |
| | | 00310 | 77139 | 04126 | | |
| | | 00900 | | | | |
| 2 | 575931 | 00391 | 00700 | 00421 | 10/1/69 | 4/1/71 |
| 3 | 575828 | 00750 | 00900 | | 12/1/69 | 12/1/70 |
| 4 | 579003 | 02107 | | | 6/1/69 | 8/1/70 |

| | |
|---|---|
| **USER:** | 2 |

**SCREEN:** ORDER NUMBER 575931

| ITEM # | DESCRIPTION | QTY. |
|--------|-------------|------|
| 00391 | MAGNETIC D EXTRACTOR 7 BR | 5 |
| 00700 | LINK ADAPTOR ADDL | 5 |
| 00421 | CTC DIRECT CONTROL | 5 |

ORDER DATE 10/1/69  DELIV DATE 4/1/71

ENTER NEW REQUIRED DELIV DATE (XX/XX/XX)

**USER:** 10/01/70

**SCREEN:** EARLIEST DELIV DATE POSSIBLE AT PRIORITY 3 IS
2/1/70

IF THIS IS REQUESTED ENTER "Y"

**USER:** Y

The great advantage of this conversation over the previous one is that it is easy for the operator. Once he is familiar with how to operate the terminal, he can hardly go wrong. The terminal tells him precisely what to do at each step, and his response is always very short.

**WHY THE DIFFERENCE?**   Why is there such a large difference between the conversation structure in these two examples? Would the systems analysts on either system adopt the conversation structure of the other if they started again? The author discussed this question with the designers and their answer was "Absolutely not!" Why, then, the difference?

The first reason relates to the operator. The operators of the airline system spend their entire working life using the terminal. They have plenty of time to become completely familiar with its functioning. They will not forget the mnemonics and formats, which they use all day. On the second system, however, most persons will use the terminal only occasionally. It will be used by a salesman, sales engineer, or other staff who would otherwise look up customer records in filing cabinets. Such personnel will not remember large numbers of mnemonics or be likely to type multi-item messages in the correct format. The conversation structure must be as simple as possible for such users, as indeed it is in the second example.

The second reason concerns the cost of the telecommunication lines. In order to minimize the network cost, the airline system attaches many terminals to the same line, as discussed later in the book. It is desirable to minimize the number of characters flowing on such a line. The first example does so. It achieves its results with a number of characters close to the minimum. Use of the technique in the second example would have resulted in many more characters transmitted. It would also have resulted in many more line turnarounds, which, as we shall see, are expensive on large networks. These considerations were particularly important in the airline case because here the lines were very lengthy and therefore expensive.

The third reason is that the airline system carries out only one application— reservations. The terminal in the second example could be used for a variety of different applications. It would have been more difficult to use single-character mnemonics in the second case because there would have been insufficient single characters. In general, many more mnemonics would have been needed for the multiple applications.

The final reason concerns the speed of the operation. The airline agents will often be talking to potential customers on the telephone at the same time that they are using the foregoing dialogue with the computer. It is desirable that the computer dialogue be quick enough and flexible enough to avoid holding up the sales conversation. In the first example above, facts can be entered as the customer states them, with the minimum of keying and in any sequence. In the second example, they must be entered in a fixed sequence, as the computer requests them, and the whole dialogue is slower.

**FACTORS AFFECTING NETWORK STRUCTURE**    Several aspects of the differences in dialogue structure affect the layout of the communication network. Let us summarize them.

### 1. Differences in Numbers of Characters

In the second of the two dialogue structures, many more characters are used. The dialogue for airline reservations systems could have been designed to be much easier for the operator to learn. It could have been a computer-initiated dialogue, such as those shown in Chapter 8. The result, however, would have been a major increase in the number of characters used, which would have meant that substantially fewer terminals could be connected to one voice-grade line. Therefore, there would have been more lines. The total cost of the telecommunication network would have been several times what is was with the dialogue shown.

### 2. Nonsymmetry in the Transmission

Some dialogue structures result in a large number of characters flowing in one direction and a small number flowing in the other direction, all on the same line. The dialogue in Figs. 8.7 to 8.10 would give a highly unbalanced character flow, for example. The result could be an inefficient usage of the line in one direction. Modems that give full-duplex operation with a much higher character rate in one direction than in the other are in existence. They might be a partial solution to the problem.

### 3. *Fixed-Frame Techniques*

The dialogue may be designed in the form of a set of unvarying responses, as discussed on page 96. The possibility then arises of storing these responses at the terminal location or at a concentrator location and of the computer transmitting merely a reference to the response rather than the response itself. In systems with display screens, the responses are sometimes referred to as "frames", a frame being the contents of one response screen. Although some systems send back an entire screen in response, others respond with a line or a few characters on a screen.

The responses may be unchanging or they may be different for each conversation. We could, in fact, categorize them as follows:

1. Responses that never change.
2. Responses that are composed in real-time as the dialogue proceeds.
3. Responses that do not change in real-time but that are changed by a maintenance procedure, perhaps one a day, perhaps infrequently when circumstances require.

Responses in categories 1 and 3 can give a clean and simple design and simplify programming. If such responses are generated at the periphery of the communication network, there can be a substantial saving in line costs; if, however, they are transmitted from the central computer, the network cost will generally be higher than if responses in category 2 were used.

When the responses are of category 3, carefully planned "display maintenance" procedures are needed. It is desirable to avoid excessive duplication of displays, and the catalog of displays will itself become a standard piece of documentation for the programmers and systems analysts.

### 4. *Compaction Techniques*

Fixed-frame techniques may not be viable; nevertheless, the responses are likely to contain many repetitive phrases that could be generated peripherally. The information transmitted could be a string of numbers for phrase generation with interspersed "literals" that must be reproduced exactly at the terminal.

Thus if three-digit numbers are used to generate phrases, and the literals are placed in parentheses, the following transmission:

123(85000)Δ491(76500)Δ007(b4019)Δ008(32481)

could result in this being printed

| | |
|---|---|
| ASSUMED VALUE OF PROPERTY | = 85000 |
| CASH ON SELLING PROPERTY | = 76500 |
| CAPITAL GAINS TAX IF SOLD | = 4019 |
| NET CASH AFTER CAPITAL GAINS TAX | = 32481 |

In this example, 123 generated the phrase ASSUMED VALUE OF PROPERTY =, 491 generated CASH ON SELLING PROPERTY =, and so on. Here Δ is a "new line" character.

This scheme would demand little complexity in the peripheral machine; thus it need not be a stored-program computer. In practice, however, a computer is often used as the peripheral machine; then more elaborate editing of the transactions may be employed than that above. Compaction techniques, in general, will be discussed in Chapter 22.

Where peripheral-phrase generation is used, the dialogue can be designed with this scheme in mind. It may be desirable to standardize the phrases used and limit their proliferation.

### 5. Dialogue in Peripheral Computers

Part of the dialogue on some systems comes from a small peripheral computer rather than the large central machine. This step saves still more line costs, because only those responses for which the central computer is essential will be transmitted to it. It will be necessary to transmit to the central computer only when its superior processing power is essential or when its data base must be referred to or updated. Many operator messages in a dialogue do not have these requirements. The proportion of messages not having them tends to be high when a prime factor in the dialogue design has been the terminal-operator psychology.

If the system designer is considering the use of peripheral computers, he might, in his thinking, divide the dialogue into two parts: that which can be executed entirely in the peripheral machine and that which needs transmission to the central machine. Let us refer to these divisions as peripheral-machine dialogue and central-machine dialogue. On some systems, a substantial amount of dialogue can be peripheral. Sometimes, for example, a major part of the dialogue is used for collecting data piece by piece from the operator or for formulating a query step by step. If this process takes place without long-distance transmission, the dialogue can be designed to be as effective as possible from the psychological point of view, with no concern about the numbers of characters or number of turnarounds. After several pairs of peripheral-machine dialogue have been used to collect the data required, the data are then transmitted in an appropriate format to the central computer, and a brief central-machine dialogue may ensue. Any transmissions between the peripheral and central computers can be in a compacted form. The balance possible between peripheral-machine dialogue and central-machine dialogue will differ greatly from one application to another. An assessment of this balance in conjunction with line costs will lead the designer to decide whether peripheral-machine dialogue is worth considering.

# 11 THREE-WAY DIALOGUE

On most systems the user communicates directly with the computer and the computer responds directly to him. There are many cases, however, when a three-way dialogue ensues. A variety of different reasons exist for this, and there are a number of possible configurations. The systems analyst should always bear it in mind as one of his possible options.

**DIALOGUE VIA A THIRD PARTY**    The person using an information system sometimes does not communicate directly with it. Instead he talks to a third party who, in turn, communicates with the computer. The reasons for this situation can be as follows:

1. The originator of the exchange does not have a terminal.
2. The originator does not know how to use the necessary dialogue or computer language.
3. The originator is barred access to the machine for security reasons.
4. The originator is barred access to the machine for proficiency reasons. Only persons with a certain level of training are allowed to modify the data base, for example.
5. The intermediary who operates the terminal has a specialized knowledge which the originator of the exchange is making use of.
6. The intermediary has access to more than one computer system.

Perhaps the most common example of three-way dialogue occurs when the public call terminal operators. If you telephone to query your electricity bill, for example, you may speak to a girl who looks up your record with a visual display. When you go into a savings bank, you may confront a teller who accesses your account record at his terminal. The same will be true in many industrial situations. The best way to provide an information service for management is not necessarily to place terminals in managers' offices but rather to give them access to specialists who use terminals.

**MESSAGE INTERCEPTION**    The next example of three-way dialogue is when an arrangement exists for certain messages to be intercepted for human attention. The intercepted message may come from a terminal operator or it may be a machine-to-machine transmission as with a message being relayed from a message-switching center. The intercept operator may be able to communicate directly with the originating operator, or the feedback may be indirect, taking place at some time after the original transmission.

The reasons for interception are likely to be the following:

1. An error is detected in the input from an operator, that cannot be corrected by two-way communication with him.
2. An error is detected in a transmission, the originator of which is no longer on line, as with a message being relayed via a message-switching center.
3. A possible security violation is detected. The violator will be automatically locked from sensitive data and an intercept message sent to a security officer, who may take action.
4. A transaction proves to be unprocessable; for example, the file record it refers to cannot be located.
5. The transaction is designed so that there will be human assistance in handling it.

**HUMAN ASSISTANCE FOR THE COMPUTER**    On some systems used for making operational decisions, not all the decisions should be left entirely to the computer. There are some for which it has insufficient information or for which it cannot be programmed adequately. Human decision-making capability is entirely different in nature to that which can easily be programmed. The objective in designing a system should be to combine the human and machine capabilities to the best effect. This does not necessarily mean making the machine do everything. There are instances when the machine should defer to human experience, flexibility, or knowledge of the situation.

The last step in making up production schedules might be passed on a screen to the shop foreman, who knows the current shop situations. The decision about overbooking on an airline flight might be referred to an experienced flight controller. In certain problem-solving situations, periodic human intervention in the decision-making process can be more effective then an attempt to make the computer do everything.

In certain man-computer dialogues, then, the originating terminal operators will ask for information or for a decision; and the computer, in processing the request, will sometimes reach a point at which a decision must be requested from a third party manning a terminal for this purpose.

**HUMAN DIALOGUE**
**VIA A COMPUTER**
A fascinating form of three-way dialogue can take place when two persons communicate with one another, but instead of doing it face-to-face, they do it via computer terminals. At MIT, Stanford Research Institute, and other institutions with advanced time-sharing systems, it has been discovered that such a dialogue can add a new dimension to human communication. The dialogue must be more disciplined, and the participants are forced to understand each other's discipline. Persons communicating on a complex subject each have a model or image in their mind representing their particular understanding of the subject. Failure to communicate adequately results when, as is often the case, the persons have different images. Part of human communication is the passing of simple facts from one person to another, but a much more difficult and quite vital part of it is the process by which one mind makes changes to its model or image of the situation. Complete communication only occurs when the different persons's models are restructured to be identical.

If persons are communicating with the aid of a computer, they will probably use a common bank of data, common programs for manipulating the data, and sometimes common mathematical models, simulations, and analytical programs. They will have to examine reports and calculations of a predetermined format, such as cash-flow analyses or PERT diagrams. Precise rather than vague communication is enforced, at least on certain aspects of the subject in question. In certain ways, people will be able to communicate more effectively via a machine than face-to-face. Pioneers in this area, Licklider and Taylor [1], state that the computer, acting as an intermediary between people, promises, surprisingly, "to bring a new depth of intellectual interchange to the fine old art of face-to-face communication."

The communicators could be in the same room or far apart. The board room of the future may have large computer screens that all can see and a staff, possibly in a different room, to help use the machines. A conference room may have individual screens, and members may have individual files and programs with their own data and models stored. An ideal arrangement might be for conference participants to have their own individual terminals placed so that they display the same data. When two or more people are editing or changing the data with a text-editing program, they are simply connected to the same computer on dial or leased lines.

**INFORMATION ROOMS**

When a third party enters a man-machine dialogue, he may be a solitary individual or a member of a group assembled in an information room. The use of groups of persons with terminals gathered together in a special room can be valuable in certain circumstances. The systems analyst will often build such rooms into his network design. Some examples were given in Chapter 5.

There are many variations on the theme of information rooms. A room with computer terminals and specialists can be an essential part of widely differing schemes. Such a facility can vary greatly in size and complexity, ranging all the way from two men on teletype machines to the Project Apollo control room at NASA's Manned Space Center. In the coming decade, industry—like the Pentagon—will have its war rooms.

Seven situations in which a room with terminals and specialized staff is an adjunct to the computer system are discussed below.

### 1. Management Information Center

This information center provides specialists and facilities to supply management with requested information. It avoids the need to place terminals in managers' offices, although in some cases a terminal may be used there because it provides the fastest means of delivering the results.

The information room concept is of value not merely in large corporations but in very small organizations as well. It should be recognized that many of the information sources will not be in computers but in manuals, letters, or microfilm. In some cases, the information may be on listings produced by batch processing. A small firm may print a weekly listing of accounts or other data rather than make such information available in real-time at a terminal. The information room staff in small firms may increasingly make use of on-line service bureau facilities, plus external information sources.

The data requested by top management will relate to all parts of the organization, and telecommunication facilities may link the information center to far-flung locations. These will be used for telephone, facsimile, and data transmission. They may be public dial lines or the organization's internal telephone network. If a line to any particular location is used frequently enough (say, more than 2 hours per day), it should be a private leased line—the break-even cost between dial and private lines depending on the tariffs.

Some of the information requests may need the use of a library. A link from the information center to a company library may be used so that the services of the librarian can be enlisted when required. In some large corporations, television screens have been installed in managers' offices, thereby providing video links to the information.

### 2. *An Input Preparation Center*

Just as persons wishing to obtain information from a computer may telephone the staff in an information center, so persons wishing to *enter* information may use a similar process. Management might telephone and say "make sure such and such an item is completed by next Monday," and the staff enter this statement into the data for computing work schedules.

In some cases, a high proportion of the input data is obtained from persons telephoning an information center. Airlines, for example, have a center in which telephone calls to make bookings on cancellations are handled. The terminal operators talk to the passenger, give him the facts he wants about flight schedules and seat availability, and then enter details of his booking into the computer.

In the future, requests from customers will be handled in this manner in many types of firms.

### 3. *An Operations Room*

Another use of an information room is as a center from which a set of operations are directed or where operational decisions are made.

The New York police use a control room in Manhattan for directing police cars, launches and ambulances. The staff of the operations room have terminals which display the current emergencies and police activities. The reader is no doubt familiar from television with the Apollo control room used in directing the moon shots. Operations centers, similar in principle but on a smaller scale, will be part of industrial systems for directing such operations as the flow of work through a job shop or the dispatching of a delivery fleet.

All the information about the state of the operation in question is made available at one location. Management, wanting to know what is happening or wanting to change it, contact this operations room. The scheduling of the operations may be done by computer, but the final control or dispatching remains in human hands. The computer may repeatedly reschedule when unanticipated events occur.

### 4. *A Chart Room*

In many companies the rooms in which managers meet are lined with charts along the walls. The charts display facts that the managers should know and that can be referred to in discussions. Typical of the information provided in this way are organization charts, PERT or GANTT charts, layout maps, diagrams of information flow, sales statistics, financial data, details of forth-coming computer systems, and so on.

The computer terminal offers the possibility of considerably extending the quantity of information that can be made available in this way. The meeting room may have one single computer terminal with lucid instructions on how to display various types of information of interest to managers. It may have more than one terminal connected to different types of computer systems. The mere presence of a display terminal can intimidate managers into learning how to use it. Elaborately constructed wall displays with lights are sometimes used. There may be a large screen or projection facility that enables groups at meetings to study and discuss displayed data. The boardroom of the future may have several such wall screens.

When a chart room with terminals is first set up, discussion should be promoted among the managers who use it, as to what information should be available. The files of such information often evolve at a rapid rate. This is one of the ways of exploring management's needs in a management information system.

In the early days of setting up a chart room with or without terminals, there will be much experimenting with displays in an attempt to provide the most useful information. Initially, therefore, the displays should perhaps be of a temporary nature. The evolution of management requirements will lead to an evolution of the computer system to provide them. This development represents an educational process by which managers can improve their understanding of the functioning of the company, plus the potentialities of data processing, and by which the computer staff improve their understanding of the needs of management.

### 5. *An Operator-Assistance Center*

Whereas top management or strategic management rarely operate today's terminals because of the diversity of their information needs, lower level or operational management having a specific and well-defined task to carry out will often use a terminal to accomplish that task. Shop-floor foremen, personnel managers, warehouse managers, and branch sales managers can all be found making use of computer terminals. Specialized staff, such as engineers, laboratory technicians, investment analysts, and architects, may use terminals in an intricate manner.

With the more elaborate applications, the terminal users may occasionally need help. Such help may come from the system itself, which might be switched into an instructional mode. Alternatively, the bewildered terminal user may be able to telephone an assistance center where an operator can monitor his actions and instruct him as to the correct ones.

The value of such human assistance should not be underrated. It is only too easy for the inexperienced terminal user to become confused at the terminal and feel too foolish to ask for help from his colleagues. Anonymous assistance and monitoring from the assistance center will be greatly appreciated and may avoid his rejecting the system (as has often happened).

### 6. *A Facility for Noncomputer Processing*

When it is decided that not all decisions shall be made by the computer but that some shall be referred to human decision makers, these persons may be gathered in a room designed for such a purpose. They may also carry out some of the other functions discussed in this chapter.

Human assistance can be built into the system in one of two ways. The first way is to intercept any transaction that falls into a range deemed to need attention and refer it to a specialist at a terminal. The specialist will often use the same real-time system in making his decision about the transaction. The second way is to have the specialist inspect the situation at intervals and set figures in the system that enable the computer to take automatic action on the transactions.

The specialists in an information control room have their own sources of data for decision making. These sources may be maintained in the same system. In one such room each specialist has two terminals. One is a low-speed printer that gives unsolicited messages from the system, and the other is an inquiry terminal from which files can be inspected and changes made. With this combination, an urgent message from the system does not interrupt the specialist in the middle of a terminal dialogue.

### 7. *A Data Control Room*

Where data are entered into the computer system by employees at distant terminals, it is desirable to ensure, as far as possible, that they are accurate.

When data are collected from a factory shop floor, for example, the data base that will be used for production scheduling and other purposes is dependent for its accuracy on the information entered by workers at the work station terminals. Tight controls can be built into the system so that any errors will be detected. However, the correcting of the errors may be best done by a central agency responsible for file accuracy rather than by the worker at his simple data-entry terminal. Staff in a data control room are informed by the computer of the suspected error. They contact the shop floor to find out the correct situation and then adjust the files accordingly.

As mentioned earlier, on some systems, security of information in the files is of great importance.  Information must not be read by unauthorized persons, and, even more vital, it must not be changed by someone who might have felonious intent. Tight security controls can be built into the system. When a possible or suspected security violation is detected by the computer, a security officer should be informed immediately. Usually the suspected violation will be simply a terminal operator using an incorrect procedure, but bringing it immediately to the attention of the security specialist will help safeguard against serious violation.

The control of security and accuracy of the files, again, may be carried on in a centralized *information* room.

---

The functions we have listed in this chapter may take place in the same room. These seven uses of information rooms once more return us to our theme of building appropriate human skills into the information processing system. Because of the lack of intelligence of the computers, their augmentation by skilled staff will help give a system the flexibility that is needed in industry. Left to its own devices, the computer can be a dangerously stupid machine in certain applications.

SECTION **III**

# TERMINAL
# CONSIDERATIONS

# 12  TERMINAL DESIGN FOR HUMAN USE

Terminal factors can be discussed in two parts: those that relate to the terminal's interface with the telecommunication network and those that relate to its interface with the user or means of handling data. These two aspects are linked together in the overall consideration of the logic or "intelligence" that is built into the terminal—and hence, to a large degree, its cost.

In the case of a man-computer dialogue system, terminal features will form an essential element of the dialogue. It is the human side of terminal design or selection that this chapter discusses.

A poorly planned terminal configuration can have a serious effect on the efficient operation of a system. It can slow down the system, lessen its usefulness, introduce errors, and significantly add to the overall cost. It is very desirable that the right terminals be selected, for they are the link between the machinery and its human users. To a major extent, the users' image of the system comes from the terminals.

Whereas there are relatively few basic types of computer to choose from, a tremendous number of different terminal devices can be attached to computers.

Most computer peripherals can be removed from the computer room and attached to a communications interface. They can then have a typewriter, a keyboard, or a screen display added, in which case they are called a conversational terminal. With a control console, they can be called an off-line data-preparation terminal; or with a cluster of manual input devices, they can be called a data-collection system. Tape cartridges or small disks can be added, as well as logic circuitry and memory in varying quantities. Microprogramming or even a stored-program mini-computer may be used. The endless variations

133

on these terminal possibilities are further increased by the fact that the components can be supplied from many hundreds of peripheral-equipment manufacturers. The units are often built in a modular fashion so that, as with a hi-fi system, a variety of differing devices may be added. The user's choice can be complex, and it is a choice that can ultimately affect every other part of the system.

The terminals may be automatic devices connected to machinery, plants, railroad lines, and so on. They may collect readings or signals from such equipment for processing; and after processing, they may use signals from the computer for controlling the equipment. Alternatively, the terminals may be devices for human communication. A man may use the keyboard or some other device for sending information to the computer. Similarly, the computer may send information to the people using it. This information may be typed or displayed on screens or in lights. It may be spoken audibly, or other means of human communication may be used.

The information, whether from automatic devices or from manually operated keyboards, may be transmitted immediately to the computer or may be stored in some medium for transmission at a later time. The preparation of data, in other words, may be *on-line* or *off-line*. Readings of instruments, for example, may be punched into paper tape that is later transmitted to the computer. Similarly, data collected from manually operated devices may be punched into paper tape. In this case, the terminal of the computer is an on-line paper-tape reader. The output may also make use of an interim medium, such as paper tape or punched cards, or it may directly control the environment in question. Very often it is necessary to make a printed copy of the computer output for later analysis. In this case, part of the terminal equipment may be a typewriter or printer.

**CHARACTERISTICS OF A DOCUMENT INPUT DEVICE**     Input to the system may come directly from instruments or keyboards, or it may come from documents onto which the data have been transcribed. Let us first examine the characteristics of a document input device.

The documents to be read may be punched cards, paper tape, magnetic tape cartridges, or other media onto which data can be transcribed conveniently. They could also be optical readers, which read writing or marks on documents. Magnetic-ink character recognition might be used; other types of documents, such as a factory worker's badge, might be read. The factors that must be analyzed in selecting a terminal of this type are discussed below.

## 1. *Type of Media*

Careful thought must be given, when planning a system, to the selection of the best type of input media. Traditionally, paper tape has been used in transmission systems because of its low cost. The designer must decide whether it should be five-channel, seven-channel, or eight-channel. The decision will depend on what checking facilities are desirable and on whether the information transmitted is purely numeric, alphabetic, or alphanumeric with special characters. It may also depend on the communication facilities available—for example, the line control unit at the computer center.

Other media are gaining in popularity. Such electronic storage as disk and magnetic-tape cartridges is dropping in cost. Punched cards are used because of the ease of sorting, merging, and storing them.

The sender may need a means of storing a small quantity of information that he can retain himself, such as a roll of paper tape, a deck of cards, or a small magnetic-tape cartridge. He may keep this in his desk drawer. On the other hand, it is becoming increasingly common for users to store their data in a remote computer file and call it from a terminal when they need it.

The medium used may be one that must be capable of being processed on other machines—for example, punched cards or magnetic-ledger cards.

It may be one that necessitates human attention at the terminal. If small pieces of paper tape are transmitted, this will be so, but not so for a large reel of tape or a deck of punched cards loaded into a hopper and temporarily left unattended. The information transmitted may be partly from documents, such as cards or plates, and partly from the human-operated keyboards. If the keyboard is used along with the document reader, the terminal must be designed so that they can easily be operated in conjunction with one another.

## 2. *Temporary Storage Prior to Transmission*

Sometimes the terminal equipment is designed to collect data off-line from the computer and transmit it at intervals in batches. The advantages are that there is less interference with the activities of the computer and the communication lines are occupied for a shorter time. An operator at a keyboard, for example, may type the contents of documents for several hours, these being stored on an appropriate medium at the terminal, such as a disk or tape cartridge. The computer is then dialed and all the data are transmitted in a 3-minute telephone call.

Again, data-collection terminals on a factory floor may be linked to a small machine where the data are stored. The data are then transmitted from this machine to a computer at intervals. The storage unit in such cases may have one terminal connected to it, or many.

### 3. *Speed of Operation*

A terminal of suitable speed must be selected. Choice of the right terminal will be determined by the volume of traffic to be transmitted and the speed of the communication lines available. Ideally a terminal will operate so that data are transmitted at the maximum rate the communication line allows, but this situation is not always possible because of other factors in the terminal design. In considering speed, the number of terminals on one communication line must be evaluated.

A thorough study is sometimes necessary to determine the amount of data that will be transmitted by the terminal. The survey must indicate not only the average use of the terminal but also how the volumes vary month by month, day by day, and hour by hour. The system must be designed to handle the peak traffic volume during the peak periods. Statistics on how rapidly the traffic builds up and dies away again are necessary. These may be important in order to determine what queues will develop. Traffic volume figures must be projected forward to indicate how the load on the terminal will vary after installation.

If the lengths of the message vary, information is needed on this point. A histogram showing the frequency of occurrences of messages of different lengths should be produced.

**TERMINALS FOR MANUAL INPUT**

When human beings are keying in data on line, many other factors must be considered. We now have a man-machine interface, often real-time. This interface must be designed to be efficient and, at the same time, as convenient as possible for its operators to use. The terminal that is somehow inconvenient or confusing for human use will considerably impair the efficiency of this system. Some of the requirements of the human users are discussed below.

### 1. *Type of Keys Provided*

The terminal may have an alphabetic keyboard like a typewriter. It may also have digits. The digits may be in a 3 by 4 matrix so that they can be operated rapidly with one hand. Special characters may be needed, or special punctuation. Many terminals have special keys with meanings characteristic of that system, such as keys with mathematical functions; date keys saying "yesterday," "today," and "tomorrow"; and keys saying "one seat," "two seats," and "three seats," "first class" and "tourist class," "book," "cancel," and "confirm" on an airline reservations system. Again, many terminals have special control keys, such as "end of message" and "cancel this transaction." Terminals using a cathode-ray tube have keys for manipulating or altering the data displayed on the screen. In many systems a single special character will replace the entering of a number of alphabetic characters or even replace a whole message.

Elaborate special-purpose keyboards are used for creating certain types of man-machine interface. One way of constructing a man-machine dialogue is to build many elements of it into the terminal hardware. The keys can be specially constructed, and if desirable, the response can be given on specially labeled lights. The disadvantage of building the dialogue into the hardware is that it can make change at a later time difficult or impossible and it can be more expensive than using off-the-shelf terminals.

The terminal may be designed so that the keys can alter their meaning from one transaction to another. A matrix of keys may be used over which a perspex sheet is placed that labels the keys according to requirements. On the early airline reservations systems, a card or plate of metal was used that represented flights to a certain set of destinations. When this card or plate was in place, the lights and keys that were lined up against it then represented the flights that were available and the cities to and from which they went. The card or plate itself had a number that was sensed by the terminal, and this number was transmitted to the computer as part of the input information.

Some terminals use levers or knobs rather than a keyboard. Some of the cheapest terminals make use of a telephone Touchtone keyboard or dial for input. A telephone, in fact, is sometimes used itself as a terminal to a real-time system. The telephone dial is used first for establishing communications with the computer and then for transmitting information. The earpiece on the telephone may be used to receive a spoken reply from the computer. Telephone dials are slow to use and prone to a surprisingly high number of operator errors, but the Touchtone telephone keyboard holds great promise for future application.

On many commercial applications, the systems analysts find a need to relabel the keys. However, on many terminals relabeling cannot be neatly and inexpensively accomplished. Simple keyboard relabeling is a valuable feature for some terminal users.

### 2. One-Finger Operation

A surprising number of terminals have needed two hands to operate them. The finger of the right hand presses one key while the left hand presses a SHIFT or ALTERNATE MEANING key. This feature is undesirable when the operator needs her left hand for something else, such as holding a telephone, pointing to an item on a document or screen, or manipulating a light pen. When a SHIFT or similar key is needed, because a typewriter-like keyboard is employed, its use should be confined to infrequently keyed items. On some terminals the ENTER operation, which is required to terminate every input, needs two hands.

### 3. *Use of Plates, Cards, and Similar Items, in Combination with a Keyboard*

On some systems it is desirable to transmit certain fixed information for which plates, cards, paper tape, and the like may be used in conjunction with variable information that may be keyed into a keyboard. Alternatively, the fixed information may be set up by means of levers or switches used in conjunction with a keyboard.

A card may be selected from a rack of cards and transmitted along with the keyed-in data. A workman may use a badge that is entered into a badge reader and its number transmitted along with keyed-in information. Analog data from instruments may be transmitted again, perhaps with manually entered data.

### 4. *Format Guidance*

When an operator keys several items into a terminal, he must do so in such a way that the computer can tell which item is which, and where one ends and another begins. The operator could *memorize* the sequence in which they are entered, but this step is only satisfactory for a simple operation that the operator carries out repetitively. The dialogue could be designed so that the computer tells him exactly what to enter and in which sequence. He may be instructed to enter the characters under a line of type giving the required format. He may enter them in preassigned positions on a screen, in which case it must be easy to move the cursor to the requisite positions. In terminals that do not give a printed response, the device itself may give guidance in formatting. On one such terminal, the input is digital from an inexpensive set of digit switches (shown in Fig. 12.1). The fields to be entered vary in nature and length and are clearly labeled in a window adjacent to the switches. The labels are attached to a cylindrical bar and thus can be changed by rotating the bar with the thumb wheel. In the top part of Fig. 12.1, a worker is going to enter setup information. He rotates the thumb wheel until the left-hand word in the window is "SETUP". The other words then tell him the positions to enter the digits for "BADGE" number, "JOB" number, "OPERATION" number, "MACHINE" number,

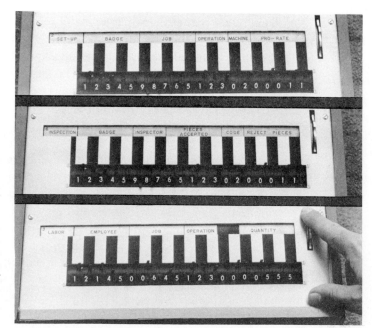

*Fig. 12.1.* A set of inexpensive digital switches with labels that can be changed using the thumb-wheel. The interchangeable labels solve the problem of field identification. (Part of a very low cost voice-answerback terminal for shop-floor data entry that did not reach the market place because of the adverse financial conditions of 1971. It was constructed by Rudolph Pola of Pola Data Associates.)

and "PRO-RATE." The other two sections of the diagram show the different fields required for entering "INSPECTION" and "LABOR" data.

### 5. *Use of Data from the Computer in Conjunction with Keyed Input*

It is often necessary to add to or modify data that are already in the memory of a computer. In this case, the data in question may be typed out or displayed in such a way that a minor modification to them can be made accurately and with as little new keyed input as possible. On a typewriter, the sequence of operator actions might be as follows: First, he keys in a message requesting the computer to display the data that he wishes to add to or modify. He then presses a key with a label such as "duplicate"; this causes the typewriter to type a copy of the record displayed. It types as long as the duplicate key is depressed; when it is released, the operator may key in the modification that he wishes to make and continue duplicating the remainder of the record. After the operator has established that the record is correct, it is reentered into the system.

When a two-way interchange between the computer and the terminal is used in this manner, a wide variety of possibilities exist for modifying the stored data by means of special keys or devices on the computer. Special keys are often devised which again are characteristic of the application in question.

A cathode-ray tube display used in conjunction with a keyboard provides a more versatile way to modify data in the machine. Most cathode-ray tube and similar display terminals have a cursor—a visible point that can be moved by the operator to any position on the screen. The cursor is usually represented on the screen by a small triangle or other character, or by a short dash underlining a character to which the cursor position currently refers. If an operator wishes to change a character in the middle of a display, he moves the cursor so that it refers to the character in question and he then takes appropriate action on the keyboard. The means for moving and utilizing the cursor differ from one device to another. Some screens have a "destructive" cursor; as it is moved horizontally across the screen, it erases everything it passes over on that line. Other screens have nondestructive cursors. Some can be switched from being destructive to nondestructive under program control.

Another device used in conjunction with a display screen is a light pen, a manually held pointer that can be directed accurately to any position on the screen. This device is used to point or "draw" on the screen, and many programming aids can assist in perfecting the drawing. Keys can be used for making lines parallel, for duplicating parts of the drawing, for rotating, diminishing, enlarging, or deleting parts of the drawing, for adding components held in the computer's storage, and so on. A curve can be drawn on the screen, and the computer will devise a mathematical expression to fit the curve, adjusting the curve very slightly if necessary. A surface can be drawn—for example, metal panels in the design of a car body—and the computer will make the surface fit certain design constraints and rotate the image so that its designer may view it from all angles. A girder construction can be drawn and figures displayed on the screen, giving the stresses on the girders in differing conditions.

Other devices are sometimes used for interacting with a screen, including a coupled "desk pad" on which the user draws with a stylus.

### 6. *Ease and Speed of Operation*

Some terminals must be operated very quickly and easily. With others, there is little or no need for speed in their operation. A terminal at a bank counter must be operated quickly because a customer is waiting for a reply. A data-collection terminal in a factory, which is only used infrequently, does not have the same requirement for speed unless it is used in such a way that lines of workers could be kept waiting—for example, to clock in at the start of the day. Rotary switches rather than a touch-typist's keyboard are generally used on a factory data-collection terminal. Terminals that handle a high volume of data must work rapidly, perhaps operated by touch-typists. If a terminal is used to answer telephone enquiries, speed is usually essential because the answer required must be obtainable in a few seconds while the enquirer is on the telephone.

The type of operator has an effect on the terminal design. Some operators are highly trained in the use of a terminal. Others, such as factory or railroad workers, are less trained or less nimble-fingered and need a terminal that is easy to operate. Some terminals have to be operated by a touch-typist in an office; others by a laborer on a building site.

The ease with which the terminal must be operated depends to some extent on what other work the operator is doing. Does she sit comfortably in front of the terminal all day, or does she only occasionally stand over it to make an entry? Does she use both hands, or is she holding a telephone in the other hand? Does she enter repetitive data by means of cards, plates, or other devices? Does an input transaction require a lot of thought and detailed checking? Does it require a conversation with the computer? In general, the terminal should be designed or selected so that it fits in with the other actions of its operator as easily as possible.

### 7. *Terminal Environment*

The surroundings of the terminal may be an important factor in its design. Does it have to fit into an elegantly designed showroom? Is it in an atmosphere of dust, or heat, or high humidity? Must it fit into a confined space or be placed on a bank counter? Will it be moved from one location to another? Is vibration a problem? Are there any restrictions on weight or electrical characteristics?

The packaging of the terminal is important in some applications but not in others. Terminals installed on the floor of the New York Stock Exchange, for example, needed careful packaging to meet limited space requirements. Terminals installed in a cellulose factory needed special flame proofing; because of the inflammable atmosphere, sparks had to be suppressed. Some terminals are located in remote or small offices, which may affect the packaging needed.

Environmental illumination is an important consideration with a screen terminal. Can the screen contents be read without eye strain? The lettering must be sufficiently bright, sharp, large, and flicker-free for the operator. If the operator uses the terminal 8 hours a day, these considerations are especially important. A badly planned screen can easily give such an operator a headache.

### 8. *Visual Input Verification*

Three types of check might be made on the data manually entered into a terminal. First, these data may be visually displayed in some way so that the operator can check them  Second, the transmission itself will be checked automatically. And third, certain programmed checks on the validity of the input might be made by the computer.

In order for the operator to check the input visually, it might be typed out or displayed on a cathode-ray tube before the computer processes it. If the terminal uses a set of switches or a matrix of keys, a complete message might be set up in them and examined by the operator before it is transmitted to the computer. The switches or keys will stay in position until the transaction is entered. If a device like a typewriter or display screen is used, each character should print as it is keyed in. The operator can then watch the line of print as a visual check for errors. If the terminal transmits one character at a time, an erroneous character will normally be transmitted before the operator detects it.

When an operator does make a mistake, she must be given an easy way to correct this error. She must be able to backspace and erase the last character transmitted or several previous characters. If the error occurred earlier in a long message, it is useful to be able to make a small correction without having to reenter the entire message. Control keys on the keyboards of some terminals give this facility. In some cases, the correction will take place in the buffer of the terminal; in others, it must be done by programming in the computer receiving the message.

### 9. *Automatic Input Verification*

Various checks can be made on the input to a real-time system. Generally the checks rely on programming and organization, but a number of features may be built into terminals to assist this process.

The terminal may have some means of allowing the computer to indicate to the operator that a message is incomplete or invalid. It might be a printed message to the operator generated by the terminal, or it might merely utilize an indicator, such as a red light or a buzzer.

Batch totals or check totals might be used to ensure that no data are lost. These can be used whether transactions are entered in batches or singly. Quantities or account numbers or some other fields are added up by a control section and also by the computer to make sure that all the transactions have been received by the computer. This technique may be facilitated by the use of a counter on the terminal itself. By using the counter the operator can ensure that all the data have been received by the computer. On many systems the use of serial numbers is employed to make certain that no message has been lost. The adding of serial numbers to messages might be an automatic function of the terminal.

10. *The Bridging of Failures*

Line failures or computer failures will occur occasionally, thereby disabling the terminal. In some systems it will be desirable that the terminal *records* transactions even when it is not connected to the computer. It will transmit these transactions later when the link is once more working correctly. A small magnetic-tape cartridge that is slow in operation, and therefore not too expensive, may be used for this purpose. Paper tape has been used on some terminals but it has the disadvantage of not being reusable. On certain systems the transactions are merely printed by the terminal and the operator transmits them manually when the computer returns. In this case, the terminal may have an accumulator so that control totals can be kept and so that there is a continuity of control totals throughout the failure period.

It may be desirable, in some applications, for the operator to use the terminal in exactly the same way whether the computer link has failed or not. In other words, when the link becomes inoperative, the terminal automatically starts recording and later the computer will read what it has recorded. This may be the case when electronic-fund-transfer terminals (the checkless society) are found in stores and restaurants. The terminal temporarily isolated from the computer network will record a customer's payment with an encoded fund transfer card. Details of the payment will be sent to the computer when it again makes contact. The only difference during the period of failure will be that the customer's credit record and bank balance will not be inspected. During this period, he may not be permitted to debit his account with more than a certain sum (say $200) and the bank may be insured against petty fraud that might occur by chance during the failure period.

11. *Security*

It is usually desirable to prevent unauthorized persons from interfering with the terminal or from entering data into it. In a banking system, for example, only an authorized teller should be able to send transactions to the computer. As for the terminal in a stockbroker's office, it would be unfortunate if the cleaning lady could play with the system and inadvertently cause a transaction to be dealt with by the computer!

There are a number of ways of maintaining adequate terminal security. One is to place a lock on the terminal. A bank teller may have his own key, and every time he enters a transaction he must insert this key and turn it. Some banking terminals have two keys so that two separate tellers can use them.

Another way of maintaining security is to allow each terminal user to have a card or badge, which he inserts into the terminal. Using this device, he must "sign in" before he can transmit data that are processed by the computer. When he has finished using the terminal, he must "sign out" the same way. The cards or badges used have different types of significance. Certain transactions may only be possible if a supervisor's card is inserted into the system. The system may operate in a training mode so that when a trainee's card is inserted, the computer will respond to the terminal in all its normal ways, but it will not change any records on its files.

Often a more secure technique is for the individuals using the terminals to enter a code number (and often their personnel number also). The terminal may be designed so that this security number is not printed or displayed like the other input, so that it cannot be seen by unauthorized eyes. The printing or display may be inhibited by a command from the computer, or by the operator pressing a key.

**DEVICES FOR OUTPUT OF INFORMATION**

Output of data in response to human input is sometimes at a machine separate from the input machine— for example, a high-speed printer, a card punch, or a large display panel. Usually, however, the input and output take place on the same device. The output is often read as it is produced, in real time, with a man-machine dialogue taking place.

The considerations that may affect the choice or design of output mechanisms appear below.

1. *Hard vs. Soft Copy*

Is a printed or punched record of the transaction needed at the terminal location? Often such a record is not necessary, especially if the transaction is logged, for example, on magnetic tape, at the computer center.

The term "soft copy" is used to describe terminals that leave no permanent record. Such terminals fall into two categories, visual and audio. Cathode-ray tubes or other display devices are the most common. These can be fairly cheap devices that display information rapidly. Their speed improvement over typewriterlike machines or teleprinters can make a significant difference to the nature of the man-machine dialogue. Displays in pictorial or graphic form capable of quick comprehension are also facilitated by visual-display terminals.

Alternatively, voice answerback provides the cheapest possible output terminal, for a normal telephone may be used. This type of reply may not be as clear as a visual display but it is often adequate. The vocabulary of spoken words must be stored by the computer. Some machines store them in analog form and thus have a limited vocabulary. They may be stored on a magnetic drum or photographically recorded strip. Others store them in a digital format.

The sound of human words is converted into computer digits or characters, which can be converted back into clear, understandable sound. The characters are then stored in the computer or on its files as normal computer records would be. An average-length human-voice word might take between 100 and 200 characters to store in this way. Sequences of human-voice words are composed by normal program instructions. By storing the words on tape or random-access files the machine acquires an unlimited vocabulary.

There are many commercial applications in which hard copy is not strictly needed; however, the administrative staff familiar with traditional methods are likely to argue that it is. Blind adherence to hard copy in some cases negates much of the economic justification for the real-time system—the removal of local paper files and the work that they incur. There are now many case histories in which the local office managers fought to retain hard-copy files, lost the fight, and today the local office operates with a "soft-copy" terminal, fewer staff, and greater efficiency. Systems analysts will frequently have this fight on their hands in the years ahead. The movement away from paperwork files will progress as the cost of on-line storage and teleprocessing drops.

It is sometimes desirable to have one hard-copy terminal backing up a group of soft-copy devices. A programmer using an on-line programming language may want his program printed after he has modified it, but he does not need the printer all the time. A commercial installation may want some form of printed report; in particular, it may need regular print-out for standby purposes in case of system failure. The printer, and possibly a punch also, may be attached to the same control unit as the soft-copy devices or attached to a concentrator unit.

### 2. *Speed*

As we discussed in Chapter 7, the response time and output speed of a terminal affects the types of thinking processes that the operator can be expected to accomplish successfully. The speed at which the response is printed or displayed depends on the terminal mechanisms. A device operating at typewriter speeds may be too slow for applications where lengthy messages or displays must be scanned quickly or where the dialogue structure requires that the operator retain certain facts in his "short-term memory" between responses. A faster printer or a display screen may be used. The display screen can be filled with information very quickly, and often the constraining factor on it is the speed at which the telecommunication line can transmit to it. A line speed of 4800 bits per second is enough for most situations in which the screen is filled with alphanumeric data (or other characters). This is close to the maximum screen contents. It is indeed fortunate that the maximum transmissions speeds of analog telephone lines are close to the maximum reading speeds of human beings. Giving the operator information at the speeds of teletype lines or typewriter mechanisms can impede his progress in a frustrating manner. It has been said that computer-assisted instruction received at these low speeds is like being taught by a teacher with a severe speech impediment.

### 3. *Amount of Data that Can be Displayed*

The next important parameter is the length of the responses that are required. With a typewriter or other continuous device, there is no limit on this factor (except perhaps operator patience when the speed is slow). If a display screen is used, however, the amount that can be displayed at one time will be an important parameter.

A display screen may be used with a program that slides the information on the screen up and down like a Biblical scroll. Use of certain keys can "wind" the scroll up or down in a flick. Alternatively, a page-flip key may switch the screen contents between consecutive pages. Similarly, the image may be moved from side to side or a graphic display can be enlarged or diminished to overcome the fact that the screen is a "window" of limited size. Some systems use a video-switching unit; it enables operators to select different "channels" as on a television set and to examine different displays generated by the computer. In some cases, the channels may also be used for visual observation via a television camera.

### 4. *Type of Data Displayed*

In order to give maximum assistance to the terminal operator, the ways in which the data are presented must be considered carefully. They must be displayed in the form that he can understand most easily. The form may be pictorial; it may consist of light displays, bar charts, or graphs. It may be tabulated or it may be a verbal reply. Display lights may be positioned beside a changeable matrix card. A graph-plotting pen may be used. A display tube may be desirable for pictorial presentation, or a typewriter may be fitted with special characters.

Familiarity to the operator is important in designing the display, if it can be achieved. For example, in a process-control application where a large control room full of meters has been partially replaced by computer-operated displays, it has been disadvantageous to use digital print-outs and tables. Some form of graphic or analog presentation is preferable, for this is familiar to the operators.

It seems likely that in the years ahead a wide diversity of display mechanisms will be used in an attempt to communicate as effectively as possible with a wide variety of managers, foremen, and other personnel. Increasing attention to this aspect of the man-machine interface will probably be needed.

### 5. Character Sets

Some applications need special characters. In some, a diverse set of special characters is needed for producing diagrams. In other systems it is desirable to have interchangeable sets of characters on a terminal. This step can be accomplished with the interchangeable "golf ball"-type head on an IBM Selectric typing mechanism. With some display screens, the character generation is in microprogramming which can be modified.

### 6. Alert Indicators

It is sometimes desirable that the operator's attention be alerted to a particular display or item on a display. An unsolicited message arriving at a display, for example, might be brought to the operator's attention by a flashing light. A particular field in the middle of a screen may be highlighted by making it blink on and off or by using a different color. On one terminal, the characters can be either white characters on a black background or black characters on white, selectable under program control. Fields or portions of a screen may be made to stand out by making them black on white when the rest of the screen is white on black.

### 7. Group vs. Individual Displays

A display may be small and designed to be read by one individual or it may be a large group display. The latter may be used at an operation control center, at a public location, such as an airport, or in a situation where several persons may discuss the display. Meeting rooms of the future may be equipped with a group display.

### 8. Operator Modification of Data

Often it is necessary for the operator to make modifications to records by displaying them, changing certain characters or factors, and sending them back to the computer. A typewriter or a display screen may be used for this purpose, a keyboard working in conjunction with it as described earlier. Controls for easy modification of data must be built into the equipment; moreover, the programs must be written to give the operator the maximum help.

Modification of data is generally easier on a visual-display terminal than on a printer terminal. The cursor controls should be designed to make modification as easy as possible. Sometimes a light pen will be used.

### 9. *Pictorial Output*

In some cases, a photographic picture or image will be displayed. This may come from a film strip, slides, microfilm, or microfiche in the terminal or its control unit. The machines for EVR (electronic video recording) and similar technologies for displaying film or still frames may become the basis of such a terminal because of the very large number of images they can hold. There are many applications for which a pictorial image is desirable at the terminal, and these may eventually constitute a large proportion of the terminal market.

### 10. *Visual Suitability*

The display size must be suitable for its audience. If a man sits immediately in front of a display screen with a bright sharp image, the lettering may be as small as the print of this book. If he is farther away or if the resolution is less good, it must be proportionately large. If two operators, for example, obtain quick answers from the same display screen, the writing must be large enough for this to be done efficiently.

The visual suitability of the display must be considered in relation to its environment. The brightness must be suitably greater than the ambient lighting. The contrast and accuracy must be sufficiently high, the distortion and flicker time sufficiently low.

In some cases, the display must fit into a confined space, as on a passenger check-in desk at an airport. Sometimes the keyboard and screen unit are better separated. The physical appearance of the unit may be of particular importance, for example, in an executive's office.

### 11. *System Activity Indicators*

When programming or carrying out some other activity at an on-line terminal, there may be periods when the system is silent as the computer executes a program possibly interleaved with operations for many other users. If the terminal is completely silent during this period, the user often becomes restless, wondering sometimes if the computer is still paying attention to him. Terminals often have a "system alert" light, showing that the terminal is still connected to the distant computer. This device is very useful, but it is psychologically desirable to have some means of indicating that the program is being run. Some terminals, for example, wink a light, make a soft bleeping noise, or type a character at intervals. This activity has been referred to as "hand holding." By using the tones of a Touchtone telephone dial or data set, a variety of different sounds could be made, if desired, to indicate to an impatient terminal operator what activity is being carried out. Audible sounds on some terminals, however, have proved distracting. If there is more than one operator and terminal in a room, they can become annoying. It may be better if a silent means of indication is used.

**SUMMARY**    At the end of the next chapter we will summarize these and other considerations by giving a checklist that the systems analyst may use when selecting a terminal. First, however, we must discuss the communication line interface.

# 13 THE INTERFACE WITH THE COMMUNICATION LINE

A teleprocessing system has three components that are incompatible in speed: the computer, the terminal, and the communication line linking them. These components are usually incompatible in other ways also. The computer and most terminals are digital devices designed to deal with bits, or square-edged pulse trains; but most communication lines are *analog* in operation, designed to transmit a continuous range of frequencies. The coding of characters used in most terminals differs from that in the computers they are connected to. The error rates encountered on most communication lines are higher than those generally acceptable in computers.

This chapter is concerned with the engineering that is used to overcome these incompatibilities.

**INCOMPATIBILITIES**   Since its earliest days the computer has had the prob-
**IN SPEED**   lem that it operates much faster than its input and output units. Being an expensive machine, it cannot afford to wait for them. The problem was solved by using *buffers*. The computer dumps a quantity of output into a storage unit, or buffer, at full speed, and then the contents of this unit are printed slowly, at the speed of the printing mechanism. When the information has been printed, the computer again refills the buffer at its own speed. The opposite process takes place for input.

A communication line is handled in a similar way. The characters from the computer will normally be transmitted one bit at a time from a buffer that is refilled periodically.

151

**TERMINAL**
**BUFFERING**

The terminal may also have a buffer. Suppose that a voice line transmits at 4800 bits per second from keyboard terminals. The operators cannot type information into the terminal at this speed; at best, they may type about three characters (21 bits) per second, but there will be lengthy pauses for thought and other activity. In this case, their keying might fill up a buffer of, say, 100 characters, the contents of which would be transmitted, in turn, over the line in one burst that would take less than one-fifth of a second. This process makes sense, however, only when the line has some other work to occupy its time when it is not transmitting from this particular terminal. If only one terminal is attached to the line, then there is no point in having a terminal buffer (at least for purposes of timing). The need for the buffer arises when more than one device is attached to the line. In practice, as we shall see, many devices can be attached to one communication line, and sometimes many terminals share the same buffer. The buffers are used both for transmissions to the computer and transmissions from it.

Paper tape has traditionally been used as a cheap form of buffer. A message is punched into paper tape and the tape placed on a tape reader to be read at the computer's convenience. This scheme is used on many message-switching systems. A buffer allows messages to be composed fully before being transmitted to the computer. If the message is long or complicated, or if it takes a long time to compose, it may be worthwhile checking to see that it is correct before transmitting any of it. If many long messages are sent to the computer without buffering at the terminal and the operator enters characters slowly—perhaps because she is talking to a client on the telephone at the same time—then a large amount of computer memory will be tied up in buffering the messages at the computer end of the communication lines. Partially completed messages will remain in computer storage for a relatively long period before being processed. When buffering is used, no single terminal will occupy the line for a long period of time, neither will it tie up the computer for a long period.

A hardware buffer may be in the terminal itself, or it may be in a unit that controls several terminals. The logic associated with it usually carries out functions other than simple buffering.

The cost of buffering in a terminal was high once but has fallen substantially in recent years. Nevertheless, at the time of writing more unbuffered than buffered terminals are installed. The cost trade-offs associated with buffering the terminals will emerge in the design calculations later in the book.

**ERROR**
**CONTROL**

A different reason for having a buffer in a terminal concerns error control. (Error control is discussed in detail in Chapter 15.) It is one of the important features that a terminal may or may not have.

Errors in the transmission may be detected by using codes designed to reveal whether any bits have been changed. A block of data normally has some extra bits (or characters) added to it; these bits are obtained by performing a logical or mathematical operation on all the other bits. In this way a unique checking pattern is generated at the transmitting machine. The same process is performed at the receiving machine; and if the pattern generated is identical, then it is assumed that no error has occurred in the transmission. The certainty of detecting an error depends on the effectiveness of the technique for generating the error pattern. Some rather complicated techniques make it highly unlikely for an error to slip through undetected.

Having detected an error, the receiving device may or may not take automatic action to correct it. The safest action is to request that the item be retransmitted. The device that originally sent the message receives an instruction to send it again. This step can be done only if the sending device still has the message. For a terminal, a buffer would be needed. The message would be retained in the buffer until it was known whether it had been received correctly or not.

If a terminal has no buffer, error checking of messages from the terminal may still take place; but when an error is found, there can be no *automatic* retransmission. Instead the operator is notified of the error and she must initiate retransmission. The terminal must be able to send and receive the signals saying whether the data were received correctly or not.

An alternative to error detection and retransmission is error *correction*. Here a code is used that makes it possible to ascertain not only that there has been an error but also what that error was. The error is corrected without retransmission; thus this operation is referred to as "forward error correction." Chapter 15 will discuss the pros and cons of error detection and forward error correction.

**SYNCHRONOUS VS. ASYNCHRONOUS TRANSMISSION**

Data transmission can be either synchronous or asynchronous. Asynchronous transmission is often referred to as start-stop. With synchronous transmission, characters are sent in a continuous stream. A block of perhaps 100 characters or more may be sent at one time, and for the duration of that block the receiving terminal must be exactly in phase with the transmitting terminal. With asynchronous transmission, one character is sent at a time. The character is initialized by a START signal, shown in Fig. 13.1 as a "O" condition on the line, and terminated by a STOP signal, here a "1" condition on the line. The pulses between these two give the bits of which the character is composed. Between characters, the line is in a "1" condition. As a START bit switches it to O, the receiving machine starts sampling the bits.

**ASYNCHRONOUS (START–STOP) TRANSMISSION**

Figure 13.1 shows the form in which a character is sent with START–STOP transmission. The two most common types of character coding are illustrated, Baudot* code and ASCII code. Most non-American teleprinters transmit Baudot code characters with five data bits plus the START and STOP elements (CCITT telegraph alphabet No. 2), as shown at the top of the figure. Most American terminals designed in recent years transmit ASCII characters, shown at the bottom of the figure, with eight data bits (of which one is often unused) plus the START and STOP elements.

START–STOP transmission is usually used on keyboard devices which do not have a buffer and on which the operator sends characters along the line at more or less random intervals as she happens to press the keys. The START pulse initiates the sampling; thus there can be an indeterminate interval between the characters. Characters are transmittted when the operator's finger presses the keys. If the operator pauses for several seconds between one keystroke and the next, the line will remain in the 1 condition for this period of time.

Start-stop machines are generally less expensive to produce than synchronous machines; for this reason, many machines that transmit card-to-card or paper tape-to-printer, card-to-computer, and so on, are also start-stop, although the character stream does not have the pauses between characters a keyboard transmission has.

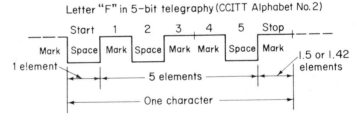

Letter "F" in 5-bit telegraphy (CCITT Alphabet No. 2)

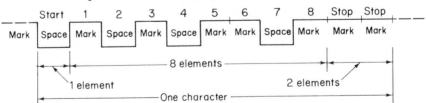

Figure "5" for 8-bit telegraph machines (ASCII code):

*Fig. 13.1.* Typical character structures for START–STOP (asynchronous) transmission.

* The name "Baudot code" has been commonly used to refer to the standard five-bit telegraph code (International Alphabet No. 2). It was, however, devised by Donald Murray, and differs substantially from Baudot's original 5-bit code.

The receiving machine has, in essence, a clocking device that starts when the START element is detected and operates for as many bits as there are in a character. With this, the receiving machine can distinguish which bit is which. The STOP element was made longer than the data bits in case the receiver clock was not operating at quite the same speed as the transmitter.

When this start-stop transmission is used, there can be an indeterminate period between one character and the next. When one character ends, the receiving device waits idly for the start of the next one. The transmitter and the receiver are then exactly in phase, and they remain in phase while the character is sent. The receiver thus is able to attach the correct meaning to each bit it receives.

When an automatic machine such as a paper-tape reader is sending START–STOP signals, the length of the STOP condition is governed by the sending machine. It is short, always 1.42 (1.5 or 2) times the other bits, so as to obtain the maximum transmission rate. When a typist uses the keyboard of a start-stop machine, on the other hand, the duration between her keystrokes varies. The transmission occurs when she presses each key, so the stop condition varies in length considerably. When a scientist uses a teleprinter on a time-sharing system, he may be doing work that involves a great amount of thinking. Occasionally there may be a very long pause between one character and another while he thinks or makes notes. The STOP "bit" will last for the duration of this period.

Teletype speeds in common use are listed in Table 13.1. Such speeds are often quoted in "words per minute." An average teletype word is considered to be five characters long. Because there is a space character between words, there are, then, six characters per word, and $x$ words per minute $= x/10$ characters per second.

**Table 13.1.** COMMONLY USED TELETYPE SPEEDS

| Speed in Bauds (bits per second) | Number of Bits in Character | Stop Bit Duration (in bits) | Information Bit Duration | Characters per Second | Words per Minute (nominal) |
|---|---|---|---|---|---|
| 45.5 | 7.42 | 1.42 | 21.97 | 6.13 | 60 |
| 50 | 7.42 | 1.42 | 20 | 6.74 | 66 |
| 50 | 7.50 | 1.50 | 20 | 6.67 | 66 |
| 74.2 | 7.42 | 1.42 | 13.48 | 10 | 100 |
| 75 | 7.50 | 1.50 | 13.33 | 10 | 100 |
| 75 | 10 | 1.00 | 13.33 | 7.5 | 75 |
| 75 | 11 | 2.00 | 13.33 | 6.82 | 68 |
| 150 | 10 | 1.00 | 6.67 | 15 | 150 |

**SYNCHRONOUS**
**TRANSMISSION**

When machines transmit to each other continuously, with regular timing, synchronous transmission can give the most efficient line utilization. Here the bits of one character are followed immediately by those of the next. There are no START or STOP bits and no pauses between characters. The stream of characters of this type is divided into blocks. All the bits in the block are transmitted at equal-time intervals. The transmitting and receiving machines must be exactly in synchronization for the duration of the block so that if the receiving machine knows which is the first bit, it will be able to tell which are the bits of each character (or words).

Devices using synchronous transmission employ a wide variety of block lengths. The block size may vary from a few characters to many hundreds of characters. Often it relates to the physical nature of the data medium. For example, in the transmission of punched cards it is convenient to use 80 characters as the maximum block length, for there are that many characters per card. Similarly, the length of print lines, the size of buffers, the number of characters in records, or some such system consideration may determine the block size. Some time is taken up between the transmission of one block and the next; therefore the larger the block length, in general, the faster the overall transmission.

With asynchronous transmission, the unit of transmission is normally the character. The operator of a teletype machine presses a key on her keyboard and one character is sent, complete with its START and STOP bits. It is independent in time of any other character. With synchronous transmission, the characters are stored until a complete block is ready to be sent. The block is sent from a buffer at the maximum speed of the line and its modems. There are no gaps between characters as there are when a teletype operator taps at her keyboard. Synchronous transmission is therefore of value when one communication line has several different terminals operating on it. In order to permit synchronous transmission, however, terminals must have buffers; consequently, they are more expensive than asynchronous devices.

The synchronization of the transmitting and receiving machines is controlled by oscillators on many systems. Before a block is sent, the oscillator of the receiving machine must be brought exactly into phase with the oscillator of the transmitting machine. This step is done by sending a synchronization pattern or character at the start of the block. If this were not done, the receiving device would not be able to tell which bit received was the first bit in a character, which the second, and so on. Once the oscillators at each end are synchronized, they will remain so until the end of the block. Oscillators do, however, drift apart slightly in frequency. This drift is very low if highly stable oscillators are used;

but with those low enough in price to be used in quantity in input-output units, the drift is significant. Oscillators in common use in these machines are likely to be accurate to about one part in 100,000. If they are sampling the transmission 2500 times per second, say, then they are likely to stay in synchronization for a time of the order of 20 seconds. Most data processing machines resynchronize their oscillators every one or two seconds for safety. Synchronization can also be maintained by "framing" blocks and carrying timing information in the frames.

On some systems, this places an upper bound on the block length, but not always, because resynchronization characters may be set in the middle of a block. The IBM range of "binary synchronous" equipment, for example, inserts two synchronization characters into the text at one-second intervals. In the U.S. ASCII code with parity checking, these characters would be coded 01101000 01101000. The receiving station is constantly looking for the synchronization pattern and so ensures that the transmitter and receiver are in step.

**BLOCK**
**STRUCTURE**
A block of bits sent by synchronous transmission must have certain features. It must, for example, start with the synchronization pattern or character. It will normally end with an error-checking pattern or character. The block length, as with other data records used by computers, may be of fixed length or variable length. Frequently it is the latter, for variable length usually allows better line utilization. It would be necessary on most systems to pad many blocks with blank characters if fixed-length blocks were used. If the block is of variable length, an end-of-block pattern must be used to tell the receiving machine to begin the actions needed when a block ends. This pattern will normally be sent immediately prior to the error-checking pattern.

Often data are sent in the form of characters or groups of (usually) 6, 7, or 8 bits. The above patterns can be 1, 2, or more characters. One transmission scheme, for example, uses six-bit characters. These are transmitted without parity checking, so that the whole block is divided up into groups of six bits. The block must start with the following characters: 111111, 111110 (in that sequence). This constitutes the synchronization pattern. A circuit in the receiving machine spends its life scanning the input for this pattern. When it finds it, then the receiving device knows that the next bit it receives is the first data bit. The synchronization pattern is unique. The coding of characters must be such that it could not occur anywhere else in the transmission.

The block ends with a six-bit error-checking pattern (one character) and immediately preceding that is the end-of-message character. When the text is being transmitted, the receiving device is generating its own error-checking pattern, which is computed from the characters received. At the same time, it is examining each character received to see whether it is the end-of message character. When this character is received, the machine knows that the next one is to be the transmitted error-checking pattern, and so it compares that with the pattern it has generated itself. If there is a difference, the receiving machine sends a message to the transmitting machine to demand a retransmission of that message.

Figure 13.2 shows the format of a block of text transmitted in this manner. It is designed for a line to which many input-output machines are attached.

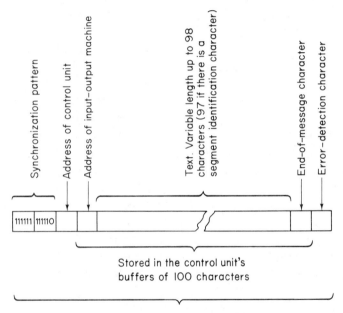

Stored in the control unit's buffers of 100 characters

The entire block is composed of six-bit characters

*Fig. 13.2.* Typical format of a block of data for synchronous transmission on a heavily loaded line with many terminals where efficient line loading is important.

These machines are arranged in groups, and each group is connected to a control unit, which itself is connected to the line which transmits data to and from the computer. After the synchronization pattern in each block comes the address of the control unit (one character) and the address of the input-output machine (one character) to which the message is going or from which the message has come. It is possible that messages transmitted to the computer may be longer than the maximum length of a block. In this case, they are divided into as many blocks as necessary, and a character is used as a segment identifier to link them. The control unit places this identifier, if it is needed, in the block immediately before the text. The text itself is again in six-bit characters and can be of any length up to 98 characters.  This maximum is imposed by the size of the buffers (100 characters) used in the control units.

There are many variations of this type of format.  Sometimes one character is designated as the "synchronization character," and a stream of these characters is sent continuously between messages when the line would otherwise be idle.  At least two such characters are necessary prior to a message to establish synchronization.  The example in Fig. 13.2 is perhaps noteworthy because it minimizes the number of bits transmitted.  Only six-bit characters are used, which is satisfactory for many applications.  On many synchronous transmission schemes, the number of bits needed has been allowed to grow much higher than in this illustration; consequently, it may be worthwhile to question the necessity for the excess bits.

**ADVANTAGES AND DISADVANTAGES**       There are two conflicting desires: to make the terminal inexpensive and to use the communication lines efficiently by putting many terminals on one line. Up until now low-cost terminals have been start-stop, with no buffers.  Buffered, synchronous terminals have been more expensive, but have given better line utilization.  Where the lines are short and inexpensive (e.g., within one city), efficient line utilization is of little importance.  When a dial-up line is used, normally there will only be one terminal on the line and start-stop operation will often be good enough.  A somewhat higher character-transmission rate could be obtained with synchronous transmission.

The other main advantage of synchronous transmission is that the error rate can be less.  Extremely good error control can be achieved with high-order error-detecting codes and a buffer in the sending machine so that retransmission can be automatically requested.

The disadvantage of synchronous operation, the fact that it is more expensive, is diminishing as the cost of logic circuitry drops.  At the same time, the reliability of logic circuitry is substantially increasing.  All the logic for a synchronous, buffered, error-checking terminal can now be constructed on one large-scale-integration chip, which can be low in cost if large quantities are mass-produced.

**EDITING**       The inexpensive start-stop terminal may contain no logic other than that for transmitting and receiving each character.  At the other end of the scale, a terminal may contain a high level of "intelligence," as will be discussed in Chapter 16.  The systems analyst must assess the value of placing intelligence in the terminal *rather than elsewhere*.

One of the functions that logic circuitry in the terminal can perform is editing. Messages from the computer may contain new line indicators, and tab or column number indicators. These will cause the data to be laid out on the screen in a neat, readable fashion without having to transmit many blank characters within the message. Similarly, the operator may construct her message in a buffer, modify it, and correct any errors she may have made, before it is transmitted. This operation may be more intricate if her responses consist of filling in or changing items on a screen already filled with data.

On a graphic terminal, there are many possible ways in which the image may be "edited." The number of bits needed to transmit a line drawing or, for that matter, any other image depends on the amount of logic in the terminal to assist in constructing the image.

## LINE DISCIPLINE

It is often desirable to attach several terminals to one line. As will be discussed in Section IV, there are many ways to organize a network so that the cost of attaching many terminals to a computer is minimized. Where one line interconnects several terminals that transmit in turn, not simultaneously, some form of line discipline is needed.

When several devices all share one communication path, only can one transmit at once, although several or all points can receive the same information. Each terminal must have an address of one or more characters, and it must have the ability to recognize a message sent to that address. A line may, for example, have 26 terminals with addresses A to Z. The computer sends down the line a message that is to be displayed by terminals A, G, and H. The message is preceded by these three addresses, and each terminal has circuitry that scans for its own address. Terminals A, G, and H recognize their addresses and display the message simultaneously. The other terminals do not recognize their address and so ignore the message. The network may also have a "broadcast" code, which causes all terminals on a line to display those messages preceded by it.

## POLLING

For transmission in the other direction, several terminals may wish to transmit at the same time. Only one can do so; the others must wait their turn. To organize this, the line will normally be polled. A polling message is sent down the line to a terminal, saying, "Terminal X, have you anything to transmit? If so, go ahead." If terminal X has nothing to send, a negative reply will be received and the next polling message will be sent, "Terminal Y, have you anything to transmit? If so, go ahead."

The device that does the polling—often a computer—will have in its memory a polling list giving the sequence in which the terminals should be polled. The polling list and its use determine the priorities with which terminals are scanned. Certain important terminals may have their address more than once on the polling list and thus they are polled twice as frequently as the others. Any number of lines may be in use at one time.

As will be seen in the calculations in Section VI, roll-call polling can sometimes degrade the response time obtained at the terminals. This is particularly true when the time taken to reverse the direction of transmission on the line is lengthy (line turnaround time). Nevertheless, there are many fast-response systems on which a large number of terminals are polled. Polling schemes other than roll-call polling can avoid many of the line turnarounds that occur in that process, thereby giving much improved response times.

There are other forms of line discipline in which a continuous stream of characters travel nonstop on the line. For any line discipline, however, appropriate logic must be built into the terminal.

**FULL DUPLEX VS.**
**HALF DUPLEX**

Over a given physical line, the terminal equipment may be designed so that it can either transmit in both directions at once, full-duplex transmission, or it can transmit in either direction but not both at the same time—half duplex.

An input-output terminal or a computer-line adapter works in somewhat different fashions, depending on which is used. Where full-duplex transmission is employed, it may be used either to send data streams in both directions at the same time or to send data in one direction and control signals in the other. The control signals govern the flow of data and are used for error control. Data at the transmitting end are held until the receiving end indicates that the data have been received correctly. If the data are not received correctly, the control signal indicates this fact and the data are retransmitted. Control signals ensure that no two terminals transmit at once on a line with many terminals, and the signals organize the sequence of transmission.

Simultaneous transmission in two directions can be obtained on a two-wire line by using two separate frequency bands. One is used for transmission in one direction and the other for the opposite direction. By keeping the signals strictly separated in frequency, they can be prevented from interfering with each other.

The two bands may not be of the same bandwidth. A much larger channel capacity is needed for sending data than for sending the return signals that control the flow of data. If, therefore, data are to be sent in one direction only, the major part of the line bandwidth can be used for data. Some schemes thus permit a high bit-rate in one direction with a very low bit-rate return path. This transmission can usually be reversed in direction so that data can be sent either way. One modem, for example, permits transmission of data at 3600 bits per second in one direction and provides a simultaneous return path for control signals at 150 bits per second.

Many data processing situations are not able to take advantage of the facility to transmit streams of data in both directions at the same time. Consequently, where full-duplex transmission is used, it is often with data traveling in one direction only, the other direction being used for control signals.

Full-duplex lines are generally more expensive than half-duplex lines, commonly 10 percent more expensive in the United States. Subsequent chapters will examine the advantage of full-duplex operation in detail.

**CHARACTER CODING**
A variety of different codes are used on transmission lines.[1] The most common ones are the 7-bit US ASCII code, the United States standard, and the 5-bit Baudot code used for international telegraphy.

All such codes use control characters to indicate start of message, end of message, error indication, and so on. The transmission cannot take place without some of these control characters. However, it is often desirable to transmit *all* of the six-, seven-, or eight-bit combinations that a computer or its peripheral device can store. A conflict therefore arises here.

The conflict is resolved by using a pair of characters for the control character, instead of one. For example, the DLE character (Data Link Escape) of the ASCII and similar codes may precede any control character, and this tells the receiving machine that the control character has its control meaning. The DLE character is regarded as not being part of the data. In order to transmit a DLE character and have the receiving machine accept it, it must *itself* be preceded by a DLE character.

This type of transmission is sometimes referred to as a *transparent code* or transmission in *transparent text mode*.

Some machines can switch backward and forward between transparent and normal text. Sequences of characters are needed for this operation, for example,

DLE STX: Initiate transparent text mode.

DLE ETB: Terminate transparent transmission.

DLE ITB: Terminate transparent text mode but continue transmission in normal mode.

[1] James Martin, *Teleprocessing Network Organization*, Chapter 2, Prentice-Hall, Englewood Cliffs, N.J., 1970.

Sometimes it is desirable to transmit more characters than there are combinations in the code. The five-bit Baudot code, for example, has $2^5 = 32$ possible combinations, but it is necessary to send the digits, letters of the alphabet, and punctuation with it. This step is done by an "escape mechanism," a character that changes the meaning of the following characters. In the case of the Baudot code, "letters shift" and "figures shift" characters indicate whether the characters following them are from a numeric set or an alphabetic set, like the use of the shift key on a typewriter.

## CODE CONVERSION

It is desirable for devices that use different codes to be able to communicate. In order to do so, some form of code conversion must be used. Code conversion most commonly takes place in the central computer system. However, it may take place in a remote line-control computer or in the terminal control unit.

## SECURITY

We mentioned security in the previous chapter. Several aspects of security may affect the interface between the terminal and the communication line. First, the terminal should be able to identify itself uniquely to the computer. This will prevent a person at a different terminal from contacting the computer and carrying out unauthorized operations. The substitute terminal could be connected to the computer by simple dialing in some cases and in other cases by wire-tapping at a private branch exchange. To identify itself, the terminal may, on interrogation, transmit a unique number, which is hard-wired into tamperproof circuiting. This step alone will not give protection from the determined intruder who has a high level of engineering capability. He could obtain the unique number by recording on a tapped wire and modify his terminal to transmit it. However, the unique terminal number combined with a related set of other measures, will defeat most attempted breaches in security.

The second technique that may be used is cryptography. The user may have a magnetic cartridge of random numbers, and the computer has the same set on its file for the user. The terminal uses these sets for encrypting the data sent and for decrypting the data received. The cartridge is changed periodically. A variety of other cryptography techniques are possible.

The terminal may be equipped with a lock so that it cannot be used by persons without a key. Some terminals have the facility to read a user's identity card. A card the size of a credit card with data encoded on a magnetic stripe is used for this purpose. Lastly, the terminal may have the ability to inhibit printing or display when the user keys in his security code.

**BANDWIDTH OF
A VOICE CHANNEL**

The signal-carrying capacity of communication links can be described in terms of the frequencies that they will carry. A certain physical link might, for example, transmit energy at frequencies ranging from 300 to 150,000 hertz. [The word hertz (Hz) has replaced "cycles per second" in describing frequency and bandwidth. Their meaning is identical.] Above 150,000 and below 300 Hz, the signal is too much attenuated to be useful. The range of frequencies is described as the bandwidth of the channel. The bandwidth is 149,700 (=150,000 − 300) Hz (or cycles per second). In fact, the upper cutoff point is not as sharp as is suggested by this, and we would probably say a bandwidth of 150 kilohertz (kHz).

Figure 13.3 shows the attenuation of different frequencies on a typical voice channel. It will be seen that between about 300 and 3400 Hz different

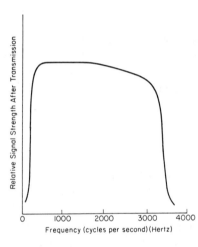

*Fig. 13.3.* Variation in signal strength with frequency after transmission over a typical voice line.

frequencies are attenuated roughly equally. Frequencies outside these limits are not usable, and therefore we would say that this channel had a bandwidth of 3100 Hz.

The quantity of data that can be transmitted over a channel is approximately proportional to the bandwidth.[2]

The frequencies transmitted in Fig. 13.3 are not sufficient to reproduce the human voice exactly. They are, however, enough to make it intelligible and to make the speaker recognizable. This is all that is demanded of the telephone system. Hi-fi enthusiasts strive to make their machines reproduce frequencies

[2] See James Martin, *Telecommunications and the Computer*, Chapters 10 and 11, Prentice-Hall, Englewood Cliffs, N.J., 1969.

from 30 to 20,000 Hz. If the telephone system could transmit this range, then we could send high-fidelity music over it. Sending music over the channel in Fig. 13.3 would clip it of its lower and higher frequencies, and it would sound less true to life than over a small transistor radio.

The physical media that are used for telecommunications all have a bandwidth much larger than that needed for one telephone conversation, so between towns one link is made to carry as many voice channels as possible. The bandwidth of one physical channel is electronically cut up into slices of 4000 Hz, and each of these slices becomes one voice channel.[3] The result is shown in Fig. 13.3. The frequencies given here fit easily into the 4000-Hz slice.

In order to transmit data over the telephone line, then, we must manipulate it electronically so that it fits into the frequencies of Fig. 13.3. This step is done by a *modem*, which will be discussed shortly.

Nonvoice channels have bandwidths different from that in Fig. 13.3— subvoice-grade channels are lower in bandwidth, and broadband channels are higher. If desirable, channels of extremely high bandwidth can be obtained.

**MODULATION**     Data entering or leaving data processing machines are normally binary in form and consist of rectangular pulses resembling those in Fig. 13.4. It is necessary to convert these pulses so that they will travel over the range of frequencies shown in Fig. 13.3, or whatever the frequencies of the line in question are.

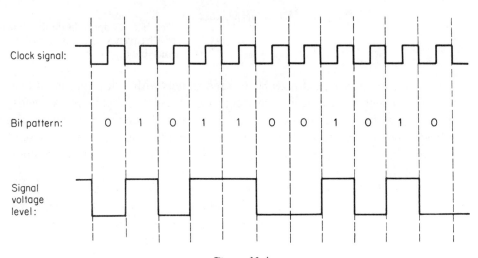

*Figure 13.4*

[3] *Telecommunications and the Computer*, Chapters 10 and 15.

Two problems become apparent. First, the line represented by Fig. 13.3 does not transmit dc current. Frequencies below 200 Hz are severely attenuated. A data pattern in which every bit is a "1," for example, would not be transmitted. Second, high frequencies are attenuated, and this fact alone would cause our square-edged pulses to become distorted. The faster the bit rate, the greater would be the distortion.

The square-edged pulse train is, therefore, manipulated electronically to make it fit as well as possible into the transmission frequencies of Fig. 13.3. In a typical system, a "carrier" is used that is a single-frequency signal in the middle of the band available for transmission. The carrier is modified in some way by the data to be sent so that it "carries" the data. This process is referred to as "modulation."

As can be seen in Fig. 13.3, a certain range of frequencies travels without much distortion over telephone circuits. A frequency of 1500 Hz, for example, is near the middle of the human voice range. Modulation employs these voice frequencies to carry data that would otherwise suffer too much distortion. Thus a sine wave of 1500 Hz may be used as a carrier on which the data to be sent are superimposed in the manner shown in Fig. 13.5.

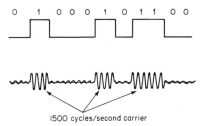

*Fig. 13.5.* Amplitude modulation of a frequency at the center of the voice band.

In addition to making it possible to send signals with a dc component over channels that will not transmit direct current, modulation achieves two ends: first, it reduces the effects of noise and distortion and, second, it increases the possible signaling speed. By using simple modulation devices, one can send computer data without undue distortion over the voice circuits and other communication lines of the world.

Figure 13.5 illustrates one type of modulation—amplitude modulation—in which a 1 is represented by a high-amplitude sine wave at the carrier frequency and a 0 is represented by a lower-amplitude wave of the same frequency. Other types of modulation are described in the next chapter.

**MODEMS AND
DATA SETS**

In order to achieve modulation, the binary output from the data processing machine must enter a "modulator," which produces the appropriate sine wave and modifies it in accordance with the data. This process produces a signal suitable for sending over voice circuits; and whatever manipulation the electronics do to the human voice, they can also do to this signal and the data will still be recoverable. At the other end of the communication line, the carrier must be "demodulated" back to binary form. The circuitry for modulating and demodulating is usually combined into one unit, referred to by the abbreviated term modem.

The modem, a unit about the size of a domestic radio set, is connected to the data-processing machine, and it is then able to transmit data over normal telephone, or other, lines as in Fig. 13.6.

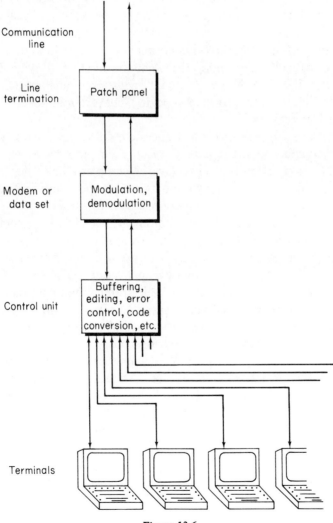

*Figure 13.6*

Modems are made both by the computer manufacturers and by the telephone companies. They are sometimes also called data sets.

The increasing choice of modems on the market and in the laboratory will give the systems engineer more scope in selecting between these criteria to suit his particular data processing environment.

**TRANSMISSION WITHOUT MODEMS**   Modems are not necessarily used on lines that are privately laid, although here, still, they can increase greatly the speed of transmission. Many computer users need to have data transmission lines within their own premises, as well as privately owned lines linking two buildings near each other. The terms *in-plant* and *out-plant* system are used. "Out-plant" system implies that common carrier lines are used. "In-plant" lines are normally a straightforward copper path, possibly coaxial cable, connecting the points in question. Private links of this type are often installed by a firm's own engineers. Sometimes they are also provided by telecommunication companies, but external to any major telecommunication network.

Devices that use these lines often operate by the simple making and breaking of relay contacts, or the sending of rectangular pulse trains, such as that in Fig. 13.4. No modulation is needed. Over a wire pair a few miles in length, dc pulses can be sent at speeds up to about 300 bits per second. The distortion of the signals makes it impractical to send data in this form at speeds much higher than 300 bits per second over an ordinary pair of wires, except over short distances or unless closely spaced repeaters reconstruct the pulse stream—a very powerful technique to be discussed later. A speed of 300 bits per second, however, is a useful one for many computer applications. The speed could be increased greatly by using small coaxial cables rather than wire pairs. In many systems, a large number of typewriter-speed terminals within a localized area, say 3 miles across, could be connected to a time-sharing system or to a concentrator without modems. Although most common carrier lines require modems today, it is possible that the wire pairs that connect a central office to all locations with a telephone could be used over a limited area for dc signaling as in the earlier days of telegraphy. A low-cost private branch exchange for data signals used in this way has been developed.

A modem for low-speed transmission typically costs about $20 or $40 monthly rental. A time-sharing system with 500 low-speed terminals (only a few of which are in use at any one time) would be likely to pay, then, about $20,000 to $40,000 per month for modems. If dc signaling could be used, this high cost would be avoided.

**TERMINAL COMPONENTS**

All the mechanisms discussed in this chapter may be in one unit, or there may be several units. Figure 13.6 shows the units on a typical visual display system attached to a leased line. Separate terminals are linked to a common control unit, which contains most of the digital logic and storage.

The control unit is attached to the modem by using a standard terminal-modem interface. In some cases, the modem is built into the packaging of the terminal itself, and terminal and modem can be tailored to each other's needs.

The termination of the telephone line is at a "patch panel," which with the aid of jack-plugs enables terminals to be switched to different lines.

In many cases, the terminal will use a public telephone dial line; then the modem must be connected to a telephone, or a data set with a telephone dial must be used.

**SUMMARY: CHECKLIST**

The following pages summarize the terminal features by giving a checklist for reference when selecting a terminal.

*Manual Input Facilities*

Typewriterlike keyboard

Keyboard with letters in alphabetic sequence

Keyboard like a Touchtone telephone

Keyboard like a calculating machine

Matrix keyboard

Keys with special labels

Keyboard with interchangeable key labels

Keyboard with overlays or templates

Lever set

Rotary switches

Pushbuttons

Light pen with display tube

Coupled stylus on "desk pad"

Pen-following mechanism

Badge reader

Punched-card reader

Matrix card holder

Can the data be keyed into a buffer and modified before transmission?

Is paper tape or any other serial medium used for buffering?

Does the keyboard give any help in formatting messages?

Does it have the necessary keys for the dialogue in question?

Does it have special facilities for when the computer fails?

Can it be operated with one hand?

Can the keys be changed?

Does a bell ring at the end of a line?

Are there good cursor controls?

Are there facilities for easy modification of computer data?

Are there skip and tab keys?

Are there page or scroll keys?

Are there YES/NO or other keys for high-speed scanning?

Is the manual correction of errors easy?

Can the numeric part of the keyboard be operated by one hand ($3 \times 4$ matrix)?

Does the keyboard have a good "feel" to a fast touch-typist?

Are HELP or INTERRUPT keys desirable in the man-machine dialogue?

Does the input means have appropriate security features?

*Document Input Facilities*

Paper-tape reader/punch

Card reader/punch

Magnetic-tape cassette

Disk

Magnetic cord reader

Does the machine in the foregoing cases have or need the facility to write or punch a document as it is being keyed in?

Can one storage media be shared by many keyboards?

Badge and credit card (identity card) reader

Optical document reader

Magnetic-ink document reader

Mark-sense card reader

Matrix plate or card reader

Can various devices be attached to one control unit?

*Output Facilities*

Typewriterlike printer

Printer that operates faster than a typewriter

Inexpensive numeric-only printer, like a calculating machine

Should the printer print on a special document, such as a bank passbook?

Should the printer have special characters—for example, for mathematics, text editing, chemical formulas, or producing diagrams?

Should the character set be interchangeable as with an IBM Selectric "golf-ball"?

Is hard copy essential or would it be possible to do without it?

Could the hard-copy facility be at the computer or concentrator rather than at the terminal?

Could a camera be used rather than an expensive copying machine?

If a printer or plotter is needed, could one such device serve many terminals?

*Visual-Display Screen* (features of visual displays are listed separately below)

Picturephone

Interface to standard television set

Light panel

Graph plotter

Strip recorder

Telephone voice answerback

Dials

Facsimile machine

Projector for slides, microfilm, microfiche, EVR frames, etc.

How rapidly must the data be printed or displayed? This factor relates to the delivery time for bulk transmission and to man-machine interaction processes in a dialogue system (see Chapter 7)?

Is there a means of alerting the operator's attention?

Is there an audible alarm?

Can certain fields be highlighted—for example, with color?

Does it have appropriate tabbing, skipping, and page-change features?

*Features of Display Screens*

Can it display enough characters?

Are the displayed characters large enough?

Are the characters easy to read?

Is it flicker-free?

Is the image bright enough? Some displays have caused operator headaches.

Is the image suitably protected from external glare?

Is the display rate fast enough for the man-machine dialogue?

Can it handle vectors or other graphic features?

Destructive or nondestructive cursor?

Can the cursor be made either destructive or nondestructive under program control?

What cursor movements are possible?

Are the keys for cursor movement straightforward?

What character insert and delete capabilities are available?

Does it have suitable special characters?

Is the character set large enough?

Should the character set be interchangeable: for example using microprogramming?

Does it have a scroll feature (text roll up and roll down)?

Does it have selectable horizontal tabs, reverse tabs, field skips, or other formatting features?

What editing capabilities are available?

Can individual fields be highlighted in some way—for example, by blinking, color, different brightness, or reverse field (either black characters on white or white characters on black)?

Can masks be stored for editing of screen contents?

Can data fields be protected (made unchangeable by the operator)?

Can the data fields be program-defined?

Are the features changeable—for example, microprogrammed?

Are spaces to the right of an "end-of-line" character transmitted?

What data compaction occurs on transmission?

Does it have line addressing so that part of a display can be changed without the rest?

Can a protected field be used for selective data entry?

Are upper- and lower-case characters needed (e.g., in text editing)?

Should images be displayed that are not composed digitally—for example, documents, signatures, photographs, diagrams? These may be stored at the terminal on film, microfilm, slides, EVR cartridges, etc.

Can such images be half-tone (like a photograph)?

Can such images be in color?

Can "panels" be stored at the terminal control unit for display or for editing purposes?

If locally stored images are displayed, should they be combined with transmitted data?

Does it have a light pen?

Is the detection of light-pen positioning fine enough?

Does it have pen tracking capability and is it fast enough?

Can light-pen field selection be allowed and disallowed under program control?

Do selectable fields brighten as the pen approaches to indicate to the operator that he may select them?

Does the light pen have a pressure-sensitive switch in its tip?

Can the images be printed?

Can the images be automatically copied onto a monitor screen?

Is a group display needed?

Is an extra–high-capacity screen needed (10,000 characters or higher)?

Can the screen image be printed?

If so is the printer at the terminal, elsewhere at the terminal location serving several users, or at a concentrator or central computer location?

What is the quality of the printing?

*Features for Security*

Unique terminal identification by the computer

Do dial-up terminals automatically transmit terminal ID?

Lockable keyboard

Nonprinting feature for when keying in security code or password.

Automatic print/display suppression of security code or password field.

Print/display suppression of other fields possible?

Identification card reader?

Cryptography feature

Physical lock and key

Feature for prevention of *copying* on other terminal or printer.

Feature for erasing buffer.

Feature to prevent terminal cable connections being switched.

Protection from effects of control unit failure?

*Features of the Communication Line Interface*

Is a standardized code used (e.g., ASCII)?
Is a compact code needed to maximize transmission efficiency?
Can *different* codes be used, for flexibility?
Can any characters be used (e.g., with an escape character mechanism)?

*Features for Control of Errors*

Erase, or backspace, key

Cancel transaction key

Automatic error detection. The code used for automatic error detection can range from relatively insecure parity checks to virtually errorproof polynomial codes of a high order.

Automatic transmission when an error is detected (which implies some form of buffer at the terminal)

Forward-error correction

Transaction logging in the terminal

Accumulators in the terminal for keeping totals

Logging facilities and/or accumulators that record details of transactions entered when the computer is inoperative

A recording mechanism (e.g., tape cassette) for recording transactions when the computer is inoperative, which can later be transmitted to it. This transmission may or may not be automatic.

Synchronous or start-stop operation?

Is full-duplex or half-duplex transmission used?

If it is full duplex, is it designed so that full advantage can be taken of simultaneous transmission in both directions?

Is there any form of interrupt mechanism?

Does the terminal have dial-up capabilities?

Can it dial a remote machine automatically?

Will it automatically redial if it first obtains a busy signal?

Is a buffer used so that transmission can be at maximum-line speed (important, as we shall see on high-performance multidrop lines)?

Can operator editing of input be done before transmission (especially with a video display)?

Is the transmission rate suitably high?

Is the transmission rate changeable for bad line conditions?

Is a modem or acoustical coupler built in?

If not, does it have a standard EIA RS232B (or other) interface with the modem?

Does it have multiplexing facilities—for example, a modulation device selecting a set portion of the available bandwidth?

Can several terminals be connected to one buffer or control unit?

Does the control unit dynamically assign buffer space?

Can there be terminal-to-terminal communication?

Does it contain logic for multidrop operation (many terminals on one line) such as polling?

If polling is used, is it roll call or hub?

If one device on a multidrop line fails, will this affect the line functioning?

What communication line turnaround time is associated with the terminal?

How does the line turnaround time affect the network organization and response time?

If it is normally attached to a leased line, can it have an alternate dial-up connection, possibly at lower speed?

Will it automatically establish a dial-up connection if a leased line fails?

Is a modem built into the terminal or separate?

Is the terminal monitored for running out of paper or other holdups?

Can unsolicited messages be sent to an idling terminal?

Can an idling terminal be dialed?

*General*

Is it portable?

Need it be battery operated (e.g., when a terminal is taken in a car and used in a public call box)?

Is it silent?

Is it compact enough?

Is it attractive?

Is it robust?

Is it reliable?

Is it designed so that it can be easily serviced?

Is the maintenance contract good enough?

Is the maintenance organization good enough?

Are there replaceable blocks of components for quick repair?

Can these blocks be changed by trained local staff so that a visit from a repairman is unnecessary?

Can the remote computer be used in terminal fault diagnosis or checkout?

Is the construction modular so that separate keyboards or other devices can be used?

Can the device be used off-line for a needed function—for example, typewriter or desk calculator?

# 14 COMPARISON OF MODULATION EQUIPMENT

Most communication lines, as we discussed in the previous chapter, are basically analog in operation (although this situation may change within the next decade). Data processing devices, on the other hand, are digital. In order to link them together, a modem is usually required.

The systems analyst is confronted with a wide range of modems and associated devices. The purpose of this chapter is to set them into perspective and give him some guidelines for his selection of this piece of equipment.

**CRITERIA FOR CHOICE**    Four major requirements will affect his choice:

1. Speed of transmission
2. Response time
3. Number of errors in transmission
4. Cost

The relative importance of these four requirements will vary from one application to another. An appropriate balance between them is required. As we discuss different types of arrangement, we will relate them to these basic requirements.

The wide selection of modulation methods is useful because the characteristics and needs of the data transmission vary widely from one situation to another. In some circumstances, speed is all important. In others, it is not a vital factor; and accuracy might be a stronger consideration. In some systems, the communication lines are very long and thus expensive. In this case, the modulation and line control methods are chosen to give the most efficient use of the expensive facility. In other cases, the modems themselves are a more significant part of the cost; therefore inexpensive modulation techniques are chosen. The noise characteristics vary considerably from one network to another; in addition, the bandwidth available also varies. Public voice circuits have a bandwidth broken up by an unusable signaling frequency.[1] Private lines, particularly when installed for data transmission, may have good noise characteristics. Public lines going through an exchange, on the other hand, usually suffer from impulse, and other, noise effects. Amplitude variations are common on some circuits. On others, there is considerable delay distortion, and so on. Private lines can be conditioned to overcome these factors in part. Public lines cannot. In some cases, fast response time will be a dominating consideration, and because polling is used, it will be highly dependent on a fast modem turnaround time.

Let us first outline the different modulation methods available to us and then again discuss the decision facing the systems analyst.

**NO MODEM**   The simplest (and cheapest) arrangement of all is not to have a modem. The square-edged pulses that emerge from the terminal are fed directly into the pair of wires that are used for transmission. This is referred to as *baseband* signaling. The pulses quickly become distorted, as shown in Fig. 14.1. If they are transmitted too far or at too

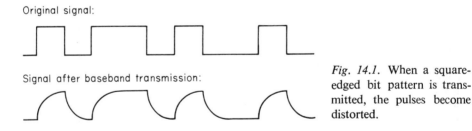

Original signal:

Signal after baseband transmission:

*Fig. 14.1.* When a square-edged bit pattern is transmitted, the pulses become distorted.

fast a speed, the distortion will become so great that the bit pattern cannot be recovered. Furthermore, they cannot be transmitted over a line with repeaters because they will not amplify the dc component of baseband signals.

However, this form of transmission is perfectly satisfactory for local operation. As mentioned previously, terminals operating at up to 300 bits per second can operate successfully over lines up to 3 miles. Much higher speeds are possible over shorter distances.

[1] James Martin, *Telecommunications and the Computer*, Prentice-Hall, Englewood Cliffs, N.J., 1969, Chapter 17.

**ACOUSTICAL COUPLERS**   When the bits are sent over greater distances than those possible without modems, or when they are sent over lines with repeaters, some method is needed to convert the bits of Fig. 13.4 so that they travel over the range of frequencies shown in Fig. 13.3 (or similar).

One inexpensive method is to use acoustical couplers. These convert the characters to be transmitted into audible tones, such as those generated by a Touchtone telephone. A machine using audible tones need not necessarily be wired to the line physically. It can make sounds that are picked up by the telephone microphone and this is referred to as acoustical coupling. The sounds used must be at those frequencies having low attenuation as in Fig. 13.3. The sounds are reproduced at the far end of the connection by a telephone earpiece and are then converted back into data signals. Acoustical coupling is somewhat less efficient than direct coupling. At the time of writing, it is used for transmitting between relatively slow machines, such as typewriterlike terminals.

In an acoustical-coupling device, the telephone handpiece fits in a special cradle. Acoustical couplers are generally less expensive than modems. Another advantage of acoustical coupling is that the terminal can easily be made portable. A small terminal could be made to transmit to a computer from a public call box. Nondigital machines also use acoustical coupling. Documents can be copied at a distance with a Xerox machine in this way.

Although there is no electrical connection to the telephone lines, it is still possible for acoustically coupled machines to interfere with the public network's signaling, as with a directly coupled device. Also, severe crosstalk can be caused on a telephone link that carries many voice channels, by the transmission of a continuous frequency, as with a repetitive data pattern. It is therefore desirable that the coupling device randomize the signal before it is sent, although most such devices do not do so today.

By 1970 acoustical couplers were extensively used in the United States. In many other countries, however, the telecommunication authorities would not permit their use. This action prohibited the variety of applications of small portable terminals, such as from public coin-operated telephones. A major advantage of acoustical couplers is the ability to use them anywhere there is a telephone, without a wired connection to the telephone line. For this reason, acoustical couplers have been built into the circuitry of some portable devices. There are many possible ways of coding the characters into sets of audible frequencies that can be used on the telephone line.

**DIRECT-TONE TRANSMISSION**   The same coding and frequencies as with an acoustical coupler could be used with the frequency-generating circuits wired directly to the telephone line. Such circuits would be cheaper to manufacture than an acoustical coupler because the telephone handset cradle with its microphone, speaker, and sound insulation, would not be required.

Some inexpensive modems operate in this way, with data being sent character by character, and the bits in each character being sent in parallel with appropriate coding into frequencies. Such a technique, although inexpensive, cannot achieve a high character rate. It is satisfactory for single typewriter-speed devices on a voice line. Parity or other checking can be used to guard against errors, but a higher error rate tends to be encountered than with other low-speed forms of modulation.

**MODULATION OF A**    There are two main purposes in using modems.
**SINE WAVE CARRIER**    *First,* they increase the possible speed over a given
circuit, such as a voice line. *Second,* they reduce the effects of noise and distortion. Many communication links would be unusable at reasonable speeds without modulation.

A variety of modems have been developed in recent years for use with data processing machines. The speed at which data can be sent over a given voice line has been steadily increasing over the last few years, and this increase is largely a result of improved modem design. It is an area that is still developing fast.

The majority of modems in operation transmit a continuous sine wave carrier. They modulate this carrier in accordance with the data that are to be sent. The sine wave has three parameters that we could modulate: its amplitude, its frequency, and its phase. There are thus three basic types of modulation in use: amplitude modulation, frequency modulation, and phase modulation. Each of these methods is in common use today. The sine wave carrier may be represented by

$$a = A \sin (2\pi ft + \theta)$$

where $a$ = the instantaneous amplitude of carrier voltage at time $t$
$A$ = the maximum amplitude of carrier voltage
$f$ = the carrier frequency
$\theta$ = the phase

The values of $A$, $f$, or $\theta$ may be varied to make the wave carry information.

The first of these modulation methods was illustrated in Fig. 13.5. All three are shown in Fig. 14.2. A sinusoidal carrier wave of, say, 1500 Hz (in the center of the telephone voice band) is modulated to carry the information bits 01000101100.

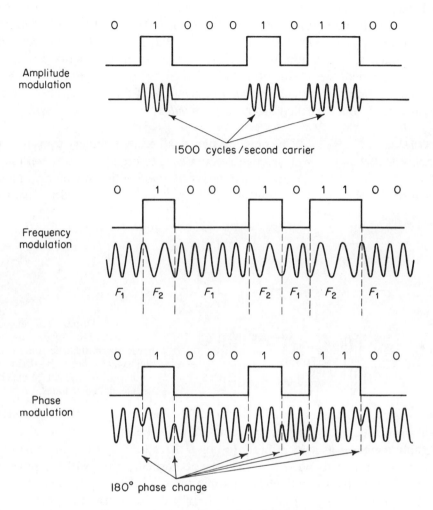

*Fig. 14.2.* The three basic methods of modulating a sine wave carrier (a simplified diagram showing only binary signals).

In the top diagram of Fig. 14.2, the amplitude is varied in accordance with the bit pattern. In the second diagram, the frequency is varied; and in the bottom one, the phase is varied. In these simplified diagrams, the channel is being operated inefficiently because far more bits could be packed into the carrier oscillations shown. The tightness of this packing determines the speed of operation.

Many variations are possible within these three main types of modulation. Different methods are possible for detecting the signal and recovering the bits.

With phase modulation, for example, a given phase condition may represent either a given bit condition or a *change* from a 1 to 0 or 0 to 1 bit. The former is referred to as *fixed-reference detection*, and the latter, *differential detection*. With frequency modulation, the maximum frequency deviation that can occur, $\triangle f$, can be varied over a wide range. The larger $\triangle f$ is the larger the bandwidth required but the greater the resiliance to the effects of noise. The ratio of $\triangle f$ to the carrier frequency is called the *modulation index*.

**MULTILEVEL TRANSMISSION**   The previous figures all relate to binary transmission. It is possible, however, to use a waveform with *more than two states* as the modulating waveform. This is shown for amplitude modulation in Fig. 14.3. "Di-bits" are used to give four

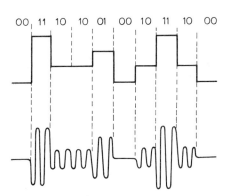

00  11  10  10  01  00  10  11  10  00

*Fig. 14.3.* Di-bits are encoded here, instead of single bits, and hence there must be four detectable signal states rather than two. Similarly, tri-bits can be encoded with eight signal states.

possible states in the modulated waveform. This process approximately doubles the transmission rate that can be achieved with the modem, but it also considerably increases its susceptibility to noise. Because amplitude modulation is already susceptible to noise, di-bits are not normally used with it; however, they are frequently used with phase modulation.

In some modems, "tri-bits" are used. In order to transmit the grouping of three bits, $2^3 = 8$ possible states are needed. Again, the susceptibility to noise and distortion is much greater. Phase modulation using di-bits is referred to as *four-phase modulation* and that using tri-bits is called *eight-phase modulation*. A few experimental modems have employed *16-phase modulation*.

**MODEMS FOR PUBLIC LINES**   On a private-leased telephone line, the machine transmitting data has the bandwidth of Fig 13.3 all to itself. On the public network, however, certain frequencies are used by the network for signaling purposes. The modem must be designed so that it cannot interfere with the signaling. Usually this means that the signaling frequencies must be avoided entirely.

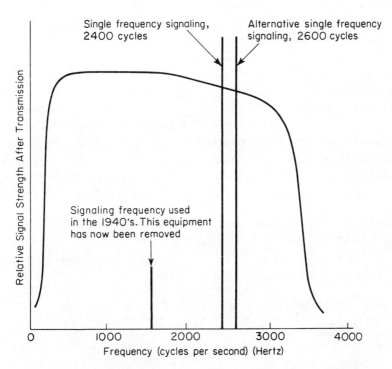

*Fig. 14.4.* In-band signaling frequencies on Bell System Telephone plant. The modem must be designed so that it does not interfere with the network signaling using these frequencies. Some different countries use different frequencies.

Figure 14.4 shows the signaling frequencies used on American telephone lines. Unfortunately, different frequencies are used in other countries. They are different on a British telephone plant, and the CCITT world standard is different from either of these. Signals are sent at these frequencies to indicate, for example, when a subscriber puts down his telephone so that the line may be disconnected.

If a data processing machine happens to transmit at the signaling frequency while sending little or no current at other frequencies, then it could interfere with the operation of the line. Many data processing machines, therefore, are designed to avoid the signaling frequencies completely. The result is to limit the bandwidth available for transmission and hence the speed at which data can be sent. It is possible to design a modem that randomizes the signal, smearing it across the available bandwidth like the human voice so that it can never be mistaken for line signaling. However, doing so increases the modem cost.

Because of the signaling frequencies, modems designed for private voice lines cannot operate on public lines. The maximum speed attainable on public lines is lower. Furthermore, modems designed for the public network in North America cannot be used in other countries and vice versa.

**MODEM PERFORMANCE IN THE PRESENCE OF BACKGROUND NOISE** All electronic processes are set against a background of "thermal" noise. The incessant random motion of electrons forms a level of noise proportional to the absolute temperature. The performance of the various modulation systems in the presence of this "white" noise can be evaluated theoretically. This is done in detail in *Data Transmission* by Bennett and Davey (McGraw-Hill, 1965). The results of this work are tabulated in Table 14.1 and give an interesting comparison between different modulation tech-

**Table 14.1.** THEORETICAL PERFORMANCE OF DIFFERENT MODULATION SYSTEMS IN THE PRESENCE OF WHITE NOISE *

| Modulation System | Number of States | Speed in Bits per Second per Cycle of Bandwidth | Average Signal-to-Noise ratio (dB) for Error Rate of 1 to $10^4$ Bits |
|---|---|---|---|
| *Amplitude Modulation, Full Carrier* | | | |
| 1. Envelope detection | 2 | 1 | 11.9 |
| 2. Synchronous detection | 2 | 1 | 11.4 |
| | 4 | 2 | 19.8 |
| | 8 | 3 | 26.5 |
| *Amplitude Modulation, Suppressed Carrier* | | | |
| 3. Synchronous detection | 2 | 1 | 8.4 |
| 4.    ″       ″ | 4 | 2 | 15.3 |
| 5.    ″       ″ | 8 | 3 | 21.3 |
| *Amplitude Modulation, Vestigial Sideband* | | | |
| 6. 50% modulation | 2 | 2 | 16.2 |
| *Frequency modulation* | | | |
| 7. | 2 | 1 | 11.7 |
| 8. | 4 | 2 | 21.1 |
| 9. | 8 | 3 | 28.3 |
| *Phase Modulation* | | | |
| 10. Fixed-reference detection | 2 | 1 | 8.4 |
| 11.   ″        ″        ″ | 4 | 2 | 11.4 |
| 12.   ″        ″        ″ | 8 | 3 | 16.5 |
| 13. Differential detection | 2 | 1 | 9.3 |
| 14.    ″         ″ | 4 | 2 | 13.7 |
| 15.    ″         ″ | 8 | 3 | 19.5 |

*Bennett and Davey, *Data Transmission*, McGraw-Hill, New York, 1965.

niques. The exact nature of the various detection schemes and variations in amplitude modulation is explained in *Telecommunications and the Computer*, Chapter 13.

It will be seen that the lowest signal-to-noise ratio is required by lines 3 and 10 of Table 14.1. These two types of modulation give the lowest error rate in the presence of thermal background noise. A higher bit rate can be attained by using multilevel transmission, but smaller differences in signal have to be detected. With four states rather than two (i.e., the transmission of di-bits as in Fig. 14.3), line 11, phase modulation with fixed-reference detection gives the lowest signal-to-noise ratio. This type of modulation is also the best with 8 states, and is often used in practice for high-speed transmission over a voice line.

**PERFORMANCE IN THE PRESENCE OF OTHER NOISE**    The most persistent and damaging defect of communication lines is the amplitude changes associated with *impulse noise* and *level changes*. This has a direct effect on any form of *amplitude* modulation and tends to render it more error-prone than frequency or phase modulation. Both frequency and phase modems use limiters, so that changes in amplitude are ignored except for the most violent ones.

Impulse noise, therefore, affects phase and frequency modulation to a lesser extent than amplitude modulation. Large impulses saturating the capacity of the electronics result in "ringing" and cause stray frequency components within the region of the carrier frequency. Because of such stray frequencies, phase modulation is generally more resistant to impulse noise than the other methods.

*Sudden phase changes* as well as sudden amplitude changes occur in the signal, and, of course, these affect phase modulation badly. However, they are far less common than amplitude changes. They will be likely to affect amplitude modulation with synchronous detection also, and frequency modulation. Frequency modulation recovers almost immediately from the effect of phase changes, but phase modulation using fixed-reference detection may not recover quickly and thus a string of erroneous bits may result. Here phase modulation with differential detection has an advantage over fixed-reference detection in that it recovers as soon as the phase change has ended; therefore for one sharp phase change only one bit will be likely to be in error.

**TESTS ON LINES**    Tests on communication lines support the theoretical conclusions that phase modulation performs better than frequency modulation in the presence of noise and that frequency modulation performs better than amplitude modulation.

Figure 14.5 shows typical results comparing frequency and phase modulation. First white noise and then impulse noise was generated artificially, adding to the distortions already present on the lines, and a number of modems were tested. The noise amplitude was varied and the resulting errors measured. The modems used were a binary frequency-modulation modem in which the modulation index and midfrequency could be varied as shown, plus a binary phase-modulation modem with fixed-reference detection and again a variable midfrequency.

The tests illustrate a high noise level and correspondingly large error rate. The generally superior performance of phase modulation can be seen. In live conditions, the signal-to-noise ratio will usually be 30 db or better.

**PERFORMANCE IN THE PRESENCE OF DISTORTION**

The precise shape of the curve in Fig. 13.3 between 300 and 3000 Hz is very important in the design of modems for a high bit rate. Over this range, the curve should be as flat as possible. In other words, the attenuation should be approximately equal at every frequency. Variation in attenuation over the range used is referred to as *attenuation distortion.* Not only should the attenuation be equal, but the delay encountered should also be equal, as far as possible. The signal at 3000 Hz should not arrive a millisecond or so before the signal at 300 Hz.

Delay distortion, in which different frequencies are delayed by different amounts, is a common and serious defect, especially on long lines not constructed with data transmission in mind. It has its worst effect on phase modulation. The relative performance of amplitude and frequency modulation depends on the characteristics of the distortion. Simple, double sideband, amplitude modulation performs quite well. Vestigial sideband amplitude modulation is badly affected by delay distortion.

**CIRCUIT CONDITIONING**

Both attenuation distortion and delay distortion can be compensated for by carefully adjusting the circuit. Compensating adjustments can, in fact, be made at the ends of the circuit where the modems are connected.

When a public circuit is dialed between two distant locations, different physical paths will be switched into the links on different occasions. With a private line, however, the path is fixed and adjustments can be made to its characteristics. In particular, it can be adjusted to have the same attenuation and the same delay, within certain limits, between the frequencies of 300 and 3000 Hz (or perhaps a rather smaller range). The attenuation and the delay are said to be "equalized" over the frequency range in question. *Equalizer* circuits achieve this by adding an artificial attenuation and an artificial delay at different

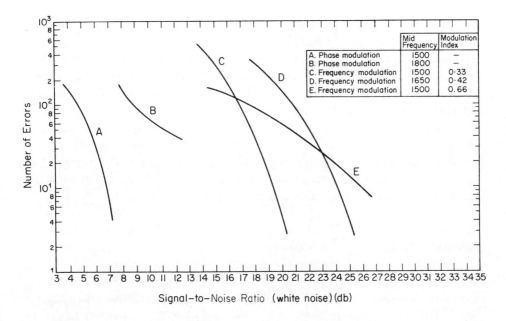

| | Mid Frequency | Modulation Index |
|---|---|---|
| A. Phase modulation | 1500 | — |
| B. Phase modulation | 1800 | — |
| C. Frequency modulation | 1500 | 0·33 |
| D. Frequency modulation | 1650 | 0·42 |
| E. Frequency modulation | 1500 | 0.66 |

Signal–to–Noise Ratio  (white noise)(db)

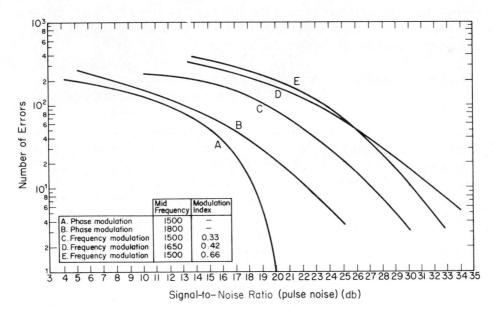

| | Mid Frequency | Modulation Index |
|---|---|---|
| A. Phase modulation | 1500 | — |
| B. Phase modulation | 1800 | — |
| C. Frequency modulation | 1500 | 0.33 |
| D. Frequency modulation | 1650 | 0.42 |
| E. Frequency modulation | 1500 | 0.66 |

Signal–to–Noise Ratio  (pulse noise) (db)

*Fig. 14.5.* Experimental tests showing the superior performance of phase modulation in the presence of noise. *Diagram redrawn from L. A. Joyce, "Comparative Tests of Modems Designed for Digital Transmission Using Frequency Modulation and Phase Modulation Techniques,"* IBM Technical Report TR04.05113.071. *April 1964, LaGaude, France.*

frequencies. The entire process can be performed by the telephone company and is then referred to as "conditioning."

Many carriers either have separate tariffs for conditioned telephone lines and unconditioned lines or charge extra for conditioning. Several grades of conditioning are available. A modem designed for a conditioned line will give a higher bit rate than that for an unconditioned line, or it will give a lower error rate.

*Private lines thus not only have the advantage of being free from network signaling but are also capable of being conditioned.* In addition, they are generally less perturbed by noise and distortion than the switched line. The switching gear can cause impulse noise that causes errors in data.

**DYNAMIC**
**EQUALIZATION**

Because of the preceding factors, the data transmission speeds available on private voice lines have usually been twice those on public lines.

The designers of modems for public lines cannot benefit from conditioning. They can, however, fight back with what is referred to as "dynamic equalization." This process refers to a circuit that measures the characteristics of the line in use and automatically adjusts the attenuation and delay so that these factors are equal, within limits, over a given range of frequencies. In this way, higher speeds can be obtained over public lines.

**DIGITAL CAPABILITY**
**IN THE MODEM**

As the cost of mass-produced digital circuitry drops, it becomes more feasible to include digital logic in the modem. We commented earlier that the modem may randomize the data that are sent, smearing them across the available bandwidth like the human voice so that they can never be mistaken for signaling. The receiving modem uses the converse logic for restoring the original bit pattern. Digital techniques can be used for shaping the signal that is sent. The digital capability may also be used for the automatic correction of errors that occur.

**FORWARD-ERROR**
**CORRECTION**

As we progress to the modulation techniques that give higher bit rates, the susceptibility to noise and distortion increases and the number of errors grows.

The number of errors does not grow proportionately to the increase in speed, but *much* faster. Typical numbers of errors occurring in the modulation process on a leased conditioned voice line before any form of error correction might be around one bit in 100,000 when the transmission rate is 2400 bits per second, one bit in 20,000 at 4800 bits per second, and one bit in 1000 at 9600 bits per second. These figures will vary substantially with the specific design of the modem and will probably improve somewhat as the state of the art develops.

The figures at the higher speeds are quite unacceptable for most systems. Modems operating at speeds of 4800 bits per second and above on a voice line often have error-correction facilities built into digital logic within the modem. The bits sent are collected into a group, and an error-checking pattern is added to this group of such a nature that most errors can be automatically corrected by the digital circuitry in the receiving modem. *Forward-error correction* of this type does not correct all the errors. Some patterns of erroneous bits will cause the error-correction logic to make an incorrect adjustment. The level of accuracy that can be achieved in this way depends on the complexity and the cost of the error-correcting codes used.

**ALTERNATE**
**SPEEDS**
Some modems are designed so that they can be switched to operate at different speeds, with consequently different error rates. One such modem, for example, is designed to operate over voice lines at 1200, 4800, or 9600 bits per second. It uses forward-error correction and is claimed by its manufacturers to have error rates of less than one bit in $10^9$, $10^6$, and $10^3$, respectively, at these speeds.

The higher error rate here is severe and would probably only be used in conjunction with terminals that have error-detection facilities and a means of retransmitting erroneous words without incurring a substantial delay. English text transmitted with an error rate of one bit in 1000 would generally be intelligible, although somewhat annoying. On short lines or in-plant lines, the error rate at 9600 bits may drop by a factor of 10 or 100. The error rate at 4800 bits per second is typical of many of today's uses of data transmission. The 1200-bit-per-second rate would be used where accuracy is the prime consideration or where the terminals do not have error-detection and retransmission facilities. The noise level on telephone lines varies substantially, and for that reason it may be worthwhile to be able to vary the degree of error protection.

One situation in which a two-speed modem is particularly valuable is where the dial-up network is used as a standby for times when leased-line failures occur. During normal conditions, the terminal may operate over a leased line at 4800 bits per second, say, but when the leased line fails, the operator will have to dial the computer over the public network. If the terminal is to have a single modem for both, it must be designed for alternate public-line or private-line operation—the former having to avoid the public signaling frequencies and to function on lines without conditioning.

**LINE
TURNAROUND TIME**
As we shall see in more detail later, it is important with some systems to be able to reverse the direction of transmission very quickly. In doing so, on a half-duplex line the two modems must set up their circuits for reverse transmission and establish synchronization. On a full-duplex line, the modems may be designed so that the transmission paths in both directions are permanently connected.

Modems using basic amplitude modulation can reverse their direction of transmission quickly. However, the high-speed modems of more recent design take longer. With phase modulation, for example, it takes some time to establish synchronization between the two machines, and this process must occur before the detection process can operate satisfactorily. The establishment of dynamic equalization takes time. Indeed, the more sophisticated processes used to achieve higher transmission speeds generally pay a penalty in increased line turnaround time. When forward-error correction is built into the modem, this factor, too, increases the turnaround time because a buffer full of data must be transmitted and checked.

The systems analyst who is designing a network sometimes forgets about line turnaround times. In the advertisements for fast modems in the technical press, the one modem characteristic often not mentioned is turnaround time. In some systems—for example, point-to-point links with full-duplex lines—it is of no importance. On others—for example, fast response systems with polling—it is extremely important.

**MODEMS ON
POLLED LINES**
A question on polled lines that concerns turnaround time is just how long it takes a terminal not currently in transmission mode to the computer, to switch to this state. One terminal sends an "end of transmission" signal, and a new terminal is instructed to transmit. The carrier must be established between the new terminal and the computer, and the new terminal must be synchronized with the receiving machine. The time needed to establish transmission is related to line turnaround time. It tends to be longer with higher-speed modems. It can degrade the response time substantially on a polled line with many terminals, especially if roll-call polling is used. Even on a full-duplex line, this time to switch the connection to a new terminal cannot be avoided.

**MODEMS BUILT
INTO THE TERMINAL**
Most modems to date have been separate from the data processing equipment. An EIA standard defines the interface between the modem and the data pro-

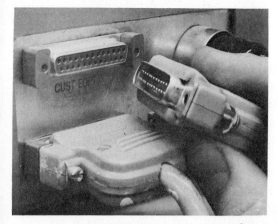

A

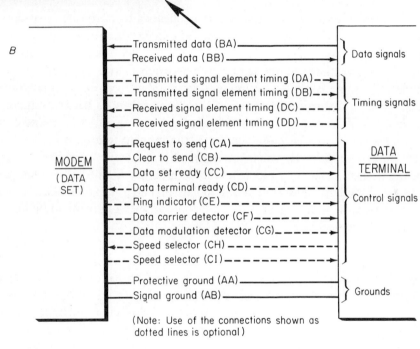

*Fig. 14.6.* The interface between the modem and the data processing equipment is a standard that is well adhered to.

B

MODEM
(DATA
SET)

Transmitted data (BA)
Received data (BB)
} Data signals

Transmitted signal element timing (DA)
Transmitted signal element timing (DB)
Received signal element timing (DC)
Received signal element timing (DD)
} Timing signals

Request to send (CA)
Clear to send (CB)
Data set ready (CC)
Data terminal ready (CD)
Ring indicator (CE)
Data carrier detector (CF)
Data modulation detector (CG)
Speed selector (CH)
Speed selector (CI)
} Control signals

DATA
TERMINAL

Protective ground (AA)
Signal ground (AB)
} Grounds

(Note: Use of the connections shown as dotted lines is optional)

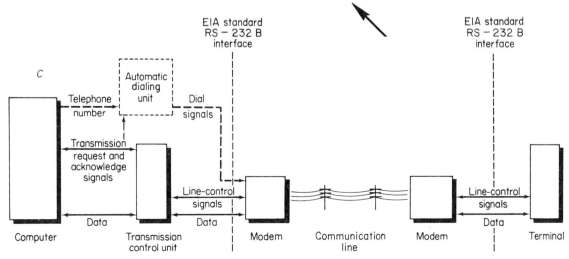

C

EIA standard
RS – 232 B
interface

EIA standard
RS – 232 B
interface

Computer

Telephone
number

Automatic
dialing
unit

Dial
signals

Transmission
request and
acknowledge
signals

Line-control
signals

Data

Transmission
control unit

Data

Modem

Communication
line

Modem

Line-control
signals

Data

Terminal

cessing machine (EIA standard RS-232B), and this standard has generally been followed (see Fig. 14.6).

There is much to be said, however, for building the modem into the terminal and into the line control unit at the computer. First, the modem and data processing machine can share common packaging and power units. With portable terminals, there is only one unit to carry. Second, the modem characteristics can be tailored to the data transmission characteristics. Third, where the modem contains digital logic, for any reason, this logic can be integrated with the terminal logic, perhaps on the same LSI chip. Where the modem uses logic for error correction, it seems particularly appropriate to combine it with the terminal's error-detection logic. It is cheaper to have one error-correcting process than two in separate machines. The logic for circumventing leased-line failures by automatically dialing on a public line involves both the terminal and the modem, because the modem must be switched to a different transmission mode. The same is true of techniques for combatting a noisy line with retries in a slower transmission mode. Such techniques can be better designed if the modem is built into the terminal. Finally, it is convenient to have one organization responsible for the maintenance of the modem and terminal. There have been many situations in which the terminal manufacturer has blamed an error on the modem, and the modem manufacturer has blamed it on the terminal. Integrated modem and terminal design can also help in fault isolation.

Let us now return again to the question of selecting from among the many modulation devices available.

## SPEED VS. SIGNAL-TO-NOISE RATIO

If the maximum amount of data is packed into a given bandwidth, this step is done at the expense of decreasing the signal-to-noise ratio. It is generally true with each type of modulation that means used for increasing the data rate also increase the susceptibility to noise.

Speed is all important on some systems, and it is desirable to pump the maximum amount of data through the available channels. This is often true where the lines used are long and therefore expensive. Where a long line is used on a dial-up basis, high-speed transmission minimizes the length of time the line is held. Where an organization has a nationwide network in America, for example, the highest possible utilization of the costly lines is desirable so that the total line mileage can be minimized. In such a case, it might be worthwhile to permit a higher error rate and to build good error-detection procedures into the system.

On the other hand, the data rate may be restricted by factors other than the transmission line. The terminal equipment may be slow. A 400-bit-per-second card punch or printer may be in use on a voice line capable of transmitting 4800 bits per second or more. The transmission may be at the speed of a girl non-synchronously pounding a typewriter. Such is often the case, and here it is advantageous for the modem to make use of the bandwidth available to help achieve the maximum reduction of errors.

Sometimes, as in the transmission of programs, accuracy is of the greatest importance and speed can be sacrificed for accuracy. The accuracy can, however, be achieved by the use of tight error-detecting codes and retransmission, as will be discussed in the next chapter.

The bandwidth of an amplitude-modulated signal can be halved if one sideband is suppressed. The width of the sideband transmitted can also be varied somewhat.[2] In this case, if the bandwidth was below a certain size, the accuracy would fall off significantly.

Frequency modulation offers greater scope than amplitude modulation for varying the signal-to-noise ratio because the range over which the frequency is modulated can be varied. When a large frequency range is used, the power required will be less. Therefore, for a given transmission power, a better signal-to-noise ratio can be obtained (because the noise energy is constant) when the range over which the frequency is modulated is high. Increased signal-to-noise ratio is bought at the cost of increased bandwidth.

With phase modulation, multilevel operation, four-phase or eight-phase, is used for increasing the data rate, and this again increases the susceptibility to noise.

If the perfect form of modulation could be found and the transmission was confronted with only white thermal noise, Shannon's formula would apply. The maximum possible number of bits per second that could be transmitted is

$$W \log_2 \left( 1 + \frac{S}{N} \right)$$

where W is the bandwidth and $S/N$ is the ratio of signal power to noise power.

Actual modems rarely achieve better than about one-third of this theoretical maximum. However, the relationship between bits per second, $W$, $S$, and $N$ follows a broadly similar pattern. The signal power can be increased only up to a certain point, beyond that it becomes more economical to employ a large bandwidth.

**MODEM COST VS. SPEED**   An all-important factor on many systems is cost, and this consideration may override all others. Modems that are designed to give the maximum speed on a given line are disproportionately more expensive than those operating at a

[2] *Telecommunications and the Computer*, Chapter 13.

lower rate. The systems analyst should evaluate the cost per bit transmitted for different modems. He will find that on short lines the minimum cost per bit is achieved when the line is being used well below its maximum. On long lines, however, it becomes worthwhile to pay for the fast modems. The trade-off depends, first, on the cost of the lines relative to that of the modems and, secondly, on whether the increased speed can be usefully employed. The latter factor, as we will discuss in Section VI, may depend on the overall structure of the network.

When very long lines are used, it becomes economically feasible to have the fastest transmission possible on that line. This process is achieved by such devices as remote concentrators and modems which make the maximum use of the bandwidth. Modem cost becomes insignificant compared with the economics of line utilization.

At the opposite extreme, a system may have many hundreds of terminals and relatively low-cost lines linking the terminals either directly to the computer or to remote concentrators. The system may have terminals that are only occasionally connected to the computer by means of public dialing—for example, terminals in users' homes or offices on a time-shared system. Here the terminal and modem cost needs to be kept low. Often when remote concentrators are used, it is best to have low-cost facilities connecting the terminals to the concentrators and high-cost, high-efficiency links connecting the concentrators to the computer center. There may be many hundreds of the former low-cost links on the system but only a few of the high-cost ones.

In some cases, high-transmission speed will be required simply to achieve the necessary response time or delivery time. With visual display units, for example, it is often worth paying for 4800-bits-per-second modems so that the screen can be quickly filled with information, tables, or charts.

**MODEM COST VS. ERROR CONTROL**

Phase modulation usually gives better resistance to noise than frequency modulation or amplitude modulation, but generally it is more expensive. Simple amplitude modulation is the cheapest form, but its resistance to noise is less than that of frequency or phase modulation. Good performance in the presence of noise costs more than poor performance.

As indicated earlier, cost is of considerable importance on some systems, whereas accuracy is vital on others. The application in question determines which factor should be stressed in selecting modems. In some cases, it may be more economical to use good error-detection and error-correction procedures than to use expensive modems. However good the modulation system, it will not put right the errors resulting from bad impulse noise; and on many lines this is the most common type of defect.

In a system like a message-switching system in which computers are used for storing and relaying verbal memoranda, transmission errors will not necessarily have any great consequence. Tight controls will be planned to prevent message loss and to facilitate the retransmission of messages found to be in error. On the other hand, transmission of programs, accountancy figures, air-traffic control data, and so on warrant careful attention to accuracy of transmission.

**ERROR RATE VS. THROUGHPUT** In order to achieve the maximum throughput, it may be worthwhile to use a high-speed modulation scheme, even though it does generate a large number of errors, and then employ a powerful error-detecting code.

To correct the errors that are found, blocks of data containing them must be retransmitted. If the block size is too great or if there are too many errors, the proportion of blocks being retransmitted will become too high. Chapter 35 illustrates calculations relating to this trade-off.

If forward-error correction is not used, then increasing the modem speed beyond a certain point results in *decreased* effective throughput, because so many data blocks have to be retransmitted. Forward-error correction becomes desirable at this point and should be backed up by the safer error-*detection* codes.

An appropriate trade-off between these factors is needed in order to maximize the throughput.

**THE CHOICE OF MODEM** It will be seen that the best choice of modem differs on different communication links, and in different data processing circumstances. Let us reiterate the four main criteria of the user.

1. *Speed of Transmission*

The fastest data rates are achieved with elaborate phase modulation schemes having multilevel coding. Conditioning is used on private lines to help achieve maximum speed. On public lines, the modem may dynamically equalize the line. At the high data rates, the modem cost increases disproportionately to the gain in speed.

2. *Response Time*

Response time, especially on a polled line, can be degraded by lengthy modem turnaround time. Phase modulation, particularly with differential detection, tends to result in lengthy turnaround times. Some modems have a turnaround time of 200 milliseconds or more, and there may be many such turnarounds within one scan of a multidrop line. The solution to this situation is improved techniques of line control.

### 3. *Number of Errors*

The most error-free modems on the majority of lines seem to be those using two-phase modulation. Fixed-reference detection may be better than differential detection. The latter scheme detects a *change* from 0 to 1 or 1 to 0, and if one such change is missed, a string of bit errors will result. Modem performance can be enhanced with built-in digital logic and forward-error correction.

### 4. *Cost*

The cheapest form of transmission uses no modems over short distances. Acoustical couplers are inexpensive, and so is directly wired signaling of the type used by acoustical couplers. The cheapest form of sine wave modulation is probably two-state amplitude modulation with envelope detection. Savings can also result from having the modem built into the terminal.

Other factors that should be examined in selecting a modem are

1. Is it compatible with the network in question? (For example, does it avoid interference with network signaling? In many countries: has it been approved by the telecommunication authorities?)
2. Is its reliability high? One manufacturer quotes a mean time between failures of 50,000 hours.
3. Can it use alternate speeds, or be switched between public and private lines?
4. Is it capable of operating with START–STOP rather than synchronous terminals?
5. Is it designed to assist in fault isolation, so that the user can determine whether the modem, the communication path, or the data-processing machine is the cause of a failure?
6. Are good maintenance facilities available?

# 15 LINE ERRORS AND THEIR TREATMENT

The control of errors is of vital importance on many data transmission systems. On others, however, it is not of great significance. The number of bits that are incorrect after data transmission (with no error correction) is typically in the range of one in 50,000 to one in 500,000. (Some high-speed modems give much higher error rates, and so do short- and long-wave radio links.)

A variety of error-correction procedures are in use, but most of those in common use still leave a number of undetected errors that is greater than the number that would be expected on other components of a computer system. Tape and file channels on a computer, for example, have an error rate very much lower than those on the telecommunication links in conventional use today.

In addition to transmission errors, the errors made by operators constitute a significant problem in the design of on-line systems. The number of errors made by the operators of the input–output devices on a large system usually far exceeds the number of errors caused by noise or distortion on the transmission lines. It is usually important that accuracy controls be devised for the human input. A tight network of controls is necessary to stop abuse or embezzlement on many systems. It is also important to ensure that nothing is lost or double-entered when hardware failures occur on the system or when switchover takes place. In this chapter we will discuss the treatment of errors arising from noise and distortion on the communication lines.

**NUMBER OF LINE ERRORS**     It is useful for the systems analyst to have a rule of thumb for estimating the numbers of errors that he is likely to encounter. He will use these figures for doing probability calculations that indicate to him the viability of different systems approaches. With them, he may answer such questions as what degree of error checking is needed and what block length he should use for transmission.

The figures in Table 15.1 are typical average error rates and might be used as the rule of thumb if the systems analyst has no more precise figures relating to his particular lines. These rule-of-thumb figures are suggested by surveying

**Table 15.1.** TYPICAL AVERAGE ERROR RATES

| Type of Channel | Transmission Rate (bits per second) | Bit Error Rate |
|---|---|---|
| 50-baud Telex | 50 | 1 in 50,000 |
| 150 or 200 baud subvoice-grade lines | 150 or 200 | 1 in 100,000 |
| Public-voice lines | 600 | 1 in 500,000 |
| | 1200 | 1 in 200,000 |
| Subject to wide variation and before the application of error correcting codes | 2400 | 1 in 100,000 |
| | 4800 | 1 in $10^4$ to $10^5$ |
| | 9600 | 1 in $10^3$ to $10^4$ |

many reports published by the International Telecommunications Union and individual common carriers. Lines of the same type in most countries appear to have about the same error rate when they are working correctly with well-adjusted data sets. Certain individual lines, however, have a large amount of noise on them that considerably exceeds the figures shown. This is usually caused by old plant, ill-adjusted equipment or by workmen on the lines. The figures for data rates above 2400 on a voice line are subject to a fairly wide variation because the modulation techniques used become far more sensitive to noise and distortion.

**POSSIBLE APPROACHES**

A variety of approaches can be used to deal with noise on transmission lines. All the approaches discussed below are found on data transmission systems in use today.

The first, and easiest, approach is to ignore the noise—and this is often done. The majority of telegraph links in operation today, for example, have no error-checking facilities at all. Part of the reason is that they normally transmit English-language text that will be read by human beings. Errors in English language caused by the changing of a bit or of a small group of bits are usually obvious to the human eye, and we correct them in the mind as we read the material. Telegrams that have figures as well as text in them commonly repeat the figures. This inexpensive approach is also taken on computer systems where the transmission handles verbal text. For example, on administrative message-switching systems, it is usually acceptable to have transmission to and from unchecked telegraph machines. If the text turns out to be unintelligible, the user can always ask for a retransmission.

An error rate of one bit in $10^5$ is perhaps not quite as bad as it sounds. Suppose that we considered transmitting the text of this book, for example, and coded it in five-bit Baudot code. If one bit in $10^5$ were in error, in the entire book there would be about 40 letters that were wrong. The book would certainly still be readable, and the majority of its readers would not notice most of these errors. The human eye has a habit of passing unperturbed over minor errors in text. The manuscript for this book was first set in galley proofs by the compositor. The proofs were then read and checked by a proofreader. It was next divided into pages and page proofs were checked for errors. By that time, most of the errors should have been deleted from the text, but, in fact, those remaining corresponded to an error rate of one bit in $2 \times 10^4$, an error level higher than that which would be found on unchecked telegraph transmission.

In any case, on most systems *some* of the errors are ignored. An error-detection procedure that catches all of them has proved too expensive. Many systems in current use might raise the level of undetected errors from one bit in $10^5$ to one bit in $10^7$ or $10^8$. It is possible to devise a coding scheme that gives much better protection than this. In fact, one that is on the market gives an undetected error rate of one bit in $10^{14}$, but it is expensive.

An error-detection rate of one bit in $10^{14}$ is much lower than needed for most practical purposes. If one had transmitted nonstop at that rate over a voice line at 2400 bits per second, for a normal working week (no vacations) since the time of Christ, one would probably not have had an error yet!

By using sufficiently powerful error-detecting codes, virtually any measure of protection from transmission errors can be achieved. The codes necessary to achieve this condition are described in Chapter 5 of the author's *Teleprocessing Network Organization*. It is hoped that some future terminals will give a very high measure of protection at reasonable cost, using "large-scale integration" circuits for encoding and error detection.

**CALCULATIONS OF THE EFFECT OF ERRORS**

In designing a computer system, it is important to know what error rate is expected. Calculations should then be done to estimate the effect of this rate on the system as a whole. On some systems the effect of infrequently occurring errors is cumulative, and it is in such situations that special care is needed in eliminating errors. For example, if messages cause the updating of files, and an error in the message causes an error to be recorded on the file, then on some systems it is possible that as the months pass, the file will accumulate a greater and greater number of inaccuracies.

Suppose, for example, that teletype transactions with one bit in $10^5$ in error update a file of ten thousand records. Suppose that, on the average, an item is updated 100 times a month and that if any one of 20 five-bit characters is in error in the transmission, then the item will be updated incorrectly. After 6 months no less than 4500 file records will be incorrect. If an error-correction procedure on the telecommunication lines reduces the rate of undetected errors to one bit in $10^7$, then 60 of the file records are likely to be incorrect at the end of 6 months. With one bit in $10^8$, six records are likely to be wrong. Probability calculations of this type need to be done on various aspects of the system when it is being designed; such calculations are illustrated in Chapter 35.

## DETECTION OF ERRORS

In order to *detect* communication errors, redundancy is built into the messages transmitted. In other words, more bits are sent than are needed for the coding of the data alone.

Redundancy can be built into individual characters. This is done by using parity checks. It is also done by using certain character codes, such as a 4-out-of-8 code. The parity check is not very effective in data transmission (although often used) because a burst of noise frequently destroys more than one bit in a character. The higher the transmission speed, the more likely is this to be true. A noise impulse 2 milliseconds in duration, for example, may destroy only one bit if the transmission rate is 600 bits per second, but at 1200 bits per second it may wipe out 2 bits; at 4800 bits per second, 4 or 5 bits may be destroyed, and so on. If an even number of bits are destroyed, the error will not be detected.

The 4-out-of-8 code and other such character codes are a little safer because, to be undetectable, errors must be compensating; in other words, if a 1 bit is changed into a 0, then a 0 bit must also be changed into a 1. This sometimes happens with the bursts of noise and oscillating effects on communication lines. It is more likely to happen at higher bit rates, and with high-speed modulation techniques.

Instead of using redundancy within a *character* in this way, it is better to use redundancy within a *block* of characters. A block of many characters will be followed by a cluster of error-checking bits—perhaps in the form of one or more error-checking characters. A block of this structure was shown in Fig.

13.2, and may have more than the one error-detection character shown. Some transmission schemes have character checking—for example, a parity bit on each character—in addition to the check on the block. It can be shown, however, that much more efficient error detection results from using all the redundant bits for block checking, not character checking.

The probability of a transmission error remaining undetected can be made very low, either by a brute-force method that gives a high degree of redundancy or, better, by an intricate method of coding. Many systems in actual usage do not employ a *very* secure error-detection scheme; instead they compromise with one that is not too expensive but that will probably let one error in a thousand or so slip through. As mass-produced logic drops in cost, it is probable that an increasing number of transmission devices will use an error-detection scheme of high quality.

**DEALING WITH**
**ERRORS**

Once the errors have been detected, the question arises: What should the system do about them? Generally it is desirable that it should take some automatic action to correct the fault. Some data transmission systems, however, do not do so and leave the fault to be corrected by human means at a later time. For example, one system that transmits data to be punched into cards causes a card to be offset in its position in the stacker when an error is detected. The offset cards are later picked out by the operator, who then arranges for retransmission. In general, it is much better to have some means of automatic retransmission rather than a manual procedure; and such a scheme is usually less expensive than employing an operator for this purpose. In some real-time terminal systems, however, automatic retransmission has not been used because it is easy for the terminal operator to reenter a message or request retransmission.

Again, on some systems, it is possible to ignore incorrect data, but it is important to know that they *are* incorrect. On such systems, error detection takes place with no attempt to correct the errors. This could be the case with statistical data where erroneous samples can be discarded without distortion. It is used on systems for reading remote instruments where the readings are changing slowly and an occasional missed reading does not matter. The advantage of a detection-only scheme is that it requires a channel in only one direction. In systems with telephone and telegraph lines, this advantage is not worthwhile, because such channels are half or full duplex. However, it is a great advantage with certain tracking and telemetry systems, and here we find detection-only schemes. Clearly, for most commercial applications, they will not suffice.

**ERROR-CORRECTING**      Automatic correction can take a number of forms.
**CODES**      First, sufficient redundancy can be built into the
transmission code so that the code itself permits
*automatic error correction* as well as detection. Because no return path is
needed, this scheme is sometimes referred to as *forward-error correction.* In
order to perform such correction effectively in the presence of *bursts* of noise, a
large proportion of redundancy bits may be needed. Codes that give safe
forward-error correction are, therefore, somewhat inefficient in their use of
communication line capacity. If the communication line permitted the transfer
of information in one direction only, then forward-error correction would be
extremely valuable. However, again, most earthbound systems use half-duplex
or full-duplex communication links. In general, error-*correcting* codes alone
on voice-grade or subvoice-grade lines do not give us as good value for money,
or value for bandwidth, as error-*detecting* codes coupled with the ability to
retransmit automatically data that are found to contain an error. Forward-error
correction becomes advantageous when the number of errors is so high that
retransmission would degrade the throughput (discussed in Chapter 35). On
higher-speed links, the argument for forward error correction becomes stronger
because the time taken for reversing the direction of transmission is equivalent
to many bits of transmission. This time is relatively high on wideband links
and on half-duplex voice-grade links with high-speed modems.

Where forward error correction is used—for example, on high-speed
modems—it is often backed up with more secure error-detection techniques
but with the advantage that less data have to be retransmitted.

**LOOP**      One method of detecting errors does not use a code
**CHECK**      at all. Instead all the bits received are retransmitted
back to their sender, and the sending machine checks
that they are still intact. If they are not, then the item in error is retransmitted.
Sometimes referred to as a loop check or echo check, this scheme is normally
used on a full-duplex line or on a continuous loop line. Again, it uses the
channel capacity less efficiently than would be possible with an error-detection
code, although often the return path of a full duplex is underutilized in a system,
for the system does not produce enough data to keep the channel loaded with
data in both directions. A loop check is most commonly found on short lines
and in-plant lines where the wastage of channel capacity is less costly. It gives
a degree of protection that is more certain than most other methods.

**RETRANSMISSION**      Many different forms of error *detection* and retrans-
**OF DATA IN ERROR**      mission are built into data-handling equipment. In a
typical high-speed paper-tape transmission system, a

"vertical" parity check—that is, a parity check on each character—is used along with a "horizontal" checking character at the end of a block of characters. At the end of each block, the receiving station sends a signal to the transmitting station saying whether the block has been received correctly or whether an error has been detected. If an error is found, both the transmitting tape reader and the receiving tape punch go into reverse and run backward to the beginning of that block. The punch then erases the incorrect data by punching a hole into every position—the *delete-character* code. The block is then retransmitted. If transmission of the same block is attempted several times (four times on much equipment) and is still incorrect, then the equipment will stop and notify its operator by means of a warning light and bell or buzzer. Other automatic facilities are usually used to detect broken or jammed paper tape and to warn when the punch is running short of tape.

Where data are being transmitted to a computer, automatic retransmission is sometimes handled under program control and sometimes by circuitry external to the main computer.

**ERROR CONTROL ON RADIO CIRCUITS**   When High Frequency radio is used for telegraphy, the mutilation of bits is normally much worse than with land-based telegraph circuits. It is subject to severe fading and distortion, especially in times of high sun-spot activity. Because of its high error rate and general unreliability, its use is avoided as far as possible for transmission of computer data. However, it is still used in some more isolated areas and in ship-to-shore links.

The system of error detection and retransmission most commonly in use for radio telegraphy is the van Duuren ARQ system. This transmits full duplex, synchronously, the characters being sent in blocks or "words," a 3-out-of-7 code being used (which permits 35 different combinations, as opposed to 32 with the five bits of normal telegraphy). The START and STOP bits of the Baudot code are stripped off, and the remaining five are recorded into 3-out-of-7 code and transmitted.

If the receiving equipment detects more or less than three bits in any character, transmission of data in the opposite direction is interrupted. An error signal is sent back to the transmitter of the data now in error. This transmitter then interrupts *its* sending, returns to the invalid word, and retransmits it. On a long radio link, one or more words may have been sent after the message that had the error, depending on the duration of the transmission path. These words are discarded by the receiver. When the transmitter receives the error indication, it stops what it is transmitting, backtracks to the word in error, and retransmits that and all following words.

High-frequency radio links can be expected to have an error rate before correction of one character in 1000—sometimes much worse. Most of these errors will be detected with the 3-out-of-7 code, but there is a certain probability of a double mutilation that makes a character incorrect while still leaving it with three 1 bits. The number of *undetected* errors in this case is approximately one character in 10,000,000. This mutilation rate can rise as high as one character in 40 or even as high as one character in 4 on bad links and at certain bad points of time. If the mutilation rate is one character in 40, the undetected error rate rises to one character in 16,000, and the effective speed of the link would drop to a speed of perhaps 90 percent of the nominal speed, depending on the word size and link retransmission time. If the mutilation rate rises to one character in four, the rate after error detection and retransmission is about one character in 160, and the effective speed is likely to drop to about half the nominal speed. This speed is still usable for human-language messages, because we can apply our own error-correction thinking.

**HOW MUCH IS**
**RETRANSMITTED?**
Systems differ in how much they require to be retransmitted when an error is detected. Some retransmit only one character when a character error is found. Others retransmit many characters or even many messages.

There are two possible advantages in retransmitting a *small* quantity of data. First, it saves time. It is quicker to retransmit 5 characters than 500 when an error is found. However, if the error rate is one character error in 20,000 (a typical figure for Telex and telegraph lines), the percentage loss in speed does not differ greatly between these two cases. It *would* be significant if a block of 5000 had to be retransmitted.

Second, when a large block is retransmitted, it has to be stored somewhere until the receiving machine has confirmed that the transmission was correct. Often there is no problem. In transmitting from paper tape, for example, the tape reader merely reverses to the beginning of that block. The paper tape is its own message storage. The same is true with transmission from magnetic tape or disk. With transmission from a keyboard, however, an auxiliary storage, or *buffer*, is needed if there is a chance that the message may have to be retransmitted automatically. On some input devices, a small core storage unit constitutes the buffer. On others, the keys themselves are the storage. They remain locked down until successful transmission is acknowledged. Again, several input devices may share a common control unit, and this unit contains the buffer storage. Buffer storage in quantity can be fairly expensive, so it may be better to check and retransmit only a small number of characters at a time. Again, when data on punched cards are transmitted, a buffer is needed for retransmission unless the machine is designed in an ingenious manner so that the card can be reread if required.

The *disadvantages* of using small blocks for retransmission are first that the error-detection codes can be more efficient on a large block of data. In other words, the ratio of the number of bits *with* the error-detection code to the number if the data were sent *without* protection is smaller for a given degree of protection if the quantity of data is large. Second, where blocks of data are sent synchronously, a period of time is taken up between blocks in control characters and line turnaround procedures. The longer the block, the less significant this wasted time.

The well-designed transmission system achieves the best compromise between these factions. Chapter 35 illustrates the calculations done for determining optimum block lengths.

Let us consider some examples of different retransmission quantities.

1. *Retransmission of one character.* Characters are individually error checked, as with a 4-out-of-8 code. As soon as a character error is detected, retransmission of that character is requested. This scheme is likely to be used only on a slow link.

2. *Retransmission of one word.* One type of British equipment uses blocks of nine characters. Figure 15.1 shows such a block. The block has a parity bit for each "row" or character, as well as for each column. A transmitting terminal has buffers that hold two such blocks. Should the receiver detect an error in row or column parity, retransmission of that block is requested.

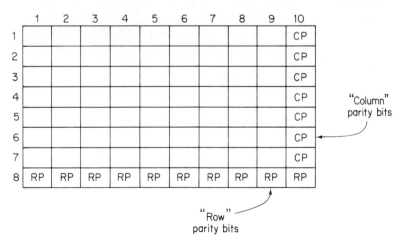

*Fig. 15.1.* A fixed format of data; nine seven-bit characters.

Some systems use smaller blocks than this. The Western Union EDAC (Error Detection Automatic Correction) System uses four-character blocks in one of its models. Four five-bit teletype-code characters are transmitted synchronously, with a five-bit error-checking pattern, from a buffer. A three-bit control signal is returned by the receiver to indicate correct reception. If this signal is mutilated, the transmitting machine repeats the transmission. It does so until it receives confirmation of correct receipt, and then the four characters in storage can be erased.

3. *Retransmission of a message or record.* The preceding "words" were both short and fixed in length. Many machines retransmit complete messages or records at one time that are much longer than the foregoing words and, more often than not, variable in length. They may have a format such as that shown in Fig. 13.2, in which an end-of-transmission character terminates the text and this is followed by the error-checking characters. The record may be retransmitted from back-spaced tape from a variable-length area in the core of computer or from a buffer in a control unit attached to the transmitting device. If a buffer is used, there may be a maximum size for the amount that can be retransmitted. If the message exceeds that size, it is broken into separate messages that are linked together with a control character indicating that a given transmission has not completed the message.

4. *Retransmission of a block of several messages or records.* When the transmission speed is high, it becomes economical on many systems to transmit the data synchronously in large blocks. These blocks may be longer than one "message" or "record." On most systems, when an error occurs in any of the records, the whole block of records is retransmitted. By using machines with good logic capabilities, it would be possible to resend only the faulty record and not all the other records in the block.

5. *Retransmission of a batch of separate records.* Sometimes a control is placed on a whole batch of records. Like the controls conventionally used in batch data processing, the computer adds up account numbers and/or certain data fields from each record to produce *hash totals.* These totals are accumulated at the sending and the receiving end and are then compared. At one of these stations, such a control might, in some cases, be produced manually on an adding machine, and it is often used to detect not only the errors in transmission but also errors in

manual preparation of data. When one computer sends a program to another computer, it is vital that there should be no undetected error in the program, so the words or groups of characters are added up into an otherwise meaningless hash total. This hash total is transmitted with the program, and only if the receiving computer obtains the same total in *its* addition is the program accepted.

Some form of batch control of this type is often used, where applicable, *as well as other* automatic transmission controls. Its use is entirely in the hands of the systems analyst and can be made as comprehensive and secure as he feels necessary.

A typical application of batch totals might be on the network shown in Fig. 15.2. Here, transactions are to be sent from many branch locations to the

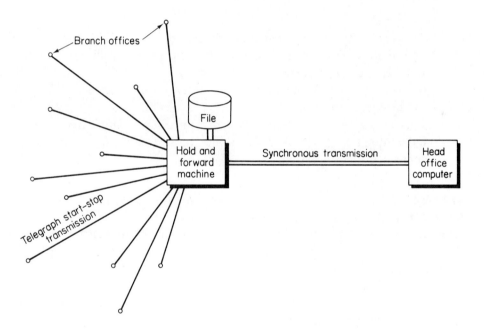

*Fig. 15.2.* Batch error control is here performed at the hold and forward machine. The batch totals so formed are relayed to the central computer.

head office computer. The transactions are punched into paper tape at the branches on a telegraph. The transactions are grouped into batches of about 50, and these are added up on an adding machine before punching. The totals obtained are punched as the last transaction of the batch.

The batches are sent on telegraph lines to a programmed hold-and-forward concentrator. This machine handles all the data from one area and forwards them periodically to the distant head office computer on a dial-up voice line using synchronous transmission. The main purpose is to reduce the cost of the communication lines.

As the concentrator receives a batch, it adds up the batch totals and compares them with the totals received. It prints a message at the branch, saying whether the totals were correct or not. If this were not done, the telegraph transmission would be unchecked. Here the batch totals are being used to check the accuracy of punching as well as the accuracy of transmission. The concentrator stores the data on its file and later dials up the head office computer to transmit the batches it has collected. This link has other error-detection facilities, but, for additional safety, the batch totals are again checked by the head office computer.

6. *Retransmission at a later time.* The batch totals in Fig. 15.2 were checked immediately; the transmission was complete and the sender was notified whether they were correct or not. Some forms of validity check might not be capable of being used until the items are processed. They may, for example, necessitate comparing transactions with a master tape. They are, nevertheless, valuable error controls, and an originating computer might keep the data in its files until a receiving computer has confirmed this validation.

**TRANSMISSION ERROR-CONTROL CHARACTERS**  In order to govern the automatic retransmission of information in which an error has been detected, a number of special characters (*control characters*) are used—sometimes sequences of characters. The ASCII code, for example, uses the codes ACK, NAK, CAN, and DEL.

The ACK code is used by the receiver to signal the transmitter that a block of code has been received correctly. Similarly, the NAK code is sent by the receiving terminal to tell the transmitter that a block of code received had an error in it. When the transmitter sends a block of code on most systems, it waits before it sends the next one until the ACK or NAK control character is received from the transmitter. If ACK is received, it proceeds normally; if NAK, it resends the block in error.

The transmitter itself commonly does some error checking on what it sends. It is possible that the circuits doing so may detect an error in a message on which transmission has already begun. The transmitter must then cancel the message, and therefore it sends a CAN character. The DEL character is normally a character that should be totally ignored. It is used to delete characters already punched in paper tape, by punching a hole in every position.

The transmitting and receiving machines have circuits designed to detect these special characters. Sometimes the special character combination of bits might itself have a meaning in the data to be sent. The data may, for example, contain the bit combination 0001100, which in the ASCII code is a CAN character. If this is a possibility, then clearly 0001100 cannot be used by itself to mean "cancel." In this case, each of the control signals is composed of two characters, the first of which is DLE (Data Link Escape, 0000100 in ASCII code). DLE CAN (0000100 0001100) is then interpreted as "cancel," and similarly with other control characters. If DLE itself is to be sent as a valid *data* character, it must be sent as DLE DLE (0000100 0000100). In this way, any combination of data bits can be sent without being confused with the control signals.

**ODD–EVEN
RECORD COUNT**    It is possible that the control characters themselves or end-of-transmission characters could be invalidated by a noise error. If this happens, then there is a danger that a complete message might be lost or two messages inadvertently joined together. It is possible that during the automatic retransmission process a message could be erroneously sent twice. To prevent these errors, an odd–even count may be kept of the records transmitted.

Sometimes, at the start of a block, a control character is sent to indicate whether this is an odd-numbered or even-numbered block. On some systems, two alternative *start-of-transmission* characters are used. With other schemes, it is the ACK characters that contain this odd-even check. Two different ACK-type signals may be sent: ACK 0 and ACK 1. On the ASCII code there is only one ACK character; so if this code is used, a two-character sequence may be employed.

If an odd-numbered block does not follow an even-numbered block, then the block following the last correct block is retransmitted. It is very improbable that two blocks could be lost together or two blocks transmitted twice in such a manner that the odd–even count would not detect the error. However, some systems use a *serial number*, instead of the odd–even count, to check that this has not happened. The serial number may be examined by hardware, but often it is a check that is applied by a computer program; one of its main values is to bridge the continuity gap when a terminal computer, or other hardware, failure occurs. During the period of recovery from such a failure, there is a danger of losing or double processing a transaction.

More detailed examples of the bits and characters that travel on communication lines for error control are given in the author's *Teleprocessing Network Organization* (Prentice-Hall, Englewood Cliffs, N.J., 1970).

**MINIMUM NUMBERS OF BITS FOR ERROR RECOVERY**   Error control need not have elaborate transmission of control characters back and forth. Some transmission schemes seem unnecessarily burdened by their use of control messages. Error control could be achieved with two control bits only, one for saying whether a message had been received correctly or not and one as an alternation bit giving an odd-even count.

It is difficult on multipoint lines to recover from *addressing* errors with certainty by means of answerback schemes with control characters. The simplest method is a scheme with positive acknowledgements *only*. The receiver simply ignores incorrect messages. The transmitter sends a message with an odd-even block count and waits for acknowledgement of its correct receipt. If no acknowledgement is received after a specified time, then it resends the message, with the same odd-even count. One of two things might have gone wrong. First, the message might have been received with an error. In this case, it is resent as would be required. Second, the positive acknowledgement might have been destroyed. In this case, when the receiver receives a second copy, he will send the positive acknowledgement again. Providing that all errors are detected by error-detecting codes, this simple scheme will be infallible on point-to-point or multipoint lines.

# 16 INTELLIGENT TERMINALS

Terminals vary from simple devices with no storage and no circuitry worth gracing with the word "logic," to highly complex machines with microprogramming or stored-program computing capability. A common terminal in the future may be "the mini-computer in the office."

The advantage of very simple terminals is that they are inexpensive. If there are many terminals and one computer on a system, it makes sense to keep the terminals cheap—and to put the logic in the computer. However, where the communication lines are expensive, a new factor enters the argument: can we lower the overall communication bill by building more logic functions into the terminals? Or, better, can we lower the overall system cost?

There are other arguments besides the question of cost. Can we create a better man-machine interface if we make the terminal more elaborate? Can we lessen the number of errors? Can we do something to lessen the inconvenience when the computer or communication line fails?

Logic capability in the terminal used to be expensive. Furthermore, it used to be somewhat unreliable, and the cost of maintenance engineers chasing round to fix the large quantity of terminals is much higher than when they are merely servicing the computers. Consequently, many unbuffered, asynchronous, simple-minded terminals are still being sold. The cost of logic, however, is dropping fast and its reliability, with the advent of large-scale integration circuitry, is becoming very high. Buffering and logic can reside on a single mass-produced silicon chip in the terminal. Mini-computers are falling in price, like other logic devices, much faster than the drop in price of communication lines. Therefore the whole question of how much intelligence should reside in the terminal is

215

being reevaluated. The systems analyst will be confronted with a much wider diversity of choice.

Let us now review the types of operations that might be performed at the terminal and do so in order of increasing logic requirement.

### 1. *Generation of Bits to Be Sent and Interpretation of Bits Received*

The terminal generates the bits to be sent, including START and STOP bits if asynchronous transmission is being used. It translates the bits received into appropriate mechanical action. In the simplest form of network, this would be the only function (other than data set functions) carried on away from the computer center. Synchronous transmission is more efficient than START–STOP, but it requires more terminal circuitry.

### 2. *Terminal Clustering*

Several different input-output devices may be attached to the same control unit. The terminal may be designed so that only one such device can operate at once, or there may be several operators using different devices simultaneously. In the latter case, some means of interleaving the separate transmissions will be necessary. This may require buffer storage. The control unit must contain the logic for addressing the different devices.

### 3. *Functions Associated with Multidrop Operation*

For reasons of economy, several terminals, often at different locations, are attached to one communication line. In a polled system, the terminal must recognize its address on messages sent to it and must ignore other messages. It must respond logically to polling, go-ahead, and end-of-transmission signals. The functions can be carried out by a control unit that serves one terminal device or several. The same is true for devices attached to a synchronously controlled loop.

Early polling schemes had minimal logic in the terminal, and many of these terminals are still being marketed. The terminal has no buffer and roll-call polling is used. To achieve fast response times on manual terminals, a buffer is needed, and hub polling is better than roll call.[1] Hub polling reduces the number of line turnarounds by making each termination relay the polling messages on to

---

[1] Hub polling is described in detail in *Teleprocessing Network Organization*, Prentice-Hall, Englewood Cliffs, N.J., 1970, Chapter 9.

the next terminal if it has nothing to transmit. This process requires more logic in the terminal; in particular, it requires a terminal to change its action when its normal addressee is inoperative.

Again a continuous loop between the terminals using synchronous transmission increases the line efficiency but also increases the terminal logic requirements.

Such increases in logic requirement do not appear so disadvantageous in the era of large-scale integration.

### 4. *Error Control and Retransmission*

As we commented in the previous chapter, certain elaborate codes can give a very high measure of protection from transmission errors. Virtually no error can slip by undetected. The most powerful error-detecting codes have not been used on the majority of terminals because of the amount of logic required. Automatic retransmission of items in error needs further logic and, in particular, requires each item to be stored until it is known that it has been received correctly. Some error-detecting terminals have not been equipped for automatic retransmission. Furthermore, during a period of noise on the line, it may be necessary for the terminal to try several times to send a message. It may vary the time between successive tries or even switch its modem to half-speed operation to improve the chances of success. How much of such logic is worth building into the terminal?

Again a combination of error-detecting codes may be used, the error-correcting code to minimize the amount of retransmission and the error-detecting code to ensure that uncorrected errors cannot slip through.

### 5. *Security*

As mentioned in Chapter 12, terminal features are needed to enhance the security of the system. The terminal may respond with a unique identification number when interrogated. Otherwise most of the logic operations associated with security may be in the central computer. If cryptography is used, as it may be for the transmission of highly confidential data, greater levels of safety will require more complex logic operations.

### 6. *Failure Protection*

When the computer becomes inoperative or inaccessible, the terminal may become useless, or it may carry on some functions of its own. Where the terminal is being used for data entry, it may be able to record data for later transmission to the computer. If it has some of the features listed below, the terminal may be able to carry on a limited dialogue with its user.

When a leased communication line fails, the terminal may automatically dial an alternate connection to the computer—switching its modem operation accordingly.

### 7. *Automatic Answering*

An idling terminal may have the ability to respond with operator attention to a signal from the computer. In this way, the computer may send unsolicited data for printing or recording.

### 8. *Editing*

A terminal operator may wish to edit his input at the terminal. He may, for example, make mistakes and want to backspace and correct them. He may want to insert words or figures into a format laid out on the terminal screen by the computer. On many systems the code for doing so—for example, two backspace characters followed by two replacement characters—travels all the way to the central computer and this computer does the editing. Some terminal control units, however, have editing logic in them. For instance, the edited message may appear on a terminal screen and be checked by the operator before it is transmitted. Editing functions could also take place in a concentrator as part of the work of assembling a message for synchronous transmission.

Editing a message from an operator before transmission slightly reduces the number of characters to be transmitted. However, the reduction may not be enough to pay for the added terminal logic that is required. On the other hand, logic for formatting the messages from the computer may bring a very substantial saving. Suppose, for the purpose of illustration, that it is desired to display on the terminal screen tables or statements such as those shown in Fig. 16.1. If the terminal or control unit has no formatting logic, then many blank characters must be transmitted in order to format the display in a readable manner. Figure 16.1 would need more blanks than other characters. If its data could be sent in a compressed form, with formatting characters but no blanks, then the number of characters transmitted would be almost halved. At the terminal or control unit (or possibly the concentrator), the formatting characters would be used to expand the data into a neat display format. Here again we have a trade-off between distributed logic hardware and communication line costs.

A R JENKINS  397 E 34 ST, APT 19B, NEW YORK 10017
073–2–037948

| DATE | PARTICULARS | PAYMENTS | RECEIPTS | BALANCES |
|------|-------------|----------|----------|----------|
| 9.24 | OPENING BALANCE | | | 2338.66 |
| 9.26 | | | 956.60 | 3295.26 |
| 9.30 | INTEREST CHARGES | 63.85 | | 3231.68 |
| 10.5 | INVESTMENTS BOUGHT | 1218.00 | | 2013.68 |
| 10.5 | ALREADY ADVISED | | 993.87 | 3007.55 |
| 10.15 | | 265.00 | | 2742.55 |
| 10.16 | | 44.00 | | 2698.55 |
| 10.16 | | 2600.00 | | 98.55 |
| 10.22 | | 100.00 | | 1.45 |
| 10.23 | CHARGES | 2.10 | | 3.55 |

*Fig. 16.1.* The blanks between fields need not be transmitted.

Formatting logic saves buffer storage as well as transmission time. The Sanders 620 Data Display System terminal, for example, has 2000 character positions on its screen but only 1000 characters of buffer storage. Formatting characters among the 1000 stored cause the display to be tabulated neatly on the 2000 available screen positions.

### 9. *Compaction*

The use of such editing is, in a sense, a form of data compaction. There are many other ways of minimizing the numbers of bits that need to be transmitted. Numeric data can be converted into binary form. Alphabetic data and most punctuation could be transmitted as five-bit characters. In fact, there is much to be said for using the five-bit Baudot code for compact data transmission.[2] It uses "letters shift" and "figures shift" characters to switch the meaning of the bit combinations between letters and figures (plus special characters), somewhat like the shift key on a typewriter. It is interesting to reflect that a five-bit code with *three* shifts could carry all the data that most users would be likely to want to transmit. A minor modification of the Baudot code could achieve this, as

[2] *Teleprocessing Network Organization*, Chapter 2.

shown in Fig. 16.2. The character 00010 has been given the meaning "transparency shift." When this character is transmitted, the characters following it

| Code | Letters Shift — CCITT standard international telegraph alphabet No. 2 | Figures Shift | Transparency Shift — Control characters or four-bit binary combinations (T) |
|------|------|------|------|
| 1 1 0 0 0 | A | — | T |
| 1 0 0 1 1 | B | ? | Control |
| 0 1 1 1 0 | C | : | Control |
| 1 0 0 1 0 | D | Who are you? | Control |
| 1 0 0 0 0 | E | 3 | T |
| 1 0 1 1 0 | F | Note 1 | Control |
| 0 1 0 1 1 | G | Note 1 | Control |
| 0 0 1 0 1 | H | Note 1 | T |
| 0 1 1 0 0 | I | 8 | T |
| 1 1 0 1 0 | J | Bell | Control |
| 1 1 1 1 0 | K | ( | Control |
| 0 1 0 0 1 | L | ) | T |
| 0 0 1 1 1 | M | . | Control |
| 0 0 1 1 0 | N | , | Control |
| 0 0 0 1 1 | O | 9 | Control |
| 0 1 1 0 1 | P | 0 | T |
| 1 1 1 0 1 | Q | 1 | T |
| 0 1 0 1 0 | R | 4 | Control |
| 1 0 1 0 0 | S | , | T |
| 0 0 0 0 1 | T | 5 | T |
| 1 1 1 0 0 | U | 7 | T |
| 0 1 1 1 1 | V | = | Control |
| 1 1 0 0 1 | W | 2 | T |
| 1 0 1 1 1 | X | / | Control |
| 1 0 1 0 1 | Y | 6 | T |
| 1 0 0 0 1 | Z | + | T |
| 0 0 0 0 0 | Blank | | T |
| 0 0 1 0 0 | Space | | T |
| 0 1 0 0 0 | Line feed | | T |
| 1 1 1 1 1 | Letters shift | | |
| 1 1 0 1 1 | Figures shift | | |
| 0 0 0 1 0 | Transparency shift | | |

*Fig. 16.2.* A compact code. A suggested modification of Baudot code to make it transmit "transparent" binary code and a wide variety of control characters.

Note 1: Not allocated internationally by CCITT; available to each country for internal use.

have the meanings shown in the rightmost column, until a "letters shift" or "figures shift" character is sent. Some of these are control characters. A variety of control characters are used on modern terminals. The remainder are four-bit binary characters, bits 1, 2, 3, and 5 being used, with the fourth (always a 0) being ignored. Any eight-bit binary character can thus be sent in two of the five-bit characters, and so programs could be transmitted in this code.

A somewhat tidier five-bit, three-shift code could be devised if the Baudot code were ignored. The Baudot code is, however, the most commonly used telegraph code outside North America. The character 00010 is "carriage return" in the Baudot code and "transparency shift" in Fig. 16.2. In order to communicate with a Baudot-code machine, a machine using the code in Fig. 16.2 need only inhibit its "transparency shift" feature and substitute "carriage return."

If a large number of machines using a five-bit, three-shift code came into use, the translation circuitry could be on one LSI chip and would not be expensive. The throughput with alphanumeric data on a given data channel would be almost 40 percent higher than with the ASCII code and almost 60 percent higher than with the eight-bit codes in use.

*Verbal* data could be compacted more tightly because of the redundancy in English language, but the cost of the compacting and uncompacting would be much higher. Suppose, for example, that a communication link transmits eight-bit characters, as when transmitting programs. Suppose that each character contains combinations of bits that represent the 200 or so most commonly used words. Suppose, also, that 32 of the 256 possible combinations indicate that this character alone does not give the word in question but that the next character is also needed. This gives $32 \times 256 = 8192$ additional words that may be encoded. Another combination of bits in the first character indicates that the word is spelled out in BCD. The machine receiving this string of data converts it into verbal English with a table look-up operation.

The cost in storage at the terminals is high. The number of characters used could easily be 64,000, but a voice line could be made to transmit as many as 40,000 words per minute. At the present cost of storage, it would probably not be economical to use such a method. During the next decade, however, schemes of this type may appear increasingly attractive.

The vocabulary required for many specific applications is small, and it may be necessary to store no more than, say, 256 words. Alternatively, such a scheme may generate not words but messages or phrases.

### 10. *Generation of Messages or Phrases*

It is highly desirable that a terminal respond to its operator in easily understood English. On many applications, the dialogue that is designed contains a number of often-repeated phrases. Such responses have been generated in most systems by the central computer. A considerable amount of verbiage then has to be sent down the communication lines. An alternative that involves less transmission time is to send only a coded reference to the responses and have the phrases, table formats, and so on generated by the terminal.

A character or group of characters may cause a stock sentence or phrase to be generated. For many applications, 128 phrases would be plenty. One character could be given the meaning: "The next character is a phrase-generating character." The next character would then generate one from a list of 128 (or 256) phrases.

It is probably on commercial systems or systems with programs for carrying out highly specialized functions that one is most likely to find a need for canned responses. However, even on general-purpose systems where the operator writes programs at the keyboard, or where the terminal functions like an elaborate desk calculator, a set of fixed responses makes the device easier to use. JOSS, the RAND Corporation time-sharing system that became famous as one of the earliest conversational computing facilities, had 40 canned responses that made it considerably easier to use.

However, whereas all of JOSS's canned responses could be stored in about 2000 characters, we are going to need a large storage if we are to store the verbiage from many specialized programs. The question arises: Would it be economically viable to have a disk file or other large storage at the terminal control unit? In some cases, it would. For most such purposes the disk could be considerably smaller and slower than the disks and drums used for data files. For such purposes, it might be worth making a very inexpensive disk unit, with a slow seek mechanism and disks the size of a 45-rpm phonograph record with no high-precision packing.

### 11. *Image Storage at the Terminal*

In some terminals entire images are stored and will be produced on the receipt of appropriate commands from the computer. A variety of different media may be used for image storage. As we discussed in Chapter 8, an entire man-machine dialogue may be constructed with fixed-frame responses. In some cases, the availability of photographs or diagrams from an image-display system entirely changes the realm of what is possible in terminal dialogue.

### 12. *Graphic Image Formation*

Many graphic applications in which the computer generates line diagrams are in use. In order to transmit the diagram, it will be broken into separate lines that will be transmitted in a coded form. Scanning the entire diagram like a television picture is scanned would need far too much communication bandwidth. The assembly of the picture from the coded information will be done by the display control unit. This unit will normally be a computer that the operator uses.

The question then arises: How much processing will be done in the terminal computer, and how much in the remote larger machine? As in nongraphic applications, the control computer may be used for library storage and large files of data, as well as for processing that is too lengthy for the terminal computer. Because of the fast response time needed with graphics, and the complex nature of some responses, the graphics terminals will almost always use a local computer—it may be an inexpensive mini-computer that relies on a remote central machine for some of the operations.

### 13. *Input Checking Operations*

When the terminal has its own mini-computer, there are many operations which it may carry out before data are sent onward to the central machine. One is the syntax or consistency checking of input data. The terminal computer may collect the data piece-by-piece from the operator, check it, and send in one message to the central machine.

### 14. *Dialogue*

It is very important to make terminal "conversations" as easy to use and unconfusing as possible, but this intention, as we discussed in Chapter 10, can result in a large amount of verbiage being transmitted. With multidrop lines, the result can be a substantial increase in the network cost.

One solution is to make the terminal control computer take over at least part of the dialogue. For example, in an airline-reservation system, the dialogue in which details of the passenger and his booking are recorded could be carried out by a peripheral computer. The peripheral computer would check the data for completeness, date-time continuity, and journey continuity and then transmit it to the central computer for filing. Earlier, when the availability of seats is being checked, the dialogue must be with the central computer because *it* keeps the necessary data.

### 15. *Language Preprocessing*

Where a terminal operator is programming a distant time-shared computer, some preprocessing of the language he uses may be done in the terminal computer. This step is worthwhile in remote job-entry systems in which the program will not be compiled and executed immediately but will wait in a conventional job stream. The preprocessing will detect some of the programmer's errors in real time and thus improve his chances of obtaining the results he needs the first time.

As with all these "intelligent terminal" schemes, the question must be asked: Where is it more economical to do this function, at the terminal location or at the central computer?

### 16. *Computing Operations Not Needing Files*

It is possible that a common use for data transmission in the future will be to provide a backup for "the mini-computer in the office." The mini-computer may have no files. It may have a small disk. It may be able to read and write tape cartridges stored on its user's shelves.

If its user performs routine calculations, it may not need any external assistance. Often, however, it will need to call on a remote program library and obtain information from distant data banks. It may need the assistance of a remote computer to compile large programs or to execute programs that need a large quantity of storage or high computing power.

In some cases, the peripheral computers will be general-purpose machines that need to be programmed by their operators. In other cases, they will be machines for carrying on a highly specialized function for operators without programming skills. Secretaries may perhaps use such machines for text editing and document preparation, the storage of documents perhaps being on a central computer. Some of the countrywide banking systems in England use terminal computers that enable the bank clerks to carry out local accounting operations and that communicate with a central computer in London which has all the customer files.

### 17. *Terminal Computers with Files*

In some cases, a small amount of file storage may be used on the terminal computers, so that records not needed centrally can be stored.

### 18. *Specialized Subsidiary Processors*

In the rapidly evolving technology of time-sharing systems, some schools of thought favor general-purpose systems, as well as highly specialized systems and software. Some of the smaller and highly specialized systems have proven very efficient and have given an impressively fast response time. It seems probable that we will see more of them and that their cost per user will remain competitive with the larger, more general systems.

A corporation may have a number of such computers in its various locations, each capable of meeting a local need. Small, specialized systems are relatively easy to implement. These systems may be designed so as to pass on transactions that they cannot handle to a larger data processing system. Typical of such systems are those providing on-line computation with languages, such as APL and BASIC, those providing secretaries with text-editing and letter-typing facilities, and small commercial enquiry and data-entry systems. Figure 16.3 shows a possible arrangement with a line from the main data processing center wandering around several small real-time systems that are self-contained for their own functions. General-purpose terminals are used. The computer at the center polls the peripheral computers periodically to see whether they have any work for the main computer.

The network, in fact, may not have a distinguishable main computer. An organization may operate several computer centers primarily dedicated to different types of work but capable of interchanging some jobs or transactions. The centers may have different files of information available to them and different programs. Transactions are routed to the appropriate location in this complex.

In this chapter we have talked about "intelligence" in the terminal, or terminal control unit. This is not the only place where intelligence can reside. It may be built into nodes of the communication network, sometimes referred to as concentrators. Line-control computers, remote both from the central computer and from the terminal, may carry out some of the functions we have discussed. Before assessing this possibility, we must discuss the communication line networks.

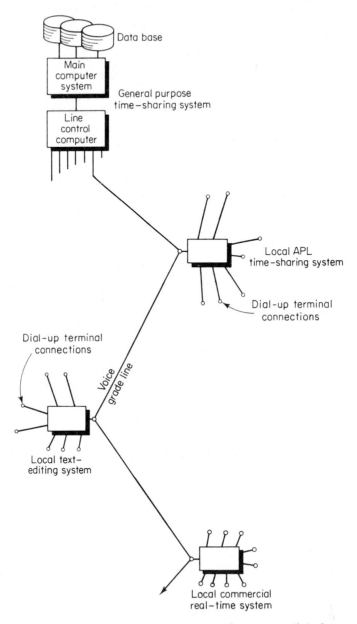

*Fig. 16.3.* Small, local, special-purpose on-line systems linked to a large central system with wider capabilities and a large data base. The nodes of the network have become self-contained systems. If the path to the main computer is used only a small part of the day, the peripheral computers may dial up the main center rather than use a leased line.

SECTION **IV**

**NETWORK**
**CONSIDERATIONS**

# 17  TYPES OF COMMUNICATION LINES

In designing a teleprocessing network, the systems analyst has a number of types of communication lines that he may use in the construction of his network. This chapter summarizes these types.

**TRANSMISSION RATES**   Perhaps the most important parameter in comparing communication lines is their transmission speed. The communication lines in use vary in transmission rate from about 50 bits per second up to more than a million. Speeds higher than those of a voice line, however, are not widely available on a dial-up basis, although switched wideband facilities now exist in some cities.

Figure 17.1 gives an estimate of the relative popularity of different data transmission time requirements and message lengths. The digits from 1 to 9 indicate the relative usage of different areas on the chart, the most popular being real-time dialogue systems with a response time of 1 to 3 seconds. Many areas on the chart not marked by a digit also have data transmission in use, but it is less common than the marked areas. As will be seen, the 50,000-bits-per-second line does not intersect any of the marked areas. Consequently, it was not surprising, perhaps, that when AT & T introduced their 50,000-bits-per-second switched service to the first few cities in 1970, there were few subscribers for it. Given some years of development, however, this situation will almost certainly change. If higher-speed lines are available at reasonable cost, the digits on this figure will migrate in a southeasterly direction.

I gave Fig. 17.1 to fifty or so systems analysts, all highly experienced in diverse areas, and asked them how they thought the digits might change in the next five years or so. Their estimates differed over a surprisingly wide range,

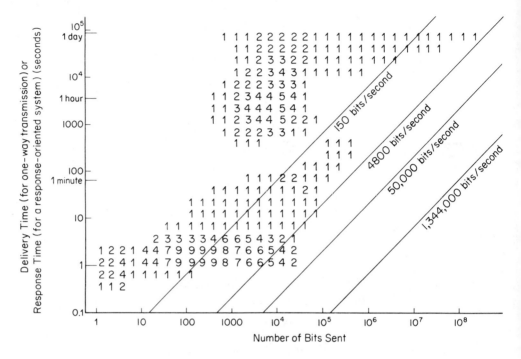

*Fig. 17.1.* An estimate of the relative popularity of different data transmission time requirements and message lengths. The figures from 1 to 9 indicate the relative usage of different areas on the chart, the most popular being real-time dialogue systems with a response time of 1 to 3 seconds. Many areas on the chart that are not marked by a digit also have data transmission in use, but it is less common than in the marked areas. The lack of digits around the line speed of 50,000 bits per second may have been caused by lack of line facilities rather than by a genuine absence of requirement.

and it became clear that they were imagining entirely different uses of data transmission. Figure 17.2 shows a composite diagram made from some of the more plausible replies. The moral seems to be that, given good line facilities, the data transmission industry will grow in many new directions, including some that are barely anticipated today.

**CATEGORIES OF LINE**

Table 17.1 lists the main types of leased and public communication links in order of increasing speed.

The speeds have been listed in terms of the number of data bits per second that may be sent over the line. Communication lines fall into one of three categories of speed.

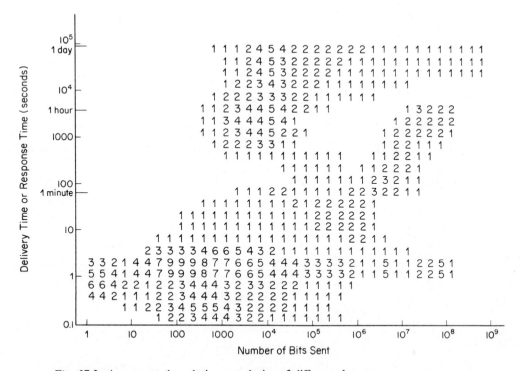

*Fig. 17.2.* A guess at the relative popularity of different data transmission uses five years hence. A group of experienced systems analysts were asked to make estimates of how Fig. 17.1 would change. Their estimates differed over a surprisingly wide range, suggesting that, given appropriate transmission facilities, a wide variety of new uses for data transmission will emerge (see text).

1. *Subvoice grade.* Lines designed for telegraph and similar machines transmitting at speeds ranging, in the United States, from 45 to 150 bits per second. Some countries have lines of higher speed than their telegraph facilities, but still much slower than the capacity of voice lines. Britain, for example, has its Datel 200 service operating at 200 bits per second. Most industrialized countries outside North America have a similar 200-bit-per-second service (a CCITT standard). All these lines are today commonly obtained by subdividing telephone channels.

2. *Voice grade.* At present, telephone channels normally transmit at speeds from 600 to 4800 bits per second. Speeds of 9600 and possibly higher may become common in the near future. Dial-up telephone lines are commonly used for speeds of 1200 or 2400 bits per second today. Speeds up to 3600, however, may soon become common on the public network.

**Table 17.1.** TYPES OF COMMUNICATION LINES AVAILABLE

*1. Public (Dial-Up) Lines*

| | Bit Rate (bits per second) | | Bandwidth (kHz) | Type of Line | | | Half Duplex or Full Duplex |
|---|---|---|---|---|---|---|---|
| | | | | United States | | United Kingdom | |
| | Fixed | Dependent on Modem | | AT & T | Western Union | | |
| Subvoice grade | 45 (6 Murray characters per second) | Up to 45 | | | TTY-TWX and CPT-TWX | | HDX |
| | | | | | CE-TWX | | HDX or FDX |
| | 50 (10 DIC characters per second) | | | | Telex | Telex | HDX |
| | 110 | Up to 150 | | | TTY-TWX and CPT-TWX | | HDX or FDX |
| | | Up to 200 | | | CE-TWX | Datel 200 | FDX |
| The public telephone network | | Up to 600 | | | | Datel 600 | FDX |
| | | Up to 1200 | | | | Datel 600 | FDX |
| | | 600 to 4800 (Certain modems achieve higher speeds.) | 3 (Not all freely usable because of network signaling.) | Public network | | Public telephone network | HDX or FDX |
| Switched wideband networks | 600 | (Other speeds will be achievable with other modems.) | 2 | | BEX (Certain cities only) | | FDX |
| | 1200 & 2400 | | 4 | | | | |
| | 4800* | | 8* | | | | |
| | 9600* | | 16* | | | | |
| | 38,400* | | 48* | | | | |
| | 50,000 | Up to 50,000 | | Dataphone 50 (few cities only) | | | FDX |

*Planned but not yet available.

232

## 2. Leased Lines

| | Bit Rate (bits per second) | | Bandwidth (kHz) | Type of Line | | | Half Duplex or Full Duplex |
| --- | --- | --- | --- | --- | --- | --- | --- |
| | Fixed | Dependent on Modem | | United States | | United Kingdom | |
| | | | | AT & T | Western Union | | |
| **Subvoice grade** | 50 | Up to 45 | | 1004 | | | HDX/FDX |
| | | | | | | Tariff H | FDX |
| | | Up to 55 | | 1002 | | | HDX/FDX |
| | | Up to 75 | | 1005 | | | HDX/FDX |
| | 100 | | | | | Datel 100 | FDX |
| | | Up to 150 | | 1006 | | | HDX/FDX |
| | | Up to 180 | | | | | HDX/FDX |
| | 200 | | | | 1006 | Datel 200 | FDX |
| **Voice-grade lines** | | Up to 600 | 3 | | | Datel 600 | FDX |
| | | Up to 1200 | 3 | | | Datel 600 | FDX |
| | | 600 to 10,500 (For the higher rates, conditioning is needed.) | 3 | 3002 (C1, C2, C4 and C5 conditioning) | | (Datel 2000 refers to conditioned or high-quality voice lines.) | HDX/FDX |
| **Wideband** | 19,200 | | 24 | 8803 | | | FDX |
| | 40,800 | | 48 | 8801 | | Special quotation | FDX |
| | 50,000 | | 48 | 8801 | | | |
| | 230,400 | | 240 | 5700 (originally TELPAK C) 5800 (originally TELPAK D) (5700 & 5800 tariffs all provide "bundles" of smaller bandwidth lines.) | | | FDX |
| | | | 1000 (approx.) | | | | |

233

A speed of 4800 is already possible with a reasonable error rate but requires elaborate modem design (Chapter 14). Telephone organizations in some other countries have not yet permitted the use of such high speeds over their telephone lines. In many countries, 600 or 1200 bits per second is still the maximum.

3. *Wideband.* Wideband lines give speeds much higher than voice channels, using facilities that carry many simultaneous telephone calls. Speeds up to about 500,000 bits per second are in use, and higher bit rates are possible if required.

All these line types may be channeled over a variety of different physical facilities. This chapter and indeed the tariffs themselves normally say nothing about the medium used for transmission. It might very well be wire, coaxial cable, microwave radio, or even satellite. The transmission over different media is organized in such a way that the channels obtained have largely the same properties—same capacity, same noise level, and same error rate. The user generally cannot tell whether he is using a microwave link, coaxial cable, or pairs of open wires stretched between telephone poles. Only satellite transmission requires different data-handling equipment, and here only because a delay of one-third of a second or so occurs in travelling the great distance.

**SWITCHED VS. LEASED LINES**

The next most important parameter about the lines is whether they are public switched lines or not. Voice lines and telegraph lines can either be switched through public exchanges (central offices) or permanently connected. Facilities for switching broadband channels are in operation in some countries, although most broadband channels today are permanent connections.

When you dial a friend and talk to him on the telephone, you speak over a line connected by means of the public exchanges. This line, referred to as a "public" or "switched" line, could be used for the transmission of data. Alternatively, a "private" or "leased" line could be connected permanently or semipermanently between the transmitting machines. The private line may be connected via the local switching office, but it would not be connected to the switchgear and signaling devices of that office. An interoffice private connection would use the same physical links as the switched circuits. It would not, however, have to carry the signaling that is needed on a switched line. As we mentioned in Chapter 14, this is one reason why it is possible to achieve a higher rate of data transmission over a private line. Another reason is that private lines can be carefully balanced to provide the high quality that makes higher-speed data transmission possible.

Just as you can either dial a telephone connection or have it permanently wired, so it is with other types of lines. Telegraph lines, for example, which have a much lower speed of transmission than is possible over voice lines, may be permanently connected or may be dialed like a telephone line via a switched public network. Telex is such a network; it exists throughout most of the world, permitting transmission at 50 bits per second. Telex users can set up international connections to other countries. Some countries have a switched public network, operating at a somewhat higher speed than Telex but at less speed than telephone lines. In the United States, the TWX network gives speeds up to 150 bits per second. TWX lines can be connected to Telex lines for overseas calls. Also, certain countries are building up a switched network for very high-speed (wideband) connections. In the United States, Western Union has installed the first sections of a system in which a user can indicate *in his dialing* what capacity link he needs.

**ADVANTAGES OF LINES LEASED**

The leased voice line has certain advantages for data transmission over the switched connections, some of which we mentioned earlier. Let us summarize these advantages.

1. If it is to be used for more than a given number of hours per day, the leased line is less expensive than the switched line. If it is used for only an hour or so per day, then it is more expensive. The breakeven point depends on the actual charges, which in turn depend on the mileage of the circuit, but it is likely to be of the order of several hours per day. This factor is clearly an important consideration in designing a data transmission network.

2. Private lines can be specially treated or "conditioned" to compensate for the distortion that is encountered on them. The common carriers charge extra for conditioning. In this way the number of data errors can be reduced or, alternatively, a higher transmission rate can be made possible. The switched connection cannot be conditioned beforehand in the same way, because it is not known what path the circuit will take. Dialing at one time is likely to set up a quite different physical path from that obtained by dialing at another time, and there are a large number of possible paths. Modems now exist that condition dynamically and adjust to whatever connection they are used on. These devices enable higher speeds to be obtained over switched circuits but they are expensive.

3. Switched voice lines usually carry signaling within the bandwidth that would be used for data (at frequencies such as those shown in Fig. 14.5). Data transmission machines must be designed so that the form in which the data are sent cannot interfere with the common carrier's signaling. With some machines, this operation also makes the capacity available for data transmission somewhat less than that over a private voice line. A common rate over a switched voice line in the 1960s was 1200 bits per second, whereas 2400 bits per second was common over a specially conditioned, leased voice line. As stated earlier, it is probable that up to 3600 bits per second over switched voice lines and 4800 to 9600 bits per second over conditioned, leased voice lines will become common in the 1970s. Already some modems transmit at higher speeds than 3600 over public voice lines.

4. The leased line may be less perturbed by noise and distortion than the switched line. The switching gear can cause impulse noise that results in errors in data. This is a third factor that contributes to a lower error rate for a given transmission speed on private lines.

The cost advantage of switched lines will dominate if the terminal has only a low usage. In addition, the ability to *dial* a distant machine gives great flexibility. Different machines can be dialed with the same terminal, perhaps offering quite different facilities. A typewriter terminal used at one time by a secretary for computer-assisted text editing may at another time be connected to a scientific time-sharing system and at still another time may dial a computer-assisted teaching program. Machine availability is another consideration. If one system is overloaded or under repair, the terminal user might dial an alternative system. Often this dialing is done over the firm's own leased tie lines.

**LINE CONDITIONING**

As has been mentioned, private leased voice lines can be *conditioned* so that they have better properties for data transmission. Tariffs specify maximum levels for certain types of distortion. *An additional charge is made by most carriers for lines that are conditioned.*

The American Telephone and Telegraph Company, for example, has three types of conditioned voice lines, the conditioning being referred to as Types C1, C2, C4 and C5. A line ideal for data transmission would have an equal drop in signal voltage for all frequencies transmitted. Also, all frequencies would have the same propagation time. This is not so in practice. Different frequencies suffer different attenuation and different signal delay. Conditioning attempts to equalize the attenuation and delay at different frequencies. Standards are laid down in the tariffs for the measure of equalization that must be achieved. The signal attenuation and delay at different frequencies must lie within certain limits for each type of conditioning. The higher the conditioning number, the narrower are the limits. The result of the conditioning is that a higher data speed can be obtained over that line, given suitable line-termination equipment (modem).

Types C1 and C2 conditioning are applicable to point-to-point and multipoint lines. Type C4 is available only on two-point, three-point and four-point lines. Type C5 conditioning can only be applied to point-to-point lines.

**TARIFFS FOR**
**WIDEBAND LINES**
**AND BUNDLES**

The North American common carriers offer several tariffs for leased wideband lines. Some of these can be subdivided by the carrier into "bundles" of lower bandwidth. Some can be subdivided into channels for voice transmission, telephotograph, teletypewriter, control, signaling, facsimile or data. With some tariffs the user pays a lower price for the bundles than for the individual channels.

The word "TELPAK" was formally used for the "bulk" communication services offered by the telephone companies and Western Union. The word has now been eliminated from the tariffs but is still found in much literature. What used to be TELPAK C is now called a Type 5700 line, and what used to be TELPAK D is now Type 5800. Both can provide a wideband channel or a bundle of lesser channels.

The TELPAK customer pays a monthly charge based on the capacity of the communications channel he selects, the number of airline miles between locations, and the type and quantity of channel terminals. He has use of this channel on a full-time basis.

Originally there were four sizes of TELPAK channels: TELPAK A, B, C, and D. However, in 1964 the Federal Communications Commission ruled that rates for TELPAK A (12 voice circuits) and TELPAK B (24 voice circuits) were discriminatory in that a large user could obtain a group of channels at lower cost per channel than a small user, who could not take advantage of the bulk rates. In 1967 the TELPAK A and B offerings were eliminated.

The Type 5700 line has a base capacity of 60 voice channels (full duplex).

The Type 5800 line has a base capacity of 240 voice channels (full duplex).

Each voice channel in these lines can itself be subdivided into one of the following:

1. Twelve teletype channels, half or full duplex (75 bits per second).
2. Six class-D channels, half or full duplex (180 bits per second).
3. Four AT & T Type 1006 channels, half or full duplex (150 bits per second).

There cannot be mixtures of these channel types in a voice channel. The Type 5700 line can transmit data at speeds up to 230,400 bits per second; the Type 5800 line has a potential transmission rate much higher. Line-termination equipment is provided with these links, and each link has a separate voice channel for coordination purposes.

The TELPAK channels thus serve two purposes. First, they provide a wideband channel over which data can be sent at a much higher rate than over a voice channel. Second, they provide a means of offering groups of voice or sub-voice lines at reduced rates—a kind of discount for bulk buying.

Suppose that a company requires a 50,000-bit-per-second link between two cities, together with 23 voice channels and 14 teletypewriter channels, or perhaps 30 voice channels and no teletypewriter links. Then it would be likely to use the Type 5700 tariff. In leasing these facilities, it would have some unused capacity. If it wishes, it can make use of this capacity at no extra charge for mileage, although there would be a terminal charge.

Government agencies and certain firms in the same business whose rates and charges are regulated by the government (e.g., airlines and railroads) may *share* bundled services. Airlines, for example, pool their needs for voice and teletypewriter channels. An intercompany organization purchases the bundled services and then apportions the channels to individual airlines. Most of the lines channeling passenger reservations to a distant office where bookings can be made are Type 5700 or 5800 lines, and so also are the lines carrying data between terminals in those offices and a distant reservations computer. There has been some demand to extend these shared facilities to other types of organizations that could benefit from them by sharing, but this is not permissible as yet.

TELPAK originally was proposed as an interstate service, but since then it has become generally available intrastate as well.

Although not a TELPAK offering, Series 8000 is another "bulk" communications service in the United States that offers wideband transmission of high-speed data, or facsimile, at rates up to 50,000 bits a second; the customer has the alternative of using the channel for voice communication up to a maximum of 12 circuits. A Type 8801 link, part of this series, provides a data link at speeds up to 50,000 bits per second with appropriate terminating data sets and a voice channel for coordination. A Type 8803 link provides a data link with a fixed speed of 19,200 bits per second and leaves a remaining capacity that can be used either for a second simultaneous 19,200-bits-per-second channel or for up to five voice channels. These links must connect only two cities. The separate channels cannot terminate at intermediate locations.

Most countries outside North America also offer tariffs similar to the Series 8000, and in most locations quotations for higher speeds can be obtained on request. Obtaining a wideband link in many such countries can be a slow process. This is particularly so if the termination is required in a small town or rural area rather than in a city to which such links already exist. Undoubtedly, as the demand for such facilities increases, the service of the common carriers in providing them will improve.

**SWITCHED**
**PRIVATE**
**SYSTEMS**
Many firms have private leased-line systems that are switched with private exchanges. It is possible to engineer these systems to the same quality as private lines and thus provide a switching system of better quality than the public network.

Some private lines are wholly owned by their users rather than leased. Users are generally prohibited from installing their own lines across public highways, and most privately installed communication links are wholly within a user's premises—for example, within a factory, office building, or laboratory. Railroads have their own communication links along their tracks. Some companies have private point-to-point microwave transmission links or other radio links. Recently infrared and optical links have proven a valuable medium for the transmission of data; line-of-sight links can be established at low cost, capable of carrying up to several million bits per second. Such links require no license, as do private microwave links. The device in Fig. 17.3 transmits and receives a quarter of a million bits per second. It is used in cities for transmission between rooftops. Its main drawback is that the link can be put out of operation for a brief period by rain downpours of abnormal intensity—and for longer periods by thick fog.

**TELEX**
Telex is a worldwide switched, public teleprinter system. It operates at 66 words per minute (50 bits per second) and uses the Murray code. It is operated in the United States by Western Union. Any teleprinter on the system can dial any other teleprinter in that country, and Telex machines can be connected internationally without speed or code conversion. The United States can dial Canada and Mexico directly, but operator intervention is needed when dialing to other countries. Some countries permit the Telex facilities to be used for other forms of dial-up data transmission. Each Telex call is billed on a time and distance basis.

*Fig. 17.3.* An OPTRAN infrared transmission device in use for transmitting data at very high rates over line-on-sight paths.

Each subscriber has an individual line and his own number, as with the conventional telephone service. His teleprinter is fitted with a dial, like a telephone, with which he can dial other subscribers. The teleprinter used may or may not have paper-tape equipment also. The teleprinter can be unattended. When a message is sent to an unattended teleprinter, it will switch itself on, print the message, and then switch itself off.

**TELETYPEWRITER EXCHANGE SERVICE**      The North American common carriers offer a service that is competitive with Telex. Again, each subscriber has a dial-up teletypewriter with his own number listed in a nationwide directory. This service is called the Teletypewriter Exchange Service (TWX), and it uses the telephone circuits combined with several TWX channels so that they can be sent over one voice channel. The combining or "multiplexing" is done at the local switching office, where the dc signals are changed to equivalent bursts of appropriate frequencies. The link between the local switching office and the subscriber is often a conventional telephone line, and in this case the teletypewriter needs a data set to convert the dc signals to appropriate frequencies in the voice range.

Other manufacturers' data transmission equipment can be connected to TWX lines and can transmit at speeds up to 150 bits per second, half or full duplex. This process requires a special terminal arrangement at additional cost. Three types of access lines to the TWX network exist.

1. TTY-TWX.
   This is an access line with a teletypewriter provided by the common carrier. The speeds of transmission are either 6 characters per second in Murray code or 10 characters per second in Data Interchange Code (DIC).

2. CPT-TWX.
   CPT stands for "customer provided terminal"; to this access line the customer can attach any device operating with one of the preceding two speeds and codes and adhering to normal TWX line control. The device could be a computer with an appropriate adapter on its input-output channel.

3. CE-TWX (formerly called "TWX Prime").
   CE stands for "customer equipment." This can now be any device and is not restricted to a specific code or character speed. Two TWX subsystems are accessible, one operating at speeds up to 45 bits per second and the other up to 150. A CE-TWX terminal can communicate only with another CE-TWX terminal.

TWX directories listing TTY-TWX and CPT-TWX subscribers are published.

**SUMMARY**  A summary of the main categories of communication link appears in Table 17.2.

**Table 17.2.** CATEGORIES OF COMMUNICATION LINE AND TARIFF

| Types of Link | Comments |
|---|---|
| Digital link | Designed for digital transmission. No modem required. Are code sensitive in some cases. |
| Analog link | Transmits a continuous range of frequencies like a voice line. Modem required. |
| Switched public | Cheaper if usage is low. Switched telephone lines are universally available. It is necessary to avoid signaling frequencies on public telephone lines. |
| Leased (sometimes called "private") | Cheaper than public lines if usage is high. May have lower error rate. Higher speeds possible on leased telephone lines than switched ones because (1) conditioning is possible and (2) no signaling to avoid. |
| Leased with private switching | May give the lowest cost. Combines the advantages of leased lines with the flexibility of switching. Public switched wideband lines may not be available, hence private switched wideband networks are built. |
| Private (non-common-carrier) | Usually only permitted within a subscriber's premises. See next item. |

**Private (Non-Common-Carrier) Links:**

| | |
|---|---|
| In-plant | Very high bit rates achievable using coaxial cables or PCM on wire pairs. |
| Microwave radio | Permissible in special cases for point-to-point links. |
| Shortwave or VHF radio | Used for transmission to and from moving vehicles or people. |
| Optical or infrared | Used for short links—e.g., between city roof-tops—at high bit rates (250,000 bps, typical). No license required. Put out of action by thick fog or *very* intense rain. |

**Table 17.2** CONTINUED

| Types of Link | Comments |
|---|---|

**Speeds**

Subvoice grade — Usually refers to speeds below 600 bits per second.

Voice grade — Usually refers to analog voice lines using modems of speeds from 600 to 10,500 bits per second.

Wideband — Speeds above those of voice lines, most commonly 19,200; 40,800; 50,000, and 240,000.

(For a detailed list see Table 17.1)

**Mode of Operation**

Simplex — Transmission in one direction only. Not normally used in data transmission except for telemetry or space applications.

Half duplex — One direction or the other; not both at once. The most common in the United States.

Full duplex — Transmission in both directions simultaneously. On the Bell System costs 10% more than half duplex and can give disproportionately higher throughput if the terminal is designed to take advantage of it.

Note: These terms sometimes describe the limitation of a machine rather than the limitation of the line it is attached to.

**Conditioning**

Applied by the telephone company to *leased* analog voice lines to achieve more uniform attenuation and delay so that higher-speed modems can be employed. Extra charge levied.

Types
- C1 } C2 — For 2-point and multipoint channels.
- C4 — For 2-point, 3-point and 4-point channels.
- C5 — For 2-point channels only.

**Tariffs**

Tariff includes data set — Common carrier provides the data set (modem) and hence the transmission rate is fixed.

Tariff simply for bandwidth — User chooses the modem. Transmission rate depends on modem design.

**DATA-PHONE Service** — An AT & T service that provides a data set with the line.

243

**Table 17.2** CONTINUED

| Types of Link | Comments |
|---|---|

**Public Telegraph Networks**

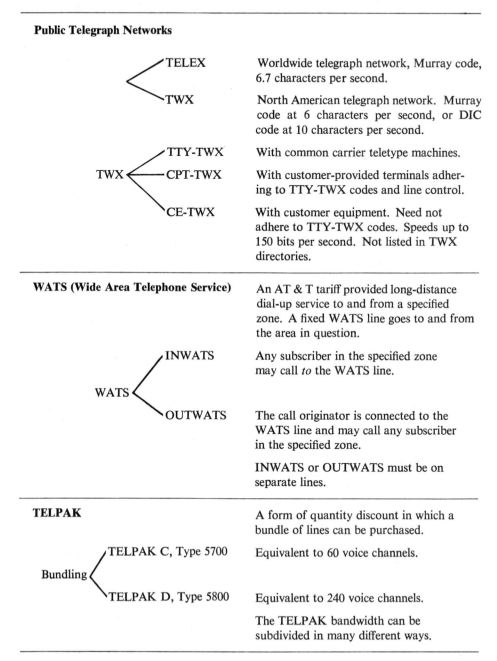

| | |
|---|---|
| TELEX | Worldwide telegraph network, Murray code, 6.7 characters per second. |
| TWX | North American telegraph network. Murray code at 6 characters per second, or DIC code at 10 characters per second. |
| TTY-TWX | With common carrier teletype machines. |
| CPT-TWX | With customer-provided terminals adhering to TTY-TWX codes and line control. |
| CE-TWX | With customer equipment. Need not adhere to TTY-TWX codes. Speeds up to 150 bits per second. Not listed in TWX directories. |

**WATS (Wide Area Telephone Service)** — An AT & T tariff provided long-distance dial-up service to and from a specified zone. A fixed WATS line goes to and from the area in question.

| | |
|---|---|
| INWATS | Any subscriber in the specified zone may call *to* the WATS line. |
| OUTWATS | The call originator is connected to the WATS line and may call any subscriber in the specified zone. |
| | INWATS or OUTWATS must be on separate lines. |

**TELPAK** — A form of quantity discount in which a bundle of lines can be purchased.

| | |
|---|---|
| TELPAK C, Type 5700 | Equivalent to 60 voice channels. |
| TELPAK D, Type 5800 | Equivalent to 240 voice channels. |
| | The TELPAK bandwidth can be subdivided in many different ways. |

# 18

## COSTS OF LINES

This chapter gives an illustration of typical costs of communication facilities and methods of working out the charges. The charges are taken from various common carrier tariffs and, of course, are likely to change. They should not be regarded as current, but rather as illustrations, and should not be used for actual planning purposes.

There are two types of methods by which charges may be made: *public*, or *switched*, lines and *private*, or *leased*, lines. The former will be charged on a basis of number of calls made, plus their duration and distance. In addition, there will usually be a periodic service charge to maintain access to the system. Leased lines have a monthly charge based on the type of line and its length. There may be a separate charge for the line termination and possibly a separate charge for that part of the line which connects the line termination to the local central office. If the line connects several points, as in Fig. 3.4, there may be a charge for each termination.

**DISTANCE
MEASURING**
Length of line enters into all line charges. The common carrier is free to route the line over any desired path and may switch the line to different paths to circumnavigate breakdowns or overloads. The charges are normally independent of the actual routing of the line and are based on the straight-line distance between the points connected.

AT & T have a system in which they have divided the United States by horizontal and vertical grid lines. By means of these lines, they give each location a vertical (V) and horizontal (H) coordinate, and these coordinates give the official way of calculating distances. Table 18.1 gives the AT & T listing of V

245

**Table 18.1.** AT&T V AND H COORDINATES FOR THE MAIN TOWNS IN NEW JERSEY*

State    NEW JERSEY

| City | V | H | City | V | H |
|------|------|------|------|------|------|
| Asbury Park | 5091 | 1340 | Metuchen | 5069 | 1429 |
| Atlantic City | 5284 | 1284 | Millburn | 5031 | 1445 |
| | | | Millville | 5338 | 1371 |
| Bayonne | 5022 | 1413 | Morristown | 5035 | 1478 |
| Belleville | 5004 | 1434 | | | |
| Boonton | 5009 | 1483 | Newark | 5015 | 1430 |
| Bound Brook | 5082 | 1454 | New Brunswick | 5085 | 1434 |
| Bridgeton | 5351 | 1401 | | | |
| Burlington | 5200 | 1435 | Orange | 5015 | 1442 |
| | | | Passaic | 4989 | 1440 |
| Camden | 5249 | 1453 | Paterson | 4984 | 1452 |
| Carteret | 5048 | 1415 | Paulsboro | 5281 | 1455 |
| Chatham | 5036 | 1458 | Perth Amboy | 5065 | 1413 |
| Clifton | 5106 | 1515 | Phillipsburg | 5122 | 1560 |
| Collingswood | 5249 | 1443 | Plainfield | 5061 | 1447 |
| Cranford | 5043 | 1437 | Pleasantville | 5288 | 1300 |
| | | | Princeton | 5132 | 1444 |
| Doner | 5028 | 1500 | | | |
| Dumont | 4962 | 1434 | Rahway | 5099 | 1427 |
| | | | Red Bank | 5073 | 1364 |
| Elizabeth | 5032 | 1426 | Ridgewood | 4967 | 1454 |
| Englewood | 4968 | 1424 | Riverside | 5217 | 1443 |
| Ewing | 5159 | 1449 | Roselle | 5038 | 1432 |
| | | | Rutherford | 4993 | 1433 |
| Fair Lawn | 4977 | 1446 | | | |
| | | | Salem | 5349 | 1453 |
| Gloucester | 5258 | 1446 | Somerville | 5089 | 1466 |
| | | | South Amboy | 5071 | 1410 |
| Hackensack | 4976 | 1432 | South Orange | 5022 | 1442 |
| Haddonfield | 5248 | 1435 | South River | 5087 | 1419 |
| Haddon Heights | 5254 | 1437 | Summit | 5038 | 1452 |
| Hammonton | 5272 | 1370 | | | |
| Hasbrouck Heights | 4984 | 1434 | Teaneck | 4974 | 1429 |
| Hawthorne | 4977 | 1455 | Trenton | 5164 | 1440 |
| | | | | | |
| Jersey City | 5006 | 1409 | Union City | 4995 | 1415 |
| | | | | | |
| Kearny | 5007 | 1431 | Verona | 5006 | 1453 |
| | | | Vineland | 5320 | 1380 |
| Lakewood | 5133 | 1350 | | | |
| Leonia | 4975 | 1422 | Westfield | 5048 | 1441 |
| Linden | 5042 | 1427 | Woodbridge | 5058 | 1420 |
| | | | Woodbury | 5271 | 1444 |
| Madison | 5035 | 1465 | | | |

*A similar list exists for each state. These form the basis for calculating distances on which charges are based.

and H coordinates for the main towns in New Jersey. Similar lists exist for other states. Most other telephone companies also adopt this method of calculating distances.

The distance is then obtained from the coordinates by Pythagoras' theorem as follows.

1. Obtain the V and H coordinates for each rate center.
2. Obtain the difference between the V coordinates of the two rate centers. Obtain the difference between the H coordinates. (*Note:* The difference is always obtained by subtracting the smaller coordinate from the larger coordinate.)
3. Square each difference obtained in case 2 above.
4. Add the squares of the V difference and the H difference obtained in case 3 above.
5. Divide the sum of the squares obtained in case 4 above by 10. Round to next higher whole number if any fraction is obtained.
6. Obtain the square root of the result obtained in case 5 above. This is the rate distance in miles. (Fractional miles being considered as full miles.)

To illustrate this, let us calculate the distance from Englewood on the New Jersey table to Las Vegas, which has a V coordinate of 8665 and an H coordinate 7411.

|   |           | V    | H    |
|---|-----------|------|------|
| 1.| Las Vegas | 8665 | 7411 |
| 2.| Englewood | 4968 | 1424 |
|   | Differences | 3697 | 5987 |

$$\text{Distance} = \sqrt{\frac{(V_1 - V_2)^2 + (H_1 - H_2)^2}{10}}$$

$$= \sqrt{\frac{3697^2 + 5987^2}{10}} = \sqrt{4{,}951{,}198}$$

$$= 2225 \text{ miles}$$

**PRIVATE LEASED LINES**

Tables 18.2 and 18.3 give typical charges for private leased lines of various speeds in the United States and Great Britain.

There are two interesting points to note. *First,* the cost is far from proportional to the bit rate. You have much better value for money in terms of cost per bit on the higher-speed lines, particularly when the

**Table 18.2.** CHARGES FOR INTERSTATE PRIVATE LEASED LINES IN THE UNITED STATES (MONTHLY CHARGES IN DOLLARS)*

| Line types | Type 1002 (up to 55 bits/sec) | | Type 1005 (up to 75 bits/sec) | | Type 1006 (up to 150 bits/sec) | | Type 3002 (Voice grade) | |
|---|---|---|---|---|---|---|---|---|
| | Half Duplex | Full Duplex | Half Duplex | Full Duplex | Half Duplex | Full Duplex | Half Duplex | Full Duplex |
| **Interexchange channel charge per mile per month** | | | | | | | | |
| First 25 miles (0–25) | 1.40 | 1.54 | 1.54 | 1.69 | 1.75 | 1.93 | 3.00 | 3.30 |
| Next 75 miles (26–100) | 1.40 | 1.54 | 1.54 | 1.69 | 1.75 | 1.93 | 2.10 | 2.31 |
| Next 150 miles (101–250) | 0.98 | 1.08 | 1.08 | 1.19 | 1.23 | 1.35 | 1.50 | 1.65 |
| Next 250 miles (251–500) | 0.56 | 0.62 | 0.62 | 0.68 | 0.70 | 0.77 | 1.05 | 1.16 |
| Next 500 miles (501–1000) | 0.42 | 0.46 | 0.46 | 0.51 | 0.53 | 0.58 | 0.75 | 0.83 |
| Thereafter (1001 and over) | 0.28 | 0.31 | 0.31 | 0.34 | 0.35 | 0.41 | 0.75 | 0.83 |
| **Charge per line termination for the first station in an exchange:** | 25.00 | 27.50 | 27.50 | 30.25 | 31.25 | 34.36 | 12.50 | 13.75 |
| **For each additional station on the same service and in the same exchange:** | 7.50 | 8.25 | 8.25 | 9.08 | 9.38 | 10.32 | 7.50 | 8.25 |

*These charges are likely to change and should be regarded as illustrations only.

lines are short. In both countries there is little difference in cost between the higher-speed and lower-speed telegraph lines. For short distances, 1200 bits per second on a voice line costs less than twice 45 or 50 bits per second on a telegraph line. *Second*, there is little difference between the charge for half-duplex and full-duplex interchange lines. *Third*, there is little difference between the charge for half-duplex and full-duplex interchange lines in the States; in Great Britain there is no difference. With the local loop from exchange to subscriber, however, the full-duplex charge is double the half-duplex charge.

The American mileage charges are interstate charges for a channel between local central offices. To this figure must be added the channel terminal charges and the charge for the local loops from the central offices to the line terminations. If the line has several terminations, there will be several of the latter type of charges.

Other, similarly structured, tariffs can be obtained for the other low-speed lines listed in Table 18.2.

In doing calculations on the optimization of networks, the systems analyst will often need to do computations in which the line costs are a parameter. The reader may like to glance ahead to page 728 where the tariffs in this chapter are translated into segments of PL/I and FORTRAN code.

**Table 18.3.** CHARGES FOR PRIVATE LEASED LINES IN GREAT BRITAIN*

| | Telegraph Lines (full duplex or half duplex) | | | Voice Line (half duplex) | |
|---|---|---|---|---|---|
| Radial Distance (miles) | Tariff H (50 bits per second) Line Charge (in pounds per year) | Tariff J (100 bits per second) Line Charge (in pounds per year) | Single Payment Connection Charge | Tariff S (up to 1200 bits per second) Line Charge (in pounds per year) | Single Payment Connection Charge |
| 5 | £88 | £88 | Varies from £5 to £35 | £88 | £5 |
| 10 | 168 | 168 | | 168 | 10 |
| 20 | 328 | 328 | | 328 | 20 |
| 50 | 500 | 650 | | 700 | 30 |
| 100 | 700 | 950 | £35 | 1200 | 40 |
| 150 | 700 | 950 | 35 | 1700 | 50 |
| 200 | 800 | 1,060 | 35 | 2200 | 50 |
| 300 | 920 | 1,220 | 35 | 3000 | 50 |

*Note:* £1 = $2.4.

*These charges are likely to change and should be regarded as illustrations only.

**MULTIPOINT**
**LINKS**
In working out the charge for a multidrop line, there may be several different ways in which the points can be connected, as shown in Fig. 18.1. The charge for the line should be based on the shortest interconnection path—for example, path 4 in the figure. (Is this the shortest?) Each segment of the line will then be priced separately, as, for example, with the charges in Table 18.2. The charges would *not* be applied to the whole line—that is, the 1190 miles of path 4. There will be a local loop and termination charge, as in Table 18.2, for each location.

**DIFFERENCES**
**BETWEEN STATE**
**CHARGES**
The charges illustrated in Table 18.2 were for *interstate* links in the United States. The rates will vary considerably within individual states, even when the facilities are all part of the same Bell Telephone System. To illustrate this variation, Table 18.4 gives the charges for Type 1002 lines in different states. The charges can vary by a factor of 2. Also, the difference between the half-duplex and full-duplex facility can be large. Similar variation occurs with other line types.

**COST OF LINE**
**CONDITIONING**
Conditioning a line incurs an extra charge as follows:

| | | |
|---|---|---|
| Type C1: | 2-point channel: | $5 per month per exchange |
| | Multipoint channel: | $10 per month per exchange |
| Type C2: | 2-point channel: | $19 per month per exchange |
| | Multipoint channel: | $28 per month per exchange |
| Type C4: | 2-point channel: | $30 per month for first station in an exchange |
| | | $9.75 per month for each additional station |
| | 3-point and 4-point channels: | $36 per month for first station in an exchange |
| | | $9.75 per month for each additional station |
| Type C5: | 2-point channel: | $37 per month per exchange. |

These data are for interstate lines. The cost for lines within individual states varies. Also if the line is arranged for key controlled switching the charge may be higher.

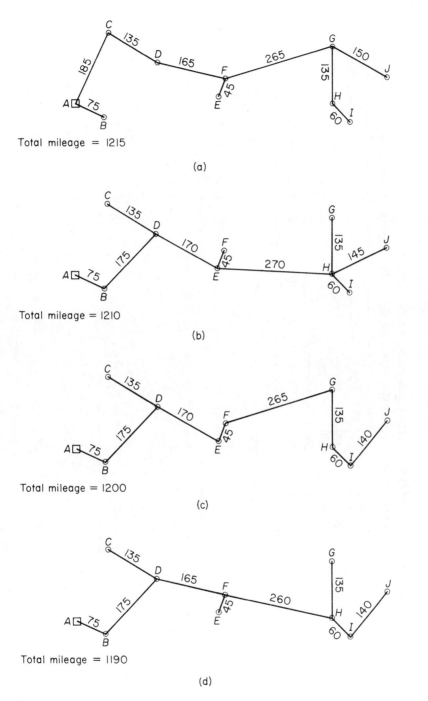

*Fig. 18.1.* There are several ways of interconnecting multiple locations with a multidrop line. The one having the lowest cost should be selected.

251

**Table 18.4.** AN ILLUSTRATION OF THE DIFFERENCES IN CHARGES BETWEEN DIFFERENT STATES IN THE U.S.A.* (CHARGES FOR TYPE 1006 SUBVOICE-GRADE LINES—150 BITS PER SECOND)

| | Illinois Bell Telephone Company | Indiana Bell Telephone Company | Michigan Bell Telephone Company | Mountain States Telephone Company | New York Telephone Company | New England Telephone and Telegraph Company | | |
|---|---|---|---|---|---|---|---|---|
| | | | | | | Mass. | Maine | Other States |
| **Interexchange mileage ($/mi/mo.)** | | | | | | | | |
| Half duplex | 250 @ $2.03 Add'l @ 1.82 | $2.24 | $3.50 | $1.98 | 225 @ 1.95 Add'l @ 1.625 | 2.10 | 2.10 | 2.10 |
| Full duplex | 250 @ 2.53 Add'l @ 2.27 | 2.80 | 4.37 | 2.48 | 225 @ 2.40 Add'l @ 2.00 | 2.625 | 2.625 | 2.625 |
| **Local channel ($/mo.)** | | | | | | | | |
| First ¼ mile | — | — | — | 1.35 | — | .75 | | |
| Each add'l 1¼ mile | — | — | — | 1.35 | — | .75 | — | |
| Flat or min. charge | 7.00 | 5.00 | 5.00 | 5.40 | 4.00 | 3.00 | 4.00 | 2.50 to 4.50 |
| Full-duplex service rate | +100% | +100% | +100% | +100% | +100% | +100% | +100% | +100% |
| **Drop charge ($/mo.)** both half and full duplex | 14.00 | 10.00 | — | 12.50 | 10.00 | 10.00 | 10.00 | 10.00 |
| **Station arrangement** both half and full duplex | 25.00 | 25.00 | 25.00 | 25.00 | 25.00 | 25.00 | 25.00 | 25.00 |

*These charges are likely to change.

**BROADBAND COSTS**    The interstate mileage charges for broadband channels in the United States are shown in Table 18.5.

**Table 18.5**

|  | Bandwidth (kilohertz) | Equivalent Voice Channels | Charge/Mile/ Month |
|---|---|---|---|
| Line Type 8801 | 48 | — | $15 first 250 miles $10.50 next 250 miles $7.50 501 miles and over |
| Line Type 5700 | 240 | 60 | $30.00 |
| Line Type 5800 | 1000 (approx.) | 240 | $85.00 |

In addition to these charges, there is an installation charge and a monthly charge for each terminal. Some typical charges are shown in Table 18.6.

**Table 18.6**

| Terminal | Speed | Equivalent Number of Voice Channels | Installation Charge | Monthly Charge |
|---|---|---|---|---|
| Type 8801 | 40,800 bits per second + one voice link for coordination | — | 200 | 425 |
| Type 5702 | 105,000 bits per second on 7-level magnetic tape + one voice link for coordination | 60 | 400 | 550 |
| Type 5801 | 500,000 bits per second on 7-level magnetic tape + one voice link for coordination | 228 | 900 | 1300 |

These charges relate to the first station installed in an exchange and may be lower for subsequent ones.

**SWITCHED**   The preceding charges were all for private leased
**LINES**     lines. When a line is only needed for a short portion
              of the day, it may be less expensive to use a switched
line. Table 18.7 gives the charges for TWX lines in the United States, operating
at speeds up to 150 bits per second. These may be compared with the charges for
leased-type 1006 lines given in Fig. 18.2.

Suppose that we transmit for $x$ minutes every day of the year except for
weekends, between two points that are 200 miles apart. The annual cost using
dial-up TWX lines is:

$$\$(0.35x \times 52 \times 5 + 12 \times 25) = \$(91x + 300) \qquad \text{(from Table 18.7)}$$

The cost using leased-type 1006 lines is:

$$\$12 \times [100 \times 1.75 + 100 \times 1.23 + 2 \times 31.25] = \$4326 \qquad \text{(from Table 18.2)}$$

These two costs become equal when

$$91x + 300 = 4326 \qquad \text{that is, } x = 44.24 \text{ minutes}$$

This is the breakeven point in cost between leased and dial 150 bps lines for
a 200-mile distance. If the user transmits for more than 44.25 minutes per day
it would be cheaper to use a leased line.

Tables 18.8 and 18.9 give the dial costs of Telex and telephone lines in
Britain. These may similarly be compared with the leased line cost in Table 18.3.

Chapter 41 contains further discussion of leased versus dial lines.

**Table 18.7.** UNITED STATES CHARGES FOR INTERSTATE TWX LINES (DIAL-UP LINES
GIVING SPEEDS UP TO 150 BITS PER SECOND) *

| Distance (miles) | Charge for Each Minute or Fraction Thereof |
|---|---|
| 0–50 | $0.20 |
| 50–110 | 0.25 |
| 110–185 | 0.30 |
| 185–280 | 0.35 |
| 280–450 | 0.40 |
| 450–800 | 0.45 |
| 800–1300 | 0.50 |
| 1300–2000 | 0.55 |
| 2000 or over | 0.60 |

*These charges are likely to change and should be regarded as illustrations only. A
monthly charge of $25 must be added to the above charges. It does not include the cost of
terminal equipment.

**Table 18.8.** UNITED KINGDOM TELEX LINE CHARGES (50 BITS PER SECOND)*

| Distance in Miles between Telex Centers | Duration of Transmission Time Bought for 1p (=$0.024) (in seconds) |
|---|---|
| Up to 35 | 60 |
| 37–75 | 30 |
| Over 75 | 15 |

*These charges are likely to change and should be regarded as illustrations only.

**Table 18.9.** UNITED KINGDOM CHARGES FOR DIAL-UP, POINT-TO-POINT (STD) HALF-DUPLEX VOICE LINES*

| Distance | Time Bought for 1p (= $0.024) | | |
|---|---|---|---|
| | Monday–Friday 9 A.M. to Noon | Monday–Friday 8 A.M. to 9 A.M. and Noon to 6 P.M. | Every night 6 P.M. to 8 P.M. and all day Saturday and Sunday |
| Local calls | 6 | 6 | 12 |
| Trunk calls | | | |
| up to 35 miles | 20 | 30 | 72 |
| 35 to 50 miles | 12 | 15 | 36 |
| over 50 miles | 8 | 10 | 36 |

*These charges are likely to change and should be regarded as illustrations only.

**WIDE AREA TELEPHONE SERVICE**

A further tariff in the United States provides long-distance dial-up facilities for a fixed monthly fee. This is called WATS, the Wide Area Telephone Service. When a subscriber is given a WATS access line, he is permitted to make as many calls as desired to a specified zone or zones. Similarly subscribers in a given zone or zones may be permitted to call a WATS line. There are two alternative methods of charging, one using a flat monthly charge and the other using a fixed hourly rate with a minimum of 15 hours.

Suppose that a subscriber in New York wishes to have a WATS line to the West Coast of the United States. He may pay a certain fixed charge per month for this service and is then free to make whatever calls he wants to the West

**Table 18.10.** UNITED STATES CHARGES FOR DIAL-UP, POINT-TO-POINT INTERSTATE VOICE LINES*

| Airline Miles | | Day — Monday thru Friday 8:00 A.M. to 5:00 P.M. | | Evening — Sunday thru Friday 5:00 P.M. to 11:00 P.M. | | Night — Every night 11:00 P.M. to 8:00 A.M. | | Week-end — Saturday 8:00 A.M. to 11:00 P.M. Sunday 8:00 A.M. to 5:00 P.M.† | |
|---|---|---|---|---|---|---|---|---|---|
| Over | Up to and Including | Initial 3 Min. | Each Additional Min. | Initial 3 Min. | Each Additional Min. | Initial 1 Min. | Each Additional Min. | Initial 3 Min. | Each Additional Min. |
| 0 | 10 | $ .15 | $ .05 | $ .15 | $ .05 | $ .10* | $ .05 | $ .15 | $ .05 |
| 10 | 16 | .20 | .05 | .20 | .05 | .10 | .05 | .20 | .05 |
| 16 | 22 | .25 | .05 | .25 | .05 | .10 | .05 | .20 | .05 |
| 22 | 30 | .30 | .10 | .30 | .10 | .10 | .05 | .20 | .05 |
| 30 | 40 | .35 | .10 | .35 | .10 | .15 | .10 | .35 | .10 |
| 40 | 55 | .40 | .10 | .40 | .10 | .15 | .10 | .35 | .10 |
| 55 | 70 | .45 | .15 | .40 | .10 | .15 | .10 | .35 | .10 |
| 70 | 85 | .50 | .15 | .40 | .10 | .15 | .10 | .35 | .10 |
| 85 | 100 | .55 | .15 | .40 | .10 | .15 | .10 | .35 | .10 |
| 100 | 124 | .60 | .15 | .45 | .15 | .15 | .10 | .35 | .10 |
| 124 | 148 | .65 | .20 | .50 | .15 | .15 | .10 | .35 | .15 |
| 148 | 196 | .70 | .20 | .55 | .15 | .20 | .15 | .50 | .15 |
| 196 | 244 | .70 | .20 | .55 | .15 | .20 | .15 | .50 | .15 |
| 244 | 292 | .75 | .25 | .55 | .15 | .20 | .15 | .50 | .15 |
| 292 | 354 | .80 | .25 | .55 | .15 | .20 | .15 | .50 | .15 |
| 354 | 430 | .85 | .25 | .60 | .20 | .20 | .15 | .50 | .15 |
| 430 | 675 | .95 | .30 | .60 | .20 | .20 | .15 | .50 | .15 |
| 675 | 925 | 1.05 | .35 | .65 | .20 | .20 | .15 | .50 | .15 |
| 925 | 1360 | 1.15 | .35 | .70 | .20 | .25 | .20 | .65 | .20 |
| 1360 | 1910 | 1.25 | .40 | .75 | .25 | .25 | .20 | .65 | .20 |
| 1910 | 3000 | 1.35 | .45 | .85 | .25 | .35 | .20 | .70 | .20 |

*Because these figures may change they should not be used for design purposes.  †For initial 2 minutes.

Coast or nearer WATS zones. The whole of the United States is divided up into six WATS zones based largely on state boundaries. Figure 18.2 shows these zones as viewed from New York. The charge for zone 2 is greater than that for zone 1, zone 3 greater than 2, and so on. If the subscriber pays for access to zone 4, he can call zones 1, 2, and 3 for that same charge, but not zones 5 and 6.

The zone numbering of Fig. 18.2 is applicable only to New York. Another state would have a map with different numbering and different charges. Figure 18.3 shows the WATS zone numbering as applicable to Missouri. The flat-rate monthly charges are given on both diagrams and it will be seen that they vary.

There are two types of WATS service: OUTWATS in which the subscriber with the WATS line may originate as many calls as he wishes to the zone in question, and INWATS in which subscribers in the zone may call the WATS line. INWATS and OUTWATS require separate lines. Both are used to help minimize data transmission costs.

WATS permits data transmission using the same data sets as normal telephone lines. It is not possible to make person-to-person, conference, third-party, credit, or collect (reverse charge) calls under the WATS tariff.

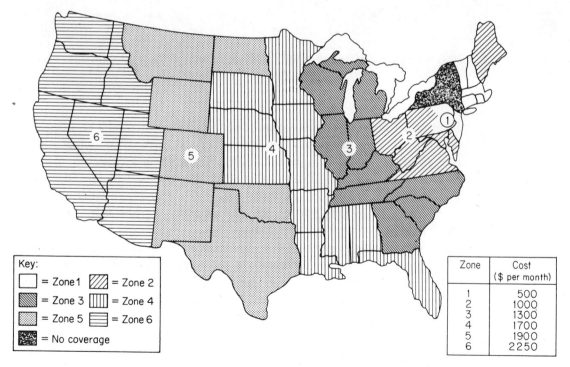

| Zone | Cost ($ per month) |
|------|--------------------|
| 1 | 500 |
| 2 | 1000 |
| 3 | 1300 |
| 4 | 1700 |
| 5 | 1900 |
| 6 | 2250 |

Key:
☐ = Zone 1   ▨ = Zone 2
▨ = Zone 3   ▥ = Zone 4
▦ = Zone 5   ▤ = Zone 6
▨ = No coverage

*Fig. 18.2.* WATS zone configuration for southeast New York subscriber.

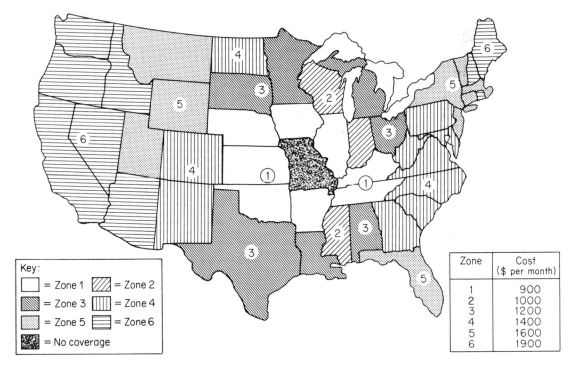

*Fig. 18.3.* WATS zone configuration for a Missouri subscriber. Note the differences in cost from Fig. 18.2.

If terminals are used to call a remote computer, the INWATS service may be used, and on some systems will give the cheapest form of communication. In order to give a suitably high probability of obtaining a free line, several WATS lines will often be installed to one zone. The calculations for determining how many lines are needed are illustrated in Chapter 33. A caller will call one number and a scanning mechanism will search for a free line in the group of WATS lines.

The lines may serve one zone. For example in Fig. 18.2, they may go from New York to zone 6, and other lines will serve the other zones. Conversely callers in lower-numbered zones may call the zone 6 lines. In the latter case the system will need more lines to zone 6 but this may give the lowest-cost configuration because this group serves everybody. Because of the choice between a line serving a unique zone and lines serving several zones, many alternative WATS configurations are possible. The user must evaluate which configuration gives him his required probability of obtaining a free line (no busy signal) at the lowest cost. This is a sufficiently complex calculation to require a computer program, as will be discussed in Chapter 41.

As we shall see in Section VI many of the network pricing calculations for data transmission require computer programs to obtain a minimum-cost network.

# 19 THE NEED FOR MULTIPLEXING

While writing this book I took part in a conference in Europe in which the participants decided to demonstrate some points by using a computer in the United States remotely. A teletype machine was employed as the terminal, and the communication link, a telephone line, was obtained with no difficulty. At the end of half an hour's use, I examined the print-out and estimated that about 3000 characters had been transmitted in total to and from the computer. This number is probably typical when using a teletype machine for time sharing.

The voice line was capable of transmitting 4800 bits per second (more than this rate could be obtained with sophisticated modems). In half an hour, then, it could transmit $1800 \times 4800 = 8,640,000$ bits; and, in fact, it had sent only $3000 \times 7 = 21,000$ bits of data. One could say that the efficiency of the way we had used it was $21,000/8,640,000 = 0.0024$, a very poor way to use such an expensive facility.

**EFFICIENCY: 0.0001** Voice lines are now being constructed by using PCM techniques in which one telephone channel becomes equivalent to 56,000 bits per second in each direction. (See details of the Bell System T1 carrier in the author's *Telecommunications and the Computer*.) This bit stream could conceivably transmit $1800 \times 56,000$ bits in half an hour, in each direction. The transmission efficiency with the above use of time sharing could then be said to be

$$\frac{21,000}{2 \times 1800 \times 56,000} = 0.0001$$

For many users the efficiency would be lower than this as they transmit far fewer than 3000 characters in half an hour.

In an industry with the logic capability of the computer industry, an efficiency of 0.0001 ought not to survive long. If we can push the efficiency up to 0.25, we have an improvement of 2500 times, and on the analog voice line used at 4800 bits per second, a one hundredfold improvement. We can secure such improvements if we can arrange for different users to share the transmission capacity simultaneously. The computer, after all, is being time-shared. We must time-share the lines also.

The need for sharing is even more pronounced with other transmission facilities. The microwave links, coaxial cables, and even wire pairs that form today's telecommunication links can be made to carry *very* much higher bit rates than the preceding ones. The wire pair of the Bell System T1 carrier transmits a potentially usable 1,344,000 bits per second. The wire pair of the T2 carrier transmits 6 million bits per second.

**SHARING THE LINES**

The sharing of transmission lines can be carried out in a variety of different ways, as we shall see later.

Basically, two problems are involved. The first is the technical problem of combining different transmissions on the same line. This is relatively easily solved. If several separate transmissions are sent over the same line *at the same time*, this process is referred to as "multiplexing." Many different *multiplexers* are available for data transmission and all achieve a high level of efficiency—0.8 to 0.9, for example.

The second problem is that of bringing together a sufficient number of users to fill the group of channels that have been derived from the line. Sometimes there are enough users within one organization. They can be brought together to share a leased line. Often this is not the case however.

**WAYS TO ORGANIZE LINE SHARING**

There are a number of ways in which the sharing of communication lines might be arranged.

### 1. *Different Users of One System*

On a system with many terminals, the communication network will be organized so that lines are shared between the terminals. A simple arrangement could be the one shown in Fig. 19.1. Here a group of terminal users do not have a computer in their building. Instead they use a distant computer by means of a voice line that is shared between them.

Sometimes the terminal users are in different buildings, scattered geographically. In this case, unshared lines may connect them to a point at which

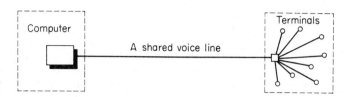

*Figure 19.1*

sharing begins. A network of this type may link many users, as shown in Fig. 2.7.

A variety of different devices and techniques are available to facilitate sharing. These are reviewed in the next chapter. It is the job of the systems analyst to select the best for his particular system, and doing so can be a complex job.

## 2. Different System Users within One Organization

Corporations that are up to date in their use of data processing have a proliferation of different systems. A data communications network that is shared by different system users may be set up within the corporation. In some cases, the network may simply be a facility that enables tie lines to be used for data. A leased TELPAK link may be split up by multiplexing equipment into many separate data links, each used for separate purposes. The data links so derived need not be of the same data rate. A variety of such multiplexing equipment is on the market.

It is probable that complex private data networks, using private-switching facilities and multiplexers, will become increasingly popular in large corporations in the years ahead. Three types of switching are in use in this way, all of which will be described briefly.

1. *Line switching*, in which circuits are switched as in the telephone network.
2. *Message switching*, in which data messages are stored at switching centers and then relayed onward.
3. *Packet switching*, in which data packets of fixed format travel through a leased line network, being routed by mini-computers like cars on a railroad.

The use of such private networks will reduce the need to overlay separate networks for separate systems, as described in Chapter 5, and so will lower the overall data-communications bill of a corporation.

### 3. *Combining the Transmissions of Separate Organizations*

A higher utilization of shared facilities may be achieved if several different organizations combine in the sharing. A network of leased lines and private-switching facilities could serve an association of several corporations at a lower cost per user than if it were designed for one corporation. Unfortunately, this practice is not permitted by the regulations controlling the use of telecommunications in most countries. In the United States, it is permitted only for certain special cases.

### 4. *Line Broking*

An entrepreneur might operate a "line broking" business in which he leases lines, voice or wideband, attaches equipment to them that permits them to be shared, and then sells the subchannels so derived to terminal users. The line broker may be one of the major users with capacity to spare. This service would be a valuable one in data transmission because, again, it would greatly lessen the wastage and hence the cost to the user. Unfortunately, line broking is also prohibited in most countries.

### 5. *Public Data Networks*

In the example used at the beginning of the chapter, no other users were available to share the line across the Atlantic; therefore it had to be used in a wasteful manner. This situation often occurs today, especially when public telephone lines are used for data. In order to avoid similar inefficiency, a switched public network, designed for data transmission, is needed. Such a network would make use of high-capacity trunks that carry many millions of bits per second. The Telex and TWX networks are examples of switched public networks, but they can only operate at low speeds. It is desirable that a switched public data network operate at speeds ranging from about 200 bits per second to 250,000 or higher.

**REQUIREMENTS FOR NEW DATA NETWORKS**   Public data-transmission networks are now being planned or built in several countries. A meeting of the International Standards Organization in Paris defined what it considered the needs of new data transmission networks, from the point of view of data processing users (ISO/-TC97/SC6).

Its main conclusions appear below.

1. *Need*

New data networks are required to overcome the following limitations of the existing networks:

1. The existing public switched telephone and Telex networks cannot give fast enough call setup times.
2. In many instances the existing public switched networks give insufficient reliability in setting up calls.
3. The existing public switched networks give inadequate data transfer rates.
4. Private networks frequently suffer from underutilization (and consequently high cost).
5. Private networks frequently have inadequate standby security because of their limited size.

2. *International Compatibility*

International compatibility and operation are prime requirements. Consequently,

1. the interface between the network and the terminal equipment must be identical for all countries—physically, electrically, functionally and procedurally.
2. the performance and transmission characteristics of a connection when established should be the same whether a national or international connection is used. It is recognized that some minor parameters of propagation delay, time to establish a connection, etc., may be different. (Many countries are now committed to the building of public data networks that are incompatible. This unfortunate circumstance will result in higher hardware and software costs for the user than if international compatibility had been achieved.)

3. *Network Compatibility*

Interworking between any new network and the existing telephone network is necessary, for a new network cannot initially serve all subscribers in a country, and perhaps never when one considers that eventually every home may have a simple data terminal—for example, a pushbutton telephone, teleprinter, or interface with a television set.

### 4. Bit-Sequence Independency

A prime requirement, especially at the higher data-signaling rates (e.g., at 2400 bits per second and above), is that the network transmit all bit sequences without any restrictions on the number of continuous "one" or "zero" bits transferred across the interface.

Bit-sequence independency is a necessity in view of the following applications:

Digit facsimile
Binary data (e.g., program loading)
Analog-to-digital converted data (e.g., process control, radar, encoded voice)
Packed numeric data
Cryptographic information
Scrambled data
Random bit sequences
Bit-framing control procedures.

### 5. Data-Signaling Rates

In considering data-signaling rates, ISO/TC 97/SC 6 gives Table 19.1 as a guide to CCITT. The selection of a set of these rates is dependent on the economics of the network design.

**Table 19.1**

| Data-Signaling Rate (bits/sec) | Synchronous | Asynchronous |
|---|---|---|
| 48,000 | Yes | No |
| 9600 | Yes | No |
| 4800 | Yes | No |
| 2400 | Yes | No |
| 1200 | Yes | All data-signaling |
| 600 | Yes | rates in this range |
| 200 | Yes | are required. |
| 0 | | |

The rates are unrelated to the bit rates of the new PCM telephone systems, such as the T1 carrier. An adjustment of the bit rates to fit in with PCM telephone standards may be desirable.

### 6. *Error Rate*

The error rate of the network should be as good as possible within the bounds of technology and economics, but it must be better than that available at present over leased circuits. The error rate should also be consistent both in the short and the long term and from connection to connection.

### 7. *Call Setup and Disconnect Times*

For an end-to-end user call setup time, including a 10-digit address, where the user data-signaling rate is 2400 bits per second, a target figure of less than 100 milliseconds should be aimed at. This figure is about three times the time required to transmit the 10-digit address at 2400 bits per second, which is reasonable. It is understood that this multiplying factor cannot be a guideline for operation at other speeds. The important factors are that the call setup times should be such that (1) the efficiency of a system handling short messages should not be unduly impaired and (2) the network caters to systems requiring fast responses. The call disconnection should be of the same order as or shorter than the call setup times.

**THE EVOLUTION OF COMPUTER NETWORKS**

It is probable that private networks with similar characteristics will be set up in large corporations. This step will depend to a large extent on the tariffs and operational date of any public data networks that are built.

In the years ahead we are likely to see an evolution of data transmission networks passing through the following stages:

1. *Private networks in which terminals are linked to one system* designed for one set of functions—for example, today's airline, banking and data-entry systems, and time-sharing systems using one computer center.

2. *Private networks in which more than one system are interlinked, within one corporation.* For example, the interlinking of separate time-sharing facilities or data-base systems; the interconnection of computer centers.

3. *Private networks in which systems in different organizations share data network facilities.* For example, interbank systems or interairline systems in which network facilities are shared, and in some cases computing services are shared; the interconnection of time-sharing systems and computer centers in different organizations, as in the ARPA network [1].

4. *Public data transmission networks that cover a portion of a country only.* Unlike the telephone network, they will be built to take advantage of digital technology and multiplexing so that the user pays a fee proportional to his data rate. For cost reasons, they will probably only cover a portion of a country at first—the profitable portion with a high density of users. Examples: the Datran System, Germany's EDS System, Britain's proposed data network.

5. *Nationwide public networks.* It may be two decades before public data networks become as ubiquitous as the telephone network. Eventually terminals in most homes and offices will be interlinked.

6. *International public data networks.* With the rapidly dropping cost of international links, it seems likely that international networks "cream-skimming" the most profitable routes may exist before national networks give full coverage to less-profitable areas. The problems we are now creating with international incompatibility will have to be solved with interface computers.

The further we progress toward nationwide data networks, the less wastage of bandwidth there will be. It has been estimated that there will be 2.5 million terminals in use in the United States by 1980. If all these terminals used their communication lines as inefficiently as the example at the start of this chapter the wastage of the available lines would be appalling. It is almost certain that sufficient communication lines to support this usage could not be provided. Private networks, as discussed in the next chapter, would be less wasteful. However, many separate private networks overlaid geographically require a much greater number of communication lines than a public data network with digital microwave links or coaxial cables and a very high level of multiplexing. Such a data network is going to become an extremely important national resource.

### REFERENCES

1. *Resource Sharing Computer Networks.* Five papers in the Spring Joint Computer Conference, 1970:
   (a) L. Roberts, *Computer Network Development to Achieve Resource Sharing.*
   (b) F. Heart, R. Kahn, S. Ornstein, W. Crowther, D. Walden, *The Interface Message Processor for the ARPA Computer Network.*
   (c) L. Kleinrock, *Analytic and Simulation Methods in Computer Network Design.*
   (d) H. Frank, I. Frisch, W. Chou, *Topological Considerations in the Design of the ARPA Network.*
   (e) S. Carr, S. Crocker, V. Cerf, *HOST–HOST Communication Protocol in the ARPA Network.*

# 20 MEANS OF LOWERING COMMUNICATION NETWORK COSTS

As increasing numbers of terminals are used with one computer system, the need to devise means of lowering the overall cost of the network grows. Data transmission lines today work with various devices that were not found on early telegraph lines. The variety and scope of such devices are growing rapidly, and the systems analyst is faced with a confusing array of different machines and claims. In order to decide between the alternative approaches, he must do some calculations, and these are illustrated in Section VI in this book.

In this chapter we will attempt to set into perspective the various approaches in organizing a network.

The purpose of much of the increased complexity is to reduce the overall network cost. The larger real-time communication networks of today would have been unthinkably expensive without the concentrators, multiplexers, or other devices that they use, and without their sometimes elaborate line-control procedures. On such systems, one can no longer simply connect each terminal by itself on a voice line, leased or dial up, to the computer.

The techniques used depend on the lengths, and hence the cost, of the communication lines and on the number of terminals. If the lines are very long, they are expensive; so techniques for minimizing the cost of the lines dominate the network design. If the lines are short, their cost is of less concern, and the cost of the terminals and devices attached to the lines is of greater importance. Where the lines are very short—for example, all in one plant, one office block, or one campus—then their cost is of little significance in the design, and we often find their bandwidth being used quite wantonly. If a system has a large number of terminals, then the terminal cost becomes of major importance, and the network organization should use schemes that enable the terminal design to be as inexpensive as possible.

## Systems with Very Short Private Lines

Let us start this discussion with the situation in which the lines are so short that we can almost ignore their cost. Bunches of wires are privately laid through a building to the terminals. We are prepared to lay many wires to one terminal if we can make the terminal cost sufficiently low.

The terminal might be a simple data entry device—for example, on the shop floor of a factory.

Often it is built from standard electrical components, such as lamps, rotary switches, and nixi tubes. It is designed to be as inexpensive as possible and may contain no elaborate logic circuits, amplifiers, or other such electronics.

Such a terminal will often have multiwire cable going to it. The total number of wires needed could be reduced by adding more logic in the terminal, but doing so increases its cost.

**TERMINAL CONTROL UNITS**   The terminals with their multiwire cable may be connected to an intermediate device that scans them and sends the data onward to the computer on lines that are more efficiently used. Figure 20.1 is an example of this. Many other types of terminal control units with remote terminals are possible. On the terminal side of the control unit, the cost of the wires is subordinated entirely or partially to the cost of the terminal. On the other hand, the control unit would have enough logic to allow the telephone line in Fig. 20.1 to be used reasonably efficiently.

If it is short, the link from the control unit to the computer may also be inefficiently used, although very much less so than the wiring to the terminals. An interesting example is the use of a loop wire carrying a high-speed pulse stream. This promising development in communications technology enables binary pulses to be sent around a simple loop consisting of a pair of wires at rates of 500,000 bits per second or higher. The wires have an inexpensive repeater every thousand feet or so, which enables the line to be very long if necessary. It will always be a private line and cannot link directly to common-carrier lines except at prohibitive cost, so we will find this pulse-carrying loop traveling around private premises and not normally beyond them. Because of the very high bit rate, the loop can wander around many control units, each with many

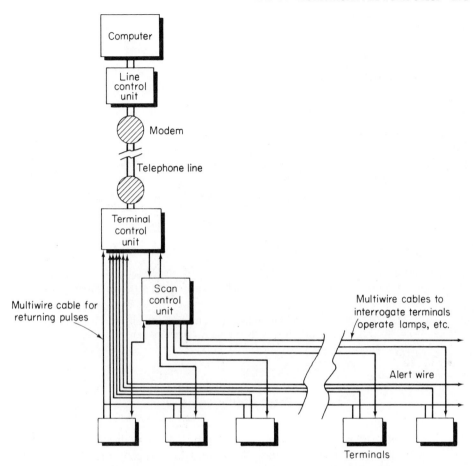

*Fig. 20.1.* The multiwire cabling, inefficiently used, enables the terminal to be as inexpensive as possible. This would only be done with relatively short in-plant wiring.

terminals attached to it (Fig. 20.2). It will carry data to, and take data from, all the control units to which it is attached. The data characters from different devices will be mixed together on the loop and then sorted out into separate transactions at the computer that controls the loop.

The total information rate to and from factory data-collection terminals on which such a system is used may be very low compared with the 500,000 bits per second that the loop can carry. This bit stream may be used at a level of efficiency staggeringly low by the conventional standards of data processing. The line-control procedures are designed with a very great overhead because a large overhead does not matter.

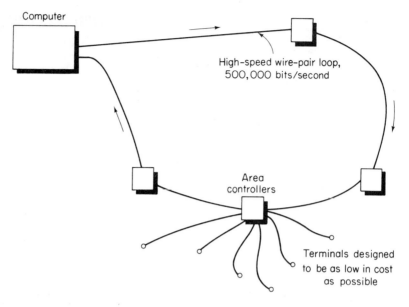

*Fig. 20.2.* A high-speed digital loop with many terminals attached to it. A simple pair of wires with frequent repeaters can be made to carry more than a million bits per second.

## Short Public Lines

We cannot be as wanton in our use of public lines or lines leased between locations from the common carrier. We would not employ multiwire connections such as those in Fig. 20.1 or the high-speed pulse stream discussed earlier. Nevertheless, on short lines, the terminal cost still dominates the design. Short public lines are still used at efficiencies far below that of which they are capable.

It is indeed intriguing to reflect on how inefficiently local telephone lines are used. The two wires from the telephone in my apartment travel to the local central office in a lead-shielded cable, which carries hundreds of other such pairs. This pair of wires is for my exclusive use as long as I pay my telephone bill. Nobody else will share it. This practice seems inefficient, for such a pair of wires has a bandwidth capable of carrying 24 or more telephone conversations at the same time. When such a pair of wires is used to link switching centers, it is common to find it carrying a "channel group" of 12 telephone conversations. Furthermore, my telephone is in use no more than an hour in total in an average week—0.6 percent utilization. One could say that the line carries a fraction $\frac{1}{24} \times (0.6/100) = 0.00025$ of the voice transmission it is capable of carrying.

Rarely in engineering can one find such an expensive facility as a nation's local telephone lines used so inefficiently. This is not true of the long-distance links. On these, great ingenuity has been expended in making full use of the bandwidth.

When one is transmitting over a public or a leased line, it is normal to use a modem. As we commented in Chapter 14, data can be transmitted without modems over short lines that do not have amplifiers. Where modems are used on short lines, the modulation technique can be different from that for long lines, and less expensive. Some manufacturers make modems that are designed for lines only a few miles in length.

A short line is often used in a point-to-point fashion, linking one terminal to a computer. Such a line may be a public or a leased line, whichever is cheaper. Acoustical coupling is often used on short lines because of its low cost and because the terminal can be connected to any telephone.

Placing a single manual terminal on a line gives a utilization of the line far below that of which it is capable. This situation is acceptable if the line is short and inexpensive, although as we shall see in Chapter 42, it is worth using multiplexing techniques on lines only a few miles in length. Often the low-line utilization is overridden by the convenience of obtaining a dial-up connection.

## Long Lines

When longer lines are used, the techniques change. Now the lines are more costly, and it is desirable to use them efficiently. If the lines are more than 100 miles or so long, line cost dominates the network design.

The first step to efficient line utilization is good modem design. Throughout the 1960s much ingenuity was expended on designing modems that would enable higher speeds to be used, especially on voice lines. Modems alone, however, do not solve our problem, except in the case of fast point-to-point operation—for example, magnetic tape-to-tape transmission or the sending of listings, invoices, etc., in quantity. On many commercial systems, we wish to connect manual terminals to the long lines, or other devices that cannot transmit at the full line speed. In spite of the high bit rates now possible, many terminals are still found using voice lines at 14.8 characters per second.

Suppose that terminals are to be situated at nine locations shown in Fig. 20.3, and connected to the computer many miles away. If the terminals have a high usage, it is cheaper to have a leased line to them rather than a dial-up line. One approach would be to have a leased line to each of them, as shown in Fig. 20.4. Such lines, however, are likely to be inefficiently utilized for the following reasons:

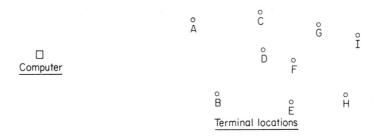

*Figure 20.3*

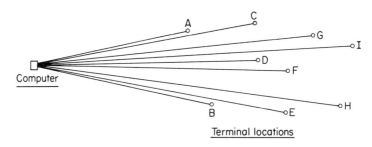

*Figure 20.4*

1. Most of the terminals will not be transmitting or receiving constantly. A high-speed printer may only be used in occasional bursts. A real-time terminal may have relatively short messages and responses, interspersed with much lengthier periods of silence while the operator "thinks," uses the response, or talks to his client. We would like to organize the line in such a way that when one terminal is inactive, another is using the line.

2. The line, equipped with suitable modems, has a certain maximum transmission speed. Most terminals are unlikely to operate at this speed. We would like to interleave the characters or messages to and from different terminals to make the most of available line speed.

3. The messages we send to the terminals may contain repetitive information or information that could be coded less redundantly. By building some form of intelligence into the network away from the computer, we could lessen this repetitive or redundant transmission.

**TECHNIQUES FOR MINIMIZING NETWORK COST**

A variety of devices and techniques are available for achieving these ends. Their objective is to minimize network cost. Without such methods a large network would have prohibitively expensive line costs. Let us now summarize some of the methods available. Combinations of the techniques below may be used in practice.

### 1. *Use of a Private Exchange*

The total line mileage can be cut greatly by using line switching. In Fig. 20.5 a switching mechanism is placed at location D. Messages from the com-

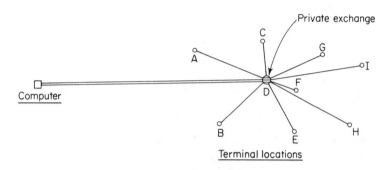

*Figure 20.5*

puter to a terminal go through this switch. The messages are preceded by addressing characters, which cause the line from the computer to be physically connected to the line to the appropriate terminal. Similarly, when the terminal sends a message to the computer, the appropriate connection must be established. There may be more than one line from the exchange to the computer, and the switching mechanism must be able to hunt for a free one.

The switching mechanism may be a privately owned switching device; it may be a private branch exchange at location D leased from the common carrier; it may be a mechanism installed in the local central office (telephone exchange) at D.

The disadvantage of using an exchange in this way is that a terminal operator may be unable to obtain a line to the computer when he wants to because they may all be busy. Figure 20.5 shows two lines from the exchange to the computer. In practice, there may be more terminals and more lines. The designer must calculate the probability of the terminal operator not being able to make a connection and being kept waiting for a long time. Chapter 33 will give examples of the calculations needed in designing systems that incorporate exchanges.

## 2. *Multidrop Lines*

The total line mileage can be cut further than in Fig. 20.5 by using a multidrop line. Multidrop (or multipoint) means that several terminals are connected to the same line. The terminals can be in different locations, with the line taking the shortest path between them, as in Fig. 20.6. It will be seen that the total line mileage in Fig. 20.6 is substantially lower than in Fig. 20.5.

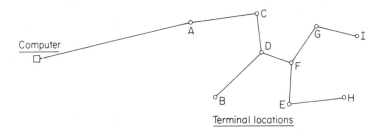

Terminal locations

*Figure 20.6*

Two terminals on a multidrop line cannot transmit or receive at the same time. A discipline must be established on the line whereby the devices wait their turns to transmit. If a terminal user wishes to transmit, he must wait until the line is free and on most systems must wait until the computer sends a signal asking that terminal if it has anything. The terminal cost will be somewhat higher because it needs circuits for recognizing its address and carrying out the line control procedures.

The terminal user may, therefore, be kept waiting on a multidrop line just as on a system using an exchange. However, he may not be kept waiting so long. A multidrop line is occupied only for the duration of one message. On the other hand, if the exchange in Fig. 20.5 is used, the connection from one terminal to the computer may remain unbroken for the duration of a "conversation." Indeed, one terminal user often has the capability of hanging on to his connection. He may do so deliberately for fear of losing his link to the computer. However, by using an exchange and not multidrop lines, the user never has to wait for the line to become free; thus he may receive somewhat faster response times.

If a user can hold his connection for the duration of a "conversation" with the computer, the long line from the exchange to the computer will be used inefficiently, for it will be idle during the time when the computer is preparing the response and when the user is reading it and thinking about his next input.

It would be possible to design an exchange (a line configuration such as that in Fig. 20.5 being used) in such a way that it switched lines quickly at the end of each message in accordance with the demands for connections. Then a user would not be kept waiting for a lengthy period. Such an exchange would be electronically operated rather than use electromechanical step-by-step switches as in most PBX's (private branch exchanges).

In Fig. 20.5 two lines are used from the terminal area to the computer, whereas only one is used in Fig. 20.6. Because of the way the users hold their connection, this result might occur in practice. In fact, more than two lines might be needed to give adequate service. The one line in Fig. 20.6, on the other hand, might be overloaded, so two lines would be multidropped to the nine terminal locations shown. This situation is illustrated in Fig. 20.7. The line configuration here is arranged to give a balanced loading and again to take the shortest path. The total line mileage is still shorter than in Fig. 20.5.

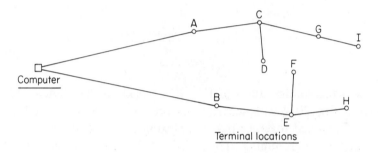

*Figure 20.7*

The systems analyst must be careful that a multidrop line configuration does not degrade his response time unduly. A fast response time (2 seconds, say) is unlikely to be achieved with unbuffered terminals, for one operator will be kept waiting while another types in data. To evaluate the response times, the systems analyst may use queuing calculations or build a simulation of the line. These are again illustrated in Section VI.

### 3. *Multiplexers*

Suppose that the terminals in the preceding illustrations are typewriter-speed devices that can operate on a 150-bit-per-second line. A conditioned voice line to the computer can carry 4800 bits per second. Such lines are commonly used today at 2400 bits per second with a not-too-expensive modem. If we could divide up this capacity, we could use the 2400 bits per second as, say, ten entirely independent 150-bit-per-second channels. This figure gives an allowance for the inefficiency of the dividing-up process. [Here it is $(150 \times 10)/2400 =$

62.5 percent efficient.] Dividing up one line into several independent channels is called "multiplexing." Use of a multiplexer with our nine terminal locations is shown in Fig. 20.8. A full-duplex line is used from the multiplexing unit to the computer so that all the terminals can be either transmitting or receiving at the same time.

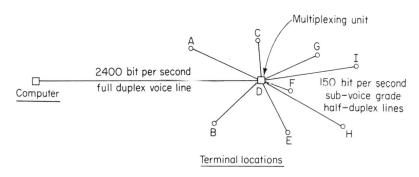

*Figure 20.8*

The way the configuration of Fig. 20.8 works can be thought of as being equivalent to Fig. 20.4, with separate lines to each terminal. The fact that the channels are grouped together by multiplexing does not affect the system performance or the programming. This is one of the attractive features of using a multiplexer. The response time or line availability is in no way degraded, as it would be with a multidrop line or a configuration using an exchange. There are no addressing or polling messages needed; no headers for operating an exchange or making a terminal recognize that a message is addressed to it. The programmer, indeed, need not know that multiplexing is being used. The multiplexing unit is transparent even to the line control units.

If 150-bit-per-second lines had been used in Fig. 20.6, however, the overall line cost of the scheme in Fig. 20.8 would have been higher.

Simple multiplexers that do not store or manipulate the data in any way have a number of advantages over other means of improving line utilization. We can summarize these advantages as follows:

1. They are relatively inexpensive, certainly more so than the concentration techniques discussed below.
2. They do not affect the programming in any way. The multiplexers are "transparent" to the programs that send and receive data and control signals on the low-speed lines as though those lines were still separate and nonmultiplexed.

3. Being simple, the multiplexing devices generally have a high reliability.
4. If it is desired to send a long continuous stream of data on some of the lines, as in a remote batch operation, the multiplexers can handle this operation without interruption of the stream or interference with other users.
5. They cause no significant increase in response time.
6. The low-speed lines are connected to the computer center at all times. The terminal user will not have to wait to obtain a line as he often does with dial-up public lines or systems using a private exchange.

More elaborate concentration techniques, on the other hand, can give a greater line saving.

### 4. Buffers

Most transmitting and receiving devices operate at their own speed—a speed that is usually different from the optimum speed of the line. An extreme example is a keyboard operator. A girl at a teletype machine presses the keys at her own rate, and the characters are transmitted at this rate regardless of the capacity of the line. An engineer at a time-sharing-system terminal may type with one finger. Worse, he pauses for lengthy periods to think about what he is going to type next. If the terminal has no buffer, he is tying up the communication line. On the other hand, if it has a buffer, his hesitant typing could be filling up the buffer without consideration of the line; the line could be transmitting other data. When he requests that the message be sent to the computer, the contents of the buffer would then be sent at the maximum speed of the line.

Communication-line buffers are clearly of value when the line has many different devices contending for transmission, for the overall time that each device will occupy the line is lessened. Terminal buffers would be of value in Figs. 20.6 and 20.7. In Figs. 20.4 and 20.8 they would be less so because here no other devices are contending for the line. Even in this case, however, the higher-speed transmission they make possible may lessen core and time usage in the computer.

The buffer increases the cost of the terminal. The cost must be balanced against the saving, and the longer the lines, the more likely it is that terminal buffers save money.

In addition to saving money, terminal buffers can have a major effect on the time an operator is kept waiting at a terminal. Suppose that a typical operator keys data into a terminal at 1.5 characters per second on a multidrop line that transmits at 15 characters per second. Suppose that an average length for a message keyed in is 75 characters and that you are waiting for another terminal to transmit. If there is no buffering, you will wait 50 seconds. With *buffering*, you will wait 5 seconds. If a voice line is used at a speed of 150 characters per second, and buffering is used, you will wait only half a second.

A cheap form of buffer is the use of paper tape. The operator punches her message into tape and places the tape in a reader to be read when the computer requests transmission. The contents of the tape are transmitted over a telegraph line at its maximum speed.

### 5. *Shared Buffers*

Where any form of electronic storage is used, terminal buffering is expensive. One method that has been used to lower the cost is to share buffers between several terminals.

The unit holding the shared buffers may allocate a fixed area of buffer space to each terminal, or it may allocate the space dynamically on the basis of demand (Chapter 34). When the device handles many terminals and randomly generated transactions of widely varying length, it is more economical for it to use dynamic buffer allocation.

### 6. *Terminal Control Units*

Where a unit is built to buffer the transaction from several terminals, other functions for controlling the terminals or improving line control may be built into the same device. Some control units, as we discussed in Chapter 16, have a substantial amount of logic in them.

The terminals are usually close to the control unit and are connected with multiwire cabling. However, they may be far away, attached by private in-plant wiring or possibly by telecommunication links.

### 7. *Concentrators*

Synchronous transmission is more efficient than start-stop transmission. In order to make the best use of a long voice line, or wide band line, we would like to transmit synchronously at its maximum speed. Many terminals are start-stop devices. Start-stop machines are simpler and less expensive than synchronous machines. Therefore we find line configurations in which start-stop lines go to a concentration point, as in Fig. 20.9, and from there on the data are carried by synchronous transmission.

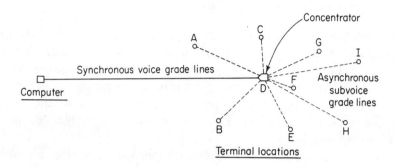

*Figure 20.9*

Similarly, a concentrator may link slow lines to a fast line—voice grade or wideband. It may link lines that are inefficiently or intermittently used to a line on which the transmission is organized as efficiently as possible.

The concentrator, as described here, is doing more than the multiplexer above, because it restructures the message or bit pattern in use. The multiplexer merely groups several transmissions on low bandwidth lines into one of higher bandwidth, without changing the structure or composition of any of them.

Common usage of the terms "concentrator" and "multiplexer" is unfortunately not always as clear-cut as this. "Multiplexer" is sometimes used to mean what we call a "concentrator" here and vice versa. In this book, however, the word "multiplexer" is restricted to devices that combine signals or bit streams but that do not change their structure.

In the past, the term concentrator has been applied to devices that do not change the speed of lines but that link many lines from terminals (or telephones) to a smaller number of on-going lines. When a terminal attempts to contact a computer, for example, the signal may reach a concentrator of this type, which then searches for a free line to the computer. Today it is more common to find the term concentrator being used to refer to devices that store messages arriving on low-speed lines and transmit them to a computer in a modified form on a more tightly organized high-speed line.

Concentrators linking lines of different speeds carry out a buffering operation. They must, therefore, hold incoming messages on the low-speed lines until they can be transmitted on the high-speed line. Similarly, outgoing messages are stored while they are transmitted on the low-speed lines. Thus such devices are sometimes called "hold-and-forward" concentrators. They do not store the messages semipermanently on secondary files, such as disk units. A message-switching system that we will discuss shortly does do so, and this system is sometimes referred to as a "store-and-forward" system.

### 8. *Concentrators with Multidrop Lines*

In the preceding material we discussed improving the efficiency of line use by building features into the terminals that increase their cost. Now as we continue down this list of increasingly expensive items, we can add complications to the concentrators. The intent, as before, is to reduce the overall network cost. The network may have far more terminal locations than in the preceding figures. Some networks have found it economical to couple 200 or more terminals to one long line.

First, the concentrators can be multidropped on one line, as were the terminals in Fig. 20.6 or 20.8. They must then have the logic necessary for responding to polling messages, recognizing messages addressed to them, and other line control functions. Second, the low-speed lines downstream of the concentrators may have several multidropped terminals on them. The logic must then exist to discipline the low-speed lines. Third, there is more than one level of concentration in some large networks. Common control units may feed voice lines that link into concentrators on wideband lines.

### 9. *Line Computers*

The complexity of the concentrator is now becoming sufficiently great for a stored-program computer to be used as the concentrator. This has been the case on many systems. The flexibility of this approach has permitted such a machine to vary its function. A line computer at regional centers has been used for concentration during the day when the system's real-time terminals are active and then as a bulk-transmission machine in the evening when the terminals close down—for example, printing listings and bills transmitted from the main computer.

### 10. *Line Computers with Files*

In many applications in which users carry on a "conversation" at a terminal, much verbiage is displayed on the screen in order to make the system easy to use. The next step in improving the efficiency with which the long lines are used is to reduce what is actually transmitted. If a stored-program machine is used either as a concentrator or a terminal-control unit, it can be used for generating terminal responses and for compacting the messages that are transmitted. Canned responses can be stored on secondary storage in a line computer so that many messages transmitted on the long lines are merely brief codes that cause the line computer to generate terminal responses.

## 11. *Line Computers with Application Program*

Giving further responsibility to the peripheral computers, these machines may have application-dependent programs for conversing with the terminal user. In many systems only a few of the transactions in a lengthy man-machine conversation need either the power of the central computer or its data base.

The philosophy on many large systems is becoming: When the lines are long, distribute the "intelligence" throughout the network so that the quantity of data transmitted is minimized.

## 12. *Message-Switching Systems*

For years message-switching systems have been used to relay cables between many locations. Now they are being used for computer data also.

Locations wishing to communicate with each other could send data directly by teleprinter links. However, where there are many widely separated locations, the cost of communications can be reduced by using some form of message-switching system. Consider the points illustrated in Fig. 20.10, which represent terminals located in eight different cities. One solution to providing telecommunications links between them would be to have direct communications between every pair of points, as in Fig. 20.11. An alternative, which uses far

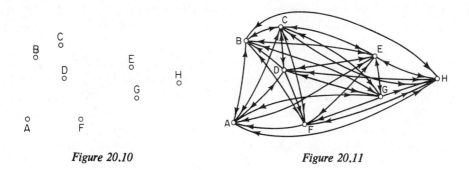

Figure 20.10                                    Figure 20.11

fewer communication lines, is to connect all the points to a switching device, as shown in Fig. 20.12.

The larger the number of locations, the greater the saving in line costs when a switching center is used. A further reduction in line costs is achieved by using *multidrop* lines, in which one line connects several terminals (Fig. 20.13). Multidrop lines could be used if the traffic volume is not too high.

There is a fundamental difference between line switching and message switching. Figures 20.10 through 20.13 could apply to either system. With line

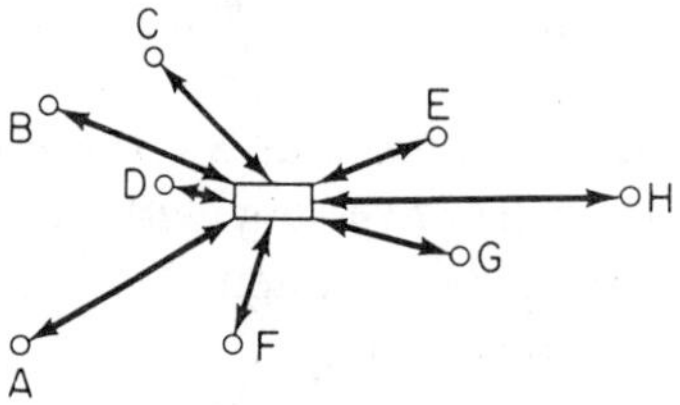

*Figure 20.12* 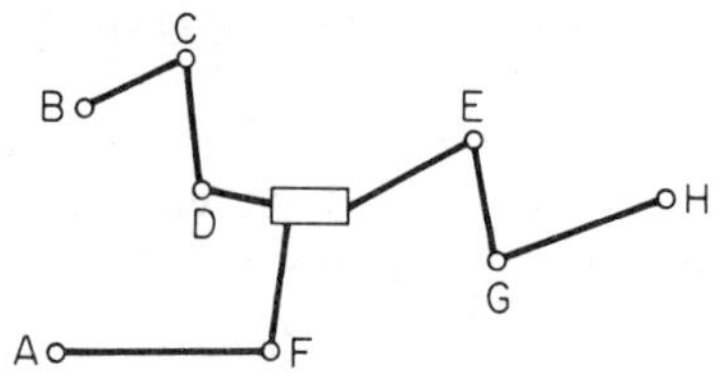                              *Figure 20.13*

switching, a physical connection is made between the circuit paths, as in a telephone exchange. With message switching, no physical connection is made; instead the message is stored and then passed on to its destination or destinations. In a message-switching system the terminals are not interconnected and enabled to respond to each other directly, in real time, as with two telephones. This system, however, can give a better line utilization than line switching.

Today, if the traffic volume is high enough to warrant it, computers are used for message switching. A message-switching system sometimes becomes an important part of a computer network.

### 13. *Packet-Switching Systems*

Message-switching systems have traditionally been used to relay messages that do not need a fast delivery time. Recently, however, some systems have been built which operate like message-switching systems but which relay their messages in a few milliseconds. Such systems have been referred to as packet-switching systems.

In such systems, the terminals or data processing computers are linked to the network via small *interface computers*. The interface computers format the data that are to be sent into "packets," often of fixed length with a fixed format header. Wideband communication links interconnect the interface computers, the network being designed so that if one of the lines fails there is always an alternate line to the interface computer. Figure 21.12 shows such a network. In this illustration the interface computers form the nodes of the network. They determine the routing for their "packets," and the packets are passed very quickly from one interface computer to another. The packet is never put in secondary storage, as in a message-switching system. The network in Fig. 21.12 uses 50,000-bit-per-second lines, and packets traverse the network in less than 100 milliseconds. Packet switching can thus be used for fast-response-time systems.[1]

---

[1] Packet-switching networks are discussed in the author's *Future Developments in Telecommunications*, Prentice-Hall, Englewood Cliffs, N.J., 1971, Chapter 10.

# 21 NETWORK RELIABILITY

Reliability is a major concern in communication-oriented systems. In more than one survey of users of large data transmission networks, almost all of them claimed that the reliability of their communication links was unsatisfactory. Many actions can be taken to correct this situation. Some of them will be taken by the common carriers; some will be taken by the equipment manufacturers; but there are many actions that the user himself can take to improve the performance of his network.

**TYPES OF UNRELIABILITY**      Communication lines can fail to give adequate service or can cause reliability problems in several different ways. It is important to differentiate between these ways clearly because the solutions to the problems they cause are entirely different. The five sources of complaint are as follows:

1. *Line errors.* Some data transmitted over the lines are garbled due to bits being added or lost.
2. *"Busy signals."* The terminal user attempts to dial the computer and cannot obtain a connection. He receives a "busy" signal ("engaged" in British parlance). In some cases, the proportion of busy signals can rise to pathological proportions, for reasons we shall discuss.
3. *Disconnections.* A much rarer event than obtaining a busy signal on a dial-up circuit is that a user is disconnected during his call.
4. *Line outages.* Many systems use leased lines rather than dial-up lines, thus avoiding the problem of busy signals. However, when leased lines

fail, an alternative path usually cannot be dialed as it can with a switched connection. Leased-line failures are a serious problem on some systems.

5. *Recovery errors.* Sometimes data are lost or a file is mistakenly updated twice when the system recovers from a line outage or disconnection. This is entirely a system problem rather than a line problem.

**TYPES OF LINES**
There are five basically different line situations, which differ in their proneness to error.

### 1. *Permanently Fixed In-Plant Wiring*

This situation is entirely under the user's control. The organization of such lines is often designed so that there is no contention and hence no possibility of busy signals or disconnections. Internal wiring should be free from line outages. The noise level on the wiring will depend on how well the wiring is shielded and whether it runs close to major sources of electrical noise. Some wiring in factories has been laid in a position in which it has picked up much electrical interference and has caused many data errors. On the other hand, well-laid or well-shielded in-plant wiring can be largely trouble free. In any case, the user has the solution to the problems in his own hands. Many users with fixed internal wiring have no complaints about it.

### 2. *Internal Dial Connections*

The internal telephone extensions pass through the user's private branch exchange. The number of paths through this exchange will be substantially lower than the number of lines connected to it, and therefore the caller can occasionally receive a busy signal from the exchange when the extension he is calling is, in fact, free. Again, the number of ports into the computer will be substantially lower than the number of users, and busy signals can result for this reason also. Chapter 33 gives examples of the design calculations needed for determining the requisite numbers of paths through an exchange and the paths into the computer. If the ratio of the number of paths to number of users is too low, then user dissatisfaction will result because of busy signals.

### 3. *Public Dial Connections*

When the call is placed on the public network, the user will seldom obtain busy signals as a result of there being no available path through the network (except in localized areas of extreme congestion where the telephone company has failed to meet its own design objectives). He will still receive busy signals from the computer occasionally because there are more users than paths into the machine. In order to find out how many paths he needs into the machine, we can use the same calculations as with internal dial connections.

With internal connections, the user has some measure of control over the noise on the lines and hence the error rate. With public lines, he is at the mercy of the network and is likely to obtain a higher error rate than with internal lines or leased external lines. If he is concerned about data accuracy, he must use error-detecting or error-correcting codes (see Chapter 15). Equipment using the most powerful error-correcting codes can make him virtually immune from undetected errors. However, much of the equipment on the market today does not give this high level of protection.

### 4. *Tie Lines*

A system in which the computer is dialed over a corporation's tie lines is likely to have the same amount of noise and subsequent errors as one using the public network, and it will usually have more trouble with busy signals. Corporate tie lines are traditionally prone to busy signals because they are designed to minimize cost. The number of tie lines necessary to achieve a particular grade of service can be calculated, and the methods for doing such calculations are given in Chapter 33.

### 5. *Leased Lines*

Where leased lines are used without private branch exchanges, there will be no network busy signals. Chapters 40, 42, and 43 show some network maps giving typical leased-line configurations. Leased lines generally give a somewhat lower error rate than public dial lines, but not low enough to mean that any different error-detecting or error-correcting codes can be used.

The problem with leased lines is that occasionally they fail, and when they do, the terminal user often has no way of contacting the computer. He cannot re-dial the computer as on a public connection, unless the system happens to have equipment that provides this alternative.

**OTHER CAUSES OF FAILURE**   There are many causes for the failure of a data transmission link other than the line itself being out. Let us summarize these causes, for the steps we take to protect our systems from line outages must also protect them from those other types of failure.

Outages or occurrences that are thought to be failures can be caused by

1. modem malfunction
2. incorrect operation of a private branch exchange
3. malfunction of the terminal
4. malfunction of the transmission control unit at the computer
5. malfunction of multiplexer or concentration equipment
6. faulty in-house cables
7. errors in the transmission control software
8. error in application program
9. central computer fault
10. line being disconnected due to an automatic time-out at the computer. The time-out is used to protect the other devices on the line when an operator does not respond. If it were not used, other terminals would be kept waiting
11. line being disconnected by the software after a given number of consecutive attempts at retransmission when errors occur
12. local power failure, including a terminal, modem, or other plug being accidentally pulled out
13. terminal-operator procedure error
14. computer-operator procedure error

**FAILURE MONITORING**

It is amazing how little is known, in a typical installation, about what causes the communication line problems. Insufficient data are collected to analyze the causes of malfunction. In many cases, the communication lines are blamed for what is in fact an operator error or software bug. Even on systems in which the reasons for failures are logged, a high proportion are recorded as being of uncertain cause. Communication failures often clear themselves before the trouble cause can be isolated. It is highly desirable that the causes of failures *should* be determined. Frequently something can be done about them. If software errors, PBX malfunctions, or operator errors are dismissed as being line faults, then, instead of being isolated and corrected, they will continue to cause trouble. It is too easy simply to blame the telephone company.

For this reason, it is desirable that the communication lines be monitored automatically. It is necessary to know how often busy signals are obtained so that exchange and tie-line capacity requirements can be assessed. However, more often than not, the proportion of busy signals is unknown. Again, it is desirable to know exactly what leased-line outages occur so that other causes of failure can be sought if necessary. It is a rare installation that, in fact, knows this.

In order to carry out network design to given standards of reliability, the proportion of leased-line failures must be estimated. If we know the proportion, we can take steps to protect the system from them, as will be discussed shortly. Very few statistics, however, have been made publicly available, and those that are available differ widely. It is desirable to have an industry standard for leased-line reliability, plus automatic monitoring of the lines to ensure that the standard is met.

**METHODS OF ENHANCING RELIABILITY**
A wide variety of steps can be taken to lessen communication line problems. We will list 35 of them in the remainder of this chapter. Different measures are applicable to different types of networks.

New networks that are specifically designed for data transmission are coming into existence. These networks are planned to have better *availability* characteristics than existing ones, as well as lower data error rates. The improvement will be significant but not enough to eliminate the need for reliability measures on systems in which reliability in a major concern. The new networks are unlikely to displace existing communication lines completely for many years, for billions of dollars of capital expenditure are tied up in present-day lines. Users who are situated in appropriate locations will be able to use the new facilities, but many will employ existing lines for years to come. Many will use existing lines as feeders to the cities where the new networks are available. The majority of users, in other words, will be concerned with some lines having the same level of reliability as today.

**LEASED LINES**
Some leased lines in use by computer systems seem to have behaved remarkably well, an outage being a rare event. On other systems, leased-line failures have been more common. Some localities seem more prone to them than others, especially, perhaps, dense metropolitan areas.

In examining reports giving statistics of leased-line failures in the United States, it was found that the figures indicated fewer failures in reports dating from the early 1960s than in recent reports. Perhaps the reason is because the American telephone network as a whole is plagued by maintenance problems at the time of writing; perhaps it is because the pioneering users of the early

1960s took more care with their leased lines. A typical figure for failures at the time of writing seems to be from two line failures per week to one failure every two weeks. The failure rate does not seem to vary much with distance. Long lines are not noticeably more failure-prone than short ones. The failure probability does vary with the time of day, becoming greater when the public telephone network is in greater use (see Fig. 21.1). If the probability of failure in a period of one hour has an *average* of 0.005, this figure might drop to 0.0025 during the night hours and rise to 0.01 during working hours, with perhaps 0.02 between 9:00 A.M. and noon.

Some of the outages are very short in duration—a few seconds or less. Many, however, are long. In one typical analysis of leased-line failures, the line is out for more than one hour in about half of the failures. The availability of leased lines in recent analyses is typically about 98 percent, that is:

$$\frac{\text{Time line is available}}{\text{Total time}} = 0.98$$

This figure is of the same order as that of many nonduplexed computer systems. In many cases, however, a real-time computer system is duplexed for reliability reasons, and its availability can become 99.6 percent. In this case, something should be done to improve the availability of the leased lines to the terminals; otherwise they become the weakest link in the system. There are many real-time computer systems working today with duplexed computers but with no steps taken to improve network availability.

**STEPS THAT MAY BE TAKEN TO IMPROVE LEASED-LINE SYSTEMS**   Certain steps may help in the operation of a leased-line network.

### 1. *Automatic Retry*

When the line fails to send the data, the sending machine tries repeatedly until the line is available again. This process would be of value for the outages of very short duration. If the machine detects that the outage lasts longer than a given period, it will notify the operator.

### 2. *Message Storage at the Terminal*

In many systems *customers* cause the origination of transactions—bank customers, department store customers, airline customers, and so forth. One cannot tell the customers to go away because the communication line has failed. Instead one takes their money or records their transaction, and details are kept

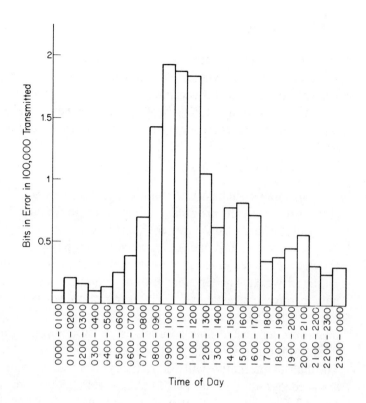

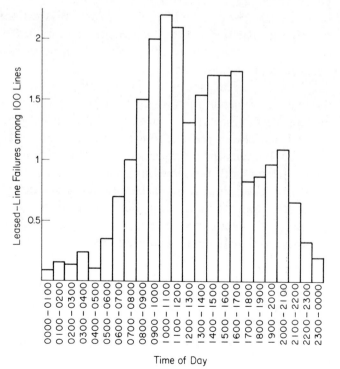

*ig. 21.1.* Both data errors and ased-line failures for telephone nes vary in number with the me of day, as shown here, being ore frequent when the telephone etwork is more highly utilized.

to be sent to the computer when the line is operating again. As we discussed in Chapter 16, it is convenient on some systems to have the operator continue to record transactions at the terminal in the same way or at least in a similar way to that which she would use when all is working well. The terminal or the terminal control unit would store the transactions for subsequent transmission.

### 3. *Alternate Dial-Up Facilities*

On some systems a line availability of 98 percent is not good enough, and storing the transactions until the line is restored is not a suitable answer when many of the outages last more than one hour.

Some form of alternate transmission capability is needed, and it is desirable to select whatever alternative is the cheapest. One possibility is to employ the public network. The terminal and the computer are equipped so that the terminal operator can establish a dial connection when the leased one fails. The transmission speed may have to be slower, but not so slow as to damage the operation seriously. This solution is satisfactory provided that the terminal does not require a speed greater than that of a voice line—and it rarely does. The dial-up alternative will add to the system cost. Sometimes different modems are needed, although modems that can work *either* over a leased line or over a public line at reduced speed are now available.

One argument for building the modem into the terminal or data processing machine is that it can then be switched automatically to lower-speed transmission if necessary, as when a terminal on a leased line dials an alternate connection on a public line.

It seems logical that the telephone company might be persuaded to provide the dial-up connection free of cost during the periods when the leased line is inoperative, but the author knows of no case in which this has happened!

It is not always possible to provide an alternate dial-up circuit. The "local loop" cable which links the subscriber's equipment to the local telephone office often contains both the leased-line connection and the dial connection. If the failure is in this cable the subscriber loses both his leased line and dial capability. Many leased-line failures occur, however, in trunks and exchanges beyond the local loop. In some cases the telephone company might be persuaded to provide the leased and dial lines in separate cables.

### 4. *Alternate Paths*

The communication lines may be duplicated in part, for reliability. In the New York SPRINT System for dispatching police cars, two sets of voice lines link the dispatchers' terminals to the computer center, one running down the East

Side of Manhattan and the other, for added safety, down the West. In some of the trans-Atlantic airline-reservation systems, two voice lines are used in separate submarine cables.

Two or more communication lines may share the load from a given location with many terminals, or from a concentration point. When one fails, the service will be degraded but not completely lost, and the system may be designed with this in mind.

### 5. *Alternate Response Capabilities*

The system may be designed so that if the main computer cannot be contacted, a limited form of response can be obtained from a subsidiary machine closer to the terminals. This machine may be at the concentrator location, *C*, or the terminal control unit location, *D*, in Fig. 21.2. The subsidiary machine for

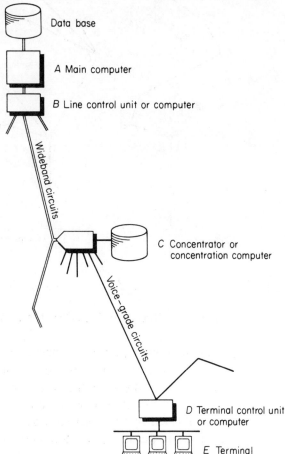

*Fig. 21.2.* When circuit from *B* to *C* fails, limited responses could be sent to the terminal from computers placed at *C* or *D*.

this purpose is likely to be a small stored-program computer capable of carrying on a dialogue with the terminal operator, capable of collecting data, but not being able to answer questions that need the information in the central data base or to carry out operations that need high-processing power. If C in Fig. 21.2 is the machine in question, there may be an alternate dial connection from D to C. The dialing may be manual or may be done automatically by machine D.

### 6. *Looped Lines*

Where one line links several terminals, or concentrators, the line availability as seen by any one terminal can vary with the line configuration. In Fig. 21.3

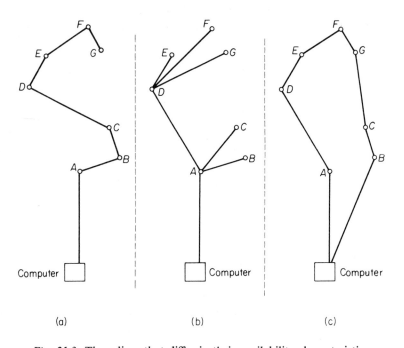

(a)                    (b)                    (c)

*Fig. 21.3.* Three lines that differ in their availability characteristics.

part (a) gives the lowest cost line connecting the seven terminals. This is the layout that most systems would use today for a polled line connecting these seven terminals. Part (b) gives a line of higher cost, because the total distance is greater, but with somewhat better availability characteristics. Terminal C, for example, is unaffected by the failure of line segments DE, DF, AB, or AC, any of which would have put it out of action in the part (a) layout. Part (b) and part

(a) use exactly the same line control hardware and software. The layout in part (c) gives the highest availability, provided that the computer can communicate with the terminals by either the left-hand side or the right-hand side of the loop. In this case, any single-line segment can fail and the terminals are still accessible. The line configuration in part (c) is of lower cost than that in part (b). However, the hardware for giving dual access to the line will be slightly more expensive, and the software must be written in such a manner that the polling and accessing of the terminals can be split at any point when a break is detected. This process should happen automatically, the software using diagnostics to determine where the line break is.

### 7. *Distributed Networks*

Figure 21.3 shows terminals that are connected by one line. Most systems have a larger number of terminals and several lines are needed. Consider the terminal locations shown in Fig. 21.4, for example. The circles in this figure

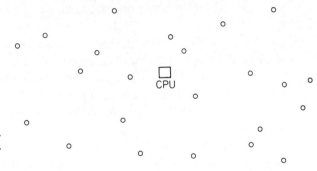

*Fig. 21.4.* Terminals to be connected to the CPU, in the following four diagrams.

could be the locations of either terminals or concentrators. In a typical system they would be connected with a minimum-cost line network, as shown in Fig. 21.5.

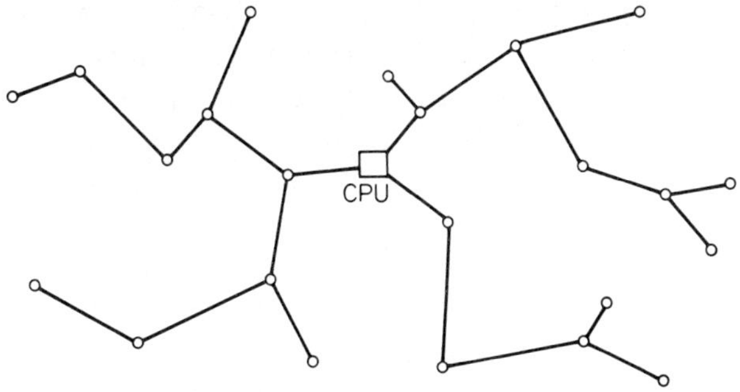

*Fig. 21.5.* Minimum distance interconnection (a tree structure).

The type of layout shown in Fig. 21.5 is referred to as a *tree structure*. The lines never loop back on themselves. Now let us suppose that we modify the Fig. 21.5 layout by saying that there must be two paths from any single terminal to the computer. Figure 21.5 shows the result. Any single line segment in Fig. 21.5 can fail, and every terminal will still be connected to the computer. The total line cost has increased by a small proportion only; it has certainly not doubled, as the cost does when the central computer is duplexed. This line configuration might be referred to as a *distributed network*.

Response-time calculations (see Section VI) might indicate that not as many terminals can be permitted on one line as in Figs. 21.5 and 21.6. In Fig. 21.6, in particular, if one of the line segments closest to the computer fails, there would be a large number of terminals effectively connected to one line. Perhaps two more lines should be added from the CPU to the terminals marked A and B. Suppose that the response time calculations indicate that no more than four terminals should be connected to any one line. Figure 21.7 shows the tree structure that meets this criterion. Now if we add to that the criterion that there must be two paths to any one terminal, we can have a distributed network like that in Fig. 21.8.

In order to facilitate addressing in a network like those in Figs. 21.6 or 21.8, some of the lines would be disconnected with a switch. Figure 21.9 is the same as Fig. 21.8 except that the dotted lines indicate which links have been switched off. This could be the normal configuration when no lines are failed. As soon as one of the line segments in use in Fig. 21.9 fails, the computer diagnostics will determine which one it is by addressing the terminals on its path.

Suppose that the line segment *CD* fails. The computer will determine where the failure is and look up a record giving details of how the network should be reconfigured. One way to do so would be to switch on line *GF*. The switch could be made manually or automatically. On most systems it is good enough to send an emergency message to the locations where the switching must be done, and have it done manually. The line control program would now read new polling instructions into main storage, for the changed line configuration. It will test the configuration and then continue normal operations on the two lines that are affected while the operators take steps to restore line segment *CD*.

The change indicated here results in a line now having eight terminals: *D, A, E, F, G, H, I*, and *J*. The result will be a temporary degradation of response time on this line. A slightly more complicated reconfiguration could have resulted in no line with more than five terminals, as shown in Fig. 21.10. For *any* failure of a single-line segment, it is always possible to reconfigure the network in this manner so that there are not more than five terminals on any line.

On systems in which nonbranching loops are used, as in Fig. 21.2, part (c), the computer can be programmed to take care of line-segment failures without

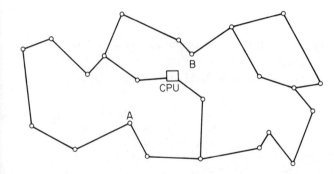

*Fig. 21.6.* Interconnection with two alternate paths to each terminal.

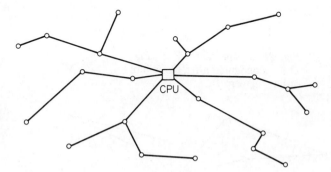

*Fig. 21.7.* Minimum-distance interconnection with no more than four terminals on each line (in order that the response-time criteria are met).

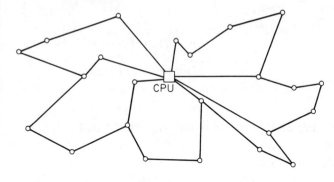

*Fig. 21.8.* A distributed network that can be split into links having no more than four terminals per link.

*Fig. 21.9.* The network of Fig. 21.8 with certain lines effectively disabled to permit simple line control.

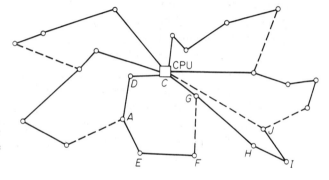

human intervention. This may be worthwhile in order to avoid the multiple manual switching used in the reconfiguration from Figs. 21.9 to 21.10. However, the total line cost becomes greater. Figure 21.11 shows the same locations linked with four-terminal loops.

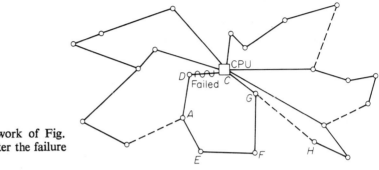

*Fig. 21.10.* The network of Fig. 21.9 reconfigured after the failure of line segment *DC*.

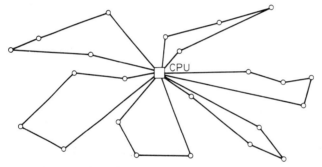

*Fig. 21.11.* Interconnection with looped lines having no more than four terminals per loop.

**THE ARPA NETWORK**

Figure 21.12 shows a nationwide distributed network of wideband lines, the ARPA network (Advanced Research Projects Association), which links computers at MIT, Caltec, the RAND Corporation, and similar locations. The lines are leased links operating at 50,000 bits per second. The nodes shown in Fig. 21.12 have small computers of high reliability linking the network to the time-sharing systems at each location. The nodal computers apply highly effective error detection and correction procedures to the transmission—so effective that in the first year of operation no uncorrected transmission error is known to have occurred. When any of the links fails, the node affected automatically routes the traffic by an alternate path. For example, the switching time is very fast, the normal network response time being less than 100 milliseconds (including switching). This order of switching speed could be achieved

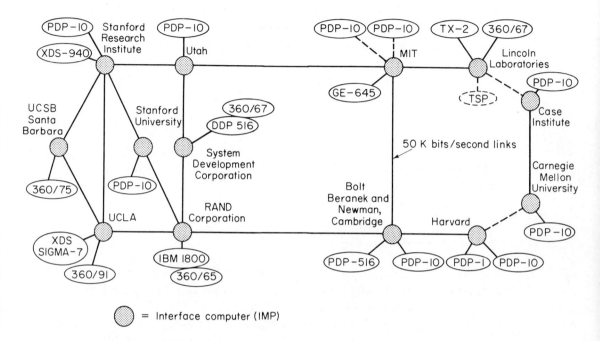

*Fig. 21.12.* The ARPA network, January, 1971. Many new facilities are likely to be added.

either with solid state line switching (as in the IBM 2750) or with packet switching (see below). The ARPA network uses packet switching.

### 8. *Store-and-Forward Systems*

Message-switching systems as we commented previously have generally been used where there was no very fast response time criterion. The data are stored in the file of the message-switching computer (or on paper tape if the system is not computerized). The message-switching system then relays the data to the requisite terminal or terminals. If the line from the system to the terminal is inoperative or if the terminal cannot be reached for any other reason, the system will store the message until the terminal is back "on the air" and then forward it.

### 9. *Packet-Switching Networks*

Packet-switching networks are used where a fast response *is* required. The data are formatted into one or more fixed-length "packets" that are routed through a leased-line network with small computers at the nodes. These computers hold the packet briefly and then send it on to the next node in the network. The packet can traverse the network in less than 100 milliseconds, bypassing any parts of the network that have failed. Packet switching can form the basis of an adaptive network that automatically adjusts the route which the packet traverses to bypass failed lines or failed nodes.

## STEPS THAT MAY BE
## TAKEN TO IMPROVE
## DIAL-UP LINE SYSTEMS

### 10. *Automatic Redialing*

When a leased line fails, the user is normally at its mercy. When a dial connection returns a busy signal, however, the user can dial again, hoping that this time he will obtain a connection. If he is dialing one single telephone and its user is busy, the probability that he will obtain a ringing tone if he dials again in 20 seconds is low. If, however, he is dialing a computer with 100 ports and receives a busy signal, there may be a good probability that one of the ports will become free within 20 seconds or less. To save him the annoyance of constantly redialing and receiving busy signals, the hardware could be designed to redial for him automatically.

This redialing capability could be located in the terminal, the terminal control unit, or in the private branch exchange. In a few locations, private branch exchanges operating under stored program control have been installed. Automatic redialing is one of the features that could be programmed on such exchanges. It will be of great convenience for telephone calls as well as data calls, especially when the party in question has to be called over congested tie lines.

### 11. *Plan Adequate PBX Facilities*

The main complaint about dial systems is that busy signals are obtained too high a proportion of the time. This happens because the ratio of system facilities to users is too low. The system designer should do calculations such as those described in Chapter 33 to determine what this ratio should be.

The first area in which the facilities may be inadequate is the private branch exchange. The calculation should determine how many registers and paths through the exchange are necessary.

## 12. *Plan an Adequate Number of Dial Lines*

The second area in which the facilities may be inadequate is the number of dial lines that are employed, particularly tie lines. Similar calculations are needed here.

## 13. *Plan an Adequate Number of Ports into the Computer*

The third area in which the facilities may be inadequate is the number of ports into the computer. Again, similar types of calculations apply.

On many telephone networks, a different type of busy signal is obtained when the user is busy than when the switching facilities or lines are busy. The American public network gives a fast busy signal to indicate switching or network facilities occupied and a slow busy signal to signify user occupied. (This may have been poor psychology for the cities with telephone congestion, because the knowledgeable users can tell that it is not the parties they are calling who are constantly busy, and sometimes they become furious at the proportion of "fast busies" they receive.) For a computer system, it can be useful to know whether the cause of the users' complaints is the network or the computer, and so they can be asked to record whether the busy signals they complain about are slow or fast.

## 14. *Prevent Users Hanging onto Lines Unnecessarily*

Sometimes on dial systems the unfortunate phenomenon begins of users failing to replace the telephone receivers when they have temporarily finished with the computer. Their reason for doing so is that they sometimes have difficulty obtaining a connection. They become frustrated with the busy signals they receive, and once they have a connection they hang onto it. On some systems users have kept their data set handpiece "off the hook" all morning or even all day to be sure that the computer was available when they turned again to their terminal.

Once this "line-hanging" behavior sets in, it spreads rapidly. A few users start it; they cause an increase in the proportion of busy signals for other users, and thus other users are forced to adopt the same tactic. The degradation can be fast and severe, for most systems have far more users than available lines. Sometimes a temporary peak of system usage for a few days can start the "line-hanging" syndrome.

User behavior of this type can be discouraged by management expressly forbidding it, as well as pointing out its danger. It tends to be encouraged if there is no financial penalty to the user in hanging onto the line, as is often the case. He should be made to pay for line time.

### 15. *Automatic Monitoring of Users*

In order to help management to enforce their dictate against line-hanging, the computer may be programmed to record how long users are connected and how much computer time they use. A listing of violators could be printed for management.

### 16. *Automatic Cutoff of Users*

Where there is no management to control the users, a more drastic step can be taken: the computer could be programmed to cut them off automatically if their lines are connected without use for more than a given period, say 5 minutes.

### 17. *Alternate Dialing Routes*

Where a corporate dialing system using tie lines is planned, the capability to switch calls along alternate routes may be built in. If one route is full, a different one will be used. The route used as the final resort may be given high capacity which is rarely exceeded. This is done on the public network.

## STEPS FOR DEALING WITH DATA ERRORS

### 18. *Use of Leased Rather Than Dial-Up Lines*

Some users of real-time systems want a very quick reaction. To them, the time delay caused by dialing can be inconvenient, and the chance that they may fail to establish the connection could be disastrous. In such cases, dialing may be avoided by using lines permanently connected, often via multiplexers or concentrators. As we will see in the calculations in Section VI, the permanently connected leased-line network is often less expensive than the use of dial lines.

### 19. *Error Detection*

As was discussed in Chapter 15, error-detecting codes are used on many data transmission links to detect errors caused by noise and distortion on the line. A powerful polynomial code can detect virtually all errors even on noisy lines. Codes in common use, however, are less secure.

## 20. *Automatic Retransmission*

The sending machine can be designed to retain the data sent until it receives verification of correct transmission; if, instead, it receives an indication that there was an error, it retransmits the data. A keyboard terminal would need a buffer in order to store the data for retransmission. A buffer increases the cost of the terminal, and many users have opted for a cheaper, nonbuffered terminal. If the terminal does not have the capability to retransmit, then the operator must be informed that an error has been detected so that he can reinitiate the transaction.

## 21. *Automatic Retransmission with Variable Time Delay*

A device using automatic retransmission will normally retransmit several times in succession if there is an error each time. Many such machines retransmit three times, then give up and call an operator. This, however, is not always the best course of action, especially with high-speed modems, because the line may be perturbed by noise for a period of time (several seconds, say) and then the noise ceases. When this is the case it will be better to attempt automatic retransmission, at first immediately and then after delays of increasing length.

## 22. *Forward-Error Correction*

The higher the transmission speed over a given analog line, the higher will be the error rate. Modems operating at 9600 bits per second over a voice line, as discussed earlier, give much higher error rates than those operating at 4800 bits per second. When the error rate becomes too great, the time lost in retransmission can be excessive. The calculations in Chapter 35 will illustrate that retransmission time can be so great as to make the 9600-bit-per-second modem effectively slower than the 4800 one. The answer is to use error-*correcting* codes rather than error *detection* which codes the need for retransmission. Forward-error correction will not catch every error; therefore, on a secure system, it may be backed up with error-*detecting* codes and retransmission. The retransmission in this case will be far more infrequent.

### 23. *Two-Speed Modems*

The error rate with the highest-speed modems may become so great that they cannot be used. Modems may have a switch on them so that they can be cut to half-speed when such conditions prevail. A modem may be able to operate, for example, at either 4800 or 9600 bits per second. It is possible that the switch could be done dynamically, like dynamic equalization, switching from 9600 to 4800 if the noise conditions are bad, or perhaps from 4800 to 2400.

### 24. *Ensuring of Correct Modem Adjustment*

Some links seem to suffer a much higher error rate than normal. It seems probable that many of them have ill-adjusted modems. Care should be taken to see that the modem is correctly adjusted. The error rate on the line should be checked; if it is higher than the expected figures, the cause should be investigated.

## IN-HOUSE WIRING

### 25. *Appropriate Precautions When Installing Internal Wiring*

Sometimes it is the in-house wiring rather than the external wiring that is the source of trouble. Much noise can be picked up on the user's premises. If security violations occur because of wiretapping, they will almost certainly be on the user's premises. Sometimes the user installs his own in-house wiring. The installation should be done only by a skilled telecommunication engineer who is aware of noise sources. The error rate on the in-house wiring should be carefully measured to ensure that it is not excessive.

## NONCOMMON-CARRIER EQUIPMENT

### 26. *Assessment of the Reliability of Network Devices*

The user may employ in his network configuration a variety of devices which are not provided by the common carrier—for example, modems, concentrators, multiplexers, and line control computers. Machines having a reliability that is in keeping with the overall reliability sought from the network should be selected. The network on page 26, for example, is highly dependent on the reliability of the concentrators used. A high level of reliability is sometimes built into the computer center by duplexing the machines; but if the concentrators (or the high-speed links) are of low reliability, then the system as a whole is out of balance. The expenditure of reliability engineering at the center is largely wasted. The system is as weak as its weakest link.

### 27. *Consideration of Alternate Power Sources*

The reliability of the power supply should be considered in the assessment of reliability. An alternate power supply might be needed. Storage batteries may be used for vital devices, such as multiplexers, as in the common carrier's plant.

### 28. *Should There Be Two Terminals per Location?*

Terminal failures will occur occasionally. Many locations require more than one terminal. A design criterion on some systems is to avoid installing a solitary terminal at any location where system availability is particularly important. When a terminal fails, then the back-up machine is there and usually operative.

## PERSONNEL CONSIDERATIONS

### 29. *Ensuring Good Operating Procedures and Training*

There is little doubt that the cause of a high proportion of communication line problems on many systems is incorrect operating procedures. The communication links are often blamed when what actually happened was that an operator has loaded the wrong software, pulled out the wrong plug, or pressed the wrong key on a terminal. In one detailed survey, a group of communication-oriented systems acknowledged to be well-managed were compared with a general cross section of communication-oriented systems. It was found that the average system had *five times* as many system interruptions as the well-managed system. The hardware of the two groups of systems was similar. The main dissimilarity lay in the training and quality of operating personnel, plus the quality of system documentation. The lesson is clear. You cannot take good photographs with a Leica without knowing exactly how to use it. Operating a communication-oriented computer is much more complex than operating a camera, and insufficient care has been taken in selecting and training operators.

### 30. *Writing Good Operating Manuals*

The operator's manuals should be precise and easy to read and understand. Often they are not.

### 31. *Planning Tight Recovery Procedures*

After a failure has occurred, the terminal operator usually has to reenter the data that were being entered and that were interrupted. It is at this time that errors are often made. The item may fail to be entered, or it may be entered twice and erroneously update a quantity field twice. The key to preventing this situation is tight recovery procedures planned to deal correctly with every possible failure. The recovery procedures must be linked to precise operator manuals telling the operator exactly what to do after the failure. Management must then ensure that the operators (especially the terminal operators) follow these instructions to the letter. Without tight control of this process, errors are bound to occur.

## OTHER CONSIDERATIONS

### 32. *Use of Standard Software Where Possible*

Some failures are caused by software errors. This problem can be lessened by thorough debugging and by the avoidance, as far as possible, of nonstandard programs. Clever programmers are sometimes given to writing highly ingenious patches or routines of a nonstandard nature to speed up or improve the operation. These can have two disadvantages: they are difficult for other programmers to understand, and they may not work when a new version of the software comes into operation. It is strongly recommended that unorthodox patching be avoided on communication-oriented systems. Its temporary advantage often gives way to serious failure problems.

### 33. *Avoidance of Frequent Changes of the Software*

When the software is working well, it is a good idea to avoid frequent changes to it. Do not cut over every new version of the operating system. Let well enough alone.

## 34. *Establishing the Reason for All Failures*

As we have seen, there are many different reasons for problems with communication lines. Often the cause is not the line itself. On most systems the majority of failures are connected with the operator, the devices attached to the line, or the software. As we commented earlier, if the causes of line failures are not known, it will not be possible to take appropriate action about them. All failures should be recorded. Steps should be taken wherever possible to establish the reasons for failure. Even on systems where this procedure is followed conscientiously, however, a high proportion of failures are still listed as being of uncertain cause. The performance of the lines will be better understood if they are automatically monitored, and this step should be done on systems in which reliability is of high concern.

## 35. *Use Equipment That Can Isolate the Causes of Failures*

When a transmission link is inoperative it is necessary to determine whether it is the terminal, modem, or line itself that has failed. Different repair men will be called for different failures. Some modems have a circuit that is like a communication line but which loops immediately back into the modem. When in TEST mode it can be determined whether a failure is with the modem or the line. Similarly, data processing machines can be designed with "wrap-around" facilities so that the user can determine whether a failure is in the data processing machine or beyond it in the modem or line. In order to be able to correct faults as quickly as possible, the user should be able to make these tests himself.

# 22 INTELLIGENCE IN THE NETWORK

In a telecommunication-based system, as we have seen, many operations must be performed on data besides the execution of the application programs that process it. A variety of housekeeping and system-control operations have been listed. There are various places in the system network where these operations could be performed. A commonly used approach has been to let the central computer control the entire network and perform all, or almost all, of the housekeeping operations. Yet this is certainly not the only approach, and it may not be the best approach, particularly when the networks in question become larger or more complex.

It may not even be desirable, as we have seen, to carry out all the application programs on the central computer. It may be more economical on a large network to have small computers at peripheral or junctional points and to use these computers to reduce drastically the amount of data that need be sent to and from the distant center. There are several ways in which the "intelligence" of the system can be distributed throughout the network, rather than all residing in the central computer. This chapter discusses these methods, together with their pros and cons.

The systems analyst, in choosing from what will become an increasingly large number of alternatives, may do so with the following ground rules:

1. *Minimum cost.* This may be the prime consideration.
2. *High reliability.* The value attached to system availability will vary from one system to another. The systems analyst must evaluate how much extra money is worth spending on duplexing, alternate routing, and reliability in general.

3. *Complexity.* Excessive complexity should be avoided. The problems multiply as the square of the complexity—or a higher-order power!

4. *Software cost.* Some means of distributing intelligence throughout a network incur a high programming expenditure. The use of stored-program peripheral machines may inflate the cost.

5. *Flexibility and expandability.* It is necessary to choose hardware and software techniques that can easily be changed and expanded later. Some approaches make this step difficult.

**LOCATIONS**
**FOR**
**SUBSYSTEMS**

Subsystems in which logic operations are performed could be in a variety of different places in the network. Figure 22.1 shows six places on a typical large network where "intelligence" can reside.

1. *In the central computer, A.* On many systems today, the central computer handles everything. The network may then contain no other expensive components. Relatively simple and inexpensive terminals may be used. The lines will be constantly in use, scanning the terminals. There may be only one terminal per line. Where the distances are very short, this may be the most economical design.

2. *In a line control unit or line control computer, B.* Many functions are necessary to control a terminal network. If the host computer performs all the operations itself, it will be constantly interrupting its main processing, and many machine cycles will be needed for line control. Some of the line control functions may be performed by a separate line control unit. In some systems, all of them are performed by a separate and specialized computer.  The ratio of which functions are performed by a line control unit, which by the host computer hardware, and which by its software varies widely from system to system. Some application programs could be performed by the subsystem computer—for example, accuracy checking and message logging.

3. *In the network concentrators, C and D.* The concentrators may take a variety of different forms. They may be relatively simple machines with unchangeable logic. They may have wired-in logic, part or all of which can be changed by an engineer. They may be microprogrammed and thus flexible in possible means of use. Or they may be stored-program computers, sometimes designed solely for concentration but sometimes also capable of other operations and equipped with files, high-speed printers, and other input-output equipment.

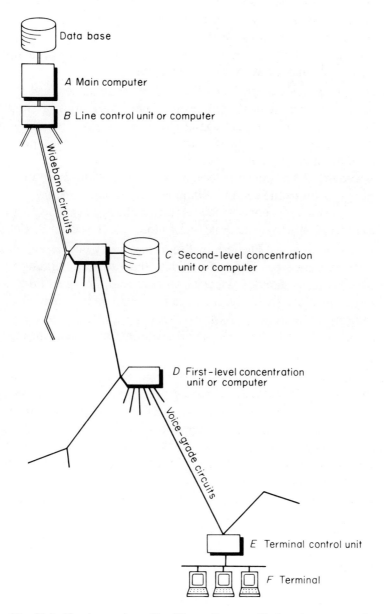

*Fig. 22.1.* Six places where "intelligence" can reside in a large network.

Sometimes a computer positioned in a network similarly to the concentrators in Fig. 22.1 may be a real-time system itself, or at least an on-line data processing system. One may, for example, have a terminal network in which this computer handles most of the responses to terminals and occasionally passes transactions onward to the main computer. It may pass large jobs on to the main computer, or it may pass transactions on when they need to obtain information from, or update, the files kept centrally at the main computer.

4. *In the terminal control unit, E.* Again, terminal control units differ greatly in their logical complexity. They range from a simple "stunt box" to a stored-program computer. They may control one terminal or many. They may be programmed to generate curves on a graphic terminal and to interact with the operator's use of the light-pen and keyboard. They may run commercial-application programs and pass messages on to the central computer only when necessary.

They may be constructed to carry out a variety of logical functions that could otherwise be done at, or closer to, the center of the network.

5. *In the terminal, F.* The terminal itself may carry out certain logic operations ranging from simple functions, such as accumulating totals in a terminal that handles financial transactions, to operations involving intricate logic. In the years ahead we will hear much discussion of "intelligent terminals." Where several terminals share a control unit, it will normally be better to put all common functions in the control unit.

**DUPLICATION OF HARDWARE**

Distributing the logic functions throughout the network increases the amount of hardware required. The lower a function is performed in Fig. 22.1, from B to F, the more duplication of hardware is necessary. The least-expensive approach, if line costs were ignored, would be to have very simple terminals linked directly to the computer center, where the main computer or line control computer handles all the necessary logic. Many systems have one teletypewriter per line linked to the computer center in this way.

As we have seen, distributing the logic throughout the network can lower the communication line cost. If there is only one teleprinter per line, the total network cost will be higher than with several per line; but in the latter case, the added line control functions will increase the hardware cost. Some large commercial systems with transactions utilizing a central data base have very costly line requirements, and need a wideband link from the concentrators to computer center, as in Fig. 22.1. When one examines their transactions and responses, one often sees that only a small fraction of them need either the power of the central machine or its data base. Every element in their man-machine conversation involves transmission to the computer center and a response from there. If this relatively simple conversation handling could be programmed at the concentrator level, the expensive wideband link might not be needed.

The length of the lines determines the best way to organize them. In a geographically dispersed system, the lines are expensive, so there is a strong argument for distributed intelligence to lower the line cost. If, on the other hand, the lines are short, the most economical design may be that with simple terminals and the logic of line control and housekeeping being done at the computer center. A system with terminals in the Wall Street area only may have one terminal per line with no elaborate network logic. The same system with terminals throughout the greater New York area may have multidrop lines and terminal control units that buffer, edit, and error-check the transactions. The same system with terminals across several states may use concentrators and possibly stored-program logic at either the concentrator or the terminal control unit to lessen the data flowing on the lines, and therefore to lower the line requirements. It is interesting to note that in order to meet all these possibilities, a manufacturer would need different sets of data transmission hardware and software in his product line.

The current trend to increase the "intelligence" in the periphery of long-distance networks could be checked somewhat when new public data transmission networks come into operation. (See the author's *Future Developments in Telecommunications.*) The prices proposed for transmission over the Datran System, for example, are fixed—independent of distance—for all links other than "local" ones. When this system is in use, there may be less need for intelligent concentrators.

**FUNCTIONS TO BE PERFORMED**  The functions that may be performed in a concentrator can be divided into two categories: those that relate to the concentration operation and those that could be performed by intelligent terminals. We are thus likely to find all the functions listed in Chapter 16 being performed at a network concentration point rather than at a terminal. It is often more economical to place these functions at the concentrator rather than at the terminal, for there can be a large number of terminals and it is desirable to keep their cost low.

The concentrator, in its simplest form, may be merely a scanning device with a smaller number of lines to the computer than to the terminals. A hold-and-forward concentrator will have the following functions:

1. Buffering messages from the low-speed lines for transmission in modified form on the high-speed line (or lines) and vice versa.
2. Allocation of storage and control of queues.
3. Receipt and transmission of messages on the low-speed lines, using the line control procedures appropriate for the terminals.
4. Receipt and transmission of messages on the higher-speed lines, using the line control procedures appropriate for the computer.
5. Polling the low-speed lines if they are multidropped or controlled by a loop configuration.
6. Responding to polling or other signals if more than one concentrator is attached to the higher-speed lines.
7. Converting the code if necessary from that used by the terminals to that used on the line to the computer. This step may involve conversion of character sequences.
8. Conversion of start-stop transmission on the low-speed lines to synchronous transmission on the higher-speed line.
9. Error detection and retransmission.
10. Responding to line failures, perhaps by establishing an alternate routing or dialed connection.

**SELECTION OF CONCENTRATORS**

Concentrators and multiplexers vary widely in cost, capability, and the number of lines they can handle. A large number of such devices are on the market, and the selection of the best one for a particular system is by no means easy. The choice will depend on the number of terminals and their distance from the computer. Given a particular set of terminal locations, line costs, and distances, it is possible to evaluate which of the various multiplexers or concentrators would give the lowest network cost. This type of calculation is illustrated in Chapters 42 and 43. The calculation is sufficiently complex for computing to be necessary.

A general conclusion from running programs like those in Chapters 42 and 43 for a variety of networks is that different systems have widely differing concentrator needs. Even systems in which the terminals are relatively close to the computer can benefit from the use of multiplexers or concentrators. It is desirable to have on the market a very broad spectrum of such devices, ranging from very small and inexpensive multiplexers to large, complex, and "intelligent" concentrators. They will find a place in the cost minimization of different networks.

**ADAPTIVE NETWORKS**

Networks for specific systems, such as airline systems, are often designed with that system exclusively in mind. The "intelligent" features of the concentrators or other network devices may be oriented, at least in part, to that particular application.

It may be thought desirable in many networks in the future to make them truly application independent. In other words, they can be used without modification of their basic logic for whatever changes may be made in the system using the network. The network involved may be regarded as one module of a complex system that remains independent and in doing so makes future development easier.

The logic in the network in such a case would be almost entirely concerned with maximizing the throughput of the network, achieving error-free operation, and providing the highest possible availability.

A packet-switching network, such as the ARPA one (Fig. 21.12), provides one method of achieving these objectives. The transmission between the nodal computers can be made virtually error free with high-power detecting codes. Computers using any different code can be attached to the network via its interface computers. Any data can be sent, from very low speeds (1 bit per hour) to the highest speeds of the network, all with reasonable efficiency because the packet operation provides an effective form of multiplexing. Each node of such a network may be designed so that at least three lines are connected to it. In other words, for every line entering the node, at least two lines leave it. A regular-shaped network of three-line nodes would be composed of hexagons, as in Fig. 22.2; but, in practice, networks are unlikely to have this uniformity. Figure 21.12 is more typical. One military network was constructed of hexagons, when the key word was "survivability" rather than "availability."

In a packet-switching network, the node computers all have a complete knowledge of the status of the network. If the status changes—for example, if a node computer fails, a line fails, or an area becomes congested—control messages indicating this fact pass throughout the entire network, and the network status tables in each node are updated. These status tables enable each node to route all packets to a destination marked in their header by an efficient routing (a choice of one of two lines in Fig. 22.2). When a node becomes temporarily congested, it sends a "shut-up" message to its neighbours who temporarily route their packets so as to avoid it.

Many different variations are possible in the disciplines or algorithms for controlling a network of this type. The main point is that the nodes of the network have the intelligence to adapt their routing to meet changing network

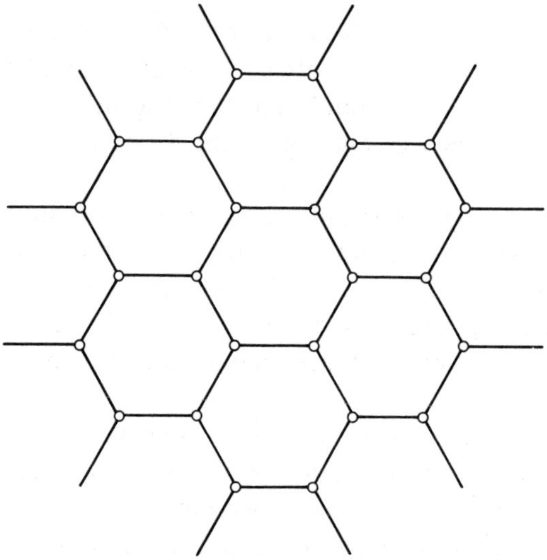

*Figure 22.2*

circumstances. As ARPA has proved, such a network can have very high availability as well as very high accuracy of transmission. [1]

Adaptive routing could also be used in a network with line switching and bit or character multiplexing if these operations were under computer control.

## REFERENCES

1. *Resource Sharing Computer Networks*. Five papers in the Spring Joint Computer Conference, 1970:

   (a) L. Roberts, *Computer Network Development to Achieve Resource Sharing.*

   (b) F. Heart, R. Kahn, S. Ornstein, W. Crowther, D. Walden, *The Interface Message Processor for the ARPA Computer Network.*

   (c) L. Kleinrock, *Analytic and Simulation Methods in Computer Network Design.*

   (d) H. Frank, I. Frisch, W. Chou, *Topological Considerations in the Design of the ARPA Network.*

   (e) S. Carr, S. Crocker, V. Cerf, *HOST–HOST Communication Protocol in the ARPA Network.*

SECTION **V**

**PROGRAMMING**
**CONSIDERATIONS**

# 23 WHAT SHOULD THE SOFTWARE BE REQUIRED TO DO?

The "intelligence" in a network, as discussed earlier, can reside almost entirely in the central computer or it can be scattered throughout the network. Logic functions may have their home

1. in the terminal
2. in the terminal-control unit handling several terminals
3. in the concentrator
4. in the line-control device attached to a computer channel
5. in the central computer itself

Any of the logic operations performed on the data transmitted may be carried out by programming if the device in question is a stored-program machine, as all the above categories of devices can be. On the other hand, the operations may be performed by logic circuitry permanently wired into the machines or by microprogramming in which the built-in logic is modifiable.

Because of this diversity of options, the programming required for control of the transmission of data varies substantially from one selection of hardware to another. The software packages available for assisting the programmer also vary widely. On some systems he has to program for the movement of every bit or character on the communication lines; on others, software packages take care of all the functions associated with data transmission.

319

**THE FUNCTIONS TO BE ACCOMPLISHED**    Let us review the functions that must be accomplished in order to control the transmission of data and then discuss the various ways they can be assigned to hardware logic, microprogramming, software packages, or code written specifically for the system.

**BASIC FUNCTIONS**    First we will examine the basic functions that are likely to be performed on a simple on-line system. A variety of other functions relating to more complex network control—line control, man-computer dialogue, and so on—will then be added.

Consider the basic system shown in Fig. 23.1, with terminals linked to a computer by permanent point-to-point lines.

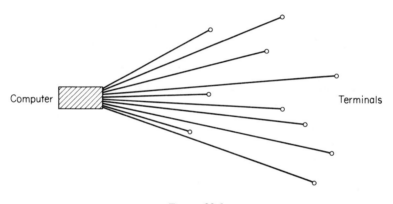

*Figure 23.1*

With any input-output unit, such as a tape or disk, the main programs in the computer receive, or prepare for output, a complete record or message. A short routine writes or reads the record and checks that it has been done correctly. This operation is also required with the communication lines, but here the input-output routine may be more complicated.

The digital information is transmitted on the communication lines a "bit" at a time. The messages to be transmitted must therefore be broken into bits, which are sent at the speed of the line. Similarly, on receiving a message, bits are assembled one at a time into characters, and the characters are assembled into messages. Both the characters and messages must be error checked and the errors corrected if possible. Suitable control signals must be generated for operating the distant terminals at the correct times.

The following functions must be carried out:

1. *To initiate and control the reception* of data from the lines. The lines may be of different speeds. Many lines may be transmitting or receiving at once. The terminals may have to be addressed to see when they are ready to transmit.
2. *To assemble the bits* into characters and characters into messages.
3. *To convert the coding* of the characters. The coding for the communication lines may be different from that used by the computer. The lines, for example, may use the Murray code, whereas the computer uses binary coded decimal.
4. *To check for errors*, both in the characters, by means of a parity check, and in the messages, by means of longitudinal redundancy checks, such as analyzing polynomial checking characters.
5. *To edit the messages* if necessary. For example, an operator may make mistakes in typing on the keyboard, use backspace, or erase characters. The message must be edited into its correct format before it is ready for processing. Control characters must be recognized and removed.
6. *To recognize end-of-record or end-of-transmission characters*, and carry out the housekeeping, preparing for another transmission if necessary. If an error was detected, the same message should be sent again.
7. *To deliver messages to the main programs*, one at a time, edited and converted.
8. *To accept messages from the main programs* when they are ready for transmission to the terminals.
9. *To prepare these messages for output*. It will be necessary to convert them from computer code to communication line code. Control characters may have to be added.
10. *To initiate the transmission* of these messages.
11. *To monitor the sending process*, repeating characters or messages if the terminal detects an error in transmission.
12. *To signal end-of-transmission* to the terminal and carry out the necessary housekeeping functions and line control functions.

If programs in the main computer carry out all these functions, the application programs will be interrupted very frequently and the performance of the computer will be degraded. If there are many lines or a high-data rate, the degradation will be severe. It is usual, therefore, to perform some of the preceding functions in an external device.

Such a device may assemble the bits into characters and feed characters to the main computer. It may assemble the characters into words or blocks and feed these to the computer. To do so substantially reduces the number of interrupts. The external device may store a whole message, recognize the end-of-transmission character, and only then interrupt the main computer. The external device may, in fact, carry out all the foregoing functions with hard-wired logic, microprogramming, or a stored program.

The choice among these approaches is determined to some extent by the number of communication lines that must be handled. If the system has only one communication line, this line may go straight into the computer or into a device with a buffer storage, which automatically assembles or disassembles a complete message. However, if there are 50 or a 100 communication lines, they are best terminated in a separate line-control computer.

**POLLING AND**
**DIALING FUNCTIONS**
Software requirements increase in complexity when a more elaborate configuration of communication lines is used than that in Fig. 23.1. The system may have polled lines, looped lines, or dial lines. The functions required to control these include the following:

1. *Dialing terminals.* The program may dial the requisite digits and establish contact with the terminal or with another computer. If the dialed station is "busy," the request for the operation may be stored and acted on later.

2. *Scanning dial-up terminals.* In some cases, a group of terminals on dial-up lines will be scanned by the program to see whether any of them have stored data to send.

3. *Answering when the computer is dialed.* When a dialed call is received from a terminal or other computer, the software should establish a connection with the device, using the requisite protocol, and should notify the necessary application program.

4. *Polling by programming.* When a line is polled, this may be done entirely by programming. The program has a list giving the terminal addresses and the sequence in which they are polled.

5. *Polling with an autopoll device.* Where an external polling device is used, the software does not send the polling messages itself; instead it gives instructions to the polling device.

6. *Controlling looped lines.* Where several devices are attached to a looped line using a synchronous stream of words, the software may assemble and disassemble the necessary bits and characters.

Once again all these functions may be handled in the central computer or in a separate machine. For flexibility, this machine may be a stored-program computer capable of handling messages of any length and capable of controlling different numbers of lines. It may have an instruction set that is different from conventional computers and that is designed for the handling of communication lines. It may have the facility to log messages on its own random-access file or tape unit. It may send English-language messages to the terminal operators as part of its control procedures. Because it is a programmable unit, its procedures may be modified as circumstances demand.

**BASIC SOFTWARE PACKAGES** The preceding functions constitute the basic essentials required for controlling the communication lines. Some software packages for line control contain these basic functions and little else. They relieve the programmers of the need to assemble bits into characters, convert codes, and perform the other functions given above. As will be illustrated in the next two chapters, the application programmer sometimes simply writes GET and PUT macroinstructions, and appropriate coding is made available to him.

Little else is required on simple systems. On larger or more complex systems, more concern is needed concerning the efficiency of organization both of the control computer and the communications network. The result leads to queuing schemes for messages and higher levels of multiprogramming, to dynamic buffer allocation, to message-compaction techniques, and to the communication-line concentrators and the other schemes discussed in earlier chapters.

**SCHEDULING AND RESOURCE ALLOCATION** Concern for efficient use of the computers is likely to lead to the following functions:

1. *Dynamic buffer allocation.* When variable-length messages are received and transmitted, the buffers that hold them can be organized in several different ways, as will be discussed in Chapter 34. The dynamic allocation of buffer storage in blocks can lessen the total storage requirement. The blocks will be chained together as required; and as soon as a block becomes free, it will be allocated again to the pool of available blocks.

2. *Handling line queues.* On a polled communication line, a queue of transactions can build up, if it is permitted to, waiting for transmission. On some simple systems, no queuing is permitted; that is, no program can send a message on a line when one is already waiting to be sent. This procedure will sometimes hold up the processing, and so a queuing mechanism is desirable.

3. *Handling queues for programs.* Similarly, queues of input messages build up, if permitted, waiting for the attention of certain programs. A similar queuing mechanism may handle input and output.

4. *Handling items for multiple destinations.* A message may be routed, not to one but to many destinations. Rather than occupying many queues simultaneously, which is wasteful, there may be one copy of the message. Control entries referencing the message would then be put into the various queue control areas.

5. *Priority scheduling.* Some messages may be given priority over others. In this case, a queue mechanism that handles multiple priorities is needed.

6. *Multiprogramming.* When application programs have to wait for telecommunication operations to be completed, it is desirable that the central processing unit should be able to switch its attention to other work. The ability to switch easily to lower-priority tasks, and back, is needed.

**FUNCTIONS CONCERNED WITH NETWORK DEVICES**   As we discussed, a variety of devices are built into communication networks, such as multiplexers, concentrators, and store-and-forward computers. The software may format data or control messages so as to interface with such devices.

1. *Blocking data.* In some systems there is an optimum block length for transmission, calculated in Chapter 35. Individual records or messages may therefore be gathered together in one block. In some cases, the network devices handle a fixed-length block or packet size, or set of sizes. The software will reformat the data to be transmitted, as required, and will extract individual records from the blocks received.

2. *Multiplexing.* Where a multiplexer is used, interleaving characters or words of different terminals, the demultiplexing at the computer center may be done by software or hardware. The converse applies to transmission *from* the computer.

3. *Data compacting.* A variety of techniques can be used for compressing the transmitted information so that it can be sent in a smaller number of characters. "Compacting" the data on transmission and "decompacting" it on reception would be a software function.

4. *Store-and-forward functions.* Some systems file messages for later transmission or later retrieval from a terminal. Software control of this operation is needed.

5. *Message switching.* All the functions normally carried out by a message-switching system may be built into the software.

## LOGGING AND
## STATISTICS GATHERING

1. *Message logging.* On some systems all messages are logged on tape or disk, for possible reference later.
2. *Statistics gathering.* An important but often neglected function is the gathering of statistics on traffic volumes, line errors, and line failures.

## RECOVERY FROM
## FAILURES

1. *Line failures.* When a line or terminal fails, the programs may record information to assist in the recovery procedures.
2. *Sequential numbering of messages.* Messages may be given sequential numbers by the front-end software to assist in recovery procedures when failures occur. The sequential numbers may be transmitted to the terminal operators.
3. *Assistance when the central computer fails.* Software in a line-control computer may record data needed for recovery when the central computer fails. It may automatically send responses to the operators.
4. *Recovery procedures.* Programs to assist in recovery from failure should be written, and these might make use of message logs or sequential number schemes.
5. *Diagnostics.* The correct functioning of various parts of the system may be checked by using diagnostic programs in the central computer. The correct operation of a terminal and its connection to the computer may be tested by calling a diagnostic program from the terminal, which checks all possible conditions.
6. *Cross-patching tests.* Cross patching, sometimes called "wraparound," means that a line leaving the computer is "patched" or jack-plugged so that it immediately reenters the computer. The reason for this step is that by sending data out and then immediately in on such a line, the capability of the computer to transmit and receive correctly is tested. By using such methods, the cause of incorrect functioning can be pinpointed, and software to do this automatically has proved of great value.

## EXTERNAL-RESPONSE GENERATION

1. *Control of an external unit that generates responses.* An external unit may store responses to be sent to the terminal and transmit these responses when it receives commands from the computer. Such an external unit may be at the computer location, at a concentrator location, or at the terminal location.

2. *Control of an external unit that formats documents or displays.* An external unit may store details of forms, tables, or charts to be printed or displayed. Information from the computer will cause the form to be generated and filled with relevant data. Often such a unit will be at the terminal location.

3. *Control of a voice-answerback unit.* Instructions may be given to a voice-answerback unit to generate selected spoken words. With some hardware, the computer sends a coded reference, or address, of each word or phrase to be sent. With other devices, a string of bits is sent, which the voice-answerback unit can convert into sound, and the answerback unit itself does not store any vocabulary.

## SECURITY FEATURES

Two security features desirable in the data-transmission software are the ability to identify positively (1) the terminal the computer is communicating with and (2) the operator of that terminal. An additional feature, less often used today, is the ability to encrypt the data being sent.

1. *Terminal identification.* Terminals designed with security in view have the capability to transmit a unique terminal-identification number. The terminals may check this number when queries are being received. Sometimes, when data are being sent, the software will first check the identification of the device it is about to send to.

2. *User identification.* The terminal user may be identified by various means, the most common of which as we discussed earlier is that he keys in a unique number or password, which is checked by the computer. The number will be changed periodically. He may alternatively insert an identification card that causes a user number to be transmitted. The programs will check whether this user is authorized to carry out the functions he is requesting.

3. *Encoding and decoding.* As protection against wiretapping or accidental misrouting of sensitive data, cryptography may be used. The transmission software may do the encryption and decryption of the messages.

4. *Security monitoring.* When violations of security occur, the software may automatically lock a terminal and notify a security officer. All potential violations should be logged by the software for later analysis or inspection.

Much data-transmission software does not yet have security features built into it. However, they will become of increasing importance in the future.

**MAN-MACHINE DIALOGUE**  Some functions related to the man-machine dialogue may be built into the software packages. These functions, however, are more likely to be application-oriented than the features discussed above.

1. *Reasonableness checks.* Range values may be placed on certain fields to assist in detection of miskeying.

2. *Completeness checks.* A record may be assembled entry by entry and then checked to ensure that no entry has been omitted.

3. *Data inspection.* Some inspection of data may take place without the data being processed in any way. This may be done using standard features in the software, without recourse to the application programs. File records may be inspected. A mass of data in many "pages" may be scanned or page-flipped, with a visual display unit. An index may be scanned, and so on.

4. *Preliminary dialogues.* A precisely defined preliminary dialogue may be used before the application programs are entered. This dialogue may step through a series of "menu" screens, as in Figs. 8.7 to 8.10, to determine which application program should be used. It may request a series of data entries from the operator to build up a record ready for the application program.

A wide variety of such preprocessing operations are possible. As we will discuss later, some of this dialogue software may reside in a stored-program concentrator or terminal-control unit rather than in the central computer.

**LEVELS OF TRANSPARENCY**  The logic for carrying out such functions can be packaged in a variety of different ways. It may be distributed between different machines.

It will become increasingly important to protect the application programmer from the complexities of the network and the terminals. In the future, we will probably see layers of software designed to make the transmission facilities as transparent as possible, while in reality they are becoming increasingly complex.

It will be important to achieve "code transparency" in a code-sensitive network. It will be important to achieve "terminal transparency" where one terminal type can be substituted for another or where incompatible terminals must communicate. It will be important to achieve "network transparency" because of increasing complexity and variety of networks. These topics will be discussed in Chapter 27.

# 24    A BASIC SOFTWARE PACKAGE

In this chapter and the next we will describe some typical teleprocessing software. In Chapter 26 future developments in software for data transmission will be discussed.

The majority of IBM users employ 360 (or 370) Operating System, OS, or Disk Operating System, DOS. Their teleprocessing software must fit into the framework of these operating systems. Two types of "access method" for teleprocessing are provided. These are typical of what is available in teleprocessing software and so we will describe them.

The first, the subject of this chapter, is a simple software package that provides the basic functions needed for controlling telecommunication lines. It is called BTAM (*Basic Telecommunications Access Method*). To send a message to a terminal, the application programmer puts a WRITE macroinstruction in his program. To obtain a message from a terminal, he uses a READ macroinstruction. This program does not control queues of transactions as would be needed on a large system with multidrop lines or concentrators; and it does not do any message editing.

The second access method is called TCAM (*Telecommunications Access Method*), and it replaces the older QTAM (*Queued Telecommunications Access Method*). TCAM maintains queues of transactions and uses its own separate control program within the operating system to schedule the operations. In order to send a message to a terminal, the application programmer writes a PUT macroinstruction in his program. To obtain a message from a terminal, he uses a GET macroinstruction. These operations then take their place in whatever queues the TCAM control program is maintaining. TCAM will be discussed in the following chapter.

**BTAM**                        BTAM carries out the functions described below.

1. *Addressing Terminals and Receiving Messages from Them*

When there is a READ macroinstruction in the application program, this results in a linkage to a BTAM routine, which addresses the terminal indicated and instructs it to transmit.

After a READ macroinstruction has been issued, the application program may continue. Eventually it reaches a point when it can go no further until it obtains the message which results from that READ. At this point, normal Assembly Language WAIT macroinstruction is written in the program. Control is then transferred by the operating-system supervisor to some other program. When the conditions of the WAIT are satisfied—in other words, when the message has been read in and is ready to be processed—the supervisor returns control to the waiting application program.

2. *Polling*

If the terminal is on a polled line, the READ macroinstruction results in the line being scanned (polled); and when a terminal indicates that it has a message, this message is read. In order to do so, the BTAM program must have a polling list telling it the addresses of the terminals and the sequence in which they must be polled. The list is given to it earlier in the program in a macroinstruction that specifies the terminal sequence and says whether it should be polled in a "wrap-around" continuous fashion or not.

As an illustration, on a line with IBM 2740s, a "READ INITIAL AND RESET" macroinstruction results in the following sequence of input-output operations:

1. *Write* three EOT characters to reset the line.
2. *Write* the polling character, giving the address of the starting terminal.
3. *Write* a space character (giving a necessary time delay).
4. *Read* the response from the terminal.
5. If the response is negative, repeat the preceding three steps for the next terminal on the list.
6. If the response is positive, *read* the text characters.
7. *Write* an EOA character, followed by three EOT characters, to terminate the operation and again reset the line.

When transmission has been completed successfully, the BTAM program notifies the application program.

### 3. *Transmitting Messages to Terminals*

Similarly, the application programmer can send a message to terminal by means of a WRITE macroinstruction.

Again, with some line control schemes it is necessary to have a sequence of messages going backward and forward in order to transmit a message to a terminal. (See *Teleprocessing Network Organization* Chapter 9.) As an illustration, again, on a line with IBM 2740s a "WRITE Initial and Reset" would result in the following sequence of operations:

1. *Write* three EOT characters to reset the line.
2. *Write* the addressing character for the terminal in question.
3. *Write* a space character (giving a necessary time delay).
4. *Read* the response from the terminal, saying whether it is ready to receive.
5. If the terminal is ready to receive, *write* an EOA character, followed by the test.
6. *Read* the acknowledgement from the terminal, saying whether the message has been received correctly.
7. *Write* three EOT characters, again to reset the line.

Again, when transmission has been successfully accomplished, the BTAM code notifies the application program.

### 4. *Handling Transmission Errors*

Where error-detecting codes are used, with automatic retransmission of erroneous messages, the BTAM code will initiate the retransmission when necessary.

If correct transmission has not been accomplished after a specified number of retries, the BTAM code will notify the application program so that it can take appropriate action.

### 5. *Organizing Buffer Pools for Variable-Length Messages*

BTAM, when working under OS 360 (or 370), allocates blocks of buffers dynamically as required. If a message is being received and fills the block allocated to it, another block will be chained to the first. This chaining process will continue until the entire message is received. The converse process takes place on output. As soon as a block is finished with, it is made free again in the pool of available blocks.

### 6. Dialing Terminals and Answering Terminals That Dial the Computer

When the terminal is on a dial line, the WRITE macroinstruction can cause the BTAM code to carry out the dialing operation. A "WRITE Initial" macroinstruction will cause the computer to dial the terminal, establish connection, and transmit the data in question. A "WRITE Continue" causes it to transmit the data without dialing (because the connection is already established). When a "busy" signal is obtained for a terminal that is dialed, the BTAM code will notify the application program.

Similarly, a READ macroinstruction may dial a terminal to see whether it has anything to send. In some cases, a dialing list will be given to BTAM, which will then dial the terminals on the list, as in a polling operation.

When a terminal user dials the computer, BTAM can be set up to accept the call, establish contact with the terminal, and notify the application program that the call has been received.

### 7. Code Conversion

BTAM provides a translation routine and a set of translation tables that convert between the code employed by the computer and the various codes employed by terminals. If necessary, the user can define a new set of terminal characters and give this translation table to the BTAM routines.

### 8. Keeping Error Statistics

BTAM maintains statistics of all transmission errors that are detected.

### 9. Providing On-Line Terminal Testing Facilities

BTAM operates on-line diagnostics that facilitate the testing of terminal equipment.

10. *Initialization of Operations*

The OPEN macroinstruction of BTAM activates a line group—that is, any defined group of lines using identical control procedures. This must be done before any message can be sent or received over the lines. Similarly, a CLOSE macroinstruction terminates the operation. The OPEN macroinstruction activates the buffer pools and executes the channel program required to initialize the telecommunication control units and modems.

**RELATIONSHIP TO OTHER PROGRAMS**   Figure 24.1 shows the linkages between BTAM and the programs using it. Two levels of priority of teleprocessing program are shown, along with a background of low-priority, non-teleprocessing programs.

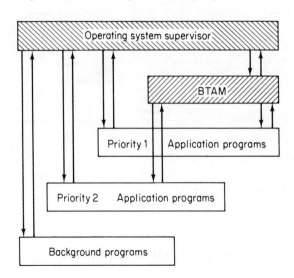

*Figure 24.1*

Figure 24.2 illustrates the events that occur in the processing of an enquiry from a terminal. The application program issues a READ macroinstruction. This is expanded by BTAM, as in point 2 above, into code that includes several input-output operations. The BTAM issues the first of these. It is executed by the supervisor and control is returned to the application program.

The application program continues with any processing that can be done prior to receiving the results of this READ. It may issue READs and WRITEs on other lines, but it is not permitted to do so on the line for which the above READ was issued. When it can do no more processing, it issues a WAIT macroinstruction.

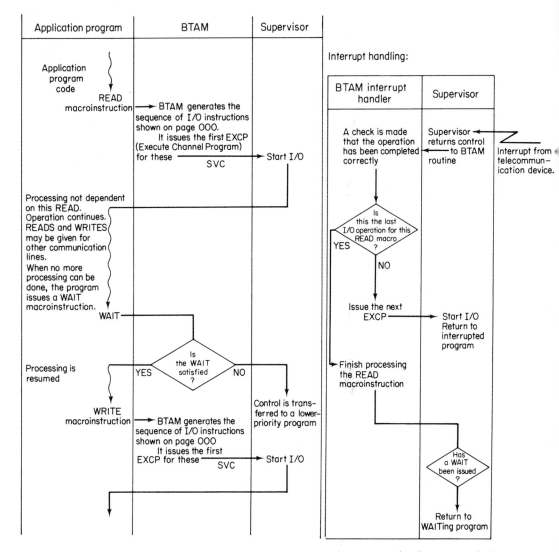

*Fig. 24.2.* The events that occur when BTAM handles an enquiry from a terminal.

Meanwhile, the input-output operation is continuing. An interrupt will be received from the telecommunications devices when an input-output command has been completed. The supervisor, processing this interrupt, will pass control to the BTAM routine again. BTAM will check that the operation was completed correctly and issue the next input-output command. A series of such interrupts will ensue until the message from the terminal has been read into core. The BTAM routine checks that there are no line errors, and then control is returned to the program that issued the WAIT.

The application program processes the message and composes a reply to it. It then sends this reply to the terminal by issuing a WRITE macroinstruction, which is expanded by BTAM into a sequence of input-output commands such as those in point 3 above. These are executed in the same manner, and the terminal receives its response.

# 25 MORE POWERFUL SOFTWARE

The level of software support outlined in the previous chapter makes tele-processing programming easier, but on complex systems the programmer is still left with difficult problems that could have been taken over by software. Some organizations have recognized this fact and have written their own software package, which fits between the application programs and the basic teleprocessing package, as shown in Fig. 25.1. Such a package may reside in the highest-priority partition of the operating systems.

The reasons for writing a subsidiary teleprocessing package like this can be to handle some standard aspect of man-machine dialogue, to give a particular treatment of errors or failures, to further simplify the input-output coding, or, a particularly important reason, to program facilities for queuing and multiple WAIT conditions in the application programs so that many asynchronous events can be processed with efficient use of the processing unit—in other words, to achieve multi-thread operation.

In this chapter we will describe a teleprocessing software package that is more comprehensive than the one given in the previous chapter. Even with comprehensive software available, there will probably be good reasons, in some cases, for users to write their own packages fitting into the software scheme as in Fig. 25.1. These reasons will sometimes relate to unique system requirements or man-machine needs. In some cases, the reasons may be the saving of money, or of computer memory or time.

**TCAM**　　　　　　　　IBM's general-purpose teleprocessing package for real-time systems is TCAM (Telecommunications Access Method), which operates under OS 360 (in a 360 or 370).

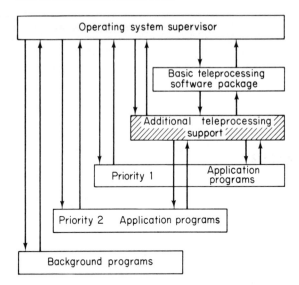

*Fig. 25.1.* Some organizations have produced a software package that fits between the teleprocessing application programs and the basic teleprocessing software. Such a package may be written for a particular class of applications.

TCAM will handle the data transmission in a system with a high degree of multiprogramming. Many transactions of different types and different categories of communications equipment may be in process simultaneously. The application programmer is isolated from the input-output operations and simply specifies them in his program with macroinstructions, such as GET and PUT. He need pay no attention to the complex queuing and timing considerations.

TCAM, unlike more basic teleprocessing software, has its own *control program*, which takes charge and schedules the traffic-handling operations. Interrupts and macroinstructions in the application programs cause control to be given to the TCAM control program. This control program resides in one partition of a system under control of OS 360. It is executed as the highest-priority job in the system. The application programs are normally executed in the lower-priority partitions, although, if necessary, some may share the highest-priority partition with the control program.

Non-real-time jobs may also be run in the same system and would normally occupy the lowest-priority partitions.

Messages reaching the TCAM control program are routed by it to the requisite destination, which may be a terminal or an application program. Often the required communication line or program will be occupied, and so the TCAM control program organizes queues of items waiting for these facilities.

**MESSAGE SWITCHING AND DATA COLLECTION** Sometimes TCAM can handle an incoming message by itself without needing to pass it to an application program. Such is the case when the message is merely to be routed to another terminal or computer, as in a message-switching system. TCAM, in fact, carries out by itself all the functions that would be found in a message-switching system. If a message from a message-switching terminal is intended for processing by an application program, the header of the message indicates this fact.

Similarly, TCAM can carry out a data collection function without reference to application programs. Terminal operators key in data that are to be collected for subsequent batch processing, rather as they might punch data into cards. TCAM will either store the data in a queue for a particular application program or else write it in secondary storage independently of an application program. In the latter case, the data will be read for batch processing at some later time by an access method unrelated to TCAM.

**MESSAGE FORMATS**
The TCAM control program thus serves as an intermediary between application programs and terminals, and sometimes between terminals and terminals, and between terminals and secondary storage devices. The terminals can be diverse in nature and can be used with different line control procedures.

The application programs no longer need refer to terminals but can refer to messages using macroinstructions such as GET and PUT.

Because of the different routing possibilities, some messages need to have a *header*, which the TCAM control program will use in directing the message to appropriate destinations. The header contains such information as:

1. a code for originating terminal
2. a code for destination or destinations
3. a message type indicator

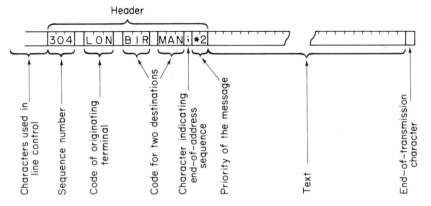

*Fig. 25.2.* A message with a header.

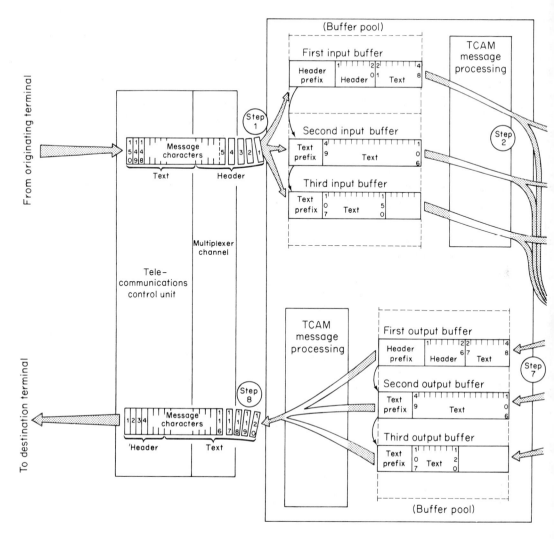

4. a sequence number (for recovering from failures with loss of messages)

5. a priority indicator

An example of a message with a header is shown in Fig. 25.2. Widely differing formats of header can be specified.

Many systems do not use a header at all on the incoming messages because all messages are destined for the same application program. In others, a one-character "action code" may be used to select the appropriate application program.

**QUEUING**    The messages may arrive at random times. Often they are not processed immediately because the processing unit is occupied; and when they have been processed, a response may not be sent immediately because the line is occupied. The TCAM control

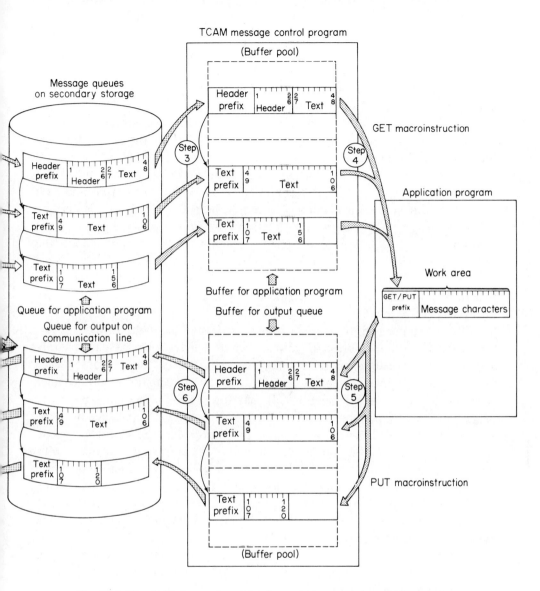

Fig. 25.3. The buffering and queuing in secondary storage used by TCAM.

program, attempting to maintain high utilization of both the processing unit and the lines, builds queues of items waiting for these facilities. The queues can be either in the computer's main memory or on secondary storage. Where a fast response time is important, it is desirable that the queues should be in main memory, not on disk, and therefore a version of the control program that achieves this step would be generated. The receiving of the input traffic, the sending of the output traffic, and serving of the application programs would then all take place asynchronously.

This is illustrated in Fig. 25.3 (on pp. 338–339) for a case in which secondary storage is being used to hold the message queues.

Step 1 of Fig. 25.3 shows the characters from the telecommunication line entering the computer on the multiplexer channel. The characters are directed into dynamically allocated blocks of buffer storage by the TCAM message-control program. The control program maintains a pool of fixed-length buffer blocks that are used both for telecommunications input and output and as a buffer to and from the application programs. The buffer blocks in this case are shorter in length than the incoming message. The message therefore occupies three blocks. The prefixes of each block contain the chaining that links the blocks, along with other control information.

The user defines the size of the buffers that he wishes the control program to allocate. Calculations to determine the optimum size for such buffers are illustrated in Chapter 34.

When a buffer is filled, TCAM begins processing the data. It may convert the code and do simple forms of editing, such as deletion of backspace characters and the preceding characters they cancel. It may check the sequence number, update a message count, add time and date information, and do other such simple user-specified functions. It may log the message onto tape. After performing these functions (step 2 in Fig. 25.3), it writes the message into secondary storage in a queue, in this case for a particular application program. It could, in a message-switching application, have been placed in a queue for output on a communication line. Each such queue is for a particular application program or a particular communication line. The user determines the routing to the appropriate application program queue either by putting its destination code in the message header or by means of macroinstructions that generate the message-control program.

For each queue in secondary storage waiting for an application program, there is a buffer in main storage, which the TCAM control program keeps filled if there are messages available (step 3 in Fig. 25.3).

When the application program issues a GET macroinstruction (step 4), TCAM moves the message from the buffer into a work area provided for that application program. The header prefix is deleted, but a small prefix remains, giving the size and chaining information for when the message exceeds one block.

The application program goes to work on the message and eventually composes a response that it makes ready for output with a PUT macroinstruction (step 5). The output queuing operations in the remaining steps are then the converse of those for input.

The queue in step 6 could have been a queue for another application program rather than a queue for a communication line.

All the queuing is handling on a first-in, first-out basis within priority groups.

**ADVANTAGES AND DISADVANTAGES**   The advantage of this type of software package over basic ones, like that discussed in the previous chapter, is that it is a higher-level macrolanguage, and hence programming time is reduced. For some systems, its complete handling of message switching or data collection is a major advantage. On many real-time systems, response time will be of prime importance, and so all of the message queuing will be in the main storage. The application programs may be placed in the same partition as the TCAM programs.

TCAM has prewritten routines for checkpointing, logging, date and time stamping, sequence numbering and checking, message interception and re-routing, and transmitting error messages. It supports a separate master terminal for the operator.

A basic package such as that in the previous chapter, on the other hand, requires less main memory and secondary storage. For this reason, it is likely to be used on small systems, especially when multithread operation is not necessary. Greater flexibility can be achieved with the basic package in return for greater programming effort. BTAM is easier to modify than TCAM.

Increasingly, in the future, the manpower saving and bug-free operation that result from using the higher-level packages are going to outweigh the costs of greater overhead.

# 26   PROGRAMMED CONTROL UNITS AND CONCENTRATORS

In the three previous chapters we discussed software in the central computer. Software can also reside in the three places shown in Fig. 26.1—in a line-control computer at the computer center, in a stored-program concentrator, and in a terminal-control unit.

**ADVANTAGES OF SEPARATE LINE-CONTROL COMPUTERS**   The prime purpose of using a separate line-control computer is to remove the burden of communication line handling from the main computer. The main computer is expensive and is equipped with instructions and facilities not needed in communication line handling. The line-control computer can be given a specialized instruction set and special facilities for data transmission. Some expensive computers at the time of writing spend as much as 60 percent of their processing time handling the various interrupts that arise from their lines and terminal devices.

Often there are other advantages in using the separate processor. Its software is especially written for it and is not subject to the constraints associated with the central computer's operating system. Microprogramming can be used in places where it could not in the main machine and can greatly enhance efficiency. Special-purpose machine instructions of great power can be designed.

The line-control computer can be designed so that it can handle a wide mix of different terminal types and line-control procedures, if necessary. When done in the main computer, this sometimes incurs substantial expense in line adaptors, and storage for line-control software routines.

An important advantage can be flexibility. The handling of telecommunications equipment often has special requirements that can require modification of

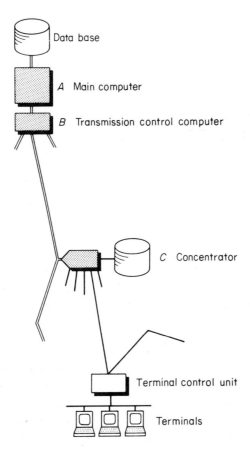

Data base

*A* Main computer

*B* Transmission control computer

*C* Concentrator

Terminal control unit

Terminals

*Fig. 26.1.* Three places where the line control software may reside.

computer line-control facilities. This is true because of the diversity of different terminal types. It is especially true for products marketed internationally rather than with one country or area such as North America. In a stored-program, line-control machine, functions may be done by programs that have otherwise been done by hardware—for example, character assembly, line recognition, and polling. The modification of such operations can be comparatively easy when it is in well-written program modules.

During operation, different programs can be read into the machine when different terminal types are dialed. If, for example, a broadband link is used for a short period to transmit batch data at high speed, then for that time the machine can become a high-speed line controller.

The secondary storage and its organization can be specifically designed for such functions as buffering, message switching, response generation, or voice answerback. This design will usually result in access speeds, mechanisms, and organizations that differ from those used in the main computer.

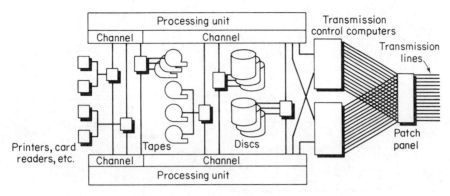

*Figure 26.2*

It may be possible to build the line-control computer to have substantially higher reliability than the central computer. Because it is smaller, less can go wrong, duplexing is cheaper, and fallback procedures can be more specialized. The line-control computer can then be programmed to take limited action of its own when the main computer fails. It can communicate with the operators and instruct them as to the correct procedures. It can dump incoming data onto a tape or disk for later processing. It can take action to ensure that no items are lost. It may have a file of data, which enables it to give its own responses to certain important but simple operator enquiries.

In systems needing high reliability, both the main computer and the line-control computer may be duplexed. The configuration in Fig. 26.2 has been used on many systems. One of the main computers in this configuration may be doing non-communication-based work until its twin fails or is taken off the air for maintenance. Both line-control computers may record the incoming traffic so that if one of these fails, no message is lost and no message need be reentered by the operator.

A less-expensive configuration giving limited protection is that in Fig. 26.3 in which the main computer can handle some of the lines itself. It can do so only in the event of failure of the line-control computer. When the latter computer fails, important lines in use at that time will be switched (often manually) to the main machine. In general, two processors offer better possibilities for graceful degradation than one.

Temporary failures in the central computer are often caused by software problems and it is sometimes necessary to carry out an *initial program load* (*IPL*) to correct them. This is much easier if the terminal network is not connected directly to the central computer. The line-control computer both makes the IPL easier and isolates the terminal user to some extent from the computer center problems.

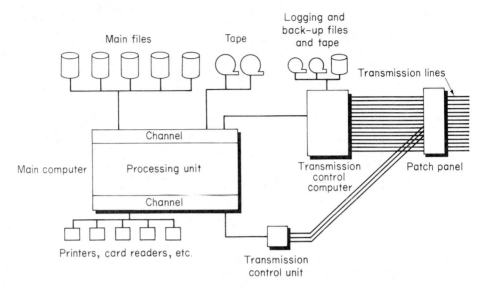

*Figure 26.3*

**DISADVANTAGES OF SEPARATE LINE-CONTROL COMPUTERS**

There are some possible disadvantages in using a separate line-control computer. First, on simple systems with few lines, the cost of taking the lines directly into the main computer may be lower.

Second, some systems have been installed in which the line-control computer came from a different manufacturer than the one who made the main machine. This situation can cause difficulties in interfacing the hardware and software. It can cause arguments about who is responsible for failures, lost messages, or garbled responses. Sometimes, indeed, three manufacturers are responsible for the central system—the manufacturer of the main computer, that of the line-control computer, and that of the modems. It is preferable if this hardware comes from one vendor.

Another possible disadvantage of the two-computer approach is that two computers in series are inherently less reliable than one. If the probabilities of the main computer and the line computer working correctly are, respectively, $P_1$ and $P_2$, then the probability that both will be operative together is $P_1 \times P_2$. Unless $P_2$ is almost 1, the combination is worse than $P_1$ alone.

**ADVANTAGES OF REMOTE LINE COMPUTERS**

The main reason for using remote computers as concentrators or terminal-control units is to reduce the cost of the communication links to the computer. The system designer could equally well have the same functions done at the computer center, and he must compare the costs of the alternatives. In some cases, the transmission requirements are excessive if an intelligent control unit is not employed. In graphic applications, for example, the transmission of images to the terminal with a fast response time would require a high bandwidth line if there were not a local machine for generating the diagrams. Generally a local computer is used for interacting with the user; and if a distant machine is used, the transmission to and from it is used only at certain points in the dialogue.

Again, as we discussed in Section II, the communication line requirements can be cut drastically in some commercial applications if a remote computer carries out those long-winded sections of dialogue that are designed with terminal-user psychology as a prime consideration. In some cases, the programs in the terminal-control unit or concentrator collect and assemble data from the terminal users for transmission in a batch at a later time. The control unit may be programmed to dial the main computer at appropriate times.

Many of the advantages just discussed for the line-control computer also apply to programmed concentrators and terminal-control units. They can take some of the work from the main computer. In some cases, this amounts to a major savings in processor time and memory, for the main computer no longer has to pay attention to the interrupts from many terminals. It does, however, have to control the line connecting the device to the computer center, and disassemble the messages if they are packed together.

The problem of handling terminals with nonstandard requirements can be taken care of in the software of the remote device, and again this can be made comparatively easy if well-documented modules are planned with such modifications in mind.

Foreign telegraph lines, shortwave radio links, and lines with special control procedures can be terminated in a stored-program concentrator that takes care of their special requirements and sends standard messages with standard control procedures to the main computer's software. There is much to be said for using such devices to protect the central computer from the eccentricities of the data transmission world. The diversity of procedures found on communication lines is increasing in spite of efforts to standardize.

**SOFTWARE IN THE LINE-CONTROL COMPUTER** How completely the line-control computer handles the telecommunications links depends to some extent on its hardware. It may, for example, not be equipped with its own input-output unit, such as tape and disk. If the machine has all the hardware necessary, it may assume all the functions associated with teleprocessing. The host may merely handle the READ and WRITE instructions of the application programs with a simple channel operation. It will often not use dynamic buffer allocation or a queuing mechanism, as described for the GET and PUT instructions in the previous chapter. The channel between the host and its line-control machine is sufficiently fast for these not to be worthwhile. The queuing and dynamic buffer allocation is all done in the line-control computer.

The main computer may, on the other hand, have substantial software on its files for when the line-control computer fails. If there is a standby line-control computer, as in Fig. 26.2, the main computer will have software to assist in the switchover. If there is an alternate communication-line path into the main machine, it will call software for controlling this path into its main memory when necessary.

The initial program load (IPL) of the line-control computer will usually be done from the main computer. This may be true for the remote computers as well as the local ones. In some complex networks with many computers, all of them have been loaded (IPLed) from the main computer. Similarly, changes to network status tables in the remote machines are sent from the main machine. In the packet-switching network of Fig. 21.12, the controlling computer sends a change to its interface computer, and the latter passes the change to those computers to which *it* is connected. These computers, in turn, pass it to *their* neighbors, and so on, like a chain letter. In a fraction of a second, the change is operative in every computer in the network. The initial program load of an entire network may take place in a similar manner.

As we discussed in the previous chapter, secondary storage, such as a disk unit, may be used for several functions in teleprocessing control, such as queuing, logging, messaging switching, and data collection. If the line-control machine does not have secondary storage, then the software functions will be split between the host computer and the line-control computer. If a package with the functions discussed in the previous chapter is employed, the operations of the left-hand page of Fig. 26.3 may be carried out in the line-control machine, and those on the right-hand page in the host computer. The application programs might, in such a case, have two possible sets of input-output macro-instructions: one that uses GET and PUT commands as shown, which result in queuing and use of secondary storage; and the other, which uses READ and WRITE commands to transfer data directly to the line-control computer without queuing in the host or use of secondary storage. In generating his system, the user can then choose to avoid the use of secondary storage for his normal input and output if he wishes.

# 27  FUTURE DEVELOPMENTS IN DATA TRANSMISSION SOFTWARE

The time it takes to write programs and the shortage of programmers are perhaps the main factors discouraging a more comprehensive use of computers. Too much of the available talent is drowning in the problems of coding and debugging. The decade ahead is going to be one of ever-increasing complexity in the design of systems, and it will be increasingly important to protect the application programmer from the monstrous complications that will entangle him if he ventures into network control, data base control, task scheduling, and so on.

Running counter to this trend is the spread of mini-computers, which many ex-programmers of 1401s and UNIVAC Is have greeted with gasps of relief. But even here one wonders how many mini-computers will exist in a decade's time without the capability to dial up distant library computers, compilation facilities, data banks, number crunchers, or specialized services.

The overhead associated with operating systems, data base management, network management, and other support is going to become very high. This situation will no doubt meet with protests from persons such as those who objected to the overhead incurred by languages like FORTRAN when they were first used, and then to the overhead of operating systems.

However, one force is moving us inexorably in the direction of increased software capability: the cost of the hardware is dropping fast. The numbers of machine instructions that can be executed for one dollar cost, or the number of bits that can be stored for one dollar, are increasing exponentially. The new techniques now emerging in the research laboratories will ensure that a near-exponential growth continues for at least the next decade (and probably much longer). In ten years' time we will probably be able to store 100 times as many bits and execute 100 times as many instructions as today—for the same price.

However, while machine capability is developing at this amazing rate, programmer capability is not. Programmers are, if anything, increasing in cost. Are there any conceivable techniques by which we could make the application programmers 100 times more productive?

**HIGH-LEVEL LANGUAGES**   The first essential is that high-level languages will be available for all data transmission applications. For programming real-time systems in the 1960s, the use of FORTRAN, ALGOL, COBOL, and PL/I was the exception rather than the rule. In the future, application programming in any language lower than those must become unthinkable, and the language arguments should revolve around languages that are even higher.

Languages like report-program generators will be used, so that an application programmer by simply specifying the format of the report can generate the code needed for producing it, or now, for producing displays on terminal screens. Data-base management software will be used for querying and searching data files and for answering questions that involve comparing and processing the data on the files. In such systems one macroinstruction will generate the code for what will sometimes be a large number of file operations. Linked to the data-base management schemes will be specific terminal-dialogue structures, and the same system will generate the code necessary for such structures.

The application programmer should be able to forget about the telecommunication network almost completely. He should use GET and PUT macroinstructions with a symbolic address for the terminal, and the "front-end" software should take care of all transmission and terminal-control questions. This will be an increasingly complex function as network organization becomes more complex.

**APPLICATION-ORIENTED SOFTWARE**   The control programs, operating systems, file management, and network management systems will in most cases (but not all) be independent of the applications they are being used for. In addition, there will probably be much development of software for specific applications. There will be packages for banking, packages for civil engineering, for stockbrokers, lawyers, statisticians, accountants, and almost every other group that can use computers. There will be packages for operations (such as the collection of factory shop-floor data) which are designed so that they can be quickly tailored to local conditions. There will be many time-sharing systems with different application packages that can be dialed, and the terminal that can be connected to them will become a most versatile instrument if its user knows how to employ it fully. In many cases, one suspects, he will not. The terminal capability will often be far ahead of the understanding of its user. Eventually, and perhaps within the next decade, the programming bottleneck will be replaced with a comprehension bottleneck.

**STANDING ON EACH OTHER'S SHOULDERS**
The first two decades of programming were characterized by "everyone doing his own thing." Only too rarely did one person learn from another's mistakes and build on another's successes. In hundreds of firms one could see application programs for the same job being written by independent groups, each claiming without validity that they were unique.

If the not-invented-here factor seemed more important than productivity, part of the reason was that other people's programs were difficult to understand and difficult to modify. They were usually ill-documented. They were usually not modular in structure and were not designed with ease of modification in mind. Some were covered in patches, and patches upon patches, and were filled with irrationally added branch instructions to stopgap routines. An attempt to modify them was more risky than attempting to change the electric wiring in an ancient building when one does not know the circuits. It was better to rip it out and start again.

A great increase in the productivity of a nation's programmers will come when the same application packages can be used in many different companies, with a few easily made modifications. Many software houses and manufacturers are now striving to produce such packages. A spectacular success was IBM's package for the airline industry, which is now working in many airlines throughout the world (most of whom originally said they were unique and could not use standard application programs). The package capitalized on the experience laboriously gained in the early airline reservation systems where, in the words of one practitioner, the programs were "hewn out of the rock." This is a case where new groups of programmers could stand on the shoulders of groups who had worked before them and could build on their experience. Without this approach, small airlines who cannot afford 200 programmers would not have the systems they have today.

**APPLICATION PROGRAM COMPILERS**
In some cases where an application package is provided, there will have to be many variations in the way it operates. Rather than being a single modifiable program package, a compiler may be employed. The user is given a specialized language for stating his needs, and this code is then compiled to produce the application program. There will be wide variations

in the languages used for such purposes, ranging from simple schemes for specifying reports or displays to application-oriented macroinstructions in programming languages.

**DIALOGUE**
**PROGRAM**
**GENERATORS**

A software tool that would take much of the work out of programming commercial real-time systems would be a dialogue program generator. The systems analyst would specify the terminal displays or printouts that he wants, the permissible responses to them from the user, and the error procedures.

When designing a dialogue, it is essential that the systems analysts try it out on live users. Furthermore, it is generally desirable that they explore the effect of alternative dialogue structures and obtain as much feedback from live users as they can. To do so, a computer is needed with the terminals in question. Sometimes a smaller computer is used than the one that is eventually installed.

The question then arises: How do we test the man-machine dialogue before we program it? How do we ensure that the dialogue structure and standards we give the programmers will in fact work? A simulator is needed for this purpose. The simulator is a general-purpose program that allows its user to specify a dialogue structure, punch details of it onto cards or enter it directly into a system, and then to try it out at terminals. The simulator will log the user's reactions in the experimental dialogue and produce a statistical summary. The simulator must be designed to be largely independent of the application and must be designed so that it can be used without a substantial programming effort.

One such program (described in the author's *Design of Man-Machine Dialogue*) allows its user to create a file of terminal displays and some branching logic associated with them. The terminal operator sees a display on the screen, enters a response, and then receives another display as a result of his response. In this way, all the dialogue associated with a particular operation can be stepped through, appearing to the operator as it would on the completed system. The operator's responses are recorded and the displays can be modified accordingly.

Such a program could be the basis for a dialogue program generator. After the simulation had been used to perfect the dialogue—a process during which many changes are usually made—the resulting card deck or file could be the input to a compiler. The compiler would generate a program that would handle such a dialogue and have an appropriate interface with the programs that process the input. Some simple dialogue program generators have already proved themselves to be very effective.

**NETWORK TRANSPARENCY**

It is desirable that the application programmer be isolated as completely as possible from the problems of the transmission network. He should give input-output macroinstructions with a symbolic terminal address and be unconcerned with how his data reach the terminal. We will refer to this facility as *network transparency*. The communication network, the term is saying, should be transparent to the programmer. He should perceive the terminal and its relation to his program, and know nothing about the layers in between.

The terminal in this case could be either local or remote, and it would make no difference to the application programs. The data would travel between the two with the same result. This capability has been referred to as *local-remote independence*.

In a system with network transparency, the application program could be transferred to a computer with a different communication-line network, and no change should be necessary. Again, the network may be changed without affecting the application program. The change may happen suddenly, for example, if a leased line fails and a dial-up connection is made, perhaps with a quite different line organization—for example, no multiplexing.

In order to achieve network transparency, some complex software for network control can be needed. The more sophisticated the network, the more software features are needed.

**TERMINAL TRANSPARENCY**

It may be desirable to have not only the network but also the terminal "transparent." If the software provides *terminal transparency*, a terminal of one type may be substituted for a terminal of another type, given the same symbolic address, and no change would be needed in the application programs. A user could dial the same program from a teletype machine, a visual display unit, an IBM 2740, or most other types of terminals. On a message-switching system, terminals of all different types could communicate.

Terminal transparency is probably not completely attainable between *all* terminals, because there is such a diversity of types. A few handle only digits; some only YES/NO or specially labeled lights. Some have elaborate editing logic or internal programming. Some handle graphics; some voice answerback.

It should be possible, however, to divide all terminals into a number of categories such that transparency is attainable within a category. This would seem a worthwhile objective in view of the increasing proliferation of terminals on the market. Many attempts at standardization have worked but within a limited group of machines, and new reasons have emerged for designing machines outside the restrictions or for inventing yet another level of standardization. The mess, as some would call it, is likely to become worse, not better; therefore there is great value in the concept of "terminal transparency."

It will be necessary to devise a mechanism or operator procedure that enables a terminal dialing in to indicate its type. For terminals on private lines, the software will be able to look up the terminal type, knowing its address.

**CODE**
**TRANSPARENCY**

A third form of transparency is *code transparency*, which occurs when a network and line-control scheme cannot transmit all possible combinations of bits. Some of the public data networks in certain countries require certain bit patterns for network functions, and these patterns must be unique. Most line-control schemes attach special significance to certain bit patterns.

To make it possible to transmit *any* bit pattern, as might occur, for example, in a computer program, the disallowed bit sequences must be broken up by the insertion of an extra bit or bits in some standard way. For instance, it may not be permissible to have more than five consecutive 1 bits. In this case, whenever five consecutive 1 bits occur, the transmission logic will always insert a zero bit after them, and the receiving logic will always delete it. In this way code transparency can be achieved.

**LOGICAL AND**
**PHYSICAL**
**TRANSMISSION**

Most systems analysts are familiar with the concept of logical and physical records on tape or disk. The *logical record* is the input or output of an application program. The *physical record* is what is actually written on tape or disk, and it often contains several logical records blocked together.

In data transmission, too, the block of data that travels over the link is different to the input-output message from the program but in more complex ways. Let us again call the program input-output item the *logical record* and the block that is transmitted the *physical transmission block.*

The logical record will have control characters and a destination address added to it in order that the destination device can receive it and operate correctly. Let us call the combination of logical record, address and control characters, the *terminal transmission block.* The terminal transmission block will in some cases have no data. It will simply be taking a controlling action as in error control or addressing. Sometimes it may have more than one address.

The *physical transmission block* may contain several terminal *transmission blocks*. It may also carry its own control bits, an address, and error detection bits.

While in many systems the characters in a terminal transmission block are contiguous, with some multiplexing schemes they are not. A simple multiplexer scans the low-speed lines that reach it, sequentially, and may compose a transmission record that has, in turn, one character from each line. Thus with a four-line multiplexer, the transmission from the multiplexer to the computer may consist of

Character from line 1
Character from line 2
Character from line 3
Character from line 4
Character from line 1
Character from line 2

.
.
.

This mixture may be demultiplexed by similar hardware at the computer, or it may be demultiplexed in the software. The converse takes place on transmission *from* the computer.

**LEVELS OF**      The levels of software producing the logical record,
**SOFTWARE**      the terminal transmission block, and the physical transmission block may be separate in systems of the future. Figure 27.1 shows possible layers of software on a teleprocessing system. On the left-hand side of the diagram is the application program which is processing transactions from a terminal on the right-hand side of the diagram. Between these are four levels of software.

Between the application programs and the telecommunication facilities are routines for handling certain types of terminal dialogue. The dialogues will take many forms on different systems. In some, they will include facilities for editing the input and output, for scanning through pages of information with a page-flip or scroll mechanism, for rapid browsing, for index searching, or other routine and well-defined operations. In other systems, the dialogue processing will be uniquely written for a particular application, perhaps with a dialogue program generator. Some of the terminal messages may be handled entirely by the dialogue-processing routines, and these routines will respond to the terminal. The routines, for example, may be carrying on a dialogue to collect data from the terminal operator, and when a complete set of information is collected about a particular transaction, it will be passed to the main application programs for processing and filing.

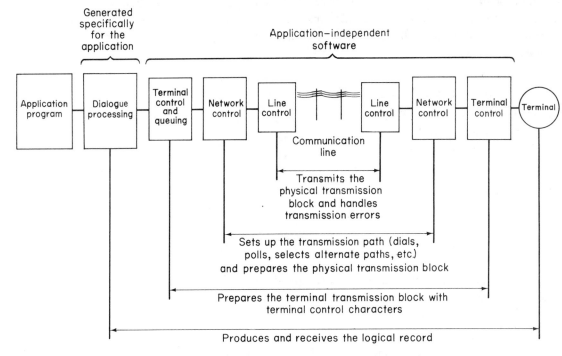

*Fig. 27.1.* Possible layers in data transmission software.

Either the application programs or their dialogue preprocessor will pass *logical records* to the telecommunications software. The records will be queued in dynamically organized buffer storage in the block labeled "terminal control and queuing." In this block the terminal control function will format the data into the *terminal transmission block*. This may be a simple operation that involves merely adding a control character and address. On the other hand, it may require code conversion or elaborate reformatting of the data. It is in this layer of software that "terminal transparency" is taken care of; and if the system handles multiple terminal types, the nature of the terminal in question is looked up, and appropriate conversion or reformatting is done.

The next software layer is the block labeled "network control." This will produce the *physical transmission block*, combining *terminal transmission blocks* if the network design requires this. The network control layer will set up the transmission path to the terminal. This may involve dialing. It may require the generation of polling messages.

When terminals dial in, the network-control software will establish communication with them and identify them.

The innermost blocks in Fig. 27.1 represent the function of line control—the actual transmission of the data. This function includes the recognition and generation of the characters used for loop control. It includes error checking and the handling of transmission errors.

**COMPLEX**
**NETWORKS**

Let us now see how these software layers might fit into line-control units, concentrators, and terminal-control units.

The three innermost layers in Fig. 27.1 are application independent and thus may be built into microprogramming or hardware logic rather than software. This is perhaps more likely to be true at the terminal end, rather than the computer end, and depends upon the relative cost of a stored-program machine. In some cases, the "terminal-control" and "network-control" functions will be trivial, as in a scheme designed for simple terminals always attached to leased voice lines.

Figure 27.2 shows a network with simple terminals connected to concentrators. The main computer has a line-control computer attached to it to handle the teleprocessing network, and therefore the software resides in three separate types of machine. The terminal-control, network-control, and line-control functions are all in the line-control computer rather than the main computer. The *physical transmission blocks* sent by the line-control computer are received by the software (firmware or hardware) in the concentrator. The network-control layer in the concentrator decomposes the *physical transmission blocks* from the computer center and forms *terminal transmission blocks*, which are sent on down the low-speed lines.

In Fig. 27.3 a more elaborate concentrator, which handles multidrop low-speed lines, is shown. The dialogue preprocessing function has been moved from the main computer to the concentration computer. The terminal-control function, in which the terminal transmission block is created, is also moved to the concentration computer. Both changes lessen the number of characters flowing on the line to the computer center and thus facilitate the attachment of the maximum numbers of terminals. The concentrator now uses two network-control layers, one for the high-speed line network and one for the low-speed network. The high- and low-speed networks may be quite incompatible in their mode of operation.

Figure 27.4 shows a wide variety of different network types and devices linked to the same computer center. The software layers are found in a variety of machines, as shown. Although many different procedures and techniques are used in the networks, the application programmer knows nothing of them

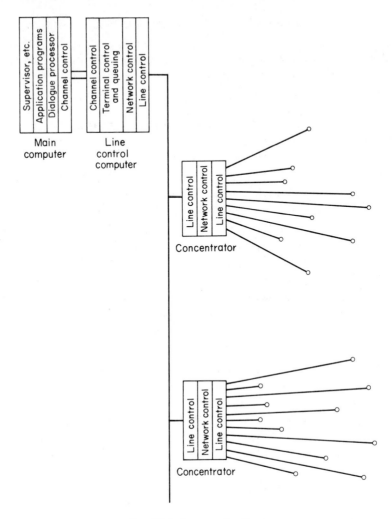

*Fig. 27.2.* Layers of software.

because network transparency, device transparency, and code transparency are achieved in software or equivalent "firmware."

Many varieties of similar schemes will probably be proposed. They will probably have in common the ability to isolate the application programmers from network complexities and to permit the changing of transmission facilities or terminals without the changing of application programs. Network transparency and terminal transparency are desirable objectives. In any complex system, modularity is essential in the design. The separate layers of software that have been shown, like the layers of an onion, are a form of modularity.

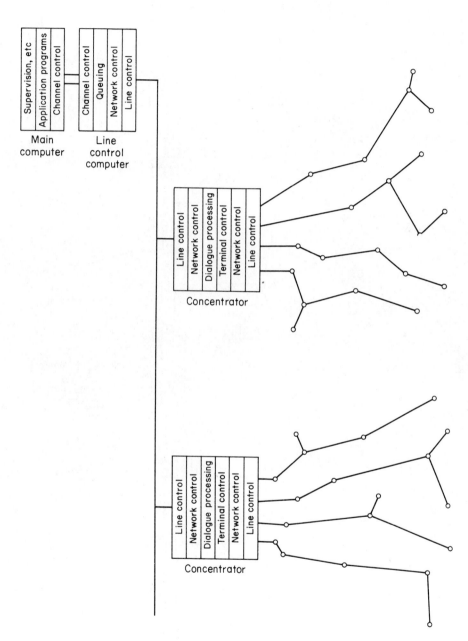

*Fig. 27.3.* Layer of software (with more functions in the concentrator than occur in Fig. 27.2).

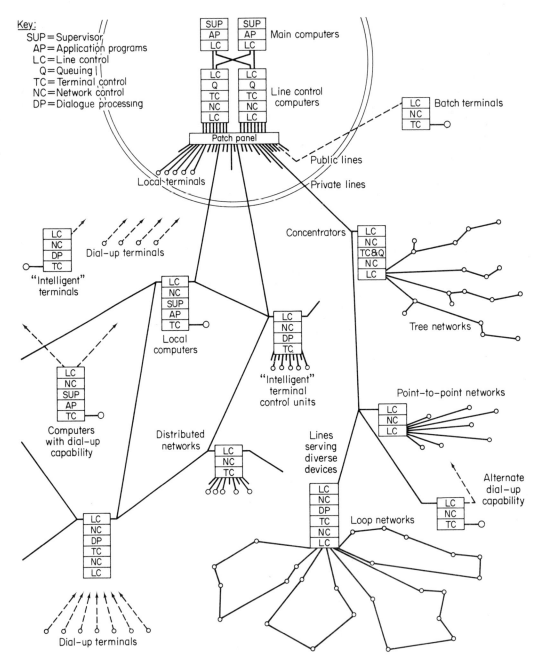

*Fig. 27.4.* The data transmission software of the future must serve all kinds of interlinked machines.

They permit one section of the system to be changed without its affecting the rest.

**ROUTING AND JOB CONTROL** An increasing number of networks are likely to connect more than one computer. There are two main reasons. The first is that *similar* computers can be connected for load sharing. This procedure, as the queuing theory of Section VI will show, can substantially decrease the turnaround time for batch jobs. The second is that computers with different facilities can be interconnected, to make a wide range of capabilities available to the user. In some cases, a job given to a small local computer will automatically be passed on to a larger or faster machine. A job requiring a particular data base may automatically be passed on to a machine having access to it.

The job-routing and job-control mechanisms of such a network will be part of future software. Perhaps a future *job control language* will be devised for users of multicomputer networks. Today, in the job control language, the user specifies parameters that enable the job to be scheduled in the job queues with appropriate priority and that enable the resources of one computer system to be allocated to it. In network systems the user may not know which computer his job is being run on but will specify parameters that enable the facilities of the network to be allocated appropriately.

**DIRECTORY FUNCTIONS** A terminal user will often have many different computer services available to him. A preliminary step in his work will be to find the right computer. At present he usually does so by dialing a known number. It may be desirable to have some form of directory services available to him at the terminal. He may type in the name of the service he needs and be automatically switched to it. He may carry on a dialogue with a directory routine to locate the facility he wants. In the future, he may have an entire "yellow pages" of computer services available to him on his terminal screen; and when he selects one, the computer he is using will automatically switch him to the machine offering that service. "Directory" software may become a standard part of computer networks.

Having selected a computer in this way, the user may not know where it is. The software in the machine his terminal is connected to may automatically route his messages to it.

**ENGINEERING DISCIPLINE** Many other new facilities will be needed in future software, especially in the intriguing area of controlling multicomputer networks.

It will become increasingly important for such software production to become a disciplined branch of engineering. As long as it is undisciplined, we will be plagued by bugs and by gross duplication of effort of different programming groups.

Often in programming there is a way to do something that is the *best* way— a best way to sift data, or do a table look-up, or invert a matrix, or search a file. However, time and again one finds individual programmers coding such operations, devising their own way of doing it, and often doing it in a far from optimal manner. To a greater degree in the years ahead, standard optimal routines for many of the basic operations of data processing must be made available, and their usage must be widely taught. Programming must change from being a cottage industry to being a scientifically planned mass-production industry. The programmers themselves should be encouraged to be highly competent professionals rather than be just promoted to administrative or systems analysis jobs as soon as they become proficient. The gospel of modular design, standardization, and clear documentation must spread through the industry so that program engineering acquires the formality of the older branches of engineering. After all, you would not build a battleship with poor planning, few engineering drawings, and hundreds of mechanics tinkering at will with their own piece of the construction. And some large programming systems are almost as complex as a battleship.

Standardization is going to increase the overhead required in core and computer time; but in view of the manpower bottleneck, it is overhead that we can ill afford to do without. Furthermore, the number of program bugs in modern software is becoming a serious problem. It is only by use of standardization and machine-generated routines that error-free software of immense complexity can be built up. As the number of lines of code in programming systems increases by a factor of ten, again, we cannot afford to let either the manpower requirements or the number of errors increase proportionately (and they tend to increase more as the square of the complexity if standardization techniques are not introduced).

A chain-reaction growth will occur when program developers learn to stand on one another's shoulders rather than, in the words of one bitter practitioner today, "standing on one another's feet."

# 28 WHAT TYPES OF CALCULATIONS ARE NEEDED?

Consider the following cautionary tales.

1. Lemming Associates, listed by *Fortune* as one of America's ten fastest-growing companies, has installed a real-time system that will enable the company to react immediately to customer demands or enquiries on the telephone. A few small cities were cut over first and the system thoroughly debugged. Now the day has arrived for the triumphant cutover of New York City. An advertising campaign has been prepared, and the company president is to attend the cutover ceremony.

New York City will increase the throughput of the system by 30 percent. The data processing manager intuitively feels that this will increase the response time by about 30 percent. The response time at present averages about 2 seconds, so this is nothing to worry about. Everyone is very pleased that such a fast response has been achieved. It is known that the central processing unit can handle several times its present load.

The New York terminals come into operation early in the morning, and it is soon apparent that the system is failing to handle the increased load as expected. The average response time drops to 4 seconds, then to 6 seconds. Some of the transactions take a quarter of a minute to receive a reply. The opening ceremony proceeds regardless, and the president is diplomatically cautioned that there is a minor and temporary technical problem.

An emergency program in the computer is brought into action, which deletes some transactions in core in the event of an overload and tells the associated terminal operators to "Repeat last message." This technique assumes

365

that the overload is a momentary one, caused perhaps by the chance occurrence of many persons entering a transaction at the same moment. Unfortunately, the operators, because of the presence of the president, are hyperalert and when told by the terminal to "Repeat last message" do so immediately. The result is that the overload is made even worse and few responses are obtained during the opening ceremony other than "Repeat last message."

Consequently, New York has to be taken off the system. The problem is that certain channels are severely overloaded, and the performance of the system degenerates rapidly when this point is reached. Correctly done design calculations would have indicated that the increment in load was enough to cause major channel queuing problems. Unfortunately, queuing had not been correctly taken into consideration in the calculations. A major redesign is needed and it is a year before New York is back on the air.

2. The Marble Trust, one of the nation's oldest and stateliest institutions, had installed a real-time savings bank system 2 years ago. The lines of customers at the teller windows, however, were longer now than before the system was installed. A junior employee submitted an idea to the bank's suggestion scheme. Take down the signs over the teller windows, he said, which direct customers to the windows on the basis of the position of their name in the alphabet (A–C, D–F, G–J, and so on). Instead, let the customers be free to go to whichever teller (and terminal) has the smallest line. After many months had elapsed (this was a big organization), the chairman of the bank saw the suggestion. Knowing no queuing theory, he dismissed it quickly as likely to cause further confusion. This, after all, was the way the teller windows had been organized for as long as he had been at the bank.

3. A time-sharing system was being installed in a Japanese electronics firm. Many of the research staff in different buildings were given inexpensive terminals at their desks. The system was brilliantly designed and programmed. The only snag was that the telephone company had initially failed to provide a sufficient number of paths through the PBX, and the users frequently obtained a busy signal.

With typical ingenuity the users rapidly discovered that they were obtaining busy signals when, in fact, not all the ports into the computer were occupied. Consequently, individuals began to look after their own interests by failing to disconnect once they had obtained a line to the computer. Instead, they would keep the line all afternoon because although they were not using it all the time, holding it would ensure its being available when they wanted it.

Finally, several months behind schedule, the telephone company enlarged the PBX. Unfortunately, the habit of failing to release the line had become ingrained, and now the PBX occupancy was several times what any design calculation would have revealed and even the new PBX was inadequate. The problem was solved by a resourceful Japanese programmer who programmed the machine to disconnect terminal users automatically if they had not transmitted for 5 minutes. It did not, however, disconnect his own terminal and he sometimes permitted close friends to use this.

4. Nathaniel Babbage, a sociology graduate from the University of East Anglia, is determined to prevent the system he is working on in England from running into the type of trouble he heard about on the other side of the Atlantic. For more than a year now he has been writing a simulation model. His great day comes when he presents its results at a monthly management meeting.

A consultant who is present at this meeting does a few calculations while examining the simulation model. He announces that he finds its results approximately correct but that, contrary to the belief of Mr. Babbage, the system is in danger of not working. Mr. Babbage indignantly asks how he can presume to check a year's simulation work with half an hour's calculations. The consultant explains that queuing equations and tables such as those in Martin's *Systems Analysis for Data Transmission* make it possible to check segments of the simulation. Mr. Babbage reflects that it had been his policy not to buy books that cost more than £3. The simulation, in fact, has been run at only one throughput value—the throughput that is forecast. At this throughput, the performance is adequate. However, queues exist such that a 20 percent increase in throughput would cause hopeless congestion and the system would cease to function.

A plot of the response time of the system against throughput would look as shown in Fig. 28.1. Simulating only one throughput value had not revealed the performance degradation that a slight increase in traffic would cause. The inaccuracy of the forecast figures, or the daily variation in traffic, might mean that the system would in fact suffer this degradation.

The consultant pointed out that the situation was easily remedied, for no use of multiplexing had been made in the line network. Instead of the large amount of time spent on simulation, a few analytical calculations and the consideration of more alternative design approaches would have been more profitable. The current configuration for the line network was twice as expensive as it need have been.

**THE USER'S POINT OF VIEW**  A good way to begin the design calculations is to start with the terminal user's point of view. What does he want from the system? What aspects of its behavior are important to him? What questions ought he to ask about the

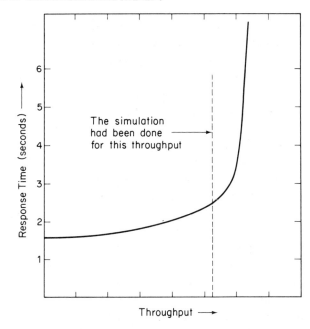

Figure 28.1

system performance? If we can determine the answers, then we can set about working out how to design the network with minimum cost. We must examine the costs and performance characteristics of alternative approaches and determine the possible trade-offs.

The user is concerned with the following factors:

1. On real-time systems, the main factor is the response time.
2. On non-real-time systems, other measures of speed are important—for example, on a batch system, the time required to transmit the batch, or the total throughput of the link, is important. On message-switching systems, the time from origination of the message to its delivery is the key factor.
3. On a real-time system or message-switching system, the time involved will vary. It is desirable to know how it varies. The *mean* time might be 3 seconds, for example; nevertheless, with some transactions the operator is kept waiting a quarter of a minute, which might be very undesirable. The data processing manager or the design team might ask for the standard deviation of response time as well as the mean or, better, the distribution of response times.
4. On some systems it is necessary to establish an interconnection with the computer before a real-time conversation begins. It may be necessary,

for example, to dial a computer. If there is only one response—a simple enquiry perhaps—the dialing and connection time may be included in the response time. If there is a lengthy conversation, the initial interconnection time may be unimportant compared to the response times once connected.

5. When dialing a computer, there is a certain probability that the call will not go through. The lines, the exchange circuits, or the ports into the computer might be fully occupied. It is worthwhile to evaluate this probability or rather to choose facilities sufficient to give the grade of service that has been decided on.

6. The user is concerned with the accuracy of the transmission. This will vary with the speed of transmission, the type of modem, and the error-detecting or correcting code that is used. Depending on these characteristics, an optimum block length can be chosen. This is particularly worthwhile in batch transmission.

**RESPONSE TIMES**

On a real-time system, the users judge the performance of the system mainly by the response times that they observe. Our calculations on such systems must be concerned with response times to a large extent.

Response time has been defined differently by different authorities. Indeed, it makes sense to define it differently on different types of systems. In our definition for real-time systems the response time may be the time between the operator's pressing the ENTER key on a display terminal and the appearance of the first character of the response on the screen. On a message-switching system, the definition might be "the time that elapses between the last action of sending a message and the start of its receipt at its correct destination."

The definitions could equally well, however, relate to the *completion* of receiving the response. On some systems, this might be thought more useful as a definition because it takes into consideration the speed of the transmission and display of the response. The response time on a typewriterlike terminal would be slower than on a screen terminal because of the slowness of printing. Again, when the terminal is used with a public line rather than a private line, the time for dialing the computer has sometimes been included in the definition of response time. It might be preferable, however, not to include it and to define interconnection time differently from response time.

Clearly, then, before calculating response times, a definition must be agreed upon. The proliferation of definitions does not matter provided that all parties involved agree on what is meant. Except where stated to the contrary, the definition given earlier (*the time that elapses between the last action the operator takes in sending the input and the start of the display of the output*) will be the one that is used for the calculations in this book.

The response time is a function of many factors. Sometimes the response time achieved is largely dominated by the communication link design, as we shall see. Sometimes, especially on systems with simple lines and one terminal per line, the transmission time is barely a factor in response time. Often much money can be saved by optimizing the mechanical structure and the geographical layout of the communication network, but this action must be taken in conjunction with detailed calculations of the effect it has on response time.

In *Design of Real-Time Computer Systems*[1] it was stressed that there are nine critical factors in the design of real-time systems. Any one of these factors could be a potential bottleneck in the flow of work through the system. Any one could be the factor that causes system degradation when certain volumes of data are encountered. The nine factors are:

1. Processing-unit core storage.
2. Processing time in the computer.
3. Peripheral file storage, for example, drums or disks.
4. Channel utilization.
5. Utilization of access mechanisms or read/write heads.
6. Communication-line utilization.
7. Utilization of the various devices used in transmission—concentrators, buffer storage, and so on.
8. Terminal utilization.
9. Capability of the terminal operators.

The first five of these are concerned exclusively with the computer center—the design of the processing unit, the channels, the supervisory programs, the file hardware, addressing and accessing methods, and so on. We shall not discuss these. We shall merely assume computer system response time, or rather a distribution of response times. Calculations and models concerning the computer center need to be tacked onto the calculations and models concerning communication lines in the following chapters.[1]

The aim in designing a real-time system is to achieve a balance between the various bottlenecks that can occur. There are many relationships between the above nine factors and these must be understood in the design process. In designing the data transmission network, there is no need to spend extra

[1] See James Martin, *Design of Real-Time Computer Systems* (Englewood Cliffs, N. J.: Prentice-Hall, 1967), Chaps. 23 ff.

money on achieving a fast response if the computer center cannot match it. On the other hand, it would be unfortunate to have a fine performance from the computer center and then have it badly degraded because of the communication network design. The author has observed the latter case on several systems of his acquaintance.

**ANSWERS IN TERMS OF PROBABILITY**     When a potential user asks such questions as: "What response time will I get at the terminals?" or "How long a delay will there be before I can enter a transaction?" the answers can only be given in terms of probability. This approach differs from many of the calculations done by a systems analyst, especially in batch-processing systems. He can calculate exactly how long it will take to read a certain tape or to print a quantity of information. The probabilistic nature of the calculations makes them considerably more difficult than on a batch-processing system.

The systems analyst must condition the users to ask the right type of question about a terminal system. It is reasonable to ask: "What is the mean response time?" or: "What is the standard deviation of response time?" It usually does not make sense to ask: "What is the maximum response time?" Transactions are entered at the whim of the human operators. Just as people make telephone calls at times of their own choosing, so in a real-time system, the times on which operators press the ENTER key, or equivalent, are not closely controlled. It is possible that all the operators could press their ENTER key at the same instant. If they did, the response time that some of them would receive would be very long. It is *extremely* improbable that this would happen on a system with many terminals; therefore we should not allow the user to ask: "What is the maximum response time?" Instead, we could give him a probability distribution of obtaining different response times. He might ask for a curve to be drawn such as the one in Fig. 28.2.

The effect of a chance peak in the system's traffic is to lengthen the response time. Momentary peaks that are greater than the system's capacity will occur now and then. Some transactions will then be delayed until the system can handle them.

Figure 28.3 illustrates the variation in message volume. It shows the peaks in traffic reaching a real-time system. The system could be designed so that its capacity is as represented by the line *AB*. It could then process all of the peaks without delay. This, however, would be wasteful, and normally systems are not designed to handle the largest peak in traffic. The system is more likely to be designed so that its capacity is represented by the line *CD*. Here the peaks cannot be processed as they occur but will be flattened by the system into the

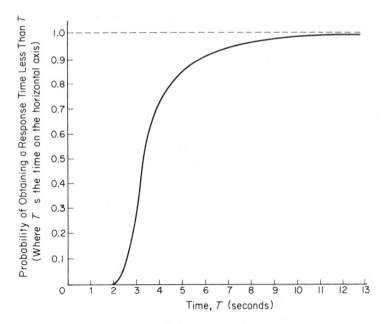

Fig. 28.2. Cumulative distribution of response times.

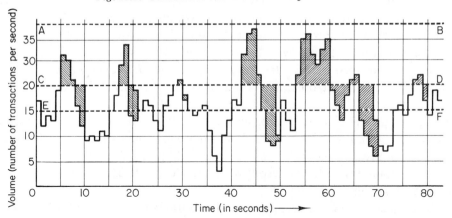

Fig. 28.3. Variation in volume of messages reaching the system. If the capacity of the system is *AB*, it can handle all the messages reaching it. If the capacity of the system is *CD*, the peaks of traffic cannot be handled as they occur but will be flattened as shown by the shaded areas below the line *CD*. This lengthens the response time as shown. If the capacity of the system is *EF*, it cannot handle all the messages reaching it.

shaded areas under the line CD. This will lengthen the time of the system's response to these transactions, as indicated by the shading. The shaded area under the line CD is equal to that above it. If the capacity of the system were represented by the line EF, then the system would be unable to process some of the transactions.

When making statements or guarantees about the performance of a real-time system, a probability statement must be used. The contract for several airline reservations systems has said, for example, that the system must be able to handle 90 percent of the transactions reaching it with a response of 3 seconds or less. It is just such a statement that will result from the estimating calculations.

**THE EFFECT OF CHANGES IN LOAD**    The behavior of most real-time systems varies with the load they handle. It varies in a different manner on different systems and it is important to understand the nature of the variation. On most real-time systems, the load varies considerably from one time to another. On some systems, the load is much higher on certain days of the year than on others. On a savings bank system, the design may be dominated by the flood of customers who come into the bank at lunchtime. On other systems, special considerations cause a very high load at certain times. A strike of airline employees in the United States, for example, can cause a very high load on international carriers. Certain market circumstances can cause a very high load on a stock market information system.

The utilization of some elements of the system does not vary uniformly with load. Queues build up. Storage areas become filled and paths through an exchange are occupied. It is therefore useful to plot the performance characteristics we are interested in against load on the system. Diagrams like those in Fig. 28.5, which show the variation in mean and standard deviation of a performance parameter with load, may be plotted. If a distribution curve is drawn as in Fig. 28.2, it should be a family of curves, rather than one curve as in Fig. 28.4.

Curves plotting the mean and standard deviation of response time as in Fig. 28.5 can assume a variety of different shapes. It is only by knowing the shape of such a curve that a designer will obtain a "feel" for the behavioral characteristics of the system he is putting together.

A skillful driver has an excellent feel for the behavioral characteristics of his car. He knows that if he depresses the accelerator too suddenly, the acceleration of the car will not immediately be proportional to the foot pressure. He knows that he can take a certain curve at 30 miles per hour in third gear, but if he drives at that speed in fourth gear he will end up in the ditch. Similarly, we need to have a feel for the behavior of the real-time computer system we are designing or thinking of purchasing. Unfortunately, we do not understand its behavioral characteristics instinctively. Often, indeed, our intuitive feeling can lead us surprisingly astray. It improves with practice, of course, but in general it is not to be trusted. It can be observed that most people's intuition about the behavior of communication-based systems leads them to make the

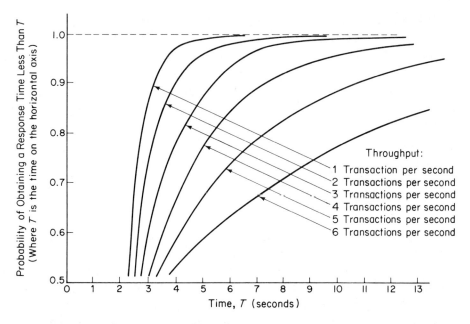

*Fig. 28.4.* Response time distributions for different throughput rates.

wrong guess sufficiently often for it to be dangerous. We need to calculate how the system will behave and to express the results of our calculations in such a way that the implications can be clearly grasped.

The curves in Fig. 28.5 showing how terminal response times vary with the system throughput are typical. The curves all swing upward as the congestion in the system increases, just as the time to drive through a city increases with

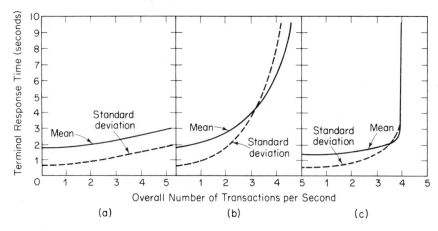

*Fig. 28.5.* The curves showing variation of response times with throughput can assume a variety of different shapes.

the number of vehicles on the streets. A number of different elements of time will have been added together to obtain these figures.

The slope of the curves gives an indication of the stability of the system. The system illustrated in diagram (a), for example, is fairly stable. Suppose that this is the system for an application that normally expects two transactions per second in the peak hour. If there is a sudden but temporary rise in the demands on the system and the throughput rises to four transactions per second for a period, the system will be able to handle this increase without a noticeably bad degradation of performance. If the system in diagram (b), however, is planned for two transactions per second, this situation will be less stable. A temporary rise to four transactions per second will provide a decided rise in the mean response time. Also, the standard deviation of response time has risen severely, and now a significant proportion of transactions will have to wait a long time for a response. By a rough approximation, 10 percent will have to wait more than 16 seconds; 5 percent will have to wait more than 22 seconds.

With the system in diagram (c), the situation is still worse. Here two transactions per second are handled comfortably with a low response time, but if the throughput doubles temporarily, the system will be completely unable to handle it. The traffic will back up endlessly like a Friday evening rush hour when the roads become blocked.

The system in diagram (c) is particularly dangerous if the designer, like Mr. Babbage in our earlier story, has not investigated the whole shape of the curve. He may have explored that part between one and three transactions per second, perhaps using the simulation technique discussed in Chapter 38. In this case, his results will look good and he will be ignorant of the fact that the system is going to seize up between three and four transactions per second. (Many of the simulation studies the author has examined have investigated only one point on the curve.)

The shape of the curve in diagram (c)—misleading though it is if you omit that part to the right of three transactions per second—is typical of many actual systems. The sudden swoop upward is often caused by one particular bottleneck that does not contribute in a major way to the overall response time when the throughput is low but nevertheless reaches its maximum throughput at this point.

**UNRELIABLE LOAD ESTIMATES**   A number of communication-based systems have notoriously overshot their design estimates. One of the causes for this is that many more messages were sent to the working system than was originally counted. A large proportion of the systems in operation have found themselves processing or being required to process substantially more transactions than were written down in the original estimates.

One of the reasons for this situation is that terminal operators of certain types of systems tend to use the terminal simply because it is there, without realizing the effect they are having on the system as a whole. This needs to be foreseen and carefully controlled. Operators must not be allowed to press keys for the sake of pressing keys. However, many systems are used more than anticipated because they are useful. Experience on some systems for storing and forwarding administrative messages has been that, after the system has been in operation for a time, the number of administrative messages is double that before the system was used. Enquiry terminals on other systems are likely to be used far more frequently than data collection based on previous facilities would indicate.

**PARKINSON'S LAW OF REAL-TIME SYSTEMS** One of my earlier books suggested a Parkinson's law of real-time systems saying that "*If operator terminals provide a useful service, their utilization will expand to fill the system capacity.*" This has undoubtedly been foreseen by the computer manufacturers wishing to sell more equipment, but it can make a mockery of the design calculations.

Indeed, since writing the preceding statement, the systems I have observed have suggested a second and somewhat more cynical Parkinsonian-type law: *If a communication-based system is sufficiently complex, it is installed before it is designed!*

It certainly appears that, with many systems, the traffic being handled by the system cannot be assessed with any accuracy until after the system has been installed. This paradoxical situation can only be resolved by installing equipment that can be expanded or, possibly, contracted, easily. The ranges of computers now available that are truly modular are essential in this field.

A business system may be deliberately planned in two models. The first may be partially an experimental system and will collect data of its own actual operation for design of the second system. In installing a system for switching administrative traffic, for example, the system may be such that it can handle what is thought to be the present-day volumes. When the system is installed, measurements will be made of the load passing through it and of any extra use that may be made of it. Its network, storage, or number of files may then be increased as required to increase the throughput, lessen the waiting times, or increase the message-storage facilities. A real-time business system should always be designed to maintain statistics about its own operation so that when a further model of the system is installed, the best design data will be available.

The design calculations in this situation should explore a wide range of possible traffic loads. They should concentrate on determining the best of the many alternative ways the system and network can be constructed. The systems analyst should concentrate to a large extent on questions like "What are the best *types* of equipment he can buy?" and "What are the best *types* of approaches he should recommend?" The techniques in the following chapters will help to answer these questions.

# 29 THE DESIGN PROCESS

When a scientist looks at the world, he is prone to build models of it. Sometimes they are physical models like the double helix representing the DNA molecule. Sometimes they are mathematical models like Newton's set of equations explaining the motions of planets in the solar system. Sometimes they are models in which simple logical ideas interact like Freud's explanations of human behavior or like a simulation of car movements on a railroad.

The scientist does not pretend that his model is an exact representation of reality. Often, he knows that he has ignored certain influencing factors. He might have used the equations of motion, for example, without taking friction into consideration. He might have modeled a nuclear reaction as though the particles involved were solid like billiard balls. However, he usually claims two things for his model: first, it gives him insight into the way the world works—insight that he could not have obtained without it; second, it is useful. It enables him to make predictions, build working products, or take actions that change events. He can build a bridge or synthesize a new drug. He can use a computer to simulate the explosion of a nuclear device without violating the test-ban treaty.

A systems analyst can also build models when he is designing a new system. He might model a parallel programming mechanism, a data base, or a proposed real-time system. We shall use models in our discussion of the design of data transmission networks, realizing, again, that these models are not always exact. We have to make assumptions that simplify the model building. We make some assumptions in practice because we do not know all the facts exactly. However, once more we make two claims for the models: they provide us with insight that is valuable in the planning of data transmission systems and they are useful. They enable us to construct networks that meet our performance criteria at near-minimum cost. They enable us to make decisions between alternate methods of operating. Indeed, when a mathematician says he has solved a problem relating to real life, he often means that he has constructed a model of the process in equations, and he solved the equations.

**THREE LEVELS**
**OF COMPLEXITY**
In practical systems engineering, calculations are likely to be done at three levels.

### 1. Scrap-Paper Calculations

In the beginning the systems analyst wants to see whether an idea is feasible. Generally he can choose among several alternative approaches. He wants to do *quick* calculations that are accurate enough to enable him to decide between approaches and test feasibility. Such calculations can be made using the tables in Appendix VIII and the methods discussed in the following chapters. In doing these approximate calculations, he will make a number of simplifying assumptions. It is often useful for a systems analyst to be able to give quick answers to questions—for example, in a monthly meeting. Some typical questions would be: "What effect would it have on the network if we had a 5-second rather than a 3-second response time?" or "What effect would it have if we used a new expensive modem that operates at 9600 bits per second rather than 4800?" or "Should type A messages be given priority over type B?" Good enough answers can often be obtained with scrap-paper calculations.

### 2. Programmed Analytical Models

For more elaborate calculations, a computer program may be written. By using a computer, the systems analyst can plot curves like those discussed in the previous chapter. The reader may glance ahead to such curves in Chapters 36, 37, and 39, which were obtained from models programmed using queuing theory. In determining the optimum geographical layout of lines, in determining which of many terminals are connected to public and which to private lines, and in determining the location of concentrators or multiplexers, we again use computer programs.

### 3. Simulation Models

The mathematical models, even when programmed, contain simplifying assumqtions. They do not represent the communication lines exactly. In order to obtain an exact representation, as with other processes in the system design, simulation may be used. This is discussed in Chapter 38.

Simulation programs take more computer time and usually take longer to write than models produced with mathematical equations. They would have to be run many times to plot curves of how a performance measure varies with throughput. Often, therefore, we can obtain more insight into what is happening by using a mathematical approach. Consequently, a designer may use mathematics to determine the overall perspective and to determine what should be simulated; he may then use simulation to explore the exact behavior of a line, with its concentrators, polling mechanisms, and so on.

A systems analyst should maintain a sense of perspective as to what technique is appropriate at what time. It is a good rule to say that he should never use simulation until he has attempted to obtain equivalent results by approximate hand calculations first. High-fidelity mathematical models of computer processes have proved difficult to construct; as a result, many analysts and designers have turned to simulation. Often, however, an approximate mathematical model can sometimes be of more value than a more exact simulation model because of the ease with which the effect of changing the variables can be explored. The accuracy needed may be a determining factor in the type of model that is used. Until a system is working, there is usually only an approximate knowledge of the input data for the design—the traffic volumes and message lengths, for example. In this case, there may be no point in striving for very high fidelity in the models. Sufficient accuracy is needed to discover which of several alternative possibilities is the best course to take.

**STEPS IN THE DESIGN PROCEDURE**

Frequently a lengthy sequence of steps is necessary in designing a data transmission network. For a large network, the geographical layout of the lines can be a complex process, but before the layout is made, decisions have to be taken about the techniques to be used on the lines—multiplexers, exchanges, concentrators, etc. Calculations must be made about the permissible loadings of whatever facilities are contemplated.

The design procedure will often be an iterative process. At first a guess as to a possible network may be made. Calculations will be done to see whether this fulfills the requirements. If it does not, the system will be adjusted until it does fulfill them. If it does, alternative approaches will be tried with a view to minimizing the network cost. Once a particular form of network has been decided upon, various computer algorithms are available for establishing an optimum configuration of that network. Figure 29.1 shows a possible sequence of steps. Designing communications facilities may be only one step in a larger process of designing a real-time system.

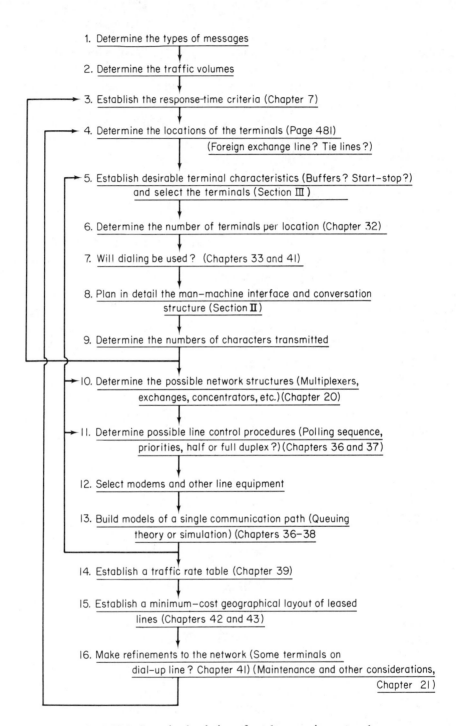

1. Determine the types of messages

2. Determine the traffic volumes

3. Establish the response-time criteria (Chapter 7)

4. Determine the locations of the terminals (Page 481)
    (Foreign exchange line? Tie lines?)

5. Establish desirable terminal characteristics (Buffers? Start-stop?)
    and select the terminals (Section III )

6. Determine the number of terminals per location (Chapter 32)

7. Will dialing be used? (Chapters 33 and 41)

8. Plan in detail the man-machine interface and conversation
    structure (Section II)

9. Determine the numbers of characters transmitted

10. Determine the possible network structures (Multiplexers,
    exchanges, concentrators, etc.)(Chapter 20)

11. Determine possible line control procedures (Polling sequence,
    priorities, half or full duplex?)(Chapters 36 and 37)

12. Select modems and other line equipment

13. Build models of a single communication path (Queuing
    theory or simulation) (Chapters 36–38

14. Establish a traffic rate table (Chapter 39)

15. Establish a minimum-cost geographical layout of leased
    lines (Chapters 42 and 43)

16. Make refinements to the network (Some terminals on
    dial-up line? Chapter 41) (Maintenance and other considerations,
    Chapter 21)

*Fig. 29.1.* Steps in the design of a teleprocessing network

**TRAFFIC PEAKS**   The process begins by determining what types of messages are to be transmitted. Then, for each type, it is necessary to determine the volumes of traffic at each location. The volumes will vary with the time of day and the day of the year. This variation must be investigated and the peak loads established. It is a good idea to plot curves showing the variation, such as those in Figs. 29.2 and 29.3.

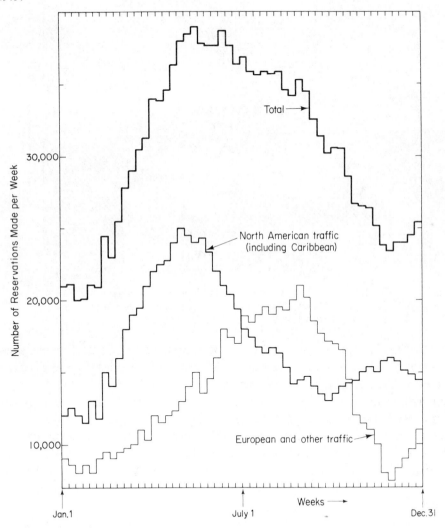

*Fig. 29.2.* The number of reservations made each week on an airline. The communications facilities must be sufficient to handle the peak traffic. The peaks on different parts of the network do not coincide here.

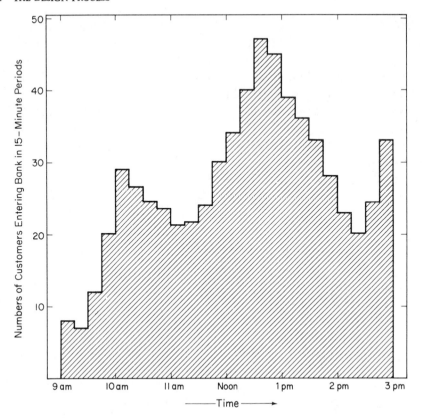

*Fig. 29.3.* The daily variation in loading in a savings bank. The figures were obtained by counting the customers entering the bank during 15-minute periods.

In Fig. 29.2 the traffic from different regions has peaks at different times of the year. This variation is helpful in the design of the central system because it means that the total peak is less severe than it would otherwise be. The communication network, however, must be designed to handle the regional peaks. It is possible that some days of the year might have a higher load than that indicated by the weekly average shown. The daily volumes should be listed to check for this possibility. Such listings will sometimes be a by-product of an existing data processing installation, although the new system will often be used in a new way and there are only indirect methods of estimating its potential traffic.

Figure 29.3 shows the variation in load within the day. Again, like Fig. 29.2, its resolution may not be fine enough. During the lunch hour, or just before closing time, there may be 5-minute periods having a substantially higher load than one-third of that of the quarter-hour periods shown. A 5-minute count might be plotted.

Abnormal circumstances may give peaks higher than those plotted. The systems designer has to make up his mind what level of peak he really wants to handle. Does he want to build a system that performs with the peak load of the peak day? If so, it may be seriously underutilized at other times. Does he want to build in enough slack to handle emergencies?

The peak 5 minutes may be many times higher than the average load on some systems. In a factory with work stations on the shop floor, for example, the period just before the workers leave for lunch or home is likely to have a massive surge of transactions. In one case this peak is 10 to 20 times the average. A system designed to handle it would be certain to have many of its components underutilized at other times. The processing unit can be occupied with background work but the line and terminal facilities cannot. In some types of systems, a local and relatively inexpensive concentrator may absorb the flood and transmit the transactions onward to the computer center at its leisure. The concentrator may be programmed to respond to the terminals. The desirability of such techniques must emerge from the design calculations.

Possible increases in the traffic must be considered whether they come from the natural growth of the organization, from temporary volume surges, or from the Parkinson's law of real-time systems in the previous chapter. The network design should therefore be done for a range of traffic volumes. The cost of the network will usually be a step function increasing discontinuously with volume because when a line or a device reaches its reasonable maximum, another line or device must be added. Again when a certain volume is reached, a structural change may be desirable. The calculations in the chapters ahead will explore the changes in cost or structure of a network with increasing volume.

**DETERMINING THE TYPE OF LINE ORGANIZATION**     Step 3 in Fig. 29.1 is the establishment of the response-time criteria as discussed in Chapter 7. This can have a major effect on the types of devices that are permissible on the communication lines.

Next we must establish where the terminals are going to be. On some systems there is little or no scope for discussion on this point. A terminal is located in each sales office, for example. On other systems it is a major question. The airlines have terminals in a limited number of locations, not in every city where bookings are made. If you telephone Pan American in Boston about your flight, for instance, your call is routed to girls at terminals in New York, on TELPAK lines shared with other airlines. Determining whether to put terminals in Boston or in other cities is a major cost trade-off calculation. It will be discussed further in Chapter 32.

Similarly, we must determine how many terminals are needed in each location to handle the traffic load. There may be lines of people requiring service from the terminal operators. The queues may be physical as at a teller's window or they may consist of telephone users becoming impatient at the supposedly smoothing tones of a prerecorded voice. There may be no queues at all; people simply go away if some types of terminal are not available when needed. The probability calculations necessary for studying these situations are discussed in Chapter 32.

Step 5 of Fig. 29.1 is to determine the desirable terminal characteristics (Chapters 12 and 13). The characteristics affecting response time are the speed of output (typewriter, higher-speed printer or screen), whether or not the device has buffers, whether it is designed for use on full-duplex lines, what control characters it needs in the transmission, whether it can be multidropped on a line and if so how it responds to polling, and how long it takes to turn around the direction of transmission.

Step 7 of Fig. 29.1 asks whether dialing will be used from the terminal to the computer. If dialing is used, it is necessary to decide on a figure for the probability of failure to establish the connection. This enables the numbers of computer ports, tie lines, paths through the exchanges, and other facilities to be determined with the probability calculations of Chapter 33. Sometimes it is quite inacceptable to use dialing because of the delay involved. When dialing is acceptable, it is sometimes economical to have some of the terminals on dial-up and some on leased lines. This is discussed in Chapter 41.

Before we can examine the operation of the line in detail and determine such factors as how many terminals can be placed on it, the lengths of the messages must be determined. A distribution of message lengths is required. If the system is one in which a conversation takes place between computer and terminal user, the structure of the conversation must be known in some detail. A detailed study of it, preferably with a man-machine simulator, will help and should provide the design figures needed.

On many systems, the detailed structure of the man-machine conversation has changed during the programming and implementation of the system. Almost invariably the total number of characters transmitted increases when this change occurs. Sometimes the number of characters in a message increases, and sometimes the number of messages increases. In either case, it is necessary to change the communication line network. In some systems, the refining of the man-machine interface has resulted in the network cost more than doubling. The designer should be alert to this danger.

When the message lengths are known, it may be necessary to reiterate the design. The cost may be too high. It may be desirable to slacken the response-time requirement or to change the terminal equipment to give more suitable facilities.

Various approximate calculations may now be made to determine whether devices such as multiplexers, private exchanges, or concentrators could be used on the lines. The list of possible means of lowering the network cost in Chapter 20 should be checked over. At the same time, the modems may be selected. As we shall see, it is important to pay attention to modem turnaround time as well as transmission speed on a multidrop line.

At this stage, models of a single communication path, from terminal to computer, may be constructed. Such models are discussed in Chapters 36, 37, and 38. The response times indicated by the models will be examined. A plot should be produced of how they, and their standard deviation, vary with throughput. The models may be adjusted to investigate the effect of differing the line organizations and the characteristics of the terminals, modems, and other equipment.

The line models that are built, whether using queuing theory or simulation, will make it possible to produce a traffic rate table (step 14 in Fig. 29.1) which states the maximum traffic loads that are permissible with different numbers of terminals on the lines. Chapter 39 discusses this.

The geographical layout can then begin. With multidrop lines spanning many cities, there are an immense number of different ways of interconnecting the terminals. With concentrators, multiplexers, and private exchanges, the problem becomes much more complex. A variety of different algorithms and techniques is in use for layout of data transmission networks. None of them (at the time of writing) is a panacea. Some compute a minimum-cost network by trial and error but fail to consider all the various devices that could be used on such a network. Some make mathematical assumptions, again, that convert the problem into a similar, but simpler, problem which is easier to solve. Nevertheless, the systems analyst, if he is able to survey the tools available to him in perspective, can fit together a network of near-minimum cost.

Having done so, he may still want to reiterate. He may want to change the design to put stored-program capability in the concentrators. He may want to change the locations of the terminals or reconsider the use of some dial-up connections. These techniques are discussed in Chapters 40 to 43.

# 30   SOME BASIC STATISTICS

As noted in Chapter 28, the results of most of our calculations on data transmission networks have to be expressed in terms of statistics. We talk about the *mean* response time, the *mean* throughput, and so on. In addition to talking about the means, we need a measure of dispersion. If possible, we would like to obtain a complete distribution of many of the quantities we deal with.

**STANDARD**
**DEVIATION**

A number of measures of dispersion will be used, the most important of which is the *standard deviation*.

Often the results of calculations will be quoted in terms of a mean and standard deviation, as in Fig. 28.7.

The standard deviation is probably the most illuminating of the various measures of dispersion. It is in the same units as the mean (unlike the variance and second moment). If the mean is in seconds, the standard deviation is also in seconds. An approximate feel for the significance of the standard deviation can be obtained from Fig. 30.1, which shows a typical distribution curve for a continuous spread of values. The area under any portion of the curve is proportional to the number of occurrences that have a value within that range. If a set of values of some parameter follows a distribution that is roughly symmetrical and unimodal (i.e., has only one hump as in Fig. 30.1), then it is usually the case that roughly two-thirds of the values lie within one standard deviation on either side of the mean. About 96 percent of the values lie within two standard deviations of the mean, and less than 1 percent of the transactions lie beyond the range of three standard deviations from the mean.

If we say, for example, that the IQs of a group of systems analysts have a mean of 135 and a standard deviation of 10, then we know that about two-thirds

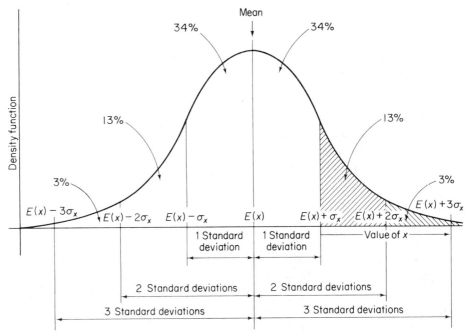

*Fig. 30.1.* If we know that a set of values follows a distribution that is fairly symmetrical and unimodal (i.e., has only one hump), we usually tend to picture a distribution that is something like the above (a normal distribution).

of the group have IQs between 125 and 145. About 2 percent of them are geniuses with an IQ above 155, and about 2 percent are struggling below 115.

The curve drawn in Fig. 30.1 is actually that of a *normal distribution.* The curve could equally well have been drawn for a situation where the standard deviation is smaller, in which case it would have been thinner; or where the standard deviation is larger, in which case it would have been more spread out. The labeling on the diagram would have been unchanged. Figure 30.2 shows six sets of values of a variable *x.* The three sets at the top half of the diagram have different means but the same standard deviation. The three sets at the bottom have the same means but different standard deviations. In any of these sets of values, however, it is true that two-thirds of the values lie within one standard deviation of the mean and about 96 percent lie within two standard deviations of the mean.

The reader who does not already automatically form a picture in his mind when he hears the words standard deviation should remember Figs. 30.1 and 30.2. If his broker then tells him that the value of his stock holdings can be expected to reach $30,000 in 2 years, but with a standard deviation of $10,000, he can picture what this means. (My broker would not dare be so precise!)

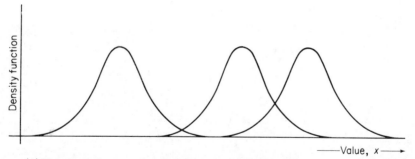

(a) Three sets of values of x with different means but the same standard deviation

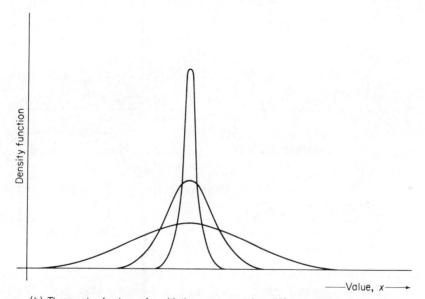

(b) Three sets of values of x with the same mean but different standard deviations

*Fig. 30.2.* For any of these six sets of values the figures in Fig. 30.1 apply, because they are all normal distributions.

**RESPONSE TIMES**    Not all the distributions we meet are normal distributions. The distribution curves sometimes have a different shape from those in Figs. 30.1 and 30.2. Many of the factors we deal with in everyday life are almost normally distributed—for example, the weights, heights, and IQs of the population, the errors made in measurement, the distance by which I miss the bull's eye on a dart board, and the daily fluctuations of the stock market. Unfortunately, most of the variables discussed in the following chapters are not *normally* distributed. The response time on communication-based systems, for example, does not follow a normal distribution. More typically, it would be distributed as in Fig. 30.3. The distribution is skewed toward the upper side. This distribution

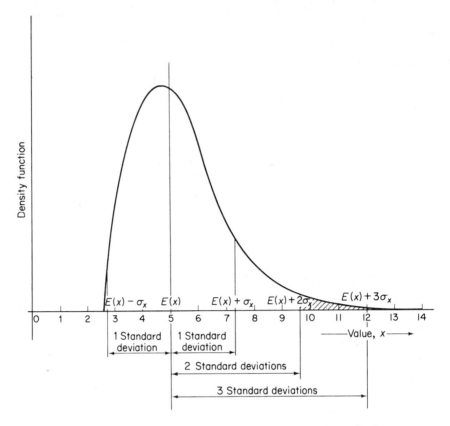

*Fig. 30.3.* Response time does not follow a normal distribution. This distribution would be more typical.

could be taller or flatter. As we shall see later, if the standard deviation is low, it will tend to be less skewed and closer to a normal distribution. If the standard deviation is higher, it will tend to be more skewed.

In order to have a complete knowledge of the set of values, we need to know the mean, the standard deviation, and the type of distribution. We shall endeavour to find these factors in subsequent chapters when evaluating response times.

Meanwhile, let us mention a very useful rule of thumb. It turns out in most of our calculations that *the 95 percentile of response time is close to the mean response time + two standard deviations.* In other words, about 5 percent of the responses take longer than this value. This rule, of course, is approximate. It will differ somewhat from system to system. However, it is surprising how often it holds true, and later we shall see some of the rationale behind it. For the moment, the reader seeking to attach a meaning to the words standard deviation may remember this rule. Look again, now, at Fig. 28.5 with the rule in mind.

**CALCULATION OF STANDARD DEVIATIONS**

Let us suppose that we have $N$ discrete values of a variable $x$ and we wish to calculate its standard deviation.

We shall always refer[1] to the mean of $x$ as $E(x)$ (the expected value of $x$). We will refer to the standard deviation of $x$ as $\sigma_x$.

The standard deviation is the root-mean-square deviation of the values. To calculate it for a set of discrete values of $x$, we carry out the following steps:

1. Calculate $E(x)$, the mean value of $x$.
2. Calculate the deviation of each value of $x$ from the mean, $[x - E(x)]$.
3. Calculate the mean value of the square of this deviation:

$$\frac{\sum [x - E(x)]^2}{N}$$

4. Calculate the square root of this mean:

$$\sigma_x = \sqrt{\frac{\sum [x - E(x)]^2}{N}} \tag{30.1}$$

The process is illustrated in Table 30.1. Here we have 20 discrete values of $x$, given in the left-hand column. Their mean is 80. The next columns calculate $[x - E(x)]$ and $[x - E(x)]^2$. Summing the right-hand column and dividing by 20 gives

$$\frac{\sum [x - E(x)]^2}{N} = 880$$

Hence $\sigma_x$ is found to be 29.66.

When a statistician is talking about *samples* taken rather than specific values, such as the preceding ones, he calculates the standard deviation dividing by $N - 1$ rather than by $N$, where $N$ is the number of samples. So we have

$$\sigma_x = \sqrt{\frac{\sum (x - \bar{x})^2}{N - 1}} \tag{30.2}$$

($\bar{x}$ is written for the sample mean.)

If the values of $x$ in the Table 30.1 were samples, then the standard deviation would be $\sqrt{926.32} = 30.24$.

---

[1] Appendix I contains a complete list of the notation used in this book.

**Table 30.1.** CALCULATION OF THE STANDARD DEVIATION OF 20 DISCRETE VALUES OF THE VARIABLE $x$

| Twenty Values of $x$ | $[x - E(x)]$ | $[x - E(x)]^2$ |
|---|---|---|
| 30 | $-50$ | 2500 |
| 50 | $-30$ | 900 |
| 120 | $+40$ | 1600 |
| 100 | $+20$ | 400 |
| 70 | $-10$ | 100 |
| 80 | 0 | 0 |
| 40 | $-40$ | 1600 |
| 140 | $+60$ | 3600 |
| 60 | $-20$ | 400 |
| 100 | $+20$ | 400 |
| 80 | 0 | 0 |
| 30 | $-50$ | 2500 |
| 110 | $+30$ | 900 |
| 90 | $+10$ | 100 |
| 60 | $-20$ | 400 |
| 70 | $-10$ | 100 |
| 120 | $+40$ | 1600 |
| 100 | $+20$ | 400 |
| 70 | $-10$ | 100 |
| 80 | 0 | 0 |
| TOTAL 1600 | | TOTAL 17,600 |

$$\text{Mean, } E(x) = \frac{1600}{20} = 80 \qquad \frac{\sum [x - E(x)]^2}{20} = 880$$

$$\sigma_x = \sqrt{880} = 29.66$$

The larger the number of samples taken, the more accurate will be the assessment, both of the mean and the standard deviation. When $N$ is large, the difference between the preceding equations becomes negligible.

**OTHER MEASURES OF DISPERSION**

Several alternative measures of dispersion exist. Thus we shall find it helpful to employ the following terms also in this book.

1. *The Variance*

The variance is the square of the standard deviation. We shall write it as Var $(x)$.

## 2. *The Second Moment*

The second moment is the mean of all of the values of the variable squared. In other words, for a set of $N$ values of the variable $x$, we square each value and take the mean of these.

$$\frac{\sum x^2}{N}$$

We will write $E(x^2)$ for second moment because this notation will remind you how it is calculated. Table 30.2 shows the calculation of the second (and third) moments of the same set of values as in Table 30.1.

**Table 30.2.** CALCULATION OF THE SECOND AND THIRD MOMENTS OF 20 DISCRETE VALUES OF THE VARIABLE $x$

| Twenty Values of $x$ | $x^2$ | $x^3$ |
|---|---|---|
| 30 | 900 | 27,000 |
| 50 | 2,500 | 125,000 |
| 120 | 14,400 | 1,728,000 |
| 100 | 10,000 | 1,000,000 |
| 70 | 4,900 | 343,000 |
| 80 | 6,400 | 512,000 |
| 40 | 1,600 | 64,000 |
| 140 | 19,600 | 2,744,000 |
| 60 | 3,600 | 216,000 |
| 100 | 10,000 | 1,000,000 |
| 80 | 6,400 | 512,000 |
| 30 | 900 | 27,000 |
| 110 | 12,100 | 1,331,000 |
| 90 | 8,100 | 729,000 |
| 60 | 3,600 | 216,000 |
| 70 | 4,900 | 343,000 |
| 120 | 14,400 | 1,728,000 |
| 100 | 10,000 | 1,000,000 |
| 70 | 4,900 | 343,000 |
| 80 | 6,400 | 512,000 |
| Total 1600 | Total 145,600 | Total 14,500,000 |

Mean, $E(x) = \dfrac{1600}{20} = 80$

Second moment
$= E(x^2) = \dfrac{145,600}{20}$
$= 7,280$

Third moment
$= E(x^3) = \dfrac{14,500,000}{20}$
$= 725,000$

## 3. *Percentiles*

A percentile states that a certain percentage of the values in question are greater than a given value. Thus if 5 percent of the response times are greater than 4 seconds, we say that the 95 percentile response time is 4 seconds.

**THE MOMENTS**     We have just discussed the second moment $E(x^2)$. The first moment is the same as the mean, $E(x)$. We can also calculate a third moment, $E(x^3)$, a fourth moment, $E(x^4)$, and so on ad infinitum. The first and second moments tell us much of what we would like to know about a set of values, but not everything. The third moment, which is in effect a measure of the skewness of a distribution, tells us more. In order to specify it *exactly*, we need to know all the moments, although the first, second, and third moments tell us enough for most practical purposes.

The third moment will appear in some of the equations used in Chapters 36 and 37. It is calculated for the set of 20 values in Table 30.2.

**USES OF**     If we know the mean and standard deviation of a set
**SECOND MOMENT**     of values, this knowledge is exactly equivalent to
**AND VARIANCE**     knowing the mean and second moment (or the mean and variance). The second moment is related to the standard deviation, in fact, by the following equation:

$$E(x^2) = E^2(x) + \sigma_x^2$$

or                                                                                  (30.3)

$$E(x^2) = E^2(x) + \text{Var}\,(x)$$

Thus we have an alternative way of computing the standard deviation (which is used in programs later on). The reader may observe that the figures for mean, standard deviation, and second moment, calculated in Tables 30.1 and 30.2 for the 20 values of $x$, obey this equation.

All three terms convey the same information; so why have we bothered to introduce the variance and the second moment into this book as well as the standard deviation? The answer is that they are going to make certain of our calculations easier. In systems analysis calculations, we are usually concerned about combinations of variables. In calculating response time, for example, we add together many different variables. In calculating file-access time, we have to know the fraction of transactions going to different files. When we manipulate combinations of variables, use of the variance and second moment will make life easier.

**COMBINATIONS OF VARIABLES**   Suppose that we require the mean and standard deviation of a variable $x$, when this variable is itself derived from other variables, $a$, $b$, $c$, and so on. We know the mean and standard deviation of $a$, $b$, $c$, ... , and from this we need to calculate these factors for $x$.

There are several cases we may consider:

1. $x = a + b + c + \cdots$

   In this case,

   $$E(x) = E(a) + E(b) + E(c) + \cdots \qquad \text{for any variables } a, b, c, \cdots,$$

   and

   $$\text{Var } (x) = \text{Var } (a) + \text{Var } (b) + \text{Var } (c) + \cdots \qquad (30.4)$$

   if $a, b, c, \ldots$ are **independent** variables.

We now have an easy rule to remember. If $x$ is the sum of a number of independent variables, then the variance of $x$ is the sum of the variances of the variables. Variances are additive in this way; standard deviations and second moments are not, which is why we introduce variance into this text.

Let us consider an example of how variance is used. The response time on a multidrop communication line may be defined as the sum of the following variables:

(a) The time spent waiting for transmission on the input line
(b) The input transmission time
(c) The time spent in the computer
(d) The time spent queuing for output transmission
(e) The output transmission time

We can obtain a figure for the mean and variance (standard deviation squared) of each of these quantities. Then we add the five means to find the mean overall response time and we add the five variances to find the variance of response time.

Academically one could argue that this procedure is not absolutely accurate because the five preceding factors are not absolutely independent. The time spent in the computer may be affected slightly by the time of input transmission and by the length of the output message. For practical purposes, however, we shall regard them as independent. The degree of interdependence is very slight. In order to obtain the variance of dependant variables, we need to use the covariance. Even if this step were worth doing, we do not know the covariance, and so we will use Eq. (30.4). This is typical of the slight approximations that are invariably made when mathematical models are constructed of real events. There will be other such approximations in subsequent chapters, but neverthe-less the models we derive pass the supreme test of being *useful* in designing systems.

**2. x = a + K where K is a constant.**

In this case, $E(x) = E(a) + K$, and $\sigma x = \sigma a$, because the standard deviation of $K$ is zero.

**3. x = K·a where K is a constant.**

In this case, $E(x) = K \cdot E(a)$.

$$\sigma x = K \sigma_a$$
$$\text{Var}(x) = K^2 \cdot \text{Var}(a)$$
$$E(x^2) = K^2 \cdot E(a^2)$$
$$E(x^3) = K^3 \cdot E(a^3).$$

**4. x is equal to one of a possible set of variables, a, b, c, . . . .**

This is a case that we meet frequently in systems analysis. Our variable, $x$, is a choice between variables of which we know the mean and standard deviation.

Let the probability of its being $a$ be $P_a$

the probability of its being $b$ be $P_b$

the probability of its being $c$ be $P_c$ . . .

For example, a message traveling on a transmission line must be one of three types: $A$, $B$, and $C$. Ten percent of the messages are $A$, 30 percent are $B$, and 60 percent are $C$. We know the means and standard deviations of the length of each type, and need to calculate the overall mean message length and its standard deviation.

Again: A transaction causes a seek to either file $A$, $B$, or $C$. Twenty-five percent of them refer to file $A$, 35 percent to file $B$, and 40 percent to file $C$. We know the means and standard deviations of the seek time for each file, and need to calculate the overall mean and standard deviation for the message.

To obtain the mean in such cases we calculate the "weighted mean":

(1)   The elapsed time is the sum of several independent times:

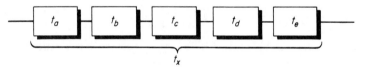

Rule:  1.   Add the means.       $E(t_x) = E(t_a) + E(t_b) + E(t_c) + E(t_d) + E(t_e)$
       2.   Add the variances.   $VAR(t_x) = VAR(t_a) + VAR(t_b) + VAR(t_c) + VAR(t_d) + VAR(t_e)$

(2)   The elapsed time is one of several independent time figures:

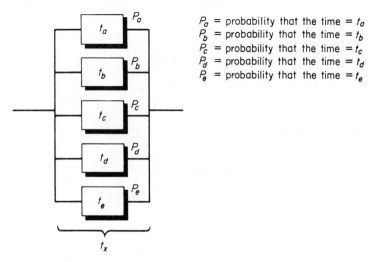

$P_a$ = probability that the time = $t_a$
$P_b$ = probability that the time = $t_b$
$P_c$ = probability that the time = $t_c$
$P_d$ = probability that the time = $t_d$
$P_e$ = probability that the time = $t_e$

Rule:  1. Calculate the weighted mean
$$E(t_x) = P_a.E(t_a) + P_b.E(t_b) + P_c.E(t_c) + P_d.E(t_d) + P_e.E(t_e)$$
       2. Calculate the weighted second moment
$$E(t_x^2) = P_a.E(t_a^2) + P_b.E(t_b^2) + P_c.E(t_c^2) + P_d.E(t_d^2) + P_e.E(t_e^2)$$
       3. Calculate the weighted third moment
$$E(t_x^3) = P_a.E(t_a^3) + P_b.E(t_b^3) + P_c.E(t_c^3) + P_d.E(t_d^3) + P_e.E(t_e^3)$$

*Fig. 30.4.* Combinations of variables.

$$E(x) = P_a \cdot E(a) + P_b \cdot E(b) + P_e \cdot E(c) + \cdots$$

The *easiest* way to deal with the dispersion is to remember that we can similarly take the weighted second moment:

$$E(x^2) = P_a \cdot E(a^2) + P_b \cdot E(b^2) + P_c \cdot E(c^2) + \cdots \qquad (30.5)$$

The third moments, and other moments, obey a similar relationship:

$$E(x^3) = P_a \cdot E(a^3) + P_b \cdot E(b^3) + P_c \cdot E(c^3) + \cdots \tag{30.6}$$

$$E(x^N) = P \cdot E(a^N) + P_b \cdot E(b^N) + P_c \cdot E(c^N) + \cdots \quad \text{(where } N \text{ is an integer)}$$

The reader should note that it is quite wrong to take the weighted variance or standard deviation! He must therefore convert these into second moments, using Eq. (30.3), carry out the above manipulation, and then convert the results back to standard deviations if so desired.

In some calculations there are many possible values that a variable could take. In such cases we may use a computer to evaluate the mean and the moments. Suppose that we have a set of $N$ possible values of a time variable. $P(K)$ is the probability of the time having a value $T(K)$, and we are able to give the computer a table for $P(K)$ and $T(K)$. The mean time is then computed as:

$$E(t) = \sum_{K=1}^{N} P(K) \cdot T(K) \tag{30.7}$$

and the second and third moments are:

$$E(t^2) = \sum_{K=1}^{N} P(K) \cdot T^2(K) \tag{30.8}$$

$$E(t^3) = \sum_{K=1}^{N} P(K) \cdot T^3(K) \tag{30.9}$$

Having computed the second moments, we may find the standard deviation:

$$\sigma_t = \sqrt{E(t^2) - E^2(t)}$$

In the above examples we have applied the variance and second moment to obtain simple rules for manipulating variables. Figure 30.4 illustrates these rules.

**Example 30.1. Message Length Statistics.** Suppose that we are designing the communication line configuration for a system that has two types of transactions, A and B. For each input message there is a response from the computer to the terminal originating that message. No other traffic travels on the line when these terminals are active. Thirty percent of the messages are of type A and 70 percent are type B.

Both the input and output message lengths can vary widely. A study of the man-machine dialogue which takes place has given the distributions of lengths shown in Tables 30.3 and 30.4.

**Table 30.3.** TRANSACTION TYPE A

| Number of Characters | Distribution<br>Fraction of Transactions of This Length | Cumulative Distribution<br>Fraction of Transactions of This Length or Less |
|---|---|---|
| **Input** | | |
| Below 6 | None | None |
| 6–10 | 0.390 | 0.390 |
| 11–15 | 0.214 | 0.604 |
| 16–20 | 0.186 | 0.790 |
| 21–40 | 0.140 | 0.930 |
| 41–60 | 0.070 | 1.000 |
| Over 60 | None | 1.000 |
| **Output** | | |
| Below 6 | None | None |
| 6–20 | 0.021 | 0.021 |
| 21–40 | 0.029 | 0.050 |
| 41–60 | 0.038 | 0.088 |
| 61–80 | 0.058 | 0.146 |
| 81–100 | 0.082 | 0.228 |
| 101–120 | 0.154 | 0.382 |
| 121–140 | 0.298 | 0.680 |
| 141–160 | 0.204 | 0.884 |
| 161–180 | 0.112 | 0.996 |
| 181–200 | 0.004 | 1.000 |
| Over 200 | None | 1.000 |

The characters in the tables are *all* of the characters transmitted in a message, including control characters and error-checking characters. There is also a constant period of time that must be added to the total message transmission time to include such factors as establishing synchronization and line turnaround. In order to use one phrase for this factor, we will refer to it as line preparation time. In this example, the line preparation time for input transmission is 0.5 second; for output transmission it is 0.7 second. An indication of how such figures are obtained will be given in Chapter 37.

Let $T_1$ be the line preparation time for input messages and $T_2$ be the line preparation time for output messages.

The overall transmission time for an input message is

$$T_{M_I} = \frac{N_I}{S} + T_1$$

**Table 30.4.** TRANSACTION TYPE B

| Number of Characters | Distribution Fraction of Transactions of This Length | Cumulative Distribution Fraction of Transactions of This Length or Less |
|---|---|---|
| **Input** | | |
| Below 6 | None | None |
| 6–10 | 0.473 | 0.473 |
| 11–15 | 0.283 | 0.756 |
| 16–20 | 0.118 | 0.874 |
| 21–40 | 0.099 | 0.973 |
| 41–60 | 0.027 | 1.000 |
| Over 60 | None | 1.000 |
| **Output** | | |
| Below 6 | None | None |
| 6–20 | 0.055 | 0.055 |
| 21–40 | 0.147 | 0.202 |
| 41–60 | 0.193 | 0.395 |
| 61–80 | 0.278 | 0.673 |
| 81–100 | 0.182 | 0.855 |
| 101–120 | 0.072 | 0.927 |
| 121–140 | 0.034 | 0.961 |
| 141–160 | 0.021 | 0.982 |
| 161–180 | 0.011 | 0.993 |
| 181–200 | 0.007 | 1.000 |
| Over 200 | None | 1.000 |

and for an output message

$$T_{M_O} = \frac{N_O}{S} + T_2$$

where $N_I$ = the number of characters in the input message
$N_O$ = the number of characters in the output message
$S$ = the line speed (characters per unit time)

The calculations that we are going to perform in the following chapters will need as input such factors as

1. The mean time that type A messages occupy the line on input.
2. The mean time that type A messages occupy the line on output.

3. The above for type B messages.
4. The mean input time for *all* messages, A and B.
5. The mean output time for *all* messages, A and B.
6. The mean time for all messages, input and output, types A and B.
7. The second moments of the preceding quantities.
8. Third moments of some of the preceding quantities.

We are going to write most of our calculations in the form of simple computer programs, so let us begin with a program to calculate the foregoing values.

**COMPUTER**          Here and in the following chapters we shall use a
**PROGRAM**           large number of different variables. It is therefore
**NOTATION**          helpful to devise a program notation in which the
                      meaning can be easily understood when reading the
code. We shall use six-character field labels for variables like the preceding ones, as well as others in the following chapters.

The first two characters of each six-character field will refer to a statistical parameter, such as a mean, standard deviation, second moment, or, in later chapters, the parameter of a gamma distribution.

The next two characters of the field will refer to a system variable, such as service time, response time, number of characters or, in later chapters, waiting time in a queue.

The last two of the six characters give the transaction or facility to which the first four characters refer—for example, the communication line, the input portion of a half-duplex communication line, the computer system, the input message type A, and so on.

Table 30.5 illustrates this notation. As an example, SMNCIA refers to the second moment (SM) of the number of characters (NC) in the input message type A (IA). EVTTCS is the expected value (EV)—mean—of the total time (TT) that a transaction spends in the computer system (CS)—a value which itself would often have to be obtained from some detailed calculations.

**Table 30.5.** SIX-CHARACTER FIELDS USED IN THE COMPUTER PROGRAMS

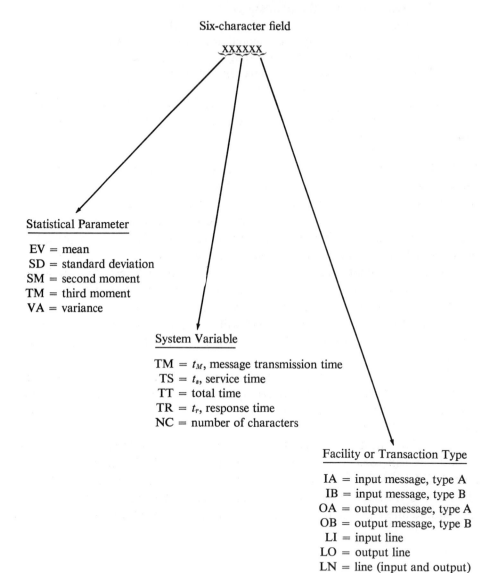

Six-character field

$$\underbrace{\text{XXXXXX}}$$

Statistical Parameter

EV = mean
SD = standard deviation
SM = second moment
TM = third moment
VA = variance

System Variable

TM = $t_M$, message transmission time
TS = $t_s$, service time
TT = total time
TR = $t_r$, response time
NC = number of characters

Facility or Transaction Type

IA = input message, type A
IB = input message, type B
OA = output message, type A
OB = output message, type B
LI = input line
LO = output line
LN = line (input and output)
CS = computer system

**Table 30.6.** THE MEANING OF THE FIELDS USED IN THE COMPUTER PROGRAMS

```
T1     =LINE PREPARATION TIME FOR INPUT MESSAGES (CONSTANT)
T2     =LINE PREPARATION TIME FOR OUTPUT MESSAGES (CONSTANT)
SPEED =SPEED OF TRANSMISSION LINE IN CHARACTERS PER SECOND
FIA(K)=FRACTION OF INPUT TRANSACTIONS TYPE A THAT HAVE K CHARACTERS
FIB(K)=FRACTION OF INPUT TRANSACTIONS TYPE B THAT HAVE K CHARACTERS
FOA(K)=FRACTION OF OUTPUT TRANSACTIONS TYPE A THAT HAVE K CHARS
FOB(K)=FRACTION OF OUTPUT TRANSACTIONS TYPE B THAT HAVE K CHARS
TIA    =TOTAL OF FIA(*)   (WHICH SHOULD = 1 )
TIB    =TOTAL OF FIB(*)   (WHICH SHOULD = 1 )
TOA    =TOTAL OF FOA(*)   (WHICH SHOULD = 1 )
TOB    =TOTAL OF FOB(*)   (WHICH SHOULD = 1 )
EVTMIA=EXPECTED VALUE OF TRANSMISSION TIME OF INPUT  MESSAGE TYPE A
EVTMIB=EXPECTED VALUE OF TRANSMISSION TIME OF INPUT  MESSAGE TYPE B
EVTMOA=EXPECTED VALUE OF TRANSMISSION TIME OF OUTPUT MESSAGE TYPE A
EVTMOB=EXPECTED VALUE OF TRANSMISSION TIME OF OUTPUT MESSAGE TYPE B
SMTMIA=SECOND MOMENT OF  TRANSMISSION TIME OF INPUT  MESSAGE TYPE A
SMTMIB=SECOND MOMENT OF  TRANSMISSION TIME OF INPUT  MESSAGE TYPE B
SMTMOA=SECOND MOMENT OF  TRANSMISSION TIME OF OUTPUT MESSAGE TYPE A
SMTMOB=SECOND MOMENT OF  TRANSMISSION TIME OF OUTPUT MESSAGE TYPE B
TMTMIA=THIRD MOMENT   OF TRANSMISSION TIME OF INPUT  MESSAGE TYPE A
TMTMIB=THIRD MOMENT   OF TRANSMISSION TIME OF INPUT  MESSAGE TYPE B
TMTMOA=THIRD MOMENT   OF TRANSMISSION TIME OF OUTPUT MESSAGE TYPE A
TMTMOB=THIRD MOMENT   OF TRANSMISSION TIME OF OUTPUT MESSAGE TYPE B
EVTMLI=EXPECTED VALUE OF TRANSMISN TIME OF INPUT   MESS, (ANY TYPE)
EVTMLO=EXPECTED VALUE OF TRANSMISN TIME OF OUTPUT  MESS, (ANY TYPE)
SMTMLI=SECOND MOMENT OF  TRANSMISN TIME OF INPUT   MESS, (ANY TYPE)
SMTMLO=SECOND MOMENT OF  TRANSMISN TIME OF OUTPUT  MESS, (ANY TYPE)
TMTMLI=THIRD  MOMENT OF  TRANSMISN TIME OF INPUT   MESS, (ANY TYPE)
TMTMLO=THIRD  MOMENT OF  TRANSMISN TIME OF OUTPUT  MESS, (ANY TYPE)
VATMLI=VARIANCE OF TRANSMISSION TIME OF INPUT   MESSAGES (ANY TYPE)
VATMLO=VARIANCE OF TRANSMISSION TIME OF OUTPUT MESSAGES (ANY TYPE)
EVTTCS=EXPECTED VALUE OF TOTAL TIME MESS SPENDS IN COMPUTER SYSTEM
VATTCS=VARIANCE OF TOTAL TIME MESSAGE SPENDS IN COMPUTER SYSTEM
VATRLN=VARIANCE OF RESPONSE TIME FOR THE LINE
EVTRLN=EXPECTED VALUE OF RESPONSE TIME FOR THE LINE
SDTRLN=STANDARD DEVIATION OF RESPONSE TIME FOR THE LINE
```

Table 30.6 gives a listing of the fields used in this chapter. Appendix II gives a complete listing for the programs used throughout the book.

**PROGRAM FOR OBTAINING TIMING STATISTICS**

Let us now compute the timing statistics for the foregoing data, for a communication line with a speed of 14.8 characters per second.*

* Note. Two versions are given of each group of program statements, a PL/I version and a FORTRAN version. The PL/I version has been written for clarity of understanding by the reader rather than for efficient machine operation. The FORTRAN version is written with machine efficiency in mind at the expense of clarity of understanding.

## In PL/I:

```
T1=.5;
T2=.7;
SPEED=14.8;

DCL FIA(6:60 );DCL FIB(6:60 );DCL FOA(6:200);DCL FOB(6:200);
DO K=6     TO 10 ;FIA(K)=.390/5  ;END;
DO K=11    TO 15 ;FIA(K)=.214/5  ;END;
DO K=16    TO 20 ;FIA(K)=.186/5  ;END;
DO K=21    TO 40 ;FIA(K)=.140/20;END;
DO K=41    TO 60 ;FIA(K)=.070/20;END;
DO K=6     TO 10 ;FIB(K)=.473/5  ;END;
DO K=11    TO 15 ;FIB(K)=.283/5  ;END;
DO K=16    TO 20 ;FIB(K)=.118/5  ;END;
DO K=21    TO 40 ;FIB(K)=.099/20;END;
DO K=41    TO 60 ;FIB(K)=.027/20;END;
DO K=6     TO 20 ;FOA(K)=.021/15;END;
DO K=21    TO 40 ;FOA(K)=.029/20;END;
DO K=41    TO 60 ;FOA(K)=.038/20;END;
DO K=61    TO 80 ;FOA(K)=.058/20;END;
DO K=81    TO 100;FOA(K)=.082/20;END;
DO K=101   TO 120;FOA(K)=.154/20;END;
DO K=121   TO 140;FOA(K)=.298/20;END;
DO K=141   TO 160;FOA(K)=.204/20;END;
DO K=161   TO 180;FOA(K)=.112/20;END;
DO K=181   TO 200;FOA(K)=.004/20;END;
DO K=6     TO 20 ;FOB(K)=.055/15;END;
DO K=21    TO 40 ;FOB(K)=.147/20;END;
DO K=41    TO 60 ;FOB(K)=.193/20;END;
DO K=61    TO 80 ;FOB(K)=.278/20;END;
DO K=81    TO 100;FOB(K)=.182/20;END;
DO K=101   TO 120;FOB(K)=.072/20;END;
DO K=121   TO 140;FOB(K)=.034/20;END;
DO K=141   TO 160;FOB(K)=.021/20;END;
DO K=161   TO 180;FOB(K)=.011/20;END;
DO K=181   TO 200;FOB(K)=.007/20;END;

TIA,TOA,TIB,TOB=0;
EVTMIA,EVTMIB,SMTMIA,SMTMIB,TMTMIA,TMTMIB,
EVTMOA,EVTMOB,SMTMOA,SMTMOB,TMTMOA,TMTMOB=0;
DO K=6 TO 60;
EVTMIA=EVTMIA+(K/SPEED+T1)*FIA(K);
SMTMIA=SMTMIA+(K/SPEED+T1)**2*FIA(K);
TMTMIA=TMTMIA+(K/SPEED+T1)**3*FIA(K);
TIA=TIA+FIA(K);
END;
DO K=6 TO 60;
EVTMIB=EVTMIB+(K/SPEED+T1)*FIB(K);
SMTMIB=SMTMIB+(K/SPEED+T1)**2*FIB(K);
TMTMIB=TMTMIB+(K/SPEED+T1)**3*FIB(K);
TIB=TIB+FIB(K);
END;
DO K=6 TO 200;
EVTMOA=EVTMOA+(K/SPEED+T2)*FOA(K);
SMTMOA=SMTMOA+(K/SPEED+T2)**2*FOA(K);
TMTMOA=TMTMOA+(K/SPEED+T2)**3*FOA(K);
TOA=TOA+FOA(K);
```

```
END;
DO K=6 TO 200;
EVTMOB=EVTMOB+(K/SPEED+T2)*FOB(K);
SMTMOB=SMTMOB+(K/SPEED+T2)**2*FOB(K);
TMTMOB=TMTMOB+(K/SPEED+T2)**3*FOB(K);
TOB=TOB+FOB(K);
END;
PUT DATA (TIA,TOA,TIB,TOB)SKIP;

PUT DATA (EVTMIA,EVTMOA,EVTMIB,EVTMOB)SKIP;
PUT DATA (SMTMIA,SMTMOA,SMTMIB,SMTMOB)SKIP;
PUT DATA (TMTMIA,TMTMOA,TMTMIB,TMTMOB)SKIP;

EVTMLI=.3*EVTMIA+.7*EVTMIB;
EVTMLO=.3*EVTMOA+.7*EVTMOB;
SMTMLI=.3*SMTMIA+.7*SMTMIB;
SMTMLO=.3*SMTMOA+.7*SMTMOB;
TMTMLI=.3*TMTMIA+.7*TMTMIB;
TMTMLO=.3*TMTMOA+.7*TMTMOB;
EVTMLN=(EVTMLI+EVTMLO)/2;
SMTMLN=(SMTMLI+SMTMLO)/2;
TMTMLN=(TMTMLI+TMTMLO)/2;
PUT DATA (EVTMLI,EVTMLO)SKIP;
PUT DATA (SMTMLI,SMTMLO)SKIP;
PUT DATA (TMTMLI,TMTMLO)SKIP;

EVTTCS=1;
VATTCS=.25;
VATMLI=SMTMLI-EVTMLI*EVTMLI;
VATMLO=SMTMLO-EVTMLO*EVTMLO;
EVTRLN=EVTMLI+EVTTCS+EVTMLO;
VATRLN=VATMLI+VATTCS+VATMLO;
SDTRLN=SQRT(VATRLN);
PUT DATA (EVTRLN,SDTRLN) SKIP;
```

In FORTRAN:

```
C....
      DIMENSION FIA(60),FIB(60),FOA(200),FOB(200)
C....
      L1=3
C
      T1=.5
      T2=.7
      SPEED=14.8
C
      CFIA=.390/5.0
      CFIB=.473/5.0
      DO 10 K= 6, 10
      FIA(K)=CFIA
   10 FIB(K)=CFIB
      CFIA=.214/5.0
      CFIB=.283/5.0
      DO 20 K= 11, 15
      FIA(K)=CFIA
   20 FIB(K)=CFIB
```

```
      CFIA=.186/5.0
      CFIB=.118/5.0
      DO  30 K= 16, 20
      FIA(K)=CFIA
   30 FIB(K)=CFIB
      CFIA=.140/20.0
      CFIB=.099/20.0
      DO  40 K= 21, 40
      FIA(K)=CFIA
   40 FIB(K)=CFIB
      CFIA=.070/20.0
      CFIB=.027/20.0
      DO  50 K= 41, 60
      FIA(K)=CFIA
   50 FIB(K)=CFIB
      CFOA=.021/15.0
      CFOB=.055/15.0
      DO  60 K=  6, 20
      FOA(K)=CFOA
   60 FOB(K)=CFOB
      CFOA=.029/20.0
      CFOB=.147/20.0
      DO  70 K= 21, 40
      FOA(K)=CFOA
   70 FOB(K)=CFOB
      CFCA=.038/20.0
      CFCB=.193/20.0
      DO  80 K= 41, 60
      FOA(K)=CFOA
   80 FOB(K)=CFCB
      CFCA=.058/20.0
      CFCB=.278/20.0
      DO  90 K= 61, 80
      FOA(K)=CFOA
   90 FOB(K)=CFCB
      CFCA=.082/20.0
      CFCB=.182/20.0
      DO 100 K= 81,100
      FOA(K)=CFCA
  100 FOB(K)=CFCB
      CFCA=.154/20.0
      CFCB=.072/20.0
      DO 110 K=101,120
      FCA(K)=CFCA
  110 FOB(K)=CFCB
      CFCA=.298/20.0
      CFCB=.034/20.0
      DO 120 K=121,140
      FOA(K)=CFCA
  120 FOB(K)=CFCB
      CFCA=.204/20.0
      CFOB=.021/20.0
      DO 130 K=141,160
      FOA(K)=CFCA
  130 FOB(K)=CFCB
      CFOA=.112/20.0
```

```
        CFCB=.011/20.0
        DO 140 K=161,180
        FCA(K)=CFCA
  140 FCB(K)=CFCB
        CFCA=.004/20.0
        CFCB=.007/20.0
        DO 150 K=181,200
        FCA(K)=CFCA
  150 FCB(K)=CFCB
C
        DATA TIA,TOA,TIB,TOB,
       1EVTMIA,EVTMIB,SMTMIA,SMTMIB,TMTMIA,TMTMIB,
       2EVTMOA,EVTMOB,SMTMOA,SMTMOB,TMTMOA,TMTMOB/16*0.0/
C
        DO 160 K=6,60
        TMI=K/SPEED+T1
        EVTMIA=EVTMIA+TMI*FIA(K)
        SMTMIA=SMTMIA+TMI**2*FIA(K)
        TMTMIA=TMTMIA+TMI**3*FIA(K)
        TIA=TIA+FIA(K)
        EVTMIB=EVTMIB+TMI*FIB(K)
        SMTMIB=SMTMIB+TMI**2*FIB(K)
        TMTMIB=TMTMIB+TMI**3*FIB(K)
  160 TIB=TIB+FIB(K)
C
        DO 170 K=6,200
        TMO=K/SPEED+T2
        EVTMOA=EVTMOA+TMO*FCA(K)
        SMTMOA=SMTMOA+TMO**2*FCA(K)
        TMTMOA=TMTMOA+TMO**3*FCA(K)
        TOA=TOA+FCA(K)
        EVTMOB=EVTMOB+TMO*FOB(K)
        SMTMOB=SMTMOB+TMO**2*FOB(K)
        TMTMOB=TMTMOB+TMO**3*FOB(K)
  170 TOB=TOB+FOB(K)
C
        WRITE (L1,180)
       1TIA,TOA,TIB,TOB,
       2EVTMIA,EVTMOA,EVTMIB,EVTMOB,
       3SMTMIA,SMTMOA,SMTMIB,SMTMOB,
       4TMTMIA,TMTMOA,TMTMIB,TMTMOB
  180 FORMAT (1H1,
       1'TIA=',E13.6,T26,'TOA=',E13.6,T50,
       2'TIB=',E13.6,T74,'TOB=',E13.6/1H
       3'EVTMIA=',E13.6,T26,'EVTMOA=',E13.6,T50,
       4'EVTMIB=',E13.6,T74,'EVTMOB=',E13.6/1H ,
       5'SMTMIA=',E13.6,T26,'SMTMOA=',E13.6,T50,
       6'SMTMIB=',E13.6,T74,'SMTMOB=',E13.6/1H ,
       7'TMTMIA=',E13.6,T26,'TMTMOA=',E13.6,T50,
       8'TMTMIB=',E13.6,T74,'TMTMOB=',E13.6)
C
        EVTMLI=.3*EVTMIA+.7*EVTMIB
        EVTMLO=.3*EVTMOA+.7*EVTMOB
        SMTMLI=.3*SMTMIA+.7*SMTMIB
        SMTMLC=.3*SMTMOA+.7*SMTMOB
        TMTMLI=.3*TMTMIA+.7*TMTMIB
```

```
      TMTMLC=.3*TMTMOA+.7*TMTMOB
      EVTMLN=(EVTMLI+EVTMLO)/2.0
      SMTMLN=(SMTMLI+SMTMLC)/2.0
      TMTMLN=(TMTMLI+TMTMLC)/2.0
      WRITE (L1,190)
     1EVTMLI,EVTMLO,
     2SMTMLI,SMTMLC,
     3TMTMLI,TMTMLC
  190 FORMAT (1H ,
     1'EVTMLI=',E13.6,T26,'EVTMLO=',E13.6/1H ,
     2'SMTMLI=',E13.6,T26,'SMTMLO=',E13.6/1H ,
     3'TMTMLI=',E13.6,T26,'TMTMLO=',E13.6)
C
      EVTTCS=1.0
      VATTCS=.25
      VATMLI=SMTMLI-EVTMLI*EVTMLI
      VATMLO=SMTMLC-EVTMLO*EVTMLO
      EVTRLN=EVTMLI+EVTTCS+EVTMLO
      VATRLN=VATMLI+VATTCS+VATMLO
      SDTRLN=SQRT(VATRLN)
      WRITE (L1,200)
     1EVTRLN,SDTRLN
  200 FORMAT (1H ,
     1'EVTRLN=',E13.6,T26,'SDTRLN=',E13.6)
      STOP
      END
```

The fields TIA, TOA, TIB, and TOB that are printed out in the preceding computation all equal 1 (to the nearest five significant figures). This serves as a check on the input.

The results are as follows (in seconds, seconds$^2$, and seconds$^3$):

| | | | |
|---|---|---|---|
| EVTMIA = 1.65 | EVTMOA = 8.88 | EVTMIB = 1.44 | EVTMOB = 5.41 |
| SMTMIA = 3.41 | SMTMOA = 85.43 | SMTMIB = 2.49 | SMTMOB = 34.71 |
| TMTMIA = 8.80 | TMTMOA = 859.99 | TMTMIB = 5.34 | TMTMOB = 255.18 |

| | |
|---|---|
| EVTMLI = 1.51 | EVTMLO = 6.45 |
| SMTMLI = 2.76 | SMTMLO = 49.93 |
| TMTMLI = 6.38 | TMTMLO = 436.59 |

| | |
|---|---|
| EVTRLN = 8.96 | SDTRLN = 3.00 |

If no queuing occurred on the system, the time for input and response could be calculated by adding the means of the input transmission time, the time spent in the computer system, and the output transmission time. Also, because these three variables are largely independent, it is reasonable to add their variances to obtain the variance of the response time and hence its standard deviation.

Suppose that we have calculated the mean time spent in the computer system by a transaction to be 1 second, with a standard deviation of 0.5 second (variance $= 0.25$ second$^2$); then (ignoring queuing) the response time would be calculated as follows:

In PL/I:

```
EVTTCS=1;
VATTCS=.25;
VATMLI=SMTMLI-EVTMLI*EVTMLI;
VATMLO=SMTMLO-EVTMLO*EVTMLO;
EVTRLN=EVTMLI+EVTTCS+EVTMLO;
VATRLN=VATMLI+VATTCS+VATMLO;
SDTRLN=SQRT(VATRLN);
PUT DATA (EVTRLN,SDTRLN) SKIP;
```

In FORTRAN:

```
EVTTCS=1.0
VATTCS=.25
VATMLI=SMTMLI-EVTMLI*EVTMLI
VATMLO=SMTMLO-EVTMLO*EVTMLO
EVTRLN=EVTMLI+EVTTCS+EVTMLO
VATRLN=VATMLI+VATTCS+VATMLO
SDTRLN=SQRT(VATRLN)
      WRITE (L1,200)
     1EVTRLN,SDTRLN
200 FORMAT (1H ,
     1'EVTRLN=',E13.6,T26,'SDTRLN=',E13.6)
```

This calculation gives a mean time of 8.96 seconds, with a standard deviation of 3.00 seconds.

The time may, in fact, be much longer because of the queuing for the line. If more than one terminal is using the line, we must add into our equation for the means *the mean time spent waiting for the line* and into our variance equation the *variance of the time spent waiting for the line*. This is the subject of the next chapter.

## REFERENCES

1. M. J. Moroney, *Facts From Figures*. London: Penguin Books, 1951. Delightfully readable nonmathematical survey of statistics. Paperback. Inexpensive.

2. J. E. Freund and F. J. Williams, *Modern Business Statistics*. Englewood Cliffs, N.J.: Prentice-Hall, Inc., 1958. Elementary introduction to statistics, nonmathematical.

3. A. M. Mood and F. A. Graybill, *Introduction to the Theory of Statistics*. New York: McGraw-Hill Book Company, 1963. More detailed introduction to statistics. Mathematics not too difficult.

4. K. A. Brownlee, *Statistical Theory and Methodology in Science and Engineering*. New York: John Wiley & Sons, Inc., 1965. Good general book on statistics. Many practical examples.

**CLASS QUESTIONS**

*Class questions for this (and other chapters) are at the end of the book. (See page 864.)*

# 31 QUEUING CALCULATIONS

In the design of communication networks, and indeed of computer systems in general, there are places at which congestion occurs. Queues build up. In planning a system to meet given performance criteria, we must take these queues into consideration and ask such questions as: "How long will a transaction have to wait before it is transmitted over a given line?" "How long will a user have to wait before he receives service at a terminal, or attention to his telephone query?" "What is the probability that all the tie lines to a particular location are busy?" The answers determine important parameters in the network design, such as how many terminals can be attached to one line or how many terminals, concentrators, or tie lines are needed in certain locations.

Such questions can be dealt with in two ways: the first is by queuing theory; the second is by simulation. In this chapter we shall discuss the relevant, basic queuing theory, and the reader will see it applied in the following chapters. In Chapter 38 the simulation approach to the same problems will be discussed.

In the first stages of the design, the systems engineer needs quick answers to a variety of questions, like: "What will be the effect on cost of tighter response-time criteria?" "What will be the effect of having fewer lines or fewer terminals?" There will usually be a large variety of different possible configurations, and a much quicker method than simulation is needed for exploring the possibilities. Later, when a configuration is tentatively selected, it can be simulated.

This chapter describes some basic alternatives to simulation that a systems analyst may use, without any knowledge of mathematics other than basic algebra. It is intended to give him a "cook book" of elementary formulas and curves with which he may size up a queuing situation. It is advocated that this *simple queuing theory should always be used before simulation is considered.* A

413

sense of perspective is needed in selecting the appropriate design tools. The chapter describes when simple queuing and probability theory is adequate and when it should be supplemented by simulation. This is a decision that must be made by the persons making design estimates for a system.

It is probable that, at the early stages, certain facts vital to the network design will be known inexactly. The numbers of messages to be transmitted may be known only very approximately. The structure of the terminal users' man-machine "conversation" may be only vaguely understood. In this case, if a simulation is made, its results will be as uncertain as these figures. It is important to translate the possible error of input into terms of possible error of results. Because of inexact knowledge of input data, some quick and easy calculations using the equations and tables in this book generally form the best way to start the design process. We can, if desirable, use simulation to refine it at a later stage.

The approach using equations and curves often gives a clearer insight into the parameters that are important in a particular network design. Even when we do not know the exact numbers and lengths of messages, it can provide an understanding of which is the best of possible alternative techniques. This knowledge is useful, particularly with the many different alternatives open to us in data communications.

The basic concepts of queuing and probability theory that are applicable are stated below in terms that may be of value to a systems engineer without a great knowledge of mathematics. Tables are given in Appendix VIII that will enable the reader to obtain a quick estimate of queue sizes, probability of given delays, and so on. In some circumstances, these tables are not applicable and will give a wrong answer. The limitations of such a method are stated below and should be noted carefully.

## THE POISSON DISTRIBUTION

The formulas and curves that follow are based on the assumption that the events causing input to the system occur *at random*. Let us clarify what we mean by this statement.

Suppose that at some random time in the future a customer walks into a bank and asks to withdraw some cash. The event causes a transaction to be sent to the computer. Ignore for the moment the question of lunchtime activity peaks, and assume that we are considering a period during which the average customer activity is constant. This event could have occurred at any time during the period we are examining. The circumstances that cause it to happen are related to the individual's private life, and as far as we can assess, it happened *at random*. In other words, the probability of its happening in that second is the same as the probability of its happening at any other second.

Now the bank has many customers, and they all walk in to make transactions at *random* times. The probability of any one *particular* customer coming in any one minute is very low, but, because of the large number of customers, several will probably walk in during that one minute.

This situation is typical of the load on many real-time systems, but not all of them. A system may have ten transactions per second reaching it, say, on average. Although this system load is fairly high, the probability that any one *particular* transaction arrives in a given second is very low and is equal to the probability of it arriving in the next second, or the next. This number of arrivals in a given time period may be described by a limiting case of the binominal distribution known as the *Poisson distribution.*

It can be shown mathematically that the probability of having *n* arrivals in a given time period is

$$P(n) = \frac{e^{-E(n)} E^n(n)}{n!} \qquad (31.1)$$

where $P(n)$ = the probability of having *n* arrivals in the time period
$E(n)$ = the mean value of *n* for the time period

$$\left[ \begin{array}{ll} n! & \text{is equal to } n \times (n-1) \times (n-2) \times \cdots \times 3 \times 2 \times 1 \\ e & \text{is equal to } 2.71828 \end{array} \right]$$

The Poisson distribution is tabulated in Table 2 of Appendix VIII.

The reader should note that this arrival pattern may be described in a variety of different ways:

A Poisson arrival pattern.

The number of events per unit time follows the Poisson distribution.

A random arrival pattern.

The interarrival times follow an exponential distribution.

An exponential arrival pattern.

An Erlang 1 arrival pattern.

These phrases, some of which are loosely worded, can all be found in the literature, and the reader is cautioned not to be confused by such terminology.

In this discussion, the probability of one *particular* customer entering the bank, or one *particular* event occurring in a given time period, follows *a uniform distribution.* In other words, the probability is the same regardless of which time period of that length is examined. The probability of having *n* such events occur in a given time period follows a *Poisson distribution;* and the probability that times between events are less than a certain figure follows an *exponential distribution*. These are all different descriptions of the same stochastic process. They are shown graphically in Fig. 31.1.

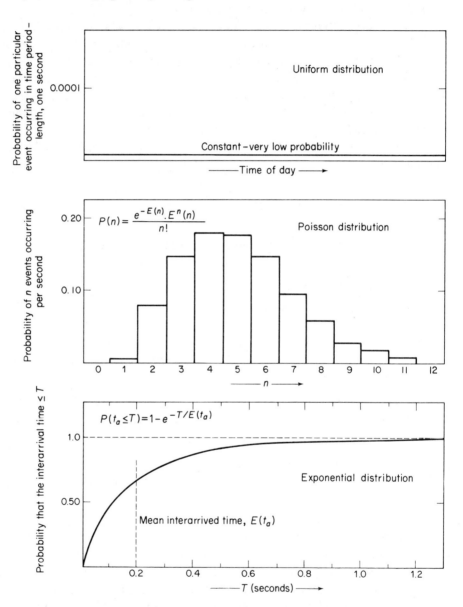

*Fig. 31.1.* Three ways of describing a random arrival process.

To illustrate, let us consider a real-time system with records relating to a large number of clients. During the peak hour of its activity, transactions are received at the average rate of two per second and follow a Poisson arrival pattern. Let us calculate the probability $P(n)$ of having $n$ arrivals per second. In the preceding formula, $E(n) = 2$. Therefore

$$P(n) = \frac{2.71828^{-2} \times 2^n}{n!}$$

Substituting $n = 0, 1, 2, 3, \ldots$, we obtain the following probabilities rounded to four decimals.

| Number of Arrivals per Second, $n$ | Probability |
|:---:|:---:|
| 0 | 0.1353 |
| 1 | 0.2707 |
| 2 | 0.2707 |
| 3 | 0.1804 |
| 4 | 0.0902 |
| 5 | 0.0361 |
| 6 | 0.0120 |
| 7 | 0.0034 |
| 8 | 0.0009 |
| 9 | 0.0002 |

It is possible to get more than nine arrivals per second, but the probability is very small (about 0.000046).

This distribution may be plotted as a histogram, as shown in Fig. 31.2.

**Example 31.1. A Device That Can Handle Three Arrivals per Second.** A device can handle three transactions per second. Transactions arrive at a mean rate of two per second and follow a Poisson arrival pattern. What proportion of the transactions will be handled as soon as they arrive?

The probability of the arrival rate being less than or equal to three per second is

$$P(n \leq 3) = \sum_{n=0}^{n=3} \frac{e^{-E(n)} E^n(n)}{n!} \tag{31.1}$$

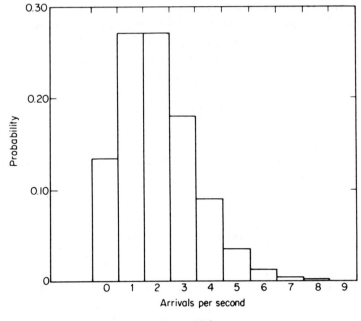

*Figure 31.2*

In this case, if the system is designed so that it can handle a maximum of three arrivals per second, the probability of its not being overloaded is

$$P(n \leq 3) = \sum_{n=0}^{n=3} \frac{2.71828^{-2} \times 2^n}{n!}$$

$$= 0.1353 + 0.2707 + 0.2707 + 0.1804$$

$$= 0.8571$$

In other words, 85.71 percent of the arrivals will be handled immediately; 14.29 percent will be delayed slightly. As is indicated by examination of Fig. 31.2, a delay greater than three times the time to handle one arrival will be rare. The time to handle one arrival is, on the average, one-third of a second. Therefore a delay greater than one second will be rare, which on most systems is quite acceptable.

The system in this case can be regarded as a facility with a certain utilization factor. In this example, it can handle a maximum of three arrivals per second but is in fact handling only two on average. It is therefore $66\frac{2}{3}$ percent utilized. The concept of *facility utilization* is used frequently in the following pages. The closer the facility utilization is to 100 percent, the greater the delays will become and the greater the queues that will build up.

**THE USE
OF POISSON
TABLES**

Using the preceding formula, tables can be computed that give values of the Poisson function. Table 3 in Appendix VIII gives the probability of having $X$ or more arrivals in a given time. For example, if the average arrival rate is 3.1 arrivals per second [i.e., $E(n) = 3.1$], then the probability of having five or more arrivals in a given second is 0.2018, using $X = 5$ from the table. Mathematically,

$$\sum_{n=5}^{n=\infty} \frac{e^{-E(n)} E^n(n)}{n!} \tag{31.2}$$

Using this equation, the systems analyst may estimate the probability that the system will fail to handle a given throughput criterion.

Often *the initial estimates may be made using a load figure such that it will not be exceeded for 90 percent of the time.* The figure may be obtained by using the Poisson tables.

Suppose that the average arrival rate $E(n)$ is 3.1 arrivals per second again. From the tables, the probability of having $X = 6$ arrivals per second or more is 0.0943. This number might therefore be taken as the throughput for making the first estimates. Similarly, if a proposed system handles an average 17 transactions per second during the peak hour, there is a 0.0953 probability of having 23 or more transactions in one second. In some cases, 23 transactions per second might be used as the preliminary design throughput, and a system that can handle this load is designed for the first iteration.

**BASIC
QUEUING
THEORY**

When transactions arrive randomly at a facility in the manner described and the facility takes a certain time to process or serve each transaction, queues will build up. Lines of bank customers wait for a teller and his terminal to become free. Lines of transactions in a computer input buffer wait for the attention of the processing unit. Lines of requests for file references wait for a file channel to become free, and so on. Lines may build up at any of the bottlenecks in a system.

The heavier the utilization of the facility in question, the longer the lines will become. As will be shown, it may be satisfactory to design a system with a *facility utilization* of 70 percent, but above 90 percent it may be too risky or give too poor a service. Thus if a file channel is 20 percent loaded, there will be hardly any items waiting for it, on average. If it is 90 percent loaded, there will normally be a queue, and at times this queue will become very large.

The facility utilization may be defined as

$$\frac{\text{The load on a facility}}{\text{The maximum load the facility can handle}}$$

$$\frac{\text{The time the facility is occupied}}{\text{The time available}}$$

For example, if a bank teller is occupied 80 percent of his time and the remainder of the time he stands idle waiting for the next customer, we can regard him as a facility with a facility utilization of 0.8. If a communication line is used to transmit 8-bit characters at a rate of 2400 bits per second so that it can transmit a maximum of 2400/8 characters per second, and we design a system in which a total of 12,000 characters from many different devices are sent down the line in a peak minute (including synchronization, end-of-message, control characters, etc.), then the facility utilization of the line during this minute is

$$\frac{12,000}{\frac{2400}{8} \times 60} = 0.667$$

Again, if a file arm makes 9000 file references in the peak hour and the arm is in use or held for an average of 300 milliseconds per reference, then the facility utilization of the arm for the peak hour is

$$\frac{9000 \times 300}{3600 \times 1000} = 0.75$$

When designing a system, we can usually produce an estimate for the utilization of the various facilities; examples will be given in subsequent chapters. Knowing this utilization, we need to be able to estimate what queues of items build up to wait for the facility. How many items will there be in the line and how long will they have to wait? These are the types of questions that queuing theory will sometimes be able to answer for us.

The queues that some of the formulas below deal with are "single-server" queues—that is, items that are waiting to be serviced by *one* facility. They may be transactions in a computer input queue waiting for the supervisory program to cause work on them to commence. They may be items at terminals contending for a multidrop communication line, and so on. They wait for this facility in much the same way automobiles arriving at a gas station wait for a solitary attendant. If, however, there were more than one attendant, this situation would constitute a *multiserver* queue, for which the analysis is rather more complex.

The formulas in the next section all relate to a situation in which the items arrive at random times. In other words, the interarrival times are exponentially distributed. The validity of this assumption is discussed later.

**SINGLE-SERVER QUEUING FORMULAS** The object of the queuing theory outlined here is to calculate the approximate average sizes of queues and the average time that transactions are kept waiting in them. We also want to estimate how often the queues exceed certain values. This knowledge will enable us to calculate, for example, how much core storage is needed to hold the queues of transactions and associated programs, how many lines are needed, what size concentrator buffers are necessary, and so on. We will be able to estimate the response times. We will obtain an idea of how customers will be kept waiting at a bank counter, or how long we may have to wait if we telephone an airline to make a booking.

Most of the queue characteristics we are interested in are plotted and tabulated in Appendix VIII, Tables 5 to 11. Each of these characteristics varies with the utilization of the facility in question. The horizontal scale of each set of curves is *facility utilization.*

It is suggested that *these curves, and the formulas behind them, should be a basic tool for making first approximation estimates of queue sizes in real-time systems.*

Let us first consider a queue with a single server as illustrated in Figure 31.3. In designing a computer system, most of the queues that we will be able to apply formulas to will be of this type.

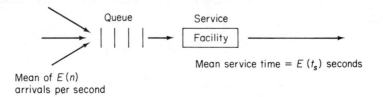

Facility utilization, $\rho = E(n) . E(t_s)$

*Fig. 31.3.* A single-server queuing situation.

Let $t_s$ be the service time of an item and $\sigma_{t_s}$ be the standard deviation of all service times.

Let $w$ be the number of items waiting at a given time for service and $q$ be the number of items in the system, both waiting service or being served, at a given time.

Let $t_w$ be the time an item waits before being served and $t_q$ be the time it spends in the system both waiting and being served.

The mean values of $w$, $q$, $t_w$, and $t_q$ are represented by $E(w)$, $E(q)$, $E(t_w)$, and $E(t_q)$. It is always true that

$$t_q = t_w + t_s \tag{31.3}$$

Therefore
$$E(t_q) = E(t_w) + E(t_s) \tag{31.4}$$

The lengths of the items waiting are independent of the lengths of the items being served. Thus

$$\text{Var } (t_q) = \text{Var } (t_w) + \text{Var } (t_s) \tag{31.5}$$

Sometimes in our calculations we will want to find $E(t_q)$ and Var $(t_q)$, and sometimes we will be interested in the waiting time before service begins: $E(t_w)$ and Var $(t_w)$.

As $E(n)$ is the mean number of items being served and we are discussing a steady-state condition,

$$E(w) = E(n)E(t_w) \tag{31.6}$$

and

$$E(q) = E(n)E(t_q) \tag{31.7}$$

Let $\rho$ be the facility utilization. Then because we have a steady-state condition,

$$\rho = E(n)E(t_s) \tag{31.8}$$

*This is the equation that is commonly used for calculating $\rho$.*

From Eqs. (31.4) and (31.7), we have

$$E(q) = E(n)E(t_q) = E(n)E(t_w) + E(n)E(t_s)$$

Substituting from Eqs. (31.6) and (31.8),

$$E(q) = E(w) + \rho \tag{31.9}$$

[A student sometimes makes the mistake of thinking that $E(q)$ must be one greater than the mean number of items waiting for service, $E(w)$. This is not true because there is not always an item being serviced. Only one is being serviced a fraction $\rho$ of the time.]

The basic theorem of single-server queuing theory was developed by Khintchine and Polloczek, and results in the following formula:

$$E(w) = \frac{\rho^2}{2(1 - \rho)}\left\{1 + \left[\frac{\sigma_{t_s}}{E(t_s)}\right]^2\right\} \qquad (31.10)$$

This formula is used to make many of the queue-size estimates in the design of computer systems. It applies to exponential interarrival times, any distribution of service times, and surprisingly, perhaps, *any dispatching discipline provided that its selection of the next item to be serviced does not depend on the service time*.

By *dispatching discipline* we mean the rules governing the selection of the next item to be serviced. A common rule, for example, is "First in, first out (FIFO)"; less useful is "Last in, first out (LIFO)." The dispatching discipline may take *priority* into consideration and service the important items before others, or it may use selection criteria based on the effect the item has on the system. Provided that the selection criteria does not depend on the service time needed, the Khintchine-Polloczek formula applies.

The reader should note that there are some queuing situations in systems design in which the dispatching discipline definitely does depend on service time. We may deliberately select the shorter items to be serviced first, for example, in some cases, because doing so gives a lower mean service time. In the control of a communication line, we may give input messages priority over output because they are shorter. In such cases we would not use the Khintchine-Polloczek equation and its derivatives, but rather equations on subsequent pages that relate to queues in which different transaction streams are dispatched with different priorities.

Substituting Eq. (31.10) into the previous equations, we obtain

$$E(q) = \rho + \frac{\rho^2}{2(1 - \rho)}\left\{1 + \left[\frac{\sigma_{t_s}}{E(t_s)}\right]^2\right\} \qquad (31.11)$$

$$E(t_w) = \frac{\rho E(t_s)}{2(1 - \rho)}\left\{1 + \left[\frac{\sigma_{t_s}}{E(t_s)}\right]^2\right\} \qquad (31.12)$$

$$E(t_q) = E(t_s) + \frac{\rho E(t_s)}{2(1 - \rho)}\left\{1 + \left[\frac{\sigma_{t_s}}{E(t_s)}\right]^2\right\} \qquad (31.13)$$

The term

$$\frac{1}{2}\left\{1 + \left[\frac{\sigma_{t_s}}{E(t_s)}\right]^2\right\}$$

appears in each of the equations describing mean queue characteristics. This term is dependent on the dispersion of the service times. Two particular cases can be noted.

1. *When the service times are constant,*

$$\sigma_{t_s} = 0$$

Therefore
$$\frac{1}{2}\left\{1 + \left[\frac{\sigma_{t_s}}{E(t_s)}\right]^2\right\} = \frac{1}{2}$$

$$E(q) = \rho + \frac{\rho^2}{2(1 - \rho)} \tag{31.14}$$

and

$$E(t_q) = E(t_s)\left[1 + \frac{\rho}{2(1 - \rho)}\right] \tag{31.15}$$

2. *When the service times are exponentially distributed,*

$$\sigma_{t_s} = E(t_s)$$

Therefore
$$\frac{1}{2}\left\{1 + \left[\frac{\sigma_{t_s}}{E(t_s)}\right]^2\right\} = 1 \tag{31.16a}$$

$$E(q) = \rho + \frac{\rho^2}{1 - \rho} = \frac{\rho}{1 - \rho} \tag{31.16b}$$

and

$$E(t_q) = E(t_s)\left[1 + \frac{\rho}{1 - \rho}\right] = \frac{E(t_s)}{1 - \rho} \tag{31.17}$$

Most service times in computing systems lie somewhere between these two cases. We rarely find service times that are entirely constant. Even a drum access to read one complete track is not constant because of the varied rotational delay in waiting for the track to position itself. The occupancy of a communication line transmitting fixed-length messages may be one case where the service time is constant.

On the other hand, we find that the dispersion of service times is not often as great as the case for random or exponentially distributed service times—$\sigma_{t_s}$ is rarely as large as $E(t_s)$. This case is sometimes regarded as a "worst case," and therefore the design is done with formulas relating to exponential service times. Such a calculation may overestimate the queue sizes and queuing times slightly, but the error at least is on the side of safety. It is certainly easy to remember the simple equations

$$E(q) = \frac{\rho}{1 - \rho}$$

and

$$E(t_q) = \frac{E(t_s)}{1 - \rho}$$

An exponential distribution of service times is certainly not the worst case that could be found in reality. However, if the service times in any queuing calculation are found to be worse than exponentially distributed, that is often a warning sign to the designer. If the standard deviation is higher than the mean, it is often an indication that some change should be made in the design. Take the following case, for example. There are six types of transactions, in equal numbers, having the following service times: 15, 20, 25, 30, 35, and 300. The standard deviation of these times is slightly higher than the mean. The last one, however, is very long compared with the others. It will cause some of the transactions to queue much longer than they would if it did not exist. It is likely that something can be done in the design to shorten it. If the figures relate to message lengths, for example, the very long messages should be chopped up into slices if possible.

Figure 31.4 gives curves plotting $E(q)$ against $\rho$ for different values of $\sigma_{t_s}$, and Fig. 31.5 plots $E(t_q)$. The uppermost curve in each is for exponential service times, which might be thought of as the worst case in reasonable design— if you are higher on the chart than the curves shown, do something about it. The lowest curve is the best case of constant service times. Most practical cases fall between these curves, so some estimate of $\sigma_{t_s}$ should be made.

From these two sets of curves, we can rapidly obtain our first estimate of certain of the queues that could build up in proposed systems, including queues

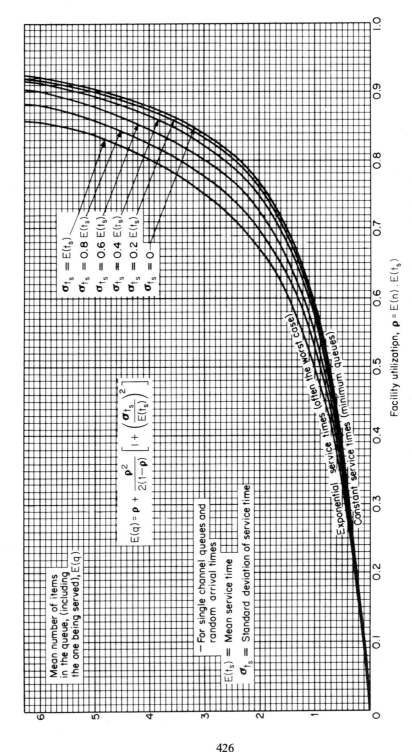

*Fig. 31.4.* Mean queue sizes for single-server queues with Poisson arrival pattern.

MEAN QUEUING TIMES FOR SINGLE-SERVER QUEUES WITH POISSON ARRIVAL PATTERN

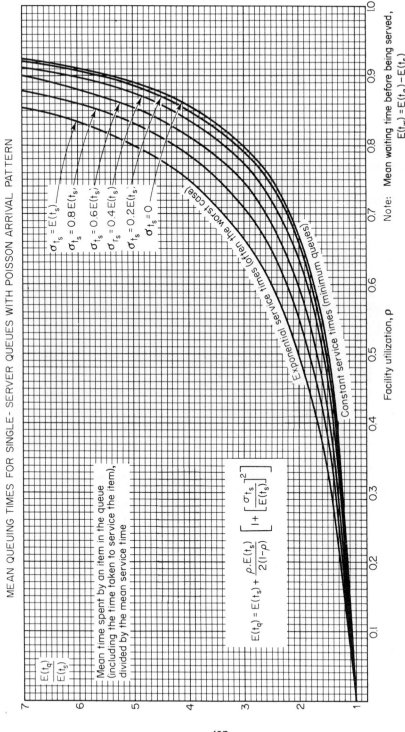

Note: Mean waiting time before being served,
$E(t_w) = E(t_q) - E(t_s)$

*Fig. 31.5.* Mean queuing times for single-server queues with Poisson arrival pattern.

427

in the computer, in the concentrators and multiplexers, and queues at the terminals. Examples of their use are given in subsequent chapters.

The mean queuing time is tabulated in Table 5 of Appendix VIII. Note that the mean waiting time before service, $E(t_w)$, may be obtained from these curves or table, using the equation:

$$E(t_w) = E(t_q) - E(t_s)$$

**Example 31.2. Queue for a Bank Teller.** In the design of a banking system, it is desirable to know how many customers will have to wait in line for a single bank teller at the peak hour.

The response time of the system and its standard deviation have been calculated, including the terminal key-in, printing, and document-insertion times.

The actions of the terminal operator have been timed. The *service time* $t_s$ is then the total time the teller takes in dealing with the transaction. The teller is the *facility* and so the *facility utilization* $\rho$ is the proportion of time the teller is occupied. If there are $E(n)$ transactions or customers in the peak hour, $\rho$ for the teller $= E(n)E(t_s)$.

Let us suppose that there are 30 customers to be handled in the peak hour. On an average, the teller takes 1.5 minutes per customer. Then

$$\rho = \frac{1.5 \times 30}{60} = 0.75$$

The teller is 75 percent utilized.

We can obtain a quick estimate of the numbers of people queuing from the curves of Fig. 31.4. We see that when $\rho = 0.75$, then $E(q)$, the mean number of people queuing at the bank counter, is between 1.88 and 3.0, depending on the standard deviation of $t_s$, the time the teller takes to handle a transaction.

Suppose that we measure the standard deviation of $t_s$ and find it to be half a minute. Then

$$\sigma_{t_s} = 0.33E(t_s)$$

Interpolating in Fig. 31.4, we find that $E(q) = 2.0$—on the average, there will be two customers at the bank counter.

The total time that the customer stands at the bank counter may be found from the curves in Fig. 31.5 or by using the formula $E(q) = E(n)E(t_q)$.

Equation (31.13) gives $E(t_q) = 4$ minutes. Table 5 in Appendix VIII tabulates mean queuing time for single servers.

Using the second moment of service time $E(t_s^2)$ rather than its standard deviation, we can write the Khintchine-Polloczek equations as follows:

$$E(w) = \frac{E^2(n)E(t_s^2)}{2(1 - \rho)} \tag{31.18}$$

$$E(q) = \rho + \frac{E^2(n)E(t_s^2)}{2(1 - \rho)} \tag{31.19}$$

$$E(t_w) = \frac{E(n)E(t_s^2)}{2(1 - \rho)} \tag{31.20}$$

$$E(t_q) = E(t_s) + \frac{E(n)E(t_s^2)}{2(1 - \rho)} \tag{31.21}$$

Table 31.2 lists the equations we are likely to use for this type of queuing situation.

**AMPLIFICATION** Inspecting the slope of the curves in Fig. 31.4, we see
**FACTOR** that *when the facility for which items are queuing becomes more than about 80 percent utilized, the lines grow at an alarming rate.* This fact is very important in the design of data transmission systems. If we design a system having facility utilizations of more than about 80 percent, then a small increase in traffic may cause severe degradation in system performance or may possibly cause the system to switch into the emergency procedures.

A small increase of $x$ percent in the input traffic will cause an increase of approximately

$$\left(E(t_s) + \frac{E(t_s)\rho(2 - \rho)}{2(1 - \rho)^2}\left\{1 + \left[\frac{\sigma_{t_s}}{E(t_s)}\right]^2\right\}\right) x \tag{31.22}$$

percent in queue size.

When the facility utilization is 50 percent, this increase is $4 \times E(t_s)$ percent for exponential service times. But when the facility utilization is 90 percent, the increase is $100 \times E(t_s)$ percent—that is, 25 times greater. A small increase in throughput at 90 percent utilization causes an effect on queue size 25 times greater than it would cause at a facility utilization of 50 percent.

Similarly, the amplifying effect in queue time is

$$\left(\frac{E^2(t_s)}{2(1 - \rho)^2}\left\{1 + \left[\frac{\sigma_{t_s}}{E(t_s)}\right]^2\right\}\right) x \tag{31.23}$$

For exponential service times, this is $4E^2(t_s)$ at a facility utilization of 50 percent but $100E^2(t_s)$ at a facility utilization of 90 percent—again 25 times worse.

Furthermore, it will be seen that the queue size is not greatly affected by differences in $\sigma_{t_s}$ for low values of facility utilization. However, for high facility utilizations, differences in $\sigma_{t_s}$ make a large difference. It is therefore more desirable to obtain an accurate knowledge of $\sigma_{t_s}$ if we are designing at high facility utilizations. The inaccuracy in an assumption that $s$ is exponential will have more effect when $\rho$ is high. Moreover, if there is an occasional long service time, as might be caused on a transmission line by a long message, the result will be heavy queuing when $\rho$ is high.

**STANDARD**
**DEVIATION**
**OF QUEUE**
**SIZES**

The previous formulas have given mean values for queue sizes and times. Besides knowing the mean, it is usually desirable to know something about the distribution of the queue sizes and times. We need to answer questions like: "How many transactions will be delayed more than such-and-such an amount?" or: "How much core do I need to hold the items in the queue (and possibly also the programs that are dealing with them)?"

Before discussing these equations further, we need to be able to evaluate the standard deviation $q$ or $t_q$, or the variance (which is the square of the standard deviation).

One way of doing so uses the *second and third moments* of service time

$$E(t_s^2) \quad \text{and} \quad E(t_s^3)$$

The variance of queue size was evaluated by Khintchine and Polloczek for a single-server queue with random arrivals and a *first-come, first-served dispatching discipline*. This latter criterion did not apply to the earlier formulas.

The variance of $q$ is

$$\text{Var}(q) = \frac{E^3(n)E(t_s^3)}{3(1-\rho)} + \frac{E^4(n)E^2(t_s^2)}{4(1-\rho)^2} + \frac{E^2(n)(3-2\rho)E(t_s^2)}{2(1-\rho)} + \rho(1-\rho) \quad (31.24)$$

The variance of $t_q$ is

$$\text{Var}(t_q) = \frac{E(n)E(t_s^3)}{3(1-\rho)} - \frac{E^2(n)E^2(t_s^2)}{2(1-\rho)^2} + \sigma_{t_s}^2 \quad (31.25)$$

For the simplified case when the service time is either exponential or constant, these equations can be greatly simplified again. Table 31.1 lists these equations.

[For exponential service times: $E(t_s^2) = 2E^2(t_s)$ and $E(t_s^3) = 6E^3(t_s)$

For constant service times:   $E(t_s^2) = t_s^2$ and $E(t_s^3) = t_s^3$]

Figures 31.6 and 31.7 plot the standard deviations of $q$ and $t_q$ against $\rho$, and Tables 6 and 7 in Appendix VIII tabulate the standard deviations of queuing

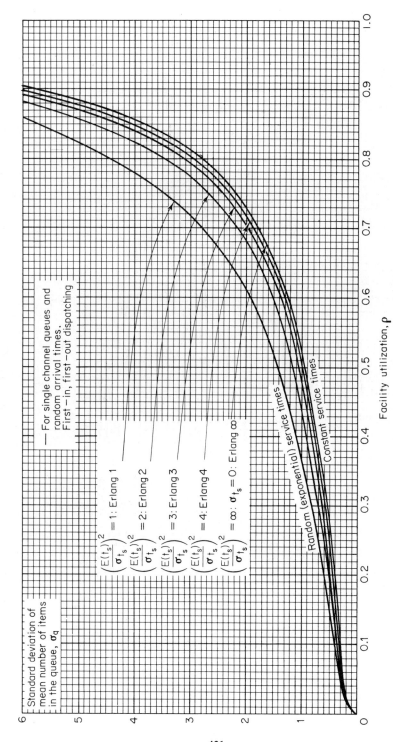

*Fig. 31.6.* Standard deviation of queue sizes in a single-server queue, with Poisson arrival times and first-in, first-out dispatching.

431

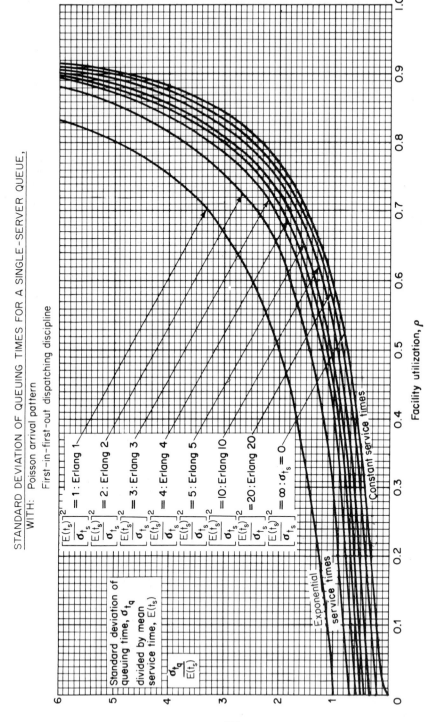

STANDARD DEVIATION OF QUEUING TIMES FOR A SINGLE - SERVER QUEUE,
WITH:  Poisson arrival pattern

First-in-first-out dispatching discipline

$\left[\dfrac{E(t_s)}{\sigma_{t_s}}\right]^2 = 1$: Erlang 1

$\left[\dfrac{E(t_s)}{\sigma_{t_s}}\right]^2 = 2$: Erlang 2

$\left[\dfrac{E(t_s)}{\sigma_{t_s}}\right]^2 = 3$: Erlang 3

$\left[\dfrac{E(t_s)}{\sigma_{t_s}}\right]^2 = 4$: Erlang 4

$\left[\dfrac{E(t_s)}{\sigma_{t_s}}\right]^2 = 5$: Erlang 5

$\left[\dfrac{E(t_s)}{\sigma_{t_s}}\right]^2 = 10$: Erlang 10

$\left[\dfrac{E(t_s)}{\sigma_{t_s}}\right]^2 = 20$: Erlang 20

$\left[\dfrac{E(t_s)}{\sigma_{t_s}}\right]^2 = \infty : \sigma_{t_s} = 0$

Standard deviation of queuing time, $\sigma_{t_q}$ divided by mean service time, $E(t_s)$

$\dfrac{\sigma_{t_q}}{E(t_s)}$

Exponential service times

Constant service times

Facility utilization, $\rho$

432

*Fig. 31.7.* Standard deviation of queuing times with single-server queues with Poisson arrival pattern.

time and waiting time in a single-server queue. These all make the assumption that the service time follows a gamma distribution, as we shall explain shortly.

**PROBABILITIES**
**OF QUEUES**
**EXCEEDING**
**GIVEN SIZES**

It is useful to be able to evaluate the probabilities that queues exceed certain sizes and times exceed certain values. We frequently want an answer to such questions as: "How often does the queue exceed six?" or: "Will 90 percent of the transactions be served in less than $x$ seconds?" It is only possible to answer such questions by mathematical methods if we can fit the service times into a known distribution.

If the service time distribution is exponential (normally our "worst case" assumption), then it can be shown that the distribution of $q$ is

$$P(q = N) = (1 - \rho)\rho^N$$

where $P(q = N)$ is the probability that $q = N$.

Hence the probability that $q$ is greater than or equal to $N$ is

$$P(q \geq N) = \sum_{q=N}^{\infty} (1 - \rho)\rho^q$$

This equation is plotted in Fig. 31.8 for various values of $N$.

The probability of queuing time $t_q$ being greater than time $T$ can also be evaluated for exponential service times.

$$P(t_q > T) = e^{-(1-\rho)T/E(t_s)} \tag{31.26}$$

This equation is plotted in Fig. 31.9.

In this case $t_q$ is, as will be seen from the foregoing equation, exponentially distributed. Such is usually not the case, however, because the service time distribution is not exponential. For many of the queuing situations resulting from actual design problems, no one has devised a precise formula for $P(q \geq N)$ or $P(t_q > T)$.

One way to obtain percentiles of response time is to use simulation. This process, however, is time consuming, and if we could devise a quicker but approximate method it would be worthwhile, especially in the early stages of the design. It turns out that gamma distribution gives us a very useful approximation.

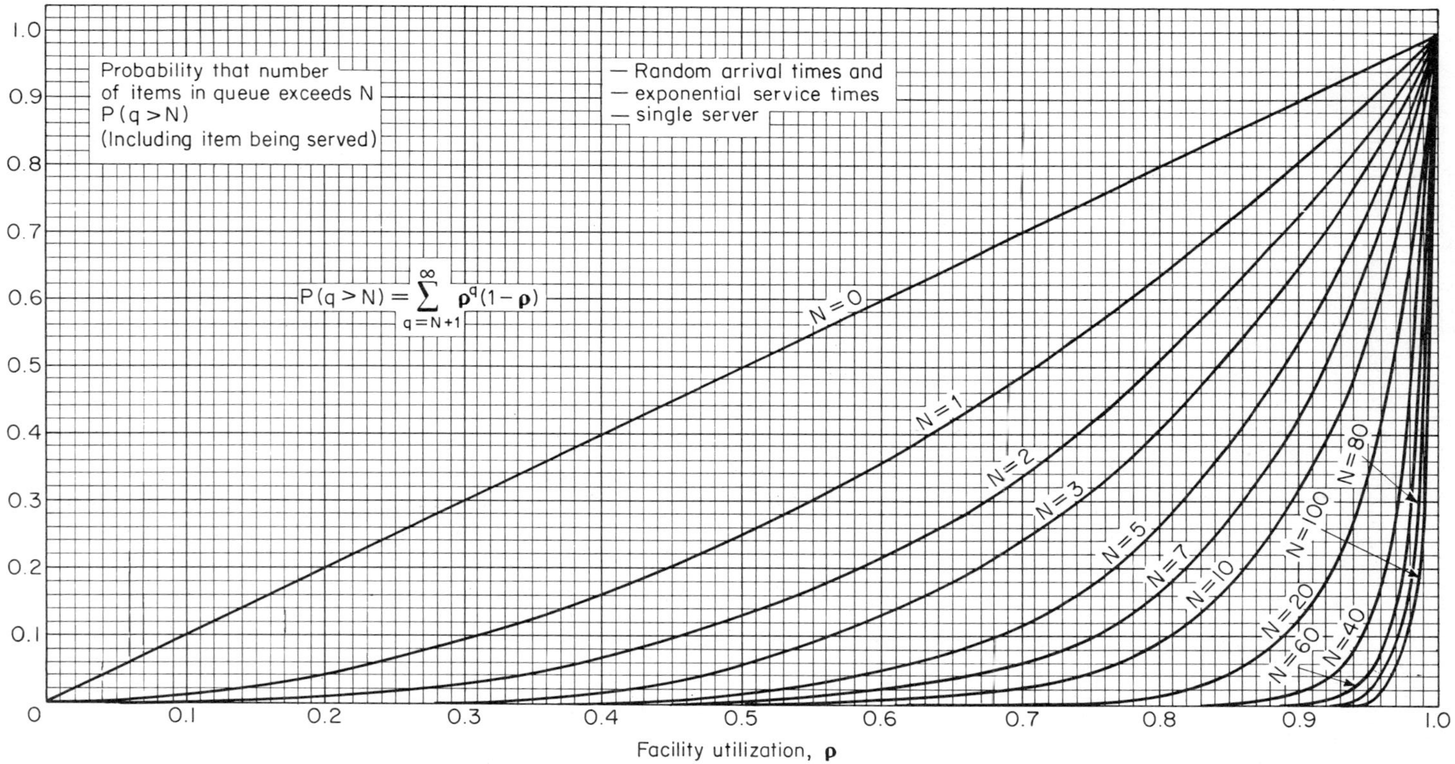
Probability that number
of items in queue exceeds N
P (q > N)
(Including item being served)
— Random arrival times and
— exponential service times
— single server
$P(q > N) = \sum_{q=N+1}^{\infty} \rho^q (1-\rho)$
N=0
N=1
N=2
N=3
N=5
N=7
N=10
N=20
N=40
N=60
N=80
N=100
1.0
0.9
0.8
0.7
0.6
0.5
0.4
0.3
0.2
0.1
0
0.1
0.2
0.3
0.4
0.5
0.6
0.7
0.8
0.9
1.0
Facility utilization, ρ

*Fig. 31.8.* Probability of exceeding certain queue sizes in a single-server queue.

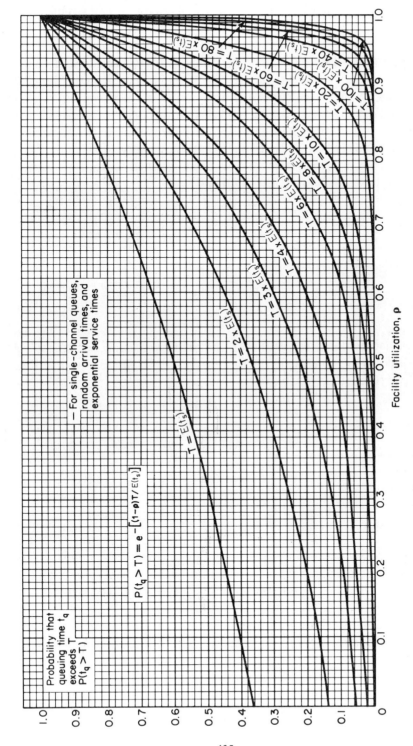

Probability that
queuing time $t_q$
exceeds T
$P(t_q > T)$

— For single-channel queues,
random arrival times, and
exponential service times

$$P(t_q > T) = e^{-\left[(1-\rho)T/E(t_s)\right]}$$

$T = E(t_s)$

$T = 2 \times E(t_s)$

$T = 3 \times E(t_s)$

$T = 4 \times E(t_s)$

$T = 6 \times E(t_s)$

$T = 8 \times E(t_s)$

$T = 10 \times E(t_s)$

$T = 20 \times E(t_s)$

$T = 40 \times E(t_s)$

$T = 60 \times E(t_s)$

$T = 80 \times E(t_s)$

$T = 100 \times E(t_s)$

Facility utilization, $\rho$

*Fig. 31.9.* Probability of exceeding certain queuing times in a single-server queue.

**THE ERLANG AND GAMMA DISTRIBUTIONS**      When we have a stream of transactions that arrive at random, the times between messages, as discussed earlier, are exponentially distributed. Many of the ways in which we could manipulate this stream of messages would result in an Erlang distribution. For example, suppose that there is a two-way switch on an input line which carries messages with exponential interarrival times. This switch is operated in such a way that alternate messages go down different paths. The result (Fig. 31.10) is that the switched message stream has interarrival times that follow an Erlang 2 distribution.

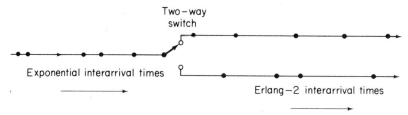

*Figure 31.10*

If we had used a three-way switch and switched messages down paths A, B, C, ... successively, then the resulting message stream would have had Erlang 3 interarrival times (Fig. 31.11).

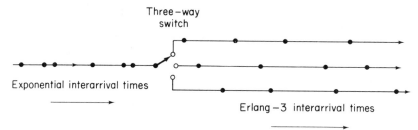

*Figure 31.11*

If we had switched them alternately down a very large number of paths, the resulting interarrival times would have become close to constant. An Erlang ∞ distribution of interarrival times means that the interarrival times are constant.

The Erlang distributions are specific cases of a more general family, the gamma distributions. For an Erlang distribution of times, $t$, the ratio $[E(t_s)/\sigma_{t_s}]^2$ is always an integer. For the gamma distribution, it can have any value. The gamma distribution has a parameter $R$, where

$$R = \left[\frac{E(t_s)}{\sigma_{t_s}}\right]^2 \qquad (31.27)$$

For the gamma distribution, the probability of $t$ being less than a given time is

$$P(t \leq T) = \frac{\int_0^T \left[\dfrac{RT}{E(t)}\right]^{R-1} e^{-RT/E(t)} \dfrac{R}{E(t)} \, dt}{\int_0^\infty \left[\dfrac{RT}{E(t)}\right]^{R-1} e^{-RT/E(t)} \dfrac{R}{E(t)} \, dt} \qquad (31.28)$$

The exponential distributions, the Erlang distributions, and a constant set of values are all specific cases of the gamma distribution. For the exponential distribution, $R = 1$. For the Erlang distributions, $R$ can be any integer. For a constant set of values, $R = \infty$.

One of the properties of the gamma distribution is that when two or more independent variables follow a gamma distribution, then the sum of these variables also follows a gamma distribution. Generally, in evaluating terminal response time, or other time parameters in a computer system, we have to add together separate time elements, as in Fig. 31.12, for example. Here time

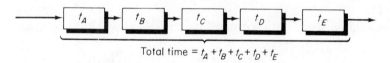

Total time $= t_A + t_B + t_C + t_D + t_E$

Fig. 31.12. If these five time elements are independent and each follows a gamma distribution, then the total time will follow a gamma distribution.

element $t_A$ might be the time spent at a terminal queuing to obtain the transmission line. Time $t_B$ is the transmission time. Time $t_C$ is the time spent in the computer system. Time $t_D$ is the time spent queuing for the output transmission, and $t_E$ is the output transmission time. The input transmission time might follow an exponential distribution and hence the queuing time for this service would be exponential. The time spent in the computer might approximate an Erlang distribution closely. The output messages, and hence their transmission time, might be of constant length. The queuing time resulting on the output line is then a reasonable fit to a gamma distribution. These times are largely, but not entirely, independent. We might therefore expect that their sum is close to a gamma distribution.

In most practical cases where we want to fit a known mathematical distribution to the response time of a data transmission system, it turns out that the gamma distribution gives a fairly good fit. In many cases, the elements of time that we have to add together can themselves be best approximated by the gamma distribution. If we add an exponential queuing time, for example, to another time that is constant, the result is a gamma distribution.

In some of our calculations it is useful to represent time values other than response times by the gamma distribution. Knowing the mean and standard deviation of message lengths or seek time, for example, we may select the gamma distribution that also has these values.

It is, in fact, this approximation that allows us to plot the standard deviations of queue sizes and queuing times in Figs. 31.6 and 31.7 and to tabulate the standard deviations of queuing times and waiting times in Appendix VIII. We assume that the service times of the queue follow a gamma distribution. If we do not use this approximation (which is quite good enough for most practical cases), then we must know the third moment of service time and use Eqs. (31.24) and (31.25).

For the gamma distribution, the third moment is

$$E(t^3) = \frac{(R+1)(R+2)}{R^2} E^3(t) \tag{31.29}$$

Using this equation, we see that Eqs. (31.24) and (31.25) contract to

$$\text{Var }(q) = \frac{1}{(1-\rho)^2} \left\{ 1 - \frac{\rho}{2} \left[ 3 - \frac{\rho(10-\rho)}{6} - \frac{3-3\rho+\rho^2}{R} - \frac{\rho(8-5\rho)}{6R^2} \right] \right\} \tag{31.30}$$

and

$$\text{Var }(t_q) = \left[ \frac{E(t_s)}{1-\rho} \right]^2 \left\{ \left[ 1 - \frac{\rho}{6}(4-\rho)\left(1 - \frac{1}{R}\right)\left(1 + \frac{1}{R}\right) - \left[ 1 - \frac{\rho}{2}\left(1 - \frac{1}{R}\right) \right]^2 \right\} \tag{31.31}$$

**ESTIMATING PROBABILITIES OF RESPONSE TIMES**

Using this approximation and Tables 6 and 7 of Appendix VIII, the systems engineer can obtain a very quick estimate of $\sigma_{t_w}$ and $\sigma_{t_q}$.

This gives a simple and useful method of answering such questions as: "Will 90 percent of the transactions have a response in 3 seconds or less?"

The procedure follows four steps:

1. Calculate the mean response time, $E(t)$.
2. Calculate the standard deviation of response time, $\sigma_t$.
3. Select a gamma distribution that has a close fit to the distribution of response times. This will be the gamma distribution with the parameter

$$R = \left[\frac{E(t)}{\sigma_t}\right]^2$$

4. Use tables of the gamma distribution to find values of Prob $(t \leq T)$ and hence answer the question.

If at a later time the system designer needs to be more exact or more rigorous, he must either plunge into a *much* higher level of mathematics or resort to simulation. The latter is probably the best approach.

The gamma distribution, unfortunately, is not so easy to handle for the purpose of calculations as are the other equations in this chapter. It is plotted in Figs. 31.13 and 31.14. The two plots are identical except that they are drawn with different scales. The useful range of the gamma distribution is tabulated in Table 4 of Appendix VIII. These plots and table are intended to form a tool that the reader can use quickly in estimating response times.

**Example 31.3. Use of the Gamma Curves and Table.** We have estimated the mean response time of a real-time system to be 3 seconds and the standard deviation to be 1.5 seconds.

1. What fraction of the transactions will have a response time greater than 6 seconds?
2. What fraction will have a response time greater than 9 seconds?
3. What fraction will have a response time greater than 12 seconds?

$$E(t) = 3$$

$$\sigma_t = 1.5$$

Therefore

$$R = \left[\frac{E(t)}{\sigma_t}\right]^2 = \left(\frac{3}{1.5}\right)^2 = 4$$

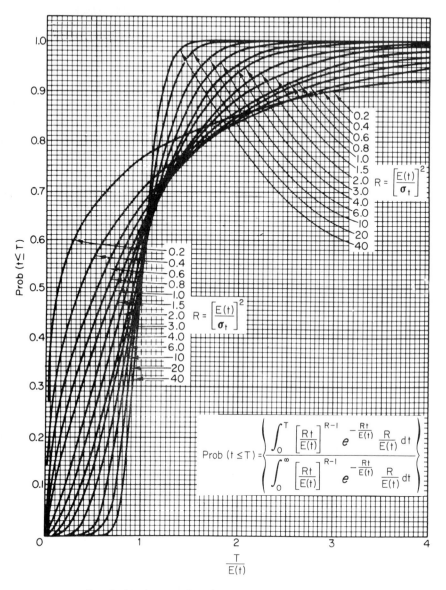

*Fig. 31.13.* A plot of the incomplete gamma function.

We will first let $T = 6$ and find Prob $(t \leq 6)$.

$$\frac{T}{E(t)} = \frac{6}{3} = 2$$

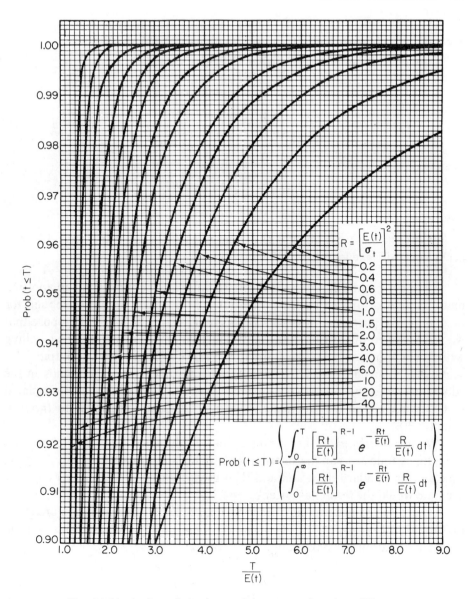

*Fig. 31.14.* A plot of the incomplete gamma function. (The top tenth of Fig. 31.13, opposite, replotted for increased accuracy.)

Using the $R = 4$ curve on either Fig. 31.13 or 31.14, we can read that for $[(T/E(t)] = 2$, Prob $(t \le T)$ is about 0.955. More accurately, from Table 4 in Appendix VIII, Prob $(t \le T) = 0.9576$.

In other words, 0.9576 of the transactions will have a response time of less than 6 seconds, i.e., 4.24 percent of them will take longer than 6 seconds.

Now let us repeat the process for 9 seconds.

$$T = 9$$

$$\left[\frac{T}{E(t)}\right] = 3$$

Therefore

$$\text{Prob } (t \leq T) = 0.9977$$

from Table 4.

In other words, only about 0.23 percent will take longer than 9 seconds. Practically none will take longer than 12 seconds.

Fitting a gamma curve to the response times is, of course, only an approximate method of answering these questions. It is usually accurate enough for most *practical* purposes, however. Let us look at a typical case. Suppose that we have a communication line on which terminals are polled. The polling sequence will be controlled by a list in the line control program. Output messages will be given priority over input, and the time a message spends in the computer center will be approximately constant. This situation is simulated in Chapter 38. The message lengths follow a distribution similar to those in Chapter 30.

We are interested in the response times at the terminals. How closely do these times follow a gamma distribution? If we had found the mean response time and its standard deviation and then used Table 4 in Appendix VIII, how accurate would the result have been?

Figure 31.15 answers this question. The results of the simulation are given in Table 38.14 on page 671. The mean response time is 1.938 seconds and the standard deviation is 0.990 second. Therefore

$$R = \left(\frac{1.938}{0.990}\right)^2 = 3.83$$

A gamma distribution curve with this value of $R$ is plotted as the solid line in Fig. 31.15. The crosses represent the distribution of response times as given by the simulation, in Table 38.14.

It will be observed that they do not follow the gamma distribution curve exactly but are close to it. This degree of closeness of fit is typical of the situa-

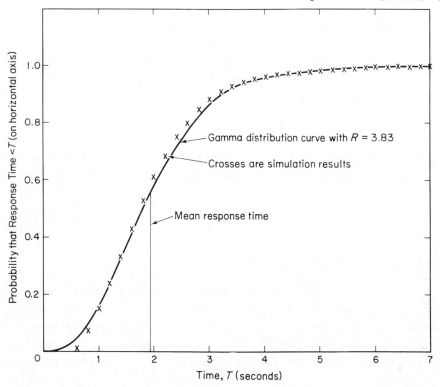

*Fig. 31.15.* Comparison of a simulation of a polled communication line (from Chapter 38) with a gamma distribution estimate. The deviation between the two is of typical magnitude.

tions in which we shall employ the gamma distribution, as well as Table 4, for estimating response time probabilities.

**Example 31.4. Dispersion of Bank Teller Queuing Time.** In Example 31.2 we calculated the mean queue size and queuing time for a bank teller. Let us calculate now the standard deviation of queue sizes and the probability of the queue exceeding certain sizes.

In order to calculate the standard deviations from Eqs. (31.24) and (31.25), we need to know the third moment of the service time. This moment could have been evaluated when the teller and terminal operations were timed. The third moment, however, is not given in Example 31.2. We are told that the service times have a mean of 1.5 minutes and standard deviation of 0.5 minute. Let us take these figures and use Eqs. (31.30) and (31.31).

$$ R = \left[ \frac{E(t_s)}{\sigma_{t_s}} \right]^2 = \left( \frac{1.5}{0.5} \right)^2 = 9 $$

The service times approximate a gamma distribution with $R = 9$.

Using $R = 9$ and knowing that the server utilization $\rho = 0.75$, we can use Figs. 31.6 and 31.7 to obtain a quick estimate of the standard deviations of queue size and queuing time. Table 6 in Appendix VIII tabulates the standard deviation of queuing time. From the table or curves,

$$\sigma_{t_q} \simeq 2.1 \times E(t_s) = 2.1 \times 1.5 = 3.15 \text{ minutes}$$

How many customers will have to stand in the queue longer than 10 minutes?

If the service times were exponential, we could use Eq. (31.26) or glance at Fig. 31.9.

$$\text{Prob}\,(t_q \geq 10) = \exp - \left[\frac{(1 - \rho) \times 10}{E(t_s)}\right] = \exp - \left[\frac{(1 - 0.75) \times 10}{1.5}\right]$$

$$= e^{-1.667} = 0.188$$

We know, however, that this answer is pessimistic because the service times have a much lower dispersion than an exponential distribution. The standard deviation is one-third of the mean, whereas for an exponential distribution it equals the mean.

Let us therefore assume that the queuing times approximate a gamma distribution with $E(t_q) = 4$ minutes, as calculated on page 428, and $\sigma_{t_q} = 3.15$ minutes, as calculated above.

$$R \text{ for this gamma distribution} = \left(\frac{4}{3.15}\right)^2 = 1.51$$

The curve in Fig. 31.13 or 31.14 with $R = 1.51$ gives us the distribution of queuing times. We are interested in the point at which $T = 10$.

$$\frac{T}{E(t_q)} = \frac{10}{4} = 2.5$$

Using Table 4 in Appendix VIII, we find that Prob $(t \leq T)$ is approximately 0.94. Six percent of the customers will stand in the queue longer than 10 minutes.

**THE EFFECT OF DIFFERENT DISPATCHING DISCIPLINES**

We noted earlier that the equations for $E(w)$, $E(q)$, $E(t_w)$, and $E(t_q)$ applied for any dispatching or scheduling discipline that chooses the next item to be served regardless of the service time. This fact is true of all the equations from (31.3) to (31.23). It is not true of (31.24) and the following equations, which apply only to "first-in, first-out" dispatching.

The standard deviations of $w$, $q$, $t_w$, and $t_q$ will be different for different dispatching disciplines. So also will be $P(q \geq N)$, $P(t_q > T)$, and other such measures. Only the *mean* values will be unaffected.

One dispatching discipline of interest is that in which the next item to be served is selected at *random* from the queue. This situation corresponds approximately to a polling situation in which a number of terminals are cyclically scanned to select the next item to be serviced. As might be expected, random dispatching gives a greater dispersion of queue sizes and times than first-in, first-out dispatching. The difference in $\sigma_q$ and $\sigma_{t_q}$ between these two disciplines becomes larger as $\rho$ becomes larger. This fact is shown in the curves in Fig. 31.16 for $\sigma_{t_q}$. These curves compare the two disciplines for constant service times and also for exponential service times.

The equation equivalent to (31.25) for random dispatching is

$$\text{Var}\ (t_q) = \frac{2E(n)E(t_s^3)}{3(1 - \rho)(2 - \rho)} + \frac{E^2(n)E^2(t_s^2)(2 + \rho)}{4(1 - \rho)^2(2 - \rho)} + E(t_s^2) - E^2(t_s) \quad (31.32)$$

For exponential service times, this equation becomes

$$\sigma_{t_q} = \frac{E(t_s)}{1 - \rho}\sqrt{\frac{2\rho^2 + 2 - \rho}{2 - \rho}} \quad (31.33)$$

and for constant service times

$$\sigma_{t_q} = \frac{E(t_s)}{1 - \rho}\sqrt{\frac{8\rho - 2\rho^2 + 3\rho^3}{12(2 - \rho)}} \quad (31.34)$$

The two equations are plotted in Fig. 31.16.

**QUEUES WITH PRIORITIES**     The queues considered so far do not give different items different priorities. Queues in which dispatching is done on the basis of priority category are important in computer and data transmission system design.

Suppose that priority 1 items are always served before priority 2 items, priority 2 before priority 3, and so on. We may be interested in the sizes of the queues and queuing times for all items, considered together, and we may also be interested in queues for individual priority categories.

Let us suppose that there are $k$ different streams of transactions entering the queue, having priority levels 1, 2, 3, . . . , $k$.

The mean arrival rate of priority $j$ items is $E(n_j)$.

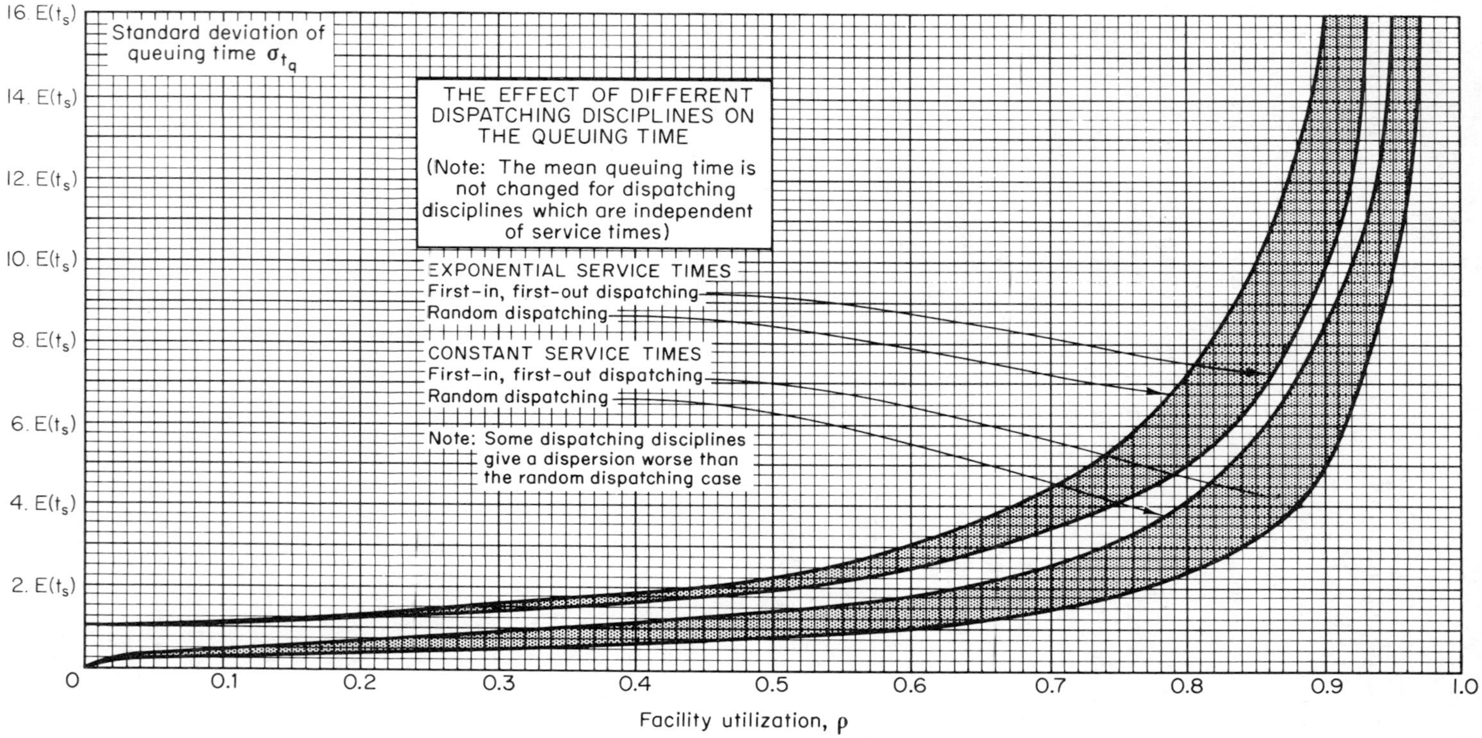
16. $E(t_s)$
14. $E(t_s)$
12. $E(t_s)$
10. $E(t_s)$
8. $E(t_s)$
6. $E(t_s)$
4. $E(t_s)$
2. $E(t_s)$
Standard deviation of queuing time $\sigma_{t_q}$
THE EFFECT OF DIFFERENT DISPATCHING DISCIPLINES ON THE QUEUING TIME
(Note: The mean queuing time is not changed for dispatching disciplines which are independent of service times)
EXPONENTIAL SERVICE TIMES
First-in, first-out dispatching
Random dispatching
CONSTANT SERVICE TIMES
First-in, first-out dispatching
Random dispatching
Note: Some dispatching disciplines give a dispersion worse than the random dispatching case
0
0.1
0.2
0.3
0.4
0.5
0.6
0.7
0.8
0.9
1.0
Facility utilization, $\rho$

*Fig. 31.16.* The effect of different dispatching disciplines on queuing time.

If the items in each class arrive independently with Poisson arrival distributions, then the total arrival rate also follows a Poisson distribution with mean $E(n)$, such that

$$E(n) = E(n_1) + E(n_2) + E(n_3) + \cdots + E(n_k)$$

Let the service time for the different priority levels be $t_{s_1}, t_{s_2}, t_{s_3}, \ldots, t_{s_k}$.

$$E(t_s) = \frac{E(n_1)}{E(n)} E(t_{s_1}) + \frac{E(n_2)}{E(n)} E(t_{s_2}) + \cdots + \frac{E(n_k)}{E(n)} E(t_{s_k}) \qquad (31.35)$$

and

$$E(t_s^2) = \frac{E(n_1)}{E(n)} E(t_{s_1}^2) + \frac{E(n_2)}{E(n)} E(t_{s_2}^2) + \cdots + \frac{E(n_k)}{E(n)} E(t_{s_k}^2) \qquad (31.36)$$

Let the fraction of facility utilization due to the priority $j$ items be $\rho_j$. Then

$$\rho_j = E(n_j)E(t_{s_j})$$

and

$$\rho = \rho_1 + \rho_2 + \rho_3 + \cdots + \rho_k \qquad (31.37)$$

The total number of items in the queue will be made up of the items of each separate priority stream.

Let the number in the queue for priority $j$ be $q_j$. Then the total number queuing is

$$q = q_1 + q_2 + \cdots + q_k \qquad (31.38)$$

Let the mean queuing time for items of priority $j$ be $E(t_q)$. Then the overall average queuing time is

$$E(t_q) = \frac{E(n_1)}{E(n)} E(t_{q_1}) + \frac{E(n_2)}{E(n)} E(t_{q_2}) + \cdots + \frac{E(n_k)}{E(n)} E(t_{q_k}) \qquad (31.39)$$

Similar relationships apply to $E(w)$ and $E(t_w)$.

**INTERRUPTS**     The queue sizes and times will be different if any *interruption* of transaction processing can take place. If no interruptions are permitted, then the highest priority items simply go to the head of the line. If interruptions are permitted, then as soon as an item arrives it breaks into the serving of any lower-priority item. The serving of the interrupted item may resume, when permitted, at the point at which it broke off, or, alternatively it may have to begin again at the beginning. We thus have three possible dispatching disciplines in different situations for priority-structured queues. In all of them, the items in any one priority category are served in a first-in, first-out manner. We shall use the following names to describe the three situations:

### 1. *"Head-of-Line" Priority Dispatching*

Priority $j$ items are served before priority $(j + 1)$ or lower-priority items. The highest priority items go to the head of the waiting line. No item interrupts the serving of any other item.

### 2. *"Preemptive Resume" Priority Dispatching*

Priority $j$ items interrupt the serving of priority $(j + 1)$ or lower-priority items. After an interrupt has occurred, the serving of the interrupted item will resume when permitted at the point at which it broke off. The top-priority stream of items obeys the Khintchine-Polloczek equations, (31.10) to (31.25), as though no other items were present.

### 3. *"Preemptive Repeat" Priority Dispatching*

Priority $j$ items interrupt the serving of priority $(j + 1)$ or lower-priority items. After an interrupt has occurred, the serving of the interrupted items will start again from the beginning when permitted. The top-priority stream of items again obeys the Khintchine-Polloczek equations as though no other items were present.

In the calculations that are done for the design of computer systems, "preemptive repeat" priority dispatching is rarely met and so will not be discussed further. "Preemptive resume" is found in the queuing of work in the processing unit, in which many operations are interrupted but resume where they left off. "Head-of-line" priority dispatching is found in several areas—for example, input transactions may have priority over output, type A transactions may have priority over type B, and so on. We will use the "head-of-line" priority equations in our discussion of the organization of transmission lines.

**HEAD-OF-LINE**    In a "head-of-line" priority dispatching case, if the
**PRIORITY**    mean service time for each priority category is the
**DISPATCHING**    same, then and only then are the preceding formulas
for the means of the overall queue sizes and times
obeyed [Eqs. (31.10) to (31.23)]. If priority 1 items require, on the average, a shorter service time than priority 2 items, then the dispatching discipline is no

longer independent of service times, and we have disobeyed this condition, which is necessary for the validity of Eqs. (31.10) to (31.23).

In fact, *if we deliberately give high priority to the items with short service times, we can reduce the mean size of the queues and queuing times.*

The way to treat this case analytically is to use a model with "head-of-line" priority dispatching.

It can be shown that the mean waiting time for priority $j$ items is

$$E(t_{w_j}) = \frac{E(n)E(t_s^2)}{2[1 - (\rho_1 + \rho_2 + \cdots + \rho_{j-1})][1 - (\rho_1 + \rho_2 + \cdots + \rho_j)]} \quad (31.40)$$

as before

$$E(t_{q_j}) = E(t_{w_j}) + E(t_{s_j}) \quad (31.41)$$

The mean number of priority $j$ items waiting is

$$E(w_j) = E(n_j)E(t_{w_j})$$

That is,

$$E(w_j) = \frac{E(n)E(n_j)E(t_s^2)}{2[1 - (\rho_1 + \rho_2 + \cdots + \rho_{j-1})][1 - (\rho_1 + \rho_2 + \cdots + \rho_j)]} \quad (31.42)$$

Where there are only two priority levels, Eq. (31.41) simplifies to

$$E(t_{q_1}) = \frac{E(n)E(t_s^2)}{2(1 - \rho_1)} + E(t_{s_1}) \quad (31.43)$$

and

$$E(t_{q_2}) = \frac{E(n)E(t_s^2)}{2(1 - \rho_1)(1 - \rho)} + E(t_{s_2}) \quad (31.44)$$

The second moment of waiting time for priority $j$ items is

$$E(t_{w_j}^2) = \frac{E(n)E(t_s^3)}{3[1 - (\rho_1 + \rho_2 + \cdots + \rho_{j-1})]^2[1 - (\rho_1 + \rho_2 + \cdots + \rho_j)]}$$
$$+ \frac{E(n)E(t_s^2)[E(n_1)E(t_{s_1}^2) + E(n_2)E(t_{s_2}^2) + \cdots + E(n_j)E(t_{s_j}^2)]}{2[1 - (\rho_1 + \rho_2 + \cdots + \rho_{j-1})]^2[1 - (\rho_1 + \rho_2 + \cdots + \rho_j)]^2} \quad (31.45)$$
$$+ \frac{E(n)E(t_s^2)[E(n_1)E(t_{s_1}^2) + E(n_2)E(t_{s_2}^2) + \cdots + E(n_{j-1})E(t_{s_{j-1}}^2)]}{2[1 - (\rho_1 + \rho_2 + \cdots + \rho_{j-1})]^3[1 - (\rho_1 + \rho_2 + \cdots + \rho_j)]}$$

The second moment of the overall waiting time for all the items is

$$E(t_w^2) = \frac{E(n_1)}{E(n)} E(t_{w1}^2) + \frac{E(n_2)}{E(n)} E(t_{w2}^2) + \cdots + \frac{E(n_k)}{E(n)} E(t_{wk}^2) \qquad (31.46)$$

From these second moments and means, the standard deviations may be calculated using

$$\sigma_{t_{w_j}} = \sqrt{E(t_{wj}^2) - E^2(t_{wj}^2)}$$

These equations simplify somewhat for the case in which the service time for the entire transaction set is assumed to be exponentially distributed

$$E(t_s^2) = 2E^2(t_s)$$

and for the case in which it is constant

$$E(t_s^2) = t_s^2$$

Table 31.3 lists formulas for these cases.

**PREEMPTIVE-RESUME**
**PRIORITY**
**DISPATCHING**

For preemptive-resume priority dispatching, in which high-priority items not only go to the head of the queue but also cause the work on a lower-priority item to be stopped immediately, Eqs. (31.35) to (31.39) still hold.

The mean waiting-line size and waiting times for the priority $j$ items are

$$E(t_{wj}) = \frac{1}{[1 - (\rho_1 + \rho_2 + \cdots + \rho_{j-1})]} [E(t_{sj})(\rho_1 + \rho_2 + \cdots + \rho_{j-1})]$$
$$+ \frac{E(n_1)E(t_{s1}^2) + E(n_2)E(t_{s2}^2) + \cdots + E(n_j)E(t_{sj}^2)}{2[1 - (\rho_1 + \rho_2 + \cdots + \rho_j)]} \qquad (31.47)$$

$$E(t_q) = E(t_w) + E(t_{sj}) = \frac{1}{[1 - (\rho_1 + \rho_2 + \cdots + \rho_{j-1})]}$$
$$\times \left\{ E(t_{sj}) + \frac{E(n_1)E(t_{s1}^2) + E(n_2)E(t_{s2}^2) + \cdots + E(n_j)E(t_{sj}^2)}{2[1 - (\rho_1 + \rho_2 + \cdots + \rho_j)]} \right\} \qquad (31.48)$$

The mean number of priority $j$ items waiting is

$$E(w_j) = E(n_j)E(t_{w_j}) = \frac{1}{[1 - (\rho_1 + \rho_2 + \cdots + \rho_{j-1})]}$$

$$\times \left\{ \rho_j(\rho_1 + \rho_2 + \cdots + \rho_{j-1}) \right. \tag{31.49}$$

$$\left. + \frac{E(n_j)[E(n_1)E(t_{s_1}^2) + E(n_2)E(t_{s_2}^2) + \cdots + E(n_j)E(t_{s_j}^2)]}{2[1 - (\rho_1 + \rho_2 + \cdots + \rho_j)]} \right\}$$

For the top priority stream, these equations condense to

$$E(t_{w_1}) = \frac{E(n_1)E(t_{s_1}^2)}{2(1 - \rho_1)}$$

and

$$E(w_1) = \frac{E^2(n_1)E(t_{s_1}^2)}{2(1 - \rho_1)}$$

If the service time for the top priority stream is exponentially distributed, these equations reduce to

$$E(t_{w_1}) = \frac{\rho_1}{1 - \rho_1} E(t_{s_1})$$

and

$$E(w_1) = \frac{\rho_1^2}{1 - \rho_1}$$

which gives

$$E(q_1) = \frac{\rho_1}{1 - \rho_1}$$

Table 31.4 lists these and other equations for preemptive-resume priority queues.

**MULTISERVER QUEUES**    Next, in this quick summary of basic queuing formulas, we shall examine the situation in which more than one server tends the items.

Suppose that a customer telephones an airline to enquire about his booking. Any one of a group of agents may handle his call. It is possible that all the agents will be busy, however, and he will have to wait. He takes his place in a line and a tape-recorded voice tells him that the first agent to become free will deal with him—this is a multiserver queuing situation. It is represented by the upper half of Fig. 31.17. The $M$ identical servers shown here are airline agents.

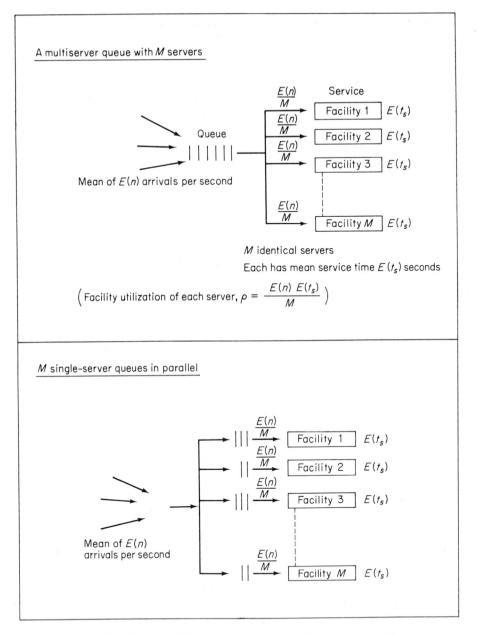

*Fig. 31.17.* The upper diagram represents a multiserver queue. The lower diagram represents $M$ single-server queues in parallel, having the same service times and arrival rate as in the upper diagram. The queue time for the multiserver case in the upper diagram is less than that for the lower diagram.

Note that he can go to any one of the servers. If he could only go to *his* particular server, then we would have a group of single-server queues, as shown in the bottom half of Fig. 31.17. The total queuing time for a group of items served by predetermined servers is greater than if they were able to choose the first of these servers who became free.

The equations that are commonly used in models involving multiserver queues make the following assumptions:

1. Arrival times follow a Poisson distribution, as before.
2. Items are served on a first-in, first-out basis.
3. The service times follow an exponential distribution.
4. All the servers have identical service time distributions. The last two assumptions make these formulas more restricted in their use than the single-server formulas.

Let us suppose that there are $M$ identical servers. The mean number of items being serviced is $E(n)$. Thus

$$\frac{E(n)}{M}$$

items go to each server. The mean service time is $E(t_s)$. Therefore the facility utilization of an individual server is

$$\rho = \frac{E(n)E(t_s)}{M} \tag{31.50}$$

As before, $\rho$ must be less than 1. As $\rho$ approaches 1, the queue sizes and times build up rapidly, although not quite as rapidly as in the single-server case with the same exponential service time.

The relationships in Eqs. (31.3) to (31.8) still hold:

$$t_q = t_w + t_s \tag{31.3}$$

$$E(t_q) = E(t_w) + E(t_s) \tag{31.4}$$

$$E(_w) = E(n)E(t_w) \tag{31.6}$$

and

$$E(q) = E(n)E(t_q) \tag{31.7}$$

Now, $t_w$, $t_q$, $w$, and $q$ relate to items waiting for any of the $M$ servers, not just to one of them.

$$E(q) = E(n)E(t_q) = E(n)E(t_w) + E(n)E(t_s)$$

Substituting from Eqs. (31.6) and (31.50), we get

$$E(q) = E(w) + M\rho \qquad (31.51)$$

It can be shown that the probability of there being $N$ items in the system at a given instant is

$$P(q = N) = \frac{(M\rho)^N}{N!} P_0 \qquad \text{if } N \leq M$$

and

$$P(q = N) = \frac{(M\rho)^N}{M!M^{N-M}} P_0 \qquad \text{if } N \geq M$$

where

$$P_0 = 1 \bigg/ \sum_{n=0}^{M-1} \frac{(M\rho)^N}{N!} + \frac{(M\rho)^M}{(1-\rho)M!} \qquad (31.52)$$

The probability of there being $K$ or more than $K$ items in the system at a given instant is

$$P(q \geq K) = \sum_{N=K}^{\infty} P(q = N)$$

This equation is plotted in Figs. 31.18 to 31.21 for 2, 3, 4, 5, and 20 servers. It is interesting to compare these figures with Fig. 31.6 for one server.

In particular, the probability of all servers being busy at a given instant is

$$B = P(q \geq M) = \sum_{N=M}^{\infty} P(q = N)$$

which can be calculated to be

$$B = \frac{1 - \left[\dfrac{\sum_{N=0}^{M-1} \dfrac{(M\rho)^N}{N!}}{\sum_{N=0}^{M} \dfrac{(M\rho)^N}{N!}}\right]}{1 - \rho \left[\dfrac{\sum_{N=0}^{M-1} \dfrac{(M\rho)^N}{N!}}{\sum_{N=0}^{M} \dfrac{(M\rho)^N}{N!}}\right]} \qquad (31.53)$$

This factor, $B$, appears in all the remaining equations for multiserver queuing (unfortunately!). It is plotted in Fig. 31.22 and tabulated in Table 8 of Appendix VIII. Note that this equation condenses to $B = \rho$ when $M = 1$.

It can be shown that in the multichannel queues described the mean number of items waiting before service begins is

$$E(w) = B\frac{\rho}{1 - \rho} \tag{31.54}$$

Thus

$$E(q) = B\frac{\rho}{1 - \rho} + M\rho \tag{31.55}$$

The standard deviation of $w$ is given by

$$\sigma_w = \frac{1}{1 - \rho} \sqrt{B\rho(1 + \rho - B\rho)} \tag{31.56}$$

The mean waiting time before service begins is

$$E(t_w) = \frac{B}{M}\frac{E(t_s)}{(1 - \rho)} \tag{31.57}$$

Therefore

$$E(t_q) = \frac{B}{M}\frac{E(t_s)}{(1 - \rho)} + E(t_s) \tag{31.58}$$

The standard deviation of waiting time is

$$\sigma_{t_w} = \frac{E(t_s)}{M(1 - \rho)} \sqrt{B(2 - B)} \tag{31.59}$$

and

$$\sigma_{t_q} = \frac{E(t_s)}{M(1 - \rho)} \sqrt{B(2 - B) + M^2(1 - \rho)^2} \tag{31.60}$$

The probability of waiting for a longer time than $t$ is given by

$$\text{Prob } (t_w \geq t) = B\,e^{-[M(1-\rho)t/E(t_s)]} \tag{31.61}$$

The mean queuing times, Eq. (31.58), and the standard deviation of queuing times, Eq. (31.60), are tabulated in Tables 9 and 10 of Appendix VIII.

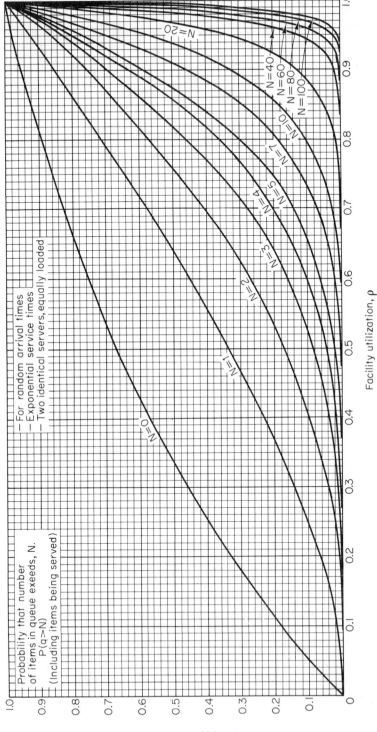

456

*Fig. 31.18.* Probability of exceeding certain queue sizes in a two-server queue.

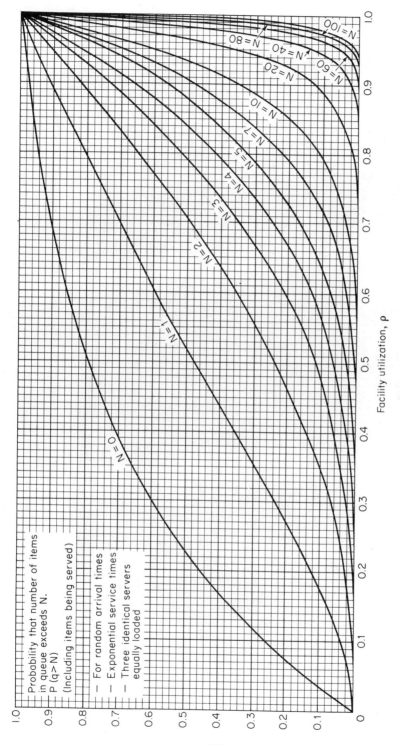

Probability that number of items
in queue exceeds N.
P (q > N)
(Including items being served)

— For random arrival times
— Exponential service times
— Three identical servers
  equally loaded

N = 0

N = 1

N = 2

N = 3

N = 4

N = 5

N = 7

N = 10

N = 20

N = 80    N = 40

N = 60

N = 100

Facility utilization, ρ

*Fig. 31.19.* Probability of exceeding certain queue sizes in a three-server queue.

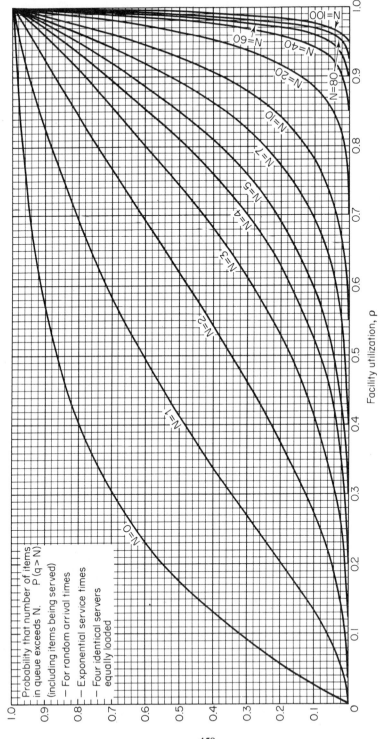

*Fig. 31.20.* Probability of exceeding certain queue sizes in a four-server queue.

458

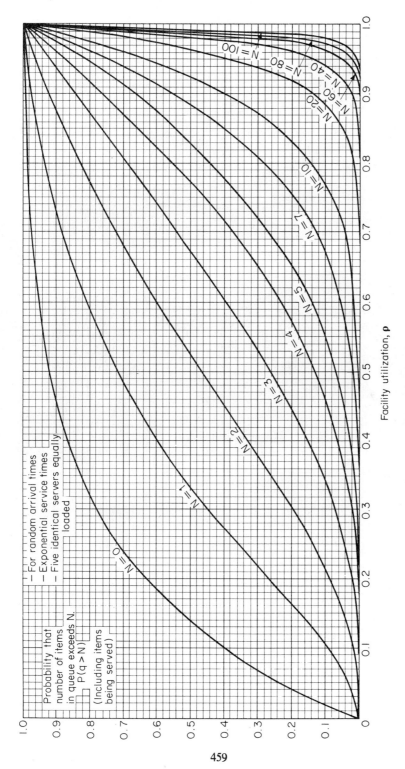

Facility utilization, ρ

*Fig. 31.21.* Probability of exceeding certain queue sizes in a five-server queue.

459

PROBABILITY THAT ALL SERVERS ARE BUSY IN A MULTI–SERVER QUEUE,

WITH: Exponential interarrival times
Exponential service times
All servers equally loaded
First–in–first–out dispatching

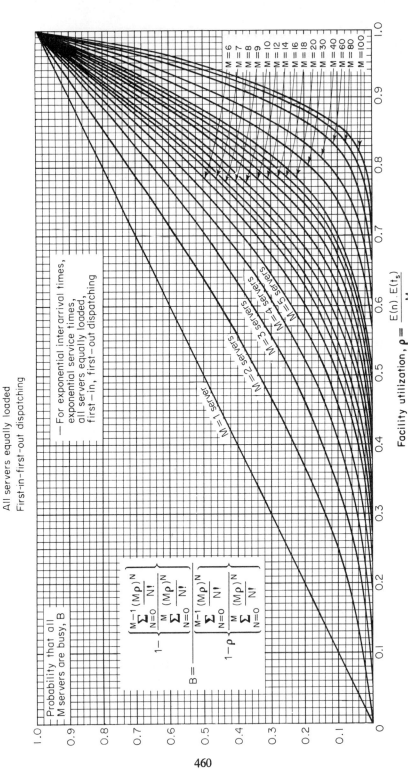

*Fig.* 31.22. Probability that all servers are busy in a multiserver queuing system.

They are plotted against $\rho$ in Figs. 31.24 and 31.25. The mean number of items in the queue is plotted against $\rho$ in Fig. 31.23.

**NONEXPONENTIAL SERVICE TIMES** All the preceding equations for multiserver queuing assume that the service times are exponentially distributed. Frequently in the cases in which we would like to use these equations, we know that the service times have a dispersion that is less than that of an exponential distribution. In such cases, the foregoing multiserver equations are pessimistic, giving a waiting time and a queue size somewhat longer than actuality. Simple general equations do not exist for queues with many servers and general waiting times. Solutions to such problems can be obtained but only by mathematical methods too elaborate for the typical systems analyst.

The systems analyst needs fairly quick techniques that will enable him to understand the behavior of the mechanisms he is devising, usually in circumstances in which his input data are inaccurate or uncertain. In such cases, the following approximation is helpful. The mean waiting time, $E(t_w)$, for a *single-server* queue with nonexponential service times is related to the mean waiting time for exponential services times, $E(t_{w\exp})$, by the following equation:

$$E(t_w) = \frac{E(t_{w\exp})}{2}\left\{1 + \left[\frac{\sigma_{t_s}}{E(t_s)}\right]^2\right\} \tag{31.62}$$

This result follows from Eqs. (31.12) and (31.17).

Similarly,

$$E(w) = \frac{E(w_{\exp})}{2}\left\{1 + \left[\frac{\sigma_{t_s}}{E(t_s)}\right]^2\right\} \tag{31.63}$$

where $E(w_{\exp})$ is the number of items waiting before service when the service time is exponential.

We can show, using simulation, that for multiserver queues, *also*, the waiting times and waiting-line sizes when the service times are not exponential are related to those when the service times *are* exponential in approximately the same ratio.

As a very quick and approximate way of estimating waiting times in multiserver queues, we suggest, therefore, that the systems analyst take the value of $E(t_q)$ from Table 9 in Appendix VIII, subtract $E(t_s)$ from it to obtain $E(t_w)$, and then multiply $E(t_w)$ by the factor

$$\frac{1}{2}\left\{1 + \left[\frac{\sigma_{t_s}}{E(t_s)}\right]^2\right\}$$

The value of $E(w)$ may be similarly obtained.

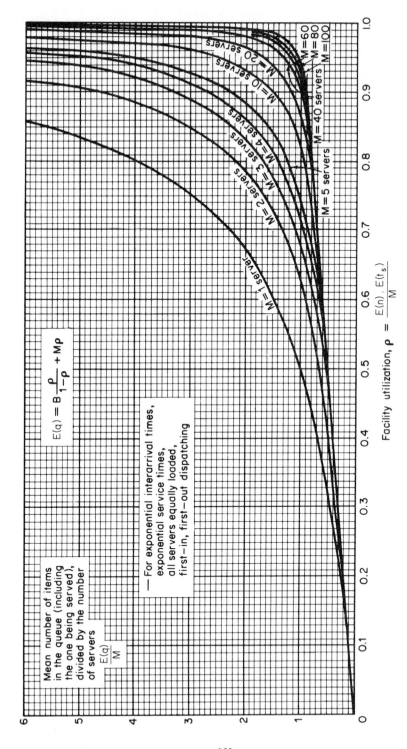

*Fig. 31.23.* Sizes of queues in a multiserver queuing system.

MEAN QUEUING TIMES FOR MULTI-SERVER QUEUES,

WITH: Exponential interarrival times
Exponential service times
All servers equally loaded
First-in-first-out dispatching

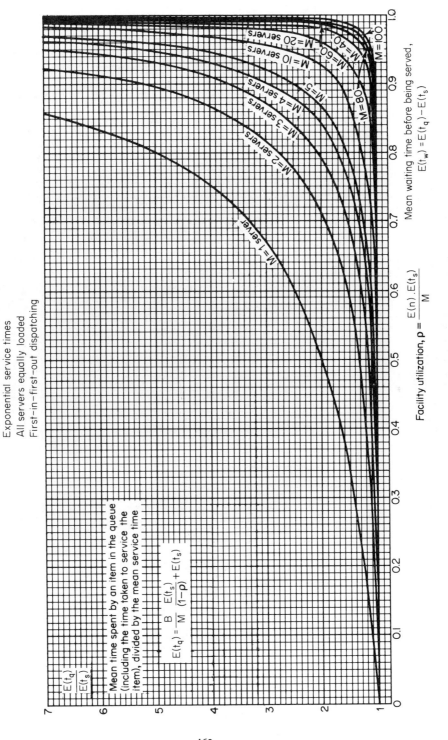

*Fig. 31.24.* Queuing times for multiserver queues.

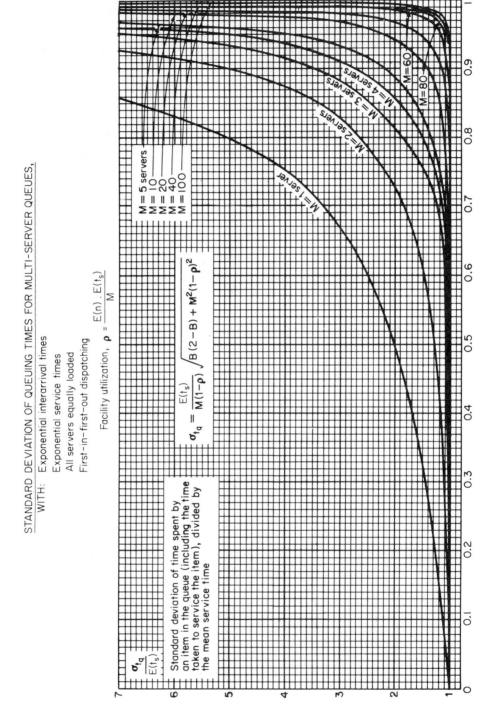

STANDARD DEVIATION OF QUEUING TIMES FOR MULTI-SERVER QUEUES,

WITH: Exponential interarrival times
Exponential service times
All servers equally loaded
First-in-first-out dispatching

Facility utilization, $\rho = \dfrac{E(n) \cdot E(t_s)}{M}$

$$\sigma_{t_q} = \frac{E(t_s)}{M(1-\rho)} \sqrt{B(2-B) + M^2(1-\rho)^2}$$

$\dfrac{\sigma_{t_q}}{E(t_s)}$

Standard deviation of time spent by an item in the queue (including the time taken to service the item), divided by the mean service time

M = 5 servers
M = 10
M = 20
M = 40
M = 100

M = 1 server

M = 2 servers

M = 3 servers

M = 4 servers

M = 60

M = 80

*Fig. 31.25.* Standard deviation of queuing times for multiserver queues.

464

**Example 31.5. Waiting for Telephone Service.** Telephone enquiries that arrive at random (Poisson interarrival time distribution) are being served by three girls using terminals. They take 6 minutes per call on the average. The calls are automatically routed to the first free girl. In the busiest half hour of the peak day, 12 calls are likely to be received. The service time is approximately exponentially distributed.

How long can a customer be expected to wait before talking to an agent? What is the standard deviation of this time?

A glance at the $M = 3$ curve in Figs. 31.24 and 31.25 gives us an approximate answer to the question and also shows us how fast the queue sizes are rising with rising traffic volume.

$$\rho = \frac{E(n)E(t_s)}{M} = \frac{\frac{12}{30} \times 6}{3} = 0.8$$

Both of the $M = 3$ curves are rising fairly rapidly when $\rho = 0.8$.

We can also obtain the answer from Tables 9 and 10 of Appendix VIII.

$$E(t_q) = 2.079 \times E(t_s)$$

and

$$\sigma_{t_s} = 1.853 \times E(t_s)$$

Therefore

$$E(t_q) = 2.079 \times 6 = 12.47 \text{ minutes}$$

and

$$\sigma_{t_q} = 1.853 \times 6 = 11.12 \text{ minutes}$$

$$t_q = t_w + t_s$$

and

$$\text{Var}(t_q) = \text{Var}(t_w) + \text{Var}(t_s)$$

The time a client waits before being dealt with has a mean of $12.47 - 6 = 6.47$ minutes and a variance of $11.12^2 - 6^2 = 87.65$ minutes$^2$, which gives a standard deviation of 9.36 minutes.

**WAITING TIME FOR ITEMS THAT ARE DELAYED** In some instances the preceding equations for waiting time, $E(t_w)$, might be a little misleading. A queuing system might have the characteristic that many of the items do not have to wait at all ($t_w = 0$), but that the few that do wait are delayed a long time. In this case, the mean waiting time for *the delayed items* is much longer than $E(t_w)$.

Suppose, for example, that you telephone an airline to check on your reservation. Ten girls with terminals deal with such calls, constituting a 10-server queuing system with a mean service time of 10 minutes. Suppose that the girls are 70 percent utilized, $\rho = 0.7$. Then the mean waiting time can be calculated from the foregoing equations to be 0.74 minute, which might seem acceptably low. However, the probability that all servers are busy, $B$, is 0.222. Hence 0.0778 percent of the callers are not kept waiting at all. Those that *are* kept waiting wait an average 3.33 minutes. Although 0.74 minute might not annoy a caller, 3.33 minutes are probably long enough to cause him to become impatient.

Let us define *mean delay time*, $E(t_d)$, as the mean time those callers who are kept waiting have to wait (ignoring those who are not kept waiting).

The probability that a caller will be kept waiting is $B$. The mean waiting time is therefore

$$E(t_w) = BE(t_d) + (1 - B)0 = BE(t_d)$$

But

$$E(t_w) = \frac{B}{M} \frac{E(t_s)}{1 - \rho} \tag{31.57}$$

Therefore

$$E(t_d) = \frac{E(t_s)}{M(1 - \rho)} \tag{31.64}$$

For single-server queues, the probability of the server being busy is $\rho$. The mean waiting time is therefore

$$E(t_w) = \rho E(t_d) + (1 - \rho)0 = \rho E(t_d)$$

Thus

$$E(t_d) = \frac{E(t_w)}{\rho} = \frac{E(t_s)}{2(1 - \rho)} \left\{ 1 + \left[ \frac{\sigma_{t_s}}{E(t_s)} \right]^2 \right\} \tag{31.65}$$

When the service times are exponentially distributed, this equation becomes

$$E(t_d) = \frac{E(t_s)}{1 - \rho}$$

**Example 31.6. Waiting for the Bank Teller.** The bank teller in Example 31.2 took a mean of 1.5 minutes to serve his customers, using a terminal on a real-time system. The mean queuing time was calculated to be 4 minutes and hence the mean waiting time is 2.5 minutes. How long, on the average, will a customer have to wait if he is not served immediately?

$$E(t_d) = \frac{E(t_w)}{\rho}$$

The utilization of the server (the bank teller) was 0.75 in this case. Therefore

$$E(t_d) = \frac{2.5}{0.75} = 3.33$$

The customer has a 25 percent chance of being served immediately and a 75 percent chance of having to wait a mean time of 3.33 minutes.

**NONQUEUING SITUATIONS** In the discussion of queues throughout this chapter it has been assumed that no items leave the system until they have been served. Another related situation that we will encounter in system design is that in which no queue can form. If an item is not served immediately, it is lost or goes away. If you encounter a busy tie-line group, for example, when calling a distant party, you are not able to wait in the queue until a line becomes free. It is probable that you will not know the full tie-line group is causing your busy signal. You will think that the party you are calling is busy. You will probably call again later, but for the time being you are a transaction lost to the system.

In this type of situation we want to know the probability of losing a call. It will equal the probability that all servers are busy, but this will be different from $B$ above for the case in which all the items join a queue.

We will write $P_B$ for the probability that all servers are busy.

Suppose, again, that we have $M$ equally loaded servers with utilization $\rho$. Once more the service time is exponential and the arrival rate follows a Poisson distribution.

It can be shown that the probability that no terminal is free is

$$P_B = \frac{(M\rho)^M}{M!} \bigg/ \sum_{N=0}^{M} \frac{(M\rho)^N}{N!} \qquad (31.66)$$

Figure 31.26 gives a plot of Eq. (31.66), and it is tabulated in Table 11 in Appendix VIII.

For values not in Table 11, Eq. (31.66) can be written in the following form, and evaluated with tables of the Poisson distribution and summed Poisson distribution:

$$P_B = \frac{(M\rho)^M e^{-M\rho}}{M!} \bigg/ \left\{ 1 - \sum_{n=M+1}^{\infty} \frac{(M\rho)^N e^{-M\rho}}{N!} \right\} \qquad (31.67)$$

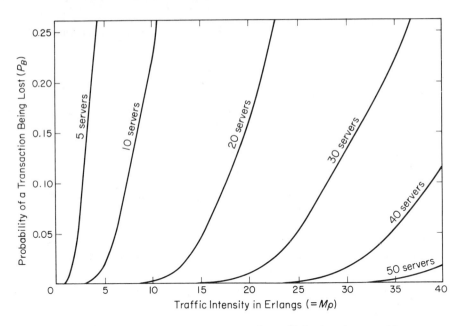

*Fig. 31.26.* Probability that a transaction will be lost in a multi-server nonqueuing situation (see page 467). Assumptions: Poisson arrival pattern; all servers are equal; if an item cannot be served immediately it is lost.

A suitable set of tables is General Electric's *Tables of the Individual and Cumulative Terms of the Poisson Distribution.*[1]

**CASES IN WHICH THE PRECEDING THEORY IS INACCURATE**

The foregoing formulas, and indeed any mathematical analysis of such problems, are approximations of the more complex situations that exist in reality. In deriving the formulas, certain assumptions were made, and the systems analyst should understand these assumptions. In most cases where applied, they will give an answer that is slightly pessimistic. In other words, they will indicate rather longer queues and delays than are actually the case. The reason is that random arrivals and sometimes exponential service times are used. A live situation may be slightly better than random. However, the discrepancy is usually small and may well be regarded as a reasonable systems analyst's safety allowance.

There are, however, two types of situation when the queues and delays will be worse than those indicated by the preceding curves.

First, for some reason superimposed on the normal behavior of the system, a sudden flood of items may arrive within a short period. For example, in a stockbroker's system certain news on the ticker tape might trigger a sudden burst of transactions.

[1] Princeton, N. J.: Van Nostrand, 1962.

Second, on occasion the service time may be considerably longer than the normal range. For example, the system may handle a few exceptionally long messages that tie up the communication lines, buffers, core, and possibly file channels. In statistics when a small number of items in a group have values much higher than the rest, the mean is of little value and even the standard deviation is misleading. The queue size might, therefore, be evaluated ignoring the long service times, and the effect of these times might be investigated afterward.

In some cases, it will be incorrect to assume that the interarrival times follow a Poisson distribution. This assumption, however, normally does not introduce too great an inaccuracy. If non-Poisson interarrival times are to be considered in detail, simulation is necessary. It should be noted, however, that most simulations done for this kind of system themselves have a Poisson distribution of input.

In the case of messages entering a system, it will generally be sufficiently valid to assume a Poisson distribution. In the case of requests for file actions, this assumption may not be true because the control program mechanisms will have acted as a filter that, to some extent, evens out the distribution of events. At peak loads the interarrival times at the file channel will be more constant than a Poisson distribution. The degree of this effect will depend on the control program mechanisms. Some mechanisms will deliberately restrict the flow of work when the queues are becoming high. Estimating the behavior of such a mechanism in fine detail requires an elaborate simulation. At the survey stage, nevertheless, an approximate estimate of queues is usually enough to specify the storage requirements of the system.

In general, any restricting element in a system, like a narrow section in a pipeline, tends to flatten the peaks of the traffic in the manner shown in Fig. 28.3. This traffic then reaching farther elements of the system has interarrival times slightly more constant than a Poisson distribution.

The structure of the queues may be more complex than those handled by the simple theory outlined earlier. Customers telephoning or queuing at windows for service may give up if they have to wait too long. In some cases, more elaborate queuing theory may be required than that in this chapter. A bibliography is provided for the reader at the end of the chapter.

In the chapters that follow, where queuing theory is used, we shall point out what assumptions are being made and discuss the level of accuracy of the calculations. We shall also point out where simulation seems to be worthwhile. Chapter 38 illustrates the use of simulation. Frequently, mathematical models of elements of data transmission systems give a clear insight into what is required to optimize the design than simulation does. Such models would be based on the equations in this chapter.

**Table 31.1.** THE NOTATION USED IN THIS CHAPTER

| | | |
|---|---|---|
| $n$ | Number of arrivals per second | |
| $E(n)$ | Average number of arrivals per second | |
| $P(n = N)$ | Probability of having $N$ arrivals in a given second | |
| $P(n \geq N)$ | Probability of having $N$ or more arrivals in a given second | |
| $t_a$ | Interarrival time | |
| $E(t_a)$ | Mean interarrival time | $E(t_a) = 1/E(n)$ |
| $t_s$ | Service time for an item | |
| $E(t_s)$ | Mean service time for all items | |
| $\rho$ | Facility utilization of one serving facility | $\rho = E(n)E(t_s)$ for a single server |
| $M$ | The number of servers in parallel on a multiserver system. | $\rho = E(n)E(t_s)/M$ for multiple servers |
| $t_\omega$ | Time an item spends waiting for service (not including time being served) | |
| $E(t_\omega)$ | Mean of $t_w$ for all items | |
| $w$ | Number of items waiting for service (not including item being served) | |
| $E(w)$ | Mean of $w$ for all items | $E(w) = E(n)E(t_w)$ |
| $t_q$ | Time an item spends in system, waiting and being served | $t_q = t_w + t_s$ |
| $E(t_q)$ | Mean of $t_q$ for all items | $E(t_q) = E(t_w) + E(t_s)$ |
| $q$ | Number of items in system, waiting and being served. | |
| $E(q)$ | Mean of $q$ for all items | $E(q) = E(n)E(t_q)$ |
| $E(t_d)$ | The mean waiting time for items which have to wait (not including items with waiting time = zero). | |
| $P(q = N)$ | Probability that $N$ items are in the system | |
| $P(q \geq N)$ | Probability that $q$ equals or is greater than integer $N$. | |
| $P(t_q > T)$ | Probability that $t_q$ is greater than a given time, $T$. | |
| $B$ | Probability that all servers are busy on a multiserver queuing system | |
| $P_B$ | Probability that all servers are busy on a multiserver system with no queuing (i.e., probability of a transaction being lost). | |
| $E(x)$ | The mean value of $x$ | |
| $E(x^2)$ | The second moment of $x$ | |
| $E(x^3)$ | The third moment of $x$ | |
| $\sigma_x$ | The standard deviation of $x$ | $\sigma_x = \sqrt{E(x^2) - E^2(x)}$ |
| $\text{Var}(x)$ | The variance of $x$ | $\text{Var}(x) = \sigma_x^2$ |
| $R$ | Parameter of a gamma distribution of $x$ | $R = \left[\dfrac{E(x)}{\sigma_x}\right]^2$ |

**Table 31.2.** FORMULAS FOR SINGLE-SERVER QUEUES

ASSUMPTIONS: 1. Poisson arrival pattern
2. Dispatching discipline does not give preference to items with shorter service times (if it does, the formulas in Table 31.3 should be used).
3. Formulas for second moment and standard deviation of queue sizes, or times, assume first-in, first-out dispatching.
4. No items leave the queue

$$\rho = E(n)E(t_s)$$

$$t_q = t_w + t_s$$

$$E(t_q) = E(t_w) + E(t_s)$$

$$E(w) = E(n)E(t_w)$$

$$E(q) = E(n)E(t_q)$$

$$E(q) = E(w) + \rho$$

$$E(\mathrm{w}) = \frac{\rho^2}{2(1-\rho)}\left[1 + \left(\frac{\sigma_{t_s}}{E(t_s)}\right)^2\right] \equiv \frac{E^2(n)E(t_s^2)}{2(1-\rho)}$$

$$E(q) = \rho + \frac{\rho^2}{2(1-\rho)}\left[1 + \left(\frac{\sigma_{t_s}}{E(t_s)}\right)^2\right] \equiv \rho + \frac{E^2(n)E(t_s^2)}{2(1-\rho)}$$

$$E(t_w) = \frac{\rho E(t_s)}{2(1-\rho)}\left[1 + \left(\frac{\sigma_{t_s}}{E(t_s)}\right)^2\right] \equiv \frac{E(n)E(t_s^2)}{2(1-\rho)}$$

$$E(t_q) = E(t_s) + \frac{\rho E(t_s)}{2(1-\rho)}\left[1 + \left(\frac{\sigma_{t_s}}{E(t_s)}\right)^2\right] \equiv E(t_s) + \frac{E(n)E(t_s^2)}{2(1-\rho)}$$

$$E(t_w^2) = \frac{E(n)E(t_s^3)}{3(1-\rho)} + \frac{E^2(n)E^2(t_s^2)}{2(1-\rho)^2}$$

$$\sigma_{t_w} = \sqrt{E(t_w^2) - E^2(t_w)}$$

$$= \sqrt{\frac{E(n)E(t_s^3)}{3(1-\rho)} - \frac{E^2(n)E^2(t_s^2)}{2(1-\rho)^2}}$$

$$E(t_q^2) = \frac{E(n)E(t_s^3) + 3E(t_s^2)}{3(1-\rho)} + \frac{E^2(n)E^2(t_s^2)}{2(1-\rho)^2}$$

$$\sigma_{t_q} = \sqrt{E(t_q^2) - E^2(t_q)}$$

$$= \sqrt{\frac{E(n)E(t_s^3)}{3(1-\rho)} - \frac{E^2(n)E^2(t_s^2)}{2(1-\rho)^2} + \sigma_{t_s}^2}$$

$$\sigma_q = \sqrt{\frac{E^3(n)E(t_s^3)}{3(1-\rho)} + \frac{E^4(n)E^2(t_s^2)}{4(1-\rho)^2} + \frac{E^2(n)(3 - 2\rho)E(t_s^2)}{2(1-\rho)} + \rho(1-\rho)}$$

## Table 31.2. CONTINUED

If the service times are either exponentially distributed or constant, the above equations for queue sizes and times simplify to the following:

| Exponential Service Times | Constant Service Times |
|---|---|
| $\sigma_{t_s} = E(t_s)$ | $\sigma_{t_s} = 0$ |
| $E(t_s^2) = 2E^2(t_s)$ | $E(t_s^2) = t_s^2$ |
| $E(w) = \dfrac{\rho^2}{1-\rho}$ | $E(w) = \dfrac{\rho^2}{2(1-\rho)}$ |
| $E(q) = \dfrac{\rho}{1-\rho}$ | $E(q) = \dfrac{\rho^2}{2(1-\rho)} + \rho$ |
| $E(t_w) = \dfrac{\rho E(t_s)}{1-\rho}$ | $E(t_w) = \dfrac{\rho t_s}{2(1-\rho)}$ |
| $E(t_q) = \dfrac{E(t_s)}{1-\rho}$ | $E(t_q) = \dfrac{t_s(2-\rho)}{2(1-\rho)}$ |
| $\sigma_q = \dfrac{\sqrt{\rho}}{1-\rho}$ | $\sigma_q = \dfrac{1}{1-\rho}\sqrt{\rho - \dfrac{3\rho^2}{2} + \dfrac{5\rho^3}{6} + \dfrac{\rho^4}{12}}$ |
| $\sigma_{jw} = \dfrac{E(t_s)}{1-\rho}\sqrt{2\rho - \rho^2}$ | $\sigma_{tw} = \dfrac{t_s}{1-\rho}\sqrt{\dfrac{\rho}{3} - \dfrac{\rho^2}{12}}$ |
| $\sigma_{t_q} = \dfrac{E(t_s)}{1-\rho}$ | $\sigma_{t_q} = \dfrac{t_s}{1-\rho}\sqrt{\dfrac{\rho}{3} - \dfrac{\rho^2}{12}}$ |
| $\text{Prob}\,(q = N) = (1-\rho)\rho^N$ | |
| $\text{Prob}\,(q \le N) = \displaystyle\sum_{i=0}^{N} (1-\rho)\rho^i$ | |
| $\text{Prob}\,(t_q \le t) = 1 - e^{-(1-\rho)t/E(t_s)}$ | |

**Table 31.3.** FORMULAS FOR QUEUES WITH PRIORITY CATEGORIES AND NO INTER-
RUPTS ("HEAD-OF-LINE" PRIORITY QUEUING DISCIPLINE)*

---

\* Priority $j$ items are serviced before priority $(j + 1)$ items. No item is interrupted while being served. Other assumptions are the same as in the previous table.

---

### 1. Formulas for queues with two priority categories

$$E(n) = E(n_1) + E(n_2)$$

$$\rho_1 = E(n_1)E(t_{s_1}); \ \rho_2 = E(n_2)E(t_{s_2})$$

$$\rho = \rho_1 + \rho_2$$

$$E(t_s) = \left[\frac{E(n_1)}{E(n)}\right]E(t_{s_1}) + \left[\frac{E(n_2)}{E(n)}\right]E(t_{s_2})$$

$$E(t_s^2) = \left[\frac{E(n_1)}{E(n)}\right]E(t_{s_1}^2) + \left[\frac{E(n_2)}{E(n)}\right]E(t_{s_2}^2)$$

$$E(w_1) = \frac{E(n)E(n_1)E(t_s^2)}{2(1 - \rho_1)}$$

$$E(w_2) = \frac{E(n)E(n_2)E(t_s^2)}{2(1 - \rho_1)(1 - \rho)}$$

$$E(w) = E(w_1) + E(w_2)$$

$$E(q_1) = E(w_1) + \rho_1$$

$$E(q_2) = E(w_2) + \rho_2$$

$$E(q) = E(q_1) + E(q_2)$$

$$E(t_{w_1}) = \frac{E(n)E(t_s^2)}{2(1 - \rho_1)}$$

$$E(t_{w_2}) = \frac{E(n)E(t_s^2)}{2(1 - \rho_1)(1 - \rho)}$$

$$E(t_w) = \frac{E(n_1)}{E(n)}E(t_{w_1}) + \frac{E(n_2)}{E(n)}E(t_{w_2})$$

$$E(t_{q_1}) = E(t_{w_1}) + E(t_{s_1})$$

$$E(t_{q_2}) = E(t_{w_2}) + E(t_{s_2})$$

$$E(t_q) = \frac{E(n_1)}{E(n)}E(t_{q_1}) + \frac{E(n_2)}{E(n)}E(t_{q_2})$$

$$E(t_{w_1}^2) = \frac{E(n)E(t_s^3)}{3(1 - \rho_1)} + \frac{E(n_1)E(n)E(t_{s_1}^2)E(t_s^2)}{2(1 - \rho_1)^2}$$

$$E(t_{w_2}^2) = \frac{E(n)E(t_s^3)}{3(1 - \rho_1)^2(1 - \rho)} + \frac{E^2(n)E^2(t_s^2)}{2(1 - \rho_1)^2(1 - \rho)^2}$$

$$+ \frac{E(n_1)E(t_{s_1}^2)E(n)E(t_s^2)}{2(1 - \rho_1)^3(1 - \rho)}$$

$$E(t_w^2) = \frac{E(n_1)}{E(n)}E(t_{w_1}^2) + \frac{E(n_2)}{E(n)}E(t_{w_2}^2)$$

$$\sigma_{t_{w_1}} = \sqrt{E(t_{w_1}^2) - E^2(t_{w_1})} \ \text{ etc.}$$

473

**Table 31.3.** CONTINUED

---

If the service times are either exponentially distributed or constant, the above equations for queue sizes and times simplify to the following:

| Exponential Service Times | Constant Service Times |
|---|---|

$$E(w_1) = \frac{\rho E(n_1)E(t_s)}{(1 - \rho_1)}$$

$$E(w_1) = \frac{\rho E(n_1)t_s}{(1 - \rho_1)}$$

$$E(w_2) = \frac{\rho E(n_2)E(t_s)}{(1 - \rho_1)(1 - \rho)}$$

$$E(w_2) = \frac{\rho E(n_2)t_s}{(1 - \rho_1)(1 - \rho)}$$

$$E(w) = E(w_1) + E(w_2)$$

$$E(w) = E(w_1) + E(w_2)$$

$$= \frac{\rho E(t_s)[E(n) - \rho E(n_1)]}{(1 - \rho_1)(1 - \rho)}$$

$$= \frac{\rho t_s[E(n) - \rho E(n_1)]}{(1 - \rho_1)(1 - \rho)}$$

$$E(t_{w_1}) = \frac{\rho}{1 - \rho_1} E(t_s)$$

$$E(t_{w_1}) = \frac{\rho t_s}{2(1 - \rho_1)}$$

$$E(t_{w_2}) = \frac{\rho}{(1 - \rho_1)(1 - \rho)} E(t_s)$$

$$E(t_{w_2}) = \frac{\rho t_s}{2(1 - \rho_1)(1 - \rho)}$$

$$E(t_w) = \frac{E(n_1)}{E(n)} E(t_{w_1}) + \frac{E(n_2)}{E(n)} E(t_{w_2})$$

$$E(t_w) = \frac{E(n_1)}{E(n)} E(t_{w_1}) + \frac{E(n_2)}{E(n)} E(t_{w_2})$$

$$= \frac{E^2(t_s)[E(n) - \rho E(n_1)]}{(1 - \rho_1)(1 - \rho)}$$

$$= \frac{t_s[E(n) - \rho E(n_1)]}{2(1 - \rho_1)(1 - \rho)}$$

$$E(t_{w_1}^2) = \frac{2\rho E(t_s)}{(1 - \rho_1)}\left[E(t_s) + \frac{\rho_1 E(t_{s_1})}{(1 - \rho_1)}\right]$$

$$E(t_{w_1}^2) = \frac{\rho t_s}{6(1 - \rho_1)}\left[2t_s + \frac{3\rho_1 t_{s_1}}{(1 - \rho_1)}\right]$$

$$E(t_{w_2}^2) = \frac{2\rho E(t_s)}{(1 - \rho_1)^2(1 - \rho)}\left[\frac{E(t_s)}{(1 - \rho)}\right.$$

$$E(t_{w_2}^2) = \frac{\rho t_s}{6(1 - \rho_1)^2(1 - \rho)}\left[\frac{(2 + \rho)t_s}{(1 - \rho)}\right.$$

$$\left. + \frac{\rho_1 E(t_{s_1})}{(1 - \rho_1)}\right]$$

$$\left. + \frac{3\rho_1 t_{s_1}}{(1 - \rho_1)}\right]$$

$$E(t_w^2) = \frac{E(n_1)}{E(n)} E(t_{w_1}^2) + \frac{E(n_2)}{E(n)} E(t_{w_2}^2)$$

$$E(t_w^2) = \frac{E(n_1)}{E(n)} E(t_{w_1}^2) + \frac{E(n_2)}{E(n)} E(t_{w_2}^2)$$

$$\text{Prob}\,(t_{w_1} \le t)$$

$$= \frac{E(n) - \rho E(n_1)}{(1 - \rho_1)} E(t_{s_1})e^{-(1-\rho_1)t/E(t_{s_1})}$$

**Table 31.3.** CONTINUED

## 2. Formulas for queues with $R$ priority categories

$$E(n) = \sum_{i=1}^{R} E(n_i)$$

$$\rho = \sum_{i=1}^{R} \rho_i$$

$$E(t_s) = \sum_{i=1}^{R} \frac{E(n_i)}{E(n)} E(t_{s_i})$$

$$E(t_s^2) = \sum_{i=1}^{R} \frac{E(n_i)}{E(n)} E(t_{s_i}^2)$$

$$E(w_j) = \frac{E(n)E(n_j)E(t_s^2)}{2\left[1 - \sum_{i=1}^{j-1} E(n_i)E(t_{s_i})\right]\left[1 - \sum_{i=1}^{j} E(n_i)E(t_{s_i})\right]}$$

$$E(w) = \sum_{i=1}^{R} E(w_i)$$

$$E(q_j) = E(w_j) + \rho_j$$

$$E(q) = \sum_{i=1}^{R} E(q_i)$$

$$E(t_{w_j}) = \frac{E(n)E(t^2)}{2\left[1 - \sum_{i=1}^{j-1} E(n_i)E(t_{s_i})\right]\left[1 - \sum_{i=1}^{j} E(n_i)E(t_{s_i})\right]}$$

$$E(t_w) = \sum_{i=1}^{R} \frac{E(n_i)}{E(n)} E(t_{w_i})$$

$$E(t_{q_j}) = E(t_{w_j}) + E(t_{s_j})$$

$$E(t_q) = \sum_{i=1}^{R} \frac{E(n_i)}{E(n)} E(t_{q_i})$$

$$E(t_{w_j}^2) = \frac{E(n)E(t_s^3)}{3\left[1 - \sum_{i=1}^{j-1} E(n_i)E(t_{s_i})\right]^2\left[1 - \sum_{i=1}^{j} E(n_i)E(t_{s_i})\right]}$$

$$+ \frac{E(n)E(t_s^2)\sum_{i=1}^{j} E(n_i)E(t_{s_i}^2)}{2\left[1 - \sum_{i=1}^{j-1} E(n_i)E(t_{s_i})\right]^2\left[1 - \sum_{i=1}^{j} E(n_i)E(t_{s_i})\right]^2}$$

$$+ \frac{E(n)E(t_s^2)\sum_{i=1}^{j-1} E(n_i)E(t_{s_i}^2)}{2\left[1 - \sum_{i=1}^{j-1} E(n_i)E(t_{s_i})\right]^3\left[1 - \sum_{i=1}^{j} E(n_i)E(t_{s_i})\right]}$$

$$E(t_w^2) = \sum_{i=1}^{R} \frac{E(n_i)}{E(n)} E(t_{w_i}^2)$$

$$\sigma_{t_{w_i}} = \sqrt{E(t_{w_i}^2) - E^2(t_{w_i})} \quad \text{etc.}$$

**Table 31.4.** FORMULAS FOR QUEUES WITH PRIORITY CATEGORIES AND INTERRUPTS. PREEMPTIVE-RESUME PRIORITY QUEUING DISCIPLINE*

---

* Priority $j$ items are served before priority $(j + 1)$ items. A higher-priority item interrupts the serving of a lower-priority item. After the serving of the higher-priority item, the serving of the lower-priority item resumes from where it was interrupted. Other assumptions are the same as in Table 31.2.

---

## 1. Formulas for queues with two priority categories

$$E(n) = E(n_1) + E(n_2)$$

$$\rho_1 = E(n_1)E(t_{s_1}); \ \rho_2 = E(n_2)E(t_{s_2})$$

$$\rho = \rho_1 + \rho_2$$

$$E(t_s) = \left[\frac{E(n_1)}{E(n)}\right]E(t_{s_1}) + \left[\frac{E(n_2)}{E(n)}\right]E(t_{s_2})$$

$$E(t_s^2) = \left[\frac{E(n_1)}{E(n)}\right]E(t_{s_1}^2) + \left[\frac{E(n_2)}{E(n)}\right]E(t_{s_2}^2)$$

$$E(w_1) = \frac{E^2(n_1)E(t_{s_1}^2)}{2(1 - \rho_1)}$$

$$E(w_2) = \frac{1}{1 - \rho_1}\left[\rho_1\rho_2 + \frac{E(n)E(n_2)E(t_s^2)}{2(1 - \rho)}\right]$$

$$E(w) = E(w_1) + E(w_2)$$

$$E(q_1) = E(w_1) + \rho_1$$

$$E(q_2) = E(w_2) + \rho_2$$

$$E(q) = E(q_1) + E(q_2)$$

$$E(t_{w_1}) = \frac{E(n_1)E(t_{s_1}^2)}{2(1 - \rho_1)}$$

$$E(t_{w_2}) = \frac{E(n)E(t_s^2)}{2(1 - \rho_1)(1 - \rho)} + \frac{\rho_1 E(t_{s_2})}{(1 - \rho_1)}$$

$$E(t_w) = \frac{E(n_1)}{E(n)}E(t_{w_1}) + \frac{E(n_2)}{E(n)}E(t_{w_2})$$

$$E(t_{q_1}) = E(t_{w_1}) + E(t_{s_1})$$

$$E(t_{q_2}) = E(t_{w_2}) + E(t_{s_2})$$

$$E(t_q) = \frac{E(n_1)}{E(n)}E(t_{q_1}) + \frac{E(n_2)}{E(n)}E(t_{q_2})$$

**Table 31.4.** CONTINUED

If the service times are either exponentially distributed or constant, the above equations for queue times and sizes simplify to the following:

### Exponential Service Times

$$E(w_1) = \frac{\rho_1^2}{1 - \rho_1}$$

$$E(w_2) = \frac{1}{1 - \rho_1}\left[\rho_1\rho_2 + \frac{\rho_1 E(n_2)E(t_{s_1}) + \rho_2^2}{(1 - \rho)}\right]$$

$$E(w) = E(w_1) + E(w_2)$$

$$= \frac{1}{1 - \rho_1}\left[\rho\rho_1 + \frac{\rho_1 E(n_2)E(t_{s_1}) + \rho^2}{(1 - \rho)}\right]$$

$$E(t_{w_1}) = \frac{\rho_1 E(t_{s_1})}{1 - \rho_1}$$

$$E(t_{w_2}) = \frac{1}{1 - \rho_1}\left[\rho_1 E(t_{s_2}) + \frac{\rho_1 E(t_{s_1}) + \rho_2 E(t_{s_2})}{(1 - \rho)}\right]$$

$$E(t_w) = \frac{1}{E(n)(1 - \rho_1)}\left[\rho\rho_1 + \frac{\rho_1 E(n_2)E(t_{s_1}) + \rho_2^2}{(1 - \rho)}\right]$$

### Constant Service Times

$$E(w_1) = \frac{\rho^2}{2(1 - \rho_1)}$$

$$E(w_2) = \frac{1}{1 - \rho_1}\left[\rho_1\rho_2 + \frac{\rho_1 E(n_2)t_{s_1} + \rho_2^2}{2(1 - \rho)}\right]$$

$$E(w) = E(w_1) + E(w_2)$$

$$= \frac{1}{1 - \rho_1}\left[\frac{\rho^2}{2} + \rho_1\rho_2 + \frac{\rho_1 E(n_2)t_{s_1} + \rho_2^2}{2(1 - \rho)}\right]$$

$$E(t_{w_1}) = \frac{\rho_1 t_{s_1}}{2(1 - \rho_1)}$$

$$E(t_{w_2}) = \frac{1}{1 - \rho_1}\left[\rho_1 t_{s_2} + \frac{\rho_1 t_{s_1} + \rho_2 t_{s_2}}{2(1 - \rho)}\right]$$

$$E(t_w) = \frac{1}{E(n)(1 - \rho_1)}\left[\frac{\rho_1^2}{2} + \rho_1\rho_2 + \frac{\rho_1 E(n_2)t_{s_1} + \rho_2^2}{2(1 - \rho)}\right]$$

**Table 31.4.** CONTINUED

## 2. Formulas for queues with $R$ priority categories

$$E(n) = \sum_{i=1}^{R} E(n_i)$$

$$\rho = \sum_{i=1}^{R} \rho_i$$

$$E(t_s) = \sum_{i=1}^{R} \frac{E(n_i)}{E(n)} E(t_{s_i})$$

$$E(t_s^2) = \sum_{i=1}^{R} \frac{E(n_i)}{E(n)} E(t_{s_i}^2)$$

$$E(w_j) = \frac{1}{\left(1 - \sum_{i=1}^{j-1} \rho_i\right)} \left[ \rho_j \sum_{i=1}^{j-1} \rho_i + \frac{E(n_j) \sum_{i=1}^{j} E(n_i) E(t_{s_i}^2)}{2\left[1 - \sum_{i=1}^{j} \rho_i\right]} \right]$$

$$E(w) = \sum_{i=1}^{R} E(w_i)$$

$$E(q_j) = E(w_j) + \rho_j$$

$$E(q) = \sum_{i=1}^{R} E(q_i)$$

$$E(t_{w_j}) = \frac{1}{\left(1 - \sum_{i=1}^{j-1} \rho_i\right)} \left[ E(t_{s_j})(\rho_1 + \rho_2 + \cdots + \rho_{j-1}) + \frac{\sum_{i=1}^{j} E(n_i) E(t_{s_i}^2)}{2\left[1 - \sum_{i=1}^{j} \rho_i\right]} \right]$$

$$E(t_w) = \sum_{i=1}^{R} \frac{E(n_i)}{E(n)} E(t_{w_i})$$

$$E(t_{q_j}) = E(t_{w_j}) + E(t_{s_j})$$

$$E(t_q) = \sum_{i=1}^{R} \frac{E(n_i)}{E(n)} E(t_{q_i})$$

**Table 31.5.** FORMULAS FOR MULTISERVER QUEUES

ASSUMPTIONS:
1. Poisson arrival pattern
2. Exponential service times
3. All servers equally loaded
4. All servers have the same mean service time
5. First-in, first-out dispatching
6. No items leave the queue

$$\rho = \frac{E(n)E(t_s)}{M}$$

$$t_q = t_w + t_s$$
$$E(t_q) = E(t_w) + E(t_s)$$
$$E(w) = E(n)E(t_w)$$
$$E(q) = E(n)E(t_q)$$
$$E(q) = E(w) + M\rho$$

Probability that all servers are busy =

$$B = \left\{ 1 - \left( \frac{\sum\limits_{N=0}^{M-1} \frac{(M\rho)^N}{N!}}{\sum\limits_{N=0}^{M} \frac{(M\rho)^N}{N!}} \right) \right\} \bigg/ \left\{ 1 - \rho \left( \frac{\sum\limits_{N=0}^{M-1} \frac{(M\rho)^N}{N!}}{\sum\limits_{N=0}^{M} \frac{(M\rho)^N}{N!}} \right) \right\}$$

$$E(w) = B\frac{\rho}{1-\rho}$$

$$E(q) = B\frac{\rho}{1-\rho} + M\rho$$

$$E(t_w) = \frac{B}{M}\frac{E(t_s)}{1-\rho}$$

$$E(t_q) = \frac{B}{M}\frac{E(t_s)}{1-\rho} + E(t_s)$$

$$\sigma_{t_w} = \frac{E(t_s)}{M(1-\rho)}\sqrt{B(2-B)}$$

$$\sigma_{t_q} = \frac{E(t_s)}{M(1-\rho)}\sqrt{B(2-B) + M^2(1-\rho)^2}$$

$$\sigma_w = \frac{1}{1-\rho}\sqrt{B\rho(1+\rho-B\rho)}$$

$$P(t_w > t) = Be^{-M(1-\rho)t/E(t_s)}$$

$$P(q \geq k) = \sum_{N=0}^{K} P(q = N) \qquad \text{where}$$

$$P(q = N) = \frac{(M\rho)^N}{N!} \bigg/ \left\{ \sum_{N=0}^{M-1} \frac{(M\rho)^N}{N!} + \frac{(M\rho)^N}{(1-\rho)M!} \right\} \quad \text{if } N < M,$$

$$\qquad = \frac{(M\rho)^N}{M!M^{(N-M)}} \bigg/ \left\{ \sum_{N=0}^{M-1} \frac{(M\rho)^N}{N!} + \frac{(M\rho)^M}{(1-\rho)M!} \right\} \quad \text{if } N \geq M$$

$$E(t_d) = \frac{E(t_s)}{M(1-\rho)}$$

**Table 31.5.** CONTINUED

---

For *M* servers when no queues form (all items not served immediately are lost). Otherwise the same assumptions:

---

$$P_B = \frac{(M\rho)^M}{M!} \bigg/ \sum_{N=0}^{M} \frac{(M\rho)^N}{N!}$$

## BIBLIOGRAPHY

1. P. M. Morse, *Queues, Inventories and Maintenance*, New York: J. Wiley & Sons, Inc., 1958. Handles simple queuing theory in clear terms.

2. D. R. Cox and W. L. Smith, *Queues*, New York: J. Wiley & Sons, Inc., 1961. Brief, concise survey of queuing theory.

3. J. Riordan, *Stochastic Service Systems*, New York: J. Wiley & Sons, Inc., 1962. Moderately mathematical queuing book by a staff member of Bell Telephone Laboratory.

4. A. Y. Khintchine, *Mathematical Methods in the Theory of Queuing*, New York: Hafner, 1960. Mathematical treatment of queuing fundamentals.

5. W. Feller, *An Introduction to Probability Theory and Its Applications*, 2nd edition, New York: J. Wiley & Sons, Inc., 1957. Short but clear derivations of the multi-server queue problems.

6. T. L. Saaty, *Elements of Queuing Theory*. New York: McGraw-Hill, Book Company, Inc., 1961. Collection of techniques and results for queuing problems, very mathematical.

7. L. Takacs, *Introduction to the Theory of Queues*. New York: Oxford University Press, 1962. Strictly for mathematicians.

8. D. Nee, *Application of Queuing Theory to Information System Design*, Stanford Research Institute Technical Documentary Report. No. ESD-TDR-64-428. A report classifying a wide variety of queuing models and queuing literature.

9. *Analysis of Some Queuing Models in Real-Time Systems*, IBM Manual Number F20-0007-0. Published by IBM, Poughkeepsie, New York, 1965. Very useful application of queuing theory to computer systems.

**CLASS QUESTIONS**   *Class questions for this (and other chapters) are at the end of the book.*

# 32 CALCULATION OF NUMBER OF TERMINALS REQUIRED

Before doing the calculations necessary in planning the communication-line network, we need to decide how many terminals are required at each location. That is the subject of this chapter.

In some cases, we must begin one step further back and decide which locations *have* terminals. This decision may be clear-cut if the terminals are used for computing. Certain people need to use the terminal and it must be available close to their locality, just as a desk calculator was in earlier days. On the other hand, where the terminal is not actually handled by the person requiring or giving information, he does not mind too much where it is located, providing that the service he receives is efficient and convenient. When you telephone an airline, for example, to make a reservation, the girl you speak to may be in your own town or in a distant city. You do not necessarily know where she is, and you do not care providing that you have no trouble or expense in contacting her. Therefore, when designing such a system, we need not have a terminal in every town but can group them in certain strategic locations and run foreign exchange lines to the towns without terminals.

Similarly, in management information systems, a terminal is not available in every manager's office. Some managers use the telephone, and some, in a more expensive scheme, have a closed-circuit television link to an information center.

The grouping together of terminals and their operators lowers the total number needed. This cost saving must be balanced against the increased cost of telephone, television and, now, Picturephone links to bring the service to its users and, in some systems, against the inconvenience of making the users come

481

to a central location. As we shall see from the equations in this chapter, some arrangements of terminals and services are better than others and give a lower waiting time or better availability of services for the same cost.

**QUEUING**
**CALCULATIONS**

In determining how many terminals and operators we need on a system, we must calculate which queues form for the use of the terminal and which form for the service of the operator. If the queue forms for one single operator or one single terminal, then single-server queuing theory will be used and the curves in Figs. 31.4 to 31.7 will apply. If the persons queuing are free to choose between several operators or terminals, thcn we will use multiserver queuing theory and the curves in Figs. 31.22 to 31.25 will apply.

If the traffic volume requires more than one server, then it is better to arrange for a free choice of servers rather than have a group of single-server queues. The arrangement in the bottom half of Fig. 32.1 is better than that in the top half. In fact, the more servers we can have grouped together in one place to handle the traffic, the better. This fact can be seen from Fig. 31.23. Suppose that the number of servers are chosen so that the facility utilization $\rho = 0.8$ and the mean service time is 10 minutes. Imagine a barber shop with 6 barbers. They take 10 minutes per customer on the average and this time is exponentially distributed. The barbers are 80 percent utilized during the period of our observations. If a customer can select the first barber who becomes free, we have a six-server queue. The mean time the customer will have to wait before being served is 4.31 minutes.

$$\frac{E(t_q)}{E(t_s)}$$

from Table 9 is 1.431. Thus

$$E(t_q) = 1.431 \times 10 = 14.31$$
$$E(t_w) = E(t_q) - E(t_s) = 14.31 - 10 = 4.31 \text{ minutes}$$

If, on the other hand, each customer goes to his own particular barber, we have six single–server queues. The facility utilization $\rho$ is the same, (0.8), but the mean time the customer waits before being served is 40 minutes. This is clearly no way to run a barber shop.

Suppose that 2 of the barbers can only do haircuts, 2 can only do rinses, and 2 can only do shaves. Suppose, also, for the sake of making the arithmetic easier, that the times for a shave, rinse, and haircut are the same and that one-third of the customers want shaves, one-third want rinses, and one-third

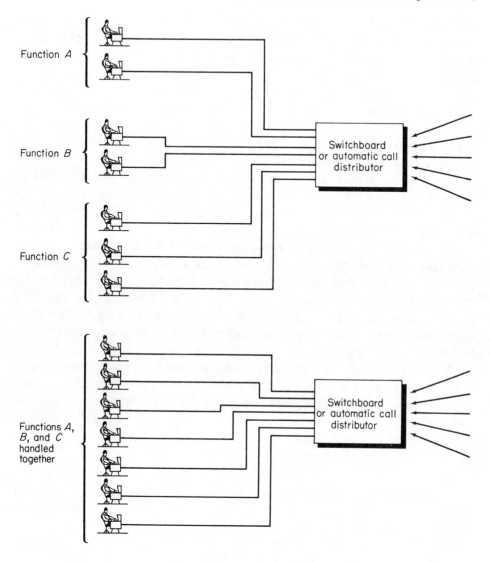

*Fig. 32.1.* Longer waiting and more calls result from the top arrangement than from the bottom.

want haircuts. We then have 3 two-server queues, with $\rho = 0.8$ again. The customers now have to wait, on the average, 17.78 minutes before their hair is cut. This is more than four times the six-server figure of 4.31 minutes. When the shop is busier and $\rho = 0.9$, the differences in the preceding times are much greater. The management would have given better customer service if it had trained all the barbers to do shaves, rinses, *and* haircuts.

The same applies to the use of terminals. When designing a system in which terminal operators handle a variety of functions for clients who telephone, it is tempting to have different operators handle different types of work. Better service could be given, however, if every terminal operator could handle *all* the functions that a telephone caller might need. This process would complicate the job of the operator and may necessitate additional training. It may be facilitated by designing the terminal language to give the maximum help to the operator. The systems analyst must calculate the benefits and determine what he considers to be the best trade-off.

One savings bank in the author's experience had teller windows labeled by alphabetic grouping A–G, H–M, and so on. The customers went to the appropriate window, depending on their name. Before automation, this practice was a good one because each teller had a more manageable file of customer records. Then a real-time system was installed and the tellers had terminals. Each terminal could access *any* customer's record. Nevertheless, the alphabetic grouping remained. The time the customers had to wait was substantially longer than if they had been able to go to *any* teller. The busier the bank, the larger were the values of $\rho$, and the worse was this difference in waiting time. After more than a year of operating this way, the bank finally removed the alphabetic grouping signs.

On some systems, the lines are a particularly sensitive issue because excessive waiting might result in lost business. This factor may be true for an airline. If you telephone an airline to make an enquiry or a reservation and are kept waiting beyond the limits of your patience, you may ring off and call a different airline. An airline would like as many customers as possible to have zero waiting time when they telephone.

**Example 32.1. Probability That a Caller Will Be Kept Waiting.** In a small city, 20 customers per hour, on the average, call an airline during its period of peak activity to enquire about flights or make reservations. Real-time terminals are being installed, and once the terminals are installed, it will take an average of 6 minutes to deal with a call. This time is approximately exponentially distributed. Each agent handling the calls is equipped with a terminal. It is considered desirable that not more than one-tenth of the callers should be kept waiting during the peak period. How many terminals will be needed to meet this criterion? If a caller *is* kept waiting, how long will the wait be?

The airline has both foreign and domestic flights. Of the 20 calls, 7 are for foreign flights and 13 are for domestic flights, on the average. Separate agents have always handled the foreign flights. What will be the effect of keeping them separate?

If a separate group of agents handles the foreign calls, the facility utilization ($\rho$) for these agents will be

$$\rho = \frac{E(n)E(t_s)}{M} = \frac{\frac{7}{60} \times 6}{M} = \frac{0.7}{M}$$

where $M$ is the number of agents.

Let us see if 2 agents will be sufficient to handle the foreign calls. We want to find $B$, the probability of all agents being busy, which is tabulated in Table 8. $B$ must be no greater than 0.1 if the customer-waiting criterion is to be satisfied.

If $M = 2$, then $\rho = 0.35$ and from Table 8 $B = 0.18$.
The criterion is not met. Let us try 3 agents.

If $M = 3$, then $\rho = 0.233$ and from Table 8 $B = 0.035$.
We thus need 3 agents for foreign calls.

Now the domestic calls:

$$\rho = \frac{E(n)E(t_s)}{M} = \frac{\frac{13}{60} \times 6}{M} = \frac{1.3}{M}$$

Try $M = 3$: $\rho = 0.433$ and $P_B = 0.17$.
Try $M = 4$: $\rho = 0.325$ and $P_B = 0.05$.

We need 4 agents for domestic calls. Thus we have a total of 7 agents (and terminals).

The 5 percent of callers who *are* kept waiting will wait

$$E(t_d) = \frac{E(t_s)}{M(1 - \rho)} \qquad \text{[Eq. (31.64)]}$$

$$= \frac{6}{4 \times (1 - 0.325)}$$

$$= 2.22 \text{ minutes}$$

The callers for foreign flights will wait

$$E(t_d) = \frac{6}{3 \times (1 - 0.233)} = 2.61 \text{ minutes}$$

Now suppose that the same agents handle *either* foreign or domestic calls. For this group, we have

$$\rho = \frac{\frac{20}{60} \times 6}{M} = \frac{2}{M}$$

Try $M = 4$: $\rho = 0.5$ and $P_B = 0.174$.
Try $M = 5$: $\rho = 0.4$ and $P_B = 0.06$.

With this arrangement, we need 5 agents instead of 7. This number, when all the cities with agents are considered, is probably a sufficient saving to justify training the agent to handle both foreign and domestic calls.

The callers who are kept waiting will now wait, on the average,

$$E(t_d) = \frac{6}{5 \times (1 - 0.4)} = 2 \text{ minutes}$$

somewhat less than in the foregoing case.

**GROUPING**
**CITIES**
**TOGETHER**

Suppose that there were five small cities not too far apart, each having this same traffic volume. If all their calls were routed to one point, there would be 100 calls per hour in the peak period. Thus

$$\rho = \frac{\frac{100}{60} \times 6}{M} = \frac{10}{M}$$

With 15 agents, we then have $\rho = 0.666$, and from Table 8 $P_B = 0.1$.

In this case, 15 agents would be sufficient instead of the preceding 25 (or 35 with foreign calls handled separately).

Customers kept waiting would have to wait only

$$\frac{6}{15 \times (1 - 0.666)} = 1.2 \text{ minutes}$$

on the average.

Here 20 such cities could be handled by 50 agents, and customers who had to wait would wait only 0.6 minute on the average. The saving in agents and terminals must be balanced against the cost of lines to route calls to the centralized location.

With terminals grouped together in this way, the system is also better protected from the effect of terminal failures or sick operators. In more than one way, there is safety in numbers.

**PHYSICAL QUEUES**
**OF PEOPLE**

An automatic call distributor is likely to be used with the above system to route calls to the agents. If no agent is free when a customer calls, a recorded voice will ask him to wait until one becomes free. On some systems for other applications this function is done by a manual switchboard. Either way, it is a multi-server queuing situation in which the calls are routed to the first free agent. Where physical queues of people form in front of counters, the situation is not quite so clear. If customers are free to select any of a group of servers, all doing identical jobs, as in a large bank, they will normally form separate queues for each server, but will switch queues if a nearby queue becomes shorter than their own, or if a nearby server becomes available. A new customer will freely select the shortest queue. It therefore seems reasonable to expect that the queue sizes will approximate those given by multiserver queuing theory, and calculations based on this assumption are used in practice for calculating the number of servers needed.

**Example 32.2. Number of Terminal Operators Needed.** A real-time system is being designed for a savings bank. In a big city branch there have been large queues of customers at lunch time, and bank management fears that it is losing customers because of this. It has set a criterion on the design of the new system that the mean queue size for each teller should not exceed 2 (including the customer being served).

The design team has made studies of customer volumes and has estimated that 20 customers in a 5-minute period can be expected during the lunch time peak. Studies of the tellers' work have indicated that when they each have a terminal their mean time to handle one customer will be 2 minutes, and that the distribution of this time will be approximately exponential.

Given this information, how many tellers (and terminals) will the bank require?

$$E(n) = \frac{20}{5} = 4 \text{ customers per minute.}$$

$$E(t_s) = 2 \text{ minutes}$$

$$\rho = \frac{E(n)E(t_s)}{M}$$

where $M$ is the number of tellers. Therefore

$$\rho = \frac{8}{M}$$

When $M = 8$, $\rho = 1$, which is too high (see Fig. 31.24).

Let us try $M = 9$. Using Table 9 this gives approximately:

$$\frac{E(t_q)}{E(t_s)} = 1.7$$

$$\therefore E(t_q) = 1.7 \times 2 = 3.4$$

$$E(q) = E(n) \times E(t_q)$$

$$\therefore E(q) = 4 \times 3.4 = 13.6$$

Therefore the mean number of customers queuing per teller is

$$\frac{13.6}{9} = 1.5$$

The design criterion is therefore satisfied by using 9 teller windows.

The time each teller takes to operate the terminal is estimated to be as follows:

| | |
|---|---|
| Insert pass-book | 5 sec |
| Key in transaction | 4 sec |
| Response time | 2 sec |
| Printing | 2 sec |
| Remove pass-book | 4 sec |
| Total: | 17 sec |

This time was included in the estimate of 2 minutes as the mean time to handle each customer. It was suggested that one terminal should be shared by 3 tellers. If it was shared by 4 or more, then some of them would have to walk a distance to the terminal. If the teller is working non-stop, handling one customer every 2 minutes, then the utilization of the terminal will be

$$\rho = E(n) \times E(t_s) = \frac{1}{2 \times 60} \times 3 \times 17 = .425$$

The time taken to use the terminal is going to be nearly constant. The standard deviation is unlikely to be higher than, say, 5 seconds. Using the $(\sigma_{t_s}/E(t_s))^2 = 0.1$ column in Table 5 we have for the terminal (single server):

$$\frac{E(t_q)}{E(t_s)} = 1.4$$

$$\therefore \frac{E(t_w)}{E(t_s)} = 0.4$$

The mean time the teller waits for the terminal is

$$0.4 \times 17 = 6.8 \text{ seconds}$$

In practice, the time will probably be less because the assumptions behind Table 5 are worse than the conditions met in this situation. There is not an infinite population of users, and the arrival rate may be smoother than a Poisson distribution.

Using this calculation, it was not felt necessary to revise upward the estimate of 2 minutes to handle one customer. The bank therefore needs 9 teller windows with 3 terminals. It was felt advisable to install a fourth terminal in case one is out of action during the peak period.

How would this situation work out in practice? Is there any practical experience that justifies the queuing model we have used? Interestingly enough, there is—and it suggests that our calculation here is not quite adequate. We shall discuss this point later in the chapter and do the preceding calculation again in the light of experience.

**NUMBER OF TERMINALS PER OPERATOR**    In savings banks, having one terminal between three tellers has worked well in practice. Some banks have no more than two tellers per terminal. In other applications, however, the "conversation" between the operator and the terminal is more complex. It may last for a longer period of time than the time the operator spends in talking to the client. There may be no client, and the operator may need to have the terminal available all the time. The counter of an airline office looks, perhaps, not dissimilar to the counter of a bank and the lines of people are similar, but the airline is likely to have one terminal per agent because the agent carries on a lengthier conversation with the machine.

The correspondence between operators and terminals must clearly be an early decision in the calculation of numbers of terminals needed and must be based on a study of the overall job of the person using the terminal.

**GROWTH IN TRAFFIC VOLUMES**    Looking again at the curves in Fig. 31.24, we see that the curve for one server rises fairly gently. If the waiting time for this single-server queue was equal to the service time—that is,

$$\frac{E(t_q)}{E(t_s)} = 2$$

this situation should not be worrisome. An increase in traffic volume of a few percent would cause an increase in waiting time of a few percent—nothing catastrophic.

On the other hand, if we had a 10-server queue and the waiting time was equal to the service time

$$\frac{E(t_q)}{E(t_s)} = 2$$

this situation would be highly dangerous. An increase in traffic volume of a few percent would send the waiting time hurtling upward.

It is important on any data transmission system or real-time computer to make measurements of the traffic volumes at the terminals, on the lines, in the processing unit, in the computer channels, and so on and to relate these measurements to the shape of the queuing curves.

**Example 32.3. The Effect of Traffic Increase.** A public utility has many enquiries from its customers and staff—querying bills and customer accounts. These questions are answered by a group of five operators using terminals with screens. The system has recently been installed and is regarded as working successfully. During a peak period, an average of 174 calls per hour are handled. It takes 1.5 minutes, on the average, to deal with one enquiry. During this peak time, a caller is kept waiting an average 1.4 minutes before talking to a terminal operator, but it is not thought worthwhile to spend money to reduce this waiting period.

The company anticipates that the number of enquiries will be 10 percent higher during the winter period. Will the present number of operators be able to handle that growth?

$$\rho = \frac{E(n)E(t_s)}{M} = \frac{\frac{174}{60} \times 1.5}{5} = 0.87$$

Using Table 9, we would expect that

$$\frac{E(t_q)}{E(t_s)} = 2.1$$

Thus
$$E(t_q) = 2.1 \times 1.5 = 3.15 \text{ minutes}$$

Therefore
$$E(t_w) = E(t_q) - E(t_s) = 3.15 - 1.5 = 1.65 \text{ minutes}$$

Multiserver queuing theory gives a mean waiting time of 1.65 minutes. The measured waiting time in the peak hour is 1.4 minutes. This waiting time may be due to the fact that the service times are not exponentially distributed, or it may be due to random fluctuations of the values measured. In any case, the theory is reasonably close to the measured result.

When the number of enquiries increases by 10 percent, we will have

$$\rho = 0.87 + 0.087 = 0.957$$

A glance at Fig. 31.24 indicates that this situation is far from healthy. The curve for $M = 5$ is streaking rapidly upward.

Table 9 gives $\qquad\qquad\qquad \dfrac{E(t_q)}{E(t_s)} = 5.5$

Hence $\qquad\qquad\qquad\qquad E(t_q) = 8.25$ minutes

which would cause considerable impatience and annoyance to most customers.

Because the system is on such an unstable part of the curve in Fig. 31.24, the data processing manager would be well advised to install at least one more terminal quickly.

With 6 terminals and a 10 percent increase in usage,

$$\rho = \frac{\frac{191}{60} \times 1.5}{6} = 0.80$$

Thus we are back to a more reasonable part of the curves of Fig. 31.24. $E(t_q)$ drops to 2.15 minutes, which gives a mean waiting time of 0.65 minute.

If, however, the winter peak is 20 percent higher than now (rather than 10 percent), $\rho$ would once again be uncomfortably high. It would be wise to have 7 terminals and operators in readiness, in addition to the spare one needed to cover illness or failure.

**NONEXPONENTIAL SERVICE TIMES**   If measurements of the service time in the foregoing calculations had indicated that it was far from exponential, then the approximation given in Eqs. (31.62) and (31.63) might have been used in calculating the queue sizes and waiting times.

$$E(w) = \frac{E(w_{\exp})}{2}\left\{1 + \left[\frac{\sigma_{t_s}}{E(t_s)}\right]^2\right\} \qquad (31.62)$$

and

$$E(t_w) = \frac{E(t_{w\exp})}{2}\left\{1 + \left[\frac{\sigma_{t_s}}{E(t_s)}\right]^2\right\} \qquad (31.63)$$

where $E(w_{\exp})$ and $E(t_{w\exp})$ are the number of items waiting and the waiting time for the case in question if its service time distribution *were* exponential.

In the preceding example we were told that the mean time to handle one call was 1.5 minutes, and we assumed that the time was exponentially distributed. We might have been given the additional information that the standard deviation of the time to handle a call was 0.75 minute. We would then have

$$\left[\frac{\sigma_{t_s}}{E(t_s)}\right]^2 = \left(\frac{0.75}{1.5}\right)^2 = \frac{1}{4}$$

Using this assumption,

$$E(t_w) = \frac{E(t_{w\exp})}{2}\left[1 + \frac{1}{4}\right] = \frac{5}{8} E(t_{w\exp}).$$

For $\rho = 0.87$, we found from Table 9 that

$$E(t_{w\exp}) = 1.65 \text{ minutes}$$

Therefore
$$E(t_w) = \tfrac{5}{8} \times 1.65 = 1.03 \text{ minutes}$$

When the number of inquiries rises by 10 percent, however, $\rho$ still rises to 0.957 and $E(t_w)$ rises to 4.22 minutes. The system is still on a highly unstable part of the curve and the same conclusions apply. Even if the service times were constant as in the lowest curve in Fig. 31.5, a utilization $\rho$ of 0.957 would be highly undesirable.

The data processing manager would certainly not be justified in feeling content with his system because the customers only wait 1.03 minutes on the average.

**NONQUEUING SITUATION**   The preceding models have related to situations in which the persons being served *queue* for the terminal or its operator. In other types of systems, if a terminal is not free the users go away. No queue forms. Laboratory personnel, for example, may go to a terminal room to use the terminal of a time-sharing system. If no terminal is free, they return to other work and come back later.

In this situation we are interested in calculating the probability that a user will not find a free terminal. The equation that is applicable is (31.66), which is plotted in Fig. 31.26 and tabulated in Table 11 of Appendix VIII.

The probability that no terminal is free is

$$P_B = \frac{(M\rho)^M}{M!} \left/ \sum_{N=0}^{M} \frac{(M\rho)^N}{N!} \right.$$

where $M$ is the number of terminals and $\rho$ is the terminal utilization.

$$M\rho = E(n)E(t_s)$$

where $n$ is the number of persons arriving to use the terminal in unit time and $t_s$ is the time the user occupies the terminal.

The equation assumes that $n$ follows a Poisson distribution and $t_s$ an exponential distribution.

**Example 32.4. Availability of Terminals on a Time-Sharing System.** A laboratory has used an experimental time-sharing system for 2 years. The service has proven itself to be of great potential, yet the staff has continually felt frustrated by not being able to have access to a terminal at the moment one is needed. They complain that much of their time has been wasted, and consequently many have resorted to batch processing. A new system is now to be installed. A design criterion is that the probability of a staff member being unable to obtain a free terminal when he needs it should be no greater than 0.01.

The duration of terminal occupancy is found to be approximately exponentially distributed with a mean of 40 minutes. It is estimated that with the new service 30 users will sign on per hour during the morning hours when activity has been observed to be highest. How many terminals are needed?

$$M\rho = E(n)\cdot E(t_s) = \frac{30}{60} \times 40 = 20$$

Using Table 11, when $M\rho = 20$, thirty terminals will give $P_B = 0.00846$. Twenty-nine terminals will give $P_B = 0.01279$. Thirty terminals are therefore needed to fill the design criterion.

This assumes that *any* of the 30 terminals will be available to a new user. If some of the terminals are in persons, offices or in separate areas, this will not be so. Just as with the earlier calculations, if all the terminals are grouped together, it lowers the total number of terminals needed (or alternatively raises the standard of service given). Making users walk to the other end of the building, or go to a different floor, may provoke complaints ("What are telecommunications for?"). However, it may result in better service because after their walk they have a higher probability of finding a terminal free than if the terminals were dispersed throughout the building.

In my own place of work, the secretaries use terminals for producing documents, text editing and so on. A variety of scientific computing systems are used by different people. Some use terminals attached to a computer in the building and others dial distant machines. However, most of these activities make use of the same type of terminal (although there are also a small number of other more specialized terminals). In many types of organization it is an advantage to employ a common type of terminal, and to pool the terminals so that secretaries and scientists alike use the same group of machines (a popular arrangement).

Figure 32.2 shows the numbers of servers needed for different traffic rates, in order to achieve a probability-of-not-obtaining-a-server of 0.1, 0.01 and 0.001. In the above example in which $M\rho = 20$ we can read from these curves that to

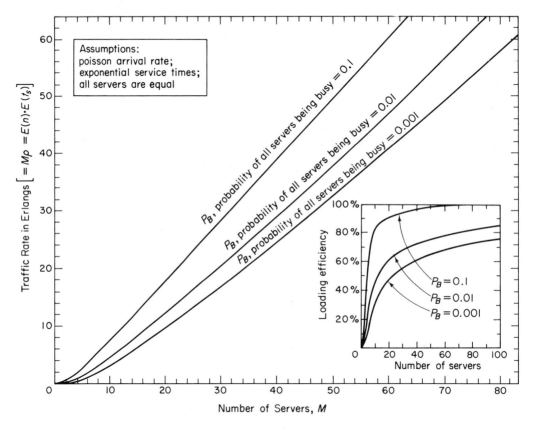

*Fig. 32.2.* The numbers of servers required to give different levels of "grade of service" on a nonqueuing multiserver system.

achieve a 0.01 chance of not finding a terminal we need 30 terminals. To achieve a 0.1 chance, we need 23 terminals; and to achieve a 0.001 chance, we need 35 terminals. The same curves can be used in the next chapter when the requirements for tie lines and exchanges are discussed.

The inset shows how the loading efficiency increases with the number of servers for a given $P_B$ criterion. Above about 40 terminals the improvement with an increased number of terminals is becoming less pronounced. For the criterion in the above example, $P_B = 0.01$, the slope of the efficiency curve is considerably steeper below 30 terminals. If there are less than 30 terminals it certainly pays to pool them and make all terminals equal.

**PRACTICAL**          How has the use of these models worked out in prac-
**EXPERIENCE**          tice? In most of the other chapters of Section VI, we
                        are talking about the behavior of mechanistic devices.
We can compare our mathematical model against a simulation of the device or, eventually, against the performance of the device itself. We can make a precise statement about the accuracy of the model because the device behaves in a mechanically determined manner. In this chapter, however, we are talking mainly about people. The users and operators who come into contact with a system have a variety of idiosyncrasies and feel under no constraint to obey the assumptions of queuing theory.

Several decades of experience have been obtained in applying queuing theory to the design of telephone exchanges and trunks, as will be discussed further in the next chapter. On the other hand, experience in observing the efficacy of queuing theory as applied to terminals and operators is limited.

The holding times for telephone calls have been found in practice to be sufficiently close to an exponential distribution to make models based on this assumption give useful results.[1] Such models have been widely employed for many years. Simulation has also been used. Before the advent of computers, special-purpose machines were built to assist in simulating the behavior of exchanges.

The use of queuing equations in telephone exchange design has five advantages in its favor which may not all be present when terminals are involved. Let us discuss these.

### 1. *Poissonian Input*

The exchange serves a *large* population of users who are truly independent of one another. This means that the traffic volume follows a Poisson distribution very closely. Some computer terminals also serve a large population of independent users—airline terminals dealing with telephone reservations, for example—and here, as one might expect, measurements of the traffic volume indicate that it is indeed Poissonian.

On certain systems, however, the nature of the work might be such that clustering of traffic occurs, which would give rise to a higher waiting time than

---

[1] Charles Clos and Roger I. Wilkinson, "Dialing Habits of Telephone Customers," *Bell System Tech. J.*, January 1952.

otherwise. In a factory when it is time for a work break, or in a university when a class ends, a cluster of transactions might arrive. Again, if the transactions are building up to some specific event, then the result may be clustering.

A. M. Lee describes a case in which the "transactions" were passengers arriving to check in for departing BEA flights at London Airport.[2] Before a flight, passengers arrived at times distributed as in Fig. 32.3. There were flights

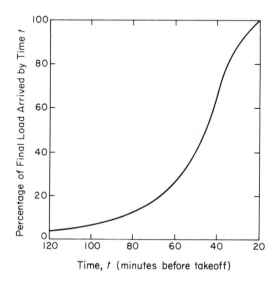

*Fig. 32.3.* Passenger arrival pattern for a flight. *Redrawn with permission from A. M. Lee,* Applied Queuing Theory, *MacMillan, London and St. Martin's Press, New York, 1966.*

with this arrival distribution every 5 to 10 minutes, and the sum of their passenger arrival rates was the input to the passenger queue. It was not clear how far such an arrival rate would deviate from the Poisson distribution, and so a count of arriving passengers was made. Figure 32.4 compares the results of this with a Poisson distribution having the same mean. It was decided in this case that it was sufficiently close to assume Poissonian input to the model.

In some systems there can be a specific cause of clustering, which the systems analyst should look out for. In others, and this is probably more common, the transactions go through some form of buffering process before they reach the queue, thus evening out the interarrival times. In a registration scheme in which terminals are used, the clients have to fill in a form at a preliminary desk before reaching the clerk with the terminal. As a result, they reach the clerk somewhat more evenly than if they had walked straight in off the street. The systems analyst who does not want to use simulation may usually claim with reasonable justification that the Poissonian arrival rate assumption errs only slightly—and errs on the side of conservatism and safety.

[2] A. M. Lee, *Applied Queuing Theory* (London: Macmillan, and New York: St. Martin's Press, 1966).

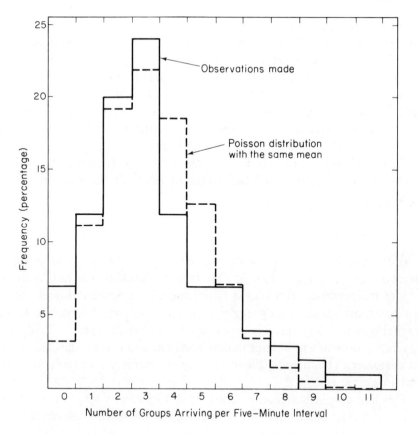

*Fig. 32.4.* The analysts felt justified in using a Poisson input distribution.

### 2. *Exceptionally Long Service Times*

If the service times are found to be not exponential, the approximation in Eq. (31.62) might be used. Occasionally, however, when *people* are involved, the service time is going to be much longer than normal. For instance, the person standing in front of us in a bank teller's line often seems to have some mysterious business that takes forever. Certain women on the telephone will defy any exponential distribution. The effect of a solitary long service time is going to be serious if there is only one server. It will cause delays if there are two or three servers. On the other hand, if there are a large number of servers, it will have very little effect. In a public telephone exchange, there are a large number of circuits that the calls can use, and thus one person who stays on the telephone all evening, will not degrade the service appreciably.

Using Table 9, if we have 20 servers and a facility utilization $\rho$ of 0.8, we have a mean waiting time of 0.064 times the mean service time. If one server is effectively taken out of action (by a long telephone call, for example) and the remainder then have a facility utilization of $0.8 \times 20/19 = 0.84$, the mean waiting time is then 0.121 times the service time. If, on the other hand, there had been 6 servers and one is taken out of action, the facility utilization rises from 0.8 to $0.8 \times 6/5 = 0.96$. The mean waiting time rises from 0.431 to 4.508 times the mean service time, and the system is dangerously close to the condition of $\rho = 1$, in which it cannot handle all the transactions.

Moral: If there are likely to be some users who tie up a server for long periods, evaluate the effect of this factor in terms of the number of servers needed.

### 3. Variation in Service Time

In the examples in this chapter we have treated service time as though it were constant. In most cases it is. One law, however, that is not found in the works of mathematical statistics is Parkinson's law. Some terminal operators, when confronted with a long queue of people, can be observed to speed up remarkably, and when there is no queue other than the person being served, they tend to slow down, indulge in conversation, and perhaps give extra help to their customer. The queuing theory version of Parkinson's law is "$t_s$ varies to maintain $\rho$ close to 1."

This human phenomenon is clearly useful in some ways, but it means that we must not take our equations too literally. If the servers are observed to be fully occupied during a nonpeak period, there is no need to panic. On the other hand it would not be a good idea to design the terminal arrangement for the minimum $t_s$ the operator was capable of.

Interestingly, the variation in operator service time does not seem to occur in the author's experience on some systems with *telephone* customers. The operator does not know how big the queue is, and therefore all customers receive equal treatment, except perhaps when there are long gaps between customers. Is this good? Not necessarily. It is often desirable to have the terminal operator speed up when there is a queue. A mechanism for flashing a red light at the terminals when telephone calls are being queued could be worthwhile.

### 4. Selection of Servers

An important assumption in multiserver queuing theory is that the transactions form *one* queue and each item in turn is served by the first server to become free. Probably the most important deviation from theory that occurs in practice is that lines of standing people do not behave this sensibly. If a bank has four tellers with identical functions, the best way to marshal the customers would be to make them form one line and then have each teller, on becoming free, take the next person standing in line. In reality, four lines form and customers tend to transfer from one line to another in order to maintain the shortest number of people in front of them. We have assumed that this freedom in queue switching gives approximately the same effect as having one queue. We could, if we had wished, have used some rather more complex queuing theory which relates to queues with jockeying. In practice, however, many people standing in lines seem remarkably reluctant to switch queues. Consequently, the mean waiting time is longer than that predicted by the equations. The equations seem to have predicted queue sizes reasonably well when there are just two servers. The inaccuracy with larger numbers of servers seems greater the greater their number.

British European Airline (BEA), in their study of queuing for passenger check-in counters, recorded passenger queuing times at two advance registration counters at London Airport. The measurements made are shown in Fig. 32.5. These measurements agree as closely as could be expected with the

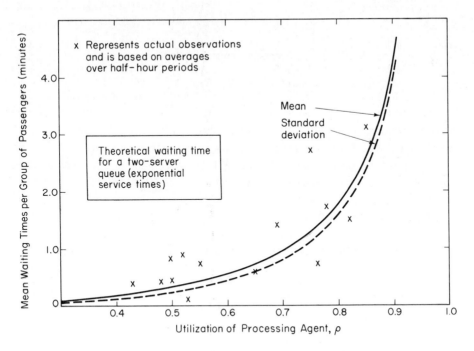

Fig. 32.5. The agreement between theory and actuality. *Redrawn with permission from A. M. Lee*, Applied Queuing Theory, *Macmillan, London, and St. Martin's Press, New York, 1966.*

two-server queuing equations. The agreement between the theory and practice was so encouraging that BEA went on to use the same equations to design check-in arrangements with more than two servers. Lee has reported the interesting way in which the theory then broke down.

Figure 32.6 shows the passenger check-in area. Counters 2 to 8 were commonly in use, and so a multiserver queuing model with seven servers might have been expected to predict the queue sizes. Such a model, however, assumes

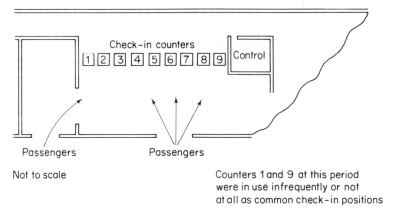

Not to scale

Counters 1 and 9 at this period were in use infrequently or not at all as common check-in positions

*Fig. 32.6.* Passenger check-in counters at London Airport. *Reproduced with permission from A. M. Lee,* Applied Queuing Theory, *Macmillan, London and St. Martin's Press, New York, 1966.*

that the passengers distribute themselves evenly between the counters, which did not happen. Figure 32.7 shows how they did distribute themselves. The counters near the doors were more popular than the more distant ones. Furthermore, the passengers seemed remarkably reluctant to leave one queue and join another, shorter one. Sometimes there was a line at counter 7, for example, and none at counters 3 and 4.

The BEA operations research team observed that

Jockeying for position in queues seemed to happen in epidemics, but even so it slowly began to dawn upon the team that it was of a formal nature. If ready to jockey at all, passengers appeared willing to move no farther than one queue to either side of their original positions, and no passenger appeared ready to move more than once. If true this would imply that irrespective of the number of counters provided, the effect insofar as the waiting time of individual passengers was concerned would be no better than that given by groups of *three* counters with limited availability.[3]

[3] A. M. Lee, *Applied Queuing Theory*, London: Macmillan and New York: St. Martin's Press, 1966.

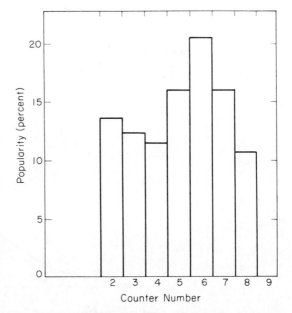

*Fig. 32.7.* As shown here, the passengers did not distribute themselves evenly over the seven counters in use. This and their reluctance to switch queues freely, gave a longer queuing time than was expected from multiserver queuing theory. *Reproduced with permission from A. M. Lee*, Applied Queuing Theory, *Macmillan, London and St. Martin's Press, New York, 1966.*

The latter conclusion seems to be supported by Fig. 32.8. Here the mean waiting times over 15-minute periods were observed, and plotted, when 4, 5, and 6 counters were in operation. The multiserver queuing model for 3 servers would have given a better prediction of the queuing times than the models for 4, 5, or 6 servers.

The reluctance to switch lines may have been partly due to the fact that the passengers were carrying luggage. It may have also been due to the fact that the British seem to observe curiously disciplined queuing behavior. However, to some extent the same phenomenon can be observed elsewhere where physical lines of people queue for the services of operators with terminals. In one New York savings bank with a dozen or so tellers using real-time terminals, it is common to see some tellers idle while others have a queue.

It is interesting to note that, again, this phenomenon does not seem to occur where the terminal operators are handling *telephone* customers. Here the calls are automatically distributed to the next free operator and the multiserver queuing equations generally agree well with actual waiting times.

### 5. *Behavior During Overloaded Periods*

If the queues at an airline check-in desk became longer than anticipated, many passengers who arrive on time fail to reach the departure desk before the

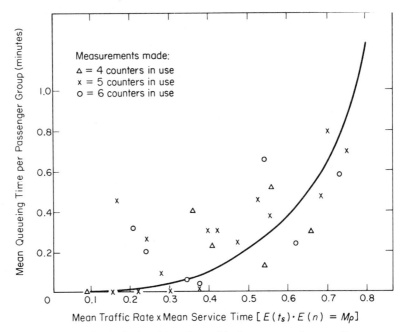

*Fig. 32.8.* Theoretical waiting time with three servers in use. *Reproduced with permission from A. M. Lee,* Applied Queuing Theory, *Macmillan, London and St. Martin's Press, New York, 1966.*

flight is closed. As a result, they complain, usually long and loud. While complaining, they sometimes block the counter, thereby increasing the delays. The overload here can be self-amplifying.

On other systems the opposite is true. If you keep a telephone caller waiting long enough, he gives up. The mean waiting time for the successful callers is then less than would be predicted, but some customers might be lost. In designing a system, it is generally desirable to work out what the effect of long waits will be.

**FACE-TO-FACE SERVICE** In general, it seems that the worst deviations from the queuing models occur when the queues are lines of people who come face-to-face with whoever serves them. In such situations, human idiosyncracies take over. Telephone queues are better disciplined and obey the queuing models better. Theory and practice seem to agree reasonably well with telephone queues except when the caller is kept waiting too long. With physical queues, it is perhaps unwise to assume an even distribution over more than four servers. Where there are many terminals, one might calculate the waiting time by using the four-server model.

**Example 32.5. Number of Terminal Operators Needed (again).** In view of what has just been said, let us take another look at the way we did Example 32.2. We concluded that nine teller windows in use would meet the design criterion that the mean queue for each teller should not exceed two customers. In reaching this conclusion, however, we used the multiserver queuing model for nine servers, which means that we were assuming, in effect, that the customers would distribute themselves evenly among the nine tellers and switch queues freely. The foregoing BEA experience indicates that such would not be the case and that the queue sizes would not be better than those for a four-server model.

Let us do the calculation again, using a four-server model.
It is still true that

$$\rho = \frac{E(n)E(t_s)}{M} = \frac{8}{M}$$

where $M$ is the number of tellers.
If we have 9 tellers,

$$\rho = \frac{8}{9} = 0.889$$

Using Table 9 again, but now taking the times for a four-server model with $\rho = 0.889$, we have approximately

$$\frac{E(t_q)}{E(t_s)} = 2.75$$

Therefore
$$E(t_q) = 2.75 \times 2 = 5.5$$

$$E(q) = E(n)E(t_q)$$

$$= 4 \times 5.5 = 22$$

We thus have 22 persons queuing for 9 tellers, which is more than 2 persons per teller, and so the design criterion is not met.
Let us try 10 tellers.

$$\rho = \frac{8}{M} = 0.8$$

From Table 9, taking the times for a four-server model with $\rho = 0.8$,

$$\frac{E(t_q)}{E(t_s)} = 1.746$$

$$E(t_q) = 2 \times 1.746 = 3.492$$

$$E(q) = E(n)E(t_q)$$

$$= 4 \times 3.492 = 14.0$$

Thus there are 1.4 persons per teller, on the average, and the design criterion is met. If we still permit no more than 3 tellers to one terminal, 10 tellers will need 4 terminals. Adding one more terminal to cover breakdowns, we obtain a total of 5 terminals on the system.

Doing the same calculation, using a three-server model, gives 1.66 persons per teller, and therefore it appears that 10 teller windows will be enough even if the customers queue as badly as London Airport passengers.

# 33
## EXCHANGE, TIE-LINE, AND
## WATS-LINE CALCULATIONS

In planning a system with an exchange, or with a group of trunks WATS lines, registers, ports, or other facilities serving a community of users, a certain class of calculation is needed. How many paths through the exchange must we make available in order to give a certain grade of service? How many tie lines do we need to a certain PBX? How many ports are necessary on a time-sharing system in a given laboratory? How many WATS lines are needed to WATS zone 6? A hold-and-forward concentrator can have different storage sizes, thus making different numbers of memory blocks dynamically available to its users. What size is needed?

The telephone companies have had to answer these types of questions long before the advent of computers. Let us reemploy their methods on computer systems and then see whether data transmission introduces any new problems.

**GRADE OF**       In telephone engineering a call will normally be lost
**SERVICE**        if, at the instant when the system tries to establish a
                  connection, there are no idle paths through an ex-
change, no available registers to set up a connection, or no available trunks in a trunk group. The caller hears a "busy" signal and puts down his telephone handset. The usual way of describing the blocking characteristics of a system, or part of a system, is to state the probability that a call will be lost when there is a given traffic load. The probability of losing a call is referred to as the "grade of service."

The grade of service in public telephone engineering typically ranges from 0.01 to 0.001. In other words, one call in 100 to one call in 1000 is lost. The subscriber generally does not know that it is the telephone company equipment that has lost his call. He hears the busy signal and assumes that the person he is calling is busy, not the exchange equipment or trunks. When he calls a computer, however, he may not be so tolerant because he then knows that it is *some* part of the system that is failing to give him service.

**ERLANGS**   The traffic volume in telephone engineering is measured in a unit called the *erlang* (after A. K. Erlang, a mathematician who developed some of the equations used in designing exchange systems). An erlang is the amount of traffic one trunk can handle in one hour if it is busy all the time—in other words, 3600 call-seconds of traffic.

The number of erlangs received is given by

$$\frac{\text{No. of calls per hour} \times \text{mean holding time per call (seconds)}}{3600}$$

If $M$ trunks or other facilities handle this traffic, then their facility utilization

$$\rho = \frac{\text{erlangs}}{M} \tag{33.1}$$

**CALLS LOST**   Two types of situation can occur when congestion
**OR DELAYED**   arises. (1) Calls can be delayed—that is, queued—until it is possible to serve them, and (2) calls can be lost when a facility they want is unattainable.

Each type of situation may be encountered when placing an ordinary telephone call. In the first case, when we pick up the telephone, we listen for a dial tone, which is normally heard almost immediately. Occasionally, however, we may have to wait for a second or so; very rarely, several seconds. The delay occurs because registers are used in handling the call. The number of registers is limited, and if all are in use the call will have to wait until one becomes free.

In the second case, we may hear a busy signal if a path to the number we called cannot be established. In this case we put the telephone down and the call is lost. The busy signal may be caused by the fact that the party we called is "busy," but, alternatively, it is possible that there are no free paths or equipments in the exchange, or the lines between exchanges are fully occupied. This case is not a queuing situation like the preceding one; no queues form.

The equations traditionally used in telephone engineering for designing exchange and trunk systems are similar to those for multiserver queuing theory as described in Chapter 31. In addition to using a Poisson arrival pattern, they make the assumption that the duration of calls follows an exponential distribution. In practice, this assumption is found to be approximate but reasonable.

Once again a mathematical model is used that resembles but does not exactly duplicate the situation we are interested in. Figure 33.1 shows a typical distribu-

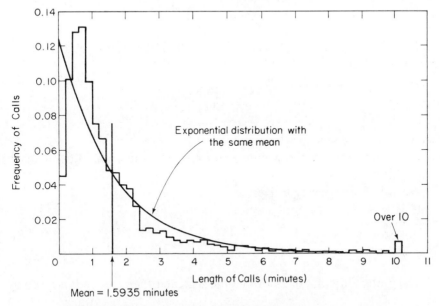

Mean = 1.5935 minutes

*Fig. 33.1.* A measurement of the lengths of telephone calls on inter-office trunks. The distribution of holding times is very close to an exponential distribution. *Reproduced with permission from R. I. Wilkinson, "The Interconnection of Telephone Systems,"* Bell System Tech. J., *October, 1931.*

tion of telephone calling times. It will be seen that it is close to an exponential distribution. There are now decades of experience in using the queuing equations in designing telephone systems, and in general they work very well. Telephone subscribers obey the rules of queuing theory much better than the airline check-in passengers discussed in the previous chapter!

**DELAYED CALLS**  For the first type of situation, in which queuing occurs, we can again employ Eqs. (31.50) to (31.60) from Chapter 31.

**Example 33.1. Number of Registers Required in an Exchange.** Callers occupy a register in an exchange when dialing a call for a mean time of 8 seconds. They do not hear a dial tone until they have gained access to such a register. It is estimated that 2000 calls will be received in the peak hour. A design objective is that not more than 1 percent of the callers have to wait more than one second for a dial tone. How many registers are needed to achieve this objective?

What is the probability that a caller will have to wait more than 2 seconds?

The traffic volume in erlangs is

$$\frac{2000 \times 8}{3600} = 4.444$$

let $M$ be the number of registers and $\rho$ be the utilization of a register. From Eq. (33.1)

$$\rho = \frac{erlangs}{M}$$

Therefore $M\rho = 4.444$.

Let us make a guess at a number of registers and then adjust it to fit the design objective.

We will first try using 9 registers.

If $M = 9$,

$$\rho = \frac{4.444}{9} = 0.494$$

The probability that the waiting time is greater than $t$ seconds is given by

$$P(t_w \geq t) = Be^{-M(1-\rho)t/E(t_s)} \tag{31.61}$$

where $B$ is the probability that all registers are busy:

$$B = 1 - \left[\sum_{N=0}^{M-1} \frac{(M\rho)^N}{N!} \middle/ \sum_{N=0}^{M} \frac{(M\rho)^N}{N!}\right] \middle/ \left\{1 - \rho\left[\sum_{N=0}^{M-1} \frac{(M\rho)^N}{N!} \middle/ \sum_{N=0}^{M} \frac{(M\rho)^N}{N!}\right]\right\} \tag{31.53}$$

Table 8 gives a value of $B$ in this case to be 0.042. Therefore

$$\text{Prob } (t_w > 1) = 0.042e^{-(9/8) \times 0.506 \times 1}$$
$$= 0.042e^{-0.569}$$
$$= 0.023$$

Thus 2.3 percent of the calls will have to wait more than 1 second.

This figure does not quite meet the requisite condition, so let us try with 10 registers.

If $M = 10$,

$$\rho = \frac{4.444}{10} = 0.4444$$

Table 8 gives a value of $B$ to be 0.017. Therefore

$$\text{Prob } (t_w > 1) = 0.017e^{-(10/8)\times 0.556\times 1}$$

$$= 0.0085$$

Here 0.85 percent of the calls will be delayed by more than 1 second. The exchange should therefore have 10 registers.

The probability that calls have to wait more than 2 seconds in this case is

$$\text{Prob } (t_w > 2) = 0.017e^{-(10/8)\times 0.556\times 2}$$

$$= 0.017e^{-1.389}$$

$$= 0.0042$$

A similar calculation can be used for other parts of the design in which transactions are queued. If, for example, data transactions queue for registers, core blocks, or lines in a group of lines, then a multiserver queuing calculation may be performed.

Now let us examine a situation in which the call is lost rather than queued.

**PROBABILITY OF LOSING A CALL**   In exchange and trunk engineering, it is assumed that a call is *lost* if no path is available when the subscriber completes dialing. The probability of losing a call (assuming an exponential distribution of call duration) is given by

$$P_B = \frac{\dfrac{(M\rho)^M}{M!}}{\displaystyle\sum_{N=0}^{M} \frac{(M\rho)^N}{N!}}$$

where $M$ is the number of facilities (or servers) and $\rho$ is the facility utilization. $M\rho$ is, then, the traffic volume in erlangs.

$$M\rho = E(n)E(t_s)$$

where $E(n)$ is the mean number of transactions arriving in unit time and $E(t_s)$ is the mean holding time for one transaction (in the same time unit).

This equation gives the probability that all $M$ servers are busy, which in this case is the probability of losing a call. No queues form, and thus it differs from the probability that all $M$ servers are busy in Eq. (31.63), which relates to the queuing situation when no calls are lost.

**Example 33.2. WATS-Line or Tie-Line Requirements.** Private leased tie lines are being planned to connect two centers of activity in a corporation. It is anticipated that 100 calls will be originated using these lines in the peak hour of an average day and that an average call will be of 180 seconds duration. When a user makes a tie-line call, he will obtain a busy signal if no tie line is available. How many lines are needed to give a grade of service of 0.001? If, due to special circumstances on one day, the peak hour is four times busier than normal, what will the grade of service be?

*Note:* The same calculations could apply to WATS lines enabling terminal users to dial into a computer center. The 100 calls, for example, could originate from WATS zone 6 in Fig. 18.2, and the question could be asked: "How many WATS lines will be needed from zone 6 to the computer in New York?"

The traffic volume in erlangs is

$$\frac{100 \times 180}{3600} = 5.0 \text{ erlangs}$$

That is,

$$M\rho = 5.0$$

where $M$ is the number of lines and $\rho$ is the line utilization. Hence

$$P_B = \frac{5.0^M/M!}{\sum_{N=0}^{M} 5.0^N/N!}$$

Using Table 11, we see that $P_B = 0.00132$ for 13 lines and 0.00047 for 14 lines. We therefore need 14 lines to give a grade of service (probability of call lost) of 0.001.

On the abnormally busy day when the traffic volume is four times the above—that is, 20 erlangs—we see that the grade of service will have dropped to 0.369.

**ADVANTAGES OF LARGER GROUPING**
When it is possible to group traffic so that a larger number of facilities is used, this grouping, as with terminals in the last chapter, will result in a more efficient employment of the facilities. Large trunk groups are more efficient than small ones for a given grade of service. The larger the value of $M$, the better. Just as in the previous chapter it was better to arrange bank tellers in one large group and gather airline reservation agents together in one location, so here it is better, where possible, to have a large trunk group, to have one large exchange rather than several small ones, and so on.

Let us use an example to illustrate this point.

**Example 33.3. Small vs. Large Trunk Groups.** Suppose that the traffic in the previous example is split into five parts, which are channeled separately. In each fraction, 20 calls will be originated, on the average, in the peak hour (the same total number of calls). How many tie lines will be needed to handle each fraction with the same grade of service? How will the total number of lines compare with the number in the previous example?

The fraction consists of

$$\frac{20 \times 180}{3600} = 1.0 \text{ erlangs}$$

Therefore

$$M\rho = 1.0 \qquad\qquad \text{(from Eq. (33.1))}$$

From Eq. (31.66), the probability of all lines being busy is therefore:

$$P_B = \frac{1/M!}{\sum\limits_{N=0}^{M} 1/N!}$$

Using Table 11, we see that $P_B = 0.00307$ for 5 lines and 0.00051 for 6 lines. Therefore we need 6 lines for each fraction in order to obtain $P_B \leq 0.001$.

A total of $6 \times 5 = 30$ lines is needed to handle the five separate fractions of the traffic, whereas only 14 lines were needed in the previous example.

If the lines were available in groups, as is often the case, the advantage of not splitting the traffic would have been still more pronounced. Suppose that groups of 5 lines each were available. The previous example would have needed 3 such groups to give the 14 lines. This example would need 10 groups, 2 for the 6 lines in each fraction.

In designing the public telephone network, the improved efficiency resulting from a larger grouping of trunks is frequently taken advantage of. This factor increases the complexity and expense of switching but results in considerable overall saving. The same will apply in some cases when designing data transmission networks.

**Example 33.4. Number of Ports and Trunks for a Time-Sharing System.** A time-sharing system is being planned that will have several hundred users with terminals in offices and laboratories. It is thought desirable to give the users a grade of service not worse than 0.01—that is, when they dial the system, they have a 99 in 100 chance of being able to use it. The usage statistics from a small pilot system suggest that when the full system is installed, an average 50 users will be connected to it at any one time during the morning hours when usage is likely to be heaviest. How many ports will the system need to give a grade of service of 0.01?

At any one time, 10 of the 50 users will be in the same building as the computer on the average. The remainder will be connected via trunks from a Centrex system. How many such trunks will be needed?

An average 50 lines are in use during the whole of the peak hour. The traffic volume is then 50 erlangs.

If the system has $M$ ports, $M\rho = 50$. Hence from Eq. (33.1)

$$P_B = \frac{50^M/M!}{\displaystyle\sum_{N=0}^{M} 50^N/N!}$$

Using Table 11 again, we see that $P_B = 0.0217$ for $M = 60$ and 0.0014 for $M = 70$. A quick computation gives 0.00109 for $M = 63$ and 0.00084 for $M = 64$. The system will need 64 ports.

Similarly, the trunks from the Centrex office carry 40 erlangs, and a similar calculation shows that 53 trunks are required.

**NONEXPONENTIAL HOLDING TIMES**
In designing exchanges and trunks to handle telephone calls, it is reasonable to assume that the call duration is exponentially distributed. With data transmission, however, the validity of this assumption is far from certain. Some measurements on specific systems have indicated that the assumption is justifiable for that system. In other cases, the assumption has proven unjustifiable *because of the presence of a few very long holding times.* Some users hog the system!

In many aspects of system design, the exponential distribution of holding times or service times represents a worst-case or near worst-case assumption. If the standard deviation of message lengths is substantially higher than the mean, then this indicates that certain long messages should be chopped into segments and sent separately to avoid blocking the line. In exchange design, however, with today's equipment, we are at the mercy of the user. If he chooses to hold his connection through the exchange all day, we cannot stop him, and we have effectively lost one path through the exchange or one trunk. With a time-sharing system, there may be a good reason why users stay at their terminal for extended periods. An attempt should be made to foresee this situation before the communication links and ports are planned. If the pattern of holding times is thought to be much worse than exponential—for example, if its coefficient of variance is much higher than 1 or if many short holding times are mixed in with long ones—then the preceding calculations will be invalid and it is probably necessary to resort to simulation as discussed in Chapter 38.

A situation that may possibly give trouble is one in which terminal users are intermixed with telephone users on the same exchange or trunking facilities. The telephone users may have a mean holding time of 3 minutes or so, and the terminal users may hold their connection for long periods. In such a situation, there is a probability that at certain times a larger than average number of terminals will be in operation. A reduced number of circuits are available for a period which is lengthy compared to the duration of a telephone call.

One way to calculate the number of circuits needed in such a situation is to do the calculations for the terminals separately from those for the telephones.

**Example 33.5. Mixed Telephone and Data Traffic.** A group of facilities is being designed to handle both terminal users and telephone users intermixed. The terminal users have very long holding times compared to the telephone users. The terminal holding times are thought likely, however, to follow an exponential distribution roughly. It is anticipated that 12 erlangs of terminal traffic and 8 erlangs of telephone traffic will be used. How many circuits are needed to handle the combined traffic and ensure a grade of service of 0.005 to the telephone users?

Let us plan to use $M_1$ circuits for the terminal traffic and $M_2$ separate circuits for the telephone traffic. If at any time the terminal traffic uses more than its $M_1$ circuits, it will encroach on the voice traffic. We want the probability of this happening to be less than 0.005.

The probability that encroachment will happen is

$$P_B = \frac{12^{M_1}/M_1!}{\sum_{N=0}^{M_1} 12^N/N!}$$

From Table 11, $P_B = 0.00557$ when $M_1 = 21$ and $0.00303$ when $M_1 = 22$. We should therefore use 22 circuits for the terminal traffic.

Similarly, for the voice traffic

$$P_B = \frac{8^{M_2}/M_2!}{\sum_{N=0}^{M_2} 8^N/N!}$$

Table 11 indicates that $M_2$ should be 16 circuits.

A total of $16 + 22 = 38$ circuits should be used for both the terminals and telephones.

If the calculation had been done for the total of $12 + 8 = 20$ erlangs (ignoring the difference in the traffic types and the fact that the combined holding times do not in any way resemble an exponential distribution), then it would have given a figure of 32 circuits needed. If 32 circuits had been used, then for 0.56 percent of the time the data traffic would consume 21 circuits, leaving only 11 circuits for the 8 erlangs of voice traffic.

**USER**
**BEHAVIOR**

In the foregoing time-sharing example, we were aiming at a grade of service of 0.01. This grade should keep most users happy. There is a danger, however, that certain user behavior patterns could severely degrade the service. As we discussed in Chapter 21, if the users find that they sometimes cannot obtain a line to the computer when they want one, they may fail to release their line once they have it. Knowing that they want to use the system again in an hour or so, they keep their data set connected to the computer. Once this "line-hanging" syndrome sets in, service will degrade rapidly. More and more users will adopt the same tactic and everyone will suffer. This practice has happened on a number of such systems, frequently because of inadequate PBX facilities.

The level of terminal usage is sometimes highly unpredictable on time-sharing systems. If a new service meets a demand that is badly felt or provides a programming facility that suddenly becomes popular in a particular laboratory, then usage could rise suddenly, thereby flooding the facilities and causing the "line-hanging" syndrome to start.

Generally the number of terminals and potential users is *much* higher than the number of lines, ports, or paths through an exchange, and thus the possibility always exists of a sudden flooding of the facilities. This situation is true of public telephone exchanges. An exchange might have several thousand lines to subscribers but expect only about 50 erlangs of traffic during a normal peak hour and so have only 70 paths available. A factor that makes this situation permissible on a telephone exchange is the predictability of the calling rate and holding times of a large group of users. This predictability may be missing on a time-sharing system; consequently, larger safety margins and the ability to add to the facilities quickly are desirable. As data transmission over the public network grows, its less predictable nature and long holding times may become a problem in public exchange design. It has been a serious factor in the clogging of some city exchanges which has infuriated American telephone subscribers. It would be advantageous to reserve a certain number of circuits for voice only, but doing so may not be possible in the United States because of the foreign attachments ruling and the use of acoustical couplers.

Some method of stopping users from hanging onto their connection when they should release it is clearly desirable. This problem has been discussed in Chapter 21.

# 34 BUFFERING

Buffering is required in modern computers for all input/output devices. In this chapter we are concerned solely with the buffer areas required for telecommunications. On a system with messages arriving and being transmitted on many lines simultaneously, the storage requirements for buffering can be high, especially if the messages are long. In addition to requiring buffer areas in the main computer, we frequently need them in line-control computers and concentrators as well.

The storage used for buffering is a fairly expensive facility and it is worthwhile minimizing it. There are various ways to do so. Unless the system has only a small number of terminals, it will not be economical to allow an input and an output storage area for each terminal or each line equal to the maximum length of the message transmitted. The calculations in this chapter will indicate ways of minimizing such storage requirements.

**USE OF PERIPHERAL MEDIA FOR BUFFERING**
On many communication-based computer systems, the processing unit storage alone is sufficient for input/output buffering of messages. Storage in the main computer may be used, or in a subsidiary line-control computer. However, on some systems it is desirable to supplement the processing unit storage with other, cheaper, storage media. Disk files, drums, or magnetic tape, for example, may be used for buffering.

It is normal to use peripheral storage on a message-switching system. Here the processing needed is slight and the traffic volumes fairly large. The computer is relatively inexpensive, and to buffer this number of messages in main memory would not be economical. As messages are received into memory, they are

515

written on a peripheral medium, usually disk files. As output messages are sent, they are read, as required, from the files into main memory for transmission.

Peripheral storage may be used like this for normal traffic flow, or it may be used only for temporary overloads. The storage allocated in the processor may be able to handle the average traffic, but when every terminal sends a long message or more terminals than normal transmit at once, then tape or disks may be used as a temporary dumping area to prevent the main storage from becoming clogged.

The economies of using peripheral storage can be strong where multidrop lines are used for output. If messages are prepared for a number of terminals on the same line, only one message can be sent at once. Instead of waiting in main storage for their turn, they may wait on drums, disks, or tape.

Such storage devices sometimes add little or nothing to the cost of the system, for they are already used for other purposes. Most real-time data processing systems have large random-access files. Many have serial files, such as tape, for logging traffic. External files may be used for fallback—to store messages for later transmission when a terminal breaks down. Similarly, they may be used for rerouting messages, storing messages with many addresses, and giving terminals a facility to retrieve messages if desirable.

**CALCULATION OF CORE REQUIRED FOR BUFFERING**

Planning the storage area required for buffering on peripheral media is generally not a critical or difficult calculation, for the areas available are large. Processing unit storage, on the other hand, is often at a premium, and buffering calculations for it must be done with care.

A message arriving at the computer and being processed may occupy the processing unit storage for the following periods of time:

1. While it is being received (which may take several seconds).
2. When it has been received completely and is queuing, waiting for the processor.
3. While it is being processed.
4. After processing is complete and the reply is queuing, waiting for the output line.
5. While the reply is being transmitted.

With some methods of storage allocation, when one message has finished with an area of storage, another, possibly from a different communication line, will use it. The length of time the area is tied up is therefore important in the calculations. The term *block-second* is used, as with relocatable program blocks, to mean one block occupied for one second.

Knowing how much storage one message takes up, the times for periods 2 and 4 above may be calculated from queuing theory, as described in Chapter 31. In order to do such calculations, the line utilization, the throughput, and the processing items must be known.

Let us now re-examine the times used during periods 1 and 5 above.

**FOUR METHODS OF CORE ALLOCATION**   There are four common methods of allocating storage for buffering on communication lines. The user may not, however, be free to choose the method that gives the most economical use as calculated below. He may be bound by other considerations; for example, he may be using a standard communication-line input/output control program that dictates how buffer storage is allocated. Even if this program does not give the optimum usage of storage, he may still wish to use it because to rewrite such a program would involve much work. In making storage estimates, one must know how such a program operates.

The four common allocation techniques are as follows:

METHOD 1. A fixed input and output area may be permanently associated with each communication line.

METHOD 2. As soon as a message is to be transmitted or received, a block of storage is taken from a pool and reserved for it. The block is held until the message is completely transmitted or received and then becomes part of the pool again. If the messages vary in length, the blocks must be equal in size to the maximum message length.

METHOD 3. Again a block is allocated as soon as a message is to be transmitted or received. This time its size corresponds to the size of the message. With messages that vary in length, the method can be used for output but cannot be easily used for input unless a concentrator or other device flags the messages to indicate their length.

METHOD 4. A pool of blocks, each smaller than the size of most messages, is used. A block is assigned to a line when the computer starts to receive a message from the line. If the block fills with characters, another block from the pool is chained to it. Blocks are assigned in this way until the complete message is received. The reverse is done on transmission.

Figure 34.1 illustrates the four methods, and from it one can see that method 4 uses the least storage.

Combinations of these methods are conceivable. For example, method 3 may be used for output messages but method 2 for input, because the size of messages is unknown when they begin to arrive.

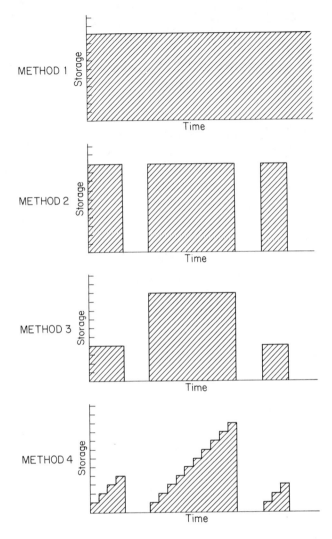

METHOD 1

METHOD 2

METHOD 3

METHOD 4

*Fig. 34.1.* Four methods of allocating buffer storage.

**CALCULATIONS FOR FIXED MESSAGE LENGTHS**

Let us suppose, initially, that the system handles messages of fixed length, and let us calculate the storage requirements for buffering with the foregoing four methods.

The calculations in this chapter assume that as soon as the reception of a message is complete, the message is removed from the buffer area into a queue, where it waits for processing or for logging on files or tape. Similarly, on output, the message is not placed in the buffer area until the line is free, ready for transmission. These assumptions may not be true. If a message is received and *cannot be processed immediately*, it may be queued in the buffering area. The same is true for output. In this case the storage utilization is greater than that used below, and the addition may be evaluated when the queue sizes are estimated.

METHOD 1. Suppose that there are $N$ lines and that the length of a message is $l$ characters.

**Note:**  The length of a message must include all the necessary control characters that are stored in the buffer. This will include the terminal address but may not include start- and end-of-message indicators.

The storage required for input is $Nl$ *characters.*

The same storage will be required also for output unless input and output share a half-duplexed line, in which case input and output may share the same buffer area.

METHOD 2. Suppose that the speed of the lines is $s$ characters per second and that the length of a message again is $l$ characters. Then the message will occupy the line for $l/s$ seconds. If a block of storage of $l$ characters is allocated when a message begins to be received and is released when reception is complete, the $l$ characters will be occupied for $l/s$ seconds.

Suppose the frequency of reception in the peak period, for which the design is done, is such that $f$ messages per hour are received on the average. Then $f$ blocks of $l$ characters will be occupied for $l/s$ seconds each. Therefore the storage required, on the average, is

$$\frac{fl(l/s)}{3600} = \frac{fl^2}{3600s} \text{ characters}$$

The choice between method 1 and method 2 may depend on the line utilization. Suppose that the overall line utilization is $\rho$.

$$\rho = \frac{\text{Actual number of characters transmitted}}{\text{Maximum possible number of characters transmitted}}$$

$$= \frac{(fl/3600)}{Ns} = \frac{fl}{3600Ns}$$

Then

$$\frac{\text{Core required for method 2}}{\text{Core required for method 1}} = \frac{N\rho l}{Nl} = \rho$$

Thus if the line utilization is close to 100 percent, method 1 may be used, for it is simple to program. The lower the line utilization, the greater the disadvantage of using an input/output control program which operates in method 1, as certain of the standardized programs made available by manufacturers do operate.

METHOD 3. For fixed–length messages, the same calculation applies to method 3 as to method 2. We will discuss variable-length messages shortly.

METHOD 4. Suppose the characters arriving on the communication lines are read into a block of core which can hold $B$ characters. When this block is full, the characters are read into another block which is chained to this one. On a machine with binary capabilities, space equivalent to one character might be sufficient for this chaining. On a machine without binary capabilities, two or more characters might be needed. On a typical system, blocks capable of holding thirty-two characters are used, but only 30 message characters are placed in one block, the remaining space being used for chaining.

Suppose that space equivalent to $(B + 2)$ characters is occupied by the block. For the receipt of one message,

$$(B + 2) \text{ characters are occupied for } \quad \frac{B}{s} \quad \text{seconds}$$

for another   $$(B + 2) \text{ characters are occupied for } \quad \frac{2B}{s} \quad \text{seconds}$$

and so on,

$$\vdots$$

$$(B + 2) \text{ characters are occupied for } \left\lceil \frac{l}{B} \right\rceil \frac{B}{s} \quad \text{seconds}^1$$

Therefore the total occupancy of storage for one message is

$$\frac{1}{2} \left\lceil \frac{l}{B} \right\rceil \left( \left\lceil \frac{l}{B} \right\rceil + 1 \right) \frac{B}{s} (B + 2) \text{ character-seconds}$$

Therefore the storage required on average is

$$\frac{\lceil l/B \rceil (\lceil l/B \rceil + 1)(B/s)(B + 2)f}{2 \times 3600} \text{ characters}$$

---

[1] ($\lceil l/B \rceil$ is used to mean $l/B$ rounded up to the nearest integer, this being the total number of blocks used to contain a message of length $l$. $\left\lfloor \frac{l}{B} \right\rfloor$ is used to mean $l/B$ rounded down to the nearest integer. $\left\lceil \frac{l}{B} \right\rceil$ is written CEIL $(L/B)$ in the programs used. $\left\lfloor \frac{l}{B} \right\rfloor$ is written FLOOR $(L/B)$.)

The ratio of storage utilization between method 2 or 3 and method 4 is as follows:

$$\frac{\text{Storage required for method 4}}{\text{Storage required for method 3}} = \frac{[l/B]([l/B] + 1)B(B + 2)}{2l^2}$$

To illustrate this with values from a typical system, suppose that blocks of 32 characters are used, giving $B = 30$, and that the messages are all 200 characters in length,

$$\frac{\text{Storage required for method 4}}{\text{Storage required for method 3}} = \frac{\left\lceil \dfrac{200}{30} \right\rceil \left( \left\lceil \dfrac{200}{30} \right\rceil + 1 \right) \times 30 \times 32}{2 \times 200^2} = 0.672$$

Figure 34.2 plots the ratio of storage needed for method 2 (or 3) to that needed for method 4, against message length $l$.

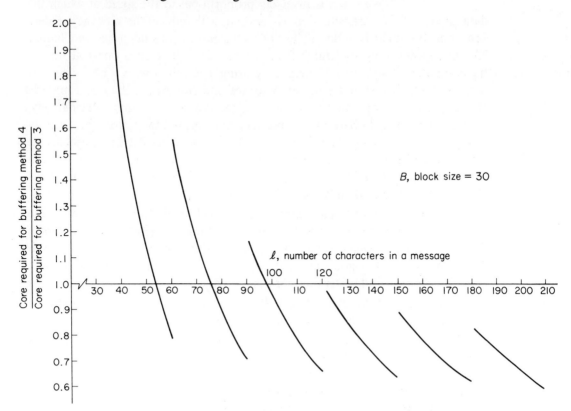

Fig. 34.2. The ratio of buffer storage required for methods 2 and 3, with a block size of 30 characters, to method 3.

It will be seen that method 4 is always the better method for messages of over a hundred characters. With short messages, however, method 4 is not necessarily the preferred one. When $l$ is slightly larger than the block size but less than four blocks, then method 2 or 3 is better — for example, if $B = 30$ and $l = 61$, method 2 or 3 is preferable. For messages that vary in length less than about three block sizes, method 2 or 3 is likely to be better. This fact is interesting because one can find dynamic buffer allocation on machines in which the mean message length is certainly less than the break-even point.

**FACTORS AFFECTING STORAGE REQUIREMENTS**

The equations above highlight a number of points that would be noted about the storage requirements for buffering.

1. The storage requirement for all except method 1 is inversely proportional to the speed at which the data arrive. If fast transmission is used, it will reduce the storage needed. Transmission might be aided by use of a concentrator, as described in Chapter 20, for concentrating the traffic from several slow lines onto one fast line to the computer. It will also be helped by using a terminal with a buffer so that there is relatively fast buffer-to-computer transmission rather than transmission at the speed of an operator pressing the keys. An operator may, alternatively, punch a message into paper tape and then transmit the tape, using a relatively fast paper tape reader. This is often done on message-switching systems. It can certainly be expensive in storage to design a system, as is so often done, in which buffering areas in the central processing unit are held while ponderous terminal users key in their data.

It should be noticed that a concentrator which sends one message at a time to the computer center at the maximum speed of the line is better in this respect than a multiplexer which sends many messages simultaneously at low speed. Again, we stress that good concentrator design can avoid the tying up of a central processing unit better used for other functions.

2. The storage requirement is still more strongly affected by the message length. It is proportional in method 3, or nearly proportional in method 4, to the *square* of message length, $l^2$. Therefore storage is saved if long messages are split up into parts and the parts sent separately. With method 4 buffering, the segment size should be an integral number of blocks. This may not be possible on systems with fixed message lengths, but it is an important consideration on systems that have variable message lengths and where a proportion of messages can be quite long.

With method 2, storage requirement is proportional to the mean message length times the *maximum* message length. Here it is clearly economical to prevent this maximum from being too high — again, probably by chopping up the long messages.

3. The distribution of message lengths on many data transmission systems has a lengthy upper tail. A small proportion of messages are *much* longer than the average. Often this case is worse than the example shown in Fig. 34.3. These

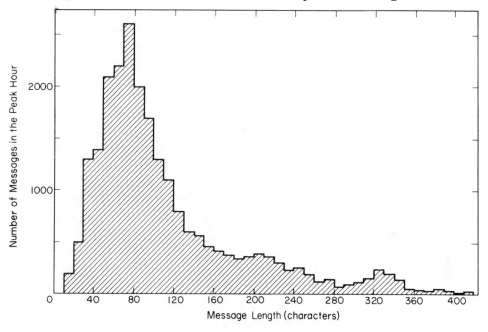

*Fig. 34.3.* A histogram showing the distribution of message lengths. The right-hand tail of the distribution causes a disproportionately large amount of storage to be tied up in the buffering schemes. It can also adversely affect the queuing for the transmission line. It would be better if a mechanism were used for dividing the long messages into separate messages of, say, not more than 150 characters.

long messages would clearly have a severe effect on methods 1 and 2. They also affect methods 3 and 4 badly because the storage requirement is roughly proportional to the square of the message length. It is desirable to find some mechanism for slicing off the upper tail of the distribution. In a system in which messages are logged directly onto a second-level store or read from a second-level store for transmission, the splitting of messages may be done automatically in the main storage of the computer under program control. With multidrop lines, the occasional long messages also degrade the response times of the system because other messages have to wait while the long ones pass. Hence it is desirable to chop them up before they are transmitted. This action may be done by a concentrator or line-control computer, or it may be inherent in the application design.

**OVERLOADS**    When using method 4 for allocating buffer storage, a temporary overload can cause a problem. Suppose that the system starts receiving and allocating blocks of storage to a number of input messages. By chance, all are long messages so that the total number of blocks available for buffering is insufficient to store them all.

As these messages flow into the computer, a point will be reached when no more blocks are available to store them. At the start of their transmission, the computer has no way of knowing their lengths and thus cannot foresee this situation. Unless some emergency action is taken, one or more of the messages will be cut off before being fully received. If the latter is the case, an estimate must be made of the number of messages that will be cut off. The computer will have to notify the terminal operator of its action and request that the message in question be retransmitted.

The overload condition might also be dealt with by temporarily dumping part of the used block chains onto an external file or tape. The computer will take this step before it completely runs out of blocks, thereby releasing blocks to hold further message characters.

**CALCULATIONS FOR**    The preceding calculations are made for systems in
**VARIABLE MESSAGE**    which all messages are the same length. Messages
**LENGTHS**    vary in length on the majority of systems. If there are two or three discrete message lengths, methods like the preceding ones may be used and the calculations done by adding together the results for each message length. Generally there is a wide variation of message length — and not a variation that can be described accurately by a common statistical distribution like the normal distribution.

Where the message lengths vary widely, the advantages of using method 4 become more pronounced. In collecting the data for system design, a histogram showing the numbers of messages of different lengths is needed, as in Fig. 34.3. Where the block size is known or can be assumed, the messages might be counted according to the numbers of blocks they occupy. The block utilization can then be evaluated for messages occupying 1 block, 2 blocks, 3 blocks, and so on. A table like Table 34.1 can be used to evaluate the average core requirement.

The table gives a wide range of message lengths. It is assumed that blocks of 32 characters, or bytes, are used and that these blocks can hold 30 message characters each. Moreover, it is assumed that communication lines are used working at a speed of 6.6 characters per second. It will therefore take $30/6.6 =$ 4.55 seconds to fill up one block. A message that fills one block will tie up one block for 4.55 seconds. A message that fills two blocks will tie up one block for $2 \times 4.55$ seconds and another block for 4.55 seconds, giving a total occupancy of $3 \times 4.55$ block-seconds, and so on. This is how the third column in the table was evaluated.

**Table 34.1**

| Message Length | Number of Messages in Peak Hour | Block Utilization per Message, in Block-Seconds | Total Block Utilization for Messages in Peak Hour, in Block-Seconds |
|---|---|---|---|
| $\left\lceil \dfrac{l}{B} \right\rceil$ Blocks | $f$ | $\dfrac{\left\lceil \dfrac{l}{B} \right\rceil\left(\left\lceil \dfrac{l}{B} \right\rceil + 1\right)}{2} \dfrac{B}{s}$ | $\dfrac{\left\lceil \dfrac{l}{B} \right\rceil\left(\left\lceil \dfrac{l}{B} \right\rceil + 1\right)}{2} \dfrac{B}{s} f$ |
| 1 block | 407 | $1 \times 4.55$ | $407 \times 4.55$ |
| 2 blocks | 2112 | $3 \times 4.55$ | $6226 \times 4.55$ |
| 3 blocks | 4350 | $6 \times 4.55$ | $26{,}100 \times 4.55$ |
| 4 blocks | 3151 | $10 \times 4.55$ | $31{,}510 \times 4.55$ |
| 5 blocks | 2711 | $15 \times 4.55$ | $40{,}665 \times 4.55$ |
| 6 blocks | 1090 | $21 \times 4.55$ | $22{,}890 \times 4.55$ |
| 7 blocks | 381 | $28 \times 4.55$ | $10{,}668 \times 4.55$ |
| 8 blocks | 140 | $36 \times 4.55$ | $5040 \times 4.55$ |
| 9 blocks | 201 | $45 \times 4.55$ | $9045 \times 4.55$ |
| 10 blocks | 64 | $55 \times 4.55$ | $3520 \times 4.55$ |
| 15 blocks | 8 | $120 \times 4.55$ | $960 \times 4.55$ |
| 20 blocks | 8 | $210 \times 4.55$ | $1680 \times 4.55$ |
| 50 blocks | 4 | $1275 \times 4.55$ | $5100 \times 4.55$ |
| 100 blocks | 4 | $5050 \times 4.55$ | $20{,}200 \times 4.55$ |

Total for all messages:

$$\sum \frac{\left\lceil \dfrac{l}{B} \right\rceil\left(\left\lceil \dfrac{l}{B} \right\rceil + 1\right)\dfrac{B}{s} f}{2} = 184{,}011 \times 4.55$$

Average storage requirement:

$$\sum \frac{\left\lceil \dfrac{l}{B} \right\rceil\left(\left\lceil \dfrac{l}{B} \right\rceil + 1\right)\dfrac{B}{s} f(B + 2)}{2 \times 3600} = \frac{184{,}011 \times 4.55 \times 32}{3600}$$

$$= 7443 \text{ characters}$$

It will be seen that the long messages cause a much larger storage occupancy than they would if split into shorter messages. The exceptional messages of 100 blocks — that is, about 3100 characters — increase the average storage requirement by nearly 1000 characters.

**PROBABILITY OF BUFFERS BEING FULL**   In method 1, an area of buffer is permanently allocated to each line. It will always be available.

In the other methods, however, segments of buffer storage are allocated from a pool, and unless the storage used is as great as that in method 1, there is a finite probability that no buffer storage will be available when a message needs it. We must calculate how much storage we need to keep this probability acceptably low.

There will often be many lines using the buffer area. For each of them, the amount of storage used will vary from time to time, and each of the lines will be independent of the others. Given these factors, we may assume the variation in usage of storage from time to time will be close to a normal distribution. If we can calculate the mean usage at any time, plus the standard deviation of it, then we can use the normal distribution to estimate the probability of running out of storage.

Let us suppose that there are $N$ lines. Let $C_i$ be the storage utilization at any instant for the $i$th line. $E(C_i)$ is the mean storage utilization for the $i$th line and Var $(C_i)$ is its variance. The total storage utilization

$$C_T = \sum_{i=1}^{N} C_i$$

The mean total storage utilization is then

$$E(C_T) = \sum_{i=1}^{N} E(C_i)$$

and the variance of total storage utilization is

$$\text{Var } (C_T) = \sum_{i=1}^{N} \text{Var } (C_i)$$

If all the lines carry a similar distribution of traffic, then

$$E(C_T) = NE(C_i)$$

and

$$\sigma_{C_T} = \sqrt{N \text{ Var } (C_i)}$$

By using the normal distribution, the 90th percentile of core utilization will be

$$E(C_T) + 1.28\sigma_{C_T}$$

The 99th percentile will be

$$E(C_T) + 2.33\sigma_{C_T}$$

and the 99.9th percentile will be

$$E(C_T) + 3.09\sigma_{C_T}$$

**COMPUTER PROGRAMS**     Where we have a histogram of the different message lengths, such as that on page 401, it is worthwhile using a computer program to evaluate the buffering requirements. Let us again use the type of notation we employed in Chapter 30. Using six-character fields as illustrated in Table 30.5, we will let

EVLBIO = the mean number of buffering characters required for a line, for input and output traffic
SMLBIO = the second moment of this number
VALBIO = the variance of this number
EVCBIO = the mean number of characters required in total or all of the lines, for input and output.
SMCBIO = the second moment of this number
VACBIO = the variance of this number
SDSCIO = the standard deviation of this number

As in Chapter 30, we will represent the message-length histogram with the following symbols:

FIA (L)     = the fraction input messages of type A with L characters
FIB (L)     = the fraction of input messages of type B with L characters
FOA (L)
and FOB (L) = the equivalent fractions of output messages
N           = the number of lines
RHO         = $\rho$, the facility utilization
B           = the number of data characters that can be stored in a core block

C               = the number of chaining or control characters required in the block

SPEED       = the speed of the line in characters per second

We will write PCT1, PCT2, and PCT3 for the 90th, 99th, and 99.9th percentiles of buffering characters respectively.

The calculations for the four methods of buffering are then written as follows:

METHOD 1. Here MAXIN and MAXOUT are the maximum numbers of characters in the input and output messages respectively.

In PL/I*:

```
MAXIN,MAXOUT=0;
DO L=1 TO 200;
IF FIA(L)>0 | FIB(L)>0 THEN MAXIN=L;
IF FOA(L)>0 | FCB(L)>0 THEN MAXOUT=L;
END;
EVCBIO=(MAXIN+MAXOUT)*N;
SDCBIO=0;
```

METHOD 2. Using the same values of MAXIN and MAXOUT,

```
SUM1,SUM2=0;
DO L=1 TO 200;
SUM1=SUM1+(.15*FIA(L)+.35*FIB(L))*MAXIN+
          (.15*FOA(L)+.35*FOB(L))*MAXOUT;
SUM2=SUM2+(.15*FIA(L)+.35*FIB(L))*MAXIN**2+
          (.15*FOA(L)+.35*FOB(L))*MAXOUT**2;
END;
EVLBIO=RHO*SUM1;
SMLBIO=RHO*SUM2;
VALBIO=SMLBIO-EVLBIO*EVLBIO;
EVCBIO=N*EVLBIO;
VACBIO=N*VALBIO;
IF VACBIO>0 THEN
SDCBIO=SQRT(VACBIO);
PCT1=EVCBIO+1.28*SDCBIO;
PCT2=EVCBIO+2.33*SDCBIO;
PCT3=EVCBIO+3.09*SDCBIO;
```

## Method 3

```
SUM1,SUM2=0;
DO L=1 TO 200;
SUM1=SUM1+(.15*FIA(L)+.35*FIB(L)+.15*FOA(L)+.35*FOB(L))*L;
SUM2=SUM2+(.15*FIA(L)+.35*FIB(L)+.15*FOA(L)+.35*FOB(L))*L**2;
END;
EVLBIO=RHO*SUM1;
SMLBIO=RHO*SUM2;
VALBIO=SMLBIO-EVLBIO*EVLBIO;
EVCBIO=N*EVLBIO;
VACBIO=N*VALBIO;
IF VACBIO>0 THEN
SDCBIO=SQRT(VACBIO);
PCT1=EVCBIO+1.28*SDCBIO;
PCT2=EVCBIO+2.33*SDCBIO;
PCT3=EVCBIO+3.09*SDCBIO;
```

## Method 4

```
SUMIA1,SUMIB1,SUMOA1,SUMOB1=0;
SUMIA2,SUMIB2,SUMOA2,SUMOB2=0;
DO L=1 TO 200;
SUM1,SUM2=0;
DO I=1 TO FLOOR(L/B);
SUM1=SUM1+(B/L)*I*(B+C);
SUM2=SUM2+(B/L)*(I*(B+C))**2;
END;
SUM1=SUM1+(1-FLOOR(L/B)*B/L)*CEIL(L/B)*(B+C);
SUM2=SUM2+(1-FLOOR(L/B)*B/L)*(CEIL(L/B)*(B+C))**2;
SUMIA1=SUMIA1+.15*FIA(L)*SUM1;
SUMIB1=SUMIB1+.35*FIB(L)*SUM1;
SUMOA1=SUMOA1+.15*FOA(L)*SUM1;
SUMOB1=SUMOB1+.35*FOB(L)*SUM1;
SUMIA2=SUMIA2+.15*FIA(L)*SUM2;
SUMIB2=SUMIB2+.35*FIB(L)*SUM2;
SUMOA2=SUMOA2+.15*FOA(L)*SUM2;
SUMOB2=SUMOB2+.35*FOB(L)*SUM2;
END;
EVLBIO=RHO*(SUMIA1+SUMIB1+SUMOA1+SUMOB1);
SMLBIO=RHO*(SUMIA2+SUMIB2+SUMOA2+SUMOB2);
VALBIO=SMLBIO-EVLBIO*EVLBIO;
EVCBIO=N*EVLBIO;
VACBIO=N*VALBIO;
SDCBIO=SQRT(VACBIO);
PCT1=EVCBIO+1.28*SDCBIO;
PCT2=EVCBIO+2.33*SDCBIO;
PCT3=EVCBIO+3.09*SDCBIO;
```

## In Fortran:

```
      DATA ZERO/0.0/
      MAXIN=ZERO
      MAXOUT=ZERO
      DO 210 L=1,200
      IF (FIA(L).GT.ZERO .OR. FIB(L).GT.ZERO) MAXIN=L
      IF (FOA(L).GT.ZERO .OR. FOB(L).GT.ZERO) MAXOUT=L
  210 CONTINUE
      EVCBIO=(MAXIN+MAXOUT)*N
      SDCBIO=ZERO


      INTEGER PCT1,PCT2,PCT3
      DATA ZERO/0.0/
  300 SUM1=ZERO
      SUM2=ZERO
      DO 310 L=1,200
      FACTOR=.15*FIA(L)+.35*FIB(L)+.15*FOA(L)+.35*FOB(L)
      SUM1=SUM1+FACTOR*L
  310 SUM2=SUM2+FACTOR*L**2
      EVLBIO=RHO*SUM1
      SMLBIO=RHO*SUM2
      VALBIO=SMLBIO-EVLBIO**2
      EVCBIO=N*EVLBIO
      VACBIO=N*VALBIO
      IF (VACBIO.GT.ZERO) SDCBIO=SQRT(VACBIO)
      PCT1=EVCBIO+1.28*SDCBIO+.5
      PCT2=EVCBIO+2.33*SDCBIO+.5
      PCT3=EVCBIO+3.09*SDCBIO+.5


      INTEGER PCT1,PCT2,PCT3,CEIL,FLOOR
      DATA ZERO/0.0/
  250 SUM1=ZERO
      SUM2=ZERO
      DO 260 L=1,200
      VAL1=(.15*FIA(L)+.35*FIB(L))*MAXIN
      VAL2=(.15*FOA(L)+.35*FOB(L))*MAXOUT
      SUM1=SUM1+VAL1+VAL2
  260 SUM2=SUM2+VAL1*MAXIN+VAL2*MAXOUT
      EVLBIO=RHO*SUM1
      SMLBIO=RHO*SUM2
      VALBIO=SMLBIO-EVLBIO**2
      EVCBIO=N*EVLBIO
      VACBIO=N*VALBIO
      IF (VACBIO.GT.ZERO) SDCBIO=SQRT(VACBIO)
      PCT1=EVCBIO+1.28*SDCBIO+.5
      PCT2=EVCBIO+2.33*SDCBIO+.5
      PCT3=EVCBIO+3.09*SDCBIO+.5
      INTEGER PCT1,PCT2,PCT3,CEIL,FLOOR
      DATA ZERO/0.0/
```

```
350 SUM11=ZERO
    SUM22=ZERO
    DO 390 L=1,200
    SUM1=ZERO
    SUM2=ZERO
    FRAC=L/B
    FLOOR=FRAC
    BDIVL=B/L
    CEIL=FRAC
    IF  (CEIL.EQ.FRAC) GO TO 360
    CEIL=CEIL+1
360 IF (FLOOR .EQ. 0) GO TO 380
    DO 370 I=1,FLOOR
    SUM1=SUM1+BDIVL*I*(B+C)
370 SUM2=SUM2+BDIVL*(I*(B+C))**2
380 VAL1=1.0-FLOOR*BDIVL
    VAL2=CEIL*(B+C)
    SUM1=SUM1+VAL1*VAL2
    SUM2=SUM2+VAL1*VAL2**2
    FACTOR=.15*FIA(L)+.35*FIB(L)+.15*FOA(L)+.35*FOB(L)
    SUM11=SUM11+FACTOR*SUM1
390 SUM22=SUM22+FACTOR*SUM2
    SUM1=SUM11
    SUM2=SUM22
    EVLBIO=RHO*SUM1
    SMLBIO=RHO*SUM2
    VALBIO=SMLBIO-EVLBIO**2
    EVCBIO=N*EVLBIO
    VACBIO=N*VALBIO
    IF (VACBIO.GT.ZERO) SDCBIO=SQRT(VACBIO)
    PCT1=EVCBIO+1.28*SDCBIO+.5
    PCT2=EVCBIO+2.33*SDCBIO+.5
    PCT3=EVCBIO+3.09*SDCBIO+.5
```

Let us apply this notation to the message-length distributions we employed in Example 30.1 on page 401.

**Example 34.1. Comparison of Buffering Methods.** Of the messages traveling to a system, 30 percent are of type A and 70 percent of type B. For every input message, an output message is sent back. This distribution of message lengths is shown (again) in Table 34.2.

The communication line speed is 14.8 characters per second. There are 50 lines operating with a utilization of 0.5.

If method 4 buffering is used, it will employ blocks of 30 data characters, plus 2 characters for chaining and control.

Compare the four buffering methods.

The program is as follows:*

```
BUFFER:  PROCEDURE CPTIONS (MAIN);
/ ****************************************************************************/
     DCL FIA(200),FIB(200),FOA(200),FOB(200);
     FIA,FIB,FOA,FOB=0;
     DC K=6      TO 10  ;FIA(K)=.390/5  ;END;
     DO K=11     TO 15  ;FIA(K)=.214/5  ;END;
     DO K=16     TO 20  ;FIA(K)=.186/5  ;END;
     DO K=21     TO 40  ;FIA(K)=.140/20;END;
     DO K=41     TO 60  ;FIA(K)=.070/20;END;
     DO K=6      TO 10  ;FIB(K)=.473/5  ;END;
     DC K=11     TO 15  ;FIB(K)=.283/5  ;END;
     DO K=16     TO 20  ;FIB(K)=.118/5  ;END;
     DO K=21     TO 40  ;FIB(K)=.099/20;END;
     DO K=41     TO 60  ;FIB(K)=.027/20;END;
     DO K=6      TO 20  ;FOA(K)=.021/15 ;END;
     DC K=21     TO 40  ;FOA(K)=.029/20;END;
     DO K=41     TO 60  ;FOA(K)=.038/20;END;
     DO K=61     TO 80  ;FOA(K)=.058/20;END;
     DO K=81     TO 100;FOA(K)=.082/20;END;
     DO K=101    TO 120;FOA(K)=.154/20;END;
     DO K=121    TO 140;FOA(K)=.298/20;END;
     DO K=141    TO 160;FOA(K)=.204/20;END;
     DO K=161    TO 180;FOA(K)=.112/20;END;
     DO K=181    TO 200;FOA(K)=.004/20;END;
     DO K=6      TO 20  ;FOB(K)=.055/15;END;
     DO K=21     TO 40  ;FOB(K)=.147/20;END;
     DC K=41     TO 60  ;FOB(K)=.193/20;END;
     CO K=61     TO 80  ;FOB(K)=.278/20;END;
     DO K=81     TO 100;FOB(K)=.182/20;END;
     DO K=101    TO 120;FOB(K)=.072/20;END;
     DO K=121    TO 140;FOB(K)=.034/20;END;
     DC K=141    TO 160;FOB(K)=.021/20;END;
     DO K=161    TO 180;FOB(K)=.011/20;END;
     DO K=181    TO 200;FOB(K)=.007/20;END;
/****************************************************************************/
     PUT SKIP EDIT ('******************************************',
     '******************************')(A,A);
     PUT SKIP EDIT (' MEAN        STANDARD      90 TH        99 TH       ',
     '   99.9 TH   ')(X(23),A,A);
     PUT SKIP EDIT (' CORE        DEVIATION    PERCENTILE    PERCENTILE',
     '   PERCENTILE')(X(23),A,A);
     PUT SKIP EDIT ('******************************************',
     '******************************')(A,A);
     N=50;  RHO=.5; B=30; C=2; SPEED=14.8;
/****************************************************************************/
     MAXIN,MAXOUT=0;
     DO L=1 TO 200;
     IF FIA(L)>0 | FIB(L)>0 THEN MAXIN=L;
```

* Like the other programs in this book, the PL/I version has been left in a form that is easy to follow rather than being contracted for greater machine efficiency.

```
IF FCA(L)>0 | FOB(L)>0 THEN MAXOUT=L:
END;
EVCBIO=(MAXIN+MAXOUT)*N;
SDCBIO=0;
PCT1,PCT2,PCT3=EVCBIO;
PUT SKIP EDIT ('BUFFERING METHOD 1',EVCBIO,SDCBIO,PCT1,PCT2,PCT3)
 (A,F(11),F(11),F(13),F(13),F(13));
PUT SKIP EDIT ('*********************************************',
 '***********************************')(A,A);
SUM1,SUM2=0;
DO L=1 TO 200;
SUM1=SUM1+(.15*FIA(L)+.35*FIB(L))*MAXIN+
           (.15*FOA(L)+.35*FOB(L))*MAXOUT;
SUM2=SUM2+(.15*FIA(L)+.35*FIB(L))*MAXIN**2+
           (.15*FOA(L)+.35*FOB(L))*MAXOUT**2;
END;
EVLBIO=RHO*SUM1;
SMLBIO=RHO*SUM2;
VALBIO=SMLBIO-EVLBIO*EVLBIO;
EVCBIO=N*EVLBIO;
VACBIO=N*VALBIO;
IF VACBIO>0 THEN
SDCBIO=SQRT(VACBIO);
PCT1=EVCBIO+1.28*SDCBIO;
PCT2=EVCBIO+2.33*SDCBIO;
PCT3=EVCBIO+3.09*SDCBIO;
PUT SKIP EDIT ('BUFFERING METHOD 2',EVCBIO,SDCBIO,PCT1,PCT2,PCT3)
 (A,F(11),F(11),F(13),F(13),F(13));
PUT SKIP EDIT ('*********************************************',
 '***********************************')(A,A);
SUM1,SUM2=0;
DO L=1 TO 200;
SUM1=SUM1+(.15*FIA(L)+.35*FIB(L)+.15*FOA(L)+.35*FOB(L))*L;
SUM2=SUM2+(.15*FIA(L)+.35*FIB(L)+.15*FOA(L)+.35*FOB(L))*L**2;
END;
EVLBIO=RHO*SUM1;
SMLBIO=RHO*SUM2;
VALBIO=SMLBIO-EVLBIO*EVLBIO;
EVCBIO=N*EVLBIO;
VACBIO=N*VALBIO;
IF VACBIO>0 THEN
SDCBIO=SQRT(VACBIO);
PCT1=EVCBIO+1.28*SDCBIO;
PCT2=EVCBIO+2.33*SDCBIO;
PCT3=EVCBIO+3.09*SDCBIO;
PUT SKIP EDIT ('BUFFERING METHOD 3',EVCBIO,SDCBIO,PCT1,PCT2,PCT3)
 (A,F(11),F(11),F(13),F(13),F(13));
PUT SKIP EDIT ('*********************************************',
 '***********************************')(A,A);
SUMIA1,SUMIB1,SUMOA1,SUMOB1=0;
SUMIA2,SUMIB2,SUMOA2,SUMOB2=0;
DO L=1 TO 200;
SUM1,SUM2=0;
DO I=1 TO FLOOR(L/B);
```

```
      SUM1=SUM1+(B/L)*I*(B+C);
      SUM2=SUM2+(B/L)*(I*(B+C))**2;
      END;
      SUM1=SUM1+(1-FLOOR(L/B)*B/L)*CEIL(L/B)*(B+C);
      SUM2=SUM2+(1-FLOOR(L/B)*B/L)*(CEIL(L/B)*(B+C))**2;
      SUMIA1=SUMIA1+.15*FIA(L)*SUM1;
      SUMIB1=SUMIB1+.35*FIB(L)*SUM1;
      SUMOA1=SUMOA1+.15*FOA(L)*SUM1;
      SUMOB1=SUMOB1+.35*FOB(L)*SUM1;
      SUMIA2=SUMIA2+.15*FIA(L)*SUM2;
      SUMIB2=SUMIB2+.35*FIB(L)*SUM2;
      SUMOA2=SUMOA2+.15*FOA(L)*SUM2;
      SUMOB2=SUMOB2+.35*FOB(L)*SUM2;
      END;
      EVLBIO=RHO*(SUMIA1+SUMIB1+SUMOA1+SUMOB1);
      SMLBIO=RHO*(SUMIA2+SUMIB2+SUMOA2+SUMOB2);
      VALBIO=SMLBIO-EVLBIO*EVLBIO;
      EVCBIO=N*EVLBIO;
      VACBIO=N*VALBIO;
      SDCBIO=SQRT(VACBIO);
      PCT1=EVCBIO+1.28*SDCBIO;
      PCT2=EVCBIO+2.33*SDCBIO;
      PCT3=EVCBIO+3.09*SDCBIO;
      PUT SKIP EDIT ('BUFFERING METHOD 4',EVCBIO,SDCBIO,PCT1,PCT2,PCT3)
       (A,F(11),F(11),F(13),F(13),F(13));
      PUT SKIP EDIT ('***************************************************',
       '******************************')(A,A);
END BUFFER;
```

In Fortran:

```
      INTEGER PCT1,PCT2,PCT3,FLOOR,CEIL
      DIMENSION FIA(200),FIB(200),FOA(200),FOB(200),
     1ASTER(21)
      DATA ASTER/21*'****'/,ZERO/0.0/,
     1FIA,FIB/200*0.0,200*0.0/,FOA/5*0.0/,FOB/5*0.0/
C
      L1=3
C
      CFIA=.390/5.0
      CFIB=.473/5.0
      DO  10 K=  6, 10
      FIA(K)=CFIA
   10 FIB(K)=CFIB
      CFIA=.214/5.0
      CFIB=.283/5.0
      DO  20 K= 11, 15
      FIA(K)=CFIA
   20 FIB(K)=CFIB
      CFIA=.186/5.0
      CFIB=.118/5.0
      DO  30 K= 16, 20
      FIA(K)=CFIA
```

```
 30 FIB(K)=CFIB
    CFIA=.140/20.0
    CFIB=.099/20.0
    DC  40 K= 21, 40
    FIA(K)=CFIA
 40 FIB(K)=CFIB
    CFIA=.070/20.0
    CFIB=.027/20.0
    DO  50 K= 41, 60
    FIA(K)=CFIA
 50 FIB(K)=CFIB
    CFOA=.021/15.0
    CFOB=.055/15.0
    DO  60 K=  6, 20
    FOA(K)=CFOA
 60 FOB(K)=CFOB
    CFOA=.029/20.0
    CFOB=.147/20.0
    DO  70 K= 21, 40
    FOA(K)=CFOA
 70 FOB(K)=CFOB
    CFOA=.038/20.0
    CFOB=.193/20.0
    DO  80 K= 41, 60
    FOA(K)=CFOA
 80 FOB(K)=CFOB
    CFOA=.058/20.0
    CFOB=.278/20.0
    DO  90 K= 61, 80
    FOA(K)=CFOA
 90 FOB(K)=CFOB
    CFOA=.082/20.0
    CFOB=.182/20.0
    DO 100 K= 81,100
    FOA(K)=CFOA
100 FOB(K)=CFOB
    CFOA=.154/20.0
    CFOB=.072/20.0
    DO 110 K=101,120
    FOA(K)=CFOA
110 FOB(K)=CFOB
    CFOA=.298/20.0
    CFOB=.034/20.0
    DO 120 K=121,140
    FOA(K)=CFOA
120 FOB(K)=CFOB
    CFOA=.204/20.0
    CFOB=.021/20.0
    DO 130 K=141,160
    FOA(K)=CFOA
130 FOB(K)=CFOB
    CFOA=.112/20.0
    CFOB=.011/20.0
```

```
      DO 140 K=161,180
      FOA(K)=CFOA
  140 FOB(K)=CFOB
      CFOA=.004/20.0
      CFOB=.007/20.0
      DO 150 K=181,200
      FOA(K)=CFOA
  150 FOB(K)=CFOB
C*******************************************************************
      WRITE (L1,200) ASTER,ASTER
  200 FORMAT (1H1,
     120A4,A3/1H ,
     224X,'MEAN       STANDARD      90 TH         99 TH         99.9 TH'/
     31H ,
     424X,'CORE       DEVIATION     PERCENTILE    PERCENTILE    PERCENTILE'/
     51H ,20A4,A3)
C....
      N=50.0
      RHO=.5
      B=30.0
      C=2.0
      SPEED=14.8
      METHOD=0
C****************METHOD 1*******************************************
      MAXIN=ZERO
      MAXOUT=ZERO
      DO 210 L=1,200
      IF (FIA(L).GT.ZERO .OR. FIB(L).GT.ZERO) MAXIN=L
      IF (FOA(L).GT.ZERO .OR. FOB(L).GT.ZERO) MAXOUT=L
  210 CONTINUE
      EVCBIO=(MAXIN+MAXOUT)*N
      SDCBIO=ZERO
      PCT1=EVCBIO
      PCT2=EVCBIO
      PCT3=EVCBIO
      GO TO 410
C****************METHOD 2*******************************************
  250 SUM1=ZERO
      SUM2=ZERO
      DO 260 L=1,200
      VAL1=(.15*FIA(L)+.35*FIB(L))*MAXIN
      VAL2=(.15*FOA(L)+.35*FOB(L))*MAXOUT
      SUM1=SUM1+VAL1+VAL2
  260 SUM2=SUM2+VAL1*MAXIN+VAL2*MAXOUT
      GO TO 400
C****************METHOD 3*******************************************
  300 SUM1=ZERO
      SUM2=ZERO
      DO 310 L=1,200
      FACTOR=.15*FIA(L)+.35*FIB(L)+.15*FOA(L)+.35*FOB(L)
      SUM1=SUM1+FACTOR*L
  310 SUM2=SUM2+FACTOR*L**2
      GO TO 400
```

```
C****************METHOD 4****************************************
  350 SUM11=ZERO
      SUM22=ZERO
      DO 390 L=1,200
      SUM1=ZERO
      SUM2=ZERO
      FRAC=L/B
      FLOOR=FRAC
      BDIVL=B/L
      CEIL=FRAC
      IF  (CEIL.EQ.FRAC) GO TO 360
      CEIL=CEIL+1
  360 IF (FLOOR .EQ. 0) GO TO 380
      DO 370 I=1,FLOOR
      SUM1=SUM1+BDIVL*I*(B+C)
  370 SUM2=SUM2+BDIVL*(I*(B+C))**2
  380 VAL1=1.0-FLOOR*BDIVL
      VAL2=CEIL*(B+C)
      SUM1=SUM1+VAL1*VAL2
      SUM2=SUM2+VAL1*VAL2**2
      FACTOR=.15*FIA(L)+.35*FIB(L)+.15*FOA(L)+.35*FOB(L)
      SUM11=SUM11+FACTOR*SUM1
  390 SUM22=SUM22+FACTOR*SUM2
      SUM1=SUM11
      SUM2=SUM22
C*************************************************************
  400 EVLBIO=RHO*SUM1
      SMLBIO=RHO*SUM2
      VALBIO=SMLBIO-EVLBIO**2
      EVCBIO=N*EVLBIO
      VACBIO=N*VALBIO
      IF (VACBIO.GT.ZERO) SDCBIO=SQRT(VACBIO)
      PCT1=EVCBIO+1.28*SDCBIO+.5
      PCT2=EVCBIO+2.33*SDCBIO+.5
      PCT3=EVCBIO+3.09*SDCBIO+.5
  410 METHOD=METHOD+1
      IEVCB=EVCBIO+.5
      ISDCB=SDCBIO+.5
      WRITE (L1,420) METHOD,IEVCB, ISDCB, PCT1,PCT2,PCT3,ASTER
  420 FORMAT(1H ,'BUFFERING METHOD ',I1,2I11,3I13/
     1        1H ,20A4,A3)
      GO TO (250,300,350,500), METHOD
C....
  500 STOP
      END
```

The following are the results of the program.

```
*****************************************************************************************
                      MEAN      STANDARD     90 TH        99 TH        99.9 TH
                      CORE      DEVIATION    PERCENTILE   PERCENTILE   PERCENTILE
*****************************************************************************************
BUFFERING METHOD 1    13000        0          13000        13000        13000
*****************************************************************************************
BUFFERING METHOD 2     3250       578          3989         4596         5035
*****************************************************************************************
BUFFERING METHOD 3     1251       294          1626         1935         2158
*****************************************************************************************
BUFFERING METHOD 4     1196       226          1486         1723         1895
*****************************************************************************************
```

**OPTIMUM BLOCK SIZE**

Where dynamic allocation of storage is used, as in buffering method 4, it is necessary to determine what the block size should be. The block allocation may be a function of the hardware, in which case the programmer or systems analyst has no say in this question, or it may be one of the options available in the software. The optimum block size is clearly going to vary from one application to another — from one mix of messages to another.

We can examine this question by using the foregoing coding and varying $B$, for example:

DO B = 1 TO 50;

**Example 34.2. The Effect of Different Block Sizes on Buffering.** For the mix of message lengths in Example 34.1, investigate the effect of different block sizes (B), in method 4 buffering, on the total storage requirements.

Table 34.3 shows the results of the program used. It will be seen that the mean core is a minimum when $B = 9$—9 data characters, giving a total of 11 in the block. The 90th percentile of storage required is a minimum when $B = 10$. The 99th and 99.9th percentile have a minimum when $B = 11$.

On some machines it will be convenient to use a block size that is a power of 2. In this case, we may take $(B + C) = 16$, giving $B = 14$ (if $C = 2$). This result will give a lower 90th percentile storage usage than $(B + C) = 8$. The 99.9th percentile storage requirement will fit inside a 16K slice of storage ( $2^{14} = 16,384$).

There is, of course, a time penalty to be paid in using a low block size. Time is required to chain the blocks together. On some concentrators and line-control computers, there will be plenty of time to spare and storage utilization will be the prime consideration. If the main control processing unit is used for buffering, time may be at a premium. Where the line speed is low, the time required for chaining will be proportionately low. The examples used in this chapter referred to a line speed of 14.8 characters per second, in which case the chaining function will occur only about once per second per line if a 16-character block size is used. This is minimal on a fast, modern machine with automatic chaining. With fast voice or broadband lines going into the central processing unit, the picture is different. Such trade-offs need to be evaluated.

**Table 34.3**

```
***********************************************************************
```

| BLOCK SIZE | MEAN CORE | STANDARD DEVIATION | 90 TH PERCENTILE | 99 TH PERCENTILE | 99.9 TH PERCENTILE |
|---|---|---|---|---|---|

```
***********************************************************************
```

| BLOCK SIZE | MEAN CORE | STANDARD DEVIATION | 90 TH PERCENTILE | 99 TH PERCENTILE | 99.9 TH PERCENTILE |
|---|---|---|---|---|---|
| 1 | 1913 | 534 | 2596 | 3157 | 3562 |
| 2 | 1301 | 358 | 1759 | 2134 | 2406 |
| 3 | 1106 | 299 | 1489 | 1804 | 2031 |
| 4 | 1016 | 271 | 1362 | 1647 | 1853 |
| 5 | 967 | 254 | 1292 | 1559 | 1752 |
| 6 | 939 | 243 | 1250 | 1506 | 1691 |
| 7 | 923 | 236 | 1225 | 1472 | 1651 |
| 8 | 915 | 231 | 1210 | 1452 | 1627 |
| 9 | 912 | 227 | 1202 | 1440 | 1612 |
| 10 | 914 | 224 | 1200 | 1435 | 1605 |
| 11 | 918 | 221 | 1202 | 1434 | 1603 |
| 12 | 925 | 220 | 1207 | 1437 | 1604 |
| 13 | 934 | 219 | 1214 | 1443 | 1609 |
| 14 | 944 | 218 | 1222 | 1451 | 1616 |
| 15 | 955 | 217 | 1233 | 1461 | 1626 |
| 16 | 968 | 217 | 1245 | 1472 | 1637 |
| 17 | 981 | 217 | 1258 | 1486 | 1650 |
| 18 | 995 | 217 | 1272 | 1500 | 1664 |
| 19 | 1010 | 217 | 1287 | 1515 | 1679 |
| 20 | 1025 | 217 | 1303 | 1531 | 1696 |
| 21 | 1041 | 218 | 1320 | 1548 | 1714 |
| 22 | 1057 | 218 | 1337 | 1566 | 1732 |
| 23 | 1074 | 219 | 1354 | 1584 | 1750 |
| 24 | 1091 | 220 | 1372 | 1603 | 1770 |
| 25 | 1108 | 221 | 1390 | 1622 | 1789 |
| 26 | 1125 | 222 | 1409 | 1641 | 1810 |
| 27 | 1143 | 223 | 1428 | 1662 | 1831 |
| 28 | 1160 | 224 | 1447 | | |
| 29 | 1178 | | | | |

# 35

## THE EFFECTS OF
## LINE ERRORS

As discussed in Chapter 15, errors occur much more frequently on transmission lines than on other data paths in computer systems. Some transmission links in use today have no error-detection equipment. Some have error-detection equipment that catches most but not all of the errors. On some lines, retransmission is necessary when an error is found.

They are two types of calculations that the systems designer should do with regard to errors. First, he should calculate the probability of the data received having undetected errors. Second, he should evaluate the effect of having to retransmit blocks of data and, where applicable, calculate the optimum block length for his particular system.

**ERROR**
**RATE**

The starting point in such calculations will be a figure for the probability that one bit, or one character, transmitted is in error. In the calculations, we shall assume that the errors occur at random and are independent of one another, which is not strictly true. We shall discuss the effect of this assumption after we have done the calculations.

As was listed earlier, typical error rates on telegraph and Telex lines[1] are 1 to 2 bit errors in 100,000 bits transmitted. On voice grade lines, the error rate varies with the speed of transmission and the type of modem used. A typical error rate for 1200-bit-per-second transmission is about one bit wrong in 200,000. At 2400 bits per second, the rate would be higher—more like one bit

[1] Figures are from *CCITT Spec. Study Group A* (*data transmission*), Contrib. 92, Annex XIII, p. 131, 1963.

wrong in 100,000. For higher transmission speeds the error rate rises rapidly unless forward-error correction is used in the modems or other equipment. At 9600 bits per second, the error rate can be very high.

**PROBABILITY OF ERROR IN MESSAGE** Suppose that the probability of one bit being in error on transmission is $P_B$.

Let $n$ be the total number of bits in the message, and let $P_M$ be the probability of there being an error in the message.

The probability of the entire message being correct is the probability that all the bits are correct:

$$(1 - P_B)^n$$

The probability of there being an error in the message is

$$P_M = 1 - (1 - P_B)^n \tag{35.1}$$

$n$ is often large; hence although this expression can be evaluated in no time at a terminal, it is useful to remember the following approximation if it is likely to be done by hand.

The binomial expansion is as follows:

$$(a + b)^n = a^n + na^{n-1}b + \frac{n(n-1)}{2!} a^{n-2}b^2 + \cdots + nab^{n-1} + b^n$$

We can then write $(1 - P_B)^n$ as follows:

$$(1 - P_B)^n = 1 - nP_B + \frac{n(n-1)}{2} P_B^2 + \cdots$$

Here $P_B$ is very small and therefore terms containing $P_B^3$, or higher powers, will be ignored.

The probability of there being an error in the message is then

$$P_M \simeq nP_B - \frac{n(n-1)}{2} P_B^2 \tag{35.2}$$

This approximation must be used with caution because if $n$ is large, the fourth and perhaps higher terms of the binomial expansion will be substantial.

**Example 35.1. Errors in Telegraph Transmission.** Transactions consisting of 100 five-bit characters are to be sent over subvoice grade lines. Telegraph terminals will be used with no error checking. What is the probability that the received message will have an error in it?

The foregoing figures for telegraph error rates should be used.

If there is one error in 100,000 bits,

$$P_B = 10^{-5}$$

If there are two errors in 100,000 bits,

$$P_B = 2 \times 10^{-5}$$

$$n = 5 \times 100 = 500$$

$$P_M = 1 - (1 - P_B)^n \qquad (35.1)$$

$$\simeq nP_B - \frac{n(n-1)}{2} P_B^2$$

For the first figure of one error in 100,000 bits,

$$P_M = 500 \times 10^{-5} - \frac{500 \times 499}{2} \times 10^{-10}$$

In general, in probability calculations of this type, there is no point whatsoever in being more accurate than two significant figures. Here and in many other such cases, we can ignore the second term of Eq. (35.2).

$$P_M = 5 \times 10^{-3}$$

One message in 200, on the average, will have an error in it.

Similarly, for the second figure of two errors in 100,000 bits, we find that $P_M = 0.01$.

Thus we can say that between 0.5 and 1 percent of the messages will have an error in them.

A more elaborate transmission scheme may employ an error-detecting code. A simple mechanism may reduce the probability of having an undetected error to $10^{-7}$, and then one message in 20,000, on the average, will have an error in it. Mechanisms based on more elaborate codes, as discussed in Chapter 15, can virtually eliminate undetected errors, but retransmission of transactions in error will still be needed.

How serious the effect of undetected errors is will vary from one application to another. The systems analyst must follow the effects through in his calculations. In some messages transmitted, the error can do little harm and is soon forgotten. In others, it may result in the file being updated incorrectly and the error may reside on the file for a long period. The system, in some cases, can act as an accumulator of errors, the files steadily becoming "dirtier."

**Example 35.2. Effect of Transmission Errors on the Files.** Real-time transactions from teleprinters with no error checking update a file of 10,000 records. On the average, an item is updated 100 times per month. If any one of 20 five-bit characters is in error in the transmission, the item will be updated incorrectly. If this process went on for 6 months, how many items on the file could be expected to be in error (assuming no other additions to or deletions from the file)?

Let us assume again that one bit in $10^5$ has a transmission error.
The probability that one message has an error in it that will damage a record is

$$P_M = 1 - (1 - P_B)^n$$

$$= 1 - (1 - 10^{-5})^{20 \times 5}$$

The record will be updated 600 times, on the average, during the 6-month period. The probability that it is correct after one update is

$$(1 - 10^{-5})^{20 \times 5}$$

The probability that it is correct after 600 updates is

$$[(1 - 10^{-5})^{20 \times 5}]^{600} = 0.55$$

After 6 months, then, only 55 percent of the records on the file would be correct; 45 percent would be in error.

If teleprinters with seven-bit characters had been used, the message error rate would have been somewhat worse, and more than half of the file would have been in error after 6 months. If we had taken the figure of two errors in 100,000 rather than one, then the preceding calculation would have given 70 percent of the file in error.

The author first did a calculation like this one when looking at a proposal for a railroad system. Unchecked teleprinter messages to the computer center would have enabled a central file to be kept of the locations and assignments of all the cars. With 70 percent of the file in error, decisions about allocation of jobs to cars would have been somewhat chaotic! The situation was not quite as bad as in this example because the errors would presumably have been discovered in a period shorter than 6 months. Nevertheless, it is no way to run a railroad.

The systems analyst must beware of using his files as an error accumulator.

The reader may like to repeat the foregoing calculation, assuming that terminals that use an error-detecting code are employed. If the undetected error rate is one in $10^7$ rather than $10^5$, the number of errors after 6 months is 0.6 percent—in other words, 60 records in the file of 10,000. This figure is more manageable, but even so some scheme for finding the errors and correcting them is clearly necessary.

**RETRANSMISSION OF**  Many data transmission systems attempt to detect
**ERROR MESSAGES**  errors in messages and retransmit them. Where unchecked teleprinters are used for sending batches of data, for example, a hash total may be formed by adding up fields in each item. This total is sent as the last item and is checked by the receiving machine.

Here we would like to decide what is a reasonable batch size, and again a similar probability calculation can be used.

**Example 35.3. Retransmission of Batches in Error.** The 100-character records in Example 35.1 are to be sent in batches with a hash total record sent at the end of the batch for checking purposes. It has been suggested that a reel of 400 records should constitute one batch, and that when such a reel is prepared, the hash total record should always be the last item on the reel. Is 400 a reasonable size for this batch?

Taking a 1 bit in 100,000 error rate again, the probability that one bit is correct is

$$(1 - 10^{-5})$$

The probability that 401 records of 500 bits each are correct is

$$(1 - 10^{-5})^{401 \times 500} = 0.134$$

In other words, 86.6 percent of the reels will have to be retransmitted. On retransmission, there is again an 86.6 percent chance of there being an error. Clearly, 400 records are far too many for one batch in this case.

Even with a batch as small as 20 records, a substantial proportion of the batches will have to be retransmitted:

$$(1 - 10^{-5})^{21 \times 500} = 0.900$$

that is, 10 percent of batches containing 20 records will have to be retransmitted.

If we know the transmission speed and the time it takes to reload a batch for retransmission, we can evaluate the overall mean transmission time per record and then choose the batch size so as to minimize this factor.

Let $N_C$ be the number of characters in a record.

Let $N_R$ be the number of data records in a block, so that $N_R + 1$ is the total number of records, including the hash total.

Let $t_L$ be the time taken to load the batch for transmission.

Let $t_R$ be the time taken to reload the batch for resending (which may be different from $t_L$), and let $S$ be the speed of the line in characters per second.

Let $P_M$ be the probability of there being an error when the batch is transmitted, $P_M^2$ be the probability of it having to be retransmitted twice, $P_M^3$ is the probability of it having to be retransmitted three times, and so on.

The mean time taken in sending a batch is then

$$t_B = t_L + \frac{N_C(N_R + 1)}{S} + \left[ t_R + \frac{N_C(N_R + 1)}{S} \right] (P_M + P_M^2 + P_M^3 + \cdots)$$

$$= t_L + t_R \frac{P_M}{1 - P_M} + \frac{N_C(N_R + 1)}{S(1 - P_M)}$$

where

$$P_M = 1 - (1 - P_B)^{5N_C(N_R+1)} \qquad \text{(from Eq. (35.1))}$$

The time per block is

$$t_M = \frac{1}{N_R + 1} \left[ t_L + t_R \frac{P_M}{1 - P_M} + \frac{N_C(N_R + 1)}{S(1 - P_M)} \right] \qquad (35.3)$$

It is desirable to select the blocking factor $N_R$ so as to minimize $t_M$.

**Example 35.4. Optimum Batch Size.** What is the optimum number of records that should be sent in one batch in Example 35.3, given that transmission speed is ten characters per second, the time taken to load a batch for transmission is 1 minute, and the time taken to reload it when an error occurs is 2 minutes.

$$P_M = 1 - (1 - 10^5)^{500(N_R+1)}$$

And from Eq. (35.3),

$$t_M = \frac{1}{N_R + 1} \left[ 60 + \frac{120 P_M + 10(N_R + 1)}{1 - P_M} \right]$$

Writing these two equations in a computer program and varying $N_R$ shows that $t_M$, the time per message, is a minimum of 14.7 seconds when $N_R = 34$. There

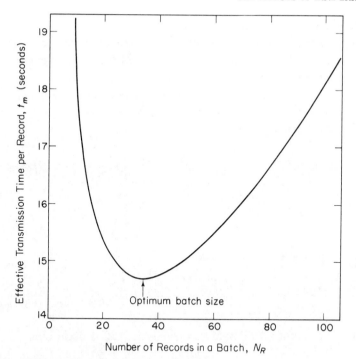

*Figure 35.1*                    Number of Records in a Batch, $N_R$

should be 34 messages in a batch. Figure 35.1 plots $t_M$ against the number of records in the batch.

**EFFECTIVE**          On links in which automatic retransmission of error
**LINE SPEED**         messages is used, the errors and line-control pro-
                       cedures effectively reduce the speed of the line. It is
advantageous to make a transmitted block long, where possible, because the overhead associated with it is then used for as much data as possible. However, if the block is too long, the time used in retransmission becomes excessive. Usually there is an optimum block length, which is a compromise between these two factors.

Again, we would like to make the transmission rate as high as possible, but as we reach the highest speeds, the error rate increases severely. If we had an error-detecting code that caught virtually all the errors, then, once more, there would be a compromise between speed of transmission and amount of retransmission due to errors. It is instructive to investigate these compromises.

Let us consider a line with automatic retransmission of blocks in error.

Let $N_C$, now, be the number of characters in a block that are used for data.

Let $N_H$ be the number of "housekeeping" characters per block that are used for purposes of line control and error detection. In the IBM STR transmission devices, for example, there are eight such characters per block. Let $t_L$ be the total turnaround time on the line that must be added to the block transmission time. The turnaround time will depend on the modem design and the line-control procedures.

Let $t_R$ be the total turnaround time that is needed when an error is detected and the block must be retransmitted. On some systems, $t_R = t_L$.

The mean time taken in sending a block is then

$$t_B = t_L + \frac{N_C + N_H}{S} + \left( t_R + \frac{N_C + N_H}{S} \right)(P_M + P_M^2 + P_M^3 + \cdots)$$

$$= t_L + \frac{N_C + N_H}{S} + \left( t_R + \frac{N_C + N_H}{S} \right)\frac{P_M}{1 - P_M}$$

The effective line speed is then

$$S_E = \frac{N_C}{t_B} = N_C \bigg/ \left\{ t_L + \frac{N_C + N_H}{S} + \left( t_R + \frac{N_C + N_H}{S} \right)\frac{P_M}{1 - P_M} \right\} \quad (35.4)$$

If we have eight-bit characters (seven-bit ASCII code plus one parity bit, for example), then

$$P_M = 1 - (1 - P_B)^{8(N_C + N_H)} \quad (35.5)$$

Using these two equations, we can explore the relations between line speeds, error rates, turnaround time, and block sizes.

Let us take the following errors rates for voice lines with different speed modems:

| Speed (bits per second) | Error Rate | |
|---|---|---|
| | 1 | 2 |
| 1200 | 1 bit in 100,000 | 1 bit in 200,000 |
| 2400 | 1 bit in  50,000 | 1 bit in 100,000 |
| 4800 | 1 bit in  12,500 | 1 bit in  25,000 |
| 9600 | 1 bit in   2,000 | 1 bit in   4,000 |

The error rates at the higher speeds are going to vary greatly with the modem design and line characteristics. At 1200 bits per second, the error rates quoted by different studies for different lines are remarkably similar. At 4800 and above, however, there seems to be wide variation. At the higher speeds, slight variations in attenuation distortion, delay distortion, and noise have an effect on the demodulation process. Another part of the reason for the variation is that the design of high-speed modems is still an evolving art. The preceding error rates may be pushed downward by better modem design.

Figure 35.2 was drawn using the first set of figures, with Eqs. (35.4) and (35.5).

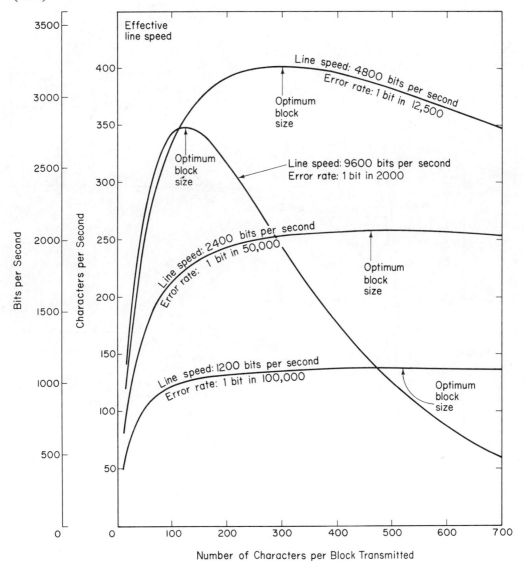

*Fig. 35.2.* Effective line speeds when control characters, turnaround, and error block retransmission are taken into consideration. Typical voice-line error rates are used.

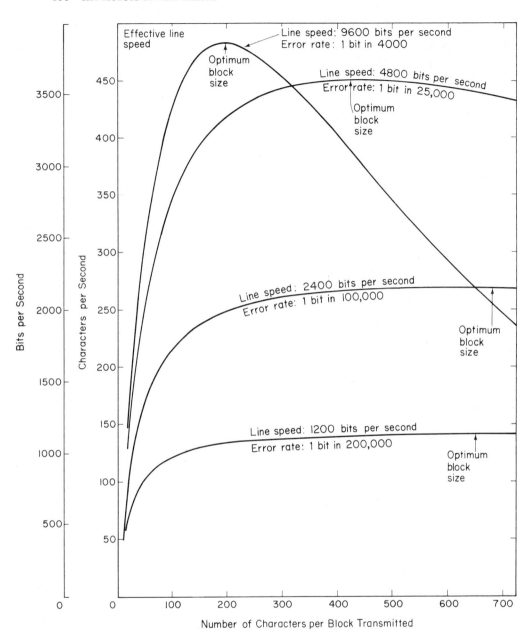

*Fig. 35.3.* Effective line speeds, with half the error rates of those in Fig. 35.2. These calculations suggest the need for forward-error correction in high-speed modems.

In the figure, $N_H$, the number of the control characters per block, was taken to be 8. $t_L$ and $t_R$, the turnaround times, were assumed to be 0.1 second each.

It will be seen that when the error rate is high, as with the two higher line speeds, there is a definite optimum block size. For the two lower speed lines, there is a wide range of block sizes that given near-optimum performance. Any block greater than 300 characters and less than 1000 is close to the optimum.

The effective line speed for the 2400-bit-per-second line is nearly twice that for the 1200-bit-per-second line. The speed for the 4800-bit-per-second line, however, is substantially less than twice that for the 2400 line. The 9600-bit-per-second line actually gives a lower effective speed than the 4800 line because its performance is dragged down by the retransmission of blocks in error. Unless something can be done to correct this we are better off with equipment at a lower speed than 9600.

Assuming that better modem design or better line conditioning might result in a lower error rate, Fig. 35.3 was drawn repeating the calculation of Fig. 35.2 but with half the error rates. Here the 9600 line gives the highest effective line speed, but only marginally so.

**FORWARD-ERROR**
**CORRECTION**
The answer to the dilemma of the 9600-bit-per-second line in Figs. 35.2 and 35.3 is to use forward-error correction. Forward-error correction is not as safe as the use of error-*detection* codes discussed in Chapter 15, and so it should be used *in addition* to error detection and retransmission. However, if the use of forward-error correction could lower the error rate of the 9600 line from 1 bit in 2000 to one bit in 100,000, then the sagging of this curve in Fig. 35.2 could be prevented. Some modems that employ forward-error correction at high transmission speeds for this reason are now on the market. They are sometimes used in conjunction with terminals and line-control machines having their own, safer error-detection and retransmission capabilities. This combination gives the highest possible effective line speed for error-free batch transmission.

# 36  MULTIDROP LINE ORGANIZATIONS

In this chapter and the next, we shall employ the queuing equations described in Chapter 31 to investigate the behavior of multidrop communication lines. Doing so will enable us to develop a table of permissible line loadings, which in turn will enable us to lay out a minimum-cost line network (in Chapter 40).

Let us begin with a simple and somewhat naive approach, then increase the sophistication of our method. The simple approach will be useful for the first look at communication line design, which a systems analyst needs to do quickly and often with many iterations.

Suppose that we are designing a line configuration for a system with two or more types of transaction. For each input message there is a response from the computer to the terminal originating that message. There is a substantial time-lapse at the terminal between the sending of consecutive messages; therefore several terminals are attached to one communication line. The line configuration might resemble the one shown in Fig. 36.1. Using the calculations in Chapter 34, we have selected terminals with some form of buffering so that characters are transmitted at the maximum speed of the terminal.

Because there are several terminals on one line, a queuing problem will exist. We want to discover the size of the delays involved in order to calculate the expected response times. We would also like to see how the delays vary with the type of line organization so that we can select the best type of line organization for the system in question.

In using queuing theory, the communication line becomes the "server." The messages wait their turn to be transmitted over the line. If we are using a full-duplex line, then there are two separate "servers," one for input and one for output. The queue for the input line will be separate from the queue for the output line. If we have a half-duplex line, there will be only one "server" handling both input and output transmission. The input and output messages will be queuing for the same facility.

The "service time" will be the total time the line is occupied by a transaction. In some cases, this period will be simply the transmission time. In other cases, the line may be occupied for a longer period. It may be held, for example, during a time when computing is done; and if so, this time must be included in the service time.

As discussed earlier, the speed at which signals are propagated on a communication line is very high. If a coaxial cable or microwave link is used, it is almost the speed of light. It is somewhat less on wire pairs but still in excess of 15,000 miles per second. Hence although a line might transmit only 150 bits per second because of bandwidth limitations, these bits flash from one point to another almost instantaneously. In our first approximate calculation of response time, we can ignore the propagation time. Consequently, the calculation is not affected by the geographical location of the terminals. In imagining our model of the communication line, we can, therefore, slide all the terminals to one location, as shown in Fig. 36.1. This process, perhaps, makes it easier to think of the

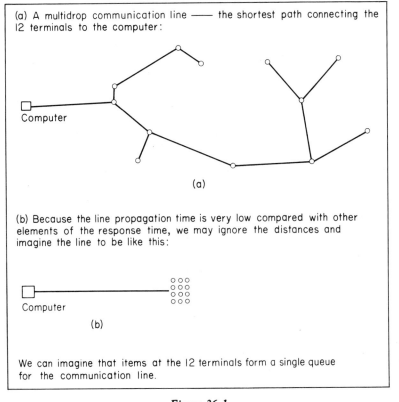

(a) A multidrop communication line —— the shortest path connecting the 12 terminals to the computer:

Computer

(a)

(b) Because the line propagation time is very low compared with other elements of the response time, we may ignore the distances and imagine the line to be like this:

Computer

(b)

We can imagine that items at the 12 terminals form a single queue for the communication line.

*Figure 36.1*

messages at the terminals as forming *one single* queue for the line, not unlike a queue of people at a box office window. Indeed, on a half-duplex line we might go one step further: transactions waiting at the computer are part of the queue for the same facility as those at the terminal.

Given this type of model, we can now apply the queuing equations. Let us consider an example.

### Example 36.1. Half-Duplex Line Held Between Input and Output Transmission.
A half-duplex line transmits at 14.8 characters per second. The terminals on the line transmit messages to the computer and await a response. The message origination rate for all the terminals on the line is 250 messages per hour. When the computer receives a message, it prepares a response ready for transmission in a mean time of 1 second, with a standard deviation of 0.5 second. During this period of time, the line is held by the computer so that it is immediately available for the output transmission.

The input and output message lengths are those used in the example on page 401 (repeated in the tables on the following two pages).

Of the transactions traveling on the line, 30 percent are of type A and 70 percent are of type B.

A line preparation time $T_1 = 0.5$ second must be included in the input message transmission time, and $T_2 = 0.7$ second must be included in the output message transmission time.

The communication line will be held for a time that includes the input transmission time, the time in the computer system, and the output transmission time.

Our calculation in Chapter 30, using these figures, told us that this holding time had a mean of 8.96 seconds and a standard deviation of 3.00 seconds. (See page 410.)

If the input line is organized in a contention fashion, then we can say that we have a single-server queue with a mean service time $E(t_s)$ of 8.96 seconds, a standard deviation of service time $\sigma_{t_s}$ of 3 seconds, and a mean arrival rate $E(n)$ of (250/3600) items per second.

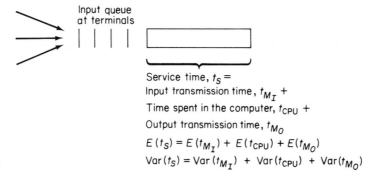

*Figure 36.2*

Input queue at terminals

Service time, $t_S =$
Input transmission time, $t_{M_I}$ +
Time spent in the computer, $t_{CPU}$ +
Output transmission time, $t_{M_O}$
$E(t_S) = E(t_{M_I}) + E(t_{CPU}) + E(t_{M_O})$
$Var(t_S) = Var(t_{M_I}) + Var(t_{CPU}) + Var(t_{M_O})$

In most systems, the input arrival pattern will be very close to a Poisson distribution. Therefore we will use the Khintchine-Polloczek equations to estimate the waiting time. If each one of the "drops" on the line can have no more than one message waiting, then, strictly, we have a queue with a limited upper bound. The Khintchine-Polloczek equations thus give only an approximate estimate of the queuing times. However, it will be close enough for practical purposes. Its inaccuracy would appear only at very high values of $\rho$, and we are unlikely to utilize a communication line with $\rho$ greater than 0.7. The results obtained from this use of queuing theory agree well with simulation studies.

**Table 36.1.** TRANSACTION TYPE A

| | Distribution | Cumulative Distribution |
|---|---|---|
| Number of Characters | Fraction of Transactions of This Length | Fraction of Transactions of This Length or Less |
| **Input** | | |
| Below 6 | None | None |
| 6–10 | 0.390 | 0.390 |
| 11–15 | 0.214 | 0.604 |
| 16–20 | 0.186 | 0.790 |
| 21–40 | 0.140 | 0.930 |
| 41–60 | 0.070 | 1.000 |
| Over 60 | None | 1.000 |
| **Output** | | |
| Below 6 | None | None |
| 6–20 | 0.021 | 0.021 |
| 21–40 | 0.029 | 0.050 |
| 41–60 | 0.038 | 0.088 |
| 61–80 | 0.058 | 0.146 |
| 81–100 | 0.082 | 0.228 |
| 101–120 | 0.154 | 0.382 |
| 121–140 | 0.298 | 0.680 |
| 141–160 | 0.204 | 0.884 |
| 161–180 | 0.112 | 0.996 |
| 181–200 | 0.004 | 1.000 |
| Over 200 | None | 1.000 |

**Table 36.2.** TRANSACTION TYPE B

| Number of Characters | Distribution<br>Fraction of Transactions<br>of This Length | Cumulative Distribution<br>Fraction of Transactions<br>of This Length or Less |
|---|---|---|
| **Input** | | |
| Below 6 | None | None |
| 6–10 | 0.473 | 0.473 |
| 11–15 | 0.283 | 0.756 |
| 16–20 | 0.118 | 0.874 |
| 21–40 | 0.099 | 0.973 |
| 41–60 | 0.027 | 1.000 |
| Over 60 | None | 1.000 |
| **Output** | | |
| Below 6 | None | None |
| 6–20 | 0.055 | 0.055 |
| 21–40 | 0.147 | 0.202 |
| 41–60 | 0.193 | 0.395 |
| 61–80 | 0.278 | 0.673 |
| 81–100 | 0.182 | 0.855 |
| 101–120 | 0.072 | 0.927 |
| 121–140 | 0.034 | 0.961 |
| 141–160 | 0.021 | 0.982 |
| 161–180 | 0.011 | 0.993 |
| 181–200 | 0.007 | 1.000 |
| Over 200 | None | 1.000 |

The facility utilization

$$\rho = E(n)E(t_s) = \frac{250 \times 8.96}{3600}$$

$$= 0.622$$

$$\left(\frac{\sigma_{t_s}}{E(t_s)}\right)^2 = \left(\frac{3.0}{8.96}\right)^2 = 0.112$$

A glance at Table 5 in Appendix VIII shows that the ratio of the mean queuing time to mean service time is about

$$\frac{E(t_q)}{E(t_s)} = 1.92$$

Therefore                                $E(t_q) = 1.92 \times 8.96$

and                                      $E(t_w) = (1.92 - 1) \times 8.96 = 8.2$

To obtain the mean response time, we must add to this the mean time for the input transmission (1.51 seconds — see EVTMLI on page 410), and the mean time in the computer system, 1 second.

Thus we obtain a mean response time $E(t_r)$ of 10.7 seconds.

The result is a somewhat lengthy response time—the penalty paid for using a slow transmission speed. It is too long to permit a slick man-computer conversation, but for many purposes it is adequate. We will do similar calculations with a voice grade line later in the chapter. Using this low-transmission speed, we could improve matters slightly, as will be seen later in the chapter, by organizing the transmission better, and we could make a major improvement by using a full-duplex line if the equipment permitted.

Table 7 in Appendix VIII gives the standard deviation of waiting time. Approximately,

$$\frac{\sigma_{t_w}}{E(t_s)} = 1.24$$

$$\sigma_{t_w} = 1.24 \times 8.96 = 11.11$$

$$\text{Var } (t_w) = 123.4 \text{ seconds}^2$$

In order to obtain the variance of response time, we must also add the variance of the input transmission time (0.494 second², calculated from the figures on page 410) and the variance of time in the computer system, $0.5^2 = 0.25$ second². (The variance in output line preparation time is 0.)

This calculation gives a variance of response time,

$$\text{Var } (t_r) = 123.4 + 0.494 + 0.25 = 124.1 \text{ seconds}^2$$

The standard deviation of response time $\sigma_{t_r}$ is then $\sqrt{124.1} = 11.2$ seconds.

This standard deviation figure indicates that a substantial variation in response time will occur. Following the 95 percentile rule of thumb discussed on page 392, we can expect that roughly 5 percent of the transactions will have to wait $E(t_r) + 2\sigma_{t_r} = 33.1$ seconds or longer for a response.

The distribution of response times will be close to a gamma distribution with parameter

$$R = \left[\frac{E(t_r)}{\sigma_{t_r}}\right]^2 = \left(\frac{10.7}{11.2}\right)^2 = 0.955$$

A glance at the curves in Fig. 31.13 tells us approximately the characteristics of such a distribution. The appropriate curve has been replotted in Fig. 36.3 by using Table 4 in Appendix VIII, and the horizontal axis has been labeled using the preceding figures. From this, or from Table 4, we see that the probability of having to wait more than 20 seconds for a response is approximately 0.16. The probability of having to wait more than 40 seconds is 0.03. It will be very rare to have to wait more than a minute.

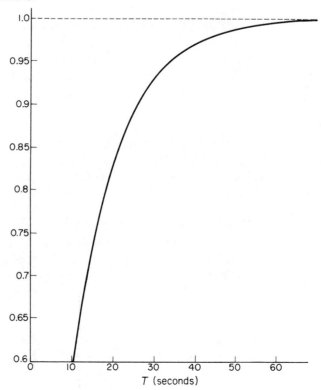

*Fig. 36.3.* Probability that response time for a transaction is greater than time 1 (on horizontal axis).

## CURVE PLOTTING

When doing such calculations, it would be ill-advised to do them for one single throughput. It is desirable to know how the system behavior varies with throughput. It is strongly recommended that the systems analyst plot curves to show how system performance varies with throughput. Doing so is the best way to adjust his design to the range of throughputs he anticipates. In this chapter the curves we will plot are smooth curves; in Chapter 38, however, they could have pronounced kinks in them.

We will use a computer to plot the curves. Most installations do not have a plotting machine; therefore the programs in this book produce the curves on a conventional alphanumeric printer.

We will again use the notation given in Table 30.5. A complete list of the notation used here is given at the end of the chapter. The curve-plotting routine is given in Appendix IV. We will call it in our programs by writing CALL GRAPH. This routine plots four curves, which it shows with lines of letters as follows:

AAAAAAAAA     represents the mean response time for type A trans-
                      actions
BBBBBBBBB     represents the mean response time for type B trans-
                      actions
SSSSSSSSS     represents the standard deviation of response time for
                      type A transactions
ZZZZZZZZZ     represents the standard deviation of response time for
                      type B transactions

All the foregoing times are in seconds. They are plotted against the mean throughput in transactions per hour.

The program feeds these variables to the plotting routine in the form of the following tables:

THRPUT (I): mean throughput
TIMEA (I): mean response time for type A transactions
TIMEB (I): mean response time for type B transactions
SIGTIMEA (I): standard deviation of response time, type A transactions
SIGTIMEB (I): standard deviation of response time, type B transactions

A vertical line of asterisks is drawn at the lowest throughput at which one of the curves goes off the top of the page. A vertical line of Xs is drawn at the absolute maximum throughput, but the asterisk line represents a more practical figure for the maximum that could be handled in reality.

Using the preceding model, the equations for the mean waiting time for the line and variance of waiting time are

$$E(t_w) = \frac{\rho E(t_s)}{2(1 - \rho)} \left(1 + \frac{1}{R}\right)$$

and

$$\text{Var}\,(t_w) = \left[\frac{E(t_s)}{1 - \rho}\right]^2 \left\{\left[1 - \frac{\rho}{6}(4 - \rho)\left(1 - \frac{1}{R}\right)\right]\left(1 + \frac{1}{R}\right)\right.$$
$$\left. - \left[1 - \frac{\rho}{2}\left(1 - \frac{1}{R}\right)\right]^2\right\} - \text{Var}\,(t_s)$$

where

$$R = \frac{E^2(t_s)}{\text{Var } (t_s)} \qquad \text{(the parameter of the gamma distribution of } t_s)$$

The mean response time for type A transactions is then

$$E(t_{r_A}) = E(t_w) + E(t_{m_{IA}}) + E(t_{\text{CPU}})$$

and for type B transactions is

$$E(t_{r_B}) = E(t_w) + E(t_{m_{IB}}) + E(t_{\text{CPU}})$$

where $t_{\text{CPU}}$ is the time the transaction spends in the computer and $E(t_{m_{IA}})$ and $E(t_{m_{IB}})$ are the transmission times for input transactions type A and type B respectively.

Similarly, the variance of response time for the two transaction types is

$$\text{Var } (t_{r_A}) = \text{Var } (t_w) + \text{Var } (t_{m_{IA}}) + \text{Var } (t_{\text{CPU}})$$

and

$$\text{Var } (t_{r_B}) = \text{Var } (t_w) + \text{Var } (t_{m_{IB}}) + \text{Var } (t_{\text{CPU}})$$

The curve-plotting program is then as follows:*

```
TIMEA,TIMEB,SIGTIMEA,SIGTIMEB=0;I,STOP=0;
DO EVNTLI=.0011574 TO .139       BY .0011574 WHILE (STOP=0);
EVTSLN=EVTMLI+EVTTCS+EVTMLO;
VATSLN=VATMLI+VATTCS+VATMLO;
GMTSLN=EVTSLN*EVTSLN/VATSLN;
EVROLN=EVNTLI*EVTSLN;
IF EVROLN >= 1 THEN STOP=1;
EVTWLN=EVROLN*EVTSLN*(1+1/GMTSLN)/(2*(1-EVROLN));
VATWLN=(EVTSLN/(1-EVROLN))**2*((1-EVROLN*(4-EVROLN)*
  (1-1/GMTSLN)/6)*(1+1/GMTSLN)-(1-EVROLN*(1-1/GMTSLN)/2)**2)-
  VATSLN;
THRPUT(I)=EVNTLI*3600;
TIMEA(I)=EVTWLN+EVTMIA+EVTTCS;
TIMEB(I)=EVTWLN+EVTMIB+EVTTCS;
SIGTIMEA(I)=SQRT(VATWLN+VATMIA+VATTCS);
SIGTIMEB(I)=SQRT(VATWLN+VATMIB+VATTCS);
MAXTHRPUT=THRPUT(I);
I=I+1;
END;
CALL GRAPH;
```

* Note again that the PL/I version of each program has been written for clarity of understanding by the reader rather than for efficient machine operation. The FORTRAN version is written with machine efficiency in mind at the expense of clarity of understanding.

**Table 36.2.** A LIST OF THE FIELDS USED IN THE COMPUTER PROGRAMS
IN THIS CHAPTER *

```
EVNTIA=MEAN ARRIVAL RATE OF INPUT  MESSAGE TYPE A
EVNTIB=MEAN ARRIVAL RATE OF INPUT  MESSAGE TYPE B
EVNTLI=MEAN ARRIVAL RATE OF INPUT  MESSAGES (ANY TYPE)
EVNTLN=MEAN TRANSACTION RATE FOR THE LINE
EVNTLO=MEAN ARRIVAL RATE OF OUTPUT MESSAGES (ANY TYPE)
EVNTOA=MEAN ARRIVAL RATE OF OUTPUT MESSAGE TYPE A
EVNTOB=MEAN ARRIVAL RATE OF OUTPUT MESSAGE TYPE B
EVROLI=FACILITY UTILIZATION OF THE LINE BY INPUT  MESS. (ANY TYPE)
EVROLN=RHO, THE FACILITY UTILIZATION OF THE LINE
EVROLO=FACILITY UTILIZATION OF THE LINE BY OUTPUT MESS. (ANY TYPE)
EVROOA=FACILITY UTILIZATION OF THE LINE BY OUTPUT MESSAGE TYPE A
EVROOB=FACILITY UTILIZATION OF THE LINE BY OUTPUT MESSAGE TYPE B
EVTMIA=EXPECTED VALUE OF TRANSMISSION TIME OF INPUT  MESSAGE TYPE A
EVTMIB=EXPECTED VALUE OF TRANSMISSION TIME OF INPUT  MESSAGE TYPE B
EVTMLI=EXPECTED VALUE OF TRANSMISN TIME OF INPUT  MESS. (ANY TYPE)
EVTMLO=EXPECTED VALUE OF TRANSMISN TIME OF OUTPUT MESS. (ANY TYPE)
EVTMOA=EXPECTED VALUE OF TRANSMISSION TIME OF OUTPUT MESSAGE TYPE A
EVTMOB=EXPECTED VALUE OF TRANSMISSION TIME OF OUTPUT MESSAGE TYPE B
EVTSLN=EXPECTED VALUE OF SERVICE TIME FOR THE LINE
EVTTCS=EXPECTED VALUE OF TOTAL TIME MESS SPENDS IN COMPUTER SYSTEM
EVTWLI=MEAN WAITING TIME FOR INPUT  MESSAGES (ANY TYPE)
EVTWLN=EXPECTED VALUE OF WAITING TIME FOR THE LINE
EVTWLO=MEAN WAITING TIME FOR OUTPUT MESSAGES (ANY TYPE)
EVTWOA=MEAN WAITING TIME FOR OUTPUT MESSAGE TYPE A
EVTWOB=MEAN WAITING TIME FOR OUTPUT MESSAGE TYPE B
GMTSLN=R, THE PARAMETER OF THE GAMMA DISTRIBUTION OF SERVICE TIME
MAXTHRPUT=MAXIMUM POSSIBLE THROUGHPUT
MAXTPT=MAXIMUM POSSIBLE THROUGHPUT
SDTRTA=STANDARD DEVIATION OF RESPONSE TIME FOR TYPE A TRANSACTIONS
SDTRTB=STANDARD DEVIATION OF RESPONSE TIME FOR TYPE B TRANSACTIONS
SIGTIMEA=STANDARD DEVIATION OF RESPONSE TIME, TYPE A TRANSACTIONS
SIGTIMEB=STANDARD DEVIATION OF RESPONSE TIME, TYPE B TRANSACTIONS
SMTMLI=SECOND MOMENT OF  TRANSMISN TIME OF INPUT  MESS. (ANY TYPE)
SMTMLO=SECOND MOMENT OF  TRANSMISN TIME OF OUTPUT MESS. (ANY TYPE)
SMTMOA=SECOND MOMENT OF  TRANSMISSION TIME OF OUTPUT MESSAGE TYPE A
SMTMOB=SECOND MOMENT OF  TRANSMISSION TIME OF OUTPUT MESSAGE TYPE B
SMTSLN=SECOND MOMENT OF SERVICE TIME FOR THE LINE
SMTWLI=SECOND MOMENT OF WAITING TIME FOR INPUT  MESSAGES (ANY TYPE)
SMTWLO=SECOND MOMENT OF WAITING TIME FOR OUTPUT MESSAGES (ANY TYPE)
SMTWOA=SECOND MOMENT OF WAITING TIME FOR OUTPUT MESSAGE TYPE A
SMTWOB=SECOND MOMENT OF WAITING TIME FOR OUTPUT MESSAGE TYPE B
SPEED =SPEED OF TRANSMISSION LINE IN CHARACTERS PER SECOND
THRPUT=MEAN THROUGHPUT
TIMEA =MEAN RESPONSE TIME FOR TYPE A TRANSACTIONS
TIMEB =MEAN RESPONSE TIME FOR TYPE B TRANSACTIONS
TMTMLI=THIRD  MOMENT OF  TRANSMISN TIME OF INPUT  MESS. (ANY TYPE)
TMTMLO=THIRD  MOMENT OF  TRANSMISN TIME OF OUTPUT MESS. (ANY TYPE)
TMTSLN=THIRD MOMENT OF SERVICE TIME FOR THE LINE
VATMIA=VARIANCE OF TRANSMISSION TIME OF INPUT  MESSAGE TYPE A
VATMIB=VARIANCE OF TRANSMISSION TIME OF INPUT  MESSAGE TYPE B
VATMLI=VARIANCE OF TRANSMISSION TIME OF INPUT  MESSAGES (ANY TYPE)
VATMLO=VARIANCE OF TRANSMISSION TIME OF OUTPUT MESSAGES (ANY TYPE)
VATSLN=VARIANCE OF SERVICE TIME FOR THE LINE
VATTCS=VARIANCE OF TOTAL TIME MESSAGE SPENDS IN COMPUTER SYSTEM
VATWLI VARIANCE OF WAITING TIME FOR INPUT  MESSAGES (ANY TYPE)
VATWLN=VARIANCE OF WAITING TIME FOR THE LINE
VATWLO=VARIANCE OF WAITING TIME FOR OUTPUT MESSAGES (ANY TYPE)
VATWOA=VARIANCE OF WAITING TIME FOR OUTPUT MESSAGE TYPE A
VATWOB=VARIANCE OF WAITING TIME FOR OUTPUT MESSAGE TYPE B
```

* Appendix II gives a complete listing for the book.

Table 36.2 lists the meaning of the notation used here. The program starts with a very low throughput and increases the throughput until $\rho = 1$. It then sets STOP $= 1$, which stops any further calculation. Figure 36.4 shows the curves produced by this program.

It will be seen from these curves that the maximum throughput is about 350 transactions per hour. However, because of the rapidly rising shape of the curves, it would probably be unwise to design a system for more than about 200 transactions per hour. As we shall see in later chapters, this conclusion will be used in helping to design a minimum cost geographical layout for the lines.

**POLLING**  The foregoing calculations referred to a contention form of line control. Polling is more common than contention, however, especially when there are a large number of terminals on a line. (Polling is discussed in the following chapter). It complicates our calculation somewhat, but if the ratio of the polling time to the message transmission time is low, we can regard its effect as an adjustment to the preceding calculations. It increases the line-holding time on input transmission by a small amount, which we can calculate. Before considering this addition, let us explore some variations on the preceding calculations.

**VARIATIONS IN**  The transmission on a multidrop line can be orga-
**LINE ORGANIZATION**  nized in a variety of ways. It is not always intuitively obvious which way is the best for a given system. Using our queuing models, we can compare the effect of the different schemes. Several questions come to mind.

1. Should we use a full-duplex or a half-duplex line? In some tariffs, at the time of writing, a full-duplex line is only 10 percent more expensive than a half-duplex line. What does this extra cost buy in terms of response time? How many extra terminals can we connect to a full-duplex line and achieve the same response time as a half-duplex line?

2. What line speed should we use? At the time of writing, an AT & T half-duplex line operating at speeds up to 150 bits per second is only slightly more expensive than a full-duplex line operating at speeds up to 75 bits per second. Which would be the better buy?

3. If we use a half-duplex line, should we program the computer so that it *holds* the line between the time when the input message is received and the time when the response is ready to be transmitted? If we do not hold the line for transaction A, then there is a chance that another input trans-

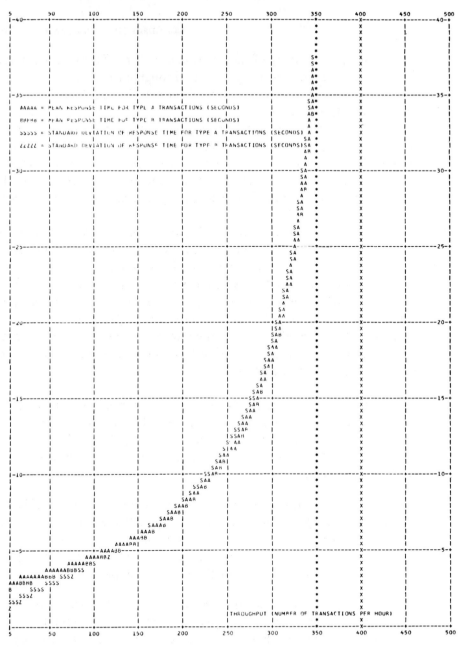

EXAMPLE FH.2.

LINE SPEED 14.8 CHARACTERS PER SECOND

|  | MEAN | STANDARD DEVIATION |
|---|---|---|
| TOTAL TRANSMISSION TIME FOR INPUT MESSAGE TYPE A (SECS) | 1.652 | 0.822 |
| TOTAL TRANSMISSION TIME FOR INPUT MESSAGE TYPE B (SECS) | 1.444 | 0.634 |
| TOTAL TRANSMISSION TIME FOR OUTPUT MESSAGE TYPE A (SECS) | 8.879 | 2.567 |
| TOTAL TRANSMISSION TIME FOR OUTPUT MESSAGE TYPE B (SECS) | 5.415 | 2.323 |
| TOTAL TIME TRANSACTION SPENDS IN COMPUTER SYSTEM (SECS) | 1.000 | 0.500 |

MODEL 1.   A HALF DUPLEX LINE HELD BY THE COMPUTER BETWEEN RECEIPT OF INPUT MESSAGE AND TRANSMISSION OF THE RESPONSE.

*Fig. 36.4.* The variation of response time, and standard deviation of response time, with throughput in Example 36.1.

action, B, might start transmitting while A is being processed. It is possible that A would then have to wait, perhaps along with other transactions, until B has been transmitted. The result is an increase in the response time for A but a decrease for B. What would be the best trade-off?

4. Should we always give output transactions priority over input on a half-duplex line? Much of today's software does so. Intuitively it may seem the best approach—send the reply to any current transaction, if it is ready, before tying up the line with new transactions. However, suppose that the output messages are longer than the input. The queuing equations, in Chapter 31, indicated that the overall queuing time is lower if short transactions are given priority over long ones. Again we ask: "Which is the best strategy?"

5. Should we give type A transactions priority over type B? Or vice versa? With today's hardware, it is difficult to give priority to a particular transaction type *on input* unless we allocate particular terminals to it. On output, however, there is no difficulty. Therefore we may be asking the question: "Should we give priority to type A transactions on output (only)?"

6. Combinations of the preceding two questions are possible. Should we give priority to both the output and to type A (or other) transactions? Could it be that the following priority scheme is the best for a half-duplex line:

> Top Priority: output messages, type A
> Priority 2: output messages, type B
> Priority 3: input messages

Our reason for giving type A messages priority might be unrelated to considerations of overall response time. It might simply be that in considering the man-machine conversation, type A *needs* as fast a response as possible, whereas there is less concern about type B. In that case, we must ask ourselves: "If we always give preference to type A messages, what will this do to the response time for type B?"

A wide variety of such questions arise during the design and implementation of a system. We can obtain some insight into the correct types of answers by using the equations in Chapter 31.

**EIGHT**
**MODELS**

Let us build a set of models for different line organizations, plot curves of response time, and compare their shapes. We will build eight models that differ in the way the line is organized for the handling of two transaction types, A and B.

MODEL 1. A half-duplex line organized as in Example 36.1. When an input message is received, the line is *held* by the computer until the output message is ready to be sent.

MODEL 2. The same as model 1 except that the line is not held after the input message is transmitted. Other input messages can seize it before the response is sent. Output messages, however, if they are waiting, are given *priority* over input.

MODEL 3. The same as model 2 except that input messages are given priority over output.

MODEL 4. The same as model 2 with the addition that type A output messages are given priority over type B. Output has priority over input. Type A and B messages are treated alike on input.

MODEL 5. The same as model 4 except that type B output messages have priority over type A.

MODEL 6. A *full-duplex* line organized in such a way that data can be transmitted on the output half of the line at the same time as data are being transmitted on the input half. No priority scheme is used.

MODEL 7. The same as model 6 except that type A output transactions have priority over type B. There is no differentiation between types A and B on input.

MODEL 8. The same as model 7 except the type B output has priority over type A.

We can quickly write a program that contains eight sets of equations corresponding to the eight models and that draws eight sets of curves so that we may compare the characteristics of the different approaches. The best choice of model will, of course, vary from one system to another.

**Example 36.2. Eight Models for Line Organization.** Using the same data as in Example 36.1, produce curves for the foregoing eight methods of organizing the lines.

MODEL 2. In the second method of organizing the line, the line is released after input transmission. The output transactions thus have to queue along

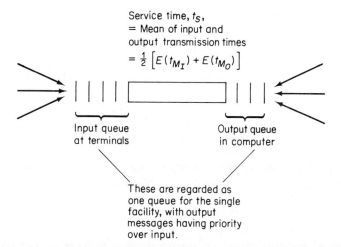

Service time, $t_S$,
= Mean of input and
output transmission times

$$= \tfrac{1}{2}\left[E(t_{M_I}) + E(t_{M_O})\right]$$

Input queue
at terminals

Output queue
in computer

These are regarded as
one queue for the single
facility, with output
messages having priority
over input.

*Figure 36.5*

with the input transactions for the same facility. The output transactions are, however, given priority.

The single-server queuing theory equations make the assumption that the arriving transaction rate follows a Poisson distribution. If we use these equations here, we are, in effect, assuming that input and output transactions together arrive in a Poisson fashion. This assumption is not quite true. The time of arrival of an output message depends on the time that transaction arrived as an input message. The combined arrival rate of input and output messages is, however, approximately Poissonian. The greater the load on the line, the closer it will be to a Poisson distribution in general. We are mainly interested in the response time when the line is rather heavily loaded. Therefore we will use the queuing equations for estimating response times, and, in fact, the results we obtain seem well justified by simulation.

The time the line is held is now simply the message transmission time, $t_{m_{IA}}$ and $t_{m_{IB}}$ for input messages and $t_{m_{OA}}$ and $t_{m_{OB}}$ for output. There is no priority differentiation between type A and B messages. The mean input line holding time is therefore

$$E(t_{m_I}) = f_A E(t_{m_{IA}}) + (1 - f_A)E(t_{m_{IB}})$$

where $f_A$ is the fraction of type A messages.

The mean output line holding time is

$$E(t_{m_O}) = f_A E(t_{m_{OA}}) + (1 - f_A)E(t_{m_{OB}})$$

These values were calculated in Chapter 30, and the section of program on page 406 forms the input to our model here.

The mean holding time of the line in this model is

$$E(t_s) = \tfrac{1}{2}[E(t_{m_I}) + E(t_{m_O})]$$

Similarly, for the second moment and third moment of holding times,

$$E(t_s^2) = \tfrac{1}{2}[E(t_{m_I}^2) + E(t_{m_O}^2)]$$

$$E(t_s^3) = \tfrac{1}{2}[E(t_{m_I}^3) + E(t_{m_O}^3)]$$

The transaction rate for the line will be the sum of the transaction rates for input and output messages.

$$E(n) = E(n_I) + E(n_O)$$

Every input message causes an output message to be sent. Therefore

$$E(n_I) = E(n_O)$$

and

$$E(n) = 2E(n_I)$$

Similarly, the facility utilization of the line, $\rho$, is the sum of the facility utilization by input messages and the facility utilization by output messages. We will call these items $\rho_I$ and $\rho_O$ respectively.

$$\rho_I = E(n_I)E(t_{m_I})$$

$$\rho_O = E(n_O)E(t_{m_O})$$

and

$$\rho = \rho_I + \rho_O$$

Because output takes priority over input, we need the equations for a single-server queue with two priorities (where the high-priority transactions do not *interrupt* any low-priority transaction). The mean waiting time for top priority (output) messages is

$$E(t_{w_O}) = \frac{E(n)E(t_s^2)}{2(1 - \rho_O)}$$

and the mean waiting time for second priority (input) messages is

$$E(t_{w_I}) = \frac{E(n)E(t_s^2)}{2(1 - \rho)(1 - \rho_O)}$$

Similarly, the second moments of waiting time for output are

$$E(t_{w_O}^2) = \frac{E(n)E(t_s^3)}{3(1 - \rho_O)} + \frac{E(n)E(t_s^2)E(n_O)E(t_{m_O}^2)}{2(1 - \rho_O)^2}$$

and for input

$$E(t_{w_I}^2) = \frac{E(n)E(t_s^3)}{3(1 - \rho)(1 - \rho_O)^2} + \frac{[E(n)E(t_s^2)]^2}{2(1 - \rho)^2(1 - \rho_O)^2} + \frac{E(n)E(t_s^2)E(n_O)E(t_{m_O}^2)}{2(1 - \rho)(1 - \rho_O)^3}$$

From these equations, the variance of waiting times can be found.

$$\text{Var } (t_{w_I}) = E(t_{w_I}^2) - E^2(t_{w_I})$$

$$\text{Var } (t_{w_O}) = E(t_{w_O}^2) - E^2(t_{w_O})$$

The mean response for type A and B transactions will then be given by

$$E(t_{r_A}) = E(t_{w_I}) + E(t_{m_{IA}}) + E(t_{\text{CPU}}) + E(t_{w_O})$$

and

$$E(t_{r_B}) = E(t_{w_I}) + E(t_{m_{IB}}) + E(t_{\text{CPU}}) + E(t_{w_O})$$

Similarly, we will add the variances.

$$\text{Var } (t_{r_A}) = \text{Var } (t_{w_I}) + \text{Var } (t_{m_{IA}}) + \text{Var } (t_{\text{CPU}}) + \text{Var } (t_{w_O})$$

and

$$\text{Var } (t_{r_B}) = \text{Var } (t_{w_O}) + \text{Var } (t_{m_{IB}}) + \text{Var } (t_{\text{CPU}}) + \text{Var } (t_{w_O})$$

Feeding these equations into a curve-plotting program, we have in PL/I:*

```
TIMEA,TIMEB,SIGTIMEA,SIGTIMEB=0;I,STOP=0;
DO EVNTLI=.0011574 TO .139       BY .0011574 WHILE (STOP=0);
EVNTLO=EVNTLI;
EVNTLN=EVNTLI*2;
EVTSLN=(EVTMLI+EVTMLO)/2;
SMTSLN=(SMTMLI+SMTMLO)/2;
TMTSLN=(TMTMLI+TMTMLO)/2;
EVROLI=EVTMLI*EVNTLI;
EVROLN=EVTSLN*EVNTLN;
IF EVROLN >= 1 THEN STOP=1;
EVTWLO=EVNTLN*SMTSLN/(2*(1-EVROLN)*(1-EVROLI));
```

* Note: The FORTRAN version of all eight models is at the end of this chapter.

```
EVTWLI=EVNTLN*SMTSLN/(2*(1-EVROLI));
SMTWLO=EVNTLN*TMTSLN/(3*(1-EVROLN)*(1-EVROLI)**2)+
 EVNTLN*SMTSLN**2/(2*(1-EVROLN)**2*(1-EVROLI)**2)+
 EVNTLN*SMTSLN*EVNTLI*SMTMLI/(2*(1-EVROLN)*(1-EVROLI)**3);
SMTWLI=EVNTLN*TMTSLN/(3*(1-EVROLI))+
 EVNTLN*SMTSLN*EVNTLI*SMTMLI/(2*(1-EVROLI)**2);
VATWLI=SMTWLI-EVTWLI*EVTWLI;
VATWLO=SMTWLO-EVTWLO*EVTWLO;
THRPUT(I)=EVNTLI*3600;
TIMEA(I)=EVTWLI+EVTMIA+EVTTCS+EVTWLO;
TIMEB(I)=EVTWLI+EVTMIB+EVTTCS+EVTWLO;
SIGTIMEA(I)=SQRT(VATWLI+VATMIA+VATTCS+VATWLO);
SIGTIMEB(I)=SQRT(VATWLI+VATMIB+VATTCS+VATWLO);
MAXTHRPUT=THRPUT(I);
I=I+1;
END;
CALL GRAPH;
```

The resulting curves are shown in Fig. 36.6.

It will be seen, when comparing these curves with Fig. 36.4, that model 1 gives slightly lower response times than model 2. With a throughput of 250 transactions per hour, model 1 gives a response time for type A transactions of approximately 7.5 seconds. Model 2 gives a response time of 10 seconds. The times for type B transactions are close. The line of asterisks giving maximum reasonable throughput is farther to the right in model 1, showing that this system can handle a throughput slightly more than 10 percent higher.

In other words, with the message times and computing times used in this example, it is better to hold the half-duplex line between input transmission and output than to give output messages priority over input and not hold it. On the other hand, if we give input messages priority over output, as in model 3, this step is better than either of the preceding cases. In general, it is always possible to find a priority scheme that will give better results than holding the line between input and output transmission. Furthermore, if the line speed was higher in comparison with the computing time, it would become much more disadvantageous to hold the line, as is clear in the subsequent examples in this chapter. Queuing models make it clear that it can sometimes pay to hold a file seek arm between reading and writing, but it does not pay to hold a communication line between receiving a message and sending its response.

MODEL 3. Model 3 is the same as model 2 except that now input is being given priority over output. The equations for the mean and second moment of waiting time therefore become

$$E(t_{w_I}) = \frac{E(n)E(t_s^2)}{2(1 - \rho_I)} \qquad E(t_{wo}) = \frac{E(n)E(t_s^2)}{2(1 - \rho)(1 - \rho_I)}$$

$$E(t_{w_I}^2) = \frac{E(n)E(t_s^3)}{3(1 - \rho_I)} + \frac{E(n)E(t_s^2)E(n_I)E(t_{m_I}^2)}{2(1 - \rho_I)^2}$$

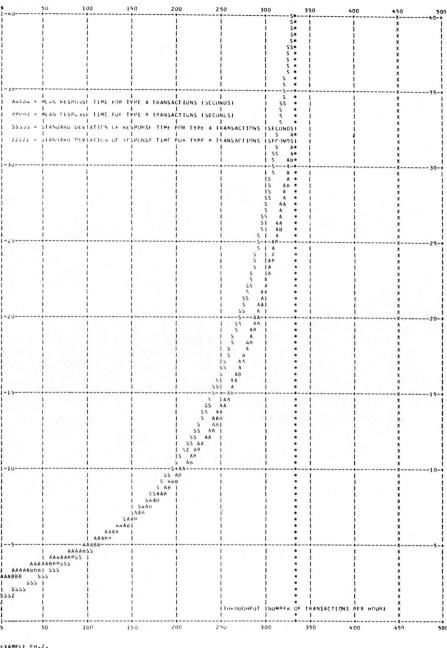

EXAMPLE FH.2.

LINE SPEED 14.8 CHARACTERS PER SECOND

| | MEAN | STANDARD DEVIATION |
|---|---|---|
| TOTAL TRANSMISSION TIME FOR INPUT MESSAGE TYPE A (SECS) | 1.652 | 0.822 |
| TOTAL TRANSMISSION TIME FOR INPUT MESSAGE TYPE B (SECS) | 1.444 | 0.634 |
| TOTAL TRANSMISSION TIME FOR OUTPUT MESSAGE TYPE A (SECS) | 8.879 | 2.567 |
| TOTAL TRANSMISSION TIME FOR OUTPUT MESSAGE TYPE B (SECS) | 5.415 | 2.323 |
| TOTAL TIME TRANSACTION SPENDS IN COMPUTER SYSTEM (SECS) | 1.000 | 0.500 |

MODEL 2.    A HALF DUPLEX LINE, NOT HELD AFTER INPUT TRANSMISSION.
OUTPUT MESSAGES HAVE PRIORITY OVER INPUT.

*Fig. 36.6.* Model 2. A half-duplex line not held after input transmission. Output messages have priority over input.

571

and

$$E(t_{wo}^2) = \frac{E(n)E(t_s^3)}{3(1-\rho)(1-\rho_I)^2} + \frac{[E(n)E(t_s^2)]^2}{2(1-\rho)^2(1-\rho_I)^2} + \frac{E(n)E(t_s^2)E(n_I)E(t_{mI}^2)}{2(1-\rho)(1-\rho_I)^3}$$

In PL/I:

```
TIMEA,TIMEB,SIGTIMEA,SIGTIMEB=0;I,STOP=0;
DO EVNTLI=.0011574 TO .139     BY .0011574 WHILE (STOP=0);
EVNTLO=EVNTLI;
EVNTLN=EVNTLI*2;
EVTSLN=(EVTMLI+EVTMLO)/2;
SMTSLN=(SMTMLL+SMTMLO)/2;
TMTSLN=(TMTMLI+TMTMLO)/2;
EVROLO=EVTMLO*EVNTLI;
EVROLN=EVTSLN*EVNTLN;
IF EVROLN >= 1 THEN STOP=1;
EVTWLI=EVNTLN*SMTSLN/(2*(1-EVROLN)*(1-EVROLO));
EVTWLO=EVNTLN*SMTSLN/(2*(1-EVROLO));
SMTWLI=EVNTLN*TMTSLN/(3*(1-EVROLN)*(1-EVROLO)**2)+
 EVNTLN*SMTSLN**2/(2*(1-EVROLN)**2*(1-EVROLO)**2)+
 EVNTLN*SMTSLN*EVNTLO*SMTMLO/(2*(1-EVROLN)*(1-EVROLO)**3);
SMTWLO=EVNTLN*TMTSLN/(3*(1-EVROLO))+
 EVNTLN*SMTSLN*EVNTLO*SMTMLO/(2*(1-EVROLO)**2);
VATWLI=SMTWLI-EVTWLI*EVTWLI;
VATWLO=SMTWLO-EVTWLO*EVTWLO;
THRPUT(I)=EVNTLI*3600;
TIMEA(I)=EVTWLI+EVTMIA+EVTTCS+EVTWLO;
TIMEB(I)=EVTWLI+EVTMIB+EVTTCS+EVTWLO;
SIGTIMEA(I)=SQRT(VATWLI+VATMIA+VATTCS+VATWLO);
SIGTIMEB(I)=SQRT(VATWLI+VATMIB+VATTCS+VATWLO);
MAXTHRPUT=THRPUT(I);
I=I+1;
END;
CALL GRAPH;
```

The output is shown in Fig. 36.7.

The response times are now lower than in either of the previous models. The row of asterisks is farther to the right. In this example, it is better to give priority to the input messages than the output, because they are shorter. This gives lower mean response times and a higher maximum throughput.

MODEL 4. In model 4 the transactions queuing for the half-duplex line are handled with three priorities:

> Top Priority: output type A
> 2nd Priority: output type B
> 3rd Priority: input

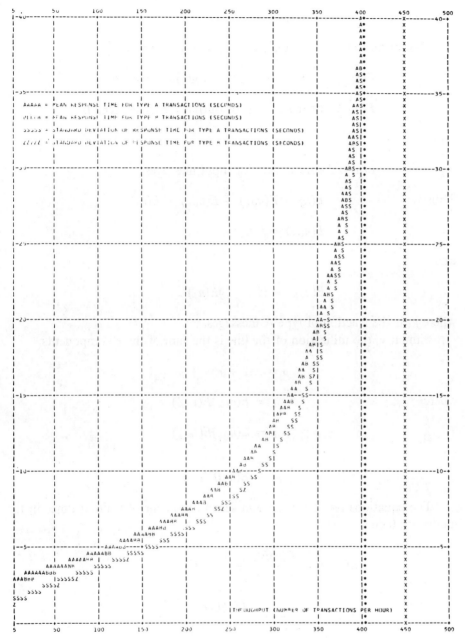

*Fig. 36.7.* Model 3. A half-duplex line, not held after input transmission. Input messages have priority over output. A somewhat higher throughput can be handled than in Fig. 36.6, indicating that it is preferable in this case to give input priority over output.

The mean traffic rate is the sum of three components:

$E(n_{OA})$: the mean rate for output messages, type A

$E(n_{OB})$: the mean rate for output messages, type B

and

$E(n_I)$: the mean rate for input messages

Thus
$$E(n) = E(n_{OA}) + E(n_{OB}) + E(n_I)$$

$$E(n_{OA}) = f_A E(n_I)$$

and

$$E(n_{OB}) = (1 - f_A)E(n_I)$$

where $f_A$ is the fraction of type A messages.

Similarly, the utilization of the line is the sum of three components

$$\rho = \rho_{OA} + \rho_{OB} + \rho_I$$

where
$$\rho_{OA} = E(n_{OA})E(t_{m_{OA}})$$

$$\rho_{OB} = E(n_{OB})E(t_{m_{OB}})$$

and

$$\rho_I = E(n_I)E(t_{m_I})$$

The equations for the mean and second moment of waiting times in this model are then

$$E(t_{w_{OA}}) = \frac{E(n)E(t_s^2)}{2(1 - \rho_{OA})}$$

$$E(t_{w_{OB}}) = \frac{E(n)E(t_s^2)}{2(1 - \rho_{OA})(1 - \rho_{OA} - \rho_{OB})}$$

$$E(t_{w_I}) = \frac{E(n)\,E(t_s^2)}{2(1 - \rho_{OA} - \rho_{OB})(1 - \rho)}$$

$$E(t_{w_{OA}}^2) = \frac{E(n)E(t_s^3)}{3(1 - \rho_{OA})} + \frac{E(n)E(t_s^2)E(n_{OA})E(t_{s_{OA}}^2)}{2(1 - \rho_{OA})^2}$$

$$E(t_{w_{OB}}^2) = \frac{E(n)E(t_s^3)}{3(1 - \rho_{OA})^2(1 - \rho_{OA} - \rho_{OB})}$$

$$+ \frac{E(n)E(t_s^2)[E(n_{OA})E(t_{s_{OA}}^2) + E(n_{OB})E(t_{s_{OB}}^2)]}{2(1 - \rho_{OA})^2(1 - \rho_{OA} - \rho_{OB})^2}$$

$$+ \frac{E(n)E(t_s^2)E(n_{OA})E(t_{s_{OA}}^2)}{2(1 - \rho_{OA})^3(1 - \rho_{OA} - \rho_{OB})}$$

and

$$E(t_{w_I}^2) = \frac{E(n)E(t_s^3)}{3(1 - \rho_{OA} - \rho_{OB})^2(1 - \rho)}$$

$$+ \frac{E^2(n)E^2(t_s^2)}{2(1 - \rho_{OA} - \rho_{OB})^2(1 - \rho)^2}$$

$$+ \frac{E(n)E(t_s^2)[E(n_{OA})E(t_{s_{OA}}^2) + E(n_{OB})E(t_{s_{OB}}^2)]}{2(1 - \rho_{OA} - \rho_{OB})^3(1 - \rho)}$$

The mean response times for type A and B transactions with this model are

$$E(t_{r_A}) = E(t_{w_I}) + E(t_{m_{IA}}) + E(t_{CPU}) + E(t_{w_{OA}})$$

and

$$E(t_{r_B}) = E(t_{w_I}) + E(t_{m_{IB}}) + E(t_{CPU}) + E(t_{w_{OB}})$$

The variances of response times are

$$\text{Var } (t_{r_A}) = \text{Var } (t_{w_I}) + \text{Var } (t_{m_{IA}}) + \text{Var } (t_{CPU}) + \text{Var } (t_{w_{OA}})$$

$$\text{Var } (t_{r_B}) = \text{Var } (t_{w_I}) + \text{Var } (t_{m_{IB}}) + \text{Var } (t_{CPU}) + \text{Var } (t_{w_{OB}})$$

In PL/I:

```
TIMEA,TIMEB,SIGTIMEA,SIGTIMEB=0;I,STOP=0;
DO EVNTLI=.0011574 TO .139      BY .0011574 WHILE (STOP=0);
EVNTLN=2*EVNTLI;
EVNTIA,EVNTOA=.3*EVNTLI;
EVNTIB,EVNTOB=.7*EVNTLI;
EVTSLN=(EVTMLI+EVTMLO)/2;
SMTSLN=(SMTMLI+SMTMLO)/2;
TMTSLN=(TMTMLI+TMTMLO)/2;
EVROLN=EVNTLN*EVTSLN;
EVROOA=EVNTOA*EVTMOA;
```

```
EVROOB=EVNTCB*EVTMOB;
IF EVROLN>1 THEN STOP=1;
 EVTWOA=EVNTLN*SMTSLN/(2*(1-EVROOA));
 EVTWCB=EVNTLN*SMTSLN/(2*(1-EVROOA)*(1-EVROOA-EVROOB));
 EVTWLI=EVNTLN*SMTSLN/(2*(1-EVROLN)*(1-EVROOA-EVROOB));
 SMTWOA=EVNTLN*TMTSLN/(3*(1-EVROOA))+
  EVNTLN*SMTSLN*EVNTOA*SMTMOA/(2*(1-EVROOA)**2);
 SMTWOB=EVNTLN*TMTSLN/(3*(1-EVROOA)**2*(1-EVROOA-EVROOB))+
  EVNTLN*SMTSLN*(EVNTOA*SMTMOA+EVNTOB*SMTMOB)/
  (2*(1-EVROOA)**2*(1-EVROOA-EVROOB)**2)+
  EVNTLN*SMTSLN*EVNTOA*SMTMOB/(2*(1-EVROOA)**3*(1-EVROOA-EVROOB));
 SMTWLI=EVNTLN*TMTSLN/(3*(1-EVROOA-EVROOB)**2*(1-EVROLN))+
  (EVNTLN*SMTSLN)**2/(2*(1-EVROOA-EVROOB)**2*(1-EVROLN)**2)+
  EVNTLN*SMTSLN*(EVNTOA*SMTMOA+EVNTOA*SMTMOB)/
  (2*(1-EVROOA-EVROOB)**3*(1-EVROLN));
 VATWLI=SMTWLI-EVTWLI*EVTWLI;
 VATWOA=SMTWOA-EVTWOA*EVTWOA;
 VATWOB=SMTWOB-EVTWOB*EVTWCB;
 THRPUT(I)=EVNTLI*3600;
 TIMEA(I)=EVTWLI+EVTMIA+EVTTCS+EVTWOA;
 TIMEB(I)=EVTWLI+EVTMIB+EVTTCS+EVTWOB;
 SIGTIMEA(I)=SQRT(VATWLI+VATMIA+VATTCS+VATWOA);
 SIGTIMEB(I)=SQRT(VATWLI+VATMIB+VATTCS+VATWOB);
 MAXTHRPUT=THRPUT(I);
 I=I+1;
 END;
 CALL GRAPH;
```

The curves plotted by this program are shown in Fig. 36.8 on p. 578.

MODEL 5. This model is the same as the last except that the priorities of output messages type A and B are interchanged. We can therefore simply interchange these messages in the program.

```
 TIMEA,TIMEB,SIGTIMEA,SIGTIMEB=0;1,STOP=0;
 DO EVNTLI=.0011574 TO .139       BY .0011574 WHILE (STOP=0);
 EVNTLN=2*EVNTLI;
 EVNTIA,EVNTOA=.3*EVNTLI;
 EVNTIB,EVNTOB=.7*EVNTLI;
 EVTSLN=(EVTMLI+EVTMLO)/2;
 SMTSLN=(SMTMLI+SMTMLO)/2;
 TMTSLN=(TMTMLI+TMTMLO)/2;
 EVROLN=EVNTLN*EVTSLN;
 EVROOA=EVNTOA*EVTMOA;
 EVROOB=EVNTOB*EVTMOB;
IF EVROLN>1 THEN STOP=1;
 EVTWOB=EVNTLN*SMTSLN/(2*(1-EVROOB));
 EVTWOA=EVNTLN*SMTSLN/(2*(1-EVROOB)*(1-EVROOA-EVROOB));
 EVTWLI=EVNTLN*SMTSLN/(2*(1-EVROLN)*(1-EVROOA-EVROOB));
```

```
SMTWOB=EVNTLN*TMTSLN/(3*(1-EVROOB))+
 EVNTLN*SMTSLN*EVNTOB*SMTMOB/(2*(1-EVROOB)**2);
SMTWOA=EVNTLN*TMTSLN/(3*(1-EVROLN)**2*(1-EVROOA-EVROOB))+
 EVNTLN*SMTSLN*(EVNTOA*SMTMOA+EVNTOB*SMTMOB)/
 (2*(1-EVROOB)**2*(1-EVROOA-EVROOB)**2)+
 EVNTLN*SMTSLN*EVNTOB*SMTMOB/(2*(1-EVROOB)**3*(1-EVROOA-EVROOB));
SMTWLI=EVNTLN*TMTSLN/(3*(1-EVROOA-EVROOB)**2*(1-EVROLN))+
 (EVNTLN*SMTSLN)**2/(2*(1-EVROOA-EVROOB)**2*(1-EVROLN)**2)+
 EVNTLN*SMTSLN*(EVNTOA*SMTMOA+EVNTOA*SMTMOB)/
 (2*(1-EVROOA-EVROOB)**3*(1-EVROLN));
VATWLI=SMTWLI-EVTWLI*EVTWLI;
VATWOA=SMTWOA-EVTWOA*EVTWOA;
VATWOB=SMTWOB-EVTWOB*EVTWOB;
THRPUT(I)=EVNTLI*3600;
TIMEA(I)=EVTWLI+EVTMIA+EVTTCS+EVTWOA;
TIMEB(I)=EVTWLI+EVTMIB+EVTTCS+EVTWOB;
SIGTIMEA(I)=SQRT(VATWLI+VATMIA+VATTCS+VATWOA);
SIGTIMEB(I)=SQRT(VATWLI+VATMIB+VATTCS+VATWOB);
MAXTHRPUT=THRPUT(I);
I=I+1;
END;
CALL GRAPH;
```

Figure 36.9 on p. 579 shows the curves for this model.

It will be seen that it is slightly better to give priority to type B messages than to type A, because they are shorter. On the other hand, model 3 was better than either of these models because input messages are much shorter than output.

In general, on a half–duplex line, it pays to give priority to the shortest messages. The type B messages do not suffer badly because type A have priority.

MODEL 6. Models 6, 7, and 8 refer to a full-duplex line. Thus we have two facilities that are independent—the input line and the output line. The queue for the input line will be separate from that of the output line.

We shall assume that the transactions arrive for both the input and the output lines with a Poisson rate of arrival. The arrivals for the output line will be dependent on input line and therefore will not *quite* be Poissonian. The dispersion of interarrival times may be somewhat less than that of an exponential distribution. However, it will be close to an exponential distribution, and the small error incurred by our assumption will at least be on the side of safety. Once again simulation gives results close to those of our model.

In our curve-plotting program, we will again start with a very small throughput and steadily increase it. When $\rho$ for either the input or output line reaches 1 we will stop the program.

IF (EVROLI > 1) | (EVROLO > 1) THEN STOP = 1;

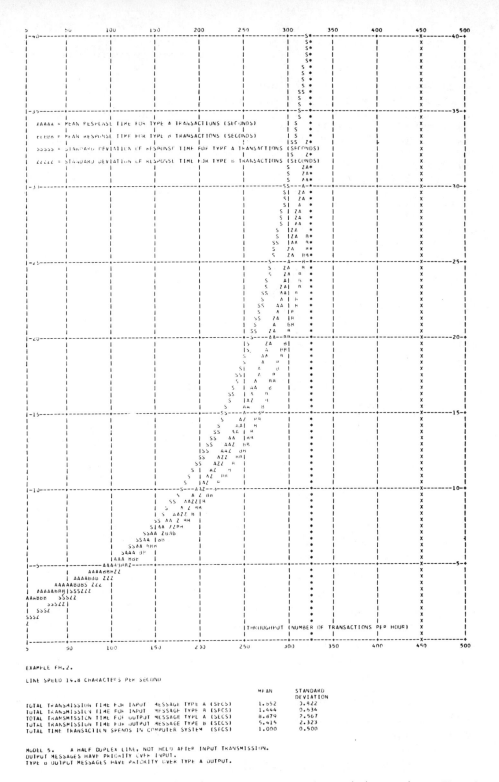

*Fig. 36.8.* Model 4. A half-duplex line. Output messages have priority over input. Type A output messages have priority over type B output.

578

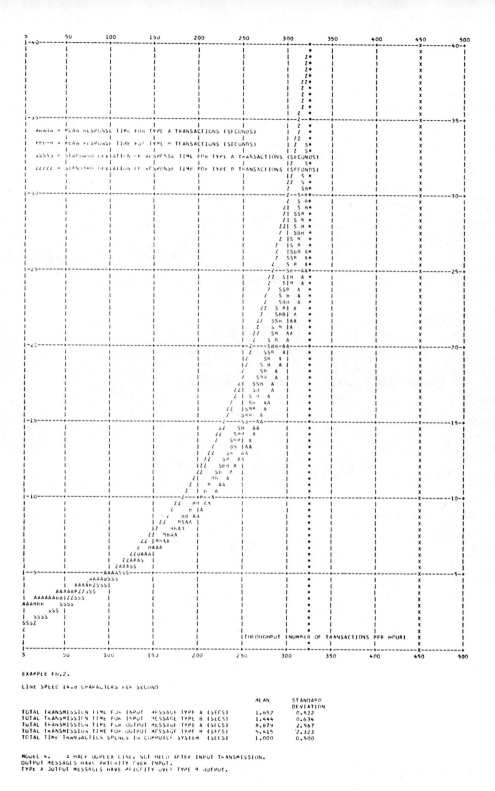

EXAMPLE FH.2.

LINE SPEED 14.8 CHARACTERS PER SECOND

| | MEAN | STANDARD DEVIATION |
|---|---|---|
| TOTAL TRANSMISSION TIME FOR INPUT MESSAGE TYPE A (SECS) | 1.652 | 0.822 |
| TOTAL TRANSMISSION TIME FOR INPUT MESSAGE TYPE B (SECS) | 1.444 | 0.634 |
| TOTAL TRANSMISSION TIME FOR OUTPUT MESSAGE TYPE A (SECS) | 8.879 | 2.567 |
| TOTAL TRANSMISSION TIME FOR OUTPUT MESSAGE TYPE B (SECS) | 5.415 | 2.323 |
| TOTAL TIME TRANSACTION SPENDS IN COMPUTER SYSTEM (SECS) | 1.000 | 0.500 |

MODEL 4.     A HALF DUPLEX LINE, NOT HELD AFTER INPUT TRANSMISSION.
OUTPUT MESSAGES HAVE PRIORITY OVER INPUT.
TYPE A OUTPUT MESSAGES HAVE PRIORITY OVER TYPE B OUTPUT.

*Fig. 36.9.* Model 5. A half-duplex line. Output messages have priority over input. Type B output messages have priority over type A.

579

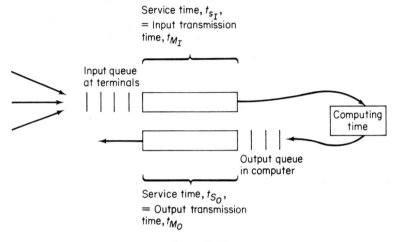

Service time, $t_{S_I}$,
= Input transmission
time, $t_{M_I}$

Input queue
at terminals

Computing
time

Output queue
in computer

Service time, $t_{S_O}$,
= Output transmission
time, $t_{M_O}$

*Figure 36.10*

The queuing equations for the input line are:

$$E(t_{w_I}) = \frac{E(n)E(t_{m_I}^2)}{2(1 - \rho_I)}$$

$$E(t_{w_I}^2) = \frac{E(n)E(t_{m_I}^3)}{3(1 - \rho_I)} + \frac{E^2(n)E^2(t_{m_I}^2)}{2(1 - \rho_I)^2}$$

and for the output line

$$E(t_{w_O}) = \frac{E(n)E(t_{m_O}^2)}{2(1 - \rho_O)}$$

$$E(t_{w_O}^2) = \frac{E(n)E(t_{m_O}^3)}{3(1 - \rho_O)} + \frac{E^2(n)E^2(t_{m_O}^2)}{2(1 - \rho_O)^2}$$

The response times for type A and type B transactions are

$$E(t_{r_A}) = E(t_{w_I}) + E(t_{m_{IA}}) + E(t_{\text{CPU}}) + E(t_{w_O})$$

and

$$E(t_{r_B}) = E(t_{w_I}) + E(t_{m_{IB}}) + E(t_{\text{CPU}}) + E(t_{w_O})$$

and the variances are

$$\mathrm{Var}\ (t_{r_A}) = \mathrm{Var}\ (t_{w_I}) + \mathrm{Var}\ (t_{m_{IA}}) + \mathrm{Var}\ (t_{\mathrm{CPU}})\ \mathrm{Var}\ (t_{w_O})$$

$$\mathrm{Var}\ (t_{r_B}) = \mathrm{Var}\ (t_{w_I}) + \mathrm{Var}\ (t_{m_{IB}}) + \mathrm{Var}\ (t_{\mathrm{CPU}}) + \mathrm{Var}\ (t_{w_O})$$

In PL/I:

```
TIMEA,TIMEB,SIGTIMEA,SIGTIMEB=0;I,STOP=0;
DO EVNTLI=.0011574 TO .139      BY .0011574 WHILE (STOP=0);
EVNTLO=EVNTLI;
EVRCLI=EVNTLI*EVTMLI;
EVROLO=EVNTLO*EVTMLO;
IF (EVRCLI>1)|(EVROLO>1) THEN STOP=1;
EVTWLI=EVNTLI*SMTMLI/(2*(1-EVROLI));
EVTWLO=EVNTLC*SMTMLO/(2*(1-EVRCLO));
SMTWLI=EVNTLI*TMTMLI/(3*(1-EVRCLI))+(EVNTLI*SMTMLI)**2/(2*(1-
   EVROLI)**2);
SMTWLO=EVNTLC*TMTMLO/(3*(1-EVRCLC))+(EVNTLC*SMTMLO)**2/(2*(1-
   EVROLO)**2);
VATWLI=SMTWLI-EVTWLI*EVTWLI;
VATWLO=SMTWLO-EVTWLO*EVTWLO;
THRPUT(I)=EVNTLI*3600;
TIMEA(I)=EVTWLI+EVTMIA+EVTTCS+EVTWLO;
TIMEB(I)=EVTWLI+EVTMIB+EVTTCS+EVTWLO;
SIGTIMEA(I)=SQRT(VATWLI+VATMIA+VATTCS+VATWLO);
SIGTIMEB(I)=SQRT(VATWLI+VATMIB+VATTCS+VATWLO);
MAXTHRPUT=THRPUT(I);
I=I+1;
END;
CALL GRAPH;
```

The curves plotted by this model are shown in Fig. 36.11.

As would be expected, the response time has dropped and the maximum throughput has increased. With model 3, the best half-duplex model for this case, a mean response time of 10 seconds is obtained at a throughput of 320 transactions per second. With model 6, this response time is obtained at a throughput of 420 transactions per seconds.

With present United States tariffs, a full-duplex line of this speed costs about 10 percent more than a half-duplex line. The improvement in throughput, as we see from our curves, is better than 10 percent. In laying a network with many terminals, we would generally be better off with full-duplex lines.

MODEL 7. In model 7 the input line is the same as that in model 6. On the output line, however, type A transactions have priority over type B.

The queuing equations for the input line remain the same.

$$E(t_{w_I}) = \frac{E(n)E(t_{m_I}^2)}{2(1 - \rho_I)}$$

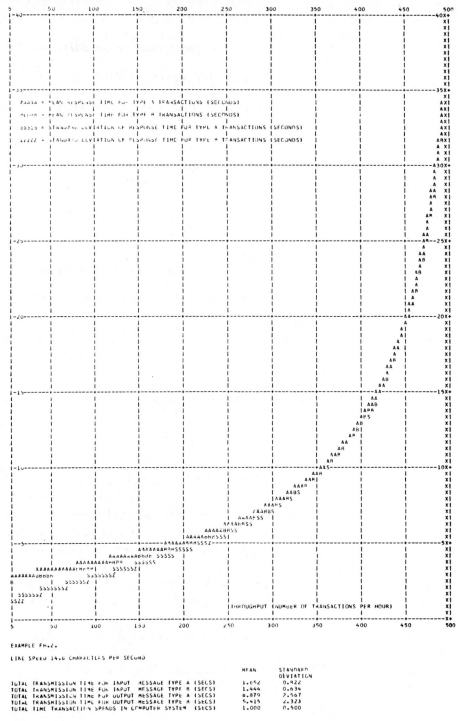

EXAMPLE FR.2.

LINE SPEED 14.8 CHARACTERS PER SECOND

|  | MEAN | STANDARD DEVIATION |
|---|---|---|
| TOTAL TRANSMISSION TIME FOR INPUT MESSAGE TYPE A (SECS) | 1.652 | 0.922 |
| TOTAL TRANSMISSION TIME FOR INPUT MESSAGE TYPE B (SECS) | 1.444 | 0.634 |
| TOTAL TRANSMISSION TIME FOR OUTPUT MESSAGE TYPE A (SECS) | 8.879 | 2.567 |
| TOTAL TRANSMISSION TIME FOR OUTPUT MESSAGE TYPE B (SECS) | 5.415 | 2.323 |
| TOTAL TIME TRANSACTION SPENDS IN COMPUTER SYSTEM (SECS) | 1.000 | 0.500 |

MODEL 6.    A FULL DUPLEX LINE WITH DATA BEING TRANSMITTED IN BOTH DIRECTIONS AT ONCE.

*Fig. 36.11.* Model 6. A full-duplex line which can transmit data in both directions at once. The throughput is higher than that with any of the half-duplex models, but not twice as high.

$$E(t_{w_I}^2) = \frac{E(n)E(t_{m_I}^3)}{3(1 - \rho_I)} + \frac{E^2(n)E^2(t_{m_I}^2)}{2(1 - \rho_I)^2}$$

For the output line, we have a two-priority queue.

$$E(t_{w_{OA}}) = \frac{E(n)E(t_{m_O}^2)}{2(1 - \rho_{OA})}$$

$$E(t_{w_{OB}}) = \frac{E(n)E(t_{m_O}^2)}{2(1 - \rho_O)(1 - \rho_{OB})}$$

where $\rho_{OA}$ is that part of the utilization of the output line due to transactions type A and $\rho_{OB}$ is that part due to transactions type B.

$$\rho_O = \rho_{OA} + \rho_{OB}$$

$$E(n) = E(n_A) + E(n_B)$$

$$\rho_O = E(n)E(t_{m_O})$$

$$\rho_{OA} = E(n_A)E(t_{m_{OA}})$$

and

$$\rho_{OB} = E(n_B)E(t_{m_{OB}})$$

The second moments of waiting time for the output line are

$$E(t_{w_{OA}}^2) = \frac{E(n)E(t_{m_O}^3)}{3(1 - \rho_{OA})} + \frac{E(n)E(t_{m_O}^2)E(n_{OA})E(t_{m_{OA}}^2)}{2(1 - \rho_{OA})^2}$$

$$E(t_{w_{OB}}^2) = \frac{E(n)E(t_{m_O}^3)}{3(1 - \rho)(1 - \rho_{OA})} + \frac{[E(n)E(t_{m_O}^2)]^2}{2(1 - \rho)^2(1 - \rho_{OA})^2}$$

$$+ \frac{E(n)E(t_{m_O}^2)E(n_{OA})E(t_{m_{OA}}^2)}{2(1 - \rho)(1 - \rho_{OA})^3}$$

The mean response times are then

$$E(t_{r_A}) = E(t_{w_I}) + E(t_{m_{IA}}) + E(t_{CPU}) + E(t_{w_{OA}})$$

and

$$E(t_{r_B}) = E(t_{w_I}) + E(t_{m_{IB}}) + E(t_{CPU}) + E(t_{w_{OB}})$$

and the variances of response times are

$$\text{Var} \, (t_{r_A}) = \text{Var} \, (t_{w_I}) + \text{Var} \, (t_{m_{IA}}) + \text{Var} \, (t_{\text{CPU}}) + \text{Var} \, (t_{w_{OA}})$$

$$\text{Var} \, (t_{r_B}) = \text{Var} \, (t_{w_I}) + \text{Var} \, (t_{m_{IB}}) + \text{Var} \, (t_{\text{CPU}}) + \text{Var} \, (t_{w_{OB}})$$

The program for this model is

```
TIMEA,TIMEB,SIGTIMEA,SIGTIMEB=0;I,STOP=0;
DO EVNTLI=.0011574 TO .139     BY .0011574 WHILE (STOP=0);
EVNTLO=EVNTLI;
EVNTOB=EVNTLI*.7;
EVNTOA=EVNTLI*.3;
EVROLI=EVTMLI*EVNTLI;
EVROLO=EVTMLO*EVNTLO;
EVROOB=EVTMOB*EVNTOB;
IF (EVROLI>1)|(EVROLO>1) THEN STOP=1;
EVTWLI=EVNTLI*SMTMLI/(2*(1-EVROLI));
EVTWOA=EVNTLI*SMTMLO/(2*(1-EVROOA));
EVTWOB=EVNTLI*SMTMLO/(2*(1-EVROOA)*(1-EVROLO));
SMTWLI=EVNTLI*TMTMLI/(3*(1-EVROLI))+(EVNTLI*SMTMLI)**2/(2*(1-
  EVROLI)**2);
SMTWOA=EVNTLO*TMTMLO/(3*(1-EVROOA))+
  EVNTLO*SMTMLO*EVNTOA*SMTMOA/(2*(1-EVROOA)**2);
SMTWOB=EVNTLO*TMTMLO/(3*(1-EVROOA)**2*(1-EVROLO))+
(EVNTLO*SMTMLO)**2/(2*(1-EVROLO)**2*(1-EVROOA)**2)+
  EVNTLO*SMTMLO*EVNTOA*SMTMOA/(2*(1-EVROLO)*(1-EVROOA)**3);
  VATWLI=SMTWLI-EVTWLI*EVTWLI;
VATWOA=SMTWOA-EVTWOA*EVTWOA;
VATWOB=SMTWOB-EVTWOB*EVTWOB;
THRPUT(I)=EVNTLI*3600;
TIMEA(I)=EVTWLI+EVTMIA+EVTTCS+EVTWOA;
TIMEB(I)=EVTWLI+EVTMIB+EVTTCS+EVTWOB;
SIGTIMEA(I)=SQRT(VATWLI+VATMIA+VATTCS+VATWOA);
SIGTIMEB(I)=SQRT(VATWLI+VATMIB+VATTCS+VATWOB);
MAXTHRPUT=THRPUT(I);
I=I+1;
END;
CALL GRAPH;
```

The output is shown in Fig. 36.12.

On the full–duplex line, unlike the half–duplex line, the type A transactions benefit greatly by being given priority over the type B transactions.

MODEL 8. This model is the same as the last except that the priorities of output messages type A and B are interchanged. Again we interchange them in the program.

Figure 36.13 shows the output.

The type B transactions benefit greatly by being given priority (unlike model 5). The overall throughput is not increased, however, by giving priority to the shorter messages because the queues for type A transactions become unacceptably large above about 510 transactions per second. The standard deviation for type A transactions also rises fast. This consideration gives a somewhat lower maximum reasonable throughput than in model 5.

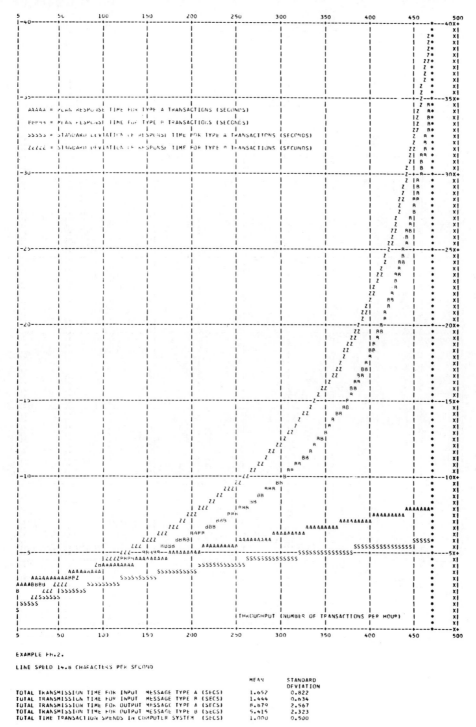

EXAMPLE FH.2.

LINE SPEED 14.8 CHARACTERS PER SECOND

| | MEAN | STANDARD DEVIATION |
|---|---|---|
| TOTAL TRANSMISSION TIME FOR INPUT MESSAGE TYPE A (SECS) | 1.652 | 0.822 |
| TOTAL TRANSMISSION TIME FOR INPUT MESSAGE TYPE B (SECS) | 1.444 | 0.634 |
| TOTAL TRANSMISSION TIME FOR OUTPUT MESSAGE TYPE A (SECS) | 8.679 | 2.567 |
| TOTAL TRANSMISSION TIME FOR OUTPUT MESSAGE TYPE B (SECS) | 5.415 | 2.323 |
| TOTAL TIME TRANSACTION SPENDS IN COMPUTER SYSTEM (SECS) | 1.000 | 0.500 |

MODEL 7.    A FULL DUPLEX LINE WITH DATA BEING TRANSMITTED IN BOTH DIRECTIONS AT ONCE.

*Fig. 36.12.* Model 7. A full-duplex line with type A output messages being given priority over type B output. The priority scheme slightly lowers the maximum throughput but gives type A transactions a short response time.

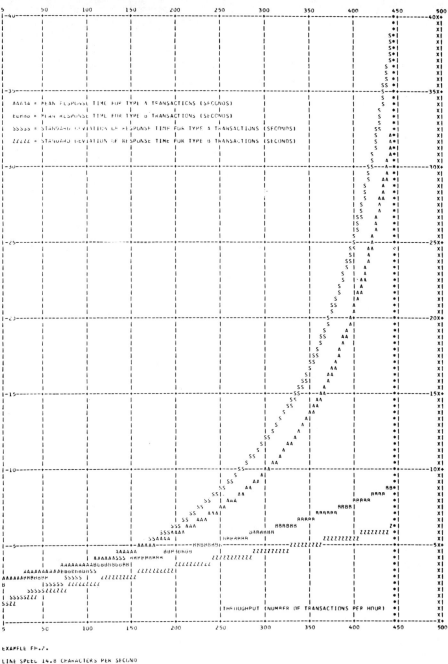

*Fig. 36.13.* Model 8. A full-duplex line with type B output messages being given priority over type A.

586

**DIFFERENT**
**MESSAGE LENGTHS**

Let us now change our line speed and mix of message lengths and see how the curves change their shape.

**Example 36.3. The Eight Models with a Higher Transmission Speed.** A transmission speed of 300 characters per second is used for messages of the following transmission times (including line preparation time):

|                                    | Mean | Standard Deviation |
|------------------------------------|------|--------------------|
| Input message type A               | 167  | 118                |
| Output response to message type A  | 67   | 47                 |
| Input message type B               | 433  | 306                |
| Output response to message type B  | 133  | 94                 |

Type A messages are again 30 percent of the total and type B are 70 percent.

The time the computer takes to process the message and prepare a response has a mean of 1 second and standard deviation of ½ second (as before).

Investigate the preceding eight line organization methods in this case.

Figures 36.14 to 36.21 show the curves plotted for this example.

MODEL 1 (Fig. 36.14). The transmission time is now a fraction of the time the transaction spends in the computer. Holding the line between input and output is therefore quite unacceptable and should not be considered.

MODELS 2 AND 3 (Figs. 36.15 and 36.16). The output messages in this example are considerably shorter than the input messages; therefore model 2 is better than model 3. The standard deviations of response time are fairly low compared with the means. Thus, there is not a very large difference in waiting time between a message that encounters a high queue and one that does not. This low standard deviation is a desirable characteristic if it can be achieved.

MODELS 4 AND 5 (Figs. 36.17 and 36.18). Type A messages are shorter than type B. However, the input messages dominate the queuing and we only allocate priority between output messages. Hence the use of a priority scheme gives so little improvement that it is hardly worth considering—unlike the other examples in this chapter. Models 4 and 5 are both better than model 3 because they give priority to output.

MODEL 6 (Fig. 36.19). This line organization gives a maximum throughput about 13 percent higher than the best of the half-duplex line organizations. Again, with this speed of line, the full-duplex line cost is about 10 percent higher than the half-duplex line cost. The full-duplex line, therefore, again seems somewhat better value for money.

Once more the standard deviation of response time is relatively low compared with the mean.

MODELS 7 AND 8 (Figs. 36.20 and 36.21). Giving priority to type A transactions produces a minor improvement in mean response time. Its effect is much less marked than in the last example or the next example (Figs. 36.27 and 36.28), in which the input messages are short compared to output. In Fig. 36.12 the standard deviation for type A transactions was high, but in Fig. 36.21 it is low.

**HIGH-SPEED LINES AND LENGTHY RESPONSES**
Where a man-machine conversation takes place on terminals with screens, the interaction is often designed in such a way that the programmer types in a relatively small number of characters, on the average, and the machine gives a lengthy response. The curves for this example are somewhat different from the preceding ones. Let us examine such a case.

**Example 36.4. The Eight Models with a Different Message Mix.** A conditioned voice line is used to transmit at 600 characters per second. The messages have the following transmission times, in milliseconds (including line preparation time):

|  | Mean | Standard Deviation |
|---|---|---|
| Input message type A (characters) | 50 | 35 |
| Output response to message type A (characters) | 750 | 530 |
| Input message type B (characters) | 50 | 35 |
| Output response to message type B (characters) | 167 | 118 |

Type A messages again represent 30 percent of the total and type B represent 70 percent.

The time spent in the computer is the same as above: mean: 1 second; standard deviation: ½ second.

Figures 36.22 to 36.28 show the curves plotted for this example.

MODEL 1. Not worth considering, for it is much worse than the other cases.

MODELS 2, 4, AND 5. The output messages in this example are much longer than the input messages. Input messages should therefore always be given priority, and any of these three models gives a worse performance than model 3.

MODEL 3. This model is the best of the half-duplex line models. Because types A and B input messages are the same length and the status in the queues is independent of type, the AAAAA curve completely masks the BBBBB curve, and the SSSSS curve completely masks the ZZZZZ curve.

MODEL 6. The full-duplex line again gives an increase in throughput sufficiently high to justify a 10 percent extra cost.

MODEL 7. Giving priority to the lengthy type A transactions is certainly wrong. The maximum throughput has dropped considerably, and the standard deviation of response time for type B transactions rises severely.

MODEL 8. Giving priority to type B transactions results in a good response time and a low standard deviation. However, it sends the response time for type A transactions and its standard deviation up somewhat higher than in model 6. Hence the maximum practical throughput is, if anything, somewhat lower than with model 6.

If type B transactions are very important and type A are not, model 8 might be a good organization to use—that is, in some "conversations." A quick response to certain short conversation elements is desirable even if other, longer responses are not sent as quickly.

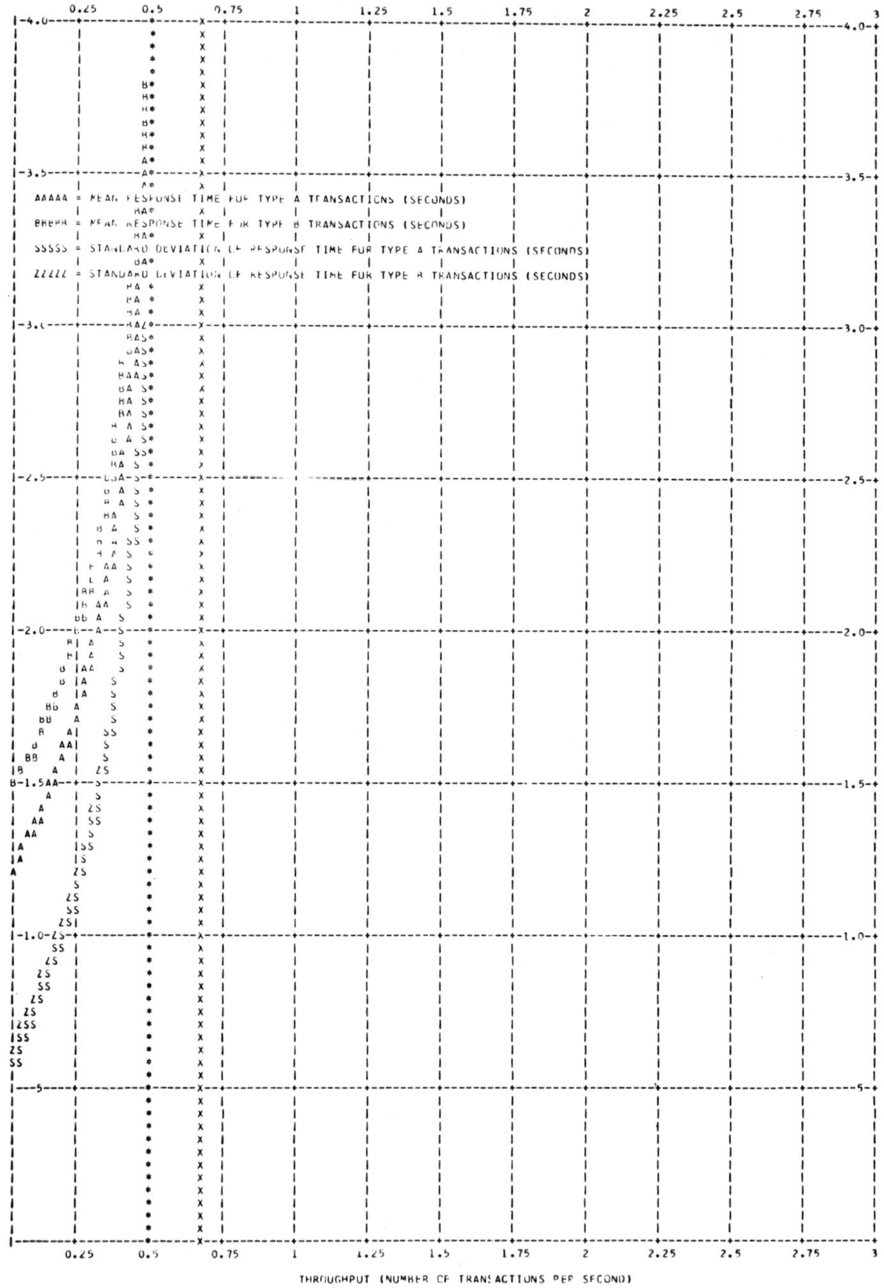

```
      0.25     0.5     0.75     1      1.25    1.5     1.75     2      2.25    2.5     2.75     3
|-4.0---+-------+-------+-------+-------+-------+-------+-------+-------+-------+-------+-------+  -4.0-+
|       |       *   X   |       |       |       |       |       |       |       |       |       |
|       |       *   X   |       |       |       |       |       |       |       |       |       |
|       |       *   X   |       |       |       |       |       |       |       |       |       |
|       |       *   X   |       |       |       |       |       |       |       |       |       |
|       |      B*   X   |       |       |       |       |       |       |       |       |       |
|       |      H*   X   |       |       |       |       |       |       |       |       |       |
|       |      H*   X   |       |       |       |       |       |       |       |       |       |
|       |      B*   X   |       |       |       |       |       |       |       |       |       |
|       |      H*   X   |       |       |       |       |       |       |       |       |       |
|       |      A*   X   |       |       |       |       |       |       |       |       |       |
|-3.5---+------A*---X---+-------+-------+-------+-------+-------+-------+-------+-------+-------+  -3.5-+
|       |      A*   X   |       |       |       |       |       |       |       |       |       |
| AAAAA = MEAN RESPONSE TIME FOR TYPE A TRANSACTIONS (SECONDS)     |       |       |       |
|       |      BA*   X   |       |       |       |       |       |       |       |       |
| BBBBB = MEAN RESPONSE TIME FOR TYPE B TRANSACTIONS (SECONDS)     |       |       |       |
|       |      BA*   X   |       |       |       |       |       |       |       |       |
| SSSSS = STANDARD DEVIATION OF RESPONSE TIME FOR TYPE A TRANSACTIONS (SECONDS)      |
|       |      BA*   X   |       |       |       |       |       |       |       |       |
| ZZZZZ = STANDARD DEVIATION OF RESPONSE TIME FOR TYPE B TRANSACTIONS (SECONDS)      |
|       |      BA *   X   |       |       |       |       |       |       |       |       |
|       |      BA *   X   |       |       |       |       |       |       |       |       |
|       |      HA *   X   |       |       |       |       |       |       |       |       |
|-3.0---+------BAZ*---X---+-------+-------+-------+-------+-------+-------+-------+-------+  -3.0-+
|       |      BAS*   X   |       |       |       |       |       |       |       |       |
|       |      BAS*   X   |       |       |       |       |       |       |       |       |
|       |    B AS*   X   |       |       |       |       |       |       |       |       |
|       |    BAAS*   X   |       |       |       |       |       |       |       |       |
|       |    BA S*   X   |       |       |       |       |       |       |       |       |
|       |    BA S*   X   |       |       |       |       |       |       |       |       |
|       |    BA S*   X   |       |       |       |       |       |       |       |       |
|       |   B A S*   X   |       |       |       |       |       |       |       |       |
|       |   B A S*   X   |       |       |       |       |       |       |       |       |
|       |   BA SS*   X   |       |       |       |       |       |       |       |       |
|       |   BA S *   X   |       |       |       |       |       |       |       |       |
|-2.5---+--BBA-S--*-------X-----+-------+-------+-------+-------+-------+-------+-------+  -2.5-+
|       |   B A S  *   X   |       |       |       |       |       |       |       |       |
|       |   B A S  *   X   |       |       |       |       |       |       |       |       |
|       |   BA  S  *   X   |       |       |       |       |       |       |       |       |
|       |   B A  S  *   X   |       |       |       |       |       |       |       |       |
|       |   B B SS  *   X   |       |       |       |       |       |       |       |       |
|       |   B A S   *   X   |       |       |       |       |       |       |       |       |
|       | B AA  S   *   X   |       |       |       |       |       |       |       |       |
|       | B A   S   *   X   |       |       |       |       |       |       |       |       |
|       |BB A   S   *   X   |       |       |       |       |       |       |       |       |
|       |B AA S     *   X   |       |       |       |       |       |       |       |       |
|-2.0---+B-A--S-----*-------X-----+-------+-------+-------+-------+-------+-------+  -2.0-+
|      B| A   S     *   X   |       |       |       |       |       |       |       |
|      B| A   S     *   X   |       |       |       |       |       |       |       |
|    B  |AA   S     *   X   |       |       |       |       |       |       |       |
|    B  |A    S     *   X   |       |       |       |       |       |       |       |
|    B  |A    S     *   X   |       |       |       |       |       |       |       |
|   BB  |A    S     *   X   |       |       |       |       |       |       |       |
|  BB   |A    S     *   X   |       |       |       |       |       |       |       |
|   B  A| SS        *   X   |       |       |       |       |       |       |       |
|  B AA | S         *   X   |       |       |       |       |       |       |       |
|BB   A | S         *   X   |       |       |       |       |       |       |       |
|B    A | ZS        *   X   |       |       |       |       |       |       |       |
|B-1.5AA-+-S---------*-------X-----+-------+-------+-------+-------+-------+  -1.5-+
|  A    | S         *   X   |       |       |       |       |       |       |
|  A    | ZS        *   X   |       |       |       |       |       |       |
|  AA   | SS        *   X   |       |       |       |       |       |       |
| AA    | S         *   X   |       |       |       |       |       |       |
|A      |SS         *   X   |       |       |       |       |       |       |
|A      |S          *   X   |       |       |       |       |       |       |
|A      | ZS        *   X   |       |       |       |       |       |       |
|       |  S        *   X   |       |       |       |       |       |       |
|       |  ZS       *   X   |       |       |       |       |       |       |
|       |  SS       *   X   |       |       |       |       |       |       |
|       |  ZS|      *   X   |       |       |       |       |       |       |
|-1.0-ZS-+----------*-------X-----+-------+-------+-------+-------+  -1.0-+
|       SS|         *   X   |       |       |       |       |       |
|       ZS|         *   X   |       |       |       |       |       |
|       ZS|         *   X   |       |       |       |       |       |
|       SS|         *   X   |       |       |       |       |       |
|       ZS|         *   X   |       |       |       |       |       |
|       ZSS|        *   X   |       |       |       |       |       |
|       ISS|        *   X   |       |       |       |       |       |
|       ZS|         *   X   |       |       |       |       |       |
|       SS|         *   X   |       |       |       |       |       |
|       |           *   X   |       |       |       |       |       |
|-------+-5---------*-------X-----+-------+-------+-------+-------+  -5-+
|       |           *   X   |       |       |       |       |       |
|       |           *   X   |       |       |       |       |       |
|       |           *   X   |       |       |       |       |       |
|       |           *   X   |       |       |       |       |       |
|       |           *   X   |       |       |       |       |       |
|       |           *   X   |       |       |       |       |       |
|       |           *   X   |       |       |       |       |       |
|       |           *   X   |       |       |       |       |       |
|       |           *   X   |       |       |       |       |       |
|       |           *   X   |       |       |       |       |       |
|       |           *   X   |       |       |       |       |       |
|-------+-+---------*-------X-----+-------+-------+-------+-------+
      0.25     0.5     0.75     1      1.25    1.5     1.75     2      2.25    2.5     2.75     3
            THROUGHPUT (NUMBER OF TRANSACTIONS PER SECOND)
```

EXAMPLE FH.3.

LINE SPEED 300 CHARACTERS PER SECOND

|  | MEAN | STANDARD DEVIATION |
|---|---|---|
| TOTAL TRANSMISSION TIME FOR INPUT MESSAGE TYPE A (SECS) | 0.167 | 0.118 |
| TOTAL TRANSMISSION TIME FOR INPUT MESSAGE TYPE B (SECS) | 0.433 | 0.306 |
| TOTAL TRANSMISSION TIME FOR OUTPUT MESSAGE TYPE A (SECS) | 0.067 | 0.047 |
| TOTAL TRANSMISSION TIME FOR OUTPUT MESSAGE TYPE B (SECS) | 0.133 | 0.094 |
| TOTAL TIME TRANSACTION SPENDS IN COMPUTER SYSTEM (SECS) | 1.000 | 0.500 |

MODEL 1.    A HALF DUPLEX LINE HELD BY THE COMPUTER BETWEEN RECEIPT OF INPUT MESSAGE AND TRANSMISSION OF THE RESPONSE.

*Fig. 36.14.* This and the following seven figures show the eight models of a line of higher transmission speed (300 characters per second, compared to 14.8 in the previous examples). At this transmission speed, model 1 above, can be rejected. The line should not be *held* between input and output if the transmission speed is high.

```
            0.25    0.5     0.75     1      1.25    1.5     1.75     2      2.25    2.5     2.75     3
  |-4.0--+-------+-------+-------+-------+-------+-------+-------+-------+-------+-------+-------+--4.0-+
  |      |       |       |       |       |       |       |  *    |   X   |       |       |       |    |
  |      |       |       |       |       |       |       |  B*   |   X   |       |       |       |    |
  |      |       |       |       |       |       |       |  B*   |   X   |       |       |       |    |
  |      |       |       |       |       |       |       |  B*   |   X   |       |       |       |    |
  |      |       |       |       |       |       |       |  B*   |   X   |       |       |       |    |
  |      |       |       |       |       |       |       | BB*   |   X   |       |       |       |    |
  |      |       |       |       |       |       |       | BA*   |   X   |       |       |       |    |
  |      |       |       |       |       |       |       | BA*   |   X   |       |       |       |    |
  |      |       |       |       |       |       |       | BA*   |   X   |       |       |       |    |
  |      |       |       |       |       |       |       | BA*   |   X   |       |       |       |    |
  |-3.5--+-------+-------+-------+-------+-------+-------+--B-A*-+---X---+-------+-------+-------+--3.5-+
  |      |       |       |       |       |       |       | B  A* |   X   |       |       |       |    |
  |  AAAAA = MEAN RESPONSE TIME FOR TYPE A TRANSACTIONS (SECONDS)  BA * |   X'  |       |       |    |
  |      |       |       |       |       |       |       | BA  * |   X   |       |       |       |    |
  |  BBBBB = MEAN RESPONSE TIME FOR TYPE B TRANSACTIONS (SECONDS)  BR A* |   X   |       |       |    |
  |      |       |       |       |       |       |       |BR A  *|   X   |       |       |       |    |
  |  SSSSS = STANDARD DEVIATION OF RESPONSE TIME FOR TYPE A TRANSACTIONS (SECONDS)  X   |       |    |
  |  ZZZZZ = STANDARD DEVIATION OF RESPONSE TIME FOR TYPE B TRANSACTIONS (SECONDS)  X   |       |    |
  |      |       |       |       |       |       |       | B  A  *|   X  |       |       |       |    |
  |      |       |       |       |       |       |       | B|A   *|   X  |       |       |       |    |
  |-3.0--+-------+-------+-------+-------+-------+-------+--B-A---*------+---X---+-------+-------+--3.0-+
  |      |       |       |       |       |       |       | B |A   * |   X   |       |       |       |    |
```

EXAMPLE FH.3.

LINE SPEED 300 CHARACTERS PER SECOND

|  | MEAN | STANDARD DEVIATION |
|---|---|---|
| TOTAL TRANSMISSION TIME FOR INPUT MESSAGE TYPE A (SECS) | 0.167 | 0.118 |
| TOTAL TRANSMISSION TIME FOR INPUT MESSAGE TYPE B (SECS) | 0.433 | 0.306 |
| TOTAL TRANSMISSION TIME FOR OUTPUT MESSAGE TYPE A (SECS) | 0.067 | 0.047 |
| TOTAL TRANSMISSION TIME FOR OUTPUT MESSAGE TYPE B (SECS) | 0.133 | 0.094 |
| TOTAL TIME TRANSACTION SPENDS IN COMPUTER SYSTEM (SECS) | 1.000 | 0.500 |

MODEL 2.    A HALF DUPLEX LINE, NOT HELD AFTER INPUT TRANSMISSION.
OUTPUT MESSAGES HAVE PRIORITY OVER INPUT.

*Fig. 36.15.* Model 2. Half-duplex line. Output has priority over input.

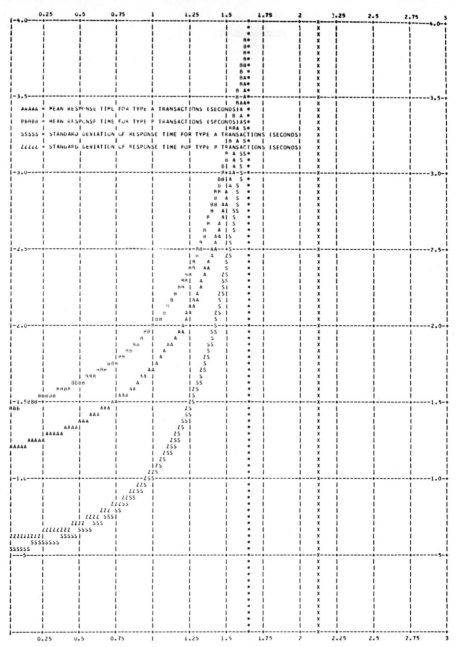

EXAMPLE FH.3.

LINE SPEED 300 CHARACTERS PER SECOND

|  | MEAN | STANDARD DEVIATION |
|---|---|---|
| TOTAL TRANSMISSION TIME FOR INPUT MESSAGE TYPE A (SECS) | 0.167 | 0.118 |
| TOTAL TRANSMISSION TIME FOR INPUT MESSAGE TYPE B (SECS) | 0.433 | 0.106 |
| TOTAL TRANSMISSION TIME FOR OUTPUT MESSAGE TYPE A (SECS) | 0.067 | 0.047 |
| TOTAL TRANSMISSION TIME FOR OUTPUT MESSAGE TYPE B (SECS) | 0.133 | 0.094 |
| TOTAL TIME TRANSACTION SPENDS IN COMPUTER SYSTEM (SECS) | 1.000 | 0.500 |

MODEL 3.    A HALF DUPLEX LINE, NOT HELD AFTER INPUT TRANSMISION.

*Fig. 36.16.* Model 3. Half-duplex line. Input has priority over output.

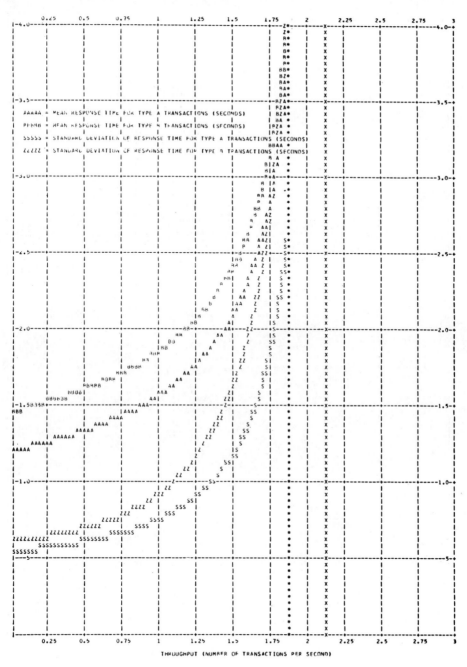

EXAMPLE FH.3.

LINE SPEED 300 CHARACTERS PER SECOND

|  | MEAN | STANDARD DEVIATION |
|---|---|---|
| TOTAL TRANSMISSION TIME FOR INPUT MESSAGE TYPE A (SECS) | 0.167 | 0.118 |
| TOTAL TRANSMISSION TIME FOR INPUT MESSAGE TYPE B (SECS) | 0.433 | 0.306 |
| TOTAL TRANSMISSION TIME FOR OUTPUT MESSAGE TYPE A (SECS) | 0.067 | 0.047 |
| TOTAL TRANSMISSION TIME FOR OUTPUT MESSAGE TYPE B (SECS) | 0.133 | 0.094 |
| TOTAL TIME TRANSACTION SPENDS IN COMPUTER SYSTEM (SECS) | 1.000 | 0.500 |

MODEL 4.   A HALF DUPLEX LINE, NOT HELD AFTER INPUT TRANSMISSION.
OUTPUT MESSAGES HAVE PRIORITY OVER INPUT.

*Fig. 36.17.* Model 4. Half-duplex line. Output has priority over input. Type A output messages have priority over type B.

593

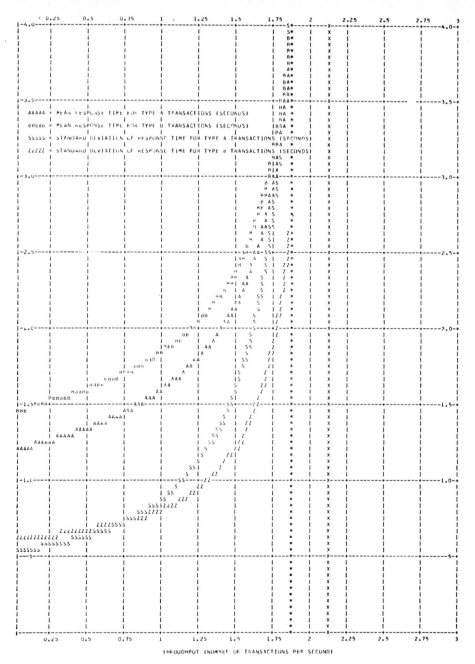

Fig. 36.18. Model 5. Half-duplex line. Output has priority over input. Type B messages have priority over type A. The models show that it is not worth having a scheme of priority by transaction in this case.

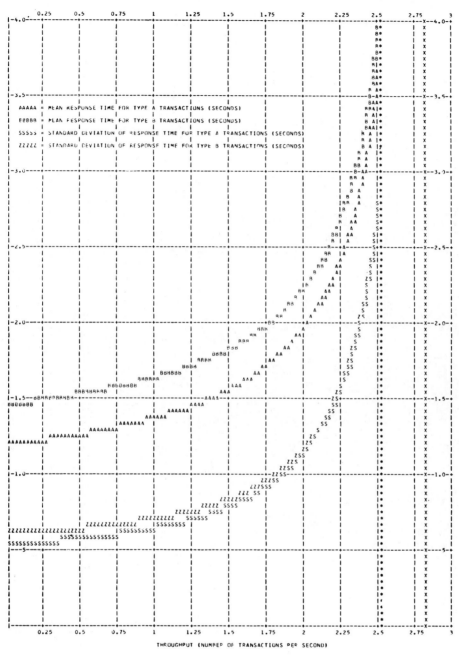

THROUGHPUT (NUMBER OF TRANSACTIONS PER SECOND)

EXAMPLE FH.3.

LINE SPEED 300 CHARACTERS PER SECOND

| | MEAN | STANDARD DEVIATION |
|---|---|---|
| TOTAL TRANSMISSION TIME FOR INPUT MESSAGE TYPE A (SECS) | 0.167 | 0.118 |
| TOTAL TRANSMISSION TIME FOR INPUT MESSAGE TYPE B (SECS) | 0.433 | 0.306 |
| TOTAL TRANSMISSION TIME FOR OUTPUT MESSAGE TYPE A (SECS) | 0.067 | 0.047 |
| TOTAL TRANSMISSION TIME FOR OUTPUT MESSAGE TYPE B (SECS) | 0.133 | 0.094 |
| TOTAL TIME TRANSACTION SPENDS IN COMPUTER SYSTEM (SECS) | 1.000 | 0.500 |

MODEL 6.    A FULL DUPLEX LINE WITH DATA BEING TRANSMITTED IN BOTH DIRECTIONS AT ONCE.

*Fig. 36.19.* Model 6. A full-duplex line. Again an improvement but not twice the throughput.

595

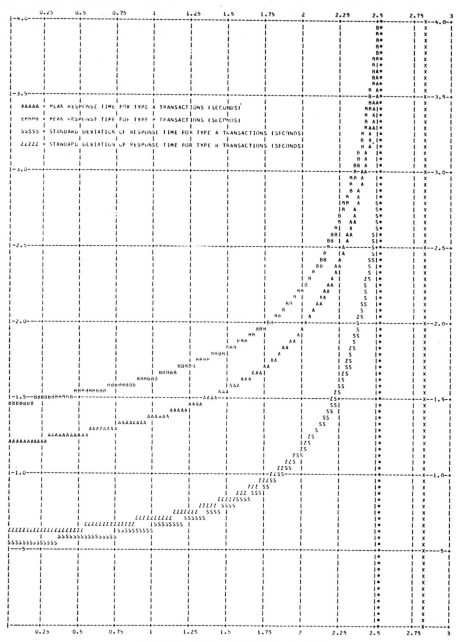

EXAMPLE FH.3.

LINE SPEED 300 CHARACTERS PER SECOND

| | MEAN | STANDARD DEVIATION |
|---|---|---|
| TOTAL TRANSMISSION TIME FOR INPUT MESSAGE TYPE A (SECS) | 0.167 | 0.118 |
| TOTAL TRANSMISSION TIME FOR INPUT MESSAGE TYPE B (SECS) | 0.433 | 0.306 |
| TOTAL TRANSMISSION TIME FOR OUTPUT MESSAGE TYPE A (SECS) | 0.067 | 0.047 |
| TOTAL TRANSMISSION TIME FOR OUTPUT MESSAGE TYPE B (SECS) | 0.133 | 0.094 |
| TOTAL TIME TRANSACTION SPENDS IN COMPUTER SYSTEM (SECS) | 1.000 | 0.500 |

MODEL 7.    A FULL DUPLEX LINE WITH DATA BEING TRANSMITTED IN BOTH DIRECTIONS AT ONCE.
TYPE A OUTPUT MESSAGES HAVE PRIORITY OVER TYPE B OUTPUT.

*Fig. 36.20.* Model 7. Full-duplex line. Type A output has priority over type B.

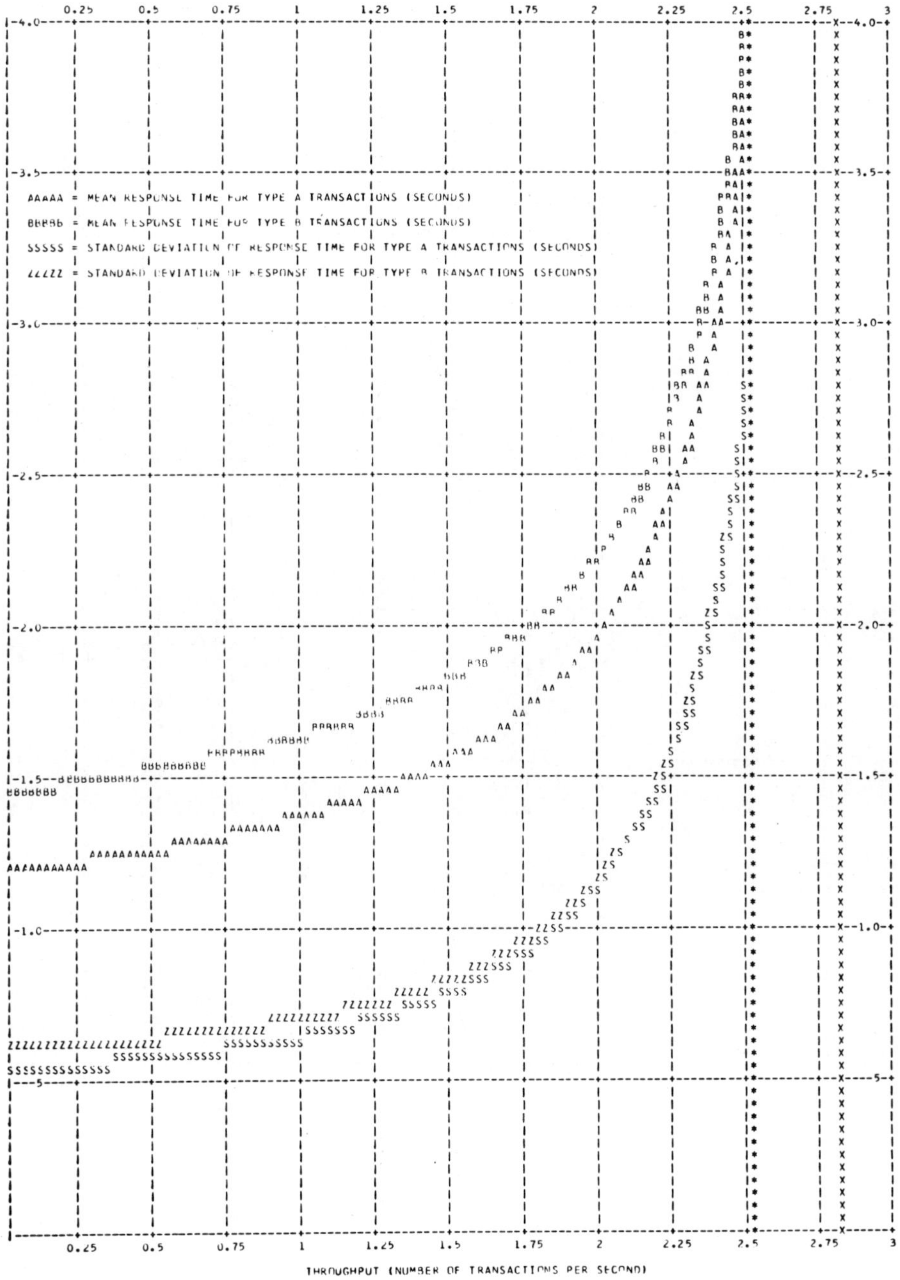

THROUGHPUT (NUMBER OF TRANSACTIONS PER SECOND)

AAAAA = MEAN RESPONSE TIME FOR TYPE A TRANSACTIONS (SECONDS)

BBBBB = MEAN RESPONSE TIME FOR TYPE B TRANSACTIONS (SECONDS)

SSSSS = STANDARD DEVIATION OF RESPONSE TIME FOR TYPE A TRANSACTIONS (SECONDS)

ZZZZZ = STANDARD DEVIATION OF RESPONSE TIME FOR TYPE B TRANSACTIONS (SECONDS)

EXAMPLE FH.3.

LINE SPEED 300 CHARACTERS PER SECOND

|  | MEAN | STANDARD DEVIATION |
|---|---|---|
| TOTAL TRANSMISSION TIME FOR INPUT MESSAGE TYPE A (SECS) | 0.167 | 0.118 |
| TOTAL TRANSMISSION TIME FOR INPUT MESSAGE TYPE B (SECS) | 0.433 | 0.306 |
| TOTAL TRANSMISSION TIME FOR OUTPUT MESSAGE TYPE A (SECS) | 0.067 | 0.047 |
| TOTAL TRANSMISSION TIME FOR OUTPUT MESSAGE TYPE B (SECS) | 0.133 | 0.094 |
| TOTAL TIME TRANSACTION SPENDS IN COMPUTER SYSTEM (SECS) | 1.000 | 0.500 |

MODEL 8.   A FULL DUPLEX LINE WITH DATA BEING TRANSMITTED IN BOTH DIRECTIONS AT ONCE.
TYPE B OUTPUT MESSAGES HAVE PRIORITY OVER TYPE A OUTPUT.

*Fig. 36.21.* Model 8. Full-duplex line. Type B output has priority over type A.

597

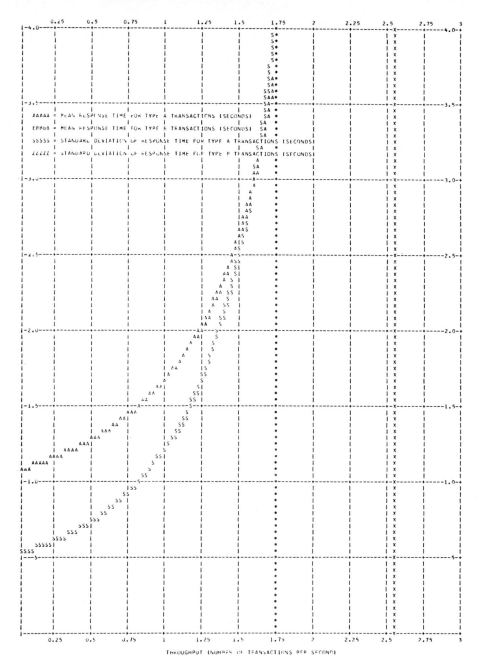

EXAMPLE FH.4.

LINE SPEED 600 CHARACTERS PER SECOND

|  | MEAN | STANDARD DEVIATION |
|---|---|---|
| TOTAL TRANSMISSION TIME FOR INPUT MESSAGE TYPE A (SECS) | 0.050 | 0.035 |
| TOTAL TRANSMISSION TIME FOR INPUT MESSAGE TYPE B (SECS) | 0.050 | 0.035 |
| TOTAL TRANSMISSION TIME FOR OUTPUT MESSAGE TYPE A (SECS) | 0.750 | 0.530 |
| TOTAL TRANSMISSION TIME FOR OUTPUT MESSAGE TYPE B (SECS) | 0.167 | 0.118 |
| TOTAL TIME TRANSACTION SPENDS IN COMPUTER SYSTEM (SECS) | 1.000 | 0.500 |

MODEL 2.    A HALF DUPLEX LINE, NOT HELD AFTER INPUT TRANSMISSION.
OUTPUT MESSAGES HAVE PRIORITY OVER INPUT.

*Fig. 36.22.* This and the following six figures relate to a line transmitting at 600 characters per second with input messages that are short compared to output. Model 2 gives priority to output.

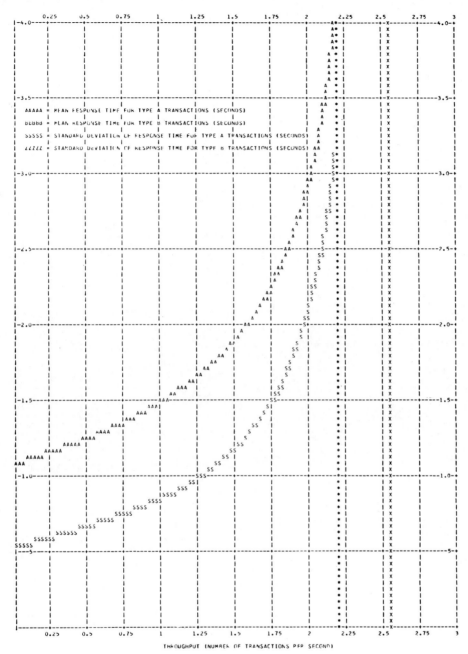

*Fig. 36.23.* Model 3 gives priority to input and because input messages are shorter, the result is better.

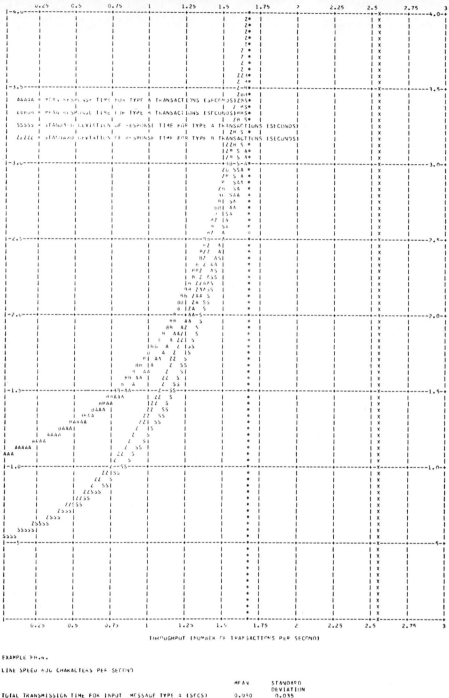

THROUGHPUT (NUMBER OF TRANSACTIONS PER SECOND)

EXAMPLE FH.4.

LINE SPEED 600 CHARACTERS PER SECOND

|  | MEAN | STANDARD DEVIATION |
|---|---|---|
| TOTAL TRANSMISSION TIME FOR INPUT MESSAGE TYPE A (SECS) | 0.050 | 0.035 |
| TOTAL TRANSMISSION TIME FOR INPUT MESSAGE TYPE B (SECS) | 0.050 | 0.035 |
| TOTAL TRANSMISSION TIME FOR OUTPUT MESSAGE TYPE A (SECS) | 0.750 | 0.530 |
| TOTAL TRANSMISSION TIME FOR OUTPUT MESSAGE TYPE B (SECS) | 0.167 | 0.118 |
| TOTAL TIME TRANSACTION SPENDS IN COMPUTER SYSTEM (SECS) | 1.000 | 0.500 |

MODEL 4.   A HALF-DUPLEX LINE, NOT HELD AFTER INPUT TRANSMISSION.
OUTPUT MESSAGES HAVE PRIORITY OVER INPUT.
TYPE A OUTPUT MESSAGES HAVE PRIORITY OVER TYPE B OUTPUT.

*Fig. 36.24.* Model 4. Half-duplex line. Output has priority over input, and type A output has priority over type B.

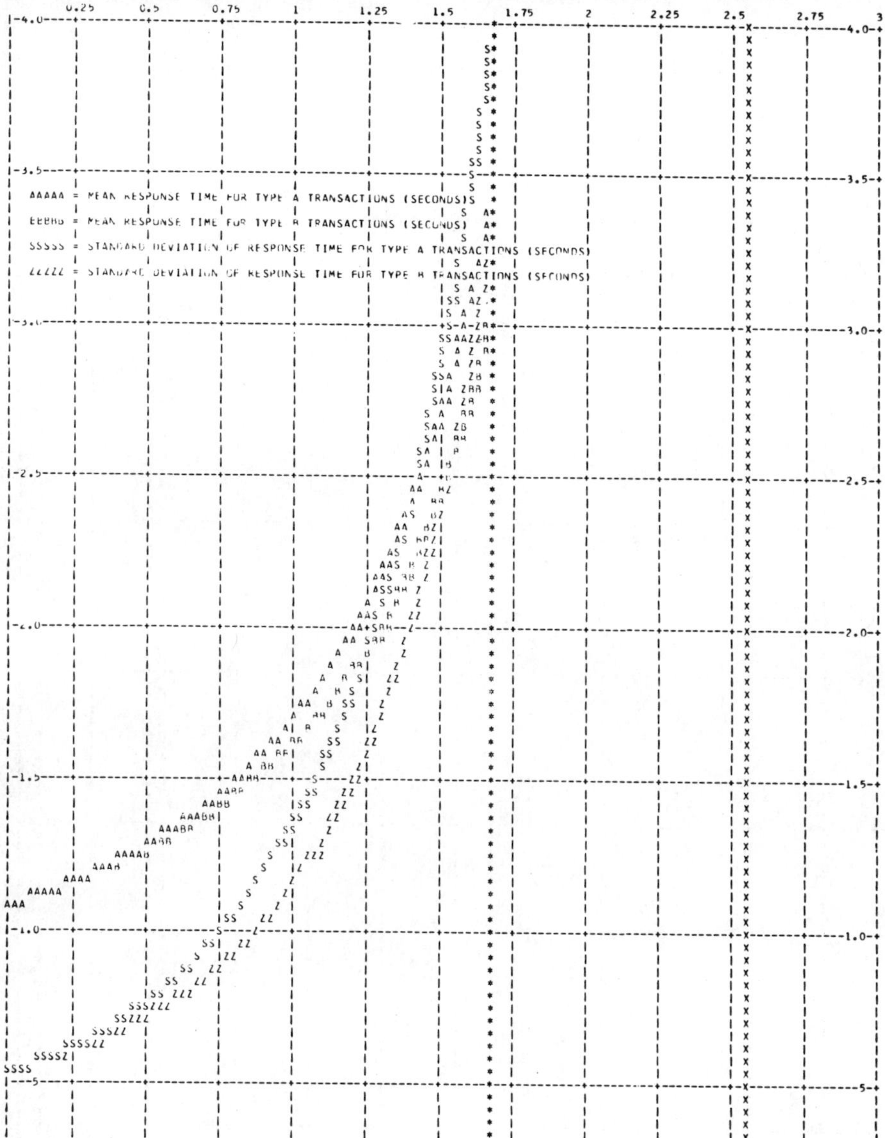

```
        0.25      0.5       0.75       1        1.25      1.5       1.75      2        2.25      2.5       2.75      3
  -4.0---+---------+---------+---------+---------+---------+---------+---------+---------+---------+--X-------+------4.0-+
```

AAAAA = MEAN RESPONSE TIME FOR TYPE A TRANSACTIONS (SECONDS)

EEEEE = MEAN RESPONSE TIME FOR TYPE B TRANSACTIONS (SECONDS)

SSSSS = STANDARD DEVIATION OF RESPONSE TIME FOR TYPE A TRANSACTIONS (SECONDS)

ZZZZZ = STANDARD DEVIATION OF RESPONSE TIME FOR TYPE B TRANSACTIONS (SECONDS)

THROUGHPUT (NUMBER OF TRANSACTIONS PER SECOND)

EXAMPLE FH.4.

LINE SPEED 600 CHARACTERS PER SECOND

|  | MEAN | STANDARD DEVIATION |
|---|---|---|
| TOTAL TRANSMISSION TIME FOR INPUT MESSAGE TYPE A (SECS) | 0.050 | 0.035 |
| TOTAL TRANSMISSION TIME FOR INPUT MESSAGE TYPE B (SECS) | 0.050 | 0.035 |
| TOTAL TRANSMISSION TIME FOR OUTPUT MESSAGE TYPE A (SECS) | 0.750 | 0.530 |
| TOTAL TRANSMISSION TIME FOR OUTPUT MESSAGE TYPE B (SECS) | 0.167 | 0.118 |
| TOTAL TIME TRANSACTION SPENDS IN COMPUTER SYSTEM (SECS) | 1.000 | 0.500 |

MODEL 5.   A HALF DUPLEX LINE, NOT HELD AFTER INPUT TRANSMISSION.
OUTPUT MESSAGES HAVE PRIORITY OVER INPUT.
TYPE B OUTPUT MESSAGES HAVE PRIORITY OVER TYPE A OUTPUT.

*Fig. 36.25.* Model 5. Half-duplex line. Output has priority over input, and type B output has priority over type A. Neither model 4 nor 5 is as good as model 3.

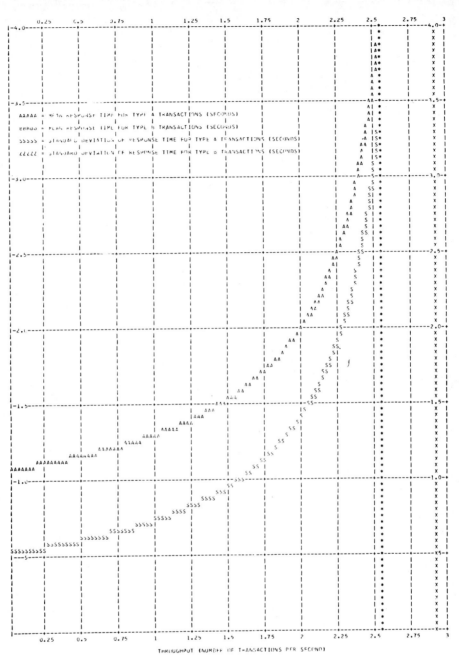

EXAMPLE FH.4.

LINE SPEED 600 CHARACTERS PER SECOND

| | MEAN | STANDARD DEVIATION |
|---|---|---|
| TOTAL TRANSMISSION TIME FOR INPUT MESSAGE TYPE A (SECS) | 0.050 | 0.035 |
| TOTAL TRANSMISSION TIME FOR INPUT MESSAGE TYPE B (SECS) | 0.050 | 0.035 |
| TOTAL TRANSMISSION TIME FOR OUTPUT MESSAGE TYPE A (SECS) | 0.750 | 0.530 |
| TOTAL TRANSMISSION TIME FOR OUTPUT MESSAGE TYPE B (SECS) | 0.167 | 0.118 |
| TOTAL TIME TRANSACTION SPENDS IN COMPUTER SYSTEM (SECS) | 1.000 | 0.500 |

MODEL 6.   A FULL DUPLEX LINE WITH DATA BEING TRANSMITTED IN BOTH DIRECTIONS AT ONCE.

*Fig. 36.26.* Model 6. A full-duplex line. No priority scheme.

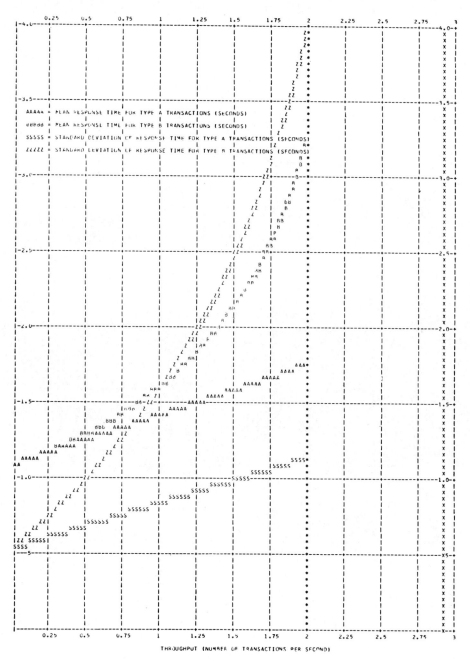

*Fig. 36.27.* Model 7. A full-duplex line. Type A output has priority over type B.

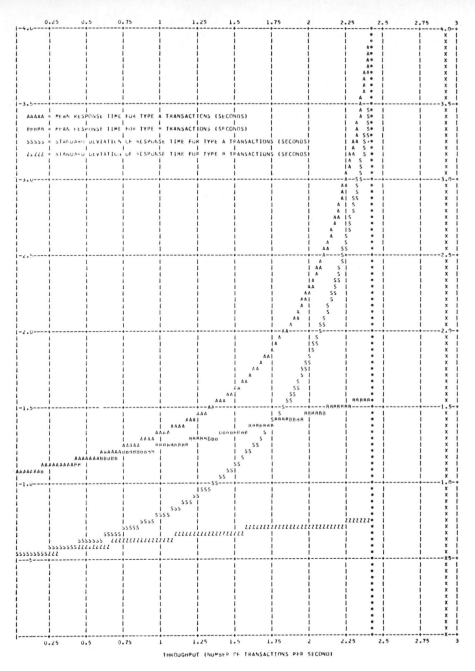

THROUGHPUT (NUMBER OF TRANSACTIONS PER SECOND)

EXAMPLE FH.4.

LINE SPEED 600 CHARACTERS PER SECOND

| | MEAN | STANDARD DEVIATION |
|---|---|---|
| TOTAL TRANSMISSION TIME FOR INPUT MESSAGE TYPE A (SECS) | 0.050 | 0.035 |
| TOTAL TRANSMISSION TIME FOR INPUT MESSAGE TYPE B (SECS) | 0.050 | 0.035 |
| TOTAL TRANSMISSION TIME FOR OUTPUT MESSAGE TYPE A (SECS) | 0.750 | 0.530 |
| TOTAL TRANSMISSION TIME FOR OUTPUT MESSAGE TYPE B (SECS) | 0.167 | 0.118 |
| TOTAL TIME TRANSACTION SPENDS IN COMPUTER SYSTEM (SECS) | 1.000 | 0.500 |

MODEL 8.    A FULL DUPLEX LINE WITH DATA BEING TRANSMITTED IN BOTH DIRECTIONS AT ONCE.
TYPE B OUTPUT MESSAGES HAVE PRIORITY OVER TYPE A OUTPUT.

*Fig. 36.28.* Model 8. Full-duplex line. Type B output has priority over type A. This is better than Model 7 because type B output messages are shorter than type A.

604

The FORTRAN listing for the eight line models:

```
      TIMEA,TIMEB,SIGTIMEA,SIGTIMEB=0;I,STOP=0;
      DO EVNTLI=.0011574 TO .139      BY .0011574 WHILE (STOP=0);
      EVNTLO=EVNTLI;
      EVNTOB=EVNTLI*.7;
      EVNTOA=EVNTLI*.3;
      EVROLI=EVTMLI*EVNTLI;
      EVROLO=EVTMLO*EVNTLO;
      EVROOB=EVTMOB*EVNTOB;
      IF (EVROLI>1)|(EVROLO>1) THEN STOP=1;
      EVTWLI=EVNTLI*SMTMLI/(2*(1-EVROLI));
      EVTWOB=EVNTLI*SMTMLO/(2*(1-EVROOB));
      EVTWOA=EVNTLI*SMTMLO/(2*(1-EVROOB)*(1-EVROLO));
      SMTWLI=EVNTLI*TMTMLI/(3*(1-EVROLI))+(EVNTLI*SMTMLI)**2/(2*(1-
       EVROLI)**2);
      SMTWOB=EVNTLO*TMTMLO/(3*(1-EVROOB))+
       EVNTLO*SMTMLO*EVNTOB*SMTMOB/(2*(1-EVROOB)**2);
      SMTWOA=EVNTLO*TMTMLO/(3*(1-EVROOB)**2*(1-EVROLO))+
      (EVNTLO*SMTMLO)**2/(2*(1-EVROLO)**2*(1-EVROOB)**2)+
       EVNTLO*SMTMLO*EVNTOB*SMTMOB/(2*(1-EVROLO)*(1-EVROOB)**3);
       VATWLI=SMTWLI-EVTWLI*EVTWLI;
      VATWOA=SMTWOA-EVTWOA*EVTWOA;
      VATWOB=SMTWOB-EVTWOB*EVTWOB;
      THRPUT(I)=EVNTLI*3600;
      TIMEA(I)=EVTWLI+EVTMIA+EVTTCS+EVTWOA;
      TIMEB(I)=EVTWLI+EVTMIB+EVTTCS+EVTWOB;
      SIGTIMEA(I)=SQRT(VATWLI+VATMIA+VATTCS+VATWOA);
      SIGTIMEB(I)=SQRT(VATWLI+VATMIB+VATTCS+VATWOB);
      MAXTHRPUT=THRPUT(I);
      I=I+1;
      END;
      CALL GRAPH;

      REAL MAXTPT
      COMMON /COMN1/TIMEA(121),TIMEB(121),SDTRTA(121),SDTRTB(121),
     1THRPUT(121),MAXTPT,SPEED,
     2VATMIA,VATMIB,VATMOA,VATMOB,VATTCS,
     3EVTMIA,EVTMIB,EVTMOA,EVTMOB,EVTTCS,
     4L1
      INTEGER STOP
      DATA ZERO/0.0/,RLIMIT/.139/,VALUE/.0011574/,MODEL/0/,IHOUR/3600/
C*******************************************************************************
C*** INITIALIZATION ***********************************************************
      ADD1=EVTMIA+EVTTCS
      ADD2=EVTMIB+EVTTCS
      ADD3=VATMIA+VATTCS
      ADD4=VATMIB+VATTCS
C*******************************************************************************
  195 MODEL=MODEL+1
      I=1
      STOP=0
      DO 200 J=1,121
      TIMEA(J)=ZERO
      TIMEB(J)=ZERO
      SDTRTA(J)=ZERO
  200 SDTRTB(J)=ZERO
      EVNTLI=ZERO
      GO TO (205,240,250,400,400,500,600,600), MODEL
C*******************************************************************************
```

```
C*MODEL 1 CALCULATIONS *****************************************************
   205 EVTSLN=EVTMLI+EVTTCS+EVTMLO
       VATSLN=VATMLI+VATTCS+VATMLO
       GMTSLN=EVTSLN*EVTSLN/VATSLN
       FACTA=1.0/GMTSLN
       FACTB=EVTSLN*(1.0+FACTA)
   210 EVNTLI=EVNTLI+VALUE
       IF (STOP.EQ.1 .OR. EVNTLI.GT.RLIMIT) GO TO 220
       EVROLN=EVNTLI*EVTSLN
       IF (EVROLN.GE.1.0) STOP=1
       FACT1=1.0-EVROLN
       EVTWLN=EVROLN*FACTB/(2.0*FACT1)
       VATWLN=(EVTSLN/FACT1)**2*((1.0-EVROLN*(4.0-EVROLN)*
      1       (1.0-FACTA)/6.0)*(1.0+FACTA)-(1.0-EVROLN*
      2       (1.0-FACTA)/2.0)**2)-VATSLN
       THRPUT(I)=EVNTLI*IHOUR
       TIMEA(I)= EVTWLN+ADD1
       TIMEB(I)= EVTWLN+ADD2
       SDTRTA(I)=SQRT(VATWLN+ADD3)
       SDTRTB(I)=SQRT(VATWLN+ADD4)
       MAXTPT=THRPUT(I)
       I=I+1
       GO TO 210
C....
   220 CALL GRAPH
       WRITE (L1,230)
   230 FORMAT (//1H ,
      1'MODEL 1.    A HALF DUPLEX LINE HELD BY THE COMPUTER BETWEEN RECEI
      2PT OF INPUT MESSAGE AND TRANSMISSION OF THE RESPONSE.')
       GO TO 195

C*************************************************************************
C*MODEL 2 AND 3 CALCULATIONS ********************************************
   240 EVTSLN=(EVTMLI+EVTMLO)/2.0
       SMTSLN=(SMTMLI+SMTMLO)/2.0
       TMTSLN=(TMTMLI+TMTMLO)/2.0
   250 EVNTLI=EVNTLI+VALUE
       IF (STOP.EQ.1 .OR. EVNTLI.GT.RLIMIT) GO TO 300
       EVNTLO=EVNTLI
       EVNTLN=EVNTLI*2.0
       EVROLN=EVTSLN*EVNTLN
       IF (EVROLN.GE.1.0) STOP=1
       FACT1=1.0-EVROLN
       FACT1S=FACT1**2
       IF (MODEL.EQ.3) GO TO 270
       EVROLO=EVTMLO*EVNTLI
       SMTVAL=SMTMLO
       FACT2=1.0-EVROLO
   260 FACT2S=FACT2**2
       EVTWLO=EVNTLN*SMTSLN/(2.0*FACT2)
       EVTWLI=EVTWLO/FACT1
       FACT3=EVNTLO*SMTVAL
       SMTWLI=EVNTLN*TMTSLN/(3.0*FACT1*FACT2S)+
      1       2.0*EVTWLI**2+EVTWLI*FACT3/FACT2S
       SMTWLO=EVNTLN*TMTSLN/(3.0*FACT2)+
```

```
      1          EVTWLO*FACT3/FACT2
         GO TO 280
  270 EVROLI=EVTMLI*EVNTLI
         SMTVAL=SMTMLI
         FACT2=1.C-EVROLI
         GO TO 260
  280 VATWLI=SMTWLI-EVTWLI**2
         VATWLO=SMTWLO-EVTWLO**2
  290 THRPUT(I)=EVNTLI*IHOUR
         TIMEA(I) =EVTWLI+EVTWLO+ADD1
         TIMEB(I) =EVTWLI+EVTWLO+ADD2
         SDTRTA(I)=SQRT(VATWLI+VATWLO+ADD3)
         SDTRTB(I)=SQRT(VATWLI+VATWLO+ADD4)
         MAXTPT=THRPUT(I)
         I=I+1
         IF (MODEL.NE.6) GO TO 250
         GO TO 500
C....
  300 CALL GRAPH
         WRITE (L1,310) MODEL
  310 FORMAT (//1H ,
     1'MODEL ',I1,'.     A HALF DUPLEX LINE, NOT HELD AFTER INPUT TRANSMI
     2SSION.')
         IF (MODEL.EQ.3) GO TO 330
         WRITE (L1,320)
  320 FORMAT (1H ,'OUTPUT MESSAGES HAVE PRIORITY OVER INPUT.')
         GO TO 195
  330 WRITE (L1,340)
  340 FORMAT (1H ,'INPUT MESSAGES HAVE PRIORITY OVER OUTPUT.')
         GO TO 195


C**************************************************************************
C*MODEL 4 AND 5 CALCULATIONS ********************************************
C*
C*EVTSLN, SMTSLN, AND TMTSLN WERE CALCULATED IN MODEL 2 AND 3 SECTION.**
C*
  400 EVNTLI=EVNTLI+VALUE
         IF (STOP.EQ.1 .OR. EVNTLI.GT.RLIMIT) GO TO 450
         EVNTLN=2.0*EVNTLI
         EVNTIA=.3*EVNTLI
         EVNTOA=EVNTIA
         EVNTIB=.7*EVNTLI
         EVNTOB=EVNTIB
         EVROLN=EVNTLN*EVTSLN
         EVROOA=EVNTOA*EVTMOA
         EVROOB=EVNTOB*EVTMOB
         IF (EVROLN.GT.1.0) STOP=1
         FACT1=1.0-EVROLN
         FACT1S=FACT1**2
         FACT3=EVNTOA*SMTMOA
         FACT4=1.0-EVROOA-EVROOB
         FACT4S=FACT4**2
         FACT5=EVNTLN*SMTSLN
         FACT6=EVNTLN*TMTSLN
```

```
      IF (MODEL.EQ.5) GO TO 410
      FACT2=1.0-EVROOA
      FACT2S=FACT2**2
      FACT7=EVNTOA
      SMTWOA=FACT6/(3.0*FACT2)+
     1         FACT5*EVNTOA*SMTMOA/(2.0*FACT2S)
  405 EVTWOA=FACT5/(2.0*FACT2)
      EVTWOB=EVTWOA/FACT4
      EVTWLI=FACT5/(2.0*FACT1*FACT4)
      SMTWOB=FACT6/(3.0*FACT1S*FACT4)+EVTWOB*(FACT3+EVNTOB*SMTMOB)/
     1        (FACT2*FACT4)+EVTWOB*FACT7*SMTMOB/FACT2S
      SMTWLI=FACT6/(3.0*FACT4S*FACT1)+
     1        2.0*EVTWLI**2+EVTWLI*(FACT3+EVNTOA*SMTMOB)/FACT4S
      IF (MODEL.EQ.4) GO TO 430
      GO TO 420
  410 FACT2=1.0-EVROOB
      FACT2S=FACT2**2
      FACT7=EVNTOB
      SMTWOA=FACT6/(3.0*FACT2)+
     1         FACT5*EVNTOB*SMTMOB/(2.0*FACT2S)
      GO TO 405
  420 SAVE=SMTWOA
      SMTWOA=SMTWOB
      SMTWOB=SAVE
      SAVE=EVTWOA
      EVTWOA=EVTWOB
      EVTWOB=SAVE
  430 VATWLI=SMTWLI-EVTWLI**2
      VATWOA=SMTWOA-EVTWOA**2
      VATWOB=SMTWOB-EVTWOB**2
  440 THRPUT(I)=EVNTLI*IHOUR
      TIMEA(I) =EVTWLI+EVTWOA+ADD1
      TIMEB(I) =EVTWLI+EVTWOB+ADD2
      SDTRTA(I)=SQRT(VATWLI+VATWOA+ADD3)
      SDTRTB(I)=SQRT(VATWLI+VATWOB+ADD4)
      MAXIPT=THRPUT(I)
      I=I+1
      IF (MODEL.LT.6) GO TO 400
      GO TO 600
C....
  450 CALL GRAPH
      WRITE (L1,310) MODEL
      WRITE (L1,320)
      IF (MODEL.EQ.5) GO TO 470
      WRITE (L1,460)
  460 FORMAT (1H ,'TYPE A OUTPUT MESSAGES HAVE PRIORITY OVER TYPE B OUTP
     1OT.')
      GO TO 195
  470 WRITE (L1,480)
  480 FORMAT (1H ,'TYPE B OUTPUT MESSAGES HAVE PRIORITY OVER TYPE A OUTP
     1OT.')
      GO TO 195
C***********************************************************************
```

```
C*MODEL 6 CALCULATIONS *********************************************************
   500 EVNTLI=EVNTLI+VALUE
       IF (STOP.EQ.1 .OR. EVNTLI.GT.RLIMIT) GO TO 510
       EVNTLO=EVNTLI
       EVROLI=EVNTLI*EVTMLI
       EVROLO=EVNTLO*EVTMLO
       IF (EVROLI.GT.1.0 .OR. EVROLO.GT.1.0) STOP=1
       FACT1=1.0-EVROLO
       FACT2=1.0-EVROLI
       EVTWLI=EVNTLI*SMTMLI/(2.0*FACT2)
       EVTWLO=EVNTLO*SMTMLO/(2.0*FACT1)
       SMTWLI=EVNTLI*TMTMLI/(3.0*FACT2)+2.0*EVTWLI**2
       SMTWLO=EVNTLO*TMTMLO/(3.0*FACT1)+2.0*EVTWLO**2
C....
C      FINAL CALCULATIONS ARE SAME AS FOR MODELS 2 AND 3
       GO TO 280
C....
   510 CALL GRAPH
       WRITE (L1,520) MODEL
   520 FORMAT (//1H ,
      1'MODEL ',I1,'.     A FULL DUPLEX LINE WITH DATA BEING TRANSMITTED I
      2N BOTH DIRECTIONS AT ONCE.')
       GO TO 195
C*****************************************************************************
C*MODEL 7 AND 8 CALCULATIONS **************************************************
   600 EVNTLI=EVNTLI+VALUE
       IF (STOP.EQ.1 .OR. EVNTLI.GT.RLIMIT) GO TO 630
       EVNTLO=EVNTLI
       EVNTOB=.7*EVNTLI
       EVNTOA=.3*EVNTLI
       EVROLI=EVTMLI*EVNTLI
       EVROLO=EVTMLO*EVNTLO
       EVROOB=EVTMOB*EVNTOB
       IF (EVROLI.GT.1.0 .OR. EVROLO.GT.1.0) STOP=1
       FACT1=1.0-EVROLI
       FACT1S=FACT1**2
       FACT3=1.0-EVROLO
       IF (MODEL.EQ.8) GO TO 620
       FACT2=1.0-EVROOA
       EVNVAL=EVNTOA
       SMTVAL=SMTMOA
   610 FACT2S=FACT2**2
       EVTWLI=EVNTLI*SMTMLI/(2.0*FACT1)
       EVTWOA=EVNTLI*SMTMLO/(2.0*FACT2)
       EVTWOB=EVTWOA/FACT3
       SMTWLI=EVNTLI*TMTMLI/(3.0*FACT1)+2.0*EVTWLI**2
       FACT4=EVNTLO*SMTMLO
       FACT5=FACT4*EVNVAL*SMTVAL
       SMTWOA=EVNTLO*TMTMLO/(3.0*FACT2)+
      1        FACT5/(2.0*FACT2S)
       SMTWOB=EVNTLO*TMTMLO/(3.0*FACT2S*FACT3)+
      1        FACT4**2/(2.0*FACT3*FACT3*FACT2S)+
      2        FACT5/(2.0*FACT3*FACT2S*FACT2)
C.....
```

```
C       FINAL CALCULATIONS ARE SAME AS FOR MODELS 4 AND 5
        IF (MODEL.EQ.8) GO TO 420
        GO TO 430
C....
  620 FACT2=1.0-EVROOB
        EVNVAL=EVNTOB
        SMTVAL=SMTMOB
        GO TO 610
C....
  630 CALL GRAPH
        WRITE (L1,520) MODEL
        IF (MODEL.EQ.8)   GO TO 640
        WRITE (L1,460)
        GO TO 195
  640 WRITE (L1,480)
        STOP
        END
```

# 37 THE EFFECT OF POLLING

Strictly speaking, the models in Chapter 36 referred to *contention* line control. The transactions competed freely for the line facility. However, most line-control schemes having a large number of terminals on the line use a *polling* scheme of line control, not contention. In these pages the models of the last chapter will be adjusted to take polling into consideration. If the polling time is low compared with the message-transmission time, there will not be too much difference, and the curves in the last chapter give a useful idea of the effect of different priority schemes and of half-duplex vs. full-duplex transmission. If the polling time is not small compared with the transmission time, then the response times are affected significantly and the relative merits of different priority schemes may also be changed.

**TIME REQUIRED FOR POLLING**
Three time elements, in addition to the message-character transmission time, must be considered on a polled communication line:

1. The time for an unsuccessful (negative) poll and its response.
2. The time for a successful (positive) poll and the acknowledgement of the message that is transmitted.
3. The time associated with output transmission, including addressing the terminal and its response, and its acknowledgement of correct receipt of the message.

Suppose that terminal C has a message to send when the computer begins its polling cycle. "Roll-call" polling is in use and the computer first polls terminal A. Terminal A returns a negative response. The computer then polls terminal B, also unsuccessfully. Terminal C is next polled and sends a positive response. The time taken by this successful poll may differ from the time taken by the unsuccessful polls.

In our calculations we will write $t_0$ for the total time for an unsuccessful poll to one terminal. When a terminal user presses the ENTER key, or an equivalent key, on his terminal, he may have to wait several times $t_0$ while other terminals are unsuccessfully polled. (Normally there is no interrupt scheme on today's communication lines.)

Following the notation used in Chapters 30 and 36, we will write $t_1$ for the time that must be added to the input transmission time, which now includes the time for successful polling and message acknowledgement. Similarly, we will write $t_2$ for the time that must be added to the output transmission time, which now includes the time for addressing the terminal and message acknowledgement.

As before, the total times for message transmission are, then, on input

$$t_{MI} = \frac{N_I}{S} + t_1$$

and on output

$$t_{Mo} = \frac{N_O}{S} + t_2$$

where $N_I$ = the number of characters in the input message
$\phantom{where }N_O$ = the number of characters in the output message
$\phantom{where }S$ = the line speed (characters per unit time)

On a half-duplex line, the message-transmission time, $T_{MI}$, will be preceded by a number of unsuccessful polls ranging from 0 to $M - 1$, where $M$ is the number of terminals on the line.

**AN EXAMPLE OF**
**THE TIMES**
**INVOLVED**

Let us consider a typical system so that the reader can see what is involved in estimating the polling times. (The following figures relate to an AT & T type 1006 line with AT & T 103F2 data sets. IBM 1050–type polling is used, and the transmission control unit is an IBM 2702 with an autopoll feature. The figures should be regarded as illustrative only.) Readers designing a transmission system should discover the latest such figures for their particular equipment.

The time elements involved (in milliseconds) in an unsuccessful poll are as follows:

1. The sending of a strobe character by the line control unit and its recognition by the data set — 80.5
2. The sending of the polling message—3 characters transmitted at 14.8 characters per second — 202.5
3. Propagation delay to the terminal — 15.0
4. Modem establishes carrier to computer — 322.0
5. The negative response—1 character transmitted at 14.8 characters per second — 67.5
6. Propagation delay to the computer — 15.0
7. If the computer was generating the individual polling signals, there would be a computer response time element here. In this case, there is not because the autopoll feature is used. — –

Total   702.5

Thus $t_0 = 702.5$ milliseconds

The propagation delay time in the foregoing example would, of course, vary with the distance. The 15 millisecond figure is for a link of 450 miles. A large part of the preceding delay is to enable the modem to establish the carrier to the computer. The 103F2 data set uses two different frequency bands simultaneously, one for each direction. As a result, there is no turnaround time when the direction of transmission is changed on the line. However, when the transmission switches from one terminal (and data set) to another, the new data set must establish its carrier frequency on the line. The 103F2 data set takes 265 milliseconds to do so, and a complete character time of 67 milliseconds elapses before transmission begins, giving the listed time of 322 milliseconds.

Some modems, particularly those that operate at higher speeds, cause a delay each time the direction of transmission on the line is changed. With some modems, this delay is small; with others, it is substantial.

When many terminals are polled on a line, the total time spent in polling will build up to several seconds. If the application was intended to be a fast response-time conversation operating on a line with a transmission speed, say, 20 times higher than the preceding one, then the polling time would be largely dependent on the modem turnaround time or the time necessary to establish its carrier. For a line with many "drops," it would be necessary (1) to use a modem with a fast turnaround in order to achieve the desired response time or (2) to use hub polling.

The time elements for a successful poll in the preceding case are as follows (in milliseconds):

1. The sending of a strobe character by the line-control unit and its recognition by the data set — 80.5
2. The sending of the polling message—3 characters transmitted at 14.8 characters per second — 202.5
3. Propagation delay to the terminal — 15.0
4. Modem establishes carrier to computer — 322.0
5. Response with text (where $N$ is the number of characters in the response, including the D, B, and longitudinal redundancy check characters)* — $N \times 67.5$
6. Propagation delay to computer — 15.0
7. Response time of line-control unit and computer — 100
8. Strobe character — 80.5
9. Positive response to terminal, 1 character time — 67.5
10. Propagation delay to terminal — 15.0
11. Line turnaround time — 79.5
12. EOT character response to computer — 67.5
13. Propagation delay to computer — 15.0
14. Response time of line-control unit and computer — 100

Total    $N \times 67.5 + 1160$

Therefore $t_1$ is 1160 milliseconds, which is added onto $t_{M1}$, the input character transmission time.

We will also have to add some time to the output-message transmission time. If the line is not released between input transmission and output (like model 1 in the previous chapter), then the added time is that for the terminal to respond saying that the message has been received correctly and for the line control unit to send the end-of-transmission character. If the line is released between input and output, the terminal must be addressed on output, and hence the time is longer.

* This form of line control is described in the author's *Teleprocessing Network Organization.*

Using the foregoing illustration, the figures for addressing a terminal and sending an output message are (in milliseconds)

| | | |
|---|---|---:|
| 1. | The strobe character | 80.5 |
| 2. | The sending of the addressing message | 202.5 |
| 3. | Propagation delay, to the terminal | 15.0 |
| 4. | Modem establishes carrier to computer | 322.0 |
| 5. | Availability response | 67.5 |
| 6. | Propagation delay, to the computer | 15.0 |
| 7. | Line control unit response time | 87.8 |
| 8. | Strobe character | 80.5 |
| 9. | Text transmission (where $N$ is the number of characters in the response, including the D and B and longitudinal redundancy check characters) | $N \times 67.5$ |
| 10. | Propagation delay, to the terminal | 15.0 |
| 11. | Positive answerback (one character) | 67.5 |
| 12. | Propagation delay, to the computer | 15.0 |
| 13. | Line control unit and computer response time | 87.8 |
| 14. | Strobe character | 80.5 |
| 15. | EOT character | 67.5 |

$$\text{Total} \qquad N \times 67.5 + 1204.1$$

Thus $t_2$ is 1204.1 milliseconds, which is added onto $t_{Mo}$, the output character transmission time.

Other systems may have different time elements—for example, after scanning through the polling list, there may be a pause before the next scan. Again, some line-control programs transmit three end-of-transmission characters, ⓒ, instead of the one in the preceding list. The reader can add the effect of such differences to the calculations that follow if such is the case on his particular system.

**MODELS OF POLLED LINES**   Mathematical models that attempt to consider polling in an exact fashion can become exceedingly complex—so complex in fact that it is easier to use a simple simulation model of a line, as will be discussed in Chapter 38. Fortunately, a short simulation program that examines the performance of *one line* can be written so that it has wide general applicability.

However, we would like to have a method of doing approximate calculations for a polled line without the added difficulty of simulation. It is useful for a systems analyst to be able to do quick approximate calculations, such as those in the previous chapters. Furthermore, it is much easier to obtain insight into the better ways to organize a line from a set of simple equations than from repeated simulation runs, even if the equations are only approximate.

Polling introduces two differences to the queuing models used in Chapter 36. First, the new messages will not be accepted on a first-come, first-served basis; in most cases, the terminals will be polled in a cyclic fashion. This process will not affect the *mean* queuing time because it does not give preferential treatment to the shorter messages. It will, however, have a slight effect on the *standard deviation* of queuing time. Figure 30.16 showed the differences between a case with first-come, first-served and random dispatching. Cyclic dispatching will lie somewhere between these two curves. Using the equations for random dispatching would give an upper limit to the standard deviation figure. In general, this result is not too important—the *mean* response time in our calculations is not affected and the standard deviation is only changed slightly.

Second, "service" time for messages on the input line must include the time taken for polling as well as the time for transmission. In order to calculate the mean service time, we want to know *how many terminals will be polled* before the one having the message is polled.

Suppose, for a start, that when an operator initiates a message, it is the only message waiting to be served on the line.

If there are $M$ terminals on the line, polled equally, then the probability of starting the scan at *one particular* terminal is $1/M$. The message in question would, by chance, be polled immediately, or it could wait while $M - 1$ other terminals are polled.

The mean number of terminals polled *before* the one in question is then

$$\sum_{N=0}^{M-1} \frac{1}{M} N = \frac{1}{M} \frac{M(M-1)}{2} = \frac{M-1}{2}$$

The mean time waiting for unsuccessful polling would then be

$$\left(\frac{M-1}{2}\right) t_0$$

($t_0$ being the time taken for the unsuccessful poll of one terminal).

Similarly, the second moment of the overall polling time is (the weighted mean of the squares of the possible polling times)

$$\sum_{N=0}^{M-1} \frac{1}{M} (Nt_0)^2 = \frac{t_0^2}{M} \frac{(M-1)M(2M-1)}{6} = \frac{(M-1)(2M-1)}{6} t_0^2$$

**Note:** *In evaluating the preceding equation, we needed to calculate $\sum_{x=0}^{M} x$ and $\sum_{x=0}^{M} x^2$. It is worthwhile noting the following summations, which are useful in this type of calculation.*[1]

$$\sum_{x=0}^{M} x = \frac{M(M+1)}{2}$$

$$\sum_{x=0}^{M} x^2 = \frac{M(M+1)(2M+1)}{6}$$

$$\sum_{x=0}^{M} x^3 = \frac{M^2(M+1)^2}{4}$$

$$\sum_{x=0}^{M} x^4 = \frac{M(M+1)(2M+1)(3M^2+3M-1)}{30}$$

$$\sum_{x=0}^{M} x^j = \sum_{x=0}^{j} (-1)^x \left(\frac{M+j+1-x}{j+1}\right) \sum_{i=0}^{j-x} (-1)^i \left(\frac{j+1}{i+x+1}\right) (M+1+i)^i$$

$$\text{for } j = 0, 1, 2, \ldots$$

[1] A book listing useful summations is V. Mangulis's *Handbook of Series.* (New York and London: Academic Press, 1965.)

Thus the variance of overall polling time is

$$\frac{(M-1)(2M-1)}{6} t_0^2 - \left[\left(\frac{M-1}{2}\right) t_0\right]^2 = \frac{M^2-1}{12} t_0^2$$

If $T_{M_I}$ is the transmission time for the input message, we could therefore use as our mean service time in the queuing equations

$$E(t_s) = E(t_{M_I}) + \frac{M-1}{2} t_0 \tag{37.1}$$

and the variance of service time

$$\text{Var}(t_s) = \text{Var}(t_{M_I}) + \frac{M^2-1}{12} t_0^2 \quad \text{or} \tag{37.2}$$

$$\sigma_{t_s} = \sqrt{\sigma_{t_{M_I}}^2 + \frac{M^2-1}{12} t_0^2} \tag{37.3}$$

[In these equations $t_{M_I}$ includes the time necessary for the successful poll and its response $= (N_I/S) + t_1.$]

If only one terminal has a message waiting, the service times will be represented accurately by the foregoing equations. On the other hand, if several terminals have messages waiting, these equations will be pessimistic because fewer terminals, on the average, will be scanned before the *next* one with a message receives a poll.

These equations are useful in enabling a systems engineer to obtain a quick estimate of the response time. If the line is not heavily loaded—for example, if $\rho \leq 0.6$—the answer will be accurate enough for most practical purposes. The lower the ratio of polling time to message transmission time, the more accurate the preceding approximation will be.

In many cases, as we shall see, the queues are dominated by the output traffic; therefore even at high-utilization figures there will only be one message waiting. In these situations, the foregoing equations for service time are accurate.

**A MORE EXACT MODEL**   Let us now calculate the effect of polling somewhat more accurately, and let us use a computer for the calculation this time.

Suppose that once again the line has $M$ terminals. Suppose, also, that $Q$ of them have a message and are waiting to be polled. The terminals that have messages are distributed at random among the $M$ terminals.

When a polling scan begins, the probability that the first terminal polled has a message is

$$P(1) = \frac{Q}{M} \tag{37.4}$$

The probability that the second terminal polled is the one to respond equals the probability that the first terminal polled does not have a message times the probability that the second terminal polled does have one.

$$P(2) = \frac{M - Q}{M} \frac{Q}{M - 1}$$

Similarly,

$$P(3) = \frac{M - Q}{M} \frac{M - Q - 1}{M - 1} \frac{Q}{M - 2}$$

And, in general, the probability that the $N$th terminal to be polled is the first one to respond is

$$P(N) = P(N - 1) \frac{M - Q - N + 2}{M - N + 1} \tag{37.5}$$

Using these probability figures, we can calculate the mean negative polling time, thus:

$$E(t_{\text{poll}}) = \sum_{N=1}^{(M-Q+1)} P(N)(N-1)t_0 \tag{37.6}$$

and the second moment of polling time

$$E(t_{\text{poll}}^2) = \sum_{N=1}^{(M-Q+1)} P(N)[(N-1)t_0]^2 \tag{37.7}$$

$$\text{Var }(t_{\text{poll}}) = E(t_{\text{poll}}^2) - E^2(t_{\text{poll}}) \tag{37.8}$$

In PL/I, writing EVTPLI for the mean polling, time on the line, SMTPLI for the second moment of polling time on the line, and VATPLI for its variance:

```
EVTPLI,SMTPLI=0;
P(1)=Q/M;
DO N=2 TO (M-Q+1);
P(N)=P(N-1)*(M-Q-N+2)/(M-N+1);
END;
DO N=1 TO (M-Q+1);
EVTPLI=EVTPLI+P(N)*(N-1)*TO;
SMTPLI=SMTPLI+P(N)*((N-1)*TO)**2;
END;
VATPLI=SMTPLI-EVTPLI*EVTPLI;
```

In Fortran:

```
10  EVTPLI=0.0
    SMTPLI=0.0
    P(1)=Q/M
    L=M-Q+1.0
    DO 20 N=2,L
20  P(N)=P(N-1)*(M-Q-N+2.0)/(M-N+1)
    DO 30 N=1,L
    EVTPLI=EVTPLI+P(N)*(N-1)*TO
30  SMTPLI=SMTPLI+P(N)*((N-1)*TO)**2
    VATPLI=SMTPLI-EVTPLI*EVTPLI
```

The mean time the input line is held by polling and transmission is

$$E(t_s) = E(t_{\text{poll}}) + E(t_{M1}) \tag{37.9}$$

The variance of this time is

$$\text{Var }(t_s) = \text{Var }(t_{\text{poll}}) + \text{Var }(t_{M1}) \tag{37.10}$$

Unfortunately, we do not have a value for $Q$, the number of terminals with a message waiting to be transmitted. $Q$ will depend on the queuing for the line, which in turn will depend to some extent on the polling time.

Let us use as our value of $Q$ the mean number of items queuing for the line as given by Eq. (37.11). We will treat the line as a single-server queue, as we did in the last chapter.

$$Q = E(n)E(t_s) + \frac{[E(n)E(t_s)]^2}{2[1 - E(n)E(t_s)]}\left[1 + \frac{\text{Var }(t_s)}{E^2(t_s)}\right] \qquad (37.11)$$

We could now treat Eqs. (37.4) to (37.11) as a set of simultaneous equations, and, solving these, obtain a value for $E(t_s)$ and Var $(t_s)$ and hence find the queuing time for the line. Let us use a computer, guess at a value of $Q$, and adjust it until the equations agree. In PL/I for a line with 12 terminals:

```
       M=12;
       TO=.7025;
       FVNTLI=.05;
       Q=1;
V1:    EVTPLI,SMTPLI=0;
       P(1)=Q/M;
       DO N=2 TO (M-Q+1);
       P(N)=P(N-1)*(M-Q-N+2)/(M-N+1);
       END;
       DO N=1 TO (M-Q+1);
       EVTPLI=EVTPLI+P(N)*(N-1)*TO;
       SMTPLI=SMTPLI+P(N)*((N-1)*TO)**2;
       END;
       VATPLI=SMTPLI-EVTPLI*EVTPLI;
       EVTSLI=EVTPLI+EVTMLI;
       VATSLI=VATPLI+VATMLI;
       EVROLI=FVNTLI*EVTSLI;
       EVNQLI=EVROLI+EVROLI**2*(1+VATSLI/EVTSLI**2)/(2*(1-EVROLI));
       IF (EVNQLI>Q)&(Q<=M) THEN DO;Q=Q+.01;GO TO V1; END;
```

IN FORTRAN:

```
       M=12
       TO=.7025
       EVNTLI=.05
       Q=1.0
C....
   10  EVTPLI=0.0
       SMTPLI=0.0
       P(1)=Q/M
       L=M-Q+1.0
       DO 20 N=2,L
   20  P(N)=P(N-1)*(M-Q-N+2.0)/(M-N+1)
       DO 30 N=1,L
       EVTPLI=EVTPLI+P(N)*(N-1)*TO
   30  SMTPLI=SMTPLI+P(N)*((N-1)*TO)**2
       VATPLI=SMTPLI-EVTPLI*EVTPLI
       EVTSLI=EVTPLI+EVTMLI
       VATSLI=VATPLI+VATMLI
       EVROLI=EVNTLI*EVTSLI
       EVNQLI=EVROLI+EVROLI**2*(1.0+VATSLI/EVTSLI**2)/(2.0*(1.0-EVROLI))
       IF (EVNQLI.LE.Q .OR. Q.GT.M) GO TO 40
       Q=Q+.01
       GO TO 10
```

Plotting a curve like those in the last chapter, we can start with a very low throughput, in which case $Q = 1$, and we can allow our initial guess of $Q$ to rise as we increase the throughput. It would be interesting to plot $E(t_{poll})$ and $\sigma(t_{poll})$ in addition to the response time. Let us add the polling timing found in this manner to the times from model 1 from the last chapter.

**Example 37.1. A Half-Duplex Line with Polling.** Consider a half-duplex line operating at 14.8 characters per second. The message-length distributions are again those of Example 36.1—that is, those in the table on page 556. The time for a negative poll, $t_0$, is 0.7025 second, from the figures given earlier in this chapter, and the line-preparation times for input and output transmission, $t_1$ and $t_2$, are 1.16 and 1.2041 seconds respectively.

How do the response times vary with the number of terminals attached to the line?

Figure 37.1 shows the results for a line with 8 terminals. Figure 37.2 is for a line with 16 terminals, and Fig. 37.3 is for 24 terminals. One can see how the response time increases and the maximum throughput drops as the number of terminals on the line is increased.

The PPPPP curves give the mean line-scanning time, $E(t_{poll})$, and the YYYYY curves give the standard deviation of this time. The line-scanning time can be seen to fall off as the queues build up, thereby resulting in a response time curve of a different shape. The curves in Fig. 37.3, for example, are much closer to a straight line than the equivalent ones without polling in Fig. 36.4 of the last chapter.

The curves have discontinuities in them at the points at which the scanning time drops. The summations in Eqs. (37.6) and (37.7) must assume an integral number of terminals with a message. As this figure changes, there is a jump in the value of the calculated response time and hence a discontinuity in the curves plotted.

On many communication lines when a terminal awaits a poll, it is the *only* terminal waiting most of the time. If this is so, the mean time waiting for a poll is $\left(\dfrac{M-1}{2}\right) \cdot t_0$, where $M$ is the number of terminals. Where the output messages are longer than the input messages, they may dominate the queuing situation, and the maximum throughput occurs at a value for which the input queue is still very low. Even when the maximum throughput is reached, we may still have to poll $(M-1)/2$ terminals on the average. In this case, the way we did the calculation in Example 37.1 is quite accurate.

Figure 37.4 illustrates this. Here the preceding calculation is repeated but using line organization model 3 from the last chapter. The half-duplex line is not held, and input messages have priority over output. Figure 37.4 is for a line

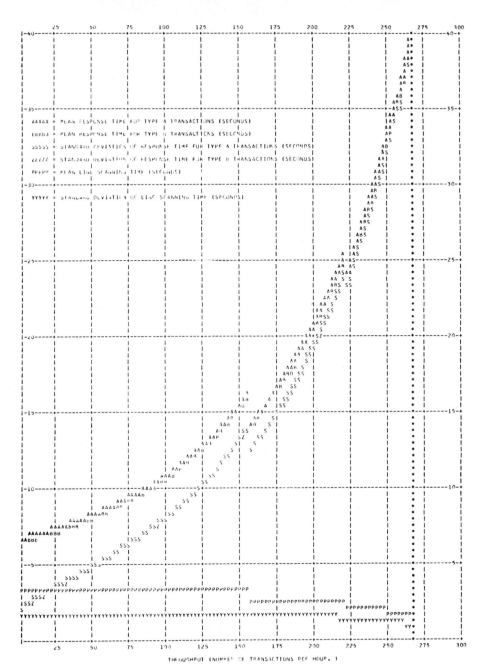

*Fig. 37.1.* Polling on a line with 8 terminals, using model 1 organization.

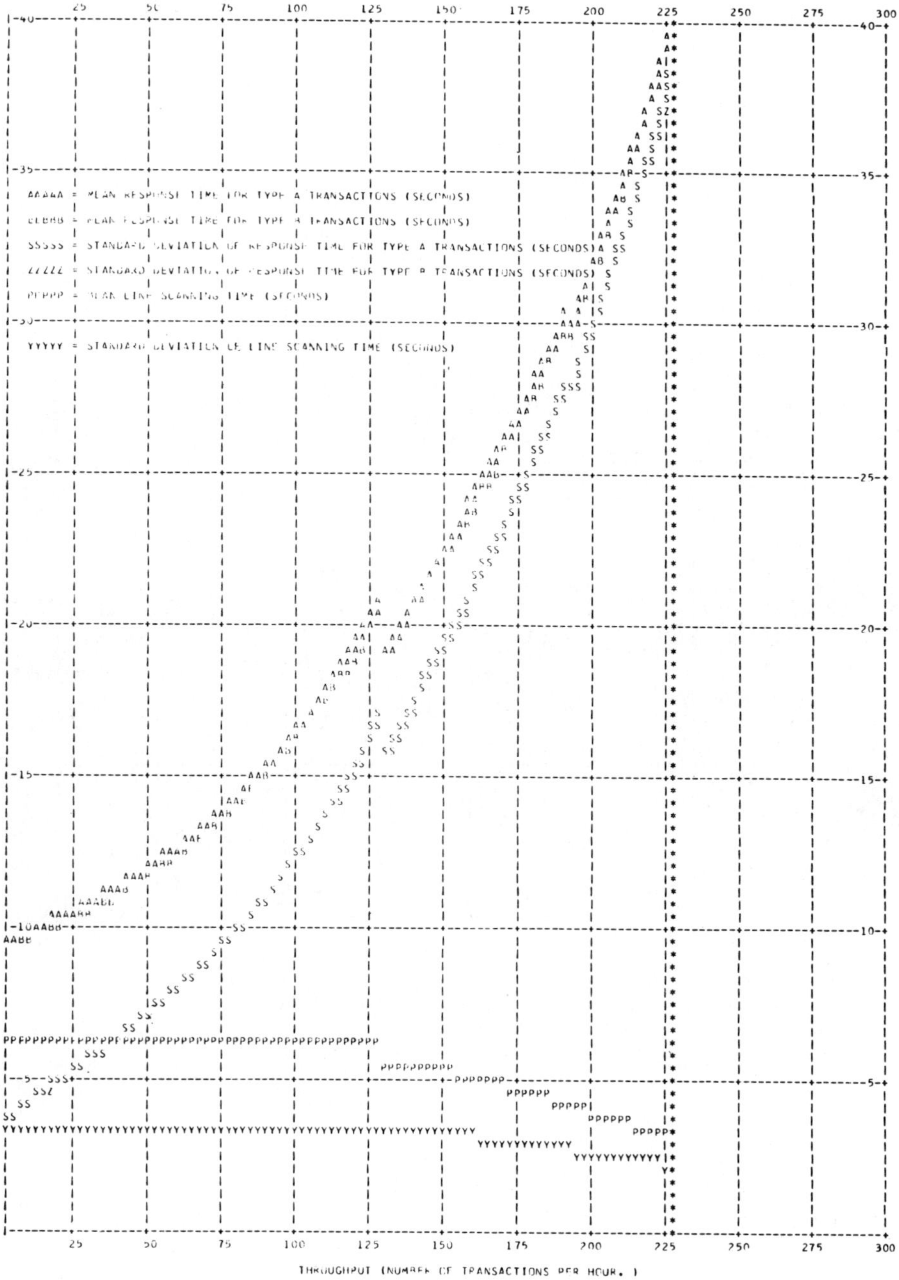

THROUGHPUT (NUMBER OF TRANSACTIONS PER HOUR. )

EXAMPLE F1.2.

LINE SPEED 14.8 CHARACTERS PER SECOND

| | MEAN | STANDARD DEVIATION |
|---|---|---|
| TOTAL TRANSMISSION TIME FOR INPUT MESSAGE TYPE A (SECS) | 2.312 | 0.822 |
| TOTAL TRANSMISSION TIME FOR INPUT MESSAGE TYPE B (SECS) | 2.104 | 0.634 |
| TOTAL TRANSMISSION TIME FOR OUTPUT MESSAGE TYPE A (SECS) | 9.383 | 2.567 |
| TOTAL TRANSMISSION TIME FOR OUTPUT MESSAGE TYPE B (SECS) | 5.910 | 2.323 |
| TOTAL TIME TRANSACTION SPENDS IN COMPUTER SYSTEM (SECS) | 1.000 | 0.500 |

MODEL 1.    A HALF DUPLEX LINE HELD BY THE COMPUTER BETWEEN RECEIPT OF INPUT MESSAGE AND TRANSMISSION OF THE RESPONSE.

*Fig. 37.2.* Polling as in Fig. 37.1 but on a line with 16 terminals.

623

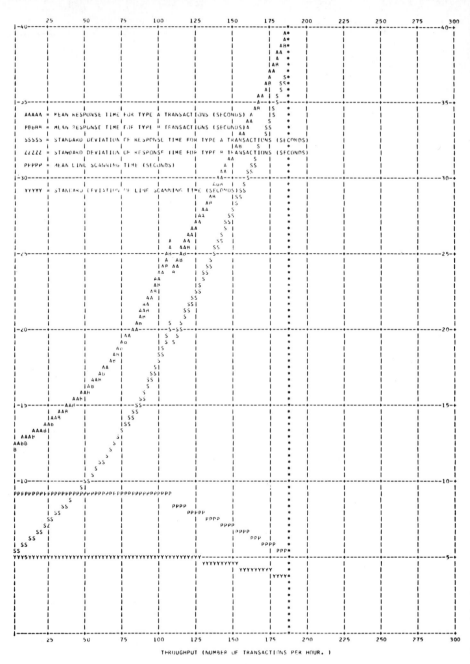

EXAMPLE F1.2.

LINE SPEED 14.8 CHARACTERS PER SECOND

| | MEAN | STANDARD DEVIATION |
|---|---|---|
| **TOTAL** TRANSMISSION TIME FOR INPUT MESSAGE TYPE A (SECS) | 2.312 | 0.822 |
| **TOTAL** TRANSMISSION TIME FOR INPUT MESSAGE TYPE B (SECS) | 2.104 | 0.434 |
| **TOTAL** TRANSMISSION TIME FOR OUTPUT MESSAGE TYPE A (SECS) | 9.383 | 2.567 |
| **TOTAL** TRANSMISSION TIME FOR OUTPUT MESSAGE TYPE B (SECS) | 5.919 | 2.323 |
| **TOTAL** TIME TRANSACTION SPENDS IN COMPUTER SYSTEM (SECS) | 1.000 | 0.500 |

MODEL 1.    A HALF DUPLEX LINE HELD BY THE COMPUTER BETWEEN RECEIPT OF INPUT MESSAGE AND TRANSMISSION OF THE RESPONSE.

*Fig. 37.3.* Polling as in Fig. 37.1 but on a line with 24 terminals.

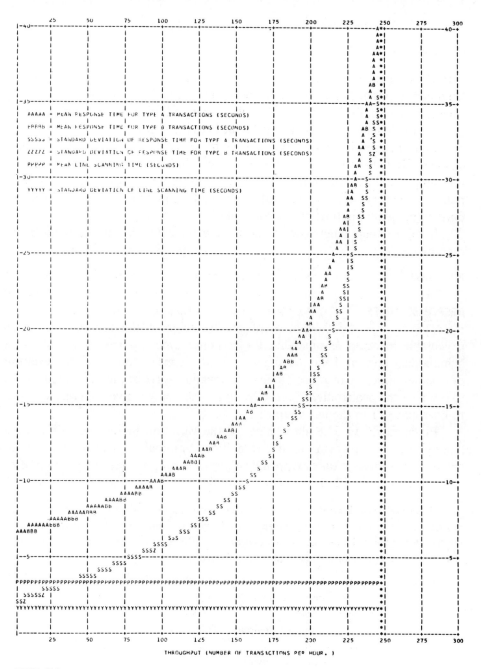

THROUGHPUT (NUMBER OF TRANSACTIONS PER HOUR. )

EXAMPLE FI.2.

LINE SPEED 14.8 CHARACTERS PER SECOND

|  | MEAN | STANDARD DEVIATION |
|---|---|---|
| TOTAL TRANSMISSION TIME FOR INPUT MESSAGE TYPE A (SECS) | 2.312 | 0.822 |
| TOTAL TRANSMISSION TIME FOR INPUT MESSAGE TYPE B (SECS) | 2.104 | 0.634 |
| TOTAL TRANSMISSION TIME FOR OUTPUT MESSAGE TYPE A (SECS) | 9.383 | 2.567 |
| TOTAL TRANSMISSION TIME FOR OUTPUT MESSAGE TYPE B (SECS) | 5.919 | 2.323 |
| TOTAL TIME TRANSACTION SPENDS IN COMPUTER SYSTEM (SECS) | 1.000 | 0.500 |

MODEL 3.     A HALF DUPLEX LINE, NOT HELD AFTER INPUT TRANSMISION.
INPUT MESSAGES HAVE PRIORITY OVER OUTPUT.

*Fig. 37.4.* Model 3 with eight terminals. The time for unsuccessful polling does not fall, as it does in model 1, Fig. 37.1.

with 8 terminals and thus may be compared directly with Fig. 37.1. Now the lengthier output messages dominate the queuing situation, and the line-scanning time curves never fall. The PPPPP curve remains a horizontal straight line.

We might have expected model 3 to be better than model 1 for this particular situation. The results in Fig. 36.6 are better than those in Fig. 36.4 in the last chapter. Here, however, the opposite is true. Model 1 permits a slightly higher throughput and the reason is that in model 3 more time is spent in unsuccessful polling. Each unsuccessful poll takes 702 milliseconds; and with 24 terminals on the line, scanning time can become high.

If the message lengths were short, model 1 could be substantially better than model 3.

**PROBABILITIES OF DIFFERENT RESPONSE TIMES**

Simulation of polled communication lines shows that the response times obtained on a given line are close to a gamma distribution. In order to obtain a quick picture of the behavior of the terminal, it seems reasonable to again assume that the response times approximately follow a gamma distribution. Then, having calculated the mean and standard deviation of response time, we may use Table 4 in Appendix VIII or the associated curves to estimate the probability of response times exceeding a given figure, as we did in Example 36.1 in the last chapter.

Figures 37.5 to 37.8 show plots of the variation in response time for a voice grade line on which the time to poll one terminal is longer than the input message transmission time. Appendix V lists the routine used for plotting these and similar figures with the gamma distribution.

**Example 37.2. Variations in Response Time.** A line operates at a speed of 300 characters per second and is organized in the fashion of model 3 in the previous chapter. The time taken for a single unsuccessful poll on it is 0.05 second. The message transmission times, including $t_1$ and $t_2$, are as follows (in milliseconds):

| | | | |
|---|---|---|---|
| Type A | input: | mean | 0.033 |
| | | standard deviation | 0.024 |
| | output: | mean | 0.033 |
| | | standard deviation | 0.024 |
| Type B | input: | mean | 0.033 |
| | | standard deviation | 0.024 |
| | output: | mean | 0.333 |
| | | standard deviation | 0.236 |

Again 30 percent of the transactions are of type A and 70 percent are of type B. The time a transaction spends in the computer system can (again) be assumed to have a mean of 1 second and a standard deviation of $\frac{1}{2}$ second.

Plot curves that give the distribution of response times and show how these vary with the number of terminals on the line.

Note that in this example *the time to poll one terminal is larger than the input-message transmission time.* Figures 37.5 to 37.8 give the curves for 10, 15, 20, and 25 terminals respectively.

**EIGHT TYPES OF**
**LINE ORGANIZATION**
**WITH POLLING**

The eight types of line organization discussed in Chapter 36 can now be reexamined for a line with polling. The models used are the same as those discussed in the last chapter except that now the mean and variance of $t_{poll}$ have been added to the mean and variance of the relevant transmission time.

**Example 37.3. Eight Ways to Organize a Polled Communication Line.** A line has 12 terminals. The message lengths and computing time are the same as in the previous example, but now the line speed is 14.8 characters per second and the time to poll one terminal is $\frac{1}{3}$ second.

Which of the eight line organization models will be the best in this case? Plot curves of the mean and standard deviation against throughput.

By now the reader can *possibly make some intelligent guesses* as to which would be the best of the eight models. After some practice with models such as those, one's intuition can become sufficiently trained to make correct judgments about design alternatives in teleprocessing.

Figures 37.9 to 37.16 show the results for the eight models. First, all the full-duplex models are better than the half-duplex ones. The best full-duplex model can handle a throughput more than 50 percent greater than the best half-duplex model. When the full-duplex line costs only 10 percent more, it is clearly the better buy if terminals that can operate in a full-duplex fashion are available.

Second, output messages type B are longer than output messages type A. Line organizations giving type A output priority over type B would therefore be expected to give a somewhat lower mean response time. There is in fact only a minor difference between models 4 and 5 for the half-duplex line but a big difference between models 7 and 8 for the full-duplex line.

Third, input messages are shorter than output on the average. We would therefore expect it to be preferable to give input messages priority over output. Model 3 is slightly better than model 2 but not as much so as with the examples in the previous chapter because now the input transmission time is effectively increased by the time taken to poll.

Finally, and this is perhaps a surprise, the best of the half-duplex line organizations is model 1. Unlike the examples in the last chapter, it is now better to hold the line between input transmission and output. Holding it gives better performance when the queues are high. Why? The PPPPP curves indicate the reason. In models 2, 3, 4, and 5 the mean line-scanning time does not fall off with increasing load. The mean number of terminals polled before the

*Fig. 37.5.* This and the following three figures show the distributions of response times for the lines in Example 37.2 with differing numbers of terminals. Here 10 terminals are attached to the line.

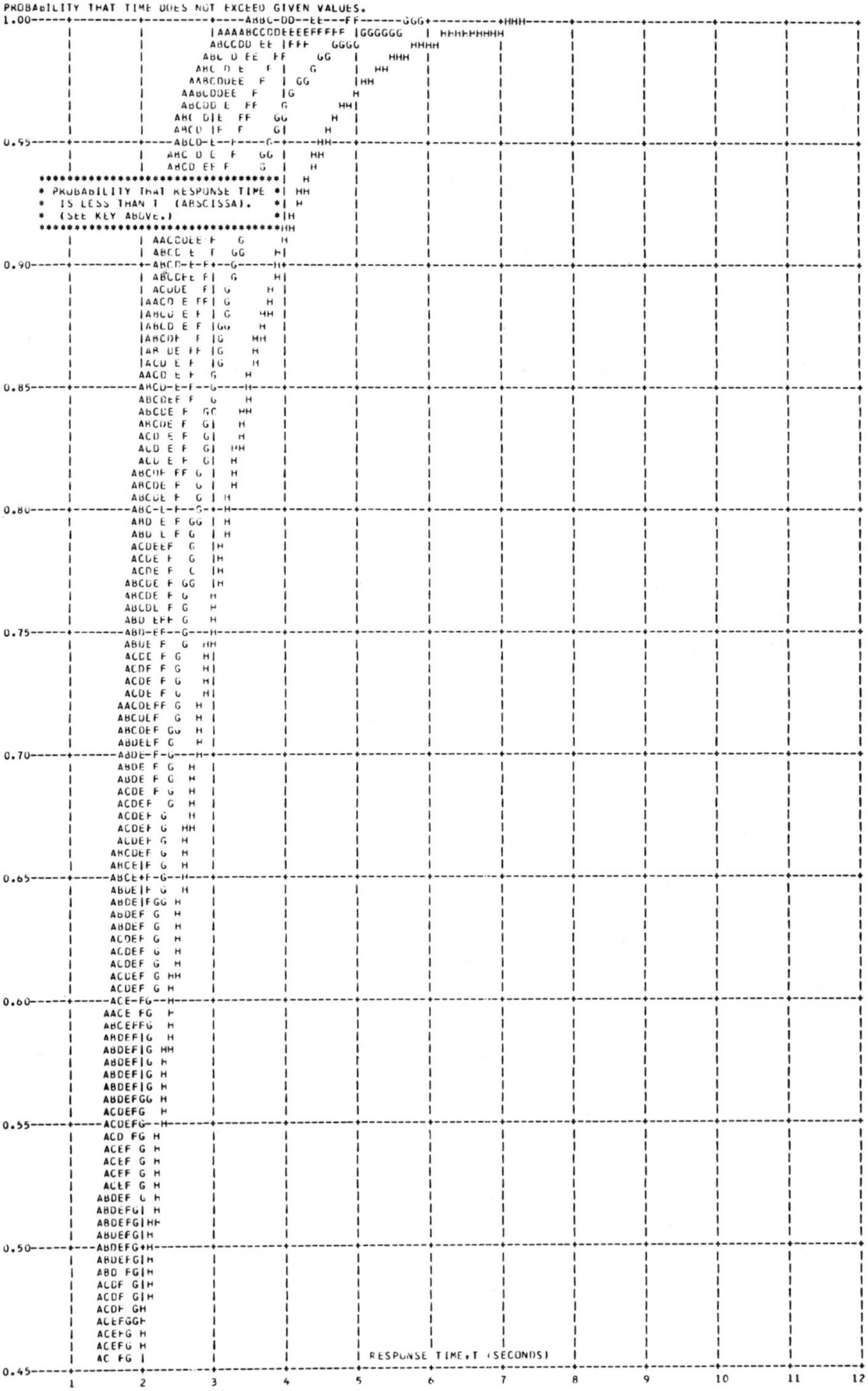

PROBABILITY THAT TIME DOES NOT EXCEED GIVEN VALUES.

PROBABILITY THAT RESPONSE TIME IS LESS THAN T (ABSCISSA). (SEE KEY ABOVE.)

RESPONSE TIME, T (SECONDS)

628

THRCUGHPUT VALUES OF CURVES BELOW
HHH = 1.20 TRANSACTIONS PER SECOND
GGG = 1.05 TRANSACTIONS PER SECOND
FFF = 0.90 TRANSACTIONS PER SECOND
EEE = 0.75 TRANSACTIONS PER SECOND
DDD = 0.60 TRANSACTIONS PER SECOND
CCC = 0.45 TRANSACTIONS PER SECOND
BBB = 0.30 TRANSACTIONS PER SECOND
AAA = 0.15 TRANSACTIONS PER SECOND

PROBABILITY THAT TIME DOES NOT EXCEED GIVEN VALUES.

```
1.00                                   A-BB-CC----DD        EE              FFF                            GGGGG
                          AAAABBCCCCDDDDDDD  EEEEEEE       FFFFFFFFFF           GGGGGGGGGGGGGGGGG
                          AABB CC  DD   EEE        FFFFF            GGGGGGGG
                         A b  C   DD    EEE        FFFF            GGGGGG
                         A B CC  DD  I   E         FF  F           GGGG
                         AABB  C   D I  EE         FF              GGG
                         ABB  C    D  I   E         F              GG
                         A  B CC  DD  I  E         F              GG                          HHHH
                         AB  C  DD  IEE         F                 GG                      HHHH
                         A  BC   D   EE                          GG                    HHH
0.95 ---------------------ABBCC--D-----F---------------GG------------------------------HHH------------
                          AAB C   D   EI      FF       F              I              HHH
                          ABB C   D  FF       F      G               I            HH
       *****************************    F              GG              I          HH
       * PROBABILITY THAT RESPONSE TIME *  FF         I G             I        HH
       * IS LESS THAN T (ABSCISSA).      *  FF         I  G            I       HH
       * (SEE KEY ABOVE.)                *  F          I   G           I      HH
       *****************************    F          I    GG          I     H
                         A  B C  D   EE        F          I     G          I    HH
                         AABBC  D     E        F          I      GG         I   HH
0.90 --------------------AB-C--D---E----FF--------GG----------------------------H---H--------------
                         AB  C   D   E       F         I    G            I        HH
                         AB  C   D   E      IF         I   G             I      H
                         A BCC  DI   F      IF         I  GG             I     H
                         AB  C  DI   E       FF        I  GG             I HH
                         AB  C  DI   E       F         I  G              I   H
                         AB  C  DDI  E       F         I  G              I  HI
                         AB  C  DI   EE      FI        IGG               I    H
                         AABC  D I  E        FI        I G               I   H
                         A BC   C I  L       FII       I G               I  H
0.85 --------------------AB-C---D--EE------------------------------------HH------------------
                         AB  C  D  IE        F  I      G I               HHH
                         AB  C D  IE        F         GG I             HH
                         A B C  D  IE        F         G  I             H
                         A MC  D   E        F         G                 IH
                         IA BC   D   E        F         G               HH
                         IABBC  DD  L        F         GG             HH
                         IAB C  D   E        F         G              HH I
                         IAB C  C   E   FF    GG        I             H  I
                         IAB C  D  FI        F         G               HH
0.80 --------------------ABCC-D--E-----F---------G------------------------------------------
                         IAB  C  D  LI  FF       G         I              H
                         IABC   C   HI   F       G         I             HH
                         A BC  D  EEI   F       GG         I            HH
                         AB C  D  C I  FF       G          I            H
                         IH C  D  F I   F       GG         I           H I
                         AB C  D  E I   F       G          I          IHH
                         AHCC  D  E I   F       G          I          HH
                         AHC  D  LL  I  F       G          I          H
                         ABC  D   L  I  F       IG         I          HI
0.75 --------------------ABC--D--E--+----------GG-------------HH-------------------------------
                         ABC  D   E  I  F       G          H I
                         AHC  D   E  IF        G          H  I
                         AB C  D   E  IF   GI        HH         I
                         AB  C  D  E  IF   GI        H I
                         AECCDD  E   IF   GI        H  I
                         ABC  D  F   IF   G         H
                         ABC  D   E   I   F       G          H I
                         ABC  D   E   I   F       G          H I
                         ABC  D   E   I   F       G          H
0.70 --------------------ABC--D--EE---I--------G--------------H-------------------------------
                         ABC  D  E   FF       G         I  H
                         AICDD  C   FI        GG        I  H
                         AAICD  E   FI        G         IH
                         ABICD  E   FI        G         HH
                         ABC  D  E   FI   GG        H
                         AHC  D  E   F I        HH
                         ABC  C  E   F I   G         HI
                         ABC  D  E   F I   G         HH
                         ABC  D  F   F I   G         H I
0.65 --------------------ABC--D--E---F---+--G---------HH--------------------------------------
                         ABCD   E  FF   I   G         H
                         ABCD   E  F  I  GG        HH I
                         ABCD  EE   F  I   G         H  I
                         A  CD  E   F  I   G         H
                         ABCCD  E   F  I   G         H
                         AHCIDD  E   F  I   GG        HH
                         ABCIDD  E   F  I   G         H
                         ABCIDD  E   F  I   G         H
                         ABCIDD  E   F  I   G         H
0.60 --------------------ABCDU-E--F----+G-----------H---------------------------------------
                         ABCD  E    F  IG        HH
                         ABCC  E  FF   IG        H
                         ABCD  E    F  IG        H
                         ABCC  E    F  GG        IH
                         ABCD  E    F   G         IH
                         AC  D  E   F    G         HH
                         AC  D E   F    G         H
                         AC  D E FF   GG        HI
                         ABC  DE  F   GI        HI
0.55 --------------------ABCD-E--F----G--------------HH------------------------------------
                         ABCDIE   F   GI        H I
                         ABCDIE   F   GG        H
                         ABCDIE   F   G I        HH
                         ABCDIE   F   G I        H
                         ABCDIE   F   G I        H
                         ABCDIE   F   G          H
                         ABCDEE   F   G          M
                         AB CE   F   G I        H
                         AC  DE  F   G I        H
0.50 --------------------ACDDE--F--G---+--H--------------------------------------------------
                         ACD E F    G   I   HH
                         ACC E F    G   I   H
                         AACD E F    G   I   H
                         ABCC E F    G   IH
                         ABCD F F  GG   IH
                         ABCDEI F    G   I  H
                         ABCDEIFF  G   IH
                         ABCDEIFF  G   IH            RESPONSE TIME,T (SECONDS)
                         A CDEI         I
0.45 ------------------------------------------------------------------------------------------------
        1       2       3       4       5       6       7       8       9       10       11       12
```

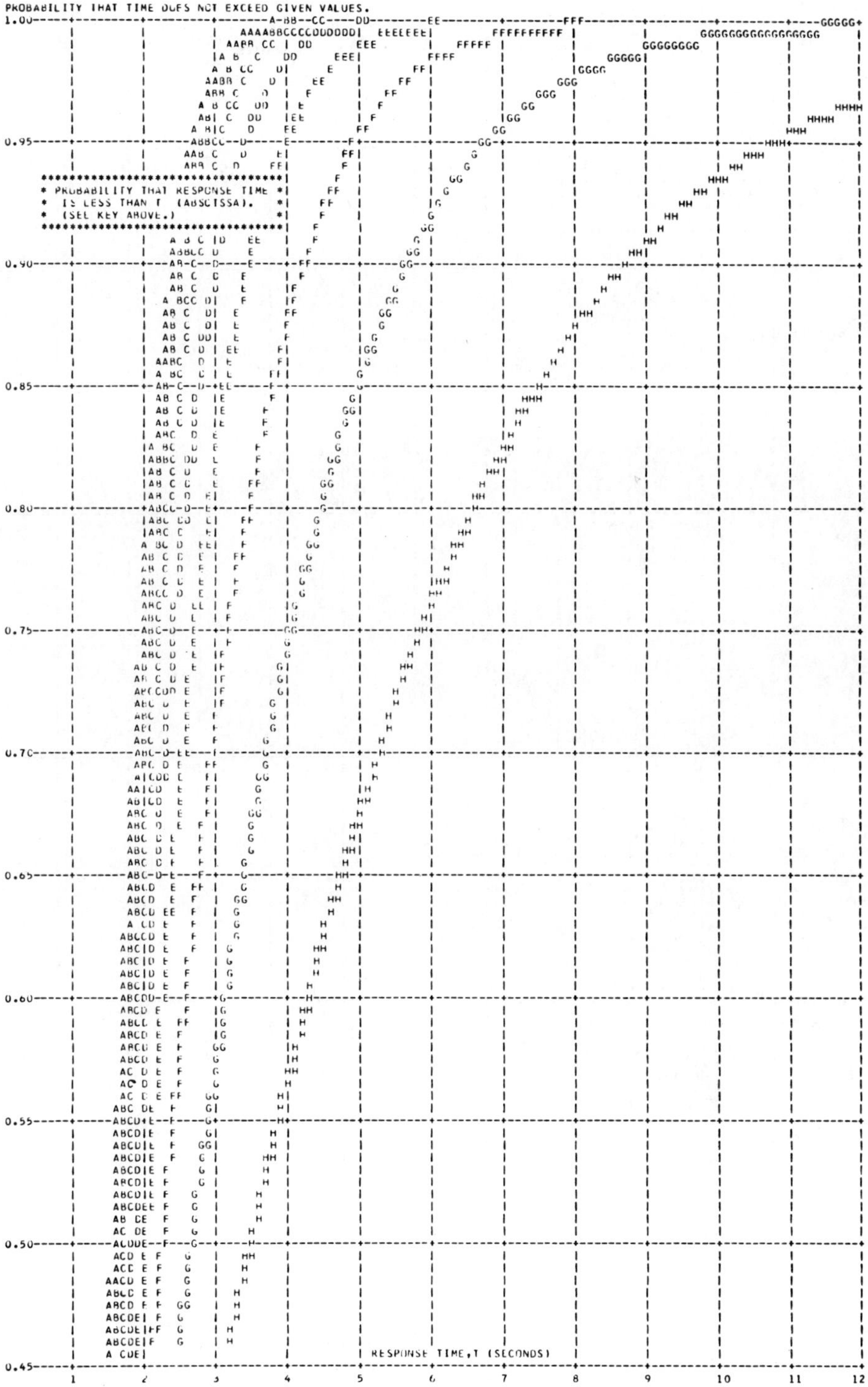

*Fig. 37.6.* The same line as in Fig. 37.5 but with 15 terminals attached.

THRCUGHPUT VALUES OF CURVES BELOW
HHH = 1.20 TRANSACTIONS PER SECUND
GGG = 1.05 TRANSACTIONS PER SECOND
FFF = 0.90 TRANSACTIONS PER SECOND
EEE = 0.75 TRANSACTIONS PER SECOND
DDD = 0.60 TRANSACTIONS PER SECOND
CCC = 0.45 TRANSACTIONS PER SECOND
BBB = 0.30 TRANSACTIONS PER SECOND
AAA = 0.15 TRANSACTIONS PER SECOND

*Fig. 37.7.* The same line as in Fig. 37.5 but with 20 terminals attached.

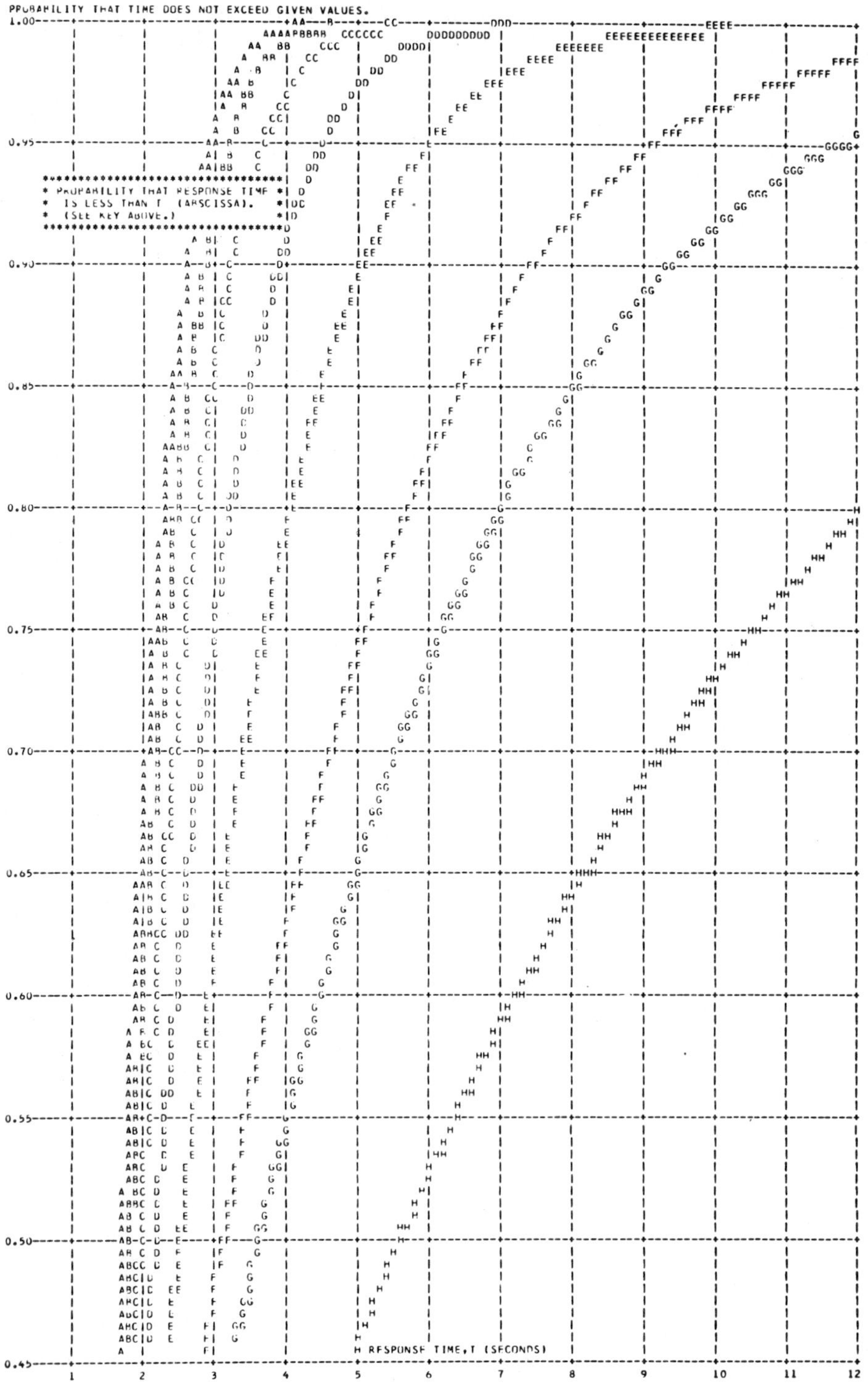

PROBABILITY THAT TIME DOES NOT EXCEED GIVEN VALUES.

```
1.00
                                    * PROBABILITY THAT RESPONSE TIME
                                    * IS LESS THAN T (ABSCISSA).
                                    * (SEE KEY ABOVE.)
0.95

0.90

0.85

0.80

0.75

0.70

0.65

0.60

0.55

0.50

                                    H RESPONSE TIME, T (SECONDS)
0.45
     1    2    3    4    5    6    7    8    9    10   11   12
```

630

THROUGHPUT VALUES OF CURVES BELOW
HHH = 1.20 TRANSACTIONS PER SECOND
GGG = 1.05 TRANSACTIONS PER SECOND
FFF = 0.90 TRANSACTIONS PER SECOND
EEE = 0.75 TRANSACTIONS PER SECOND
DDD = 0.60 TRANSACTIONS PER SECOND
CCC = 0.45 TRANSACTIONS PER SECOND
BBB = 0.30 TRANSACTIONS PER SECOND
AAA = 0.15 TRANSACTIONS PER SECOND

*Fig. 37.8.* The same line as in Fig. 37.5 but with 25 terminals attached.

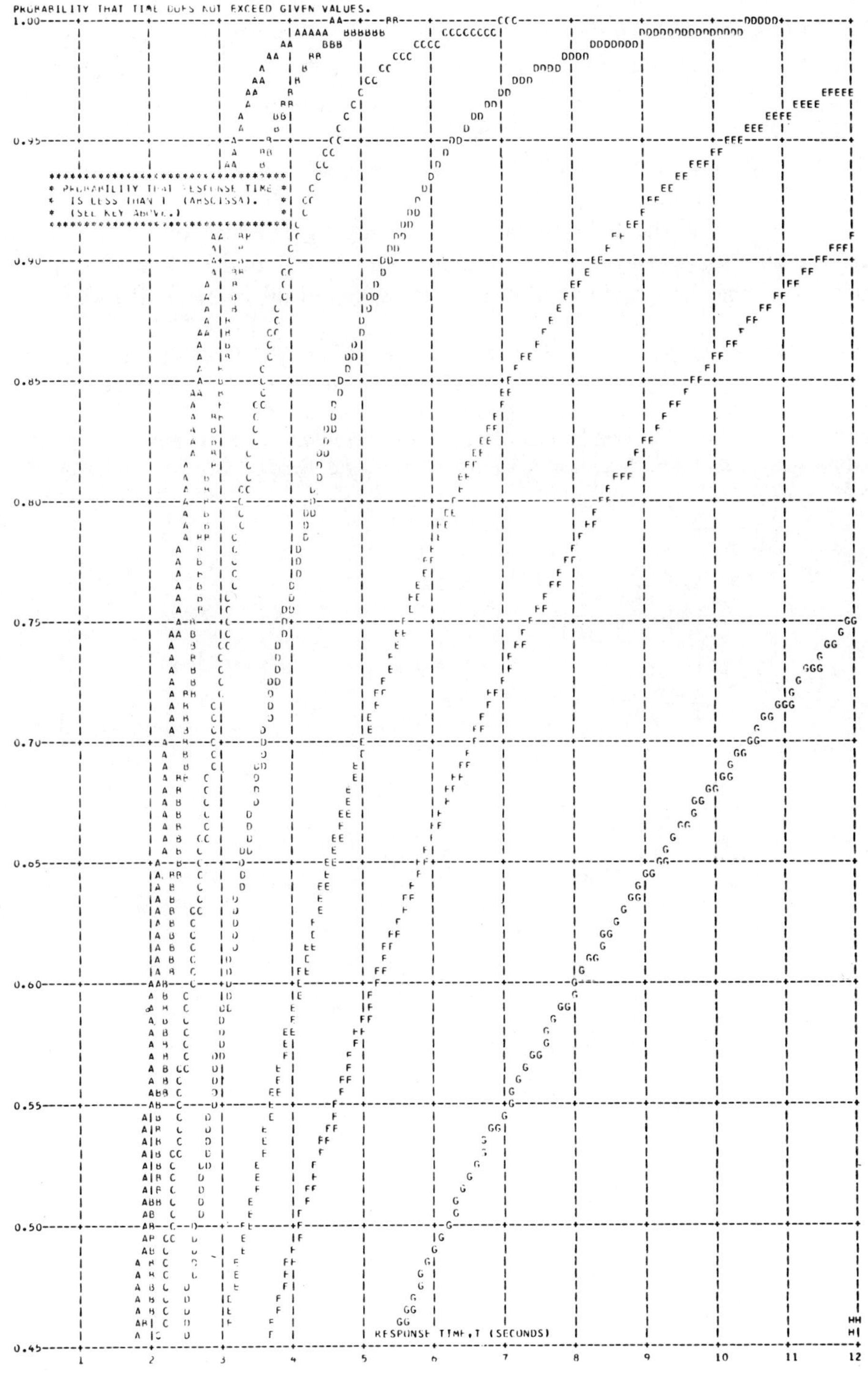

PROBABILITY THAT TIME DOES NOT EXCEED GIVEN VALUES.

```
PROBABILITY THAT TIME DOES NOT EXCEED GIVEN VALUES.
1.00                                        AA    BB              CCC                      DDDD
                              AAAAA  BBBBB      CCCCCCC              DDDDDDDDDDDDDD
                           AA    BBB      CCCC            DDDDDDD
                           A   B      CC            DDDD
                          AA  B     CC         DDD
                          AA  B    C        DD                                              EEEE
                          A   BB    C      DD                                          EEEE
                          A  BB   C       DD                                       EEE
0.95                      A   BB    CC      DD                                    FFF
                         AA   B    CC       D                                 FF
         * PROBABILITY THAT RESPONSE TIME   *  C                           EF
         * IS LESS THAN T (ABSCISSA).       *  CC                        EE
         * (SEE KEY ABOVE.)                 *  C      DD                F
                                               CC     DD             EF
                         AA  BB    C           DD                  FF                    FFF
                         A   B     C           DD                EF                    FFF
0.90                     A   BB    C       DD                  E              E         FF
                         A  B     CC      D                  FF                      FF
                         A  B     C       DD                F                      FF
                         A  B     C       D               E                      FF
                         AA  B    CC      D              E                     FF
                         A  B     C       D            F                    FF
                         A  B     C       DD         FF                   FF
                         A  B     C       D        F                   FF
0.85                     A  B     C       D        F                  FFF
                         AA  B    C       D       FF               F
                         A  B     C       DD       FF            F
                         A  B     C       DD       FF          FF
                         A  B     C       DD      EE         FF
                         A  B     C       DD      EE        FF
                         A  B     C       D        EE      FFF
                         A  B     CC      D        F      F
0.80                     A  B     C       DD       EE      FF
                         A  B     C       D        FF      FF
                         A  BB    C       D        F       F
                         A  B     C       D        FF      FF
                         A  B     C       D        F       F
                         A  B     C       D        E       FF
                         A  B     C       D        EE       F
                         A  B     C       DD       F        FF
0.75                     AA B     C       D        FF       F                              GG
                         A  B     CC      D        E        FF                          GG
                         A  B     C       D        E        FF                          G
                         A  B     C       D        F                                   GGG
                         A  B     C       DD       F                                   G
                         A  BB    C       D        FF                                IG
                         A  B     C       D        F                                GGG
                         A  B     C       D        E        F                      GG
                         A  B     C       D        E        FF                     G
0.70                     A  B     C       D        E                              GG
                         A  B     C       D        F        FF                   GG
                         A  BB    C       DD       E        FF                  IGG
                         A  B     C       D        E        FF                 GG
                         A  B     C       D        E        F                GG
                         A  B     C       D        EE       F               GG
                         A  B     C       D        E        FF             GG
                         A  B     CC      D        EE       F            GG
                         A  B     C       DD       E        FF          G
0.65                     A  BB    C       D        E        F          GG
                         A  B     C       D        FE       F          GI
                         A  B     C       D        F        FF         GG
                         A  B     CC      D        E        F          G
                         A  B     C       D        E        FF        GG
                         A  B     C       D        E        FF        G
                         A  B     C       D        EE       FF        GG
                         A  B     C       D        E        F        IG
0.60                     AAB     C       D        E        F        G
                         A  B     C       DD       E        F        GG
                         A  B     C       D        F        FF       G
                         A  B     C       D        EE       FF       G
                         A  B     C       DD       FF       F        GG
                         A  B     CC      D        E        F        G
                         A  B     CC      D        E        FF       G
                         A  BB    C       D        EE       F        IG
0.55                     A  B     C       D        F        F        G
                         A  B     C       D        E        FF      GG
                         A  B     C       D        FF       F
                         A  B    CC      D        F        F        G
                         A  B     C       D        E        F        G
                         A  B     C       D        E        F       G
                         A  B     C       D        F        FF      G
                         ABB    C       D        E        F        G
                         AB     C       D        E        F        G
0.50                     AB  CC    D        E        FF       F
                         AB  C     D        E        F        G
                         A  B  C       D        E        FF       GI
                         A  B  C       D        E        FF       G
                         A  B  C       D        E        FF       G
                         A  B  C       D        IE       F        G
                         A  B  C       DD       E        GG       
                         ABB  C       D        E        F        HH
                         A  C  D       E        F                 HI
0.45
         2        3        4        5        6        7        8        9       10       11       12
                                    RESPONSE TIME, T (SECONDS)
```

one with a message is $(M - 1)/2$, where $M$ is the number of terminals on the line (in this case 12). In model 1 the input queue is somewhat higher and there is no output queue. Because the input queue is higher, fewer terminals are polled before the one with a message. The line-scanning time therefore drops as the load increases as shown in Fig. 37.9. It does not drop in Figs. 37.10 to 37.13. Model 1, then, performs somewhat better because less time is consumed in unsuccessful polling.

As before, if the transmission speed was higher—and hence the transmission time low compared with the compute time—model 1 would lose the advantage it has here and would become the worst of the eight models.

**Note.**   *In these calculations we did not change the values of* $t_0$, $t_1$, *and* $t_2$. *In reality they would be likely to be different for half-duplex and full-duplex lines. Full-duplex operation may, for example, eliminate the delay involved in line turnaround time, although it is necessary to re-establish synchronization as the transmission switches from one terminal and modem to another. Such factors must be built individually into the values of* $t_0$, $t_1$ *and* $t_2$.

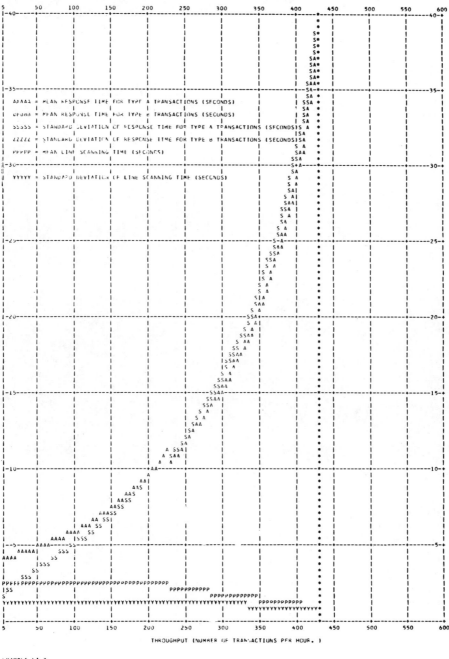

THROUGHPUT (NUMBER OF TRANSACTIONS PER HOUR. )

EXAMPLE F1.2.

LINE SPEED 14.8 CHARACTERS PER SECOND

| | MEAN | STANDARD DEVIATION |
|---|---|---|
| TOTAL TRANSMISSION TIME FOR INPUT MESSAGE TYPE A (SECS) | 0.676 | 0.478 |
| TOTAL TRANSMISSION TIME FOR INPUT MESSAGE TYPE B (SECS) | 0.676 | 0.478 |
| TOTAL TRANSMISSION TIME FOR OUTPUT MESSAGE TYPE A (SECS) | 0.676 | 0.478 |
| TOTAL TRANSMISSION TIME FOR OUTPUT MESSAGE TYPE B (SECS) | 6.757 | 4.778 |
| TOTAL TIME TRANSACTION SPENDS IN COMPUTER SYSTEM (SECS) | 1.000 | 0.500 |

MODEL 1.   A HALF DUPLEX LINE HELD BY THE COMPUTER BETWEEN RECEIPT OF INPUT MESSAGE AND TRANSMISSION OF THE RESPONSE.

*Fig. 37.9.* Model 1. This and the following seven sets of curves show the behavior of the eight models on a polled line operating at 14.8 characters per second, with 12 terminals.

633

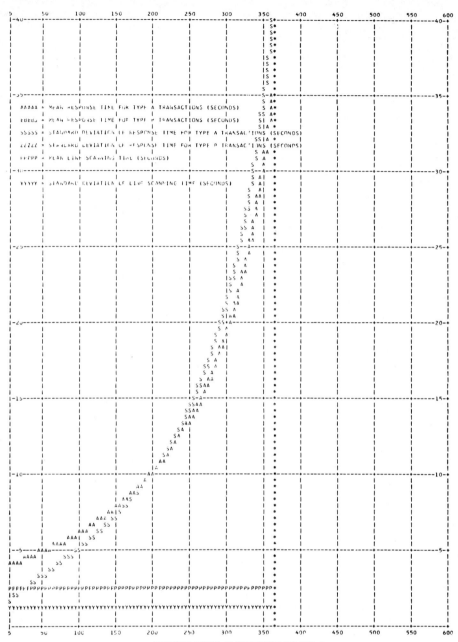

| | MEAN | STANDARD DEVIATION |
|---|---|---|
| TOTAL TRANSMISSION TIME FOR INPUT MESSAGE TYPE A (SECS) | 0.676 | 0.478 |
| TOTAL TRANSMISSION TIME FOR INPUT MESSAGE TYPE B (SECS) | 0.676 | 0.478 |
| TOTAL TRANSMISSION TIME FOR OUTPUT MESSAGE TYPE A (SECS) | 0.676 | 0.478 |
| TOTAL TRANSMISSION TIME FOR OUTPUT MESSAGE TYPE B (SECS) | 6.757 | 4.778 |
| TOTAL TIME TRANSACTION SPENDS IN COMPUTER SYSTEM (SECS) | 1.000 | 0.500 |

•

MODEL 2. A HALF DUPLEX LINE, NOT HELD AFTER INPUT TRANSMISSION. OUTPUT MESSAGES HAVE PRIORITY OVER INPUT.

*Fig. 37.10.* Model 2. Half-duplex line. Output has priority over input.

634

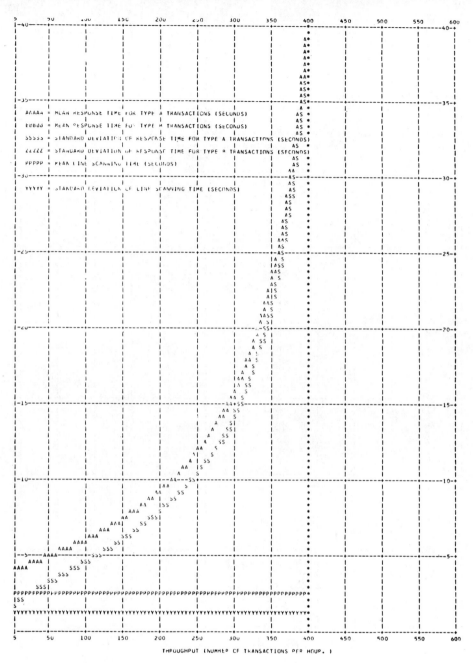

EXAMPLE F1.2.

LINE SPEED 14.8 CHARACTERS PER SECOND

|  | MEAN | STANDARD DEVIATION |
|---|---|---|
| TOTAL TRANSMISSION TIME FOR INPUT MESSAGE TYPE A (SECS) | 0.676 | 0.478 |
| TOTAL TRANSMISSION TIME FOR INPUT MESSAGE TYPE B (SECS) | 0.676 | 0.478 |
| TOTAL TRANSMISSION TIME FOR OUTPUT MESSAGE TYPE A (SECS) | 0.676 | 0.478 |
| TOTAL TRANSMISSION TIME FOR OUTPUT MESSAGE TYPE B (SECS) | 6.757 | 4.778 |
| TOTAL TIME TRANSACTION SPENDS IN COMPUTER SYSTEM (SECS) | 1.000 | 0.500 |

MODEL 3. A HALF DUPLEX LINE, NOT HELD AFTER INPUT TRANSMISSION.
INPUT MESSAGES HAVE PRIORITY OVER OUTPUT.

*Fig. 37.11.* Model 3. Half-duplex line. Input has priority over output. This is somewhat better than model 2 because the input message length is shorter.

635

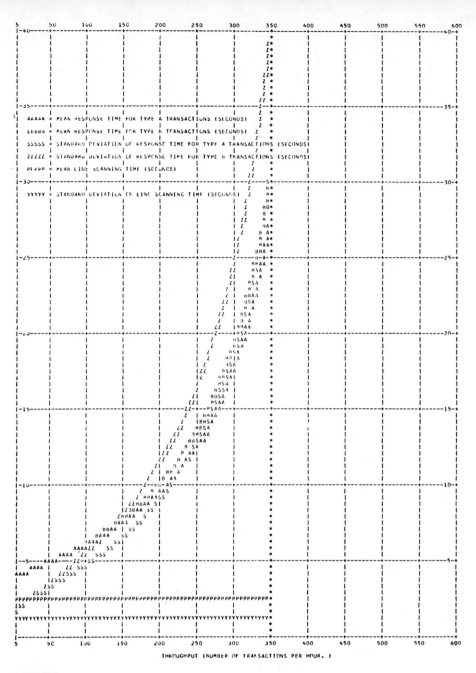

THROUGHPUT (NUMBER OF TRANSACTIONS PER HOUR.)

EXAMPLE F1.2.

LINE SPEED 14.8 CHARACTERS PER SECOND

| | MEAN | STANDARD DEVIATION |
|---|---|---|
| TOTAL TRANSMISSION TIME FOR INPUT MESSAGE TYPE A (SECS) | 0.676 | 0.478 |
| TOTAL TRANSMISSION TIME FOR INPUT MESSAGE TYPE B (SECS) | 0.676 | 0.478 |
| TOTAL TRANSMISSION TIME FOR OUTPUT MESSAGE TYPE A (SECS) | 0.676 | 0.478 |
| TOTAL TRANSMISSION TIME FOR OUTPUT MESSAGE TYPE B (SECS) | 6.757 | 4.778 |
| TOTAL TIME TRANSACTION SPENDS IN COMPUTER SYSTEM (SECS) | 1.000 | 0.500 |

MODEL 4.    A HALF DUPLEX LINE, NOT HELD AFTER INPUT TRANSMISSION.
OUTPUT MESSAGES HAVE PRIORITY OVER INPUT.
TYPE A OUTPUT MESSAGES HAVE PRIORITY OVER TYPE B OUTPUT.

*Fig. 37.12.* Model 4. Half-duplex line. Output messages type A have priority over output type B.

636

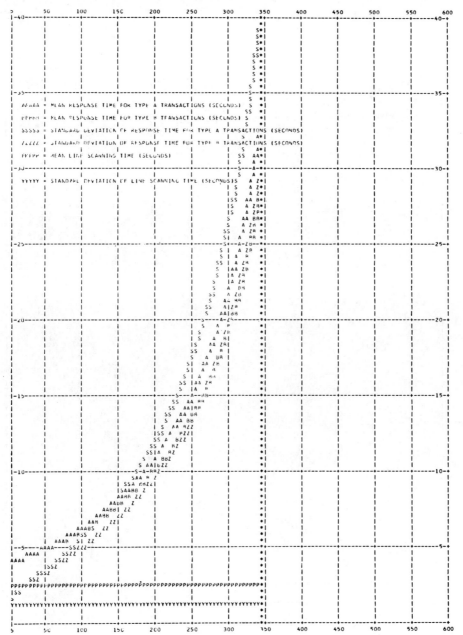

THROUGHPUT (NUMBER OF TRANSACTIONS PER HOUR.)

EXAMPLE F1.2.

LINE SPEED 14.8 CHARACTERS PER SECOND

|  | MEAN | STANDARD DEVIATION |
|---|---|---|
| TOTAL TRANSMISSION TIME FOR INPUT MESSAGE TYPE A (SECS) | 0.676 | 0.478 |
| TOTAL TRANSMISSION TIME FOR INPUT MESSAGE TYPE B (SECS) | 0.676 | 0.478 |
| TOTAL TRANSMISSION TIME FOR OUTPUT MESSAGE TYPE A (SECS) | 0.676 | 0.478 |
| TOTAL TRANSMISSION TIME FOR OUTPUT MESSAGE TYPE B (SECS) | 6.757 | 4.778 |
| TOTAL TIME TRANSACTION SPENDS IN COMPUTER SYSTEM (SECS) | 1.000 | 0.500 |

MODEL 5. A HALF DUPLEX LINE, NOT HELD AFTER INPUT TRANSMISSION.
OUTPUT MESSAGES HAVE PRIORITY OVER INPUT.
TYPE B OUTPUT MESSAGES HAVE PRIORITY OVER TYPE A OUTPUT.

*Fig. 37.13.* Model 5. Half-duplex line. Input messages type B have priority over input messages type A. The message priority scheme is not worth using. Compare this, however, with models 6 and 7 for a full-duplex line.

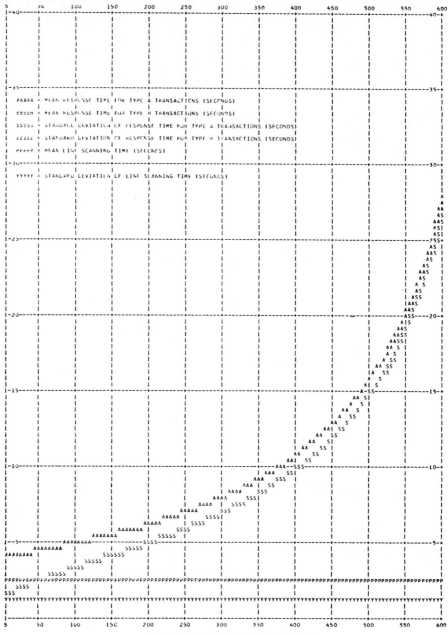

EXAMPLE FT.2.

LINE SPEED 14.8 CHARACTERS PER SECUND

|  | MEAN | STANDARD DEVIATION |
|---|---|---|
| TOTAL TRANSMISSICN TIME FOR INPUT MESSAGE TYPE A (SECS) | 0.676 | 0.478 |
| TOTAL TRANSMISSION TIME FOR INPUT MESSAGE TYPE B (SECS) | 0.676 | 0.478 |
| TOTAL TRANSMISSION TIME FCF OUTPUT MESSAGE TYPE A (SECS) | 0.676 | 0.478 |
| TOTAL TRANSMISSION TIME FOR OUTPUT MESSAGE TYPE B (SECS) | 5.757 | 4.778 |
| TOTAL TIME TRANSACTION SPENDS IN COMPUTER SYSTEM (SECS) | 1.000 | 0.500 |

MODEL 6.    A FULL DUPLEX LINE WITH DATA BEING TRANSMITTED IN BOTH DIRECTIONS AT ONCE.

*Fig. 37.14.* Model 6. A full-duplex line. No priorities. Note: The full-duplex line models assume that the terminals can take full advantage of the line, transmitting data in both directions simultaneously.

638

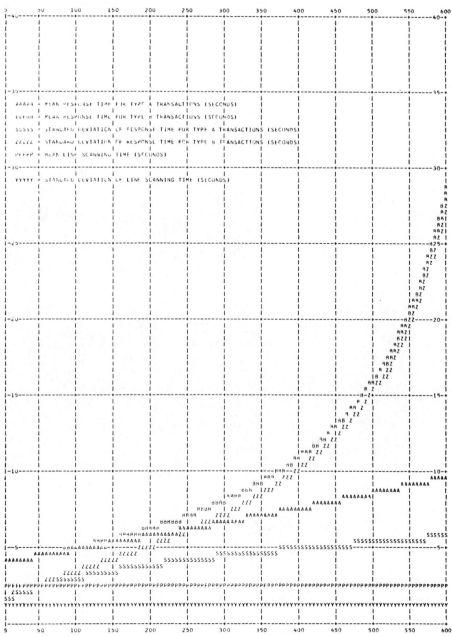

THROUGHPUT (NUMBER OF TRANSACTIONS PER HOUR. )

EXAMPLE F1.2.

LINE SPEED 14.8 CHARACTERS PER SECOND

|  | MEAN | STANDARD DEVIATION |
|---|---|---|
| TOTAL TRANSMISSION TIME FOR INPUT MESSAGE TYPE A (SECS) | 0.676 | 0.478 |
| TOTAL TRANSMISSION TIME FOR INPUT MESSAGE TYPE B (SECS) | 0.676 | 0.478 |
| TOTAL TRANSMISSION TIME FOR OUTPUT MESSAGE TYPE A (SECS) | 0.676 | 0.478 |
| TOTAL TRANSMISSION TIME FOR OUTPUT MESSAGE TYPE B (SECS) | 6.757 | 4.778 |
| TOTAL TIME TRANSACTION SPENDS IN COMPUTER SYSTEM (SECS) | 1.000 | 0.500 |

MODEL 7. A FULL DUPLEX LINE WITH DATA BEING TRANSMITTED IN BOTH DIRECTIONS AT ONCE.
TYPE A OUTPUT MESSAGES HAVE PRIORITY OVER TYPE B OUTPUT.

*Fig. 37.15.* Model 7. A full-duplex line. Output type A has priority over output type B. Type A transactions benefit without substantially affecting type B.

639

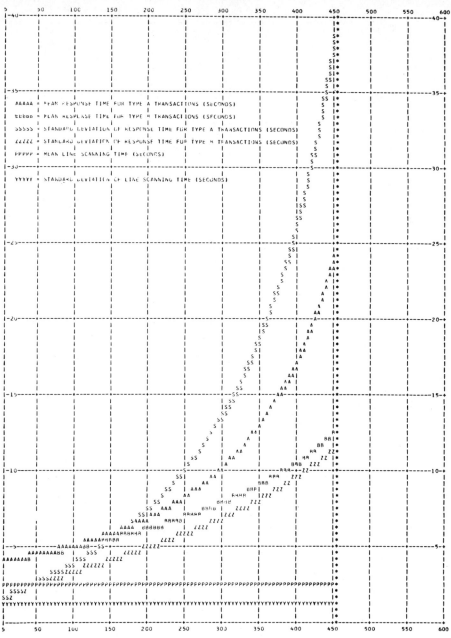

THROUGHPUT (NUMBER OF TRANSACTIONS PER HOUR.)

EXAMPLE F1.2.

LINE SPEED 14.8 CHARACTERS PER SECOND

| | MEAN | STANDARD DEVIATION |
|---|---|---|
| TOTAL TRANSMISSION TIME FOR INPUT MESSAGE TYPE A (SECS) | 0.676 | 0.478 |
| TOTAL TRANSMISSION TIME FOR INPUT MESSAGE TYPE B (SECS) | 0.676 | 0.478 |
| TOTAL TRANSMISSION TIME FOR OUTPUT MESSAGE TYPE A (SECS) | 0.676 | 0.478 |
| TOTAL TRANSMISSION TIME FOR OUTPUT MESSAGE TYPE B (SECS) | 6.757 | 4.778 |
| TOTAL TIME TRANSACTION SPENDS IN COMPUTER SYSTEM (SECS) | 1.000 | 0.500 |

MODEL 8.    A FULL DUPLEX LINE WITH DATA BEING TRANSMITTED IN BOTH DIRECTIONS AT ONCE.
TYPE B OUTPUT MESSAGES HAVE PRIORITY OVER TYPE A OUTPUT.

*Fig. 37.16.* Model 8. Full-duplex line. Type B output messages have priority over type A. This is disadvantageous because type B output messages are substantially longer than type A.

# 38

## SIMULATION OF
## COMMUNICATION LINES

One of the most powerful tools that can be used in estimating the requirements of a system is simulation.

A program is written on an existing computer to act as a model of the system in question. It behaves in some aspects like the system but is vastly simplified. A few program steps may represent, for example, transactions entering a buffer area and being allocated a core block; others represent file channels, file seek mechanisms, characters flowing on a communication line, or customers walking into a bank. When the model is built, input will be fed to it for a period of time representing the volumes and types of traffic that the actual operational system will have to deal with. The simulation program then prints out certain statistics about the behavior of the model, such as what queues develop, what response times are obtained, and how heavily the various critical factors are loaded.

A model may be built in this way of the entire system or of parts of the system. There may be a model of the communications network alone, of the file channels, the read/write mechanism, and so on. The model will specify the speed or size of the various elements, the logical interaction between the units, and the time transactions spend tying up various facilities—for example, program times and seek times. The input will fluctuate in the same way as the input to the actual operational system; hence queue lengths and response times will vary from moment to moment. The model will produce statistics on how they vary, show what proportion of transactions are delayed, by what amount, and so forth.

Typical of the output of a simulator program will be:

1. The maximum and average queue sizes wherever queues occur.
2. A histogram of the transit or response times between selected points in the system.
3. The facility utilization or extent to which various elements of the system are loaded.
4. The storage requirements for buffering or queuing.
5. The maximum throughput of the model.

The models, once built, can be adjusted and experimented with easily and endlessly. Different volumes and perhaps types of throughput can be fed to a model to see how it behaves. The effects of changes can be easily investigated. Extra communication lines can be added, storage sizes changed, channels speeded up, and programming mechanisms modified. The models can form a tool for deciding between alternative modes of operation. They may be used to settle arguments as to the merits of different programming techniques or file configurations. As the various design factors of the system come more sharply into focus, the models can be refined. More accurate program estimates become available, and the models present an increasingly accurate representation of the system.

Simulation is thus a valuable technique for monitoring and assisting the *implementation* of a system. As programming work proceeds and the network design is refined, the effects on the system of any changes can be investigated by simulation.

At the *survey* stage, however, it is often difficult to construct a model of the entire system because of time pressures and manpower shortages. Programming such a model with sufficient detail can take a long time. Furthermore, in the early stages the input may not be sufficiently good for this elaborate technique.

## SIMULATION OF COMMUNICATION LINES

When attempting to do mathematical calculations of system behavior, there may be certain areas in which we feel that a mathematical model is too difficult to construct or to approximate in its representation of the system. As pointed out in the last few chapters, a model based on queuing theory has certain assumptions buried in the mathematics. These assumptions may be accurate representations of reality; they may be approximations that are acceptably close; or they may be a convenience that makes the mathematics possible but that are likely to give results deviating seriously from actual system behavior. In the last case, we may replace the mathematics by simulation, either to investigate the behavior of that part of the mathematical model or to replace it. At the survey stage we may simulate not the entire system but one or more aspects of it that enable us to perform the overall design more accurately. We may wish to know, for example, the effect of sifting small groups of file transactions into an optimum sequence before "seeking" them in a direct-access file unit. This question is difficult to answer mathematically; therefore we simulate that aspect of the design. The simulation, in this case, is a relatively short and simple one. The remainder of the design may be done by mathematical calculation. Simulation at this stage is thus used only to bridge a gap in the calculations where our answers would otherwise have been inaccurate. We may decide to use simulation in a similar way in communication network design.

In Chapters 36 and 37 we used queuing theory to determine the response times for different line configurations or, alternatively, to determine what line loadings could be tolerated with given response criteria. If a contention form of line control is used, the results are accurate. If polling is utilized, the accuracy is less good but the equations give a useful approximation, especially when the polling time is small compared to the message transmission time. When the polling represents a significant proportion of the time, the queuing model becomes less accurate. The attempt to produce a better mathematical model leads to complications, and a level of complexity is reached at which a simple simulation model begins to appear the *easiest* way of finding permissible line loadings.

Our overall design may therefore be a patchwork of mathematical calculations and results from simulation runs. We will use simulation here to examine polled lines. The results will then plug into an algorithm in subsequent chapters for laying out a minimum-cost network connecting many cities.

**TYPES OF SIMULATOR PROGRAM**
Three levels of simulator program exist. First, a complete simulator program for the type of equipment in question may be available. By compiling it with appropriate parameter and control cards, the desired model is produced without any program writing. The traffic pattern under consideration is fed to it, and it will produce the required statistics.

Some computer manufacturers produce programs of this type for parts of their equipment. A number of simulators have been written, for example, for examining the behavior of communication lines, certain types of file systems, and software packages. Simulators have been written for certain specific applications—for example, airline reservations.

If such a complete simulator exists for the type of data transmission we are interested in, it can be used with little effort to produce the necessary design figures. Frequently, however, when such a simulator is available, it still leaves unanswered questions. It can simulate, perhaps, a certain specific type of line organization, but the user wants to know what would happen with a different organization. Usually there are many variations on a theme in communication-based systems design. What would be the effect if we gave type 1 transactions priority over type 2? What is the effect of holding the line during the processing of the transaction? What improvement do full-duplex lines give? What about multiplexers, concentrators . . .? What happens if we mix two types of terminals on the same line . . . or on the same concentrator? In order to investigate such questions, we may want to write our own simulation.

In addition, the internal workings of today's design packages are often unclear. Sometimes we are not quite sure which question the program has answered.

Second, at the other extreme, the model can be programmed in a normal computer language such as PL/I or FORTRAN. We will give an example later in the chapter. This type of simulator program is a useful way to answer limited design questions like "Do we sift file transactions before we seek them, and how many should we sift?" Building a large and complex model this way, however, could be tedious, and it would be preferable to use a language designed for simulation.

Finally, a variety of general-purpose simulation languages are available. These are languages that permit the system to be described with relative ease and from which the model may be compiled. They can be highly flexible and can simulate almost any system mechanism. Adjustments to the logic of the flow of work through the system can be examined easily. A model written in such a language can be steadily increased in complexity or detail until it represents the behavior of a system accurately.

Use of a simulation language is the most common method of tackling simulations today. Several such languages are available. One commonly used language is IBM's General Purpose Systems Simulator, GPSS (described later). Other simulation languages are referenced at the end of this chapter, including SIMSCRIPT, SIMPAC, SIMULA, CSL, plus several others that are less widely used.

## SIMULATION BY HAND

It is possible to carry out simulation without the use of a computer. We could in fact do it by using an adding machine. We would write down the various events that can occur, and then time them, making sure that we do not generate any conflicts, such as two transactions using a facility at the same time. Figure 38.1 shows the result of such an exercise with a half-duplex line on which 12 terminals are polled.

```
POLL TERMINAL    1.                              0.50
POLL TERMINAL    2.                              2.00
POLL TERMINAL    3.                              3.50
POLL TERMINAL    4.                              5.00
POLL TERMINAL    5.                              6.50
POLL TERMINAL    6.                              8.00
POLL TERMINAL    7.                              9.50
POLL TERMINAL    8.                             11.00
POLL TERMINAL    9.                             12.50
POLL TERMINAL   10.                             14.00
POLL TERMINAL   11.                             15.50
POLL TERMINAL   12.                             17.00
POLL TERMINAL    1.                             18.50
POLL TERMINAL    2.                             20.00
    INPUT MESSAGE    1.    TYPE A               22.70
POLL TERMINAL    3.                             24.20
    INPUT MESSAGE    2.    TYPE B               27.85
    OUTPUT MESSAGE         TYPE A               27.85
    OUTPUT MESSAGE         TYPE B               30.55
POLL TERMINAL    4.                             38.55
POLL TERMINAL    5.                             40.05
POLL TERMINAL    6.                             41.55
POLL TERMINAL    7.                             43.05
POLL TERMINAL    8.                             44.55
POLL TERMINAL    9.                             46.05
POLL TERMINAL   10.                             47.55
POLL TERMINAL   11.                             49.05
    INPUT MESSAGE    3.    TYPE A               49.93
POLL TERMINAL   12.                             51.43
    OUTPUT MESSAGE         TYPE A               51.43
POLL TERMINAL    1.                             54.16
POLL TERMINAL    2.                             55.66
POLL TERMINAL    3.                             57.16
    INPUT MESSAGE    4.    TYPE B               63.45
POLL TERMINAL    4.                             64.95
    OUTPUT MESSAGE         TYPE B               64.95
POLL TERMINAL    5.                             70.04
POLL TERMINAL    6.                             71.54
POLL TERMINAL    7.                             73.04
POLL TERMINAL    8.                             74.54
POLL TERMINAL    9.                             76.04
POLL TERMINAL   10.                             77.54
    INPUT MESSAGE    5.    TYPE B               84.64
POLL TERMINAL   11.                             86.14
    OUTPUT MESSAGE         TYPE B               86.14
POLL TERMINAL   12.                             91.64
POLL TERMINAL    1.                             93.14
    INPUT MESSAGE    6.    TYPE A               93.68

POLL TERMINAL    2.                             95.18
    OUTPUT MESSAGE         TYPE A               95.18
POLL TERMINAL    3.                             99.05
POLL TERMINAL    4.                            100.55
    INPUT MESSAGE    7.    TYPE A              101.91
POLL TERMINAL    5.                            103.41
    OUTPUT MESSAGE         TYPE A              103.41
```

*Figure 38.1*

```
POLL  TERMINAL   6.                              105.73
POLL  TERMINAL   7.                              107.23
POLL  TERMINAL   8.                              108.73
POLL  TERMINAL   9.                              110.23
POLL  TERMINAL  10.                              111.73
     INPUT MESSAGE     8.    TYPE B              118.22
POLL  TERMINAL  11.                              119.72
     OUTPUT MESSAGE          TYPE B              119.72
POLL  TERMINAL  12.                              126.77
POLL  TERMINAL   1.                              128.27
POLL  TERMINAL   2.                              129.77
POLL  TERMINAL   3.                              131.27
POLL  TERMINAL   4.                              132.77
POLL  TERMINAL   5.                              134.27
POLL  TERMINAL   6.                              135.77
POLL  TERMINAL   7.                              137.27
POLL  TERMINAL   8.                              138.77
POLL  TERMINAL   9.                              140.27
POLL  TERMINAL  10.                              141.77
     INPUT MESSAGE     9.    TYPE A              142.92
POLL  TERMINAL  11.                              144.42
     OUTPUT MESSAGE          TYPE A              144.42
POLL  TERMINAL  12.                              150.46
POLL  TERMINAL   1.                              151.96
POLL  TERMINAL   2.                              153.46
POLL  TERMINAL   3.                              154.96
POLL  TERMINAL   4.                              156.46
POLL  TERMINAL   5.                              157.96
POLL  TERMINAL   6.                              159.46
POLL  TERMINAL   7.                              160.96
     INPUT MESSAGE    10.    TYPE B              168.80
POLL  TERMINAL   8.                              170.30
     INPUT MESSAGE    11.    TYPE B              174.01
     OUTPUT MESSAGE          TYPE B              174.01
     OUTPUT MESSAGE          TYPE B              182.05
POLL  TERMINAL   9.                              184.85
POLL  TERMINAL  10.                              186.35
POLL  TERMINAL  11.                              187.85
     INPUT MESSAGE    12.    TYPE B              193.53
POLL  TERMINAL  12.                              195.03
     OUTPUT MESSAGE          TYPE B              195.03
POLL  TERMINAL   1.                              200.32
POLL  TERMINAL   2.                              201.82
     INPUT MESSAGE    13.    TYPE A              203.58
POLL  TERMINAL   3.                              205.08
     OUTPUT MESSAGE          TYPE A              205.08
POLL  TERMINAL   4.                              210.45
POLL  TERMINAL   5.                              211.95
POLL  TERMINAL   6.                              213.45
POLL  TERMINAL   7.                              214.95
POLL  TERMINAL   8.                              216.45
     INPUT MESSAGE    14.    TYPE B              222.80
POLL  TERMINAL   9.                              224.30
```

*Figure 38.1 continued*

Unfortunately, we would have to time a large number of events before our results became reasonably accurate. As we shall see, running as many as 10,000 transactions through such a simulation model gives results with a good deal of scatter, particularly when the queues are large. Furthermore, the line has to be polled many times between each transaction. Consequently, if we used an adding machine, we would have to sit at it for a long time before valid results were obtained.

We could, however, write a program that does all the additions—and that (as the reader might have suspected) is how the listing in Fig. 38.1 was obtained. Figure 38.2 gives the block diagram for such a program.

**SIMULATION WITHOUT A SPECIALIZED LANGUAGE**    Figure 38.3 gives a PL/I listing of a program that carries out the simulation shown in Fig. 38.2. (On pp. 654-655 is the equivalent FORTRAN listing.) The instruction tables correspond to the block numbers of Fig. 38.2.

In this example a field labeled CLOCK is used to keep the time of everything that is happening on the line. The program cycles repetitively around the loop in Fig. 38.2, adding to the value of CLOCK on the basis of what events take place. Before the main simulation loop begins, a stream of transactions is created, giving the time and terminal at which each originates. As the value of CLOCK is advanced throughout the simulation, this list will be inspected each time a poll is made to see whether a transaction is ready at the terminal in question. This step takes place in block S10 of Fig. 38.2.

When a response to a transaction is transmitted from the computer, the time at which that transaction originated is subtracted from the value of CLOCK, and this figure gives the response time. This step is done in blocks S2 and S5. The response times for several thousand transactions are collected and can then be statistically analyzed as desired.

**SIMULATION OF A HALF-DUPLEX LINE**    Let us discuss the use of this program for inspecting the behavior of a polled half-duplex line organized like model 4 in the last chapter.

**Example 38.1. Simulation of a Half-Duplex Line With Two Output Priorities.**
A half-duplex line transmits at 14.8 characters per second. Two types of transactions, A and B, are sent from this terminal to the computer, and each causes a response to be sent back to the terminal. Output traffic on the line is given priority over input. Type A output messages are given priority over type B. Because of the polling scheme used,

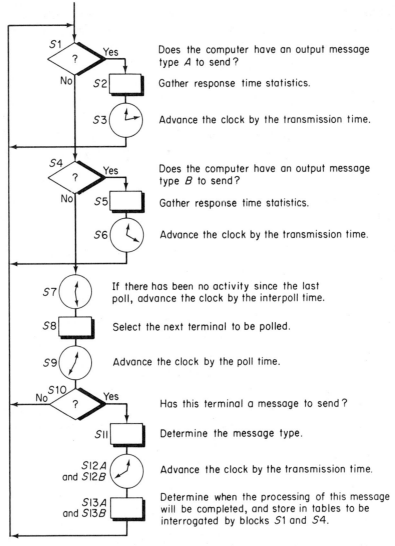

*Fig. 38.2.* Simulation of a half-duplex communication line with two message priorities, without the use of a simulation language. This is easily programmed in a language like FORTRAN or PL/I.

there is no way to give type A messages priority on input. We thus have three priority levels for data messages on the line:

> Top Priority: output type A
> Priority 2:    output type B
> Priority 3:    input type A or B

The lengths of the messages are, again, those given in Tables 30.3 and 30.4. The time taken to poll the line is 0.33 second (for a successful or an unsuccessful poll). There is no wait between successive unsuccessful polls.

**MESSAGE LENGTHS**

The lengths of the messages transmitted are given to the program in the form of a cumulative distribution as follows:

CIA(K) is the fraction of input messages, type A, with $K$ characters or less.

COA(K) is the fraction of output messages, type A, with $K$ characters or less.

CIB(K) is the fraction of input messages, type B, with $K$ characters or less.

COB(K) is the fraction of output messages, type B, with $K$ characters or less.

In PL/I:

```
DCL CIA(6:60);DCL COA(6:200);DCL CIB(6:60 ),COB(6:200);
CIA(6)=.390/5;
DO K=7   TO 10;CIA(K)=CIA(K-1)+.390/5;  END;
DO K=11  TO 15;CIA(K)=CIA(K-1)+.214/5;  END;
DO K=16  TO 20;CIA(K)=CIA(K-1)+.186/5;  END;
DO K=21  TO 40;CIA(K)=CIA(K-1)+.140/20;END;
DO K=41  TO 60;CIA(K)=CIA(K-1)+.070/20;END;
COA(6)=.021/15;
DO K=7   TO 20;COA(K)=COA(K-1)+.021/15;END;
DO K=21  TO 40;COA(K)=COA(K-1)+.029/20;END;
DO K=41  TO 60;COA(K)=COA(K-1)+.038/20;END;
DO K=61  TO 80;COA(K)=COA(K-1)+.058/20;END;
DO K=81  TO 100;COA(K)=COA(K-1)+.082/20;END;
DO K=101 TO 120;COA(K)=COA(K-1)+.154/20;END;
DO K=121 TO 140;COA(K)=COA(K-1)+.298/20;END;
DO K=141 TO 160;COA(K)=COA(K-1)+.204/20;END;
DO K=161 TO 180;COA(K)=COA(K-1)+.112/20;END;
DO K=181 TO 200;COA(K)=COA(K-1)+.004/20;END;
CIB(6)=.473/5;
DO K=7   TO 10  ;CIB(K)=CIB(K-1)+.473/5 ;END;
DO K=11  TO 15  ;CIB(K)=CIB(K-1)+.283/5 ;END;
DO K=16  TO 20  ;CIB(K)=CIB(K-1)+.118/5 ;END;
DO K=21  TO 40  ;CIB(K)=CIB(K-1)+.099/20;END;
DO K=41  TO 60  ;CIB(K)=CIB(K-1)+.027/20;END;
COB(6)=.055/15;
DO K=7   TO 20  ;COB(K)=COB(K-1)+.055/15;END;
DO K=21  TO 40  ;COB(K)=COB(K-1)+.147/20;END;
DO K=41  TO 60  ;COB(K)=COB(K-1)+.193/20;END;
DO K=61  TO 80  ;COB(K)=COB(K-1)+.278/20;END;
DO K=81  TO 100 ;COB(K)=COB(K-1)+.182/20;END;
```

```
DC K=101 TO 120;COB(K)=COB(K-1)+.072/20;END;
DO K=121 TO 140;COB(K)=COB(K-1)+.034/20;END;
DO K=141 TO 160;COB(K)=COB(K-1)+.021/20;END;
DO K=161 TO 180;COB(K)=COB(K-1)+.011/20;END;
DC K=181 TO 200;COB(K)=COB(K-1)+.007/20;END;
PUT DATA (CIA(60),CCA(200),CIB(60 ),COB(200))
```

## In Fortran:

```
      IMPLICIT REAL*8 (A-H, O-Z)
      DIMENSION CIA(60),COA(200),CIB(60),COB(200)
      L1=5
      CONA=.390/5.0
      CONB=.473/5.0
      CIA(6)=CONA
      CIB(6)=CONB
      DO 10 K= 7, 10
      CIA(K)=CIA(K-1)+CONA
   10 CIB(K)=CIB(K-1)+CONB
      CONA=.214/5.0
      CONB=.285/5.0
      DC 20 K= 11, 15
      CIA(K)=CIA(K-1)+CONA
   20 CIB(K)=CIB(K-1)+CONB
      CONA=.186/5.0
      CONB=.118/5.0
      DC 30 K=16, 20
      CIA(K)=CIA(K-1)+CONA
   30 CIB(K)=CIB(K-1)+CONB
      CONA=.140/20.0
      CONB=.099/20.0
      DO 40 K= 21, 40
      CIA(K)=CIA(K-1)+CONA
   40 CIB(K)=CIB(K-1)+CONB
      CONA=.070/20.0
      CONB=.027/20.0
      DO 50 K= 41, 60
      CIA(K)=CIA(K-1)+CONA
   50 CIB(K)=CIB(K-1)+CONB

      CONA=.021/15.0
      CONB=.055/15.0
      COA(6)=CONA
      COB(6)=CONB
      DO 60 K= 7, 20
      COA(K)=CCA(K-1)+CONA
   60 COB(K)=COB(K-1)+CONB
      CONA=.029/20.0
      CONB=.147/20.0
      DO 70 K= 21, 40
      COA(K)=CCA(K-1)+CONA
   70 COB(K)=COB(K-1)+CONB
      CONA=.038/20.0
      CONB=.193/20.0
```

```
      DO   80 K= 41, 60
      COA(K)=COA(K-1)+CONA
 80   COB(K)=COB(K-1)+CONB
      CONA=.058/20.0
      CONB=.278/20.0
      DO   90 K= 61, 80
      COA(K)=COA(K-1)+CONA
 90   COB(K)=COB(K-1)+CONB
      CONA=.082/20.0
      CONB=.182/20.0
      DO  100 K= 81,100
      COA(K)=COA(K-1)+CONA
100   COB(K)=COB(K-1)+CONB
      CONA=.154/20.0
      CONB=.072/20.0
      DO  110 K=101,120
      COA(K)=COA(K-1)+CONA
110   COB(K)=COB(K-1)+CONB
      CONA=.298/20.0
      CONB=.034/20.0
      DO  120 K=121,140
      COA(K)=COA(K-1)+CONA
120   COB(K)=COB(K-1)+CONB
      CONA=.204/20.0
      CONB=.021/20.0
      DO  130 K=141,160
      COA(K)=COA(K-1)+CONA
130   COB(K)=COB(K-1)+CONB
      CONA=.112/20.0
      CONB=.011/20.0
      DO  140 K=161,180
      COA(K)=COA(K-1)+CONA
140   COB(K)=COB(K-1)+CONB
      CONA=.004/20.0
      CONB=.007/20.0
      DO  150 K=181,200
      COA(K)=COA(K-1)+CONA
150   COB(K)=COB(K-1)+CONB
C
      WRITE (L1,160) CIA(60),COA(200),CIB(60),COB(200)
160   FORMAT (1H1,
     1'CIA(60)=',E13.6,T26,'COA(200)=',E13.6,T50,
     2'CIB(60)=',E13.6,T74,'COB(200)=',E13.6)
```

The PUT statement confirms that the figures have been entered correctly by printing out four values that should each be equal to 1.

**PRIORITIES**          Priorities are taken care of in the model by making tests to see if there is anything to be transmitted and then acting upon them in the desired sequence. The sequence of blocks in Fig. 38.2 gives priority handling as is required in this example.

**GENERATION OF RANDOM NUMBERS**   The first requirement in most simulation models is a means for generating random numbers. A number will be selected at random between 0 and 1, and this number will be used for determining the times of the input transactions, assigning a terminal for the input transaction, and determining the transaction type, as well as the input and output lengths.

The random-number generator need not be very elaborate, but it should be fast because it is used many times in the program. For this reason, an assembler-language random-number generator is used in the programs in this chapter. The statement CALL RANDOM (RAN) produces a number labeled RAN, which is chosen at random between 0 and 1. The assembler-language listing for this is given in Appendix III.

**THE POISSON ARRIVAL PROCESS**   The transactions will be generated, for the reasons given in Chapter 31, with an exponential interarrival time.

If $E(t_a)$ is the mean interarrival time, the fraction of interarrival times that are greater than a value $t_a$ is given by:

$$\text{PROB (interarrival time} > \ t_a) = e^{-t_a/E(t_a)}$$

We shall use our random number between 0 and 1 to give a value for this probability:

$$\text{RAN} = e^{-t_a/E(t_a)}$$

Hence $$t_a = - \ E(t_a) \log_e \text{RAN}.$$

To give the arrival time of a transaction in the simulation we therefore add $-E(t_a) \log_e \text{RAN}$ to the arrival time of the previous transaction.

Before beginning the simulation, let us construct a table for each terminal, giving the times at which the transactions originate. The random-number generator will be used twice, once to advance the clock by the time between successive arrivals:

```
CALL RANDCM (RAN)
CLCCK=CLCCK-DLOG(RAN)*EVTALI
```

and again to assign a terminal to the transaction. On a line with 12 terminals, the terminal number J will be:

```
CALL RANDOM (RAN)
VALUE=RAN*12.0
J=VALUE
IF (J.NE.VALUE) J=J+1
```

We will construct a two-dimensional table called BEGIN, which gives the arrival times of messages, in sequence, for each terminal.

In PL/I:

```
      DIMENSION NEXT(12),BEGIN(12,2000)
      DATA ZERO/0.0/
      CLOCK=ZERO
      DO 180 I=1,12
180   NEXT(I)=ZERO
      DO 190 J=1,2000
      DO 190 I=1,12
190   BEGIN(I,J)=ZERO
      DO 210 I=1,18000
      CALL RANDOM (RAN)
      CLOCK=CLOCK-DLOG(RAN)*EVTALI
      CALL RANDOM (RAN)
      VALUE=RAN*12.0
      J=VALUE
      IF (J.NE.VALUE) J=J+1
      NEXT(J)=NEXT(J)+1
210   BEGIN(J,NEXT(J))=CLOCK
```

This gives us 18,000 transactions to run through the model.

**SELECTION OF MESSAGE TYPES AND LENGTHS**

The random-number generator is used again to assign message types and lengths. A random number between 0 and 1 is generated. If it is less than 0.3, then the message is considered to be type A; otherwise the message is type B.

A second random number is used to look up the appropriate message length in the preceding table giving the cumulative distribution of message lengths. The message length so obtained is divided by the line speed (SPEED) to obtain the transmission time. This amount is then added to the clock time.

In PL/I:

```
  S11:CALL RANDOM (RAN);
      IF RAN < .3 THEN DO;
 S12A:CALL RANDOM (RAN);
      DO X=6 TO 60    WHILE(RAN>CIA(X));END;
      CLOCK=CLOCK+X/SPEED;
      END;
      ELSE DO;
 S12B:CALL RANDOM (RAN);
      DO X=6 TO 200   WHILE(RAN>CIB(X));END;
      CLOCK=CLOCK+X/SPEED;
      END;
```

IN FORTRAN:

```
C.S11
   440 CALL RANDOM (RAN)
       IF (RAN.GE..3) GO TO 470
CS12A
       CALL RANDOM (RAN)
       DO 450 IX=6,60
       IF (RAN.LE.CIA(IX)) GO TO 460
   450 CONTINUE
   460 CLOCK=CLOCK+IX/SPEED
       GO TO 1000
CS12B
   470 CALL RANDOM (RAN)
       DO 480 IX=6,200
       IF (RAN.LE.CIB(IX)) GO TO 490
   480 CONTINUE
   490 CLOCK=CLOCK+IX/SPEED
  1000 CONTINUE
```

## THE CODING
## OF THE MODEL

The main loop of the simulation is the code between the two lines of asterisks in Fig. 38.3. The labels on the statements correspond to those on the blocks in Fig. 38.2.

```
    SPEED=14.8;
    T0=.7025;
    T1=1.16;
    T2=1.2041;
    T3=0;
    DCL ANEW(1:20),BNEW(1:20);
    DCL CPUA(1:20),CPUB(1:20);
    CPUA,CPUB=999999;
  I,SUM1,SUM2,SUM3,SUM4,SUM5,SUM6,CLOCK=0;NEXT=1;M,N=1;
/****************************************************************/
 S1:I=I+1;
    IF I=100 THEN DO; SUM1,SUM2,SUM3,SUM4,SUM5,SUM6=0;END;
    IF I=9110 THEN GO TO S14;
    K1=1;
    DO K=2 TO 20;
    IF CPUA(K)<CPUA(K1) THEN K1=K; END;
    IF CLOCK<CPUA(K1) THEN GO TO S4;

 S2: SUM1=SUM1+1;
    SUM2=SUM2+CLOCK-ANEW(K1);
    SUM3=SUM3+(CLOCK-ANEW(K1))**2;
    CPUA(K1)=999999;

 S3:CALL RANDOM (RAN);
    DO X=6 TO 200   WHILE(RAN>COA(X));END;
    CLOCK=CLOCK+X/SPEED+T2;
    GO TO S1;
```

```
S4: K1=1;
    DO K=2 TO 20;
    IF CPUB(K)<CPUB(K1) THEN K1=K; END;
    IF CLOCK<CPUB(K1) THEN GO TO S7;

S5: SUM4=SUM4+1;
    SUM5=SUM5+CLOCK-BNEW(K1);
    SUM6=SUM6+(CLOCK-BNEW(K1))**2;
    CPUB(K1)=999999;

S6: CALL RANDOM (RAN);
    DO X=6 TO 200    WHILE(RAN>COB(X));END;
    CLOCK=CLOCK+X/SPEED+T2;
    GO TO S1;

S7: IF M=12 THEN CLOCK=CLOCK+T3;

S8:  IF M=12 THEN M=1; ELSE M=M+1;

S9:  CLOCK=CLOCK+TO;

S10: IF CLOCK<BEGIN(M,NEXT(M)) THEN GO TO S1;
     IF N=20 THEN N=1;   ELSE N=N+1;
S11:CALL RANDOM (RAN);
     IF RAN < .3 THEN DO;

S12A:CALL RANDOM (RAN);
     DO X=6 TO 60     WHILE(RAN>CIA(X));END;
     CLOCK=CLOCK+X/SPEED+T1-TO;
     ANEW(N)=BEGIN(M,NEXT(M));

S13A:CPUA(N)=CLOCK+1;
     END;
     ELSE DO;

S12B:CALL RANDOM (RAN);
     DO X=6 TO 200    WHILE(RAN>CIB(X));END;
     CLOCK=CLOCK+X/SPEED+T1-TO;
     BNEW(N)=BEGIN(M,NEXT(M));

S13B:CPUB(N)=CLOCK+1;
     END;
     NEXT(M)=NEXT(M)+1;
     GO TO S1;
 /*********************************************/
 S14:EVTRLA=SUM2/SUM1;
     SMTRLA=SUM3/SUM1;
     EVTRLB=SUM5/SUM4;
     SMTRLB=SUM6/SUM4;
     SDTRLA=SQRT(SMTRLA-EVTRLA*EVTRLA);
     SDTRLB=SQRT(SMTRLB-EVTRLB*EVTRLB);
     PUT DATA(EVTRLA,SDTRLA,EVTRLB,SDTRLB)SKIP;
     END;
```

*Figure 38.3*

In Fortran:

```
      IMPLICIT REAL*8 (A-H, O-Z)
      DIMENSION ANEW(20),BNEW(20),CPUA(20),CPUB(20)
      DATA SPEED,   TO,  T1,    T2, T3
     1    / 14.8,.7025,1.16,1.2041,0.0/
      DO 220 I=1,20
      ANEW(I)=ZERO
      BNEW(I)=ZERO
      CPUA(I)=999999.0
  220 CPUB(I)=999999.0
      I=0
      CLOCK=ZERO
      DO 230 II=1,12
  230 NEXT(II)=1
      M=1
      N=1
C*****************************************************
C..S1
  250 I=I+1
      IF (I.NE.1 .AND. I.NE.100) GO TO 260
      SUM1=ZERO
      SUM2=ZERO
      SUM3=ZERO
      SUM4=ZERO
      SUM5=ZERO
      SUM6=ZERO
  260 IF (I.EQ.9110) GO TO 550
      K1=1
      DO 270 K=2,20
  270 IF (CPUA(K).LT.CPUA(K1)) K1=K
      IF (CLOCK.LT.CPUA(K1))    GO TO 320
C..S2
      SUM1=SUM1+1.0
      SUM2=SUM2+CLOCK-ANEW(K1)
      SUM3=SUM3+(CLOCK-ANEW(K1))**2
      CPUA(K1)=999999.0
C..S3
      CALL RANDOM (RAN)
      DO 300 IX=6,200
      IF (RAN.LE.COA(IX)) GO TO 310
  300 CONTINUE
  310 CLOCK=CLOCK+IX/SPEED+T2
      GO TO 250
C..S4
  320 K1=1
      DO 330 K=2,20
  330 IF (CPUB(K).LT.CPUB(K1)) K1=K
      IF (CLOCK.LT.CPUB(K1))    GO TO 380
C..S5
      SUM4=SUM4+1.0
      SUM5=SUM5+CLOCK-BNEW(K1)
      SUM6=SUM6+(CLOCK-BNEW(K1))**2
      CPUB(K1)=999999.0
C..S6
      CALL RANDOM (RAN)
      DO 360 IX=6,200
      IF (RAN.LE.COB(IX)) GO TO 370
```

```
   360 CONTINUE
   370 CLOCK=CLOCK+IX/SPEED+T2
       GO TO 250
C..S7
   380 IF (M.EQ.12) CLOCK=CLOCK+T3
C..S8
       IF (M.EQ.12) GO TO 400
       M=M+1
       GO TO 410
   400 M=1
C..S9
   410 CLOCK=CLOCK+TO
C.S10
       IF (CLOCK.LT.BEGIN(M,NEXT(M))) GO TO 250
       IF (N.EQ.20) GO TO 430
       N=N+1
       GO TO 440
   430 N=1
C.S11
   440 CALL RANDOM (RAN)
       IF (RAN.GE..3) GO TO 470
CS12A
       CALL RANDOM (RAN)
       DO 450 IX=6,60
       IF (RAN.LE.C1A(IX)) GO TO 460
   450 CONTINUE
   460 CLOCK=CLOCK+IX/SPEED+T1-TO
       ANEW(N)=BEGIN(M,NEXT(M))
CS13A
       CPUA(N)=CLOCK+1.0
       GO TO 510
CS12B
   470 CALL RANDOM (RAN)
       DO 480 IX=6,200
       IF (RAN.LE.C1B(IX)) GO TO 490
   480 CONTINUE
   490 CLOCK=CLOCK+IX/SPEED+T1-TO
       BNEW(N)=BEGIN(M,NEXT(M))
CS13B
       CPUB(N)=CLOCK+1.0
C
   510 NEXT(M)=NEXT(M)+1
       GO TO 250
C
C****************************************************
CS14
   550 EVTRLA=SUM2/SUM1
       SMTRLA=SUM3/SUM1
       EVTRLB=SUM5/SUM4
       SMTRLB=SUM6/SUM4
       SDTRLA=DSQRT(SMTRLA-EVTRLA*EVTRLA)
       SDTRLB=DSQRT(SMTRLB-EVTRLB*EVTRLB)
       WRITE (L1,560) EVTRLA,SDTRLA,EVTRLB,SDTRLB
   560 FORMAT (1H ,
      1'EVTRLA=',E13.6,T26,'SDTRLA=',E13.6,T50,
      2'EVTRLB=',E13.6,T74,'SDTRLB=',E13.6)
```

*Figure 38.4*

**A GENERAL-PURPOSE SIMULATOR LANGUAGE**   Let us look now at a simulation language. The advantage of using such a language, rather than a general-computing language, is that it does much of the work for us. We do not have to code up the clocks, random-number generators, and statistics-gathering routines. Once a simulation language is learned, it is easier to obtain quick results from it than by coding in a general-computing language. On the other hand, it can lack the flexibility that we obtain when we code in, for example, PL/I.

We will use IBM's GPSS to illustrate the planning of communication links with a simulation language. In order to produce a model with GPSS, a block diagram may first be drawn using specially shaped blocks. Some of the common block types are illustrated in Fig. 38.7, and a model using them is given in Fig. 38.8. The mechanisms, capacities, and timings of the system to be simulated are built into such a model.

The block diagram is coded into punched cards block by block, using coding sheets of a suitable format. Cards that specify the input to the system and say how long the model should be run are included. Certain transactions can be given priorities and peak loads studied. The output of the program will give statistics about the utilization of the various parts of the system. It will say how many transactions occupy parts of the system at one time, what queues develop, what response times are obtained, and so on.

The simulator operates by effectively moving transactions through the model a block at a time. These events occur in the same time sequence as they would in the actual system. The program maintains a record of the elapsed clock time at which each event would occur on the working system. It thus updates a clock record appropriately.

Certain blocks have a time period associated with them. For example, a group of blocks representing the seek action of a random-access file have a block that gives the time of this factor. This time may not be constant. It may not even be predictable, for it may depend on the previous setting of the seek mechanism. The time may therefore have a range of values, or it may be given by a function. It is often given as a mean and a spread; thus for a seek time ranging from 40 to 120, it is $80 \pm 40$.

A transaction leaving one block normally passes to the next. However, a TRANSFER block can be used to direct the transaction to any other block. This transfer may be unvarying, or it may be a choice that is determined by a variety of conditions. For example, a certain proportion of the transactions may always go one way. Various logic conditions may determine the route taken: a route representing the transmission of a message may not be taken until a polling message has reached the terminal at which that message originates. A transaction may LOOP around a certain path several times, the way a computer program does. Again, the transaction may always go to Block A, but if Block A cannot accept it, it goes to Block B.

When a transaction enters a block, the particular event specified by that block occurs immediately. Afterward, the transaction attempts to move to the next block. However, if the program cannot execute the action called for in this next block, the transaction remains where it is until the condition causing the delay changes. It could in this way, for example, represent a car waiting for a traffic light to change or an item in a computer waiting for a file reference to be completed. The transactions jerk their way through the model with the program simulating the delays and queues that would be found in actuality.

The items of equipment to be simulated are divided into two categories. Certain items can only handle one transaction at a time—for instance, a communication line can, in most cases, only transmit one record. This type of item is referred to as a facility. If a facility is occupied, other transactions for this facility have to wait, and so a queue forms.

Alternatively, an item of equipment may be able to have multiple occupancy; it is then referred to as a storage. A storage has a capacity of so many transactions. This capacity is stated in the cards defining the model. Examples of storages are an area of dynamically allocated core and a message concentrator that can hold a limited number of messages.

A number of block types relate to facilities. A SEIZE block is one that initiates the use of the facility by a transaction. If the facility is already in use, the SEIZE block cannot be entered. The transaction must wait in the previous block until the facility becomes free, and it will then immediately enter the SEIZE block. Often the block immediately preceding a SEIZE block is a QUEUE block. This block will measure statistics about the transactions queuing for the facility. The block after the SEIZE block will then normally be a DEPART block, saying that the transaction has obtained the facility and thus is no longer in the queue. The transaction can, if so desired, hold the facility for a long period of time while other operations take place. When it eventually leaves the facility, this departure is denoted by a RELEASE block for that facility.

This procedure is illustrated simply in Fig. 38.5. Here Facility 5 is a communication line. The computer wants to send a message down the line, but the line may be busy. The GPSS transaction representing the message waits in Block 1 until the line is free. It can then enter Block 2. It passes immediately through Block 3 to Block 4. Blocks 1 and 3 have measured the length of time the transaction queued for the line, and statistics of this queue will be tabulated under the heading of Queue Number 3, as marked in the blocks. Block 4 represents the time taken to transmit the message. In this example, the *mean* time is 167 (probably milliseconds), and the time follows a distribution given by Function 6, as marked in Block 4. Function 6 is specified in detail elsewhere in the program. When the message has been transmitted, the line is released by RELEASE Block 5. Facility 5 can then be used by other transactions. All the blocks relating to a facility give the number of that facility.

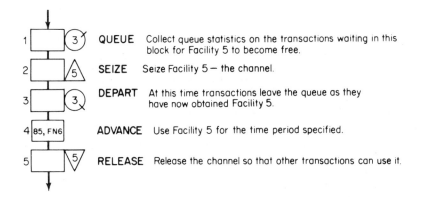

1   QUEUE   Collect queue statistics on the transactions waiting in this block for Facility 5 to become free.

2   SEIZE   Seize Facility 5 — the channel.

3   DEPART   At this time transactions leave the queue as they have now obtained Facility 5.

4   ADVANCE   Use Facility 5 for the time period specified.

5   RELEASE   Release the channel so that other transactions can use it.

*Figure 38.5*

Storages are handled in a similar manner. An ENTER block causes a transaction to enter a specified storage. If the storage is already full to capacity, the transaction must wait; it cannot enter the ENTER block until another transaction leaves the storage. Again QUEUE and DEPART blocks may be used to measure the queues that form. A transaction may occupy a storage for some time while other operations go on, and then it leaves by means of a LEAVE block. As we saw earlier, these blocks give the number of the storage in question.

Figure 38.6 illustrates the use of a storage. This figure might illustrate, for example, a remote buffer or concentrator relaying messages from a computer. The storage of the device can hold, say, 20 messages. We therefore represent it by a storage of capacity 20. The messages try to enter Storage 1 in Block 2. If Storage 1 is already full, they will have to wait, and we again use QUEUE and DEPART Blocks 1 and 3 to collect statistics on the delay. Block 4 gives the time it takes the message to enter the concentrator. The mean time is 85 (milliseconds), and this time is multiplied by Function 6 to represent the dis-

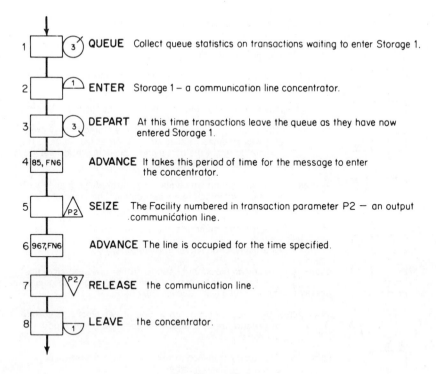

1  QUEUE  Collect queue statistics on transactions waiting to enter Storage 1.

2  ENTER  Storage 1 – a communication line concentrator.

3  DEPART  At this time transactions leave the queue as they have now
entered Storage 1.

4 85, FN6  ADVANCE  It takes this period of time for the message to enter
the concentrator.

5  SEIZE  The Facility numbered in transaction parameter P2 — an output
communication line.

6 967,FN6  ADVANCE  The line is occupied for the time specified.

7  RELEASE  the communication line.

8  LEAVE  the concentrator.

*Figure 38.6*

tribution of message lengths. When it is in the concentrator, it must SEIZE
an outgoing line. This step is done in Block 5. The line selected has the number
in Parameter 2 of the message, which causes the appropriate facility to be
seized. The facility may be already occupied by other traffic, possibly incoming
traffic; in this case, the message waits in the concentrator until the facility
becomes free. Block 6 gives the time it takes the message to be transmitted out.
This time is on a slower line and so the mean time is higher: 967 (milliseconds).
The mean time is multiplied by the same Function 6 representing the distribution of message lengths. The communication line is then released—Block 7—
and the area the message occupied is freed for other use with a LEAVE block,
Block 8. This, of course, is an unrealistically simplified example of the mechanism of a concentrator. One message may occupy several relocatable core
blocks, and considerations like line control would complicate the model.

Other major block types are shown in Fig. 38.7. It is suggested that the
reader examine these types and then read on to see how a line with polling may
be studied with GPSS.

| | | |
|---|---|---|
| GENERATE | Creates new transactions and enters them into the system. A variety of ways of specifying time intervals are possible. |
| TERMINATE | Removes transactions from the system. |
| ADVANCE | A transaction can enter this block unconditionally and remains for the time period stated. |
| SEIZE | The transaction takes control of the stated facility if it is free. |
| RELEASE | The transaction releases control of the facility. |
| PREEMPT | The transaction takes control of the stated facility even if it was previously occupied by another transaction. It cannot do this if the occupying transaction had itself preempted the facility. |
| RETURN | The transaction which gained control of the facility with the PREEMPT block releases control. The preempt transaction resumed control. |
| ENTER | The transaction enters the stated store if there is room. |
| LEAVE | The transaction leaves the stated store. |
| QUEUE | These two blocks are used to gather queueing statistics The first is used when the transaction begins to queue, |
| DEPART | the second when it leaves the queue. |
| TRANSFER | The transaction may go to one of two blocks. A variety of criteria are permissible for specifying which path is taken. |
| LOOP | Causes the transaction to loop through a section of program a given number of times. |
| LOGIC | When a transaction enters this block, logic switches are set which may be tested elsewhere in the model. |
| GATE | A GATE block regulates the flow of transactions through the system depending upon certain logic conditions. A variety of logic conditions can be tested, for example, storage full or empty facility in use or not, facility preempted or not, logic switches set, and so on. One type of GATE block bars the path of transactions; another transfers them to specified blocks. |
| MARK | The time when the transaction enters this block is marked in it and can later be tabulated. |
| ASSIGN | This block assigns value to a parameter. For example it is used in Fig. 25.5 to select which file unit the transaction is to update. |
| SPLIT | One transaction enters this block. Two or more identical transactions leave it. The duplicates thus created go to the block specified. |
| ASSEMBLE | Re-combines duplicate transactions created by a SPLIT block. When a specified number of the identical transactions have arrived, one leaves and the others are destroyed. |
| GATHER | Similar to an ASSEMBLE block but all of the transactions leave. |

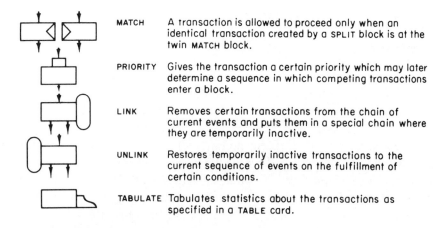

MATCH    A transaction is allowed to proceed only when an identical transaction created by a SPLIT block is at the twin MATCH block.

PRIORITY    Gives the transaction a certain priority which may later determine a sequence in which competing transactions enter a block.

LINK    Removes certain transactions from the chain of current events and puts them in a special chain where they are temporarily inactive.

UNLINK    Restores temporarily inactive transactions to the current sequence of events on the fulfillment of certain conditions.

TABULATE    Tabulates statistics about the transactions as specified in a TABLE card.

*Fig. 38.7.* Some of the block types used by IBM's GPSS III simulator language. The use of this is illustrated in the following three figures.

## SIMULATION OF A LINE ON WHICH CONCENTRATORS ARE POLLED

**Example 38.2. Simulation of Concentrators Multidropped on a Half-Duplex Line.** Consider a half-duplex voice line with some form of concentration device attached to it. The devices may be concentrators handling other low-speed lines to terminals, or they may be control units handling display screens. The messages are entered from the display screens or terminals with a Poisson distribution, and because many terminals are attached to one concentration point, the traffic volumes on the line can become quite high.

It is intended to make one voice line service 12 concentration points, thereby giving a traffic volume of between 2400 and 3000 messages per hour. The concentrators are polled in a sequence determined by the computer software.

The line-control program has a list of terminals to be polled. Each time the line is repolled, the concentrator (or control unit) addressed will be the next one in this list. Some measure of priority can be given to a terminal by including it more than once in the list. When a device is polled, its message will be sent if it has one. Only one message will be sent at a time. Nothing else can then take place on the line until the transmission is complete. When it is complete, the line will be released (not held until the reply has been sent). The next concentration point will then be polled.

Output messages will be given priority over input. In other words, when an output message becomes ready for transmission, the line will be seized as soon as the present transmission on it ends, and the output message will be sent.

During those periods when there are no messages to be sent, the polling signals will be sent down the line constantly, scanning the devices on the polling list.

Transmission takes place on the line at 300 characters per second. The message length distribution is that for the type A messages in Table 30.1. The time taken for one poll, successful or unsuccessful, is 100 milliseconds. There is a 10-millisecond interval between polls.

Assume that the processing time in the computer is 500 milliseconds. The output begins to be displayed on the terminal screen as soon as it is received at the concentrator. Investigate the response times and the distribution of response times.

Two types of activity are taking place on the line: (1) the creation and transmission of messages and (2) the polling. The messages are created at times quite independent of the polling. The input messages must wait, however, until their terminal is polled. We can construct our model in two parts, one representing what happens to the polling signal and the other representing what happens to the messages. There will never be more than one polling signal active at one time. Therefore we can have in our model just one polling signal, which travels round and round its portion of the model, occasionally causing a data message in the other half of the model to be transmitted.

This is shown in Fig. 38.8. The polling is represented by the left-hand side of the diagram, the message transmission by the right–hand side. The first act of the model is to generate one single polling signal in Block 1. Block 2 assigns a terminal to it. Thereafter this transaction travels round and round the loop shown. Each time it arrives at Block 3 a new terminal address is assigned to it. This step is done by examining the terminal address currently assigned to it and then selecting the next one in the polling list. The polling list is represented by Function 2, thus:

| | | | | | ┌ Input: the terminal last polled. | | | | | |
|---|---|---|---|---|---|---|---|---|---|---|---|---|
| | | | | | | | | ┌ Output: the terminal to be polled next. | | | | |
| 1 | | 2 | 2 | | 3 | 3 | | 4 | 4 | | 5 | 5 | | 6 | 6 | | 7 |
| 7 | | 8 | 8 | | 9 | 9 | | 10 | 10 | | 11 | 11 | | 12 | 12 | | 1 |

The transaction carries around with it, in a storage location referred to as *parameter number* 1 (P1), the number of the terminal currently being polled. Function 2 has 12 pairs of numbers. The first of each pair is the transaction now being polled (in P1). The second is the number of the terminal to be polled next. This second number is inserted into P1 by Block 3 in Fig. 38.8. In this way the terminals are polled one after another, according to the sequence of numbers in Function 2. The model thus imitates exactly the polling list mechanism in the software. Function 2, as shown in the figure, represents a polling list in which the terminals are polled cyclically. Any sequence could in fact be used.

Block 4 in Fig. 38.8 seizes the communication line (Facility 1). Block 5 advances the clock in the model for this transaction by an amount that represents the time needed for polling. Block 6 tests to see whether the terminal being polled actually does have a message to send. If it does not, then Block S8

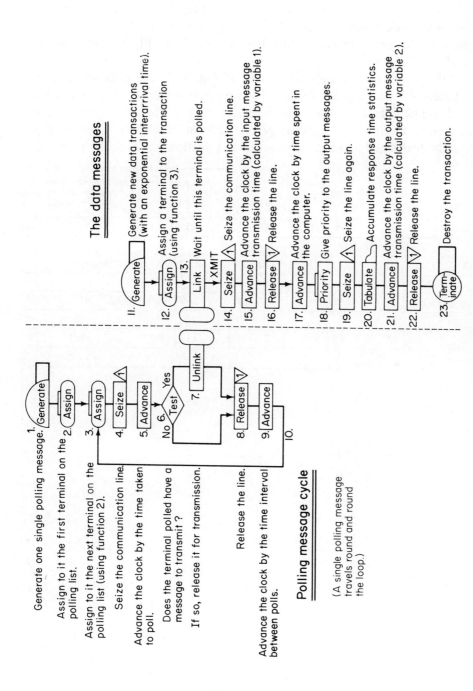

## The data messages

11. Generate — Generate new data transactions (with an exponential interarrival time).

12. Assign — Assign a terminal to the transaction (using function 3).

13. Link — Wait until this terminal is polled.

XMIT

14. Seize — Seize the communication line.

15. Advance — Advance the clock by the input message transmission time (calculated by variable 1).

16. Release — Release the line.

17. Advance — Advance the clock by time spent in the computer.

18. Priority — Give priority to the output messages.

19. Seize — Seize the line again.

20. Tabulate — Accumulate response time statistics.

21. Advance — Advance the clock by the output message transmission time (calculated by variable 2).

22. Release — Release the line.

23. Terminate — Destroy the transaction.

1. Generate — Generate one single polling message.

2. Assign — Assign to it the first terminal on the polling list.

3. Assign — Assign to it the next terminal on the polling list (using function 2).

4. Seize — Seize the communication line.

5. Advance — Advance the clock by the time taken to poll.

6. Test — Does the terminal polled have a message to transmit?

No / Yes

7. Unlink — If so, release it for transmission.

8. Release — Release the line.

9. Advance — Advance the clock by the time interval between polls.

10.

### Polling message cycle

(A single polling message travels round and round the loop.)

*Fig.* 38.8. Simulation of a polled half-duplex communication line, using GPSS.

665

releases the line (which could then be seized by the computer to send an output message). Block 9 advances the clock for this transaction by an amount that represents the pause between polls. We then return to Block 3 and the cycle repeats.

Meanwhile, on the right-hand side of Fig. 38.8, the data messages are generated and transmitted. Block 11 creates new messages. The line of code representing this block will state the mean time between the creation of messages. This time is multiplied by numbers generated from Function 1 which are exponentially distributed and have a mean of 1. Function 1 is as follows:

Input: Random numbers between 0 and 1

Output: Numbers following an exponential distribution with a mean of 1

| .0 | 0 | .1 | .104 | .2 | .222 | .3 | .355 | .4 | .509 | .5 | .690 |
|---|---|---|---|---|---|---|---|---|---|---|---|
| .6 | .915 | .7 | 1.20 | .75 | 1.38 | .8 | 1.60 | .84 | 1.83 | .88 | 2.12 |
| .9 | 2.30 | .92 | 2.52 | .94 | 2.81 | .95 | 2.99 | .96 | 3.2 | .97 | 3.5 |
| .98 | 3.9 | .99 | 4.6 | .995 | 5.3 | .998 | 6.2 | .999 | 7 | .9997 | 8 |

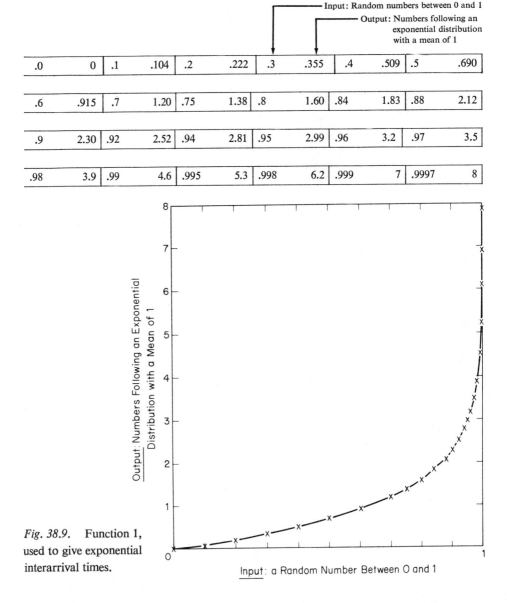

*Fig. 38.9.* Function 1, used to give exponential interarrival times.

Output: Numbers Following an Exponential Distribution with a Mean of 1

Input: a Random Number Between 0 and 1

The computer generates a random number between 0 and 1 and uses this number as the input. The output consists of numbers following an exponential distribution with a mean of 1. The mean interarrival times are multiplied by this output. The mean remains unchanged, but the interarrival times are exponentially distributed.

We are thus making the same assumption about the arrival pattern as we did in order to use the queuing theory equations in earlier chapters. The transactions are generated at random. The number of messages per second follows a Poisson distribution. This assumption is normally the only one we can make, and it is very close to actuality.

The next step is to assign a terminal to the messages that have been generated. This step is done by Block 12. Function 3 indicates what proportion of the traffic originates at each of the 12 terminals. The input to Function 3, like Function 1, is a number between 0 and 1 selected at random (an equal probability of any value between 0 and 1). Using this input, the associated output value is selected, which gives the number of the terminal to which the message is assigned from Function 3.

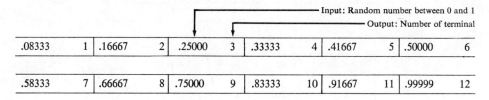

| | | | | | | | | | | | |
|---|---|---|---|---|---|---|---|---|---|---|---|
| .08333 | 1 | .16667 | 2 | .25000 | 3 | .33333 | 4 | .41667 | 5 | .50000 | 6 |

| | | | | | | | | | | | |
|---|---|---|---|---|---|---|---|---|---|---|---|
| .58333 | 7 | .66667 | 8 | .75000 | 9 | .83333 | 10 | .91667 | 11 | .99999 | 12 |

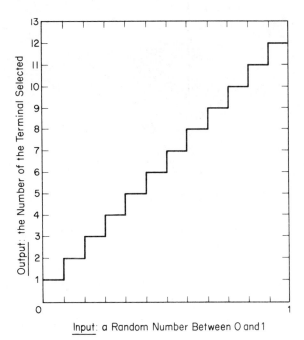

*Fig. 38.10.* Function 3, used for assigning one of twelve terminals to a transaction.

The transaction representing the data message then enters Block 13, the LINK block. It cannot pass beyond this block until "unlinked" by a polling message at Block 7, which represents that terminal being polled.

Once on its way, the message seizes the line (Facility 1) in SEIZE Block 14. The clock for this message is advanced by the message transmission time in Block 15, and then the line is released (Block 16).

The input message time is given in Variable 1 (V1). It is the number of characters in the message divided by the speed of the line. The number of characters in the input message is given by Function 4. Similarly, Variable 2 (V2) and Function 5 give the output-message transmission time.

Suppose that the output message lengths are those given in Table 30.1 for message type A. They would be translated into Function 5 as follows:

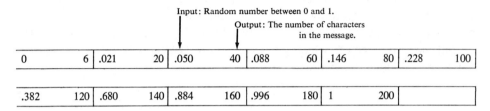

| 0 | | 6 | .021 | 20 | .050 | 40 | .088 | 60 | .146 | 80 | .228 | 100 |
|---|---|---|------|----|------|----|------|----|------|----|------|-----|
| .382 | | 120 | .680 | 140 | .884 | 160 | .996 | 180 | 1 | 200 | | |

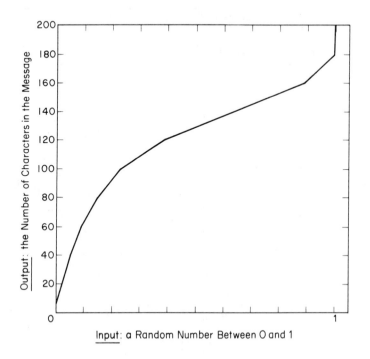

Fig. 38.11. Function 5 gives the lengths of output messages.

As the transactions flow through the model, the distribution of output message lengths will be the same as that in Table 30.1 (given a sufficiently large volume of transactions). Function 4 gives the input message lengths in a similar manner.

After the ADVANCE block for input transmission, the line is released by Block 16. It could then be seized by a polling message or by an output transaction.

In Block 17 the clock advances by the time taken in the computer to process the message and prepare a reply.

It is possible that the output message will have to queue for the line. We do, however, want it to have priority over input or polling messages. Block 18 gives it this priority. Block 19 seizes the line again.

We would like to obtain a complete set of statistics about the response times on this line. We therefore insert a TABULATE block into our model after the line has been seized for output—this is Block 20. We will look at what it produces shortly. The block tabulates the clock times from message origination to the moment when the messages reach this block. These times are response times (in the way we defined response times on page 000, that is, *not* including output transmission times). The block will give us mean and standard deviation of these times, a histogram, and a cumulative distribution.

Block 21 advances the clock for the time taken for output transmission, Facility 1, the line, being held throughout this time. Block 22 releases the line, and Block 23 terminates the lives of the transactions.

**CODING**     Figure 38.12 shows the coding used for this model. All lines with an asterisk in the first position are comments cards, inserted for clarity. The five functions used are listed first,

```
**********************************************************************************
**EXPONENTIAL FUNCTION *********************************************************
 1       FUNCTION   RN1,C24
0      0      .1     .104   .2     .222   .3     .355   .4     .509   .5     .69
.6     .915   .7     1.2    .75    1.38   .8     1.6    .84    1.83   .88    2.12
.9     2.3    .92    2.52   .94    2.81   .95    2.99   .96    3.2    .97    3.5
.98    3.9    .99    4.6    .995   5.3    .998   6.2    .999   7      .9997  8
**********************************************************************************
**NUMBER OF TERMINALS AND POLLING LIST****************************************
 2       FUNCTION   P1,D12
1      2      2      3      3      4      4      5      5      6      6      7
7      8      8      9      9      10     10     11     11     12     12     1
**********************************************************************************
**FRACTION OF MESSAGES FROM EACH TERMINAL************************************
 3       FUNCTION   RN1,D12
.083331        .166672        .25    3      .333334        .416675        .5     6
.583337        .666678        .75    9      .8333310       .9166711       .9999912
**********************************************************************************
```

```
**LENGTH OF INPUT TRANSACTIONS *****************************************
   4      FUNCTION   RN1,C6
   0      6     .390  10    .604  15    .790  20    .930  40    1     60
*********************************************************************
**LENGTH OF OUTPUT TRANSACTIONS ****************************************
   5      FUNCTION   RN1,C11
   0      6     .021  20    .050  40    .088  60    .146  80    .228  100
 .382   120   .680  140   .884  160   .996  180   1     200
*********************************************************************
**** POLLING MESSAGE CYCLE ********************************************
 1            GENERATE   1,,,1          GENERATE ONE POLLING MESSAGE ONLY
 2            ASSIGN     1,K1           FIRST TERMINAL ON POLLING LIST
 3    POLL    ASSIGN     1,FN2          ASSIGN NEXT TERMINAL ON POLLING LIST
 4            SEIZE      1              SEIZE LINE
 5            ADVANCE    K100           HOLD LINE FOR DURATION OF POLL
 6            TEST NE    CH*1,K0,REL    DOES THIS TERMINAL HAVE A MESSAGE?
 7            UNLINK     P1,XMIT,1      RELEASE ONE MESSAGE FROM TERMINAL
 8    REL     RELEASE    1              RELEASE THE LINE
 9            ADVANCE    K10            TIME INTERVAL BETWEEN POLLS
10            TRANSFER   ,POLL          POLL THE LINE AGAIN
*********************************************************************
**** THE DATA MESSAGES **********************************************
11            GENERATE   X1,FN1         GENERATE NEW MESSAGES AT TERMINALS
12            ASSIGN     1,FN3          ASSIGN A TERMINAL TO EACH MESSAGE
13            LINK       P1,FIFO        MSG WAITS UNTIL THAT TERML IS POLLED
14    XMIT    SEIZE      1              SEIZE LINE
15            ADVANCE    V1             INPUT MESSAGE TRANSMISSION TIME
16            RELEASE    1              RELEASE THE LINE
17            ADVANCE    K500           COMPUTER TIME TO PROCESS THE MESSAGE
18            PRIORITY   1              OUTPUT MESG HAS PRIORITY OVER INPUT
19            SEIZE      1              SEIZE LINE
20            TABULATE   1              GATHER RESPONSE TIME STATISTICS
21            ADVANCE    V2             OUTPUT MESSAGE TRANSMISSION TIME
22            RELEASE    1              RELEASE THE LINE
23            TERMINATE  1              DESTROY THE TRANSACTION
 *
 1    TABLE      M1,0,200,40            DISTRIBUTION TABLE FOR RESPONSE TIME
 1    VARIABLE   FN4*10/3               CALCULATION OF INPUT TRANSMIT TIME
 2    VARIABLE   FN5*10/3               CALCULATION OF OUTPUT TRANSMIT TIME
*********************************************************************
      INITIAL    X1,K1500               INTERARRIVAL TIME  (2400 MESS/HR)
      START      500,NP
      RESET
      START      5000
      RESET
*********************************************************************
      INITIAL    X1,K1400               INTERARRIVAL TIME  (2571.4 MESS/HR)
      START      5000
      RESET
      INITIAL    X1,K1300               INTERARRIVAL TIME  (2769.2 MESS/HR)
      START      5000
      RESET
      INITIAL    X1,K1200               INTERARRIVAL TIME  (3000 MESS/HR)
      START      5000
      RESET
      INITIAL    X1,K1100               INTERARRIVAL TIME  (3272.7 MESS/HR)
      START      5000
      END
```

*Figure 38.12*

then the two halves of the model. The lines of code in the model are given numbers that correspond to those in Fig. 38.8.

X1 is the mean time between messages being generated and hence determines the message rate. It is set by an INITIAL card. It is first set to a constant value, 1500 (shown as K1500). The time unit with which this model is operating is one millisecond, and thus the INITIAL card gives a mean arrival rate of one transaction every 1.5 seconds.

The model is run five times and reset after each time. Each run has an INITIAL card with a different value. We will therefore see how the performance of the line varies with changing load.

**OUTPUT OF THE MODEL**     The TABULATE block causes a distribution of response times to be printed. Figure 38.13 shows the first of these response time distributions—for 2400 messages per hour. It will be seen that the mean response time is 1.84 seconds. The standard deviation of response time is 0.908 second. The distribution shows that the 90th percentile of response time is about 3.00 seconds. Only 0.2 percent take longer than 6 seconds.

Figure 38.14 shows the equivalent table for 2571.4 messages per hour, and Fig. 38.15 illustrates response times for 2769.2 messages per hour. The 90th percentile response time is now somewhat higher than 3 seconds. If a 90th percentile of 3 seconds is to be maintained, the throughput should not be higher than 2400 messages per hour.

TABLE 1
ENTRIES IN TABLE
5000

MEAN ARGUMENT
1840.358

STANDARD DEVIATION
908.000

| UPPER LIMIT | OBSERVED FREQUENCY | PER CENT OF TOTAL | CUMULATIVE PERCENTAGE | CUMULATIVE REMAINDER | MULTIPLE OF MEAN |
|---|---|---|---|---|---|
| 0 | 0 | .00 | .0 | 100.0 | -.000 |
| 200 | 0 | .00 | .0 | 100.0 | .108 |
| 400 | 0 | .00 | .0 | 100.0 | .217 |
| 600 | 14 | .27 | .2 | 99.7 | .326 |
| 800 | 338 | 6.75 | 7.0 | 92.9 | .434 |
| 1000 | 442 | 8.83 | 15.8 | 84.1 | .543 |
| 1200 | 497 | 9.93 | 25.8 | 74.1 | .652 |
| 1400 | 513 | 10.25 | 36.0 | 63.9 | .760 |
| 1600 | 484 | 9.67 | 45.7 | 54.2 | .869 |
| 1800 | 515 | 10.29 | 56.0 | 43.9 | .978 |
| 2000 | 477 | 9.53 | 65.5 | 34.4 | 1.086 |
| 2200 | 398 | 7.95 | 73.5 | 26.4 | 1.195 |
| 2400 | 301 | 6.01 | 79.5 | 20.4 | 1.304 |
| 2600 | 222 | 4.43 | 84.0 | 15.9 | 1.412 |
| 2800 | 163 | 3.25 | 87.2 | 12.7 | 1.521 |
| 3000 | 127 | 2.53 | 89.8 | 10.1 | 1.630 |
| 3200 | 126 | 2.51 | 92.3 | 7.6 | 1.738 |
| 3400 | 75 | 1.49 | 93.8 | 6.1 | 1.847 |
| 3600 | 61 | 1.21 | 95.0 | 4.9 | 1.956 |
| 3800 | 53 | 1.05 | 96.1 | 3.8 | 2.064 |
| 4000 | 31 | .61 | 96.7 | 3.2 | 2.173 |
| 4200 | 29 | .57 | 97.3 | 2.6 | 2.282 |
| 4400 | 29 | .57 | 97.8 | 2.1 | 2.390 |
| 4600 | 20 | .39 | 98.2 | 1.7 | 2.499 |
| 4800 | 21 | .41 | 98.7 | 1.2 | 2.608 |
| 5000 | 20 | .39 | 99.1 | .8 | 2.716 |
| 5200 | 11 | .21 | 99.3 | .6 | 2.825 |
| 5400 | 7 | .13 | 99.4 | .5 | 2.934 |
| 5600 | 6 | .11 | 99.5 | .4 | 3.042 |
| 5800 | 6 | .11 | 99.7 | .2 | 3.151 |
| 6000 | 2 | .03 | 99.7 | .2 | 3.260 |
| 6200 | 3 | .05 | 99.8 | .1 | 3.368 |
| 6400 | 1 | .01 | 99.8 | .1 | 3.477 |
| 6600 | 2 | .03 | 99.8 | .1 | 3.586 |
| 6800 | 1 | .01 | 99.8 | .1 | 3.694 |
| 7000 | 2 | .03 | 99.9 | .0 | 3.803 |
| 7200 | 1 | .01 | 99.9 | .0 | 3.912 |
| 7400 | 1 | .01 | 99.9 | .0 | 4.020 |
| 7600 | 1 | .00 | 99.9 | .0 | 4.129 |
| OVERFLOW | 1 | .01 | 100.0 | 0 | |

*Figure 38.13*

672

TABLE 1
ENTRIES IN TABLE 5000    MEAN ARGUMENT 1938.094    STANDARD DEVIATION 990.000

| UPPER LIMIT | OBSERVED FREQUENCY | PER CENT OF TOTAL | CUMULATIVE PERCENTAGE | CUMULATIVE REMAINDER | MULTIPLE OF MEAN |
|---|---|---|---|---|---|
| 0 | 0 | .00 | .0 | 100.0 | -.000 |
| 200 | 0 | .00 | .0 | 100.0 | .103 |
| 400 | 0 | .00 | .0 | 100.0 | .206 |
| 600 | 37 | .73 | .7 | 99.2 | .309 |
| 800 | 312 | 6.23 | 6.9 | 93.0 | .412 |
| 1000 | 389 | 7.77 | 14.7 | 85.2 | .515 |
| 1200 | 458 | 9.15 | 23.9 | 76.0 | .619 |
| 1400 | 461 | 9.21 | 33.1 | 66.8 | .722 |
| 1600 | 477 | 9.53 | 42.6 | 57.3 | .825 |
| 1800 | 484 | 9.67 | 52.3 | 47.6 | .928 |
| 2000 | 448 | 8.95 | 61.3 | 38.6 | 1.031 |
| 2200 | 339 | 6.77 | 68.0 | 31.9 | 1.135 |
| 2400 | 337 | 6.73 | 74.8 | 25.1 | 1.238 |
| 2600 | 253 | 5.05 | 79.8 | 20.1 | 1.341 |
| 2800 | 218 | 4.35 | 84.2 | 15.7 | 1.444 |
| 3000 | 187 | 3.73 | 87.9 | 12.0 | 1.547 |
| 3200 | 131 | 2.61 | 90.6 | 9.3 | 1.651 |
| 3400 | 84 | 1.67 | 92.2 | 7.7 | 1.754 |
| 3600 | 75 | 1.49 | 93.7 | 6.2 | 1.857 |
| 3800 | 58 | 1.15 | 94.9 | 5.0 | 1.960 |
| 4000 | 46 | .91 | 95.8 | 4.1 | 2.063 |
| 4200 | 39 | .77 | 96.6 | 3.3 | 2.167 |
| 4400 | 30 | .59 | 97.2 | 2.7 | 2.270 |
| 4600 | 30 | .59 | 97.8 | 2.1 | 2.373 |
| 4800 | 17 | .33 | 98.1 | 1.8 | 2.476 |
| 5000 | 19 | .37 | 98.5 | 1.4 | 2.579 |
| 5200 | 10 | .19 | 98.7 | 1.2 | 2.683 |
| 5400 | 10 | .19 | 98.9 | 1.0 | 2.786 |
| 5600 | 11 | .21 | 99.1 | .8 | 2.889 |
| 5800 | 8 | .15 | 99.3 | .6 | 2.992 |
| 6000 | 7 | .13 | 99.4 | .5 | 3.095 |
| 6200 | 8 | .15 | 99.6 | .3 | 3.199 |
| 6400 | 1 | .01 | 99.6 | .3 | 3.302 |
| 6600 | 5 | .09 | 99.7 | .2 | 3.405 |
| 6800 | 3 | .05 | 99.8 | .1 | 3.508 |
| 7000 | 1 | .01 | 99.8 | .1 | 3.611 |
| 7200 | 2 | .03 | 99.8 | .1 | 3.714 |
| 7400 | 0 | .00 | 99.8 | .1 | 3.818 |
| 7600 | 0 | .00 | 99.8 | .1 | 3.921 |
| OVERFLOW | 5 | .09 | 100.0 | .0 | |

*Figure 38.14*

673

TABLE 1
ENTRIES IN TABLE 5000

MEAN ARGUMENT 1993.590

STANDARD DEVIATION 1032.000

| UPPER LIMIT | OBSERVED FREQUENCY | PER CENT OF TOTAL | CUMULATIVE PERCENTAGE | CUMULATIVE REMAINDER | MULTIPLE OF MEAN |
|---|---|---|---|---|---|
| 0 | 0 | .00 | .0 | 100.0 | -.000 |
| 200 | 0 | .00 | .0 | 100.0 | .100 |
| 400 | 0 | .00 | .0 | 100.0 | .200 |
| 600 | 25 | .49 | .4 | 99.5 | .300 |
| 800 | 277 | 5.53 | 6.0 | 93.9 | .401 |
| 1000 | 380 | 7.59 | 13.6 | 86.3 | .501 |
| 1200 | 426 | 8.51 | 22.1 | 77.8 | .601 |
| 1400 | 443 | 8.85 | 31.0 | 68.9 | .702 |
| 1600 | 458 | 9.15 | 40.1 | 59.8 | .802 |
| 1800 | 502 | 10.03 | 50.2 | 49.7 | .902 |
| 2000 | 430 | 8.59 | 58.8 | 41.1 | 1.003 |
| 2200 | 396 | 7.91 | 66.7 | 33.2 | 1.103 |
| 2400 | 318 | 6.35 | 73.0 | 26.9 | 1.203 |
| 2600 | 264 | 5.27 | 78.3 | 21.6 | 1.304 |
| 2800 | 244 | 4.87 | 83.2 | 16.7 | 1.404 |
| 3000 | 186 | 3.71 | 86.9 | 13.0 | 1.504 |
| 3200 | 113 | 2.25 | 89.2 | 10.7 | 1.605 |
| 3400 | 113 | 2.25 | 91.4 | 8.5 | 1.705 |
| 3600 | 87 | 1.73 | 93.2 | 6.7 | 1.805 |
| 3800 | 68 | 1.35 | 94.5 | 5.4 | 1.906 |
| 4000 | 36 | .71 | 95.3 | 4.6 | 2.006 |
| 4200 | 39 | .77 | 96.0 | 3.9 | 2.106 |
| 4400 | 34 | .67 | 96.7 | 3.2 | 2.207 |
| 4600 | 25 | .49 | 97.2 | 2.7 | 2.307 |
| 4800 | 29 | .57 | 97.8 | 2.1 | 2.407 |
| 5000 | 24 | .47 | 98.3 | 1.6 | 2.508 |
| 5200 | 7 | .13 | 98.4 | 1.5 | 2.608 |
| 5400 | 18 | .35 | 98.8 | 1.1 | 2.708 |
| 5600 | 10 | .19 | 99.0 | .9 | 2.809 |
| 5800 | 10 | .19 | 99.2 | .7 | 2.909 |
| 6000 | 7 | .13 | 99.3 | .6 | 3.009 |
| 6200 | 4 | .07 | 99.4 | .5 | 3.109 |
| 6400 | 5 | .09 | 99.5 | .4 | 3.210 |
| 6600 | 2 | .03 | 99.5 | .3 | 3.310 |
| 6800 | 4 | .07 | 99.6 | .2 | 3.410 |
| 7000 | 4 | .07 | 99.7 | .2 | 3.511 |
| 7200 | 2 | .03 | 99.7 | .1 | 3.611 |
| 7400 | 1 | .01 | 99.8 | .0 | 3.711 |
| 7600 | 0 | .00 | 99.8 |  | 3.812 |
| OVERFLOW | 9 | .17 | 100.0 |  |  |

Figure 38.15

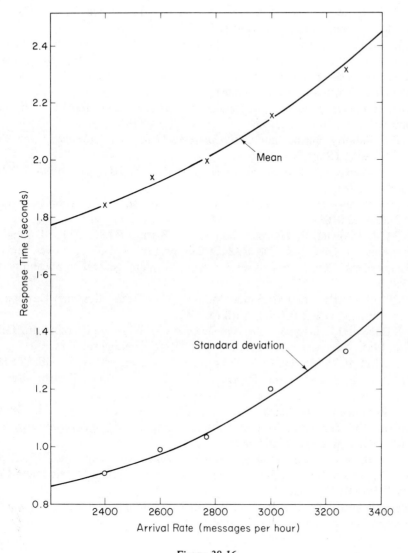

*Figure 38.16*

Figure 38.16 plots the variation in the results for the mean and standard deviation response time from these five simulation runs. The degree to which the points deviate from the smooth curve is a measure of the inaccuracy of the simulation. In order to bring the points more closely into a smooth curve, a larger number of transactions would have to be run.

# REFERENCES

1. H. S. Krasnow, and R. Merikallio, "The Past, Present and Future of General Simulation Languages," *Management Science*, November 1964.
2. K. D. Tocher, *The Art of Simulation*, Princeton, N.J.: D. Van Nostrand, 1963.
3. C. W. Churchman, "An Analysis of the Concept of Simulation," *Symposium on Simulation Models*. Edited by Austin C. Hoggatt and Frederick E. Balderston. Cincinnati: South-Western Publishing Co., 1963.
4. J. M. Hammersley, and D. C. Handscomb, *Monte Carlo Methods*. New York: John Wiley and Sons, Inc., 1964.
5. Naylor, Balintfy, Burdick and Chu, *Computer Simulation Techniques*. New York: John Wiley and Sons, Inc., 1966.
6. *General Purpose Systems Simulator* III, *Introduction*. IBM Corporation Manual Number B30-0001-0.
7. *General Purpose Systems Simulator* III, *User's Manual*. IBM Corporation Manual Number H20-0163-1.
8. H. M. Markowitz, B. Hausner, and H. W. Karr, *SIMSCRIPT: A Simulation Programming Language*. The RAND Corporation RM-3310, November 1962. (An excellent FORTRAN-based language of more general applicability than GPSS.)
9. SIMPAC User's Manual. Santa Monica, California: Systems Development Corporation, TM 602/000/00, April 15, 1962.
10. O-J. Dahl, and K. Nygaard, *The Simula Language*, Norwegian Computing Centre, Oslo, 1964. A convenient language for simulating queuing processes.
11. C. C. Holt, R. W. Shirey, D. V. Steward, J. L. Midler, and A. Stroud, "Program SIMULATE, a User's and Programmer's Manual," Social Systems Research Institute, University of Wisconsin, May 1964 (Mimeographed).
12. J. N. Buxton and J. G. Laski, "Control and Simulation Language," *The Computer Journal*, October 1962. (A useful discrete simulation language comparable to SIMSCRIPT, widely used in Europe.)
13. K. Young, *A User's Experience with Three Simulation Languages* (*GPSS, SIMSCRIPT, and SIMPAC*), Santa Monica, California: System Development Corp., TM-1755/000/00, 1963.
14. *Bibliography on Simulation* (a KWIC index). International Business Machines Corporation, Manual Number 320-0924, 1966.

# 39    ESTABLISHING A
TRAFFIC RATE TABLE

Before the systems analyst can carry out the final step of geographically laying out his communication network, he must establish the maximum traffic that each line can handle. Where the line has multidrop or concentration facilities, he wants to put as many terminals on the line as possible within the constraints of his response-time requirements. Some terminals generate more traffic than others on most systems, and as will be seen in the next chapter, the task of laying out the network sometimes involves selecting which terminals are attached to a line on the basis of their traffic volumes. The total traffic on the line must not exceed a certain amount, and this acceptable maximum usually varies with the number of terminals on the line. Hence a traffic rate table is needed.

A typical traffic rate table for a multidrop line might look like Table 39.1.

In this case, the maximum rate is quoted in terms of messages per minute. It is assumed that all terminals are likely to produce the same mix of message lengths. In the design of many systems this assumption is tenable; in practice, a traffic rate table of this type has been used in laying out the network for a wide variety of systems—airline reservation systems, hire-purchase systems, systems for insurance companies, message-switching systems, and many others. If, however, different terminal types or terminal locations produce messages of different lengths, then the traffic rate table may quote the maximum permissible line utilization for data messages (not including polling), $\rho = E(n)E(t_m)$. The program or person laying out the network would then have to calculate $\rho$ for the various configurations of terminals tried on a line, instead of merely adding up the numbers of messages.

There are three ways in which the systems analyst might set about obtain-

**Table 39.1.** A TYPICAL TRAFFIC RATE TABLE

| Number of Terminals Attached to the Line | Maximum Permissible Traffic Rate (messages per minute) |
|:---:|:---:|
| 1 | 8.01 |
| 2 | 7.85 |
| 3 | 7.73 |
| 4 | 7.59 |
| 5 | 7.46 |
| 6 | 7.34 |
| 7 | 7.21 |
| 8 | 7.09 |
| 9 | 6.96 |
| 10 | 6.85 |
| 11 | 6.74 |
| 12 | 6.63 |
| 13 | 6.53 |
| 14 | 6.44 |
| 15 | 6.33 |
| 16 | 6.21 |
| 17 | 6.15 |
| 18 | 6.07 |
| 19 | 5.98 |
| 20 | 5.89 |
| 21 | 5.82 |
| 22 | 5.74 |
| 23 | 5.66 |
| 24 | 5.57 |
| 25 | 5.50 |
| 26 | 5.43 |
| 27 | 5.36 |
| 28 | 5.30 |
| 29 | 5.22 |
| 30 | 5.15 |

ing his traffic rate table. First, he might use queuing calculations, as in Chapters 36 and 37. Second, he might use simulation, as in Chapter 38; and third, he might find a program that calculates a traffic rate table available from a computer manufacturer or consultant and might perhaps use it to establish a minimum-cost network. IBM has such a program available—CNDP (Communication Network Design Program). The program uses queuing models to establish its traffic rate table.

When a package program of this type is used for developing the traffic rate, the systems analyst must be sure that the assumptions it is using are assumptions applicable to his particular system. Often the queuing model in such a program does not fit a particular situation too well. The systems analyst might obtain a better table, and possibly a less expensive network, by tailoring a queuing model or simulation to his special requirement. CNDP recognizes this point by permitting its users to feed it their own traffic rate table. The use of programs like CNDP will be discussed further in the next chapter.

One advantage of using queuing models such as those given in earlier chapters is that the pros and cons of different line organizations can be brought to light. The curves in earlier chapters illustrated this.

**THE EFFECT OF COMPUTING TIME**    In our queuing calculations, we required a figure for the time the transactions spent in the computer—the elapsed time between receiving the input and beginning to transmit the output. We assumed a mean and variance for this figure. In reality, the figure is likely to vary with the throughput. It is itself dependent on the queues that build up for the processing unit and for the file arms and channels.

In our earlier examples, the maximum throughput was limited by the transmission line queues. This is not necessarily the case. On many systems the processing unit or the file mechanisms or channels are the bottlenecks that ultimately limit system throughput. This factor would affect the shapes of the curves drawn in Chapters 36 and 37, as well as the traffic rate table.

Figure 39.1 gives curves for a particular system showing how the time spent by transactions *in the computer* varies with the throughput. In this case, the queues are largely caused by the file arms and channel. Queuing models for analyzing file and channel queues are beyond the scope of the book and are discussed in the author's *Design of Real-Time Computer Systems*. As with the communication lines, the response time of the file subsystem swings rapidly upward when throughput becomes high enough to cause large queues.

Figure 39.2 gives curves covering the same range of throughput values, calculated for the communication lines as in Chapter 37. These curves ignore the time spent in the computer and are concerned solely with the line queues. The throughput in this diagram is the throughput of *all* the lines feeding the computer, not just one of them, as in previous curves. It is drawn this way so that its throughput may be compared directly with Fig. 39.1. The transactions from all the lines meet and together form the queues for the computer and files. Figure 39.3 shows the distribution of response times that correspond to the curves in Fig. 39.2.

In the previous chapters, a figure that was independent of the throughput was assumed for the time spent in the computer (e.g., EVTTCS, mean compute time = 1 second; SDTTCS, standard deviation of compute time = $\frac{1}{2}$ second). This figure must now be replaced with a set of figures as represented by Fig. 39.1. We replace the lines of code giving EVTTCS = 1, SDTTCS = 0.5 by an entire queuing calculation. When we do so in this case, the file subsystem reaches its maximum throughput before the communication line subsystem, and Fig. 39.4 gives the combined effect of the two.

It is from a calculation such as the one represented by Fig. 39.3 that the traffic rate table will be computed. Using the assumption that the response times follow a gamma distribution (again using simulation, this distribution appears a reasonable way to obtain practical working figures), Fig. 39.5 was obtained. It gives the distribution of response times corresponding to Fig. 39.4, and we can see that here the file subsystem bottleneck makes a major difference.

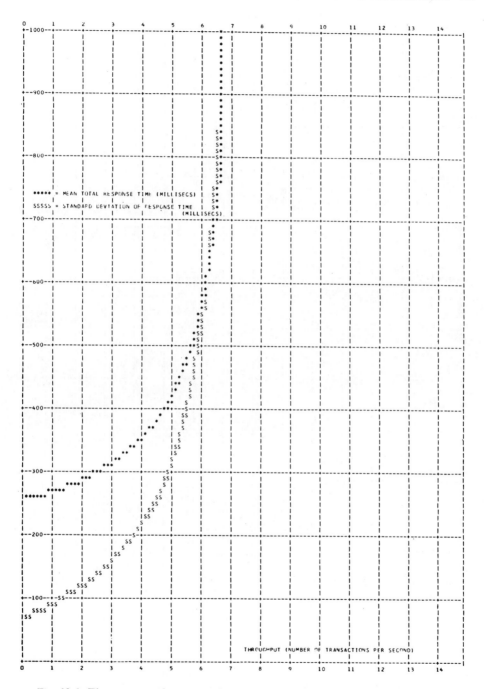

*Fig. 39.1.* The segment of response time caused by the computer and file subsystem.

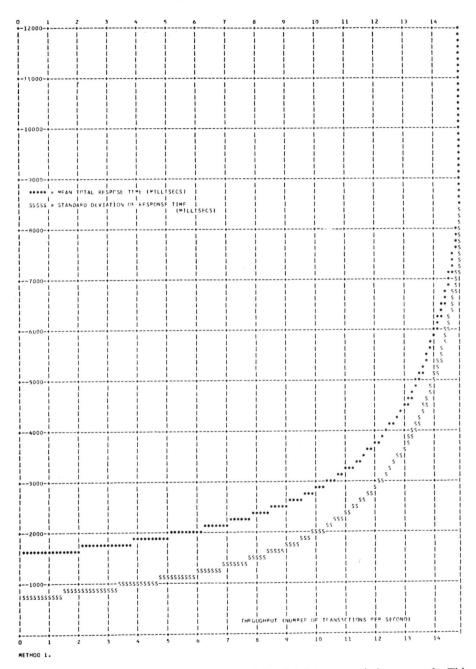

METHOD 1.

*Fig. 39.2.* The segment of response time caused by the data transmission network. This calculation is for the same system as that in the previous figure. The overall response time will be a combination of these two effects, as shown in Fig. 39.4. (Note that the vertical scales in Figs. 39.1 and 39.2 are different.)

THROUGHPUT VALUES OF CURVES BELOW
NNN = 14.5 TRANSACTIONS PER SECOND
MMM = 13.5 TRANSACTIONS PER SECOND
LLL = 12.5 TRANSACTIONS PER SECOND
KKK = 11.5 TRANSACTIONS PER SECOND
JJJ = 10.5 TRANSACTIONS PER SECOND
III =  9.5 TRANSACTIONS PER SECOND
HHH =  8.5 TRANSACTIONS PER SECOND
GGG =  7.5 TRANSACTIONS PER SECOND
FFF =  6.5 TRANSACTIONS PER SECOND

*Fig. 39.3.* The distribution of the response times of the teleprocessing subsystem—that is, a distribution corresponding to the response times shown in Fig. 39.2.

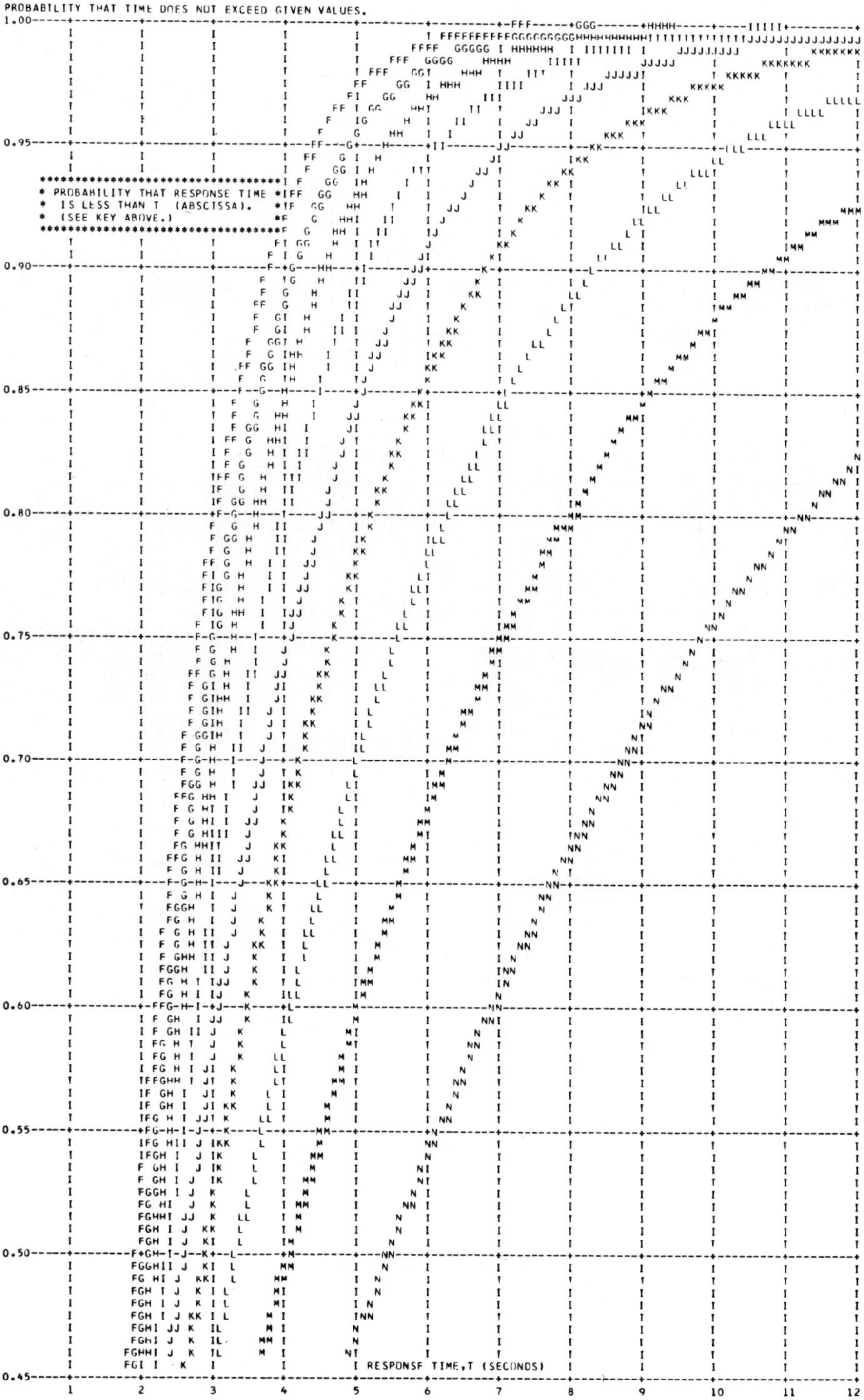

PROBABILITY THAT TIME DOES NOT EXCEED GIVEN VALUES.

*(Chart)* PROBABILITY THAT RESPONSE TIME T IS LESS THAN T (ABSCISSA). (SEE KEY ABOVE.)

RESPONSE TIME, T (SECONDS)

Vertical axis values: 1.00, 0.95, 0.90, 0.85, 0.80, 0.75, 0.70, 0.65, 0.60, 0.55, 0.50, 0.45

Horizontal axis values: 1, 2, 3, 4, 5, 6, 7, 8, 9, 10, 11, 12

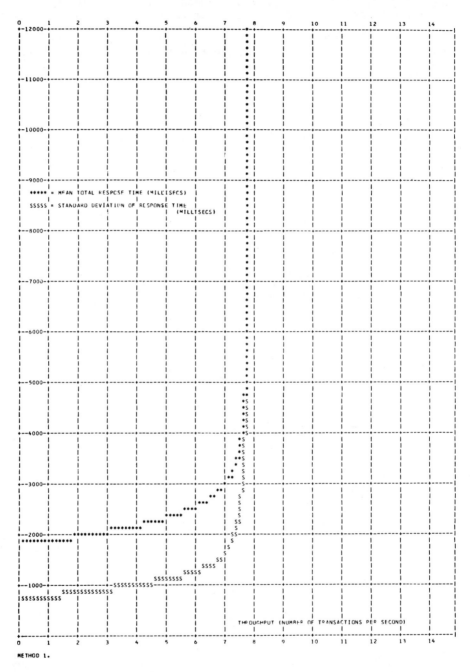

*Fig. 39.4.* The overall response time—the combined effect of the subsystem response times shown in Figs. 39.1 and 39.2.

THROUGHPUT VALUES OF CURVES BELOW
GGG = 7.5 TRANSACTIONS PER SECOND
FFF = 6.5 TRANSACTIONS PER SECOND
EEE = 5.5 TRANSACTIONS PER SECOND
DDD = 4.5 TRANSACTIONS PER SECOND
CCC = 3.5 TRANSACTIONS PER SECOND
BBB = 2.5 TRANSACTIONS PER SECOND
AAA = 1.5 TRANSACTIONS PER SECOND

*Fig. 39.5.* The distribution of overall response times—that is, a distribution corresponding to the response times shown in Fig. 39.4.

PROBABILITY THAT TIME DOES NOT EXCEED GIVEN VALUES.

```
1.00                                          AAA BB   CC  DD     FF        FFF
          I       I       I       I   AAAAABBBBCCCCCDDDDDEEEEEEE IFFFFFFFFFI
          I       I       I       IAA BBBCCCIDDDD EEEE    FFFFF           I       I       I       I
          I       I       I       AA BB CC  DD    FFF   I FFF    I       I       I       I              GGGG
          I       I       I       A IB  C  DD I EE       FFF     I       I       I       I     IGGGGGG  I
          I       I       I       A  B CC  D   IE      FI        I       I       I       I GGGGG        I
          I       I       I     AA BIC   D   FE      FF I        I       I       I     GGGG             I
          I       I       I     AA BBIC   D   E I    F  I        I       I       I  GGGG                I
          I       I       I     A BB  CC DD  EE I   FF  I        I       I    GGG I                     I
          I       I       I     A BB CC DD  EE  I  F    I        I       I GGG I                        I
0.95                                A B  C ID   F    IFF         I       I   GGG                        
          I       I       I A  B  C  D   E   IF       I        I       I  GG  I       I       I       I
          I       I       I A  B C   D   E   IF       I        I    GG  I       I       I       I
          ********************************D  EE       F         I     G  I       I       I       I
          * PROBABILITY THAT RESPONSE TIME *I  E      FF        I    GG  I       I       I       I
          * IS LESS THAN T (ABSCISSA).     *I E      FFI        I  GG  I       I       I       I
          * (SEE KEY ABOVE.)               *I E     F I         I IG  I       I       I       I
          ********************************IF    E        I        I GG  I       I       I       I
          I       I      IAB  C D  IE      FF  I         I        I  G  I       I       I       I
          I       I      AAB C  D  E    F  I             I        I   G  I       I       I
0.90                           A B C DD  E    F          I       I GG   I       
          I       I      APBCC D  EE      F   I          I       I  GG   I       I       I       I
          I       I      AAB C  D  EI      F  I          I       I G    I       I       I       I
          I       I      AIB C D   EI    F    I          I       I  G   I       I       I       I
          I       I      AIB C D  E I   FF    I          I       IGG    I       I       I       I
          I       I      AB C  D  F I   F     I          I       G     I       I       I       I
          I       I      AAB C  DD EE I  F    I          I       GG    I       I       I       I
          I       I      A B C D  E  I F      I          I       GGI   I       I       I       I
          I       I      A BCC D  E  I F      I          I     GG I    I       I       I       I
          I       I      AABC DD EE IFF       I          I     G  I    I       I       I       I
0.85                          AB C D  E    IF           I       G                
          I       I      A BIC D  E   IF      I          I     GG  I    I       I       I       I
          I       I      A BCC D EE    F      I          I   GG   I     I       I       I       I
          I       I      ABBC D  E     F      I          I   G    I     I       I       I       I
          I       I      AB  C D  F    F      I          I   G    I     I       I       I       I
          I       I      AB  C D  F   FI      I          I  G     I     I       I       I       I
          I       I      AB  C D F    FI      I          IGG     I     I       I       I       I
          I       I      A BC1DD E    FI      I          I  G    I      I       I       I       I
          I       I      A BCID  E    FFI     I          I  G    I      I       I       I       I
          I       I      AB C1D  E    F I     I          IGG     I      I       I       I       I
0.80                          AB C I D  E     F          I       G                
          I       I      AB C1D E   FF I      I          I  G  I   I    I       I       I       I
          I       I      ABCCD   F   F I      I          I GG  I   I    I       I       I       I
          I       I      AABC D  E   F  I     I          I G   I   I    I       I       I       I
          I       I      ABBC D EE   F  I     I          I  G  I   I    I       I       I       I
          I       I      AB C D E    F  I     I          I  G  I   I    I       I       I       I
          I       I      AB  C D E   F     I           I  G   I    I    I       I       I       I
          I       I      ABCCDI E    F  I     I          I G   I   I    I       I       I       I
          I       I      ABC DI E    F  I     I          I G   I   I    I       I       I       I
          I       I      AABC DIF    F  I     I          I GG  I   I    I       I       I       I
0.75                          AB CDIE      F          I  G                       
          I       I      AB C DIE    F     I          I  G    I   I    I       I       I       I
          I       I      AB CDCIE    F     I          I  G    I   I    I       I       I       I
          I       I      ABCCD IF    F     I          IGG     I   I    I       I       I       I
          I       I      ABC D E    F     I          IG      I   I    I       I       I       I
          I       I      ABC D E    F     I          I       G    I    I       I       I       I
          I       I      ABC D E    F     I          I G     I    I    I       I       I       I
          I       I      A BC D E   FF     I          IGG     I    I    I       I       I       I
          I       I      I AB CD  E  F     I          I GI    I    I    I       I       I       I
          I       I      I AB CD EE F      I          I GI    I    I    I       I       I       I
0.70                          I ABC D E    F          I  G                      
          I       I      I ABC D EI F     I          I  GI    I    I    I       I       I       I
          I       I      I ABC D EI F     I          IGG  I    I    I    I       I       I       I
          I       I      I ABC D EI F     I          I G  I    I    I    I       I       I       I
          I       I      I ABCDDEEI F     I          IGG   I    I    I    I       I       I       I
          I       I      I AABCD  E I F     I          I G   I    I    I    I       I       I       I
          I       I      I AB CD  E IFFF   I          I  G   I    I    I    I       I       I       I
          I       I      I ABCCD  E IF     I          I  G   I    I    I    I       I       I       I
          I       I      I ABC D E IF     I          I  G   I    I    I    I       I       I       I
          I       I      I ABC D E IF     I          I GG   I    I    I    I       I       I       I
0.65                          I ABCD F IF           I  GG                       
          I       I      I ABCD E F     I          I GG   I    I    I    I       I       I       I
          I       I      I ABCD E F     I          I G    I    I    I    I       I       I       I
          I       I      IAB CD F  F    I          I G    I    I    I    I       I       I       I
          I       I      IAB C D E  F   I          I G    I    I    I    I       I       I       I
          I       I      IABC DE  F     I          I G    I    I    I    I       I       I       I
          I       I      IAB C DEE FF   I          IGG    I    I    I    I       I       I       I
          I       I      IABCD E  FI    I          IG     I    I    I    I       I       I       I
          I       I      IABCD E  FI    I          IG     I    I    I    I       I       I       I
0.60                          IABCD E  FI           I G                         
          I       I      IAACD E   FI    G           I    I    I    I    I       I       I       I
          I       I      IAACD F  FI     GG          I    I    I    I    I       I       I       I
          I       I      IACCDEE F I     GI          I    I    I    I    I       I       I       I
          I       I      IABC DE  F I    GI          I    I    I    I    I       I       I       I
          I       I      IARCDDE  F I    G I         I    I    I    I    I       I       I       I
          I       I      IABCD E  F I    G I         I    I    I    I    I       I       I       I
          I       I      IABCD E  F I    G I         I    I    I    I    I       I       I       I
          I       I      IABCD E FF I    G  I        I    I    I    I    I       I       I       I
          I       I      IABCD E F  I    G  I        I    I    I    I    I       I       I       I
0.55                          IABCDEEF I    G                                    
          I       I      IABCDE  F I   GG  I        I    I    I    I    I       I       I       I
          I       I      IAB DE  F I    G  I        I    I    I    I    I       I       I       I
          I       I      IACD F  F I    G  I        I    I    I    I    I       I       I       I
          I       I      IACD E  F I   G   I        I    I    I    I    I       I       I       I
          I       I      IABCD E F I   G   I        I    I    I    I    I       I       I       I
          I       I      IABCD E F I   G   I        I    I    I    I    I       I       I       I
          I       I      IABCDE  F I   GG  I        I    I    I    I    I       I       I       I
          I       I      IABCDE  F I   G   I        I    I    I    I    I       I       I       I
          I       I      IABCDE  F I   G   I        I    I    I    I    I       I       I       I
0.50                          IARCDE  F I  GG                                    
          I       I      IABCDE FF I   G   I        I    I    I    I    I       I       I       I
          I       I      IACD E  F I  G    I        I    I    I    I    I       I       I       I
          I       I      IACD E  F I  G    I        I    I    I    I    I       I       I       I
          I       I      IACD F  F I  G    I        I    I    I    I    I       I       I       I
          I       I      IAACDE  F I  G    I        I    I    I    I    I       I       I       I
          I       I      IABCDE  F I  G    I        I    I    I    I    I       I       I       I
          I       I      IABCDE FF IGG     I        I    I    I    I    I       I       I       I
          I       I      IARCDE F  IG      I        I    I    I    I    I       I       I       I
          I       I      IC       I        I RESPONSE TIME,T (SECONDS)  I        I       I       I
0.45
            1       2       3       4       5       6       7       8       9      10      11      12
```

# 40 MINIMAL-COST NETWORK LAYOUT

Given the common carriers' catalog of line prices, the systems analyst has the task of laying out a minimum-cost network. In doing so he may use concentrators, multiplexors, multidrop lines, private exchanges, and any of the other devices discussed earlier. He can choose from a wide variety of different line types and tariffs. The physical layout of the lines can have a considerable effect on the cost of the system, particularly if the lines are long. On some systems, it is not too difficult to find an optimum layout; it can be done by hand. On other systems, complicated computing techniques are needed to obtain a minimum-cost solution.

Algorithms have been produced by a number of organizations for telecommunication network layout. Optimal network layout has been the subject of a number of Ph.D. theses. Many mathematical algorithms, however, oversimplify the problem. They usually fail to consider the various alternative structures for networks, and do not take into consideration the diversity of tariffs available. Some ignore the effects of traffic loading and some make assumptions that simplify but invalidate the mathematics—for example: Line cost is proportional to distance. The designer needs to use the available techniques with caution and common sense, and must be aware of the shortcomings of each method. With a combination of techniques, as described in this and the following chapters, he can explore the relative merits of alternative networks. Whatever calculations he performs, he must use the actual tariff cost tables, which generally cannot be represented by a simple mathematical function, and he must use his own particular traffic volumes.

Let us begin by discussing the problem without concentrators, exchanges, or similar equipment and talk about connecting the terminals directly to the computer center on leased multidrop lines. We will again begin with a simple method and then sophisticate our approach.

The next chapter refines this approach by discussing the use of dial-up lines and leased lines in the same network to help minimize the cost. Chapters 42 and 43 discuss the use of concentrators and multiplexers in the network. Meanwhile the reader should note that *many* of today's networks consist of leased lines without concentrators or multiplexers and so are like the examples used in this chapter.

Line cost increases with the length of the connection. In most cases the minimum-distance interconnection path is also the minimum-cost one. If there are not too many points to be interconnected, the minimum-distance path can be worked out by hand. This process can be aided by using a map drawn so that its paper distances are proportional to land mileage. Most map projections do not have this property; therefore, unless the distances are very small, it is important to select the right type of map. On a *conformal conic* projection, the scale is proportional to distance in all directions. Telephone companies sometimes print such a map which is useful for line layout calculations. Figure 40.1 shows a portion of a map of the United States published by AT & T, one that is useful for laying out data transmission networks. It appears to be somewhat distorted because of the projection used. Miami, for example, seems to be north of Houston. The scales refer to coordinates used by telephone companies in Mexico, the United States, and Canada in establishing line costs.[1] Their tariffs give a four-digit coordinate to every city from which distances may be calculated using Pythagoras' theorem as in Chapter 18. Using these coordinates, the designer may check that he has planned a minimum line-mileage routing.

**Example 40.1. Lowest-Cost Path Between Cities.** A single communication line is to be used to connect terminals in the following cities to a computer in Chicago. What is the minimum-cost interconnection path? See Table 40.1.

**Table 40.1**

| City | Coordinates V | Coordinates H | City | Coordinates V | Coordinates H |
|------|------|------|------|------|------|
| Birmingham, Alabama | 7518 | 2446 | Raleigh, North Carolina | 6344 | 1436 |
| Miami, Florida | 8351 | 0527 | Charleston, South Carolina | 7021 | 1281 |
| Jacksonville, Florida | 7649 | 1276 | Nashville, Tennessee | 7010 | 2710 |
| Springfield, Illinois | 6539 | 3513 | Austin, Texas | 9005 | 3996 |
| Cedar Rapids, Iowa | 6261 | 4021 | Houston, Texas | 8934 | 3536 |
| Louisville, Kentucky | 6529 | 2772 | Dallas, Texas | 8436 | 4034 |
| New Orleans, Louisiana | 8483 | 2638 | Richmond, Virginia | 5906 | 1472 |
| Kansas City, Missouri | 7027 | 4203 | Little Rock, Arkansas | 7721 | 3451 |

[1] Superscript numbers cite references at end of chapter.

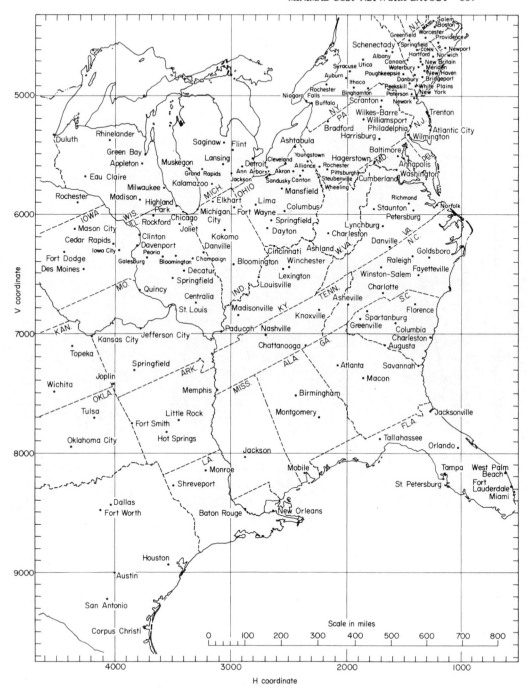

·*Fig. 40.1.* Part of a map published by AT & T for use in communication network layout. The distances on the map are proportional to airline mileages. The common carrier *V* and *H* coordinates are shown.

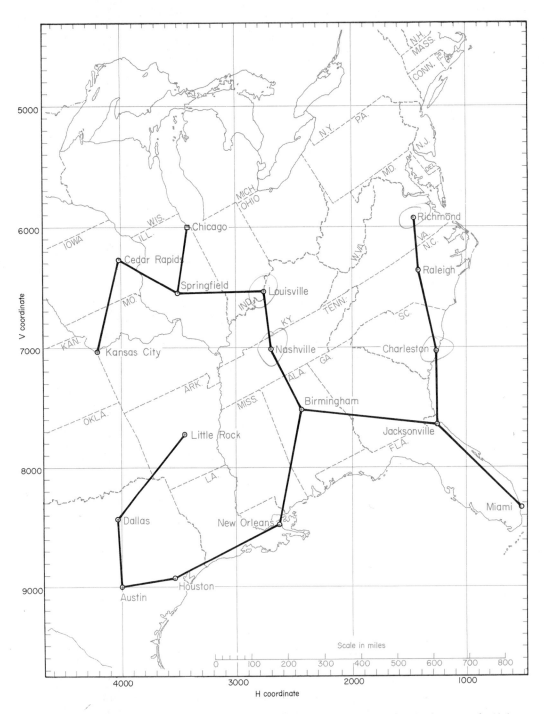

*Fig. 40.2.* The minimum-distance interconnection between the cities in Example 40.1.

We can tackle this problem by making measurements on the map in Fig. 40.1. The solution is shown in Fig. 40.2. It takes some trial and error to obtain the solution by hand, for there are many reasonable ways to interconnect the cities. In my first attempt by hand, I connected Kansas City to Little Rock instead of connecting Houston to New Orleans but then noticed that the latter is shorter. Instead of connecting Birmingham to New Orleans, we might have connected it to Little Rock. The distance is so similar that instead of measuring it on the map, we might have calculated it from the coordinates, using the Pythagorean theorem as on page 247. The distance between Birmingham and Little Rock calculated this way is

$$\sqrt{\frac{(V_1 - V_2)^2 + (H_1 - H_2)^2}{10}} = \sqrt{\frac{(7518 - 7721)^2 + (2446 - 3451)^2}{10}} = 324 \text{ miles}$$

The distance between Birmingham and New Orleans is 312 miles; hence the layout shown.

**MULTIPLE LINES**  Generally our problem is more involved than in the preceding example because not all of the cities can be attached to one line. It is necessary to choose which cities go on which line and still give a minimum-cost network. The line loading generally needs to be taken into consideration. One well-known algorithm called the *minimum spanning tree* method, developed at the Bell Telephone Laboratories, lays out a minimum-cost network without considering line loading. This is generally not suitable for data processing systems other than those with a *very* light loading. As we have seen, response time varies with line loading, and moving terminals from one line to another affects the load.

A hand method for simple networks might be as follows:

1. Determine the traffic load from each location.
2. Determine the number of terminals in use at each location.
3. Determine the maximum load the line can handle and still meet the response-time requirements. This calculation should usually be in the form of a traffic rate table, as discussed in Chapter 39.
4. Mark the locations on a map having a suitable projection.
5. Starting at the farthest points from the computer, one can link the locations together until those linked have the maximum permitted load or the maximum number of terminals permissible within the addressing scheme used. The group will then be linked to the computer. The total line distance in doing this will be kept to a minimum. Different combinations should be tried in an attempt to minimize the total line mileage.
6. Having established a reasonable set of interconnections, one can obtain the exact distances from the $V$ and $H$ coordinates or other tables, and exact costs can then be obtained from the tariff tables.

**Example 40.2. A Network Needing Several Lines.** A network is to be designed again connecting the foregoing 16 cities to a data processing center at Chicago. It has been determined that the maximum traffic any one line will be designed for is 300 messages per hour. (A calculation such as that shown in Fig. 36.7 might give this figure.)

The traffic volumes anticipated from the cities are shown in Table 40.2.

**Table 40.2**

| City | Number of Messages per Hour | |
|------|:---:|:---:|
| | To Computer | From Computer |
| Birmingham, Alabama | 13.02 | 19.20 |
| Miami, Florida | 42.96 | 63.60 |
| Jacksonville, Florida | 3.42 | 5.10 |
| Springfield, Illinois | 21.24 | 31.38 |
| Cedar Rapids, Iowa | 5.88 | 8.64 |
| Louisville, Kentucky | 5.34 | 7.92 |
| New Orleans, Louisiana | 33.42 | 35.10 |
| Kansas City, Missouri | 43.14 | 63.90 |
| Raleigh, North Carolina | 13.86 | 20.52 |
| Charleston, South Carolina | 14.70 | 21.72 |
| Nashville, Tennessee | 17.10 | 25.26 |
| Austin, Texas | 9.18 | 13.56 |
| Houston, Texas | 13.14 | 19.50 |
| Dallas, Texas | 12.60 | 18.66 |
| Richmond, Virginia | 22.86 | 33.84 |
| Little Rock, Arkansas | 10.32 | 15.24 |

It is still not too difficult to find the shortest-distance network that meets these constraints, by hand.

The best method is to begin at the locations farthest from the computer center and work inward. Starting at Miami, we can put Jacksonville, Charleston, Raleigh, and Richmond on one line without exceeding our maximum of 300 messages per hour. We could connect Louisville to the same line, but if we add Louisville and Nashville to it, the maximum is exceeded. The total number of messages per hour, input and output, adds up to 685. Therefore we need three lines. The question then becomes: "What is the shortest path with which we can connect the remaining cities (with or without Louisville) to Chicago?"

Juggling the connections in this manner leads to the minimum-line-distance solution shown in Fig. 40.3. In this network, the Miami line carries 242.6 messages per hour; the Texas line carries 268.6; and the Kansas line carries 174.2. This situation is a little unbalanced. Terminals on the Kansas line will

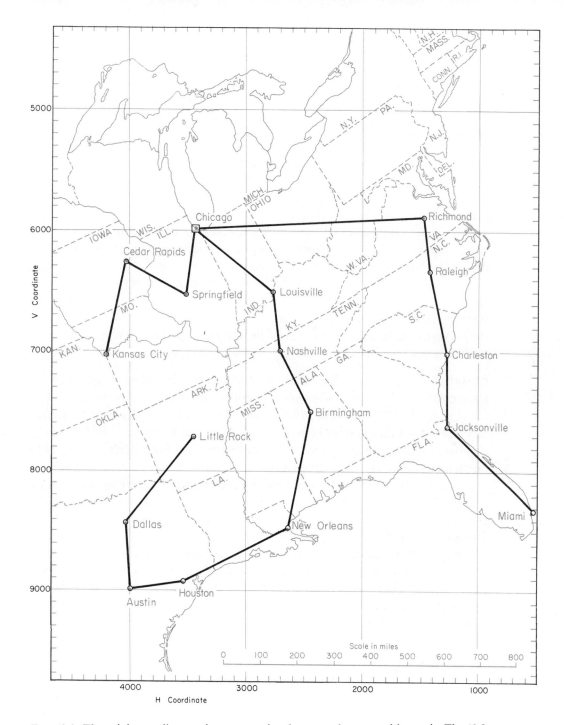

*Fig. 40.3.* The minimum-distance interconnection between the same cities as in Fig. 40.2, with the constraint that no line can handle more than 300 messages per hour. (See Example 40.2.)

have a slightly better response time. This could be adjusted at very little extra cost by putting Little Rock on the Kansas line, which drops the load on the Texas line to 243.1. The Texas line could then tolerate a throughput about 10 percent higher.

**DIFFERING LINE COSTS**

The minimum-distance solution to such problems is usually, but not always, the minimum-cost solution. Some countries have different prices for lines in different areas. The United States, for example, has separate charges for lines within certain cities, lines within one state, and lines crossing state boundaries. If the network has lines at different charges, then it is necessary to work out the cost of the links when trying out different interconnections.

If a multidrop line crosses a state boundary, then it is priced according to the interstate tariff. This tariff generally costs less than the state tariffs; thus it is advantageous to make sure that the linkages are connected in such a way that they do cross state boundaries. All of them do in Fig. 40.3. We are not paying the Texas price for the Dallas–Austin–Houston links.

**COMPLEX NETWORKS**

In actual practice, data transmission networks are often more complex than the preceding ones. Frequently they are too complex for the systems analyst to obtain a minimum-cost layout by hand methods. There may be a large number of cities to interconnect, different line charges for different areas, and a permissible traffic rate that varies with the number of terminals on a line. The network designer then needs a computer. Linear programming approaches for tackling this problem have been described, but the most commonly used and generally useful method is probably that of IBM's Communication Network Design Program.[2]

Figure 40.4 shows the network-layout algorithm that this program uses. The algorithm operates by repetitively evaluating the cost savings given by replacing a link between a location and the computer center with a link that has one extra location attached to it. A link between location $A$ and the computer may be replaced by a link to $A$ and $B$ as in Fig. 40.5.

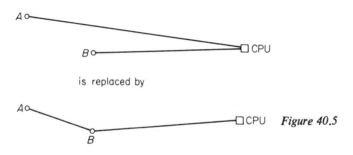

*Figure 40.5*

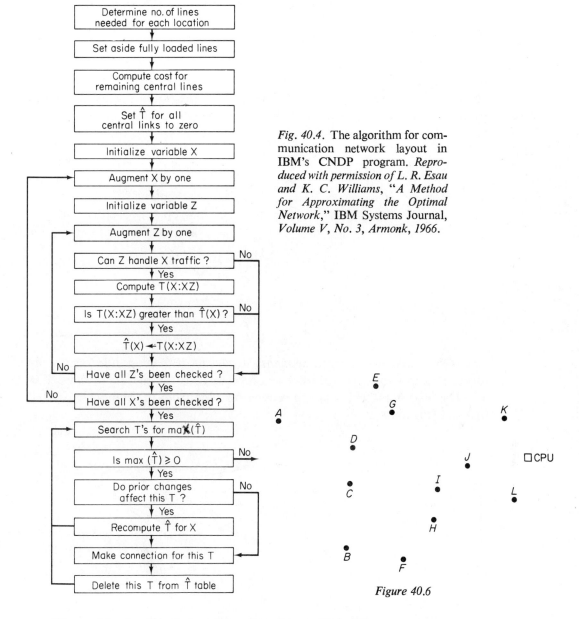

*Fig. 40.4.* The algorithm for communication network layout in IBM's CNDP program. *Reproduced with permission of L. R. Esau and K. C. Williams, "A Method for Approximating the Optimal Network,"* IBM Systems Journal, *Volume V, No. 3, Armonk, 1966.*

*Figure 40.6*

The cost trade-off in doing so is referred to as $T(A:AB)$.

There may be many locations to which $A$ could be connected in this way, each with its own cost trade-off. The maximum such trade-off for location $A$ that is permissible within the line-loading constraints is referred to as $\hat{T}(A)$.

Suppose that we have 12 locations to be connected to a central processing unit in Fig. 40.6.

Beginning letters—*A, B, C,* etc.—in this diagram represent locations farther from the computer.

Let us follow the steps taken by the CNDP algorithm in linking these locations. First, the traffic volumes are inspected to see whether any location has enough traffic to fill one line. In this case, locations $H$ and $K$ have that much traffic. Therefore $H$ and $K$ are set aside, for no other terminals can be connected to these lines (see Fig. 40.7).

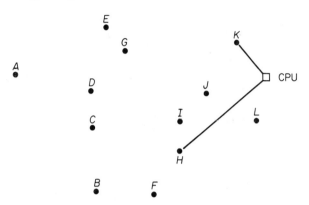

Figure 40.7

In some systems it may be necessary to have more than one line to a heavily loaded location—not in this illustration, however.

The algorithm begins by connecting one line from the computer to each location (Fig. 40.8).

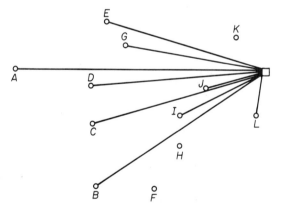

Figure 40.8

This "maximum-cost" position will now be modified step-by-step until the minimum-cost network is arrived at.

Starting with $A$, the most distant location, the trade-off costs for modifying the preceding layout are found (Figs. 40.9 and 40.10). The connection of $A$ to each of the other locations is examined to discover whether it meets the traffic load constraints and if so what the cost saving is.

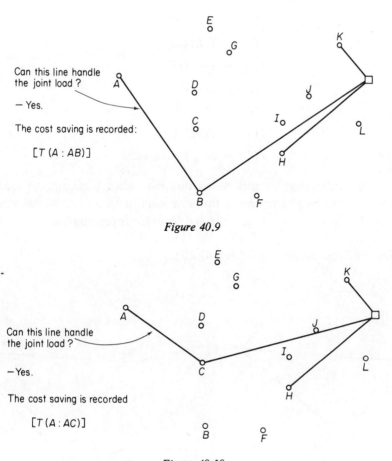

Can this line handle
the joint load ?
— Yes.
The cost saving is recorded:
[T (A : AB)]
A
B
C
D
E
F
G
H
I
J
K
L

*Figure 40.9*

Can this line handle
the joint load ?
—Yes.
The cost saving is recorded
[T (A : AC)]
A
B
C
D
E
F
G
H
I
J
K
L

*Figure 40.10*

This step is taken for all locations that $A$ could be connected to, and the maximum cost saving is found: $\hat{T}(A)$. In this case, the connection $A$ to $D$ gives the maximum saving.

$$\hat{T}(A) = T(A{:}AD)$$

Now the same is done with location $B$ to find $\hat{T}(B)$, then with each of the other locations except $H$ and $K$. The results are as follows in order of decreasing cost saving:

$$\hat{T}(A) = T(A{:}AD)$$
$$\hat{T}(B) = T(B{:}BF)$$
$$\hat{T}(C) = T(C{:}CD)$$

$$\hat{T}(D) = T(D:DC)$$
$$\hat{T}(E) = T(E:EG)$$
$$\hat{T}(G) = T(G:GE)$$
$$\hat{T}(F) = T(F:FB)$$
$$\hat{T}(I) = T(I:IJ)$$
$$\hat{T}(J) = T(J:JI)$$
$$\hat{T}(L) = \text{no positive value}$$

The algorithm now works down this list—always taking the maximum trade-off, max $(T)$—and connects the terminals in question. When a connection is made, the trade-off value is deleted from the foregoing list.

First $A$ is connected to $D$ (Fig. 40.11).

Then $B$ is connected to $F$ (Fig. 40.12).

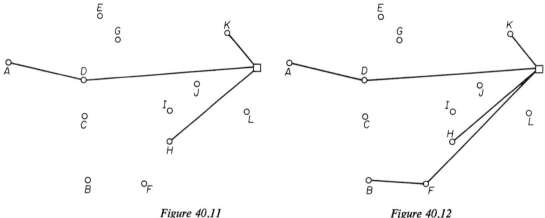

Figure 40.11                    Figure 40.12

If $\hat{T}(X) = T(X:XZ)$ in the earlier calculation, this result is not necessarily still valid if either $X$ or $Z$ has been connected to another location. In this case, $\hat{T}(X)$ must be recomputed. In looking at location $C$ now, we must recompute $\hat{T}(C)$ because location $D$ is connected to $A$.

Suppose that we now find that $C$ cannot be connected to $D$ because doing so would overload that line. $\hat{T}(C)$ is recomputed to be $T(C:CB)$. A line connecting $C$, $B$, and $F$ could handle the load. $C$ is therefore connected to $B$ (Fig. 40.13).

Next it is $D$'s turn. $\hat{T}(D)$ must be recomputed. It is now found to be $T(D:DG)$. The maximum trade-off on the list, max $(T)$, is then $\hat{T}(D)$, and so $D$ is connected to $G$ (Fig. 40.14).

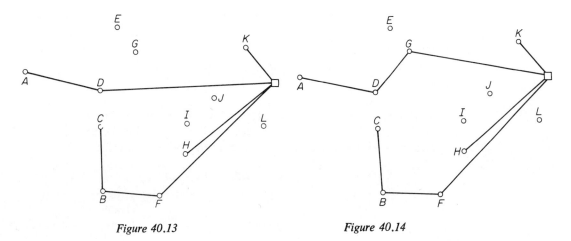

*Figure 40.13*                    *Figure 40.14*

Next it is the turn of $E$. $\hat{T}(E)$ is recomputed and is again $T(E:EG)$. $\hat{T}(E)$ remains at the top of the trade-off list and so $E$ is connected to $G$ (Fig. 40.15).

Now we turn to $G$. $\hat{T}(G)$ is recomputed, and it is found that $A$ cannot be connected to $I$ or $J$ because doing so would exceed the traffic load. There would be no saving in connecting it to $L$. Therefore the connection between $G$ and the computer remains unchanged.

$\hat{T}(F)$ must now be recomputed, and it is found that $F$ cannot be connected to $I$, $J$, or $L$ because of overloading.

$\hat{T}(I)$ is now at the top of the trade-off list and $\hat{T}(I) = T(I:IJ)$. Therefore $I$ is connected to $J$. $\hat{T}(J)$ is recomputed and $J$ is connected to $L$. The minimum-cost network in this case is shown in Fig. 40.16.

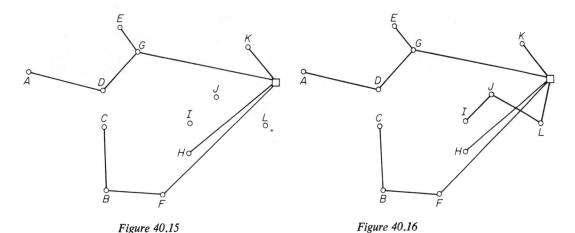

*Figure 40.15*                    *Figure 40.16*

This algorithm does not always give absolutely the minimum-cost network, but it is always very close and has the advantage over other methods of requiring a modest amount of computing time. Practical applications have shown it to be very valuable and many systems have been designed with it.

Let us now look at an example of its use.

**Example 40.3. A Network Too Complex to Optimize by Hand.** Again a network is to be designed to handle data from terminals connected to a data processing center in Chicago. Now, however, there are 187 terminal locations, as shown in Table 40.3.

**Table 40.3***

| City | Coordinates | | Traffic Volume (messages/hour) | |
|------|-----|-----|-----|-----|
| | *V* | *H* | Input | Output |
| MONTGOMERY   ALA | 7692 | 2247 | 2.09 | 3.10 |
| MOBILE   ALA | 8167 | 2367 | 1.92 | 2.84 |
| BIRMINGHAM   ALA | 7518 | 2446 | 2.17 | 3.20 |
| MERIDEN   CONN | 4740 | 1358 | 2.20 | 3.26 |
| WATERBURY   CONN | 4761 | 1391 | 2.67 | 3.95 |
| HARTFORD   CONN | 4687 | 1373 | 3.72 | 5.51 |
| NORWICH   CONN | 4668 | 1263 | 5.30 | 7.84 |
| NEW BRITAIN   CONN | 4715 | 1373 | 3.05 | 4.51 |
| NEW HAVEN CONN | 4792 | 1342 | 0.43 | 0.64 |
| DANBURY   CONN | 4829 | 1423 | 3.51 | 5.20 |
| BRIDGEPORT   CONN | 4841 | 1360 | 5.85 | 8.65 |
| CANAAN   CONN | 4703 | 1485 | 2.07 | 3.06 |
| WILMINGTON   DEL | 5326 | 1485 | 2.81 | 4.16 |
| WASHINGTON DC | 5622 | 1583 | 7.21 | 10.68 |
| ORLANDO   FLA | 7954 | 1031 | 1.44 | 2.13 |
| WEST PALM BEACH FLA | 8166 | 0607 | 2.90 | 4.29 |
| TAMPA FLA | 8173 | 1147 | 1.60 | 2.37 |
| TALLAHASSE   FLA | 7877 | 1716 | 1.43 | 2.12 |
| ST. PETERSBURG FLA | 8224 | 1159 | 0.57 | 0.85 |
| MIAMI   FLA | 8351 | 0527 | 7.16 | 10.60 |
| JACKSONVILLE   FLA | 7649 | 1276 | 0.57 | 0.85 |
| FORT LAUDERDALE FLA | 8282 | 0557 | 5.40 | 8.00 |
| MACON   GA | 7364 | 1865 | 0.43 | 0.64 |
| SAVANNAH   GA | 7266 | 1379 | 2.13 | 3.15 |
| AUGUSTA   GA | 7089 | 1674 | 0.63 | 0.94 |
| ATLANTA GA | 7260 | 2083 | 0.89 | 1.32 |
| CENTRALIA   ILL | 6744 | 3311 | 1.99 | 2.94 |
| JOLIET   ILL | 6088 | 3454 | 2.75 | 4.07 |
| HIGHLAND PARK   ILL | 5940 | 3480 | 3.01 | 4.45 |
| SPRINGFIELD   ILL | 6539 | 3513 | 3.54 | 5.23 |
| ROCKFORD   ILL | 6022 | 3675 | 3.44 | 5.09 |

*Note: These are the cities marked on the map in Fig. 40.1.

| City | Coordinates | | Traffic Volume (messages/hour) | |
|------|:---:|:---:|:---:|:---:|
| | V | H | Input | Output |
| QUINCY  ILL | 6642 | 3790 | 0.98 | 1.44 |
| PEORIA ILL | 6362 | 3592 | 3.50 | 5.18 |
| GALESBURG  ILL | 6369 | 3732 | 2.16 | 3.20 |
| DECATUR  ILL | 6478 | 3413 | 2.22 | 3.28 |
| DANVILLE  ILL | 6322 | 3245 | 2.97 | 4.39 |
| CHICAGO B ZONE 1 | 5986 | 3426 | 5.25 | 7.77 |
| CHICAGO D ZONE 2 | 5971 | 3443 | 4.52 | 6.69 |
| CHICAGO F ZONE 2 | 5971 | 3443 | 2.70 | 3.99 |
| CHICAGO H ZONE 3 | 5979 | 3455 | 3.02 | 4.47 |
| CHICAGO J ZONE 4 | 5981 | 3437 | 8.10 | 11.99 |
| CHICAGO L ZONE 5 | 5991 | 3449 | 3.65 | 5.41 |
| CHICAGO N ZONE 6 | 5998 | 3431 | 4.22 | 6.24 |
| CHICAGO P ZONE 7 | 6007 | 3412 | 3.45 | 5.11 |
| CHICAGO R ZONE 8 | 6011 | 3424 | 4.14 | 6.13 |
| CHICAGO S ZONE 9 | 6014 | 3397 | 7.46 | 11.04 |
| CHICAGO U ZONE 10 | 6022 | 3407 | 3.16 | 4.67 |
| CHICAGO X ZONE 11 | 5988 | 3474 | 0.69 | 1.02 |
| CHAMPAIGN  ILL | 6371 | 3336 | 3.37 | 4.99 |
| BLOOMINGTON  ILL | 6358 | 3483 | 1.69 | 2.49 |
| MICHIGAN CITY  IND | 5962 | 3301 | 4.01 | 5.94 |
| KOKOMO  IND | 6135 | 3063 | 1.10 | 1.63 |
| FORT WAYNE  IND | 5942 | 2982 | 5.65 | 8.36 |
| ELKHART  IND | 5895 | 3168 | 2.29 | 3.39 |
| BLOOMINGTON  IND | 6417 | 2984 | 1.90 | 2.81 |
| MASON CITY  IOWA | 6136 | 4352 | 0.57 | 0.85 |
| CLINTON  IOWA | 6180 | 3793 | 0.43 | 0.64 |
| FORT DODGE  IOWA | 6328 | 4438 | 0.59 | 0.88 |
| IOWA CITY  IOWA | 6313 | 3972 | 1.44 | 2.13 |
| DES MOINES  IOWA | 6471 | 4275 | 3.38 | 5.01 |
| DAVENPORT  IOWA | 6273 | 3817 | 2.08 | 3.08 |
| CEDAR RAPIDS  IOWA | 6261 | 4021 | 0.98 | 1.44 |
| WICHITA  KAN | 7489 | 4520 | 0.43 | 0.64 |
| TOPEKA  KAN | 7110 | 4369 | 2.05 | 3.04 |
| MADISONVILLE  KY | 6845 | 2942 | 0.59 | 0.88 |
| LEXINGTON  KY | 6459 | 2562 | 2.87 | 4.25 |
| WINCHESTER  KY | 6441 | 2509 | 2.20 | 3.26 |
| ASHLAND  KY | 6220 | 2334 | 0.63 | 0.94 |
| PADUCAH  KY | 6982 | 3088 | 0.63 | 0.94 |
| LOUISVILLE KY | 6529 | 2772 | 0.89 | 1.32 |
| MONROE  LA | 8148 | 3218 | 1.44 | 2.13 |
| SHREVEPORT LA | 8272 | 3495 | 0.43 | 0.64 |
| NEW ORLEANS LA | 8483 | 2638 | 0.57 | 0.85 |
| BATON ROUGE  LA | 8476 | 2874 | 1.56 | 2.31 |
| HAGERSTOWN  MD | 5555 | 1772 | 3.39 | 5.01 |
| CUMBERLAND  MD | 5650 | 1916 | 2.72 | 4.03 |
| BALTIMORE  MD | 5510 | 1575 | 8.95 | 13.24 |
| ANNAPOLIS  MD | 5555 | 1519 | 1.66 | 2.46 |
| SPRINGFIELD  MASS | 4620 | 1408 | 4.45 | 6.59 |

| City | Coordinates | | Traffic Volume (messages/hour) | |
|---|---|---|---|---|
| | V | H | Input | Output |
| BOSTON MASS | 4422 | 1249 | 5.63 | 8.33 |
| GREENFIELD MASS | 4537 | 1475 | 2.04 | 3.03 |
| WORCESTER MASS | 4513 | 1330 | 3.47 | 5.13 |
| SALEM MASS | 4378 | 1251 | 2.75 | 4.07 |
| JACKSON MICH | 5663 | 3009 | 3.72 | 5.51 |
| ANN ARBOR MICH | 5602 | 2918 | 3.55 | 5.26 |
| MUSKEGON MICH | 5622 | 3370 | 1.93 | 2.86 |
| LANSING MICH | 5584 | 3081 | 2.52 | 3.74 |
| KALAMAZOO MICH | 5749 | 3177 | 2.27 | 3.35 |
| GRAND RAPIDS MICH | 5628 | 3261 | 2.40 | 3.55 |
| FLINT MICH | 5461 | 2993 | 3.58 | 5.31 |
| SAGINAW MICH | 5404 | 3074 | 0.57 | 0.85 |
| DETROIT 1 MICH | 5536 | 2828 | 9.43 | 13.95 |
| DETROIT 2 MICH | 5536 | 2828 | 4.93 | 7.30 |
| ROCHESTER MINN | 5916 | 4326 | 0.71 | 1.04 |
| DULUTH MINN | 5352 | 4530 | 0.63 | 0.94 |
| JACKSON MISS | 8035 | 2880 | 0.43 | 0.64 |
| ST LOUIS MO | 6807 | 3482 | 1.23 | 1.82 |
| JEFFERSON CITY MO | 6963 | 3782 | 2.87 | 4.25 |
| JOPLIN MO | 7421 | 4015 | 1.49 | 2.21 |
| SPRINGFIELD MO | 7310 | 3836 | 3.58 | 5.29 |
| KANSAS CITY MO | 7027 | 4203 | 7.19 | 10.65 |
| OKLAHOMA CITY OKLA | 7947 | 4373 | 1.76 | 2.61 |
| TULSA OKLA | 7707 | 4173 | 0.85 | 1.26 |
| ATLANTIC CITY NJ | 5284 | 1284 | 3.14 | 4.64 |
| NEWARK NJ | 5015 | 1430 | 6.10 | 9.04 |
| PATERSON NJ | 4984 | 1452 | 3.79 | 5.61 |
| TRENTON NJ | 5164 | 1440 | 2.86 | 4.23 |
| AUBURN NY | 4858 | 2030 | 1.23 | 1.82 |
| PEEKSKILL NY | 4894 | 1470 | 3.74 | 5.54 |
| WHITE PLAINS NY | 4921 | 1416 | 6.35 | 9.40 |
| NIAGARA FALLS NY | 5053 | 2377 | 3.26 | 4.82 |
| NEW YORK CITY 1 | 4972 | 1408 | 6.09 | 9.01 |
| NEW YORK CITY 2 | 5004 | 1392 | 3.08 | 4.55 |
| NEW YORK CITY 3 | 4975 | 1387 | 4.75 | 7.02 |
| NEW YORK CITY 4 | 4970 | 1379 | 7.43 | 11.00 |
| NEW YORK CITY 5 | 5000 | 1358 | 6.29 | 9.30 |
| NEW YORK CITY 6 | 5054 | 1407 | 5.17 | 7.66 |
| UTICA NY | 4701 | 1878 | 5.46 | 8.08 |
| SYRACUSE NY | 4798 | 1990 | 3.43 | 5.07 |
| SCHENECTADY NY | 4629 | 1675 | 4.67 | 6.91 |
| ROCHESTER NY | 4913 | 2195 | 8.95 | 13.25 |
| POUGHKEEPSIE NY | 4821 | 1526 | 4.62 | 6.84 |
| ITHACA NY | 4938 | 1958 | 2.25 | 3.34 |
| BUFFALO NY | 5075 | 2326 | 9.58 | 14.18 |
| BINGHAMTON NY | 4943 | 1837 | 4.99 | 7.38 |
| ALBANY NY | 4639 | 1629 | 0.63 | 0.94 |
| GOLDSBORO NC | 6352 | 1290 | 2.07 | 3.06 |
| ASHEVILLE NC | 6749 | 2001 | 2.61 | 3.86 |
| WINSTON SALEM NC | 6440 | 1710 | 2.08 | 3.07 |
| RALEIGH NC | 6344 | 1436 | 2.31 | 3.42 |
| FAYETTEVILLE NC | 6501 | 1385 | 1.62 | 2.39 |
| CHARLOTTE NC | 6657 | 1698 | 0.43 | 0.64 |
| MANSFIELD OHIO | 5783 | 2575 | 2.26 | 3.35 |
| CLEVELAND OHIO | 5574 | 2543 | 3.09 | 4.58 |

| City | Coordinates V | H | Traffic Volume (messages/hour) Input | Output |
|------|------|------|------|------|
| YOUNGSTOWN OHIO | 5557 | 2353 | 3.66 | 5.42 |
| STEUBENVILLE OHIO | 5689 | 2262 | 2.35 | 3.48 |
| SPRINGFIELD OHIO | 6049 | 2666 | 3.13 | 4.64 |
| SANDUSKY OHIO | 5670 | 2682 | 1.58 | 2.33 |
| LIMA OHIO | 5921 | 2799 | 1.88 | 2.78 |
| DAYTON OHIO | 6113 | 2705 | 2.72 | 4.03 |
| COLUMBUS OHIO | 5972 | 2555 | 4.26 | 6.31 |
| CINCINNATI 2 OHIO | 6263 | 2679 | 2.52 | 3.73 |
| CINCINNATI 1 OHIO | 6263 | 2679 | 4.56 | 6.75 |
| CANTON OHIO | 5676 | 2419 | 0.43 | 0.64 |
| ASHTABULA OHIO | 5429 | 2462 | 1.61 | 2.39 |
| ALLIANCE OHIO | 5629 | 2395 | 3.14 | 4.65 |
| AKRON OHIO | 5637 | 2472 | 0.89 | 1.32 |
| WILLIAMSPORT PENN | 5201 | 1876 | 0.43 | 0.64 |
| SCRANTON PENN | 5042 | 1715 | 1.72 | 2.54 |
| HARRISBURG PENN | 5363 | 1733 | 1.76 | 2.61 |
| BRADFORD PENN | 5221 | 2182 | 1.68 | 2.49 |
| WILKES-BARRE PENN | 5093 | 1723 | 2.14 | 3.17 |
| PHILADELPHIA PENN | 5251 | 1458 | 8.91 | 13.19 |
| PITTSBURGH PENN | 5621 | 2185 | 8.85 | 13.09 |
| ROCHESTER PENN | 5589 | 2251 | 0.85 | 1.26 |
| NEWPORT RI | 4596 | 1160 | 3.45 | 5.10 |
| PROVIDENCE RI | 4550 | 1219 | 4.13 | 6.11 |
| FLORENCE SC | 6744 | 1417 | 0.86 | 1.28 |
| SPARTENBURG SC | 6811 | 1833 | 0.63 | 0.94 |
| CHARLESTON SC | 7021 | 1281 | 2.45 | 3.62 |
| GREENVILLE SC | 6873 | 1894 | 1.99 | 2.95 |
| COLUMBIA SC | 6901 | 1589 | 2.17 | 3.21 |
| NASHVILLE TENN | 7010 | 2710 | 2.85 | 4.21 |
| KNOXVILLE TENN | 6801 | 2251 | 0.63 | 0.94 |
| MEMPHIS TENN | 7471 | 3125 | 1.23 | 1.82 |
| CHATTANOOGA TENN | 7098 | 2366 | 2.54 | 3.76 |
| AUSTIN TEX | 9005 | 3996 | 1.53 | 2.26 |
| SAN ANTONIO TEX | 9225 | 4062 | 2.89 | 4.28 |
| HOUSTON TEX | 8934 | 3536 | 2.19 | 3.25 |
| FORT WORTH TEX | 8479 | 4122 | 1.05 | 1.55 |
| CORPUS CHRISTI TEX | 9475 | 3739 | 1.97 | 2.92 |
| DALLAS TEX | 8436 | 4034 | 2.10 | 3.11 |
| DANVILLE VA | 6270 | 1640 | 0.63 | 0.94 |
| STAUNTON VA | 5953 | 1781 | 1.19 | 1.76 |
| RICHMOND VA | 5906 | 1472 | 3.81 | 5.64 |
| PETERSBURG VA | 5961 | 1429 | 2.06 | 3.05 |
| NORFOLK VA | 5918 | 1223 | 3.14 | 4.65 |
| LYNCHBURG VA | 6093 | 1703 | 1.62 | 2.40 |
| WHEELING W VA | 5755 | 2241 | 1.43 | 2.12 |
| CHARLESTON W VA | 6152 | 2174 | 1.85 | 2.74 |
| EAU CLAIRE WIS | 5698 | 4261 | 1.39 | 2.06 |
| GREEN BAY WIS | 5512 | 3747 | 1.49 | 2.21 |
| APPLETONN WIS | 5589 | 3776 | 1.44 | 2.13 |
| MILWAUKEE WIS | 5788 | 3589 | 9.52 | 14.08 |
| MADISON WIS | 5887 | 3796 | 0.63 | 0.94 |
| RHINELANDER WIS | 5394 | 4053 | 1.23 | 1.82 |
| FORT SMITH ARK | 7752 | 3855 | 1.23 | 1.82 |
| LITTLE ROCK ARK | 7721 | 3451 | 1.72 | 2.54 |
| HOT SPRINGS ARK | 7827 | 3554 | 1.19 | 1.76 |

Table 40.3 gives the coordinates of the terminal locations, plus the traffic volumes that the network is to be designed for. In this case, there are more output messages than input. The reason is that some input messages cause a response to be sent to more than one terminal. Also the computer sends some unsolicited messages.

The terminals that are to be used operate over a half-duplex line at 14.8 characters per second. Not more than 26 terminals can be attached to one such line. Line loading and queuing calculations, such as those used in the previous chapters, have resulted in the traffic rate table shown in Table 40.4.

## Table 40.4

| Number of Terminals per Line | Maximum Traffic Rate (messages/hour) |
|:---:|:---:|
| 1 | 350.300 |
| 2 | 343.300 |
| 3 | 336.200 |
| 4 | 329.400 |
| 5 | 322.800 |
| 6 | 318.600 |
| 7 | 310.400 |
| 8 | 304.500 |
| 9 | 298.600 |
| 10 | 293.000 |
| 11 | 287.600 |
| 12 | 282.300 |
| 13 | 277.200 |
| 14 | 272.200 |
| 15 | 267.400 |
| 16 | 262.700 |
| 17 | 258.100 |
| 18 | 253.500 |
| 19 | 249.000 |
| 20 | 244.800 |
| 21 | 240.700 |
| 22 | 236.800 |
| 23 | 232.800 |
| 24 | 228.800 |
| 25 | 225.100 |
| 26 | 221.500 |

A first step in laying out the network is to determine how many terminals will be in use simultaneously at each location. A study of the operator's work in this example led to the criterion that if there are less than 24 messages per hour, only one active terminal will be needed. Similarly, if there are between 24 and 48 messages per hour, 2 terminals will be needed. If there are between 48 and 72 messages per hour, 3 will be needed and so on. A few locations will have an extra terminal for reliability, but this factor does not affect the traffic rate table, for only one will be connected to the line at one time. With the traffic volumes listed above, no location need have more than one terminal in use at one time. However, we will repeat this example with higher traffic volumes and then some locations will need several terminals.

The network was designed for Bell System type 1006 lines. The resulting configuration is shown in Fig. 40.17. Eight lines are needed, some of which have the maximum of 26 locations connected to them. The cost of the network (at the time of writing), including the channel terminal charges, is $25,890 per month.

**INCREASING THE TRAFFIC VOLUME**

Let us repeat our Example 40.3 with different traffic volumes. First, we will double the traffic volume. The resulting network is shown in Fig. 40.18. Now 11 lines are needed, including one that does not leave Chicago. Although the traffic volume has doubled, the network cost has increased by only about 4.4 percent. The reason is that some of the lines with 26 drops were not fully loaded in Fig. 40.17. Furthermore, the new interconnections shown in Fig. 40.18 have increased the total mileage by only 10.5 percent.

Next the traffic volume of Fig. 40.17 is multiplied by eight, which means that many of the locations must now have more than one terminal. The resulting network is shown in Fig. 40.19. There are now 38 lines, including 3 from New York and 3 that do not leave Chicago. The total line cost is $39,000. Although the traffic volume has gone up by 800 percent, the total line mileage has increased by only slightly more than double. The number of line terminations, including those at Chicago (and hence the channel terminal charges), have increased by only 47 percent.

Figure 40.20 plots the variation in line cost for interconnecting these cities against the traffic volume. It will be seen that the cost rises only slowly at low-traffic volumes. It will then perhaps be worthwhile to design the network with some slack in it so that the network can handle abnormally high peak loads.

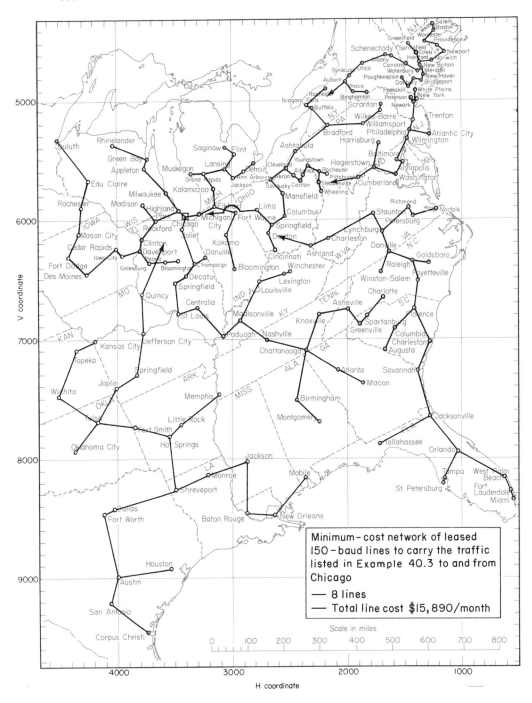

*Fig. 40.17.* The minimum-cost network for Example 40.3.

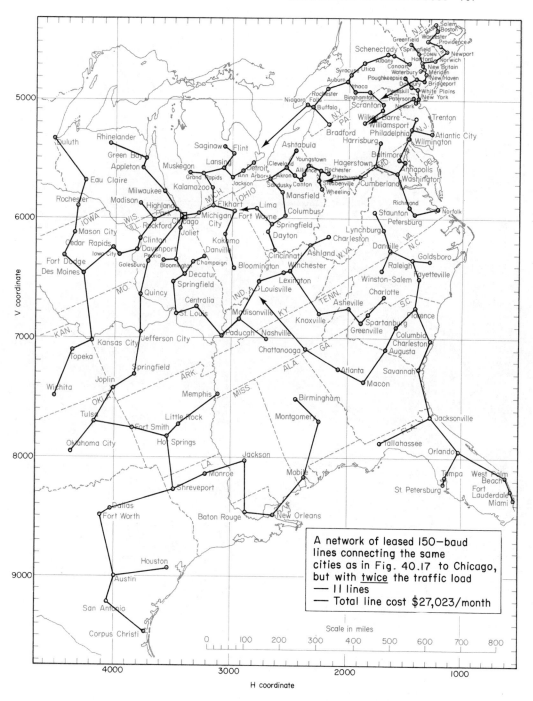

*Fig. 40.18.* A network for the same cities as in Fig. 40.17, but with twice the traffic load.

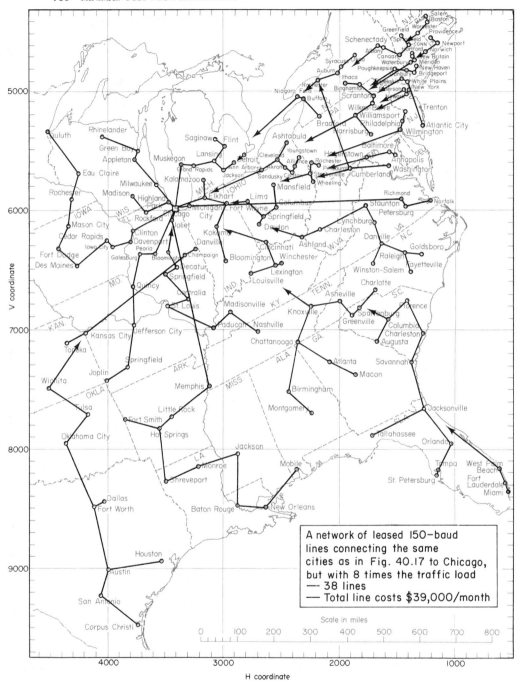

A network of leased 150–baud
lines connecting the same
cities as in Fig. 40.17 to Chicago,
but with 8 times the traffic load
—- 38 lines
— Total line costs $39,000/month

*Fig. 40.19.* A network for the same cities as in Fig. 40.17 but with eight times the traffic load.

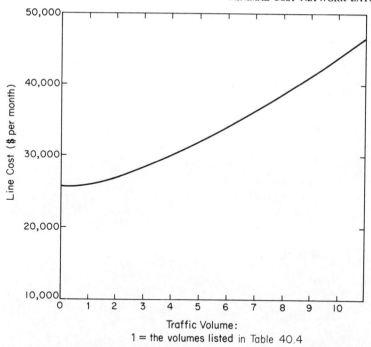

*Fig. 40.20.* The variation of cost with traffic volume for a leased line network connecting the cities in Fig. 40.17 to Chicago.

## REFERENCES

1. A List of Rate Centers and Control Offices, USA Tariff, FCC #255, filed by American Telephone and Telegraph Company.
2. The CNDP algorithm is described by L. R. Esau and K. C. Williams in "A Method for Approximating the Optimal Network," *IBM Systems Journal*, Vol. 5, No. 3, Armonk, 1966.

# 41    DIAL-UP VS. LEASED LINES

As indicated in Chapter 17, a basic decision made early in the design process is whether the terminals should be on leased or dial-up lines. If line usage is high—more than 3 hours per day, for example—then the leased-line tariff will normally prove the less expensive. If it is used infrequently, it will be cheaper to dial whenever the connection is needed.

On some systems, dialing would be quite unsatisfactory because of fast response-time requirements. Sales agents using a terminal to answer customers' telephone requests may not have the time to *dial* the computer; they want access to it almost immediately. On airline reservation systems, for example, the delay associated with dialing has generally been considered inacceptable. Dialing may add 20 seconds or so onto what would otherwise be a response time of 2 seconds. On the other hand, many systems do not need this frantic speed. On some systems, a lengthy man-machine conversation is going to ensue once the connection is made, and the addition of 20 seconds dialing time to a 20-minute conversation is negligible. Where *batches* of work are to be sent, a dialed connection is often used. However, as noted earlier, the transmission speed on a public line is generally less than on a leased line, and so here, too, the overall costs will favor the leased line if more than a certain quantity of data is to be sent.

In this chapter we will discuss systems where a dial-up connection *would* be used if it were cheaper; there is no objection to it in terms of response time or the inconvenience of dialing.

There are two types of systems in which public dial-up lines are used. The most common type is where the operator originates the calls and dials the computer (sometimes dials another terminal). The second is where the computer

711

originates the call and an automatic dialing unit establishes the connection. In the first case, if the computer has no out-dialing facility, it cannot send unsolicited messages to a terminal until the operator of that terminal dials in. In the second case, the system may be designed so that the operator can dial in addition to the computer dialing out. In some systems, however, this situation does not exist, and the computer originates all calls. The operator may load cards or tapes at the terminal, and the terminal awaits a dial-up signal from the computer. This practice occurs, for example, in some message-switching systems. The computer is programmed to dial the terminals one by one to see if they have anything to send—a scanning operation that is slow because of the time taken to dial.

When the computer originates the calls, WATS lines are somctimes used, for they allow an unlimited number of calls to a given area. When the operator originates the calls, the network may be designed with a variety of different line types—Telex, TWX, INWATS, and private branch exchanges with leased lines, as was discussed in Chapter 17. Often telephone lines are used because of the ubiquitous convenience of the public network.

**TIMING CALCULATIONS**   Figure 41.1 shows the elements of time that must be added when an operator dials a computer on the public network.

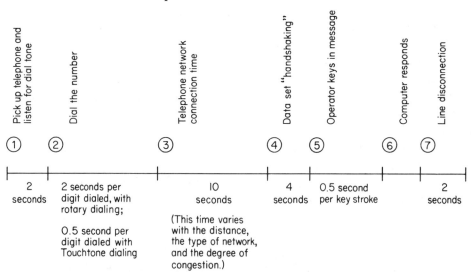

Fig. 41.1. Typical times involved in an operator dialing a computer and obtaining a response. The connection and data set hand-shaking times should be assessed specifically for the data set and connections in question.

1. The operator picks up the telephone and receives a dial tone. On some data sets, she will press the TALK button at this time.

2. She dials the number of the computer. The time taken to do so varies with the number of digits dialed and with operator dexterity. A conservative time to use in the calculations might be 2 seconds per digit for a device with a rotary dial. Timing myself on my office telephone, I find that I take 1.5 seconds per digit dialing random numbers, 2.1 seconds per digit dialing all 9s, and 0.75 second per digit dialing all 1s.

   With a Touch-Tone telephone, a reasonable time to allow is 0.5 second per digit.

3. After the dialing is completed, the equipment in the switching centers takes an additional period of time to complete the connection. This period can vary from about 1 second up to 20 seconds or more. From my telephone in Manhattan, I find that the interval between the end of dialing and the first ring of the dialed party is usually between 1 and 5 seconds. Occasionally it is longer. When calling numbers more than 500 miles away, the delay is typically about 10 seconds, but again it will occasionally be longer, sometimes 30 seconds or more. An appropriate figure can be established for the dial-up links in question.

4. On many data sets the operator hears a "data tone" when the connection is completed; she presses the DATA key and hangs up. A time of 4 seconds might be used in the calculations for this action.

5. and 6. In Fig. 41.1, (5) and (6) are the normal times for message transmission and computer response.

7. The time for disconnecting the line. Until this time element is complete, the computer cannot accept another call on the same line.

The response time may now be defined to include time elements 1 through 6 above. The total time the line into the computer is occupied includes elements 4 through 7. During this time, the line appears busy to another incoming call. This is the time period that would be used in calculations of the number of lines needed, such as those in Chapter 33. Knowing this time period, the systems analyst can calculate the probability of succeeding in obtaining service from the computer—the "grade of service."

A user might specify that the response time, including dialing, should not exceed 30 seconds, for example, and that the probability of obtaining a busy signal from the computer should not exceed 0.01. The systems analyst would use the foregoing timing figures to design a system that meets these requirements.

**COMPUTER**
**DIALING OUT**
The computer may be equipped with an automatic dialing unit that will enable it to send unsolicited messages to terminals over the public network and to scan terminals on WATS or other suitably tariffed lines to see whether they have data ready to send.

Figure 41.2 shows typical times involved when the computer dials out.

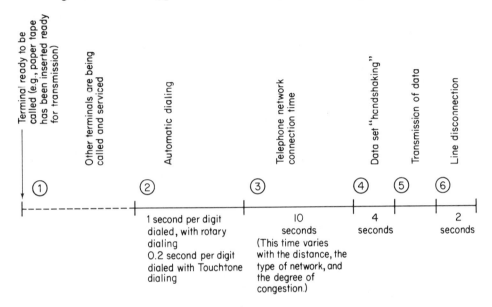

*Fig. 41.2.* Typical times involved when the computer automatically dials terminals. The connection and data set hand-shaking times should be assessed specifically for the data set and connection in question.

1. At the beginning of time element 1, the terminal is ready to transmit. The computer, or its transmission control unit, however, is busy dialing other terminals. Eventually it dials the terminal in question.

2. The dialing time, as in the previous case, varies with the number and value of digits dialed. It is at least twice as fast as manual dialing. If the systems analyst cannot obtain exact figures for the equipment in question, he might assume 1 second per digit for rotary dialing and 0.2 second per digit for Touchtone.

3. The same comments as before apply to the telephone network connection time.

4. When the connection is established, the terminal must respond to the "ringing," and a data set handshaking operation takes place. The time

for thus establishing the data path will vary from one type of equipment to another. A typical figure of 4 seconds is given in Fig. 41.2.

5. The time for the transmission of data must include the necessary control characters and timeout intervals, if any.

6. Finally, there is the disconnection time, from the end of transmission of data to the time the next call can be initiated—typically about 2 seconds.

The line-control equipment at the computer is tied up for time elements 2 through 6 above. The transaction response time for incoming transactions will include items 1 through 7.

The mean response time can be found in the following way.

Let us consider a system in which the computer dials $M$ terminals. It dials them in sequence to see whether they have data to send.

Let $t_M$ equal the time for dialing a terminal and reading its data (in seconds), $t_0$ equal the time for dialing and disconnecting a terminal that has nothing to send (seconds), and $n$ equal the number of transactions per hour handled by the system.

The proportion of the time spent servicing terminals that *have* data to send is

$$\frac{nt_M}{3600}$$

The proportion of the time spent scanning terminals that do not have data to send is

$$1 - \frac{nt_M}{3600}$$

The mean time to service one terminal is therefore

$$\frac{nt_M}{3600}\, t_M + \left(1 - \frac{nt_M}{3600}\right) t_0 = \frac{nt_M(t_M - t_0)}{3600} + t_0 \qquad (41.1)$$

A terminal having data to send may be lucky and not have to wait before it is serviced. On the other hand, it may be unlucky and have to wait while $M - 1$ terminals are serviced. The probability of it having to wait while $J$ terminals are serviced (where $0 \leq J \leq M - 1$) is $1/M$.

The mean waiting time is then

$$\sum_{J=0}^{M-1} \frac{1}{M} J \left[\frac{nt_M(t_M - t_0)}{3600} + t_0\right] = \frac{M - 1}{2} \left[\frac{nt_M(t_M - t_0)}{3600} + t_0\right]$$

The mean response time is therefore

$$E(t_R) = t_M + \frac{M-1}{2}\left[\frac{nt_M(t_M-t_0)}{3600} + t_0\right] \tag{41.2}$$

**Example 41.1. A System with Computer–Originated Dialing.** A sales-order entry system has 200 terminals in different sales offices. Data and queries about orders are entered into these terminals. The computer will dial the terminals, read what data has been entered, and send back a response. When a terminal with no data is dialed, the line into the transmission control unit will be tied up for 17 seconds. When a terminal with data is dialed, the operation, including the response to the terminal, takes 35 seconds on the average. The peak volume expected is 400 transactions per hour. How many lines into the transmission control unit are needed in order to achieve a mean response time no greater than 5 minutes?

We have

$$t_0 = 17 \quad \text{and} \quad t_M = 35$$

Let $L$ be the number of lines that are used. The maximum number of terminals per line is

$$M = \left\lceil\frac{200}{L}\right\rceil$$

The maximum number of transactions per hour per line is

$$n = \left\lceil\frac{400}{L}\right\rceil$$

(assuming that the traffic volume can be distributed evenly between the lines. A detailed knowledge of the traffic breakdown would give an exact figure for the highest value of $n$.)

From Eq. (41.2) we have the mean response time

$$E(t_R) = 35 + \frac{[200/L]-1}{2}\left\{\frac{[400/L] \times 35 \times (35-17)}{3600} + 17\right\}$$

With $L = 9$, $E(t_R) = 308.6$ seconds—slightly too high. With $L = 10$, $E(t_R) = 229.8$ seconds.

Therefore 10 lines into the transmission control unit are needed.

**RELATIVE**
**COSTS**

Assuming that there is no systems objection to dial-up lines, the systems analyst must calculate whether or not they are lower in cost than leased lines.

Figures 41.3 and 41.4 indicate the variation in cost with distance of voice-grade and subvoice-grade lines. The tariffs are likely to change and these dia-

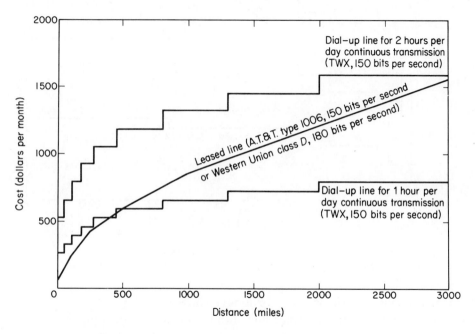

*Fig. 41.3.* A comparison of leased and dial subvoice-grade lines. Note: The costs are likely to change.

grams should only be taken as typical of relative costs. The dial-up lines in Fig. 41.3 are TWX lines used for continuous transmission (i.e., not for short, separate transmissions). On this basis, it will be seen that the leased line is always cheaper than the dial-up connection for 2 hours worth of transmission per day. For one hour of transmission per day, it is still cheaper below distances of about 400 miles. Figure 41.4 is a similar plot for voice lines. It will be seen that the break even point varies considerably with distance.

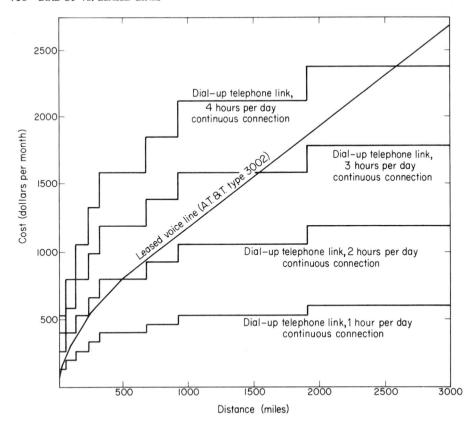

*Fig. 41.4.* A comparison of leased and dial voice-grade lines. Note:
The costs are likely to change. Dial-up costs are lower at off-peak
hours.

Surprisingly, perhaps, the two figures show that the dial-up voice-grade
line is cheaper than the subvoice line, although it has a much higher capacity.
The TWX line should therefore not be used for *continuous* transmission.

Telex rates are lower than toll telephone rates for most locations in the
United States, but are sufficiently close for it to be generally uneconomical to
use Telex either for continuous transmission. Normally Telex is used for sending
relatively short transmissions of not more than a few hundred characters. The
minimum charge[1] for such a connection is 20 to 60 cents for one minute of transmission, depending on distance (at 15 characters per second, this is 900 characters). We should therefore evaluate the cost of the subvoice-grade lines on the
basis of the number of short calls. Figure 41.5 compares dial-up cost with

---

[1] Note that all charges quoted are subject to change.

leased line cost on this basis, and Fig. 41.6 does the same for a voice line. The minimum charge on a voice line is 30 cents to $1.70 for 3 minutes. On this basis, the TWX line is substantially cheaper than toll telephone, especially for long distances. Once again the reader should note that the tariffs are likely to change.

Figures 41.7 and 41.8 show similar costs for lines in Great Britain. Here the Telex line is more expensive than the voice line for *continuous* transmission. The minimum charge for a short connection is 1p for either Telex or STD telephone lines. The time that this 1p pays for is shown in tabular form.

| Distance (miles) | Telex (seconds) | STD Telephone (seconds) |
|---|---|---|
| Up to 35 | 60 | 30 (6 minutes for local calls) |
| 35 to 50 | 30 | 15 |
| 50 to 75 | 30 | 10 |
| Over 75 | 15 | 10 |

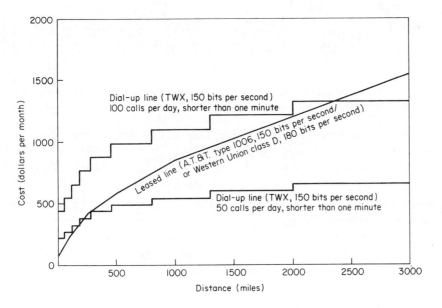

*Fig. 41.5.* A comparison of leased and dial subvoice-grade lines for short message transmission. Note: The costs are likely to change.

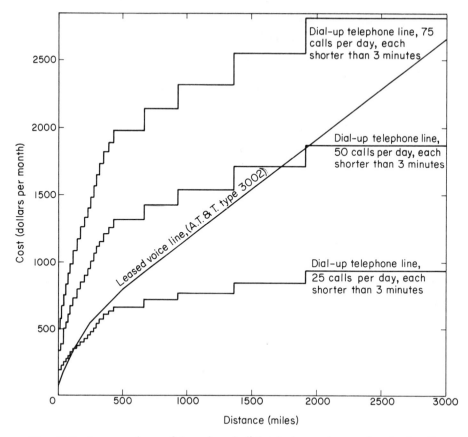

*Fig. 41.6.* A comparison of leased and dial telephone charges for short calls. Note: The charges are likely to change. Dial-up charges are lower for off-peak hours.

A "short" connection over 75 miles on Telex is therefore 15 seconds or less, in which 100 characters or less can be transmitted.

The break-even point in cost between private and public lines varies with the distance of the link as well as with the amount of time the line is used. Figures 41.9 and 41.10 illustrate this. Figure 41.10 charts the break-even point between leased and dial voice lines. Figure 41.9 shows the break-even point between leased subvoice-grade lines (Type 1006) and dial voice lines. Voice lines were used in this plot rather than TWX lines because they are cheaper for continuous transmission. In both cases the dial-up tariff looks more favorable at a long distance.

Figure 41.11 compares the WATS tariff cost with leased voice line costs. Except at long distances the monthly flat rate for the WATS line is higher than that for the leased voice line.

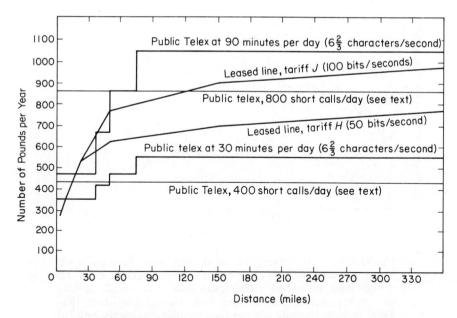

*Fig. 41.7.* Cost comparison of dial-up Telex and leased telegraph lines in Britain.

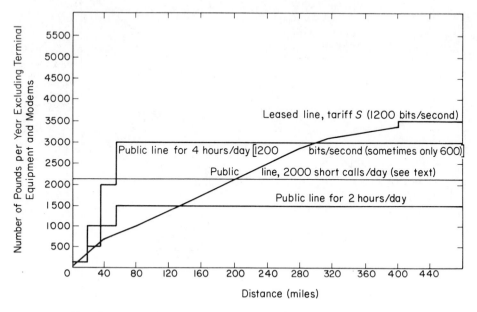

*Fig. 41.8.* Cost comparison of dial-up and leased telephone lines in Britain.

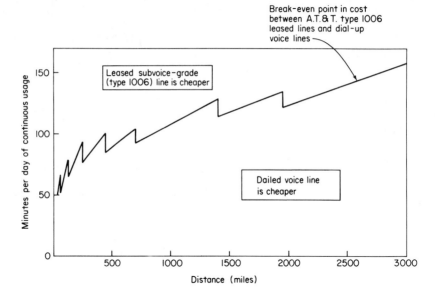

*Fig. 41.9.* A curve showing the break-even point in cost between leased subvoice-grade (Type 1006, 150-bit-per-second) lines and dial-up voice lines. Note: The calculations assumed 22 working days in the month. Dial-up voice lines were plotted rather than TWX because they are *cheaper* for continuous transmission. The price figures used are subject to change.

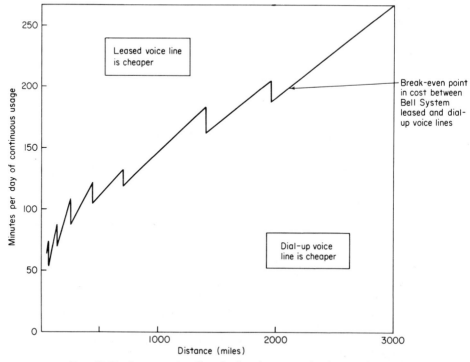

*Fig. 41.10.* A curve showing the break-even point in cost between leased and dial-up line costs on Bell System interstate voice-grade lines. Note: The calculations assumed 22 working days in the month. The price figures used in plotting the curve are subject to change.

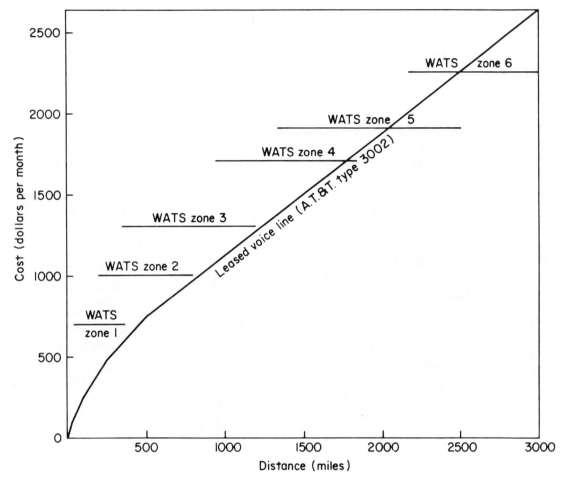

*Fig. 41.11.* A comparison of WATS line costs with those of a leased voice line. WATS lines to Southeast New York were used (see map in Fig. 18.2).

**COMPLEX NETWORKS**

For a point-to-point link, there is no difficulty in working out relative costs if the volume of data to be transmitted is known. Where many terminals are involved, however, the situation is more complex.

Sometimes the tariffs and networks indicate clearly that all the links should be dial-up. Sometimes it is clear that all of them should be leased lines. Often, however, the lowest-cost solution is to have some dial-up connections and some leased. This solution is sometimes not considered by the network designers. There is a tendency to make the network entirely one or the other.

Let us reexamine Example 40.3 from the previous chapter.

**Example 41.2. A Network with Both Dial-Up and Leased Lines.** Consider Example 40.3 of Chapter 40 again, with the possibility of using dial-up TWX connections from some of the cities to the computer center at Chicago, thereby excluding them from the leased-line network.

All the transactions are sufficiently short so that a message and its response will not occupy a 150-band line for more than one minute. If TWX lines were used, we would therefore pay for one minute of time for each message plus response. Some of the messages are unsolicited output from the computer, and these messages would also need a payment for one minute of line time. The volume figures quoted in Example 40.3 are for the peak hour. The peak-hour volume in this example is one-fourth of the daily volume.

In deciding whether a city should be on a dial-up line, we must compare the monthly cost of its dialing Chicago with the incremental cost of including it on the leased-line network. This incremental cost will depend on which nearby city it might be connected to on the leased-line network. Unfortunately, this factor cannot be assessed simply because the structure of the leased-line network is going to change severely.

It would be useful to have a program that tackles calculations of this type. A development of the CNDP algorithm described in Chapter 40 could do just that. At each step it would examine the trade-off between making a leased-line interconnection and removing the city in question from the leased-line network. No such program existed at the time this book was written. The systems designer, indeed, is often faced with situations in which the exact design tools he needs do not exist. He can either produce such tools himself, which in this case is a very lengthy process, or he can find a quicker but approximate expedient.

An approximate solution was produced in this case by H. M. Krouse at the IBM Systems Research Institute. He used an algorithm that assigns locations to dial-up lines in the following manner:

1. Starting with the city farthest from the computer center and not yet assigned to a dial-up line, find the closest neighbor that has also not yet been assigned to a dial-up line.

2. Calculate the cost of a leased line interconnecting these two cities. Only one channel-terminal charge should be added to this calculation.

3. Calculate the cost of using a dial-up line from the city in question to the computer, taking the daily volumes into consideration.

4. If the dial-up line is the less expensive of the foregoing alternatives, then assign the city to a dial-up line.

5. Repeat the preceding four steps for all the cities that will have a terminal.

6. It is possible that some cities not assigned to a dial-up line in the fore-going process have now become eligible for one. Their nearest city in step 1 may itself have now been assigned to dial up, and earlier steps must be done again, taking this factor into consideration. Therefore repeat steps 1 to 5.

7. Repeat the preceding steps until a cycle is reached in which no more cities become assigned to a dial-up line.

8. Make a list of the leased-line interconnections that were finally assumed in the foregoing calculation.

9. The minimum-cost leased-line configuration must now be found for the cities not assigned to dial-up lines. This step is done with a program using the CNDP algorithm described in Chapter 40.

The reason why this algorithm is not exact is that occasionally a leased-line segment does not connect a location to the nearest neighbor that is also on a leased line. A glance ahead at Fig. 41.14 makes this point clear. Cumberland, Maryland, is not connected to Pittsburgh, Penn., for example. The city inter-connection listing produced in step 9 is nevertheless close to the optimum net-work. As we shall see below, additional minor refinements can be made by hand.

In the program used for this algorithm, the costs are evaluated as follows (where D is the distance in miles and LCOST is the leased-line cost in dollars per month):

In PL/I:

```
IF D>1000 THEN DO;
   COST=862.0 + CEIL(D-1000)*.350;GO TO B3;END;
IF D>500  THEN DO;
   COST=597.0 + CEIL(D-500 )*.53 ;GO TO B3;END;
IF D>250  THEN DO;
   COST=422.0 + CEIL(D-250 )*.700;GO TO B3;END;
IF D>100  THEN DO;
   COST=237.5 + CEIL(D-100 )*1.23 ;GO TO B3;END;
   COST= 62.5 + CEIL(D)*1.75;
B3:
```

IN FORTRAN:

```
DIMENSION DISTC(5),PRICEC(5),PRCNTC(5)
DATA DISTC /1000.,500.0,250.,100.,  0.0/,
1     PRICEC/862.0,597.0,422.0,237.5, 62.55/,
2     PRCNTC/ .350,  .530,  .700, 1.230, 1.75/
C
   DO 140 I=1,5
   IF (D.LE.DISTC(I)) GO TO 140
   LCOST=PRICEC(I)+(D-DISTC(I))*PRCNTC(I)
   GO TO 150
140 CONTINUE
150 CONTINUE
```

For the dial-up, TWX lines, TIME is the time of connection and DCOST is the cost in dollars per month. In PL/I:

```
IF D>2000 THEN DO;DCOST=.60*CEIL(TIME);GO TO B4;END;
IF D>1300 THEN DO;DCOST=.55*CEIL(TIME);GO TO B4;END;
IF D>800  THEN DO;DCOST=.50*CEIL(TIME);GO TO B4;END;
IF D>450  THEN DO;DCOST=.45*CEIL(TIME);GO TO B4;END;
IF D>280  THEN DO;DCOST=.40*CEIL(TIME);GO TO B4;END;
IF D>185  THEN DO;DCOST=.35*CEIL(TIME);GO TO B4;END;
IF D>110  THEN DO;DCOST=.30*CEIL(TIME);GO TO B4;END;
IF D>50   THEN DO;DCOST=.25*CEIL(TIME);GO TO B4;END;
                 DCOST=.20*CEIL(TIME);
B4:
```

In Fortran:

```
      DIMENSION DISTD(9),PRCNTD(9)
      DATA DISTD /2000.,1300.,800.,450.,280.,185.,110., 50., 0./,
     1     PRCNTD/ .60,  .55,.50,.45,.40,.35,.30,.25,.20/
C
      DO 180 I=1,9
      IF (D.LE.DISTD(I)) GO TO 180
      DCOST=PRCNTD(I)*MINS
      GO TO 210
  180 CONTINUE
  210 CONTINUE
```

Similar segments of code could be used for other tariffs. Here, for example, are subroutines for voice-grade lines used in plotting Fig. 41.10.

For toll telephone connections, where MINS is the number of minutes (of continuous transmission) per day: In PL/I:

```
TIME=MINS-3;
IF D>1910 THEN DO;DCOST=1.35+.45*CEIL(TIME);GO TO B2;END;
IF D>1360 THEN DO;DCOST=1.25+.40*CEIL(TIME);GO TO B2;END;
IF D> 925 THEN DO;DCOST=1.15+.35*CEIL(TIME);GO TO B2;END;
IF D> 675 THEN DO;DCOST=1.05+.35*CEIL(TIME);GO TO B2;END;
IF D> 430 THEN DO;DCOST=.95 +.30*CEIL(TIME);GO TO B2;END;
IF D> 354 THEN DO;DCOST=.85 +.25*CEIL(TIME);GO TO B2;END;
IF D> 292 THEN DO;DCOST=.80 +.25*CEIL(TIME);GO TO B2;END;
IF D> 244 THEN DO;DCOST=0.70+.25*CEIL(TIME);GO TO B2;END;
IF D> 196 THEN DO;DCOST=0.70+.20*CEIL(TIME);GO TO B2;END;
IF D> 148 THEN DO;DCOST=0.70+.20*CEIL(TIME);GO TO B2;END;
IF D> 124 THEN DO;DCOST=0.65+.20*CEIL(TIME);GO TO B2;END;
IF D> 100 THEN DO;DCOST=0.60+.15*CEIL(TIME);GO TO B2;END;
IF D>  85 THEN DO;DCOST=0.55+.15*CEIL(TIME);GO TO B2;END;
IF D>  70 THEN DO;DCOST=0.50+.15*CEIL(TIME);GO TO B2;END;
IF D>  55 THEN DO;DCOST=0.45+.15*CEIL(TIME);GO TO B2;END;
IF D>  40 THEN DO;DCOST=0.40+.10*CEIL(TIME);GO TO B2;END;
IF D>  30 THEN DO;DCOST=0.35+.10*CEIL(TIME);GO TO B2;END;
IF D>  22 THEN DO;DCOST=0.30+.10*CEIL(TIME);GO TO B2;END;
IF D>  16 THEN DO;DCOST=0.25+.05*CEIL(TIME);GO TO B2;END;
IF D>  10 THEN DO;DCOST=0.20+.05*CEIL(TIME);GO TO B2;END;
                 DCOST=0.15+.05*CEIL(TIME);
B2:
```

In Fortran:

```
DIMENSION DISTB(21),PRICEB(21),PRCNTB(21)
DATA DISTB /1910.,1360.,925.,675.,430.,354.,292.,244.,196.,148.,
1              124.,100., 85., 70., 55., 40., 30., 22., 16., 10.,
2              0./,
3      PRICEB/1.35,1.25,1.15,1.05, .95, .85, .80, .70, .70, .70,
4              .65, .60, .55, .50, .45, .40, .35, .30, .25, .20,
5              .15/,
6      PRCNTB/ .45, .40, .35, .35, .30, 3*.25, 3*.20, 4*.15, 3*.10,
7              3*.10/,


C
       DO 50 I=1,23
       IF (D.LE.DISTB(I)) GO TO 50
       DCOST=PRICEB(I)+PRCNTB(I)*(MINS-3)
       GO TO 100
    50 CONTINUE
   100 CONTINUE
```

For leased interstate telephone lines with conditioning:

```
IF D>500 THEN DO;
 LCOST=745.0+CEIL(D-500)*0.75; GO TO B1; END;
IF D>250 THEN DO;
 LCOST=482.5+CEIL(D-250)*1.05; GO TO B1; END;
IF D>100 THEN DO;
 LCOST=257.5+CEIL(D-100)*1.50; GO TO B1; END;
IF D>25  THEN DO;
 LCOST=100  +CEIL(D-25 )*2.10; GO TO B1; END;
 LCOST=25   +CEIL(D)*3;
B1:
```

In Fortran:

```
DIMENSION DISTA(5),PRICEA(5),PRCNTA(5)
DATA DISTA /500.0,250.0,100.0, 25.0,  0.0/,
1      PRICEA/745.0,482.5,257.5,100.0,25.0/,
2      PRCNTA/ .75, 1.05, 1.50, 2.10, 3.00/
C
       DO 20 I=1,5
       IF (D.LE.DISTA(I)) GO TO 20
       LCOST=PRICEA(I)+(D-DISTA(I))*PRCNTA(I)
       GO TO 30
    20 CONTINUE
    30 CONTINUE
```

The program that was used reads the cards prepared for the CNDP runs described in Chapter 40.

Its results indicate that when the message rates are as indicated in the table of the previous chapter, it would pay to have 99 of the 187 terminal locations on TWX lines rather than on leased lines.

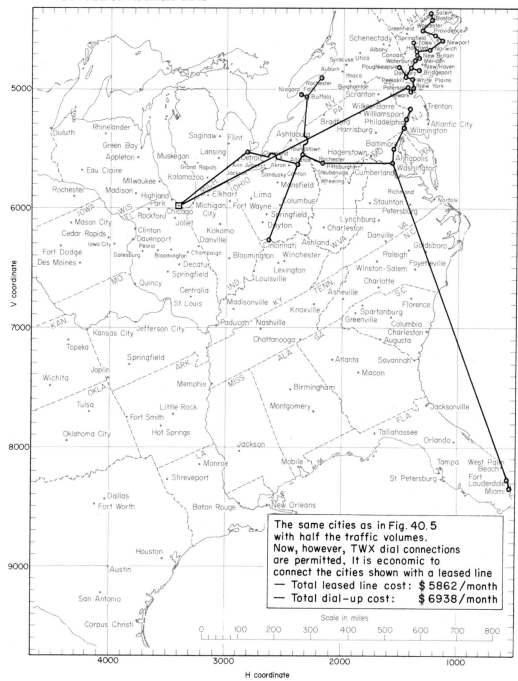

The same cities as in Fig. 40.5
with half the traffic volumes.
Now, however, TWX dial connections
are permitted. It is economic to
connect the cities shown with a leased line
— Total leased line cost: $5862/month
— Total dial-up cost: $6938/month

Scale in miles
0    100   200   300   400   500   600   700   800

*Fig. 41.12.* The lowest-cost network. The cities marked on the map
with no line going to them use TWX dialing.

The resulting network produced by CNDP for the terminals remaining on leased lines is as shown in Fig. 41.13.

The leased line costs are $10,066 per month, as opposed to $25,890 for the network in Fig. 41.5. The total TWX cost is $7968 per month, so the saving is worthwhile.

If the traffic volumes were lower, then the cost calculation would favor dial-up lines more strongly. Figure 41.12 shows the result with half the traffic volumes. There are now only two lines. The leased-line cost has dropped to $5862 per month. The dial-up cost is $6938 per month.

The leased line in Fig. 41.12 passed almost directly over some cities that are not connected to it, such as Richmond, Goldsborough, and West Palm Beach. If we could connect these cities to the line, then we could save the dial-up charges for these cities. Indeed, we can now take another look at any of the cities close to the leased-line path. We may not be able to connect them because the leased line may be fully loaded. Let us see.

There are 23 terminals on the line, including several at Chicago. Adding up the input and output load from all these terminals, we find that the total load on the line is 161.03 messages per hour. If we contemplate adding one of the terminals, our traffic rate table (Table 40.4) tells that the maximum load permissible for 24 terminals is 228.8 messages per hour. We should start with a location close to the line and as far from the computer counter as possible. West Palm Beach is the best candidate. This location has a traffic load of 7.19 messages per hour, input and output. It was allocated to a dial-up line because this load is relatively small. If we connect it to the leased line that happens to pass close to it, the total load on this line becomes 168.22, which is acceptable.

We can contemplate adding one more city—that will give the maximum number of terminals permissible on the line. Our traffic rate table says that the maximum load for 25 terminals is 225.1. Goldsborough has 5.13 messages per hour. Richmond has 9.45 messages per hour. The cost saving of dial-up calls would be greater if Richmond were added.

Similarly, we can make a minor manual adjustment to the network designed by the programs. When the traffic volume is doubled, the program allocates 143 terminal locations to leased lines with 44 using dial-up. The resulting line configuration is shown in Fig. 41.14. The monthly cost of the leased-line configuration is now $20,085, as opposed to $27,023 when all the cities were on leased lines. The total monthly TWX line bill is $4204. Consequently, there has still been a worthwhile saving, but substantially less than in the previous cases.

When the traffic is eight times the volume listed, the program allocates all terminal locations except two to leased lines. Only Wichita, Kansas, and Jackson, Miss., are allocated to dial-up lines, both cities having very low traffic vol-

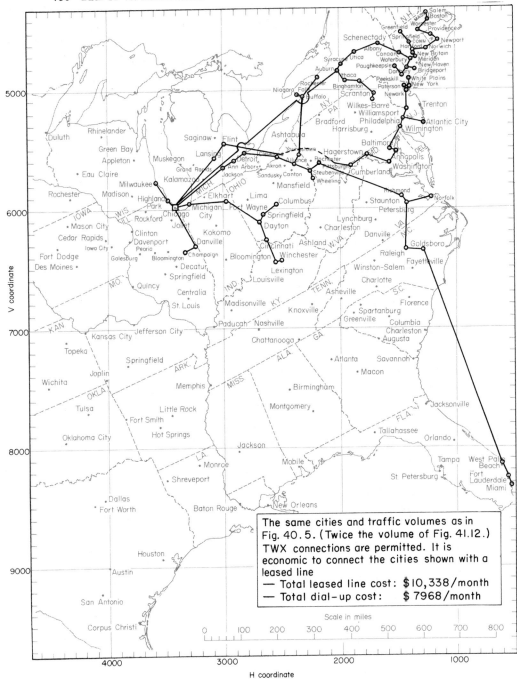

The same cities and traffic volumes as in
Fig. 40.5. (Twice the volume of Fig. 41.12.)
TWX connections are permitted. It is
economic to connect the cities shown with a
leased line
— Total leased line cost: $10,338/month
— Total dial-up cost:    $7968/month

*Fig. 41.13.* The lowest-cost network with traffic volumes twice those
of Fig. 41.12.

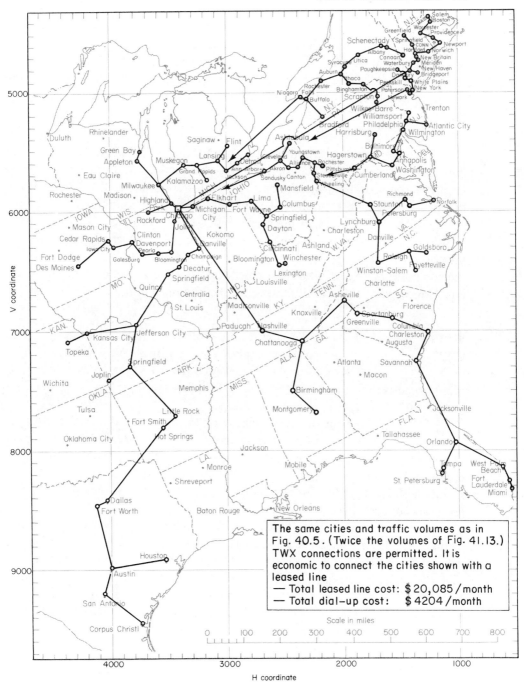

*Fig. 41.14.* The lowest-cost network with traffic volumes twice those of Fig. 41.13.

umes and being fairly distant from any other city on a leased line. The saving to be made from having these two cities connected separately is slight, perhaps nonexistent, when the cost of a line adaptor for dial-up lines at the computer is considered. In this case, a network may well be used in which all terminals are on the leased lines. The line configuration and cost will then be as shown in Fig. 40.19.

There are many variations on this theme. Some systems have no need for immediate processing of transactions, and transactions can be saved up at the terminals for periodic transmission. This factor could lower the TWX cost, or other dial-up line cost, because the first minute or three minutes must be paid for regardless of whether they are used or not.

Again, the dial-up lines may not go directly to the computer, as in the illustration in this chapter. They may go to concentration points connected to the computer on leased lines—possibly leased voice-grade lines with multiplexing. Concentration and multiplexing will be discussed in the next two chapters.

**WATS
LINES**
Considerations similar to those discussed in this chapter apply to WATS lines. As will be seen from Fig. 41.11, a WATS line to a zone is usually slightly more expensive than a leased voice line. In a few areas, at large distances, the WATS line is cheaper than the leased line.

WATS calculations are complicated by the fact that the WATS line can serve many different locations. The designer must be concerned with the *grade of service* that he requires, or the probability of failing to obtain a connection. Example 33.2 illustrated this form of probability calculation for a WATS line. Example 33.3 illustrated the advantage of having larger, rather than smaller, groupings of such lines.

The question then arises: "Should the zone 6 lines, for example zone 6 in Fig. 18.2, serve zone 5 also, or should zone 5 have its own lines?" If zone 5 has its own lines, they are lower in cost than if the zone used zone 6 lines—in Fig. 18.2 zone 5 lines are $1900 per month, compared to $2250 for zone 6. However, if zone 5 and zone 6 are combined, fewer lines will be needed to achieve a given grade of service because of the larger grouping. Which, then, is cheaper? It depends on the traffic volumes in zones 5 and 6, and only a detailed calculation can provide an answer.

If we now consider zone 4 also, there are five different possible arrangements:

1. Handle all three zones with the same zone 6 line group.
2. Handle zones 4 and 6 with the zone 6 line group and zone 5 with a zone 5 line group.
3. Handle zones 5 and 6 with the zone 6 line group and zone 4 with a zone 4 line group.
4. Handle zones 4 and 5 with a zone 5 line group and zone 6 with its own line group.
5. Handle each zone with its own line group.

Again, only a detailed calculation with the traffic volumes for each zone will reveal which of these alternatives gives the required grade of service at the lowest cost.

If we consider all six zones there are many different combinations possible. A computer program is needed which takes the traffic volumes in erlangs for each zone and does a calculation like that in Example 33.2 for each possible combination. The combination with the lowest resulting cost would be used.

In performing such a calculation, the resulting cost will be substantially lower if the grade of service (probability of line busy signal) is set at, say, 0.05 rather than 0.005 because more lines will be needed. However, a grade of service in which 5 per cent of the callers receive line busy signals would not be acceptable for most systems. The possibility arises of designing the equipment so that it automatically dials on the public network when a busy signal is received from the WATS network. The cost of combined WATS and direct distance dialing would then have to be evaluated, and a grade of service for the WATS network that would minimize the combined cost determined.

**Example 41.3. Design of a WATS Network** [1]. Various locations throughout the United States must be given facilities to dial a location at Paterson, N.J. The calls may, for example, be telephone enquiries to a room of terminal operators. (The same calculation would apply to data traffic or any other form of traffic on voice-grade lines.) The traffic volumes in erlangs from the New Jersey WATS zones are estimated to be as follows:

|  |  |
|---|---|
| Zone 1: | 7.29 erlangs |
| Zone 2: | 3.58 erlangs |
| Zone 3: | 8.73 erlangs |
| Zone 4: | 5.77 erlangs |
| Zone 5: | 3.88 erlangs |
| Zone 6: | 5.95 erlangs |
| Intrastate traffic: | 1.22 erlangs |

The grade of service required is 0.05. What combination of dial facilities will give the lowest cost?

The monthly costs of the WATS lines from New Jersey are as follows:

Zone 1:   $500
Zone 2:   $650
Zone 3:   $1250
Zone 4:   $1550
Zone 5:   $1700
Zone 6:   $1900

Because the points of origination of the calls are not stated, the cost of telephoning on the direct distance dialing network cannot be calculated exactly. An approximate calculation indicates that the cost will be between $200,000 and $300,000. This is much higher than the cost of using WATS.

Let us first calculate the cost of using a separate group of WATS lines to each zone. We will use the equation

$$P_B = \frac{\dfrac{(M\rho)^M}{M!}}{\displaystyle\sum_{N=0}^{M} \dfrac{(M\rho)^N}{N!}} \tag{31.66}$$

Where:   $M\rho = E(n)E(t_s)$ = number of erlangs of traffic
$M$ = the number of lines, and
$P_B$ = the grade of service (probability that all lines are busy) = 0.95.

Solving this equation, or using Table 11 in Appendix VIII, we find that the number of lines required to each zone are as follows:

| Zone | Number of Lines | Cost ($ per month) |
|------|-----------------|--------------------|
| 1 | 12 | 6,000 |
| 2 | 7 | 4,550 |
| 3 | 13 | 16,250 |
| 4 | 10 | 15,500 |
| 5 | 8 | 13,600 |
| 6 | 10 | 19,000 |

Four intrastate WATS lines are also needed to handle the traffic within New Jersey at a cost of $1300. The total cost therefore adds up to $76,200.

Now let us calculate the cost with a zone 6 line group handling all of the zones. This group will handle a total of 35.2 erlangs of traffic. From the above equation we can calculate that this needs 41 zone 6 lines, costing $77,900. Adding the intrastate line cost of $1300, we have a total of $79,200.

There are many possible combinations of WATS zones. A computer program is needed to perform the above type of calculation for the various combinations. Running such a program, the result indicated that the lowest cost configuration was to have a zone 6 line group handling the traffic from zones 4, 5, and 6, and the other zones being served by unique line groups. The cost was as follows:

|  | Number of Lines | Cost ($ per month) |
|---|---|---|
| Zone 1 | 12 | 6,000 |
| Zone 2 | 7 | 4,550 |
| Zone 3 | 13 | 16,250 |
| Zone 4 | 0 | 0 |
| Zone 5 | 0 | 0 |
| Zone 6 | 21 | 39,900 |
| New Jersey |  | 1,300 |
| Total |  | 68,000 |

The total cost, not including the cost of modems, is thus $68,000 per month.

**Example 41.4. Choice of WATS or Leased Network** [1]. The 159 terminal locations shown in Fig. 41.15 are to be connected to Paterson, N.J. This time the terminal locations are known, so dial or leased lines can be used. The time associated with dialing is acceptable. The terminals operate at less than 150 bits per second.

This example is an actual commercial network now in operation. The costs were evaluated for leased and dial links, both voice-grade and subvoice-grade, as follows:

| Type of Line | Cost/Month |
|---|---|
| **Subvoice-grade:** | |
| Leased: AT & T type 1006 lines, point-to-point | $104,472 |
| Leased: AT & T type 1006 lines, multipoint | 20,100 |
| Dial:    TWX-CE network | 20,626 |
| **Voice-grade:** | |
| Leased: AT & T type 3002 lines, point-to-point | $153,552 |
| Leased: AT & T type 3002 lines, multipoint | 29,700 |
| Dial:    Public telephone network | 45,978 |
| Dial:    WATS group of zone 6 lines | 17,750 |
| Dial:    WATS unique line group to each zone | 30,000 |
| Dial:    Lowest-cost combination of WATS groups | 17,750 |

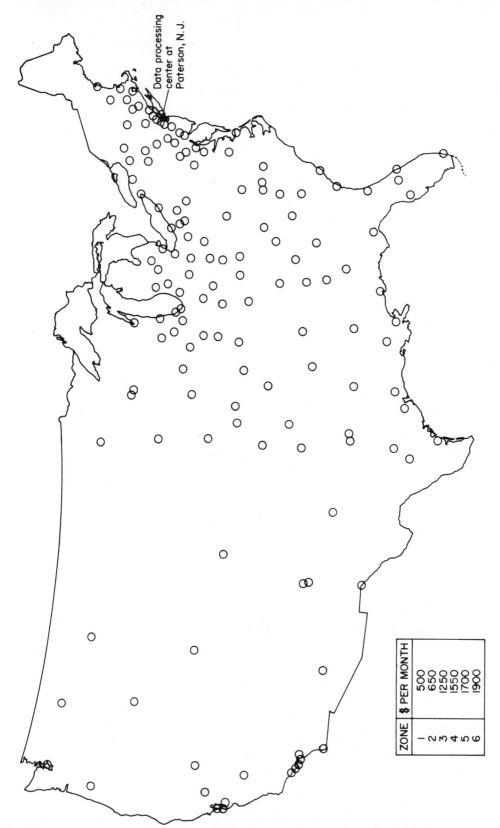

| ZONE | $ PER MONTH |
|------|-------------|
| 1 | 500 |
| 2 | 650 |
| 3 | 1250 |
| 4 | 1550 |
| 5 | 1700 |
| 6 | 1900 |

*Fig. 41.15.* The 159 terminal locations marked are to be connected to the data processing center at Paterson, N. J., using the WATS tariff.

It will be seen that the WATS tariff gives the lowest cost—lower than subvoice-grade lines. The best WATS combination is that in which a group of zone 6 lines serves all the terminals.

## REFERENCE

1. T. A. Puorro, of IBM System Research Institute, "What's with WATS," paper unpublished as yet.

# 42  CONCENTRATORS AND MULTIPLEXERS

We laid out our communication-line network in the previous two chapters without using multiplexers or any form of concentrator. At the time of writing, a large number of networks use multidrop lines in this way—without concentration—and there will be many more in the future, especially on small networks, message switching networks, and networks on which response time is of little concern. The cost of concentrators and multiplexers is dropping, however; as it drops, the likelihood improves that such devices will produce the lowest-cost network.

The manufacturers of the most suitable concentrators or multiplexers sometimes do not manufacture multidrop terminal equipment, and vice versa. Consequently, the network designs done by the manufacturers may not use the optimum combination of such equipment. The user must do some fairly elaborate calculations if he is to discover the best configuration and layout for his particular circumstances.

There are, as earlier chapters indicated, two ways in which concentrators can be used. They can be used on networks with point-to-point lines only or they can be used on networks with multidrop lines, as in Figs. 3.6 or 3.7. In this chapter we will discuss calculations involving point-to-point lines, and in the next chapter multidrop lines.

We would like to use subvoice-grade lines on many systems because of their low cost. For the same reason we would often like to use start–stop, unbuffered terminals operating at speeds comparable to those of an electric typewriter. It is with such components that reasonably low-cost data transmission systems have been built. Unfortunately, however, if we use such terminals in a multidrop fashion on subvoice-grade lines, we are in danger of degrading the response times. The curves of mean response times for systems shown in Chapters 36 and 37 swing upward into the regions of 10, 20, or sometimes 30 seconds. These figures would be higher if the messages were longer. If two teletype machines on a line are transmitting or receiving messages of 75 characters at a speed of 7.5 characters per second, then one machine may have to wait 10 seconds for its transmission. If there are more than two machines, the delay could be proportionately high. The *mean* delay will be low if the line utilization is low, but the possibility of encountering a long delay always exists.

A way out of this dilemma is to use point-to-point, low-speed lines downstream of a concentrator or multiplexer. The lines have been used in this way on systems where response time is critical. They have been used, for example, on the SABRE generation of airline reservation systems where responses of less than 3 seconds were required at start–stop terminals. The practice makes sense today on time-sharing systems using teletype machines or other low-speed terminals.

In designing a network with concentrators and point-to-point lines, two problems must be solved: first, the selection of the concentrator and, second, its geographical positioning in the network. Where multidrop lines are used, a third problem exists—the layout of the multidrop connections.

Let us first examine the question of selecting a concentrator or multiplexer.

**Example 42.1. Selection of Concentrator or Multiplexer.** Seven devices that combine traffic from several 150-baud teletype lines onto a leased-conditioned voice line are on the market. The costs of the devices are shown in the following table:

| Device | Number of Low-Speed Lines | Monthly Cost of Concentrator |
|--------|---------------------------|------------------------------|
| 1 | 4 | 100 |
| 2 | 8 | 200 |
| 3 | 14 | 400 |
| 4 | 16 | 700 |
| 5 | 20 | 1000 |
| 6 | 30 | 2000 |
| 7 | 50 | 3000 |

*Note:* Prices were invented for this example but were typical at the time of writing.

Tabulate which of these devices are the best ones to use for different sets of circumstances.

In these chapters we are judging the devices solely on a basis of minimizing the overall systems cost. Of course, in practice, other criteria need to be examined. The most important criteria in selecting a concentrator are reliability, maintainability, transmission accuracy, and the effect, if any, that the concentrator has on programs.

Looking at the concentrators from the cost point of view, however, we may be able to eliminate some factors from this list before attempting to position them in our particular network. We would like to evaluate the overall cost of connecting a terminal to the computer via each concentrator and would like to select the device that gives the lowest cost. This cost will vary with the distance of the concentrator from computer and with the number of terminals that are to be attached to it. It will not vary in a simple fashion, however, because communication-line tariffs are involved.

Glancing quickly at the prices of the machines, we might be tempted to eliminate device number 4. This device costs $700 per month and handles 16 lines, whereas two of device number 2 would also handle 16 lines but would cost only $400 per month. However, two of device number 2 would need two high-speed lines. If the concentration point were a long distance from the computer, this factor would override the device cost advantage. We cannot eliminate device 4 unless we know this distance.

Again, device 4, handling 16 terminals for $700, might seem poorer value for money than device 3, which handles 14 terminals for only $400. Device 3 gives a lower cost per terminal. Still, there may *be* 16 terminals; therefore if we use device 3, we will either need two concentrators or we will have to run low-speed lines from two of the terminals to the computer. Device 4 does not look like a very promising candidate, but there may be certain circumstances in which it gives the lowest cost.

Let us, then, draw up a table showing the distances of the concentrator (or multiplexer) from the computer, plus the number of terminals that will be attached to it. We will assume that the terminals are situated close to the concentrator. For each such pair of parameters, we will select the best of the seven concentrators.

Let $M$ be the number of terminals to be connected and $N_L$ be the number of low-speed lines the concentrator can handle.

The number of concentrators used at that location will be either[1]

$$\left\lceil \frac{M}{N_L} \right\rceil \quad \text{or} \quad \left\lfloor \frac{M}{N_L} \right\rfloor$$

[1] $\lceil M/N \rceil$ means $M/N$ rounded up the nearest integer. It is written CEIL $(M/N)$ in the programs. $\lfloor M/N \rfloor$ means $M/N$ rounded down to the nearest integer. It is written FLOOR $(M/N)$ in the programs.

If it is

$$\left\lceil \frac{M}{N_L} \right\rceil$$

then all of the terminals will be connected via the concentrator. If it is

$$\left\lfloor \frac{M}{N_L} \right\rfloor$$

then some terminals may be left out, and they would have to be connected directly to the computer on low-speed lines. Whichever of these methods is the cheaper must be used in our calculations.

The cost of the terminal connection from the concentration location to the computer may be regarded as whichever is the lowest of the following:

1. (Cost of concentrator plus cost of high-speed line from concentrator to computer) $\times \left\lceil \dfrac{M}{N_L} \right\rceil$

2. (Cost of concentrator plus cost of high-speed line from concentrator to computer) $\times \left\lfloor \dfrac{M}{N_L} \right\rfloor +$ (incremental cost of taking a low-speed line from the concentrator location to the computer) $\times \left( M - N_L \left\lfloor \dfrac{M}{N_L} \right\rfloor \right)$

Because the tariff calculations are elaborate, we will use a computer; and in our program we will write these two statements as

$$\text{CST} = (\text{CONCOST(N)} + \text{SHCOST(D)})*\text{CEIL(M/NL(N))};$$

and

$$\text{CST} = (\text{CONCOST(N)} + \text{SHCOST(D)})*\text{FLOOR(M/NL(N))}$$
$$+ (\text{M} - \text{FLOOR(M/NL(N))}*\text{NL(N)})*\text{SLCOST(D)};$$

where CONCOST(N) = the cost of the $N$th concentrator
NL(N) = the number of lines attached to the $N$th concentrator
SHCOST(D) = the cost of the high-speed line, where D is the distance it spans
SLCOST(D) = the incremental cost of running the low-speed line over additional distance, D

In reality, the terminals may not be very close to the concentrator, and an unconcentrated low-speed line will go directly to the computer. Because we do not know the terminal's location in this example, we do not know the cost of a direct low-speed line exactly and hence are assuming that the terminals are close to the concentrator. Nevertheless, the program will give us a fairly good table for comparing the devices.

The complete program follows. It uses United States interstate tariffs.

In PL/I:

```
DCL CONCOST(10), NL(10), TCST(0:10);
DCL Z CHAR (1);
/*****************************************************************************/
/*** CONCENTRATOR DETAILS **************************************************/
     CONCOST(1)=100 ; NL(1)=4 ;
     CONCOST(2)=200 ; NL(2)=8 ;
     CONCOST(3)=400 ; NL(3)=14;
     CONCOST(4)=700 ; NL(4)=16;
     CONCOST(5)=1000; NL(5)=20;
     CONCOST(6)=2000; NL(6)=30;
     CONCOST(7)=3000; NL(7)=50;
/*****************************************************************************/
     PUT PAGE EDIT ('DIST- *    NUMBER OF TERMINALS TO BE CONCENTRATED')
     (A);
     PUT SKIP EDIT ('ANCE  *  1  2  3  4  5  6  7  8  9 10 11 12 13',
     ' 14 15 16 17 18 19 20 21 22 23 24 25 26 27 28 29 30 31 32 33 34')
     (A,A);
     PUT SKIP EDIT ('*************************************************',
     '*************************************************')
     (A,A);
     DO D=1, 5 TO 100 BY 5, 125 TO 500 BY 25, 550 TO 1000 BY 50;
     PUT SKIP EDIT (D,' *')(F(5),A);
     DO M=1 TO 34;
     A=9999999;
     DO N=1 TO 7;
     J= CEIL(M/NL(N));
     CST=(CONCOST(N)+SHCOST(D))*J;
     IF CST<A THEN DO; A=CST; KC=N; J1=J; END;
     J=FLOOR(M/NL(N));
     CST=(CONCOST(N)+SHCOST(D))*J+SLCOST(D)*(M-J*NL(N));
     IF CST<A THEN DO; A=CST; KC=N; J1=J;
     IF J=0 THEN KC=0; END;
     END;
     IF J1>1 THEN Z='*'; ELSE Z=' ';
     PUT EDIT (Z,KC)(X(1),A,F(1));
     END;
     END;
/*****************************************************************************/
     PUT PAGE EDIT ('DIST- *    NUMBER OF TERMINALS TO BE CONCENTRATED')
     (A);
     PUT SKIP EDIT ('ANCE  * 35 36 37 38 39 40 41 42 43 44 45 46 47',
     ' 48 49 50 51 52 53 54 55 56 57 58 59 60 61 62 63 64 65 66 67 68')
     (A,A);
     PUT SKIP EDIT ('*************************************************',
```

```
'************************************************************************')
(A,A);
DO D=1, 5 TO 100 BY 5, 125 TO 500 BY 25, 550 TO 1000 BY 50;
PUT SKIP EDIT (D,' *')(F(5),A);
DO M=35 TO 68;
A=9999999;
DO N=1 TO 7;

   J= CEIL(M/NL(N));
   CST=(CONCOST(N)+SHCOST(D))*J;
   IF CST<A THEN DO; A=CST; KC=N; J1=J; END;
   J=FLOOR(M/NL(N));
   CST=(CONCOST(N)+SHCOST(D))*J+SLCOST(D)*(M-J*NL(N));
   IF CST<A THEN DO; A=CST; KC=N; J1=J;
   IF J=0 THEN KC=0; END;
   END;
   IF J1>1 THEN Z='*'; ELSE Z=' ';
   PUT EDIT (Z,KC)(X(1),A,F(1));
   END;
   END;
/************************************************************************/
/************************************************************************/
/**CALCULATE COST OF HIGH SPEED LINE ********************************/
 SHCOST: PROC(D);
   IF D=0 THEN DO; COST=0; GO TO B1; END;
   IF D>500 THEN DO;
     COST=745.0+CEIL(D-500)*0.75; GO TO B1; END;
   IF D>250 THEN DO;
     COST=482.5+CEIL(D-250)*1.05; GO TO B1; END;
   IF D>100 THEN DO;
     COST=257.5+CEIL(D-100)*1.50; GO TO B1; END;
   IF D>25   THEN DO;
     COST=100  +CEIL(D-25 )*2.10; GO TO B1; END;
     COST=25   +CEIL(D)*3;
 B1: RETURN(COST);
  END SHCOST;
/************************************************************************/
/**CALCULATE COST OF LOW SPEED LINE ********************************/
 SLCOST: PROC(D);
   IF D=0 THEN DO; COST=0; GO TO B2; END;
   IF D>1000 THEN DO;
     COST=862.0 + CEIL(D-1000)*.350;GO TO B3;END;
   IF D>500   THEN DO;
     COST=597.0 + CEIL(D-500 )*.53 ;GO TO B3;END;
   IF D>250   THEN DO;
     COST=422.0 + CEIL(D-250 )*.700;GO TO B3;END;
   IF D>100   THEN DO;
     COST=237.5 + CEIL(D-100 )*1.23 ;GO TO B3;END;
     COST= 62.5 + CEIL(D)*1.75;
 B3: RETURN(COST);
  END SLCOST;
/************************************************************************/
```

In Fortran:

```
      DIMENSION CONCST (10),NL(10),TCST(11),KC(68)
      LOGICAL*1 Z(68),ASTER/'*'/,SPACE/' '/,LASTER*4(28)/28*'****'/
C**************************************************************************
C*** CONCENTRATOR DETAILS ***********************************************
      DATA CONCST/100.,200.,400.,700.,1000.,2000.,3000.,3*0./,
     1     NL   / 4,   8,  14,  16,   20,    30,    50, 3*0 /
      L1=3
C**************************************************************************
   10 FORMAT (1H1,
     1'DIST- *    NUMBER OF TERMINALS TO BE CONCENTRATED')
   20 FORMAT (1H ,
     1'ANCE  *  1  2  3  4  5  6  7  8  9 10 11 12 13 14 15 16 17 18 19
     220 21 22 23 24 25 26 27 28 29 30 31 32 33 34'/1H ,27A4,A1)
   30 FORMAT (1H ,
     1'ANCE  * 35 36 37 38 39 40 41 42 43 44 45 46 47 48 49 50 51 52 53
     254 55 56 57 58 59 60 61 62 63 64 65 66 67 68'/1H ,27A4,A1)
      PAGE=1.0
      ISTART=1
      IEND=34
   90 WRITE (L1,10)
      IF (PAGE.EQ.2) GO TO 100
      WRITE (L1,20) LASTER
      GO TO 110
  100 WRITE (L1,30) LASTER
  110 D=0.0
      LIMIT=1
      INC=1
      GO TO 140
  115 D=0.0
      LIMIT=100
      INC=5
      GO TO 140
  120 LIMIT=500
      INC=25
      GO TO 140
  130 LIMIT=1000
      INC=50
C
  140 D=D+INC
      DO 200 M=ISTART,IEND
      A=9999999.0
      DO 180 N=1,7
      FM=M
      FRAC=FM/NL(N)
      J=FRAC
      IF (J.EQ.FRAC) GO TO 160
      J=J+1
  160 CST=(CONCST(N)+SHCOST(D))*J
      IF (CST.GE.A) GO TO 170
      A=CST
      KC(M)=N
      J1=J
  170 J=FRAC
      CST=(CONCST(N)+SHCOST(D))*J+SLCOST(D)*(M-J*NL(N))
```

```
      IF (CST.GE.A) GO TO 180
      A=CST
      KC(M)=N
      J1=J
      IF (J.EQ.0) KC(M)=0
180 CONTINUE
      IF (J1.GT.1) GO TO 190
      Z(M)=SPACE
      GO TO 200
190 Z(M)=ASTER
200 CONTINUE
      ID=D
      WRITE (L1,210) ID,ASTER,(Z(I),KC(I), I=ISTART,IEND)
210 FORMAT (1H ,
     115,1X,A1,34(1X,A1,I1))
      IF (D.LT.LIMIT) GO TO 140
      IF (LIMIT.EQ.1000) GO TO 220
      IF (LIMIT-100) 115,120,130
220 IF (PAGE.EQ.2) GO TO 230
      PAGE=2.0
      ISTART=35
      IEND=68
      GO TO 90
230 STOP
      END
C***********************************************************
C**CALCULATE COST OF HIGH SPEED LINE ********************
      FUNCTION SHCOST (D)
C
      DIMENSION DISTA(5),PRICEA(5),PRCNTA(5)
      DATA DISTA /500.0,250.0,100.0, 25.0,  0.0/,
     1      PRICEA/745.0,482.5,257.5,100.0,25.0/,
     2      PRCNTA/ .75, 1.05, 1.50, 2.10, 3.00/
C
      DO 20 I=1,5
      IF (D.LE.DISTA(I)) GO TO 20
      SHCOST=PRICEA(I)+(D-DISTA(I))*PRCNTA(I)
      GO TO 30
   20 CONTINUE
   30 RETURN
      END
C***********************************************************
C**CALCULATE COST OF LOW SPEED LINE ********************
      FUNCTION SLCOST (D)
C
      DIMENSION DISTC(5),PRICEC(5),PRCNTC(5)
      DATA DISTC /1000.,500.0,250.,100.,  0.0/,
     1      PRICEC/862.0,597.0,422.0,237.5, 62.55/,
     2      PRCNTC/ .350, .530, .700, 1.230, 1.75/
      DO 140 I=1,5
      IF (D.LE.DISTC(I)) GO TO 140
      SLCOST=PRICEC(I)+(D-DISTC(I))*PRCNTC(I)
      GO TO 150
  140 CONTINUE
  150 RETURN
      END
```

746

**RESULTS**

Table 42.1 shows the results of the program. The distances of the concentration point from the computer are listed vertically, and the numbers of terminals to be dealt with are listed horizontally. In each position of the table, there is one digit that gives the best device for that distance and number of terminals. If the digit has an asterisk in front of it, this means that more than one of that device is used at the concentration location, with, consequently, more than one high-speed line to the computer. If the digit is zero, then no concentrator should be used.

The first fact of interest is that all the devices find a place on the table. Good news for the concentrator salesman—whichever of these machines he is selling, he can find some circumstance in which it is better than any of the others. Device number 4 did not seem very promising, but in fact it appears on the table in many places. Device 6 does not appear anywhere on the table at distances closer to the computer than 325 miles. Device 7, however, is found as close as 200 miles. At one point device 5 is found 45 miles from the computer. Device 7 is not found with less than 33 terminals, and device 6 is not found with less than 29.

Device 3 tops the popularity poll. It would have been difficult to guess it from the list of device characteristics. Device 3 has a higher cost per line than either device 1 or 2; however, it appears far more times on the table than any of the other devices. If we do not know the exact numbers of terminals and distances in our network, we can say that device 3 is the concentrator most likely to succeed.

There are very few zeros on the table, also good news for the concentrator salesman. I have often heard the comment that concentrators are only useful on very large networks. In England I recall a data transmission specialist telling me that concentrators and multiplexers were viable only in America, with its vast distances. The table indicates that this statement is not true. Even when very close to the computer, concentrators and multiplexers can save money.

**LOCATION OF CONCENTRATORS**

Precisely which concentrator we pick for a particular situation will depend on the location of the terminals. Let us turn to the question of the geographical location of the concentrators. As we have not succeeded in eliminating any of the seven devices above we will do our calculations for each of these devices and then determine which one gives the lowest overall cost.

**Example 42.2. Location of Concentrators.** The 187 terminal locations listed in Table 40.3 are each to have one low-speed terminal connected to the computer center in Chicago. A delay no greater than a few seconds in obtaining a response at the terminal is desired; therefore low-speed multidrop lines will not be used. Instead, multiplexers or

**Table 42.1.** SELECTION OF THE CONCENTRATOR OR MULTIPLEXER THAT GIVES THE LOWEST COST CONNECTION (EXAMPLE 42.1)

| DIST- | NUMBER OF TERMINALS TO BE CONCENTRATED | | | | | | | | | | | | | | | | | | | | | | | | | | | | | | | | | |
|---|---|---|---|---|---|---|---|---|---|---|---|---|---|---|---|---|---|---|---|---|---|---|---|---|---|---|---|---|---|---|---|---|---|---|
| ANCE | 1 | 2 | 3 | 4 | 5 | 6 | 7 | 8 | 9 | 10 | 11 | 12 | 13 | 14 | 15 | 16 | 17 | 18 | 19 | 20 | 21 | 22 | 23 | 24 | 25 | 26 | 27 | 28 | 29 | 30 | 31 | 32 | 33 | 34 |
| 1 | 0 | 0 | 0 | 0 | 0 | 0 | 0 | 0 | 0 | 0 | 0 | 0 | 0 | 0 | 0 | 0 | 0 | 0 | 0 | 0 | 0 | 0 | 0 | 0 | 0 | 0 | 0 | 0 | 0 | 0 | 0 | 0 | 0 | 0 |
| 5 | 0 | 0 | 0 | 0 | 0 | 0 | 0 | 2 | 2 | 2 | 2 | 2 | 2 | 3 | 3 | 3 | 3 | 3 | 3 | 3 | 3 | 3 | 3 | *2 | *2 | *2 | *3 | *3 | *3 | *3 | *3 | *3 | *3 | *3 |
| 10 | 0 | 0 | 0 | 0 | 0 | 0 | 2 | 2 | 2 | 2 | 2 | 2 | 3 | 3 | 3 | 3 | 3 | 3 | 3 | 3 | 3 | 3 | *2 | *2 | *2 | *3 | *3 | *3 | *3 | *3 | *3 | *3 | *3 | *3 |
| 15 | 0 | 0 | 0 | 1 | 1 | 2 | 2 | 2 | 2 | 2 | 2 | 3 | 3 | 3 | 3 | 3 | 3 | 3 | 3 | 3 | 3 | *2 | *2 | *2 | *2 | *3 | *3 | *3 | *3 | *3 | *3 | *3 | *3 | *3 |
| 20 | 0 | 0 | 0 | 1 | 1 | 2 | 2 | 2 | 2 | 2 | 2 | 3 | 3 | 3 | 3 | 3 | 3 | 3 | 3 | 3 | 3 | *2 | *2 | *2 | *3 | *3 | *3 | *3 | *3 | *3 | *3 | *3 | *3 | *3 |
| 25 | 0 | 0 | 0 | 1 | 1 | 2 | 2 | 2 | 2 | 2 | 3 | 3 | 3 | 3 | 3 | 3 | 3 | 3 | 3 | 3 | *2 | *2 | *2 | *2 | *3 | *3 | *3 | *3 | *3 | *3 | *3 | *3 | *3 | *3 |
| 30 | 0 | 0 | 0 | 1 | 1 | 2 | 2 | 2 | 2 | 2 | 3 | 3 | 3 | 3 | 3 | 3 | 3 | 3 | 3 | 3 | *2 | *2 | *2 | *2 | *3 | *3 | *3 | *3 | *3 | *3 | *3 | *3 | *3 | *3 |
| 35 | 0 | 0 | 0 | 1 | 1 | 2 | 2 | 2 | 2 | 2 | 3 | 3 | 3 | 3 | 3 | *2 | *2 | *2 | *2 | *2 | *2 | *2 | *2 | *2 | *3 | *3 | *3 | *3 | *3 | *3 | *3 | *2 | *2 | *2 |
| 40 | 0 | 0 | 1 | 1 | 2 | 2 | 2 | 2 | 2 | 3 | 3 | 3 | 3 | 3 | 3 | *2 | *2 | *2 | *2 | *2 | *2 | *2 | *2 | *2 | *3 | *3 | *3 | *3 | *3 | *3 | *3 | *2 | *2 | *2 |
| 45 | 0 | 0 | 1 | 1 | 2 | 2 | 2 | 2 | 2 | 3 | 3 | 3 | 3 | 3 | 3 | *2 | *2 | *2 | *2 | 5 | *3 | *3 | *3 | *3 | *3 | *3 | *3 | *3 | *3 | *3 | *3 | *2 | *2 | *3 |
| 50 | 0 | 0 | 1 | 1 | 2 | 2 | 2 | 2 | 2 | 3 | 3 | 3 | 3 | 3 | 3 | *2 | *2 | *2 | *2 | 5 | *3 | *3 | *3 | *3 | *3 | *3 | *3 | *3 | *3 | *3 | *3 | *2 | *2 | *3 |
| 55 | 0 | 0 | 1 | 1 | 2 | 2 | 2 | 2 | 2 | 3 | 3 | 3 | 3 | 3 | 3 | *2 | *2 | *2 | 5 | 5 | *3 | *3 | *3 | *3 | *3 | *3 | *3 | *3 | *3 | *3 | *3 | *2 | *2 | *3 |
| 60 | 0 | 0 | 1 | 1 | 2 | 2 | 2 | 2 | 2 | 3 | 3 | 3 | 3 | 3 | 3 | *2 | *2 | *2 | 5 | 5 | *3 | *3 | *3 | *3 | *3 | *3 | *3 | *3 | *3 | *3 | *3 | *2 | *2 | *3 |
| 65 | 0 | 0 | 1 | 1 | 2 | 2 | 2 | 2 | 2 | 3 | 3 | 3 | 3 | 3 | 3 | *2 | *2 | *2 | 5 | 5 | *3 | *3 | *3 | *3 | *3 | *3 | *3 | *3 | *3 | *3 | *3 | *2 | *2 | *3 |
| 70 | 0 | 0 | 1 | 1 | 2 | 2 | 2 | 2 | 2 | 3 | 3 | 3 | 3 | 3 | 3 | *2 | *2 | *2 | 5 | 5 | *3 | *3 | *3 | *3 | *3 | *3 | *3 | *3 | *3 | *3 | *3 | *2 | *3 | *3 |
| 75 | 0 | 0 | 1 | 1 | 2 | 2 | 2 | 2 | 2 | 3 | 3 | 3 | 3 | 3 | 3 | *2 | *2 | *2 | 5 | 5 | *3 | *3 | *3 | *3 | *3 | *3 | *3 | *3 | *3 | *3 | *3 | *2 | *3 | *3 |
| 80 | 0 | 0 | 1 | 1 | 2 | 2 | 2 | 2 | 2 | 3 | 3 | 3 | 3 | 3 | 3 | *2 | *2 | 5 | 5 | 5 | *3 | *3 | *3 | *3 | *3 | *3 | *3 | *3 | *3 | *3 | *3 | *2 | *3 | *3 |
| 85 | 0 | 0 | 1 | 1 | 2 | 2 | 2 | 2 | 2 | 3 | 3 | 3 | 3 | 3 | 3 | *2 | *2 | 5 | 5 | 5 | *3 | *3 | *3 | *3 | *3 | *3 | *3 | *3 | *3 | *3 | *3 | *2 | *3 | *3 |
| 90 | 0 | 0 | 1 | 1 | 2 | 2 | 2 | 2 | 2 | 3 | 3 | 3 | 3 | 3 | 3 | *2 | *2 | 5 | 5 | 5 | *3 | *3 | *3 | *3 | *3 | *3 | *3 | *3 | *3 | *3 | *3 | *2 | *3 | *3 |
| 95 | 0 | 0 | 1 | 1 | 2 | 2 | 2 | 2 | 2 | 3 | 3 | 3 | 3 | 3 | 3 | 4 | 4 | 5 | 5 | 5 | *3 | *3 | *3 | *3 | *3 | *3 | *3 | *3 | *3 | *3 | *3 | *4 | *3 | *3 |
| 100 | 0 | 0 | 1 | 1 | 2 | 2 | 2 | 2 | 3 | 3 | 3 | 3 | 3 | 3 | 3 | 4 | 4 | 5 | 5 | 5 | *3 | *3 | *3 | *3 | *3 | *3 | *3 | *3 | *3 | *3 | *4 | *4 | *3 | *3 |
| 125 | 0 | 1 | 1 | 1 | 2 | 2 | 2 | 2 | 3 | 3 | 3 | 3 | 3 | 3 | 3 | 4 | 4 | 5 | 5 | 5 | *3 | *3 | *3 | *3 | *3 | *3 | *3 | *3 | *3 | *3 | *4 | *4 | *3 | *3 |
| 150 | 0 | 1 | 1 | 1 | 2 | 2 | 2 | 2 | 3 | 3 | 3 | 3 | 3 | 3 | 3 | 4 | 4 | 5 | 5 | 5 | *3 | *3 | *3 | *3 | *3 | *3 | *3 | *3 | *3 | *3 | *4 | *4 | *3 | *3 |
| 175 | 0 | 1 | 1 | 1 | 2 | 2 | 2 | 2 | 3 | 3 | 3 | 3 | 3 | 3 | 3 | 4 | 4 | 5 | 5 | 5 | *3 | *3 | *3 | *3 | *3 | *3 | *3 | *3 | *3 | *3 | *4 | *4 | *3 | *3 |
| 200 | 0 | 1 | 1 | 1 | 2 | 2 | 2 | 2 | 3 | 3 | 3 | 3 | 3 | 3 | 4 | 4 | 5 | 5 | 5 | 5 | *3 | *3 | *3 | *3 | *3 | *3 | *3 | *3 | *3 | *4 | *4 | *4 | *3 | *3 |
| 225 | 0 | 1 | 1 | 1 | 2 | 2 | 2 | 2 | 3 | 3 | 3 | 3 | 3 | 3 | 4 | 4 | 5 | 5 | 5 | 5 | *3 | *3 | *3 | *3 | *3 | *3 | *3 | *3 | *3 | *4 | *4 | *4 | *3 | *3 |
| 250 | 0 | 1 | 1 | 1 | 2 | 2 | 2 | 2 | 3 | 3 | 3 | 3 | 3 | 3 | 4 | 4 | 5 | 5 | 5 | 5 | *3 | *3 | *3 | *3 | *3 | *3 | *3 | *3 | *3 | *4 | *4 | *4 | *3 | *3 |
| 275 | 0 | 1 | 1 | 1 | 2 | 2 | 2 | 2 | 3 | 3 | 3 | 3 | 3 | 3 | 4 | 4 | 5 | 5 | 5 | 5 | *3 | *3 | *3 | *3 | *3 | *3 | *3 | *3 | *3 | *4 | *4 | *4 | *3 | *3 |
| 300 | 0 | 1 | 1 | 1 | 2 | 2 | 2 | 2 | 3 | 3 | 3 | 3 | 3 | 3 | 4 | 4 | 5 | 5 | 5 | 5 | *3 | *3 | *3 | *3 | *3 | *3 | *3 | *3 | *3 | *4 | *4 | *4 | *3 | *3 |
| 325 | 0 | 1 | 1 | 1 | 2 | 2 | 2 | 2 | 3 | 3 | 3 | 3 | 3 | 3 | 4 | 4 | 5 | 5 | 5 | 5 | *3 | *3 | *3 | *3 | *3 | *3 | *3 | *3 | *3 | 5 | *4 | *4 | *3 | *3 |
| 350 | 0 | 1 | 1 | 1 | 2 | 2 | 2 | 2 | 3 | 3 | 3 | 3 | 3 | 3 | 4 | 4 | 5 | 5 | 5 | 5 | *3 | *3 | *3 | *3 | *3 | *3 | *3 | *3 | *3 | 5 | *4 | *4 | *3 | *3 |
| 375 | 0 | 1 | 1 | 1 | 2 | 2 | 2 | 2 | 3 | 3 | 3 | 3 | 3 | 3 | 4 | 4 | 5 | 5 | 5 | 5 | *3 | *3 | *3 | *3 | *3 | *3 | *3 | *3 | *3 | 6 | *4 | *4 | *3 | *3 |
| 400 | 0 | 1 | 1 | 1 | 2 | 2 | 2 | 2 | 3 | 3 | 3 | 3 | 3 | 3 | 4 | 4 | 5 | 5 | 5 | 5 | 5 | *3 | *3 | *3 | *3 | *3 | *3 | *3 | *3 | 5 | *4 | *4 | *4 | *3 |
| 425 | 0 | 1 | 1 | 1 | 2 | 2 | 2 | 2 | 3 | 3 | 3 | 3 | 3 | 3 | 4 | 4 | 5 | 5 | 5 | 5 | 5 | *3 | *3 | *3 | *3 | *3 | *3 | *3 | 6 | 6 | *4 | *4 | *4 | *3 |
| 450 | 0 | 1 | 1 | 1 | 2 | 2 | 2 | 2 | 3 | 3 | 3 | 3 | 3 | 3 | 4 | 4 | 5 | 5 | 5 | 5 | 5 | *3 | *3 | *3 | *3 | *3 | *3 | *3 | 5 | 5 | *4 | *4 | *4 | *3 |
| 475 | 0 | 1 | 1 | 1 | 2 | 2 | 2 | 2 | 3 | 3 | 3 | 3 | 3 | 3 | 4 | 4 | 5 | 5 | 5 | 5 | 5 | *3 | *3 | *3 | *3 | *3 | *3 | *3 | 6 | 6 | *4 | *4 | *4 | *3 |
| 500 | 0 | 1 | 1 | 1 | 2 | 2 | 2 | 2 | 3 | 3 | 3 | 3 | 3 | 3 | 4 | 4 | 5 | 5 | 5 | 5 | 5 | *3 | *3 | *3 | *3 | *3 | *3 | *3 | 5 | 5 | *4 | *4 | *4 | *5 |
| 550 | 0 | 1 | 1 | 1 | 2 | 2 | 2 | 2 | 3 | 3 | 3 | 3 | 3 | 3 | 4 | 4 | 5 | 5 | 5 | 5 | 5 | *3 | *3 | *3 | *3 | *3 | *3 | *3 | 6 | 5 | *4 | *4 | *4 | *5 |
| 600 | 0 | 1 | 1 | 1 | 2 | 2 | 2 | 2 | 3 | 3 | 3 | 3 | 3 | 3 | 4 | 4 | 5 | 5 | 5 | 5 | 5 | *3 | *3 | *3 | *3 | *3 | *3 | *3 | 6 | 6 | *4 | *4 | *5 | *5 |
| 650 | 0 | 1 | 1 | 1 | 2 | 2 | 2 | 2 | 3 | 3 | 3 | 3 | 3 | 3 | 4 | 4 | 5 | 5 | 5 | 5 | 5 | *3 | *3 | *3 | *3 | *3 | *3 | *3 | 6 | 5 | *4 | *4 | *5 | *5 |
| 700 | 0 | 1 | 1 | 1 | 2 | 2 | 2 | 2 | 3 | 3 | 3 | 3 | 3 | 3 | 4 | 4 | 5 | 5 | 5 | 5 | 5 | *3 | *3 | *3 | *3 | *3 | *3 | *3 | 6 | 6 | *4 | *4 | *5 | *5 |
| 750 | 0 | 1 | 1 | 1 | 2 | 2 | 2 | 2 | 3 | 3 | 3 | 3 | 3 | 3 | 4 | 4 | 5 | 5 | 5 | 5 | 5 | *3 | *3 | *3 | *3 | *3 | *3 | *3 | 6 | 5 | *4 | *4 | *5 | *5 |
| 800 | 0 | 1 | 1 | 1 | 2 | 2 | 2 | 2 | 3 | 3 | 3 | 3 | 3 | 3 | 4 | 4 | 5 | 5 | 5 | 5 | 5 | *3 | *3 | *3 | *3 | *3 | *3 | *3 | 6 | 6 | *4 | *4 | 7 | 7 |
| 850 | 0 | 1 | 1 | 1 | 2 | 2 | 2 | 2 | 3 | 3 | 3 | 3 | 3 | 3 | 4 | 4 | 5 | 5 | 5 | 5 | 5 | *3 | *3 | *3 | *3 | *3 | *3 | *3 | 5 | 5 | *4 | *4 | 7 | 7 |
| 900 | 0 | 1 | 1 | 1 | 2 | 2 | 2 | 2 | 3 | 3 | 3 | 3 | 3 | 3 | 4 | 4 | 5 | 5 | 5 | 5 | 5 | *3 | *3 | *3 | *3 | *3 | *3 | *3 | 6 | 5 | *4 | *4 | 7 | 7 |
| 950 | 0 | 1 | 1 | 1 | 2 | 2 | 2 | 2 | 3 | 3 | 3 | 3 | 3 | 3 | 4 | 4 | 5 | 5 | 5 | 5 | 5 | *3 | *3 | *3 | *3 | *3 | *3 | *3 | 5 | 5 | *4 | *4 | 7 | 7 |
| 1000 | 0 | 1 | 1 | 1 | 2 | 2 | 2 | 2 | 3 | 3 | 3 | 3 | 3 | 3 | 4 | 4 | 5 | 5 | 5 | 5 | 5 | *3 | *3 | *3 | *3 | *3 | *3 | *3 | 6 | 5 | *4 | *4 | 7 | 7 |

# Table 42.1. CONTINUED

DIST- * NUMBER OF TERMINALS TO BE CONCENTRATED

| ANCE | 35 | 36 | 37 | 38 | 39 | 40 | 41 | 42 | 43 | 44 | 45 | 46 | 47 | 48 | 49 | 50 | 51 | 52 | 53 | 54 | 55 | 56 | 57 | 58 | 59 | 60 | 61 | 62 | 63 | 64 | 65 | 66 | 67 | 68 |
|---|---|---|---|---|---|---|---|---|---|---|---|---|---|---|---|---|---|---|---|---|---|---|---|---|---|---|---|---|---|---|---|---|---|---|
| 1 | | | | | | | | | | | | | | | | | | | | | | | | | | | | | | | | | | |
| 5 | | | | | | | | | | | | | | | | | | | | | | | | | | | | | | | | | | |
| 10 | | | | | | | | | | | | | | | | | | | | | | | | | | | | | | | | | | |
| 15 | | | | | | | | | | | | | | | | | | | | | | | | | | | | | | | | | | |
| 20 | | | | | | | | | | | | | | | | | | | | | | | | | | | | | | | | | | |
| 25 | | | | | | | | | | | | | | | | | | | | | | | | | | | | | | | | | | |
| 30 | | | | | | | | | | | | | | | | | | | | | | | | | | | | | | | | | | |
| 35 | | | | | | | | | | | | | | | | | | | | | | | | | | | | | | | | | | |
| 40 | | | | | | | | | | | | | | | | | | | | | | | | | | | | | | | | | | |
| 45 | | | | | | | | | | | | | | | | | | | | | | | | | | | | | | | | | | |
| 50 | | | | | | | | | | | | | | | | | | | | | | | | | | | | | | | | | | |
| 55 | | | | | | | | | | | | | | | | | | | | | | | | | | | | | | | | | | |
| 60 | | | | | | | | | | | | | | | | | | | | | | | | | | | | | | | | | | |
| 65 | | | | | | | | | | | | | | | | | | | | | | | | | | | | | | | | | | |
| 70 | | | | | | | | | | | | | | | | | | | | | | | | | | | | | | | | | | |
| 75 | | | | | | | | | | | | | | | | | | | | | | | | | | | | | | | | | | |
| 80 | | | | | | | | | | | | | | | | | | | | | | | | | | | | | | | | | | |
| 85 | | | | | | | | | | | | | | | | | | | | | | | | | | | | | | | | | | |
| 90 | | | | | | | | | | | | | | | | | | | | | | | | | | | | | | | | | | |
| 95 | | | | | | | | | | | | | | | | | | | | | | | | | | | | | | | | | | |
| 100 | | | | | | | | | | | | | | | | | | | | | | | | | | | | | | | | | | |
| 125 | | | | | | | | | | | | | | | | | | | | | | | | | | | | | | | | | | |
| 150 | | | | | | | | | | | | | | | | | | | | | | | | | | | | | | | | | | |
| 175 | | | | | | | | | | | | | | | | | | | | | | | | | | | | | | | | | | |
| 200 | | | | | | | | | | | | | | | | | | | | | | | | | | | | | | | | | | |
| 225 | | | | | | | | | | | | | | | | | | | | | | | | | | | | | | | | | | |
| 250 | | | | | | | | | | | | | | | | | | | | | | | | | | | | | | | | | | |
| 275 | | | | | | | | | | | | | | | | | | | | | | | | | | | | | | | | | | |
| 300 | | | | | | | | | | | | | | | | | | | | | | | | | | | | | | | | | | |
| 325 | | | | | | | | | | | | | | | | | | | | | | | | | | | | | | | | | | |
| 350 | | | | | | | | | | | | | | | | | | | | | | | | | | | | | | | | | | |
| 375 | | | | | | | | | | | | | | | | | | | | | | | | | | | | | | | | | | |
| 400 | | | | | | | | | | | | | | | | | | | | | | | | | | | | | | | | | | |
| 425 | | | | | | | | | | | | | | | | | | | | | | | | | | | | | | | | | | |
| 450 | | | | | | | | | | | | | | | | | | | | | | | | | | | | | | | | | | |
| 475 | | | | | | | | | | | | | | | | | | | | | | | | | | | | | | | | | | |
| 500 | | | | | | | | | | | | | | | | | | | | | | | | | | | | | | | | | | |
| 550 | | | | | | | | | | | | | | | | | | | | | | | | | | | | | | | | | | |
| 600 | | | | | | | | | | | | | | | | | | | | | | | | | | | | | | | | | | |
| 650 | | | | | | | | | | | | | | | | | | | | | | | | | | | | | | | | | | |
| 700 | | | | | | | | | | | | | | | | | | | | | | | | | | | | | | | | | | |
| 750 | | | | | | | | | | | | | | | | | | | | | | | | | | | | | | | | | | |
| 800 | | | | | | | | | | | | | | | | | | | | | | | | | | | | | | | | | | |
| 850 | | | | | | | | | | | | | | | | | | | | | | | | | | | | | | | | | | |
| 900 | | | | | | | | | | | | | | | | | | | | | | | | | | | | | | | | | | |
| 950 | | | | | | | | | | | | | | | | | | | | | | | | | | | | | | | | | | |
| 1000 | | | | | | | | | | | | | | | | | | | | | | | | | | | | | | | | | | |

concentrators are to be used. Seven such devices should be considered—the same seven as in the previous example. Which one of these devices should be selected, and where should such devices be positioned?

**SENSITIVITY OF POSITIONING**
Before we begin, one fact worth noting is that the network cost is not too sensitive to the exact concentrator positioning. We can move the concentrator within a zone several miles across, and only a small difference in cost occurs.

To illustrate this point, we took the 32 cities south of Atlanta, Georgia, from the list of cities and connected them to one concentrator (assuming that it could handle 32 lines). We then moved the concentrator around to observe the cost variation. Table 42.2 shows the result. The vertical scale of this table is the A.T. & T. vertical coordinate and the horizontal scale is their horizontal coordinate. The figures in the table are the total line cost. It will be seen that the smallest cost figure on the table is $15,060, representing the best position for the concentrator. The cost figures for nearby locations do not rise rapidly.

Figure 42.1 shows this on a map. The concentrator can be placed anywhere in the innermost ring, with a variation in total line cost of only 1 percent. This ring is approximately 190 miles across. If the concentrator is placed anywhere in the second ring, the cost will vary by up to 5 percent, and the outermost ring represents a variation of 10 percent from the minimum cost.

Because of this fact, we will position our concentrators at a terminal location rather than at a location not presently on the network. It would be inconvenient to create another place to service whenever we site a concentrator.

**RANKING THE POSSIBLE LOCATIONS**
We have, then, 187 possible locations where we could position a concentrator. In fact, we can consider slightly less than this number because some of the locations are in the same cities.

It is desirable to locate the concentrators at those cities where there is substantial local traffic to justify their existence. We would like to rank the cities, in fact, on a basis of the potential cost saving to be gained from siting a concentrator there.

In order to do so, a cost factor is evaluated for each city pair. It is written FACTOR (I,J) in the programs we will use. FACTOR (I,J) is the line cost saving, if any, that would accrue from connecting city J to the computer via a concentrator located at city I. In other words,

$$\text{FACTOR (I,J)} = C_c - (C_a + C_b) \quad \text{(if this is positive)}$$

where $C_c$ = the cost of a low-speed line from the terminal at city J to the computer

**Table 42.2.** THE COST SENSITIVITY OF CONCENTRATOR POSITIONING

| | 3380 | 3340 | 3300 | 3260 | 3220 | 3180 | 3140 | 3100 | 3060 | 3020 | 2980 | 2940 | 2900 | 2860 | 2820 | 2780 | 2740 | 2700 |
|---|---|---|---|---|---|---|---|---|---|---|---|---|---|---|---|---|---|---|
| 7800 | 15296 | 15295 | 15295 | 15299 | 15302 | 15304 | 15306 | 15314 | 15319 | 15321 | 15324 | 15332 | 15354 | 15376 | 15401 | 15429 | 15465 | 15504 |
| 7810 | 15292 | 15282 | 15284 | 15285 | 15287 | 15290 | 15293 | 15300 | 15305 | 15303 | 15305 | 15318 | 15329 | 15359 | 15387 | 15414 | 15451 | 15489 |
| 7820 | 15283 | 15282 | 15272 | 15274 | 15273 | 15290 | 15278 | 15284 | 15289 | 15287 | 15286 | 15295 | 15315 | 15342 | 15368 | 15397 | 15439 | 15471 |
| 7830 | 15277 | 15270 | 15263 | 15259 | 15261 | 15264 | 15265 | 15270 | 15271 | 15270 | 15271 | 15280 | 15296 | 15323 | 15352 | 15385 | 15417 | 15460 |
| 7840 | 15271 | 15263 | 15253 | 15253 | 15247 | 15253 | 15252 | 15254 | 15253 | 15252 | 15255 | 15261 | 15278 | 15303 | 15337 | 15369 | 15401 | 15445 |
| 7850 | 15267 | 15252 | 15244 | 15239 | 15237 | 15253 | 15248 | 15235 | 15253 | 15237 | 15238 | 15261 | 15260 | 15289 | 15319 | 15354 | 15391 | 15431 |
| 7860 | 15266 | 15246 | 15230 | 15229 | 15224 | 15235 | 15228 | 15226 | 15223 | 15223 | 15221 | 15228 | 15244 | 15274 | 15308 | 15340 | 15377 | 15421 |
| 7870 | 15257 | 15240 | 15226 | 15217 | 15211 | 15213 | 15225 | 15212 | 15211 | 15205 | 15209 | 15216 | 15230 | 15255 | 15292 | 15316 | 15365 | 15405 |
| 7880 | 15255 | 15232 | 15218 | 15206 | 15201 | 15201 | 15218 | 15212 | 15195 | 15195 | 15196 | 15199 | 15216 | 15242 | 15277 | 15316 | 15354 | 15399 |
| 7890 | 15250 | 15223 | 15208 | 15200 | 15188 | 15188 | 15191 | 15182 | 15184 | 15180 | 15179 | 15186 | 15203 | 15231 | 15262 | 15301 | 15344 | 15388 |
| 7900 | 15245 | 15219 | 15200 | 15190 | 15181 | 15182 | 15177 | 15169 | 15165 | 15169 | 15165 | 15172 | 15190 | 15218 | 15254 | 15294 | 15333 | 15378 |
| 7910 | 15242 | 15214 | 15197 | 15181 | 15173 | 15171 | 15165 | 15162 | 15156 | 15150 | 15156 | 15158 | 15178 | 15205 | 15242 | 15282 | 15322 | 15370 |
| 7920 | 15239 | 15209 | 15187 | 15176 | 15166 | 15162 | 15155 | 15149 | 15141 | 15141 | 15132 | 15148 | 15161 | 15190 | 15224 | 15276 | 15308 | 15360 |
| 7930 | 15236 | 15206 | 15182 | 15170 | 15150 | 15149 | 15145 | 15140 | 15130 | 15129 | 15130 | 15137 | 15149 | 15178 | 15221 | 15264 | 15308 | 15351 |
| 7940 | 15236 | 15204 | 15179 | 15157 | 15149 | 15140 | 15133 | 15128 | 15124 | 15116 | 15122 | 15124 | 15139 | 15168 | 15210 | 15258 | 15298 | 15345 |
| 7950 | 15234 | 15203 | 15175 | 15159 | 15144 | 15132 | 15124 | 15118 | 15111 | 15110 | 15113 | 15114 | 15130 | 15159 | 15201 | 15249 | 15291 | 15339 |
| 7960 | 15234 | 15197 | 15172 | 15151 | 15137 | 15114 | 15117 | 15112 | 15098 | 15091 | 15103 | 15107 | 15119 | 15147 | 15195 | 15244 | 15284 | 15334 |
| 7970 | 15236 | 15196 | 15169 | 15152 | 15129 | 15114 | 15105 | 15106 | 15087 | 15091 | 15095 | 15098 | 15114 | 15138 | 15182 | 15223 | 15281 | 15330 |
| 7980 | 15233 | 15198 | 15166 | 15144 | 15123 | 15108 | 15100 | 15096 | 15087 | 15085 | 15090 | 15093 | 15101 | 15132 | 15175 | 15231 | 15277 | 15325 |
| 7990 | 15232 | 15196 | 15167 | 15138 | 15117 | 15101 | 15095 | 15090 | 15082 | 15081 | 15082 | 15086 | 15094 | 15121 | 15171 | 15227 | 15274 | 15323 |
| 8000 | 15232 | 15193 | 15166 | 15133 | 15110 | 15098 | 15087 | 15081 | 15076 | 15077 | 15077 | 15079 | 15088 | 15114 | 15166 | 15221 | 15272 | 15317 |
| 8010 | 15232 | 15195 | 15152 | 15132 | 15102 | 15091 | 15087 | 15077 | 15073 | 15073 | 15071 | 15074 | 15078 | 15103 | 15163 | 15221 | 15269 | 15315 |
| 8020 | 15236 | 15193 | 15159 | 15126 | 15102 | 15086 | 15077 | 15072 | 15068 | 15068 | 15070 | 15074 | 15078 | 15101 | 15162 | 15217 | 15269 | 15315 |
| 8030 | 15238 | 15191 | 15161 | 15123 | 15100 | 15083 | 15074 | 15067 | 15064 | 15064 | 15066 | 15071 | 15076 | 15103 | 15161 | 15215 | 15273 | 15316 |
| 8040 | 15235 | 15192 | 15155 | 15121 | 15096 | 15081 | 15070 | 15064 | 15063 | 15065 | 15063 | 15073 | 15073 | 15106 | 15164 | 15216 | 15274 | 15319 |
| 8050 | 15240 | 15192 | 15155 | 15120 | 15091 | 15078 | 15070 | 15062 | 15062 | 15062 | 15067 | 15076 | 15085 | 15114 | 15165 | 15219 | 15277 | 15322 |
| 8060 | 15242 | 15195 | 15158 | 15119 | 15089 | 15080 | 15070 | 15063 | 15061 | 15064 | 15070 | 15079 | 15092 | 15120 | 15170 | 15225 | 15279 | 15324 |
| 8070 | 15244 | 15197 | 15155 | 15119 | 15089 | 15075 | 15067 | 15060 | 15060 | 15066 | 15075 | 15082 | 15098 | 15129 | 15176 | 15230 | 15285 | 15333 |
| 8080 | 15249 | 15201 | 15156 | 15117 | 15089 | 15076 | 15069 | 15064 | 15061 | 15069 | 15085 | 15091 | 15108 | 15140 | 15186 | 15238 | 15290 | 15333 |
| 8090 | 15254 | 15200 | 15158 | 15117 | 15090 | 15076 | 15073 | 15058 | 15068 | 15073 | 15080 | 15099 | 15117 | 15146 | 15191 | 15243 | 15293 | 15343 |
| 8100 | 15260 | 15205 | 15161 | 15120 | 15091 | 15081 | 15070 | 15058 | 15068 | 15073 | 15085 | 15106 | 15117 | 15158 | 15204 | 15251 | 15306 | 15347 |
| 8110 | 15255 | 15212 | 15164 | 15123 | 15095 | 15080 | 15079 | 15074 | 15073 | 15076 | 15092 | 15106 | 15140 | 15167 | 15211 | 15256 | 15306 | 15355 |
| 8120 | 15270 | 15219 | 15168 | 15125 | 15092 | 15087 | 15081 | 15078 | 15078 | 15084 | 15096 | 15115 | 15149 | 15180 | 15221 | 15268 | 15314 | 15364 |
| 8130 | 15275 | 15224 | 15174 | 15130 | 15095 | 15094 | 15091 | 15082 | 15087 | 15090 | 15104 | 15126 | 15162 | 15195 | 15232 | 15278 | 15324 | 15370 |
| 8140 | 15286 | 15232 | 15181 | 15134 | 15098 | 15101 | 15095 | 15090 | 15093 | 15100 | 15113 | 15131 | 15176 | 15202 | 15243 | 15289 | 15334 | 15376 |
| 8150 | 15296 | 15239 | 15185 | 15144 | 15106 | 15108 | 15103 | 15101 | 15097 | 15108 | 15121 | 15144 | 15186 | 15218 | 15255 | 15299 | 15345 | 15388 |
| 8160 | 15305 | 15251 | 15199 | 15155 | 15117 | 15117 | 15114 | 15111 | 15111 | 15117 | 15131 | 15165 | 15197 | 15230 | 15259 | 15309 | 15353 | 15396 |
| 8170 | 15313 | 15260 | 15207 | 15166 | 15130 | 15130 | 15128 | 15121 | 15124 | 15126 | 15143 | 15186 | 15207 | 15242 | 15268 | 15319 | 15365 | 15405 |
| 8180 | 15324 | 15268 | 15223 | 15180 | 15143 | 15143 | 15140 | 15133 | 15133 | 15142 | 15151 | 15197 | 15219 | 15257 | 15283 | 15324 | 15365 | 15415 |
| 8190 | 15335 | 15281 | 15235 | 15194 | 15159 | 15159 | 15154 | 15146 | 15161 | 15162 | 15164 | 15210 | 15229 | 15269 | 15295 | 15344 | 15373 | 15427 |
| 8200 | 15348 | 15294 | 15247 | 15215 | 15168 | 15178 | 15168 | 15159 | 15161 | 15162 | 15175 | 15222 | 15241 | 15280 | 15305 | 15363 | 15383 | 15436 |
| 8210 | 15362 | 15306 | 15262 | 15228 | 15207 | 15193 | 15183 | 15178 | 15173 | 15178 | 15190 | 15210 | 15256 | 15289 | 15313 | 15373 | 15393 | 15436 |
| 8220 | 15362 | 15322 | 15278 | 15245 | 15222 | 15211 | 15203 | 15190 | 15190 | 15195 | 15202 | 15222 | 15268 | 15298 | 15327 | 15360 | 15403 | 15449 |
| 8230 | 15374 | 15322 | 15294 | 15262 | 15238 | 15229 | 15218 | 15207 | 15204 | 15207 | 15217 | 15241 | 15282 | 15314 | 15346 | 15383 | 15413 | 15453 |
| 8240 | 15386 | 15338 | 15294 | 15278 | 15259 | 15247 | 15233 | 15231 | 15240 | 15224 | 15233 | 15254 | 15291 | 15316 | 15359 | 15383 | 15423 | 15466 |
| 8250 | 15397 | 15369 | 15330 | 15299 | 15279 | 15263 | 15256 | 15250 | 15257 | 15241 | 15246 | 15267 | 15306 | 15322 | 15353 | 15392 | 15437 | 15481 |
| 8260 | 15415 | 15369 | 15330 | 15316 | 15294 | 15285 | 15276 | 15256 | 15257 | 15265 | 15265 | 15279 | 15306 | 15346 | 15355 | 15401 | 15445 | 15495 |
| 8270 | 15429 | 15335 | 15345 | 15337 | 15311 | 15304 | 15292 | 15283 | 15293 | 15280 | 15285 | 15298 | 15336 | 15359 | 15377 | 15413 | 15457 | 15510 |
| 8280 | 15449 | 15402 | 15367 | 15352 | 15331 | 15320 | 15310 | 15299 | 15313 | 15291 | 15298 | 15314 | 15349 | 15367 | 15385 | 15424 | 15470 | 15519 |
| 8290 | 15466 | 15425 | 15385 | 15374 | 15353 | 15340 | 15332 | 15320 | 15313 | 15308 | 15313 | 15328 | 15355 | 15367 | 15396 | 15436 | 15483 | 15522 |
| 8300 | 15507 | 15463 | 15427 | 15396 | 15374 | 15360 | 15349 | 15337 | 15329 | 15324 | 15333 | 15348 | 15363 | 15379 | 15408 | 15448 | 15494 | 15544 |

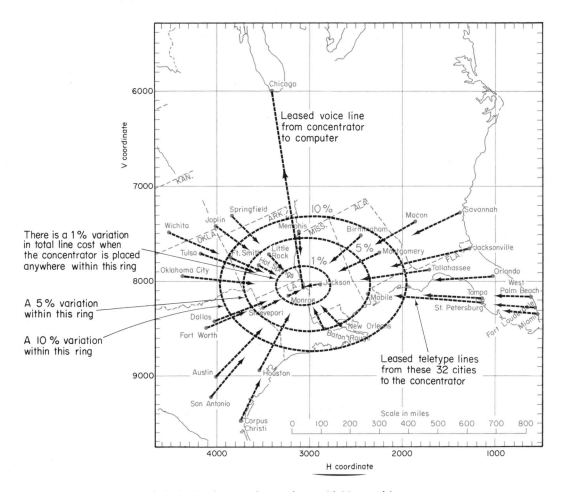

*Fig. 42.1.* Total network cost is not highly sensitive to exact concentrator positioning. The variation in total line cost when the concentrator is anywhere within the inner ring is 1%, and this ring is 190 miles across.

$C_a$ = the cost of a low-speed line from the terminal at city J to a concentrator at city I

$C_b$ = the cost of a high-speed line from the concentrator to the computer, divided by the number of terminals that will be sharing it—that is, the number of terminals that can be connected to the concentrator

If $C_c - (C_a + C_b)$ is not positive, then there will be no point in connecting city J via the concentrator at city I. It would be better to connect it directly to the computer. In this case, FACTOR (I,J) = O.

This is coded as follows, in PL/I:

```
DO I=1 TO NCITY;
DO J=1 TO NCITY;
ACOST=SLCOST(DIST(I,J));
BCOST=SHCOST(DIST(1,I))/NL;
CCOST=SLCOST(DIST(1,J));
IF (ACOST+BCOST) < CCOST THEN FACTOR(I,J)=CCOST-(ACOST+BCOST);
END;
END;
```

In Fortran:

```
   DO 5 I=1,NCITY
   BCOST=SHCOST(DIST(1,I))/NL
   DO 5 J=1,NCITY
   ACOST=SLCOST(DIST(I,J))
   CCOST=SLCOST(DIST(1,J))
   ABCOST=ACOST+BCOST
 5 IF (ABCOST.LT.CCOST) FACTOR(I,J)=CCOST-ABCOST
```

Here DIST (I,J) is the distance in miles between city I and city J, this table having been initially calculated for all city pairs. Thus SLCOST (DIST (I,J)) is the cost of a low-speed line from city I to city J, and SHCOST is the cost of a high-speed line (using United States interstate voice-grade line tariffs). NL is the number of low-speed lines that can be connected to the concentrator.

Having established this cost factor for each city pair, the program now examines every city in turn to see what saving would result from locating a concentrator there. If the concentrator in question is at city X, then the computer scans through the values of FACTOR (X,J) for every city J and picks those terminals for which it is highest until no more terminals can be connected to that concentrator. In other words, if the concentrator is at city X, the program selects the best terminals for it to concentrate and then works out the total line saving that would result, if any.

This operation is done for each city where a concentrator could be positioned, and then the computer picks the location that gives the most saving.

In PL/I, this is as follows:

```
SAVMAX=0;
DO I=1 TO NCITY;
  TAG=0; SAVING=0;
  TAG(1)=1;
  DO M=1 TO (NL-1);
    FACMAX=0;
    DO J=1 TO NCITY;
      IF TAG(J)=0 & FACTOR(I,J)>FACMAX THEN DO;
      FACMAX=FACTOR(I,J); N=J;
      END;
    END;
  END;
```

```
     IF FACMAX > 0 THEN DO;
     TAG(N)=1;
     SAVING=SAVING+SLCOST(DIST(1,N))-SLCOST(DIST(I,N));
     END;
   END;
   SAVING=SAVING+SLCOST(DIST(1,I))-CONCOST-SHCOST(DIST(1,I));
   IF SAVING>SAVMAX THEN DO;
   SAVMAX=SAVING; K=I;
   END;
END;
```

In Fortran:

```
     SAVMAX=0.0
     DO 50 I=1,NCITY
     DO 10 J=2,NCITY
10   TAG(J)=.FALSE.
     SAVING=0.0
     TAG(1)=.TRUE.
     LIMIT=NL-1
     DO 30 M=1,LIMIT
     FACMAX=0.0
     DO 20 J=1,NCITY
     IF (TAG(J) .OR. FACTOR(I,J).LE.FACMAX) GO TO 20
     FACMAX=FACTOR(I,J)
     N=J
20   CONTINUE
     IF (FACMAX.LE.0.0) GO TO 30
     TAG(N)=.TRUE.
     SAVING=SAVING+SLCOST(DIST(1,N))-SLCOST(DIST(I,N))
30   CONTINUE
     SAVING=SAVING+SLCOST(DIST(1,I))-CONCST-SHCOST(DIST(1,I))
     IF (SAVING.LE.SAVMAX) GO TO 50
     SAVMAX=SAVING
     K=I
50   CONTINUE
```

Here I is the number of the proposed concentrator location, and it is varied from 1 to NCITY, where NCITY is the total number of city locations. J is the location of a city that may be connected to that concentrator, and it is also varied from 1 to NCITY, missing out I because it is assumed that the terminals at I will be connected to the concentrator at I. TAG (J) is set to 1 when a decision is provisionally made to connect city J to the concentrator.

The total saving is added up for each concentrator location (I). The value of I that gives the maximum saving is found, and this value gives the proposed concentrator location.

Having found the best location for a concentrator and assigned terminals to be concentrated, the program then repeats the operation, looking for the best location for a second such device. This process continues until no more concentrators can be economically sited.

We now have a near-optimum set of locations for the concentrators. It is worth taking a second look, however, at which cities are connected to which concentrators. In the foregoing process, it is possible that some of the cities allocated to the first concentrator could have been more cheaply connected to the second one, and so on. The program therefore enters a second phase in which the concentrator locations are fixed and the terminal locations are scanned, starting with the one farthest from the computer and connecting each to the concentrator that gives the cheapest interconnection.

The two phases of the program are illustrated in Fig. 42.2.

**MAP PRINTING**    The programs discussed here (and in the following chapters, as well as the previous one) use a subroutine that prints a crude map on the computer printer. This process gives a quick pictorial idea of what the program is doing and has proved useful in developing and debugging these tools. Figures 42.3 to 42.7 illustrate the progress of the program in its Phase I operation—selecting the positions for concentrator type 6.

The location of concentrator type 6 that gives the most saving is Danbury, Conn. A letter C on Fig. 42.3 indicates this location. The positions of the letter Y show the cities that would be connected to Danbury. The letter N shows cities that would be connected to Danbury if the concentrator there had sufficient capacity; however, they are not connected there because the concentrator can only handle 30 lines.

After the cities connected to Danbury are deleted from the list, the next best place to locate a concentrator is at Columbia, S.C. This site is shown by the letter C in Fig. 42.4. Again the Y cities in this figure are connected to it.

After Columbia, the next best location is Williamsport, Penn., shown in Fig. 42.5. Then Hot Springs, Ark., is selected (Fig. 42.6). There are no Ns in Fig. 42.6 because only 26 locations can be economically connected via Hot Springs. Springfield, Ohio, is the next concentrator city (Fig. 42.7). Now 39 cities are left unconnected via concentrators. Using a further concentrator for these cities does not result in any savings.

A similar operation is done for each concentrator type and reveals that concentrators number 2 and 3 gave the lowest-cost network (as might have been expected from Table 42.1). Twenty-one concentrators of type number 2 were selected. The ranking of the seven devices is tabulated in Table 42.3.

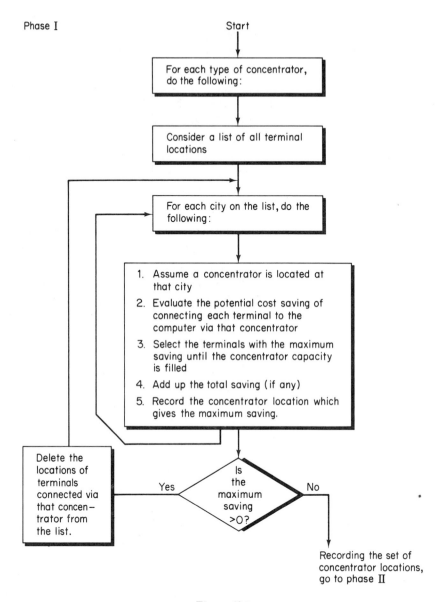

*Figure 42.2*

Phase II

Start

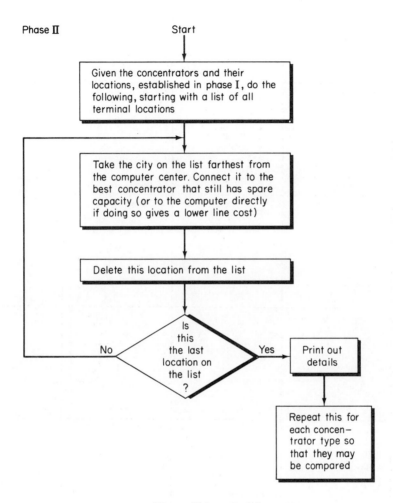

Figure 42.2 continued

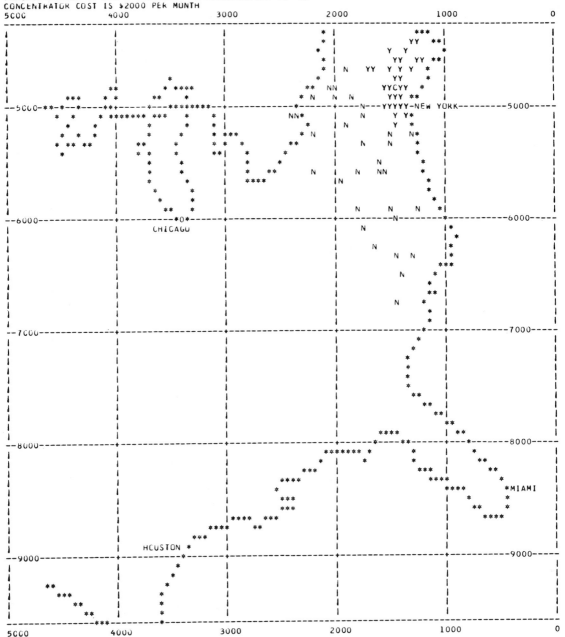

CASE NUMBER 1
MAP NUMBER 1
MAXIMUM NUMBER OF LOW SPEED LINES ON CONCENTRATOR IS 30
CONCENTRATOR COST IS $2000 PER MONTH

A MAP SHOWING THE 30 LOCATIONS CONNECTED TO THE CONCENTRATOR AT DANBURY  CONN

KEY:     O = COMPUTER CENTER
         C = CONCENTRATOR
         Y = CITIES CONNECTED TO THAT CONCENTRATOR
         N = CITIES NOT CONNECTED TO THAT CONCENTRATOR BUT WHICH
             WOULD HAVE BEEN IF IT HAD HAD THE CAPACITY

*Fig. 42.3.* This and the following four figures are maps printed by the concentrator positioning program to show the steps it is taking. Appendix VII gives the map composing routine. The maps relate to concentrator 6 in Example 42.2. The first concentrator is positioned at Danbury, Conn. (above).

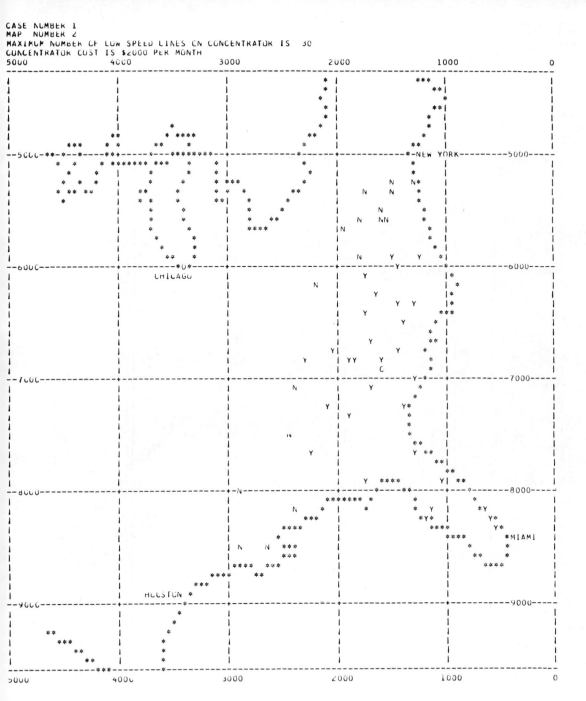

CASE NUMBER 1
MAP NUMBER 2
MAXIMUM NUMBER OF LOW SPEED LINES ON CONCENTRATOR IS  30
CONCENTRATOR COST IS $2000 PER MONTH

A MAP SHOWING THE 30 LOCATIONS CONNECTED TO THE CONCENTRATOR AT COLUMBIA  SC

KEY:     0 = COMPUTER CENTER
         C = CONCENTRATOR
         Y = CITIES CONNECTED TO THAT CONCENTRATOR
         N = CITIES NOT CONNECTED TO THAT CONCENTRATOR BUT WHICH
             WOULD HAVE BEEN IF IT HAD HAD THE CAPACITY

*Fig. 42.4.* The second concentrator is positioned at Columbia, S. C.

759

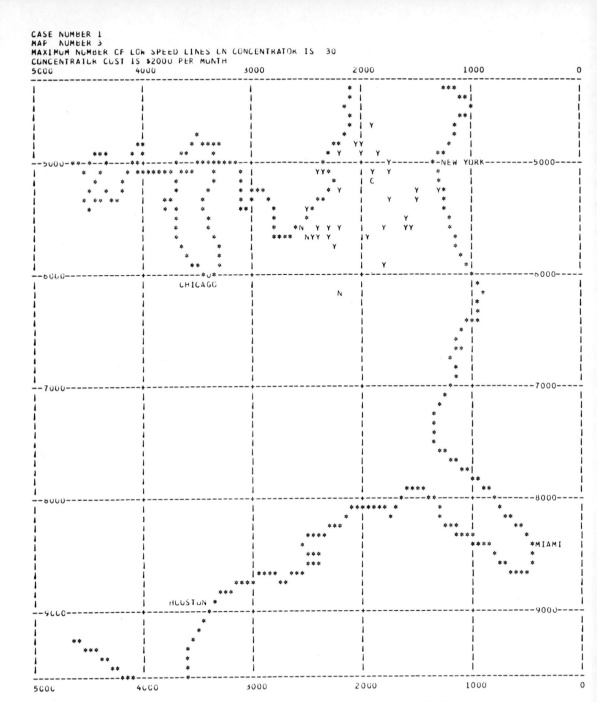

A MAP SHOWING THE 30 LOCATIONS CONNECTED TO THE CONCENTRATOR AT WILLIAMSPORT   PENN

KEY:     U = COMPUTER CENTER
         C = CONCENTRATOR
         Y = CITIES CONNECTED TO THAT CONCENTRATOR
         N = CITIES NOT CONNECTED TO THAT CONCENTRATOR BUT WHIC
             WOULD HAVE BEEN IF IT HAD HAD THE CAPACITY

*Fig. 42.5.* The third concentrator is positioned at Williamsport, Penn.

760

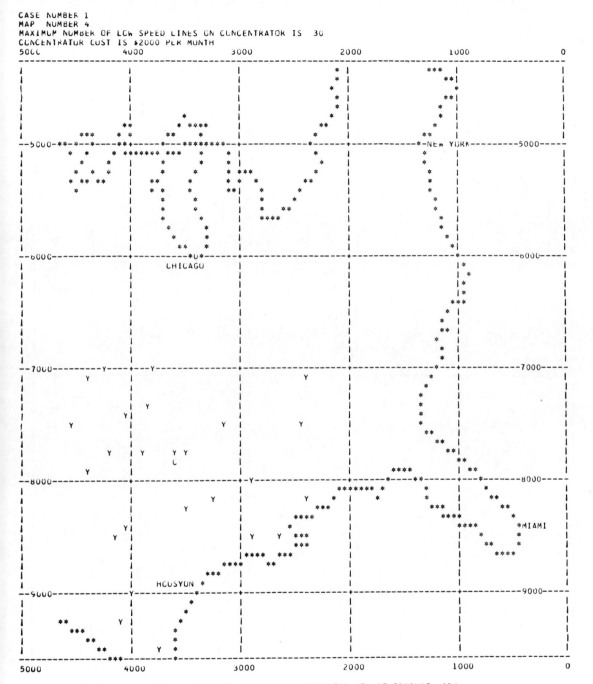

CASE NUMBER 1
MAP   NUMBER 4
MAXIMUM NUMBER OF LOW SPEED LINES ON CONCENTRATOR IS   30
CONCENTRATOR COST IS $2000 PER MONTH

*Fig. 42.6.* The fourth concentrator is positioned at Hot Springs, Ark.

761

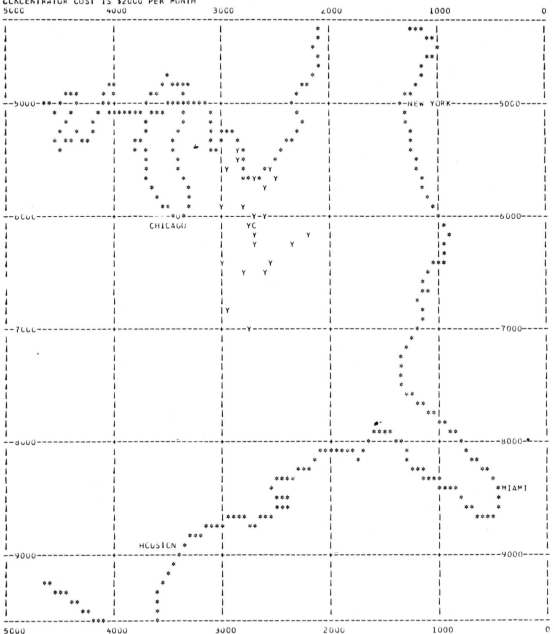

A MAP SHOWING THE 22 LOCATIONS CONNECTED TO THE CONCENTRATOR AT SPRINGFIELD OHIO

KEY:     C = COMPUTER CENTER
         C = CONCENTRATOR
         Y = CITIES CONNECTED TO THAT CONCENTRATOR
         N = CITIES NOT CONNECTED TO THAT CONCENTRATOR BUT WHICH
             WOULD HAVE BEEN IF IT HAD HAD THE CAPACITY

*Fig. 42.7.* The last concentrator in this case is positioned at Springfield, Ohio. Now phase II of the program begins. The total cost, however, is greater than with concentrators 1 to 5.

**Table 42.3**

| Concentrator Number | Concentrator Cost | Number of Lines per Concentrator | Number of Concentrators in the Network | Overall Network Cost ($ thousand) |
|---|---|---|---|---|
| 1 | 100 | 4 | 42 | 59 |
| 2 | 200 | 8 | 21 | 50 |
| 3 | 400 | 14 | 13 | 52 |
| 4 | 700 | 16 | 16 | 55 |
| 5 | 1000 | 20 | 8 | 58 |
| 6 | 2000 | 30 | 5 | 63 |
| 7 | 3000 | 50 | 4 | 67 |
| A point-to-point network with no concentrators: | | | | 95 |

The final configuration using concentrator type 2 is mapped in Fig. 42.8.

**MULTIPLE CONCENTRATOR TYPES**

In the preceding program we assumed that all the concentrators used would be of the same type. Most *existing* networks today do seem to use identical concentrators. However, the lowest-cost configuration would sometimes use more than one type of concentrator in the same network. If the concentrators are polled by the computer, they have to be compatible. Some programming considerations place restrictions on diversity. Nevertheless, many of the devices we are discussing are not polled but carry out a simple multiplexing operation that is transparent to the programs. In this case, there is little disadvantage in concentrator diversity.

With the seven concentrators and the city locations in the above example, a lower-cost network results if the concentrators used are intermixed. A program that will design such a network needs a straightforward modification to the above technique. Obtaining an optimum solution, however, takes substantially more computer time.

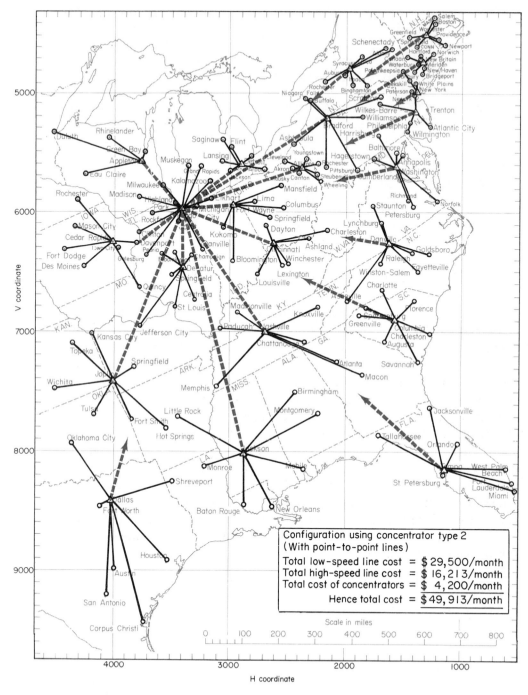

Fig. 42.8. The final configuration for Example 42.2 using concentrator 2 positioned as shown.

# 43    CONCENTRATORS WITH MULTIDROP LINES

As discussed in Chapter 20, the high-speed lines may have more than one concentrator attached to them in a multidrop fashion. Again, the low-speed lines from a concentrator or multiplexer may have several terminals attached to them. Consequently, we must not only select the concentration device and its location but we must also establish a minimum-cost multipoint linkage.

In the former case, we may proceed in two stages.

1. Use a program like that in Chapter 42 to select and position the concentrators. We do not know the cost of the high-speed line exactly yet, so we will make an estimate of it and divide its cost between the concentrators attached to it.

2. Use a multipoint linkage program like that in Chapter 40 to interconnect the concentrators. The traffic rate table will be obtained in the same way as in Chapter 39, but concentrators rather than terminals are now the subject of the queuing calculations or simulation, whichever is used. It is generally a good idea to use simulation where concentrators and multidrop lines are involved. The complete data path from the computer to the terminal will be simulated.

**Example 43.1. Concentrators on Multidrop High-Speed Lines.** A concentrator that can handle 16 terminals on subvoice-grade lines is available. It can itself be attached to a voice-grade line in a multidrop fashion. It costs $1000 per month.

Design a network using it to connect the 187 cities in the previous examples to the computer center at Chicago. Simulation indicates that three such concentrators could be attached to a voice-grade line with the message lengths in question, without degrading the response times unduly. (Note that this process is much better than using *low-speed* multi-drop lines because the voice line in this case transmits about 35 times faster than the low-speed line. Sometimes the ratio is higher.)

Does the use of this device result in a lower-cost network than the devices in the previous chapter?

The voice-line mileage to connect three locations to the computer will vary with their positioning. If the locations were clustered together, the mileage could be almost equal to their mean distance. On the other hand, with some configurations it could be three times their mean distance, although this is unlikely. In the first run of our concentrator location program, we do not know this ratio; therefore we will make a guess and assume that the total line mileage from the computer to the three concentrators is twice their mean distance. We can refine this guess later if we feel that the addition accuracy is worthwhile.

The high-speed line cost from computer to concentrator in Chapter 42 was written in PL/I as SHCOST (DIST(1,I)), I being the number of the concentrator city and 1 being the number of the computer city. This cost must now be apportioned between the concentrators, and so we write SHCOST (DIST (1,I))*2/3. Otherwise the program for positioning the concentrators is the same.

In practice, the inaccuracy of the preceding guess has only a minor effect on the concentrator placement; and with multidrop voice lines, the network cost is less sensitive to concentrator placement than it was in the previous chapter. Nevertheless it should be adjusted when the final linkage of the concentrators reveals the line costs.

The program positions the concentrators in the following locations in order of maximum saving:

1. Hartford, Conn.
2. New York, N. Y.
3. Columbia, S.C.
4. Ithaca, N.Y.
5. Shreveport, La.
6. Steubenville, Ohio
7. Atlanta, Ga.
8. Cincinnati, Ohio
9. Quincy, Ill.
10. Lansing, Mich.

Cities not connected to these concentrators are on lines direct to Chicago.

The total low-speed line cost is $40,670 and the cost of the ten concentrators is $10,000.

We must now interconnect these concentrators with multidrop voice lines. In order to do so, the CNDP program discussed in Chapter 40 is used. It connects them as shown in Fig. 43.1. The total voice-grade line cost is $4915. The total cost is therefore $55,585.

The cost is higher than with the concentrators in Fig. 42.8, and no advantage is gained. The multidrop high-speed lines are, in fact, a disadvantage. The configuration in Fig. 42.8 would therefore be used in preference to this one.

**LOW-SPEED**　　　　　　Now let us consider the case where it is the low-
**MULTIDROP LINES**　　　speed lines that are multipoint.

**Example 43.2. Concentrators with Multidrop Low-Speed Lines.** Again the 187 cities of the previous examples must be connected to Chicago. This time devices are used that concentrate the traffic from low-speed multipoint lines.

Concentrators or multiplexers having the following characteristics are to be considered:

| | Cost of Device | Number of Low-Speed Lines |
|---|---|---|
| Device 1 | 200 | 4 |
| Device 2 | 400 | 7 |
| Device 3 | 700 | 12 |

For simplicity and ease of maintenance, it has been decided that all the concentrators on the network must be of the same type.

Which concentrator should be used, and where should it be positioned?

The CNDP algorithm in Chapter 40 will now be used for interconnecting the low-speed lines, once we have determined the concentrator locations. The algorithm has one feature that was not discussed earlier. It can be given several locations to connect the terminals to, rather than just one. If more than one computer center existed, for example, it would connect each terminal to whichever center would result in the lowest overall network cost. Here we will give it the concentrator locations we select.

Because we will use CNDP in this way, we will dispense with Phase II of our concentrator-locating program. We want to obtain from it only the concentrator locations and an estimate of costs.

The low-speed line costs cannot be calculated exactly now by the concentrator-positioning program, as they could with the point-to-point lines in the previous chapter. It will not be known exactly how many locations they interconnect or with what layout. We do know the traffic volume from each city and the maximum traffic volume of the lines. Therefore we will apportion

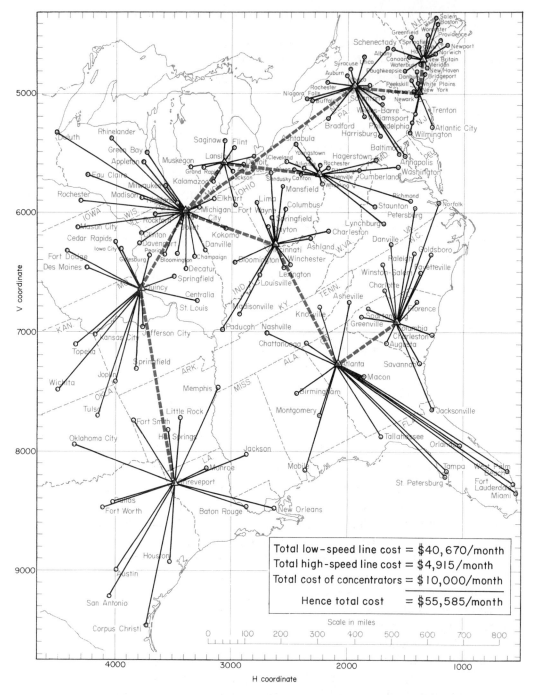

Total low–speed line cost = $40,670/month
Total high–speed line cost = $4,915/month
Total cost of concentrators = $10,000/month
Hence total cost = $55,585/month

Scale in miles

*Fig. 43.1.* The solution with the concentrator in Example 43.1. The
cost is higher than that for the network in Fig. 42.8.

the line cost out to the cities on this basis and calculate a "cost density" factor rather than an exact cost.

The program considers each city as a possible concentrator location, I. The number of lines going into this concentrator is NL (in the program notation). It then scans outward from this concentrator, assigning cities to lines until each line capacity is filled—and hence until the concentrator capacity is filled.

The cities thus assigned are noted. Their mean distance from the computer center (DCPU), as well as their mean distance from the concentrator (DCON), is calculated. The number of low-speed lines they are attached to is noted, (LIN). (This could be less than the number of lines into the concentrator, NL.)

It is then estimated that the cost of the low-speed lines into the concentrator is that of LIN lines of distance DCON and that the cost of the low-speed lines into the computer would have been that of LIN line of distance DCPU if no concentrator had been used.

The "cost density" factor, an estimate of the line cost saving, is then LIN *times* the cost of a low-speed line of length DCPU *minus* the cost of a low-speed line of length DCON *minus* the cost of a high-speed concentrator to the computer center.

In PL/I:

DENS (I) = LIN*(SLCOST (DCPU) – SLCOST (DCON)) – SHCOST (DIST (1,I));

This cost density factor, DENS (I), is evaluated for every possible concentrator location, I.

In PL/I:

```
DENS=0;
DO I=1 TO NCITY;
TLIN=0;
CONC=0;
NUM,DCPU,DCON=0;
A1:  DMIN=10000;
DO J=1 TO NCITY;
D1=DIST(I,J);
IF D1<DMIN & CONC(J)=0 THEN DO;
DMIN=D1;
L=J;
END;END;
DO M=1 TO NL;
IF SLMAX-TLIN(M)>TRAF(L) & CONC(L)=0 THEN DO;
TLIN(M)=TLIN(M)+TRAF(L);
CONC(L)=1;
NUM=NUM+1;
```

```
DCPU=DCPU+DIST(I,L);
DCON=DCON+DIST(I,L);
LIN=M;
GO TO A1; END;
END;
DCPU=DCPU/NUM;
DCCN=DCCN/NUM;
DENS(I)=LIN*(SLCOST(DCPU)-SLCOST(DCON))-SHCOST(DIST(1,I));
```

IN FORTRAN:

```
        DO 170 I=1,NCITY
170 DENS(I)=0.0D0
        DO 250 I=1,NCITY
        DO 180 II=1,30
180 TLIN(II)=0.0D0
        DO 190 II=1,NCITY
190 CONC(II)=.FALSE.
        NUM=0
        DCPU=0.0
        DCCN=0.0
200 DMIN=10000.0
        DO 210 J=1,NCITY
        D1=DIST(I,J)
        IF (D1.GE.DMIN .OR. CONC(J)) GO TO 210
        DMIN=D1
        L=J
210 CONTINUE
C
        DO 220 M=1,NL
        IF (SLMAX-TLIN(M).LE.TRAF(L) .OR. CONC(L)) GO TO 220
        TLIN(M)=TLIN(M)+TRAF(L)
        CONC(L)=.TRUE.
        NUM=NUM+1
        DCPU=DCPU+DIST(I,L)
        DCON=DCON+DIST(I,L)
        LIN=M
        GO TO 200
220 CONTINUE
C
        DCPU=DCPU/NUM
        DCCN=DCCN/NUM
        DENS(I)=LIN*(SLCOST(DCPU)-SLCOST(DCON))-SHCOST(DIST(1,I))
250 CONTINUE
```

Here DIST(I,J) is again the distance between cities I and J.

TRAF (L) is the traffic volume from city L. SLMAX is the maximum traffic permissible on a low-speed line, and TLIN (M) is the traffic allocated to the Mth line.

NUM is the number of cities assigned to the concentrator.

The city with the highest cost density factor is then found, and a concentrator is considered for that location.

In PL/I:

```
MAX=0;
DO I=1 TO NCITY;
IF DENS(I)>MAX & FLAG(I)=0
         THEN DO;
                MAX=DENS(I); K=I;
                END;
END;
PUT PAGE EDIT ('CONCENTRATOR IS CONSIDERED AT ',CITY(K))(A,A(20));
```

IN FORTRAN:

```
    MAX=0
    DO 260 I=1,NCITY
    IF (DENS(I).LE.MAX .OR. FLAG(I)) GO TO 260
    MAX=DENS(I)
    K=I
260 CONTINUE
    WRITE (L1,270) (CITY(K,II), II=1,5)
270 FORMAT (1H1,
   1'CONCENTRATOR IS CONSIDERED AT ',4A4,A3)
```

If a concentrator placed at this city does in fact result in an overall saving when the cost of the concentrator is taken into account, a concentrator is then assigned to that location. The cities connected to that concentrator are deleted from the list, and the entire process is repeated to find the next concentrator location.

The overall network cost saving is estimated. This step is done for each concentrator type. If the results seem to give a worthwhile saving, then the concentrator locations are used in a CNDP program, as described above, to establish the optimum geographic layout of the low-speed lines.

In this case, the calculation was done using eight times the traffic volumes quoted in Example 40.3. The ranking of the three concentrators in this case is as follows:

| Device Type | Number of Low-Speed Lines | Device Cost | Number of Devices | Estimated Network Cost |
|---|---|---|---|---|
| 2 | 7 | 400 | 4 | 33,129 |
| 3 | 12 | 700 | 2 | 33,967 |
| 1 | 4 | 200 | 6 | 34,158 |

It will be seen that concentrator type 2 is the best, but that there is not much to choose between the three of them.

The network using concentrator type 2 is shown in Fig. 43.2. The total cost of the lines and concentrators is $33,129 per month, compared with $39,000

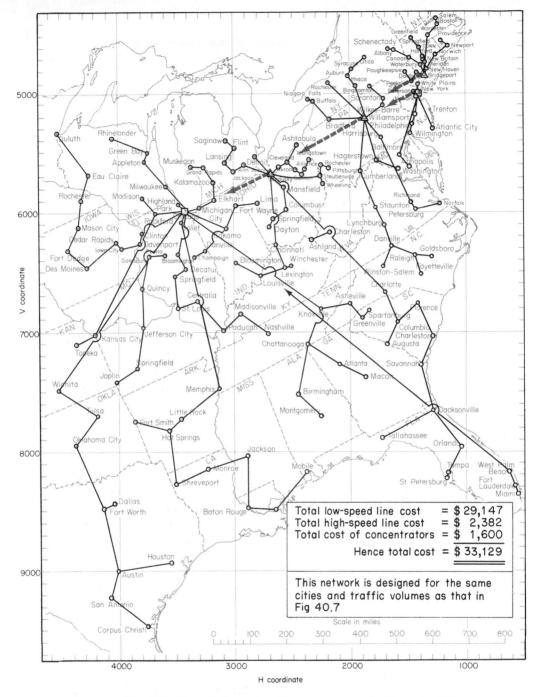

Total low-speed line cost     = $ 29,147
Total high-speed line cost    = $  2,382
Total cost of concentrators   = $  1,600
          Hence total cost    = $ 33,129

This network is designed for the same cities and traffic volumes as that in Fig 40.7

*Fig. 43.2.* The solution using the concentrators in Example 43.2. The cost is lower than that of the networks in Figs. 42.8 or 43.1. However, because the low-speed lines are multidropped (rather than high-speed as in Fig. 43.1) the response times are longer.

for the network in Fig. 40.7, which handles the same traffic volumes. Fig. 43.2, in fact, is the lowest-cost network of all our examples handling this traffic volume.

The concentrators in this case are all located in the northeastern part of the network, where the terminal locations are closer together and the traffic volumes are high. The density in the south was not enough to warrant a concentrator of this type.

Once again some benefit could have been derived from having more than one concentrator type. If device type 1 had now been used in the network of Fig. 43.2, this four-line machine situated at Spartanburg, S.C., would have made a small additional saving. No other such machine would have been added.

**CLUSTERING**    Let us again stress that our example here has very little clustering of terminals. Networks with a higher degree of terminal clustering would have benefited much more from concentrator techniques. Some terminal control units are designed for clusters of terminals and carry out the functions of a concentrator.

# 44 CASE STUDIES

This chapter presents two case studies and takes the reader through the stages which the systems analysts' thinking evolved through in designing the transmission network.

Both systems are concerned with the placing of terminals in the sales offices and storage depots of a nationwide organization in the United States. The terminals in both cases are to be used for entering new orders and enquiring about the status of current orders. Central data banks of customer and order information will be maintained. These facilities will be used in the stock control procedures, and eventually the computers will execute a variety of sales-office data-processing functions. In both systems it is thought necessary for terminal users to interact in real time with the computers.

The design of the man-machine interface, however, differs greatly on the two systems. In the first case, the product being sold is not very complex although it comes in many varieties. The ordering process is relatively straightforward. The terminal selected was a teletypewriter operating at 75 baud.

The second case deals with a highly complex engineering product that is custom built by the assembly of standard parts. To plan the order for one product, an engineer had to spend many hours with the equipment manuals. It is intended that he should now do this operation at a terminal. The computer would interrogate him in much the same way as in the example in Figs. 8.7 to 8.10. The computer would check the validity of the configuration he was ordering and would help to ensure that he did not forget possible options. An elaborate and lengthy man-machine conversation, with the computer often providing "menus" of alternatives from which the user must select, is required. The computer responses were so long that typewriter-speed terminals were ruled out because of speed. Screen display terminals would be used, and frequently the computer response filled the whole screen.

Two cases having the same category of application have been selected because many other application types have similar sets of problems.

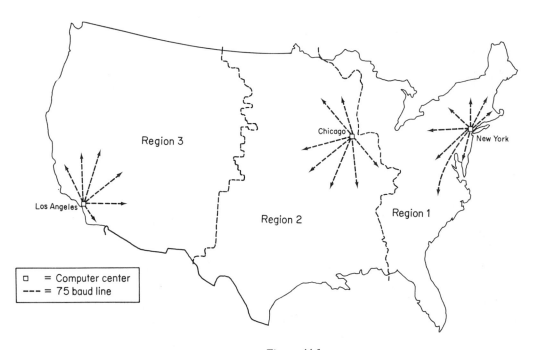

*Figure 44.1*

**CASE 1**

The operation of the Case 1 corporation is divided into three regions, as shown in Fig. 44.1, with head offices at Los Angeles, Chicago, and New York. (The divisions are the boundaries between time zones.)

The initial thinking of the systems design team was that the three regions should be handled quite separately with separate computers and data bases in the three head office locations.

A fast response time is considered desirable, particularly because many of the orders will be taken and many inquiries will be answered via the telephone. These calls should not be kept waiting. As a result, the team dislikes the idea of using the TWX network. It prefers leased lines so that the dialing times will be avoided. Some network layout and cost calculations must be done to see how viable this is.

Initially, a polling system was considered, with leased multidrop teletype lines to the three computers. However, some quick calculations were made, like those at the beginning of Chapter 36, and the mean response time obtained was about 30 seconds. The response time distribution curve was, in fact, somewhat worse than that in Fig. 36.3. This time was deemed too long, and the possibility of multidrop teletype lines was ruled out for this application. There must only be one terminal per line.

A computer program was quickly written to add up the cost of running teletype lines directly to the computer centers, as in Fig. 44.1. Its main loop was as follows (in PL/I):

```
COST = 0;
DO I = 2 TO NCITY;

D = SORT((((CV(J) — CV(1))**2 + (CH(J) — CH(1))**2)/10);
COST = COST + SLCOST(D);
END;
```

where CV(J) and CH(J) are the AT & T vertical and horizontal coordinates of the cities and CV(1) and CH(1) are the coordinates of the computer center. SLCOST is the procedure used in Chapter 42 for calculating the low-speed line cost from the common-carrier tariffs.

The total line cost came to $167,000 per month.

The possibility of having one computer center rather than three was also discussed. This factor, however, gave a prohibitively high line cost of $304,000 per month, and hence was forgotten.

An investigation of possible techniques for lowering this high cost of the line network in Fig. 44.1 began.

A range of relatively inexpensive multiplexers was investigated. One type, which permitted the signals on 12 teletype lines to be combined and sent together over one full-duplex voice line, was selected. At first, the position for the multi-plexers was chosen by manually examining the map of terminal locations. This process gave promising cost figures, and thus a more detailed investigation of multiplexer locations was done with a program like the one at the beginning of the previous chapter. The locations in Fig. 44.2 were selected, giving a total network cost—including the multiplexers—of $94,000 per month.

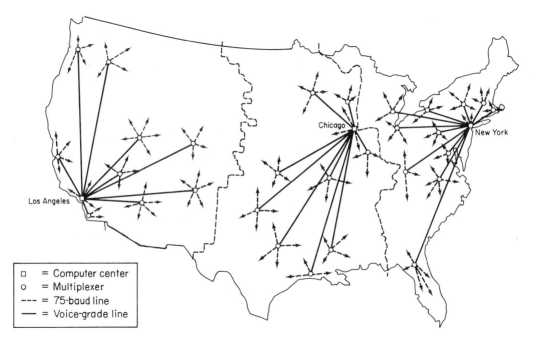

Figure 44.2

It was suggested that the line cost could be lowered further by moving the computer centers away from the head offices and siting them closer to the bulk of the multiplexers. A slight addition to the above program enabled it to try out different computer locations and discover which was the lowest in cost. The result gave computer locations at Las Vegas, St. Louis, and Pittsburgh. The total network cost dropped from $94,000 to $86,000 per month (see Fig. 44.3).

The proposal to locate the computer centers in these cities caused much argument and consternation among the top-management group responsible for data processing facilities. It was uncertain as yet whether this suggestion would be accepted, and so the network design team decided to work with two networks for the time being.

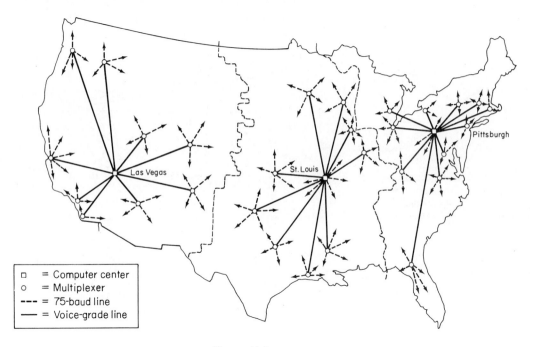

Figure 44.3

The next major step in the team's thinking was to examine all the other multiplexers and concentrators that seemed likely to be applicable. A program like the one described in Example 42.2 was used. A concentrator that handled 20 low-speed lines was found to give the lowest-cost network, and the price with the new computer center locations was now $81,000 per month.

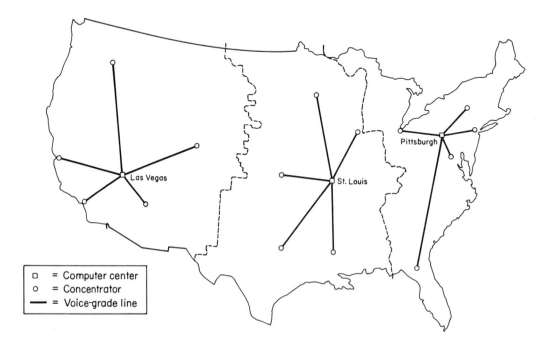

*Figure 44.4*

The team then decided to evaluate the effect of a more expensive type of concentrator, one having the capability of doing a limited form of processing on the messages. It could edit messages and store "canned" responses to the terminal, which the computer would generate by sending a two-character code. A transmission speed of 7200 bits per second could be used on the leased voice lines to the computer. A polling scheme enabled more than one concentrator to be used on each voice line. The resulting configuration (Fig. 44.5) turned out to be more expensive than the previous scheme, because of the high cost of the concentrator. The total cost came to $97,000 per month. It was pointed out, however, that with this machine it might now become feasible to use one computer center instead of three.

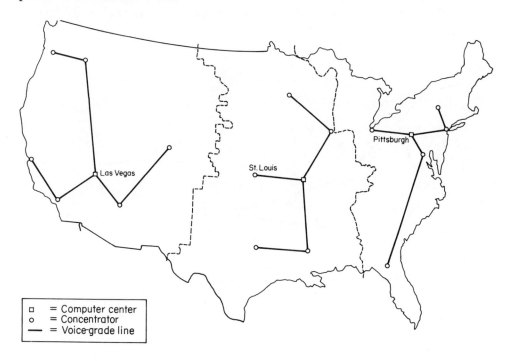

Figure 44.5

A queuing model was used to establish how many concentrators could be attached to one high-speed line. Calculations similar to those in Chapter 37 were used. A conservative estimate set the maximum as 4. A network layout program was then employed to determine which lines the concentrators should be attached to. (This was the CNDP program discussed in Chapter 40.) The program was given a traffic rate table, as in Chapter 39, rather than being allowed to establish its own. The result was the network shown in Fig. 44.6.

There was considerable saving in having one computer center rather than three, not only in the machine cost but also in building and staff savings. It was also appealing from the systems point of view to have the entire corporation data base on one computer, on which it could be processed and interrogated as a whole. Some members of the team, however, were sorry to lose the idea of a computer center at Las Vegas!

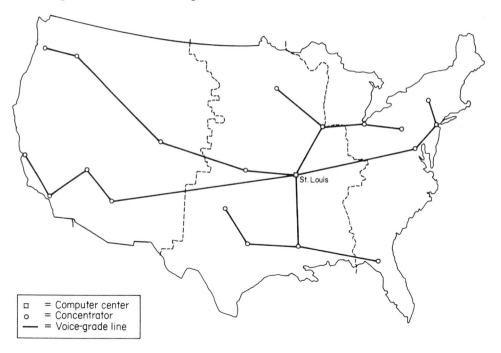

□   = Computer center
o   = Concentrator
——  = Voice-grade line

*Figure 44.6*

The single-computer-center solution was greeted with general enthusiasm; consequently, a more detailed study was made of how this network cost could be minimized. One member of the team wrote a simulation model, as in Chapter 38, representing the low-speed line, concentrator, and voice grade line with its polling of other concentrators. At the same time, another member produced a detailed analytical model of the same linkage. At first, the two models did not agree closely and so they were compared in detail. Close examination revealed that both had inaccuracies. The simulation model had a logic error in it which misrepresented the polling sequence. This error had not been detected as the model gave plausible results. The queuing model, on the other hand, neglected to include modem synchronization time. When these factors had both been corrected, the models agreed within about 3 percent, and a team began to obtain a fairly clear understanding of the effect of different factors in this type of network design.

A series of CNDP-type runs indicated that if seven concentrators could be attached to one voice line, and if the computer center were sited at Kansas City, then three voice lines would be sufficient with the configuration shown in Fig. 44.7. This configuration uses two less concentrators than in Fig. 44.6. The two that have been removed are both in locations of relatively low traffic density, and the terminals that were connected to them have been switched to nearby concentrators.

The queuing and simulation models indicated that the key to achieving this lay in two areas. First, the polling discipline must have as little idle time on the line as possible. Hub go-ahead polling rather than roll-call polling was desirable and the "hand-shaking" or synchronization time of the modems must be low. Second, the man-machine conversation should be designed to make maximum use of the concentrators' editing ability and the ability to generate "canned" responses. These considerations could be used to minimize the numbers of characters flowing on the voice lines.

The latter consideration was impressed upon the team designing the man-machine conversation. As this became worked out in greater detail it became more certain that the configuration in Fig. 44.7 would work and would give a mean response time of between two and three seconds.

One member of the team observed that for *many* nationwide organizations the best place to locate a computer center for minimum network cost must be in or near to Kansas City, this being near the geographical center of the United States. Perhaps one should buy real estate in Kansas City!

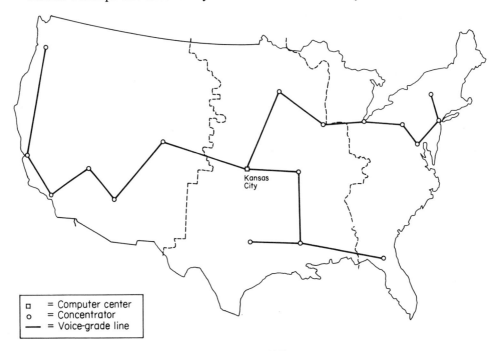

□  = Computer center
o  = Concentrator
── = Voice-grade line

*Figure 44.7*

**CASE 2**                    In the Case 2 corporation it was clear from the beginning that there would be one single on-line computer center. This fact was dictated by the desirability of having one data base that could be processed and updated centrally. Many of the planned functions of the system would have been very difficult to control with parts of the corporation sales and inventory data in different locations.

There was never any doubt in the minds of the network design team that the least expensive location for the center would have been near the geographical center of the United States—perhaps Kansas City again. The top management who made this level of decision, however, decreed that the computer center should be located at what was perhaps the most expensive place that could possibly have been found for it—the corporation's head office in Manhattan. Considerations of prestige overrode those of economics. The head of the design team did not push the network cost case, for he had no desire to live in Kansas City.

A short response time was desirable for this application because of the complex nature of the man-machine conversation. A figure agreed upon was that not more than 10 percent of the responses should take more than 5 seconds. Thus a mean response time of slightly less than 3 seconds was required. Although this figure was set as the design criterion, it was recognized that a shorter response time was desirable if it could be achieved.

The visual displays in each location were attached to a control unit, which itself was attached to a leased voice line operating at 4800 bits per second. Several control units could be attached to one voice line. It was thought that an average response from the computer was about 120 characters in length. Together with tabbing, skipping, and new characters, this length would often produce a table that almost filled the screen. A message of this length took about $\frac{1}{4}$ second to transmit, not including polling and line turnaround times. The message from the operator to the computer was fully buffered in the control unit and was much shorter. The response time of the computer itself was less than $\frac{1}{2}$ second for most messages, although messages that required considerable file accessing sometimes spent as long as 2 seconds in the computer. The mean was about $\frac{3}{4}$ second. Many such messages would be processed in parallel.

From these figures it was clear that several terminals—indeed, several control units—could be attached to one voice line. A study was made, using the queuing model of Chapter 37. If roll-call polling was used, the modem turnaround time was a major factor. The choice of modems with a reasonably low turnaround was important. It was found that about four typical cities could be connected with one voice line and meet the response-time requirements. Where the traffic was heavy, only three and sometimes only two could be connected.

Where the traffic was light, five could be connected, but for the moment the maximum was set at four. Using the queuing model, a traffic rate table was drawn up as in Chapter 39.

Because of the very high network cost, it was decided not to connect all the cities to the leased-line network. Some of the smaller and remoter locations would not have a terminal. Instead, they would telephone the nearest city with a terminal and communicate with the computer via a clerk at that city. The clerk would enter their details into his terminal and read the responses.

The network design was now done using the CNDP algorithm discussed in Chapter 37. The resulting network is shown in Fig. 44.8; it cost $324,000.

For simplicity of drawing, not all terminal locations are shown

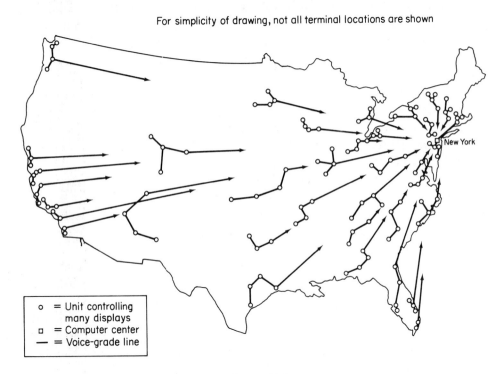

o = Unit controlling
    many displays
□ = Computer center
— = Voice-grade line

*Figure 44.8*

The cost of the network in Fig. 44.8 was so high that a search began immediately for ways of reducing it. The lines used were already operating at 4800 bits per second; thus any multiplexer or concentrator must use broadband lines. Before any such device was selected, it became clear that a Bell System 8000 series line linking the computer center to the West Coast, the Midwest, and the South would save much of the cost.

A network design using a broadband multiplexer was made. This machine operated at each end of a Bell System-type 8801 line, which transmits at 40,800 bits per second, effectively dividing it by time-division multiplexing into a group of channels operating at near voice-line speed. A program like the one in Chapter 42 was used for locating the optimum locations for the multiplexers. Considerable adjustment was made to these locations, in order to place the devices where rapid maintenance was ensured in the event of failure. The cities selected were San Francisco, Los Angeles, Cleveland, Chicago, Albany, Worcester, Mass., Charleston, Memphis, and Atlanta. Positioning the concentrators in these cities rather than in the optimum geographical locations added about 1.5 percent to the network cost. However, speed of maintenance was considered vitally important on devices affecting such a large number of the terminals. The overall cost was now $183,000 per month.

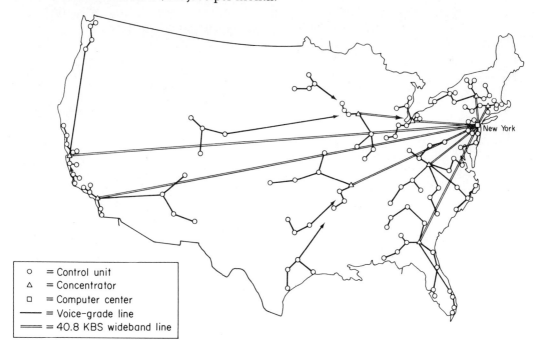

| | |
|---|---|
| o | = Control unit |
| △ | = Concentrator |
| ▢ | = Computer center |
| —— | = Voice-grade line |
| ══ | = 40.8 KBS wideband line |

*Figure 44.9*

The corporation has regional head offices at San Francisco, Los Angeles, Chicago, Cleveland, Memphis, and Atlanta. For this reason, these locations had been convenient for the termination of the broadband lines. The system approach considered next was to locate small computers, instead of the multiplexers, in these cities. The computers would be used by day for handling traffic on the real-time network; by night they would be used for batch processing and for printing invoices transmitted from the New York computer center. In general, they would provide a fast data link enabling the regions to use the New York center.

When in use as concentrators, the regional computers would edit the messages, thus cutting down the numbers of characters flowing on the broadband links. They would handle polling on the voice lines, cutting down the high-line turnarounds, and they could be multidropped on the broadband lines. A simulation was done of a linkage of this type; the conclusion was drawn that the same numbers of cities could be attached to the voice lines and that three concentration computers could be attached to type 8801 lines, as above.

The solution particularly appealed to the computer manufacturer because he did not make the multiplexers in Fig. 44.9. It appealed to the New York data processing manager because it might increase the amount of processing done in New York rather than the regions. The overall cost was somewhat higher, but it was thought that more was being bought for the money.

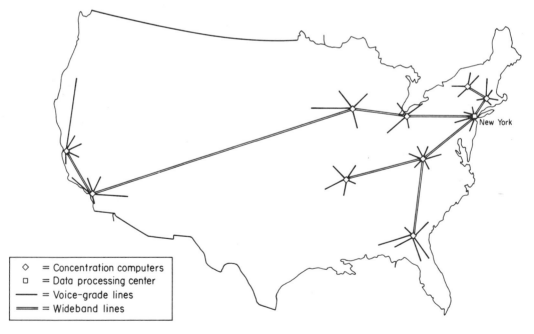

◇ = Concentration computers
□ = Data processing center
—— = Voice-grade lines
══ = Wideband lines

*Figure 44.10*

The detailed program specification and program writing now began. It took more than a year to specify the exact structure of the man-machine conversation. A laboratory environment was utilized, and one of the main criteria was that the system must be easy to use by the operator. It was intended that office clerks, salesmen, and engineers, who spent most of their time doing other work, should be able to converse easily with the distant computer. Moreover, a variety of different applications would eventually be handled, which necessitated a conversation format that did not require great training or skill. The eventual result of this highly commendable attitude was that the numbers of characters required in the machine responses became higher than the anticipated mean of 120, and the number of messages per conversation became much higher than estimated.

The multidrop broadband lines became overloaded. It was felt that a redesign of the network was needed, but at this stage anything requiring a major programming change was ruled out because of the pressure to have the system operating with as little slippage as possible. The same concentrators were kept, for the time being, but point-to-point broadband links had to be used, as shown in Fig. 44.11. The overall cost of the network and concentrators rose to $310,000 per month.

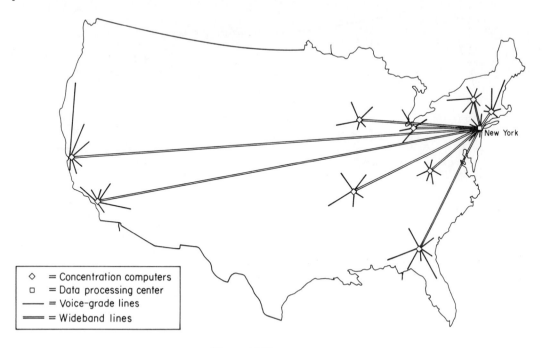

◇  = Concentration computers
□  = Data processing center
── = Voice-grade lines
══ = Wideband lines

*Figure 44.11*

A much discussed solution to the problem of the increased conversation length was to program parts of the conversation handling in the concentration computers rather than in the New York machines. Clearly, many characters were being sent back and forth that need not be sent if this action were taken. To transmit them seemed a waste when lines were so long and expensive. Furthermore, using the concentration computers in this way would relieve the central machines of considerable interrupt handling and processing time. Such a change, however, seemed a radical step because it meant putting application programs in the remote machines.

No action was taken on this suggestion until cutover started on the system represented by Fig. 44.11. As soon as this system began to work satisfactorily, program manpower became available to tackle developments of the system that would be built into a model 2 version. At the same time, a new computer that was more suitable for use as the concentration machine became available. It was lower in cost and had more core available for programming those elements of the conversation that did not require access to the data files.

The configuration now returned to that shown in Fig. 44.12, which dropped the overall network cost to $220,000 per month.

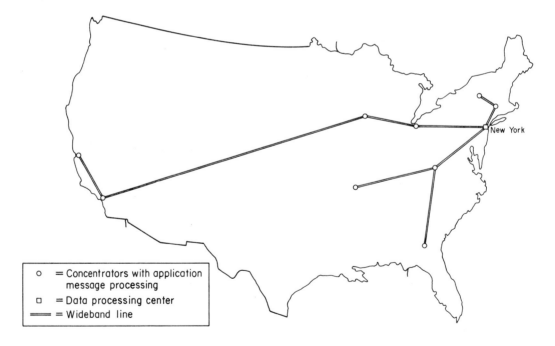

Figure 44.12

The conversation length was not the only escalation that occurred. Once the system was working well, managers of branch offices not connected to it began to complain that they also needed this facility. The number of locations to have display screens increased. It was suggested that some of the small remote offices should have teletype terminals rather than screens and that they should be content with a very slow conversation. The concentration computers now had the capability to handle teletype lines as well as the voice lines.

The system sometimes gave lengthier response times than had been intended. The reason lay in the programming and file accessing in the central computers, in the increased message lengths, and in the fact that many of the voice lines into the concentration computers now served five or even six cities. It seemed desirable, considering the current load figures and message lengths, that these voice lines should be cut back to a maximum of three cities and, in some cases, two. The voice lines were redesigned to incorporate a multiplexer that gave 7200-bit-per-second full-duplex transmission. The network now, in effect, had two stages of concentration, as shown in Fig. 44.13.

For simplicity of drawing, not all terminal locations are shown

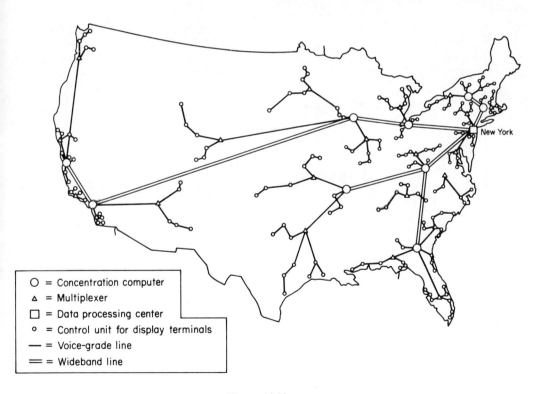

O  = Concentration computer
∆  = Multiplexer
□  = Data processing center
o  = Control unit for display terminals
—  = Voice-grade line
= = Wideband line

*Figure 44.13*

The network operated using the configuration of Fig. 44.13. It slowly became clear, however, that the corporation needed to ration its entire usage of telecommunications. Several data processing facilities had been designed independently, like those discussed in Chapter 5. A corporate data network could serve most of these and be designed along with the corporate internal telephone trunks to take the maximum advantage of "bundles" such as the Type 5700 and 5800 tariffs. Possibly new electronic private branch exchange facilities could also be employed to switch both voice and data lines. It became clear that many further network design activities lay ahead.

# APPENDICES

# I THE MATHEMATICAL NOTATION
# USED IN THIS BOOK

| | | |
|---|---|---|
| $E(x)$ | The mean value of $x$ | |
| $E(x^2)$ | The second moment of $x$ | |
| $E(x^3)$ | The third moment of $x$ | |
| $\sigma_x$ | The standard deviation of $x$ | $\sigma_x = \sqrt{E(x^2) - E^2(x)}$ |
| Var $(x)$ | The variance of $x$ | Var $(x) = \sigma_x^2$ |
| $R$ | Parameter of a gamma distribution of $x$ | $R = \left[ \dfrac{E(x)}{\sigma_x} \right]^2$ |

---

| | |
|---|---|
| $B$ | Probability that all servers are busy on a multiserver queuing system. |
| $B$ | Number of characters held by a buffer block. |
| $C_i$ | Buffer storage utilization for the $i$th line. |
| $C_T$ | Total buffer storage utilization. |
| $E(t_d)$ | The mean waiting time for items which have to wait (not including items with waiting time = zero). |
| $f$ | Number of messages per hour in a buffering scheme. |
| $f_A$ | Fraction of messages that are of type A. |
| $l$ | Size of a buffer storage block (characters). |
| $M$ | The number of servers in parallel on a multiserver system. It is used for number of terminals, number of ports and number of communication lines. $\rho = E(n)E(t_s)/M$ for multiple servers. |
| $N_c$ | Number of characters in a block that are used for data. |
| $N_H$ | Number of characters in a block that are used for "housekeeping." |
| $N_I$ | Number of characters in input message. |

795

| | |
|---|---|
| $N_{IA}$ | Number of characters in input message type A. |
| $N_L$ | Number of low-speed lines entering a concentrator. |
| $N_O$ | Number of characters in output message. |
| $N_{OA}$ | Number of characters in output message type A. |
| $N_R$ | Number of records in a block. |
| $n$ | Number of arrivals per second. |
| $P_B$ | Probability that all servers are busy on a multiserver system with no queuing (i.e., probability of a transaction being lost). |
| $P_B$ | Probability of one bit being in error after transmission. |
| $P_M$ | Probability of a message being in error after transmission. |
| $P(n = N)$ | Probability of having $N$ arrivals in a given second. |
| $P(n \geq N)$ | Probability of having $N$ or more arrivals in a given second. |
| $P(q = N)$ | Probability that $N$ items are in the system. |
| $P(q \geq N)$ | Probability that $q$ equals or is greater than integer $N$. |
| $P(t_q > T)$ | Probability that $t_q$ is greater than a given time, $T$. |
| $q$ | Number of items in system, waiting and being served. |
| $S$ | Speed of line (characters per second). |
| $T_1$ | Line preparation time for input messages. |
| $T_2$ | Line preparation time for output messages. |
| $t_a$ | Interarrival time. |
| $t_{cpu}$ | Time transaction spends in CPU. |
| $t_M$ | Time for message transmission. |
| $t_{MI}$ | Time for input message transmission. |
| $t_{MIA}$ | Time for transmission of input message type A. |
| $t_{MO}$ | Time for output message transmission. |
| $t_{MOA}$ | Time for transmission of output message type A. |
| $t_O$ | Time taken for unsuccessful poll. |
| $t_{poll}$ | Overall polling time for one message. |
| $t_q$ | Time an item spends in system, waiting and being served. $t_q = t_w + t_s$. |
| $t_r$ | Response time. |
| $t_{rA}$ | Response time for type A messages. |
| $t_s$ | Service time for an item. |
| $t_w$ | Time an item spends waiting for service (not including time being served). |
| $w$ | Number of items waiting for service (not including item being served). |
| $\rho$ | Facility utilization of one serving facility. $\rho = E(n)E(t_s)$ for a single server. |
| $\rho_I$ | $\rho$ for input messages only. |
| $\rho_{IA}$ | $\rho$ for input messages of type A only. |
| $\rho_O$ | $\rho$ for output messages only. |
| $\rho_{OA}$ | $\rho$ for output messages of type A only. |

# II THE MEANINGS OF THE FIELDS USED IN THE COMPUTER PROGRAMS IN THIS BOOK

```
ACOST  =COST OF LOW SPEED LINE FROM TERMINAL TO CONCENTRATOR
ANEW   =ORIGINATION TIME OF TYPE A TRANSACTION
BCOST  =COST OF HIGH SPEED LINE FROM CONCENTRATOR TO COMPUTER / NL
BEGIN  =TABLE OF ARRIVAL TIMES OF MESS IN SEQUENCE FOR EACH TERMINAL
BNEW   =ORIGINATION TIME OF TYPE B TRANSACTION
CCOST  =COST OF LOW SPEED LINE FROM TERMINAL TO COMPUTER
CEIL   =THE SMALLEST INTEGER GREATER THAN OR EQUAL TO A GIVEN VALUE
CFIA   =FRACTION OF INPUT  TRANSACTIONS TYPE A
CFIB   =FRACTION OF INPUT  TRANSACTIONS TYPE B
CFOA   =FRACTION OF OUTPUT TRANSACTIONS TYPE A
CFOB   =FRACTION OF OUTPUT TRANSACTIONS TYPE B
CIA(K)=FRACTION OF INPUT   MESSAGES TYPE A WITH K CHARACTERS OR LESS
CIB(K)=FRACTION OF INPUT   MESSAGES TYPE B WITH K CHARACTERS OR LESS
CLOCK  =KEEPS THE TIME OF EVERYTHING HAPPENING ON THE LINE
COA(K)=FRACTION OF OUTPUT MESSAGES TYPE A WITH K CHARACTERS OR LESS
COB(K)=FRACTION OF OUTPUT MESSAGES TYPE B WITH K CHARACTERS OR LESS
CONCST=COST OF CONCENTRATOR
CONCOST=COST OF CONCENTRATOR
CPUA   =TIME PROCESSING ENDS ON TYPE A TRANSACTION
CPUB   =TIME PROCESSING ENDS ON TYPE B TRANSACTION
D      =DISTANCE IN MILES BETWEEN TWO CITIES
DCON   =MEAN DISTANCE OF A GROUP OF CITIES FROM THE CONCENTRATOR
DCOST  =DIAL-UP TWX LINE COST IN $ PER MONTH
DCPU   =MEAN DISTANCE OF A GROUP OF CITIES FROM THE COMPUTER CENTER
DENS   =COST DENSITY FACTOR, ESTIMATE OF LINE COST SAVING
DIST(I,J)=DISTANCE IN MILES BETWEEN CITIES I AND J
EVCBIO=MEAN NO. OF BUFFERING CHARS IN TOTAL OF ALL LINES FOR I/O
EVLBIO=MEAN NUMBER OF BUFFERING CHARS FOR I/O TRAFFIC ON A LINE
EVNQLI=MEAN NUMBER OF ITEMS QUEUEING FOR INPUT MESSAGES (ANY TYPE)
EVNTIA=MEAN ARRIVAL RATE OF INPUT  MESSAGE TYPE A
EVNTIB=MEAN ARRIVAL RATE OF INPUT  MESSAGE TYPE B
```

```
EVNTLI=MEAN ARRIVAL RATE OF INPUT  MESSAGES (ANY TYPE)
EVNTLN=MEAN TRANSACTION RATE FOR THE LINE
EVNTLO=MEAN ARRIVAL RATE OF OUTPUT MESSAGES (ANY TYPE)
EVNTOA=MEAN ARRIVAL RATE OF OUTPUT MESSAGE TYPE A
EVNTOB=MEAN ARRIVAL RATE OF OUTPUT MESSAGE TYPE B
EVROLI=FACILITY UTILIZATION OF THE LINE BY INPUT  MESS, (ANY TYPE)
EVROLN=RHO, THE FACILITY UTILIZATION OF THE LINE
EVROLO=FACILITY UTILIZATION OF THE LINE BY OUTPUT MESS, (ANY TYPE)
EVROOA=FACILITY UTILIZATION OF THE LINE BY OUTPUT MESSAGE TYPE A
EVROOB=FACILITY UTILIZATION OF THE LINE BY OUTPUT MESSAGE TYPE B
EVTALI=MEAN NUMBER OF TRANSACTIONS PER SECOND ON THE INPUT LINE
EVTMIA=EXPECTED VALUE OF TRANSMISSION TIME OF INPUT  MESSAGE TYPE A
EVTMIB=EXPECTED VALUE OF TRANSMISSION TIME OF INPUT  MESSAGE TYPE B
EVTMLI=EXPECTED VALUE OF TRANSMISN TIME OF INPUT  MESS, (ANY TYPE)
EVTMLO=EXPECTED VALUE OF TRANSMISN TIME OF OUTPUT MESS, (ANY TYPE)
EVTMOA=EXPECTED VALUE OF TRANSMISSION TIME OF OUTPUT MESSAGE TYPE A
EVTMOB=EXPECTED VALUE OF TRANSMISSION TIME OF OUTPUT MESSAGE TYPE B
EVTPLI=MEAN POLLING TIME ON THE LINE
EVTRLA=MEAN RESPONSE TIME FOR TYPE A TRANSACTIONS
EVTRLB=MEAN RESPONSE TIME FOR TYPE B TRANSACTIONS
EVTRLN=EXPECTED VALUE OF RESPONSE TIME FOR THE LINE
EVTSLI=MEAN TIME THE INPUT LINE IS HELD BY POLLING AND TRANSMISSION
EVTSLN=EXPECTED VALUE OF SERVICE TIME FOR THE LINE
EVTTCS=EXPECTED VALUE OF TOTAL TIME MESS SPENDS IN COMPUTER SYSTEM
EVTWLI=MEAN WAITING TIME FOR INPUT  MESSAGES (ANY TYPE)
EVTWLN=EXPECTED VALUE OF WAITING TIME FOR THE LINE
EVTWLO=MEAN WAITING TIME FOR OUTPUT MESSAGES (ANY TYPE)
EVTWOA=MEAN WAITING TIME FOR OUTPUT MESSAGE TYPE A
EVTWOB=MEAN WAITING TIME FOR OUTPUT MESSAGE TYPE B
FACTOR(I,J)=LINE COST SAVING FROM CONNECTING CITY J TO COMPUTER VIA
            CONCENTRATOR AT CITY I
FIA(K)=FRACTION OF INPUT TRANSACTIONS TYPE A THAT HAVE K CHARACTERS
FIB(K)=FRACTION OF INPUT TRANSACTIONS TYPE B THAT HAVE K CHARACTERS
FLOOR =THE LARGEST INTEGER THAT DOES NOT EXCEED A GIVEN VALUE
FOA(K)=FRACTION OF OUTPUT TRANSACTIONS TYPE A THAT HAVE K CHARS
FOB(K)=FRACTION OF OUTPUT TRANSACTIONS TYPE B THAT HAVE K CHARS
GMTSLN=R, THE PARAMETER OF THE GAMMA DISTRIBUTION OF SERVICE TIME
LCOST = LEASED LINE COST IN $ PER MONTH
LIN   =NUMBER OF LOW SPEED LINES ACTUALLY FEEDING THE CONCENTRATOR
L1    =DATA SET REFERENCE NUMBER FOR PRINT OUTPUT
MAXIN =MAXIMUM NUMBER OF CHARACTERS IN INPUT  MESSAGE
MAXOUT=MAXIMUM NUMBER OF CHARACTERS IN OUTPUT MESSAGE
MAXTHRPUT=MAXIMUM POSSIBLE THROUGHPUT
MAXTPT=MAXIMUM POSSIBLE THROUGHPUT
MINS  =NUMBER OF MINUTES OF CONTINUOUS TOLL TELEPHONE TRANSMISSION
NCITY =NUMBER OF CITIES TO BE CONCENTRATED
NL    =NUMBER OF LOW SPEED LINES THAT A CONCENTRATOR CAN HANDLE
NUM   =NUMBER OF CITIES ASSIGNED TO THE CONCENTRATOR
P(N)  =PROBABILITY THAT THE NTH TERMINAL POLLED IS FIRST TO RESPOND
PCT1  =90TH   PERCENTILE OF BUFFERING CHARACTERS
PCT2  =99TH   PERCENTILE OF BUFFERING CHARACTERS
PCT3  =99.9TH PERCENTILE OF BUFFERING CHARACTERS
RAN   =A NUMBER CHOSEN AT RANDOM BETWEEN 0 AND 1
RHO   =FACILITY UTILIZATION OF THE LINE
SDCBIO=STAND DEV. OF BUFFERING CHARS IN TOTAL OF ALL LINES FOR I/O
```

```
SDTIME=STANDARD DEVIATION OF RESPONSE TIME, ANY TYPE TRANSACTION
SDTMIA=STAND DEV. OF TRANSMISSION TIME FOR INPUT  MESSAGE TYPE A
SDTMIB=STAND DEV. OF TRANSMISSION TIME FOR INPUT  MESSAGE TYPE B
SDTMOA=STAND DEV. OF TRANSMISSION TIME FOR OUTPUT MESSAGE TYPE A
SDTMOB=STAND DEV. OF TRANSMISSION TIME FOR OUTPUT MESSAGE TYPE B
SDTRLA=STANDARD DEVIATION OF RESPONSE TIME FOR TYPE A TRANSACTIONS
SDTRLB=STANDARD DEVIATION OF RESPONSE TIME FOR TYPE B TRANSACTIONS
SDTRLN=STANDARD DEVIATION OF RESPONSE TIME FOR THE LINE
SDTRTA=STANDARD DEVIATION OF RESPONSE TIME FOR TYPE A TRANSACTIONS
SDTRTB=STANDARD DEVIATION OF RESPONSE TIME FOR TYPE B TRANSACTIONS
SDTTCS=STAND DEV. OF TOTAL TIME MESSAGE SPENDS IN COMPUTER SYSTEM
SIGTIME=STANDARD DEVIATION OF RESPONSE TIME, ANY TYPE TRANSACTION
SIGTIMEA=STANDARD DEVIATION OF RESPONSE TIME, TYPE A TRANSACTIONS
SIGTIMEB=STANDARD DEVIATION OF RESPONSE TIME, TYPE B TRANSACTIONS
SHCOST(D)=COST OF HIGH SPEED LINE WHERE D IS THE DISTANCE IT SPANS
SLCOST(D)=COST OF LOW  SPEED LINE WHERE D IS THE DISTANCE IT SPANS
SLMAX =MAXIMUM TRAFFIC PERMISSIBLE ON A LOW SPEED LINE
SMCBIO=2ND MOMENT OF BUFFERING CHARS IN TOTAL OF ALL LINES FOR I/O
SMLBIO=2ND MOMENT OF BUFFERING CHARACTERS FOR I/O TRAFFIC ON A LINE
SMTMIA=SECOND MOMENT OF  TRANSMISSION TIME OF INPUT  MESSAGE TYPE A
SMTMIB=SECOND MOMENT OF  TRANSMISSION TIME OF INPUT  MESSAGE TYPE B
SMTMLI=SECOND MOMENT OF  TRANSMISN TIME OF INPUT  MESS, (ANY TYPE)
SMTMLO=SECOND MOMENT OF  TRANSMISN TIME OF OUTPUT MESS, (ANY TYPE)
SMTMOA=SECOND MOMENT OF  TRANSMISSION TIME OF OUTPUT MESSAGE TYPE A
SMTMOB=SECOND MOMENT OF  TRANSMISSION TIME OF OUTPUT MESSAGE TYPE B
SMTPLI=SECOND MOMENT OF POLLING TIME ON THE LINE
SMTRLA=SECOND MOMENT OF RESPONSE TIME FOR TYPE A TRANSACTIONS
SMTRLB=SECOND MOMENT OF RESPONSE TIME FOR TYPE B TRANSACTIONS
SMTSLN=SECOND MOMENT OF SERVICE TIME FOR THE LINE
SMTWLI=SECOND MOMENT OF WAITING TIME FOR INPUT  MESSAGES (ANY TYPE)
SMTWLO=SECOND MOMENT OF WAITING TIME FOR OUTPUT MESSAGES (ANY TYPE)
SMTWOA=SECOND MOMENT OF WAITING TIME FOR OUTPUT MESSAGE TYPE A
SMTWOB=SECOND MOMENT OF WAITING TIME FOR OUTPUT MESSAGE TYPE B
SPEED =SPEED OF TRANSMISSION LINE IN CHARACTERS PER SECOND
THRPUT=MEAN THROUGHPUT
TIA    =TOTAL OF FIA(*)   (WHICH SHOULD = 1 )
TIB    =TOTAL OF FIB(*)   (WHICH SHOULD = 1 )
TIME   =TIME OF A DIAL-UP CONNECTION
TIMEA  =MEAN RESPONSE TIME FOR TYPE A TRANSACTIONS
TIMEB  =MEAN RESPONSE TIME FOR TYPE B TRANSACTIONS
TLIN(M)=TRAFFIC ALLOCATED TO THE MTH LINE
TMI    =OVERALL TRANSMISSION TIME OF INPUT  MESSAGE (ANY TYPE)
TMO    =OVERALL TRANSMISSION TIME OF OUTPUT MESSAGE (ANY TYPE)
TMTMIA=THIRD MOMENT  OF  TRANSMISSION TIME OF INPUT  MESSAGE TYPE A
TMTMIB=THIRD MOMENT  OF  TRANSMISSION TIME OF INPUT  MESSAGE TYPE B
TMTMLI=THIRD  MOMENT OF  TRANSMISN TIME OF INPUT  MESS, (ANY TYPE)
TMTMLO=THIRD  MOMENT OF  TRANSMISN TIME OF OUTPUT MESS, (ANY TYPE)
TMTMOA=THIRD MOMENT  OF  TRANSMISSION TIME OF OUTPUT MESSAGE TYPE A
TMTMOB=THIRD MOMENT  OF  TRANSMISSION TIME OF OUTPUT MESSAGE TYPE B
TMTSLN=THIRD MOMENT OF SERVICE TIME FOR ·THE LINE
TOA    =TOTAL OF FOA(*)   (WHICH SHOULD = 1 )
TOB    =TOTAL OF FOB(*)   (WHICH SHOULD = 1 )
TRAF(L)=TRAFFIC VOLUME FROM CITY L
TO     =TOTAL TIME FOR AN UNSUCCESSFUL POLL TO ONE TERMINAL (CONST)
```

```
T1     =LINE PREPARATION TIME FOR INPUT MESSAGES (CONSTANT)
T2     =LINE PREPARATION TIME FOR OUTPUT MESSAGES (CONSTANT)
T3     =INTERPOLL TIME
VACBIO=VARIANCE OF BUFFERING CHARS IN TOTAL OF ALL LINES FOR I/O
VALBIO=VARIANCE OF BUFFERING CHARACTERS FOR I/O TRAFFIC ON A LINE
VATMIA=VARIANCE OF TRANSMISSION TIME OF INPUT  MESSAGE TYPE A
VATMIB=VARIANCE OF TRANSMISSION TIME OF INPUT  MESSAGE TYPE B
VATMLI=VARIANCE OF TRANSMISSION TIME OF INPUT  MESSAGES (ANY TYPE)
VATMLO=VARIANCE OF TRANSMISSION TIME OF OUTPUT MESSAGES (ANY TYPE)
VATMOA=VARIANCE OF TRANSMISSION TIME FOR OUTPUT MESSAGE TYPE A
VATMOB=VARIANCE OF TRANSMISSION TIME FOR OUTPUT MESSAGE TYPE B
VATPLI=VARIANCE OF POLLING TIME ON THE LINE
VATPLN=VARIANCE OF RESPONSE TIME FOR THE LINE
VATSLI=VARIANCE OF TIME INPUT LINE IS HELD BY POLLING & TRANSMISSN
VATSLN=VARIANCE OF SERVICE TIME FOR THE LINE
VATTCS=VARIANCE OF TOTAL TIME MESSAGE SPENDS IN COMPUTER SYSTEM
VATWLI=VARIANCE OF WAITING TIME FOR INPUT  MESSAGES (ANY TYPE)
VATWLN=VARIANCE OF WAITING TIME FOR THE LINE
VATWLO=VARIANCE OF WAITING TIME FOR OUTPUT MESSAGES (ANY TYPE)
VATWOA=VARIANCE OF WAITING TIME FOR OUTPUT MESSAGE TYPE A
VATWOB=VARIANCE OF WAITING TIME FOR OUTPUT MESSAGE TYPE B
XAX    =MAXIMUM VALUE REPRESENTED ON X-AXIS
XDIV   =VALUE OF A UNIT ON THE X-AXIS
YAX    =MAXIMUM VALUE REPRESENTED ON Y-AXIS
YDIV   =VALUE OF A UNIT ON THE Y-AXIS
****************************************************************
```

# III  RANDOM-NUMBER GENERATOR ROUTINE

The following listing shows the random-number generator routine called by the statement CALL RANDOM (RAN) in the PL/I programs of Chapter 36. It uses the power residue method and is programmed in IBM 360 assembler language.

```
POWER RESIDUE RANDOM NUMBER GENERATOR

LOC    OBJECT CODE      ADDR1 ADDR2  STMT   SOURCE STATEMENT

000000                                  3 RANDOM    START   0
000000                                  4           USING   *,15
000000 9002 D00C        0000C           5           STM     0,2,12(13)
000004 582C 1000        00000           6           L       2,0(0,1)
000008 5810 F034        00034           7           L       1,RAND+4
00000C 541C F044        00044           8           N       1,MASK
000010 5CC0 F040        00040           9           M       0,MULT
000014 5010 F034        00034          10           ST      1,RAND+4
000018 68C0 F038        00038          11           LD      0,ZERO
00001C 6AC0 F030        00030          12           AD      0,RAND
000020 7000 2000        00000          13           STE     0,0(0,2)
000024 98C2 D00C        0000C          14           LM      0,2,12(13)
000028 07FE                            15           BCR     15,14

000030                                 17           DS      0D
00003C 46C00001AFD498D                 18 RAND      DC      X'460000001AFD498D'
000038 46C000C00C000000                19 ZERO      DC      X'46C000000000000'
00004C 1AFD498D                        20 MULT      DC      X'1AFD498D'
000044 7FFFFFFF                        21 MASK      DC      X'7FFFFFFF'

                                       23           END
```

801

# IV GRAPH-PLOTTING ROUTINE

The following listing shows the graph-plotting routine used in line-loading calculations in Chapters 36 and 37. This routine is called by the statement CALL GRAPH. The data to be plotted are passed to the routine in the following tables:

THRPUT (I): mean throughput

TIME A(I): mean response time for type A transactions

TIME B(I): mean response time for type B transactions

SIGTIME A(I): standard deviation of response time for type A transactions

SIGTIME B(I): standard deviation of response time for type B transactions

MAXTHRPUT is the maximum possible throughput.

In PL/I:

```
/****************************************************************************/
/****************************************************************************/
 GRAPH: PROCEDURE;
    ON ENDPAGE (SYSPRINT);
/*PREPARE GRAPH ***********************************************************/
    DCL PL(0:96 ,0:119) CHAR(1); PL=' ';
    DO J=11 TO 119 BY 12;PL(*,J)='|';END;
    DO J=0 TO 96  BY 12;PL(J,*)='-';END;
    DO J=11 TO 119 BY 12;DO K=0 TO 96 BY 12;PL(K,J)='+';END;END;
    PL(*,0)='|';
    A2=TIMEA(1);B2=TIMEB(1);S2=SIGTIMEA(1);Z2=SIGTIMEB(1);
    XAX=500;YAX=40;
    C,G=0;
```

```
      DO J=0 TC 119  WHILE((G¬=1)&(D¬=1));
        A1=TIMEA(J);B1=TIMEB(J);S1=SIGTIMEA(J);Z1=SIGTIMEB(J);U=THRPUT(J);
        IF ((A1<0  )|(B1<0  ))|((S1<0  )|(Z1<0  )) THEN G=1;
        IF ((A1>YAX)|(B1>YAX))|((S1>YAX)|(Z1>YAX)) THEN D=1;
        IF (D=1)|(G=1) THEN GO TC FE;
        XDIV=XAX/120;YDIV=YAX/96;
   FA: IF Z1<YAX THEN
        PL((96-Z1/YDIV),(U/XDIV-1))='Z';
        IF (Z1-Z2)>YDIV THEN GO TC FV;
   FB: IF S1<YAX THEN
        PL((96-S1/YDIV),(U/XDIV-1))='S';
        IF (S1-S2)>YDIV THEN GU TO FW;
   FC: PL((96-B1/YDIV),(U/XDIV-1))='B';
        IF (B1-B2)>YDIV THEN GO TO FX;
   FD: PL((96-A1/YDIV),(U/XDIV-1))='A';
        IF (A1-A2)>YDIV THEN GO TC FY;
        A2=TIMEA(J);B2=TIMEB(J);S2=SIGTIMEA(J);Z2=SIGTIMEB(J);
        GO TO FE;
   FV: Z1=Z1-YDIV; GC TC FA;
   FW: S1=S1-YDIV; GO TC FB;
   FX: B1=B1-YDIV; GO TO FC;
   FY: A1=A1-YDIV; GC TC FD;
   FE: END;
        IF D=1 THEN PL(*,(U/XDIV-1))='*';
        IF MAXTHRPUT<XAX THEN PL(*,(MAXTHRPUT/XDIV-1))='X';
        DCL MSA CHAR(60);
       MSA='AAAAA = MEAN RESPONSE TIME FOR TYPE A TRANSACTICNS (SECONDS)';
        DCL MSB CHAR(60);
       MSB='BBBBB = MEAN RESPONSE TIME FOR TYPE B TRANSACTIONS (SECONDS)';
        DCL MSS CHAR(77);
       MSS='SSSSS = STANDARD CEVIATION OF RESPONSE TIME FOR TYPE A TRANSAC
   TIONS (SECONDS)';
        DCL MSZ CHAR(77);
       MSZ='ZZZZZ = STANDARD DEVIATION OF RESPONSE TIME FOR TYPE B TRANSAC
   TIONS (SECONDS)';
        DO J=1 TO 60;PL(14,J+2)=SUBSTR(MSA,J,1);END;
        DU J=1 TO 60;PL(16,J+2)=SUBSTR(MSB,J,1);END;
        DO J=1 TO 77;PL(18,J+2)=SUBSTR(MSS,J,1);END;
        DO J=1 TO 77;PL(20,J+2)=SUBSTR(MSZ,J,1);END;
        CCL MS2 CHAR(46);
       MS2='THROUGHPUT (NUMBER CF TRANSACTIONS PER HOUR)';
        DO J=1 TO 46;PL(94 ,J+59)=SUBSTR(MS2,J,1); END;
        DO K=0 TO 90  BY 24; PL(K,3)='0';PL((K+12),3)='5';END;
        DU K=0 TU 90  BY 24; PL(K,117)='0';PL((K+12),117)='5';END;
        DCL MS3 CHAR(7 ); MS3='4332211';
        DO J=0 TU 6 ;PL(12 *J,2)=SUBSTR(MS3,J+1,1);END;
        DU J=0 TU 6 ;PL(12 *J,116)=SUBSTR(MS3,J+1,1);END;
   /***********************************************************************/
   /*PRINT GRAPH ********************************************************/
        PUT EDIT ('5               50             100           150           200    '
         ,'    250            300            350           400           450    '
       , '     500')(PAGE,A,A,A);
        PUT EDIT (PL) (SKIP,120 A(1));
        PUT EDIT ('5               50             100           150           200    '
```

```
,'        250           300          350         400          450    '
, '       500')(SKIP,A,A,A);
    PUT EDIT('EXAMPLE FH.2.')(SKIP(3),A);
    PUT EDIT('LINE SPEED ',SPEED,' CHARACTERS PER SECOND')
     (SKIP(2),A,F(4,1),A);
    PUT EDIT('MEAN        STANDARD','DEVIATION')(SKIP(2),COLUMN(64),
     A,SKIP,COLUMN(74),A);
    SDTMIA=SQRT(VATMIA);
    SDTMIB=SQRT(VATMIB);
    SDTMOA=SQRT(VATMOA);
    SDTMOB=SQRT(VATMOB);
    SDTTCS=SQRT(VATTCS);
    PUT EDIT('TOTAL TRANSMISSION TIME FOR INPUT  MESSAGE TYPE A (SECS)
',EVTMIA,SDTMIA )(SKIP,A,F(11,3),F(11,3));
    PUT EDIT('TOTAL TRANSMISSION TIME FOR INPUT  MESSAGE TYPE B (SECS)
',EVTMIB,SDTMIB )(SKIP,A,F(11,3),F(11,3));
    PUT EDIT('TOTAL TRANSMISSION TIME FOR OUTPUT MESSAGE TYPE A (SECS)
',EVTMOA,SDTMOA )(SKIP,A,F(11,3),F(11,3));
    PUT EDIT('TOTAL TRANSMISSION TIME FOR OUTPUT MESSAGE TYPE B (SECS)
',EVTMOB,SDTMOB )(SKIP,A,F(11,3),F(11,3));
    PUT EDIT('TOTAL TIME TRANSACTION SPENDS IN COMPUTER SYSTEM  (SECS)
',EVTTCS,SDTTCS )(SKIP,A,F(11,3),F(11,3));
    END GRAPH;
```

## In Fortran:

```
    SUBROUTINE GRAPH
C....
    REAL MAXTPT,
   1MSA*8(8) /'AAAAA = ','MEAN RES','PONSE TI','ME FOR T',
   2         'YPE A TR','ANSACTIO','NS (SECO','NDS)    '/,
   3MSB*8(8) /'BBBBB = ','MEAN RES','PONSE TI','ME FOR T',
   4         'YPE B TR','ANSACTIO','NS (SECO','NDS)    '/,
   5MSS*8(10)/'SSSSS = ','STANDARD',' DEVIATI','ON OF RE','SPONSE T',
   6         'IME FOR ','TYPE A T','RANSACTI','ONS (SEC','ONDS)'/,
   7MSZ*8(10)/'ZZZZZ = ','STANDARD',' DEVIATI','ON OF RE','SPONSE T',
   8         'IME FOR ','TYPE B T','RANSACTI','ONS (SEC','ONDS)'/
    INTEGER XSUB
C....
    LOGICAL*1 PL(97,120),VRTCL/'|'/,HRZNTL/'-'/,PLUS/'+'/,Z/'Z'/,
   1S/'S'/,B/'B'/,A/'A'/,ASTER/'*'/,X/'X'/,SPACE/' '/,
   2MS3(8)/'4','3','3','2','2','1','1','-'/,
   3MS4(8)/'0','5','0','5','0','5','0','5'/
C....
    COMMON /COMN1/TIMEA(121),TIMEB(121),SDTRTA(121),SDTRTB(121),
   1THRPUT(121),MAXTPT,SPEED,
   2VATMIA,VATMIB,VATMOA,VATMOB,VATTCS,
   3EVTMIA,EVTMIB,EVTMOA,EVTMOB,EVTTCS,
   4L1
C....
    DATA ZERO/0.0/
C....
C***************************************************************************
C***************************************************************************
```

```
C*PREPARE GRAPH ***************************************************
C....
      DO 10 J=2,119
      DO 10 I=2,96
   10 PL(I,J)=SPACE
      DO 20 J=12,120,12
      DO 20 I=2,96
   20 PL(I,J)=VRTCL
      DO 30 I=1,97
   30 PL(I,1)=VRTCL
      DO 40 J=2,119
      DO 40 I=1,97,12
   40 PL(I,J)=HRZNTL
      DO 50 J=12,120,12
      DO 50 I=1,97,12
   50 PL(I,J)=PLUS
C....
      A2=TIMEA(2)
      B2=TIMEB(2)
      S2=SDTRTA(2)
      Z2=SDTRTB(2)
      XAX=500.0
      YAX=40.0
      XDIV=XAX/120.0
      YDIV=YAX/ 96.0
      D=ZERO
      G=ZERO
C....
      DO 190 J=1,120
      IF(G.EQ.1.0 .OR. D.EQ.1.0) GO TO 200
      A1=TIMEA(J)
      B1=TIMEB(J)
      S1=SDTRTA(J)
      Z1=SDTRTB(J)
      U=THRPUT(J)
      XSUB=U/XDIV
      IF (XSUB.LE.0) GO TO 190
      IF (A1.LT.ZERO .OR. B1.LT.ZERO .OR.
     1    S1.LT.ZERO .OR. Z1.LT.ZERO) G=1.0
      IF (A1.GT.YAX  .OR. B1.GT.YAX   .OR.
     1    S1.GT.YAX  .OR. Z1.GT.YAX ) D=1.0
      IF (D .EQ.1.0  .OR.  G.EQ.1.0 ) GO TO 190
  100 IF (Z1.LT.YAX) PL(97.0-Z1/YDIV,XSUB)=Z
      IF (Z1-Z2 .GT. YDIV) GO TO 140
  110 IF (S1.LT.YAX) PL(97.0-S1/YDIV,XSUB)=S
      IF (S1-S2 .GT. YDIV) GO TO 150
  120 PL(97.0-B1/YDIV,XSUB)=B
      IF (B1-B2 .GT. YDIV) GO TO 160
  130 PL(97.0-A1/YDIV,XSUB)=A
      IF (A1-A2 .GT. YDIV) GO TO 170
      A2=TIMEA(J)
      B2=TIMEB(J)
      S2=SDTRTA(J)
      Z2=SDTRTB(J)
      GO TO 190
  140 Z1=Z1-YDIV
      GO TO 100
```

```
  150 S1=S1-YDIV
      GO TO 110
  160 B1=B1-YDIV
      GO TO 120
  170 A1=A1-YDIV
      GO TO 130
  190 CONTINUE
  200 IF (D.NE.1.0) GO TO 220
      DO 210 I=1,97
  210 PL(I,XSUB)=ASTER
  220 IF (MAXTPT.GE.XAX) GO TO 240
      DO 230 I=1,97
  230 PL(I,MAXTPT/XDIV)=X
C....
  240 CONTINUE
      DO 250 I=1,8
      K=I*12-11
      DO 250 J=3,117,114
      PL(K,J)=MS3(I)
  250 PL(K,J+1)=MS4(I)
C**********************************************************************
C*PRINT GRAPH *******************************************************
C....
  300 FORMAT (1H1,'5',10X,'50',9X,'100',9X,'150',9X,'200',9X,'250',9X,
     1'300',9X,'350',9X,'400',9X,'450',9X,'500')
  310 FORMAT (1H ,120A1)
  330 FORMAT (1H ,3A1,7A8,A4,57A1)
  340 FORMAT (1H ,3A1,9A8,A5,40A1)
  350 FORMAT (1H ,60A1,'THROUGHPUT (NUMBER OF TRANSACTIONS PER HOUR)',
     116A1)
  360 FORMAT (1H ,'5',10X,'50',9X,'100',9X,'150',9X,'200',9X,'250',9X,
     1'300',9X,'350',9X,'400',9X,'450',9X,'500')
      WRITE (L1,300)
      DO 380 I=1,14
  380 WRITE (L1,310) (PL(I,J), J=1,120)
      WRITE (L1,330) (PL(15,J), J=1,3),MSA,(PL(15,J), J=64,120)
      WRITE (L1,310) (PL(16,J), J=1,120)
      WRITE (L1,330) (PL(17,J), J=1,3),MSB,(PL(17,J), J=64,120)
      WRITE (L1,310) (PL(18,J), J=1,120)
      WRITE (L1,340) (PL(19,J), J=1,3),MSS,(PL(19,J), J=81,120)
      WRITE (L1,310) (PL(20,J), J=1,120)
      WRITE (L1,340) (PL(21,J), J=1,3),MSZ,(PL(21,J), J=81,120)
      DO 390 I=22,94
  390 WRITE (L1,310) (PL(I ,J), J=1,120)
      WRITE (L1,350) (PL(95,J), J=1,60),(PL(95,J), J=105,120)
      DO 400 I=96,97
  400 WRITE (L1,310) (PL(I, J), J=1,120)
      WRITE (L1,360)
      WRITE (L1,410) SPEED
  410 FORMAT(//1H ,
     1'EXAMPLE FH.2.'//1H ,
     2'LINE SPEED ',F4.1,' CHARACTERS PER SECOND'//1H ,T65,
     3'MEAN      STANDARD'/1H ,T75,
     4'DEVIATION')
      SDTMIA=SQRT(VATMIA)
      SDTMIB=SQRT(VATMIB)
      SDTMOA=SQRT(VATMOA)
```

```
      SDTMOB=SQRT(VATMOB)
      SDTTCS=SQRT(VATTCS)
      WRITE (L1,420)
     1EVTMIA,SDTMIA,EVTMIB,SDTMIB,
     2EVTMOA,SDTMOA,EVTMOB,SDTMOB,
     3EVTTCS,SDTTCS
  420 FORMAT (1H ,
     1'TOTAL TRANSMISSION TIME FOR INPUT   MESSAGE TYPE A (SECS) ',
     2    2F11.3/1H ,
     3'TOTAL TRANSMISSION TIME FOR INPUT   MESSAGE TYPE B (SECS) ',
     4    2F11.3/1H ,
     5'TOTAL TRANSMISSION TIME FOR OUTPUT MESSAGE TYPE A (SECS) ',
     6    2F11.3/1H ,
     7'TOTAL TRANSMISSION TIME FOR OUTPUT MESSAGE TYPE B (SECS) ',
     8    2F11.3/1H ,
     9'TOTAL TIME TRANSACTION SPENDS IN COMPUTER SYSTEM  (SECS) ',
     A    2F11.3)
      RETURN
      END
```

# V ROUTINE FOR PLOTTING DISTRIBUTION OF RESPONSE TIMES

The following listing shows the program used for plotting the distribution of response times in Chapters 36 and 37, using the assumption that the response times approximately follow a gamma distribution. This routine is called by the statement CALL PROBAB. Data are passed to the routine in the following tables:

THRPUT (I): mean throughput

TIME (I): mean response time

SIGTIME (I): standard deviation of response time

MAXTHRPUT is the maximum possible throughput.

In PL/I:

```
/********************************************************************************/
 PROBAB: PROCEDURE;
    CN ENDPAGE (SYSPRINT);
    DCL PK(0:110,0:119) CHAR(1); PK=' ';
    DO J=0 TO 110 BY 10; PK(J,*)='-';END;
    DO J=0 TO 120 BY 10; PK(*,(J-1))='I';END;
    DO J=10 TO 120 BY 10;DO K=0 TO 110 BY 10;PK(K,(J-1))='+';END;END;
/********************************************************************************/
/*CALCULATE PROBABILITIES **************************************************/
    DCL LET CHAR(26); LET='ABCDEFGHIJKLMNOPQRSTUVWXYZ';
    PUT EDIT ('THROUGHPUT VALUES OF CURVES BELOW')
    (PAGE,A,SKIP(2));
    LO K= (MAXTHRPUT-4),(MAXTHRPUT-5), (MAXTHRPUT-6) TO (MAXTHRPUT-18)
    BY -2 WHILE (K>0);
    J=4*K+16;
    IF ((TIME(J)<=0)|(SIGTIME(J)<=0))   THEN GO TO EN;
    PUT EDIT (SUBSTR(LET,K,1),SUBSTR(LET,K,1),SUBSTR(LET,K,1),' = ',
    THRPUT(J), ' TRANSACTIONS PER SECOND ')(SKIP,4 A,F(4,1),A);
```

```
    R=(TIME(J)/SIGTIME(J))**2;
    IF R > 50 THEN R = 50;
    PTTO=.45;
    DO AATTSS = 100 TO 11900 BY 100 WHILE (PTTO<.998);
    TOTB = AATTSS/TIME(J);
    WN=R*TOTB;
    IF (WN>50 ) THEN GO TO EM;
    IF (TOTB<.5) THEN GO TO EM;
  CALL GAMA (R,WN,GAM,B,ER);
    PTT=1-GAM;
    PTTN=PTT;
BP:IF PTT<.455 THEN GO TO EX;
    PK((201-(PTT+.0025)*200),(AATTSS/100   )    )=SUBSTR(LET,K,1);
    IF (PTT-PTTO)>.005 THEN GO TO BQ;
EX:PTTO=PTTN;
    GO TO EM;
BQ:PTT=PTT-.005;GO TO BP;
EM:END;
EN:END;
/*PRINT PROBABILITY GRAPH ***************************************************/
/*************************************************************************/
    DCL MSH CHAR(34);MSH='*********************************';
    DCL MSI CHAR(34);MSI='* PROBABILITY THAT RESPONSE TIME *';
    DCL MSJ CHAR(34);MSJ='*  IS LESS THAN T  (ABSCISSA).   *';
    DCL MSK CHAR(34);MSK='*  (SEE KEY ABOVE.)              *';
    DO J=1 TO 34; PK(13,J+4)=SUBSTR(MSH,J,1);
                  PK(14,J+4)=SUBSTR(MSI,J,1);
                  PK(15,J+4)=SUBSTR(MSJ,J,1);
                  PK(16,J+4)=SUBSTR(MSK,J,1);
                  PK(17,J+4)=SUBSTR(MSH,J,1); END;
    DCL MSL CHAR(25);MSL='RESPONSE TIME,T (SECONDS)';
    DO J=1 TO 25;PK(109,J+50)=SUBSTR(MSL,J,1);END;
    DO J=0 TO 110 BY 10;PK(J,0)='0';END;PK(0,0)='1';
    DO J=0 TO 110 BY 10;PK(J,1)='.';END;
    DCL MSM CHAR(12);MSM='099887766554';
    DO J=0 TO 11;PK(10*J,2)=SUBSTR(MSM,J+1,1); END;
    DCL MSO CHAR(12);MSO='050505050505';
    DO J=0 TO 11;PK(10*J,3)=SUBSTR(MSO,J+1,1); END;
    PUT EDIT ('PROBABILITY THAT TIME DOES NOT EXCEED GIVEN VALUES.')
    (SKIP(3),A);
    PUT EDIT (PK)(SKIP    ,120 A('1'));
    PUT EDIT('           1               2          3          4          5',
    '         6        7          8          9         10         11',
    '          12')(SKIP,A,A,A);
    END PROBAB;
/*************************************************************************/
```

IN FORTRAN:

```
      SUBROUTINE PROBAB
C....
      REAL*8
     1MSH(5)    /5*'*********'/,
     2MSI(5)    /'* PROBAB','ILITY TH','AT RESPO','NSE TIME',' *    '/,
     3MSJ(5)    /'*  IS LE','SS THAN ','T  (ABSC','ISSA).  ',' *    '/,
     4MSK(5)    /'*  (SEE ','KEY ABOV','E.)     ','        ',' *    '/,
     5MSL(4)    /'RESPONSE',' TIME,T ','(SECONDS',')'/
      INTEGER AATTSS
```

```
      DATA ZERC/0.0/
C....
      LOGICAL*1 PK(121,120),SPACE/' '/,II/'I'/,HRZNTL/'-'/,PLUS/'+'/,
     1ALPHA(26)/'A','B','C','D','E','F','G','H','I','J','K','L','M',
     2         'N','O','P','Q','R','S','T','U','V','W','X','Y','Z'/,
     3OH/'O'/,ONE/'1'/,DOT/'.'/,
     4MSM(12)   /'0','9','9','8','8','7','7','6','6','5','5','4'/,
     5MSO(12)   /'0','5','0','5','0','5','0','5','0','5','0','5'/
C....
      COMMON /COMN1/TIME(120),SDTIME(120),THRPUT(120)
     1        /COMN2/PK
     2        /COMN3/MAXTPT
C....
C
      L1=3
      DO 30 J=1,120
      DC 10 I=1,111
   10 PK(I,J)=SPACE
      DO 20 I=1,111,10
   20 PK(I,J)=HRZNTL
   30 CONTINUE
      DO 60 J=10,120,10
      DO 40 I=1,111
   40 PK(I,J)=II
      DO 50 I=1,111,10
   50 PK(I,J)=PLUS
C
      DC 60 I=1,111,10
      PK(I,1)=OH
      PK(I,2)=DCT
      ISUB=I/10+1
      PK(I,3)=MSM(ISUB)
   60 PK(I,4)=MSO(ISUB)
      PK(1,1)=ONE
C*******************************************************************
C* CALCULATE PROBATILITIES ***************************************
      WRITE (L1,100)
  100 FORMAT (1H1,
     1'THROUGHPUT VALUES OF CURVES BELOW')
      K=MAXTPT-4
      IEND=MAXTPT-6
      INC=-1
      GO TO 120
  110 K=MAXTPT-8
      IEND=MAXTPT-18
      INC=-2
  120 IF (K.LE.C) GO TO 300
      J=4*K+16
      IF (TIME(J).LE.0.0 .OR. SDTIME(J).LE.0.0) GO TO 260
      WRITE (L1,130) ALPHA(K),ALPHA(K),ALPHA(K),THRPUT(J)
  130 FORMAT (1H ,
     13A1,' = ',F4.1,' TRANSACTIONS PER SECOND')
      R=(TIME(J)/SDTIME(J))**2
      IF (R.GT.50.C) R=50.0
      PTC=.45
      DO 250 AATTSS= 10C,11900,100
```

```
      IF (PTTO.GE..998) GO TO 260
      TOTB=AATTSS/TIME(J)
      WN=R*TOTB
      IF (WN.GT.50.0) GO TO 250
      IF (TOTB.LT..5) GO TO 250
      CALL GAMA (R,WN,GAM,B,ER)
      PTT=1.0-GAM
      PTTN=PTT
  170 IF (PTT.LT..455) GO TO 180
      PK(202.0-(PTT+.0025)*200.0,AATTSS/100+1)=ALPHA(K)
      IF (PTT-PTTO.GT..005) GO TO 190
  180 PTTO=PTTN
      GO TO 250
  190 PTT=PTT-.005
      GO TO 170
  250 CONTINUE
  260 K=K+INC
      IF (K.GE.IEND) GO TO 120
      IF (INC.EQ.-1) GO TO 110
C******************************************************************************
C* PRINT PROBABILITY GRAPH ***************************************************
C
  300 WRITE (L1,310)
  310 FORMAT (///1H ,
     1'PROBABILITY THAT TIME DOES NOT EXEEED GIVEN VALUES.')
  320 FORMAT (1H ,120A1)
  330 FORMAT (1H ,5A1,4A8,A2,81A1)
  340 FORMAT (1H ,51A1,3A8,A1,44A1)
      DO 360 I=1,13
  360 WRITE (L1,320) (PK(I   ,J), J=1   ,120)
      WRITE (L1,330) (PK(14 ,J), J=1   ,5  ),MSH,(PK(14 ,J), J=40,120)
      WRITE (L1,330) (PK(15 ,J), J=1   ,5  ),MSI,(PK(15 ,J), J=40,120)
      WRITE (L1,330) (PK(16 ,J), J=1   ,5  ),MSJ,(PK(16 ,J), J=40,120)
      WRITE (L1,330) (PK(17 ,J), J=1   ,5  ),MSK,(PK(17 ,J), J=40,120)
      WRITE (L1,330) (PK(18 ,J), J=1   ,5  ),MSH,(PK(18 ,J), J=40,120)
      DO 370 I=19,109
  370 WRITE (L1,320) (PK(I   ,J), J=1   ,120)
      WRITE (L1,340) (PK(110,J), J=1   , 51),MSL,(PK(110,J), J=77,120)
      WRITE (L1,320) (PK(111,J), J=1   ,120)
      WRITE (L1,380)
  380 FORMAT (1H ,9X,'1',9X,'2',9X,'3',9X,'4',9X,'5',9X,'6',9X,'7',
     1           9X,'8',9X,'9',9X,'10',8X,'11',8X,'12')
      RETURN
      END
```

# VI A PROGRAM FOR EVALUATING THE INCOMPLETE GAMMA FUNCTION

This program* evaluates the normalized incomplete gamma function:

$$\text{Gam}\,(R,\,T) = \frac{\displaystyle\int_{T}^{\infty}\left[\frac{Rt}{E(t)}\right]^{R-1}e^{-Rt/E(t)}\,\frac{R}{E(t)}\,dt}{\displaystyle\int_{0}^{\infty}\left[\frac{Rt}{E(t)}\right]^{R-1}e^{-Rt/E(t)}\,\frac{R}{E(t)}\,dt}$$

This equation is used by the program in Appendix 5, where it is called by the statement CALL GAMA (R, WN, GAM, B, ER), in which $R$ is the gamma parameter in the preceding equation and WN is T. GAM is the result, Gam $(R, T)$. B is the associated Poisson term, Gam $(R + 1, T) -$ Gam $(R, T)$, and $ER$ is an error indication.

If a time value, $t$ follows a gamma distribution

$$\text{Prob}\,(t \leq T) = 1 - \text{Gam}\,(R,\,T)$$

where

$$R = \frac{E^2(t)}{\text{Var}\,(t)}$$

This equation is plotted in Fig. 31.13 and tabulated in Table 4 of Appendix VIII.

*The method is taken from a FORTRAN program in the SHARE library, No. SDA3141, programmed by John R. B. Whittlesey.

## In PL/I:

```
GAMA:   PROCEDURE (A,X,GAM,B,ER);
   DCL NVB (5) FLOAT (15);
        ER=0;
        IF  X=0 | (X>0 & A>0) THEN DO;
             CALL GAMMA (A,X,GAM,B,NVB);
             IF NVB(2)>=4 THEN ER=NVB(2);RETURN;END;
        IF X>0 & A<=0 & A<TRUNC (A) | X<0 THEN ER=2;
        GAM,B=0;
END1:   END GAMA;
WHICH:  PROCEDURE (X,A,ASYMC,CNTFR,GAUSW,IBB,NVB,Z,B,N11);
   DCL NVB (5) FLOAT (15);
   DCL (N11,IBB) FLOAT (15);
        IBB=100;
        A1=2;
        NVB(2),NVB(5)=0;
     INSERT CARD  ***   NVB(4)=1;   ***   IF PRINTOUT IS DESIRED
        IF (X>=200) |
           (X<200 & A=TRUNC(A) & A>20 & X<A) |
           (X<200 & A¬=TRUNC(A) & A+X<=13) |
           (X<200 & A¬=TRUNC(A) & A+X>13 & X<A) THEN DO;
           ASYMC=0; GO TO F104; END;
        IF (X<200 & A=TRUNC(A) & A<=20) THEN N11=150/A;
F100:   ASYMC=1;
F104:   IF (X<A) | X>=A & X<=1 THEN CNTFR=0; ELSE CNTFR=1;
        IF X<500 THEN DO; GAUSW=0;RETURN;END;
        TRD=.333333333;
        A9=9*A;
        Z=((X/A)**TRD-1+ 1/A9-2/(A9*A9))*SQRT(A9);
        IF ABS(Z)<=A1 THEN GAUSW=1;ELSE GAUSW=0;
END2:   END WHICH;
GAMMA:  PROCEDURE (A,X,GAM,B,NVB);
   DCL NVB (5) FLOAT (15),   AS (8);
        IF A=0 THEN DO; GAM=0; RETURN; END;
        N11=1;
        IF SWX=1.111 THEN GO TO F120;
        AS(1)=-.577191652;
        AS(2)=0.988205891;
        AS(3)=-.897056937;
        AS(4)=0.918206857;
        AS(5)=-.756704078;
        AS(6)=0.482199394;
        AS(7)=-.193527818;
        AS(8)=0.035868343;
        E=2.718281828;

        TPI=6.283185300;
        CZP=-35.0;
        CZ=10.0**CZP;
        CZR=1./CZ;
        SWX=1.111;
F120:   AFR=A-TRUNC(A);
        DEM=A+1;
        F=1.0;
        XP=-7;
        SWS=0;
```

```
         SWT,SWW,SWR,SFS,SWG,Z,NVB(2),NS,NT,NR=0;
         BT=.4342944819;
         X1=(SQRT(A))*(11+5*(BT*LOG(A)-.9)**2);
F148:    IF X <=CZ THEN DO; B=0; GAM,GAMT,SWT=1; GO TO F400;END;
F149:    IF X/A >.05 THEN GO TO F150;
         IF (A<=0.5 & X<=85) | (A>0.5 & A<=38 & X<=X1) THEN GO TO F156;
         IF A>38 THEN GO TO F190; ELSE GO TO F153;
F150:    IF (A<=0.5 & X<=85) | (A>0.5 & A<=40 & X<=X1) THEN GO TO F156;
         IF A>40 THEN GO TO F190;
F153:    B=0;
F154:    GAM=0;
         SWW=1;
       GO TO F400;
/*CALCULATION OF THE POISSON TERM B(X,A)                              */
F156:    DO I=1 TO 50;
         DEM=DEM-1;
         IF DEM=1 THEN DO F=X*F;  GO TO F175;END;
         IF DEM<1 THEN GO TO F175;
         F=(X/DEM)*F;
         IF F<CZ THEN GO TO F153;
         END;
F171:    PUT EDIT ('LOOP IN CALC. OF B') (SKIP,A);
         RETURN;
F175:    EXPX=E**X;
         GGF=LOG (F/EXPX);
F176:    GS=0;
         DO JS=8 TO 1 BY -1;
(NOUNDERFLOW): F180:    GS=GS*AFR + AS(JS); END;
         GA=1+GS*AFR;
F181:    GGB=AFR*LOG(X)+GGF-LOG(GA);
         GO TO F193;
F187:    BAM,B=0;
         GO TO F196;
/* STIRLING APPROXIMATION EXTENDED                                    */
F190:    WPT=LOG(X)-LOG(A)+1-X/A;
         GGB=A*WPT-.5*(LOG(TPI)+LOG(A))-1/(12*A)+1/(360*A**3);
F193:    IF GGB<-85 THEN GO TO F187;
F194:    B=E**GGB;
F195:    BAM=A/X*B;
F196:    CALL WHICH (X,A,ASYMC,CNTFR,GAUSW,IBB,NVB,Z,B,N11);
         NVB(1)=0;
         V=NVB(1);
         IF NVB(1)¬=0 THEN XP=-ABS(V);
F130:    P=2*10**XP;
         IUB=IBB+100;
F198:    IF ASYMC>0 THEN GO TO F300;
F199:    IF CNTFR>0 THEN GO TO F600;
/* CONVERGENT SERIES FOR SMALL X                                      */
F200:    SWT,T,SUMT=1;
         DO ZT=1 TO IUB;
(NOUNDERFLOW):    T=T*X/(A+ZT);
            RAT=T/SUMT;
            IF RAT<=P THEN GO TO F240;
            SUMT=SUMT+T;
            IF SUMT>CZR THEN GO TO F235; END;
         PUT EDIT ('UPPER BOUND ON ITERATION COUNT REACHED IN GAMMA')
```

```
                        (SKIP,A);
          NVB(2)=5;
          GO TO F240;
F235:     NVB(2)=6;
F240:     GAMT=1-B*SUMT;
          GAM=GAMT;
          GO TO F400;
/* ASYMPTOTIC SERIES FOR LARGE X, A GREATER THAN 1                      */
F300:     SWS,S,SUMS=1;
          XM=-X;
F315:     DO ZS=1 TO IUB;
             CE=(ZS-A)/XM;
             NACE=ABS(CE);
             IF NACE>=N11 THEN GO TO F340;
             S=CE*S;
             RAS=ABS(S/SUMS);
             IF RAS<=P THEN GO TO F350;
             SUMS=SUMS+S;END;
          PUT EDIT ('UPPER BOUND ON ITERATION COUNT REACHED IN GAMMA')
                        (SKIP,A);
          NVB(2)=4;
F340:        GAMS=BAM*SUMS;
          GO TO F199;
F350:        GAMS=BAM*SUMS;
          GAM=GAMS;
          IF NVB(5)<=2 THEN GO TO F400; ELSE GO TO F199;
/* CONTINUED FRACTION APPROX. TO GAMMA FOR X LARGE RELATIVE TO A         */
F600:     SWR,BBM=1;
F601:     AAM=1/X;
F603:     AA=(X+1)/X/X;
F604:     BB=(X+2-A)/X;
F605:     APPX=AA/BB;
F620:     DO SN=2 TO IUB;
F622:        AC=-(SN-1)*(SN-A)/X/X;
F623:        BC=(X+2*SN-A)/X;
F624:        AAP=BC*AA+AC*AAM;
F625:        AAA=ABS(AAP);
F642:        IF AAA>CZR THEN GO TO F655;
F644:        BBP=BC*BB+AC*BBM;
F645:        BBB=ABS(BBP);
F632:        IF BBB>CZR THEN GO TO F655;
F634:           AAM=AA;
F635:        AA=AAP;
F636:        BBM=BB;
F637:        BB=BBP;
F638:        APPXM=APPX;
F639:        APPX=AA/BB;
             RAR=ABS((APPX-APPXM)/APPXM);
F641:        IF RAR<=P THEN GO TO F650;END;
(NOUNDERFLOW): F650: NR=3*N;
          CFCT=A*APPX;
          GO TO F660;
F655:     GAMR=B*A*APPX;
F661:     SFS=1;
```

```
         NVB(2)=3;
         NR=3*N;
F662:    CNTFR=0;
         GO TO F300;
F660:    GAMR=B*CFCT;
         IF CFCT<=0 THEN GO TO F661;
         GAM=GAMR;
         IF NVB(5)> 3 THEN GO TO F662; ELSE GO TO F400;
F400:    NVB(3)=NS+NT+NR;
END3:    END GAMMA;
```

# VII   MAP COMPOSING ROUTINE

In PL/I:

```
/***********************************************************************/
/**** MAP COMPOSING ROUTINE ********************************************/
GRID:PROC;
     DCL (S1,S2) CHAR(548);
  S1='12121312111111121314151617161615161615141312111010111213131313'||
     '13131312111111C09101010101011121212121213131314151616171718192021 22'||
     '23232424242221201918171615141312121212131415161717161515151617'||
     '18192020202019191817161615141312111010090807060504040404050506'||
     'C70708091011111213141516171819202122232425262728292930313232'||
     '33343536373839404142434344444545464647474849505051515253545556'||
     '56565655555453535353532525252525151515049484847474747484950494949'||
     '494949495051515152525252535454545455555555656565757565656565757'||
     '57585858596061626364656667676767666665656464646363 23';
  S2='07080910111213131211110091011121314151616171818192020191920 2122'||
     '23242526272829303132333433333323130292827262625242426262 62728'||
     '293031323334343332323131323333334353637383838383839404041424344'||
     '444444454647484950515253545554535455565758585758587576777879 80'||
     '79787777767574737474757575767677777879808182818181807978777877'||
     '767777675747373737475767778798081828384858687888990919191 90'||
     '89888786858483828180807978777776757474737271706968676665646362'||
     '616059585756555453525150495051525251504948474645444342414039 38'||
     '37363534333231302928282828181716151413121110090807 34';
     MAP=' ';
     DO JR=0 TO 100 BY 20; MAP(*,JR)='|'; END;
     DO JC=12 TO 67 BY 12; MAP(JC,*)='-'; END;
     MAP(3,*)='-';         MAP(67,*)='-';
     DO JR=12 TO 60 BY 12;
         DO JC=20 TO 90 BY 20;
         MAP(JR,JC)='+';
         END;
     END;
     DO JJ=1 TO 547 BY 2;
```

819

```
      MV=SUBSTR(S1,JJ,2);
      MH=SUBSTR(S2,JJ,2);
      MAP(MV,MH)='*';
      END;
      DCL MS CHAR(5) INITIAL ('56789');
      DO M=5 TO 9;
      MSUB=(M-4)*12;
      MAP(MSUB,92),
      MAP(MSUB, 2)=SUBSTR(MS,(M-4),1);
      DO N=1 TO 3;
      MAP(MSUB,92+N),
      MAP(MSUB, 2+N)='0';
      END; END;
      DCL CITIES CHAR(32) INITIAL
         ('CHICAGO HOUSTON MIAMI   NEW YORK');
      DO M=1 TO 8;
      MAP(25,26+M)=SUBSTR(CITIES,       M,1);
      MAP(59,24+M)=SUBSTR(CITIES, (8+M),1);
      MAP(53,91+M)=SUBSTR(CITIES,(16+M),1);
      MAP(12,74+M)=SUBSTR(CITIES,(24+M),1);
      END;
      MAP(24,32)='0';
      END GRID;
  /******************************************************************/

C****************************************************************************
C****************************************************************************
C**** MAP COMPOSING ROUTINE ************************************************
      SUBROUTINE GRID
      LOGICAL*1 MAP(67,101),VRTCL/'|'/,HRZNTL/'-'/,PLUS/'+'/,ASTER/'*'/,
     1SPACE/' '/,OH/'0'/,
     2MS1(5)/'5','6','7','8','9'/,
     3MS2(8)/'C','H','I','C','A','G','O',' '/,
     4MS3(8)/'H','O','U','S','T','O','N',' '/,
     5MS4(8)/'M','I','A','M','I',' ',' ',' '/,
     6MS5(8)/'N','E','W',' ','Y','O','R','K'/
C
      INTEGER*2 S1(274)
     1/ 12,12,13,12, 3*11,12,13,14,15,16,17,16,16,15,16,16,15,14,13,12,
     2  11,10,10,11,    12, 7*13,12,11,11,10, 9, 4*10,11, 4*12, 3*13,14,
     3  15,16,16,17,17,18,19,20,21,22,23,23,     3*24,    22,21,20,19,18,
     4  17,16,15,14,13, 4*12,13,14,15,16,17,17,    16, 3*15,16,17,18,19,
     54*20,19,19,18,17,16,16,15,14,13,12,11,2*10,9,8, 7, 6, 5, 4* 4, 5,
     6   5, 6, 7, 7, 8, 9,10,11,11,12,13,14,15,16,17,18,19,20,21,22,23,
     7  24,25,26,27,28, 3*29,30,31,32,32,33,34,35,36,37,38,39,40,41,42,
     82*43,44,44,45,45,46,46,47,47,48,49,50,50,51,51,52,53,54,55, 4*56,
     9  55,55,54, 4*53, 4*52, 3*51,50,49,48,48, 4*47,48,49,50, 7*49,50,
     A3*51, 4*52,    53, 3*54, 3*55, 3*56,57,57, 4*56, 4*57, 3*58,59,60,
     B  61,62,63,64,65,66, 4*67,66,66,65,65, 3*64,63,63,23/
C
      INTEGER*2 S2(274)
     1/ 7, 8, 9,10,11,12,13,13,12,11,10, 9,10,11,12,13,14,15,16,16,17,
     2  18,18,19,20,20,19,19,20,21,22,23,24,25,26,27,28,29,30,31,32,33,
     3  34,33,33,32,31,30,29,28,27,26,26,25,24,24, 4*26,27,28,29,30,31,
```

```
     4    32,33,34,34,33,32,32,31,31,32,33,33,34,35,36,37, 5*38,39,40,40,
     5    41,42,43, 4*44,45,46,47,48,49,50,51,52,53,54,55,54,53,54,55,56,
     6    57,58,58,57,58,58,75,76,77,78,79,80,79,78,77,77,76,75,74,73,74,
     7    74, 3*75,76,76,77,77,78,79,80,81,82, 3*81,80,79,78,77,78,77,76,
     8    77,77,76,75,74, 4*73,74,75,76,77,78,79,80,81,82,83,84,85,86,87,
     9    88,89,90, 3*91,90,89,88,87,86,85,84,83,82,81,80,80,79,78,77,77,
     A    76,75,74,74,73,72,71,70,69,68,67,66,65,64,63,62,61,60,59,58,57,
     B    56,55,54,53,52,51,50,49,50,51,52,52,51,50,49,48,47,46,45,44,43,
     C    42,41,40,39,38,37,36,35,34,33,32,31,30,29, 4*28,18,17,16,15,14,
     D    13,12,11,10, 9, 8, 7, 34/
C
       COMMON /CCMN1/MAP
C*******************************************************************************
       DO 10 J=2,100
       DO 10 I=4,66
    10 MAP(I,J)=SPACE
       DO 20 JR=1,101,20
       DO 20 JC=3,67
    20 MAP(JC,JR)=VRTCL
       DO 30 JR=1,101
       DO 30 JC=12,67,12
    30 MAP(JC,JR)=HRZNTL
       DO 40 JR=1,101
       MAP( 3,JR)=HRZNTL
    40 MAP(67,JR)=HRZNTL
       DO 50 JR=21,91,20
       DO 50 JC=12,60,12
    50 MAP(JC,JR)=PLUS
       DO 60 I=1,274
    60 MAP(S1(I),S2(I)+1)=ASTER
       DO 80 M=5,9
       MSUB=(M-4)*12
       MAP(MSUB,93)=MS1(M-4)
       MAP(MSUB, 3)=MS1(M-4)
       DO 70 N=1,3
       MAP(MSUB,93+N)=OH
    70 MAP(MSUB, 3+N)=OH
    80 CONTINUE
       DO 90 M=1,8
       MAP(25,27+M)=MS2(M)
       MAP(59,25+M)=MS3(M)
       MAP(53,92+M)=MS4(M)
    90 MAP(12,75+M)=MS5(M)
       MAP(24,33)=OH
       RETURN
       END
```

# VIII

## TABLES USED IN THE DESIGN CALCULATIONS

**Table 1.** RANDOM NUMBERS

| | | | | |
|---|---|---|---|---|
| 22 17 68 65 84 | 68 95 23 92 35 | 87 02 22 57 51 | 61 09 43 95 06 | 58 24 82 03 47 |
| 19 36 27 59 46 | 13 79 93 37 55 | 39 77 32 77 09 | 85 52 05 30 62 | 47 83 51 62 74 |
| 16 77 23 02 77 | 09 61 87 25 21 | 28 05 24 25 93 | 16 71 13 59 78 | 23 05 47 47 25 |
| 78 43 76 71 61 | 20 44 90 32 64 | 97 67 63 99 61 | 46 38 03 93 22 | 69 81 21 99 21 |
| 03 28 28 26 08 | 73 37 32 04 05 | 69 30 16 09 05 | 88 69 58 28 99 | 35 07 44 75 47 |
| | | | | |
| 93 22 53 64 39 | 07 10 63 76 35 | 87 03 04 79 88 | 08 13 13 85 51 | 55 34 57 72 69 |
| 78 76 58 54 74 | 92 38 70 96 92 | 52 06 79 79 45 | 82 63 18 27 44 | 69 66 92 19 09 |
| 23 68 35 26 00 | 99 53 93 61 28 | 52 70 05 48 34 | 56 65 05 61 86 | 90 92 10 70 80 |
| 15 39 25 70 99 | 93 86 52 77 65 | 15 33 59 05 28 | 22 87 26 07 47 | 86 96 98 29 06 |
| 58 71 96 30 24 | 18 46 23 34 27 | 85 13 99 24 44 | 49 18 09 79 49 | 74 16 32 23 02 |
| | | | | |
| 57 35 27 33 72 | 24 53 63 94 09 | 41 10 76 47 91 | 44 04 95 49 66 | 39 60 04 59 81 |
| 48 50 86 54 48 | 22 06 34 72 52 | 82 21 15 65 20 | 33 29 94 71 11 | 15 91 29 12 03 |
| 61 96 48 95 03 | 07 16 39 33 66 | 98 56 10 56 79 | 77 21 30 27 12 | 90 49 22 23 62 |
| 36 93 89 41 26 | 29 70 83 63 51 | 99 74 20 52 36 | 87 09 41 15 09 | 98 60 16 03 03 |
| 18 87 00 42 31 | 57 90 12 02 07 | 23 47 37 17 31 | 54 08 01 88 63 | 39 41 88 92 10 |
| | | | | |
| 88 56 53 27 59 | 33 35 72 67 47 | 77 34 55 45 70 | 08 18 27 38 90 | 16 95 86 70 75 |
| 09 72 95 84 29 | 49 41 31 06 70 | 42 38 06 45 18 | 54 84 73 31 65 | 52 53 37 97 15 |
| 12 96 88 17 31 | 65 19 69 02 83 | 60 75 86 90 68 | 24 64 19 35 51 | 56 61 87 39 12 |
| 85 94 57 24 16 | 92 09 84 38 76 | 22 00 27 69 85 | 29 81 94 78 70 | 21 94 47 90 12 |
| 38 64 43 59 98 | 98 77 87 68 07 | 91 51 67 62 44 | 40 98 05 93 78 | 23 32 65 41 18 |
| | | | | |
| 53 44 09 42 72 | 00 41 86 79 79 | 68 47 22 00 20 | 35 55 31 51 51 | 00 83 63 22 55 |
| 40.76 66 26 84 | 57 99 99 90 37 | 36 63 32 08 58 | 37 40 13 68 97 | 87 64 31 07 83 |
| 02 17 79 18 05 | 12 59 52 57 02 | 22 07 90 47 03 | 28 14 11 30 79 | 20 69 22 40 98 |
| 95 17 82 06 53 | 31 51 10 96 46 | 92 06 88 07 77 | 56 11 50 81 69 | 40 23 72 51 39 |
| 35 76 22 42 92 | 96 11 83 44 80 | 34 68 35 48 77 | 33 42 40 90 60 | 73 96 53 97 86 |
| | | | | |
| 26 29 13 56 41 | 85 47 04 66 08 | 34 72 57 59 13 | 82 43 80 46 15 | 38 26 61 70 04 |
| 77 80 20 75 82 | 72 82 32 99 90 | 63 95 73 76 63 | 89 73 44 99 05 | 48 67 26 43 18 |
| 46 40 66 44 52 | 91 36 74 43 53 | 30 82 13 54 00 | 78 45 63 98 35 | 55 03 36 67 68 |
| 37 56 08 18 09 | 77 53 84 46 47 | 31 91 18 95 58 | 24 16 74 11 53 | 44 10 13 85 57 |
| 61 65 61 68 66 | 37 27 47 39 19 | 84 83 70 07 48 | 53 21 40 06 71 | 95 06 79 88 54 |
| | | | | |
| 93 43 69 64 07 | 34 18 04 52 35 | 56 27 09 24 86 | 61 85 53 83 45 | 19 90 70 99 00 |
| 21 96 60 12 99 | 11 20 99 45 18 | 48 13 93 55 34 | 18 37 79 49 90 | 65 97 38 20 46 |
| 95 20 47 97 97 | 27 37 83 28 71 | 00 06 41 41 74 | 45 89 09 39 84 | 51 67 11 52 49 |
| 97 86 21 78 73 | 10 65 81 92 59 | 58 76 17 14 97 | 04 76 62 16 17 | 17 95 70 45 80 |
| 69 92 06 34 13 | 59 71 74 17 32 | 27 55 10 24 19 | 23 71 82 13 74 | 63 52 52 01 41 |
| | | | | |
| 04 31 17 21 56 | 33 73 99 19 87 | 26 72 39 27 67 | 53 77 57 68 93 | 60 61 97 22 61 |
| 61 06 98 03 91 | 87 14 77 43 96 | 43 00 65 98 50 | 45 60 33 01 07 | 98 99 46 50 47 |
| 85 93 85 86 88 | 72 87 08 62 40 | 16 06 10 89 20 | 23 21 34 74 97 | 76 38 03 29 63 |
| 21 74 32 47 45 | 73 96 07 94 52 | 09 65 90 77 47 | 25 76 16 19 33 | 53 05 70 53 30 |
| 15 69 53 82 80 | 79 96 23 53 10 | 65 39 07 16 29 | 45 33 02 43 70 | 02 87 40 41 45 |

SOURCE: This table is reprinted with permission from Random Numbers III and IV of Table XXXIII of R. A. Fisher and F. Yates, *Statistical Tables for Biological, Agricultural, and Medical Research* (Edenburg: Oliver & Boyd, Ltd.).

**Table 1.** (CONTINUED)

| | | | | |
|---|---|---|---|---|
| 02 89 08 04 49 | 20 21 14 68 86 | 87 63 93 95 17 | 11 29 01 95 80 | 35 14 97 35 33 |
| 87 18 15 89 79 | 85 43 01 72 73 | 08 61 74 51 69 | 89 74 39 82 15 | 94 51 33 41 67 |
| 98 83 71 94 22 | 59 97 50 99 52 | 08 52 85 08 40 | 87 80 61 65 31 | 91 51 80 32 44 |
| 10 08 58 21 66 | 72 68 49 29 31 | 89 85 84 46 06 | 59 73 19 85 23 | 65 09 29 75 63 |
| 47 90 56 10 08 | 88 02 84 27 83 | 42 29 72 23 19 | 66 56 45 65 79 | 20 71 53 20 25 |
| | | | | |
| 22 85 61 68 90 | 49 64 92 85 44 | 16 40 12 89 88 | 50 14 49 81 06 | 01 82 77 45 12 |
| 67 80 43 79 33 | 12 83 11 41 16 | 25 58 19 68 70 | 77 02 54 00 52 | 53 43 37 15 26 |
| 27 62 50 96 72 | 79 44 61 40 15 | 14 53 40 65 39 | 27 31 58 50 28 | 11 39 03 34 25 |
| 33 78 80 87 15 | 38 30 06 38 21 | 14 47 47 07 26 | 54 96 87 53 32 | 40 36 40 96 76 |
| 13 13 92 66 99 | 47 24 49 57 74 | 32 25 43 62 17 | 10 97 11 69 84 | 99 63 22 32 98 |
| | | | | |
| 10 27 53 96 23 | 71 50 54 36 23 | 54 31 04 82 98 | 04 14 12 15 09 | 26 78 25 47 47 |
| 28 41 50 61 88 | 64 85 27 20 18 | 83 36 36 05 56 | 39 71 65 09 62 | 94 76 62 11 89 |
| 34 21 42 57 02 | 59 19 18 97 48 | 80 30 03 30 98 | 05 24 67 70 07 | 84 97 50 87 46 |
| 61 81 77 23 23 | 82 82 11 54 08 | 53 28 70 58 96 | 44 07 39 55 43 | 42 34 43 39 28 |
| 61 15 18 13 54 | 16 86 20 26 88 | 90 74 80 55 09 | 14 53 90 51 17 | 52 01 63 01 59 |
| | | | | |
| 91 76 21 64 64 | 44 91 13 32 97 | 75 31 62 66 54 | 84 80 32 75 77 | 56 08 25 70 29 |
| 00 97 79 08 06 | 37 30 28 59 85 | 53 56 68 53 40 | 01 74 39 59 73 | 30 19 99 85 48 |
| 36 46 18 34 94 | 75 20 80 27 77 | 78 91 69 16 00 | 08 43 18 73 68 | 67 69 61 34 25 |
| 88 98 99 60 50 | 65 95 79 42 94 | 93 62 40 89 96 | 43 56 47 71 66 | 46 76 29 67 02 |
| 04 37 59 87 21 | 05 02 03 24 17 | 47 97 81 56 51 | 92 34 86 01 82 | 55 51 33 12 91 |
| | | | | |
| 63 62 06 34 41 | 94 21 78 55 09 | 72 76 45 16 94 | 29 95 81 83 83 | 79 88 01 97 30 |
| 78 47 23 53 90 | 34 41 92 45 71 | 09 23 70 70 07 | 12 38 92 79 43 | 14 85 11 47 23 |
| 87 63 62 15 43 | 53 14 36 59 25 | 54 47 33 70 15 | 59 24 48 40 35 | 50 03 42 99 36 |
| 47 60 92 10 77 | 88 59 53 11 52 | 66 25 69 07 04 | 48 68 64 71 06 | 61 65 70 22 12 |
| 56 88 87 59 41 | 65 28 04 67 53 | 95 79 88 37 31 | 50 41 06 94 76 | 81 83 17 16 33 |
| | | | | |
| 02 57 45 86 67 | 73 43 07 34 48 | 44 26 87 93 29 | 77 09 61 67 84 | 06 69 44 77 75 |
| 31 54 14 13 17 | 48 62 11 90 60 | 68 12 93 64 28 | 46 24 79 16 76 | 14 60 25 51 01 |
| 28 50 16 43 36 | 28 97 85 58 99 | 67 22 52 76 23 | 24 70 36 54 54 | 59 28 61 71 96 |
| 63 29 62 66 50 | 02 63 45 52 38 | 67 63 47 54 75 | 83 24 78 43 20 | 92 63 13 47 48 |
| 45 65 58 26 51 | 76 96 59 38 72 | 86 57 45 71 46 | 44 67 76 14 55 | 44 88 01 62 12 |
| | | | | |
| 39 65 36 63 70 | 77 45 85 50 51 | 74 13 39 35 22 | 30 53 36 02 95 | 49 34 88 73 61 |
| 73 71 98 16 04 | 29 18 94 51 23 | 76 51 94 84 86 | 79 93 96 38 63 | 08 58 25 58 94 |
| 72 20 56 20 11 | 72 65 71 08 86 | 79 57 95 13 91 | 97 48 72 66 48 | 09 71 17 24 89 |
| 75 17 26 99 76 | 89 37 20 70 01 | 77 31 61 95 46 | 26 97 05 73 51 | 53 33 18 72 87 |
| 37 48 60 82 29 | 81 30 15 39 14 | 48 38 75 93 29 | 06 87 37 78 48 | 45 56 00 84 47 |
| | | | | |
| 68 08 02 80 72 | 83 71 46 30 49 | 89 17 95 88 29 | 02 39 56 03 46 | 97 74 06 56 17 |
| 14 23 98 61 67 | 70 52 85 01 50 | 01 84 02 78 43 | 10 62 98 19 41 | 18 83 99 47 99 |
| 49 08 96 21 44 | 25 27 99 41 28 | 07 41 08 34 66 | 19 42 74 39 91 | 41 96 53 78 72 |
| 78 37 06 08 43 | 63 61 62 42 29 | 39 68 95 10 96 | 09 24 23 00 62 | 56 12 80 73 16 |
| 37 21 34 17 68 | 68 96 83 23 56 | 32 84 60 15 31 | 44 73 67 34 77 | 91 15 79 74 58 |
| | | | | |
| 14 29 09 34 04 | 87 83 07 55 07 | 76 58 30 83 64 | 87 29 25 58 84 | 86 50 60 00 25 |
| 58 43 28 06 36 | 49 52 83 51 14 | 47 56 91 29 34 | 05 87 31 06 95 | 12 45 57 09 09 |
| 10 43 67 29 70 | 80 62 80 03 42 | 10 80 21 38 84 | 90 56 35 03 09 | 43 12 74 49 14 |
| 44 38 88 39 54 | 86 97 37 44 22 | 00 95 01 31 76 | 17 16 29 56 63 | 38 78 94 49 81 |
| 90 69 59 19 51 | 85 39 52 85 13 | 07 28 37 07 61 | 11 16 36 27 03 | 78 86 72 04 95 |

## Table 1. (CONTINUED)

| | | | | |
|---|---|---|---|---|
| 41 47 10 25 62 | 97 05 31 03 61 | 20 26 36 31 62 | 68 69 86 95 44 | 84 95 48 46 45 |
| 91 94 14 63 19 | 75 89 11 47 11 | 31 56 34 19 09 | 79 57 92 36 59 | 14 93 87 81 40 |
| 80 06 54 18 66 | 09 18 94 06 19 | 98 40 07 17 81 | 22 45 44 84 11 | 24 62 20 42 31 |
| 67 72 77 63 48 | 84 08 31 55 58 | 24 33 45 77 58 | 90 45 67 93 82 | 75 70 16 08 24 |
| 59 40 24 13 27 | 79 26 88 86 30 | 01 31 60 10 39 | 53 58 47 70 93 | 85 81 56 39 38 |
| | | | | |
| 05 90 35 89 95 | 01 61 16 96 94 | 50 78 13 69 36 | 37 68 53 37 31 | 71 26 35 03 71 |
| 44 43 80 69 98 | 46 68 05 14 82 | 90 78 50 05 62 | 77 79 13 57 44 | 59 60 10 39 56 |
| 61 81 31 96 82 | 00 57 25 60 59 | 46 72 60 18 77 | 55 66 12 62 11 | 08 99 55 64 57 |
| 42 88 07 10 05 | 24 98 65 63 21 | 47 21 61 88 32 | 27 80 30 21 60 | 10 92 35 36 12 |
| 77 94 30 05 39 | 28 10 99 00 27 | 12 73 73 99 12 | 49 99 57 94 82 | 96 88 57 17 91 |
| | | | | |
| 78 83 19 76 16 | 94 11 68 84 26 | 23 54 20 86 85 | 23 86 66 99 07 | 36 37 34 92 09 |
| 87 76 59 61 81 | 43 63 64 61 61 | 65 76 36 95 90 | 18 48 27 45 68 | 27 23 65 30 72 |
| 91 43 05 96 47 | 55 78 99 95 24 | 37 55 85 78 78 | 01 48 41 19 10 | 35 19 54 07 73 |
| 84 97 77 72 73 | 09 62 06 65 72 | 87 12 49 03 60 | 41 15 20 76 27 | 50 47 02 29 16 |
| 87 41 60 76 83 | 44 88 96 07 80 | 83 05 83 38 96 | 73 70 66 81 90 | 30 56 10 48 59 |

## Table 2. POISSON DISTRIBUTION

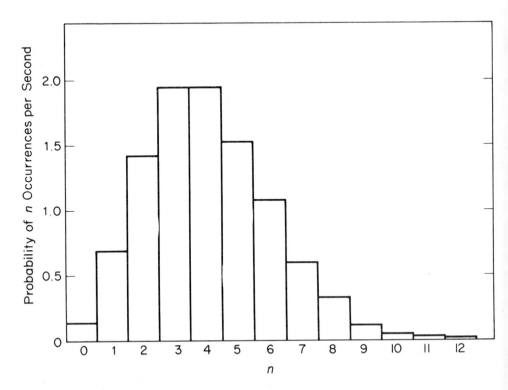

## Table 2. POISSON DISTRIBUTION

The table presents individual Poisson probabilities for the number of occurrences $n$ per unit of measurement, for selected values of $E(n)$, the mean number of occurrences per unit of measurement.
A blank space is left for values less than 0.0005.

$$P(n) = \frac{e^{-E(n)} \cdot E^n(n)}{n!}$$

Example:
For 4.0 occurrences per second:

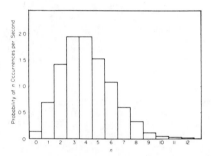

Values of E(n):

| $n$ | .001 | .002 | .003 | .004 | .005 | .006 | .007 | .008 | .009 | .01 | .02 | .03 | .04 | .05 | .06 | .07 | .08 | .09 | .10 | .15 | $n$ |
|---|---|---|---|---|---|---|---|---|---|---|---|---|---|---|---|---|---|---|---|---|---|
| 0 | 999 | 998 | 997 | 996 | 995 | 994 | 993 | 992 | 991 | 990 | 980 | 970 | 961 | 951 | 942 | 932 | 923 | 914 | 905 | 861 | 0 |
| 1 | 001 | 002 | 003 | 004 | 005 | 006 | 007 | 008 | 009 | 010 | 020 | 030 | 038 | 048 | 057 | 065 | 074 | 082 | 090 | 129 | 1 |
| 2 | | | | | | | | | | | | | 001 | 001 | 002 | 002 | 003 | 004 | 005 | 010 | 2 |

Values of E(n):

| $n$ | .20 | .25 | .30 | .40 | .50 | .60 | .70 | .80 | .90 | 1.0 | 1.1 | 1.2 | 1.3 | 1.4 | 1.5 | 1.6 | 1.7 | 1.8 | 1.9 | 2.0 | $n$ |
|---|---|---|---|---|---|---|---|---|---|---|---|---|---|---|---|---|---|---|---|---|---|
| 0 | 819 | 779 | 741 | 670 | 607 | 549 | 497 | 449 | 407 | 368 | 333 | 301 | 273 | 247 | 223 | 202 | 183 | 165 | 150 | 135 | 0 |
| 1 | 164 | 195 | 222 | 268 | 303 | 329 | 348 | 359 | 366 | 368 | 366 | 361 | 354 | 345 | 335 | 323 | 311 | 298 | 284 | 271 | 1 |
| 2 | 016 | 024 | 033 | 054 | 076 | 099 | 122 | 144 | 165 | 184 | 201 | 217 | 230 | 242 | 251 | 258 | 264 | 268 | 270 | 271 | 2 |
| 3 | 001 | 002 | 003 | 007 | 013 | 020 | 028 | 038 | 049 | 061 | 074 | 087 | 100 | 113 | 126 | 138 | 150 | 161 | 171 | 180 | 3 |
| 4 | | | | 001 | 002 | 003 | 005 | 008 | 011 | 015 | 020 | 026 | 032 | 039 | 047 | 055 | 063 | 072 | 081 | 090 | 4 |
| 5 | | | | | | | 001 | 001 | 002 | 003 | 004 | 006 | 008 | 011 | 014 | 018 | 022 | 026 | 031 | 036 | 5 |
| 6 | | | | | | | | | | 001 | 001 | 001 | 002 | 003 | 004 | 005 | 006 | 008 | 010 | 012 | 6 |
| 7 | | | | | | | | | | | | | 001 | 001 | 001 | 001 | 002 | 003 | 003 | 7 |
| 8 | | | | | | | | | | | | | | | | | | 001 | 001 | 8 |

Values of E(n):

| $n$ | 2.1 | 2.2 | 2.3 | 2.4 | 2.5 | 2.6 | 2.7 | 2.8 | 2.9 | 3.0 | 3.1 | 3.2 | 3.3 | 3.4 | 3.5 | 3.6 | 3.7 | 3.8 | 3.9 | 4.0 | $n$ |
|---|---|---|---|---|---|---|---|---|---|---|---|---|---|---|---|---|---|---|---|---|---|
| 0 | 122 | 111 | 100 | 091 | 082 | 074 | 067 | 061 | 055 | 050 | 045 | 041 | 037 | 033 | 030 | 027 | 025 | 022 | 020 | 018 | 0 |
| 1 | 257 | 244 | 231 | 218 | 205 | 193 | 181 | 170 | 160 | 149 | 140 | 130 | 122 | 113 | 106 | 098 | 091 | 085 | 079 | 073 | 1 |
| 2 | 270 | 268 | 265 | 261 | 257 | 251 | 245 | 238 | 231 | 224 | 216 | 209 | 201 | 193 | 185 | 177 | 169 | 162 | 154 | 147 | 2 |
| 3 | 189 | 197 | 203 | 209 | 214 | 218 | 220 | 222 | 224 | 224 | 224 | 223 | 221 | 219 | 216 | 212 | 209 | 205 | 200 | 195 | 3 |
| 4 | 099 | 108 | 117 | 125 | 134 | 141 | 149 | 156 | 162 | 168 | 173 | 178 | 182 | 186 | 189 | 191 | 193 | 194 | 195 | 195 | 4 |
| 5 | 042 | 048 | 054 | 060 | 067 | 074 | 080 | 087 | 094 | 101 | 107 | 114 | 120 | 126 | 132 | 138 | 143 | 148 | 152 | 156 | 5 |
| 6 | 015 | 017 | 021 | 024 | 028 | 032 | 036 | 041 | 045 | 050 | 056 | 061 | 066 | 072 | 077 | 083 | 088 | 094 | 099 | 104 | 6 |
| 7 | 004 | 005 | 007 | 008 | 010 | 012 | 014 | 016 | 019 | 022 | 025 | 028 | 031 | 035 | 039 | 042 | 047 | 051 | 055 | 060 | 7 |
| 8 | 001 | 002 | 002 | 002 | 003 | 004 | 005 | 006 | 007 | 008 | 010 | 011 | 013 | 015 | 017 | 019 | 022 | 024 | 027 | 030 | 8 |
| 9 | | | 001 | 001 | 001 | 001 | 002 | 002 | 003 | 003 | 004 | 005 | 006 | 007 | 008 | 009 | 010 | 012 | 013 | 9 |
| 10 | | | | | | | | | | 001 | 001 | 001 | 001 | 002 | 002 | 002 | 003 | 003 | 004 | 005 | 005 | 10 |
| 11 | | | | | | | | | | | | | | 001 | 001 | 001 | 001 | 001 | 002 | 002 | 11 |
| 12 | | | | | | | | | | | | | | | | | | 001 | 001 | 12 |

# Table 2. (CONTINUED) VALUES OF $p(n) = \dfrac{e^{-E(n)} E^n(n)}{n!}$

## Values of $E(n)$

| n | 4.1 | 4.2 | 4.3 | 4.4 | 4.5 | 4.6 | 4.7 | 4.8 | 4.9 | 5.0 | 5.1 | 5.2 | 5.3 | 5.4 | 5.5 | 5.6 | 5.7 | 5.8 | 5.9 | 6.0 | n |
|---|-----|-----|-----|-----|-----|-----|-----|-----|-----|-----|-----|-----|-----|-----|-----|-----|-----|-----|-----|-----|---|
| 0 | 017 | 015 | 014 | 012 | 011 | 010 | 009 | 008 | 007 | 007 | 006 | 006 | 005 | 005 | 004 | 004 | 003 | 003 | 003 | 002 | 0 |
| 1 | 068 | 063 | 058 | 054 | 050 | 046 | 043 | 040 | 036 | 034 | 031 | 029 | 026 | 024 | 022 | 021 | 019 | 018 | 016 | 015 | 1 |
| 2 | 139 | 132 | 125 | 119 | 112 | 106 | 100 | 095 | 089 | 084 | 079 | 075 | 070 | 066 | 062 | 058 | 054 | 051 | 048 | 045 | 2 |
| 3 | 190 | 185 | 180 | 174 | 169 | 163 | 157 | 152 | 146 | 140 | 135 | 129 | 124 | 119 | 113 | 108 | 103 | 098 | 094 | 089 | 3 |
| 4 | 195 | 194 | 193 | 192 | 190 | 188 | 185 | 182 | 179 | 175 | 172 | 168 | 164 | 160 | 156 | 152 | 147 | 143 | 138 | 134 | 4 |
| 5 | 160 | 163 | 166 | 169 | 171 | 173 | 174 | 175 | 175 | 175 | 175 | 175 | 174 | 173 | 171 | 170 | 168 | 166 | 163 | 161 | 5 |
| 6 | 109 | 114 | 119 | 124 | 128 | 132 | 136 | 140 | 143 | 146 | 149 | 151 | 154 | 156 | 157 | 158 | 159 | 160 | 160 | 161 | 6 |
| 7 | 064 | 069 | 073 | 078 | 082 | 087 | 091 | 096 | 100 | 104 | 109 | 113 | 116 | 120 | 123 | 127 | 130 | 133 | 135 | 138 | 7 |
| 8 | 033 | 036 | 039 | 043 | 046 | 050 | 054 | 058 | 061 | 065 | 069 | 073 | 077 | 081 | 085 | 089 | 092 | 096 | 100 | 103 | 8 |
| 9 | 015 | 017 | 019 | 021 | 023 | 026 | 028 | 031 | 033 | 036 | 039 | 042 | 045 | 049 | 052 | 055 | 059 | 062 | 065 | 069 | 9 |
| 10 | 006 | 007 | 008 | 009 | 010 | 012 | 013 | 015 | 016 | 018 | 020 | 022 | 024 | 026 | 029 | 031 | 033 | 036 | 039 | 041 | 10 |
| 11 | 002 | 003 | 003 | 004 | 004 | 005 | 006 | 006 | 007 | 008 | 009 | 010 | 012 | 013 | 014 | 016 | 017 | 019 | 021 | 023 | 11 |
| 12 | 001 | 001 | 001 | 001 | 002 | 002 | 002 | 003 | 003 | 003 | 004 | 005 | 005 | 006 | 007 | 007 | 008 | 009 | 010 | 011 | 12 |
| 13 |     |     |     | 001 | 001 | 001 | 001 | 001 | 001 | 001 | 002 | 002 | 002 | 002 | 003 | 003 | 004 | 004 | 005 | 005 | 13 |
| 14 |     |     |     |     |     |     |     |     |     |     | 001 | 001 | 001 | 001 | 001 | 001 | 001 | 002 | 002 | 002 | 14 |
| 15 |     |     |     |     |     |     |     |     |     |     |     |     |     |     |     |     | 001 | 001 | 001 | 001 | 15 |

## Values of $E(n)$

| n | 6.1 | 6.2 | 6.3 | 6.4 | 6.5 | 6.6 | 6.7 | 6.8 | 6.9 | 7.0 | 7.1 | 7.2 | 7.3 | 7.4 | 7.5 | 8.0 | 8.5 | 9.0 | 9.5 | 10.0 | n |
|---|-----|-----|-----|-----|-----|-----|-----|-----|-----|-----|-----|-----|-----|-----|-----|-----|-----|-----|-----|------|---|
| 0 | 002 | 002 | 002 | 002 | 002 | 001 | 001 | 001 | 001 | 001 | 001 | 001 | 001 | 001 | 001 |     |     |     |     |      | 0 |
| 1 | 014 | 013 | 012 | 011 | 010 | 009 | 008 | 008 | 007 | 006 | 006 | 005 | 005 | 005 | 004 | 003 | 002 | 001 | 001 |      | 1 |
| 2 | 042 | 039 | 036 | 034 | 032 | 030 | 028 | 026 | 024 | 022 | 021 | 019 | 018 | 017 | 016 | 011 | 007 | 005 | 003 | 002  | 2 |
| 3 | 085 | 081 | 077 | 073 | 069 | 065 | 062 | 058 | 055 | 052 | 049 | 046 | 044 | 041 | 039 | 029 | 021 | 015 | 011 | 008  | 3 |
| 4 | 129 | 125 | 121 | 116 | 112 | 108 | 103 | 099 | 095 | 091 | 087 | 084 | 080 | 076 | 073 | 057 | 044 | 034 | 025 | 019  | 4 |
| 5 | 158 | 155 | 152 | 149 | 145 | 142 | 138 | 135 | 131 | 128 | 124 | 120 | 117 | 113 | 109 | 092 | 075 | 061 | 048 | 038  | 5 |
| 6 | 160 | 160 | 159 | 159 | 157 | 156 | 155 | 153 | 151 | 149 | 147 | 144 | 142 | 139 | 137 | 122 | 107 | 091 | 076 | 063  | 6 |
| 7 | 140 | 142 | 144 | 145 | 146 | 147 | 148 | 149 | 149 | 149 | 149 | 148 | 147 | 146 | 140 | 129 | 117 | 104 | 090 |      | 7 |
| 8 | 107 | 110 | 113 | 116 | 119 | 121 | 124 | 126 | 128 | 130 | 132 | 134 | 135 | 136 | 137 | 140 | 138 | 132 | 123 | 113  | 8 |
| 9 | 072 | 076 | 079 | 082 | 086 | 089 | 092 | 095 | 098 | 101 | 104 | 107 | 110 | 112 | 114 | 124 | 130 | 132 | 130 | 125  | 9 |
| 10 | 044 | 047 | 050 | 053 | 056 | 059 | 062 | 065 | 068 | 071 | 074 | 077 | 080 | 083 | 086 | 099 | 110 | 119 | 124 | 125  | 10 |
| 11 | 024 | 025 | 029 | 031 | 033 | 035 | 038 | 040 | 043 | 045 | 048 | 050 | 053 | 056 | 059 | 072 | 085 | 097 | 107 | 114  | 11 |
| 12 | 012 | 014 | 015 | 016 | 018 | 019 | 021 | 023 | 025 | 026 | 028 | 030 | 032 | 034 | 037 | 048 | 060 | 073 | 084 | 095  | 12 |
| 13 | 006 | 007 | 007 | 008 | 009 | 010 | 011 | 012 | 013 | 014 | 015 | 017 | 018 | 020 | 021 | 030 | 040 | 050 | 062 | 073  | 13 |
| 14 | 003 | 003 | 003 | 004 | 004 | 005 | 005 | 006 | 006 | 007 | 008 | 009 | 009 | 010 | 011 | 017 | 024 | 032 | 042 | 052  | 14 |
| 15 | 001 | 001 | 001 | 002 | 002 | 002 | 002 | 003 | 003 | 003 | 004 | 004 | 005 | 005 | 006 | 009 | 014 | 019 | 027 | 035  | 15 |
| 16 |     |     | 001 | 001 | 001 | 001 | 001 | 001 | 001 | 001 | 002 | 002 | 002 | 002 | 003 | 005 | 007 | 011 | 016 | 022  | 16 |
| 17 |     |     |     |     |     |     |     | 001 | 001 | 001 | 001 | 001 | 001 | 001 | 001 | 002 | 004 | 006 | 009 | 013  | 17 |
| 18 |     |     |     |     |     |     |     |     |     |     |     |     |     |     |     | 001 | 002 | 003 | 005 | 007  | 18 |
| 19 |     |     |     |     |     |     |     |     |     |     |     |     |     |     |     |     | 001 | 001 | 002 | 004  | 19 |
| 20 |     |     |     |     |     |     |     |     |     |     |     |     |     |     |     |     |     | 001 | 001 | 002  | 20 |
| 21 |     |     |     |     |     |     |     |     |     |     |     |     |     |     |     |     |     |     | 001 | 21 |

SOURCE: Reproduced from *Statistical Analysis for Business Decisions* by Spurr and Bonini. Homewood, Ill.: 1967.

**Table 3.** THE SUMMED POISSON DISTRIBUTION FUNCTION

This table contains values of

$$P(n \geq X) = \sum_{n=X}^{n=\infty} \frac{e^{-E(n)}E^n(n)}{n!}$$

probability of having $X$ or more arrivals in a given time for which the mean arrival rate is $(n)$.

For example, if $E(n) = 1.8$ arrivals per second, the probability of having four or more arrivals per second is 0.1087.

|   |   |   |   |   | $E(n)$ |   |   |   |   |   |
|---|---|---|---|---|---|---|---|---|---|---|
| $X$ | 0.1 | 0.2 | 0.3 | 0.4 | 0.5 | 0.6 | 0.7 | 0.8 | 0.9 | 1.0 |
| 0 | 1.0000 | 1.0000 | 1.0000 | 1.0000 | 1.0000 | 1.0000 | 1.0000 | 1.0000 | 1.0000 | 1.0000 |
| 1 | .0952 | .1813 | .2592 | .3297 | .3935 | .4512 | .5034 | .5507 | .5934 | .6321 |
| 2 | .0047 | .0175 | .0369 | .0616 | .0902 | .1219 | .1558 | .1912 | .2275 | .2642 |
| 3 | .0002 | .0011 | .0036 | .0079 | .0144 | .0231 | .0341 | .0474 | .0629 | .0803 |
| 4 | .0000 | .0001 | .0003 | .0008 | .0018 | .0034 | .0058 | .0091 | .0135 | .0190 |
| 5 | .0000 | .0000 | .0000 | .0001 | .0002 | .0004 | .0008 | .0014 | .0023 | .0037 |
| 6 | .0000 | .0000 | .0000 | .0000 | .0000 | .0000 | .0001 | .0002 | .0003 | .0006 |
| 7 | .0000 | .0000 | .0000 | .0000 | .0000 | .0000 | .0000 | .0000 | .0000 | .0001 |

|   |   |   |   |   | $E(n)$ |   |   |   |   |   |
|---|---|---|---|---|---|---|---|---|---|---|
| $X$ | 1.1 | 1.2 | 1.3 | 1.4 | 1.5 | 1.6 | 1.7 | 1.8 | 1.9 | 2.0 |
| 0 | 1.0000 | 1.0000 | 1.0000 | 1.0000 | 1.0000 | 1.0000 | 1.0000 | 1.0000 | 1.0000 | 1.0000 |
| 1 | .6671 | .6988 | .7275 | .7543 | .7769 | .7981 | .8173 | .8347 | .8504 | .8647 |
| 2 | .3010 | .3374 | .3732 | .4082 | .4422 | .4751 | .5068 | .5372 | .5663 | .5940 |
| 3 | .0996 | .1205 | .1429 | .1665 | .1912 | .2166 | .2428 | .2694 | .2963 | .3233 |
| 4 | .0257 | .0338 | .0431 | .0537 | .0656 | .0788 | .0932 | .1087 | .1253 | .1429 |
| 5 | .0054 | .0077 | .0107 | .0143 | .0186 | .0237 | .0296 | .0364 | .0441 | .0527 |
| 6 | .0010 | .0015 | .0022 | .0032 | .0045 | .0060 | .0080 | .0104 | .0132 | .0166 |
| 7 | .0001 | .0003 | .0004 | .0006 | .0009 | .0013 | .0019 | .0026 | .0034 | .0045 |
| 8 | .0000 | .0000 | .0001 | .0001 | .0002 | .0003 | .0004 | .0006 | .0008 | .0011 |
| 9 | .0000 | .0000 | .0000 | .0000 | .0000 | .0000 | .0001 | .0001 | .0002 | .0002 |

|   |   |   |   |   | $E(n)$ |   |   |   |   |   |
|---|---|---|---|---|---|---|---|---|---|---|
| $X$ | 2.1 | 2.2 | 2.3 | 2.4 | 2.5 | 2.6 | 2.7 | 2.8 | 2.9 | 3.0 |
| 0 | 1.0000 | 1.0000 | 1.0000 | 1.0000 | 1.0000 | 1.0000 | 1.0000 | 1.0000 | 1.0000 | 1.0000 |
| 1 | .8775 | .8892 | .8997 | .9093 | .9179 | .9257 | .9328 | .9392 | .9450 | .9502 |
| 2 | .6204 | .6454 | .6691 | .6916 | .7127 | .7326 | .7513 | .7689 | .7854 | .8009 |
| 3 | .3504 | .3773 | .4040 | .4303 | .4562 | .4816 | .5064 | .5305 | .5540 | .5768 |
| 4 | .1614 | .1806 | .2007 | .2213 | .2424 | .2640 | .2859 | .3081 | .3304 | .3528 |
| 5 | .0621 | .0725 | .0838 | .0959 | .1088 | .1226 | .1371 | .1523 | .1682 | .1847 |
| 6 | .0204 | .0249 | .0300 | .0357 | .0420 | .0490 | .0567 | .0651 | .0742 | .0839 |
| 7 | .0059 | .0075 | .0094 | .0116 | .0142 | .0172 | .0206 | .0244 | .0287 | .0335 |
| 8 | .0015 | .0020 | .0026 | .0033 | .0042 | .0053 | .0066 | .0081 | .0099 | .0119 |
| 9 | .0003 | .0005 | .0006 | .0009 | .0011 | .0015 | .0019 | .0024 | .0031 | .0038 |
| 10 | .0001 | .0001 | .0001 | .0002 | .0003 | .0004 | .0005 | .0007 | .0009 | .0011 |
| 11 | .0000 | .0000 | .0000 | .0000 | .0001 | .0001 | .0001 | .0002 | .0002 | .0003 |
| 12 | .0000 | .0000 | .0000 | .0000 | .0000 | .0000 | .0000 | .0000 | .0001 | .0001 |

SOURCE: Reproduced from, *Handbook of Mathematical Tables*, Chemical Rubber Company. Reprinted by permission of the publisher.

**Table 3.** (CONTINUED)

| X | 3.1 | 3.2 | 3.3 | 3.4 | E(n) 3.5 | 3.6 | 3.7 | 3.8 | 3.9 | 4.0 |
|---|---|---|---|---|---|---|---|---|---|---|
| 0 | 1.0000 | 1.0000 | 1.0000 | 1.0000 | 1.0000 | 1.0000 | 1.0000 | 1.0000 | 1.0000 | 1.0000 |
| 1 | .9550 | .9592 | .9631 | .9666 | .9698 | .9727 | .9753 | .9776 | .9798 | .9817 |
| 2 | .8153 | .8288 | .8414 | .8532 | .8641 | .8743 | .8838 | .8926 | .9008 | .9082 |
| 3 | .5988 | .6201 | .6406 | .6603 | .6792 | .6973 | .7146 | .7311 | .7469 | .7619 |
| 4 | .3752 | .3975 | .4197 | .4416 | .4634 | .4848 | .5058 | .5265 | .5468 | .5665 |
| 5 | .2018 | .2194 | .2374 | .2558 | .2746 | .2936 | .3128 | .3322 | .3516 | .3712 |
| 6 | .0943 | .1054 | .1171 | .1295 | .1424 | .1559 | .1699 | .1844 | .1994 | .2149 |
| 7 | .0388 | .0446 | .0510 | .0579 | .0653 | .0733 | .0818 | .0909 | .1005 | .1107 |
| 8 | .0142 | .0168 | .0198 | .0231 | .0267 | .0308 | .0352 | .0401 | .0454 | .0511 |
| 9 | .0047 | .0057 | .0069 | .0083 | .0099 | .0117 | .0137 | .0160 | .0185 | .0214 |
| 10 | .0014 | .0018 | .0022 | .0027 | .0033 | .0040 | .0048 | .0058 | .0069 | .0081 |
| 11 | .0004 | .0005 | .0006 | .0008 | .0010 | .0013 | .0016 | .0019 | .0023 | .0028 |
| 12 | .0001 | .0001 | .0002 | .0002 | .0003 | .0004 | .0005 | .0006 | .0007 | .0009 |
| 13 | .0000 | .0000 | .0000 | .0001 | .0001 | .0001 | .0001 | .0002 | .0002 | .0003 |
| 14 | .0000 | .0000 | .0000 | .0000 | .0000 | .0000 | .0000 | .0000 | .0001 | .0001 |

| X | 4.1 | 4.2 | 4.3 | 4.4 | E(n) 4.5 | 4.6 | 4.7 | 4.8 | 4.9 | 5.0 |
|---|---|---|---|---|---|---|---|---|---|---|
| 0 | 1.0000 | 1.0000 | 1.0000 | 1.0000 | 1.0000 | 1.0000 | 1.0000 | 1.0000 | 1.0000 | 1.0000 |
| 1 | .9834 | .9850 | .9864 | .9877 | .9889 | .9899 | .9909 | .9918 | .9926 | .9933 |
| 2 | .9155 | .9220 | .9281 | .9337 | .9389 | .9437 | .9482 | .9523 | .9561 | .9596 |
| 3 | .7762 | .7898 | .8026 | .8149 | .8264 | .8374 | .8477 | .8575 | .8667 | .8753 |
| 4 | .5858 | .6046 | .6228 | .6406 | .6577 | .6743 | .6903 | .7058 | .7207 | .7350 |
| 5 | .3907 | .4102 | .4296 | .4488 | .4679 | .4868 | .5054 | .5237 | .5418 | .5595 |
| 6 | .2607 | .2469 | .2633 | .2801 | .2971 | .3142 | .3316 | .3490 | .3665 | .3840 |
| 7 | .1214 | .1325 | .1442 | .1564 | .1689 | .1820 | .1954 | .2092 | .2233 | .2378 |
| 8 | .0573 | .0639 | .0710 | .0786 | .0866 | .0951 | .1040 | .1133 | .1231 | .1334 |
| 9 | .0245 | .0279 | .0317 | .0358 | .0403 | .0451 | .0503 | .0558 | .0618 | .0681 |
| 10 | .0095 | .0111 | .0129 | .0149 | .0171 | .0195 | .0222 | .0251 | .0283 | .0318 |
| 11 | .0034 | .0041 | .0048 | .0057 | .0067 | .0078 | .0090 | .0104 | .0120 | .0137 |
| 12 | .0011 | .0014 | .0017 | .0020 | .0024 | .0029 | .0034 | .0040 | .0047 | .0055 |
| 13 | .0003 | .0004 | .0005 | .0007 | .0008 | .0010 | .0012 | .0014 | .0017 | .0020 |
| 14 | .0001 | .0001 | .0002 | .0002 | .0003 | .0003 | .0004 | .0005 | .0006 | .0007 |
| 15 | .0000 | .0000 | .0000 | .0001 | .0001 | .0001 | .0001 | .0001 | .0002 | .0002 |
| 16 | .0000 | .0000 | .0000 | .0000 | .0000 | .0000 | .0000 | .0000 | .0001 | .0001 |

| X | 5.1 | 5.2 | 5.3 | 5.4 | E(n) 5.5 | 5.6 | 5.7 | 5.8 | 5.9 | 6.0 |
|---|---|---|---|---|---|---|---|---|---|---|
| 0 | 1.0000 | 1.0000 | 1.0000 | 1.0000 | 1.0000 | 1.0000 | 1.0000 | 1.0000 | 1.0000 | 1.0000 |
| 1 | .9939 | .9945 | .9950 | .9955 | .9959 | .9963 | .9967 | .9970 | .9973 | .9975 |
| 2 | .9628 | .9658 | .9686 | .9711 | .9734 | .9756 | .9776 | .9794 | .9811 | .9826 |
| 3 | .8835 | .8912 | .8984 | .9052 | .9116 | .9176 | .9232 | .9285 | .9334 | .9380 |
| 4 | .7487 | .7619 | .7746 | .7867 | .7983 | .8094 | .8200 | .8300 | .8396 | .8488 |

**Table 3.** (CONTINUED)

| | | | | | $E(n)$ | | | | | |
|---|---|---|---|---|---|---|---|---|---|---|
| $X$ | 5.1 | 5.2 | 5.3 | 5.4 | 5.5 | 5.6 | 5.7 | 5.8 | 5.9 | 6.0 |
| 5 | .5769 | .5939 | .6105 | .6267 | .6425 | .6579 | .6728 | .6873 | .7013 | .7149 |
| 6 | .4016 | .4191 | .4365 | .4539 | .4711 | .4881 | .5050 | .5217 | .5381 | .5543 |
| 7 | .2526 | .2676 | .2829 | .2983 | .3140 | .3297 | .3456 | .3616 | .3776 | .3937 |
| 8 | .1440 | .1551 | .1665 | .1783 | .1905 | .2030 | .2159 | .2290 | .2424 | .2560 |
| 9 | .0748 | .0819 | .0894 | .0974 | .1056 | .1143 | .1234 | .1328 | .1426 | .1528 |
| 10 | .0356 | .0397 | .0441 | .0488 | .0538 | .0591 | .0648 | .0708 | .0772 | .0839 |
| 11 | .0156 | .0177 | .0200 | .0225 | .0253 | .0282 | .0314 | .0349 | .0386 | .0426 |
| 12 | .0063 | .0073 | .0084 | .0096 | .0110 | .0125 | .0141 | .0160 | .0179 | .0201 |
| 13 | .0024 | .0028 | .0033 | .0038 | .0045 | .0051 | .0059 | .0068 | .0078 | .0088 |
| 14 | .0008 | .0010 | .0012 | .0014 | .0017 | .0020 | .0023 | .0027 | .0031 | .0036 |
| 15 | .0003 | .0003 | .0004 | .0005 | .0006 | .0007 | .0009 | .0010 | .0012 | .0014 |
| 16 | .0001 | .0001 | .0001 | .0002 | .0002 | .0002 | .0003 | .0004 | .0004 | .0005 |
| 17 | .0000 | .0000 | .0000 | .0001 | .0001 | .0001 | .0001 | .0001 | .0001 | .0002 |
| 18 | .0000 | .0000 | .0000 | .0000 | .0000 | .0000 | .0000 | .0000 | .0000 | .0001 |

| | | | | | $E(n)$ | | | | | |
|---|---|---|---|---|---|---|---|---|---|---|
| $X$ | 6.1 | 6.2 | 6.3 | 6.4 | 6.5 | 6.6 | 6.7 | 6.8 | 6.9 | 7.0 |
| 0 | 1.0000 | 1.0000 | 1.0000 | 1.0000 | 1.0000 | 1.0000 | 1.0000 | 1.0000 | 1.0000 | 1.0000 |
| 1 | .9978 | .9980 | .9982 | .9983 | .9985 | .9986 | .9988 | .9989 | .9990 | .9991 |
| 2 | .9841 | .9854 | .9866 | .9877 | .9887 | .9897 | .9905 | .9913 | .9920 | .9927 |
| 3 | .9423 | .9464 | .9502 | .9537 | .9570 | .9600 | .9629 | .9656 | .9680 | .9704 |
| 4 | .8575 | .8658 | .8736 | .8811 | .8882 | .8948 | .9012 | .9072 | .9129 | .9182 |
| 5 | .7281 | .7408 | .7531 | .7649 | .7763 | .7873 | .7978 | .8080 | .8177 | .8270 |
| 6 | .5702 | .5859 | .6012 | .6163 | .6310 | .6453 | .6594 | .6730 | .6863 | .6993 |
| 7 | .4098 | .4258 | .4418 | .4577 | .4735 | .4892 | .5047 | .5201 | .5353 | .5503 |
| 8 | .2699 | .2840 | .2983 | .3127 | .3272 | .3419 | .3567 | .3715 | .3864 | .4013 |
| 9 | .1633 | .1741 | .1852 | .1967 | .2084 | .2204 | .2327 | .2452 | .2580 | .2709 |
| 10 | .0910 | .0984 | .1061 | .1142 | .1226 | .1314 | .1404 | .1498 | .1505 | .1695 |
| 11 | .0469 | .0514 | .0563 | .0614 | .0668 | .0726 | .0786 | .0849 | .0916 | .0985 |
| 12 | .0224 | .0250 | .0277 | .0307 | .0339 | .0373 | .0409 | .0448 | .0490 | .0534 |
| 13 | .0100 | .0113 | .0127 | .0143 | .0160 | .0179 | .0199 | .0221 | .0245 | .0270 |
| 14 | .0042 | .0048 | .0055 | .0063 | .0071 | .0080 | .0091 | .0102 | .0115 | .0128 |
| 15 | .0016 | .0019 | .0022 | .0026 | .0030 | .0034 | .0039 | .0044 | .0050 | .0057 |
| 16 | .0006 | .0007 | .0008 | .0010 | .0012 | .0014 | .0016 | .0018 | .0021 | .0024 |
| 17 | .0002 | .0003 | .0003 | .0004 | .0004 | .0005 | .0006 | .0007 | .0008 | .0010 |
| 18 | .0001 | .0001 | .0001 | .0001 | .0002 | .0002 | .0002 | .0003 | .0003 | .0004 |
| 19 | .0000 | .0000 | .0000 | .0000 | .0001 | .0001 | .0001 | .0001 | .0001 | .0001 |

| | | | | | $E(n)$ | | | | | |
|---|---|---|---|---|---|---|---|---|---|---|
| $X$ | 7.1 | 7.2 | 7.3 | 7.4 | 7.5 | 7.6 | 7.7 | 7.8 | 7.9 | 8.0 |
| 0 | 1.0000 | 1.0000 | 1.0000 | 1.0000 | 1.0000 | 1.0000 | 1.0000 | 1.0000 | 1.0000 | 1.0000 |
| 1 | .9992 | .9993 | .9993 | .9994 | .9994 | .9995 | .9995 | .9996 | .9996 | .9997 |
| 2 | .9933 | .9939 | .9944 | .9949 | .9953 | .9957 | .9961 | .9964 | .9967 | .9970 |
| 3 | .9725 | .9745 | .9764 | .9781 | .9797 | .9812 | .9826 | .9839 | .9851 | .9862 |
| 4 | .9233 | .9281 | .9326 | .9368 | .9409 | .9446 | .9482 | .9515 | .9547 | .9576 |

**Table 3.** (CONTINUED)

| X | 7.1 | 7.2 | 7.3 | 7.4 | E(n) 7.5 | 7.6 | 7.7 | 7.8 | 7.9 | 8.0 |
|---|---|---|---|---|---|---|---|---|---|---|
| 5 | .8359 | .8445 | .8527 | .8605 | .8679 | .8751 | .8819 | .8883 | .8945 | .9004 |
| 6 | .7119 | .7241 | .7360 | .7474 | .7586 | .7693 | .7797 | .7897 | .7994 | .8088 |
| 7 | .5651 | .5796 | .5940 | .6080 | .6218 | .6354 | .6486 | .6616 | .6743 | .6866 |
| 8 | .4162 | .4311 | .4459 | .4607 | .4754 | .4900 | .5044 | .5188 | .5330 | .5470 |
| 9 | .2840 | .2973 | .3108 | .3243 | .3380 | .3518 | .3657 | .3796 | .3935 | .4075 |
| 10 | .1798 | .1904 | .2012 | .2123 | .2236 | .2351 | .2469 | .2589 | .2710 | .2834 |
| 11 | .1058 | .1133 | .1212 | .1293 | .1378 | .1465 | .1555 | .1648 | .1743 | .1841 |
| 12 | .0580 | .0629 | .0681 | .0735 | .0792 | .0852 | .0915 | .0980 | .1048 | .1119 |
| 13 | .0297 | .0327 | .0358 | .0391 | .0427 | .0464 | .0504 | .0546 | .0591 | .0638 |
| 14 | .0143 | .0159 | .0176 | .0195 | .0216 | .0238 | .0261 | .0286 | .0313 | .0342 |
| 15 | .0065 | .0073 | .0082 | .0092 | .0101 | .0114 | .0127 | .0141 | .0156 | .0173 |
| 16 | .0028 | .0031 | .0036 | .0041 | .0046 | .0052 | .0059 | .0066 | .0074 | .0082 |
| 17 | .0011 | .0013 | .0015 | .0017 | .0020 | .0022 | .0026 | .0029 | .0033 | .0037 |
| 18 | .0004 | .0005 | .0006 | .0007 | .0008 | .0009 | .0011 | .0012 | .0014 | .0016 |
| 19 | .0002 | .0002 | .0002 | .0003 | .0003 | .0004 | .0004 | .0005 | .0006 | .0006 |
| 20 | .0001 | .0001 | .0001 | .0001 | .0001 | .0001 | .0002 | .0002 | .0002 | .0003 |
| 21 | .0000 | .0000 | .0000 | .0000 | .0000 | .0000 | .0000 | .0001 | .0001 | .0001 |

| X | 8.1 | 8.2 | 8.3 | 8.4 | E(n) 8.5 | 8.6 | 8.7 | 8.8 | 8.9 | 9.0 |
|---|---|---|---|---|---|---|---|---|---|---|
| 0 | 1.0000 | 1.0000 | 1.0000 | 1.0000 | 1.0000 | 1.0000 | 1.0000 | 1.0000 | 1.0000 | 1.0000 |
| 1 | .9997 | .9997 | .9998 | .9998 | .9998 | .9998 | .9998 | .9998 | .9999 | .9999 |
| 2 | .9972 | .9975 | .9977 | .9979 | .9981 | .9982 | .9984 | .9985 | .9987 | .9988 |
| 3 | .9873 | .9882 | .9891 | .9900 | .9907 | .9914 | .9921 | .9927 | .9932 | .9938 |
| 4 | .9604 | .9630 | .9654 | .9677 | .9699 | .9719 | .9738 | .9756 | .9772 | .9788 |
| 5 | .9060 | .9113 | .9163 | .9211 | .9256 | .9299 | .9340 | .9379 | .9416 | .9450 |
| 6 | .8178 | .8264 | .8347 | .8427 | .8504 | .8578 | .8648 | .8716 | .8781 | .8843 |
| 7 | .6987 | .7104 | .7219 | .7330 | .7348 | .7543 | .7645 | .7744 | .7840 | .7932 |
| 8 | .5609 | .5746 | .5881 | .6013 | .6144 | .6272 | .6398 | .6522 | .6643 | .6761 |
| 9 | .4214 | .4353 | .4493 | .4631 | .4769 | .4906 | .5042 | .5177 | .5311 | .5443 |
| 10 | .2959 | .3085 | .3212 | .3341 | .3470 | .3600 | .3731 | .3863 | .3994 | .4126 |
| 11 | .1942 | .2045 | .2150 | .2257 | .2366 | .2478 | .2591 | .2406 | .2822 | .2940 |
| 12 | .1193 | .1269 | .1348 | .1429 | .1513 | .1600 | .1689 | .1780 | .1874 | .1970 |
| 13 | .0687 | .0739 | .0793 | .0850 | .0909 | .0971 | .1035 | .1102 | .1171 | .1242 |
| 14 | .0372 | .0405 | .0439 | .0476 | .0514 | .0555 | .0597 | .0642 | .0689 | .0739 |
| 15 | .0190 | .0209 | .0229 | .0251 | .0274 | .0299 | .0325 | .0353 | .0383 | .0415 |
| 16 | .0092 | .0102 | .0113 | .0125 | .0138 | .0152 | .0168 | .0184 | .0202 | .0220 |
| 17 | .0042 | .0047 | .0053 | .0059 | .0066 | .0074 | .0082 | .0091 | .0101 | .0111 |
| 18 | .0018 | .0021 | .0023 | .0027 | .0030 | .0034 | .0038 | .0043 | .0048 | .0053 |
| 19 | .0008 | .0009 | .0010 | .0011 | .0013 | .0015 | .0017 | .0019 | .0022 | .0024 |
| 20 | .0003 | .0003 | .0004 | .0005 | .0005 | .0006 | .0007 | .0008 | .0009 | .0011 |
| 21 | .0001 | .0001 | .0002 | .0002 | .0002 | .0002 | .0003 | .0003 | .0004 | .0004 |
| 22 | .0000 | .0000 | .0001 | .0001 | .0001 | .0001 | .0001 | .0001 | .0002 | .0002 |
| 23 | .0000 | .0000 | .0000 | .0000 | .0000 | .0000 | .0000 | .0000 | .0001 | .0001 |

**Table 4.** THE INCOMPLETE GAMMA FUNCTION

$$\text{Prob}\,(t \leq T) = \left\{ \dfrac{\displaystyle\int_0^T \left[\dfrac{Rt}{E(t)}\right]^{R-1} e^{-Rt/E(t)}\,\dfrac{R}{E(t)}\,dt}{\displaystyle\int_0^\infty \left[\dfrac{Rt}{E(t)}\right]^{R-1} e^{-Rt/E(t)}\,\dfrac{R}{E(t)}\,dt} \right\}$$

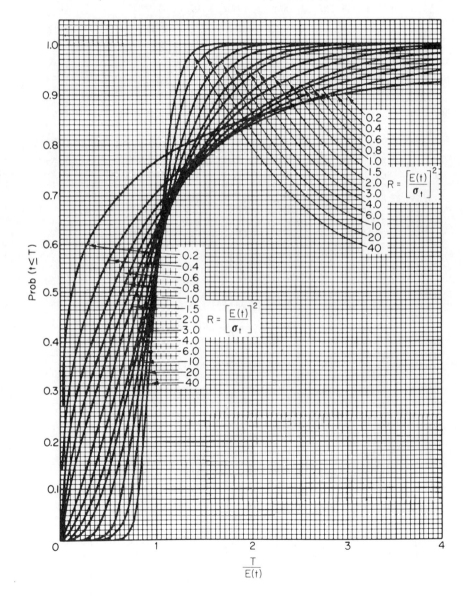

**Table 4.** (CONTINUED)   Values of Prob $(t \leq T)$

$$\frac{T}{E(t)} \qquad\qquad R = \left(\frac{E(t)}{\sigma_t}\right)^{\cdot 2}$$

| | .2 | .4 | .6 | .8 | 1.0 | 1.2 | 1.4 | 1.6 | 1.8 | 2.0 |
|---|---|---|---|---|---|---|---|---|---|---|
| 0.05 | 0.4329 | 0.2344 | 0.1350 | 0.0803 | 0.0488 | 0.0300 | 0.0187 | 0.0117 | 0.0074 | 0.0047 |
| 0.10 | 0.4964 | 0.3075 | 0.2023 | 0.1374 | 0.0952 | 0.0668 | 0.0473 | 0.0338 | 0.0243 | 0.0175 |
| 0.15 | 0.5375 | 0.3596 | 0.2552 | 0.1868 | 0.1393 | 0.1052 | 0.0802 | 0.0616 | 0.0476 | 0.0369 |
| 0.20 | 0.5683 | 0.4012 | 0.3000 | 0.2311 | 0.1813 | 0.1440 | 0.1154 | 0.0931 | 0.0755 | 0.0616 |
| 0.25 | 0.5933 | 0.4362 | 0.3393 | 0.2716 | 0.2212 | 0.1823 | 0.1516 | 0.1269 | 0.1068 | 0.0902 |
| 0.30 | 0.6143 | 0.4667 | 0.3744 | 0.3089 | 0.2592 | 0.2200 | 0.1882 | 0.1621 | 0.1403 | 0.1219 |
| 0.35 | 0.6326 | 0.4936 | 0.4063 | 0.3436 | 0.2953 | 0.2566 | 0.2248 | 0.1980 | 0.1753 | 0.1558 |
| 0.40 | 0.6486 | 0.5179 | 0.4356 | 0.3760 | 0.3297 | 0.2921 | 0.2608 | 0.2342 | 0.2112 | 0.1912 |
| 0.45 | 0.6630 | 0.5399 | 0.4625 | 0.4063 | 0.3624 | 0.3264 | 0.2962 | 0.2702 | 0.2475 | 0.2275 |
| 0.50 | 0.6760 | 0.5601 | 0.4876 | 0.4349 | 0.3935 | 0.3594 | 0.3306 | 0.3057 | 0.2837 | 0.2642 |
| 0.55 | 0.6879 | 0.5788 | 0.5109 | 0.4617 | 0.4230 | 0.3912 | 0.3641 | 0.3405 | 0.3196 | 0.3010 |
| 0.60 | 0.6989 | 0.5961 | 0.5328 | 0.4871 | 0.4512 | 0.4216 | 0.3964 | 0.3744 | 0.3549 | 0.3374 |
| 0.65 | 0.7091 | 0.6122 | 0.5533 | 0.5110 | 0.4780 | 0.4508 | 0.4276 | 0.4074 | 0.3894 | 0.3732 |
| 0.70 | 0.7185 | 0.6273 | 0.5726 | 0.5336 | 0.5034 | 0.4786 | 0.4576 | 0.4392 | 0.4229 | 0.4082 |
| 0.75 | 0.7273 | 0.6415 | 0.5908 | 0.5551 | 0.5276 | 0.5053 | 0.4863 | 0.4699 | 0.4553 | 0.4422 |
| 0.80 | 0.7356 | 0.6548 | 0.6080 | 0.5754 | 0.5507 | 0.5307 | 0.5139 | 0.4994 | 0.4865 | 0.4751 |
| 0.85 | 0.7434 | 0.6675 | 0.6242 | 0.5947 | 0.5726 | 0.5549 | 0.5402 | 0.5276 | 0.5166 | 0.5068 |
| 0.90 | 0.7508 | 0.6794 | 0.6396 | 0.6131 | 0.5934 | 0.5780 | 0.5653 | 0.5546 | 0.5453 | 0.5372 |
| 0.95 | 0.7578 | 0.6907 | 0.6543 | 0.6305 | 0.6133 | 0.6000 | 0.5893 | 0.5804 | 0.5728 | 0.5662 |
| 1.00 | 0.7644 | 0.7014 | 0.6682 | 0.6470 | 0.6321 | 0.6209 | 0.6121 | 0.6050 | 0.5990 | 0.5940 |
| 1.05 | 0.7707 | 0.7117 | 0.6814 | 0.6628 | 0.6501 | 0.6408 | 0.6338 | 0.6283 | 0.6240 | 0.6204 |
| 1.10 | 0.7767 | 0.7214 | 0.6940 | 0.6778 | 0.6671 | 0.6598 | 0.6545 | 0.6505 | 0.6476 | 0.6454 |
| 1.15 | 0.7825 | 0.7307 | 0.7060 | 0.6920 | 0.6834 | 0.6777 | 0.6740 | 0.6716 | 0.6701 | 0.6691 |
| 1.20 | 0.7880 | 0.7395 | 0.7175 | 0.7056 | 0.6988 | 0.6948 | 0.6926 | 0.6916 | 0.6913 | 0.6916 |
| 1.25 | 0.7932 | 0.7480 | 0.7284 | 0.7186 | 0.7135 | 0.7111 | 0.7102 | 0.7105 | 0.7113 | 0.7127 |
| 1.30 | 0.7983 | 0.7561 | 0.7388 | 0.7309 | 0.7275 | 0.7265 | 0.7269 | 0.7283 | 0.7303 | 0.7326 |
| 1.35 | 0.8031 | 0.7639 | 0.7488 | 0.7427 | 0.7408 | 0.7411 | 0.7427 | 0.7452 | 0.7481 | 0.7513 |
| 1.40 | 0.8077 | 0.7713 | 0.7583 | 0.7539 | 0.7534 | 0.7550 | 0.7577 | 0.7611 | 0.7649 | 0.7689 |
| 1.45 | 0.8122 | 0.7785 | 0.7675 | 0.7646 | 0.7654 | 0.7681 | 0.7718 | 0.7761 | 0.7807 | 0.7854 |
| 1.50 | 0.8165 | 0.7853 | 0.7762 | 0.7748 | 0.7769 | 0.7806 | 0.7852 | 0.7903 | 0.7955 | 0.8009 |
| 1.55 | 0.8207 | 0.7919 | 0.7846 | 0.7846 | 0.7878 | 0.7924 | 0.7979 | 0.8036 | 0.8095 | 0.8153 |
| 1.60 | 0.8247 | 0.7983 | 0.7926 | 0.7939 | 0.7981 | 0.8037 | 0.8098 | 0.8161 | 0.8225 | 0.8288 |
| 1.65 | 0.8286 | 0.8044 | 0.8003 | 0.8028 | 0.8079 | 0.8143 | 0.8211 | 0.8279 | 0.8348 | 0.8414 |
| 1.70 | 0.8323 | 0.8102 | 0.8076 | 0.8112 | 0.8173 | 0.8244 | 0.8317 | 0.8390 | 0.8462 | 0.8532 |
| 1.75 | 0.8359 | 0.8159 | 0.8147 | 0.8194 | 0.8262 | 0.8339 | 0.8417 | 0.8495 | 0.8569 | 0.8641 |
| 1.80 | 0.8394 | 0.8213 | 0.8214 | 0.8271 | 0.8347 | 0.8429 | 0.8512 | 0.8592 | 0.8670 | 0.8743 |
| 1.85 | 0.8428 | 0.8266 | 0.8279 | 0.8345 | 0.8428 | 0.8515 | 0.8601 | 0.8684 | 0.8763 | 0.8838 |
| 1.90 | 0.8461 | 0.8316 | 0.8342 | 0.8416 | 0.8504 | 0.8596 | 0.8685 | 0.8771 | 0.8851 | 0.8926 |
| 1.95 | 0.8492 | 0.8365 | 0.8402 | 0.8483 | 0.8577 | 0.8673 | 0.8764 | 0.8851 | 0.8933 | 0.9008 |
| 2.00 | 0.8523 | 0.8412 | 0.8459 | 0.8548 | 0.8647 | 0.8745 | 0.8839 | 0.8927 | 0.9009 | 0.9084 |
| 2.10 | 0.8582 | 0.8502 | 0.8568 | 0.8669 | 0.8775 | 0.8879 | 0.8976 | 0.9065 | 0.9146 | 0.9220 |
| 2.20 | 0.8638 | 0.8585 | 0.8668 | 0.8779 | 0.8892 | 0.8999 | 0.9097 | 0.9185 | 0.9265 | 0.9337 |
| 2.30 | 0.8691 | 0.8664 | 0.8761 | 0.8880 | 0.8997 | 0.9106 | 0.9204 | 0.9291 | 0.9368 | 0.9437 |
| 2.40 | 0.8740 | 0.8737 | 0.8846 | 0.8972 | 0.9093 | 0.9202 | 0.9298 | 0.9383 | 0.9458 | 0.9523 |
| 2.50 | 0.8788 | 0.8805 | 0.8926 | 0.9057 | 0.9179 | 0.9287 | 0.9382 | 0.9464 | 0.9535 | 0.9596 |
| 2.60 | 0.8833 | 0.8870 | 0.8999 | 0.9135 | 0.9257 | 0.9364 | 0.9456 | 0.9534 | 0.9601 | 0.9658 |
| 2.70 | 0.8875 | 0.8930 | 0.9068 | 0.9206 | 0.9328 | 0.9433 | 0.9521 | 0.9596 | 0.9658 | 0.9711 |
| 2.80 | 0.8916 | 0.8987 | 0.9131 | 0.9271 | 0.9392 | 0.9494 | 0.9579 | 0.9649 | 0.9708 | 0.9756 |
| 2.90 | 0.8954 | 0.9040 | 0.9190 | 0.9330 | 0.9450 | 0.9549 | 0.9630 | 0.9696 | 0.9750 | 0.9794 |
| 3.00 | 0.8991 | 0.9090 | 0.9244 | 0.9385 | 0.9502 | 0.9597 | 0.9674 | 0.9736 | 0.9786 | 0.9826 |
| 3.10 | 0.9026 | 0.9137 | 0.9295 | 0.9435 | 0.9550 | 0.9641 | 0.9714 | 0.9772 | 0.9817 | 0.9854 |
| 3.20 | 0.9060 | 0.9182 | 0.9342 | 0.9481 | 0.9592 | 0.9680 | 0.9749 | 0.9802 | 0.9844 | 0.9877 |
| 3.30 | 0.9092 | 0.9224 | 0.9386 | 0.9523 | 0.9631 | 0.9715 | 0.9779 | 0.9829 | 0.9867 | 0.9897 |
| 3.40 | 0.9123 | 0.9263 | 0.9427 | 0.9562 | 0.9666 | 0.9746 | 0.9806 | 0.9852 | 0.9887 | 0.9913 |
| 3.50 | 0.9152 | 0.9301 | 0.9465 | 0.9597 | 0.9698 | 0.9773 | 0.9830 | 0.9872 | 0.9903 | 0.9927 |

**Table 4.** (CONTINUED)        Values of Prob $(t \leq T)$

$$\frac{T}{E(t)} \qquad\qquad R = \left(\frac{E(t)}{\sigma_t}\right)^2$$

| | .2 | .4 | .6 | .8 | 1.0 | 1.2 | 1.4 | 1.6 | 1.8 | 2.0 |
|---|---|---|---|---|---|---|---|---|---|---|
| 3.60 | 0.9180 | 0.9336 | 0.9501 | 0.9630 | 0.9727 | 0.9798 | 0.9851 | 0.9889 | 0.9918 | 0.9939 |
| 3.70 | 0.9207 | 0.9370 | 0.9534 | 0.9660 | 0.9753 | 0.9820 | 0.9869 | 0.9904 | 0.9930 | 0.9949 |
| 3.80 | 0.9233 | 0.9401 | 0.9564 | 0.9687 | 0.9776 | 0.9840 | 0.9885 | 0.9917 | 0.9940 | 0.9957 |
| 3.90 | 0.9258 | 0.9431 | 0.9593 | 0.9713 | 0.9798 | 0.9857 | 0.9899 | 0.9929 | 0.9949 | 0.9964 |
| 4.00 | 0.9282 | 0.9459 | 0.9620 | 0.9736 | 0.9817 | 0.9873 | 0.9912 | 0.9938 | 0.9957 | 0.9970 |
| 4.10 | 0.9305 | 0.9486 | 0.9644 | 0.9757 | 0.9834 | 0.9887 | 0.9922 | 0.9947 | 0.9963 | 0.9975 |
| 4.20 | 0.9327 | 0.9511 | 0.9668 | 0.9777 | 0.9850 | 0.9899 | 0.9932 | 0.9954 | 0.9969 | 0.9979 |
| 4.30 | 0.9348 | 0.9535 | 0.9689 | 0.9795 | 0.9864 | 0.9910 | 0.9940 | 0.9960 | 0.9974 | 0.9982 |
| 4.40 | 0.9369 | 0.9558 | 0.9709 | 0.9811 | 0.9877 | 0.9920 | 0.9948 | 0.9966 | 0.9978 | 0.9985 |
| 4.50 | 0.9388 | 0.9579 | 0.9728 | 0.9826 | 0.9889 | 0.9929 | 0.9954 | 0.9971 | 0.9981 | 0.9988 |
| 4.60 | 0.9407 | 0.9600 | 0.9746 | 0.9840 | 0.9899 | 0.9937 | 0.9960 | 0.9975 | 0.9984 | 0.9990 |
| 4.70 | 0.9425 | 0.9619 | 0.9762 | 0.9853 | 0.9909 | 0.9944 | 0.9965 | 0.9978 | 0.9986 | 0.9991 |
| 4.80 | 0.9443 | 0.9638 | 0.9778 | 0.9865 | 0.9918 | 0.9950 | 0.9969 | 0.9981 | 0.9988 | 0.9993 |
| 4.90 | 0.9460 | 0.9655 | 0.9792 | 0.9876 | 0.9926 | 0.9955 | 0.9973 | 0.9984 | 0.9990 | 0.9994 |
| 5.00 | 0.9476 | 0.9671 | 0.9805 | 0.9886 | 0.9933 | 0.9960 | 0.9976 | 0.9986 | 0.9992 | 0.9995 |
| 5.10 | 0.9492 | 0.9687 | 0.9818 | 0.9895 | 0.9939 | 0.9965 | 0.9979 | 0.9988 | 0.9993 | 0.9996 |
| 5.20 | 0.9507 | 0.9702 | 0.9829 | 0.9903 | 0.9945 | 0.9968 | 0.9982 | 0.9990 | 0.9994 | 0.9997 |
| 5.30 | 0.9522 | 0.9716 | 0.9840 | 0.9911 | 0.9950 | 0.9972 | 0.9984 | 0.9991 | 0.9995 | 0.9997 |
| 5.40 | 0.9536 | 0.9730 | 0.9851 | 0.9918 | 0.9955 | 0.9975 | 0.9986 | 0.9992 | 0.9996 | 0.9998 |
| 5.50 | 0.9550 | 0.9742 | 0.9860 | 0.9924 | 0.9959 | 0.9978 | 0.9988 | 0.9993 | 0.9996 | 0.9998 |
| 5.60 | 0.9563 | 0.9755 | 0.9869 | 0.9930 | 0.9963 | 0.9980 | 0.9989 | 0.9994 | 0.9997 | 0.9998 |
| 5.70 | 0.9576 | 0.9766 | 0.9877 | 0.9936 | 0.9967 | 0.9982 | 0.9991 | 0.9995 | 0.9997 | 0.9999 |
| 5.80 | 0.9588 | 0.9777 | 0.9885 | 0.9941 | 0.9970 | 0.9984 | 0.9992 | 0.9996 | 0.9998 | 0.9999 |
| 5.90 | 0.9600 | 0.9788 | 0.9892 | 0.9946 | 0.9973 | 0.9986 | 0.9993 | 0.9996 | 0.9998 | 0.9999 |
| 6.00 | 0.9611 | 0.9797 | 0.9899 | 0.9950 | 0.9975 | 0.9988 | 0.9994 | 0.9997 | 0.9998 | 0.9999 |
| 6.10 | 0.9623 | 0.9807 | 0.9906 | 0.9954 | 0.9978 | 0.9989 | 0.9995 | 0.9997 | 0.9999 | 0.9999 |
| 6.20 | 0.9633 | 0.9816 | 0.9912 | 0.9958 | 0.9980 | 0.9990 | 0.9995 | 0.9998 | 0.9999 | 0.9999 |
| 6.30 | 0.9644 | 0.9824 | 0.9917 | 0.9961 | 0.9982 | 0.9991 | 0.9996 | 0.9998 | 0.9999 | 1.0000 |
| 6.40 | 0.9654 | 0.9833 | 0.9922 | 0.9964 | 0.9983 | 0.9992 | 0.9996 | 0.9998 | 0.9999 | 1.0000 |
| 6.50 | 0.9664 | 0.9840 | 0.9927 | 0.9967 | 0.9985 | 0.9993 | 0.9997 | 0.9999 | 0.9999 | 1.0000 |
| 6.60 | 0.9673 | 0.9848 | 0.9932 | 0.9970 | 0.9986 | 0.9994 | 0.9997 | 0.9999 | 0.9999 | 1.0000 |
| 6.70 | 0.9682 | 0.9855 | 0.9936 | 0.9972 | 0.9988 | 0.9995 | 0.9998 | 0.9999 | 1.0000 | 1.0000 |
| 6.80 | 0.9691 | 0.9861 | 0.9940 | 0.9974 | 0.9989 | 0.9995 | 0.9998 | 0.9999 | 1.0000 | 1.0000 |
| 6.90 | 0.9700 | 0.9868 | 0.9944 | 0.9976 | 0.9990 | 0.9996 | 0.9998 | 0.9999 | 1.0000 | 1.0000 |
| 7.00 | 0.9708 | 0.9874 | 0.9947 | 0.9978 | 0.9991 | 0.9996 | 0.9998 | 0.9999 | 1.0000 | 1.0000 |
| 7.10 | 0.9716 | 0.9880 | 0.9951 | 0.9980 | 0.9992 | 0.9997 | 0.9999 | 0.9999 | 1.0000 | 1.0000 |
| 7.20 | 0.9724 | 0.9885 | 0.9954 | 0.9981 | 0.9993 | 0.9997 | 0.9999 | 0.9999 | 1.0000 | 1.0000 |
| 7.30 | 0.9732 | 0.9890 | 0.9957 | 0.9983 | 0.9993 | 0.9997 | 0.9999 | 1.0000 | 1.0000 | 1.0000 |
| 7.40 | 0.9739 | 0.9895 | 0.9959 | 0.9984 | 0.9994 | 0.9998 | 0.9999 | 1.0000 | 1.0000 | 1.0000 |
| 7.50 | 0.9746 | 0.9900 | 0.9962 | 0.9986 | 0.9994 | 0.9998 | 0.9999 | 1.0000 | 1.0000 | 1.0000 |
| 7.60 | 0.9753 | 0.9905 | 0.9964 | 0.9987 | 0.9995 | 0.9998 | 0.9999 | 1.0000 | 1.0000 | 1.0000 |
| 7.70 | 0.9760 | 0.9909 | 0.9967 | 0.9988 | 0.9995 | 0.9998 | 0.9999 | 1.0000 | 1.0000 | 1.0000 |
| 7.80 | 0.9766 | 0.9913 | 0.9969 | 0.9989 | 0.9996 | 0.9999 | 0.9999 | 1.0000 | 1.0000 | 1.0000 |
| 7.90 | 0.9773 | 0.9917 | 0.9971 | 0.9990 | 0.9996 | 0.9999 | 1.0000 | 1.0000 | 1.0000 | 1.0000 |
| 8.00 | 0.9779 | 0.9921 | 0.9972 | 0.9990 | 0.9997 | 0.9999 | 1.0000 | 1.0000 | 1.0000 | 1.0000 |
| 8.10 | 0.9785 | 0.9924 | 0.9974 | 0.9991 | 0.9997 | 0.9999 | 1.0000 | 1.0000 | 1.0000 | 1.0000 |
| 8.20 | 0.9790 | 0.9928 | 0.9976 | 0.9992 | 0.9997 | 0.9999 | 1.0000 | 1.0000 | 1.0000 | 1.0000 |
| 8.30 | 0.9796 | 0.9931 | 0.9977 | 0.9993 | 0.9998 | 0.9999 | 1.0000 | 1.0000 | 1.0000 | 1.0000 |
| 8.40 | 0.9801 | 0.9934 | 0.9979 | 0.9993 | 0.9998 | 0.9999 | 1.0000 | 1.0000 | 1.0000 | 1.0000 |
| 8.50 | 0.9807 | 0.9937 | 0.9980 | 0.9994 | 0.9998 | 0.9999 | 1.0000 | 1.0000 | 1.0000 | 1.0000 |
| 8.60 | 0.9812 | 0.9940 | 0.9981 | 0.9994 | 0.9998 | 0.9999 | 1.0000 | 1.0000 | 1.0000 | 1.0000 |
| 8.70 | 0.9817 | 0.9942 | 0.9982 | 0.9995 | 0.9998 | 0.9999 | 1.0000 | 1.0000 | 1.0000 | 1.0000 |
| 8.80 | 0.9822 | 0.9945 | 0.9984 | 0.9995 | 0.9998 | 1.0000 | 1.0000 | 1.0000 | 1.0000 | 1.0000 |
| 8.90 | 0.9826 | 0.9947 | 0.9985 | 0.9995 | 0.9999 | 1.0000 | 1.0000 | 1.0000 | 1.0000 | 1.0000 |
| 9.00 | 0.9831 | 0.9950 | 0.9985 | 0.9996 | 0.9999 | 1.0000 | 1.0000 | 1.0000 | 1.0000 | 1.0000 |

**Table 4.** (CONTINUED)    Values of Prob $(t \leq T)$

$$\frac{T}{E(t)} \qquad\qquad R = \left(\frac{E(t)}{\sigma_t}\right)^2$$

| | 2.2 | 2.4 | 2.6 | 2.8 | 3.0 | 3.5 | 4.0 | 4.5 | 5.0 | 5.5 |
|---|---|---|---|---|---|---|---|---|---|---|
| 0.05 | 0.0030 | 0.0019 | 0.0012 | 0.0008 | 0.0005 | 0.0002 | 0.0001 | 0.0000 | 0.0000 | 0.0000 |
| 0.10 | 0.0127 | 0.0092 | 0.0067 | 0.0049 | 0.0036 | 0.0017 | 0.0008 | 0.0004 | 0.0002 | 0.0001 |
| 0.15 | 0.0288 | 0.0225 | 0.0176 | 0.0138 | 0.0109 | 0.0060 | 0.0034 | 0.0019 | 0.0011 | 0.0006 |
| 0.20 | 0.0503 | 0.0413 | 0.0340 | 0.0280 | 0.0231 | 0.0144 | 0.0091 | 0.0058 | 0.0037 | 0.0023 |
| 0.25 | 0.0765 | 0.0650 | 0.0554 | 0.0473 | 0.0405 | 0.0276 | 0.0190 | 0.0131 | 0.0091 | 0.0064 |
| 0.30 | 0.1063 | 0.0929 | 0.0814 | 0.0715 | 0.0629 | 0.0459 | 0.0338 | 0.0250 | 0.0186 | 0.0139 |
| 0.35 | 0.1389 | 0.1241 | 0.1112 | 0.0998 | 0.0897 | 0.0692 | 0.0537 | 0.0420 | 0.0329 | 0.0259 |
| 0.40 | 0.1736 | 0.1580 | 0.1441 | 0.1317 | 0.1205 | 0.0971 | 0.0788 | 0.0643 | 0.0527 | 0.0433 |
| 0.45 | 0.2097 | 0.1938 | 0.1794 | 0.1664 | 0.1546 | 0.1292 | 0.1087 | 0.0919 | 0.0780 | 0.0664 |
| 0.50 | 0.2467 | 0.2309 | 0.2165 | 0.2033 | 0.1912 | 0.1648 | 0.1429 | 0.1245 | 0.1088 | 0.0954 |
| 0.55 | 0.2841 | 0.2687 | 0.2546 | 0.2417 | 0.2296 | 0.2031 | 0.1806 | 0.1614 | 0.1446 | 0.1300 |
| 0.60 | 0.3214 | 0.3069 | 0.2934 | 0.2810 | 0.2694 | 0.2435 | 0.2213 | 0.2019 | 0.1847 | 0.1695 |
| 0.65 | 0.3584 | 0.3449 | 0.3323 | 0.3207 | 0.3098 | 0.2853 | 0.2640 | 0.2452 | 0.2283 | 0.2132 |
| 0.70 | 0.3948 | 0.3824 | 0.3710 | 0.3603 | 0.3504 | 0.3278 | 0.3081 | 0.2904 | 0.2746 | 0.2601 |
| 0.75 | 0.4302 | 0.4192 | 0.4091 | 0.3996 | 0.3907 | 0.3705 | 0.3528 | 0.3369 | 0.3225 | 0.3092 |
| 0.80 | 0.4646 | 0.4551 | 0.4462 | 0.4380 | 0.4303 | 0.4128 | 0.3975 | 0.3837 | 0.3712 | 0.3597 |
| 0.85 | 0.4979 | 0.4898 | 0.4823 | 0.4754 | 0.4689 | 0.4544 | 0.4416 | 0.4302 | 0.4199 | 0.4104 |
| 0.90 | 0.5298 | 0.5232 | 0.5171 | 0.5116 | 0.5064 | 0.4948 | 0.4848 | 0.4759 | 0.4679 | 0.4606 |
| 0.95 | 0.5604 | 0.5553 | 0.5506 | 0.5463 | 0.5424 | 0.5338 | 0.5265 | 0.5202 | 0.5146 | 0.5096 |
| 1.00 | 0.5896 | 0.5858 | 0.5825 | 0.5795 | 0.5768 | 0.5711 | 0.5665 | 0.5627 | 0.5595 | 0.5567 |
| 1.05 | 0.6174 | 0.6150 | 0.6129 | 0.6111 | 0.6096 | 0.6066 | 0.6046 | 0.6032 | 0.6022 | 0.6016 |
| 1.10 | 0.6438 | 0.6425 | 0.6416 | 0.6410 | 0.6406 | 0.6402 | 0.6406 | 0.6414 | 0.6425 | 0.6438 |
| 1.15 | 0.6687 | 0.6686 | 0.6688 | 0.6692 | 0.6698 | 0.6718 | 0.6743 | 0.6771 | 0.6801 | 0.6832 |
| 1.20 | 0.6922 | 0.6932 | 0.6944 | 0.6958 | 0.6973 | 0.7014 | 0.7058 | 0.7103 | 0.7149 | 0.7195 |
| 1.25 | 0.7144 | 0.7163 | 0.7184 | 0.7206 | 0.7229 | 0.7289 | 0.7350 | 0.7410 | 0.7470 | 0.7529 |
| 1.30 | 0.7352 | 0.7380 | 0.7409 | 0.7439 | 0.7469 | 0.7544 | 0.7619 | 0.7692 | 0.7763 | 0.7832 |
| 1.35 | 0.7548 | 0.7583 | 0.7619 | 0.7655 | 0.7691 | 0.7781 | 0.7867 | 0.7950 | 0.8030 | 0.8105 |
| 1.40 | 0.7731 | 0.7773 | 0.7815 | 0.7856 | 0.7898 | 0.7998 | 0.8094 | 0.8184 | 0.8270 | 0.8351 |
| 1.45 | 0.7902 | 0.7949 | 0.7996 | 0.8043 | 0.8088 | 0.8198 | 0.8300 | 0.8396 | 0.8486 | 0.8570 |
| 1.50 | 0.8062 | 0.8114 | 0.8165 | 0.8215 | 0.8264 | 0.8380 | 0.8488 | 0.8587 | 0.8679 | 0.8764 |
| 1.55 | 0.8211 | 0.8267 | 0.8322 | 0.8375 | 0.8426 | 0.8547 | 0.8658 | 0.8759 | 0.8851 | 0.8936 |
| 1.60 | 0.8349 | 0.8409 | 0.8466 | 0.8521 | 0.8575 | 0.8699 | 0.8811 | 0.8912 | 0.9004 | 0.9087 |
| 1.65 | 0.8478 | 0.8540 | 0.8600 | 0.8656 | 0.8711 | 0.8836 | 0.8948 | 0.9049 | 0.9138 | 0.9218 |
| 1.70 | 0.8598 | 0.8662 | 0.8722 | 0.8780 | 0.8835 | 0.8961 | 0.9072 | 0.9170 | 0.9256 | 0.9333 |
| 1.75 | 0.8709 | 0.8774 | 0.8836 | 0.8894 | 0.8949 | 0.9074 | 0.9182 | 0.9277 | 0.9360 | 0.9432 |
| 1.80 | 0.8813 | 0.8878 | 0.8940 | 0.8998 | 0.9052 | 0.9175 | 0.9281 | 0.9372 | 0.9450 | 0.9518 |
| 1.85 | 0.8908 | 0.8974 | 0.9035 | 0.9093 | 0.9147 | 0.9267 | 0.9368 | 0.9455 | 0.9529 | 0.9592 |
| 1.90 | 0.8996 | 0.9062 | 0.9123 | 0.9180 | 0.9232 | 0.9349 | 0.9446 | 0.9528 | 0.9597 | 0.9656 |
| 1.95 | 0.9078 | 0.9143 | 0.9203 | 0.9259 | 0.9310 | 0.9422 | 0.9515 | 0.9592 | 0.9656 | 0.9710 |
| 2.00 | 0.9154 | 0.9218 | 0.9276 | 0.9331 | 0.9380 | 0.9488 | 0.9576 | 0.9648 | 0.9707 | 0.9756 |
| 2.10 | 0.9288 | 0.9349 | 0.9405 | 0.9455 | 0.9502 | 0.9600 | 0.9677 | 0.9739 | 0.9789 | 0.9829 |
| 2.20 | 0.9402 | 0.9459 | 0.9512 | 0.9558 | 0.9600 | 0.9688 | 0.9756 | 0.9808 | 0.9849 | 0.9881 |
| 2.30 | 0.9498 | 0.9552 | 0.9600 | 0.9643 | 0.9680 | 0.9758 | 0.9816 | 0.9859 | 0.9893 | 0.9918 |
| 2.40 | 0.9580 | 0.9630 | 0.9673 | 0.9712 | 0.9745 | 0.9813 | 0.9862 | 0.9898 | 0.9924 | 0.9943 |
| 2.50 | 0.9648 | 0.9694 | 0.9734 | 0.9768 | 0.9797 | 0.9856 | 0.9897 | 0.9926 | 0.9947 | 0.9961 |
| 2.60 | 0.9706 | 0.9748 | 0.9783 | 0.9813 | 0.9839 | 0.9889 | 0.9923 | 0.9946 | 0.9963 | 0.9974 |
| 2.70 | 0.9755 | 0.9792 | 0.9824 | 0.9850 | 0.9873 | 0.9915 | 0.9943 | 0.9961 | 0.9974 | 0.9982 |
| 2.80 | 0.9796 | 0.9829 | 0.9857 | 0.9880 | 0.9900 | 0.9935 | 0.9958 | 0.9972 | 0.9982 | 0.9988 |
| 2.90 | 0.9830 | 0.9860 | 0.9884 | 0.9904 | 0.9921 | 0.9950 | 0.9969 | 0.9980 | 0.9988 | 0.9992 |
| 3.00 | 0.9859 | 0.9885 | 0.9906 | 0.9924 | 0.9938 | 0.9962 | 0.9977 | 0.9986 | 0.9991 | 0.9995 |
| 3.10 | 0.9883 | 0.9906 | 0.9924 | 0.9939 | 0.9951 | 0.9971 | 0.9983 | 0.9990 | 0.9994 | 0.9997 |
| 3.20 | 0.9903 | 0.9923 | 0.9939 | 0.9952 | 0.9962 | 0.9978 | 0.9988 | 0.9993 | 0.9996 | 0.9998 |
| 3.30 | 0.9919 | 0.9937 | 0.9951 | 0.9962 | 0.9970 | 0.9984 | 0.9991 | 0.9995 | 0.9997 | 0.9998 |
| 3.40 | 0.9933 | 0.9949 | 0.9961 | 0.9970 | 0.9977 | 0.9988 | 0.9993 | 0.9997 | 0.9998 | 0.9999 |
| 3.50 | 0.9945 | 0.9958 | 0.9968 | 0.9976 | 0.9982 | 0.9991 | 0.9995 | 0.9998 | 0.9999 | 0.9999 |

# Table 4. (CONTINUED)  Values of Prob $(t \leq T)$

$$\frac{T}{E(t)} \qquad\qquad R = \left(\frac{E(t)}{\sigma_t}\right)^2$$

| | 2.2 | 2.4 | 2.6 | 2.8 | 3.0 | 3.5 | 4.0 | 4.5 | 5.0 | 5.5 |
|---|---|---|---|---|---|---|---|---|---|---|
| 3.60 | 0.9954 | 0.9966 | 0.9975 | 0.9981 | 0.9986 | 0.9993 | 0.9997 | 0.9998 | 0.9999 | 1.0000 |
| 3.70 | 0.9962 | 0.9972 | 0.9980 | 0.9985 | 0.9989 | 0.9995 | 0.9998 | 0.9999 | 0.9999 | 1.0000 |
| 3.80 | 0.9969 | 0.9977 | 0.9984 | 0.9988 | 0.9991 | 0.9996 | 0.9998 | 0.9999 | 1.0000 | 1.0000 |
| 3.90 | 0.9974 | 0.9982 | 0.9987 | 0.9991 | 0.9993 | 0.9997 | 0.9999 | 0.9999 | 1.0000 | 1.0000 |
| 4.00 | 0.9979 | 0.9985 | 0.9990 | 0.9993 | 0.9995 | 0.9998 | 0.9999 | 1.0000 | 1.0000 | 1.0000 |
| 4.10 | 0.9983 | 0.9988 | 0.9992 | 0.9994 | 0.9996 | 0.9998 | 0.9999 | 1.0000 | 1.0000 | 1.0000 |
| 4.20 | 0.9986 | 0.9990 | 0.9993 | 0.9995 | 0.9997 | 0.9999 | 1.0000 | 1.0000 | 1.0000 | 1.0000 |
| 4.30 | 0.9988 | 0.9992 | 0.9995 | 0.9996 | 0.9998 | 0.9999 | 1.0000 | 1.0000 | 1.0000 | 1.0000 |
| 4.40 | 0.9990 | 0.9994 | 0.9996 | 0.9997 | 0.9998 | 0.9999 | 1.0000 | 1.0000 | 1.0000 | 1.0000 |
| 4.50 | 0.9992 | 0.9995 | 0.9997 | 0.9998 | 0.9999 | 0.9999 | 1.0000 | 1.0000 | 1.0000 | 1.0000 |
| 4.60 | 0.9993 | 0.9996 | 0.9997 | 0.9998 | 0.9999 | 1.0000 | 1.0000 | 1.0000 | 1.0000 | 1.0000 |
| 4.70 | 0.9995 | 0.9997 | 0.9998 | 0.9999 | 0.9999 | 1.0000 | 1.0000 | 1.0000 | 1.0000 | 1.0000 |
| 4.80 | 0.9996 | 0.9997 | 0.9998 | 0.9999 | 0.9999 | 1.0000 | 1.0000 | 1.0000 | 1.0000 | 1.0000 |
| 4.90 | 0.9996 | 0.9998 | 0.9999 | 0.9999 | 0.9999 | 1.0000 | 1.0000 | 1.0000 | 1.0000 | 1.0000 |
| 5.00 | 0.9997 | 0.9998 | 0.9999 | 0.9999 | 1.0000 | 1.0000 | 1.0000 | 1.0000 | 1.0000 | 1.0000 |
| 5.10 | 0.9998 | 0.9999 | 0.9999 | 0.9999 | 1.0000 | 1.0000 | 1.0000 | 1.0000 | 1.0000 | 1.0000 |
| 5.20 | 0.9998 | 0.9999 | 0.9999 | 1.0000 | 1.0000 | 1.0000 | 1.0000 | 1.0000 | 1.0000 | 1.0000 |
| 5.30 | 0.9998 | 0.9999 | 0.9999 | 1.0000 | 1.0000 | 1.0000 | 1.0000 | 1.0000 | 1.0000 | 1.0000 |
| 5.40 | 0.9999 | 0.9999 | 1.0000 | 1.0000 | 1.0000 | 1.0000 | 1.0000 | 1.0000 | 1.0000 | 1.0000 |
| 5.50 | 0.9999 | 0.9999 | 1.0000 | 1.0000 | 1.0000 | 1.0000 | 1.0000 | 1.0000 | 1.0000 | 1.0000 |
| 5.60 | 0.9999 | 1.0000 | 1.0000 | 1.0000 | 1.0000 | 1.0000 | 1.0000 | 1.0000 | 1.0000 | 1.0000 |
| 5.70 | 0.9999 | 1.0000 | 1.0000 | 1.0000 | 1.0000 | 1.0000 | 1.0000 | 1.0000 | 1.0000 | 1.0000 |
| 5.80 | 0.9999 | 1.0000 | 1.0000 | 1.0000 | 1.0000 | 1.0000 | 1.0000 | 1.0000 | 1.0000 | 1.0000 |
| 5.90 | 1.0000 | 1.0000 | 1.0000 | 1.0000 | 1.0000 | 1.0000 | 1.0000 | 1.0000 | 1.0000 | 1.0000 |
| 6.00 | 1.0000 | 1.0000 | 1.0000 | 1.0000 | 1.0000 | 1.0000 | 1.0000 | 1.0000 | 1.0000 | 1.0000 |
| 6.10 | 1.0000 | 1.0000 | 1.0000 | 1.0000 | 1.0000 | 1.0000 | 1.0000 | 1.0000 | 1.0000 | 1.0000 |
| 6.20 | 1.0000 | 1.0000 | 1.0000 | 1.0000 | 1.0000 | 1.0000 | 1.0000 | 1.0000 | 1.0000 | 1.0000 |
| 6.30 | 1.0000 | 1.0000 | 1.0000 | 1.0000 | 1.0000 | 1.0000 | 1.0000 | 1.0000 | 1.0000 | 1.0000 |
| 6.40 | 1.0000 | 1.0000 | 1.0000 | 1.0000 | 1.0000 | 1.0000 | 1.0000 | 1.0000 | 1.0000 | 1.0000 |
| 6.50 | 1.0000 | 1.0000 | 1.0000 | 1.0000 | 1.0000 | 1.0000 | 1.0000 | 1.0000 | 1.0000 | 1.0000 |
| 6.60 | 1.0000 | 1.0000 | 1.0000 | 1.0000 | 1.0000 | 1.0000 | 1.0000 | 1.0000 | 1.0000 | 1.0000 |
| 6.70 | 1.0000 | 1.0000 | 1.0000 | 1.0000 | 1.0000 | 1.0000 | 1.0000 | 1.0000 | 1.0000 | 1.0000 |
| 6.80 | 1.0000 | 1.0000 | 1.0000 | 1.0000 | 1.0000 | 1.0000 | 1.0000 | 1.0000 | 1.0000 | 1.0000 |
| 6.90 | 1.0000 | 1.0000 | 1.0000 | 1.0000 | 1.0000 | 1.0000 | 1.0000 | 1.0000 | 1.0000 | 1.0000 |
| 7.00 | 1.0000 | 1.0000 | 1.0000 | 1.0000 | 1.0000 | 1.0000 | 1.0000 | 1.0000 | 1.0000 | 1.0000 |
| 7.10 | 1.0000 | 1.0000 | 1.0000 | 1.0000 | 1.0000 | 1.0000 | 1.0000 | 1.0000 | 1.0000 | 1.0000 |
| 7.20 | 1.0000 | 1.0000 | 1.0000 | 1.0000 | 1.0000 | 1.0000 | 1.0000 | 1.0000 | 1.0000 | 1.0000 |
| 7.30 | 1.0000 | 1.0000 | 1.0000 | 1.0000 | 1.0000 | 1.0000 | 1.0000 | 1.0000 | 1.0000 | 1.0000 |
| 7.40 | 1.0000 | 1.0000 | 1.0000 | 1.0000 | 1.0000 | 1.0000 | 1.0000 | 1.0000 | 1.0000 | 1.0000 |
| 7.50 | 1.0000 | 1.0000 | 1.0000 | 1.0000 | 1.0000 | 1.0000 | 1.0000 | 1.0000 | 1.0000 | 1.0000 |
| 7.60 | 1.0000 | 1.0000 | 1.0000 | 1.0000 | 1.0000 | 1.0000 | 1.0000 | 1.0000 | 1.0000 | 1.0000 |
| 7.70 | 1.0000 | 1.0000 | 1.0000 | 1.0000 | 1.0000 | 1.0000 | 1.0000 | 1.0000 | 1.0000 | 1.0000 |
| 7.80 | 1.0000 | 1.0000 | 1.0000 | 1.0000 | 1.0000 | 1.0000 | 1.0000 | 1.0000 | 1.0000 | 1.0000 |
| 7.90 | 1.0000 | 1.0000 | 1.0000 | 1.0000 | 1.0000 | 1.0000 | 1.0000 | 1.0000 | 1.0000 | 1.0000 |
| 8.00 | 1.0000 | 1.0000 | 1.0000 | 1.0000 | 1.0000 | 1.0000 | 1.0000 | 1.0000 | 1.0000 | 1.0000 |
| 8.10 | 1.0000 | 1.0000 | 1.0000 | 1.0000 | 1.0000 | 1.0000 | 1.0000 | 1.0000 | 1.0000 | 1.0000 |
| 8.20 | 1.0000 | 1.0000 | 1.0000 | 1.0000 | 1.0000 | 1.0000 | 1.0000 | 1.0000 | 1.0000 | 1.0000 |
| 8.30 | 1.0000 | 1.0000 | 1.0000 | 1.0000 | 1.0000 | 1.0000 | 1.0000 | 1.0000 | 1.0000 | 1.0000 |
| 8.40 | 1.0000 | 1.0000 | 1.0000 | 1.0000 | 1.0000 | 1.0000 | 1.0000 | 1.0000 | 1.0000 | 1.0000 |
| 8.50 | 1.0000 | 1.0000 | 1.0000 | 1.0000 | 1.0000 | 1.0000 | 1.0000 | 1.0000 | 1.0000 | 1.0000 |
| 8.60 | 1.0000 | 1.0000 | 1.0000 | 1.0000 | 1.0000 | 1.0000 | 1.0000 | 1.0000 | 1.0000 | 1.0000 |
| 8.70 | 1.0000 | 1.0000 | 1.0000 | 1.0000 | 1.0000 | 1.0000 | 1.0000 | 1.0000 | 1.0000 | 1.0000 |
| 8.80 | 1.0000 | 1.0000 | 1.0000 | 1.0000 | 1.0000 | 1.0000 | 1.0000 | 1.0000 | 1.0000 | 1.0000 |
| 8.90 | 1.0000 | 1.0000 | 1.0000 | 1.0000 | 1.0000 | 1.0000 | 1.0000 | 1.0000 | 1.0000 | 1.0000 |
| 9.00 | 1.0000 | 1.0000 | 1.000 | 1.0000 | 1.0000 | 1.0000 | 1.0000 | 1.0000 | 1.0000 | 1.0000 |

**Table 4.** (CONTINUED)     Values of Prob ($t \leq T$)

$$\frac{T}{E(t)} \qquad\qquad R = \left(\frac{E(t)}{\sigma_t}\right)^2$$

| $\frac{T}{E(t)}$ | 6.0 | 6.5 | 7.0 | 7.5 | 8.0 | 8.5 | 9.0 | 9.5 | 10.0 | 15.0 |
|---|---|---|---|---|---|---|---|---|---|---|
| 0.05 | 0.0000 | 0.0000 | 0.0000 | 0.0000 | 0.0000 | 0.0000 | 0.0000 | 0.0000 | 0.0000 | 0.0000 |
| 0.10 | 0.0000 | 0.0000 | 0.0000 | 0.0000 | 0.0000 | 0.0000 | 0.0000 | 0.0000 | 0.0000 | 0.0000 |
| 0.15 | 0.0003 | 0.0002 | 0.0001 | 0.0001 | 0.0000 | 0.0000 | 0.0000 | 0.0000 | 0.0000 | 0.0000 |
| 0.20 | 0.0015 | 0.0010 | 0.0006 | 0.0004 | 0.0003 | 0.0002 | 0.0001 | 0.0001 | 0.0001 | 0.0000 |
| 0.25 | 0.0045 | 0.0031 | 0.0022 | 0.0016 | 0.0011 | 0.0008 | 0.0006 | 0.0004 | 0.0003 | 0.0000 |
| 0.30 | 0.0104 | 0.0078 | 0.0059 | 0.0044 | 0.0033 | 0.0025 | 0.0019 | 0.0015 | 0.0011 | 0.0001 |
| 0.35 | 0.0205 | 0.0162 | 0.0128 | 0.0102 | 0.0081 | 0.0065 | 0.0052 | 0.0041 | 0.0033 | 0.0004 |
| 0.40 | 0.0357 | 0.0295 | 0.0244 | 0.0203 | 0.0168 | 0.0140 | 0.0017 | 0.0097 | 0.0081 | 0.0014 |
| 0.45 | 0.0567 | 0.0486 | 0.0416 | 0.0358 | 0.0308 | 0.0265 | 0.0229 | 0.0198 | 0.0171 | 0.0042 |
| 0.50 | 0.0839 | 0.0739 | 0.0653 | 0.0577 | 0.0511 | 0.0453 | 0.0403 | 0.0358 | 0.0318 | 0.0103 |
| 0.55 | 0.1171 | 0.1057 | 0.0956 | 0.0866 | 0.0786 | 0.0714 | 0.0649 | 0.0590 | 0.0538 | 0.0219 |
| 0.60 | 0.1559 | 0.1436 | 0.1325 | 0.1225 | 0.1133 | 0.1050 | 0.0974 | 0.0904 | 0.0839 | 0.0415 |
| 0.65 | 0.1994 | 0.1869 | 0.1754 | 0.1648 | 0.1551 | 0.1460 | 0.1377 | 0.1299 | 0.1226 | 0.0711 |
| 0.70 | 0.2469 | 0.2346 | 0.2233 | 0.2128 | 0.2030 | 0.1938 | 0.1852 | 0.1771 | 0.1695 | 0.1121 |
| 0.75 | 0.2971 | 0.2858 | 0.2752 | 0.2653 | 0.2560 | 0.2472 | 0.2389 | 0.2311 | 0.2236 | 0.1648 |
| 0.80 | 0.3490 | 0.3391 | 0.3297 | 0.3210 | 0.3127 | 0.3048 | 0.2973 | 0.2902 | 0.2834 | 0.2280 |
| 0.85 | 0.4016 | 0.3934 | 0.3857 | 0.3784 | 0.3715 | 0.3650 | 0.3587 | 0.3528 | 0.3470 | 0.2996 |
| 0.90 | 0.4539 | 0.4476 | 0.4418 | 0.4363 | 0.4311 | 0.4261 | 0.4214 | 0.4169 | 0.4126 | 0.3767 |
| 0.95 | 0.5050 | 0.5008 | 0.4970 | 0.4933 | 0.4900 | 0.4868 | 0.4838 | 0.4809 | 0.4782 | 0.4560 |
| 1.00 | 0.5543 | 0.5522 | 0.5503 | 0.5486 | 0.5470 | 0.5456 | 0.5443 | 0.5432 | 0.5421 | 0.5344 |
| 1.05 | 0.6012 | 0.6011 | 0.6010 | 0.6011 | 0.6013 | 0.6016 | 0.6020 | 0.6024 | 0.6029 | 0.6089 |
| 1.10 | 0.6453 | 0.6469 | 0.6486 | 0.6504 | 0.6522 | 0.6540 | 0.6558 | 0.6576 | 0.6595 | 0.6775 |
| 1.15 | 0.6863 | 0.6895 | 0.6927 | 0.6959 | 0.6990 | 0.7021 | 0.7052 | 0.7082 | 0.7112 | 0.7387 |
| 1.20 | 0.7241 | 0.7286 | 0.7330 | 0.7373 | 0.7416 | 0.7457 | 0.7498 | 0.7537 | 0.7576 | 0.7919 |
| 1.25 | 0.7586 | 0.7641 | 0.7695 | 0.7747 | 0.7798 | 0.7847 | 0.7895 | 0.7941 | 0.7986 | 0.8370 |
| 1.30 | 0.7897 | 0.7961 | 0.8022 | 0.8080 | 0.8137 | 0.8191 | 0.8243 | 0.8293 | 0.8342 | 0.8743 |
| 1.35 | 0.8178 | 0.8246 | 0.8312 | 0.8374 | 0.8434 | 0.8491 | 0.8546 | 0.8598 | 0.8647 | 0.9045 |
| 1.40 | 0.8427 | 0.8499 | 0.8567 | 0.8632 | 0.8693 | 0.8750 | 0.8805 | 0.8857 | 0.8906 | 0.9284 |
| 1.45 | 0.8648 | 0.8722 | 0.8790 | 0.8855 | 0.8915 | 0.8972 | 0.9025 | 0.9075 | 0.9122 | 0.9471 |
| 1.50 | 0.8843 | 0.8916 | 0.8984 | 0.9047 | 0.9105 | 0.9159 | 0.9210 | 0.9257 | 0.9301 | 0.9614 |
| 1.55 | 0.9014 | 0.9085 | 0.9150 | 0.9210 | 0.9266 | 0.9317 | 0.9364 | 0.9408 | 0.9448 | 0.9722 |
| 1.60 | 0.9162 | 0.9230 | 0.9292 | 0.9349 | 0.9401 | 0.9448 | 0.9491 | 0.9531 | 0.9567 | 0.9802 |
| 1.65 | 0.9290 | 0.9355 | 0.9413 | 0.9466 | 0.9513 | 0.9556 | 0.9595 | 0.9631 | 0.9663 | 0.9860 |
| 1.70 | 0.9401 | 0.9462 | 0.9516 | 0.9564 | 0.9607 | 0.9645 | 0.9680 | 0.9711 | 0.9739 | 0.9903 |
| 1.75 | 0.9496 | 0.9552 | 0.9602 | 0.9645 | 0.9684 | 0.9718 | 0.9748 | 0.9775 | 0.9799 | 0.9933 |
| 1.80 | 0.9577 | 0.9629 | 0.9674 | 0.9713 | 0.9747 | 0.9777 | 0.9803 | 0.9826 | 0.9846 | 0.9954 |
| 1.85 | 0.9647 | 0.9693 | 0.9733 | 0.9768 | 0.9798 | 0.9824 | 0.9847 | 0.9866 | 0.9883 | 0.9969 |
| 1.90 | 0.9705 | 0.9747 | 0.9783 | 0.9814 | 0.9840 | 0.9862 | 0.9881 | 0.9897 | 0.9911 | 0.9979 |
| 1.95 | 0.9755 | 0.9792 | 0.9824 | 0.9851 | 0.9873 | 0.9892 | 0.9908 | 0.9922 | 0.9933 | 0.9986 |
| 2.00 | 0.9797 | 0.9830 | 0.9858 | 0.9881 | 0.9900 | 0.9916 | 0.9929 | 0.9941 | 0.9950 | 0.9991 |
| 2.10 | 0.9861 | 0.9887 | 0.9908 | 0.9925 | 0.9939 | 0.9950 | 0.9959 | 0.9966 | 0.9972 | 0.9996 |
| 2.20 | 0.9906 | 0.9925 | 0.9941 | 0.9953 | 0.9963 | 0.9970 | 0.9976 | 0.9981 | 0.9985 | 0.9998 |
| 2.30 | 0.9937 | 0.9951 | 0.9962 | 0.9971 | 0.9978 | 0.9983 | 0.9987 | 0.9990 | 0.9992 | 0.9999 |
| 2.40 | 0.9958 | 0.9968 | 0.9976 | 0.9982 | 0.9987 | 0.9990 | 0.9993 | 0.9994 | 0.9996 | 1.0000 |
| 2.50 | 0.9972 | 0.9980 | 0.9985 | 0.9989 | 0.9992 | 0.9994 | 0.9996 | 0.9997 | 0.9998 | 1.0000 |
| 2.60 | 0.9982 | 0.9987 | 0.9991 | 0.9994 | 0.9995 | 0.9997 | 0.9998 | 0.9998 | 0.9999 | 1.0000 |
| 2.70 | 0.9988 | 0.9992 | 0.9994 | 0.9996 | 0.9997 | 0.9998 | 0.9999 | 0.9999 | 0.9999 | 1.0000 |
| 2.80 | 0.9992 | 0.9995 | 0.9997 | 0.9998 | 0.9999 | 0.9999 | 0.9999 | 1.0000 | 1.0000 | 1.0000 |
| 2.90 | 0.9995 | 0.9997 | 0.9998 | 0.9999 | 0.9999 | 0.9999 | 1.0000 | 1.0000 | 1.0000 | 1.0000 |
| 3.00 | 0.9997 | 0.9998 | 0.9999 | 0.9999 | 1.0000 | 1.0000 | 1.0000 | 1.0000 | 1.0000 | 1.0000 |
| 3.10 | 0.9998 | 0.9999 | 0.9999 | 1.0000 | 1.0000 | 1.0000 | 1.0000 | 1.0000 | 1.0000 | 1.0000 |
| 3.20 | 0.9999 | 0.9999 | 1.0000 | 1.0000 | 1.0000 | 1.0000 | 1.0000 | 1.0000 | 1.0000 | 1.0000 |
| 3.30 | 0.9999 | 1.0000 | 1.0000 | 1.0000 | 1.0000 | 1.0000 | 1.0000 | 1.0000 | 1.0000 | 1.0000 |
| 3.40 | 0.9999 | 1.0000 | 1.0000 | 1.0000 | 1.0000 | 1.0000 | 1.0000 | 1.0000 | 1.0000 | 1.0000 |
| 3.50 | 1.0000 | 1.0000 | 1.0000 | 1.0000 | 1.0000 | 1.0000 | 1.0000 | 1.0000 | 1.0000 | 1.0000 |

**Table 4.** (CONTINUED)     Values of Prob $(t \le T)$

| $\dfrac{T}{E(t)}$ | $R = \left(\dfrac{E(t)}{\sigma_t}\right)^2$ | | | | |
|---|---|---|---|---|---|
| | 20 | 25 | 30 | 35 | 40 |
| 0.05 | 0.0000 | 0.0000 | 0.0000 | 0.0000 | 0.0000 |
| 0.10 | 0.0000 | 0.0000 | 0.0000 | 0.0000 | 0.0000 |
| 0.15 | 0.0000 | 0.0000 | 0.0000 | 0.0000 | 0.0000 |
| 0.20 | 0.0000 | 0.0000 | 0.0000 | 0.0000 | 0.0000 |
| 0.25 | 0.0000 | 0.0000 | 0.0000 | 0.0000 | 0.0000 |
| 0.30 | 0.0000 | 0.0000 | 0.0000 | 0.0000 | 0.0000 |
| 0.35 | 0.0001 | 0.0000 | 0.0000 | 0.0000 | 0.0000 |
| 0.40 | 0.0003 | 0.0000 | 0.0000 | 0.0000 | 0.0000 |
| 0.45 | 0.0011 | 0.0003 | 0.0001 | 0.0000 | 0.0000 |
| 0.50 | 0.0035 | 0.0012 | 0.0003 | 0.0001 | 0.0001 |
| 0.55 | 0.0093 | 0.0040 | 0.0018 | 0.0008 | 0.0004 |
| 0.60 | 0.0213 | 0.0112 | 0.0059 | 0.0032 | 0.0017 |
| 0.65 | 0.0427 | 0.0261 | 0.0162 | 0.0102 | 0.0064 |
| 0.70 | 0.0765 | 0.0532 | 0.0374 | 0.0266 | 0.0190 |
| 0.75 | 0.1248 | 0.0960 | 0.0747 | 0.0586 | 0.0463 |
| 0.80 | 0.1878 | 0.1568 | 0.1321 | 0.1121 | 0.0956 |
| 0.85 | 0.2637 | 0.2347 | 0.2104 | 0.1897 | 0.1717 |
| 0.90 | 0.3491 | 0.3262 | 0.3065 | 0.2892 | 0.2737 |
| 0.95 | 0.4394 | 0.4257 | 0.4139 | 0.4035 | 0.3941 |
| 1.00 | 0.5297 | 0.5266 | 0.5243 | 0.5225 | 0.5210 |
| 1.05 | 0.6157 | 0.6226 | 0.6293 | 0.6358 | 0.6419 |
| 1.10 | 0.6940 | 0.7090 | 0.7227 | 0.7353 | 0.7469 |
| 1.15 | 0.7623 | 0.7827 | 0.8007 | 0.8165 | 0.8307 |
| 1.20 | 0.8197 | 0.8428 | 0.8621 | 0.8786 | 0.8927 |
| 1.25 | 0.8664 | 0.8896 | 0.9081 | 0.9231 | 0.9354 |
| 1.30 | 0.9032 | 0.9246 | 0.9409 | 0.9533 | 0.9630 |
| 1.35 | 0.9313 | 0.9500 | 0.9632 | 0.9728 | 0.9798 |
| 1.40 | 0.9522 | 0.9676 | 0.9779 | 0.9847 | 0.9894 |
| 1.45 | 0.9674 | 0.9796 | 0.9871 | 0.9918 | 0.9947 |
| 1.50 | 0.9781 | 0.9874 | 0.9927 | 0.9957 | 0.9975 |
| 1.55 | 0.9856 | 0.9924 | 0.9959 | 0.9978 | 0.9988 |
| 1.60 | 0.9907 | 0.9955 | 0.9978 | 0.9989 | 0.9995 |
| 1.65 | 0.9940 | 0.9974 | 0.9989 | 0.9995 | 0.9998 |
| 1.70 | 0.9963 | 0.9985 | 0.9994 | 0.9998 | 0.9999 |
| 1.75 | 0.9977 | 0.9992 | 0.9997 | 0.9999 | 1.0000 |
| 1.80 | 0.9986 | 0.9996 | 0.9999 | 1.0000 | 1.0000 |
| 1.85 | 0.9991 | 0.9998 | 0.9999 | 1.0000 | 1.0000 |
| 1.90 | 0.9995 | 0.9999 | 1.0000 | 1.0000 | 1.0000 |
| 1.95 | 0.9997 | 0.9999 | 1.0000 | 1.0000 | 1.0000 |
| 2.00 | 0.9998 | 1.0000 | 1.0000 | 1.0000 | 1.0000 |
| 2.10 | 0.9999 | 1.0000 | 1.0000 | 1.0000 | 1.0000 |
| 2.20 | 1.0000 | 1.0000 | 1.0000 | 1.0000 | 1.0000 |
| 2.30 | 1.0000 | 1.0000 | 1.0000 | 1.0000 | 1.0000 |
| 2.40 | 1.0000 | 1.0000 | 1.0000 | 1.0000 | 1.0000 |
| 2.50 | 1.0000 | 1.0000 | 1.0000 | 1.0000 | 1.0000 |
| 2.60 | 1.0000 | 1.0000 | 1.0000 | 1.0000 | 1.0000 |
| 2.70 | 1.0000 | 1.0000 | 1.-000 | 1.0000 | 1.0000 |
| 2.80 | 1.0000 | 1.0000 | 1.0000 | 1.0000 | 1.0000 |
| 2.90 | 1.0000 | 1.0000 | 1.0000 | 1.0000 | 1.0000 |
| 3.00 | 1.0000 | 1.0000 | 1.0000 | 1.0000 | 1.0000 |
| 3.10 | 1.0000 | 1.0000 | 1.0000 | 1.0000 | 1.0000 |
| 3.20 | 1.0000 | 1.0000 | 1.0000 | 1.0000 | 1.0000 |
| 3.30 | 1.0000 | 1.0000 | 1.0000 | 1.0000 | 1.0000 |
| 3.40 | 1.0000 | 1.0000 | 1.0000 | 1.0000 | 1.0000 |
| 3.50 | 1.0000 | 1.0000 | 1.0000 | 1.0000 | 1.0000 |

**Table 5.** MEAN QUEUING TIME FOR SINGLE-SERVER QUEUES WITH POISSON ARRIVAL PATTERN.

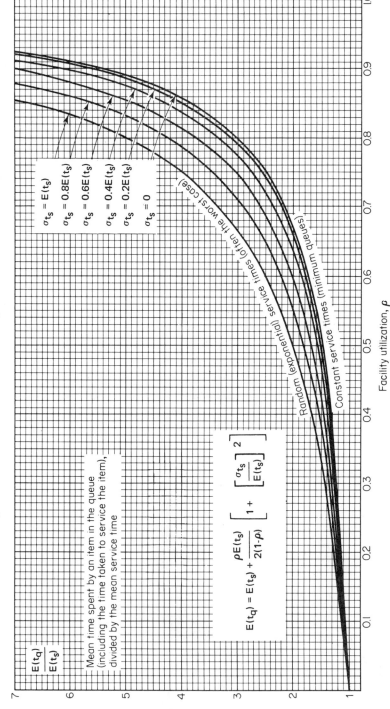

Note: Mean waiting time before being served, $E(t_w) = E(t_q) - E(t_s)$.

Curves tabulated on the following two pages.

# Table 5. (CONTINUED)

$$\text{Values of } \frac{E(t_q)}{E(t_s)}$$

Facility Utilization

Coefficient of Variation, Squared, for Service Time, $\left[\dfrac{\sigma_{t_s}}{E(t_s)}\right]^2$

| $\rho$ | 0.0 | 0.05 | 0.10 | 0.15 | 0.20 | 0.25 | 0.30 | 0.35 | 0.40 | 0.45 | 0.50 |
|---|---|---|---|---|---|---|---|---|---|---|---|
| 0.00 | 1.000 | 1.000 | 1.000 | 1.000 | 1.000 | 1.000 | 1.000 | 1.000 | 1.000 | 1.000 | 1.000 |
| 0.02 | 1.010 | 1.011 | 1.011 | 1.012 | 1.012 | 1.013 | 1.013 | 1.014 | 1.014 | 1.015 | 1.015 |
| 0.04 | 1.021 | 1.022 | 1.023 | 1.024 | 1.025 | 1.026 | 1.027 | 1.028 | 1.029 | 1.030 | 1.031 |
| 0.06 | 1.032 | 1.034 | 1.035 | 1.037 | 1.038 | 1.040 | 1.041 | 1.043 | 1.045 | 1.046 | 1.048 |
| 0.08 | 1.043 | 1.046 | 1.048 | 1.050 | 1.052 | 1.054 | 1.057 | 1.059 | 1.061 | 1.063 | 1.065 |
| 0.10 | 1.056 | 1.058 | 1.061 | 1.064 | 1.067 | 1.069 | 1.072 | 1.075 | 1.078 | 1.081 | 1.083 |
| 0.12 | 1.068 | 1.072 | 1.075 | 1.078 | 1.082 | 1.085 | 1.089 | 1.092 | 1.095 | 1.099 | 1.102 |
| 0.14 | 1.081 | 1.085 | 1.090 | 1.094 | 1.098 | 1.102 | 1.106 | 1.110 | 1.114 | 1.118 | 1.122 |
| 0.16 | 1.095 | 1.100 | 1.105 | 1.110 | 1.114 | 1.119 | 1.124 | 1.129 | 1.133 | 1.138 | 1.143 |
| 0.18 | 1.110 | 1.115 | 1.121 | 1.126 | 1.132 | 1.137 | 1.143 | 1.148 | 1.154 | 1.159 | 1.165 |
| 0.20 | 1.125 | 1.131 | 1.137 | 1.144 | 1.150 | 1.156 | 1.162 | 1.169 | 1.175 | 1.181 | 1.187 |
| 0.22 | 1.141 | 1.148 | 1.155 | 1.162 | 1.169 | 1.176 | 1.183 | 1.190 | 1.197 | 1.204 | 1.212 |
| 0.24 | 1.158 | 1.166 | 1.174 | 1.182 | 1.189 | 1.197 | 1.205 | 1.212 | 1.221 | 1.229 | 1.237 |
| 0.26 | 1.176 | 1.184 | 1.193 | 1.202 | 1.211 | 1.220 | 1.228 | 1.237 | 1.246 | 1.255 | 1.264 |
| 0.28 | 1.194 | 1.204 | 1.214 | 1.224 | 1.233 | 1.243 | 1.253 | 1.262 | 1.272 | 1.282 | 1.292 |
| 0.30 | 1.214 | 1.225 | 1.236 | 1.246 | 1.257 | 1.268 | 1.279 | 1.289 | 1.300 | 1.311 | 1.321 |
| 0.32 | 1.235 | 1.247 | 1.259 | 1.271 | 1.282 | 1.294 | 1.306 | 1.318 | 1.329 | 1.341 | 1.353 |
| 0.34 | 1.258 | 1.270 | 1.283 | 1.296 | 1.309 | 1.322 | 1.335 | 1.348 | 1.361 | 1.373 | 1.386 |
| 0.36 | 1.281 | 1.295 | 1.309 | 1.323 | 1.337 | 1.352 | 1.366 | 1.380 | 1.394 | 1.408 | 1.422 |
| 0.38 | 1.306 | 1.322 | 1.337 | 1.352 | 1.368 | 1.383 | 1.398 | 1.414 | 1.429 | 1.444 | 1.460 |
| 0.40 | 1.333 | 1.350 | 1.367 | 1.383 | 1.400 | 1.417 | 1.433 | 1.450 | 1.467 | 1.483 | 1.500 |
| 0.42 | 1.362 | 1.380 | 1.398 | 1.416 | 1.434 | 1.453 | 1.471 | 1.489 | 1.507 | 1.525 | 1.543 |
| 0.44 | 1.393 | 1.412 | 1.432 | 1.452 | 1.471 | 1.491 | 1.511 | 1.530 | 1.550 | 1.570 | 1.589 |
| 0.46 | 1.426 | 1.447 | 1.469 | 1.490 | 1.511 | 1.532 | 1.554 | 1.575 | 1.596 | 1.618 | 1.639 |
| 0.48 | 1.462 | 1.485 | 1.508 | 1.531 | 1.554 | 1.577 | 1.600 | 1.623 | 1.646 | 1.669 | 1.692 |
| 0.50 | 1.500 | 1.525 | 1.550 | 1.575 | 1.600 | 1.625 | 1.650 | 1.675 | 1.700 | 1.725 | 1.750 |
| 0.52 | 1.542 | 1.569 | 1.596 | 1.623 | 1.650 | 1.677 | 1.704 | 1.731 | 1.758 | 1.785 | 1.812 |
| 0.54 | 1.587 | 1.616 | 1.646 | 1.675 | 1.704 | 1.734 | 1.763 | 1.792 | 1.822 | 1.851 | 1.880 |
| 0.56 | 1.636 | 1.668 | 1.700 | 1.732 | 1.764 | 1.795 | 1.827 | 1.859 | 1.891 | 1.923 | 1.955 |
| 0.58 | 1.690 | 1.725 | 1.760 | 1.794 | 1.829 | 1.863 | 1.898 | 1.932 | 1.967 | 2.001 | 2.036 |
| 0.60 | 1.750 | 1.787 | 1.825 | 1.862 | 1.900 | 1.937 | 1.975 | 2.012 | 2.050 | 2.087 | 2.125 |
| 0.62 | 1.816 | 1.857 | 1.897 | 1.938 | 1.979 | 2.020 | 2.061 | 2.101 | 2.142 | 2.183 | 2.224 |
| 0.64 | 1.889 | 1.933 | 1.978 | 2.022 | 2.067 | 2.111 | 2.156 | 2.200 | 2.244 | 2.289 | 2.333 |
| 0.66 | 1.971 | 2.019 | 2.068 | 2.116 | 2.165 | 2.213 | 2.262 | 2.310 | 2.359 | 2.407 | 2.456 |
| 0.68 | 2.062 | 2.116 | 2.169 | 2.222 | 2.275 | 2.328 | 2.381 | 2.434 | 2.487 | 2.541 | 2.594 |
| 0.70 | 2.167 | 2.225 | 2.283 | 2.342 | 2.400 | 2.458 | 2.517 | 2.575 | 2.633 | 2.692 | 2.750 |
| 0.72 | 2.286 | 2.350 | 2.414 | 2.479 | 2.543 | 2.607 | 2.671 | 2.736 | 2.800 | 2.864 | 2.929 |
| 0.74 | 2.423 | 2.494 | 2.565 | 2.637 | 2.708 | 2.779 | 2.850 | 2.921 | 2.992 | 3.063 | 3.135 |
| 0.76 | 2.583 | 2.662 | 2.742 | 2.821 | 2.900 | 2.979 | 3.058 | 3.137 | 3.217 | 3.296 | 3.375 |
| 0.78 | 2.773 | 2.861 | 2.950 | 3.039 | 3.127 | 3.216 | 3.305 | 3.393 | 3.482 | 3.570 | 3.659 |
| 0.80 | 3.000 | 3.100 | 3.200 | 3.300 | 3.400 | 3.500 | 3.600 | 3.700 | 3.800 | 3.900 | 4.000 |
| 0.82 | 3.278 | 3.392 | 3.506 | 3.619 | 3.733 | 3.847 | 3.961 | 4.075 | 4.189 | 4.303 | 4.417 |
| 0.84 | 3.625 | 3.756 | 3.887 | 4.019 | 4.150 | 4.281 | 4.412 | 4.544 | 4.675 | 4.806 | 4.937 |
| 0.86 | 4.071 | 4.225 | 4.379 | 4.532 | 4.686 | 4.839 | 4.993 | 5.146 | 5.300 | 5.454 | 5.607 |
| 0.88 | 4.667 | 4.850 | 5.033 | 5.217 | 5.400 | 5.583 | 5.677 | 5.950 | 6.133 | 6.317 | 6.500 |
| 0.90 | 5.500 | 5.725 | 5.950 | 6.175 | 6.400 | 6.625 | 6.850 | 7.075 | 7.300 | 7.525 | 7.750 |
| 0.92 | 6.750 | 7.037 | 7.325 | 7.612 | 7.900 | 8.187 | 8.475 | 8.762 | 9.050 | 9.337 | 9.625 |
| 0.94 | 8.833 | 9.225 | 9.617 | 10.008 | 10.400 | 10.792 | 11.183 | 11.575 | 11.967 | 12.358 | 12.750 |
| 0.96 | 13.000 | 13.600 | 14.200 | 14.800 | 15.400 | 16.000 | 16.600 | 17.200 | 17.800 | 18.400 | 19.000 |
| 0.98 | 25.500 | 26.725 | 27.950 | 29.175 | 30.400 | 31.625 | 32.850 | 34.075 | 35.300 | 36.525 | 37.750 |

# Table 5. (CONTINUED)

$$\text{Values of } \frac{E(t_q)}{E(t_s)}$$

| Facility Utilization $\rho$ | Coefficient of Variation, Squared, for Service Time, $\left[\dfrac{\sigma_{t_s}}{E(t_s)}\right]^2$ | | | | | | | | | |
|---|---|---|---|---|---|---|---|---|---|---|
| | 0.55 | 0.60 | 0.65 | 0.70 | 0.75 | 0.80 | 0.85 | 0.90 | 0.95 | 1.00 |
| 0.00 | 1.000 | 1.000 | 1.000 | 1.000 | 1.000 | 1.000 | 1.000 | 1.000 | 1.000 | 1.000 |
| 0.02 | 1.016 | 1.016 | 1.017 | 1.017 | 1.018 | 1.108 | 1.019 | 1.019 | 1.020 | 1.020 |
| 0.04 | 1.032 | 1.033 | 1.034 | 1.035 | 1.036 | 1.037 | 1.039 | 1.040 | 1.041 | 1.042 |
| 0.06 | 1.049 | 1.051 | 1.053 | 1.054 | 1.056 | 1.057 | 1.059 | 1.061 | 1.062 | 1.064 |
| 0.08 | 1.067 | 1.070 | 1.072 | 1.074 | 1.076 | 1.078 | 1.080 | 1.083 | 1.085 | 1.087 |
| 0.10 | 1.086 | 1.089 | 1.092 | 1.094 | 1.097 | 1.100 | 1.103 | 1.106 | 1.108 | 1.111 |
| 0.12 | 1.106 | 1.109 | 1.112 | 1.116 | 1.119 | 1.123 | 1.126 | 1.130 | 1.133 | 1.136 |
| 0.14 | 1.126 | 1.130 | 1.134 | 1.138 | 1.142 | 1.147 | 1.151 | 1.155 | 1.159 | 1.163 |
| 0.16 | 1.148 | 1.152 | 1.157 | 1.162 | 1.167 | 1.171 | 1.176 | 1.181 | 1.186 | 1.190 |
| 0.18 | 1.170 | 1.176 | 1.181 | 1.187 | 1.192 | 1.198 | 1.203 | 1.209 | 1.214 | 1.220 |
| 0.20 | 1.194 | 1.200 | 1.206 | 1.212 | 1.219 | 1.225 | 1.231 | 1.237 | 1.244 | 1.250 |
| 0.22 | 1.219 | 1.226 | 1.233 | 1.240 | 1.247 | 1.254 | 1.261 | 1.268 | 1.275 | 1.282 |
| 0.24 | 1.245 | 1.253 | 1.261 | 1.268 | 1.276 | 1.284 | 1.292 | 1.300 | 1.308 | 1.316 |
| 0.26 | 1.272 | 1.281 | 1.290 | 1.307 | 1.307 | 1.316 | 1.325 | 1.334 | 1.343 | 1.351 |
| 0.28 | 1.301 | 1.311 | 1.321 | 1.331 | 1.340 | 1.350 | 1.360 | 1.369 | 1.379 | 1.389 |
| 0.30 | 1.332 | 1.343 | 1.354 | 1.364 | 1.375 | 1.386 | 1.396 | 1.407 | 1.418 | 1.429 |
| 0.32 | 1.365 | 1.376 | 1.388 | 1.400 | 1.412 | 1.424 | 1.435 | 1.447 | 1.459 | 1.471 |
| 0.34 | 1.399 | 1.412 | 1.425 | 1.438 | 1.451 | 1.464 | 1.477 | 1.489 | 1.502 | 1.515 |
| 0.36 | 1.436 | 1.450 | 1.464 | 1.478 | 1.492 | 1.506 | 1.520 | 1.534 | 1.548 | 1.562 |
| 0.38 | 1.475 | 1.490 | 1.506 | 1.521 | 1.536 | 1.552 | 1.567 | 1.582 | 1.598 | 1.613 |
| 0.40 | 1.517 | 1.533 | 1.550 | 1.567 | 1.583 | 1.600 | 1.617 | 1.633 | 1.650 | 1.667 |
| 0.42 | 1.561 | 1.579 | 1.597 | 1.616 | 1.634 | 1.652 | 1.670 | 1.688 | 1.706 | 1.724 |
| 0.33 | 1.609 | 1.629 | 1.648 | 1.668 | 1.687 | 1.707 | 1.727 | 1.746 | 1.766 | 1.786 |
| 0.46 | 1.660 | 1.681 | 1.703 | 1.724 | 1.745 | 1.767 | 1.788 | 1.809 | 1.831 | 1.852 |
| 0.48 | 1.715 | 1.738 | 1.762 | 1.785 | 1.808 | 1.831 | 1.854 | 1.877 | 1.900 | 1.923 |
| 0.50 | 1.775 | 1.800 | 1.825 | 1.850 | 1.875 | 1.900 | 1.925 | 1.950 | 1.975 | 2.000 |
| 0.52 | 1.840 | 1.876 | 1.894 | 1.921 | 1.948 | 1.975 | 2.002 | 2.029 | 2.056 | 2.083 |
| 0.54 | 1.910 | 1.939 | 1.968 | 1.998 | 2.027 | 2.057 | 2.086 | 2.115 | 2.145 | 2.174 |
| 0.56 | 1.986 | 2.018 | 2.050 | 2.082 | 2.114 | 2.145 | 2.177 | 2.209 | 2.241 | 2.273 |
| 0.58 | 2.070 | 2.105 | 2.139 | 2.174 | 2.208 | 2.243 | 2.277 | 2.312 | 2.346 | 2.381 |
| 0.60 | 2.162 | 2.200 | 2.237 | 2.275 | 2.312 | 2.350 | 2.387 | 2.425 | 2.462 | 2.500 |
| 0.62 | 2.264 | 2.305 | 2.346 | 2.387 | 2.428 | 2.468 | 2.509 | 2.550 | 2.591 | 2.632 |
| 0.64 | 2.378 | 2.422 | 2.467 | 2.511 | 2.556 | 2.600 | 2.644 | 2.689 | 2.733 | 2.778 |
| 0.66 | 2.504 | 2.553 | 2.601 | 2.650 | 2.699 | 2.747 | 2.796 | 2.844 | 2.893 | 2.941 |
| 0.68 | 2.647 | 2.700 | 2.753 | 2.806 | 2.859 | 2.912 | 2.966 | 3.019 | 3.072 | 3.125 |
| 0.70 | 2.808 | 2.867 | 2.925 | 2.983 | 3.042 | 3.100 | 3.158 | 3.217 | 3.275 | 3.333 |
| 0.72 | 2.993 | 3.057 | 3.121 | 3.186 | 3.250 | 3.314 | 3.379 | 3.443 | 3.507 | 3.571 |
| 0.74 | 3.206 | 3.277 | 3.348 | 3.419 | 3.490 | 3.562 | 3.633 | 3.704 | 3.775 | 3.846 |
| 0.76 | 3.454 | 3.533 | 3.612 | 3.692 | 3.771 | 3.850 | 3.929 | 4.008 | 4.087 | 4.167 |
| 0.78 | 3.748 | 3.836 | 3.925 | 4.014 | 4.102 | 4.191 | 4.280 | 4.368 | 4.457 | 4.545 |
| 0.80 | 4.100 | 4.200 | 4.300 | 4.400 | 4.500 | 4.600 | 4.700 | 4.800 | 4.900 | 5.000 |
| 0.82 | 4.531 | 4.644 | 4.758 | 4.872 | 4.986 | 5.100 | 5.214 | 5.328 | 5.442 | 5.556 |
| 0.84 | 5.069 | 5.200 | 5.331 | 5.462 | 5.594 | 5.725 | 5.856 | 5.987 | 6.119 | 6.250 |
| 0.86 | 5.761 | 5.914 | 6.068 | 6.221 | 6.375 | 6.529 | 6.682 | 6.836 | 6.989 | 7.143 |
| 0.88 | 6.683 | 6.867 | 7.050 | 7.233 | 7.417 | 7.600 | 7.783 | 7.967 | 8.150 | 8.333 |
| 0.90 | 7.975 | 8.200 | 8.425 | 8.650 | 8.875 | 9.100 | 9.325 | 9.550 | 9.775 | 10.000 |
| 0.92 | 9.912 | 10.200 | 10.487 | 10.775 | 11.062 | 11.350 | 11.637 | 11.925 | 12.212 | 12.500 |
| 0.94 | 13.142 | 13.533 | 13.925 | 14.317 | 14.708 | 15.100 | 15.492 | 15.883 | 16.275 | 16.667 |
| 0.96 | 19.600 | 20.200 | 20.800 | 21.400 | 22.000 | 22.600 | 23.200 | 23.800 | 24.400 | 25.000 |
| 0.98 | 38.975 | 40.200 | 41.425 | 42.650 | 43.875 | 45.100 | 46.325 | 47.550 | 48.775 | 50.000 |

**Table 6.** STANDARD DEVIATION OF QUEUING TIMES FOR A SINGLE-SERVER QUEUE, WITH POISSON ARRIVAL PATTERN AND FIRST-IN, FIRST-OUT DISPATCHING DISCIPLINE

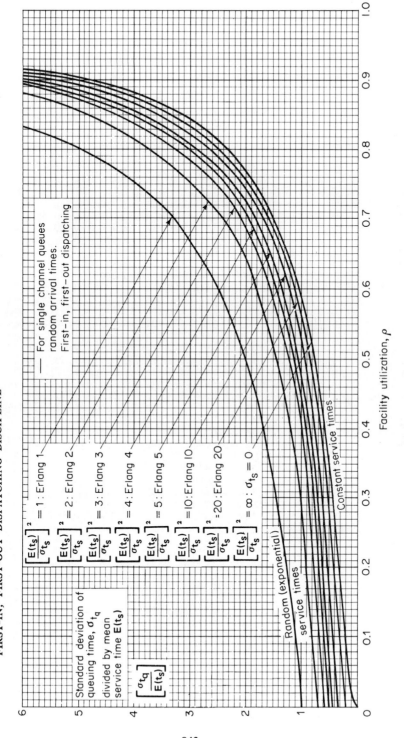

These curves are tabulated on the following two pages.

**Table 6.** (CONTINUED)

Values of $\dfrac{\sigma_{t_q}}{E[t_s]}$

| Facility Utiliza-tion | Coefficient of Variation, Squared, for Service Time, $\left[\dfrac{\sigma_{t_s}}{E(t_s)}\right]^2$ | | | | | | | | | | |
|---|---|---|---|---|---|---|---|---|---|---|---|
| | 0.0 | 0.05 | 0.10 | 0.15 | 0.20 | 0.25 | 0.30 | 0.35 | 0.40 | 0.45 | 0.50 |
| 0.00 | 0.000 | 0.224 | 0.316 | 0.387 | 0.447 | 0.500 | 0.548 | 0.592 | 0.632 | 0.671 | 0.707 |
| 0.02 | 0.083 | 0.241 | 0.330 | 0.400 | 0.460 | 0.513 | 0.561 | 0.605 | 0.646 | 0.685 | 0.722 |
| 0.04 | 0.120 | 0.258 | 0.345 | 0.414 | 0.473 | 0.526 | 0.574 | 0.619 | 0.660 | 0.699 | 0.737 |
| 0.06 | 0.149 | 0.275 | 0.360 | 0.428 | 0.487 | 0.540 | 0.588 | 0.633 | 0.675 | 0.715 | 0.752 |
| 0.08 | 0.176 | 0.293 | 0.375 | 0.443 | 0.501 | 0.554 | 0.603 | 0.648 | 0.690 | 0.731 | 0.769 |
| 0.10 | 0.200 | 0.310 | 0.391 | 0.458 | 0.516 | 0.569 | 0.618 | 0.664 | 0.707 | 0.747 | 0.786 |
| 0.12 | 0.224 | 0.328 | 0.407 | 0.473 | 0.532 | 0.585 | 0.634 | 0.680 | 0.724 | 0.765 | 0.804 |
| 0.14 | 0.247 | 0.346 | 0.424 | 0.490 | 0.548 | 0.602 | 0.651 | 0.698 | 0.741 | 0.783 | 0.823 |
| 0.16 | 0.269 | 0.365 | 0.441 | 0.507 | 0.565 | 0.619 | 0.669 | 0.716 | 0.760 | 0.802 | 0.843 |
| 0.18 | 0.292 | 0.384 | 0.460 | 0.525 | 0.583 | 0.637 | 0.687 | 0.735 | 0.780 | 0.823 | 0.864 |
| 0.20 | 0.315 | 0.404 | 0.478 | 0.543 | 0.602 | 0.656 | 0.707 | 0.755 | 0.800 | 0.844 | 0.886 |
| 0.22 | 0.337 | 0.425 | 0.498 | 0.563 | 0.622 | 0.676 | 0.727 | 0.776 | 0.822 | 0.867 | 0.909 |
| 0.24 | 0.361 | 0.446 | 0.519 | 0.583 | 0.642 | 0.697 | 0.749 | 0.798 | 0.845 | 0.890 | 0.934 |
| 0.26 | 0.385 | 0.468 | 0.540 | 0.605 | 0.664 | 0.720 | 0.772 | 0.822 | 0.869 | 0.915 | 0.960 |
| 0.28 | 0.409 | 0.491 | 0.563 | 0.628 | 0.687 | 0.743 | 0.796 | 0.846 | 0.895 | 0.942 | 0.987 |
| 0.30 | 0.434 | 0.515 | 0.587 | 0.651 | 0.711 | 0.768 | 0.821 | 0.873 | 0.922 | 0.970 | 1.016 |
| 0.32 | 0.461 | 0.541 | 0.612 | 0.677 | 0.737 | 0.794 | 0.848 | 0.900 | 0.951 | 0.999 | 1.046 |
| 0.34 | 0.488 | 0.567 | 0.638 | 0.703 | 0.764 | 0.822 | 0.877 | 0.930 | 0.981 | 1.031 | 1.079 |
| 0.36 | 0.516 | 0.595 | 0.666 | 0.731 | 0.793 | 0.852 | 0.908 | 0.961 | 1.014 | 1.064 | 1.114 |
| 0.38 | 0.546 | 0.624 | 0.695 | 0.761 | 0.824 | 0.883 | 0.940 | 0.995 | 1.048 | 1.100 | 1.151 |
| 0.40 | 0.577 | 0.655 | 0.726 | 0.793 | 0.856 | 0.917 | 0.975 | 1.031 | 1.085 | 1.138 | 1.190 |
| 0.42 | 0.610 | 0.688 | 0.760 | 0.827 | 0.891 | 0.953 | 1.012 | 1.069 | 1.125 | 1.179 | 1.233 |
| 0.44 | 0.645 | 0.723 | 0.795 | 0.864 | 0.929 | 0.991 | 1.051 | 1.110 | 1.167 | 1.223 | 1.278 |
| 0.46 | 0.682 | 0.760 | 0.833 | 0.902 | 0.969 | 1.032 | 1.094 | 1.154 | 1.213 | 1.270 | 1.327 |
| 0.48 | 0.722 | 0.800 | 0.874 | 0.944 | 1.012 | 1.077 | 1.140 | 1.202 | 1.262 | 1.321 | 1.379 |
| 0.50 | 0.764 | 0.843 | 0.918 | 0.989 | 1.058 | 1.125 | 1.190 | 1.253 | 1.315 | 1.376 | 1.436 |
| 0.52 | 0.809 | 0.889 | 0.965 | 1.038 | 1.109 | 1.117 | 1.244 | 1.309 | 1.373 | 1.436 | 1.498 |
| 0.54 | 0.858 | 0.939 | 1.017 | 1.091 | 1.163 | 1.234 | 1.302 | 1.370 | 1.436 | 1.501 | 1.565 |
| 0.56 | 0.911 | 0.993 | 1.072 | 1.149 | 1.223 | 1.295 | 1.366 | 1.436 | 1.504 | 1.572 | 1.638 |
| 0.58 | 0.968 | 1.052 | 1.133 | 1.212 | 1.288 | 1.363 | 1.436 | 1.508 | 1.579 | 1.649 | 1.719 |
| 0.60 | 1.031 | 1.117 | 1.200 | 1.281 | 1.360 | 1.437 | 1.513 | 1.588 | 1.662 | 1.735 | 1.807 |
| 0.62 | 1.100 | 1.188 | 1.274 | 1.358 | 1.439 | 1.520 | 1.599 | 1.677 | 1.754 | 1.830 | 1.905 |
| 0.64 | 1.176 | 1.276 | 1.356 | 1.443 | 1.528 | 1.611 | 1.693 | 1.775 | 1.855 | 1.935 | 2.014 |
| 0.66 | 1.261 | 1.355 | 1.447 | 1.537 | 1.626 | 1.713 | 1.799 | 1.885 | 1.969 | 2.053 | 2.136 |
| 0.68 | 1.355 | 1.454 | 1.550 | 1.644 | 1.737 | 1.828 | 1.919 | 2.008 | 2.097 | 2.185 | 2.273 |
| 0.70 | 1.462 | 1.565 | 1.665 | 1.764 | 1.862 | 1.958 | 2.054 | 2.148 | 2.242 | 2.335 | 2.428 |
| 0.72 | 1.584 | 1.692 | 1.798 | 1.902 | 2.005 | 2.107 | 2.208 | 2.309 | 2.408 | 2.507 | 2.606 |
| 0.74 | 1.724 | 2.838 | 1.950 | 2.061 | 2.170 | 2.279 | 2.387 | 2.494 | 2.600 | 2.706 | 2.811 |
| 0.76 | 1.887 | 2.008 | 2.128 | 2.246 | 2.363 | 2.479 | 2.595 | 2.710 | 2.824 | 2.937 | 3.051 |
| 0.78 | 2.080 | 2.209 | 2.337 | 2.464 | 2.591 | 2.716 | 2.841 | 2.965 | 3.088 | 3.211 | 3.334 |
| 0.80 | 2.309 | 2.449 | 2.588 | 2.726 | 2.864 | 3.000 | 3.136 | 3.271 | 3.406 | 3.540 | 3.674 |
| 0.82 | 2.590 | 2.743 | 2.895 | 3.047 | 3.197 | 3.347 | 3.497 | 3.646 | 3.794 | 3.942 | 4.090 |
| 0.84 | 2.939 | 3.109 | 3.278 | 3.447 | 3.614 | 3.781 | 3.948 | 4.114 | 4.280 | 4.445 | 4.610 |
| 0.86 | 3.388 | 3.580 | 3.771 | 3.961 | 4.150 | 4.339 | 4.528 | 4.716 | 4.904 | 5.092 | 5.279 |
| 0.88 | 3.986 | 4.207 | 4.427 | 4.646 | 4.865 | 5.083 | 5.301 | 5.519 | 5.737 | 5.954 | 6.171 |
| 0.90 | 4.822 | 5.083 | 5.344 | 5.605 | 5.865 | 6.125 | 6.385 | 6.644 | 6.903 | 7.162 | 7.420 |
| 0.92 | 6.074 | 6.398 | 6.721 | 7.043 | 7.365 | 7.687 | 8.009 | 8.331 | 8.652 | 8.974 | 9.295 |
| 0.94 | 8.160 | 8.587 | 9.013 | 9.440 | 9.866 | 10.292 | 10.717 | 11.143 | 11.568 | 11.994 | 12.419 |
| 0.96 | 12.329 | 12.963 | 13.598 | 14.232 | 14.866 | 15.500 | 16.134 | 16.768 | 17.401 | 18.035 | 18.668 |
| 0.98 | 24.831 | 26.090 | 27.349 | 28.608 | 29.866 | 31.125 | 32.384 | 33.642 | 34.901 | 36.159 | 37.417 |

**Table 6.** (CONTINUED)     Values of $\dfrac{\sigma_{t_q}}{E[t_s]}$

| Facility Utiliza-tion | Coefficient of Variation, Squared, for Service Time, $\left[\dfrac{\sigma_{t_s}}{E(t_s)}\right]^2$ | | | | | | | | | |
|---|---|---|---|---|---|---|---|---|---|---|
| $\rho$ | 0.55 | 0.60 | 0.65 | 0.70 | 0.75 | 0.80 | 0.85 | 0.90 | 0.95 | 1.00 |
| 0.00 | 0.742 | 0.775 | 0.806 | 0.837 | 0.866 | 0.894 | 0.922 | 0.949 | 0.975 | 1.000 |
| 0.02 | 0.757 | 0.790 | 0.822 | 0.853 | 0.883 | 0.912 | 0.940 | 0.968 | 0.994 | 1.020 |
| 0.04 | 0.772 | 0.806 | 0.839 | 0.871 | 0.901 | 0.931 | 0.960 | 0.988 | 1.015 | 1.042 |
| 0.06 | 0.788 | 0.823 | 0.856 | 0.889 | 0.920 | 0.950 | 0.980 | 1.008 | 1.036 | 1.064 |
| 0.08 | 0.806 | 0.841 | 0.875 | 0.908 | 0.939 | 0.970 | 1.001 | 1.030 | 1.059 | 1.087 |
| 0.10 | 0.823 | 0.859 | 0.894 | 0.927 | 0.960 | 0.992 | 1.023 | 1.053 | 1.082 | 1.111 |
| 0.12 | 0.842 | 0.879 | 0.914 | 0.948 | 0.981 | 1.014 | 1.045 | 1.076 | 1.107 | 1.136 |
| 0.14 | 0.862 | 0.899 | 0.935 | 0.970 | 1.004 | 1.037 | 1.069 | 1.101 | 1.132 | 1.163 |
| 0.16 | 0.882 | 0.920 | 0.957 | 0.993 | 1.027 | 1.061 | 1.095 | 1.127 | 1.159 | 1.190 |
| 0.18 | 0.904 | 0.943 | 0.980 | 1.017 | 1.052 | 1.087 | 1.121 | 1.154 | 1.187 | 1.220 |
| 0.20 | 0.927 | 0.966 | 1.004 | 1.042 | 1.078 | 1.114 | 1.149 | 1.183 | 1.217 | 1.250 |
| 0.22 | 0.951 | 0.991 | 1.030 | 1.068 | 1.106 | 1.142 | 1.178 | 1.213 | 1.248 | 1.282 |
| 0.24 | 0.976 | 1.017 | 1.057 | 1.096 | 1.134 | 1.172 | 1.209 | 1.245 | 1.281 | 1.316 |
| 0.26 | 1.003 | 1.045 | 1.086 | 1.126 | 1.165 | 1.203 | 1.241 | 1.278 | 1.315 | 1.351 |
| 0.28 | 1.031 | 1.074 | 1.116 | 1.157 | 1.197 | 1.237 | 1.275 | 1.314 | 1.352 | 1.389 |
| 0.30 | 1.061 | 1.105 | 1.148 | 1.190 | 1.231 | 1.272 | 1.312 | 1.351 | 1.390 | 1.429 |
| 0.32 | 1.093 | 1.137 | 1.182 | 1.225 | 1.267 | 1.309 | 1.350 | 1.391 | 1.431 | 1.471 |
| 0.34 | 1.126 | 1.172 | 1.217 | 1.262 | 1.306 | 1.349 | 1.391 | 1.433 | 1.474 | 1.515 |
| 0.36 | 1.162 | 1.209 | 1.256 | 1.301 | 1.346 | 1.391 | 1.434 | 1.478 | 1.520 | 1.562 |
| 0.38 | 1.200 | 1.249 | 1.297 | 1.343 | 1.390 | 1.435 | 1.481 | 1.525 | 1.569 | 1.613 |
| 0.40 | 1.241 | 1.291 | 1.340 | 1.388 | 1.436 | 1.483 | 1.530 | 1.576 | 1.621 | 1.667 |
| 0.42 | 1.285 | 1.336 | 1.387 | 1.437 | 1.486 | 1.534 | 1.583 | 1.630 | 1.677 | 1.724 |
| 0.44 | 1.332 | 1.385 | 1.437 | 1.488 | 1.539 | 1.589 | 1.639 | 1.688 | 1.737 | 1.786 |
| 0.46 | 1.382 | 1.437 | 1.490 | 1.544 | 1.596 | 1.648 | 1.700 | 1.751 | 1.802 | 1.852 |
| 0.48 | 1.436 | 1.493 | 1.548 | 1.603 | 1.658 | 1.712 | 1.765 | 1.818 | 1.871 | 1.923 |
| 0.50 | 1.495 | 1.553 | 1.611 | 1.668 | 1.725 | 1.780 | 1.836 | 1.891 | 1.946 | 2.000 |
| 0.52 | 1.559 | 1.619 | 1.679 | 1.738 | 1.797 | 1.855 | 1.913 | 1.970 | 2.027 | 2.083 |
| 0.54 | 1.628 | 1.691 | 1.753 | 1.814 | 1.875 | 1.936 | 1.996 | 2.056 | 2.115 | 2.174 |
| 0.56 | 1.704 | 1.769 | 1.834 | 1.898 | 1.961 | 2.024 | 2.087 | 2.149 | 2.211 | 2.273 |
| 0.58 | 1.787 | 1.855 | 1.922 | 1.989 | 2.055 | 2.121 | 2.187 | 2.252 | 2.316 | 2.381 |
| 0.60 | 1.879 | 1.949 | 2.020 | 2.089 | 2.159 | 2.228 | 2.296 | 2.364 | 2.432 | 2.500 |
| 0.62 | 1.980 | 2.054 | 2.127 | 2.201 | 2.273 | 2.346 | 2.417 | 2.489 | 2.560 | 2.632 |
| 0.64 | 2.092 | 2.170 | 2.247 | 2.324 | 2.400 | 2.477 | 2.552 | 2.628 | 2.703 | 2.778 |
| 0.66 | 2.218 | 2.300 | 2.381 | 2.462 | 2.543 | 2.623 | 2.703 | 2.783 | 2.862 | 2.941 |
| 0.68 | 2.360 | 2.446 | 2.532 | 2.618 | 2.703 | 2.788 | 2.873 | 2.957 | 3.041 | 3.125 |
| 0.70 | 2.520 | 2.612 | 2.703 | 2.794 | 2.885 | 2.975 | 3.065 | 3.155 | 3.244 | 3.333 |
| 0.72 | 2.704 | 2.802 | 2.899 | 2.996 | 3.092 | 3.189 | 3.285 | 3.380 | 3.476 | 3.571 |
| 0.74 | 2.916 | 3.021 | 3.125 | 3.229 | 3.332 | 3.435 | 3.538 | 3.641 | 3.744 | 3.846 |
| 0.76 | 3.164 | 3.276 | 3.388 | 3.500 | 3.612 | 3.723 | 3.834 | 3.945 | 4.056 | 4.167 |
| 0.78 | 3.456 | 3.578 | 3.700 | 3.821 | 3.943 | 4.064 | 4.184 | 4.305 | 4.425 | 4.545 |
| 0.80 | 3.808 | 3.941 | 4.074 | 4.207 | 4.340 | 4.472 | 4.604 | 4.736 | 4.868 | 5.000 |
| 0.82 | 4.238 | 4.385 | 4.532 | 4.679 | 4.825 | 4.972 | 5.118 | 5.264 | 5.410 | 5.556 |
| 0.84 | 4.775 | 4.940 | 5.104 | 5.268 | 5.432 | 5.596 | 5.760 | 6.923 | 6.087 | 6.250 |
| 0.86 | 5.466 | 5.653 | 5.840 | 6.026 | 6.213 | 6.399 | 6.585 | 6.771 | 6.957 | 7.143 |
| 0.88 | 6.388 | 6.605 | 6.821 | 7.038 | 7.254 | 7.470 | 7.686 | 7.902 | 8.118 | 8.333 |
| 0.90 | 7.679 | 7.937 | 8.195 | 8.454 | 8.712 | 8.969 | 9.227 | 9.485 | 9.742 | 10.000 |
| 0.92 | 9.616 | 9.936 | 10.257 | 10.578 | 10.898 | 11.219 | 11.539 | 11.860 | 12.180 | 12.500 |
| 0.94 | 12.844 | 13.269 | 13.694 | 14.119 | 14.544 | 14.968 | 15.393 | 15.818 | 16.242 | 16.667 |
| 0.96 | 19.302 | 19.935 | 20.568 | 21.201 | 21.835 | 22.468 | 23.101 | 23.734 | 24.367 | 25.000 |
| 0.98 | 38.676 | 39.934 | 41.192 | 42.451 | 43.709 | 44.967 | 46.225 | 47.484 | 48.742 | 50.000 |

# Table 7. STANDARD DEVIATION OF WAITING TIME PRIOR TO SERVICE IN A SINGLE-SERVER QUEUE, WITH POISSON ARRIVAL PATTERN AND FIRST-IN, FIRST-OUT DISPATCHING DISCIPLINE

Values of $\dfrac{\sigma_{t_w}}{E(t_s)}$

Coefficient of Variation, Squared, for Service Time, $\left[\dfrac{\sigma_{t_s}}{E(t_s)}\right]^2$

| Facility Utilization $\rho$ | 0.0 | 0.05 | 0.10 | 0.15 | 0.20 | 0.25 | 0.30 | 0.35 | 0.40 | 0.45 | 0.50 |
|---|---|---|---|---|---|---|---|---|---|---|---|
| 0.00 | 0.000 | 0.000 | 0.000 | 0.000 | 0.000 | 0.000 | 0.000 | 0.000 | 0.000 | 0.000 | 0.000 |
| 0.02 | 0.082 | 0.089 | 0.095 | 0.102 | 0.108 | 0.114 | 0.120 | 0.126 | 0.132 | 0.138 | 0.144 |
| 0.04 | 0.120 | 0.129 | 0.137 | 0.146 | 0.155 | 0.163 | 0.172 | 0.181 | 0.189 | 0.198 | 0.207 |
| 0.06 | 0.149 | 0.160 | 0.171 | 0.182 | 0.193 | 0.204 | 0.214 | 0.225 | 0.236 | 0.246 | 0.257 |
| 0.08 | 0.176 | 0.189 | 0.201 | 0.214 | 0.227 | 0.239 | 0.252 | 0.265 | 0.277 | 0.290 | 0.302 |
| 0.10 | 0.200 | 0.215 | 0.229 | 0.244 | 0.258 | 0.273 | 0.287 | 0.301 | 0.315 | 0.329 | 0.344 |
| 0.12 | 0.224 | 0.240 | 0.256 | 0.272 | 0.288 | 0.304 | 0.320 | 0.336 | 0.352 | 0.367 | 0.383 |
| 0.14 | 0.247 | 0.265 | 0.282 | 0.300 | 0.317 | 0.335 | 0.352 | 0.370 | 0.387 | 0.404 | 0.422 |
| 0.16 | 0.269 | 0.289 | 0.308 | 0.327 | 0.346 | 0.365 | 0.384 | 0.403 | 0.422 | 0.440 | 0.459 |
| 0.18 | 0.292 | 0.313 | 0.333 | 0.354 | 0.375 | 0.395 | 0.415 | 0.436 | 0.456 | 0.476 | 0.497 |
| 0.20 | 0.315 | 0.337 | 0.359 | 0.381 | 0.403 | 0.425 | 0.447 | 0.469 | 0.491 | 0.512 | 0.534 |
| 0.22 | 0.337 | 0.361 | 0.385 | 0.408 | 0.432 | 0.455 | 0.479 | 0.502 | 0.525 | 0.548 | 0.572 |
| 0.24 | 0.361 | 0.386 | 0.411 | 0.436 | 0.461 | 0.486 | 0.511 | 0.536 | 0.560 | 0.585 | 0.610 |
| 0.26 | 0.385 | 0.411 | 0.438 | 0.465 | 0.491 | 0.518 | 0.544 | 0.570 | 0.596 | 0.623 | 0.649 |
| 0.28 | 0.409 | 0.437 | 0.466 | 0.494 | 0.522 | 0.550 | 0.578 | 0.605 | 0.633 | 0.661 | 0.688 |
| 0.30 | 0.434 | 0.464 | 0.494 | 0.524 | 0.553 | 0.583 | 0.612 | 0.642 | 0.671 | 0.700 | 0.729 |
| 0.32 | 0.461 | 0.492 | 0.523 | 0.555 | 0.586 | 0.617 | 0.648 | 0.679 | 0.710 | 0.741 | 0.771 |
| 0.34 | 0.488 | 0.521 | 0.554 | 0.587 | 0.620 | 0.652 | 0.685 | 0.718 | 0.750 | 0.783 | 0.815 |
| 0.36 | 0.516 | 0.551 | 0.586 | 0.620 | 0.655 | 0.689 | 0.724 | 0.758 | 0.792 | 0.826 | 0.861 |
| 0.38 | 0.546 | 0.583 | 0.619 | 0.655 | 0.692 | 0.728 | 0.764 | 0.800 | 0.836 | 0.872 | 0.908 |
| 0.40 | 0.577 | 0.616 | 0.654 | 0.692 | 0.730 | 0.768 | 0.806 | 0.844 | 0.882 | 0.920 | 0.957 |
| 0.42 | 0.610 | 0.651 | 0.691 | 0.731 | 0.771 | 0.811 | 0.851 | 0.890 | 0.930 | 0.970 | 1.010 |
| 0.44 | 0.645 | 0.688 | 0.730 | 0.772 | 0.814 | 0.856 | 0.898 | 0.939 | 0.981 | 1.023 | 1.064 |
| 0.46 | 0.682 | 0.727 | 0.771 | 0.815 | 0.859 | 0.903 | 0.947 | 0.991 | 1.035 | 1.079 | 1.123 |
| 0.48 | 0.772 | 0.768 | 0.815 | 0.861 | 0.908 | 0.954 | 1.000 | 1.046 | 1.092 | 1.138 | 1.184 |
| 0.50 | 0.764 | 0.813 | 0.862 | 0.910 | 0.959 | 1.008 | 1.056 | 1.105 | 1.153 | 1.202 | 1.250 |
| 0.52 | 0.809 | 0.861 | 0.912 | 0.963 | 1.014 | 1.066 | 1.117 | 1.168 | 1.219 | 1.270 | 1.320 |
| 0.54 | 0.858 | 0.912 | 0.966 | 1.020 | 1.074 | 1.128 | 1.182 | 1.235 | 1.289 | 1.343 | 1.396 |
| 0.56 | 0.911 | 0.968 | 1.025 | 1.082 | 1.138 | 1.195 | 1.252 | 1.308 | 1.365 | 1.421 | 1.478 |
| 0.58 | 0.968 | 1.028 | 1.088 | 1.148 | 1.208 | 1.268 | 1.328 | 1.388 | 1.447 | 1.507 | 1.566 |
| 0.60 | 1.031 | 1.094 | 1.158 | 1.221 | 1.285 | 1.348 | 1.411 | 1.474 | 1.537 | 1.600 | 1.663 |
| 0.62 | 1.100 | 1.167 | 1.234 | 1.301 | 1.368 | 1.435 | 1.502 | 1.569 | 1.636 | 1.702 | 1.769 |
| 0.64 | 1.176 | 1.247 | 1.318 | 1.390 | 1.461 | 1.532 | 1.602 | 1.673 | 1.744 | 1.815 | 1.886 |
| 0.66 | 1.261 | 1.336 | 1.412 | 1.488 | 1.563 | 1.639 | 1.714 | 1.789 | 1.865 | 1.940 | 2.015 |
| 0.68 | 1.355 | 1.436 | 1.517 | 1.597 | 1.678 | 1.758 | 1.839 | 1.919 | 1.999 | 2.080 | 2.160 |
| 0.70 | 1.462 | 1.549 | 1.635 | 1.721 | 1.807 | 1.893 | 1.979 | 2.065 | 2.151 | 2.237 | 2.323 |
| 0.72 | 1.584 | 1.677 | 1.770 | 1.862 | 1.955 | 2.047 | 2.139 | 2.232 | 2.324 | 2.416 | 2.508 |
| 0.74 | 1.724 | 1.824 | 1.924 | 2.024 | 2.124 | 2.223 | 2.323 | 2.422 | 2.522 | 2.621 | 2.721 |
| 0.76 | 1.887 | 1.996 | 2.104 | 2.212 | 2.320 | 2.428 | 2.536 | 2.644 | 2.752 | 2.860 | 2.968 |
| 0.78 | 2.080 | 2.198 | 2.316 | 2.434 | 2.552 | 2.669 | 2.787 | 2.905 | 3.023 | 3.141 | 3.258 |
| 0.80 | 2.309 | 2.439 | 2.569 | 2.699 | 2.828 | 2.958 | 3.088 | 3.217 | 3.347 | 3.476 | 3.606 |
| 0.82 | 2.590 | 2.734 | 2.878 | 3.022 | 3.166 | 3.310 | 3.454 | 3.597 | 3.741 | 3.885 | 4.029 |
| 0.84 | 2.939 | 3.101 | 3.263 | 3.425 | 3.586 | 3.748 | 3.910 | 4.071 | 4.233 | 4.394 | 4.556 |
| 0.86 | 3.388 | 3.573 | 3.757 | 3.942 | 4.126 | 4.310 | 4.495 | 4.679 | 4.863 | 5.047 | 5.232 |
| 0.88 | 3.986 | 4.201 | 4.415 | 4.630 | 4.844 | 5.059 | 5.273 | 5.487 | 5.702 | 5.916 | 6.131 |
| 0.90 | 4.822 | 5.078 | 5.335 | 5.592 | 5.848 | 6.105 | 6.361 | 6.617 | 6.874 | 7.130 | 7.387 |
| 0.92 | 6.074 | 6.394 | 6.713 | 7.032 | 7.352 | 7.671 | 7.991 | 8.310 | 8.629 | 8.948 | 9.268 |
| 0.94 | 8.160 | 8.584 | 9.008 | 9.432 | 9.856 | 10.280 | 10.703 | 11.127 | 11.551 | 11.975 | 12.399 |
| 0.96 | 12.329 | 12.961 | 13.594 | 14.227 | 14.859 | 15.492 | 16.125 | 16.757 | 17.390 | 18.022 | 18.655 |
| 0.98 | 24.831 | 26.089 | 27.347 | 28.605 | 29.863 | 31.121 | 32.379 | 33.637 | 34.895 | 36.153 | 37.411 |

**Table 7.** (CONTINUED)

Values of $\dfrac{\sigma_{t_w}}{E(t_s)}$

| Facility Utiliza-tion | Coefficient of Variation, Squared, for Service Time, $\left[\dfrac{\sigma_{t_s}}{E(t_s)}\right]^2$ | | | | | | | | | |
|---|---|---|---|---|---|---|---|---|---|---|
| $\rho$ | 0.55 | 0.60 | 0.65 | 0.70 | 0.75 | 0.80 | 0.85 | 0.90 | 0.95 | 1.0 |
| 0.00 | 0.000 | 0.000 | 0.000 | 0.000 | 0.000 | 0.000 | 0.000 | 0.000 | 0.000 | 0.000 |
| 0.02 | 0.150 | 0.156 | 0.162 | 0.167 | 0.173 | 0.179 | 0.185 | 0.191 | 0.197 | 0.203 |
| 0.04 | 0.215 | 0.224 | 0.232 | 0.241 | 0.249 | 0.258 | 0.266 | 0.275 | 0.283 | 0.292 |
| 0.06 | 0.268 | 0.278 | 0.289 | 0.300 | 0.310 | 0.321 | 0.331 | 0.342 | 0.352 | 0.363 |
| 0.08 | 0.314 | 0.327 | 0.339 | 0.352 | 0.364 | 0.377 | 0.389 | 0.401 | 0.414 | 0.426 |
| 0.10 | 0.358 | 0.372 | 0.386 | 0.400 | 0.414 | 0.428 | 0.442 | 0.456 | 0.470 | 0.484 |
| 0.12 | 0.399 | 0.415 | 0.430 | 0.446 | 0.462 | 0.477 | 0.493 | 0.509 | 0.524 | 0.540 |
| 0.14 | 0.439 | 0.456 | 0.473 | 0.490 | 0.508 | 0.525 | 0.542 | 0.559 | 0.576 | 0.593 |
| 0.16 | 0.478 | 0.497 | 0.515 | 0.534 | 0.553 | 0.571 | 0.590 | 0.609 | 0.627 | 0.646 |
| 0.18 | 0.517 | 0.537 | 0.557 | 0.577 | 0.598 | 0.618 | 0.638 | 0.658 | 0.678 | 0.698 |
| 0.20 | 0.556 | 0.577 | 0.599 | 0.621 | 0.642 | 0.664 | 0.685 | 0.707 | 0.728 | 0.750 |
| 0.22 | 0.595 | 0.618 | 0.641 | 0.664 | 0.687 | 0.710 | 0.733 | 0.756 | 0.779 | 0.802 |
| 0.24 | 0.634 | 0.659 | 0.684 | 0.708 | 0.733 | 0.757 | 0.782 | 0.806 | 0.831 | 0.855 |
| 0.26 | 0.675 | 0.701 | 0.727 | 0.753 | 0.779 | 0.805 | 0.831 | 0.857 | 0.833 | 0.909 |
| 0.28 | 0.716 | 0.744 | 0.771 | 0.799 | 0.826 | 0.854 | 0.881 | 0.909 | 0.936 | 0.964 |
| 0.30 | 0.758 | 0.788 | 0.817 | 0.846 | 0.875 | 0.904 | 0.933 | 0.962 | 0.991 | 1.020 |
| 0.32 | 0.802 | 0.833 | 0.864 | 0.894 | 0.925 | 0.956 | 0.986 | 1.017 | 1.048 | 1.078 |
| 0.34 | 0.848 | 0.880 | 0.912 | 0.945 | 0.977 | 1.009 | 1.042 | 1.074 | 1.106 | 1.138 |
| 0.36 | 0.895 | 0.929 | 0.963 | 0.997 | 1.031 | 1.065 | 1.099 | 1.133 | 1.167 | 1.201 |
| 0.38 | 0.944 | 0.980 | 1.015 | 1.051 | 1.087 | 1.123 | 1.158 | 1.194 | 1.230 | 1.265 |
| 0.40 | 0.995 | 1.033 | 1.070 | 1.108 | 1.146 | 1.183 | 1.221 | 1.258 | 1.296 | 1.333 |
| 0.42 | 1.049 | 1.089 | 1.128 | 1.168 | 1.207 | 1.247 | 1.286 | 1.326 | 1.365 | 1.405 |
| 0.44 | 1.106 | 1.148 | 1.189 | 1.231 | 1.272 | 1.314 | 1.355 | 1.397 | 1.438 | 1.479 |
| 0.46 | 1.166 | 1.210 | 1.254 | 1.297 | 1.341 | 1.384 | 1.428 | 1.472 | 1.515 | 1.559 |
| 0.48 | 1.230 | 1.276 | 1.322 | 1.368 | 1.414 | 1.460 | 1.505 | 1.551 | 1.597 | 1.643 |
| 0.50 | 1.298 | 1.347 | 1.395 | 1.443 | 1.491 | 1.539 | 1.588 | 1.636 | 1.684 | 1.732 |
| 0.52 | 1.371 | 1.422 | 1.473 | 1.524 | 1.574 | 1.625 | 1.676 | 1.726 | 1.777 | 1.828 |
| 0.54 | 1.450 | 1.503 | 1.557 | 1.610 | 1.663 | 1.717 | 1.770 | 1.824 | 1.877 | 1.930 |
| 0.56 | 1.534 | 1.591 | 1.647 | 1.703 | 1.760 | 1.816 | 1.872 | 1.928 | 1.985 | 2.041 |
| 0.58 | 1.626 | 1.685 | 1.745 | 1.804 | 1.864 | 1.923 | 1.983 | 2.042 | 2.101 | 2.161 |
| 0.60 | 1.726 | 1.789 | 1.852 | 1.915 | 1.977 | 2.040 | 2.103 | 2.166 | 2.229 | 2.291 |
| 0.62 | 1.836 | 1.902 | 1.969 | 2.035 | 2.102 | 2.168 | 2.235 | 2.301 | 2.368 | 2.434 |
| 0.64 | 1.956 | 2.027 | 2.098 | 2.168 | 2.239 | 2.309 | 2.380 | 2.450 | 2.521 | 2.592 |
| 0.66 | 2.090 | 2.165 | 2.241 | 2.316 | 2.391 | 2.466 | 2.541 | 2.616 | 2.691 | 2.766 |
| 0.68 | 2.240 | 2.320 | 2.400 | 2.480 | 2.561 | 2.641 | 2.721 | 2.801 | 2.881 | 2.961 |
| 0.70 | 2.409 | 2.494 | 2.580 | 2.666 | 2.752 | 2.837 | 2.923 | 3.009 | 3.094 | 3.180 |
| 0.72 | 2.600 | 2.692 | 2.784 | 2.877 | 2.969 | 3.061 | 3.153 | 3.245 | 3.337 | 3.429 |
| 0.74 | 2.820 | 2.920 | 3.019 | 3.118 | 3.218 | 3.317 | 3.416 | 3.515 | 3.615 | 3.714 |
| 0.76 | 3.076 | 3.183 | 3.291 | 3.399 | 3.507 | 3.614 | 3.722 | 3.830 | 3.937 | 4.045 |
| 0.78 | 3.376 | 3.494 | 3.611 | 3.729 | 3.846 | 3.964 | 4.081 | 4.199 | 4.317 | 4.434 |
| 0.80 | 3.735 | 3.864 | 3.994 | 4.123 | 4.252 | 4.382 | 4.511 | 4.640 | 4.770 | 4.899 |
| 0.82 | 4.172 | 4.316 | 4.460 | 4.603 | 4.747 | 4.890 | 5.034 | 5.178 | 5.321 | 5.465 |
| 0.84 | 4.717 | 4.879 | 5.040 | 5.201 | 5.363 | 5.524 | 5.685 | 5.847 | 6.008 | 6.169 |
| 0.86 | 5.416 | 5.600 | 5.784 | 5.968 | 6.152 | 6.336 | 6.520 | 6.704 | 6.888 | 7.073 |
| 0.88 | 6.345 | 6.559 | 6.773 | 6.988 | 7.202 | 7.416 | 7.630 | 7.845 | 8.059 | 8.273 |
| 0.90 | 7.643 | 7.899 | 8.156 | 8.412 | 8.668 | 8.925 | 9.181 | 9.437 | 9.694 | 9.950 |
| 0.92 | 9.587 | 9.906 | 10.225 | 10.545 | 10.864 | 11.183 | 11.502 | 11.822 | 12.141 | 12.460 |
| 0.94 | 12.823 | 13.246 | 13.670 | 14.094 | 14.518 | 14.942 | 15.365 | 15.789 | 16.213 | 16.637 |
| 0.96 | 19.287 | 19.920 | 20.552 | 21.185 | 21.817 | 22.450 | 23.082 | 23.715 | 24.347 | 24.980 |
| 0.98 | 38.669 | 39.927 | 41.185 | 42.442 | 43.700 | 44.958 | 46.216 | 47.474 | 48.732 | 49.990 |

**Table 8.** PROBABILITY THAT ALL SERVERS ARE BUSY IN A MULTISERVER QUEUE, WITH EXPONENTIAL INTERARRIVAL TIMES, EXPONENTIAL SERVICE TIMES, ALL SERVERS EQUALLY LOADED, AND FIRST-IN, FIRST-OUT DISPATCHING

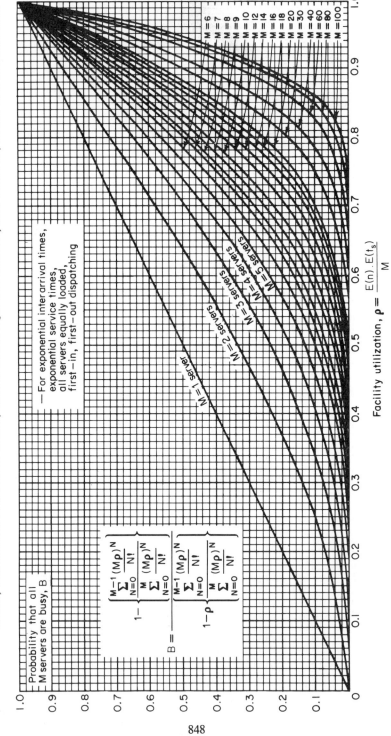

848

**Table 8.** (CONTINUED)

Values of Probability that All $M$ Servers Are Busy, $B$

Facility
Utiliza-
tion

Number of Servers, $M$

| $\rho$ | $M=1$ | $M=2$ | $M=3$ | $M=4$ | $M=5$ | $M=6$ | $M=7$ | $M=8$ | $M=9$ | $M=10$ | $M=11$ |
|---|---|---|---|---|---|---|---|---|---|---|---|
| 0.00 | 0.000 | 0.000 | 0.000 | 0.000 | 0.000 | 0.000 | 0.000 | 0.000 | 0.000 | 0.000 | 0.000 |
| 0.02 | 0.020 | 0.001 | 0.000 | 0.000 | 0.000 | 0.000 | 0.000 | 0.000 | 0.000 | 0.000 | 0.000 |
| 0.04 | 0.040 | 0.003 | 0.000 | 0.000 | 0.000 | 0.000 | 0.000 | 0.000 | 0.000 | 0.000 | 0.000 |
| 0.06 | 0.060 | 0.007 | 0.001 | 0.000 | 0.000 | 0.000 | 0.000 | 0.000 | 0.000 | 0.000 | 0.000 |
| 0.08 | 0.080 | 0.012 | 0.002 | 0.000 | 0.000 | 0.000 | 0.000 | 0.000 | 0.000 | 0.000 | 0.000 |
| 0.10 | 0.100 | 0.018 | 0.004 | 0.001 | 0.000 | 0.000 | 0.000 | 0.000 | 0.000 | 0.000 | 0.000 |
| 0.12 | 0.120 | 0.026 | 0.006 | 0.002 | 0.000 | 0.000 | 0.000 | 0.000 | 0.000 | 0.000 | 0.000 |
| 0.14 | 0.140 | 0.034 | 0.009 | 0.003 | 0.001 | 0.000 | 0.000 | 0.000 | 0.000 | 0.000 | 0.000 |
| 0.16 | 0.160 | 0.044 | 0.014 | 0.004 | 0.001 | 0.000 | 0.000 | 0.000 | 0.000 | 0.000 | 0.000 |
| 0.18 | 0.180 | 0.055 | 0.019 | 0.007 | 0.002 | 0.001 | 0.000 | 0.000 | 0.000 | 0.000 | 0.000 |
| 0.20 | 0.200 | 0.067 | 0.025 | 0.010 | 0.004 | 0.002 | 0.001 | 0.000 | 0.000 | 0.000 | 0.000 |
| 0.22 | 0.220 | 0.079 | 0.032 | 0.013 | 0.006 | 0.003 | 0.001 | 0.001 | 0.000 | 0.000 | 0.000 |
| 0.24 | 0.240 | 0.093 | 0.040 | 0.018 | 0.008 | 0.004 | 0.002 | 0.001 | 0.000 | 0.000 | 0.000 |
| 0.26 | 0.260 | 0.107 | 0.049 | 0.023 | 0.011 | 0.006 | 0.003 | 0.001 | 0.001 | 0.000 | 0.000 |
| 0.28 | 0.280 | 0.122 | 0.059 | 0.030 | 0.015 | 0.008 | 0.004 | 0.002 | 0.001 | 0.001 | 0.000 |
| 0.30 | 0.300 | 0.138 | 0.070 | 0.037 | 0.020 | 0.011 | 0.006 | 0.004 | 0.002 | 0.001 | 0.001 |
| 0.32 | 0.320 | 0.155 | 0.082 | 0.046 | 0.026 | 0.015 | 0.009 | 0.005 | 0.003 | 0.002 | 0.001 |
| 0.34 | 0.340 | 0.173 | 0.095 | 0.055 | 0.033 | 0.020 | 0.012 | 0.007 | 0.005 | 0.003 | 0.002 |
| 0.36 | 0.360 | 0.191 | 0.110 | 0.066 | 0.040 | 0.025 | 0.016 | 0.010 | 0.007 | 0.004 | 0.003 |
| 0.38 | 0.380 | 0.209 | 0.125 | 0.078 | 0.049 | 0.032 | 0.021 | 0.014 | 0.009 | 0.006 | 0.004 |
| 0.40 | 0.400 | 0.229 | 0.141 | 0.091 | 0.060 | 0.040 | 0.027 | 0.018 | 0.013 | 0.009 | 0.006 |
| 0.42 | 0.420 | 0.248 | 0.158 | 0.105 | 0.071 | 0.049 | 0.034 | 0.024 | 0.017 | 0.012 | 0.009 |
| 0.44 | 0.440 | 0.269 | 0.177 | 0.120 | 0.084 | 0.059 | 0.043 | 0.031 | 0.022 | 0.016 | 0.012 |
| 0.46 | 0.460 | 0.290 | 0.196 | 0.137 | 0.098 | 0.071 | 0.052 | 0.039 | 0.029 | 0.022 | 0.016 |
| 0.48 | 0.480 | 0.311 | 0.216 | 0.155 | 0.114 | 0.084 | 0.064 | 0.048 | 0.037 | 0.028 | 0.022 |
| 0.50 | 0.500 | 0.333 | 0.237 | 0.174 | 0.130 | 0.099 | 0.076 | 0.059 | 0.046 | 0.036 | 0.028 |
| 0.52 | 0.520 | 0.356 | 0.259 | 0.194 | 0.149 | 0.115 | 0.090 | 0.072 | 0.057 | 0.046 | 0.037 |
| 0.54 | 0.540 | 0.379 | 0.281 | 0.216 | 0.168 | 0.133 | 0.106 | 0.086 | 0.069 | 0.057 | 0.046 |
| 0.56 | 0.560 | 0.402 | 0.305 | 0.238 | 0.190 | 0.153 | 0.124 | 0.102 | 0.084 | 0.069 | 0.058 |
| 0.58 | 0.580 | 0.426 | 0.330 | 0.262 | 0.212 | 0.174 | 0.144 | 0.120 | 0.100 | 0.084 | 0.071 |
| 0.60 | 0.600 | 0.450 | 0.355 | 0.287 | 0.236 | 0.197 | 0.165 | 0.140 | 0.119 | 0.101 | 0.087 |
| 0.62 | 0.620 | 0.475 | 0.381 | 0.313 | 0.262 | 0.221 | 0.188 | 0.161 | 0.139 | 0.120 | 0.105 |
| 0.64 | 0.640 | 0.500 | 0.408 | 0.340 | 0.289 | 0.247 | 0.213 | 0.185 | 0.162 | 0.142 | 0.125 |
| 0.66 | 0.660 | 0.525 | 0.435 | 0.369 | 0.317 | 0.275 | 0.241 | 0.212 | 0.187 | 0.166 | 0.148 |
| 0.68 | 0.680 | 0.550 | 0.463 | 0.398 | 0.347 | 0.305 | 0.270 | 0.240 | 0.215 | 0.193 | 0.173 |
| 0.70 | 0.700 | 0.576 | 0.492 | 0.429 | 0.378 | 0.336 | 0.301 | 0.271 | 0.245 | 0.222 | 0.202 |
| 0.72 | 0.720 | 0.603 | 0.522 | 0.460 | 0.410 | 0.369 | 0.334 | 0.303 | 0.277 | 0.254 | 0.233 |
| 0.74 | 0.740 | 0.629 | 0.552 | 0.493 | 0.444 | 0.404 | 0.369 | 0.339 | 0.312 | 0.288 | 0.267 |
| 0.76 | 0.760 | 0.656 | 0.583 | 0.526 | 0.480 | 0.440 | 0.406 | 0.376 | 0.349 | 0.326 | 0.304 |
| 0.78 | 0.780 | 0.684 | 0.615 | 0.561 | 0.516 | 0.478 | 0.445 | 0.416 | 0.390 | 0.366 | 0.345 |
| 0.80 | 0.800 | 0.711 | 0.647 | 0.596 | 0.554 | 0.518 | 0.486 | 0.458 | 0.432 | 0.409 | 0.388 |
| 0.82 | 0.820 | 0.738 | 0.680 | 0.633 | 0.593 | 0.559 | 0.529 | 0.502 | 0.478 | 0.455 | 0.435 |
| 0.84 | 0.840 | 0.767 | 0.713 | 0.670 | 0.634 | 0.602 | 0.574 | 0.548 | 0.525 | 0.504 | 0.485 |
| 0.86 | 0.860 | 0.795 | 0.747 | 0.709 | 0.675 | 0.646 | 0.621 | 0.597 | 0.576 | 0.556 | 0.538 |
| 0.88 | 0.880 | 0.824 | 0.782 | 0.748 | 0.718 | 0.693 | 0.669 | 0.648 | 0.629 | 0.611 | 0.594 |
| 0.90 | 0.900 | 0.853 | 0.817 | 0.788 | 0.762 | 0.740 | 0.720 | 0.702 | 0.687 | 0.669 | 0.654 |
| 0.92 | 0.920 | 0.882 | 0.853 | 0.829 | 0.808 | 0.789 | 0.772 | 0.757 | 0.743 | 0.729 | 0.717 |
| 0.94 | 0.940 | 0.911 | 0.889 | 0.870 | 0.854 | 0.840 | 0.827 | 0.815 | 0.803 | 0.793 | 0.783 |
| 0.96 | 0.960 | 0.940 | 0.925 | 0.913 | 0.902 | 0.892 | 0.883 | 0.874 | 0.866 | 0.859 | 0.852 |
| 0.98 | 0.980 | 0.970 | 0.962 | 0.956 | 0.950 | 0.945 | 0.940 | 0.936 | 0.932 | 0.928 | 0.924 |

**Table 8.** (CONTINUED)

| $\rho$ | M=12 | M=13 | M=14 | M=15 | M=16 | M=17 | M=18 | M=19 | M=20 | M=25 | M=30 |
|---|---|---|---|---|---|---|---|---|---|---|---|
| 0.30 | 0.000 | 0.000 | 0.000 | 0.000 | 0.000 | 0.000 | 0.000 | 0.000 | 0.000 | 0.000 | 0.000 |
| 0.32 | 0.001 | 0.000 | 0.000 | 0.000 | 0.000 | 0.000 | 0.000 | 0.000 | 0.000 | 0.000 | 0.000 |
| 0.34 | 0.001 | 0.001 | 0.000 | 0.000 | 0.000 | 0.000 | 0.000 | 0.000 | 0.000 | 0.000 | 0.000 |
| 0.36 | 0.002 | 0.001 | 0.001 | 0.001 | 0.000 | 0.000 | 0.000 | 0.000 | 0.000 | 0.000 | 0.000 |
| 0.38 | 0.003 | 0.002 | 0.001 | 0.001 | 0.001 | 0.000 | 0.000 | 0.000 | 0.000 | 0.000 | 0.000 |
| 0.40 | 0.004 | 0.003 | 0.002 | 0.002 | 0.001 | 0.001 | 0.001 | 0.001 | 0.000 | 0.000 | 0.000 |
| 0.42 | 0.006 | 0.005 | 0.003 | 0.002 | 0.002 | 0.001 | 0.001 | 0.001 | 0.000 | 0.000 | 0.000 |
| 0.44 | 0.009 | 0.007 | 0.005 | 0.004 | 0.003 | 0.002 | 0.002 | 0.001 | 0.001 | 0.000 | 0.000 |
| 0.46 | 0.012 | 0.009 | 0.007 | 0.005 | 0.004 | 0.003 | 0.002 | 0.002 | 0.001 | 0.000 | 0.000 |
| 0.48 | 0.017 | 0.013 | 0.010 | 0.008 | 0.006 | 0.005 | 0.004 | 0.003 | 0.002 | 0.001 | 0.000 |
| 0.50 | 0.022 | 0.018 | 0.014 | 0.011 | 0.009 | 0.007 | 0.006 | 0.005 | 0.004 | 0.001 | 0.000 |
| 0.52 | 0.029 | 0.024 | 0.019 | 0.016 | 0.013 | 0.010 | 0.009 | 0.007 | 0.006 | 0.002 | 0.001 |
| 0.54 | 0.038 | 0.031 | 0.026 | 0.021 | 0.018 | 0.015 | 0.012 | 0.010 | 0.008 | 0.003 | 0.001 |
| 0.56 | 0.048 | 0.040 | 0.034 | 0.028 | 0.024 | 0.020 | 0.017 | 0.015 | 0.012 | 0.005 | 0.002 |
| 0.58 | 0.060 | 0.051 | 0.044 | 0.037 | 0.032 | 0.027 | 0.024 | 0.020 | 0.017 | 0.008 | 0.004 |
| 0.60 | 0.075 | 0.064 | 0.056 | 0.048 | 0.042 | 0.036 | 0.032 | 0.028 | 0.024 | 0.012 | 0.007 |
| 0.62 | 0.091 | 0.080 | 0.070 | 0.061 | 0.054 | 0.048 | 0.042 | 0.037 | 0.033 | 0.018 | 0.010 |
| 0.64 | 0.110 | 0.098 | 0.087 | 0.077 | 0.068 | 0.061 | 0.055 | 0.049 | 0.044 | 0.025 | 0.015 |
| 0.66 | 0.112 | 0.118 | 0.106 | 0.095 | 0.086 | 0.077 | 0.070 | 0.063 | 0.057 | 0.035 | 0.022 |
| 0.68 | 0.156 | 0.142 | 0.128 | 0.117 | 0.106 | 0.097 | 0.088 | 0.081 | 0.074 | 0.048 | 0.032 |
| 0.70 | 0.184 | 0.168 | 0.154 | 0.141 | 0.130 | 0.119 | 0.110 | 0.101 | 0.094 | 0.064 | 0.044 |
| 0.72 | 0.214 | 0.198 | 0.183 | 0.169 | 0.157 | 0.146 | 0.135 | 0.126 | 0.117 | 0.083 | 0.060 |
| 0.74 | 0.248 | 0.231 | 0.215 | 0.201 | 0.188 | 0.176 | 0.165 | 0.154 | 0.145 | 0.107 | 0.080 |
| 0.76 | 0.285 | 0.267 | 0.251 | 0.236 | 0.223 | 0.210 | 0.198 | 0.187 | 0.177 | 0.136 | 0.105 |
| 0.78 | 0.325 | 0.307 | 0.291 | 0.276 | 0.262 | 0.248 | 0.236 | 0.225 | 0.214 | 0.169 | 0.136 |
| 0.80 | 0.369 | 0.351 | 0.335 | 0.319 | 0.305 | 0.292 | 0.279 | 0.267 | 0.256 | 0.209 | 0.173 |
| 0.82 | 0.416 | 0.399 | 0.382 | 0.367 | 0.353 | 0.339 | 0.327 | 0.315 | 0.303 | 0.255 | 0.217 |
| 0.84 | 0.467 | 0.450 | 0.434 | 0.419 | 0.405 | 0.392 | 0.380 | 0.368 | 0.356 | 0.307 | 0.268 |
| 0.86 | 0.521 | 0.505 | 0.490 | 0.476 | 0.462 | 0.450 | 0.438 | 0.426 | 0.415 | 0.367 | 0.327 |
| 0.88 | 0.579 | 0.564 | 0.550 | 0.537 | 0.524 | 0.513 | 0.501 | 0.490 | 0.480 | 0.434 | 0.395 |
| 0.90 | 0.640 | 0.627 | 0.614 | 0.603 | 0.591 | 0.581 | 0.570 | 0.560 | 0.551 | 0.508 | 0.471 |
| 0.92 | 0.705 | 0.694 | 0.683 | 0.673 | 0.663 | 0.654 | 0.645 | 0.636 | 0.628 | 0.590 | 0.557 |
| 0.94 | 0.773 | 0.765 | 0.756 | 0.748 | 0.740 | 0.732 | 0.725 | 0.718 | 0.711 | 0.680 | 0.653 |
| 0.96 | 0.845 | 0.839 | 0.833 | 0.827 | 0.822 | 0.816 | 0.811 | 0.806 | 0.801 | 0.779 | 0.759 |
| 0.98 | 0.921 | 0.918 | 0.914 | 0.911 | 0.908 | 0.905 | 0.903 | 0.900 | 0.897 | 0.885 | 0.874 |

| $\rho$ | M=35 | M=40 | M=45 | M=50 | M=55 | M=60 | M=65 | M=70 | M=80 | M=90 | M=100 |
|---|---|---|---|---|---|---|---|---|---|---|---|
| 0.52 | 0.000 | 0.000 | 0.000 | 0.000 | 0.000 | 0.000 | 0.000 | 0.000 | 0.000 | 0.000 | 0.000 |
| 0.54 | 0.001 | 0.000 | 0.000 | 0.000 | 0.000 | 0.000 | 0.000 | 0.000 | 0.000 | 0.000 | 0.000 |
| 0.56 | 0.001 | 0.001 | 0.000 | 0.000 | 0.000 | 0.000 | 0.000 | 0.000 | 0.000 | 0.000 | 0.000 |
| 0.58 | 0.002 | 0.001 | 0.001 | 0.000 | 0.000 | 0.000 | 0.000 | 0.000 | 0.000 | 0.000 | 0.000 |
| 0.60 | 0.003 | 0.002 | 0.001 | 0.001 | 0.000 | 0.000 | 0.000 | 0.000 | 0.000 | 0.000 | 0.000 |
| 0.62 | 0.006 | 0.003 | 0.002 | 0.001 | 0.001 | 0.000 | 0.000 | 0.000 | 0.000 | 0.000 | 0.000 |
| 0.64 | 0.009 | 0.006 | 0.003 | 0.002 | 0.001 | 0.001 | 0.001 | 0.000 | 0.000 | 0.000 | 0.000 |
| 0.66 | 0.014 | 0.009 | 0.006 | 0.004 | 0.002 | 0.002 | 0.001 | 0.001 | 0.000 | 0.000 | 0.000 |
| 0.68 | 0.021 | 0.014 | 0.010 | 0.007 | 0.005 | 0.003 | 0.002 | 0.002 | 0.001 | 0.000 | 0.000 |
| 0.70 | 0.031 | 0.022 | 0.015 | 0.011 | 0.008 | 0.006 | 0.004 | 0.003 | 0.002 | 0.001 | 0.000 |
| 0.72 | 0.044 | 0.032 | 0.024 | 0.018 | 0.013 | 0.010 | 0.008 | 0.006 | 0.003 | 0.002 | 0.001 |
| 0.74 | 0.061 | 0.046 | 0.036 | 0.028 | 0.021 | 0.017 | 0.013 | 0.010 | 0.006 | 0.004 | 0.003 |
| 0.76 | 0.083 | 0.065 | 0.052 | 0.042 | 0.034 | 0.027 | 0.022 | 0.018 | 0.012 | 0.008 | 0.005 |
| 0.78 | 0.110 | 0.090 | 0.074 | 0.061 | 0.051 | 0.042 | 0.035 | 0.029 | 0.021 | 0.015 | 0.011 |
| 0.80 | 0.144 | 0.121 | 0.102 | 0.087 | 0.074 | 0.063 | 0.054 | 0.047 | 0.035 | 0.026 | 0.020 |
| 0.82 | 0.186 | 0.160 | 0.139 | 0.121 | 0.106 | 0.093 | 0.081 | 0.072 | 0.056 | 0.044 | 0.035 |
| 0.84 | 0.235 | 0.208 | 0.184 | 0.164 | 0.147 | 0.131 | 0.118 | 0.106 | 0.087 | 0.071 | 0.059 |
| 0.86 | 0.293 | 0.265 | 0.240 | 0.218 | 0.199 | 0.182 | 0.167 | 0.153 | 0.130 | 0.110 | 0.094 |
| 0.88 | 0.361 | 0.332 | 0.307 | 0.284 | 0.264 | 0.246 | 0.229 | 0.214 | 0.187 | 0.165 | 0.146 |
| 0.90 | 0.440 | 0.412 | 0.386 | 0.364 | 0.343 | 0.325 | 0.307 | 0.291 | 0.263 | 0.238 | 0.217 |
| 0.92 | 0.529 | 0.503 | 0.479 | 0.458 | 0.438 | 0.420 | 0.404 | 0.388 | 0.359 | 0.334 | 0.312 |
| 0.94 | 0.629 | 0.607 | 0.587 | 0.568 | 0.551 | 0.535 | 0.519 | 0.505 | 0.479 | 0.455 | 0.434 |
| 0.96 | 0.740 | 0.724 | 0.709 | 0.694 | 0.681 | 0.669 | 0.657 | 0.645 | 0.624 | 0.605 | 0.587 |
| 0.98 | 0.864 | 0.855 | 0.846 | 0.838 | 0.831 | 0.823 | 0.816 | 0.810 | 0.797 | 0.786 | 0.775 |

**Table 9.** MEAN QUEUING TIMES FOR MULTISERVER QUEUES, WITH EXPONENTIAL INTERARRIVAL TIMES, EXPONENTIAL SERVICE TIMES, ALL SERVERS EQUALLY LOADED, AND FIRST-IN, FIRST-OUT DISPATCHING

Mean waiting time before being served, $E(t_w) = E(t_q) - E(t_s)$

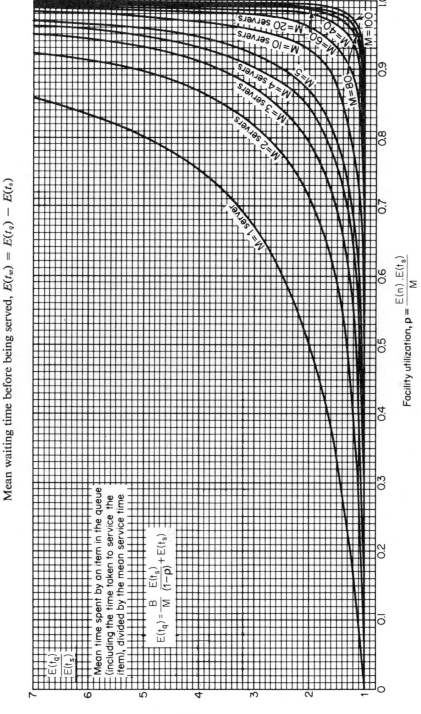

# Table 9. (CONTINUED)

Values of $\dfrac{E(t_q)}{E(t_s)}$

Facility Utilization

Number of Servers, $M$

| $\rho$ | $M=1$ | $M=2$ | $M=3$ | $M=4$ | $M=5$ | $M=6$ | $M=7$ | $M=8$ | $M=9$ | $M=10$ | $M=11$ |
|---|---|---|---|---|---|---|---|---|---|---|---|
| 0.00 | 1.000 | 1.000 | 1.000 | 1.000 | 1.000 | 1.000 | 1.000 | 1.000 | 1.000 | 1.000 | 1.000 |
| 0.02 | 1.020 | 1.000 | 1.000 | 1.000 | 1.000 | 1.000 | 1.000 | 1.000 | 1.000 | 1.000 | 1.000 |
| 0.04 | 1.042 | 1.002 | 1.000 | 1.000 | 1.000 | 1.000 | 1.000 | 1.000 | 1.000 | 1.000 | 1.000 |
| 0.06 | 0.064 | 1.004 | 1.000 | 1.000 | 1.000 | 1.000 | 1.000 | 1.000 | 1.000 | 1.000 | 1.000 |
| 0.08 | 1.087 | 1.006 | 1.001 | 1.000 | 1.000 | 1.000 | 1.000 | 1.000 | 1.000 | 1.000 | 1.000 |
| 0.10 | 1.111 | 1.010 | 1.001 | 1.000 | 1.000 | 1.000 | 1.000 | 1.000 | 1.000 | 1.000 | 1.000 |
| 0.12 | 1.136 | 1.015 | 1.002 | 1.000 | 1.000 | 1.000 | 1.000 | 1.000 | 1.000 | 1.000 | 1.000 |
| 0.14 | 1.163 | 1.020 | 1.004 | 1.001 | 1.000 | 1.000 | 1.000 | 1.000 | 1.000 | 1.000 | 1.000 |
| 0.16 | 1.190 | 1.026 | 1.005 | 1.001 | 1.000 | 1.000 | 1.000 | 1.000 | 1.000 | 1.000 | 1.000 |
| 0.18 | 1.220 | 1.033 | 1.008 | 1.002 | 1.001 | 1.000 | 1.000 | 1.000 | 1.000 | 1.000 | 1.000 |
| 0.20 | 1.250 | 1.042 | 1.010 | 1.003 | 1.001 | 1.000 | 1.000 | 1.000 | 1.000 | 1.000 | 1.000 |
| 0.22 | 1.282 | 1.051 | 1.014 | 1.004 | 1.001 | 1.001 | 1.000 | 1.000 | 1.000 | 1.000 | 1.000 |
| 0.24 | 1.316 | 1.061 | 1.017 | 1.006 | 1.002 | 1.001 | 1.000 | 1.000 | 1.000 | 1.000 | 1.000 |
| 0.26 | 1.351 | 1.073 | 1.022 | 1.008 | 1.003 | 1.001 | 1.001 | 1.000 | 1.000 | 1.000 | 1.000 |
| 0.28 | 1.389 | 1.085 | 1.027 | 1.010 | 1.004 | 1.002 | 1.001 | 1.000 | 1.000 | 1.000 | 1.000 |
| 0.30 | 1.429 | 1.099 | 1.033 | 1.013 | 1.006 | 1.003 | 1.001 | 1.001 | 1.000 | 1.000 | 1.000 |
| 0.32 | 1.471 | 1.114 | 1.040 | 1.017 | 1.008 | 1.004 | 1.002 | 1.001 | 1.001 | 1.000 | 1.000 |
| 0.34 | 1.515 | 1.131 | 1.048 | 1.021 | 1.010 | 1.005 | 1.003 | 1.001 | 1.001 | 1.000 | 1.000 |
| 0.36 | 1.562 | 1.149 | 1.057 | 1.026 | 1.013 | 1.007 | 1.004 | 1.002 | 1.001 | 1.001 | 1.000 |
| 0.38 | 1.613 | 1.169 | 1.067 | 1.031 | 1.016 | 1.009 | 1.005 | 1.003 | 1.002 | 1.001 | 1.001 |
| 0.40 | 1.667 | 1.190 | 1.078 | 1.038 | 1.020 | 1.011 | 1.006 | 1.004 | 1.002 | 1.001 | 1.001 |
| 0.42 | 1.724 | 1.214 | 1.091 | 1.045 | 1.025 | 1.014 | 1.008 | 1.005 | 1.003 | 1.002 | 1.001 |
| 0.44 | 1.786 | 1.240 | 1.105 | 1.054 | 1.030 | 1.018 | 1.011 | 1.007 | 1.004 | 1.003 | 1.002 |
| 0.46 | 1.852 | 1.268 | 1.121 | 1.063 | 1.036 | 1.022 | 1.014 | 1.009 | 1.006 | 1.004 | 1.003 |
| 0.48 | 1.923 | 1.299 | 1.138 | 1.074 | 1.044 | 1.027 | 1.017 | 1.012 | 1.008 | 1.005 | 1.004 |
| 0.50 | 2.000 | 1.333 | 1.158 | 1.087 | 1.052 | 1.033 | 1.022 | 1.015 | 1.010 | 1.007 | 1.005 |
| 0.52 | 2.083 | 1.371 | 1.180 | 1.101 | 1.062 | 1.040 | 1.027 | 1.019 | 1.013 | 1.009 | 1.007 |
| 0.54 | 2.174 | 1.412 | 1.204 | 1.117 | 1.073 | 1.048 | 1.033 | 1.023 | 1.017 | 1.012 | 1.009 |
| 0.56 | 2.273 | 1.457 | 1.231 | 1.135 | 1.086 | 1.058 | 1.040 | 1.029 | 1.021 | 1.016 | 1.012 |
| 0.58 | 2.381 | 1.507 | 1.262 | 1.156 | 1.101 | 1.069 | 1.049 | 1.036 | 1.027 | 1.020 | 1.015 |
| 0.60 | 2.500 | 1.562 | 1.296 | 1.179 | 1.118 | 1.082 | 1.059 | 1.044 | 1.033 | 1.025 | 1.020 |
| 0.62 | 2.632 | 1.624 | 1.334 | 1.206 | 1.138 | 1.097 | 1.071 | 1.053 | 1.041 | 1.032 | 1.025 |
| 0.64 | 2.778 | 1.694 | 1.377 | 1.236 | 1.160 | 1.114 | 1.085 | 1.064 | 1.050 | 1.039 | 1.032 |
| 0.66 | 2.941 | 1.772 | 1.427 | 1.271 | 1.186 | 1.135 | 1.101 | 1.078 | 1.061 | 1.049 | 1.040 |
| 0.68 | 3.125 | 1.860 | 1.483 | 1.311 | 1.217 | 1.159 | 1.120 | 1.094 | 1.075 | 1.060 | 1.049 |
| 0.70 | 3.333 | 1.961 | 1.547 | 1.357 | 1.252 | 1.187 | 1.143 | 1.113 | 1.091 | 1.074 | 1.061 |
| 0.72 | 3.571 | 2.076 | 1.621 | 1.411 | 1.293 | 1.220 | 1.170 | 1.135 | 1.110 | 1.091 | 1.076 |
| 0.74 | 3.846 | 2.210 | 1.708 | 1.474 | 1.342 | 1.259 | 1.203 | 1.163 | 1.133 | 1.111 | 1.093 |
| 0.76 | 4.167 | 2.367 | 1.810 | 1.548 | 1.400 | 1.306 | 1.242 | 1.196 | 1.162 | 1.136 | 1.115 |
| 0.78 | 4.545 | 2.554 | 1.932 | 1.637 | 1.469 | 1.362 | 1.289 | 1.236 | 1.197 | 1.166 | 1.142 |
| 0.80 | 5.000 | 2.778 | 2.079 | 1.746 | 1.554 | 1.431 | 1.347 | 1.286 | 1.240 | 1.205 | 1.176 |
| 0.82 | 5.556 | 3.053 | 2.259 | 1.879 | 1.659 | 1.518 | 1.420 | 1.349 | 1.295 | 1.253 | 1.220 |
| 0.84 | 6.250 | 3.397 | 2.486 | 2.047 | 1.792 | 1.627 | 1.512 | 1.428 | 1.365 | 1.315 | 1.275 |
| 0.86 | 7.143 | 3.840 | 2.780 | 2.265 | 1.965 | 1.770 | 1.633 | 1.533 | 1.457 | 1.397 | 1.349 |
| 0.88 | 8.333 | 4.433 | 3.172 | 2.558 | 2.197 | 1.962 | 1.797 | 1.675 | 1.582 | 1.509 | 1.450 |
| 0.90 | 10.000 | 5.263 | 3.724 | 2.969 | 2.525 | 2.234 | 2.029 | 1.877 | 1.761 | 1.669 | 1.594 |
| 0.92 | 12.500 | 6.510 | 4.553 | 3.589 | 3.019 | 2.644 | 2.379 | 2.183 | 2.031 | 1.912 | 1.815 |
| 0.94 | 16.667 | 8.591 | 5.938 | 4.626 | 3.847 | 3.333 | 2.968 | 2.697 | 2.488 | 2.321 | 2.186 |
| 0.96 | 25.000 | 12.755 | 8.711 | 6.705 | 5.508 | 4.716 | 4.152 | 3.732 | 3.407 | 3.148 | 2.937 |
| 0.98 | 50.000 | 25.253 | 17.041 | 12.950 | 10.503 | 8.877 | 7.718 | 6.851 | 6.178 | 5.641 | 5.202 |

# Table 9. (CONTINUED)

$$\text{Values of } \frac{E(t_q)}{E(t_s)}$$

Facility Utilization

Number of Servers, $M$

| $\rho$ | $M=12$ | $M=13$ | $M=14$ | $M=15$ | $M=16$ | $M=17$ | $M=18$ | $M=19$ | $M=20$ | $M=25$ | $M=30$ |
|---|---|---|---|---|---|---|---|---|---|---|---|
| 0.40 | 1.001 | 1.000 | 1.000 | 1.000 | 1.000 | 1.000 | 1.000 | 1.000 | 1.000 | 1.000 | 1.000 |
| 0.42 | 1.001 | 1.001 | 1.000 | 1.000 | 1.000 | 1.000 | 1.000 | 1.000 | 1.000 | 1.000 | 1.000 |
| 0.44 | 1.001 | 1.001 | 1.001 | 1.000 | 1.000 | 1.000 | 1.000 | 1.000 | 1.000 | 1.000 | 1.000 |
| 0.46 | 1.002 | 1.001 | 1.001 | 1.001 | 1.000 | 1.000 | 1.000 | 1.000 | 1.000 | 1.000 | 1.000 |
| 0.48 | 1.003 | 1.002 | 1.001 | 1.001 | 1.001 | 1.001 | 1.000 | 1.000 | 1.000 | 1.000 | 1.000 |
| 0.50 | 1.004 | 1.003 | 1.002 | 1.002 | 1.001 | 1.001 | 1.001 | 1.000 | 1.000 | 1.000 | 1.000 |
| 0.52 | 1.005 | 1.004 | 1.003 | 1.002 | 1.002 | 1.001 | 1.001 | 1.001 | 1.001 | 1.000 | 1.000 |
| 0.54 | 1.007 | 1.005 | 1.004 | 1.003 | 1.002 | 1.002 | 1.001 | 1.001 | 1.001 | 1.000 | 1.000 |
| 0.56 | 1.009 | 1.007 | 1.005 | 1.004 | 1.003 | 1.003 | 1.003 | 1.002 | 1.001 | 1.000 | 1.000 |
| 0.58 | 1.012 | 1.009 | 1.007 | 1.006 | 1.005 | 1.004 | 1.003 | 1.003 | 1.002 | 1.001 | 1.000 |
| 0.60 | 1.016 | 1.012 | 1.010 | 1.008 | 1.007 | 1.005 | 1.004 | 1.004 | 1.003 | 1.001 | 1.001 |
| 0.62 | 1.020 | 1.016 | 1.013 | 1.011 | 1.009 | 1.007 | 1.006 | 1.005 | 1.004 | 1.002 | 1.001 |
| 0.64 | 1.026 | 1.021 | 1.017 | 1.014 | 1.012 | 1.010 | 1.008 | 1.007 | 1.006 | 1.003 | 1.001 |
| 0.66 | 1.032 | 1.027 | 1.022 | 1.019 | 1.016 | 1.013 | 1.011 | 1.010 | 1.008 | 1.004 | 1.002 |
| 0.68 | 1.041 | 1.034 | 1.029 | 1.024 | 1.021 | 1.018 | 1.015 | 1.013 | 1.012 | 1.006 | 1.003 |
| 0.70 | 1.051 | 1.043 | 1.037 | 1.031 | 1.027 | 1.023 | 1.020 | 1.018 | 1.016 | 1.008 | 1.005 |
| 0.72 | 1.064 | 1.054 | 1.047 | 1.040 | 1.035 | 1.031 | 1.027 | 1.024 | 1.021 | 1.012 | 1.007 |
| 0.74 | 1.079 | 1.068 | 1.059 | 1.051 | 1.045 | 1.040 | 1.035 | 1.031 | 1.028 | 1.016 | 1.010 |
| 0.76 | 1.099 | 1.086 | 1.075 | 1.066 | 1.058 | 1.051 | 1.046 | 1.041 | 1.037 | 1.023 | 1.015 |
| 0.78 | 1.123 | 1.107 | 1.094 | 1.084 | 1.074 | 1.066 | 1.060 | 1.054 | 1.049 | 1.031 | 1.021 |
| 0.80 | 1.154 | 1.135 | 1.119 | 1.106 | 1.095 | 1.086 | 1.077 | 1.070 | 1.064 | 1.042 | 1.029 |
| 0.82 | 1.193 | 1.170 | 1.152 | 1.136 | 1.122 | 1.111 | 1.101 | 1.092 | 1.084 | 1.057 | 1.040 |
| 0.84 | 1.243 | 1.216 | 1.194 | 1.175 | 1.158 | 1.144 | 1.132 | 1.121 | 1.111 | 1.077 | 1.056 |
| 0.86 | 1.310 | 1.277 | 1.250 | 1.227 | 1.206 | 1.189 | 1.174 | 1.160 | 1.148 | 1.105 | 1.078 |
| 0.88 | 1.402 | 1.362 | 1.327 | 1.298 | 1.273 | 1.251 | 1.232 | 1.215 | 1.200 | 1.145 | 1.110 |
| 0.90 | 1.533 | 1.482 | 1.439 | 1.402 | 1.370 | 1.342 | 1.317 | 1.295 | 1.275 | 1.203 | 1.157 |
| 0.92 | 1.734 | 1.667 | 1.610 | 1.561 | 1.518 | 1.481 | 1.448 | 1.419 | 1.392 | 1.295 | 1.232 |
| 0.94 | 2.074 | 1.980 | 1.900 | 1.831 | 1.771 | 1.718 | 1.671 | 1.630 | 1.593 | 1.453 | 1.363 |
| 0.96 | 2.761 | 2.614 | 2.488 | 2.379 | 2.284 | 2.200 | 2.126 | 2.061 | 2.001 | 1.779 | 1.632 |
| 0.98 | 4.838 | 4.529 | 4.266 | 4.038 | 3.839 | 3.663 | 3.507 | 3.368 | 3.243 | 2.770 | 2.457 |

| $\rho$ | $M=35$ | $M=40$ | $M=45$ | $M=50$ | $M=55$ | $M=60$ | $M=65$ | $M=70$ | $M=80$ | $M=90$ | $M=100$ |
|---|---|---|---|---|---|---|---|---|---|---|---|
| 0.64 | 1.001 | 1.000 | 1.000 | 1.000 | 1.000 | 1.000 | 1.000 | 1.000 | 1.000 | 1.000 | 1.000 |
| 0.66 | 1.001 | 1.001 | 1.000 | 1.000 | 1.000 | 1.000 | 1.000 | 1.000 | 1.000 | 1.000 | 1.000 |
| 0.68 | 1.002 | 1.001 | 1.001 | 1.000 | 1.000 | 1.000 | 1.000 | 1.000 | 1.000 | 1.000 | 1.000 |
| 0.70 | 1.003 | 1.002 | 1.001 | 1.001 | 1.000 | 1.000 | 1.000 | 1.000 | 1.000 | 1.000 | 1.000 |
| 0.72 | 1.004 | 1.003 | 1.002 | 1.001 | 1.001 | 1.001 | 1.000 | 1.000 | 1.000 | 1.000 | 1.000 |
| 0.74 | 1.007 | 1.004 | 1.003 | 1.002 | 1.002 | 1.001 | 1.001 | 1.001 | 1.000 | 1.000 | 1.000 |
| 0.76 | 1.010 | 1.007 | 1.005 | 1.003 | 1.003 | 1.002 | 1.001 | 1.001 | 1.001 | 1.000 | 1.000 |
| 0.78 | 1.014 | 1.010 | 1.007 | 1.006 | 1.004 | 1.003 | 1.002 | 1.002 | 1.001 | 1.001 | 1.000 |
| 0.80 | 1.021 | 1.015 | 1.011 | 1.009 | 1.007 | 1.005 | 1.004 | 1.003 | 1.002 | 1.001 | 1.001 |
| 0.82 | 1.029 | 1.022 | 1.017 | 1.013 | 1.011 | 1.009 | 1.007 | 1.006 | 1.004 | 1.003 | 1.002 |
| 0.84 | 1.042 | 1.032 | 1.026 | 1.021 | 1.017 | 1.014 | 1.011 | 1.009 | 1.007 | 1.005 | 1.004 |
| 0.86 | 1.060 | 1.047 | 1.038 | 1.031 | 1.026 | 1.022 | 1.018 | 1.016 | 1.012 | 1.009 | 1.007 |
| 0.88 | 1.086 | 1.069 | 1.057 | 1.047 | 1.040 | 1.034 | 1.029 | 1.025 | 1.020 | 1.015 | 1.012 |
| 0.90 | 1.126 | 1.103 | 1.086 | 1.073 | 1.062 | 1.054 | 1.047 | 1.042 | 1.033 | 1.026 | 1.022 |
| 0.92 | 1.189 | 1.157 | 1.133 | 1.115 | 1.100 | 1.088 | 1.078 | 1.069 | 1.056 | 1.046 | 1.039 |
| 0.94 | 1.299 | 1.253 | 1.217 | 1.189 | 1.167 | 1.149 | 1.133 | 1.120 | 1.100 | 1.084 | 1.072 |
| 0.96 | 1.529 | 1.452 | 1.394 | 1.347 | 1.310 | 1.279 | 1.253 | 1.230 | 1.195 | 1.168 | 1.147 |
| 0.98 | 2.234 | 2.069 | 1.940 | 1.838 | 1.755 | 1.686 | 1.628 | 1.578 | 1.498 | 1.437 | 1.388 |

**Table 10.** STANDARD DEVIATION OF QUEUEING TIMES FOR MULTISERVER QUEUES WITH EXPONENTIAL INTERARRIVAL TIMES. EXPONENTIAL SERVICE TIMES. ALL SERVERS EQUALLY LOADED, AND FIRST-IN, FIRST-OUT DISPATCHING

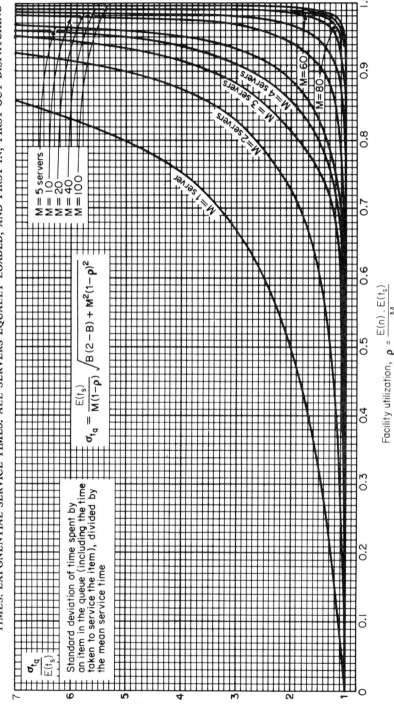

$\dfrac{\sigma_{t_q}}{E(t_s)}$

Standard deviation of time spent by an item in the queue (including the time taken to service the item), divided by the mean service time

$$\sigma_{t_q} = \frac{E(t_s)}{M(1-\rho)} \sqrt{B(2-B) + M^2(1-\rho)^2}$$

M = 5 servers
M = 10
M = 20
M = 40
M = 100

M = 1 server
M = 2 servers
M = 3 servers
M = 4 servers
M = 60
M = 80

Facility utilization, $\rho = \dfrac{E(n) \cdot E(t_s)}{M}$

# Table 10. (CONTINUED)

Values of $\dfrac{\sigma_{t_q}}{E(t_s)}$

Facility Utiliza-tion

Number of Servers, $M$

| $\rho$ | $M=1$ | $M=2$ | $M=3$ | $M=4$ | $M=5$ | $M=6$ | $M=7$ | $M=8$ | $M=9$ | $M=10$ | $M=11$ |
|---|---|---|---|---|---|---|---|---|---|---|---|
| 0.00 | 1.000 | 1.000 | 1.000 | 1.000 | 1.000 | 1.000 | 1.000 | 1.000 | 1.000 | 1.000 | 1.000 |
| 0.02 | 1.020 | 1.000 | 1.000 | 1.000 | 1.000 | 1.000 | 1.000 | 1.000 | 1.000 | 1.000 | 1.000 |
| 0.04 | 1.042 | 1.001 | 1.000 | 1.000 | 1.000 | 1.000 | 1.000 | 1.000 | 1.000 | 1.000 | 1.000 |
| 0.06 | 1.064 | 1.002 | 1.000 | 1.000 | 1.000 | 1.000 | 1.000 | 1.000 | 1.000 | 1.000 | 1.000 |
| 0.08 | 1.087 | 1.003 | 1.000 | 1.000 | 1.000 | 1.000 | 1.000 | 1.000 | 1.000 | 1.000 | 1.000 |
| 0.10 | 1.111 | 1.006 | 1.001 | 1.000 | 1.000 | 1.000 | 1.000 | 1.000 | 1.000 | 1.000 | 1.000 |
| 0.12 | 1.136 | 1.008 | 1.001 | 1.000 | 1.000 | 1.000 | 1.000 | 1.000 | 1.000 | 1.000 | 1.000 |
| 0.14 | 1.163 | 1.011 | 1.001 | 1.000 | 1.000 | 1.000 | 1.000 | 1.000 | 1.000 | 1.000 | 1.000 |
| 0.16 | 1.190 | 1.015 | 1.002 | 1.000 | 1.000 | 1.000 | 1.000 | 1.000 | 1.000 | 1.000 | 1.000 |
| 0.18 | 1.220 | 1.020 | 1.003 | 1.001 | 1.000 | 1.000 | 1.000 | 1.000 | 1.000 | 1.000 | 1.000 |
| 0.20 | 1.250 | 1.025 | 1.004 | 1.001 | 1.000 | 1.000 | 1.000 | 1.000 | 1.000 | 1.000 | 1.000 |
| 0.22 | 1.282 | 1.031 | 1.006 | 1.001 | 1.000 | 1.000 | 1.000 | 1.000 | 1.000 | 1.000 | 1.000 |
| 0.24 | 1.316 | 1.038 | 1.007 | 1.002 | 1.001 | 1.000 | 1.000 | 1.000 | 1.000 | 1.000 | 1.000 |
| 0.26 | 1.351 | 1.045 | 1.010 | 1.003 | 1.001 | 1.000 | 1.000 | 1.000 | 1.000 | 1.000 | 1.000 |
| 0.28 | 1.389 | 1.054 | 1.012 | 1.004 | 1.001 | 1.000 | 1.000 | 1.000 | 1.000 | 1.000 | 1.000 |
| 0.30 | 1.429 | 1.064 | 1.015 | 1.005 | 1.002 | 1.001 | 1.000 | 1.000 | 1.000 | 1.000 | 1.000 |
| 0.32 | 1.471 | 1.075 | 1.019 | 1.006 | 1.002 | 1.001 | 1.000 | 1.000 | 1.000 | 1.000 | 1.000 |
| 0.34 | 1.515 | 1.087 | 1.023 | 1.008 | 1.003 | 1.001 | 1.001 | 1.000 | 1.000 | 1.000 | 1.000 |
| 0.36 | 1.562 | 1.100 | 1.028 | 1.010 | 1.004 | 1.002 | 1.001 | 1.000 | 1.000 | 1.000 | 1.000 |
| 0.38 | 1.613 | 1.115 | 1.033 | 1.012 | 1.005 | 1.002 | 1.001 | 1.001 | 1.000 | 1.000 | 1.000 |
| 0.40 | 1.667 | 1.132 | 1.040 | 1.015 | 1.006 | 1.003 | 1.002 | 1.001 | 1.000 | 1.000 | 1.000 |
| 0.42 | 1.724 | 1.150 | 1.047 | 1.018 | 1.008 | 1.004 | 1.002 | 1.001 | 1.001 | 1.000 | 1.000 |
| 0.44 | 1.786 | 1.171 | 1.056 | 1.022 | 1.010 | 1.005 | 1.003 | 1.002 | 1.001 | 1.001 | 1.000 |
| 0.46 | 1.852 | 1.194 | 1.065 | 1.027 | 0.013 | 1.007 | 1.004 | 1.002 | 1.001 | 1.001 | 1.000 |
| 0.48 | 1.923 | 1.219 | 1.076 | 1.032 | 1.016 | 1.008 | 1.005 | 1.003 | 1.002 | 1.001 | 1.001 |
| 0.50 | 2.000 | 1.247 | 1.089 | 1.039 | 1.019 | 1.010 | 1.006 | 1.004 | 1.002 | 1.001 | 1.001 |
| 0.52 | 2.083 | 1.279 | 1.103 | 1.046 | 1.024 | 1.013 | 1.008 | 1.005 | 1.003 | 1.002 | 1.001 |
| 0.54 | 2.174 | 1.314 | 1.120 | 1.055 | 1.029 | 1.016 | 1.010 | 1.006 | 1.004 | 1.003 | 1.002 |
| 0.56 | 2.273 | 1.353 | 1.139 | 1.066 | 1.035 | 1.020 | 1.012 | 1.008 | 1.005 | 1.003 | 1.002 |
| 0.58 | 2.381 | 1.396 | 1.160 | 1.078 | 1.042 | 1.025 | 1.015 | 1.010 | 1.007 | 1.005 | 1.003 |
| 0.60 | 2.500 | 1.446 | 1.185 | 1.092 | 1.051 | 1.030 | 1.019 | 1.013 | 1.009 | 1.006 | 1.004 |
| 0.62 | 2.632 | 1.501 | 1.214 | 1.108 | 1.061 | 1.037 | 1.024 | 1.016 | 1.011 | 1.008 | 1.006 |
| 0.64 | 2.778 | 1.564 | 1.248 | 1.128 | 1.074 | 1.045 | 1.030 | 1.020 | 1.014 | 1.010 | 1.007 |
| 0.66 | 2.941 | 1.635 | 1.286 | 1.151 | 1.088 | 1.055 | 1.037 | 1.025 | 1.018 | 1.013 | 1.010 |
| 0.68 | 3.125 | 1.717 | 1.331 | 1.179 | 1.106 | 1.068 | 1.045 | 1.032 | 1.023 | 1.017 | 1.013 |
| 0.70 | 3.333 | 1.811 | 1.384 | 1.212 | 1.128 | 1.083 | 1.056 | 1.040 | 1.029 | 1.022 | 1.017 |
| 0.72 | 3.571 | 1.920 | 1.447 | 1.251 | 1.154 | 1.101 | 1.070 | 1.050 | 1.037 | 1.028 | 1.021 |
| 0.74 | 3.846 | 2.047 | 1.521 | 1.299 | 1.187 | 1.125 | 1.087 | 1.063 | 1.047 | 1.036 | 1.028 |
| 0.76 | 4.167 | 2.197 | 1.611 | 1.357 | 1.227 | 1.154 | 1.109 | 1.080 | 1.060 | 1.046 | 1.036 |
| 0.78 | 4.545 | 2.377 | 1.719 | 1.429 | 1.278 | 1.191 | 1.137 | 1.101 | 1.077 | 1.060 | 1.048 |
| 0.80 | 5.000 | 2.594 | 1.853 | 1.519 | 1.342 | 1.238 | 1.173 | 1.129 | 1.100 | 1.078 | 1.063 |
| 0.82 | 5.556 | 2.862 | 2.019 | 1.634 | 1.425 | 1.300 | 1.221 | 1.167 | 1.130 | 1.103 | 1.083 |
| 0.84 | 6.250 | 3.199 | 2.232 | 1.782 | 1.534 | 1.383 | 1.285 | 1.219 | 1.172 | 1.138 | 1.112 |
| 0.86 | 7.143 | 3.636 | 2.511 | 1.979 | 1.681 | 1.497 | 1.375 | 1.291 | 1.231 | 1.187 | 1.154 |
| 0.88 | 8.333 | 4.222 | 2.890 | 2.250 | 1.886 | 1.657 | 1.504 | 1.397 | 1.319 | 1.261 | 1.216 |
| 0.90 | 10.000 | 5.045 | 3.426 | 2.640 | 2.185 | 1.895 | 1.697 | 1.557 | 1.453 | 1.375 | 1.314 |
| 0.92 | 12.500 | 6.286 | 4.241 | 3.237 | 2.649 | 2.269 | 2.006 | 1.816 | 1.674 | 1.565 | 1.479 |
| 0.94 | 16.667 | 8.360 | 5.611 | 4.251 | 3.446 | 2.919 | 2.549 | 2.278 | 2.073 | 1.913 | 1.785 |
| 0.96 | 25.000 | 12.518 | 8.370 | 6.306 | 5.075 | 4.261 | 3.685 | 3.258 | 2.929 | 2.669 | 2.460 |
| 0.98 | 50.000 | 25.009 | 16.685 | 12.528 | 10.038 | 8.381 | 7.200 | 6.317 | 5.632 | 5.086 | 4.641 |

# Table 10. (CONTINUED)

Values of $\dfrac{\sigma_{t_q}}{E(t_s)}$

Facility
Utiliza-
tion

Number of Servers, $M$

| $\rho$ | $M=12$ | $M=13$ | $M=14$ | $M=15$ | $M=16$ | $M=17$ | $M=18$ | $M=19$ | $M=20$ | $M=25$ | $M=30$ |
|---|---|---|---|---|---|---|---|---|---|---|---|
| 0.40 | 1.000 | 1.000 | 1.000 | 1.000 | 1.000 | 1.000 | 1.000 | 1.000 | 1.000 | 1.000 | 1.000 |
| 0.42 | 1.000 | 1.000 | 1.000 | 1.000 | 1.000 | 1.000 | 1.000 | 1.000 | 1.000 | 1.000 | 1.000 |
| 0.44 | 1.000 | 1.000 | 1.000 | 1.000 | 1.000 | 1.000 | 1.000 | 1.000 | 1.000 | 1.000 | 1.000 |
| 0.46 | 1.000 | 1.000 | 1.000 | 1.000 | 1.000 | 1.000 | 1.000 | 1.000 | 1.000 | 1.000 | 1.000 |
| 0.48 | 1.000 | 1.000 | 1.000 | 1.000 | 1.000 | 1.000 | 1.000 | 1.000 | 1.000 | 1.000 | 1.000 |
| 0.50 | 1.001 | 1.000 | 1.000 | 1.000 | 1.000 | 1.000 | 1.000 | 1.000 | 1.000 | 1.000 | 1.000 |
| 0.52 | 1.001 | 1.001 | 1.000 | 1.000 | 1.000 | 1.000 | 1.000 | 1.000 | 1.000 | 1.000 | 1.000 |
| 0.54 | 1.001 | 1.001 | 1.001 | 1.000 | 1.000 | 1.000 | 1.000 | 1.000 | 1.000 | 1.000 | 1.000 |
| 0.56 | 1.002 | 1.001 | 1.001 | 1.001 | 1.000 | 1.000 | 1.000 | 1.000 | 1.000 | 1.000 | 1.000 |
| 0.58 | 1.002 | 1.002 | 1.001 | 1.001 | 1.001 | 1.001 | 1.000 | 1.000 | 1.000 | 1.000 | 1.000 |
| 0.60 | 1.003 | 1.002 | 1.002 | 1.001 | 1.001 | 1.001 | 1.001 | 1.000 | 1.000 | 1.000 | 1.000 |
| 0.62 | 1.004 | 1.003 | 1.002 | 1.002 | 1.001 | 1.001 | 1.001 | 1.001 | 1.001 | 1.000 | 1.000 |
| 0.64 | 1.006 | 1.004 | 1.003 | 1.003 | 1.002 | 1.002 | 1.001 | 1.001 | 1.001 | 1.000 | 1.000 |
| 0.66 | 1.007 | 1.006 | 1.004 | 1.003 | 1.003 | 1.002 | 1.002 | 1.001 | 1.001 | 1.000 | 1.000 |
| 0.68 | 1.010 | 1.008 | 1.006 | 1.005 | 1.004 | 1.003 | 1.003 | 1.002 | 1.002 | 1.001 | 1.000 |
| 0.70 | 1.013 | 1.010 | 1.008 | 1.006 | 1.005 | 1.004 | 1.004 | 1.003 | 1.002 | 1.001 | 1.001 |
| 0.72 | 1.017 | 1.013 | 1.011 | 1.009 | 1.007 | 1.006 | 1.005 | 1.004 | 1.004 | 1.002 | 1.001 |
| 0.74 | 1.022 | 1.018 | 1.014 | 1.012 | 1.010 | 1.008 | 1.007 | 1.006 | 1.005 | 1.002 | 1.001 |
| 0.74 | 1.022 | 1.018 | 1.014 | 1.012 | 1.010 | 1.008 | 1.007 | 1.006 | 1.005 | 1.002 | 1.001 |
| 0.76 | 1.029 | 1.024 | 1.019 | 1.016 | 1.013 | 1.011 | 1.010 | 1.008 | 1.007 | 1.004 | 1.002 |
| 0.78 | 1.038 | 1.031 | 1.026 | 1.022 | 1.018 | 1.015 | 1.013 | 1.011 | 1.010 | 1.005 | 1.003 |
| 0.80 | 1.051 | 1.042 | 1.035 | 1.029 | 1.025 | 1.021 | 1.018 | 1.016 | 1.014 | 1.007 | 1.004 |
| 0.82 | 1.068 | 1.057 | 1.048 | 1.040 | 1.034 | 1.030 | 1.026 | 1.022 | 1.020 | 1.011 | 1.007 |
| 0.84 | 1.093 | 1.078 | 1.066 | 1.056 | 1.048 | 1.042 | 1.036 | 1.032 | 1.028 | 1.016 | 1.010 |
| 0.86 | 1.128 | 1.108 | 1.092 | 1.079 | 1.069 | 1.060 | 1.052 | 1.046 | 1.041 | 1.024 | 1.015 |
| 0.88 | 1.182 | 1.154 | 1.133 | 1.115 | 1.100 | 1.088 | 1.077 | 1.069 | 1.061 | 1.037 | 1.024 |
| 0.90 | 1.267 | 1.229 | 1.198 | 1.172 | 1.151 | 1.134 | 1.119 | 1.106 | 1.095 | 1.059 | 1.039 |
| 0.92 | 1.411 | 1.356 | 1.310 | 1.273 | 1.241 | 1.215 | 1.192 | 1.173 | 1.156 | 1.099 | 1.068 |
| 0.94 | 1.682 | 1.598 | 1.527 | 1.468 | 1.418 | 1.376 | 1.339 | 1.307 | 1.279 | 1.183 | 1.128 |
| 0.96 | 2.288 | 2.145 | 2.025 | 1.922 | 1.834 | 1.758 | 1.691 | 1.633 | 1.581 | 1.397 | 1.286 |
| 0.98 | 4.272 | 3.961 | 3.696 | 3.468 | 3.269 | 3.094 | 2.940 | 2.803 | 2.680 | 2.224 | 1.932 |

| $\rho$ | $M=35$ | $M=40$ | $M=45$ | $M=50$ | $M=55$ | $M=60$ | $M=65$ | $M=70$ | $M=80$ | $M=90$ | $M=100$ |
|---|---|---|---|---|---|---|---|---|---|---|---|
| 0.64 | 1.000 | 1.000 | 1.000 | 1.000 | 1.000 | 1.000 | 1.000 | 1.000 | 1.000 | 1.000 | 1.000 |
| 0.66 | 1.000 | 1.000 | 1.000 | 1.000 | 1.000 | 1.000 | 1.000 | 1.000 | 1.000 | 1.000 | 1.000 |
| 0.68 | 1.000 | 1.000 | 1.000 | 1.000 | 1.000 | 1.000 | 1.000 | 1.000 | 1.000 | 1.000 | 1.000 |
| 0.70 | 1.000 | 1.000 | 1.000 | 1.000 | 1.000 | 1.000 | 1.000 | 1.000 | 1.000 | 1.000 | 1.000 |
| 0.72 | 1.000 | 1.000 | 1.000 | 1.000 | 1.000 | 1.000 | 1.000 | 1.000 | 1.000 | 1.000 | 1.000 |
| 0.74 | 1.001 | 1.000 | 1.000 | 1.000 | 1.000 | 1.000 | 1.000 | 1.000 | 1.000 | 1.000 | 1.000 |
| 0.76 | 1.001 | 1.001 | 1.000 | 1.000 | 1.000 | 1.000 | 1.000 | 1.000 | 1.000 | 1.000 | 1.000 |
| 0.78 | 1.002 | 1.001 | 1.001 | 1.000 | 1.000 | 1.000 | 1.000 | 1.000 | 1.000 | 1.000 | 1.000 |
| 0.80 | 1.003 | 1.002 | 1.001 | 1.001 | 1.001 | 1.000 | 1.000 | 1.000 | 1.000 | 1.000 | 1.000 |
| 0.82 | 1.004 | 1.003 | 1.002 | 1.001 | 1.001 | 1.001 | 1.001 | 1.000 | 1.000 | 1.000 | 1.000 |
| 0.84 | 1.007 | 1.005 | 1.003 | 1.002 | 1.002 | 1.001 | 1.001 | 1.001 | 1.001 | 1.000 | 1.000 |
| 0.86 | 1.010 | 1.007 | 1.005 | 1.004 | 1.003 | 1.002 | 1.002 | 1.001 | 1.001 | 1.001 | 1.000 |
| 0.88 | 1.017 | 1.012 | 1.009 | 1.007 | 1.005 | 1.004 | 1.003 | 1.003 | 1.002 | 1.001 | 1.001 |
| 0.90 | 1.028 | 1.020 | 1.015 | 1.012 | 1.009 | 1.008 | 1.006 | 1.005 | 1.004 | 1.003 | 1.002 |
| 0.92 | 1.048 | 1.036 | 1.028 | 1.022 | 1.018 | 1.014 | 1.012 | 1.010 | 1.007 | 1.005 | 1.004 |
| 0.94 | 1.093 | 1.071 | 1.055 | 1.044 | 1.036 | 1.030 | 1.025 | 1.021 | 1.016 | 1.012 | 1.009 |
| 0.96 | 1.215 | 1.167 | 1.132 | 1.108 | 1.089 | 1.074 | 1.063 | 1.054 | 1.041 | 1.032 | 1.026 |
| 0.98 | 1.733 | 1.590 | 1.485 | 1.405 | 1.343 | 1.293 | 1.254 | 1.221 | 1.172 | 1.138 | 1.112 |

**Table 11.** PROBABILITY THAT A TRANSACTION WILL BE LOST IN A MULTISERVER, NONQUEUING SITUATION. ASSUMPTIONS: POISSON ARRIVAL PATTERN; ALL SERVERS ARE EQUAL; IF AN ITEM CANNOT BE SERVED IMMEDIATELY, IT IS LOST

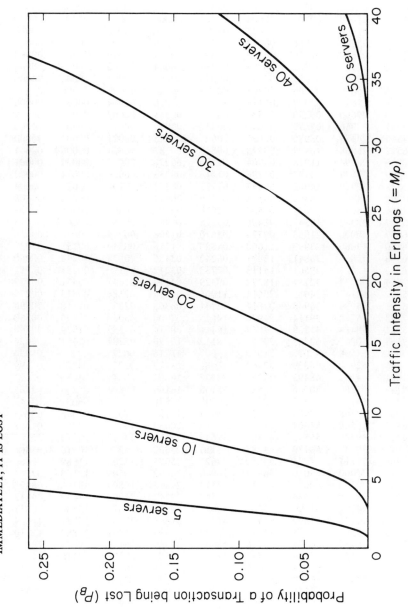

**Table 11.** (CONTINUED) Probability of a Transaction Being Lost, $P_B$

| Traffic Rate in Erlangs ($=M\rho$) | Number of Servers, $M$ | | | | | | | | | |
|---|---|---|---|---|---|---|---|---|---|---|
| | $M=1$ | 2 | 3 | 4 | 5 | 6 | 7 | 8 | 9 | 10 |
| 0.10 | .09091 | .00452 | .00015 | .00000 | .00000 | .00000 | .00000 | .00000 | .00000 | .00000 |
| 0.20 | .16667 | .01639 | .00109 | .00005 | .00000 | .00000 | .00000 | .00000 | .00000 | .00000 |
| 0.30 | .23077 | .03346 | .00333 | .00025 | .00002 | .00000 | .00000 | .00000 | .00000 | .00000 |
| 0.40 | .28571 | .05405 | .00716 | .00072 | .00006 | .00000 | .00000 | .00000 | .00000 | .00000 |
| 0.50 | .33333 | .07692 | .01266 | .00158 | .00016 | .00001 | .00000 | .00000 | .00000 | .00000 |
| 0.60 | .37500 | .10112 | .01982 | .00296 | .00036 | .00004 | .00000 | .00000 | .00000 | .00000 |
| 0.70 | .41176 | .12596 | .02855 | .00497 | .00070 | .00008 | .00001 | .00000 | .00000 | .00000 |
| 0.80 | .44444 | .15094 | .03869 | .00768 | .00123 | .00016 | .00002 | .00000 | .00000 | .00000 |
| 0.90 | .47368 | .17570 | .05007 | .01114 | .00200 | .00030 | .00004 | .00000 | .00000 | .00000 |
| 1.00 | .50000 | .20000 | .06250 | .01538 | .00307 | .00051 | .00007 | .00001 | .00000 | .00000 |
| 1.10 | .52381 | .22366 | .07579 | .02042 | .00447 | .00082 | .00013 | .00002 | .00000 | .00000 |
| 1.20 | .54545 | .24658 | .08978 | .02623 | .00625 | .00125 | .00021 | .00003 | .00000 | .00000 |
| 1.30 | .56522 | .26868 | .10429 | .03278 | .00845 | .00183 | .00034 | .00006 | .00001 | .00000 |
| 1.40 | .58333 | .28994 | .11918 | .04004 | .01109 | .00258 | .00052 | .00009 | .00001 | .00000 |
| 1.50 | .60000 | .31034 | .13433 | .04796 | .01418 | .00353 | .00076 | .00014 | .00002 | .00000 |
| 1.60 | .61538 | .32990 | .14962 | .05647 | .01775 | .00471 | .00108 | .00022 | .00004 | .00001 |
| 1.70 | .62963 | .34861 | .16496 | .06551 | .02179 | .00614 | .00149 | .00032 | .00006 | .00001 |
| 1.80 | .64286 | .36652 | .18027 | .07503 | .02630 | .00783 | .00201 | .00045 | .00009 | .00002 |
| 1.90 | .65517 | .38363 | .19547 | .08496 | .03128 | .00981 | .00265 | .00063 | .00013 | .00003 |
| 2.00 | .66667 | .40000 | .21053 | .09524 | .03670 | .01208 | .00344 | .00086 | .00019 | .00004 |
| 2.20 | .68750 | .43060 | .23999 | .11660 | .04880 | .01758 | .00549 | .00151 | .00037 | .00008 |
| 2.40 | .70588 | .45860 | .26841 | .13871 | .06242 | .02436 | .00828 | .00248 | .00066 | .00016 |
| 2.60 | .72222 | .48424 | .29561 | .16118 | .07733 | .03242 | .01190 | .00385 | .00111 | .00029 |
| 2.80 | .73684 | .50777 | .32154 | .18372 | .09329 | .04172 | .01641 | .00571 | .00177 | .00050 |
| 3.00 | .75000 | .52941 | .34615 | .20611 | .11005 | .05216 | .02186 | .00813 | .00270 | .00081 |
| 3.20 | .76190 | .54936 | .36948 | .22814 | .12741 | .06363 | .02826 | .01118 | .00396 | .00127 |
| 3.40 | .77273 | .56778 | .39154 | .24970 | .14515 | .07600 | .03560 | .01490 | .00560 | .00190 |
| 3.60 | .78261 | .58484 | .41239 | .27069 | .16311 | .08914 | .04383 | .01934 | .00768 | .00276 |
| 3.80 | .79167 | .60067 | .43209 | .29102 | .18112 | .10290 | .05291 | .02451 | .01024 | .00388 |
| 4.00 | .80000 | .61538 | .45070 | .31068 | .19907 | .11716 | .06275 | .03042 | .01334 | .00531 |
| 4.20 | .80769 | .62910 | .46829 | .32963 | .21685 | .13179 | .07328 | .03705 | .01699 | .00709 |
| 4.40 | .81481 | .64191 | .48493 | .34786 | .23437 | .14667 | .08441 | .04436 | .02123 | .00925 |
| 4.60 | .82143 | .65389 | .50066 | .36538 | .25158 | .16169 | .09605 | .05234 | .02605 | .01184 |
| 4.80 | .82759 | .66513 | .51555 | .38221 | .26843 | .17678 | .10811 | .06092 | .03147 | .01488 |
| 5.00 | .83333 | .67568 | .52966 | .39834 | .28487 | .19185 | .12052 | .07005 | .03746 | .01838 |
| 5.20 | .83871 | .68560 | .54304 | .41382 | .30088 | .20683 | .13318 | .07967 | .04401 | .02237 |
| 5.40 | .84375 | .69495 | .55573 | .42865 | .31645 | .22167 | .14603 | .08973 | .05109 | .02685 |
| 5.60 | .84848 | .70377 | .56779 | .44287 | .33156 | .23632 | .15900 | .10015 | .05866 | .03181 |
| 5.80 | .85294 | .71211 | .57926 | .45650 | .34621 | .25075 | .17202 | .11089 | .06669 | .03724 |
| 6.00 | .85714 | .72000 | .59016 | .46957 | .36040 | .26492 | .18505 | .12188 | .07514 | .04314 |
| 6.20 | .86111 | .72748 | .60055 | .48210 | .37414 | .27882 | .19804 | .13306 | .08397 | .04948 |
| 6.40 | .86486 | .73458 | .61045 | .49411 | .38743 | .29242 | .21095 | .14439 | .09312 | .05624 |
| 6.60 | .86842 | .74132 | .61990 | .50565 | .40028 | .30571 | .22375 | .15583 | .10255 | .06339 |
| 6.80 | .87179 | .74774 | .62892 | .51671 | .41271 | .31868 | .23639 | .16731 | .11223 | .07090 |
| 7.00 | .87500 | .75385 | .63755 | .52734 | .42472 | .33133 | .24887 | .17882 | .12210 | .07874 |
| 7.20 | .87805 | .75967 | .64579 | .53756 | .43633 | .34366 | .26116 | .19031 | .13213 | .08687 |
| 7.40 | .88095 | .76523 | .65369 | .54737 | .44755 | .35566 | .27325 | .20176 | .14229 | .09526 |
| 7.60 | .88372 | .77054 | .66125 | .55681 | .45839 | .36734 | .28512 | .21313 | .15253 | .10388 |
| 7.80 | .88636 | .77562 | .66850 | .56589 | .46887 | .37870 | .29676 | .22441 | .16281 | .11269 |
| 8.00 | .88889 | .78049 | .67546 | .57464 | .47901 | .38975 | .30816 | .23557 | .17314 | .12166 |
| 8.20 | .89130 | .78515 | .68214 | .58305 | .48881 | .40049 | .31933 | .24660 | .18346 | .13077 |
| 8.40 | .89362 | .78962 | .68856 | .59117 | .49828 | .41093 | .33026 | .25748 | .19376 | .13997 |
| 8.60 | .89583 | .79390 | .69474 | .59899 | .50745 | .42108 | .34094 | .26821 | .20401 | .14926 |
| 8.80 | .89796 | .79802 | .70068 | .60653 | .51632 | .43094 | .35139 | .27877 | .21419 | .15860 |
| 9.00 | .90000 | .80198 | .70640 | .61381 | .52491 | .44052 | .36158 | .28916 | .22430 | .16796 |
| 9.20 | .90196 | .80579 | .71191 | .62084 | .53322 | .44983 | .37154 | .29936 | .23431 | .17734 |
| 9.40 | .90385 | .80945 | .71722 | .62762 | .54127 | .45887 | .38126 | .30939 | .24422 | .18671 |
| 9.60 | .90566 | .81299 | .72234 | .63418 | .54907 | .46766 | .39075 | .31922 | .25401 | .19604 |
| 9.80 | .90741 | .81639 | .72729 | .64053 | .55663 | .47621 | .40001 | .32886 | .26368 | .20534 |
| 10.00 | .90909 | .81967 | .73206 | .64666 | .56395 | .48451 | .40904 | .33832 | .27321 | .21458 |

**Table 11.** (CONTINUED)  Probability of a Call Being Lost, $P_B$

Traffic
Rate of
Erlangs

Number of Servers, $M$

| $(=M\rho)$ | $M=11$ | $M=12$ | $M=13$ | $M=14$ | $M=15$ | $M=16$ | $M=17$ | $M=18$ | $M=19$ | $M=20$ |
|---|---|---|---|---|---|---|---|---|---|---|
| 1.50 | .00000 | .00000 | .00000 | .00000 | .00000 | .00000 | .00000 | .00000 | .00000 | .00000 |
| 2.00 | .00001 | .00000 | .00000 | .00000 | .00000 | .00000 | .00000 | .00000 | .00000 | .00000 |
| 2.50 | .00005 | .00001 | .00000 | .00000 | .00000 | .00000 | .00000 | .00000 | .00000 | .00000 |
| 3.00 | .00022 | .00006 | .00001 | .00000 | .00000 | .00000 | .00000 | .00000 | .00000 | .00000 |
| 3.50 | .00073 | .00021 | .00006 | .00001 | .00000 | .00000 | .00000 | .00000 | .00000 | .00000 |
| 4.00 | .00193 | .00064 | .00020 | .00006 | .00002 | .00000 | .00000 | .00000 | .00000 | .00000 |
| 4.50 | .00427 | .00160 | .00055 | .00018 | .00005 | .00002 | .00000 | .00000 | .00000 | .00000 |
| 5.00 | .00829 | .00344 | .00132 | .00047 | .00016 | .00005 | .00001 | .00000 | .00000 | .00000 |
| 5.25 | .01107 | .00482 | .00194 | .00073 | .00025 | .00008 | .00003 | .00001 | .00000 | .00000 |
| 5.50 | .01442 | .00657 | .00277 | .00109 | .00040 | .00014 | .00004 | .00001 | .00000 | .00000 |
| 5.75 | .01839 | .00873 | .00385 | .00158 | .00060 | .00022 | .00007 | .00002 | .00001 | .00000 |
| 6.00 | .02299 | .01136 | .00522 | .00223 | .00089 | .00033 | .00012 | .00004 | .00001 | .00000 |
| 6.25 | .02823 | .01449 | .00692 | .00308 | .00128 | .00050 | .00018 | .00006 | .00002 | .00001 |
| 6.50 | .03412 | .01814 | .00899 | .00416 | .00180 | .00073 | .00028 | .00010 | .00003 | .00001 |
| 6.75 | .04062 | .02234 | .01147 | .00550 | .00247 | .00104 | .00041 | .00015 | .00005 | .00002 |
| 7.00 | .04772 | .02708 | .01437 | .00713 | .00332 | .00145 | .00060 | .00023 | .00009 | .00003 |
| 7.25 | .05538 | .02827 | .01773 | .00910 | .00438 | .00198 | .00084 | .00034 | .00013 | .00005 |
| 7.50 | .06356 | .03821 | .02157 | .01142 | .00568 | .00265 | .00117 | .00049 | .00019 | .00007 |
| 7.75 | .07221 | .04456 | .02588 | .01412 | .00724 | .00350 | .00159 | .00068 | .00028 | .00011 |
| 8.00 | .08129 | .05141 | .03066 | .01722 | .00910 | .00453 | .00213 | .00094 | .00040 | .00016 |
| 8.25 | .09074 | .05872 | .03593 | .02073 | .01127 | .00578 | .00280 | .00128 | .00056 | .00023 |
| 8.50 | .10051 | .06646 | .04165 | .02466 | .01378 | .00727 | .00362 | .00171 | .00076 | .00032 |
| 8.75 | .11055 | .07460 | .04781 | .02901 | .01664 | .00902 | .00462 | .00224 | .00103 | .00045 |
| 9.00 | .12082 | .08309 | .05439 | .03379 | .01987 | .01105 | .00582 | .00290 | .00137 | .00062 |
| 9.25 | .13126 | .09188 | .06137 | .03897 | .02347 | .01338 | .00723 | .00370 | .00180 | .00083 |
| 9.50 | .14184 | .10095 | .06870 | .04454 | .02744 | .01603 | .00888 | .00466 | .00233 | .00110 |
| 9.75 | .15251 | .11025 | .07637 | .05050 | .03178 | .01900 | .01078 | .11581 | .00297 | .00145 |
| 10.00 | .16323 | .11974 | .08434 | .05682 | .03650 | .02230 | .01295 | .00714 | .00375 | .00187 |
| 10.25 | .17398 | .12938 | .09257 | .06347 | .04157 | .02594 | .01540 | .00869 | .00467 | .00239 |
| 10.50 | .18472 | .13914 | .10103 | .07044 | .04699 | .02991 | .01814 | .01047 | .00575 | .00301 |
| 10.75 | .19543 | .14899 | .10969 | .07768 | .05274 | .03422 | .02118 | .01249 | .00702 | .00376 |
| 11.00 | .20608 | .15889 | .11851 | .08519 | .05880 | .03885 | .02452 | .01477 | .00848 | .00464 |
| 11.25 | .21666 | .16883 | .12748 | .09292 | .06515 | .04380 | .02817 | .01730 | .01014 | .00567 |
| 11.50 | .22714 | .17877 | .13655 | .10085 | .07177 | .04905 | .03212 | .02011 | .01202 | .00687 |
| 11.75 | .23752 | .18869 | .14570 | .10896 | .07864 | .05460 | .03636 | .02319 | .01414 | .00824 |
| 12.00 | .24777 | .19857 | .15490 | .11721 | .08573 | .06041 | .04090 | .02654 | .01649 | .00980 |
| 12.25 | .25788 | .20839 | .16414 | .12559 | .09302 | .06648 | .04572 | .03017 | .01908 | .01155 |
| 12.50 | .26786 | .21815 | .17739 | .13406 | .10049 | .07279 | .05080 | .03408 | .02193 | .01352 |
| 12.75 | .27768 | .22782 | .18263 | .14261 | .10811 | .07932 | .05615 | .03825 | .02503 | .01570 |
| 13.00 | .28735 | .23740 | .19185 | .15121 | .11587 | .08604 | .06173 | .04268 | .02838 | .01811 |
| 13.25 | .29686 | .24687 | .20103 | .15985 | .12373 | .09294 | .06755 | .04737 | .03198 | .02074 |
| 13.50 | .30621 | .25622 | .21016 | .16850 | .13168 | .10000 | .07357 | .05229 | .03582 | .02361 |
| 13.75 | .31539 | .26545 | .21922 | .17716 | .13971 | .10719 | .07978 | .05744 | .03991 | .02671 |
| 14.00 | .32441 | .27456 | .22820 | .18580 | .14799 | .11451 | .08617 | .06281 | .04424 | .03004 |
| 14.25 | .33325 | .28353 | .23711 | .19442 | .15590 | .12192 | .09272 | .06839 | .04879 | .03359 |
| 14.50 | .34193 | .29237 | .24591 | .20299 | .16404 | .12942 | .09941 | .07415 | .05355 | .03738 |
| 14.75 | .35045 | .30107 | .25462 | .21152 | .17218 | .13699 | .10623 | .08008 | .05853 | .04138 |
| 15.00 | .35879 | .30963 | .26322 | .21998 | .18032 | .14460 | .11315 | .08617 | .06270 | .04559 |
| 15.50 | .37499 | .32631 | .28009 | .23670 | .19652 | .15993 | .12726 | .09876 | .07456 | .05463 |
| 16.00 | .39055 | .34242 | .29649 | .25309 | .21257 | .17531 | .14163 | .11181 | .03606 | .06441 |
| 16.50 | .40548 | .35796 | .31240 | .26910 | .22840 | .19064 | .15614 | .12521 | .09807 | .07485 |
| 17.00 | .41981 | .37293 | .32781 | .28472 | .24396 | .20585 | .17071 | .13884 | .11050 | .08586 |
| 17.50 | .43356 | .38736 | .34273 | .29992 | .25921 | .22089 | .18526 | .15262 | .12325 | .09734 |
| 18.00 | .44675 | .40124 | .35715 | .31469 | .27411 | .23569 | .19972 | .16647 | .13623 | .10921 |
| 18.50 | .45942 | .41461 | .37108 | .32902 | .28866 | .25024 | .21403 | .18031 | .14935 | .12138 |
| 19.00 | .47158 | .42748 | .38453 | .34291 | .30282 | .26449 | .22816 | .19409 | .16254 | .13376 |
| 19.50 | .48325 | .43987 | .39752 | .35637 | .31660 | .27843 | .24206 | .20775 | .17575 | .14629 |
| 20.00 | .49447 | .45179 | .41005 | .36940 | .33000 | .29203 | .25571 | .22126 | .18891 | .15889 |

859

**Table 11.** (CONTINUED)     Probability of a Call Being Lost, $P_B$

Traffic
Rate in                                                  Number of Servers, $M$
Erlangs

| $(= M\rho)$ | $M=21$ | $M=22$ | $M=23$ | $M=24$ | $M=25$ | $M=26$ | $M=27$ | $M=28$ | $M=29$ | $M=30$ |
|---|---|---|---|---|---|---|---|---|---|---|
| 6.00 | .00000 | .00000 | .00000 | .00000 | .00000 | .00000 | .00000 | .00000 | .00000 | .00000 |
| 6.50 | .00000 | .00000 | .00000 | .00000 | .00000 | .00000 | .00000 | .00000 | .00000 | .00000 |
| 7.00 | .00001 | .00000 | .00000 | .00000 | .00000 | .00000 | .00000 | .00000 | .00000 | .00000 |
| 7.50 | .00003 | .00001 | .00000 | .00000 | .00000 | .00000 | .00000 | .00000 | .00000 | .00000 |
| 8.00 | .00006 | .00002 | .00001 | .00000 | .00000 | .00000 | .00000 | .00000 | .00000 | .00000 |
| 8.50 | .00013 | .00005 | .00002 | .00001 | .00000 | .00000 | .00000 | .00000 | .00000 | .00000 |
| 9.00 | .00026 | .00011 | .00004 | .00002 | .00001 | .00000 | .00000 | .00000 | .00000 | .00000 |
| 9.50 | .00050 | .00022 | .00009 | .00004 | .00001 | .00000 | .00000 | .00000 | .00000 | .00000 |
| 10.00 | .00089 | .00040 | .00018 | .00007 | .00003 | .00001 | .00000 | .00000 | .00000 | .00000 |
| 10.50 | .00150 | .00072 | .00033 | .00014 | .00006 | .00002 | .00001 | .00000 | .00000 | .00000 |
| 11.00 | .00242 | .00121 | .00058 | .00027 | .00012 | .00005 | .00002 | .00001 | .00000 | .00000 |
| 11.50 | .00375 | .00195 | .00098 | .00047 | .00022 | .00010 | .00004 | .00002 | .00001 | .00000 |
| 12.00 | .00557 | .00303 | .00158 | .00079 | .00038 | .00017 | .00008 | .00003 | .00001 | .00001 |
| 12.50 | .00798 | .00452 | .00245 | .00127 | .00064 | .00031 | .00014 | .00006 | .00003 | .00001 |
| 13.00 | .01109 | .00651 | .00367 | .00198 | .00103 | .00051 | .00025 | .00011 | .00005 | .00002 |
| 13.50 | .01495 | .00909 | .00531 | .00298 | .00160 | .00083 | .00042 | .00020 | .00009 | .00004 |
| 14.00 | .01963 | .01234 | .00745 | .00433 | .00242 | .00130 | .00067 | .00034 | .00016 | .00008 |
| 14.50 | .02516 | .01631 | .01018 | .00611 | .00353 | .00197 | .00105 | .00055 | .00027 | .00013 |
| 15.00 | .03154 | .02105 | .01354 | .00839 | .00501 | .00288 | .00160 | .00086 | .00044 | .00022 |
| 15.50 | .03876 | .02658 | .01760 | .01124 | .00692 | .00411 | .00235 | .00130 | .00069 | .00036 |
| 16.00 | .04678 | .03290 | .02238 | .01470 | .00932 | .00570 | .00337 | .00192 | .00106 | .00056 |
| 16.50 | .05555 | .03999 | .02789 | .01881 | .01226 | .00772 | .00470 | .00276 | .00157 | .00086 |
| 17.00 | .06499 | .04782 | .03414 | .02361 | .01580 | .01023 | .00640 | .00387 | .00226 | .00128 |
| 17.50 | .07503 | .05632 | .04109 | .02909 | .01996 | .01326 | .00852 | .00530 | .00319 | .00185 |
| 18.00 | .08560 | .06545 | .04873 | .03526 | .02476 | .01685 | .01111 | .00709 | .00438 | .00262 |
| 18.50 | .09660 | .07513 | .05699 | .04208 | .03020 | .02103 | .01421 | .00930 | .00590 | .00362 |
| 19.00 | .10796 | .08528 | .06582 | .04952 | .03627 | .02582 | .01785 | .01197 | .00778 | .00490 |
| 19.50 | .11959 | .09584 | .07515 | .05755 | .04296 | .03121 | .02205 | .01512 | .01007 | .00650 |
| 20.00 | .13144 | .10673 | .08493 | .06610 | .05022 | .03720 | .02681 | .01879 | .01279 | .00846 |
| 20.50 | .14342 | .11789 | .09508 | .17512 | .05802 | .04375 | .03215 | .02299 | .01599 | .01081 |
| 21.00 | .15548 | .12924 | .10554 | .08454 | .06631 | .05083 | .03803 | .02773 | .01969 | .01359 |
| 21.50 | .16758 | .14072 | .11625 | .09432 | .07503 | .05842 | .04445 | .03301 | .02389 | .01683 |
| 22.00 | .17960 | .15230 | .12715 | .10439 | .08413 | .06646 | .05137 | .03880 | .02859 | .02054 |
| 22.50 | .19168 | .16390 | .13818 | .11469 | .09356 | .07490 | .05875 | .04508 | .03380 | .02472 |
| 23.00 | .20361 | .17550 | .14930 | .12517 | .10327 | .08370 | .06656 | .05184 | .03949 | .02939 |
| 23.50 | .21542 | .18706 | .16046 | .13578 | .11319 | .09281 | .07474 | .05903 | .04565 | .03452 |
| 24.00 | .22709 | .19855 | .17162 | .14648 | .12329 | .10217 | .08326 | .06661 | .05225 | .04012 |
| 24.50 | .23860 | .20993 | .18275 | .15723 | .13351 | .11175 | .09207 | .07455 | .05925 | .04616 |
| 25.00 | .24993 | .22119 | .19382 | .16798 | .14382 | .12149 | .10112 | .08281 | .06663 | .05260 |
| 25.50 | .26107 | .23231 | .20481 | .17872 | .15418 | .13136 | .11037 | .09133 | .07434 | .05943 |
| 26.00 | .27201 | .24326 | .21568 | .18940 | .16456 | .14131 | .11978 | .10009 | .08235 | .06661 |
| 26.50 | .28274 | .25405 | .22643 | .20001 | .17493 | .15131 | .12931 | .10904 | .09061 | .07411 |
| 27.00 | .29327 | .26466 | .23704 | .21053 | .18525 | .16134 | .13893 | .11814 | .09909 | .08188 |
| 27.50 | .30358 | .27509 | .24750 | .22094 | .19552 | .17136 | .14860 | .12736 | .10776 | .08990 |
| 28.00 | .31367 | .28532 | .25780 | .23122 | .20570 | .18135 | .15830 | .13666 | .11657 | .09812 |
| 28.50 | .32355 | .29535 | .26792 | .24137 | .21578 | .19129 | .16799 | .14602 | .12550 | .10652 |
| 29.00 | .33322 | .30519 | .27788 | .25137 | .22576 | .20115 | .17767 | .15542 | .13451 | .11507 |
| 29.50 | .34267 | .31483 | .28765 | .26121 | .23561 | .21094 | .18730 | .16481 | .14358 | .12372 |
| 30.00 | .35190 | .32426 | .29724 | .27090 | .24533 | .22062 | .19687 | .17419 | .15268 | .13246 |
| 30.50 | .36093 | .33350 | .30664 | .28041 | .25490 | .23019 | .20637 | .18354 | .16180 | .14126 |
| 31.00 | .36975 | .34255 | .31586 | .28977 | .26433 | .23964 | .21577 | .19283 | .17090 | .15009 |
| 31.50 | .37838 | .35139 | .32490 | .29895 | .27361 | .24896 | .22508 | .20225 | .17997 | .15894 |
| 32.00 | .38680 | .36005 | .33375 | .30796 | .28274 | .25815 | .23428 | .21120 | .18900 | .16778 |
| 32.50 | .39503 | .36851 | .34242 | .31680 | .29170 | .26720 | .24336 | .22025 | .19797 | .17659 |
| 33.00 | .40307 | .37679 | .35091 | .32546 | .30051 | .27611 | .25232 | .22921 | .20687 | .18537 |
| 33.50 | .41092 | .38489 | .35922 | .33396 | .30916 | .28486 | .26114 | .23806 | .21569 | .19410 |
| 34.00 | .41860 | .39281 | .36736 | .34229 | .31764 | .29348 | .26984 | .24680 | .22441 | .20277 |
| 34.50 | .42610 | .40055 | .37532 | .35045 | .32597 | .30194 | .27840 | .25542 | .23304 | .21136 |
| 35.00 | .43342 | .40812 | .38312 | .35845 | .33414 | .31025 | .28682 | .26391 | .24157 | .21987 |

**Table 11.** (CONTINUED)  Probability of a call being lost, $P_B$

Traffic
Rate in                                                      Number of Servers, $M$:
Erlangs

| $(=M\rho)$ | 35 | 40 | 45 | 50 | 55 | 60 | 70 | 80 | 90 | 100 |
|---|---|---|---|---|---|---|---|---|---|---|
| 15.00 | .00000 | .00000 | .00000 | .00000 | .00000 | .00000 | .00000 | .00000 | .00000 | .00000 |
| 16.00 | .00002 | .00000 | .00000 | .00000 | .00000 | .00000 | .00000 | .00000 | .00000 | .00000 |
| 17.00 | .00005 | .00000 | .00000 | .00000 | .00000 | .00000 | .00000 | .00000 | .00000 | .00000 |
| 18.00 | .00013 | .00000 | .00000 | .00000 | .00000 | .00000 | .00000 | .00000 | .00000 | .00000 |
| 19.00 | .00031 | .00001 | .00000 | .00000 | .00000 | .00000 | .00000 | .00000 | .00000 | .00000 |
| 20.00 | .00069 | .00003 | .00000 | .00000 | .00000 | .00000 | .00000 | .00000 | .00000 | .00000 |
| 21.00 | .00139 | .00007 | .00000 | .00000 | .00000 | .00000 | .00000 | .00000 | .00000 | .00000 |
| 22.00 | .00262 | .00017 | .00001 | .00000 | .00000 | .00000 | .00000 | .00000 | .00000 | .00000 |
| 23.00 | .00458 | .00037 | .00002 | .00000 | .00000 | .00000 | .00000 | .00000 | .00000 | .00000 |
| 24.00 | .00751 | .00075 | .00004 | .00000 | .00000 | .00000 | .00000 | .00000 | .00000 | .00000 |
| 25.00 | .01165 | .00141 | .00009 | .00000 | .00000 | .00000 | .00000 | .00000 | .00000 | .00000 |
| 26.00 | .01715 | .00250 | .00020 | .00001 | .00000 | .00000 | .00000 | .00000 | .00000 | .00000 |
| 27.00 | .02413 | .00418 | .00041 | .00002 | .00000 | .00000 | .00000 | .00000 | .00000 | .00000 |
| 28.00 | .03261 | .00662 | .00077 | .00005 | .00000 | .00000 | .00000 | .00000 | .00000 | .00000 |
| 29.00 | .04253 | .00999 | .00137 | .00011 | .00001 | .00000 | .00000 | .00000 | .00000 | .00000 |
| 30.00 | .05377 | .01444 | .00232 | .00022 | .00001 | .00000 | .00000 | .00000 | .00000 | .00000 |
| 31.00 | .06617 | .02006 | .00375 | .00042 | .00003 | .00000 | .00000 | .00000 | .00000 | .00000 |
| 32.00 | .07954 | .02689 | .00579 | .00076 | .00006 | .00000 | .00000 | .00000 | .00000 | .00000 |
| 33.00 | .09367 | .03493 | .00856 | .00130 | .00012 | .00001 | .00000 | .00000 | .00000 | .00000 |
| 34.00 | .10838 | .04412 | .01219 | .00212 | .00023 | .00002 | .00000 | .00000 | .00000 | .00000 |
| 35.00 | .12348 | .05435 | .01677 | .00334 | .00042 | .00003 | .00000 | .00000 | .00000 | .00000 |
| 36.00 | .13883 | .06550 | .02234 | .00504 | .00072 | .00007 | .00000 | .00000 | .00000 | .00000 |
| 37.00 | .15428 | .07742 | .02893 | .00734 | .00120 | .00013 | .00000 | .00000 | .00000 | .00000 |
| 38.00 | .16972 | .08996 | .03650 | .01034 | .00192 | .00023 | .00000 | .00000 | .00000 | .00000 |
| 39.00 | .18506 | .10299 | .04501 | .01411 | .00295 | .00040 | .00000 | .00000 | .00000 | .00000 |
| 40.00 | .20023 | .11637 | .05436 | .01870 | .00439 | .00068 | .00000 | .00000 | .00000 | .00000 |
| 41.00 | .21517 | .12998 | .06445 | .02416 | .00631 | .00110 | .00001 | .00000 | .00000 | .00000 |
| 42.00 | .22984 | .14372 | .07519 | .03047 | .00880 | .00172 | .00002 | .00000 | .00000 | .00000 |
| 43.00 | .24420 | .15749 | .08644 | .03760 | .01193 | .00260 | .00004 | .00000 | .00000 | .00000 |
| 44.00 | .25823 | .17123 | .09811 | .04551 | .01576 | .00382 | .00007 | .00000 | .00000 | .00000 |
| 45.00 | .27192 | .18487 | .11009 | .05412 | .02032 | .00543 | .00013 | .00000 | .00000 | .00000 |
| 46.00 | .28526 | .19837 | .12229 | .06336 | .02561 | .00752 | .00022 | .00000 | .00000 | .00000 |
| 47.00 | .29824 | .21167 | .13463 | .07313 | .03164 | .01014 | .00036 | .00000 | .00000 | .00000 |
| 48.00 | .31086 | .22475 | .14703 | .08335 | .03837 | .01335 | .00058 | .00001 | .00000 | .00000 |
| 49.00 | .32313 | .23760 | .15943 | .09393 | .04576 | .01719 | .00090 | .00001 | .00000 | .00000 |
| 50.00 | .33505 | .25018 | .17178 | .10479 | .05374 | .02166 | .00137 | .00002 | .00000 | .00000 |
| 51.00 | .34662 | .26250 | .18404 | .11586 | .06226 | .02679 | .00202 | .00004 | .00000 | .00000 |
| 52.00 | .35785 | .27453 | .19618 | .12707 | .07124 | .03255 | .00289 | .00007 | .00000 | .00000 |
| 53.00 | .36876 | .28628 | .20815 | .13836 | .08061 | .03891 | .00405 | .00012 | .00000 | .00000 |
| 54.00 | .37934 | .29775 | .21995 | .14967 | .09030 | .04584 | .00554 | .00019 | .00000 | .00000 |
| 55.00 | .38962 | .30893 | .23155 | .16097 | .10024 | .05328 | .00741 | .00031 | .00001 | .00000 |
| 56.00 | .39960 | .31983 | .24295 | .17222 | .11037 | .06119 | .00971 | .00048 | .00001 | .00000 |
| 57.00 | .40928 | .33045 | .25412 | .18338 | .12065 | .06950 | .01247 | .00073 | .00001 | .00000 |
| 58.00 | .41869 | .34079 | .26507 | .19442 | .13101 | .07815 | .01572 | .00107 | .00002 | .00000 |
| 59.00 | .42782 | .35087 | .27579 | .20534 | .14141 | .08708 | .01947 | .00155 | .00004 | .00000 |
| 60.00 | .43669 | .36068 | .28628 | .21611 | .15182 | .09625 | .02374 | .00220 | .00006 | .00000 |
| 61.00 | .44531 | .37024 | .29653 | .22671 | .16220 | .10560 | .02851 | .00304 | .00010 | .00000 |
| 62.00 | .45368 | .37955 | .30656 | .23714 | .17253 | .11508 | .03377 | .00412 | .00016 | .00000 |
| 63.00 | .46183 | .38861 | .31635 | .24739 | .18278 | .12466 | .03950 | .00548 | .00026 | .00000 |
| 64.00 | .46974 | .39744 | .32592 | .25745 | .19292 | .13428 | .04566 | .00716 | .00039 | .00001 |
| 65.00 | .47744 | .40604 | .33527 | .26732 | .20296 | .14393 | .05222 | .00917 | .00058 | .00001 |
| 66.00 | .48493 | .41441 | .34439 | .27700 | .21287 | .15357 | .05914 | .01157 | .00084 | .00002 |
| 67.00 | .49222 | .42257 | .35330 | .28648 | .22263 | .16318 | .06637 | .01436 | .00120 | .00003 |
| 68.00 | .49931 | .43053 | .36201 | .29578 | .23226 | .17273 | .07388 | .01755 | .00167 | .00006 |
| 69.00 | .50621 | .43828 | .37050 | .30487 | .24172 | .18221 | .08162 | .02117 | .00230 | .00009 |
| 70.00 | .51294 | .44584 | .37880 | .31378 | .25104 | .19160 | .08956 | .02520 | .00309 | .00014 |
| 71.00 | .51949 | .45320 | .38690 | .32250 | .26019 | .20089 | .09765 | .02963 | .00409 | .00021 |
| 72.00 | .52587 | .46039 | .39481 | .33104 | .26917 | .21007 | .10587 | .03446 | .00532 | .00031 |
| 73.00 | .53209 | .46740 | .40254 | .33939 | .27800 | .21913 | .11418 | .03966 | .00682 | .00046 |
| 74.00 | .53815 | .47423 | .41009 | .34756 | .28666 | .22806 | .12256 | .04521 | .00860 | .00065 |
| 75.00 | .54407 | .48091 | .41746 | .35556 | .29515 | .23686 | .13097 | .05107 | .01069 | .00092 |

# CLASS QUESTIONS

## PART I TEST OF GENERAL UNDERSTANDING

1.1  What is the difference between "bauds" and "bits-per-second"?

1.2  What are half-duplex and full-duplex lines?

1.3  A full-duplex line in the United States is commonly 10 per cent more expensive than a half-duplex line. What facilities should the terminals have to take *maximum* advantage of full-duplex transmission? When is the expense of such facilities warranted?

1.4  What does modulation mean? What are the common methods of modulation?

1.5  What is the difference between synchronous and asynchronous transmission? Draw a typical message format for each. What are the relative advantages of each?

1.6  What could be the advantages of integrating modems into the terminal electronics?

1.7  When is it desirable to have buffers in terminals? List several cases. When are unbuffered terminals adequate?

1.8  What is the difference between line-switching, message-switching and packet-switching? When are message-switching systems used?

1.9  Under what circumstances would you use WATS?

1.10 What is a multidrop circuit? When would you use it? When would you avoid using it?

1.11 Higher speeds have generally been used on leased voice lines than on public voice lines. Why? (More than one reason.)

1.12 What electronic mechanisms can be employed to obtain transmission speeds on public telephone lines as high as those on leased voice lines?

1.13 On what types of system would you recommend the use of TWX? On what types of system would you not use it?

1.14  What is TELPAK C?  When would you employ it?

1.15  If polling is to be used with a high measure of reliability, what features should a terminal have?

1.16  Select a polling mechanism and specify in detail the characters that flow in both directions on the line.

1.17  What are the advantages of hub polling over roll-call polling?  What are its disadvantages?  When would you recommend its use?  When would you not recommend its use?

1.18  What are the advantages of a simple time-division multiplexer over other means of lowering network cost?

1.19  What mechanisms can offer greater network cost savings than a simple time-division multiplexer?  Why?

1.20  Most mechanisms other than simple multiplexing for lowering network cost entail certain risks, such as the risk of obtaining "busy" signals.  What different risks are associated with different mechanisms?

1.21  What tariffs and mechanisms would you consider for the nine cases indicated in the table below?
(a) for teletype machines
(b) for visual display units

| Number of different places called or from which calls originate: | Number of calls per day: | | |
|---|---|---|---|
| | FEW | MANY | VERY MANY |
| FEW | | | |
| MANY | | | |
| VERY   MANY | | | |

1.22  What are the functions required at the computer center for transmission control?  Consider when they might be done by hardware, and when by software.

1.23  Real-time terminals are to be installed for student registration at a university.  What terminal features would you recommend?  What form of dialogue structure would be best suited for this application?

1.24  In what ways can a communication link fail or be unreliable?  List measures that may be used to protect systems from communication unreliability.

1.25  Define response time.  What elements of time must be added into the overall response time?  Which of these are variable and which could lead to a high standard deviation of response time?

1.26 Given a choice, which would you rather design for:
(a) A mean response time of 10 seconds,
(b) 50% of the response times are equal to or less than 10 seconds.
Why?

## PART II STATISTICS QUESTIONS (CHAPTER 30)

2.1   Messages travelling on a transmission line to a computer have the following numbers of characters:

| Percentage of Messages | Number of Characters |
|:---:|:---:|
| 20 | 80 |
| 10 | 100 |
| 30 | 120 |
| 20 | 160 |
| 20 | 280 |

Calculate: (a) the mean number of characters in a message
(b) the standard deviation of number of characters
(c) the variance of number of characters.

2.2   The transmission rate is 20 characters per second.  Calculate:
(a) the mean message transmission time
(b) the standard deviation of message transmission time
(c) the variance of message transmission time.

2.3   When the above messages have completed transmission, the time to process them and send a reply to the operator has a mean of 8.5 seconds with a standard deviation of 7 seconds.
   The total transaction time is defined by the customer as the time to transmit the message to the computer, process it and send the reply to the operator. Calculate:
(a) the mean total transaction time
(b) the standard deviation of the total transaction time
(c) the variance of the total transaction time.

2.4   The rotation time of a disk is 25 msec.  After a seek it is necessary for the disk to position itself before the read commences.  Calculate:
(a) the mean rotational delay
(b) the standard deviation of rotational delay
(c) the variance of rotational delay.

2.5   The file reference time is here defined as seek time + rotational delay + record read time.  The read time for the above records is a constant 6 msec.  The mean seek time for a given set of records is 40msec. and the standard deviation is 12 msec. Calculate approximately:

(a) the mean file reference time

(b) the standard deviation of file reference time

(c) the variance of file reference time.

2.6 Transactions are a mixture of four types, A, B, C, and D. The mean response times for these transactions, and their second moments, are as follows:

| Transaction Type | Percentage of this Type | Mean Response Time (sec) | Second Moment of Response Time (sec$^2$) |
|---|---|---|---|
| A | 10 | 10 | 120 |
| B | 20 | 5 | 50 |
| C | 30 | 10 | 100 |
| D | 40 | 8 | 100 |

For the entire transaction group, what is:

(a) the mean response time

(b) the standard deviation of the response time

(c) the variance of the response time?

2.7 Transactions are a mixture of three types, A, B, and C, which make access to different files as follows:

| Transaction Type | Percentage of this Type | Mean File Reference Time (msec) | Standard Deviation of File Reference Time (msec) |
|---|---|---|---|
| A | 60 | 100 | 20 |
| B | 30 | 120 | 25 |
| C | 10 | 80 | 15 |

For the entire transaction group, what is:

(a) the mean file reference time

(b) the standard deviation of file reference time

(c) the variance of file reference time?

## PART III QUESTIONS ON THE POISSON AND EXPONENTIAL DISTRIBUTIONS*

3.1 A communication line services two terminals in different towns. Transactions arrive at each terminal randomly. The mean number of transactions per second at one terminal is higher than the mean at the other. However, the transaction

* To save work you should use tables where needed.

rate at each follows a Poisson distribution. Will the combined arrival rate be a Poisson distribution or not?

3.2  The requests for access on a file arm arrive at random (Poisson arrival rate). The mean number of requests per second is 2. What will be the standard deviation, variance and second moment of number of requests per second?

3.3  In London during the V2 attacks, these missiles land at random within a given area. (The time interval between explosions follows an exponential distribution.) The mean time between explosions is 3 hours. Covent Garden is doing a performance of Parsifal which lasts 6 hours. What is the probability that there will not be an explosion during the performance? This can be done in two ways: using the exponential distribution or using the Poisson distribution. Do it both ways and check that your answers agree.

3.4  In the above question what is the probability that there will be 3 or more explosions during the performance?

3.5  A computer system has a mean time to failure of 20 hours. What is the probability that it will fail during a demonstration lasting 2 hours?

3.6  A certain facility is unable to handle more than 12 transactions per minute. Transactions having an exponential interarrival time distribution arrive at a mean rate of 7.1 per minute. What proportion of the time will 13 or more transactions arrive in one minute?

## PART IV  QUEUING THEORY QUESTIONS

4.1  Customers walk into a sales office at random. Their requests are answered by one operator at a terminal. The time she takes to service each customer follows an exponential distribution with a mean of 30 seconds. A queue forms for the service of this operator. Plot a curve (approximately) showing the mean number of customers in the queue (vertical axis) against the rate of arrival of customers (horizontal axis).

4.2  A computer has a full-duplex communication line network with display terminals. The mean length of the output message is 480 characters. The line speed is 120 characters per second. Three lines service 40, 60, and 100 terminals, respectively. Assume that the message length is exponentially distributed, and that the output to each terminal is an equal fraction of the whole. Assume also that the output messages arrive with an exponential interarrival time. (Is this realistic?)

Plot a curve showing the number of messages in the core buffer for output transmission (vertical) against the number of messages per hour from each terminal. Note: As this question refers to full-duplex lines this input need not be considered in answering this question.

4.3 A computer channel has six drums attached to it. Nothing else is in use on this channel. Requests for drum reads occur at random (Poisson) during the peak period, at a rate of 50 per second. The rotational delay and read time give a drum access time that has a mean of 15 milliseconds and a standard deviation of 10 milliseconds. Only one drum access can take place at once on the channel. What is the mean time for a drum access, including the time spent queuing for that access.

4.4 Passengers telephone an airline reservation office at random. In the busiest half hour of the peak day, 12 calls are received. The calls are routed automatically to the first free agent in an office with three agents. The agent takes six minutes on average to deal with a typical customer. Make the worst-case assumption that this service time is exponentially distributed, and calculate how long a customer can be expected to wait before talking to an agent. Assume that no customer rings off before being serviced. What will be the waiting time when this peak is 10% higher than expected?

4.5 You are to install a group of time-sharing terminals to serve a group of 200 people. A design criterion is that a person coming to the terminal room should have a 0.99 probability of finding a terminal free. The terminal occupancy is approximately exponentially distributed with a mean of 30 minutes. It is estimated that 20 users will sign on per hour during the peak times (the 0.99 probability applies to the peak times).

How many terminals will you install?

4.6 Telephone callers occupy a register in an exchange when dialing a call for a mean time of 8 seconds. They do not hear a dial tone until they have gained access to such a register. It is estimated that 1000 calls will be received in the peak hour. A design objective is that not more than 1 percent of the callers have to wait more than one second for a dial tone. How many registers are needed to achieve this objective?

What is the probability that a caller will have to wait more than 2 seconds?

4.7 Private-leased tie lines are being planned to connect two centers of activity in a corporation. It is anticipated that 200 calls will be originated using these lines in the peak hour of an average day and that an average call will be of 4 minutes duration. When a user makes a tie-line call, he will obtain a busy signal if no tie-line is available. How many lines are needed to give a grade of service of 0.005?

If, due to special circumstances on one day, the peak hour is four times busier, what will be the probability of not getting through?

4.8 A time-sharing system is being planned that will have several hundred users with terminals in offices and laboratories. It is thought desirable to give the users a grade of service not worse than 0.01—that is, when they dial the system, they have a 99 in 100 chance of being able to use it. The usage statistics from a small pilot system suggest that when the full system is installed, an average 35 users will be connected to it at any one time during the morning hours when usage is likely to be heaviest. How many ports will the system need to give a grade of service of 0.01?

At any one time 8 of the 35 users will be in the same building as the computer on the average. The remainder will be connected via trunks from a Centrex system. How many such trunks will be needed?

4.9 Table A.1 is the output of a typical GPSS Simulation run of a real-time system. The argument of the table is the response time (listed in the left-hand column). Investigate how closely the response times can be approximated by the incomplete gamma function. Note: A quick way to do this is to plot the values on the curves in Figs. 31.13 and 31.14. No calculation is needed.

4.10 The initial design of an airline reservation system is calculated to give a mean response time of 1.7 seconds with a standard deviation of 1.2 seconds. The customer wants a contract which says that 90% of the transactions will have a response in less than 3 seconds. Is this condition met? (Assume that the response times approximately follow a gamma distribution.)

4.11 An operator is using a terminal on a multidrop line. Calculations show that when she presses the key requesting attention she waits, on average, 9.6 seconds before she can transmit, with a standard deviation of 6.4 seconds. During the sending of 100 transactions how many times, approximately, will she have to wait more than half a minute before she gains attention? (Again assume that the times approximately follow a gamma distribution.)

4.12 Figure 36.12 gives the results of a computation of the response time of a system. A design criterion on this system is that only 5% of the responses for type A transactions are to exceed 10 seconds. What, approximately, is the maximum throughput the system can handle and still meet this criterion?

## PART V QUESTIONS ON TRANSMISSION ERRORS

The teletype messages are sent over "public" lines on which it can be expected that one bit in $10^5$ has a transmission error. To simplify the following calculations assume that each error affects only one bit and that the errors are independent of one another. Note: The question should be answered to an accuracy of two significant figures *only*.

5.1 If a teletype transaction consists of 200 five-bit characters (with no checking), what is the probability that it has an error in it?

5.2 A manufacturer proposes to send the above teletype messages in batches of 400 transactions. A hash total is taken of each batch, which is also 200 characters in length. What is the probability that the batch will have to be retransmitted?

5.3 Real-time teletype transactions (with no error checking) will update a file of 10,000 records. On average an item is updated 100 times per month. If any one

**Table A.1.** MEAN RESPONSE TIME = 321.134. STANDARD DEVIATION OF RESPONSE TIME = 237.004.

| Response Time Upper Limit | Observed Frequency | Per Cent of Total | Cumulative Percentage | Multiple of Mean |
|---|---|---|---|---|
| 100 | 420 | 2.99 | 3.0 | .311 |
| 150 | 2385 | 17.00 | 20.0 | .467 |
| 200 | 2705 | 19.28 | 39.3 | .623 |
| 250 | 1788 | 12.74 | 52.0 | .778 |
| 300 | 1334 | 9.51 | 61.5 | .934 |
| 350 | 1045 | 7.45 | 69.0 | 1.090 |
| 400 | 842 | 6.00 | 75.0 | 1.246 |
| 450 | 651 | 4.64 | 79.6 | 1.401 |
| 500 | 543 | 3.87 | 83.5 | 1.557 |
| 550 | 408 | 2.91 | 86.4 | 1.713 |
| 600 | 338 | 2.41 | 88.8 | 1.868 |
| 650 | 320 | 2.28 | 91.1 | 2.024 |
| 700 | 207 | 1.48 | 92.5 | 2.180 |
| 750 | 197 | 1.40 | 93.9 | 2.335 |
| 800 | 173 | 1.23 | 95.2 | 2.491 |
| 850 | 115 | .82 | 96.0 | 2.647 |
| 900 | 120 | .86 | 96.9 | 2.803 |
| 950 | 79 | .56 | 97.4 | 2.958 |
| 1000 | 68 | .48 | 97.9 | 3.114 |
| 1050 | 62 | .44 | 98.3 | 3.270 |
| 1100 | 49 | .35 | 98.7 | 3.425 |
| 1150 | 31 | .22 | 98.9 | 3.581 |
| 1200 | 28 | .20 | 99.1 | 3.737 |
| 1250 | 28 | .20 | 99.3 | 3.892 |
| 1300 | 21 | .15 | 99.5 | 4.048 |
| 1350 | 12 | .09 | 99.6 | 4.204 |
| 1400 | 5 | .04 | 99.6 | 4.360 |
| 1450 | 9 | .06 | 99.7 | 4.515 |
| 1500 | 4 | .03 | 99.7 | 4.671 |
| 1550 | 1 | .01 | 99.7 | 4.827 |
| 1600 | 6 | .04 | 99.7 | 4.982 |
| 1650 | 2 | .01 | 99.7 | 5.138 |
| 1700 | 5 | .04 | 99.8 | 5.294 |
| 1750 | 3 | .02 | 99.8 | 5.449 |
| 1800 | 3 | .02 | 99.8 | 5.605 |
| 1850 | 0 | .00 | 99.8 | 5.761 |
| 1900 | 3 | .02 | 99.8 | 5.917 |
| 1950 | 1 | .01 | 99.9 | 6.072 |
| 2000 | 3 | .02 | 99.9 | 6.228 |
| 2050 | 3 | .02 | 99.9 | 6.384 |
| 2100 | 5 | .04 | 99.9 | 6.539 |
| 2150 | 4 | .03 | 100.0 | 6.695 |
| 2200 | 1 | .01 | 100.0 | 6.851 |
| 2250 | 2 | .01 | 100.0 | 7.006 |
| 2300 | 3 | .02 | 100.0 | 7.162 |

of 30 characters is in error in the transmission, the item will be updated incorrectly. After six months of this how many items on the file can be expected to be incorrect?

5.4   What is the answer to the above question if the messages have error checking, and now one bit in $10^7$ is an undetected error?

## PART VI QUESTIONS REQUIRING COMPUTATION

6.1   An organization has many offices with clustered terminals. The numbers of terminals per office differ widely. A terminal control unit will be used to connect the terminals to a leased line and to carry out certain editing and control functions. One control unit requires one line, but different models of the control unit connect different numbers of terminals, as in the following table:

| Model | Price (monthly rental) | Maximum number of terminals that may be connected |
|-------|------------------------|---------------------------------------------------|
| 1 | 80 | 1 |
| 2 | 220 | 4 |
| 3 | 380 | 8 |
| 4 | 640 | 16 |
| 5 | 990 | 32 |

Model 1 control unit requires one type 1006 sub-voice-grade line.

Model 2 control unit requires one voice-grade line without conditioning.

Models 3, 4 and 5 control units require one voice-grade line with C2 conditioning.

The choice of control unit will depend upon the distance from the computer center as well as the number of terminals. Compute a table showing the minimum cost control unit selection for different distances and number of terminals.

6.2   We have no simple analytical method of finding the queuing time for a multiserver queue with general (or Erlang) service times. The following approximate equation is suggested, however:

$$E(t_w) = \frac{E(t_{w\exp})}{2} \left[ 1 + \frac{(\sigma_{t_s})^2}{E(t_s)} \right]$$

or

$$E(t_w) = \frac{E(t_{w\exp})}{2} \left[ 1 + \frac{1}{K} \right]$$

for an Erlang $K$ distribution of service times.

$E(t_{w\exp})$ is the waiting time for the situation when the service times are exponential.

You are asked to test this equation using simulation. Find out from your simulation when the above approximation is accurate and when it deviates from the actual waiting times. Investigate this with different numbers of servers.

6.3 A network such as that in Fig. 3.7 can use either hub or roll-call polling. Write a simulation program to compare the two when the numbers of concentrators per line vary from 2 to 12. Typical figures for transmission rate, line turnaround time and message lengths may be assumed. A detailed description of the character flow for hub and roll-call polling can be found in the author's book, *Teleprocessing Network Organization*.

6.4 159 cities are listed below, along with their A.T.&T. vertical and horizontal coordinates. The cities are to be connected to a computer center at Detroit, Michigan (which has coordinates: vertical 5536 and horizontal 2828). The cities are shown in the figure. The listing gives the numbers of messages per hour that are expected from the cities. For each message there will normally be a response from the computer. A set of questions follows which relates to different networks interconnecting these cities.

| | City | Vertical Coordinate | Horizontal Coordinate | Number of Messages per hour |
|---|---|---|---|---|
| 1 | WALDWICK-RIDGE NJ | 4967 | 1451 | 19.00 |
| 2 | ALBANY NY | 4649 | 1629 | 13.50 |
| 3 | BOSTON MASS (MKT) | 4422 | 1249 | 57.00 |
| 4 | CONCORD NH | 4326 | 1426 | 10.30 |
| 5 | HARTFORD CONN | 4687 | 1373 | 12.70 |
| 6 | NEW HAVEN CONN | 4792 | 1342 | 10.10 |
| 7 | PORTLAND MA | 4121 | 1334 | 5.30 |
| 8 | PROVIDENCE RI | 4550 | 1219 | 10.50 |
| 9 | SPRINGFLD MASS | 4620 | 1408 | 8.20 |
| 10 | WORCESTER MASS | 4513 | 1330 | 5.80 |
| 11 | BRKLYN NY | 4997 | 1406 | 9.70 |
| 12 | MANH DWTWN NY | 4997 | 1406 | 46.90 |
| 13 | MANH MID NY | 4997 | 1406 | 52.10 |
| 14 | MANH UPT NY | 4997 | 1406 | 48.20 |
| 15 | QUEENS NY | 4999 | 1406 | 9.10 |
| 16 | BETHLEHM PENN | 5157 | 1574 | 5.70 |
| 17 | HARRISBG PENN | 5363 | 1733 | 10.10 |
| 18 | PHILA PENN | 5251 | 1458 | 53.60 |

| | City | | | Vertical Coordinate | Horizontal Coordinate | Number of Messages per hour |
|---|---|---|---|---|---|---|
| ✓ 19 | PITTSBG | PENN | | 5621 | 2185 | 29.70 |
| 20 | READING | PENN | | 5258 | 1612 | 4.80 |
| ✓ 21 | SCRANTN | PENN | | 5042 | 1715 | 3.90 |
| 22 | TRENTON | NJ | | 5164 | 1440 | 15.10 |
| 23 | WILLMINGTN | DEL | | 5326 | 1485 | 9.50 |
| 24 | YORK | PENN | | 5402 | 1674 | 5.00 |
| 25 | BALTIMRE | MD | | 5510 | 1575 | 19.40 |
| 26 | CHARLOTTE | NC | | 6657 | 1698 | 9.20 |
| 27 | GREENSBRO | NC | | 6400 | 1638 | 6.90 |
| 28 | HAGERSTWN | MD | | 5555 | 1772 | 3.90 |
| 29 | NORFORK | VG | | 5936 | 1198 | 11.10 |
| 30 | RALEIGH | NC | | 6344 | 1436 | 13.30 |
| 31 | RICHMOND | VG | | 5906 | 1472 | 14.00 |
| 32 | ROANOKE | VG | | 6196 | 1801 | 6.50 |
| 33 | WASHINGTN | DC | (MSC) | 5622 | 1583 | 46.50 |
| 34 | WASHINGTN | DC | (FED) | 5622 | 1583 | 53.60 |
| 35 | WINSTON SAL | NC | | 6440 | 1710 | 6.20 |
| ✓ 36 | ATLANTA | GEO | | 7260 | 2083 | 35.10 |
| 37 | BIRMINGHM | ALA | | 7518 | 2446 | 9.60 |
| 38 | CPKENNEDY | FLA | | 7925 | 903 | 4.80 |
| 39 | CHATTANOOGA | TENN | | 7098 | 2366 | 6.00 |
| 40 | COLUMBIA | SC | | 6901 | 1589 | 8.80 |
| 41 | GREENVILLE | SC | | 6873 | 1894 | 7.30 |
| 42 | HUNTSVILLE | ALA | | 7267 | 2535 | 6.60 |
| 43 | JACKSONVILLE | FLA | | 7649 | 1276 | 10.50 |
| ✓ 44 | MIAMI | FLA | | 8351 | 527 | 24.90 |
| ✓ 45 | MOBILE | ALA | | 8167 | 2367 | 5.60 |
| 46 | MONTGOMERY | ALA | | 7692 | 2247 | 4.90 |
| 47 | ORLANDO | FLA | | 7954 | 1031 | 7.80 |
| 48 | SAVANNAH | GA | | 7266 | 1379 | 7.30 |
| 49 | TALLAHASSEE | FLA | | 7877 | 1716 | 7.20 |
| ✓ 50 | TAMPA | FLA | | 8173 | 1147 | 14.90 |
| 51 | CHARLESTON | SC | | 7021 | 1281 | 12.90 |
| ✓ 52 | CINCINNATI | OHIO | | 6263 | 2679 | 15.60 |
| ✓ 53 | COLUMBUS | OHIO | | 5972 | 2555 | 14.70 |

| | City | Vertical Coordinate | Horizontal Coordinate | Number of Messages per hour |
|---|---|---|---|---|
| 54 | DAYTON OHIO | 6113 | 2705 | 9.90 |
| 55 | EVANSVILLE IND. | 6729 | 3019 | 4.50 |
| 56 | FORT WAYNE IND | 5942 | 2982 | 6.00 |
| 57 | INDIANAPOLIS IND | 6272 | 2992 | 17.60 |
| 58 | KINGSPORT TENN | 6570 | 2107 | 3.80 |
| 59 | KNOXVILLE TENN | 6801 | 2251 | 6.60 |
| 60 | LAFAETTE IND | 6202 | 3167 | 3.40 |
| 61 | LEXINGTON KY | 6459 | 2562 | 8.20 |
| 62 | LOUISVILLE KY | 6529 | 2772 | 10.40 |
| 63 | NASHVILLE TENN | 7010 | 2710 | 9.20 |
| 64 | TERRE HAUTE IND | 6428 | 3145 | 3.50 |
| 65 | AKRON OHIO | 5637 | 2472 | 8.70 |
| 66 | BUFFALO NY | 5075 | 2326 | 13.30 |
| 67 | CANTON OHIO | 5676 | 2419 | 3.20 |
| 68 | CLEVELAND OHIO | 5574 | 2543 | 28.90 |
| 69 | DETROIT N MICH | 5536 | 2828 | 51.90 |
| 70 | ERIE PA | 5321 | 2397 | 4.40 |
| 71 | FLINT MICH | 5461 | 2993 | 9.20 |
| 72 | GRAND RAPIDS MICH | 5628 | 3261 | 2.40 |
| 73 | KALAMAZOO MICH | 5749 | 3177 | 5.70 |
| 74 | LANSING MICH | 5584 | 3081 | 9.40 |
| 75 | LIMA NY | 4958 | 2163 | 2.80 |
| 76 | MANSFIELD OHIO | 5783 | 2575 | 2.70 |
| 77 | TOLEDO OHIO | 5704 | 2820 | 9.30 |
| 78 | YOUNGSTONW OHIO | 5557 | 2353 | 7.00 |
| 79 | AURORA ILL | 6062 | 3511 | 12.00 |
| 80 | CHICAGO DT ILL | 5986 | 3426 | 47.20 |
| 81 | CHICAGO ILL | 5986 | 3426 | 28.10 |
| 82 | CHICAGO WEST ILL | 6058 | 3387 | 23.90 |
| 83 | MOLINE ILL | 6272 | 3807 | 6.00 |
| 84 | PEORIA ILL | 6362 | 3592 | 6.70 |
| 85 | RIVER OAKS TX | 8479 | 4122 | 11.50 |
| 86 | ROCKFORD ILL | 6022 | 3675 | 5.60 |
| 87 | SOUTH BEND IND | 5918 | 3206 | 8.40 |
| 88 | SPRINGFIELD ILL | 6539 | 3513 | 11.20 |

| | City | Vertical Coordinate | Horizontal Coordinate | Number of Messages per hour |
|---|---|---|---|---|
| 89 | JACKSON MISS | 8035 | 2880 | 10.50 |
| 90 | KANSAS CITY KANSAS | 7028 | 4212 | 22.50 |
| 91 | JEFFERSON CITY MO | 6963 | 3782 | 6.90 |
| 92 | LITTLE ROCK ARK | 7721 | 3451 | 10.30 |
| 93 | MEMPHIS TENN | 7471 | 3125 | 15.20 |
| 94 | OAKLAHOMA CY OKLA | 7947 | 4373 | 14.60 |
| 95 | STLOUIS MO | 6807 | 3482 | 32.80 |
| 96 | SPRINGFIELD MO | 7310 | 3836 | 4.00 |
| 97 | TOPEKA KA | 7110 | 4369 | 5.30 |
| 98 | TULSA OKLA | 7707 | 4173 | 11.40 |
| 99 | WICHITA KAN | 7489 | 4520 | 8.30 |
| 100 | AUSTIN TX | 9005 | 3996 | 11.20 |
| 101 | BATON ROUGE LA | 8476 | 2874 | 7.80 |
| 102 | BEAUMONT TX | 8777 | 3344 | 4.40 |
| 103 | CORPUS CHRISTI TX | 9475 | 3739 | 6.50 |
| 104 | DALLAS TX | 8436 | 4034 | 31.20 |
| 105 | EL PASO TX | 9231 | 5655 | 5.20 |
| 106 | FORT WORTH TX | 8479 | 4122 | 12.50 |
| 107 | HOUSTON TX | 8938 | 3536 | 36.60 |
| 108 | LUBBOCK TX | 8598 | 4962 | 10.00 |
| 109 | NEW ORLEANS LA | 8483 | 2638 | 14.70 |
| 110 | SAN ANTONIO TX | 9225 | 4062 | 12.10 |
| 111 | SHREVEPORT LA | 8272 | 3495 | 12.10 |
| 112 | ANAHEIM CAL | 9250 | 7810 | 25.90 |
| 113 | GLENDALE CAL | 9193 | 7883 | 23.50 |
| 114 | LA EAST CAL | 9213 | 7878 | 13.90 |
| 115 | LA WESTCH CAL | 9213 | 7878 | 26.00 |
| 116 | LA WILSHIRE CAL | 9213 | 7878 | 41.20 |
| 117 | RIVERSIDE CAL | 9202 | 7717 | 19.00 |
| 118 | SAN DIEGO CAL | 9468 | 7629 | 16.10 |
| 119 | SANTA BARB CAL | 9171 | 8150 | 8.60 |
| 120 | ALBUQUER NM | 8549 | 5887 | 10.70 |
| 121 | FRESNO CAL | 8669 | 8239 | 6.90 |
| 122 | PER OAKS NM | 8549 | 5887 | 21.40 |
| 123 | PHOENIX AR | 9135 | 6748 | 20.40 |

| | City | | Vertical Coordinate | Horizontal Coordinat | Number of Messages per hour |
|---|---|---|---|---|---|
| 124 | RENO | NEV | 8064 | 8323 | 3.70 |
| 125 | REDWD CITY | CAL | 8556 | 8682 | 11.80 |
| 126 | SACRAMENTO | CAL | 8304 | 8580 | 17.20 |
| 127 | SAN FRAN | CAL | 8492 | 8719 | 32.40 |
| 128 | SAN JOSE | CAL | 8583 | 8619 | 17.20 |
| 129 | BOISE | ID | 7096 | 7869 | 5.30 |
| 130 | DENVER | COL | 7501 | 5899 | 29.30 |
| 131 | HELENA | MONT | 6336 | 7348 | 6.20 |
| 132 | PORTLAND | ORE | 6799 | 8914 | 13.60 |
| 133 | SALEM | ORE | 6929 | 8958 | 6.60 |
| 134 | SALT LK CY | UTA | 7576 | 7065 | 13.40 |
| 135 | SEATTLE | WAS | 6336 | 8896 | 22.20 |
| 136 | SPOKANE | WAS | 6247 | 8180 | 8.60 |
| 137 | TACOMA | WAS | 6415 | 8906 | 3.70 |
| 138 | CEDAR RAP | IO | 6261 | 4021 | 6.60 |
| 139 | DES MOINES | IO | 6471 | 4275 | 10.70 |
| 140 | FARGO | ND | 5615 | 5182 | 6.20 |
| 141 | GRN BAY | WIS | 5512 | 3747 | 8.50 |
| 142 | LINCOLN | NEB | 6823 | 4674 | 6.80 |
| 143 | MADISON | WIS | 5887 | 3796 | 9.20 |
| 144 | MILWAUKEE | WIS | 5788 | 3589 | 23.10 |
| 145 | MINNEAPLIS | MINN | 5781 | 4525 | 21.10 |
| 146 | OMAHA | NEB | 6687 | 4595 | 11.40 |
| 147 | ST PAUL | MINN | 5776 | 4498 | 15.10 |
| 148 | SIOUX FLS | SD | 6279 | 4900 | 4.40 |
| 149 | BRIDGEPT | CONN | 4841 | 1360 | 6.60 |
| 150 | CRANFORD | NJ | 5043 | 1437 | 16.90 |
| 151 | ELMIRA | NY | 5029 | 1953 | 5.20 |
| 152 | ENDICOTT | NY | 4956 | 1855 | 5.00 |
| 153 | NEWARK | NJ | 5015 | 1430 | 23.00 |
| 154 | POK | NY | 4821 | 1526 | 6.20 |
| 155 | ROCHESTER | NY | 4913 | 2195 | 12.90 |
| 156 | SYRACUSE | NY | 4798 | 1990 | 10.00 |
| 157 | UTICA | NY | 4701 | 1878 | 3.40 |
| 158 | WH PLAINS | NY | 4921 | 1416 | 16.80 |
| 159 | WH PLAINS II | NY | 4921 | 1416 | 4.20 |

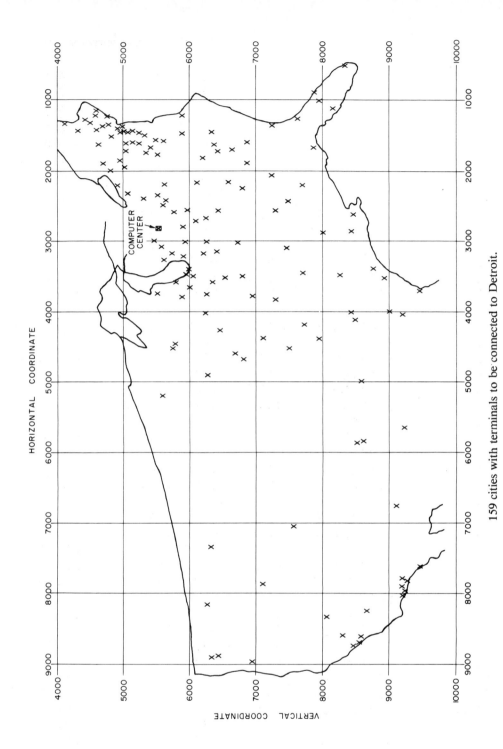

HORIZONTAL COORDINATE

VERTICAL COORDINATE

COMPUTER
CENTER

159 cities with terminals to be connected to Detroit.

A variety of networks could be designed for these cities differing with the types of terminals, messages and response time requirements. The following questions relate to the same set of cities, but the answers will be different.

**Case 1. Slow Terminals; No Tight Response-Time Requirements.** Each city in the above list is to have a typewriter-speed terminal. There is no requirement for a fast response-time; 60 seconds is adequate.

*a* Discussion:    What techniques or aspects of the design might be used to minimize the overall cost of the network.

*b* Discussion:    List those types of network structures that you feel should be costed in detail.

*c* Computation: Design a minimum-cost network assuming that the message lengths will be as follows (in characters):

|  | Input | Output |
|---|---|---|
| Mean | 48 | 106 |
| Standard Deviation | 15 | 88 |

The terminal speed is 10 characters per second.

**Case 2. Typewriter-Speed Dialogue.** A typewriter-speed terminal is again required in each city in the above list. Now, however, it will be used for man–computer dialogue in which a short response-time is needed. Ninety percent of the responses must be within 3 seconds, and to achieve this the mean response-time must be within $1\frac{1}{2}$ seconds.

*a* Discussion:    What techniques or aspects of the design can be used to minimize the cost of communication? How do they differ from the previous case?

*b* Discussion:    List those types of network structures that you feel should be costed in detail.

*c* Computation: Design a minimum-cost network assuming that the message lengths will be the same as in the previous case, and that the terminal speed is 15 characters per second.

**Case 3. Voice-Grade Dialogue.** A terminal is to be used at each location which because of the nature of the dialogue must transmit at 4,800 bits per second. In this case typewriter-speed dialogue would be far too slow. The responses from the computer will often be short—only a few characters—but occasionally will be long, transmitting an entire screenfull of information.

*a* Discussion:   What techniques or aspects of the design would now be preferable? How do they differ from the previous case?

*b* Discussion:   List those types of network structures that you feel should be costed in detail.

*c* Computation:   Design a minimum cost network assuming that the message lengths will be as follows:

To the computer:  Mean: 10 characters
                  Standard Deviation: 5 characters

From the computer:  15%: 1 character
                    12%: 2 to 4 characters
                     8%: 5 to 10 characters
                    10%: 11 to 30 characters
                    15%: 31 to 100 characters
                    10%: 101 to 200 characters
                    10%: 201 to 400 characters
                    10%: 401 to 600 characters
                    15%: A full screen of 1000 characters

**Case 4. High-Volume Voice-Grade Dialogue.**  This case is the same as the previous one, except that now the volume of messages from each city is 25 times greater. This means that some cities will need several terminals. Assume that the operator's activities when using the terminal set a maximum message rate per terminal of 120 messages per hour. Answer the same questions as before.

**Case 5. Differing Requirements.**  In this case the cities differ in their requirements. Some want teletype machines; some want a fast display unit dialogue; a few want a hard copy print-out of high volume. What types of network structure could serve these differing needs? What features or aspects of the design would be effective in lowering the cost?

## PART VII  THOUGHT-PROVOKERS

7.1 A corporation has a number of different teleprocessing systems which were implemented at different times. The figures in Chapter 5 show the different systems. The overall cost of data transmission in the corporation could be much less if these networks were integrated. A project is now being set up to study ways in which this could be done. In rationalizing the transmission facilities, it is necessary to plan a network structure that can better incorporate future needs and expansion. Discuss the techniques and approaches that might be possible for serving the data transmission needs of this corporation.

7.2 A network of leased wideband lines is to be set up to interconnect a number of computer installations all of which have real-time terminals as well as batch operations. It seems desirable that the network in question should be able to carry data of widely differing rates, including 15 characters per second for typewriter-like terminals, 600 characters per second for visual display units, and speeds in excess of 15,000 characters per second for tape-to-tape and computer-to-computer transmission. What techniques might be used in the future for combining these speed requirements on one wideband line?

7.3 One of the Federal Reserve Banks carried out a study on the future of the American payments mechanism. A growth is anticipated in the volume of checks so great that it cannot economically be absorbed. Credit cards have problems associated with them, give an alarmingly high cost per transaction (which the consumer pays indirectly and unknowingly), and do little to reduce the overall quantity of paperwork.

The solution is an electronic fund transfer (EFT) system. Using this, the consumer would have a magnetically encoded card with which he would make payments directly. The card would be inserted into an EFT terminal, and the transaction would be transmitted to a bank where the consumer's record would be updated in real-time if he had the funds available.

It was estimated that when EFT becomes as widely used as credit cards are today, the terminal cost could be less than $300. The cost per transaction would be *much* lower than with credit cards. Most stores, offices and restaurants would have an EFT terminal. Some consumers might have one in their home. It was thought possible that at some time in the 1980's there might be more than a million EFT terminals in use in the United States.

1. Discuss what telecommunication facilities are needed for EFT.
2. Will the present-day type of facilities be adequate? If not, what improvement is needed?
3. What methods could minimize the transmission costs?
4. How would you build provisions for reliability into the system?

7.4 A major data-processing manufacturer is attempting to determine what teleprocessing products and services it should market in the time frame of 3 years hence to 7 years hence. What recommendations would you make? What needs do teleprocessing users have which are not filled today? How will their needs change in the future? What new opportunities can be created in this market area? Develop a brief statement of strategy which should guide the development work in such a corporation.

7.5 An industrial nation smaller than the United States wants to set up a Government-controlled, switched, public, data-transmission network. There are many ways in which such a network could be designed. What recommendations would you make?

# GLOSSARY

There is little point in redefining the wheel, and where useful the definitions in this glossary have been taken from other recognized glossaries.

A suffix "2" after a definition below indicates that it is the CCITT definition, published in *List of Definitions of Essential Telecommunication Terms,* International Telecommunication Union, Geneva.

A suffix "1" after a definition below indicates that the definition is taken from the *Data Communications Glossary,* International Business Machines Corporation, Poughkeepsie 1967 (Manual number C20–1666).

**Address.** A coded representation of the destination of data, or of their originating terminal. Multiple terminals on one communication line, for example, must have unique addresses. Telegraph messages reaching a switching center carry an address before their text to indicate the destination of the message.

**Alphabet** (telegraph or data). A table of correspondence between an agreed set of characters and the signals which represent them. (2).

**Alternate routing.** An alternative communications path used if the normal one is not available. These may be one or more possible alternative paths.

**Amplitude modulation.** One of three ways of modifying a sine wave signal in order to make it "carry" information. The sine wave, or "carrier," has its amplitude modified in accordance with the information to be transmitted.

**Analog data.** Data in the form of *continuously variable* physical quantities. (Compare with **Digital data.**) (1).

**Analog transmission.** Transmission of a continuously variable signal as opposed to a discretely variable signal. Physical quantities such as temperature are continuously variable and so are described as "analog." Data characters, on the other hand, are coded in discrete separate pulses or signal levels, and are referred to as "digital." The normal way of transmitting a telephone, or voice, signal has been analog; but now digital encoding (using PCM) is coming into use over trunks.

**Application program.** The working programs in a system may be classed as *application programs* and *supervisory programs.* The application programs are the main data-processing programs. They contain no input-output coding except in the form of macroinstructions that transfer control to the supervisory programs. They are usually unique to one type of application, whereas the supervisory programs could be used for a variety of different application types. A number of different terms are used for these two classes of program.

**ARQ** (Automatic Request for Repetition). A system employing an error-detecting code and so conceived that any false signal initiates a repetition of the transmission of the character incorrectly received. (2).

**ASCII** (American Standard Code for Information Interchange). Usually pronounced "ask'-ee." An eight-level code for data transfer adopted by the American Standards Association to achieve compatibility between data devices. (1).

**Asynchronous transmission.** Transmission in which each information character, or sometimes each word or small block, is individually synchronized, usually by the use of start and stop elements. The gap between each character (or word) is not of a necessarily fixed length. (Compare with **Synchronous transmission.**) Asynchronous transmission is also called *start-stop transmission.*

**Attended operation.** In data set applications, individuals are required at both stations to establish the connection and transfer the data sets from talk (voice) mode to data mode. (Compare **Unattended operation.**) (1).

**Attenuation.** Decrease in magnitude of current, voltage, or power of a signal in transmission between points. May be expressed in decibels. (1).

**Attenuation equalizer.** (See **Equalizer.**)

**Audio frequencies.** Frequencies that can be heard by the human ear (usually 30 to 20,000 cycles per second). (1).

**Automatic calling unit** (ACU). A dialing device supplied by the communications common carrier, which permits a business machine to automatically dial calls over the communication networks. (1).

**Automatic dialing unit** (ADU). A device capable of automatically generating dialing digits. (Compare with **Automatic calling unit.**) (1).

**Bandwidth.** The range of frequencies available for signaling. The differences expressed in cycles per second (hertz) between the highest and lowest frequencies of a band.

**Baseband signaling.** Transmission of a signal at its original frequencies, i.e., a signal not changed by modulation.

**Baud.** Unit of signaling speed. The speed in bauds is the number of discrete conditions or signal events per second. (This is applied only to the actual signals on a communication line.) If each signal event represents only one bit condition, baud is the same as bits per second. When each signal event represents other than one bit (e.g., see **Dibit**), baud does not equal bits per second. (1).

**Baudot code.** A code for the transmission of data in which five equal-length bits represent one character. This code is used in most DC teletypewriter machines where 1 start element and 1.42 stop elements are added. (See page 109.) (1).

**Bel.** Ten decibels, q.v.

**BEX.** Broadband exchange, q.v.

**Bias distortion.** In teletypewriter applications, the uniform shifting of the beginning of all marking pulses from their proper positions in relation to the beginning of the start pulse. (1).

**Bias distortion, asymmetrical distortion.** Distortion affecting a two-condition (or binary) modulation (or restitution) in which all the significant conditions have longer or shorter durations than the corresponding theoretical durations. (2).

**Bit.** Contraction of "binary digit," the smallest unit of information in a binary system. A bit represents the choice between a mark or space (one or zero) condition.

**Bit rate.** The speed at which bits are transmitted, usually expressed in bits per second. (Compare with **Baud.**)

**Broadband.** Communication channel having a bandwidth greater than a voice-grade channel, and therefore capable of higher-speed data transmission. (1).

**Broadband exchange** (BEX). Public switched communication system of Western Union, featuring various bandwidth FDX connections. (1).

**Buffer.** A storage device used to compensate for a difference in rate of data flow, or time of occurrence of events, when transmitting data from one device to another. (1).

**Cable.** Assembly of one or more conductors within an enveloping protective sheath, so constructed as to permit the use of conductors separately or in groups. (1).

**Carrier.** A continuous frequency capable of being modulated, or impressed with a second (information carrying) signal. (1).

**Carrier, communications common.** A company which furnishes communications services to the general public, and which is regulated by appropriate local, state, or federal agencies. The term strictly includes truckers and movers, bus lines, and airlines, but is usually used to refer to telecommunication companies.

**Carrier system.** A means of obtaining a number of channels over a single path by modulating each channel on a different carrier frequency and demodulating at the receiving point to restore the signals to their original form.

**Carrier telegraphy, carrier current telegraphy.** A method of transmission in which the signals from a telegraph transmitter modulate an alternating current. (2).

**Central office.** The place where communications common carriers terminate customer lines and locate the switching equipment which interconnects those lines. (Also referred to as an *exchange, end office,* and *local central office.*)

**Chad.** The material removed when forming a hole or notch in a storage medium such as punched tape or punched cards.

**Chadless tape.** Perforated tape with the chad partially 'attached, to facilitate interpretive printing on the tape.

**Channel.** 1. (CCITT and ASA standard) A means of one-way transmission. (Compare with **Circuit.**)
2. (Tariff and common usage) As used in the tariffs, a path for electrical transmission between two or more points without common-carrier-provided terminal equipment. Also called *circuit, line, link, path,* or *facility.* (1).

**Channel, analog.** A channel on which the information transmitted can take any value between the limits defined by the channel. Most voice channels are analog channels.

**Channel, voice-grade.** A channel suitable for transmission of speech, digital or analog data, or facsimile, generally with a frequency range of about 300 to 3400 cycles per second.

**12-channel group** (of carrier current system). The assembly of 12 telephone channels, in a carrier system, occupying adjacent bands in the spectrum, for the purpose of simultaneous modulation or demodulation. (2).

**Character.** Letter, figure, number, punctuation or other sign contained in a message. Besides such characters, there may be characters for special symbols and some control functions. (1).

**Characteristic distortion.** Distortion caused by transients which, as a result of the modulation, are present in the transmission channel and depend on its transmission qualities.

**Circuit.** A means of both-way communication between two points, comprising associated "go" and "return" channels. (1).

**Circuit, four-wire.** A communication path in which four wires (two for each direction of transmission) are presented to the station equipment. (1).

**Circuit, two-wire.** A metallic circuit formed by two conductors insulated from each other. It is possible to use the two conductors as either a one-way transmission path, a half-duplex path, or a duplex path. (1).

**Common carrier.** (*See* **Carrier, communications common.**)

**Compandor.** A compandor is a combination of a compressor at one point in a communication path for reducing the volume *range* of signals, followed by an expandor at another point for restoring the original volume range. Usually its purpose is to improve the ratio of the signal to the interference entering in the path between the compressor and expandor. (2).

**Compressor.** Electronic device which compresses the volume range of a signal, used in a compandor (q.v.). An "expandor" restores the original volume range after transmission.

**Conditioning.** The addition of equipment to a leased voice-grade channel to provide minimum values of line characteristics required for data transmission. (1).

**Contention.** This is a method of line control in which the terminals request to transmit. If the channel in question is free, transmission goes ahead; if it is not free, the terminal will have to wait until it becomes free. The queue of contention requests may be built up by the computer, and this can either be in a prearranged sequence or in the sequence in which the requests are made.

**Control character.** A character whose occurrence in a particular context initiates, modifies, or stops a control operation—e.g., a character to control carriage return. (1).

**Control mode.** The state that all terminals on a line must be in to allow line control actions, or terminal selection to occur. When all terminals on a line are in the control mode, characters on the line are viewed as control characters performing line discipline, that is, polling or addressing. (1).

**Cross-bar switch.** A switch having a plurality of vertical paths, a plurality of horizontal paths, and electromagnetically operated mechanical means for interconnecting any one of the vertical paths with any of the horizontal paths. See page 326. (2).

**Cross-bar system.** A type of line-switching system which uses cross-bar switches.

**Cross talk.** The unwanted transfer of energy from one circuit, called the *disturbing* circuit, to another circuit, called the *disturbed* circuit. (2).

**Cross talk, far-end.** Cross talk which travels along the disturbed circuit in the same direction as the signals in that circuit. To determine the far-end cross talk between two pairs, 1 and 2, signals are transmitted on pair 1 at station A, and the level of cross talk is measured on pair 2 at station B. (1).

**Cross talk, near-end.** Cross talk which is propagated in a disturbed channel in the direction opposite to the direction of propagation of the current in the disturbing channel. Ordinarily, the terminal of the disturbed channel at which the near-end cross talk is present is near or coincides with the energized terminal of the disturbing channel. (1).

**Dataphone.** Both a service mark and a trademark of AT & T and the Bell System. As a service mark it indicates the transmission of data over the telephone network. As a trademark it identifies the communications equipment furnished by the Bell System for data communications services. (1).

**Data set.** A device which performs the modulation/demodulation and control functions necessary to provide compatibility between business machines and communications facilities. (*See also* **Line adapter, Modem,** *and* **Subset.**) (1).

**Data-signaling rate.** It is given by $\sum_{i=1}^{m} \frac{1}{T_i} \log_2 n_i$, where $m$ is the number of parallel channels, $T$ is the minimum interval for the $i$th channel, expressed in seconds,

$n$ is the number of significant conditions of the modulation in the $i$th channel. Data-signaling rate is expressed in bits per second. (2).

**Dataspeed.** An AT & T marketing term for a family of medium-speed paper tape transmitting and receiving units. Similar equipment is also marketed by Western Union. (1).

**DDD.** (*See* **Direct distance dialing,** q.v.)

**Decibel** (db). A tenth of a bel. A unit for measuring relative strength of a signal parameter such as power, voltage, etc. The number of decibels is ten times the logarithm (base 10) of the ratio of the measured quantity to the reference level. The reference level must always be indicated, such as 1 milliwatt for power ratio. (1). See Fig. 9.5.

**Delay distortion.** Distortion occurring when the envelope delay of a circuit or system is not constant over the frequency range required for transmission.

**Delay equalizer.** A corrective network which is designed to make the phase delay or envelope delay of a circuit or system substantially constant over a desired frequency range. (*See* **Equalizer.**) (1).

**Demodulation.** The process of retrieving intelligence (data) from a modulated carrier wave; the reverse of modulation. (1).

**Diagnostic programs.** These are used to check equipment malfunctions and to pinpoint faulty components. They may be used by the computer engineer or may be called in by the supervisory programs automatically.

**Diagnostics, system.** Rather than checking one individual component, system diagnostics utilize the whole system in a manner similar to its operational running. Programs resembling the operational programs will be used rather than systematic programs that run logical patterns. These will normally detect overall system malfunctions but will not isolate faulty components.

**Diagnostics, unit.** These are used on a conventional computer to detect faults in the various units. Separate unit diagnostics will check such items as arithmetic circuitry, transfer instructions, each input-output unit, and so on.

**Dial pulse.** A current interruption in the DC loop of a calling telephone. It is produced by the breaking and making of the dial pulse contacts of a calling telephone when a digit is dialed. The loop current is interrupted once for each unit of value of the digit. (1).

**Dial-up.** The use of a dial or pushbutton telephone to initiate a station-to-station telephone call.

**Dibit.** A group of two bits. In four-phase modulation, each possible dibit is encoded as one of four unique carrier phase shifts. The four possible states for a dibit are 00, 01, 10, 11.

**Differential modulations.** A type of modulation in which the choice of the significant condition for any signal element is dependent on the choice for the previous signal element. (2).

**Digital data.** Information represented by a code consisting of a sequence of discrete elements. (Compare with **Analog data.**) (1).

**Digital signal.** A discrete or discontinuous signal; one whose various states are discrete intervals apart. (Compare with **Analog transmission.**) (1).

**Direct distance dialing** (DDD). A telephone exchange service which enables the telephone user to call other subscribers outside his local area without operator assistance. In the United Kingdom and some other countries, this is called *Subscriber Trunk Dialing* (STD).

**Disconnect signal.** A signal transmitted from one end of a subscriber line or trunk to indicate at the other end that the established connection should be disconnected. (1).

**Distortion.** The unwanted change in waveform that occurs between two points in a transmission system. (1).

**Distributing frame.** A structure for terminating permanent wires of a telephone central office, private branch exchange, or private exchange, and for permitting the easy change of connections between them by means of cross-connecting wires. (1).

**Double-current transmission, polar direct-current system.** A form of binary telegraph transmission in which positive and negative direct currents denote the significant conditions. (2).

**Drop, subscriber's.** The line from a telephone cable to a subscriber's building. (1).

**Duplex transmission.** Simultaneous two-way independent transmission in both directions. (Compare with **Half-duplex transmission.** Also called *full-duplex transmission.*) (1).

**Duplexing.** The use of duplicate computers, files or circuitry, so that in the event of one component failing an alternative one can enable the system to carry on its work.

**Echo.** An echo is a wave which has been reflected or otherwise returned with sufficient magnitude and delay for it to be perceptible in some manner as a wave distinct from that directly transmitted.

**Echo check.** A method of checking data transmission accuracy whereby the received data are returned to the sending end for comparison with the original data.

**Echo suppressor.** A line device used to prevent energy from being reflected back (echoed) to the transmitter. It attenuates the transmission path in one direction while signals are being passed in the other direction. (1).

**End distortion.** End distortion of start-stop teletypewriter signals is the shifting of the end of all marking pulses from their proper positions in relation to the beginning of the start pulse.

**End office.** (*See* **Central office.**)

**Equalization.** Compensation for the attenuation (signal loss) increase with frequency. Its purpose is to produce a flat frequency response while the temperature remains constant. (1).

**Equalizer.** Any combination (usually adjustable) of coils, capacitors, and/or resistors inserted in transmission line or amplifier circuit to improve its frequency response. (1).

**Equivalent four-wire system.** A transmission system using frequency division to obtain full-duplex operation over only one pair of wires. (1).

**Error-correcting telegraph code.** An error-detecting code incorporating sufficient additional signaling elements to enable the nature of some or all of the errors to be indicated and corrected entirely at the receiving end.

**Error-detecting and feedback system, decision feedback system, request repeat system, ARQ system.** A system employing an error-detecting code and so arranged that a signal detected as being in error automatically initiates a request for retransmission of the signal detected as being in error. (2).

**Error-detecting telegraph code.** A telegraph code in which each telegraph signal conforms to specific rules of construction, so that departures from this construction in the received signals can be automatically detected. Such codes necessarily require more signaling elements than are required to convey the basic information.

**ESS.** (Electronic Switching System). Bell System term for computerized telephone exchange. ESS 1 is a central office. ESS 101 gives private branch exchange (PBX) switching controlled from the local central office. (*See* Chapter 19.)

**Even parity check (odd parity check).** This is a check which tests whether the number of digits in a group of binary digits is even (even parity check) or odd (odd parity check). (2).

**Exchange.** A unit established by a communications common carrier for the administration of communication service in a specified area which usually embraces a city, town, or village and its environs. It consists of one or more central offices together with the associated equipment used in furnishing communication service. (This term is often used as a synonym for "central office," q.v.)

**Exchange, classes of.** Class 1 (*see* **Regional center**); class 2 (*see* **Sectional center**); class 3 (*see* **Primary center**); class 4 (*see* **Toll center**); class 5 (*see* **End office**).

**Exchange, private automatic** (PAX). A dial telephone exchange that provides private telephone service to an organization and that does *not* allow calls to be transmitted to or from the public telephone network.

**Exchange, private automatic branch** (PABX). A private automatic telephone exchange that provides for the transmission of calls to and from the public telephone network.

**Exchange, private branch** (PBX). A manual exchange connected to the public telephone network on the user's premises and operated by an attendant supplied by the user. PBX is today commonly used to refer also to an automatic exchange.

**Exchange, trunk.** An exchange devoted primarily to interconnecting trunks.

**Exchange service.** A service permitting interconnection of any two customers' stations through the use of the exchange system.

**Expandor.** A transducer which for a given amplitude range or input voltages produces a larger range of output voltages. One important type of expandor employs the information from the envelope of speech signals to expand their volume range. (Compare **Compandor.**) (1).

**Facsimile** (FAX). A system for the transmission of images. The image is scanned at the transmitter, reconstructed at the receiving station, and duplicated on some form of paper. (1).

**Fail softly.** When a piece of equipment fails, the programs let the system fall back to a degraded mode of operation rather than let it fail catastrophically and give no response to its users.

**Fall-back, double.** Fall-back in which two separate equipment failures have to be contended with.

**Fall-back procedures.** When the equipment develops a fault the programs operate in such a way as to circumvent this fault. This may or may not give a degraded service. Procedures necessary for fall-back may include those to switch over to an alternative computer or file, to change file addresses, to send output to a typewriter instead of a printer, to use different communication lines or bypass a faulty terminal, etc.

**FCC.** Federal Communications Commission, q.v.

**FD** or **FDX.** Full duplex. (*See* **Duplex.**)

**FDM.** Frequency-division multiplex, q.v.

**Federal Communications Commission** (FCC). A board of seven commissioners appointed by the President under the Communication Act of 1934, having the power to regulate all interstate and foreign electrical communication systems originating in the United States. (1).

**Figures shift.** A physical shift in a teletypewriter which enables the printing of numbers, symbols, upper-case characters, etc. (Compare with **Letters shift.**) (1).

**Filter.** A network designed to transmit currents of frequencies within one or more frequency bands and to attenuate currents of other frequencies. (2).

**Foreign exchange service.** A service which connects a customer's telephone to a telephone company central office normally not serving the customer's location. (Also applies to TWX service.) (1).

**Fortuitous distortion.** Distortion resulting from causes generally subject to random laws (accidental irregularities in the operation of the apparatus and of the moving parts, disturbances affecting the transmission channel, etc.). (2).

**Four-wire circuit.** A circuit using two pairs of conductors, one pair for the "go" channel and the other pair for the "return" channel. (2).

**Four-wire equivalent circuit.** A circuit using the same pair of conductors to give "go" and "return" channels by means of different carrier frequencies for the two channels. (2).

**Four-wire terminating set.** Hybrid arrangement by which four-wire circuits are terminated on a two-wire basis for interconnection with two-wire circuits.

**Frequency-derived channel.** Any of the channels obtained from multiplexing a channel by frequency division. (2).

**Frequency-division multiplex.** A multiplex system in which the available transmission frequency range is divided into narrower bands, each used for a separate channel. (2).

**Frequency modulation.** One of three ways of modifying a sine wave signal to make it "carry" information. The sine wave or "carrier" has its frequency modified in accordance with the information to be transmitted. The frequency function of the modulated wave may be continuous or discontinuous. In the latter case, two or more particular frequencies may correspond each to one significant condition.

**Frequency-shift signaling, frequency-shift keying** (FSK). Frequency modulation method in which the frequency is made to vary at the significant instants. 1. By smooth transitions: the modulated wave and the change in frequency are continuous at the significant instants. 2. By abrupt transitions: the modulated wave is continuous but the frequency is discontinuous at the significant instants. (2).

**FSK.** Frequency-shift keying, q.v.

**FTS.** Federal Telecommunications System.

**Full-duplex** (FD or FDX) **transmission.** (*See* **Duplex transmission.**)

**Half-duplex** (HD or HDX) **circuit.**
1. CCITT definition: A circuit designed for duplex operation, but which, on account of the nature of the terminal equipments, can be operated alternately only.
2. Definition in common usage (the normal meaning in computer literature): A circuit designed for transmission in either direction but not both directions simultaneously.

**Handshaking.** Exchange of predetermined signals for purposes of control when a connection is established between two data sets.

**Harmonic distortion.** The resultant presence of harmonic frequencies (due to non-liner characteristics of a transmission line) in the response when a sinusoidal stimulus is applied. (1).

**HD or HDX.** Half duplex. (*See* **Half-duplex circuit.**)

**Hertz** (Hz). A measure of frequency or bandwidth. The same as cycles per second.

**Home loop.** An operation involving only those input and output units associated with the local terminal. (1).

**In-house.** *See* **In-plant system.**

**In-plant system.** A system whose parts, including remote terminals, are all situated in one building or localized area. The term is also used for communication systems spanning several buildings and sometimes covering a large distance, but in which no common carrier facilities are used.

**International Telecommunication Union** (ITU). The telecommunications agency of the United Nations, established to provide standardized communications procedures and practices including frequency allocation and radio regulations on a world-wide basis.

**Interoffice trunk.** A direct trunk between local central offices.

**Intertoll trunk.** A trunk between toll offices in different telephone exchanges. (1).

**ITU.** International Telecommunication Union, q.v.

**Keyboard perforator.** A perforator provided with a bank of keys, the manual depression of any one of which will cause the code of the corresponding character or function to be punched in a tape. (2).

**Keyboard send/receive.** A combination teletypewriter transmitter and receiver with transmission capability from keyboard only.

**KSR.** Keyboard send/receive, q.v.

**Leased facility.** A facility reserved for sole use of a single leasing customer. (*See also* **private line.**) (1).

**Letters shift.** A physical shift in a teletypewriter which enables the printing of alphabetic characters. Also, the name of the character which causes this shift. (*Compare* with **Figures shift.**) (1).

**Line switching.** Switching in which a circuit path is set up between the incoming and outgoing lines. Contrast with message switching (q.v.) in which no such physical path is established.

**Link communication.** The physical means of connecting one location to another for the purpose of transmitting and receiving information. (1).

**Loading.** Adding inductance (load coils) to a transmission line to minimize amplitude distortion. (1).

**Local exchange, local central office.** An exchange in which subscribers' lines terminate. (Also referred to as *end office.*)

**Local line, local loop.** A channel connecting the subscriber's equipment to the line terminating equipment in the central office exchange. Usually metallic circuit (either two-wire or four-wire). (1).

**Longitudinal redundancy check** (LRC). A system of error control based on the formation of a block check following preset rules. The check formation rule is applied in the same manner to each character. In a simple case, the LRC is created by forming a parity check on each bit position of all the characters in the block (e.g., the first bit of the LRC character creates odd parity among the one-bit positions of the characters in the block).

**Loop checking, message feedback, information feedback.** A method of checking the accuracy of transmission of data in which the received data are returned to the sending end for comparison with the original data, which are stored there for this purpose. (2).

**LRC.** Longitudinal redundancy check.

**LTRS.** Letters shift, q.v. (*See* **Letters shift.**)

**Mark.** Presence of signal. In telegraph communications a mark represents the closed condition or current flowing. A mark impulse is equivalent to a binary 1. (*See* page 394.)

**Mark-hold.** The normal no-traffic line condition whereby a steady mark is transmitted.

**Mark-to-space transition.** The transition, or switching from a marking impulse to a spacing impulse.

**Mark-hold.** The normal no-traffic line condition whereby a steady mark is transmitted. This may be a customer-selectable option. (Compare with **Space-hold.**) (1).

**Master station.** A unit having control of all other terminals on a multipoint circuit for purposes of polling and/or selection. (1).

**Mean time to failure.** The average length of time for which the system, or a component of the system, works without fault.

**Mean time to repair.** When the system, or a component of the system, develops a fault, this is the average time taken to correct the fault.

**Message reference block.** When more than one message in the system is being processed in parallel, an area of storage is allocated to each message and remains uniquely associated with that message for the duration of its stay in the computer. This is called the *message reference block* in this book. It will normally contain the message and data associated with it that are required for its processing. In most systems, it contains an area of working storage uniquely reserved for that message.

**Message switching.** The technique of receiving a message, storing it until the proper outgoing line is available, and then retransmitting. No direct connection between the incoming and outgoing lines is set up as in line switching (q.v.).

**Microwave.** Any electromagnetic wave in the radio-frequency spectrum above 890 megacycles per second. (1).

**Modem.** A contraction of "modulator-demodulator." The term may be used when the modulator and the demodulator are associated in the same signal-conversion equipment. (*See* **Modulation** *and* **Data set.**) (1).

**Modulation.** The process by which some characteristic of one wave is varied in accordance with another wave or signal. This technique is used in data sets and moderns to make business machine signals compatible with communications facilities. (1).

**Modulation with a fixed reference.** A type of modulation in which the choice of the significant condition for any signal element is based on a fixed reference. (2).

**Multidrop line.** Line or circuit interconnecting several stations. (Also called *multipoint line.*) (1).

**Multiplex, multichannel.** Use of a common channel in order to make two or more channels, either by splitting of the frequency band transmitted by the common channel into narrower bands, each of which is used to constitute a distinct channel (frequency-division multiplex), or by allotting this common channel in turn, to constitute different intermittent channels (time-division multiplex). (2).

**Multiplexing.** The division of a transmission facility into two or more channels either by splitting the frequency band transmitted by the channel into narrower bands, each of which is used to constitute a distinct channel (frequency-division multiplex), or by allotting this common channel to several different information channels, one at a time (time-division multiplexing). (2).

**Multiplexor.** A device which uses several communication channels at the same time, and transmits and receives messages and controls the communication lines. This device itself may or may not be a stored-program computer.

**Multipoint line.** (*See* **Multidrop line.**)

**Neutral transmission.** Method of transmitting teletypewriter signals, whereby a mark is represented by current on the line and a space is represented by the absence of current. By extension to tone signaling, neutral transmission is a method of signaling employing two signaling states, one of the states representing both a space condition and also the absence of any signaling. (Also called *unipolar.* Compare with **Polar transmission.**) (1).

**Noise.** Random electrical signals, introduced by circuit components or natural disturbances, which tend to degrade the performance of a communications channel. (1).

**Off hook.** Activated (in regard to a telephone set). By extension, a data set automatically answering on a public switched system is said to go "off hook." (Compare with **On hook.**) (1).

**Off line.** Not in the line loop. In telegraph usage, paper tapes frequently are punched "off line" and then transmitted using a paper tape transmitter.

**On hook.** Deactivated (in regard to a telephone set). A telephone not in use is "on hook." (1).

**On line.** Directly in the line loop. In telegraph usage, transmitting directly onto the line rather than, for example, perforating a tape for later transmission. (*See also* **On-line computer system.**)

**On-line computer system.** An on-line system may be defined as one in which the input data enter the computer directly from their point of origin and/or output data are transmitted directly to where they are used. The intermediate stages such as punching data into cards or paper tape, writing magnetic tape, or off-line printing, are largely avoided.

**Open wire.** A conductor separately supported above the surface of the ground—i.e., supported on insulators.

**Open-wire line.** A pole line whose conductors are principally in the form of open wire.

**PABX.** Private automatic branch exchange. (*See* **Exchange, private automatic branch.**)

**Parallel transmission.** Simultaneous transmission of the bits making up a character or byte, either over separate channels or on different carrier frequencies on the channel. (1). The simultaneous transmission of a certain number of signal elements constituting the same telegraph or data signal. For example, use of a code according to which each signal is characterized by a combination of 3 out of 12 frequencies simultaneously transmitted over the channel. (2).

**Parity check.** Addition of noninformation bits to data, making the number of ones in a grouping of bits either always even or always odd. This permits detection of bit groupings that contain single errors. It may be applied to characters, blocks, or any convenient bit grouping. (1).

**Parity check, horizontal.** A parity check applied to the group of certain bits from every character in a block. (*See also* **Longitudinal redundancy check.**)

**Parity check, vertical.** A parity check applied to the group which is all bits in one character. (Also called *vertical redundancy check*.) (1).

**PAX.** Private automatic exchange. (*See* **Exchange, private automatic.**)

**PBX.** Private branch exchange. (*See* **Exchange, private branch.**)

**PCM.** (*See* **Pulse code modulation.**)

**PDM.** (*See* **Pulse duration modulation.**)

**Perforator.** An instrument for the manual preparation of a perforated tape, in which telegraph signals are represented by holes punched in accordance with a predetermined code. Paper tape is prepared off line with this. (Compare with **Reperforator.**) (2).

**Phantom telegraph circuit.** Telegraph circuit superimposed on two physical circuits reserved for telephony. (2).

**Phase distortion.** (*See* **Distortion, delay.**)

**Phase equalizer, delay equalizer.** A delay equalizer is a corrective network which is designed to make the phase delay or envelope delay of a circuit or system substantially constant over a desired frequency range. (2).

**Phase-inversion modulation.** A method of phase modulation in which the two significant conditions differ in phase by $\pi$ radians. (2).

**Phase modulation.** One of three ways of modifying a sine wave signal to make it "carry" information. The sine wave or "carrier," has its phase changed in accordance with the information to be transmitted.

**Pilot model.** This is a model of the system used for program testing purposes which is less complex than the complete model, e.g., the files used on a pilot model may contain a much smaller number of records than the operational files; there may be few lines and fewer terminals per line.

**Polar transmission.** A method for transmitting teletypewriter signals, whereby the marking signal is represented by direct current flowing in one direction and the spacing signal is represented by an equal current flowing in the opposite direction. By extension to tone signaling, polar transmission is a method of transmission employing three distinct states, two to represent a mark and a space and one to represent the absence of a signal. (Also called *bipolar*. Compare with **Neutral transmission.**)

**Polling.** This is a means of controlling communication lines. The communication control device will send signals to a terminal saying, "Terminal A. Have you anything to send?" if not, "Terminal B. Have you anything to send?" and so on. Polling is an alternative to contention. It makes sure that no terminal is kept waiting for a long time.

**Polling list.** The polling signal will usually be sent under program control. The program will have in core a list for each channel which tells the sequence in which the terminals are to be polled.

**PPM.** (*See* **Pulse position modulation.**)

**Primary center.** A control center connecting toll centers; a class 3 office. It can also serve as a toll center for its local end offices.

**Private automatic branch exchange.** (*See* **Exchange, private automatic branch.**)

**Private automatic exchange.** (*See* **Exchange, private automatic.**)

**Private branch exchange** (PBX). A telephone exchange serving an individual organization and having connections to a public telephone exchange. (2).

**Private line.** Denotes the channel and channel equipment furnished to a customer as a unit for his exclusive use, without interexchange switching arrangements. (1).

**Processing, batch.** A method of computer operation in which a number of similar input items are accumulated and grouped for processing.

**Processing, in line.** The processing of transactions as they occur, with no preliminary editing or sorting of them before they enter the system. (1).

**Propagation delay.** The time necessary for a signal to travel from one point on a circuit to another.

**Public.** Provided by a common carrier for use by many customers.

**Public switched network.** Any switching system that provides circuit switching to many customers. In the U.S.A. there are four such networks: Telex, TWX, telephone, and Broadband Exchange. (1).

**Pulse-code modulation** (PCM). Modulation of a pulse train in accordance with a code. (2).

**Pulse-duration modulation** (PDM) (**pulse-width modulation**) (**pulse-length modulation**). A form of pulse modulation in which the durations of pulses are varied. (2).

**Pulse Modulation.** Transmission of information by modulation of a pulsed, or intermittent, carrier. Pulse width, count, position, phase, and/or amplitude may be the varied characteristic.

**Pulse-position modulation** (PPM). A form of pulse modulation in which the positions in time of pulses are varied, without modifying their duration. (2).

**Pushbutton dialing.** The use of keys or pushbuttons instead of a rotary dial to generate a sequence of digits to establish a circuit connection. The signal form is usually multiple tones. (Also called *tone dialing, Touch-call, Touch-Tone.*) (1).

**Real time.** A real-time computer system may be defined as one that controls an environment by receiving data, processing them, and returning the results sufficiently quickly to affect the functioning of the environment at that time.

**Reasonableness checks.** Tests made on information reaching a real-time system or being transmitted from it to ensure that the data in question lie within a given range. It is one of the means of protecting a system from data transmission errors.

**Recovery from fall-back.** When the system has switched to a fall-back mode of operation and the cause of the fall-back has been removed, the system must be restored to its former condition. This is referred to as *recovery from fall-back.* The recovery process may involve updating information in the files to produce two duplicate copies of the file.

**Redundancy check.** An automatic or programmed check based on the systematic insertion of components or characters used especially for checking purposes. (1).

**Redundant code.** A code using more signal elements than necessary to represent the intrinsic information. For example, five-unit code using all the characters of International Telegraph Alphabet No. 2 is not redundant; five-unit code using only the figures in International Telegraph Alphabet No. 2 is redundant; seven-unit code using only signals made of four "space" and three "mark" elements is redundant. (2).

**Reference pilot.** A reference pilot is a different wave from those which transmit the telecommunication signals (telegraphy, telephony). It is used in carrier systems to facilitate the maintenance and adjustment of the carrier transmission system. (For example, automatic level regulation, synchronization of oscillators, etc.) (2).

**Regenerative repeater.** (*See* **Repeater, regenerative.**)

**Regional center.** A control center (class 1 office) connecting sectional centers of the telephone system together. Every pair of regional centers in the United States has a direct circuit group running from one center to the other. (1).

**Repeater.**
1. A device whereby currents received over one circuit are automatically repeated in another circuit or circuits, generally in an amplified and/or reshaped form.
2. A device used to restore signals, which have been distorted because of attenuation, to their original shape and transmission level.

**Repeater, regenerative.** Normally, a repeater utilized in telegraph applications. Its function is to retime and retransmit the received signal impulses restored to their original strength. These repeaters are speed- and code-sensitive and are intended for use with standard telegraph speeds and codes. (Also called *regen.*) (1).

**Repeater, telegraph.** A device which receives telegraph signals and automatically retransmits corresponding signals. (2).

**Reperforator** (receiving perforator.) A telegraph instrument in which the received signals cause the code of the corresponding characters or functions to be punched in a tape. (1).

**Reperforator/transmitter** (RT). A teletypewriter unit consisting of a reperforator and a tape transmitter, each independent of the other. It is used as a relaying device and is especially suitable for transforming the incoming speed to a different outgoing speed, and for temporary queuing.

**Residual error rate, undetected error rate.** The ratio of the number of bits, unit elements, characters or blocks incorrectly received but undetected or uncorrected by the error-control equipment, to the total number of bits, unit elements, characters or blocks sent. (2).

**Response time.** This is the time the system takes to react to a given input. If a message is keyed into a terminal by an operator and the reply from the computer, when it comes, is typed at the same terminal, response time may be defined as the time interval between the operator pressing the last key and the terminal typing the first letter of the reply. For different types of terminal, response time may be defined similarly. It is the interval between an event and the system's response to the event.

**Ringdown.** A method of signaling subscribers and operators using either a 20-cycle AC signal, a 135-cycle AC signal, or a 100-cycle signal interrupted 20 times per second. (1).

**Routing.** The assignment of the communications path by which a message or telephone call will reach its destination. (1).

**Routing, alternate.** Assignment of a secondary communications path to a destination when the primary path is unavailable. (1).

**Routing indicator.** An address, or group of characters, in the heading of a message defining the final circuit or terminal to which the message has to be delivered. (1).

**RT.** Reperforator/transmitter, q.v.

**Saturation testing.** Program testing with a large bulk of messages intended to bring to light those errors which will only occur very infrequently and which may be triggered by rare coincidences such as two different messages arriving at the same time.

**Sectional center.** A control center connecting primary centers; a class 2 office. (1).

**Seek.** A mechanical movement involved in locating a record in a random-access file. This may, for example, be the movement of an arm and head mechanism that is necessary before a read instruction can be given to read data in a certain location on the file.

**Selection.** Addressing a terminal and/or a component on a selective calling circuit. (1).

**Selective calling.** The ability of the transmitting station to specify which of several stations on the same line is to receive a message. (1).

**Self-checking numbers.** Numbers which contain redundant information so that an error in them, caused, for example, by noise on a transmission line, may be detected.

**Serial transmission.** Used to identify a system wherein the bits of a character occur serially in time. Implies only a single transmission channel. (Also called *serial-by-bit*.) (1). Transmission at successive intervals of signal elements constituting the same telegraph or data signal. For example, transmission of signal elements by a standard teleprinter, in accordance with International Telegraph Alphabet No. 2; telegraph transmission by a time-divided channel. (2).

**Sideband.** The frequency band on either the upper or lower side of the carrier frequency within which fall the frequencies produced by the process of modulation. (2).

**Signal-to-noise ratio** (S/N). Relative power of the signal to the noise in a channel. (1).

**Simplex circuit.**
1. CCITT definition: A circuit permitting the transmission of signals in either direction, but not in both simultaneously.
2. Definition in common usage (the normal meaning in computer literature): A circuit permitting transmission in one specific direction only.

**Simplex mode.** Operation of a communication channel in one direction only, with no capability for reversing. (1).

**Simulation.** This is a word which is sometimes confusing as it has three entirely different meanings, namely:

*Simulation for design and monitoring.* This is a technique whereby a model of the working system can be built in the form of a computer program. Special computer languages are available for producing this model. A complete system may be described by a succession of different models. These models can then be adjusted easily and endlessly, and the system that is being designed or monitored can be experimented with to test the effect of any proposed changes. The simulation model is a program that is run on a computer separate from the system that is being designed.

*Simulation of input devices.* This is a program testing aid. For various reasons it is undesirable to use actual lines and terminals for some of the program testing. Therefore, magnetic tape or other media may be used and read in by a special program which makes the data appear as if they came from actual lines and terminals. Simulation in this sense is the replacement of one set of equipment by another set of equipment and programs, so that the behavior is similar.

*Simulation of supervisory programs.* This is used for program testing purposes when the actual supervisory programs are not yet available. A comparatively simple program to bridge the gap is used instead. This type of simulation is the replacement of one set of programs by another set which imitates it.

**Single-current transmission,** (inverse) **neutral direct-current system.** A form of telegraph transmission effected by means of unidirectional currents. (2).

**Space.** 1. An impulse which, in a neutral circuit, causes the loop to open or causes absence of signal, while in a polar circuit it causes the loop current to flow in a direction opposite to that for a mark impulse. A space impulse is equivalent to a binary 0. 2. In some codes, a character which causes a printer to leave a character width with no printed symbol. (1).

**Space-hold.** The normal no-traffic line condition whereby a steady space is transmitted. (Compare with **Mark-hold.**) (1).

**Space-to-mark transition.** The transition, or switching, from a spacing impulse to a marking impulse. (1).

**Spacing bias.** *See* **Distortion, bias.**

**Spectrum.** 1. A continuous range of frequencies, usually wide in extent, within which waves have some specific common characteristic. 2. A graphical representation of the distribution of the amplitude (and sometimes phase) of the components of a wave as a function of frequency. A spectrum may be continuous or, on the contrary, contain only points corresponding to certain discrete values. (2).

**Start element.** The first element of a character in certain serial transmissions, used to permit synchronization. In Baudot teletypewriter operation, it is one space bit. (1).

**Start-stop system.** A system in which each group of code elements corresponding to an alphabetical signal is preceded by a start signal which serves to prepare the receiving mechanism for the reception and registration of a character, and is followed by a stop signal which serves to bring the receiving mechanism to rest in preparation for the reception of the next character. (Contrast with **Synchronous system.**) (Start-stop transmission is also referred to as *asynchronous transmission,* q.v.)

**Station.** One of the input or output points of a communications system—e.g., the telephone set in the telephone system or the point where the business machine interfaces the channel on a leased private line. (1).

**Status maps.** Tables which give the status of various programs, devices, input-output operations, or the status of the communication lines.

**Step-by-step switch.** A switch that moves in synchronism with a pulse device such as a rotary telephone dial. Each digit dialed causes the movement of successive selector switches to carry the connection forward until the desired line is reached. (Also called *stepper switch*. Compare with **Line switching** and **Cross-bar system**.) (1).

**Step-by-step system.** A type of line-switching system which uses step-by-step switches. (1).

**Stop bit.** (See **Stop element.**)

**Stop element.** The last element of a character in asynchronous serial transmissions, used to ensure recognition of the next start element. In Baudot teletypewriter operation it is 1.42 mark bits. (*See also* **Start-stop transmission.**) (1).

**Store and forward.** The interruption of data flow from the originating terminal to the designated receiver by storing the information enroute and forwarding it at a later time. (*See* **Message switching.**)

**Stunt box.** A device to 1. control the nonprinting functions of a teletypewriter terminal, such as carriage return and line feed; and 2. a device to recognize line control characters (e.g., DCC, TSC, etc.). (1).

**Subscriber trunk dialing.** (*See* **direct distance dialing.**)

**Subscriber's line.** The telephone line connecting the exchange to the subscriber's station. (2).

**Subscriber's loop.** (*See* **Local loop.**)

**Subset.** A subscriber set of equipment, such as a telephone. A modulation and demodulation device. (Also called *data set,* which is a more precise term.) (1).

**Subscriber's loop.** (*See* **Local loop.**)

**Subvoice-grade channel.** A channel of bandwidth narrower than that of voice-grade channels. Such channels are usually subchannels of a voice-grade line. (1).

**Supergroup.** The assembly of five 12-channel groups, occupying adjacent bands in the spectrum, for the purpose of simultaneous modulation or demodulation. (2).

**Supervisory programs.** Those computer programs designed to coordinate service and augment the machine components of the system, and coordinate and service application programs. They handle work scheduling, input-output operations, error actions, and other functions.

**Supervisory signals.** Signals used to indicate the various operating states of circuit combinations. (1).

**Supervisory system.** The complete set of supervisory programs used on a given system.

**Support programs.** The ultimate operational system consists of supervisory programs and application programs. However, a third set of programs are needed to install the system, including diagnostics, testing aids, data generator programs, terminal simulators, etc. These are referred to as *support programs.*

**Suppressed carrier transmission.** That method of communication in which the carrier frequency is suppressed either partially or to the maximum degree possible. One or both of the sidebands may be transmitted. (1).

**Switch hook.** A switch on a telephone set, associated with the structure supporting the receiver or handset. It is operated by the removal or replacement of the receiver or handset on the support. (*See also* **Off hook** *and* **On hook.**) (1).

**Switching center.** A location which terminates multiple circuits and is capable of interconnecting circuits or transferring traffic between circuits; may be automatic, semiautomatic, or torn-tape. (The latter is a location where operators tear off the incoming printed and punched paper tape and transfer it manually to the proper outgoing circuit.) (1).

**Switching message.** (*See* **Message switching.**)

**Switchover.** When a failure occurs in the equipment a switch may occur to an alternative component. This may be, for example, an alternative file unit, an alternative communication line or an alternative computer. The switchover process may be automatic under program control or it may be manual.

**Synchronous.** Having a constant time interval between successive bits, characters, or vents. The term implies that all equipment in the system is in step.

**Synchronous system.** A system in which the sending and receiving instruments are operating continuously at substantially the same frequency and are maintained, by means of correction, if necessary, in a desired phase relationship. (Contrast with **Start-stop system.**) (2).

**Synchronous transmission.** A transmission process such that between any two significant instants there is always an integral number of unit intervals. (Contrast with **Asynchronous** or **Start-stop transmission.**) (1).

**Tandem office.** An office that is used to interconnect the local end offices over tandem trunks in a densely settled exchange area where it is uneconomical for a telephone company to provide direct interconnection between all end offices. The tandem office completes all calls between the end offices but is not directly connected to subscribers. (1).

**Tandem office, tandem central office.** A central office used primarily as a switching point for traffic between other central offices. (2).

**Tariff.** The published rate for a specific unit of equipment, facility, or type of service provided by a communications common carrier. Also the vehicle by which the regulating agencies approve or disapprove such facilities or services. Thus the tariff becomes a contract between customer and common carrier.

**TD.** Transmitter-distributor, q.v.

**Teleprocessing.** A form of information handling in which a data-processing system utilizes communication facilities. (Originally, but no longer, an IBM trademark.) (1).

**Teletype.** Trademark of Teletype Corporation, usually referring to a series of different types of teleprinter equipment such as tape punches, reperforators, page printers, etc., utilized for communications systems.

**Teletypewriter exchange service** (TWX). An AT&T public switched teletypewriter service in which suitably arranged teletypewriter stations are provided with lines to a central office for access to other such stations throughout the U.S.A. and Canada. Both Baudot- and ASCII-coded machines are used. Business machines may also be used, with certain restrictions. (1).

**Telex service.** A dial-up telegraph service enabling its subscribers to communicate directly and temporarily among themselves by means of start-stop apparatus and of circuits of the public telegraph network. The service operates world wide. Baudot equipment is used. Computers can be connected to the Telex network.

**Terminal.** Any device capable of sending and/or receiving information over a communication channel. The means by which data are entered into a computer system and by which the decisions of the system are communicated to the environment it affects. A wide variety of terminal devices have been built, including teleprinters, special keyboards, light displays, cathode tubes, thermocouples, pressure gauges and other instrumentation, radar units, telephones, etc.

**TEX.** (*See* **Telex service.**)

**Tie line.** A private-line communications channel of the type provided by communications common carriers for linking two or more points together.

**Time-derived channel.** Any of the channels obtained from multiplexing a channel by time division.

**Time-division multiplex.** A system in which a channel is established in connecting intermittently, generally at regular intervals and by means of an automatic distribution, its terminal equipment to a common channel. At times when these connections are not established, the section of the common channel between the distributors can be utilized in order to establish other similar channels, in turn.

**Toll center.** Basic toll switching entity; a central office where channels and toll message circuits terminate. While this is usually one particular central office in a city, larger cities may have several central offices where toll message circuits terminate. A class 4 office. (Also called "toll office" and "toll point.") (1).

**Toll circuit** (American). *See* **Trunk circuit** (British).

**Toll switching trunk** (American). *See* **Trunk junction** (British).

**Tone dialing.** (*See* **Pushbutton dialing.**)

**Touch-call.** Proprietary term of GT&E. (*See* **Pushbutton dialing.**)

**Touch-tone.** AT&T term for pushbutton dialing, q.v.

**Transceiver.** A terminal that can transmit and receive traffic.

**Translator.** A device that converts information from one system of representation into equivalent information in another system of representation. In telephone equipment, it is the device that converts dialed digits into call-routing information. (1).

**Transmitter-distributor** (TD). The device in a teletypewriter terminal which makes and breaks the line in timed sequence. Modern usage of the term refers to a paper tape transmitter.

**Transreceiver.** A terminal that can transmit and receive traffic. (1).

**Trunk circuit** (British), **toll circuit** (American). A circuit connecting two exchanges in different localities. *Note:* In Great Britain, a trunk circuit is approximately 15 miles long or more. A circuit connecting two exchanges less than 15 miles apart is called a *junction circuit.*

**Trunk exchange** (British), **toll office** (American). An exchange with the function of controlling the switching of trunk (British) [toll (American)] traffic.

**Trunk group.** Those trunks between two points both of which are switching centers and/or individual message distribution points, and which employ the same multiplex terminal equipment.

**Trunk junction** (British), **toll switching trunk** (American). A line connecting a trunk exchange to a local exchange and permitting a trunk operator to call a subscriber to establish a trunk call.

**Unattended operations.** The automatic features of a station's operation permit the transmission and reception of messages on an unattended basis. (1).

**Vertical parity (redundancy) check.** (*See* **Parity check, vertical.**)

**VOGAD** (Voice-Operated Gain-Adjusting Device). A device somewhat similar to a compandor and used on some radio systems; a voice-operated device which removes fluctuation from input speech and sends it out at a constant level. No restoring device is needed at the receiving end. (1).

**Voice-frequency, telephone-frequency.** Any frequency within that part of the audio-frequency range essential for the transmission of speech of commercial quality, i.e., 300–3400 c/s. (2).

**Voice-frequency carrier telegraphy.** That form of carrier telegraphy in which the carrier currents have frequencies such that the modulated currents may be transmitted over a voice-frequency telephone channel. (1).

**Voice-frequency multichannel telegraphy.** Telegraphy using two or more carrier currents the frequencies of which are within the voice-frequency range. Voice-frequency telegraph systems permit the transmission of up to 24 channels over a single circuit by use of frequency-division multiplexing.

**Voice-grade channel.** (*See* **Channel, voice-grade.**)

**Voice-operated device.** A device used on a telephone circuit to permit the presence of telephone currents to effect a desired control. Such a device is used in most echo suppressors. (1).

**VRC.** Vertical redundancy check. (*See also* **Parity check.**)

**Watchdog timer.** This is a timer which is set by the program. It interrupts the program after a given period of time, e.g., one second. This will prevent the system from going into an endless loop due to a program error, or becoming idle because of an equipment fault. The Watchdog timer may sound a horn or cause a computer interrupt if such a fault is detected.

**WATS** (Wide Area Telephone Service). A service provided by telephone companies in the United States which permits a customer by use of an access line to make calls to telephones in a specific zone in a dial basis for a flat monthly charge. Monthly charges are based on the size of the area in which the calls are placed, not on the number or length of calls. Under the WATS arrangement, the U.S. is divided into six zones to be called on a full-time or measured-time basis. (1).

**Word.** 1. In telegraphy, six operations or characters (five characters plus one space). ("Group" is also used in place of "word.") 2. In computing, a sequence of bits or characters treated as a unit and capable of being stored in one computer location. (1).

**WPM** (Words per minute). A common measure of speed in telegraph systems.

# INDEX*

## A

Amplitude modulation, 167, 181 et seq.,
esp. 185–186, 189–194
Analog transmission, 33, 139, 145–146,
152 et seq., 181
Application programming, 349 et seq., 362
ARPA network, 267, 298–299
ARQ, 207–208
ASCII code, 155, 158, 163, 212–213, 221
Asynchronous transmission, 154–157,
160, 266
and costs, 160
Attenuation, 165, 166–167, 183, 188–191

## B

Badge reader and response, 69, 94, 106,
139
Badges, 106, 144–145
Bandwidth, 162, 165–166, 182, 186,
196, 206
Basic Teleprocessing Access Method
(BTAM), 329 et seq.
Batch transmission, 8, 10, 15, 33, 44–45,
134–136
and error control, 101 et seq.
with real-time systems, 47

Baudot code, 154, 162, 163, 203, 207,
219–221
Bell System T1 Carrier, 14, 28
Binary synchronous transmission, 158
and optimum block size, 538
Bit-sequence independency, 266
Broadcast code, 161
BTAM, 329 et seq.
Buffering, 515 et seq. (*see also* Buffers)
and core space, 516–539
and cost reduction, 515 et seq.
and peripheral media, 515 et seq.
for telecommunications only, 515 et seq.
Buffers, 70–71, 152 et seq., esp. 160,
194, 208–210, 215, 219, 278–280
calculation of optimum block size,
524–539
and dynamic allocation of core, 323,
331 et seq., 515–518, 520–522,
524, 539
Bursts of noise, 201 et seq.
Busy signal, 29–31, 58, 285 et seq.

## C

CATV, 97
Carrier-sine wave, 184–185
CCITT, 155, 187, 266
"Centrex," 511–513

---

Where page numbers are followed by "et seq.," the discussion of the entry continues for the
remainder of the chapter.

904